D1564553

MELVILLE
SEA DICTIONARY

MELVILLE
SEA DICTIONARY

A Glossed Concordance and
Analysis of the
Sea Language in
Melville's Nautical Novels

JILL B. GIDMARK

Greenwood Press
Westport, Connecticut • London, England

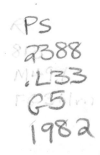

Library of Congress Cataloging in Publication Data

Gidmark, Jill B.
  Melville sea dictionary.

  Bibliography: p.
  1. Melville, Herman, 1819-1891—Language—Glossaries,
etc. 2. Melville, Herman, 1819-1891—Concordances.
3. Sea in literature. 4. Naval art and science—
Terminology. 5. Sea stories, American—Concordances.
I. Title.
PS2388.L33G5   813'.3   82-6122
ISBN 0-313-23330-6 (lib. bdg.)   AACR2

Library of Congress Catalog Card Number: 82-6122
ISBN: 0-313-23330-6

First published in 1982

Greenwood Press
A division of Congressional Information Service, Inc.
88 Post Road West, Westport, Connecticut 06881

Printed in the United States of America

10 9 8 7 6 5 4 3 2 1

To the memory of my father,
John Harris Barnum,
former Chief Petty Officer in the United States Navy,
with whom I once sailed the mighty Pacific

Contents

Acknowledgments

Newton Arvin has remarked that Melville's favorite words "color the fabric" of Moby-Dick as strongly as the use of a favorite range of hues affects the manner of a painter. On a scale less grandiose but no less true, I can say that the fabric of the present study is stronger, its hues brighter and clearer, due to insights and directions and support that many people have given me. To Joseph Smeall, who envisioned the project and guided me from its beginning, I feel profound gratitude for the hundreds of hours he gave to wrestling with Melville and with language with me, for showing me, more clearly than White Jacket could have done, that "A snuff of the sea . . . is inspiration," and for tempering my enthusiasm with his wisdom and perceptions. To Hennig Cohen, editor of the prestigious three-volume concordance of Moby-Dick, gratitude for his initial encouragement of and interest in my work. To Mary Ellen Gee--dear friend, colleague, partner in things of music and things of the sea, and typist of the present volume--overwhelming thanks for the thorough patience of Taji, a finely critical eye, and all manner of kindnesses. To my other friends and colleagues at the General College of the University of Minnesota, who indulged me with a teaching schedule that allowed for revision of this work, thanks for their friendship and good humor and support.

Most of all, I thank my son, Benjamin, who loves whales nearly as much as I do, and my husband, John, who, whenever my mind hovers over Descartian or other vortices, is always my sure Keel of the Ages.

Introduction

Melville's experience at sea formed a solid base for his art. At nineteen, he shipped out for Liverpool on the packet St. Lawrence as a "boy." Two years later, he signed articles aboard the whaling ship Acushnet (subsequently jumping ship) and then the Lucy Ann (subsequently mutinying). He had experience aboard the Charles and Henry as a harpooner and aboard the frigate United States as ordinary seaman before returning home. To his half dozen years as a crew member should be added his sea experience as a passenger to and from London in order to negotiate publication of White-Jacket personally. During this time, his journal tells us, he had much opportunity to recall the old emotions of being at the masthead. Melville's years at sea gave him a reality and a language far more immediate and direct than mere reading could have, affecting his life and writing profoundly.

Melville's first six novels--Typee, Omoo, Mardi, Redburn, White-Jacket, and Moby-Dick--transmute such experience into art and form a unified corpus of important sea literature. In them we discover, among other things, much about nineteenth-century seamen, nautical language, sea creatures, and Melville's perspective about the sea itself. While none of Melville's later works is so directly nautical, he did not completely abandon the theme of the sea after writing the epilogue to Moby-Dick. The short stories "The Encantadas," "Benito Cereno," and "Billy Budd," the novel Israel Potter, and the epic poem Clarel all use the sea in unique ways. These works, however, stand apart from the six sea novels in several respects: they are not as directly about the sea or sea adventures, chronologically they do not form as discrete a unit (other writings on other subjects intervene), and they are not as clearly autobiographical.

The present study is an identification and exploration of the nautical language revealed in the pages of a magnificent nautical author. The study isolates, in a glossed concordance, the vocabulary that Melville used in naming the sea, its geography and meteorology, its flora and fauna, and the men and ships that cross it. The study also analyzes the sea language etymologically, morphologically, and contextually, revealing both semantic and syntactic patterns. It deals with the sea word as a lexical item, as an element within a sentence, and as an element within a chapter.

What becomes apparent from the study is that Melville uses an extraordinarily varied and extraordinarily vigorous nautical vocabulary. When Melville refers, in his first sea novel, to "the concise, point-blank phrase of the sailors," or has the protagonist of his last sea novel observe that "Something of the salt sea yet lingered in Old Bildad's language," we are ready, mindful of Melville's sea career, to settle back and believe that the man is talking about what he knows intimately and reveres.

Melville's sea vocabulary is, on its own merits, an elaborate one. There are solid Anglo-Saxon words (<u>fin</u>, <u>bay</u>), sailor words (<u>sea-pie</u>, <u>landlubber</u>), technical words (<u>kentledge</u>, <u>marling-spike</u>), scientific words (<u>cetology</u>, <u>ichthyology</u>), geographical words (<u>isthmus</u>, <u>Galapagos Islands</u>), and poetic words (<u>billows</u>, <u>tempest</u>). Most of the words are nouns, and most of their uses are specific and referential.

What Melville does with such a set of terms is also elaborate. He shifts their functions from one part of speech to another. He adds affixes and forms compounds to stretch semantic potential. And he flexes the vocabulary with vigorous descriptions and with figurative language. A good deal of this sort of craft makes manifest the close, mysterious, and essential association between the land and the sea, specifically between mankind and the sea.

In organizing the sea vocabulary into both syntactic and semantic categories and in analyzing Melville's linguistic performance within those categories, this study reveals progressively more frequent and progressively more conscious and imaginative use of the sea vocabulary from the first through the sixth novel, with the exception that <u>Mardi</u> (the third novel) frequently vies with <u>Moby-Dick</u> in intricacy and beauty. There are, of course, similarities in content as well between these two works, which may bear on the similarities in language: they both involve a purposeful and singular voyage by sea which is a hunt after an object (a beloved woman in the first case, a hated whale in the second); the hunt is adventuresome and fraught with people who seem "evil" (Hautia and the flower maidens, Fedallah and his tiger-yellow crew); and of all the sea novels, <u>Mardi</u> and <u>Moby-Dick</u> were the books that Melville felt the most compelled to write and with which he was most satisfied.

Melville in his sea novels becomes increasingly aware of the power of the word. There is, generally, an increasing frequency, from sea novel to sea novel, of those words identifying the sea itself and a general decline of those words naming the geographical environment of the sea, the junctures of the sea with the land. Melville uses many terms for the nonhuman animate and inanimate items that interact with the sea (flora and fauna, weather, sea craft and their parts), depicting an environment teeming with life and energy. The terms referring to roles that man assumes when interacting with the sea generally increase from the first sea novel to the last; man seems to take an increasingly active and various role in his dealings with the sea.

Compiled as a research tool, this study offers in Chapter 1 an overview of the 345 nautical words that Melville uses, discussing their etymologies, their references, their figurative uses, and their compounds. The chapter also classifies and examines the words in terms of four semantic groups. Chapter 2 considers the words as parts of speech and analyzes their emergence, progression, and adaptability from sea novel to sea novel. Chapter 3, in describing the words in their contexts, explores one noun from each semantic group in light of the sentences in the sea novels where it appears. It then concentrates on one chapter from each of the sea novels, describing the syntactic and semantic

activities of a particular sea term within it. Finally, the word "sea"
is examined for patterns of frequency and complexity of function
throughout the sea novel canon.

The final chapter of the study presents a glossed concordance of
Melville's sea vocabulary words, giving definitions culled from
dictionaries compiled by nineteenth-century seamen, identifying parts of
speech, and listing a short contextual phrase for every appearance of
each word. The five appendices that follow the concordance contain
semantic and syntactic classifications of the words, their compounds,
their figurative use, and the sets of sentences referred to in Chapter 3.
The bibliography is a compilation of sources directly cited in the text
that illuminate Melville's use of language as well as sources more
biographical that illuminate Melville's sea adventures, his publications,
or his milieu.

MELVILLE
SEA DICTIONARY

1
The Words
of the
Sea Vocabulary

And what did you know, you bumpkin! Before you came on board the
Andrew Miller? What knew you of gun-deck, or orlop, or mustering
round the capstan, beating to quarters, and piping to dinner? Did
you ever roll to grog on board your greasy ballyhoo of blazes? Did
you ever winter at Mahon? Did you ever "lash and carry?" Why, what
are even a merchant-seaman's sorry yarns of voyages to China after
tea-caddies, and voyages to the West Indies after sugar puncheons,
and voyages to the Shetlands after seal-skins--what are even these
yarns, you Tubbs, you! to high life in a man-of-war?
                                                    --White-Jacket

Method of Analysis

Studying each of the six sea novels in the order of their composition,
I derived a sea lexicon of 345 words. Since there exist no manuscripts
for any of the sea novels, I used the most authoritative texts to date--
Northwestern Newberry editions for Typee (1968), Omoo (1968), Mardi
(1970), Redburn (1969), and White-Jacket (1970), and since Moby-Dick will
not appear in that series for several years, the Hayford-Parker edition
of that novel (1967), on which the forthcoming Northwestern Newberry
edition will be based.

The vocabulary was not one that I had formulated before coming to the
works, but one that arose out of my perusal of the texts themselves. As
new words appeared from book to book, they were added to my list. I tried
not to be arbitrary about what constituted "sea vocabulary," but included
all words that signaled sea in their definitions or in their associations.
I was particular about omitting words like "river," "pond," and "glacier"
(although "stream" was included when the reference meant ocean stream,
and "liquid" was included on the basis of its appearance in Mardi in the
phrase liquid sphere, in which context the term clearly denotes the
ocean). I ignored the proper names of navigators and historians that I

came across because they seem to tell us more about Melville's reading than about Melville's experiences with the phenomena of the sea. But mythological and scientific terms (for example, of sea gods or of species of sea life)--and there are fewer of both kinds in Melville's writings than one might expect--were included, since Melville may have come upon such terms in conversing with his shipmates.

Each word was noted on one five-by-eight card, or on more than one-- <u>sea</u>, for example, running to fifty-eight cards. I thus recorded all occurrences of each term, novel by novel, giving the page number of the occurrence, certain grammatical data (number and part of speech for the nouns, tense for the verbs), and enough of each word's context to preserve the word's grammatical and semantic environment, usually five to ten words, though some words occur in sentences of only two or three words--for example, "A sea-toss?" in <u>Mardi</u>, p. 44, and "The rigging lived." in <u>Moby-Dick</u>, p. 455--in which case the entries give no additional context.

Characteristics of the Words

Etymology

In seeking etymologies for the sea vocabulary, I consulted, first, Webster's 1828 <u>American Dictionary of the English Language</u>, since Melville had access to that volume. If a word was not listed there, or if no derivation was given (and this was the case for approximately fifty of the terms), I then consulted <u>Webster's Third New International Dictionary</u>, <u>The Oxford Dictionary of the English Language</u>, the <u>Oxford English Dictionary</u> (OED), or the <u>American Heritage Dictionary</u>. I found that, etymologically, Melville's sea vocabulary was a mixed lot. Nearly two-thirds of the terms proved to be derivatives of Old English or of Latin-- and of that fraction, half were Old English and half were Latin. And there is a small group of words that claims heritage from both sources-- <u>cat-head</u>, <u>dock</u>, <u>ferry</u>, <u>fin</u>, <u>fish</u>, <u>foam</u>, <u>gangway</u>. Approximately fifty terms were of Middle English origin, which comprised the third largest etymological group. There were frequent occurrences of words of Scandinavian, French, Spanish, and Portuguese derivations, and far less frequently Russian, Greek, Irish, Cornish, Dutch, and Icelandic words. The most exotic words, in terms of derivation, were <u>atoll</u> (Maldive), <u>catamaran</u> (Tamil), <u>dinghy</u> (Hindi), <u>proa</u> and <u>prow</u> (Malay), and <u>terrapin</u> (Algonquin). For three of the words--<u>gale</u>, <u>shark</u>, and <u>squid</u>--derivation was not given in four of the dictionaries, and the <u>OED</u> characterized the origin as "obscure" or "uncertain." <u>Gurry</u> and <u>schooner</u> originated in the United States, and several other words--<u>bob-stays</u>, <u>gam</u>, <u>jib</u>, <u>kentledge</u>, <u>lugger</u>, <u>spanker</u>, and <u>yaw</u>--were described etymologically only as "nautical." None of the dictionaries cited either <u>boneeta</u> or <u>try-works</u>, and the origin of <u>skrimshander</u> was not given.

One interesting etymology of the sea vocabulary is <u>specksynder</u>. The spelling (and the sea novels are not fastidious about this) is Melville's,[1] and it is not included in that form in any of the dictionaries. But "specksioneer" does occur, both in <u>Funk and Wagnalls</u> and in the <u>OED</u>, where it is described as having Dutch origin. In whaling, the word named the

chief harpooner, the man in charge of "flensing" or stripping the
blubber off the whale, and it is an important word for Melville in
Moby-Dick, since he used it as the title of his thirty-third chapter and
took some time to ponder over it lexically on page twenty-eight
("Literally this word means Fat-Cutter") and was bold enough to call
"specksioneer" the "corrupted" title of specksynder. Melville's spelling
reflected an Old English etymology that would derive "-synder" from
syndrian or sundrian, "to cut apart." The Melvillian etymology reflects
that mixing of experience (it is more probable that Melville heard the
word than that he ever saw it in print) with bookishness ("-synder" is
Old English) which characterizes Melville's creativity.

Sailor Jargon

The vocabulary that Melville uses is a colorful one, drawn from many
nations and peoples whose lives were, as his was, caught up in the sea.
Whaling terminology, the vocabulary of sailors, is exclusive territory,
beyond the comprehension of landsmen. Yet Melville does not flaunt this
privileged language. Directions for adjusting sails or steering ships
are generally confined to dialogue, and what words Melville does use of
this nature are not, generally, beyond the grasp of the landsman, for, as
White Jacket muses, "the men who talk the most sea lingo are the least
sailor-like in reality" (p. 308), and Melville is a thorough sailor.

Melville uses both the arcane words and the more common sea terms
with equal alacrity, and his vocabulary, given the context in which he
uses it, neither confounds the reader nor condescends to him. Rather, he
seems ever conscious of his (or of his narrator's) position within an
exclusive realm of experience not shared by all of his readers, for
phrases such as "according to sea usages" (Omoo, p. 71), "so called by
sailors" (Mardi, p. 40), or "this was an old man-of-war's phrase" (White-
Jacket, p. 91) are common throughout the sea novels. White-Jacket, in
fact, may be read as an instruction manual for getting along on a man-of-
war--there are chapters entitled "Publishing Poetry in a Man-of-War,"
"Wash-day, and House Cleaning in a Man-of-war," and "How they Bury a Man-
of-War's-man at Sea." And Moby-Dick includes explicit, epic-like
directions for harpooning a whale and disposing most efficiently of its
carcass.

Definition and Reference

Lexically, as well as etymologically, there is an interesting
diversity among the words of Melville's sea vocabulary. There are common
words with straightforward meanings (dock, coral, frog), common words
that may be used in a nautical way but also exist with independent
meanings in the vocabulary of landsmen (boom, shroud, canvas), words that
have two independent sea meanings (brig, shoal, reef), terminology
specifically and exclusively of the sea (cat-head, bob-stays, kentledge),
and scientific words with very specific meanings (chondropterygii,
glyptolepis, pterichthys). Melville was aware that he was not writing a
scientific treatise; yet, while he was conscious of appealing to an
audience broader than sailors or scientists, that audience contained the
learned as well as the ignorant.

And there are other classes of words whose groupings are less defined.
Melville uses a vocabulary that carries poetic connotations (billows,
abyss, brine), mythologic (Neptune, Torf-Egill), and exotic (Caribbean,
Polynesia). All such words are evocative, contrasting with the very
literal references by sailors to their work and tools.

Overwhelmingly, all of Melville's sea words have reference to
phenomena or to constructs of the physical world. The waters of the
Atlantic and, more important, of the Pacific (both of which Melville
traversed), the craft in which he journeyed, the tools and the men of his
trade--all exist in his pages. Melville began with experience (the sea)
and out of that emerged the symbol. Melville did not intend any sea term
that he uses to stand for anything else; its face value was its intent
and meaning. He told Sophia Hawthorne (in a letter dated January 8,
1852) that he did not before the fact design those parcels of "allegories"
commonly attributed to his books (specifically to Moby-Dick). Symbol was
a possibility; reference to his sea experience was the reality.

> I had some vague idea while writing it [Moby-Dick], that the
> whole book was susceptible of an allegoric construction, &
> also that parts of it were--but the speciality of many of the
> particular subordinate allegories, were first revealed to me,
> after reading Mr Hawthorne's letter, which, without citing
> any particular examples, yet intimated the part-&-parcel
> allegoricalness of the whole.[2]

Moreover, since life for Melville, for an important time was the sea,
to his mind and purpose it was as natural to infuse sea properties and
descriptions into land objects as it was to describe sea objects in terms
of land (or, at least, of nonsea) attributes. The two realities became
merged in Melville's mind. Syntactically this led to compounding, one of
Melville's favorite grammatical techniques (see below), and semantically
it led to figurative language.

Description by Simile and Metaphor

In Melville's sea novel canon, I found slightly more than fifty
instances where Melville referred to a land object in terms of the sea,
and nearly sixty instances where a sea object was given land terminology
or comparison, the majority in both cases appearing in Moby-Dick (see
Appendix D). There were no occurrences in Typee of either phenomenon,
only two in Omoo of land objects ascribed sea names, and none in that
novel of sea objects given land terminology. Of the remaining three
novels, White-Jacket had the second highest frequency of sea objects
given nonsea terms, and Mardi the second highest frequency of land
objects described in sea terms.

When Melville used sea vocabulary for objects that were not directly
a part of the sea, both the terms and the constructions that he used are
of interest. Places are thus described in Moby-Dick: Nantucket is "more
lonely than the Eddystone lighthouse," Spain is a "great whale stranded
on the shores of Europe," and a Spanish land breeze can "turn . . .
sailor" and go to sea. Sailors (even apprentice sailors, like
Wellingborough Redburn) describe and direct with nautical diction,
placing things verbally under the "lee" of a rock or a warehouse,
indicating a warehouse that is "on our starboard." Buildings or rooms
are so handled: the Spouter Inn has walls like "bulwarks" and a small
room that is "cold as a clam"; pews are called "hatches" and a pulpit is
both a "mast-head" and the "world's prow." More cosmically, the
commonwealth is a "Leviathan"; stars of the Milky Way are "white
breakers"; the sky and air can be "vast out-bellying sails." In Mardi
thought breaks over Taji like "billows," recollections like "foam."
Very often, sounds are given nautical characteristics. In Redburn
organ notes resemble "oars" in bubbling brooks, or "spray" dashed in the
face, while hornpipe music in Moby-Dick is "a sharp but a noiseless

squall." Yoomy's verses come bubbling out "like water" (Mardi), dancing
is worse than "pulling after whales in a calm" (Moby-Dick). Harmony can
come in a "flood-tide" in Redburn. ("Scented reminiscences" also come
that way in White-Jacket, as do "fragrances" in Mardi--and wine is at
once "flood-tide" and "soul-tide" in Mardi and a "purple tide" in White-
Jacket.) Sound, in fact, is "a liquid sea" (Redburn). Mosquitoes can
eddy (Omoo) and rumors can be set afloat (White-Jacket); a railway is a
leviathan (Moby-Dick), and Perth's sparks fly in his "wake" (Moby-Dick).
    Finally, the earth is a frigate (Moby-Dick) the world is a "ship on
its passage out" (Moby-Dick). Life has seas (Moby-Dick) or an ocean
(Redburn), is "an unsounded ocean" (Moby-Dick), and God has "inscrutable
tides" (Moby-Dick). The following passage from White-Jacket is perhaps
the best analogy of this sort:
    We mortals are all on board a fast-sailing, never-sinking
    world-frigate, of which God was the shipwright; and she is
    but one craft in a Milky-Way fleet, of which God is the Lord
    High Admiral. . . . And believe not the hypochondriac dwellers
    below hatches, who will tell you, with a sneer, that our
    world-frigate is bound to no final harbor whatever; that our
    voyage will prove an endless circumnavigation of space (p. 398).
    Ships, marine life, and the sea are the three most common categories
of nautical entities given descriptions or comparisons in land terms. In
all three categories the range of description is amazingly broad (see
Appendix D). The black hull of the Neversink butts the white sea like
"a ram" (White-Jacket). A three-decker is a city (White-Jacket),
merchant ships are "extension bridges" (Moby-Dick), a man-of-war is a
city, a town, a house, a theatre (White-Jacket), and a frigate is a
"black world" (White-Jacket). And a ship in general is described in
White-Jacket as "a bit of terra firma," a great city, a heart of oak, a
vast wash-tub--and a "Gomorrah . . . of the deep." In Moby-Dick parts of
a ship are exotically characterized--mast-heads are like the "tops of
tall palms," while masts buckle "like Indian canes," poise like "three
Horatii on a steed," or stand "stiff as spines of old kings of Cologne,"
the path of a ship resembling "the furrow of a cannon-ball."
    Sharks are "vultures" in Moby-Dick and appear as "a spirit in the
water" in Mardi. All manner of animate and inanimate objects characterize
the whale, and not surprisingly they all occur in Moby-Dick. Various
species of whales are grouped by size and compared to folio, octavo, and
duodecimo volumes. The whale is a phantom, a "snow hill." Pods of whales
are "horses in a ring." A whale can be kitten-like, playing on an ocean
as if it were a hearth. And even in the teeth of disaster, playful feline
imagery prevails--on the first day of the chase, the white whale shakes
Ahab's boat in his jaws as a cat would a mouse.
    But most of the land terms, even in Moby-Dick, are channeled into
descriptions of the sea. In Moby-Dick, the sea is smooth as "gold-beater's
skin"; waves roll "like scrolls of silver" or blush like wine, and in
Mardi every wave-crest is "a flame." Waves are "fullers" which bleach
sea craft white as "walrus skeletons" (Moby-Dick). The sea is like a
"harvest plain" (Mardi), a "watery prairie" (Redburn), a carpet and a
meadow (Moby-Dick). A squall is "a white fire" upon a prairie (Moby-Dick).
But far more often the sea is invested with animate--more specifically,
with animal--characteristics. In terms of metaphor, sea is an even more
important concept for Melville than whale. It certainly is described
more vividly. There is a playful description of the sea--waves are like
"hearth-stone cats" (Moby-Dick), and a comic one--the sea is a "huge
cheese with maggots [sharks] in it" (Moby-Dick). In three novels, the

sea is given equestrian imagery: it neighs and snorts in Redburn, it paws
white hoofs in White-Jacket, and in Moby-Dick it is a battle steed, torn
and enraged waves forming Moby Dick's "mane." Mardi has one brutal image
of the sea, where waters clash like lions, but Moby-Dick has many more:
the ocean is a tiger, the sea is a "savage tigress," waves curl and hiss
like "enraged serpents." And as the beginning and ending of Melville's
experience as a sailor, as the overwielding and omnipresent cause and
effect of experiences of all of the sailors in his novels, the sea is
"the stable of brute monsters," and it is "the true Tophet" (White-Jacket).

Occurring less frequently than either of these two types of
description, but also important when assessing how Melville's sea
experiences formed the foundation of his writing, are Melville's
metaphors, similes, or allusions that equate sea things with other sea
things (see Appendix D). Sailing craft of various sorts, or parts
thereof, and marine life, whales specifically, are most often described
in this way. Moby-Dick contains the vast majority of such constructions,
although Redburn does describe a Liverpool dock as an archipelago, a ship
as an island, and says that sea grass was fastened to the planks of the
Highlander like leeches. The Highlander is also said to rise like a vast
buoy, but almost exclusively all the remaining references to craft are in
terms of animate sea life. In Moby-Dick, for instance, sails are compared
to feathers of an albatross, the boom to the lower jaw of the whale.
Whale boats (and this is the only occurrence in Omoo of a sea object so
described, and there are no descriptions of this sort in Typee) are
tortoises on the beach; Mardi describes both fleets of canoes and Ziani's
feluccas as "frightened water-fowl" and a shallop as a "gull over a smooth
lagoon." In Moby-Dick, a boat flies through the water like "a shark all
fins."

Interestingly enough, almost all the references to fish or to whales
are given in terms of inanimate craft. A porpoise has a stem and a stern,
and a fish is "a floating island" (Moby-Dick). A whale is said to have a
"fore" part as well as a "fathom-deep life"; his jaw is compared to the
jib-boom of a ship (two hundred pages after the reverse comparison was
made, in Moby-Dick), and his intestines to "the great cables and hausers"
in the orlop deck of a line-of-battle ship (Moby-Dick). A whale is as
big as a ship in Redburn; a whale afloat in Moby-Dick is a launched line-
of-battle ship or a waterlogged, dismantled ship.

Descriptions of the sea itself in metaphor or simile are more elusive,
and all appear in Moby-Dick. Waves on the whale's flank are like "surf
on a beach"; a swell at the whale's muzzle is dashed as a swell "where
two hostile currents meet." Finally, in the closing sentence of the book,
the sea is "a great shroud . . . [which] rolls on as it rolled five
thousand years ago."

Personification and Nautical Imposition

Two other categories of verbal manipulation give further clues about
Melville's relationship with the sea. One is the way in which he
personified the sea, fish, and ships, a phenomenon which does not occur
at all in Typee and Omoo, very seldom in Mardi, Redburn, and White-Jacket,
and only twenty times in Moby-Dick. The other is the reverse of this,
Melville's practice of describing men in terms of the sea (see Appendix D).
The isles of Polynesia can confess a truth and a whale can toss himself
"sailor-like" to heaven (Moby-Dick). Mastheads are "tufted with arms and
legs" (Moby-Dick), rigging can "live" (Moby-Dick) and paddles "play"
(Redburn), and a frigate has "bones," which can break (White-Jacket).

The ocean, too, has bones (<u>Moby-Dick</u>)--it is both "maternal" and "robust and man-like," heaving "with long, strong, lingering swells, as Samson's chest in his sleep" (<u>Moby-Dick</u>). The "masculine" sea thinks "murderous" thoughts.

As well as partaking of both sexes, the sea to Melville displays both positive and negative emotions. Foam plays in <u>Mardi</u>; the sea is magnanimous in <u>Moby-Dick</u> and "blue, boundless, dimpled, laughing, sunny" in <u>White-Jacket</u>; the "hand-clappings" of the waves in <u>Moby-Dick</u> are "suspended by exceeding rapture." But beneath the flippant "such a funny, sporty, gamy, jesty, joky, hoky-poky lad, is the ocean, oh!" is the "black" face of the ocean (<u>White-Jacket</u>), the sea's "mad gales of passions" (<u>Mardi</u>), and billows that are "baffled," "envious," and "panther-like" (<u>Moby-Dick</u>). The sea "rebels," and "sea-stirrings seem to speak of some hidden awful soul beneath" (<u>Moby-Dick</u>); but "the black sea heaved as if its vast tides were a conscience; and the great mundane soul were in anguish and remorse for the long sin and suffering it had bred" (<u>Moby-Dick</u>).

Descriptions of men in sea terms, what I will call "nautical imposition," are nearly three times as frequent as personification of the sea and its inhabitants (see Appendix D). All of the sea novels use this construction at least once, with over one-half of the occurrences appearing in <u>Moby-Dick</u>. What is interesting is that there is a gradual progression in terms of frequency of this construction from novel to novel: I counted only one instance of it in <u>Typee</u> and nearly fifty in <u>Moby-Dick</u>, with the numbers gradually increasing from the earliest to the latest sea novel.

Such "nautical imposition" is of three sorts. It is, first of all, used to describe either the appearance or the behavior of specific crew members. Mad Jack has muscles like ship's shrouds, a chest like a bulkhead, and a nose like a keel (<u>White-Jacket</u>). Uhia's voice is "sonorous as a conch," his arm strong as the backbone of a shark (<u>Mardi</u>). Jack Blunt in <u>Redburn</u> looks like "a fat porpoise, standing on end. He had a round face, too, like a walrus." Ishmael clings to Queequeg, at the beginning of <u>Moby-Dick</u>, "like a barnacle." Stubb is "fish-like" and "gay as a frigate's pennant"; Starbuck is like "a patient chronometer, his interior vitality . . . warranted to do well in all climates." And Ahab resembles both his "dismasted craft" and "a mute and maned sea-lion," although he is the Lord "and keel" of the <u>Pequod</u>; his brow is gaunt and ribbed, like the black sand beach after some stormy tide has been gnawing it. He describes himself as a dying whale, his final jets being the "strongest and fullest of trouble."

Secondly--and this category overlaps to some extent with the first-- such description can be more a matter of the narrator's natural turn of phrase than a characteristic of the person he is describing. For example, in <u>Redburn</u>, sailors "come to anchor" before a bar. Members of the band aboard the <u>Neversink</u> play once in a while "to stir the stagnant current in our poor old Commodore's torpid veins." The mess cook tells the crew to "sail away" from the galley, and the Master-at-arms tells Leggs to "top your boom and sail large." In <u>Moby-Dick</u> Ishmael "sounds" his pockets with "anxious grapnels." And the same novel calls men and women "silent islands" and records an incident about a gentleman harpooning a lady and then "re-harpooning" her. The crew sets all their "sterns" on the gunwhale to eat, and Queequeg taps the "stern" of a young sailor who mimics him.

A third category consists of proverbs or aphorisms in which some truth or remonstrance about life is told with sea terminology. In <u>White-Jacket</u>, every man-of-war's-man is said to roll around the world like a

billow; men have ribbed chests, like the ribbed bows of a frigate, to act
as bulkheads to dam off an onset. In Mardi Taji speculates, "Like
helmless vessels, tempest-tossed, our only anchorage is when we founder."
In Moby-Dick, sailors are like "rootless seaweed," people are like oysters
"observing the sun through water," all men are "enveloped in whale-lines,"
and furthermore, they are turned round and round in this world like a
windlass, with Fate as the handspike. Ishmael urges his readers to
retain, like a great whale, a consistent temperature in all seasons, to
live in the world without being of it. Two hundred pages earlier,
temperance had been the theme of Father Mapple's sermon as well: ". . .
top gallant delight is to him . . . whom all the waves of the billows of
the seas of the boisterous mob can never shake from this sure Keel of the
Ages" (p. 51).
    Melville's interplay between man and the sea, between realities of
the land and those of the sea, proves an important point beyond what
lexical definitions and etymological analysis can come to. The sea is
not a force separate from human life for Melville but is inextricably
linked with it, the sea sporting traits of humanity as readily as
humanity accrues traits of the sea. In 1903 William P. Trent was
criticizing Moby-Dick for certain flaws, but in spite of them, remarked
that "the breath of the sea is in it."[3]

Classification of the Vocabulary

    The body of Melville's sea vocabulary is large and assorted but may
be given form and pattern in two ways--semantically and syntactically.
Syntactically, we can use the traditional form classes--noun, verb,
adjective, and adverb--to categorize the sea vocabulary (see Chapter 3).
This method would seem simple and direct, although it is not entirely
discrete. One sea term, for example, may appear in two or even three
form classes.
    Additionally, classification of another sort may be used to provide
other insights into Melville's sea vocabulary. This system is "semantic"
in that it uses meaning to catalog the terms, but consequently the
classifications emerge more subjective and tenuous. The major semantic
clusters that emerge from studying Melville's sea vocabulary involve the
sea itself, its geographical environment, the nonhuman animate and
inanimate items that associate with it (flora and fauna, meteorology, the
craft and its parts), and the human roles man assumes when interacting
with the sea. There is overlap here, too--the same word may, in various
passages in the sea novels, participate in several semantic classes,
though such overlap is less frequent than that in the syntactic system.

Primary Sea Terms (1)

    What I will call the primary sea terms, and there are forty of them,
signal the sea itself. These words are lexically closest to the sea and
either rename it as a whole or refer to parts or manifestations of it,
either directly or obliquely. Seas are properly named by the words
Atlantic, Pacific, or Caribbean. Common nouns for the whole are the

deep, deluge, flood, and ocean, and less directly, abyss. Words
referring to parts of the sea are breaker, brine, bubble, crest, current,
eddy, foam, ripple, scud, spray, stream, surf, swell, tide, trough, wake,
and wave. References to qualities or manifestations of the sea are made
by aquatic, depth, fathom, fluid, liquid, marine, maritime, nautical, and
simply water. Billows, vortex, maelstrom, and whirlpool have the
additional property of being poetic. Many of these terms are used
figuratively: they may appear in metonymy, simile, metaphor, apostrophe,
enthymeme, and thus can be symbols as well as purely referential terms.

Throughout the composition of his novels, Melville used the primary
sea terms with increasing frequency. Almost consistently, these terms
occur most often in Moby-Dick, and if there is a novel in which one does
not appear, that novel will usually by Typee, Omoo, or Redburn. In Mardi
we see the only exception to this pattern of increasing frequency, for
Mardi is second only to Moby-Dick in its wealth of the primary sea terms.

Secondary Sea Terms (2)

There are slightly fewer secondary sea terms (twenty-seven) than
primary sea terms in Melville's sea novels. These secondary sea terms
refer to geographical associations of land and sea, either by naming a
juncture of the two or by describing some protuberance of the land into
the sea or of the sea into the land. Sea and land join in the references
of beach, coast, cove, delta, harbor, port, shore, and strand; and land
or sea geographically intrude into each other in archipelago, atoll, bay,
cape, gulf, inlet, island and isle, isthmus, lagoon, peninsula, quay,
reef, sand-bar, shoal, and strait. Some of these intrusions are referred
to by proper names--Gallipagos or Polynesia, for example. Ashore and
sound(-ing) also are classed with this group.

In frequency and pattern throughout the sea novels, there seems to be
a general decline in the use of this set of terms, a reversal of the
tendency noted for the previous class. For example, Omoo, Melville's
second sea novel, includes most of the occurrences of ashore, beach,
isthmus, lagoon, peninsula, and Polynesia(-n). Moby-Dick, in contrast,
leads the other sea novels only in one word--sound(-ing)--and is missing
many of the other words (for example, atoll, canal, delta, inlet, isthmus,
sand-bar). With each novel, Melville seems to have concentrated less on
the periphery of the sea, its borders and boundaries, and more on the
thing itself, the brunt of its power and force, the fullness of its
effects, its distance and difference from the land.

Tertiary Sea Terms (3A, 3B, 3C)

The tertiary sea terms compose the largest referential category to
Melville's sea vocabulary. Included here are terms naming those animate
or inanimate objects which either affect or traverse the sea. These can
be divided into three subgroups. The first (3A) includes terms naming
animate but nonhuman life that exists within or around the sea, and
consists of eighty-nine terms. This group names not only different
varieties of fish (for example, alewives, mollymeaux, silver-heads) and
other forms of sea life (barnacle, coral, leech) but parts of these
(baleen, fin, gill), products thereof (blubber, spermaceti, nippers), and
activities thereof (blow, spout, roll). Among these terms are those of
scientific nomenclature (Xiphius Platypterus, chondropterygii, glyptolepis)
and obsolete terms (ork, kraken).

Melville uses this plethora of terms, I believe, to suggest that the
sea is a very vital and energetic place, teeming with life and activity,
and that it has been such since the beginning of time. It is interesting
to note that none of these words (with the exception of whale) is used
with much frequency (half a dozen or fewer occurrences per novel is the
average), but there are nearly three times as many different words
denoting sea life as there are words referring to the sea itself. What
is also interesting is the distribution of these terms, which follows a
pattern quite different from that of either the primary or the secondary
sea terms. That is, rather than a progression, there is a concentration:
most of these words occur in either Mardi or Moby-Dick exclusively, in
both of those novels exclusively, or in both of those novels and in some
combination of the other novels. Mardi is the only novel where, for
example, cockles, crocodile, and leech occur; Moby-Dick is the only novel
where cod, ork, and sprat occur; ambergris, kelp, nautilus, and other of
the terms occur in both of those novels and none of the others.
The second class of the tertiary sea terms (3B) consists of only six
members and names those inanimate meteorological forces affecting the sea:
calm, gale, sou'-wester, squall, tempest, and trade (winds). Moby-Dick
includes all these terms except the last one (which appears in Mardi and
Omoo) and includes as well the majority of the references of the other
six terms, especially those of tempest. Gale appears most frequently in
White-Jacket, and both White-Jacket and Moby-Dick have the majority of
occurrences of calm and squall.
The final class of the tertiary sea terms (3C) has members that are
both inanimate and nonhuman, naming the craft that traverse the sea,
parts of such craft, objects aboard such craft that are used exclusively
at sea, actions of such craft, and direction words specifying position in
relation to such craft. This class of words is the richest, containing
the largest number of items of the sea vocabulary--nearly twice that of
the second largest category. In the six novels there are nearly fifty
different words for various kinds of ships and boats alone. What is more,
Melville seems to use, from novel to novel, an increasing number of
different terms to name his craft. And he includes all manner of craft,
from the very common (ship, boat, canoe) to the outmoded (ark, galleon)
and exotic (felucca, junk, proa); those craft that are equipped for war
(corvette, frigate, man-of-war), for trade (drogher, merchantman, packet),
and for pleasure (yacht). And names for collections of craft are used--
fleet, flotilla, navy. Actions or stance of the craft (adrift, afloat,
anchor, cruise, dive, dock, drift, drown, float, gam, heave to, launch,
moor, passage, pitch, roll, row, sheer, sound, stave, tack, voyage, yaw)
are not exceptional, except that they include members of a variety of
form classes--nouns, verbs, and adjectives. Parts of the craft and/or
objects on board account for half of the members of this class and abound
with specific terms for decks (for example, orlop), ropes (brail), sails
(spanker), masts (sampson-post), and other equipment. Besides directions
(windward, larboard, astern) and measurements (fathom, offing, knot), the
other terms included in this group are for four objects that are not craft
but which are inanimate constructs that have the sea as their environment--
buoy, pier, lighthouse, and wharf.

Quaternary Sea Terms (4)

The quaternary sea terms, a class that numbers almost exactly as many
members as the first class of sea terms, names or characterizes the human
roles that man assumes when relating to the sea. White-Jacket and Moby-

Dick are the novels where most of these terms occur, and Typee includes
the least. All manner of men are named, from criminals of the sea--
buc(c)anier, corsair, mutineer, pirate, privateer to gods--Neptune, Torf-
Egill. And many ranks of seamen abound--land-lubber, sailor, mariner,
mate, salt, tar, merchantman, harpooner, skrimshander, steersman, skipper,
captain. There are mermaids, mermen, and castaways to complete Melville's
world. Also of note are the many additional human roles that Melville
concocts by compounding (for example, sea-monarch, sea-dog, sea-Socrates),
discussed below.

The sea words, then, are Melville's "verbal palette,"[4] his experience
that becomes the hallmark of his language. No one novel is consistently
richer in images or words of the sea than the others, but different sets
of sea terms appear uniquely in each of the books and to different
advantage. It is an intense and special vocabulary, a creation out of
which Melville further creates. Citing these words suggests how
intimately and infinitely expressive they may be. But the difficult
things that Melville had to say with this characteristic set of words he
said by using their literal meanings and by plumbing their syntactic and
semantic depths. He combined and invented words, he "foregrounded" words
and attached affixes to them, so that his sea vocabulary emerged as
unconformable to conventional standards, but remained at its roots very
basic.

Compounding

Nautical life is one of naming: naming the many types of craft, the
complex minutiae of a ship, its many special activities and maneuvers,
and naming all the novelties that are experienced aboard. And there are
times when such naming becomes one of combining terms that are already at
hand, of compounding. As even a rapid perusal of Gershom Bradford's The
Mariner's Dictionary[5] or the glossary of Austin Knight's Modern Seamanship[6]
will testify, nautical language is even recently one of many compounds.

Compounding is one of Melville's favorite grammatical manipulations.
He conceives of a world of associations. These associations--some logical,
others not immediately so--occur with surprising aplomb and are the naming
words of new experience. When Melville is not satisfied that the
expression or character of a single term would adequately do, he uses two,
infusing the connotations from two joined entities into the minds of his
readers, making a new reality (or set of associations) from two existing
ones. In punctuating this new reality he is indiscriminate. At times he
will name a concept with a hyphenated compound; at other times (even in
the same novel) he will use the same terms in a solid compound, or
completely separate the terms so that they appear as two form classes
(for example, adjective and noun) rather than one. Though there are
irregularities, the two terms that Melville compounds are generally
joined by a hyphen, and although again there are exceptions, the compounds
that Melville forms overwhelmingly are composed of and function as nouns.

All the sea novels show compounding, but not to the same extent or
advantage (see Appendix C). Furthermore, Melville in an important respect
sets up a different compound vocabulary for each of the sea novels, since

a large number of the compound words are novel-specific, appearing in
only one of the sea novels. Finally, comparing Melville's compounding
practices with those of both turn-of-the-century grammarians and more
modern linguists yields some insights into Melville's characteristic
compounding habits. Melville's compounding appears to fit no pattern
exactly; it eludes classification by school or decade. If it abides by
many prescribed rules, it also breaks many, and what evolves for any
given contextual instance of compounding is usually Melville's (or his
printer's) whim, rather than conscious obedience to a linguistic code.

Progression in the Novels

     In Typee (abbreviated T in following references) there are fifty
different sea words that are compounds. Nearly 40 percent of these
appear exclusively in that novel. Typee includes the fewest compounds
constructed of the primary sea terms of any of the sea novels--only nine
different compounds in the book use sea and only three use water. Unique
to the book are certain compounds of coral, fish, shell, canoe, and oar.
     In Omoo (abbreviated O), the number of compounds based on sea-word
roots more than doubles, and so does the number of compounds exclusive to
that novel. Omoo seems grammatically more experimental and imaginative
than Typee, even though the books have a continuous narrative line and
are generally taken to be companion pieces. In Omoo there is a slight
increase in compounds having more than two terms and compounds using
water, a doubling of the number of compounds of sea, an increase in the
compounds using the secondary sea terms, and a continuance of the trend
to use novel-specific terms involving fish and canoe.
     In Mardi (abbreviated M), the third sea novel, there are twice as
many different sea compounds as in Omoo, and the percentage of that
number which appears exclusively in Mardi is 66 percent, the largest
proportion of novel-specific compounds in all of the sea novels. Mardi
is one of the two sea novels (White-Jacket is the other) that use the
greatest number and variety of sea compounds (nearly fifty). More
nautical flora and fauna appear in the compounds (for example, sea-moss,
frigate-birds, sea-snakes), many of them novel-specific. There are
several proper nouns as well (Fidus-Achates-ship, Froth-of-the-Sea), and
some common nouns whimsically capitalized (Paddle-Song, Fish-ponds).
Nearly a dozen different compounds include -fish and almost as many
involve water-, so the compounding vocabulary of Mardi is very active
indeed.
     Redburn (abbreviated R) contains roughly forty fewer sea compounds
than Mardi and half of those occur only in Redburn. Redburn has perhaps
a dozen fewer compounds of sea than Mardi does but roughly as many as
Moby-Dick. The book, a tale of Melville's apprenticeship, includes in
its sea compounds much sailor jargon and nautical lingo, a few anomalies
(sea compounds with clowns, ocean with elephants), and the longest
compounds in the sea novels, two of them running to six terms each
(larboard-fore-top-sail-clew-line and starboard-main-top-gallant-bow-line).
     White-Jacket (abbreviated WJ) can boast the largest number of sea
compounds, 60 percent of which are unique to that novel. In White-Jacket,
the sea, the craft that sail it, and the men that man the craft are
subjects of most of the compounds, and among them are such novelties as
sail-proud, frigate-executives, and sea-dandies.
     Moby-Dick (abbreviated MD) has more conservative compounding--there
are no untoward capitalizations, few fanciful compounds, only two
hyphenated titles, and only one compound place-name; but for all its

subtlety, Moby-Dick has an insistent assortment of sea compounds. The word sea itself hooks up with -traditions, -pastures, -storm, and -god as easily as with -port and -coast; foam combines with -flakes and -fountains. Shark-white, ocean-wide, tide-beating, ocean-perishing, and fathom-deep are all indicative of the powerful sea compounds in the book.

Man and the Sea

Sea compounds that refer to human roles occur in all of the novels and are of the most divergent types. Only one, however, has anything to do with race--negro-sailor (R). None directly names an actual woman; the environment Melville creates in the sea novels is overwhelmingly male. Fayaway and Hautia, for example, have little importance or substance, and Aunt Charity's ginger-jub is not a serious intrusion into the masculine realm. The feminine principle does appear nominally, at least, in mermaids (in all the novels except WJ), alewives (MD), she-shark (M), and an "incomprehensible story about a sort of fairy sea-queen" (R). Except for cabin-boy (R, WJ) and sailor-boy (R), "man" is either stated or implied in the following words: boatswain (O, R, WJ), boatswain's-mate (WJ), bowsman (M), Cape-Cod-man (MD), Coast-of-Guinea-Man (R), forecastle-man (WJ), gig-men (WJ), helmsmen (T, R), mast-man (WJ), mizen-top-men (WJ), oarsmen (O, WJ, MD), after-oarsmen (MD), fellow-sailor (O, WJ), sailor-man (R), seaman (all the novels), able-seaman (R, WJ), ordinary-seaman (R), ship's-yeoman (WJ), and ship-master (MD). This is not to mention the many other roles, such as messmate (R, WJ) and horse-marine (WJ), that do not overtly designate sex. The word sea is the first term of an assortment of morphologically and vocationally diverse role compounds: sea-nymphs (WJ), sea-god (M, MD), sea-sage (M), sea-king (M, WJ, MD), sea-queen (R), sea-lord (WJ), sea-dog (M, WJ, MD), sea-tyrant (R), sea-clown (R), sea-dandies (WJ), sea-citizens (WJ), sea-fencibles (WJ), sea-warriors (WJ), sea-patriots (WJ), sea-wardens (WJ), and even sea-Socrates (WJ). (Note that Mardi even uses Shark-Syllogism!)

Melville and the Manuals

Three major typographical studies on the compounding of English words that were written during the half-century between 1891, the year of Melville's death, and 1941 all set up synthetic rules for the formation and punctuation of compounds that are interesting to compare with Melville's practices insofar as they describe the state of the language when Melville was using it. Melville follows most of the rules, but he also breaks a good many of them, and his sense of grammar seems not very closely allied with any one grammarian as it coasts on a sea all its own. Any "patterns" that become discernible in his compounding he frequently deviates from. What can be concluded is that in his prolific compounding, Melville very frequently joins some objects with others, and the combinations that result are not always predictable.

F. Horace Teall. F. Horace Teall, who based his study of compounding primarily on Webster's 1882 dictionary, lamented the "laxity"[7] of lexicographers in developing a consistent system for punctuating word pairs in English, and he noted the "curious crankiness"[8] of Richard Paul Jodrell's Philology on the English Language (1820), which was based on a premise that two words, if joined at all, should be solidified into one continuous word, generating such idiosyncracies as "camelswallower,"

"pulpitsophistry," and "tapestryhanging." Teall also noted that a more
recent dictionary, Cassell's Encyclopedic Dictionary,[9] customarily
printed as hyphenated compounds any phrases where the first term was
subordinate to the second, so that "penitential-canons" and "physical-
geography" were typical entries. A principle Teall believed to be
unimpeachable with respect to compounding was that

> The ordinary hyphened compound in English is a sort of
> transition between the phrasal form and that of the
> continuous word, and the hyphen when properly used marks
> the fact that the words joined by it are arbitrarily
> associated in literal meaning, thereby becoming a
> compound instead of a grammatically constructed phrase.[10]

And the hyphen, he asserted, was a useful punctuation because it made
"the component words visibly distinct."[11]

A convention among English writers and readers, Teall pointed out,
was to shun the use of the hyphen because "brevity . . . imparts a
certain strength and beauty to language."[12] But Teall himself believed
that "almost as frequently the reverse method is better."[13] He did,
however, voice a distaste for "needless or improper joinings" between an
adjective and a noun, a difficulty because logic conflicts with grammar,
and grammar should determine word forms.[14] Among the types of phrases
that he cited as needlessly compounded but that Melville did hyphenate
were such words as able seaman, man of war's man, salt water, and
Samson's post.

Teall set down five rules for the proper compounding of nouns,[15] all
of which Melville followed. The first stated that two nouns used
together, except in apposition, and naming one thing, are considered a
compound; one of Teall's examples, sand-bar, Melville uses in that
hyphenated form in Mardi. Rule two stated that when the second term of a
two-noun phrase "expresses direct action upon the first" and ends in
"-ing," "-er," or "-or," a compound results.[16] Melville uses this form
frequently--for example, beach-comber (O), boat-steerer (MD), and canoe-
building (O, M). Teall's third rule allowed for a verbal noun (one
ending in "-ing") and the substantive following it to be compounded, and
in the sea novels are such forms as fishing-boat (R), winding-sheets (M),
and whaling-fleet (MD).[17] The fourth fule stated that a construction is
properly considered compound when the members were so arbitrarily linked
together that, if separated, they would have no inherent significance;
Teall's examples of crow's-nest and man-of-war appear in Melville's
pages.[18] Teall's final rule was similar to the fourth, stating that two
words used in arbitrary association in a name, when they have no primary
relation to each other, constitute a compound.[19] Melville uses Teall's
example of between-decks in Redburn. Teall added a sixth rule for
compounds other than nouns, which allowed for compounding two terms when
their joint implication might be misunderstood were they left as separate
words, and cut-water (T), castaway (M, MD), and try-works (MD) are thus
permitted.[20]

Teall believed, as apparently Melville (and/or his printer) did not,
since he is inconsistent, that there were real differences between
compounds that were hyphenated and those that had a solid form. He
reasoned that both groups of words may have members that are equally
"permanent" and that may, in fact, demonstrate the same accent pattern.
So, after determining that dictionaries were consistently inconsistent on
this point, Teall formulated three rules to govern solid compounds, the
first two dealing with arbitrariness and inseparability of the joined
members, the third concerning a word used in a particular and literal

sense followed by one of a general nature. Some of the words that fit
into the final category still retain the hyphen, according to Teall
(Melville shows, for example, seal-skin--O, WJ, MD), but still others,
Teall affirmed, have dropped the hyphen (Melville's boatswain--O, R, WJ--
does this).

Teall offered over a hundred pages of what he felt to be a definitive
list of inseparable compounds; nearly seventy of these turn up in
Melville's sea novels. That is, they are in Melville's books but not
always in the form that Teall would have them take. In three of the
words on Teall's list--inlet (T), larboard and starboard (both occurring
in all of the sea novels)--I feel the two terms are so inseparable that I
would hesitate to call them "compounds" at all. Of Teall's remaining
words, nearly half appear in Melville consistently as solid words. These
are boatswain (O, R, WJ), bowline (R, M), bowman (as bowsman only, in M),
bowsprit (T, M, R, WJ, MD), breakwater (O, MD), bulkhead (T, O, M, R, WJ),
castaway (M, MD), codfish (MD), fisherman (O, MD), forecastle (all of the
novels), foresail (M), gunwhale (T, O, M, R, MD), helmsman (R)--keelman
appears in Teall, but not in Melville; oarsman appears in O, WJ, and MD,
but not in Teall), merchantman (R, WJ), midship(s) (M), seaman (all the
novels), seasickness (R), shipboard (WJ), shipmate (O, R, WJ), shipwreck
(M, WJ, R), shipyard (MD), steersman (M, R), thwartship(s) (as
athwartships only, in MD), topsail (WJ), whalebone (T, MD), and whaleman
(M).

There is a nearly equal number of words that Teall considers
inseparable compounds that consistently appear as hyphenated in Melville:
bobstay (T), bumboat (WJ), cathead (R), cutwater (T), figurehead (T, R,
WJ, MD), finback (only as Fin-back, in R and MD), fishlike (MD, where
eel-like and salmon-like also appear), foretop (O, M, R, WJ), foretopmast
(WJ), goldfish (M, WJ, MD), mainsail (M, WJ, MD), mainroyalmast (as
main-royal-mast in WJ; as main-royalmast in MD), maintop (M), maintopsail
(WJ), masthead (M, R, WJ, MD), mastman (WJ), sailboat (O, MD), sailmaker
(WJ), sailorlike (O, M, WJ, and MD, where lubber-like also occurs),
seacoast (WJ, MD), sealskin (O, WJ, MD), seashore (T, O, M), seasick (R,
MD), steerageway (WJ), topgallantmast (R), topmast (WJ), and trysail (WJ).
Names for sails appear in Teall consistently as solid forms:
foretopgallantmast, mainroyal, mainstaysail, maintopgallantmast,
maintopmast. Melville, however, consistently hyphenates such words:
fore-top-gallant-yard (M), fore-topsail (O), top-gallant-mast (R), and
main-topsail-yard (WJ, which includes a wide assortment of similar terms).

In a considerably smaller number of words that Teall records as solid
compounds, Melville's usage is inconsistent. Bargeman occurs in White-
Jacket both with and without the hyphen (bread-barge also occurs in that
novel). Foremast has a solid form in Mardi and Redburn, but a hyphenated
one in White-Jacket and Moby-Dick; and mainmast is also solid in Redburn,
but hyphenated in White-Jacket. Seaport is hyphenated in Omoo and White-
Jacket, but solid in Redburn and Moby-Dick. Both seaside (a solid word
in Moby-Dick) and shipshape (a solid word in White-Jacket) are hyphenated
in Mardi. Steamboat is a solid word in Omoo and Redburn and hyphenated
in White-Jacket. Waterfall appears as a solid word in Typee and a
hyphenated one in Typee's companion novel, Omoo. And yardarm is solid in
Omoo but hyphenated in Redburn, White-Jacket, and Moby-Dick.

So Melville appears to follow no pattern with these inconsistencies.
It would be a neat statement to say that as Melville composes the sea
novels, he uses increasingly more hyphenation in his compounds, or
increasingly less, but that would be contrary to fact.

Frederick W. Hamilton. Nearly thirty years after Teall's book was published, Frederick W. Hamilton, the educational director of the United Typothetae of America, came out with a brief study on compounding which began by stressing the constant change in the evolution of the language, emphasizing a clear progress toward eliminating the hyphen. Both Chaucer and Shakespeare, Hamilton asserted, used compound words and phrases frequently, but Shakespeare used the hyphen far less than Chaucer did.[21] Hamilton based his principles on Teall's set of rules, which was then supplemented by "more specific rules"[22] that analyzed compounds by part of speech. Hamilton gave ten ways to construct "compounds having the force of nouns,"[23] nine rules for generating adjectival compounds, four that elicit verbs, and seven that allow for adverbs.

Among the compound nouns of Melville's sea vocabulary, the most common are noun-noun combinations, although adjective-noun (for example, first-cutter--O), noun-verb (tide-rip--MD), and verb-noun (fishing-pole--T, O) compounds also appear. Adjectives that are compounds are also frequently of the noun-noun variety, although noun-verb compounds (scroll-prowed--M), adjective-noun combinations (fresh-water--M, WJ), and even a verb-adverb (go-ashore--T, a type that Hamilton does not consider) occur. Melville may, in fact, use verb combinations, although they are not specifically members of his sea vocabulary, and the only adverb compound in the sea vocabulary is oceanward (M).

The final section of Hamilton's book set forth forty-one rules for using the hyphen, twelve of which apply to Melville's sea compounds. Although the rules are consistent with Teall's, Hamilton rephrased them and added a goodly number of his own. All of the rules but one and part of another are applicable to the sea vocabulary that Melville follows, hyphenating nouns in an objective relationship to each other (for example, canoe-building--O, M), a present participle and a noun (cruising-ground--O), words denoting occupation (fish-hunter--O, compounds of "fellow" (fellow-sailor--O, WJ) and of "life" and "world" (world-frigate--WJ), compounds with numerals (three-decker--T, O, M, WJ) or including a possessive noun (crow's-nest--MD), and compounds where a noun is used as an adjective to specify color (sea-blue--M, R; sea-green--WJ). And, as Hamilton suggested, Melville omits the hyphen in compounds ending with "man" or "woman" (seaman--all the novels).

Two more of Hamilton's rules apply to the sea vocabulary. Melville does not comply with one of them--Hamilton suggested that compounds of "skin" with words of one syllable be printed as solid, but both seal-skin (O, WJ, MD) and shark-skin (M, MD) usually appear hyphenated in Melville. Melville does follow, in part, Hamilton's rule that a noun preceding "like" not take a hyphen if the noun is a monosyllable, except when it ends in "-l," but if the noun contains more than one syllable a hyphen should be used. Melville used eel-like (MD), lubber-like (MD), sailor-like (O, M, WJ, MD), and salmon-like (MD), all of which follow Hamilton in some respect--but also fish-like (MD), which violates Hamilton. Hamilton's last caution lists thirty-one "words of everyday occurrence" that should be hyphenated and do not fall under any of the above classifications, among them man-of-war.[24]

Alice Morton Ball. A lecturer on editing at George Washington University and then on the staff of the Government Printing Office and the Department of State, Alice Morton Ball published a compounding manual similar to Teall's and Hamilton's in 1941.[25] Ball's guide tied up loose ends from the previous guides. It was a terse caveat against compounding certain words and an explicit and systematic aid to joining and hyphenating

other words. It was better organized and more methodic than either
Teall's or Hamilton's works and, like Hamilton's, contained a
"comprehensive" alphabetical list of "properly compounded" words.
      In the first several pages of her text, Ball firmly recorded her
philosophy about compounding, stating that the "only legitimate" reason
for compounding was to avoid ambiguity, and the "only legitimate" reason
for using the hyphen was to give "visual intelligibility" and "temporary
expediency."[26] She followed Hamilton in surveying lexicographers, whom
she proved "conclusively" to be erratic authorities concerning
compounding.[27] Like Hamilton, she noted that the trend of the language
was toward the simplicity of the solid forms of compounds, but also
stated that current practice favored keeping words apart if the meaning
was clear without compounding. In other words, to her the hyphen in
compounds seemed a vanishing species. To Melville it was a useful and
preferred punctuation.
      Ball's comprehensive list of compounding rules began with a section
headed "Words preferably not compounded,"[28] most of which Melville breaks.
The two that he follows concern, first, a possessive noun and a preceding
numeral, which, according to Ball, should not be compounded (her example
was "two weeks' pay") unless the two words are used jointly as one part
of speech. Melville uses two ships'-lengths in Mardi, but the compound
there is functioning as the object of the preposition "within." The
other rule that Melville follows involves a gerund and a noun, when one
clearly functions as an adjective of the other. The pair is to be
compounded only if they qualify another noun, and Melville's adjective
sea-faring (O, R) does this. Ball preferred that when two nouns occur
together, one of them obviously functioning as an adjective of the other,
the pair not be compounded, as in "boy king," but Melville uses both
sailor-boy (R) and sea-king (M). And neither, says Ball, should an
adjective and the noun it modifies be compounded when they are in
juxtaposition, but we can find rose-pearl in Mardi.
      Melville does, however, follow all of Ball's rules for properly
compounded words, although three rules involving numerals do not apply to
the sea vocabulary.[29] Ball suggested, as Teall and Hamilton had, that
words be compounded, either with or without the hyphen, when the idea
they express is not properly conveyed by two separate words. This can
involve a pair of nouns when neither functions as an adjective (canoe-
building--O, M); words used together as a conventional or improvised unit
(try-works--MD), as a composite title (damn-my-eyes-tar--WJ), or as a
proper name (Coast-of-Guinea-Man--R); a possessive and its noun (crow's-
nest--MD), or a prepositional phrase (man-of-war--T, O, WJ, MD) when
joined arbitrarily or nonliterally.
      Proper uses of the hyphen Ball designated in eight rules, seven of
which apply to the sea vocabulary and with which Melville concurs.[30]
Thus, doubling a vowel (sea-alcove--WJ), combining letters in a confusing
way (starboard-quarter--WJ), and mispronouncing (go-ashore--T) are all
prevented. An apostrophe is allowed to be retained (boatswain's-mate--WJ)
and words of duplicating (whale-fish--MD) or conflicting terms (sea-beach--
M) are joined without confusion. Hyphenated words also include color
terms (foam-white--M), complex compounds that have two primary accents
(main-deck-batteries--WJ), and compounds both conventional (port-hole--R,
WJ) and improvised (bob-stay--T).
      Ball's fourth group of rules designated other uses of the hyphen, and
in Melville there is at least one example of all five of these rules:
compound nouns beginning with a gerund (whaling-cruise--O), compound
nouns ending in an adverb or a preposition (castaway--M, MD), compound

nouns of three or more simple words (The-Heart-of-Black-Coral--M),
compound nouns naming the same person or thing with two words (merchant-
captain--WJ), and compound technical units of measurement (fathom-deep--
MD).[31]

Ball deals with compound adjectives in three rules that apply to the
sea vocabulary.[32] Such terms are hyphenated, said Ball, when the second
element is a participle (wide-foaming--M), when the second element is a
coined word in the form of a participle (scroll-prowed--M), or when the
modifier is an improvised unit (life-buoy-coffin--MD).

Solid compounds were not allotted as many formation rules as
hyphenated words,[33] and of those that apply to the sea vocabulary, an
important one that Melville breaks concerns compound words with only one
primary accent that have developed by accretion from other solid
compounds. Ball's example was "topgallantmast," which consistently
appears in Melville with two hyphens (in R). But Melville does concur
with other of Ball's rules--a word is a solid compound if it has only one
primary accent (alewife--MD) and if the first word is the equivalent of a
prefix (forecastle--all novels). Finally, in both Ball and Melville, a
derivative of a compound word follows the form (solid or hyphenated) of
the original compound (man-of-war's-man--O, R, WJ): Hamilton preferred
to drop the final hyphen in that term).

According to Ball, the following words, which Melville chooses to
hyphenate, should be solid compounds: bobstay, cathead, cofferdam,
figurehead, knighthead, landlubber, sandbar, stateroom, bargeman,
beachcomber, seabeach, boathook, lifeboat, whaleboat, sailboat, steamboat
(hyphenated in WJ but one word in O and R), longboat, tugboat, gunboat,
bumboat, boatload, boatheader, jollyboat, bowshot, canoeload, clamshell,
halfdeck, drydock (Melville puts both "d's" in the upper case), dockyard,
flyingfish, goldfish, starfish, fishhook, shellfish, fishbone, floodgate,
foretop, foretopmast, bullfrog, topgallant, galleyslave, helmsman,
keelhauling, leeway, maintop, mainbrace, masthead, mainmast, mizzenmast,
topgallantmast, mastman, quartermaster, topmast, watchmate, messmate,
mizzentop, mizzentopman, pierhead, porthole, seaport, doublereef,
mainroyal, mainroyalmast, mainsail, foretopsail (in O there are two
hyphens; in M and WJ only one, after "fore"), maintopsail (in O there is
a hyphen after the first syllable only; in WJ there are two hyphens),
sailboat (in R this is solid; in O and MD, hyphenated), moonsail,
sailmaker (WJ also shows the first letter in both the upper and the lower
cases), sailcloth, sailorman, seamonster (solid in O; hyphenated in T),
seashore, seaside, seashell, shellwork, shipshape, shipbuilding, flagship,
shipwork, shipmaster, offshore, steerageway, maintop, foretop, topblock,
watertight, waterfowl, waterside, waterspout, cutwater, waterproof,
watergate, waterline, headwater, and whaleboat.

Ball and Melville agree on the form for the following sea vocabulary
words: alewife, bulkhead, crow's-nest, gangway, gunwhale, hatchway,
landsman (although Ball omits the "s"), lighthouse, man-of-war, outrigger,
steersman, topsail, whirlpool, yellow-back, bowsman (Ball omits the "s"),
bowline, bowsprit, lee-bow, clipper-built, codfish, quarter-deck, three-
decker, swordfish (Ball, O, and M have this as a solid compound; M also
shows it in two words; in WJ and MD it is hyphenated), foam-white, lee-bow,
jury-mast, shipmate, oarsman, ocean-wide, mother-of-pearl, running-rigging,
topsail (a solid word in Ball, M, and R; a hyphenated word in M, O, WJ,
and MD), seaman, sea-god, sea-girt, sea-green, sea-mark, shipwreck(ed),
ship-owner, shipboard (solid in Ball and WJ, hyphenated in MD), shipyard,
water-logged, waterfall (solid in Ball and T, hyphenated in O),
watercourse, breakwater, whaleman, and whalebone.

Castaway and tortoiseshell (solid in T, hyphenated in R) are words that Ball prefers to hyphenate and Melville usually uses as a solid compound.

Melville's remaining compound words, which constitute the majority of Melville's sea compounds, are not mentioned in Ball. Melville hyphenates all of those remaining words except five: dockgate, foremast, foresail, merchantman, and sailaway.

Melville and the Linguists

What turn-of-the-century grammarians had to say about compounding we saw to be useful practically in that, in a definite way, their approach was a semantic one. They did not lose sight of that referential entity that a certain word would signal, and such reality dictated many of their grammatical decisions. It may be that the further removed we become from that actual and experiential realm that language describes, the less effective we can be in analyzing Melville's compounds.

What certain major linguists have to say about compounding does not concentrate on definiteness or appropriateness of meaning or even on the use of the hyphen (which so consumed the grammarians), but on syntax. In so far as Melville's compounding is a reflection of his sea experience-- and I believe it largely is--Melville attends far less to syntax (his syntax is to a large degree conventional and consequently not so revealing of his art) and punctuation than to the specificity and appropriateness of the terms he combined.

Leonard Bloomfield. Leonard Bloomfield, for example, felt that using meaning as a criterion for compounding was a mistake, that the pattern of stress between the compound members should be the determining factor. He used a single high stress to distinguish what he wished to call a compound word from what he would call a two-word phrase.[34] This works on most of Melville's sea compounds of two terms, except that the grammatical environment of the sentence at times can modify that stress pattern. And Melville's compounds of three or more terms may have a variety of stress patterns--fish-at-arms, stander-of-mastheads, sail-of-the-line, damn-my-eyes-tar, fore-top-gallant-yard. Such, for Melville, are the in inadequacies of this system.

Bloomfield's lines of classifying compounds involved the relationship of a compound as a whole to its individual members as well as its use the sentence. These prove, for our purposes, not much more helpful than his ideas about stress. The types of compounds Bloomfield isolates are "exocentric" (where the head word of the compound would function differently in a sentence than the compound as a whole--one of his examples was the plant name "bittersweet," where the word's coordinated members are both adjectives, but the word itself is a noun--compare Melville's adjective go-ashore, in the phrase "his go-ashore traps," where the head word is a verb) and as "endocentric" (where the compound as a whole functions in the same manner as the head word, as in the adjective "bittersweet"--compare Melville's adjective long-boat). Bloomfield's "syntactic" compounds have members that stand to each other in the same grammatical relation as they would were they not compounded (as "blackbird" or "whitecap"--compare Melville's castaway, silver-head). "Asyntactic" compounds have members that do not combine in syntactic construction (as "door-knob" or "horsefly"--compare Melville's try-works, out-rigger, and gangway). "Semisyntactic" compounds deviate slightly from normal syntactic patterns (as with the verb "housekeep" or the noun "turnkey"--or Melville's three-decker or first-cutter).[35]

Otto Jespersen. Because Otto Jespersen does not dismiss meaning
entirely when discussing compounds, what he had to say is more applicable
to an investigation of Melville's sea compounds than what Bloomfield had
to say. In fact, Jespersen took Bloomfield's stress theory to task on
the basis that pronunciation varies from individual to individual and
that, because it depends on the rhythm of the sentence, it is basically
unstable anyway.[36] We must fall back on semantics: we have a compound
"if the meaning of the whole cannot be logically deduced from the meaning
of the elements separately."[37] Rather than trying to decide which compou
compounds should be admissible and which should not, Jespersen described
instead the types of compounds that were. Concrete, material objects
seemed to him to produce the least difficulty and seemed to Melville to
be the most useful raw material for his sea compounds.

Jespersen discussed his compounds by part of speech and devoted
nearly as many pages to the noun-noun variety (which he called substantive
compounds) as to all other combinations combined. Melville's sea
compounds are overwhelmingly of this variety, and most follow Jespersen's
first pattern, AB = B modified by A (boat-hook--M, T, MD). The second, AB = A
modified by B, is not as common (sloop-of-war--O, R, WJ, MD). Jespersen's
third type, which he noted was very sparse in English (AB = A + B--the
copulative compound), is only represented in the sea vocabulary by Torf-
Egill (M). Type four, where the compound members in some sense identify
each other (AB means at the same time A and B) is more common, allowing
for sailor-boy (R). Bahuvrihi compounds, Jespersen's fifth group, were
based on the stylistic trick of metonymy ("redcoat," "blue-beard") and
are not represented in the sea vocabulary, although his final substantive
category, in which the two elements are joined with a preposition, is
mother-of-pearl--T, O, WJ).

Robert B. Lees. While Jespersen evaded designing neat physical or
semantic criteria for compounds, Robert B. Lees inferred that such
criteria need not exist, that linguists should formulate grammatical
descriptions and not classify physical or semantic objects.[38] Lees
distinguished forty-nine types or subtypes of nominal compounds and
designed optional transformational rules to generate the compounds. His
work, however, resulted in a problem that Lees himself anticipated and
one that we must acknowledge concerning Melville:

. . . in a great many cases it will be possible to construct
on the basis of the given transformations an indefinitely
large number of compounds which do not occur in any extant
corpus of English . . . because of various conventions of
usage and of historical vicissitudes . . . they are
grammatical, but, for some accidents of cultural history,
they happen not to have come into use.[39]

So a rule that produces bullfrog from The frog is like a bull, reasoned
Lees, will also produce the ungrammatical frog animal from The animal is
like a frog. Interesting, however, is that Lees marked the similarly
generated flounder fish as ungrammatical in English (would he do the same
with tuna fish?), though Melville uses whale-fish quite unapologetically
in Moby-Dick. So, ultimately, Lees is inadequate to a complete
description of Melville's compounding.

The English language, as may be inferred from perusing these linguists,
can be both vastly subtle and vastly complex, and Melville uses both
potentialities to great advantage when fashioning the language of his
tales, although he uses it in a way that is characteristically his own,
not aligning itself completely with any one linguistic or grammatical
school of thought.

Notes

1. Since there are no extant manuscripts for any of the sea novels, we can never determine whether the many inconsistencies in spelling and in compounding were due to oversights of Melville or of his printer.

2. Merrill R. Davis and William H. Gilman, eds., The Letters of Herman Melville (New Haven: Yale University Press, 1960), p. 146.

3. William P. Trent, A History of American Literature, 1607-1865 (New York: D. Appleton, 1903), p. 390.

4. Newton Arvin, Herman Melville (n.p.: William Sloan Associates, Inc., 1950), p. 162.

5. Austin M. Knight, Modern Seamanship (New York: D. Van Nostrand Co., Inc., 1943).

6. Gershom Bradford, The Mariner's Dictionary (New York: Weathervane Books, 1952).

7. Horace Teall, The Compounding of English Words: When and Why Joining or Separation is Preferable, with Concise Rules and Alphabetical Lists (New York: John Ireland, 1891).

8. Ibid., p. 18.

9. The entry in the National Union Catalog for this book reads: "The Encyclopaedic dictionary: an original work of reference to the words in the English language, giving a full account of their origin, meaning, pronunciation and use; with colored plates and numerous illustrations in the text, also a supplementary volume containing new words." Since the dictionary ran to eight volumes, it is possible that Cassell released a few of them before the final publication date which the National Union Catalog sets at 1903, or that Teall saw all or part of the work before it went to press. Indeed he would have to have seen it in some form to be referring to the work in 1891.

10. Teall, Compounding of English Words, p. 31.

11. Ibid.

12. Ibid, p. 67.

13. Ibid.

14. Ibid., pp. 137-39.

15. Teall formulated his rules after discounting such superficial rules based entirely on accentuation as earlier grammarians had proposed, such as the Rev. Matthew Harrison in his The Rise, Progress, and Present Structure of the English Language, which was published in 1850, a year before Moby-Dick.

16. Teall, Compounding of English Words, p. 145.

17. Ibid., p. 147.

18. Ibid., p. 149.

19. Ibid., p. 150.

20. Ibid., p. 157.

21. Frederick W. Hamilton, Compound Words: A study of the Principles of Compounding, the Components of Compounds, and the Use of the Hyphen (Chicago: Committee on Education, United Typothetae of America, 1918), p. 2.

22. Ibid., p. 4.

23. Ibid., pp. 7-8.

24. Ibid., p. 14.

25. Alice Morton Ball, Compounding in the English Language: A Comparative Review of Variant Authorities with a Rational System for General Use and a Comprehensive Alphabetic List of Compound Words (New York: The H. W. Wilson Co., 1941).

26. Ibid., p. 3.

27. Ibid., pp. 6-43.

28. Ibid., p. 69.

29. Ibid., pp. 70-72.

30. Ibid., pp. 72-73.

31. Ibid., p. 73.

32. Ibid., p. 74.

33. Ibid., pp. 75-77.

34. Leonard Bloomfield, Language (New York: Holt, Rinehart, and Winston, 1933), p. 228.

35. Ibid., pp. 227-35.

36. Otto Jespersen, A Modern Grammar on Historical Principles (Copenhagen: Ejnar Munksgaard, 1942), 6: 135-36.

37. Ibid., p. 137.

38. Robert B. Lees, The Grammar of English Nominalizations (Bloomington: Indiana University Press, 1968), p. xxiv. This book was also published eight years earlier as a monograph.

39. Ibid., p. 121.

2
The Words as Parts of Speech

> . . . he talked little else than sailor phrases, which sounded
> whimsically enough.
>
> --<u>Omoo</u>

The Nouns

According to Josephine Miles, nineteenth-century prose tended to use
fewer verbs and more nouns than prose written earlier.[1] At the same time,
especially in America, writers tended to use a more sensory vocabulary,
their prose theoretically, as well as literally, expressing man's
expanding experience with Nature. Melville's sea vocabulary is a good
example of both of these tendencies. Of the 345 glossary items, 316 are
either nouns or used as nouns. As we have seen in the previous section
on compounding, Melville is very conscious of connecting man with Nature--
specifically, with the sea.

Composition and Versatility

Over one half of Melville's sea nouns function exclusively as nouns.[2]
But Melville manipulates his vocabulary, using its potential to cross
distinctions between parts of speech. In slightly over one hundred of
the vocabulary entries, Melville uses a sea term in a nominal role as
well as at least one other function. The simplest of these other
functions involves using a term as both a noun and its possessive
(<u>brigantine</u>, <u>canoe</u>, <u>captain</u>, <u>craft</u>, <u>crew</u>, <u>cutter</u>, <u>dolphin</u>, <u>gig</u>, <u>mate</u>,
<u>mermaid</u>, <u>mutineer</u>, <u>schooner</u>, <u>shallop</u>, <u>sheet</u>, and <u>vessel</u>). And there are
instances where Melville uses a sea term in a nominal and an attributive
function, as a premodifier of another noun: in the construction "bowsprit
bitts" and "windlass chorus," for example, the first term in each case
is functioning attributively. The following terms also occur in the sea
novels exclusively in those two ways: <u>cabin</u>, <u>cape</u>, <u>capstan</u>, <u>conch</u>, <u>coral</u>,

eel, forecastle, galley, harbor, hawse, lighthouse, marine, mizzen, navy, ocean, oyster, Pacific, porpoise, royal, salt, scupper, shell, spar, sperm, steerage, turtle, wave, wharf, and yard. And then there are five terms that function as nouns and as adjectives, but may require a suffix in their conversion into adjectives: brine(-y), pearl(-y and zero morpheme), Polynesia(-n), tar(-ry), tempest(-uous and zero morpheme). Tide appears in the novels as both a noun and an adjective, but the adjective constructions are compound forms: "half-tide rocks" and "tide-beating heart."

The language allows for certain words to function as either nouns or verbs with no other change in the word's form than perhaps a tense and/or number marker, and Melville's sea novels use several words in both capacities: anchor, beach, bubble, coast, crest, cruise, dive, dock, fish, flood, foam, harpoon, keel, moor, mutiny, paddle, reef, ripple, sail, scud, ship, shoal, sound, spout, tack, and voyage. Row and navigate should also be considered here, since they appear in the novels as both nouns and verbs--but with the distinction that the nominal form uses a suffix: row becomes rower and navigate becomes navigator.

Grammatically very versatile are dive, dock, navigate, reef, and sail, which appear throughout the novels as nouns, verbs, and adjectives. Forms of deck, jib, larboard, lee, sea, shore, squall, stern, and water appear as nouns, adjectives, and adverbs. Cruise and voyage are both used as nouns, verbs, and noun adverbs. Fore and aft are adverbs, prepositions, and nouns, and in addition fore appears as an adjective. But the most active words for Melville are fish, foam, and ship, which, of all the sea vocabulary, are root words for the formation of nouns, verbs, adjectives, and adverbs. The patterns of affixes required in each case will be discussed in the subsequent sections on each part of speech.

The only proper names included in the concordance are two denoting person (Neptune, Torf-Egill), five of place (Atlantic, Caribbean, Gallipagos, Pacific, and Polynesia), and six of scientific nomenclature (Cephalaspis, Chondropterygii, Glyptolepis, Mollusca, Pterichthys, and Xiphius Platypterus). The rest of the vocabulary consists of common nouns, which appear in the singular and plural, with the exception of a group of singular nouns that do not form the plural in any of the sea novels (cachalot, kelson, mussel, nautilus, and ork) and a group of plural nouns that usually, even for Melville, are not singular (alewives, billows--but note the discussion of billows in the following chapter-- bob-stays, boneetas, cockles, flounders, halyards, knight-heads, nippers, silver-heads, snatch-blocks, try-works, wriggle-tails, and yellow-backs).

The nouns are all, by selection, concrete, although certain words (such as abyss, lee, vortex) and some of the meteorological terminology of the tertiary sea terms may be marginally categorized as abstract.

As might be expected, there are over ten times as many count nouns in Melville's sea vocabulary as there are mass nouns, with water and canvas belonging to both categories.[3]

Type and Function

The nouns in Melville's sea vocabulary form a strongly conventional category. Unlike the classes of verbs, adjectives, and adverbs, other parts of speech do not become nouns by adding an affix or by shifting the word's position in the sentence. Melville's nouns do the things that nouns conventionally do--functioning as subjects and objects, naming or specifying targets of reference, and relating in rule-governed ways with prefixes, suffixes, and function words. Words in the possessive case or those functioning as adverbs are not considered here, as a consequence, to be nouns. Melville is, furthermore, conventional in his use of his sea nouns in that he is alert to the primary semantic ties between nouns and objects in the world. His creativity, his craft, is always anchored in his actual experience of his sailor world. His nouns of address become apostrophes; his predicate nominatives connect the tangible with the intangible; his appositives display some unusual improvisations.

Predicate Nominatives. Melville used the predicate nominative construction frequently and conventionally in all six of the novels, but in Mardi, White-Jacket, and Moby-Dick idealization quickens. An island is a "canto" (Mardi, p. 642), a ship is an "island" (Redburn, p. 165), or it is "the great leviathan himself" (Moby-Dick, p. 357). Stubbs' spine is a "keel" (Moby-Dick, p. 454), Azzageddi is a "lobster" or a "mackerel" (Mardi, p. 507), and the narrator aboard the becalmed Highlander senses that the crew is the ship: "We were a most puissant man-of-war" (White-Jacket, p. 325). Near the end of Melville's last two sea novels, some unusual predicate nominatives occur: in White-Jacket (p. 398), the narrator muses that, since this world is a frigate ("world-frigate"), God is the shipwright; and near the close of Moby-Dick (p. 423), Ishmael finds that the sea is "a crucible of molten gold, that bubblingly leaps with light and heat."

Appositives. The appositives that Melville constructs from his sea nouns commonly identify people, places, and craft, often restrictively; but idealizing, nonrestrictive appositives occur, especially in three of the last sea novels. We find a frigate, the bosom of a sailor's home (White-Jacket, p. 290); and a flag-ship, lord and master of its crew (White-Jacket, p. 195). In Mardi (p. 482) there are state canoes, "sea-snakes, all." There is the Brown Shark, a "sea-attorney" (Mardi, p. 40), and to the crew "theology, or amber, or ambergris" are all the same (Mardi, p. 375).

But the sea itself (identified by the primary sea terms) accumulates the most appositives. An inland ocean is called "a smooth expanse" (Mardi, p. 554), and a long-rolling chant is "a sea of sounds" (Mardi, p. 366). Friends of a diver who died in Mardi carry his remains "to their sepulchre, the sea" (Mardi, p. 300). And Ishmael muses about an essential factor for the whale-hunter, "the proverbial evanescence of a thing writ in water, a wake" (Moby-Dick, p. 453).

Nominatives of Address. Typical phrases of nominatives of address appear in many pages of the sea novels--to captains, gallant fore-top-men, surgeons of the fleet, sheet-anchor-men, gunners mates, sea-fencibles, mariners, lubbers, paddlers, shipmates, tars, and voyagers. All of the sea novels use the convention, though unequally. Paddlers and voyagers are addressed most often in Mardi, for example, shipmates in Typee, tars in White-Jacket, and captain dominates all of the novels.

Apostrophes. The constructions that are most unique and poetic, apostrophes, expanding the language of the sea to uncharted bounds, are used only in three of the last sea novels. In Mardi (p. 546), sandbars are ordered to "rise, and stay the tide!" and in White-Jacket (p. 295) "hidden reefs and rocks" are given a similar charge. White-Jacket also includes this exclamation: "Archipelago Rio! ere Noah on old Ararat anchored his ark, there lay anchored in you all these green, rocky isles I now see. But God did not build on you, isles!" (p. 211). More common to White-

Jacket are cries like "Away! Second, Third, and Fourth Cutters, away!"
(p. 71) or, of the ignoble white jacket, "Sink! sink! oh shroud!" (p. 394).
In Mardi, fish are often addressed: ". . . merry fins, swim away!"
(p. 150), "Pipe away, merry fish" (p. 150), "Bright fish!" (p. 167).   In
Moby-Dick, an important group of exhortations falls to the whale:
> But that pipe, poor whale, was thy last. (p. 242)
> Yet calm, enticing calm, oh whale! thou glidest on. (p. 447)
> . . . blow on and split your spout, O whale! (p. 454)
> I grin at thee, thou grinning whale! (p. 467)
> Towards thee I roll, thou all-destroying but unconquerable
> whale. (p. 468)
Taji reminisces about his ship in Mardi: "Good old Arcturion!
Maternal craft . . . Old ship!" (p. 24). And addressing ships or parts
of them becomes one of the two major themes of the apostrophes in
Moby-Dick:
> Good-by, mast-head--keep a good eye upon the whale. (p. 462)
> He's looking this way--come, oakum; quick! (p. 432)
> "Ah, noble ship"; the angel seemed to say, "beat on . . . thou
> noble ship." (p. 43)
> Ship, old ship! my old head shakes to think of thee! (p. 362)
> Oh! ye three unsurrendered spires of mine; thou uncracked keel;
> and only god-bullied hull; thou firm deck, and haughty helm,
> and Pole-pointed prow,--death-glorious ship! (p. 468)
To the sea is accorded a group of apostrophes in three of the last
sea novels that are emotionally as varied as the moods of the sea. The
sea throughout is idealized as almost a deity, and a sailor responds to
that power by venerating or blasting it (sometimes both on the same page),
but more often than not he is awed. And so, in prayer or in despair, to
forestall some fate or to reverberate exuberance, the sea is addressed by
Melville's sailors in Mardi, White-Jacket, and Moby-Dick. There are,
first of all, compounds of the sea that are used. In Mardi: "Now, old
sea-king!" (p. 483). In White-Jacket: "Let me snuff thee up, sea-breeze!"
(p. 77) and "Forbid it, sea-gods!" (p. 77). And in Moby-Dick, Ahab
addresses the sun: "Thou sea-mark!" (p. 411).
> There are apostrophes of praise in Mardi and in Moby-Dick for the sea:
> Oh, Ocean, when thou choosest to smile, more beautiful thou art
> than flowery mead or plain. (Mardi, p. 50)
> Then hail, for ever hail, O sea, in whose eternal tossings the
> wild fowl finds his only rest! (Moby-Dick, pp. 409-10)
There are prayers both exuberant--"Let me feel thee again, old sea!"
(White-Jacket, p. 77)--and, more frequently, desperate:
> Slope downwards to thy depths, O sea. (Moby-Dick, p. 467)
> Drive, drive in your nails, Oh ye waves! to their uttermost
> heads drive them in! (Moby-Dick, p. 464)
> . . . cork-screw whirlpools, suck us down! (White-Jacket, p. 295)
In Moby-Dick, though, another phenomenon emerges that displays the sea
not only as akin to human life, but inextricably linked with it. Both of
these references appear in the last seventy pages of the book and represent
Melville's philosophy that there is an important respect in which the sea
and man are one: ". . . though hill and valley mothered me, ye billows
are my foster-brothers!" (Moby-Dick, p. 410) and "ho, ho! from all your
furthest bounds, pour ye now in, ye bold billows of my whole foregone
life, and top this one piled comber of my death!" (Moby-Dick, p. 468).
    The fact is that the concept of the sea for Melville becomes
increasingly more complex from novel to novel--and the increasing semantic
complexity is reflected by an increasing syntactic complexity. For

example, in Typee and Omoo, the word "sea" is used primarily as a
prepositional object, although Omoo contains some occurrences of sea as
nominative, attributive, and objective as well. In Mardi, sea appears in
many mixed parts of speech. Redburn, likewise, uses sea in varied
grammatical ways, and furthermore, there are far more occurrences of the
term there than in Mardi. Sea begins to be used more frequently as a
subject in White-Jacket--that is, more frequently than in previous novels,
but still relatively seldom when compared with the other parts of speech.
The same trend continues in Moby-Dick, where sea appears with approximately
the same frequency as it does in White-Jacket and with the same relative
distribution of parts of speech.

In none of the novels, then, is sea presented grammatically as much
of an agent of design and identity separate from Melville's crews. But
it is a supremely important power to those crews. If the men are at times
only remotely conscious of it, it is imminent all the same, interacting
with them, forming the ground of their existence and sustenance.

The Verbs

A perusal of Melville's sea vocabulary shows many words that function
both as nouns and as verbs without any form change. Such dual function
words are anchor, beach, bubble, coast, cruise, dive, dock, eddy, fish,
float, flood, foam, harpoon, heel, hull, keel, mutiny, paddle, reef,
ripple, roll, sail, scud, ship, shoal, sound, spout, swell, swim, tack,
voyage, and wash. On the other hand, Melville uses some words exclusively
as verbs. They are blow, breach, broach to, drift, drown, embark, gally,
heave to, moor, navigate, pitch, rig, row, sheer, stave, wade, and yaw.
Note that all of these verbs are dynamic, transitional-event, activity
verbs. None state merely perception or relation. Yet, note as well that
most of these verbs can be converted to noun usages with affixes, which
Melville chooses to do to the following words: moor (moorings--Omoo),
navigate (navigator--all the novels; circumnavigator--Typee, Mardi, White-
Jacket; navigation--Omoo, Mardi, White-Jacket; circumnavigation--Typee,
Mardi, White-Jacket, Moby-Dick), rig (riggers--Redburn, Moby-Dick; out-
rigger--Typee, Mardi; rigging--all the novels; fore-rigging--Mardi;
running-rigging--Mardi; main-rigging--Omoo, Moby-Dick; standing-rigging--
Redburn), row (rowers--Typee), and sail (sailor--all the novels).

Melville's language here may be seen to be not only a language that
reported an experience, but a language that reported an active experience--
a language of doing as against one of feeling or perceiving. His verbs
are nominalized to name agents of actions or receivers of action, or are
given a gerundive suffix to name actions per se.

Class, Voice, Tense, and Mood

All of the sea verbs that Melville uses may be described as dynamic--
activity verbs (for example, to harpoon), transitional-event verbs (to
beach), or momentary verbs (to bubble). None are stative verbs of mere
perception or cognition or relation.[4] This is, however, not unusual for
such an active trade as seafaring. Of the verbs that also function as

nouns, all are regular in their tense formations except <u>swim</u>, a Class 7
irregular verb. Of the pure verbs, <u>blow</u> is an irregular Class 6 verb;
<u>breach</u>, <u>heave to</u>, and <u>stave</u> are irregular in Melville's usage, but would
probably be considered regular today; and the remaining verbs are regular.
    Melville places his sea verbs most often in the active voice. His
vocabulary is active and immediate, and that is how he usually uses it.
The few verbs that are given the passive voice mainly have <u>fish</u> (usually
indicating the whale) or <u>ship</u> as their grammatical subject, and the
implication is that mankind (some member of a ship's crew) is the agent
of the action on those subjects. <u>Moby-Dick</u> records the largest number of
verbs in the passive voice (<u>Typee</u> the fewest), but the total number is
slight.
    The subject of each verb determines the person of the verb and often
dictates to what semantic class (see the previous chapter) the verb
belongs. Melville uses the verbs of his sea vocabulary in ways that are
both unusually active and very predictable. Although all grammatical
persons are used, the third person is the most common, because words
reporting actions by persons or things other than the speaker are most
common. Primary sea terms and the first subset of the tertiary sea terms
(3A, animate and nonhuman sea life) contain the fewest, though even so a
substantial number of the verbs. The quaternary sea terms present the
second highest humber of verbs, approximately two-thirds the number of
the largest category. Not all of the verbs in this class take the third
person. There are, for example, many first-person references in the
dialogue Melville uses, and a number of second-person imperatives. The
remaining two semantic classes of sea terms (2--geography, and 3B--
meteorology) contain no sea verbs.
    Although a majority of the sea verbs appears in the simple past tense,
and the future tense has the fewest numbers (it does not occur at all in
<u>White-Jacket</u> and very rarely in the other novels; the number of infinitives
is only slightly larger than the number of future-tense verbs, and it
remains fairly constant from novel to novel), all tenses are represented.
All of the novels are consistent in using sea verbs in the past tense most
frequently and, in all cases except for <u>Moby-Dick</u>, present participles
nearly as frequently. They form, in fact, a bridge between present and
past time, since the identical "-ing" form occurs, usually in a free verb
phrase modifier, whether or not the sense of the base clause is present
or past.
    In <u>Moby-Dick</u>, sea verbs occur more frequently in the historical
present than in any other novel. The book is Melville's masterpiece, and
he uses an immediate word form to create and recall a most immediate
experience. Allowing for the length of <u>Mardi</u>, there is proportionately
an increase, from the earliest sea novel to the last, in the amount of
historical present tense that Melville uses. There seems to be no
corresponding pattern to the frequency of the past tense from novel to
novel: <u>Mardi</u> and <u>Moby-Dick</u> use it more than <u>Omoo</u> and <u>White-Jacket</u> do, and
<u>Typee</u> and <u>Redburn</u> use it less than that. All in all, there is a general
tendency for Melville to use proportionately and increasingly more sea
verbs in each sea novel that he writes, integrating even more completely
the sea words with the world of words, of audience, of the land.
    Although most of the verbs appear, naturally, in the indicative mood,
Melville uses the subjunctive on occasion with his sea verbs, with equal
frequency in all of the novels except for <u>Omoo</u> and <u>Redburn</u>, where it is
less common. The imperative mood appears in the sea novels only slightly
more frequently than the subjunctive, but with more of an observable
pattern. Three of the first novels--<u>Typee</u>, <u>Omoo</u>, and <u>Redburn</u>--have sea

verbs that use the imperative, but only once or twice. Mardi, White-Jacket, and Moby-Dick use it much more frequently--White-Jacket, that invective against naval discipline, the most frequently of all.

Frequency, Distribution, and Variants

Many of the sea verbs occur only once or twice in the entire canon of Melville's sea novels. These are bubble (M), broach to (WJ), drift (M), gally (O, MD), heel (MD), pitch (O, MD), scud (WJ), sheer (O), shoal (M), swell (MD), wade (M), and wash (MD). The verbs that are used most often are float (T, M, R, WJ, MD), sail (all of the novels), swim (all). and swim (all).

The types of verbs most active in each novel vary considerably and go a long way to indicate the subject matter of each tale. Typee, Omoo, and Redburn are the novels with the fewest sea verbs. Cruise in Typee, beach and paddle in Omoo, and dock in Redburn are the most frequent in those novels. In Mardi, verbs that connote quiet or calm activity (coast, drift, float, flood, ripple), as well as words of a more technical or arcane language (navigate, shoal, yaw) are the most frequent. The verbs that are used the most in White-Jacket are anchor, reef, ship, and tack. And Moby-Dick's most common verbs designate the activities both of the whale and of the sea (breach, roll, sail, spout, stave, swell) and are as violent as the verbs in Mardi are placid.

Melville uses two variant spellings, a number of different affixes, and several archaisms in conjunction with his verb phrases. The verb cruise follows the noun spelling of the same form in all occurrences except for those on page twenty-two of Typee, where it appears both as the infinitive to cruize and as the present participle cruizing. The verb reef appears, in the present tense for three pages of White-Jacket (pp. 391-94), as reeve and reeving, and in the past tense as reeved, rove, and reefed. Among the affixes present in the sea verbs are compound forms--wide-foaming (M), pitch-poling (MD), and ship-wrecked (R). The verbs that make the most use of affixes are navigate (as circumnavigate--M, R, WJ) and ship (unship--M, WJ), and outsail occurs once, as a present participle in Mardi.

A number of verbal archaisms occur in bound or free modifiers--introduced by the subordinate conjunction "ere": some of them in Jespersen's time period of "before-past"[5]--"ere Noah . . . anchored his ark" (WJ, p. 211), "a week would elapse ere the Julia sailed" (O, p. 140); others in the period of "before-future"--"stave in your spirit-casks, ere rigging the life-boat" (M, p. 107), "ere the Pequod's weedy hull rolls side by side with the barnacled hulls of the leviathan" (MD, p. 116). Archaisms also involve the auxiliary of a sea verb and, notably, they all occur in Mardi: "thou didst dive into the deeps of things" (p. 385), "did'st ever dive in deep waters, Taji?" (p. 650), "doth the maiden swim" (p. 267)--or the formal use of the second person singular pronoun with the imperative: "Dive thou" (p. 651) and the formal second-person possessive pronoun: "in rafts thy murdered float" (p. 552). On the same page spoken by the same king are these two phrases: "comst thou to fish" and "come you to fish" (p. 166). Unusual sentence orders that emphasize the verbs, a poetic archaism, occur as do most other forms of archaism, in Mardi: "Bright fish! diving deep as high soars the lark" (p. 267) and "To swim, it's exceedingly pleasant" (p. 150).

Semantics and Figurative Language

Most of the sea verbs are used in a purely straightforward,
referential way, but even so, the language allows for a wide latitude in
the types of subjects an individual verb can take. For example, in Omoo,
"our captain . . . anchored alongside of her" (p. 19) and "to have the
ship snugly anchored" (p. 83) may indicate nearly the same thing; no one
would deduce that it was the person of the captain that was being
anchored in the first case, distinct from the ship in the second. In
fact, in certain verbs where crossing the water is implied, a person or
an assembly of people is often used as a metonymy for the larger reality
of the entire vessel and its complete crew that is indeed underway. In
Mardi, "we floated" (p. 266) and "canoes floated" (p. 285), "we keeled
the beach" (p. 589) and "our canoes keeled the bottom" (p. 201), and the
meaning of the statement is exactly the same. In Omoo, both "vessels"
(p. xiii) and a "mate" (p. 51) navigate (the vessels, though, navigate
the ocean, and the mate the ship, so the identity is not as close as in
the first example). The verb sail, however, is most active in this
flexibility. Mardi records subjects of that verb, within a matter of only
a few pages, as "I" (p. 64), "we" (p. 57), the "brigantine" (p. 57), and
the "captain" (p. 69), and the action implied is all of the same piece.
What varies is the focus, even though the other activities are simultaneous
and concurrent, as overtones and harmonics are in a note of music.
    Figurative language involving the sea verbs occurs in every one of
the sea novels, although Typee, Omoo, and Redburn use it very little.
The simile and metaphors Typee does have concern birds "sailing aloft"
(p. 10), canoes floating "gracefully as a swan" (p. 132), and suggest
retiring for the night by saying "mooring ourselves" (p. 45). In Omoo,
mosquitoes "eddy" (p. 201) around the crew. Redburn's metaphors both
involve members of the crew--death means to heave up "anchor for the
world to come" (p. 138), and the captain walking the decks looks like a
dandy "circumnavigating the dress-circle" (p. 294).
    As would be expected, the poetic Mardi and the masterful Moby-Dick
both teem with figurative language. Mardi's examples are either very
picturesque or very philosophical or something in between. Arrows "dive"
(p. 422) through the water like red-hot bars, fish "float" (p. 121) on
the sea like constellations in the heavens, and lava "floods" (p. 499)
the forest. Birds and clouds, but also worlds and spirits, "sail" (pp. 8,
148, 469, 633). We, in fact, "sail blithely through life" (p. 52), and
advice is given to "stave in your spirit-casks, ere rigging the life-boat"
(p. 107). Moby-Dick has the same types of simile and metaphor, and new
varieties as well. First of all, such language makes vivid description--
a painting in the Spouter Inn has lines "floating in a nameless yeast"
(p. 20), and once on the sea the horizon floats, as do "a little isle of
sunlight" (p. 43), "milky-ways of coral isles" (p. 325), and even "an oily
calmness" (p. 49). The language adds philosophical or psychological
dimensions when Melville writes that "nameless imminglings float beneath
me here" (p. 409), or "there floated into my inmost soul, endless
processions of the whale" (p. 16), or "reminiscences" (p. 23) floated in
the deep shadows of someone's eyes, or Jonah's deep sea-line sounds
incredible "depths of the soul" (p. 45). Beyond these conventions,
Melville is colloquial and humorous when he spins the tale of a gentleman
harpooning a lady and then reharpooning her (p. 332), a man "swimming
like a dog" (p. 61), or Ishmael sounding his pockets "with anxious
grapnels" (p. 17). He illustrates again the identity of man with the sea
when he writes, "the noble negro to every roll of the sea harmoniously

rolled his fine form" (p. 191). Whales are, like people, also identified with the sea (they "swim in a sea of water, and have a sea of oil swimming in them"--p. 4) and with ships ("did whale ever yaw[6] so before?"--p. 296). But, almost religiously, the whale is identified with a profound and immutable spirit--"the ghost is spouted up" (p. 358), "the eternal whale will . . . spout his frothed defiance to the skies" (p. 385).

White-Jacket, a relatively bitter polemic, contains a surprising amount of metaphor and simile, most of which involves ships or people. With fifty thousand gallons of water-casks in her bowels, the Neversink seemed to have a "huge Lake Ontario" in her and resembled "the united continent of the Eastern Hemisphere--floating in a vast ocean herself, and having a Mediterranean floating in her" (p. 175). The Neversink sailed "like a shooting-star" (p. 272), and conversely, there were stars "sailing in heaven's blue, as we on the azure main" (p. 77). As a companion piece to Redburn, White-Jacket has a bit of the language that Melville would characterize as belonging to a "damn-my-eyes-tar, that is, a humbug" (p. 349). For example, a count is described as "mincingly circumnavigating a shot-box" (p. 238). And at various places in the novel, some of the crew is ordered to "sail away out of this [the cook's galley], and let me clear up the wreck" (p. 59), and to "top your boom and sail large now" (p. 308). Mothers of sailors are advised to hold fast to their sons,

. . . all those who have not yet weighed their anchors for the Navy--round and round, hitch over hitch, bind your leading-strings on them, and, clinching a ring-bolt into your chimney-jam, moor your boys fast to that best of anchors, the hearth-stone (p. 229).

The novel ends with a two-page extended analogy that begins:

As a man-of-war that sails through the sea, so this earth that sails through the air. We mortals are all on board a fast-sailing, never-sinking world-frigate, of which God was the shipwright; and she is but one craft in a Milky-Way fleet, of which God is the Lord High Admiral. The port we sail from is forever astern. And though far out of sight of land, for ages and ages we continue to sail with sealed orders, and our last destination remains a secret to ourselves and our officers; yet our final haven was predestined ere we slipped from the stocks at Creation (p. 398. Note further discussion in the next chapter.)

The Adjectives

Nearly one-third of the sea vocabulary involves, in one form or another, the adjective. That is nearly twice the number of words that have verbal characteristics. Although the adjectival activity of the vocabulary is less focused and restricted than that of the verbal, it is also less intense. That is, there is a very close similarity in the total number of sea adjectives and sea verbs in the novels, but a far greater variety of different adjectives than verbs.

What follows is an analysis of the forms that Melville's sea adjectives take. It would be, in a semantic sense, as fruitless to

discuss the adjectives in isolation from the nouns they modify as it
would have been to discuss the verbs entirely apart from their nominal
subjects, and so, from Melville's examples, the adjectives are at times
identified in conjunction with what they modify.

Seven Adjectival Forms

Considering the forms and frequencies of adjectives, it is surprising
to find that White-Jacket, the bitterest, most serious, and least "poetic"
of the sea canon, far surpasses the other books in the number of
adjectives used. But perhaps the phenomenon can be explained in terms of
possession (the possessive construction), ownership and dominance being
prominent motifs in the novel. Moby-Dick slightly leads Mardi in
containing the second greatest number of sea adjectives, but White-Jacket
has nearly twice as many as either of those books. Redburn is not far
behind Mardi in the frequency of adjectives, and Omoo and Typee have the
fewest.

Possessive Construction. The form of Melville's adjectives for which
he shows the most preference is the possessive construction. White-Jacket,
mainly because of the heavy use of boatswain's and captain's, records more
than twice as many possessive forms as any other sea novel. Mardi is
second, with frequent usage of boat's and ship's. Omoo, Redburn, and
Moby-Dick use roughly the same number of possessives, and Typee uses the
fewest of any of the novels, although the possessive is the most important
adjectival form in that book. Melville's earliest record of his
adventures, Typee, uses far fewer sea adjectives than any other sea novel.
Melville's second novel, Omoo, uses more than twice as many. But White-
Jacket uses ten times as many.

Noun Conversion. The second most common form of Melville's sea
adjectives is the adaptation of a noun to the adjective class without
adding a suffix. When nouns are used in this premodifying capacity, they
very closely resemble the head term in a compound noun. Two of the
notable features that Randolph Quirk mentions about such nouns are that
they usually appear in their singular form and usually have the accent
pattern of the two-word phrase.[7] The pattern of singularity is consistent
in Melville's premodifying nouns with the exception of the phrase
Sandwich Islands Mission.
The accentual pattern is another thing. When the premodifying noun
is one term, the accent is generally on that term ("anchor button,"
"cabin people," "whale statements"), but not always ("starboard
carronades," "leviathan gore," "bowsprit bitts"). Frequently the accent
is on the premodifying noun when the noun being modified is compound ("lee
fore-brace") or when the premodifying noun is compound ("gun-boat actions,"
"Quarter-deck lords"), but not always ("ocean-wide renown," "salt-sea
life"). When the noun head is part of a title ("the Island Queen," "a
Man-of-War Hermit," "Pearl Shell Islands"), when the combination of
premodifying noun plus noun is unusual or bizarre ("submarine bridal
chambers and nurseries," "sailor boarding-house"), or when a noun plus a
participle together act as one premodifying term and probably should be
hyphenated anyway ("foam beaded rim"), the accent is on the noun that is
modified and not on the premodifier.

Affixes. A third common way for Melville to convert nouns into
adjectives is with the addition of one or more affixes. This method

Melville uses less than two-fifths as frequently as noun conversion, but it is nevertheless popular with him. White-Jacket has more of this type of adjective than any other sea novel, with Moby-Dick following close behind and Mardi, Typee, Omoo, and Redburn trailing at some distance.

The suffix that appears most frequently, with the most different adjectives, is "-y." All of the novels use it, but Mardi (billowy, finny, foamy, pearly, watery) and Moby-Dick most of all. Redburn (briney, fishy, tarry, watery), White-Jacket (foamy, squally, watery), Typee (briney, foamy, watery), and Omoo (watery) use it less frequently. The single most prevalent suffix is "-al" which, as naval in White-Jacket, occurs over fifty times. The word occurs in every other sea novel as well, but rarely more than once or twice in each.

The only other suffix Typee uses with the sea adjectives is "-n" in Polynesian, but it occurs very frequently in both Typee and Omoo, once in Mardi, and twice in White-Jacket. The only adjectival affixes appearing in Redburn are "trans-" (transatlantic) and "-like," as unseamanlike in Redburn and Mardi, as sailor-like in Omoo, Redburn, and White-Jacket. The same words occur in Mardi; sailor-like, billow-like, eel-like, and salmon-like in Moby-Dick; unsailorlike and unseaworthy in Omoo. The suffix "-ward" is the only additional affix White-Jacket uses, in leeward, which Moby-Dick records as well; Mardi shows seaward. Tideless occurs in Mardi, harborless and shoreless in Moby-Dick. No other affix appears in Mardi, except for the prefixes "sub-" (attached to -marine, in both Mardi and Moby-Dick) and "un-" (see above). Omoo contains a suffix none of the other sea novels uses with the sea vocabulary, "-able" (navigable), and two that appear only in Moby-Dick, "-ous" (mutinous in Omoo, tempestuous in Moby-Dick) and "-ish" (sharkish in both). Moby-Dick, the most active novel regarding suffixes, records the only superlative ("fishiest of all fishy places"), uses two suffixes to coin nonce words, "-ic" (leviathanic) and "-wise" (whale-wise), and converts a verb into an adjective by using a prefix (afloat).

Compound Adjectives. The next major group of adjectives in terms of frequency is the compound adjective. Except for White-Jacket (which has the most varieties of compound adjectives and the largest total number of them) and Moby-Dick (which is second to White-Jacket in both respects), the frequency of compound adjectives gradually increases with each novel. That is, from Typee to Omoo to Mardi to Redburn it gradually increases, and then it doubles in the last two novels. White-Jacket, Moby-Dick, and Redburn far surpass the other novels in the number of compound sea adjectives they use.

Most of the adjective compounds have two members, and in most cases, both are nouns. Examining the novels in order of their increasing number of exceptions, I found that in Omoo the compounds are exclusively nominal. In Redburn the only exception is the combination of noun plus adjective, which occurs in two terms (sea-sick, sea-blue). Typee has two types of exceptions, an adjective plus a noun (South-Sea) and a prepositional phrase (mother-of-pearl). Moby-Dick has three exceptions: two of them are noun-plus-adjective (ocean-wide, shark-white), one is adjective-plus-noun (wild-ocean, which incidentally modifies two participles--"born" and "nurtured") and the other a prepositional phrase (Sky-Sail-Pole). White-Jacket has the most deviances from the nominal pattern--there is one prepositional phrase (mother-of-pearl), two cases of adjective-plus-noun (main-deck, fresh-water), three nouns-plus-adjective (sail-proud, sea-green, sea-sick), and four three-word compounds, two of them noun-noun-noun (fore-top-mast, mizzen-top-sail) and two of them adjective-noun-noun (main-top=mast, main-top-sail).

The order of the members of the compounds is another important aspect of their composition. I found a fairly even balance among the compounds as to whether a certain sea word functions as the head word of the term or whether it is the final term. In only one novel is there a large preference for one pattern--Redburn, with its heavy use of compounds beginning with sea, generally records more sea terms in the initial position, and Moby-Dick records a slight tendency of this sort. White-Jacket uses many words beginning with sail- or sea- and ending with -mast or -deck, and so the proportion of the sea words is evenly balanced between the two positions. In Mardi, Omoo, and Typee, the use of sea words as the final member of the compound adjective has a slight edge.

Verb Conversion. The fifth most important type of adjective for Melville involves the conversion of a verbal form into an adjective--a participle used in a modifying capacity. The overall pattern in the sea novels of this phenomenon shows a gradual increase from Typee through White-Jacket and then a doubling of it in Moby-Dick. Fishing is the only participial adjective I found in Typee, and whaling the only one in Omoo, except that that adjective occurs roughly half a dozen times in Omoo and only once in Typee. Floating, which appears in all of the novels except for Typee and Omoo, occurs in Mardi nearly ten times, far more frequently than in any other novel, although Redburn and White-Jacket use it substantially. Melville prefers present participial adjectives to past participial adjectives by a ratio of fifty-five to one. Mardi, Redburn, and Moby-Dick are the only novels that use the past form, and those vary with each book: becalmed (Mardi), shipped (Redburn), and sharked and unshored (Moby-Dick, where both words refer to the sea).

Adjectives both Participial and Compound. There is a group of adjectives that Melville is fond of using, which are simultaneously participial and compound. This set of words has slightly over half the number of members of the participial group and slightly more than one-fourth the number of members of the compound group but demonstrates an interesting wordplay on Melville's part. The words represent an assortment of adjectives that are very common (water-logged--Mardi; ship-wrecked--Mardi, White-Jacket; sea-going--Redburn, White-Jacket, Moby-Dick) as well as adjectives that probably appear on the pages of no other author (foam-flaked--Mardi, ocean-tombed--Mardi, water-smitten--Moby-Dick). As would be expected, the unique compounds appear once only, and the more common compounds far more often.

The pattern of the compounds is usually noun-plus-participle, although Redburn has two adjective-plus-participles (one-masted, fast-sailing) and White-Jacket has one (double-reefed). There are nearly twice as many past participles used in the compounds as there are present participles, although Melville's tendency, as he wrote the sea novels, was to use increasingly more present participial sea compounds. In Typee I recorded two past forms and no present ones, in Moby-Dick one past and four present.

With very few exceptions, the participial compounds are terms of two members (Typee's mother-of-pearl-handled is one of the exceptions) where the sea word is the initial term (for example, canoe-shaped--T, sea-girt--M, tide-beating--MD). Mardi's scroll-prowed, Redburn's one-masted and fast-sailing, and White-Jacket's double-reefed are the prominent exceptions. Melville's adjectival compounding, his building up of term upon term, seems to be a very conscientious rhythmic device akin to the motion of the waves. Just as the Pacific, Melville's favorite ocean, seemed to Ishmael "the tide-beating heart of earth" (MD, p. 400), so the advertisements that caught Redburn's eye for the departure of "superior fast-sailing, coppered and copper-fastened ships" (R, p. 192), and the slumbering of the absolute monarch of Juam--"the universe-rounded, zodiac-belted, royalty-girdled, arm-clasped, self-hugged, indivisible Donjalolo" (M, p. 240)--scan with similar rise and fall.

Pure Adjectives. The adjectives left to consider are the "pure" adjectives, those that exist independently of the other form classes, with neither suffix nor adjoining member. This group consists of those words far enough removed from a nominal counterpart so that a nominal root is not visible. Naval, for example, was tallied as a noun-plus-suffix because the root "nav-" readily identified its relationship to navy, and Polynesian is only a single letter away from Polynesia. Insular, however, is distinct enough from island in phonemic form (not, however, in meaning or etymology, in which the terms are very close) to be classified a pure adjective. There are not even ten such pure adjectives, and they are of three sorts.

The first group contains geographical terms, and its members are Pacific (an adjective as used in Typee to modify "station" but not necessarily adjectival as used in conjunction with or reference to ocean, which happens frequently in the novels and where it is taken to be one title--much like Captain Bob--rather than an adjective-plus-noun phrase) and Caribbean (in Mardi, where it modifies canoe). A second group consists of pure adjectives that are all Latin derivations: nautical (appearing in all the novels except Moby-Dick, and usually half a dozen times or so per novel), maritime (appearing in all of the novels except Typee and Redburn), and insular (White-Jacket). The final grouping is sailor jargon: fore and aft when they assume roles of modification (more often they are nouns) and the construction (referred to by Admiral W. H. Smyth in his 1867 Sailor's Word-Book as a "comparative adjective"[8]) after.[9]

Usually each sea word will be used in only one or two of the adjectival forms: boat, for example, is mainly possessive, though there are several occurrences of noun conversion; brine always appears adjectivally as a noun with the suffix "-y"; and coral usually as a converted noun, once as a compound adjective, and twice as a compound participial adjective. Not surprisingly, sea and water are the most adjectivally adaptable and active of the words, both appearing in all of the adjectival forms except for the pure adjective. There are several sea terms that are used as adjectives only once in the sea novel canon: bow (O--noun conversion), calm (M--participle), Caribbean (M--pure adjective), clipper and coast (both R--participial compounds), conch (M--noun conversion), dolphin (R--possessive), hawse (WJ--noun conversion), jib (O--noun conversion; in other cases it is either a noun or hyphenated to boom, sheets, halyards, flying, or stay), lighthouse (WJ--noun conversion), mutiny (O--noun-plus-suffix), Pacific (T--pure adjective), salt (WJ--noun conversion), scupper (R--noun conversion), sheet (WJ--compound possessive), sou'-wester (R--noun conversion), spar (WJ--noun conversion), squall (WJ--noun-plus-suffix, tar (R--noun-plus-suffix), trade (M--noun conversion), wave (M--noun conversion), wharf (WJ--noun conversion), and windlass (O--noun conversion). In many ways the most unusual of the sea adjectives, go-ashore also appears only once, in the first sea novel that Melville wrote, in "he preserved his go-ashore traps" (T, p. 35), as a compound consisting of a verb plus an adverb.

The Adjective Phrase

The great majority of Melville's sea adjectives are in the attributive position, whether Melville is speaking, for example, of "the boatswain's locker" (R, p. 268) or of "the whale's gastric juices" (MD, p. 306). The use of the complementary sea adjective is uncommon, although it does occur in four ways: as a predicate adjective (for example, "They are becalmed"--M, p. 48, "Sometimes it [coffee] tastes fishy"--R, p. 43, "myriads that were ocean-tombed"--M, p. 192, "The attention was sailor-like"--O, p. 7; and where the adjectives ship-shape--WJ, and sea-sick--O, R, WJ occur), as the object of a preposition (shore-cap of the captain's"--M, p. 101), as an elliptical construction with only an implied reference ("least sailor-like of the crew"--WJ, p. 10; "eyes . . . fixed in its head, like a whale's"--M, p. 395), and in a transposed word order ("the highest truth, shoreless, indefinite as God"--MD, p. 97).

Foregrounding

A major curiosity, involving the linguistic concept of "foregrounding," emerges when analyzing Melville's adjectives and helps to explain some of the delicacies and innuendos of Melville's sea language. Geoffrey N. Leech remarks about foregrounding:
> Foregrounding or motivated deviation from linguistic, or
> other socially accepted norms, has been claimed to be a
> basic principle of aesthetic communication. . . . The
> norms of the language are in the dimension of analysis
> regarded as a "background," against which features which
> are prominent because of their abnormality are placed in focus.[9]

Four years after he published the article from which this passage was excerpted, Leech included a chapter entitled "Foregrounding and Interpretation" in his book A Linguistic Guide to English Poetry, which explains the concept further:
> . . . deviations from linguistic or other socially accepted
> norms have been given the special name of "foregrounding,"
> which involves the analogy of a figure seen against a
> background. The artistic deviation "sticks out" from its
> background, the automatic system, like a figure in the
> foreground of a visual field. . . . The foregrounded
> figure is the linguistic deviation, and the background is
> the language--the system taken for granted in any talk of
> "deviation."[10]

Melville uses a number of degrees of such "foregrounding" in his sea novels. A very elementary degree, a bridge between linguistic norm and poetic deviation, would be where modification is used not for a simple noun but with something less precise than that, usually a participle. Examples are numerous: "without the captain's speaking to me"--R, p. 68; "the fact of the captain's not showing any leniency"--WJ, p. 276; "of every sailor's saving it [the soul]"--WJ, p. 155; "the seaman's inadvertently saying sir"--WJ, p. 162; "the vessel's sinking outright"--M, p. 119.

True foregrounding occurs in the sea novels when Melville jarringly juxtaposes two words in an adjective phrase that are not commonly thought of in conjunction. The simplest of these are also very quaint. The combination is novel, and it delights: "the Cape Horn theatricals"--WJ, p. 276; "no quarter-deck dignity"--M, p. 5; "the gun-deck gossip"--WJ, p. 398; "all is glee, fishy glee"--M, p. 149; "forecastle choir" and "forecastle boudoir"--M, pp. 5, 81; man-of-war "epic," "vice," and

"scourge"--WJ, pp. 270, 308, 345; "nautical fragrancies"--R, p. 273;
"our sail-proud braggadocio of an Indiaman"--WJ, p. 105; "Sky-Sail-Pole
lyrics"--M, p. 384; "with a sailor's blessing"--O, p. 99; "a sailor
superstition"--WJ, p. 332; "with some sea joke"--O, p. 47; "this sea
cake-basket"--M, p. 64; shore "pomp" and "delights"--WJ, pp. 165, 391;
"submarine bridal-chambers and nurseries"--MD, p. 327; "Steelkilt was
wild-ocean born, and wild-ocean nurtured"--MD, p. 210; "small crabs,
shell-fish, and other sea candies and macaroni"--MD, p. 230; "that old
sea hearth-stone"--M, p. 5.

Whenever watery is joined to a noun as an adjective, the resulting
modification is strange and wonderful, giving us Melville's perspective
of seeing all things through nautical glasses. He uses watery in all of
his sea novels, combining it with such words as "path" (T, p. 5), "grave"
(O, p. 40), "waste," "zone," "hollows," "cliff," "obsequies," "opinions,"
and "nations" (M, pp. 10, 25, 30, 37, 192, 245, 368), "highlands,"
"prairie," and "inn" (R, pp. 116, 294, 166), "wilderness" (WJ, p. 214),
and "circle," "world," "spaces," "locality," "region," "moors," "wrinkles,"
"Potter's Fields," "defile," and "doom" (MD, pp. 121, 148, 156, 199, 208,
356, 446, 399, 321, 307).

At a level more complex, foregrounding in the sea novels attains a
poetic character, either due to some manner of animation or personification
or because it is vaguely metaphysical. Among examples at this level are
"the billows' throng" (M, p. 214), "in billowy battalions charge they"
(M, p. 273), "give me . . . this briny, foamy life" (R. p. 66), "they
shipped their quarter-deck faces" (WJ, pp. 95, 103, 276), "foam-flaked
dromedary-humps" (M, p. 543), "foamy fleeces" (M, p. 549), "foamy
confusion" (MD, p. 257), "the island's throbbing heart" (M, p. 191), "the
leviathanic brotherhood" (MD, p. 119), "young Leviathan amours" (MD,
p. 326), ocean "reveries" and "skin" (MD, pp. 12, 405), "the ocean's utmost
bones" (MD, p. 50), "a boat bounded on the sea's back" (M, p. 28), "the
ship's live-oak knees" (WJ, p. 233), "the ship's navel" (MD, p. 363), "the
Pacific . . . seems the tide-beating heart of earth" (MD, p. 400), the
deep's "unshored, harborless immensities" (MD, p. 116), the "liquid sphere"
(M, p. 85), and "the ocean's immeasurable burning-glass" (MD, p. 411).

The Adverbs

Perhaps least satisfactory of the form classes for grammarians, due to
its heterogeneity, the adverb class is also, for Melville, the smallest.
Most traditionally, and most commonly for the sea vocabulary, the
distinction between the adverb and other form classes is a morphological
one; an affix is joined to a word from another form class, usually a noun.
That is the most frequent but not the exclusive method of adverb formation.

Adverbial Form

Affixes. Adverbs with prefixes are more prevalent in the sea novels
than adverbs with suffixes, and the adverbial prefix that appears exclusively in the sea novel canon is "a-," attaching to either a noun or a
verb. Quirk points out that words beginning with "a-" are problematic for

grammarians, some of whom classify them as adjectives and others as
adverbs. They usually function predicatively and only a few can be used
attributively. Quirk's guideline for classification is that if a word can
function predicatively only after "be," it is usually an adverb, since
adjectives may be used with other intensive verbs, for example, "seem,"
as well.[11]

Melville's adverbs that are a combination of "a-" plus a noun, in
basically descending order of frequency, are ashore, astern, alee, abeam,
afoam, and amain. Ashore, in fact, is the most frequent of all Melville's
sea adverbs, occurring in his sea novels at least two hundred times more
often than any other adverb. The pattern of its usage is neither
predictable nor ordered, appearing most often in Omoo and White-Jacket,
in Redburn next most frequently, and in Typee, Mardi, and Moby-Dick far
fewer times. Astern is used most often in Mardi, approximately one-third
as many times in White-Jacket and Redburn, only occasionally in Moby-Dick,
once in Omoo, and not at all in Typee. The most "exotic" of the "a-"
adverbs is alee, used once in Mardi and once in Moby-Dick. Abeam, afoam,
and amain all have a singular appearance in the sea novels, abeam in
White-Jacket and afoam and amain in Moby-Dick.

An additional form of the "a-" adverbs appears when the prefix is
combined with a verb, as in adrift and afloat. Afloat is nearly six times
as prevalent as adrift in the sea novels, and its concentration is overwhelmingly in White-Jacket. Adrift has scattered and only occasional
usage--in Mardi, White-Jacket, and Moby-Dick. Although most dictionaries
classify afloat as both an adjective and an adverb, Quirk labels it an
adjective,[12] but its use in the sea novels is adverbial. It is exclusively
predicative except for three attributive occurrences as a free modifier.

Suffixes are also important in adverb formation, and "-ward" is the
most common. It attaches to sea terms that are primary (oceanward--M;
seaward--O, M, WJ; waterward--MD), secondary (shoreward--M, R, WJ), and
tertiary (sternward--M). The "-ly" suffix occurs in conjunction with two
nouns (piratically--O; squally--MD) and one adjective (nautically--M).
Occurring either as an adverbial free modifier or in a bound and
predicative position, words composed of a noun plus "-like" or "-wise"
are adverbs of manner; sailor-like--O, R, WJ; fish-like, salmon-like, and
harpoon-wise--MD.

Compounding. Melville's sea adverbs also appear as varieties of
compound words. One of these subgroups is semantically akin to the "-ly"
adverbs of manner, consisting of a noun plus either "-fashion" (sailor-
fashion--O) or "-shape" (ship-shape--WJ). Another subgroup has one member,
the adverb of opposition, in which "off-" as the initial term is in a
semantical sense counter to the noun it precedes--off-shore (MD).

There are two divisions to the final, and marginally compound,
subgroup of adverbs of direction, in which prepositions are a key element.
In the first, an unusual preposition is joined to the plural noun:
amidships (R, WJ), athwartships (O, R, MD). In the second, a common
preposition (usually "to," although "from" also appears) is placed in
front of the noun as a separate word: to larboard (M, MD), to leeward
(O, M, R, WJ), to or from windward (T, O, R, WJ, MD), from aft (M).

The Noun Adverb. The construction of the noun adverb is one that
Melville uses a good deal, and in several different ways. As a one-word
phrase, aft (O, M, R, WJ, MD) and cruise (O, WJ) and with modification,
voyage (the whole voyage--O, R; last voyage--MD), wake (ten wakes round
the world--MD), fin (fin out--MD), deck (three decks down--WJ), fathom

(fathoms down--M, R, WJ, MD; fifty fathoms, a thousand fathoms down--WJ; a thousand fathoms, ten thousand fathoms down--MD), and sea (three seas off--MD) appear regularly.

Melville also uses a more complex noun adverb form, where a noun is repeated and the repetitions are joined with a copula (jib-boom-and-jib-boom--R; gunwhale and gunwhale--M, MD) or a preposition (deck on deck--M, deck under deck--WJ, ripple after ripple--M, cruise after cruise--WJ, stunsail on stunsail--MD). There is a variation of this, where two nouns in a prescribed pattern, joined with a copula, together function as a noun adverb phrase. One of these phrases is very common in the sea novels and employs nouns of relatively equal degrees of abstraction--fore and aft (O, R, WJ, MD); another, ship-shape and Bristol fashion, occurs once (in WJ), but is so predictable that it became an idiom of land as well as of sea jargon; the last, heart and helm, also occurs only once, in Moby-Dick, but is striking for its joining (and, therefore, its melding) of two very unequal substances, warm emotion and inanimate object, another case of Melville's linking man with the sea.

Modification and Contrast. A vast majority of Melville's sea adverbs are an independent modification of either dynamic action verbs (for example, "cutting adrift the last fragments"--M, p. 120; "ridden fore and aft on a rail"--WJ, p. 102; "swept ashore in a gale"--R, p. 115) or stative be verbs (for example, "we'll be all afloat"--M, p. 6; "he is braced up fore and aft"--WJ, p. 34; "when they ought to be ashore"--O, p. 48). Very few of them either modify words that are not verbs (for example, "nautically submissive"--M, p. 91) or are themselves modified by another adverb (for example, "far" or "forever" astern--WJ, pp. 112, 398; all the cruise--WJ, p. 351; the whole cruise--WJ, p. 351; last cruise--O, p. 289; three decks down--WJ, p. 10.

Another consideration is Quirk's concept of adverbial contrast in alternative interrogation and alternative negation. Whether or not an adverb can participate in such contrast, says Quirk, determines whether or not the adverb is an adjunct (as opposed to a disjunct or a conjunct).[13] Adjunctive contrast occurs from time to time in the sea novels, usually in connection with afloat, although ashore, astern, and abeam are also occasionally involved. Several examples will demonstrate how integrated the contrastive phrase is into the sentence: in White-Jacket (p. 34)--"on shore at least, Jack might bouse away as much as he pleased; but afloat it will not do at all"; in Redburn (p. 309)--"this remarkable crew, who were so clever ashore and so craven afloat"; and again in White-Jacket (p. 44)--"with the wind astern or abeam."

Beyond placement, direction, and manner, Melville's adverbs may be significant in a deeper semantic sense, to display to the reader the contrast in Melville's mind between shore and land. The adverb ashore gives one part of the picture. Ashore is where there are "soldiers" (T, p. 16), a place where one is "impatient to get" or "on liberty" (T, pp. 28, 33), where sailors are "lovers of fun" (O, p. 41). It can also be a place of "general dissatisfaction" (O, p. 75), where there is "no lack of idle sailors" (O, p. 147), a place to be beckoned to ("Come ashore!"--M, p. 162), to "drift" to (M, p. 68), even to "jump" to (R, p. 14). "Eating and drinking" (R, p. 31), "laying idle" (R, p. 46), and other manner of "indulging" (R, p. 32) occur there. What is not spoken of is "what too many seamen are when ashore" (WJ, p. 375), but what can be said in defense is that "ashore . . . [a man is] no longer a sailor" (WJ, p. 390).

In the early sea novels, the contrast between "ashore" and "afloat" was one to mark but to make light of at the same time; men were afloat,

outward bound, until their ship's barrels were full of whale oil, and
then the home and the hearth were their destination. Only in Moby-Dick
does the "ashore/at sea" contrast take on a more serious, more symbolic,
more mysterious cast. Starbuck verbalizes a situation that is pregnant
with meaning because of idiosyncracies of the Pequod's crew and its cruise:

> The gale that now hammers at us to stave us, we can turn it
> into a fair wind that will drive us towards home. Yonder,
> to windward, all is blackness of doom; but to leeward,
> homeward--I see it lightens up there; but not with lightning
> (p. 414).

Figurative Language

The final consideration to make about Melville's adverbs is to what
extent they are involved in figurative language. Of the half dozen or so
recorded instances, the majority of the phrases are similes and compare a
sea object with something on the land. Early in Omoo, porpoises and other
fish sport under the Julia's bows "like pups ashore" (p. 34), and there
is a time when, because of her short keel, the Julia begins "spinning to
windward like a top" (p. 90). In White-Jacket, the Highlander's seamen,
"while pitching the shot up the hatchway from hand to hand, [are] like
schoolboys playing ball ashore" (p. 207).

Perhaps Melville fashions his similes this way out of his attention
for his landlubber audience, so that they might identify what they do not
know in terms of what they do, or perhaps he is making yet another subtle
remark about how similar the land and the sea really are, how akin men to
the ocean. In addition to the similes, one metaphor appears, in which a
sailor's manner of dress is compared to a ship's rigging (Mad Jack "is
braced up fore and aft, like a ship on the wind"--WJ, p. 34), and one
glorious personification, in Father Mapple's sermon in Moby-Dick, in
which man, ship, and sea all syntactically combine ("Wave after wave thus
leaps into the ship, and . . . runs roaring fore and aft"--p. 48).

Notes

1. Josephine Miles, Style and Proportion: The Language of Prose and
Poetry (Boston: Little, Brown & Co., 1967), pp. 68, 72.

2. The words functioning in this way are abyss, albatross, albicore,
alewives, alligator, ambergris, archipelago, argosy, ark, Atlantic, atoll,
baleen, barnacle, barge, bark, binnacle, blubber, bob-stays, boneeta,
boom, brail, breaker, brig, brit, buc(c)anier, bulkhead, bulwark, buoy,
caboose, cachalot, canal, canvas, cat-head, cephalaspis, cetology, chart,
chevalier, chondropterygii, chronometer, clam, cockles, cod, coffer-dam,
compass, corsair, corvette, crab, crocodile, crow's-nest, current, davit,
delta, deluge, depth, dinghy, drogher, duck, felucca, ferry, figure-head,
flipper, flotilla, flounders, frog, gaff, gale, galleon, gallant, galliot,
gill, glyptolepis, grampus, gulf, gurry, halyard, hatch, helm,
hermaphrodite, herring, hold, ichthyology, inlet, isthmus, junk, kelp,
kelson, kentledge, knight-head, knot, kraken, lagoon, landsman, lanyard,

launch, lay, leech, liner, lobster, lugger, mackerel, maelstrom, marling, mollusca, mullet, mussel, nautilus, oar, offing, ork, orlop, outrigger, passage, peninsula, periwinkle, pier, plank, polyp, pontoon, poop, port, privateer, proa, pterichthys, quadrant, quay, rib, rudder, run, Sampson-Post, sand-bar, scale, scuttle, seine, sextant, shad, sheer, shrimp, silver-heads, skiff, skrimshander, sloop, snatch-blocks, spanker, specksynder, spile, sprat, spray, state-room, steamer, stem, steward, strait, strand, stream, sturgeon, surf, swan, swell, tadpole, taffrail, terrapin, tiller, top, transom, trick, trout, truck, try-works, tug, vortex, walrus, wash, whirlpool, wriggle-tail, Xiphius Platypterus, yacht, yawl, and yellow-back.

3. The mass nouns are ambergris, baleen, blubber, brit, canvas, cetology, coral, foam, gurry, herring, ichthyology, kentledge, lee, mackerel, oakum, rigging, salmon, shrimp, skrimshander, spermaciti, squid, steerage, sturgeon, surf, trout, and water.

4. The classes of dynamic and stative verbs are well illustrated in Randolph Quirk, Sidney Greenbaum, Geoffrey Leech, and Jim Svartvik, A Grammar of Contemporary English (New York: Seminar Press, 1972), pp. 95-96.

5. Otto Jespersen, A Modern English Grammar on Historical Principles (Copenhagen: Ejnar Munksgaard, 1949), 4: 2.

6. According to Richard Henry Dana's The Seaman's Friend (Boston: Thomas Groom & Co., 1857), p. 130, the word "yaw" refers to "the motion of a vessel when she goes off from her course."

7. Quirk et al., A Grammar of Contemporary English, pp. 914-15.

8. W. H. Smyth, The Sailor's Word-Book: An Alphabetical Digest of Nautical Terms (London: Blackie & Son, 1867), p. 24.

9. Geoffrey Leech, "'This bread I break'--Language and Interpretation," A Review of English Literature 6 (1965): 68.

10. Geoffrey Leech, A Linguistic Guide to English Poetry (London: Longman Group Ltd., 1969), p. 57.

11. Quirk et al., A Grammar of Contemporary English, p. 235.

12. Ibid., p. 236.

13. Ibid, p.. 268-69.

3
The Words in Their Contexts

They say Homer himself was once a tar, even as his hero,
Ulysses, was both a sailor and a shipwright. I'll swear
Shakespeare was once a captain of the forecastle. . . .
And the world-finder, Christopher Columbus, was a sailor!
and so was Camoens, who went to sea with Gama. . . . Then
there's Falconer, whose "Shipwreck" will never founder,
though he himself, poor fellow, was lost at sea in the
Aurora frigate. Old Noah was the first sailor. And St.
Paul, too, knew how to box the compass, my lad! . . .
There's Shelley, he was quite a sailor. . . . And was not
Byron a sailor? . . . I say, White-Jacket, d'ye mind me?
there never was a very great man yet who spent all his life
inland.

--<u>White-Jacket</u>

A Word Within Its Sentences

    Now that characteristics of the sea vocabulary have been set forth
and classification systems for it proposed, and the function and the
composition of the words themselves have been examined, extending the
scope of the grammatical investigation to the contexts in which Melville
places his words would seem appropriate. The primary unit of integrity
and significance which Melville uses is the sentence, and the sea
vocabulary appears in all types, from the simplest three-word independent
base clause to magnificent, modified, multiclaused elaborations that run
to half a page. Examining all the sentences that use sea vocabulary in
all of the sea novels would be, of course, impractical and so to impose
some method to such an immense body of data, I have chosen to focus on
six important sea vocabulary terms, one from each semantic class--
<u>billows</u> (1), <u>shore</u> (2), <u>fin</u> (3A), <u>squall</u> (3B), <u>anchor</u> (3C), and <u>tar</u> (4).

These terms were selected primarily on the basis of two criteria:
first that they belong exclusively to their class and to none other
(fathom, for example, spans four classes, and several of the other words
participate in at least two), and second that they be in some semantic or
syntactic way curious, overtly illustrating something of the facility and
art of which Melville is capable. After choosing my terms, I listed the
sentences in all of the sea novels where they appeared, and then went
about an analysis of how each term was used throughout those novels.
Appendix E should be consulted for the sets of sentences wherein each of
the six words occurs. These sentences will be referred to in the text by
an initial for each novel followed by a citation number, numbering the
sentences of that novel where the word in question occurs. Thus, R-5
indicates the fifth sentence in Redburn where a particular word appears;
MD-13, the thirteenth sentence in Moby-Dick that uses the term in question,
and so on; the specific page references are given in Appendix E. Such a
system, first of all, indicates progression of the words more immediately
than page numbers (since it is not uncommon for one page to contain more
than one of the words under examination), and secondly, the citations
appear less cluttered.

Billows (1)

Primary sea terms function in interesting, symbolic ways more
frequently than secondary sea terms. This is not simply because the
vocabulary of the primary group significantly outnumbers that of the
secondary group, but in part because Melville, as he made his way through
the pages of the sea novels, became more conscious, I think, of the
linguistic and artistic possibilities of the primary sea terms.
According to Smyth's The Sailor's Word-Book, the primary sea term
billows is "more in use among poets than seamen,"[1] and certainly the two
most "poetic" of the sea novels, Mardi and Moby-Dick, each contain at
least three times more uses of the word than the other sea novels do.
The word appears in Mardi's pages as a straight referential indicator, as
a metonymy for the sea, and most provocatively, as a symbol. Melville is
careful with his overtly poetic terms--if he had used them more frequently
than he does, their foregrounding would not have been as effective, and
so we do not see billows nearly as often in the sea novels as, for
example, the secondary sea term shore.
Melville's uses of billows in the referential sense are prolific and
diffuse within his sentences. There are three basic tenses in which the
term is employed, and all three involve action. With participles--
"tossed" (T-1),[2] "flashing" (T-2), "heaving" (O-1), "raised and lowered"
(MD-19); verbs--"beat" (M-23), "smote" (M-26), "lifts" (MD-6), "recoil"
(MD-21); and adjectives--"black" (M-11), "wild" (M-14), "panther" (MD-2),
"destroying" (MD-24), the word designates a force that is active, nonhuman,
frightening.
"Billows" are precursors of doom or danger. In Mardi the word is
correlated by coordination with a prowling shark (M-2). Much later in
the book, "the blue billows" that "gush in glittering foam" tempt Taji to
Hautia's bower (M-30). In Moby-Dick, billows are "envious" of Ahab's
passing because they want to "whelm" his track (MD-7). By means of a
simile in four of the novels, the word is hooked up with a bomb (M-17),
people dying aboard ship (R-5), whatever evil nature or man can deal out
(the sea or war--WJ-8), the lulling effect of a Nantucketer's sails (MD-4),
stars (MD-15), a giant's palms (MD-17), and Ahab (MD-22). The sea, taking
charge of man, undulates "in milk-white billows of foam" (WJ-3) over "lee

carronades on the quarter-deck and forecastle." And as, or perhaps because, the Neversink, heedless, bounds over the billows, "a black cloud rises out of the sea; the sun drops down from the sky; a horrible mist far and wide spreads over the water" (WJ-2). Father Mapple recalls, in his sermon, how much of a panther a billow can be, as it leapt over the bulwarks, springing on Jonah (MD-2).

At least twice in the sea novels Melville uses a sentence to associate billows with thought, and once with life itself. In Mardi, "recollections" break over Taji "like returning billows on a beach long bared" (M-9). And in Melville's next book, young Redburn, hearing a great bell tolling in the mist, associates it with the "solemn roll of the billows" as he approaches Liverpool (R-1). Ahab, in an anguished exhortation, presses all the "bold" billows of his "whole foregone life" to pour in "from all your furthest bounds" to cover "this one piled comber of my death" (MD-23).

Billows, it seems, are inevitable, ineluctable, and cyclical. They are both "returning" (M-9) and "circling" (M-27), "immense long-extended and long rolling" (M-6), and "enormous" (M-12). They can, however, be "lost"--swallowed up by "the brow of a beetling crag" (M-13)--but only in some phenomenon of nature. Man is powerless against them. To him, billows are "destroying" (MD-24). In themselves, they are certain, something to swear by (M-18); a vehicle by which to direct ships, as the white light of their foam indicated Hamora's western shore to Taji (M-25); a phenomenon that has been rolling on "speechless and unspoken to" "for long Chinese ages" (MD-15).

Billows may imply what is positive, playful, even as they themselves are harsh and foreboding, but not as often. The spectral shadow that is cast "over the heaving billows" turns out to be dawn (O-1). Interestingly, all occurrences of unquestionably positive associations of the term occur in Mardi except for two. Mardi is, according to Melville, a romance, different from anything he had written, and in that genre the reality of a harsh sea becomes muted and transmuted into a more gentle illusion. Twice the billows "lave" (M-1, 29), and in the first of these, do so mildly with a "cadence." Taji records, almost affectionately, how "our little sea-goat" bounded "over the billows" (M-5). The billows in Mardi can roll by "listlessly" (M-8), become a playmate of surfers (M-16), or softly "lap" (M-20). They are "bowling" (M-24) and "silvery" (M-22). In White-Jacket the billows are described with equal felicity--"we were gradually rolled by the smooth, sliding billows" (WJ-6)--but in this instance the billows are, ominously, "broad out upon the deep." In Moby-Dick, duodecimo whales, a lucky omen, "invariably come from the breezy billows to windward" (MD-5). And the fine tale of Jonah is dubbed "billow-like and boisterously grand" (MD-1).

On the occasions where Melville uses billows as a metonymy for sea, the tone is more subdued than either of these extremes. Billows are something that Tommo pines for (O-2) as Ishmael will do later; yet, as White Jacket reads in Waller's verse, one must occasionally have a reprieve from them (WJ-5), substantiating what Lemsford says in the closing pages of the book, "I venerate the sea, and venerate it so highly, shipmates, that ever more I shall abstain from crossing it" (p. 389). Melville is factual about what he says of billows when using this form of the word-- islands rise up from them (M-7); fishermen brave them for food (R-2); squid, "unearthly, formless, chance-like apparition[s] of life," undulate on them (MD-11). His tone is appropriate--the billows' "low moan" and the sad sigh of the breeze is a fitting eulogy for a dead diver whose body is committed to the sea (M-19). Finally, Melville is wistful; by prepositional construction, White Jacket nostalgically associates Jack

Chase with the "blue billows" (WJ-1) near the beginning of the book, a
foreshadowing of the prepositional construction Jack uses much later to
connect them both with the billows (WJ-7).

Finally, there are occurrences of the word billows--all in Mardi and
Moby-Dick--that have a clearly symbolic sense, where their contexts infuse
them with unusual associations. Half of those in Mardi are put into the
voice of someone other than the protagonist. Three connote military or
political agitation--"bright billows of cuirassiers" charging at Waterloo
(M-15), Babbalanja recalling Lombardo tossing his great mane in "hairy
billows" (M-28), and Mohi, in the final pages of the book, prophesying
the impending doom of the state, over which "combing billows must break"
(M-31). The other occurrence in Mardi is the most interesting of all,
for Melville first associates the currents of various rivers (the
Mississippi, the Ohio, the Missouri, and the Arkansas) with "all the past
and present pouring in me [Taji]" and immediately thereafter states, "I
roll down my billow from afar" (M-21). The possessive marker as well as
the singular number (of the seventy-four occurrences of billows in the
sea novels, only a dozen are singular, and nearly half of these occur in
Moby-Dick) are unusual, and Moby-Dick uses both. There are metaphysical
billows which are "of" Ahab's foregone life (MD-23) and billows which are
Ahab's "foster-brothers," since he was "suckled by the sea" (MD-17). And
Ahab, near the end of his life, feels "like a billow that's all one
crested comb" (MD-22). A billow breaks (MD-13) and leaps (MD-2) in the
singular and, also in the singular, as we have seen, takes the suffix
"-like" (MD-1).

In his best creation, Moby-Dick, Melville thus assembles a number of
linguistic tricks in connection with the term billows and plays them all
to wonderful advantage.

Shore (2)

The secondary sea term shore, the juncture of nautical and terrestrial
realms, is prevalent in the sea novels, occurring roughly three times as
often as the primary sea term billows. There seems to be no pattern of
progression in Melville's use of shore in the novels; it is used least in
Moby-Dick, Typee, and Redburn; more often in White-Jacket and Omoo; and
in Mardi at least twice as often as in any other novel. The common
background uses of shore are those repeated, bare references that are
almost adverbial, peripheral to a more important business of a sentence.
Such occurrences are directional or positional, where shore is the object
of any number of localizing prepositions: "to," "near," "of," "with,"
"from," "between"--and where no other elements in the sentence modify or
illuminate the word or the concept. In these cases, shore always occurs
with a definite article and is more frequently singular than plural.

Two smaller categories are also relatively insignificant to an analysis
of the grammatical peculiarities of shore. One of these is where shore,
again adverbial, as a locational target, functions as the direct object
of certain verbs: "gained," "reaching," "rounding," "touched," "visited,"
"leave," "laves," The other minor category is where shore is a locational
subject of the sentence but without modification and in a manner that
seems neither unusual nor atypical--for example, "the shores of Diranda
were in sight" (Mardi, p. 439) or "the shore was lined with multitudes
pushing off wildly in canoes" (Mardi, p. 499).

The set of sentences that foreground shore to some degree, which are
recorded in Appendix E, is distinguished by the presence of adjectival
modofications or by an offer of information that is less specifically

locational. About one-half of the sentences belong to this set. Within
the set, as might be expected, number, part of speech, degree of
reference or symbolism, and modification vary considerably.

In Omoo, Redburn, White-Jacket, and Moby-Dick, shore appears
overwhelmingly in the singular, but in Typee and Mardi singular and plural
appear equally often. There seems to be a distinct difference between
the singular, which is more directly locational in reference, and the
plural, which even by plurality ceases to be exclusively locational and
is foregrounded to some degree by the very fact of its plurality. In the
sentences of Typee where shore is foregrounded, the word is most often
the object of a preposition (except for T-1 and T-3, where it is a
subject). The word is used in sentences that are descriptive--shore
"recedes, describes a semi-circle" (T-1), is "beautiful" (T-2), "elevated"
(T-6), and "indented" (T-3). A "lofty" shore (T-4) has "shadows," which
may prepare Typee's reader for the symbolical "dimly looming shores of
Paradise" (T-8) which Tommo imagines while visiting the chief's mausoleum.
While there are no overtly symbolic uses of shore in Omoo, there are two
instances when the word is used as a metonymy for the people or nation
that inhabit(s) the shore--in those sentences, the narrator's concern is
"communication with the shore" (O-3) and "any word even from the shore"
(O-11). The remaining sentences either involve description--"the shore,
which was margined with foam" (O-5); use one of several adjectives with
shore--"bold . . . undulating" (O-6), "strange" (O-13), "farthest" (O-16),
"lake" (O-17), "southern" (O-20), "green" (O-21); hook shore up with an
interesting noun phrase--"Formed by a bold sweep of the shore" (O-12); or
introduce shore as an adjective--of "scenery" (O-1), "doctor(s)" (O-4, 14),
"boat" (O-8, 10), "physician" (O-9). At least one of these is overtly a
simile--"Like shore doctors, he did not eschew his own medicines" (O-4).

Mardi adds two additional forms of shore as parts of speech not found
in Typee or Omoo, displays a provocative array of modification for shore,
and uses shore in three ways--reference, metonymy, and symbol. Shore in
this novel appears as a verbal--"shoals . . . shoreing the white reef of
the Milky Way" (M-27); an adverb--"shoreward" (M-2, 41); and a unique
adjective--"shoreless" (M-3)--in addition to its appearance as subject
(M-17, 24, 26, 38, 45, the latter of which is a modified simile: "As if
Mardi were a poem, and every island a canto, the shore now in sight was
called Flozella-a-Nina, or The-Last-Verse-of-the-Song"), or direct object
(M-5, 6, 12, 13, 17, 23, 32, 33, 37, 39, 42, 44), or as object of a
preposition (M-7, 11, 14, 15, 18, 20, 21, 25, 28, 29, 30, 31, 34, 35, 36,
40, 43), or predicate nominative (M-8), fragment nominative (M-9), or
appositive (M-4). When shore does appear as a noun, it may be modified
by common adjectives--"bright" (M-4, 7), "neighboring" (M-12, 13, 40),
"remote" (M-10), "uninhabited" (M-28), and "distant" (M-35); by vivid
adjectives--"grand" (M-36), "glorious" (M-33), "bold" (M-29, 30), and
"pleasant" (M-18, 44); by unusual adjectives--"violet" (M-11), "russet"
(M-16), "willowy" (M-17), and "unhappy" (M-31); by positional adjectives--
"Kolumba's western" (M-34), "Hamora's western" (M-37), "Hamora's northern"
(M-38), and "long, verdant, northern" (M-15); and by adjective pairs--
"green, teacherous" (M-15), "dark and bold" (M-22), "lofty and insulated"
(M-23), and "silent and forlorn" (M-24).

As in the first two novels, the use of shore in Mardi is primarily
referential. There are two instances of metonymy--M-31, "the feud between
Dominora and this unhappy shore" and M-39, "since leaving Piko's shore of
spears." One of three uses of shore as symbol is in a chapter entitled
"Dreams," so that the surrealistic imagery of "Shoals, like nebulous
vapors, shoreing the white reef of the Milky Way" (M-27) fits the context.

The other two instances of symbol involve Taji's beloved, Yillah, who for a good deal of the novel is not much more than a dream herself. Taji calls her "my shore and my grove" (M-8), implying that finding her would give his life permanence and peace; yet, at the book's frenzied close, he must despairingly feel as he had admitted earlier in his fruitless pursuit: "Enough: no shore for me yet" (M-9).

Besides the semantic interest of relating a sentence to the theme of the book, there is syntactic interest within several sentences of Mardi where shore is involved in some way in coordinating alliterations (M-16, "Oh! russet shores of Rhine and Rhone!"; M-1, "neither sail or shore was in sight") and in assonance (M-8, "Was not Yillah my shore and my grove?"). And then there is the sentence that, because of its coordination, approaches zeugma: "Though once attained, all three--red rose, bright shore, and soft heart--are full of love, bloom, and all manner of delights" (M-4).

In the first four sea novels, possessive pronouns often introduce the word shore. In Typee, natives see a European craft approaching "their" shores (T-5), and in Omoo pagans of Tahiti have Protestant missionaries arrive to and depart from "their" shores (O-7). Melville uses the widest variety of possessives with shore: "thy," "their," "our," and "its" (where the shore can belong to the breeze--M-42, as well as to a particular land--M-14, M-26). In Redburn, "our" and "his" are found with shore, but neither White-Jacket nor Moby-Dick shows possessive pronouns associating with the noun. What they do show is possessive pronouns (in Redburn, a possessive noun is used in this way--R-9) combining with the adjective shore to modify another noun--for example, "his shore sympathies" (WJ-10), "their shore friends" (MD-3).

Naturally, when Melville uses shore, his most frequent meaning is "shore of the sea." However, he does not use the specific term "sea-shore" very often. When it does occur, it contributes in a substantial and even jocular way to modifying the tone of the sentence, in a way that shore alone would not. The first occurrence is in Typee (T-7), where the verb "hie" and a reflexive "him," coming before the shore compound, have already gotten the reader in a good humor: "old Marheyo himself would hie him away to the sea-shore." And, before the sentence ends, Melville, proud of the rhythm he has begun in his sentence, echoes the compound with another: ". . . for the purpose of collecting various species of rare sea-weed." The other occurrences of sea-shore may not please quite as much, although they do seem purposeful; the compound makes possible a greater degree of explicitness than the pure form shore would have done. In Omoo, for example, the narrator would leave no question in an incredulous reader's mind that the cocoa palm is found "right on the sea-shore, where its roots are actually washed" (O-19). In Mardi, the two members of the compound appear together without a hyphen, and grow out of a humorous simile: the Ranger calls several fish by name and pats their scales "like St. Anthony, in ancient Coptic, instilling virtuous principles into his finny flock on the sea shore" (O-20). And in Redburn the compound (also without the hyphen) is one of the many devices within a sentence that aids in poking fun at the narrator's naiveté:

> Reverentially folding this map, I pass a plate of the Town
> Hall, and come upon the Title Page, which, in the middle,
> is ornamented with a piece of landscape, representing a
> loosely clad lady in sandals, pensively seated upon a
> bleak rock on the sea shore, supporting her head with one
> hand, and with the other, exhibiting to the stranger an
> oval sort of salver, bearing the figure of a strange

bird, with this motto elastically stretched for a border--
"Deus nobis haec otia fecit" (R-10).

All of the novels except Typee show several other shore compounds,
most of which (unlike sea-shore) appear only once. In Omoo the compound
is used as an adjective in the base clause: "we got our off-shore tacks
aboard" (O-2). In Mardi the compound appears as the subject of the
sentence: "Its main-shore was a steep acclivity" (M-26). Redburn shows
the compound in an initial free modifier--"in the shore-bloom that came
to us" (R-14)--and White-Jacket has it in the final free modifier slot--
"in a service so galling to all shore-manhood as the Navy" (WJ-17). A
marble tablet near the pulpit of New Bedford's Whaleman's Chapel carries
the sentence that includes the final shore compound, which appears as a
final modifier to an initial modifier--"on the Off-shore Ground in the
Pacific" (MD-1).

Thus, shore appears in many guises. Besides the affixes already
mentioned, the prefix "a-" joins shore more than two hundred times
throughout the sea novels. Ashore has not been discussed here because
it is consistently adverbial, with the exception of "go-ashore traps" in
Typee, which was mentioned in the adjective section of the previous
chapter. Ashore has no other extraordinary occurrences.

Fin (3A)

The first division of the tertiary sea terms, that involving animate,
nonhuman life of the sea, has many members that might be analyzed for
their syntactic and semantic peculiarities, among which are albatros(s),
fish, shark, and whale. What is surprising is that even a word that one
would expect to be relatively tame and void of much complexity, such as
fin, is not. Melville's manipulations are at play even here. The word's
distribution is unlike that of either billows or shore, occurring in only
four of the sea novels. There is a singular occurrence in both Omoo and
Redburn, and an equal multiplicity of occurrences in both Mardi and
Moby-Dick.

A most striking semantic feature about fin (common to other words
from this group as well) is the amount of anthropomorphizing Melville
does with it, or at least the number of times he uses the term in
connection with humanity. The word first occurs in Omoo, in a sentence
that describes a tattoo of a blue shark, "nothing but fins from head to
tail," (O-1) on a strange renegade's forehead.

But Mardi is the novel that shows this feature most distinctly. Forty
pages into the book, a "dainty" blue shark "lounged by with a careless
fin and an indolent tail" (M-1), and from there, the tendency to instill
some human character into fin takes many turns. In one instance the
narrator examines boneetas examining him and remarks, ". . . they behold
our limber fins, our speckled and beautiful scales" (M-15). A page later
he puts a song into the mouths of the fish, one verse of which is: "We
fish, we fish, we merrily swim,/ We care not for friend nor foe:/ Our fins
are stout,/ Our tails are out,/ As through the seas we go" (M-17). The
other pointedly anthropomorphic sentence in Mardi describes the Ranger
"instilling virtuous principles into his finny flock" (M-20). Three other
sentences in Mardi also connect fins with humanity. One of them
physically joins the two worlds by ingestion--"finny things, of flavor
rare, but hard to mouth for bones" (M-24). In another, Babbalanja is
conjecturing about people of strange races, who may "have fins or wings
for arms" (M-26). The final sentence connects something of a land animal
with something of a sea creature by a conjunction and applies both to a

dwarf on Hooloomooloo, the Isle of Cripples, who, "furnished with feelers
or fins, rolled himself up in a ball, bowling over the ground in advance"
(M-28). So Melville has compared a man to a fish as well as a fish to a
man.

Moby-Dick's sentences involving the anthropomorphism of fin are
subtler. One of the sentences is a quotation from Charles Lamb, which
calls the whale "the finny people's king" (MD-1), another comments on how
"gregarious" the fin-back whale is (MD-7), and still another explains that
"Tall-Spout and Long-John" are also names for that whale (MD-2). An infant
whale's "delicate side-fins" are compared to a "baby's ears" (MD-22) in
another sentence and, more metaphysically, "every dimly-discovered,
uprising fin of some undiscernable form" is compared to "the embodiment
of . . . elusive thoughts" (MD-11).

Another semantic feature of the word fin concerns its implication.
Fin is used overwhelmingly as a direct referent in the four sea novels
where it appears, and in Mardi alone is there any deviation from that
norm. There the word appears five times as a metonymy for "fish" (M-4, 9,
11, 13, 15) and once as a metaphor for "arms" (M-15).

A third semantic peculiarity to note about the fin sentences is that
Melville liberally couches figurative language in them. There are three
cases of formally poetic verse (M-17, 19; MD-1) and at least six similes.
In Mardi dorsal fins are compared to spokes of a wheel (M-2) and a cocked
trigger of a gun (M-8). Along with the comparison already alluded to of
side-fins and a baby's ears (MD-22), Moby-Dick also notes the similarity
between fins and "a lost sheep's ear" (MD-13), and between a "fin-bone"
and a harpoon (MD-25). The most engaging simile, though, is part of a
more extended analogy, and involves an inanimate object:

When the sea is moderately calm, and slightly marred with
spherical ripples, and this gnomon-like fin stands up and
casts shadows upon the wrinkled surface, it may well be
supposed that the watery circle surrounding it somewhat
resembles a dial, with its style and wavy hour-lines
graved on it (MD-6).

Fin is used, furthermore, in alliteration--"fins and flippers fricasseed"
(M-25), "furnished with feelers or fins" (M-28) and in zeugma--"all is . . .
light hearts and light fins" (M-12).

Syntactically, fin appears, with varying degrees of frequency, in all
of the major form classes except for the finite verb (there is, however,
a past participle which functions in a compound as an appositive--M-27).
It is most often a noun, commonly an adjective and even occasionally an
adverb. Primarily the nominal office of fin is as an object of the
prepositions "with," "without," "at," "from," "for," "to," "of," "upon,"
and "like," which construction occurs in Mardi slightly more frequently
(M-1, 5, 8, 9, 10, 12, 14, 19, 23, 28) than in Moby-Dick (where all of
the forms are singular--MD-2, 9, 15, 19, 24, 25). The subject of a base
clause is the second most frequent function of the forms of fin which are
nouns, and those occurrences as well are split between Mardi (all plural
forms: M-11, 17, 18) and Moby-Dick (MD-3, 5, 7, 8, 11, 13, 21, 22).
Direct objects are also numerous (M-15, 22, 26; R-1; MD-14, 16, 18, 26).
Fin has a limited appearance as an appositive (M-27; MD-4, 10, 23), the
subject of an absolute (M-2, 25, both plural), the subject of a
subordinate clause (MD-6, 17, both singular), and singular appearances as
a predicate nominative (R-1, a plural form) and as the subject of a noun
phrase (O-1, plural).

All of the adjectival forms of fin have an "-ny" suffix. The
construction finny is a strangely poetic one and, not surprisingly,

occurs more times in the strangely poetic novel Mardi than anywhere else.
There, the word modifies "tribes" (M-3, 6), "creatures" (M-7), "flock"
(M-20), and "things" (M-24). One of the Moby-Dick occurrences is in a
quotation from Charles Lamb's Triumph of the Whale, where it is used to
modify a possessive adjective--"the finny people's king" (MD-1) and the
last occurrence echoes the dual image in Mardi, "finny tribes" (M-22).[3]

The two adverbial occurrences of fin are noun adverbs and appear
without affix. They also both refer to whales. In Mardi Taji is
discussing various species of whales "fighting, fin for fin" (M-4) and in
Moby-Dick Ahab exhorts his crew to hunt the white whale until he "spouts
black blood and rolls fin out" (MD-12).

Melville does a moderate amount of compounding with the word fin.
Fin-back, with various combinations of upper and lower case letters for
the "f" and the "b," is the most prevalent of the compounds, occurring in
Mardi (M-21), Redburn (R-1, twice in the same sentence), and Moby-Dick
(MD-2, 3, 7, 8). Melville's additional compound shows fin in the past
participial form, finned-lions (M-27). Moby-Dick has fin as the initial
member of the compound, fin-bone (MD-25), as well as the final member--
back-fin (MD-10), side-fins (MD-21, 22).

There is also a moderate amount of modification that is associated
with fin in Mardi and in Moby-Dick. Some of this is positional ("dorsal"--
M-2, 8; "ventral"--M-5; "starboard"--MD-15), much of it is possessive
(M-2, 5, 8, 10, 15, 17, 20; MD-13, 15, 17, 18, 21, 24, 25, 26). The more
unusual occurrences in Mardi are: "careless" (M-1), "myriad" (M-11),
"fiery" (M-21), and "bright and twittering" (M-19). Moby-Dick's peculiar
modifiers for fin include: "gnomon-like" (MD-6), "shuddering" (MD-14),
"delicate" (MD-22), and "scolloped" (MD-23). And two of Moby-Dick's
sentences show fin described by many modifiers--one of them, for all its
modification, still relatively straightforward, "His broad fins are bored,
and scolloped out like a lost sheep's ear!" (MD-13). The other
modification sentence rather obscures than illuminates fin, sublimating
it in the same Descartian vortices that tempt and beckon the water gazer
who is the subject of the sentence:

Perhaps they were; or perhaps there might have been shoals
of them in the far horizon; but lulled into such an opium-
like listlessness of vacant, unconscious reverie is this
absent-minded youth by the blending cadence of waves with
thoughts, that at last he loses his identity; takes the
mystic ocean at his feet for the visible image of that
deep, blue, bottomless soul, pervading mankind and nature;
and every strange, half-seen, gliding, beautiful thing
that eludes him; every dimly-discovered, uprising fin of
some undiscernable form, seems to him the embodiment of
those elusive thoughts that only people the soul by
continually flitting through it (MD-11).

Semantically and syntactically, then, even a supposedly trivial sea
vocabulary item can be seen to be vigorous and active. This is one of
the strengths and beauties of Melville's prose: he does not neglect to
sound the grammatical possibilities of something small.

Squall (3B)

Squall appears in all the sea novels except the first, and unlike the
other five vocabulary terms under consideration, is used progressively
more often and in progressively more important ways from novel to novel.
Most of its occurrences are referential, and there is, at least in the

middle novels of <u>Mardi</u>, <u>Redburn</u>, and <u>White-Jacket</u> a fairly equal
distribution between the singular and the plural numbers, while <u>Omoo</u> and
<u>Moby-Dick</u> are fairly consistent in using the singular. The uses of the
word seem confined to those of the noun and the adjective, and only one
suffix ("-y") and one compound (<u>snow-squall</u>) were tallied in connection
with <u>squall</u>. The word, thus, is not among the most active or flexible of
Melville's sea vocabulary, but its importance resides in its value as
simile, as symbol, and as solid meteorological referent for Melville and
for the characters in his books.

Of the three occurrences of <u>squall</u> in <u>Omoo</u>, the first two are trivial
and the final one is an interesting simile. The action of water or wind
on the ship, the effects of the squall, are grammatically more important
than the squall itself, which is relegated to an unadorned object of a
preposition in <u>O</u>-1 and <u>O</u>-2. But in <u>O</u>-3 Melville not so subtly combines
humanity with the sea storm, as a "passionate old man" is described as
making "as much fuss as a white squall aboard the Flying Dutchman."

The sentences of <u>Mardi</u> using <u>squall</u> run to the same number as those
of <u>Omoo</u>, but they are more intense because of the modification in each of
them and because of a type of simile reversal in the first one. That is,
in <u>M</u>-1, the squall, or more specifically, what it brings with it (the
trade winds) is compared to "favors snappishly conferred" and is the more
important element of the comparison, instead of comparing something else
(an old man's behavior, which is the more important element of the
comparison in the <u>Omoo</u> example) to the squall. But, because "favors"
ultimately generate exclusively from a human source, the point is again
made that the sea and humanity connect. In this novel, <u>squalls</u> are both
"cold" and "fierce" (<u>M</u>-2) and "very sharp" (<u>M</u>-1), and a hypothetical
"shade of a ship, full of sailor's ghosts" would dissolve in a
"supernatural" squall (<u>M</u>-3).

Most of the <u>squall</u> sentences in <u>Redburn</u> are background terms, using
<u>squall</u> in either the singular or the plural as a simple referent in a
prepositional construction. Among such uses, the word takes on one
adjectival modifier, "hard" (<u>R</u>-2), and connects by coordination with
either "hurricanes" (<u>R</u>-1) or "rains" (<u>R</u>-7). (Contrast this with the
sentence in <u>Moby-Dick</u> that combines <u>squall</u> with "whale" and "harpoon"--
<u>MD</u>-10). The word has one unusual occurrence, in a religious metaphor
about earth and heaven: "sailors . . . have plenty of squalls here below,
but fair weather aloft" (<u>R</u>-3).

<u>White-Jacket</u>'s treatment of squalls is somehow more ingenious. There
are here the trivial background constructions (<u>WJ</u>-2, 3, 7), but, for the
first time in the sea novels, a "black" squall is mentioned (<u>WJ</u>-4) and,
for the second time, a "white" squall is mentioned (the other reference is
(<u>O</u>-3), this time in conjunction with "living gales and Typhoons" (<u>WJ</u>-1).
In another sentence, an Indiaman is "tossed about in the squalls" like a
football (<u>WJ</u>-6). Squall is modified by "hard" (<u>WJ</u>-8) as it had been in
the previous novel. <u>White-Jacket</u> shows one of the two occurrences of
<u>squall</u> as an adjective in "the squally Cape" (<u>WJ</u>-5); the other is <u>MD</u>-14),
and the only occurrence of <u>squall</u> in a compound, "I hailed every snow-
squall" (<u>WJ</u>-9).

The most frequent, the most imaginative, and the most descriptive
appearances of <u>squall</u> are in <u>Moby-Dick</u>. There are, first of all, sentences
where the word has a fairly trivial and referential sense--<u>MD</u>-1, 5 (where
it is the object of "kill"), 6, 7 (where, in a sentence fragment, it acts
as an interjection), 12 (where it is modified by "foggy"), and 13 (where,
with "capsizings," it is a compound subject of a subordinate clause). Two
of <u>squall</u>'s appearances as objects of the preposition "of" are unique

because they are in some way descriptive of the word's physical referent: MD-13, "in the teeth of a squall" and MD-9, "into the white curdling cream of the squall." There are three metaphorical uses of squall--one referring to Peleg's rages (MD-2, another to Ahab's outbursts (MD-15), and the third to Flask's antics ("he strikes into a sharp but noiseless squall of a hornpipe"--MD-3). The "White Squall" is what "the gauntleted ghost of the Southern Seas" is dubbed (MD-8). Two important similes involve squall--one characterizing the movements of a whale ("he fantails like a split jib in a squall"--MD-4), the other, in flamboyant description, personifying and animating the word in a dual simile: ". . . the whole squall roared, forked, and crackled around us like a white fire upon the prairie, in which, unconsumed, we were burning; immortal in these jaws of death!" (MD-11).

Squall is, therefore, a powerful sea word semantically and symbolically, though it is quite tame syntactically. To seamen it is always vicious (note the sentences using the descriptive words "teeth" and "jaws"), and the best that can be said about it in reality is what is said symbolically about Peleg's anger: "Whew! . . . the squall's gone off to leeward, I think" (MD-2).

Anchor (3C)

Since the last division of the tertiary sea terms is the largest by at least twice of any other group of the sea vocabulary, selecting a single term to analyze was difficult. The scope of the terms is very broad, some occurring only once in any of the sea novels (for example, coffer-dam, lugger, felucca) and others (such as bow, frigate, hawse) used by Melville to great advantage. Anchor was selected because it has a good distribution within all of the novels and because it is fairly typical of a good many of the words in this division that Melville uses both referentially and symbolically.

White-Jacket and Redburn each contain more sentences with anchor than any other sea novel, White-Jacket with over twice the number in Redburn. Mardi has the fewest occurrences of anchor (over a third of which are, incidentally, symbolic). Of the referential occurrences of anchor, the overwhelming majority are nominal, although verbal and adjectival uses are occasionally found in the sentences as well. Of the nominal functions, anchor occurs most often as an object of a preposition and as a direct object. The singular number of the word predominates ten to one over the plural.

Typee's nominal uses of anchor are entirely referential; there is nothing complex or figurative in them. All of the occurrences except two (which have a suffix and, consequently, will be discussed shortly) are as the pure form anchor, the only accompanying modification being the possessive pronoun "her" (T-7). The uses are either as the object of a preposition ("at"--T-1, 6; "to"--T-4, 5) or the direct object of a verb ("dropped"--T-7; "ordered"--T-9).

Objects of the preposition also predominate in Omoo's uses of anchor ("to"--O-2, 3, 8, 13; "at"--O-5; "for"--O-18). There are direct objects as well (of "find"--O-1; "let go"--O-4, 9; "catted"--O-15; "drops"--O-22). And Omoo introduces new nominal functions: subordinate-clause subject (O-10, 12, 16) and base-clause subject (O-7, 14, 17, 23).

Mardi shows no sentences where anchor is used as a direct object, although anchor as object of a preposition (M-4, the phrase is "profoundly at anchor," and M-16) and as subject of the base clause (M-3, where it is inverted in a question) do exist. Mardi does one thing that the first

two novels do not and that will be important in novels to come: it uses
anchor in an appositive noun phrase (M-1).

Redburn's contribution to the grammatical palette of anchor is the
use of the word as the subject of an absolute clause (R-1, 5; WJ-6 is the
only other sentence in the sea novels where this happens). Other than
that, anchor appears most frequently as a prepositional object (R-2, 4, 6,
9, 10, 11, 13, 14, 15, 19, 21, 22, 23, 24, 27, 29, 30). With less
frequency, anchor is used as the subject of a base clause (R-8, with the
modofication of "her starboard"; R-17; as an inverted subject in R-16 and
R-28), as the subject of a subordinate clause (R-3), as a direct object
(of "had"--R-7; of "catted"--R-25; of "weigh"--R-26), and in an
appositive noun phrase (R-18, 20).

Since White-Jacket has such a large assortment of sentences using
anchor (the word even occurs three times in one of the sentences--WJ-15,
and in over sixty sentences throughout the book), it is not surprising
that all of the nominal capacities are in use. Only half of the words,
moreover, are the pure form anchor; the others show the word in some
compound or with some affix. When anchor occurs unadorned, it is as a
direct object (WJ-1, 10, 15, 20, 26, 27, 39, 42, 43, 47, 60), as an
object of the preposition (WJ-2, 3, 4, 5, 8, 24, 33, 34, 38, 40, 46, 48,
56, 58, 59), as the subject of a base clause (WJ-61, 64), and as a
nominative in a sentence fragment (WJ-63, a chapter title).

Moby-Dick contributes the predicate nominative to anchor's uses
(MD-14) and shows anchor most frequently as an object of the preposition
(MD-2, 3, 4, 5--where it is modified by "great," 6, 7, 8--modified by
"approaching," 10, 11--modified by "frigate's," 15, 17). There are
singular appearances of anchor as the subject of a base clause (MD-16),
the subject of a subordinate clause (MD-9), and a direct object (MD-12).

The adjectival appearances of anchor are rare; I recorded only three
cases, and they all have unique forms. Of the two in White-Jacket, one
is a possessive adjective: "the sheet-anchor-man's integrity" (WJ-31),
and the other shows the nominal form functioning as an adjective: "he
with the anchor button" (WJ-45). The adjective of anchor in Moby-Dick is
a compound participle: "this corner-anchored old ark" (MD-1).

All the novels except Moby-Dick (including Moby-Dick if the above
participle is allowed) use anchor infrequently in a verbal capacity to
refer to a number of sailing craft. In Typee, it is "a whale ship" which
was "anchored" (T-8), in Omoo, simply, "the ship" (O-11). Redburn leaves
the craft out of the phrase, though one is implied: "not long after
anchoring" (R-12). White-Jacket's three sentences that use anchor in
this way all refer to different craft: "like another man-of-war, fast
anchored in the bay" (WJ-23); "though his vessel be anchored a mile from
shore" (WJ-28); "ere Noah . . . anchored his ark" (WJ-37). One of Mardi's
sentences of this type uses anchor fairly straightforwardly, though note
the modification: "the fated brig lay anchored" (M-2). The other is
sufficiently interesting to quote in full. In it, "a mighty rock" is the
subject of "anchored," but the word is attended by several other noun
phrases and does not receive its verb until the end of the sentence: "On
our left, Porpheero's southwest point, a mighty rock, long tiers of
galleries within, deck on deck; and flag-staffs, like an admiral's masts:
a line-of-battleship, all purpose stone, and anchored in the sea" (M-7).

The suffix "-age," when added to anchor, semantically (Melville is
consistent here) converts an instrument into a place. Anchorage occurs
in all of the sea novels except Moby-Dick, occasionally with modification.
The unadorned word occurs in the following sentences--T-2, O-20, 21. It
is also shown modified by "good and secure" (T-3), "safe" (O-6), "their"
(O-19), "our only" (O-8), and "our" (WJ-22).

The single most important compound involving anchor is sheet-anchor-man, and the word appears exclusively in White-Jacket. It is commonly used in a dialogue tag, usually as an inverted subject (WJ-7, 12, 14, 36, 57, 62), but also as the subject of a base clause (WJ-11, 18--modified by "one rheumatic old," 30--by "a knowing old," 32; as an inverted subject--WJ-6), as the subject of a subordinate clause (WJ-44), as a direct object (WJ-16), as an object of a preposition (WJ-19, 49--modified by "some old"), as a predicate nominative (WJ-51), as a nominative of address (WJ-35, 54), and, importantly, as an appositive (WJ-13, 17, 21, 25, 50, 53). Sheet-anchor-man, in fact, is the word that so staggeringly inflates the total number of times that anchor is used in White-Jacket.

Of the other compound words using anchor, one appears in Moby-Dick (anchor-watch, MD-13) and the rest are in White-Jacket. These are: anchor-button (WJ-9, 55), anchor-buoy (WJ-29), and best-bower-anchors (WJ-52; and in WJ-41 without the second hyphen, so that the words seem to be a compound adjective and a noun).

Besides being grammatically creative with anchor, Melville also uses the word to figurative and symbolic advantage. In three of the novels--Mardi, White-Jacket, and Moby-Dick--it is used in a simile. Half of these are comparisons involving humanity (another link in Melville's connection between the sea and man). The earliest of these is the most philosophical: "Like helmless vessels, tempest-tossed, our only anchorage is when we founder" (M-8). In White-Jacket, the narrator, weighted down by his rain-soaked apparel, feels as if he were "weighing the anchor" (WJ-1). A sheet-anchor-man's integrity is later compared to "a rock" (WJ-31). And in Moby-Dick, Father Mapple compares Jonah to an anchor, "taken up . . . and dropped into the sea" (MD-3). Other similes use anchor in comparisons with the landscape (M-6, WJ-23), with the jaw of a whale (MD-14), and with a curved blubber-hook and the crotch of an apple tree (MD-15).

Of the anchor sentences using symbolism (and this involves all of the sea novels except the first) that is not directly simile, all but three of the examples involve human behavior. Two of the exceptions speak of islands being anchored (M-4, WJ-37), and in the last, marginally a symbol, the narrator would use "a frigate's anchors" for "bridle-bits" to ride the constellation Cetus (MD-11). In Omoo, when the mate declares that "The captain's anchor is pretty nigh atrip" (O-7) he means that the man is near death; but when Landless sings, "His anchor's atrip when his money's all spent" (WJ-61), the implication is not nearly as serious. Two occurrences in Redburn involve the profound meaning of an afterlife--"till he hove up anchor for the world to come" (R-15) and "the harbor where they never weigh anchor" (R-26), and a third is very earthbound--"all came to anchor before the bar" (R-30). When Ishmael inquires about the absent man who will be his bedfellow at the Spouter Inn, the landlord responds that the man must have "come to anchor" somewhere else (MD-2). Finally, White Jacket, well acquainted with all the horrors in a man-of-war, addresses a few sentences to "Mothers of men!" whom he admonishes to hold their sons fast if they have any who have not already "weighed their anchors for the Navy" (WJ-43).

Anchor, then, in literal compound or in figurative symbol, is useful to Melville semantically both as an indispensible ship's tool and as an indicator of human or geographic behavior. He also referentially expands the dictionary definition of the word by referring to the object as some mode of adornment or embellishment (see M-1; R-14, 19; WJ-10, 26, 27, 41, 45, 56) or using it in the name of an eating establishment (R-22, 23, 24, 29). It is not the most frequent vocabulary word in its class, but it indicates what Melville can do with a word of its sort.

Tar (4)

The sea words of the quaternary class, those naming the roles in
which human beings interact with the sea, generally are less symbolic
than members of the previous classes. That is, they do not represent or
imply anything beyond their literal meanings. It is not that the words
pale when compared to their counterparts in other classes, but that their
syntactic and semantic activity is of a different sort.

The word tar, for example, occurs in all of the sea novels and is
important in its sentences less for its syntax and grammar (it functions
most frequently as a noun, once as an adjective) than for its semantics,
for the extent to which the sentences define the word itself--both by
adjectival modification and by broader context.

It is not surprising that Redburn and White-Jacket, the two novels
that explain in detail what being a sailor is all about, each use tar
more often, by a substantial margin, than any of the other sea novels.
There are, in fact, only three or fewer sentences in each of the other
four books that contain the word at all. The total number of tar's
appearances is evenly divided between the singular and the plural. Most
of the sentences tend to make some statement about the demeanor,
behavior, and/or habits of tars in general; only a minority focus on one
specific tar, and then the actions of that individual are in some way
characteristic of the entire group of tars anyway.

Syntactically, the one occurrence of tar as an adjective is in
Redburn (R-6, "some tarry captain of a forecastle") and the noun forms of
the word are varied and show no particular pattern. As an object of a
preposition, the largest category, tar makes its first and last
appearance (T-1; R-5, 7, 8, 9, 11, 12, 14, 15; WJ-1, 2, 3, 4, 8, 9, 11,
13, 15, 24, 25, 27, 28, 29, 32; MD-2). As the direct object of a verb
("becomes"--O-1, "feed"--R-3, "claimed to be"--R-10, "leading"--R-3,
"alarmed"--WJ-6, "altered to suit"--WJ-10, "hauling"--WJ-12, and "call"--
WJ-26), as a nominative of address (WJ-16, 17, 18, 19, 20, 21, 22), as a
base-clause subject (O-2, 3; WJ-7, 23--in a dialogue tag, where it is
inverted, 30, 33, 36), and as the subject of a subordinate clause (M-1--
the only occurrence of tar in that book; R-4; WJ-5, 14) tar appears with
relatively equal frequency. The word has two appearances in an
appositive noun phrase (R-2; WJ-31), where the phrase, an initial free
modifier, inverts normal sentence order) and one as a simple nominative
in an exclamatory sentence fragment (WJ-35). Except for the adjective
and the singular compound "damn-my-eyes-tar" (WJ-26), tar occurs in all
of the sentences in its pure form.

Semantically, the literal meaning of tar is illuminated by direct
modofication of the word and by those lexical contributions other elements
of the sentence make. The portrait of a tar which is compiled by tar's
modification is both sympathetic and realistic. A tar is, after all, a
"perfect" sailor, according to Smyth's sense of the word,[4] and the
adjectives that Melville chose to surround tar bear that out, although he
does not overly glorify the breed. In fact, according to "state-room
sailors" (the term is a bit of a condescension) tars are "good-for-
nothing" (T-1), and man-of-war's-men have coined the phrase "damn-my-eyes-
tar" for a counterfeit tar who pretends, with an affected swagger, that he
is the real thing (WJ-26). The true tar is "honest" and "good-natured"
(M-1), "grinning" (R-14), "strong" and "healthy" (R-5), "noble" (WJ-1, 16,
18, 21, 22), "admiring" of good character (WJ-3), "jolly" (WJ-7),
"enterprising" (WJ-14), "gallant" (WJ-20), "fine" (WJ-28, 33), and "all
American" (WJ-10). When tars become "old" (O-3; M-1; R-1, 8; WJ-15, 25,

30, 31), they may be "less careful" of holding on to the rigging than a
landsman (R-1), and may even become "decrepit or rheumatic" (WJ-25), but
they are still "reverend old tars" (WJ-31).

There is more to the picture. Melville does not hesitate to inform
us that there is a "boisterousness . . . common to tars" (WJ-2). They
may be "reckless" (WJ-13, 32), "Bowery-boys tars" (WJ-9), and not
infrequently given to drink (R-13; WJ-35, 36; MD-2). However, Melville
would have us know that "the modern tar is not quite so gross as
heretofore" (R-4). What is at once a compliment and an acknowledgment of
the limitations of this class of sailor is Melville's remark that "a
thorough tar is unfit for anything else" (O-2).

Aside from the direct modification associated with tar, the remainder
of the sentences are helpful in defining the habits and customs of such
men. The maturation of a mere "boy" into a tar means that he has become
valiant--ready, "cutlass in hand," to take on a dozen of the enemy and
dash them "pell-mell" (O-1). Tars are usually hatless (WJ-24), and
instead of "the old-fashioned Lord Rodney cue, which they used to wear
some fifty years ago," tars of Melville's day sport "love curls, worn at
the side of the head, just before the ear" (WJ-29). They may wear a
small purse or "monkey-bag . . . round their necks, tucked out of sight"
(WJ-5). It is a good bet that tars will not be able to read (R-5) and
so may be duped by all manner of scurvy knaves haunting the docks (R-11).
Or they may be the "luckless" objects of their country's economy, one
which does not allow for a decent hot meal while their ships lie in
dock. What is shown to most "dreadfully alarm" tars is the rumor that
their supply of grog is waning or is depleted (WJ-6). But the strain is
a proud one of long heritage--Homer was once a tar (WJ-23), and
furthermore, tars can do much to "voluntarily improve" the "evils" of
their "condition" (R-4). A "true tar" is a "man of valor" (WJ-8). The
highest compliment White Jacket can pay a friend is to say that he "was
expressly created and labelled for a tar" (WJ-4). A verse of a "fine
song" that Neversink's tars sing about themselves comments, in adjacent
base clauses and in the subsequent connection of the nominal elements of
the first line, on their strength and their identity with the sea:

Hearts of oak are our ships, jolly tars are our men,
We always are ready, steady boys, steady,
To fight and to conquer, again and again (WJ-7).

Along with the literal meaning of tar, the figurative language
Melville uses is valuable to the definition of the word. Two metaphors
are used which describe a tar's behavior in terms of a meteorological
disturbance--in Mardi, when a tar becomes provoked, he is "swept through
and through with a terrible typhoon of passion" (M-1); in White-Jacket,
the surge of a sudden shower is "hailed by the reckless tars with a
hurricane of yells" (WJ-13). Melville uses one simile in connection with
tar, and it compares "a noisy irruption of cherry-cheeked young tars" [5]
with "so many curly spaniels" emerging from a kennel (R-7). Hypallage
occurs once, in the prepositional phrase "into the astonished hands of
tars" (R-11), where the transposition of the adjective from the more
natural position before "tars" to the more unique spot before "hands"
gives the sentence its vigor. Irony occurs with White-Jacket's two final
uses of the term tar, where the narrator berates his colleagues, calling
them "fine fellows" and "generous-hearted tars" when he means (and also
says) that they are "the greatest curmudgeons afloat! it's the bottle
that's generous, not they!" (WJ-35, 36).

Tar is, then, a word that is more robust semantically than
grammatically, a word important to Melville because becoming what the

word implies (if we can believe that portions of <u>Redburn</u> and <u>White-Jacket</u> are autobiographical) involved a long and painful process that he survived. Attaining that level of perfect seamanship, Melville was early at that pinnacle of life that he would spend six novels glorifying.

A Word Within a Chapter

Besides the sentence, the other discrete and discernible unit of composition that Melville uses is the chapter. The paragraph does not seem to be developed with as much care and attention as either the sentence or the chapter; some paragraphing, in fact, especially in <u>Mardi</u>, <u>Redburn</u>, and <u>White-Jacket</u> (compare, for example, <u>Mardi</u>, Chapter 37; <u>Redburn</u>, Chapter 38; <u>White-Jacket</u>, Chapter 46), seems randomly done, after every sentence or two.

The chapter's development throughout the sea novels is one of the magnificent signs of the evolution of Melville's craft. The chapter seems to have more integrity and focus with each novel Melville writes until, in <u>Moby-Dick</u>, he arrived at the perfect balance between length and scope.

Melville preferred short chapters. In <u>Typee</u>, the first and shortest book that Melville wrote, the chapters average only seven and one-half pages, and those are Melville's longest chapters, on the average. The shortest are in <u>Mardi</u>, the middle novel, where the chapters average three and one-third pages. In <u>Moby-Dick</u> the chapters average nearly four pages.

The manner in which Melville names his chapters also changes from novel to novel and tells something about how his artistic vision became clearer. The chapters in <u>Typee</u> sport a variety of titles and illustrate how diversified and rambling Melville's scope is. The table of contents shows Chapter 26, for example, designated in the following way:

Chapter 26. King Mehevi. Allusions to his Hawaiian Majesty. Conduct of Marheyo and Mehevi in certain delicate matters. Peculiar system of Marriage. Number of Population. Uniformity. Embalming. Places of Sepulture. Funeral obsequies at Nukuheva. Number of Inhabitants in Typee. Location of the Dwellings. Happiness enjoyed in the Valley. A Warning. Some ideas with regard to the Civilization of the Islands. Reference to the Present state of the Hawaiians. Story of a Missionary's Wife. Fashionable Equipage at Oahu. Reflections.

Melville must have recognized the unwieldiness of that, for none of the other sea novels has chapters titled so tortuously. By the time he came to write <u>Mardi</u>, there is still diversity among the titles, but there is also much more focus, examples of the extremes in length being the titles of Chapter 184, "Morning," and Chapter 116, "Landing to visit Hivohitee the Pontiff, they encounter an extraordinary old Hermit; with whom Yoomy has a confidential Interview, but learns little." When he is ready to write the chapters of <u>Moby-Dick</u>, Melville is also ready with the most succinct and clear-cut names for them--"Chowder," "A Squeeze of the Hand," "The Symphony."

Taking one chapter from each sea novel and examining Melville's treatment of a certain word or group of words will help to clarify what a chapter is for Melville, what it can do, how Melville uses its unity to focus and to augment the meaning of his sea vocabulary. The chapters I have chosen to analyze were not randomly selected but represent those chapters which use the sea vocabulary in a substantial and especially effective way.

Typee--Chapter 2: Passage from the Cruising Ground to the Marquesas. Sleepy times aboard Ship. South Sea Scenery. Land ho! The French Squadron discovered at Anchor in the Bay of Nukuheva. Strange Pilot. Escort of Canoes. A Flotilla of Cocoa-Nuts. Swimming Visitors. The Dolly boarded by them. State of affairs that ensue.

Many of the chapters in Typee are straight narration, of seemingly unconnected events. Some of them end with a twist of philosophy or morality, a tactic that reaches its highest art in Moby-Dick. The development of the individual sea word itself flounders in Typee's chapters: Melville has not yet, in this his first novel, fully discovered the power of the word or his power to give it new associations.

In the fledgling novel, however, Melville's chapters are certainly not without sea terms. Chapter 2, for example, is endowed with eighty-two different varieties of them, most occurring once or twice, but several (notably island, which appears nineteen times) more often. Compounds and affixed forms of the pure sea terms exist: sea-fowl, sea-pacer, anchorage, whaling, cut-water, waterfall, fore-peak, out-rigger. The sea terms are well distributed throughout the chapter, although they decrease toward the end of the chapter, the final four paragraphs showing the smallest number of any section of equal length in the chapter.

Because island is so frequent in Typee and, specifically, in this second chapter, its development, pattern, and accumulation of modification and affixes in that chapter are worth considering. Discounting the title, it is the second sea term to appear in the chapter (preceded by trade-winds in the first paragraph) and the penultimate sea term as well (followed by ocean in the final paragraph). Within that frame, the four paragraphs before the last are void of island entirely, the next group of five paragraphs from the beginning and the next group of five from the end each have at least one reference to island, and the middle paragraph of the book has none. Whether or not that peculiarly patterned concentration was planned, it does exist and begins to imply that elaborate, formed positionings of the word island may well be more impressive than its syntactic considerations.

In the first occurrence of island and in its appearances in the five paragraphs immediately preceding the middle of the chapter, the plural form predominates eight to five over the singular, and those are the only forms of island in that section. In the five paragraphs that immediately follow the middle paragraph of the chapter, the plural is less clearly dominant (occurring twice, the singular once). The word with the affix "-er" occurs once in the singular and twice in the plural.

The occurrences of island before the middle of the chapter (those in paragraphs one and six to ten equaling thirteen occurrences) are twice as numerous as those occurring in the latter half of the chapter (in paragraphs twelve through sixteen and in paragraph twenty-one, where island occurs six times), but more grammatically predictable. That is,

in the first and larger group, there is less foregrounding of the terms,
fewer surprises in the modifications, than in the second, smaller group.
The first group shows island functioning ten times as the object of a
preposition, twice as a subject, and once as a direct object; the second
group uses island as the object of a preposition three times, and as a
direct object, a predicate nominative, and the subject of a subordinate
clause once each. Apart from definite articles, the modifications "other,"
"adjacent," "these," and "this" are found with island in the first group,
but the singular phrase "some yet undiscovered island" appears in the
second.

The islands referred to in the first paragraph of the chapter in
question, and indeed in the entire first half of the chapter, are
specifically the Marquesas. But the level of meaning alters in the
second half of the chapter. The first of that group of island
references is no longer restricted to the Marquesas, but has expanded to
all "the islands of the Pacific." Islanders seemingly "on the point of
flying at one another's throats" and "the head of an islander" are the
next two references in this group, and the concept of island is thus
circling into some new sphere of significance until the final, poignant
sentence of the chapter: "Thrice happy are they who, inhabiting some
yet undiscovered island in the midst of the ocean, have never been
brought into contaminating contact with the white man." Heretofore,
Typee has given us cameos of islanders, happy and frolicking in their
tropical paradise. In the final paragraph of the second chapter, however,
a strong sense of morality infuses itself into Melville's prose as the
Dolly's crew, with "the grossest licentiousness and the most shameful
inebriety," take advantage of the innocent islanders. The paradise that
had been so idyllically described and factually plotted in the first half
of the chapter has now become a purity violated, and whatever paradise
might still exist is now a mythical one uncharted, a hypothetical one
identified by the indefinite pronoun "some."

Omoo--Chapter 17: The Coral Islands

Of all the sea novels, Omoo and Mardi have by far the most occurrences
of coral. The word appears approximately thirty times in each of those
two books, and since Omoo is less than half the length of Mardi, the
position of coral in Omoo is a prominent one indeed.

Over one-quarter of Omoo's instances of coral appear in the three-
and-one-half page chapter near the beginning of the novel that uses coral
in its title and that describes the process of coral formation. Although
islands thus formed are by title the subject of the chapter, they do not
appear until approximately the middle of the chapter.

The frame for them, a unit of five paragraphs on either side of the
concentration of the coral entries, is a curious one. What precedes
their appearance is a narrator's uncertainty about where exactly, between
Marquesas and Tahiti, he is; a navigator's drunken staggering about the
deck as he attempts to determine his ship's position by sighting his
"rusty-old" quadrant on the sun, the moon, and the stars; and a crew
member's chance sighting of land as he darns a rent in a fore-top-sail.
Such a prologue is humorous and good-natured. All three men are comic
and bumbling, and contrast with the beauty and awesomeness of the islands
themselves. They help to temper the description of the islands'
evolution, geographical formation, population and terrain, and economy.
There are no colors used in the initial frame itself, but in the island
section proper appear "emerald," "green," and "verdure" (while not a color,

it nevertheless suggests color), an ease and peace for readers' eyes and
imaginations, and a neat backdrop for the word coral.

The final half of the frame to the coral island section, the five
paragraphs that end the chapter, returns somewhat to meteorology, but the
tone has become subdued and mysterious. The colors have sharpened.
Evening has just begun in the "blue" lagoon, the sunset making one of the
islands flame "like a vast dyed oriel illuminated." The universe, as if
in a vision, is transformed in a reverie that affects both its inanimate
and its animate elements. The trade winds fill "swooning sails" and,
inhaling the "languid" and fragrant air, one of the crew, ill with scurvy,
crying out in pain, is carried below. A "foam that sparkled," a blue
lagoon, and "strange shapes" compose a vision for the narrator--"No living
thing was seen." His "fancy" quickened; and he fell to "dreaming of the
endless grottoes and galleries, far below the reach of the mariner's
lead." Mermaids people his dreams, "chasing each other in and out of
coral cells, and catching their long hair in the coral twigs!"

Such a chapter ending is whimsical and fanciful, setting the minds of
Melville's readers adrift on the seas of revery that Melville himself
must have experienced when gazing from the ship. The same sort of
imaginative stimuli occur, for example, at the end of Chapter 41, where
the narrator and his cohorts go "out into the moonlight" for a "nocturnal
picknick," and at the end of Chapter 56, when it is concluded that "the
water-sprites had rolled our stone out of its noose."

The fact that Omoo lacks a certain cohesiveness that is present in
Typee (the encompassing plan of Typee--that of escape-captivity-escape--
is but one such indication) is perhaps symbolized by the lack of unity
and imaginative power Melville injects into the individual terms of his
sea vocabulary. Consequently, the syntax of the word coral pales somewhat
in comparison with the semantics of its frame. As a part of speech, the
word is fairly monochromatic, almost exclusively an adjective (that is,
if, in the phrase "Coral Islands," it be allowed as adjective; if the two
words so appearing together in a title, which happens three times in the
chapter, be taken as one grammatical unit instead of as two, then coral's
parts of speech are expanded by a nominative fragment, a direct object,
and a subject) and once as the object of a preposition. In the chapter
under consideration, coral appears independent of affix or compound
member or even modification. Besides "islands," the word is used to
modify "insect," "formations," "cells," and "twigs."

The pattern of coral's appearances in Chapter 17 is not complex. It
unifies the chapter in a very literal way, being the first word to appear
(after "the" in the title) and the last word but one (before "twigs") to
conclude the chapter. After the title, six paragraphs elapse before the
word is seen again, and before the final sentence of the chapter (where
the word occurs twice) there is a distance of seven paragraphs between
occurrences of coral. Coral concentrates in the middle of the chapter,
paragraphs seven through thirteen, where it is seen once in paragraphs
seven, nine, and thirteen and twice in paragraph ten, paragraphs eight,
eleven, and twelve being void of the word.

The Coral Islands are significant because, in Melville's words, they
are "perhaps the most remarkable and interesting in the Pacific." Their
position in the seventeenth chapter of Omoo, framed initially by anecdotes
of very earthy humor and finally by apparently miraculous vision, enables
them to assume desirable qualities of both worlds and to be preserved in
the reader's mind as a novel place indeed.

Mardi--Chapter 38:   The Sea on Fire

    Melville's third novel, besides telling mythical adventures and
harboring philosophical speculation, also contains lovely descriptive
passages about the sea: Chapter 36, "The Parki gives up the Ghost,"
about surviving a sudden squall that follows a long, hot calm, and
Chapter 165, "They round the stormy Cape of Capes," about navigating in
an ice storm, are examples. But Chapter 38, "The Sea on Fire," is perhaps
the best, with its variety and concentration of primary sea terms. Given
the proliferation of that class of sea terms (thirty-seven total
occurrences of some thirteen separate sea vocabulary items) in a chapter
that scarcely spans three pages, selecting one word for analysis would
not give a complete picture of how that referent was being developed
descriptively in Melville's prose. What I chose to do, then, was to
deviate slightly from the treatment given individual words in the
preceding or in the following novel chapters, and select those primary
sea terms that are the most synonymous with each other, according to
Melville's usage of them in the chapter, examining them as a unit.
    Five words, then, emerge as important in this way; in order of
decreasing frequency they are sea (thirteen times), water (six times),
ocean (four times), fluid (twice), and brine (twice). Whichever term
Melville uses, the referent is the same. The choice seems to be a
stylistic one--for example, if Melville is using a figure of speech in a
phrase, he rounds it out with the most poetic sea word, providing us with
"as we parted the pallid brine" (paragraph five). Or he may use a
different word simply for variety, since the concept is referred to so
very often and he would maintain the reader's interest and curiosity
about it. Sea and water tend to be used when Melville is tossing off a
prepositional clause of position, when other elements of the sentence
really contain the interest. Fluid, however, a slightly uncommon
synonym, is used when Melville wants a firm and highlighted identification,
for example, "that the fluid itself becomes charged with the luminous
principle" (paragraph fourteen). The other primary sea terms occurring
in the chapter--wake, foam, billows, marine, wave, Atlantic, Pacific, and
crest--each merge in various ways with the meaning of the five synonyms of
sea, but their scope and use is sufficiently different to exclude them
from the assembly of true synonyms.
    The identical sentence fragment (the chapter title) and the final
sentence of the chapter both contain the unmodified word sea, which at
once provides unity and delineation to the subject matter of the chapter.
In fact, of the nineteen paragraphs of the chapter, sea occurs in ten, in
every paragraph where there are primary sea terms (paragraphs two, three,
four, five, ten, eleven, twelve, fourteen, fifteen, nineteen) except
paragraph fourteen. This one does, nevertheless, include fluid, water,
and ocean. Of the five synonyms, sea occurs as the sole primary sea term
in paragraphs thirteen and nineteen; in conjunction with one other in
paragraphs three and ten (with water), four (with fluid), eleven (with
ocean), twelve (with waters), and fifteen (with brine); and with two
others in paragraphs two (with water and ocean) and five (with brine and
water). Well over one-half of the total number of times that these five
synonyms occur are as objects of a preposition, although there are
several cases of direct objects and subordinate clause subjects, and one
base-clause subject and one nominative fragment as well.
    Except for one instance of seamen (the suffix transforms the primary
sea term sea into a quaternary one, and thus the form is disregarded in
the present investigation) and one of waters (the plural form occurs but

once in the chapter; the singular five times), the five synonyms occur in
pure form, without affixes, compound associates, and even without much
adjectival modification. Sea, for example, is given no modification. It
is interesting that the three primary sea vocabulary synonyms that are
modified in the chapter (fluid, brine, ocean) are given modifiers that
themselves, in their contexts, are synonyms. Thus we have "luminous fluid"
(paragraph four), "pallid brine" (paragraph five), and "phosphorescent
ocean" (paragraph fourteen).

There are other words and phrases, however, that are associated in an
integral way with the five sea synonyms either by prepositional
construction, by verbal complement or subject, or by some other grammatical
coalescence within the sentence. Overwhelmingly, these are an elaboration
of what exists in the chapter title, where sea is juxtaposed with "fire."
Either in hue or in brilliancy, and relatively as frequently as they
occur, the five sea synonyms mirror something of the essence of fire.
Thus in the context of sea, besides "fire" (sea's first association) are
the words "constellations," "fountains of fire," "radiant" vapor,
"sparkling luminosity," "pallidness," "phosphorescence," "seeming
ignition," and the simile "white as a shroud." In ocean's contextual
environment are "pallid white color," "corruscating . . . with tiny
golden sparkles," and "luminous." Water hooks up with "cadaverous gleam,"
"illuminations," and "irradiate"; fluid with "contrasting . . .
brilliancy" and "charged with the luminous principle"; and brine with
"kindle a fire."

There is something in "fire" antithetical to sea:[6]   one destroys life
and yet illuminates that around it, and the other sustains life and yet
obscures that within it; one is transient, the other very nearly eternal.
When thus juxtaposed, as by Melville, to describe a very real natural
phenomenon, marine phosphorescence,[7] the sea takes on the properties of
fire--it then illuminates and is akin to manifestations of death (sea--
"shroud," water--"cadaver")--and passes quickly away.

These characteristics are interesting but have a true significance
only in the final sentence of the chapter, when fish, a nautical subject
of importance only to sea, merges grammatically with both sea and "fire":
"But, alas, thrice alas, for the poor little fire-fish of the sea, whose
radiance but reveals them to their foes, and lights the way to their
destruction." Something else is also infused here--at least a pathetic
fallacy and at best a philosophical axiom. Mixing descriptions of
inanimate nature with twists of morality is one tactic for ending
chapters that reaches a high level of art in Moby-Dick, and we can begin
to see Melville experimenting with it in Mardi.

Redburn--Chapter 24: He Begins to Hop About in the Rigging Like a
                      Saint Jago's Monkey
         Chapter 34: The Irrawaddy

Redburn, composed in just ten weeks, is not often tallied among
Melville's great creations, though, in passages of both humor and
gothicism, it can be as energetic as any book Melville wrote. Its
chapters are focused to the extent that some of them are highly episodic,
becoming set pieces from a landlubber's perspective (which the narrator,
an apprentice sailor, is for a good deal of the novel) about a sailor's
"strange" manner of naming things (Chapter 13, "He has a Fine Day at Sea")
or about what being a sailor really entails (Chapter 26, "A Sailor a Jack
of All trades").

Though a slight book in many ways, one that Melville later scoffed at, one of its strengths is its very self-conscious use of a sea terminology concerned with parts and furnishings of a ship, to which Wellingborough Redburn becomes gradually accustomed. His initial wonderment and naiveté are parts of both the book's humor and its charm for a lubbery audience, who, knowing little or nothing of the sea themselves, can so readily sympathize with his blunders in a new world.

Rigging is perhaps one of the most general terms and yet it is one of the most important concepts Redburn was to come across in his adventure. For the novel it is pivotal indeed, occurring more often and with more areas of concentration than in any other sea novel. While there are scarcely ten pages of Redburn that lapse without the word appearing, there are two chapters where the uses of the word are most concentrated and functional--in the subjective Chapter 24, where Redburn boasts of his adeptness in the rigging, and in the objective Chapter 34, where Redburn discusses the rigging of an Indian ship.

The treatment of the word rigging contrasts both syntactically and semantically in the two chapters. The word is, first of all, used only in the first half of Chapter 24, and its occurrences (even in the title) are exclusively as objects of a preposition. It is modified only by one word, "old," in the third paragraph, and it never appears in compound or with affix. In Chapter 34, the word does not appear at all until the fifth paragraph, and then only one other time (paragraph thirteen) before its flowering in the final three paragraphs of the chapter. Here it is usually an object of a preposition, although it does appear as a base-clause subject once (paragraph nineteen) and as a direct object (paragraph twenty-one). Its second occurrence is accompanied by possessive modification ("the Highlander's rigging," paragraph thirteen), and its three final occurrences by modification and compounding ("running rigging"--paragraph twenty; "standing-rigging"--twice in paragraph twenty-one).

Semantically, however, the occurrences of rigging in the earlier chapter are more interesting. For one thing, of the seven occurrences of rigging in Chapter 24, four of them are attended in some way by a simile. Three of these are Redburn's impressions of being in the rigging: he hops about "like a Saint Jago's monkey" (chapter title), he is as nimble "as a monkey" (paragraph five), and he hovers "like a judgment angel" (paragraph nine). The other simile is less important for what it tells us about Redburn's antics but more important for the insight it gives us into Melville's creative process. The reference of the subject is to a "clumsy sort of twine, called spun-yarn" that the sailors on board manufacture: "For material, they use odds and ends of old rigging called 'junk,' the yarns of which are picked to pieces, and then twisted into new combinations, something as most books are manufactured" (paragraph three). We know that, in spinning this and other of his sea stories, Melville extensively borrowed from contemporary travel books, from nautical histories, from Polynesian travelogues, and even from Spenser, so that the sentence is an analogy of his method of "reprocessing" new books from old.

The references to rigging in Chapter 34 are void of simile and metaphor. The only figurative language it can boast is alliteration ("ropes and rigging"--paragraph nineteen; "running rigging"--paragraph twenty; "shrouds and standing-rigging of a ship" and "setting up or slacking off her standing-rigging"--both in paragraph twenty-one), and the earlier chapter has that as well ("running up the rigging"--paragraph six). Hence, Chapter 34, which is on the surface the more exotic chapter,

since its topic is the rigging of a huge Bombay "country ship," has, in
one sense at least, less grammatical excitement than a chapter about a
"boy" becoming accustomed to the rigging on an American packet-ship.

White-Jacket--Chapter 94: The End

The final chapter of White-Jacket is the most provocative symbolically,
the chapter that most obviously joins the world of the sea with that of
the land, that couches a virulent outrage in analogy.

Although frigate occurs in all of the sea novels, in none is it so
apparent as in White-Jacket, where it is seen nearly two hundred times.
But only in the final chapter of the book is the word both so consistently
compounded (it occurs in compound in all five of its appearances) and so
consistently symbolic. In Mardi the word is compounded once (frigate-
birds), and earlier in White-Jacket, it occurs in four compounds each of
which has a single appearance (in order throughout the book, they are:
frigate-executives, frigate-merchantman, fighting-frigate, frigate-action).
In the final chapter of White-Jacket, the word occurs five times, each
time in the compound world-frigate.

The compound first appears in the second sentence of the chapter,
anticipated by an enthymeme of two subordinate clauses of an "as-so"
construction, a simile, and a resultant clause, each containing a
synonymic form of one of the compound members of world-frigate: "As a
man-of-war that sails through the sea, so this earth that sails through
the air." The terms man-of-war in the first subordinate clause and the
earth in the second are, in the first case, more general and, in the
second, more specific than the two elements of the compound world-frigate
that derives from them. Man-of-war refers to any vessel of a nation's
navy, while frigate is a specific class of vessel within that navy;
earth refers specifically either to our globe or to the land of it, while
the meaning of world can encompass both the earth with its inhabitants
and the universe of which that earth and the other planets are a part, the
latter seemingly the sense Melville is employing. The merging and melding
of the terms, each taken from separate adjoining dependent clauses and
then combined in the ensuing independent clause, is a tactic that
heightens syntactic and semantic interest and renders all-encompassing
(if the universe is under scrutiny, what could possibly be excluded?)
and, therefore, more poignant Melville's entire discussion.

Besides occurring in the first paragraph, world-frigate closes the
analogy with an appearance in the last paragraph of the chapter, where
it is sandwiched between two other "world-" compounds that use "mate" as
their second member. Since, according to Smyth, "ship-mate" once
denoted someone dearer than a brother,[8] we can transfer some of that
meaning to world-mate by association, since the two compounds appear
together in both occurrences, joined with a copula. The fact that both
occurrences are nominatives of address is a further indication of their
substantial connection.

Finally, world-frigate appears twice in the second paragraph and once
in the seventh, and between those two paragraphs the analogy becomes
highly developed. Both the terrestrial and the nautical universe,
Melville is saying, are "oppressed by illiberal laws," the violators of
which are degraded ("legalized sin") in their own eyes and in everyone
else's. Furthermore, the helplessly ill are shut up beneath hatches,
while "we still sport our gay streamer aloft." Our craft, says Melville,
our world, is a lie, but perhaps the fault is our own: "There are no
mysteries out of ourselves."

The adjectival modification which attends world-frigate provides a
very specific identification and ownership. It is as if Melville were
making quite certain there would be no questions as to his meaning. The
earliest occurrence of the compound, as the analogy is being presented,
is a double compound participle which is really a dual identification of
a primary characteristic of frigate ("fast-sailing") and of world
("never-sinking"). The indefinite article is the only one Melville uses
with the compound, and the only time he uses one. The analogy has now
been established, and subsequently, the world-frigate is introduced by
either the demonstrative adjective "this" (once) or the possessive "our"
(three times).

The craft on which Melville sailed--the universe that he loved and
the peace that he saw violated by man's inhumanity to man--he chose to
present as the world, so that his landlocked audience could, with the
most ease and facility, understand his outcry. By consistently coupling
the words world and frigate in Chapter 94, Melville made both his analogy
and his invective inescapably obvious, and by ending White-Jacket on that
very symbolic and yet very concrete point, he captured a people's
sympathies and ignited their outrage from his own.

Moby-Dick--Chapter 35: The Mast-Head

In Moby-Dick's thirty-fifth chapter, the tertiary sea term mast
becomes important for its accumulation of cultural associations and
symbolic implication. Melville does in this chapter what he does as well
in many others, focuses on a word that accumulates, in the set of sentences
that is the chapter, more and more semantic, linguistic, and contextual
richness, so that by the end of the chapter the word resonates with new
Melvillian meaning, which thereafter, in the subsequent one hundred
chapters of the book, retains that meaning.

The narrator is, of course, Ishmael, and this chapter, unlike many
others in Moby-Dick, is ostensibly in the first person, giving us a
predominant fact about Ishmael's personality: he is, like Bulkington
(like Melville?) one of the eternal water gazers, so enraptured by the
sea that while at his stand he keeps "but sorry guard," so sorry, in fact,
that he "movingly admonish[es]" the ship owners of Nantucket not to enlist
"any [similar] lad with lean brow and hollow eye; given to unseasonable
meditativeness." Through these eyes, then, and with such thoughts, we
are given a masthead reverie about a masthead reverie, a stream-of-
conscious musing from Ishmael as his eyes are held by the sea, which
verifies and symbolizes once again the bond between man and the sea, the
interrelationships between the marine world and the terrestrial.

The term mast, either in this form or, more commonly, with an affix,
appears twenty-four times in the brief Chapter 35. Three of the
occurrences are as mast, all of which are nouns (one joined to "summit"
by prepositional construction) and only one of which has any modification:
"that great stone mast." T'-gallant-mast (in a prepositional phrase
introduced by the word "head") and main-mast (modified by "his towering")
are the only other occasional forms. All other uses of mast are compound
constructions followed by "-head." Of these, half contain various forms
of the verb "stand." There are "standing mast-heads," "standers of mast-
heads" (once modified by "earliest," once by "all"), "stander(s)-of-mast-
heads" (modified by either "a dauntless" or "modern"), "mast-head
standers" (twice, once the subject of "a nation of"), and even "stood his
mast-head." So, linguistically, the word is very active, although it is
not at all predictable. That is, the word's sequence throughout the

chapter is not from simple (<u>mast</u>) to complex (<u>stander-of-mast-heads</u>), since, for example, <u>mast</u> appears in that pure form in one of the three final references and as <u>mast-head</u> in the first six references; no predictable pattern of the word's form is apparent.

What is apparent and significant, though, is the word's distribution. Of the eight pages of the chapter, the word (in one form or another) appears the following number of times: page 135 (ten), page 136 (seven), page 137 (three), page 138 (three), page 139 (one), page 140 (none). The literal, referential use of the word, then, steadily declines throughout the chapter until it disappears, while, inversely, the symbolic, figurative meanings develop toward the chapter's splendid philosophical climax.

The frame for the chapter, both on the initial, literal level and on the final, symbolic level, is pleasant weather. But as <u>mast</u> accumulates its associations, the tone within that frame changes. Ishmael begins informatively and conversationally and ends exhortatively and didactically. Grammatically, there is an increase in the use of inverted elements, of adjectives, and of the subjunctive mood toward the end of the chapter, a tendency to use language that is at once more elaborate, more archaic, and more indefinite than it was at the beginning.

And what of those symbolic associations that <u>mast</u> takes on? It begins innocuously enough, Ishmael stating that it was his turn for his first masthead, explaining to the lay reader what significance the standing of mastheads had in American whalers, and then drawing in historical references both from inland (ancient: Egyptian pyramids, the tower of Babel, the pillar of the Christian hermit Saint Stylites, and modern: Napoleon, Washington, Admiral Nelson) and from the coast (spars erected on the coasts of early Nantucket and New Zealand). Before turning to "the one proper mast-head, that of a whale-ship at sea," Ishmael affirms that it is truly warrantable "to couple . . . the mast-head standers of the land with those of the sea," one of the major themes of the chapter and, in a more general way, one of the major themes of all of Melville's sea literature. Ishmael at this point returns momentarily to the rotation of masthead duties among the seamen (with the difference that, in the first instance of such figurative language in the chapter, he compares standing a masthead to wearing gigantic stilts while "the hugest monsters of the sea"--note the hyperbole--swim "between your legs," which creatures he in turn compares to ancient ships sailing "between the boots of the famous Colossus at old Rhodes") and then explains in detail his emotional state while manning a masthead: "lost in the infinite series of the sea . . . a sublime uneventfulness invests you." In a parody of a book he plunders (William Scoresby, Jr.'s <u>An Account of the Arctic Regions</u>), Melville then humorously digresses on crow's nests and accoutrements therein.

It is then that the philosophical shift comes about that allows Melville to transmute factual and fanciful history into metaphysical and religious speculation. Getting from a ship's timber to a sailor's soul (to say nothing of "the inscrutable tides of God") is touchy business, but Ishmael, "with the problem of the universe revolving in me," does in one short chapter. The sailor's "opium-like listlessness" while crossing "seductive seas . . . watery pastures" brings an important archetype to the fore. Waves and thoughts blend in a cadence until the sailor loses his spiritual identity and his physical balance: he "takes the mystic ocean at his feet for the visible image of that deep, blue, bottomless soul pervading mankind and nature." The Pantheism (the word "Pantheists" ends the chapter), symbolized by Wickliffe's ashes strewn and diffused on the shore, is the world-soul of Emerson, which would reappear as an American religion in Clarel, and which divinely focuses the man-and-the-ocean marriage that Melville held so dear. The sea, perhaps the giver of life, certainly the sustainer of it, is intimately apprehended only in such a dream state, and the language that Melville uses in Chapter 35-- imprecise, poetic--reveals that dream.

The Word *Sea*

Any examination of Melville's vocabulary of the sea would not be complete without a consideration of the word sea itself. Whether or not Melville was conscious of it, the word's wavelike pattern of frequency, symbolic compounding, and generally mounting complexity of associations become apparent when examining the uses of the word from sea novel to sea novel. These three phenomena, then--pattern of frequency, compounding, and complexity of associations--will be the basis of the following analysis.

The sheer bulk of the references involving sea is staggering. No other vocabulary item is so consistently popular, novel after novel. Some words, however, are indigenous to specific books. The word whale, for example, is very common in Moby-Dick, but scarcely appears in earlier novels. Man-of-war and frigate are the backbone of White-Jacket, but are not important at all in the other books. Sea, however, dominates all six novels.

The word is, first of all, all-consuming and all-encompassing, the elemental unity and ground of being that exists at the beginning and at the end of each book, a literal and metaphorical frame. It occurs in the initial sentence of Omoo, Mardi, and Redburn (after also appearing in the title of the first chapter), in the first paragraph of Typee, in the prefatory note of White-Jacket, and on the title page of Moby-Dick (in an epigraph from Paradise Lost). Likewise, it is seen in the final chapter of Omoo and White-Jacket, on the last page of Typee, Redburn, and Moby-Dick (in an epilogue), and as the final word in Mardi. Within this framework, in each novel, the word scarcely fails to emerge, in some form, every ten pages, and usually far more often.

The relative frequency of sea from novel to novel can be said to take on the pattern of a wave. Typee is the lowest ebb of the "wave," containing the fewest occurrences of sea. At Omoo the swell begins, the total occurrences of sea increasing by three times, heightening the wave's level. Mardi elevates the surge considerably, to nearly twice that of Omoo. In Redburn the surge abates by half, elevates slightly in White-Jacket, and then, with a final rush of energy, crests and breaks in Moby-Dick at its summit.

The compounding of sea is spectacular in terms of the words with which it combines. Melville compounds, as we have seen in a previous chapter, in three not always distinct and not always exclusive ways: combining two terms into one solid word, joining two terms with a hyphen, and using two separate words in an adjective-noun relationship that is close enough (or at least as close as some of his hyphenated compounds) to be considered compound. Generally, the compounds, as well as the pure form sea, occur as nouns, occasionally as adjectives. The only

marginally adverbial form of sea is seaward, and its functions are as a
prepositional object (Omoo--once, Mardi--three times), as an adjective
(Mardi--once, Moby-Dick--once), and as a pure adverb (Omoo--three times,
Mardi--three times, Moby-Dick--once).

The group of solid sea compounds that Melville uses is much smaller
than the hyphenated group; Typee has none, and the earliest one in Omoo
is also what a landsman would expect to be the most common--seamen, or
seaman. The word occurs at least a dozen additional times in Omoo, but
only once (hyphenated) in Mardi, twice in Redburn (where able-seaman and
and ordinary-seaman also occur), twice in White-Jacket (modified by "able"
or by "ordinary"), and not at all in Moby-Dick, substantiating Smyth's
claim that the term is "seldom bestowed among seafaring men upon their
associates."[9] There is, however, also a smattering of seamanship
occurrences (O--three, M and R--one), one of unseaworthy (O), one of
seamanlike (M), and one of unseamanlike (WJ). The only other appearances
of sea as a solid compound are seamonsters (M; this word occurs two other
times in the sea novels, in Typee and in Moby-Dick, where it is
hyphenated), Anglesea (M), and Mayor Seafull (WJ).

Melville's hyphenated compounds are prolific, notable in that they
seem to reinforce the theme of each of the sea novels. Typee's compounds
are exotic and pleasant (South-sea, sea-shore, sea-weed, sea-shell). Omoo
shows more concern with human roles (sea-captain, sea-prophets, sea-jockey),
coupling more realities of ordinary living with the sea (Sea-Parlour,
sea-clothing, sea-boots, sea-chests, sea-beef, sea-potations, sea-sick,
and most encompassingly, sea-day and sea-life), although some of the
pleasantry and exoticism are carried over from Typee (South-Sea, sea-canoes,
sea-port, sea-breeze, sea-faring, sea-voyage).

Mardi, a book that is perhaps more haunting than Moby-Dick and in
many ways as beautiful, owes part of its whimsy to its compounded names
for marine flora and fauna (sea-moss, sea-gull, sea-chamois, sea-serpent,
sea-slugs, sea-hawks, sea-goat--used figuratively for the ship Little
Jule--sea-kite, sea-kelp, sea-fowl, sea-grass, sea-nettle, sea-urchin,
sea-weed, sea-kraken, sea-beeves, sea-noddy, sea-porcupine, sea-thyme).
In Mardi we see human roles denominated more imaginatively and more
regally than in the first two novels (sea-dog, sea-tailor, sea-monarchs,
sea-god, sea-sage, Sea-king--three times, sea-hunters). There are
references to mythic battle (sea-equipage, sea-cavalry, sea-fight) and
several new characteristics or accoutrements of the sea itself (sea-blue,
sea-ripples, sea-dingle, sea-winds, sea-cavern, sea-water). In Mardi,
finally, the longest novel, exist the longest sea compounds (Froth-of-
the-Sea and deep-sea-lead).

Redburn is void of the poetic language of Mardi; the only nonhuman
marine life it mentions is sea-horses, sea-beef, sea-fowl, and--in a
simile in which sailors are compared to it--sea-weed. The compoundings
of the novel indicate that here is a no-nonsense book that wants to get
down to the business at hand, capturing from a greenhorn's point of view
what life at sea is all about. Consequently, the sea-career, sea-life,
and sea-service are to the fore. Nautical paintings are twice labeled
sea-pieces, part of a sea-ditty is quoted, sea-ports are passed, sea-
sickness is experienced, and the indignant narrator finds himself at the
beck of illiterate sea-tyrants, who would reduce Isaac Newton and Lord
Bacon in similar circumstances to sea-clowns.

White-Jacket and its hyphenated compounds are devoted almost
exclusively to the classifications of the men aboard a man-of-war and
their sea-actions as the Neversink rolls in her sea-way. The whole
company of the crew are sea-citizens, sea-patriots, who may at turns be

flattered by being called noble sea-fencibles and trusty sea-warriors,
be sneered at as sea-dandies, or be blasted as a "sea-tallow strainer."
There are aboard ship the sea-commoners, and there are sea-kings and
sea-lords. Sea-officers may include sea-Lieutenants, a sea-martinet (the
captain), a sea-commander, and sea-heroes. Other names White Jacket
ascribes to members of the crew are sea-barbers (who have sea-legs),
sea-vagabond, sea-tutor, sea-undertaker. The book is written to expose
the horrifying sea-statutes and sea-laws, which convert the naval frigate
into "a sort of sea-Newgate."

Moby-Dick uses proportionately fewer hyphenated compounds than the
previous novels do, the author having by this time recognized that there
can be an "intense artificialness" in sea-usages. Several occur in echo
of former novels (sea-captain, sea-dogs, sea-faring, sea-officers, sea-king,
sea-coal, sea-toss, sea-fowl, sea-side) and the hyphenated compounds that
are unique either describe specific marine life (sea-gudgeon, sea-unicorn,
sea-lion, sea-raven, sea-vulture, sea-ivory) or--and this is a
characteristic of the novel generally--describe some aspect or implication
of the sea itself (sea-storm, salt-sea, sea-traditions, sea-pastures,
sea-mark, sea-crashing).

On those relatively few occasions when Melville uses sea as an
adjective, the word is doing one of two things--it is either a possessive
construction, which happens twice ("sea's back"--Mardi; "sea's
landlessness"--Moby-Dick), or in conjunction with the noun it precedes,
it is serving in roughly the same capacity as a compound and might as
well be hyphenated. In fact, all of the novels contain pairs of separate
words with sea as the adjective that elsewhere in the sea canon are
hyphenated compounds. In Omoo, "sea parlance" (hyphenated in Mardi) and
"South Sea voyages" (hyphenated in Typee) are separate words. Mardi
contains "sea moss" and "sea shore" which are both hyphenated elsewhere
in the novel. Redburn's "sea shore" is hyphenated in Typee, and "sea
outfit" is hyphenated in Moby-Dick. "Sea parlance" appears as two
separate words in White-Jacket but as a hyphenated compound in Mardi.
And "sea captain," hyphenated in Redburn, as well as "sea fowls,"
hyphenated in Redburn and Mardi, are separate words in Moby-Dick.

Typee contains no instances of sea as adjective, though the other
novels show a range of from five (White-Jacket) to eleven (Moby-Dick.
The phenomenon, then, is not a major grammatical venture for Melville;
yet, for the record, the additional nouns that employ sea as their
adjective are listed. "South Sea" in Omoo modifies "voyages" and
"yachting," and sea is used as well to modify "vessel," "joke," "usages,"
"phrase," and "stock of fruits." In Redburn the word modifies "sideboard,"
"murders," and "reminiscences." The three remaining novels employ, in
one or more cases, adjectival modification in addition to sea; White-Jacket
uses "raw" with sea to modify "air," and then shows "parlance," "coal-
hole," "sexagenerian," and "saying" each following sea. Moby-Dick has
two phrases of extended modification--"crazy old sea chest" and "yellowish
sea charts"--as well as an assortment of nouns that use sea as their
single adjective: "carpenters," "coopers," "blacksmiths," "turtles,"
"creature" (twice), "bannisters." Finally, Mardi shows three phrases of
extended modification using sea, all fairly poetic--"wild sea song,"
"moonless sea midnight," and "old sea hearth-stone" (a metaphor for the
Arcturion's fore-hatch). Besides those terms, sea in isolation modifies
"engagements" (though "sea-battles" is hyphenated in Omoo), "boat," "moss,"
"groves and mosses," and "Elephant."

As a noun, the concept "sea" is focused and defined. There are two
very interesting functions and some interesting modification that sea

takes on in order to do this. <u>Sea</u> can be, first of all, used in apostrophe. This phenomenon occurs only in the final two books of the sea novel canon, <u>White-Jacket</u> and <u>Moby-Dick</u>, three times in each book. In <u>White-Jacket</u>, the references are all accompanied by metaphor and are introduced by the narrator telling us he has seated himself on one of the upper yards for a bit of reflection. He is overcome by "a very fine feeling, and one that fuses us into the universe of things, and makes us a part of the All" (p. 76). With such a rapture, he would, in a sense, fuse himself with the sea. He desires to "feel thee again, old sea" and "snuff thee up, sea-breeze." The final half of each apostrophe uses a horse-and-rider metaphor, though in the first case it is the sea that is the horse--"let me leap into thy saddle once more"--and in the second it seems to be the narrator--"let me . . . whinny in thy spray" (p. 77). Is the narrator just confusing his metaphorical line or, in crossing it, is he stating an important identity, that he feels at one with the sea? Grammatically, it seems to be the latter. In the novel's third use of <u>sea</u> as apostrophe, White Jacket begs the <u>sea-gods</u> to intercede with Neptune so that "the tomb that swallowed up Pharoah and all his hosts" will be his as well.

In one of <u>Moby-Dick</u>'s apostrophes to the sea, Ahab uses <u>sea</u> in a compound, "<u>sea-mark</u>," that actually refers to the sun, consulting it as an augur: "thou tellest me truly where I <u>am</u>--but canst thou cast the least hint where I shall be?" (p. 411). The other two both contain "O sea," one voiced in praise and reverence--"Then hail, for ever hail" (p. 409), the other in vehemence and despair--"Slope downwards to thy depths . . . that . . . Ahab may slide this last, last time upon his mark!" (p. 467). All of the apostrophes venerate the sea, ascribe to it superhuman powers, elevating it to the level of a deity.

In contrast, the two times that <u>sea</u> appears as a noun adverb, both in <u>Moby-Dick</u>, are more earthbound, though perhaps less referentially literal. That is, the sea itself is less important primarily as a referent than it is as an incidental term in a nautical manner of speech. Flask says, with an exasperation that is comic, "I can't see three seas off" (p. 191). And, finally, the captain of the <u>Samuel Enderby</u> recounts how he was put to bed "half seas over" (p. 366), or in Smyth's words, "nearly intoxicated."[10]

Although there is no steady novel-to-novel progression of the <u>amount</u> of modification that hooks up with <u>sea</u>, there is a chronological development concerning the <u>type</u> of modification that Melville uses with the word. A development and expansion of the character of the sea, its versatility and variety, and yet its consistency novel after novel gradually comes into focus, until in <u>Moby-Dick</u> a wonderful and awesome force emerges that is very nearly alive and eternal.

<u>Typee</u> modifies <u>sea</u> one time, late in the novel, and while part of that modification personifies <u>sea</u>, it is nevertheless not an uncommon epithet--"chopping angry seas" (p. 251). Curiously enough, the final modifier of the final word <u>sea</u> in the final sea novel is akin to that initial noun phrase in the first sea novel--"the sledge-hammering seas" (<u>MD</u>, p. 467). Of the dozen modifiers that are associated with <u>sea</u> in <u>Omoo</u>, all are befitting an expansive and pleasurable Polynesian adventure. The seas there are "considerable" (p. 95), "tremendous" (p. 59), but "generally tranquil" (p. 58), and the worst that can be said about them is that they are "alive with large whales" (p. 35). Other than that, the sea is "smooth" (p. 34), "open" (p. 3), "bright blue" (p. 115), and "serene" (p. 212).

The modifications that <u>Mardi</u> uses with <u>sea</u> are substantial, outnumbered only by those of <u>Moby-Dick</u>. In this novel unusual adjectives begin to associate with <u>sea</u>, <u>sea</u> begins to take on modification of symbolic proportions, and phrasal modification of <u>sea</u> begins to happen. <u>Sea</u>'s modification in this novel is, by turns, pleasant ("mild, warm seas"--p. 7, "frolicsome sea"--p. 560, "sunny, summer seas"--p. 636) and unpleasant ("his frigid seas"--p. 467, "the seething sea"--p. 499, "an angry sea"--p. 617). Against that ambivalent backdrop, unusual characteristics of the sea are highlighted: it is "wild and remote" (p. 97), "sociable" (p. 256), "quicksilver" (p. 547), and "fresh-born" (p. 502).

It is a short step from there to a certain twist of the truth that indicates that something larger than life, some mythic sense, is being attributed to the sea through its modification, for the sea is not literally "waveless" (p. 416), "tideless" (p. 554), "diluvian" (p. 555), "sunless" (p. 638), "shoreless" (pp. 38, 74), or "endless" (pp. 38, 654); yet, the presence of those adjectives suspends credibility so that, in the strange romance of <u>Mardi</u>, the sea indeed might be what the adjectives affirm. And there is one overtly symbolic possessive modifier that is used with <u>sea</u>, in the sadly provocative sentence in which Taji mourns the loss of Yillah: "There are thoughts that lie and glitter deep: tearful pearls beneath life's sea, that surges still, and rolls sunlit, whatever it may hide" (p. 194). Melville's practice of using attributive phrasal modification is in its infancy in <u>Mardi</u>, though the book does yield such constructions as "southern and most genial seas" (p. 6), "a high, slow-rolling sea" (p. 37), and "the bottomless, bottomless sea" (p. 303). Both <u>White-Jacket</u> and <u>Moby-Dick</u> see a flowering of that art.

Both <u>Redburn</u> and <u>White-Jacket</u> each contain fewer than twenty instances where <u>sea</u> is modified, but they seem at once a summation and an extension of the sort of sea modification that has gone before. For instance, in both <u>Mardi</u> and <u>Redburn</u>, the sea is "pleasant" (<u>M</u>--p. 11; <u>R</u>--p. 290); in both <u>Mardi</u> and <u>White-Jacket</u> the seas are "summer" seas (<u>M</u>--p. 636, <u>WJ</u>--p. 323). There are also echoes of texture and color: in <u>Omoo</u> the sea is "smooth" (p. 34), and in <u>White-Jacket</u> it is "tolerably smooth" (p. 97). It is "glassy" in both <u>Mardi</u> (pp. 116, 117) and <u>Redburn</u> (pp. 9, 292), where it is also "endless" (<u>M</u>--p. 654, <u>R</u>--p. 66). In <u>Omoo</u> the only color attributed to the sea is "blue" (pp. 115, 212). It is "blue" in <u>Mardi</u> (p. 101) and "violet" as well (p. 632). In <u>Redburn</u> it is "blue" (p. 298), "bright-blue" (p. 6), "deep blue" (p. 74), "midnight" (p. 244), "violet" (p. 298), and "green" (p. 9) besides. In <u>White-Jacket</u> yet another color is introduced--"white" (p. 270), and two of the previous colors are repeated--"green" (p. 114) and "blue" (p. 280). The unique sea modification in <u>Redburn</u> is more ominous than enticing--"calamitous sea" (p. 9), "violent sea" (p. 171), "damp night sea" (p. 245), and (note the indefinite pronoun) "some reluctant, sedgy sea" (p. 230). Although <u>White-Jacket</u> shows the sea to be "torrid, monotonous" (p. 223) and "yeasting" (p. 106), the majority of its <u>sea</u> modifications are positive: "the calm sea" (p. 392), "a placid sea" (p. 322), "a jubilant sea" (p. 287), and "the goodlie South Sea" (p. 98). It is here that Melville is busy spewing his invective at mankind--he has no quarrel with nature (the sea) at this point. He is, in fact, openly curious about it and about its effect on the human spirit:

> The reason of the mirthfulness of these top-men was, that
> they always looked out upon the blue, boundless, dimpled,
> laughing, sunny sea. Nor do I hold, that it militates
> against this theory, that of a stormy day, when the face

of the ocean was black, and overcast, that some of them
would grow moody, and chose to sit apart (p. 47).
And so, if the sea is not to be feared at this point, it is to be marveled
at, and given its due. It is, and this is the major connection between
the sea modification of White-Jacket and that of the succeeding novel,
"thrice holy" (p. 16).

"Holy" is the initial sea adjective in both White-Jacket and Moby-Dick,
and in the latter novel it gives some idea of how "limitless" and
"uncharted" (p. 159) are not only the seas, but the host of adjectives
connected with the seas. In every way the most interesting sea
adjectives in the sea novel canon are found in Moby-Dick. It is the book
that expends the most effort in describing the sea and the book that reaps
the advantage of the practice done in the previous five novels in
constructing vivid and rhetorically appropriate (if not always literally
comprehensible) sea modifications.

The unique color adjective that Moby-Dick uses to describe the sea is
"yellow," which occurs as a proper noun ("Yellow Sea"--p. 167), a common
noun (p. 234), and a synonym ("that same golden sea"--p. 406). The
phenomenon of using a color in both proper and common noun slots with sea
is unique, and occurs in Moby-Dick on two other occasions--with "white"
("White Sea"--p. 167; "a milky sea"--p. 169) and "black" ("Black Sea"--
p. 20; "the black sea"--p. 201). The sea in Moby-Dick is also, as it has
been previously, "green" (p. 95) and "blue" ("a dark blue sea"--p. 159,
"a midnight sea"--p. 168, "the blue morning sea"--p. 221).

As the tendency of Moby-Dick's color adjectives indicates, Moby-Dick
echoes sea adjectives from previous novels as well as readily constructing
new forms. Generally, the modification that is repeated is a single word
(sometimes a single syllable) rather than a phrase, a conventional sea
adjective rather than one that is outstanding or unexpected. So, in
Moby-Dick, as in the novels before it, the seas are "salt" (MD--p. 85,
O--p. 92, M--p. 12), "high" (MD--p. 36; M--p. 373; WJ--pp. 312, 352),
"calm" (MD--p. 121, 314, 346; WJ--p. 392), "summer" (MD--p. 140; M--
pp. 24, 636), "tropical" (MD--pp. 314, 448; M--p. 632, as "tropic"),
"seething" (MD--p. 415, M--p. 499), and "rolling" (MD--pp. 300, 395, 413,
442; M--p. 37; R--p. 289). As in Mardi (p. 161), the sea in Moby-Dick is
"fathomless" (p. 203), and as in Omoo (p. 35), it is "live" (MD--p. 235).
In Mardi we were told the sea was "frigid" (p. 467) and "wintry" (p. 543;
Moby-Dick elaborates on that characteristic in the phrases "the frozen
seas" (p. 137), "those Icy Seas" (p. 343), "those shuddering, icy seas"
(p. 261), and "those frigid Polar Seas" (p. 372). What in Mardi were
"wild and remote seas" are in Moby-Dick "wild and distant seas" (p. 16)
and later in the novel "the remotest and most savage seas" (p. 201).

Two remarkable features become evident about the sea modification
specific to Moby-Dick. One is that such modification describes a
phenomenon that is overwhelmingly active. Early in the book, the sea is
described (in a predicate adjective) as "still" (p. 49), as "vacant"
(p. 239), and three times as "calm" (see above), but far more frequently,
and unprecedentedly, it is just the opposite. Nearly halfway through the
novel the references begin, with the adjective "rising" (p. 194).
Chronologically, the sea is "perilous" (p. 202), "turbid" (p. 257),
"shuddering" (p. 216), "swashing" (p. 415), and, among the last
modification that appears with sea, "breaking" (p. 450), "swarming"
(p. 463), and "weltering" (p. 466).

The other notable feature about Moby-Dick's sea modification is the
array of human emotions ascribed to the sea. Not surprisingly, the
modification in this group overlaps with the previous one, for in such

personification of the sea as "lawless" (p. 126), "uncivilized" (pp. 155, 387), "savage" (pp. 201, 210), "audacious" (p. 193), "crazy" (p. 267), "mad" (p. 427), and "most riotously perverse" (p. 191), there is a good deal of activity as well. Moby-Dick is the only novel to venture any gender for the sea, and for Melville the sea has qualities that are both feminine ("his maternal sea"--p. 210) and masculine ("the robust and man-like sea" and "the masculine sea"--both p. 426). It might even be conjectured that the three color adjectives used as proper names of the sea--white, yellow, black (see above)--could be a subtle acknowledgement of the races of mankind, and if so, Melville is drawing both a sexual and a racial parallel between humanity and the sea.

But in the set of adjectives of the sea, we must conclude that the sea, though it may contain comparisons with and vestiges of humanity, transcends them to something religious, something "holy" (see above). It is (knowledge of it is?) "forbidden" (p. 16), "profound" (p. 378), "uncontaminated" (p. 396), even "incorruptible" (p. 265). It is an innocence that no mere man can violate, a state of being that no mortal mind can comprehend.

The final characteristic to be noted about the attributive modification of sea in Moby-Dick is grammatical. We have seen that Melville's mastery of the single word in constructing his modification is an enticement to his reader. The words that he foregrounds prompt speculation about what we think Melville's attitude toward the sea was and what we think he wanted that of his audience to be. The adjectival phrases that he uses to describe the sea contain elements that are active, emotional, and just as provocative as the adjectival words. Both "a sleepy, vapory, mid-day sea" (p. 336) and "those most candid and impartial seas" (p. 409) beckon the reader to an open, perhaps favorable opinion about the sea, but the phrases "the creamy, sidelong-rushing sea" (p. 426), "the most riotously perverse and cross-running seas" (p. 191), and "a discolored, rolling, and oftentimes tumultous and bursting sea" (p. 263) elicit awe for an amazing power.

Besides the use of adjectival modification, sea associates with words in its immediate grammatical context in two important ways: by combining with words or phrases in prepositional construction and by joining with them by means of a copula. The first of these two tactics is by far the most numerous. Investigation of this set is limited primarily to those constructions using only the preposition "of" (that use "_____ of the sea" or, rarely, "the sea of_____"); since "of" is the preposition that most nearly denotes ownership or possession (relationship or integration of some degree), analysis of such constructions may shed light on how Melville views the sea's involvement with objects external to it.

As with other grammatical peculiarities, the most fascinating and numerous prepositional constructions involving sea are in Moby-Dick and Mardi; the fewest, the tamest, and the most predictable are in Typee and Omoo. In Typee's only construction of this sort, occurring in the novel's opening paragraph, the "privations and hardships of the sea" (p. 3) prepare for the ensuing escapade on land to be more attractive. Omoo's initial "routine of sea-life" (p. 34) gives way to an extension of the Polynesian idyll, interspersed by "a trough" (p. 58), "the action" (p. 63), "the waves" (p. 111), and "the swell" (p. 263) of the sea, as well as "those marvelous tales" (p. 46) of the sea.

Mardi also shows the "trough" of the sea (p. 72) and the "action" of the sea (p. 374), but those are the book's only simple constructions. The swell of the sea here recorded is a "great swell" (p. 141), there is a "roar" of the sea (p. 118), "an extraordinary rolling" (p. 216), and it

is the "season of high sea" (pp. 235, 373). Mardi's very first "of" sea
construction, "this phenomenon of the sea" (p. 9), indicates what a
transformation has taken place between Melville's sensibilities in his
first two novels and those in his third. There is something noteworthy,
something more than literal here, for his audience to sit up and observe
about the sea. It may not ever before have crossed their minds to
consider the ship's crew as "a fixture" (p. 111) on the sea, or fish
"locusts" (p. 148) of the sea, or the pupils of a young Polynesian's eyes
"floating isles in the sea" (p. 226), but Mardi leads them to do that.
Of the sea also--and this is a nearer approach to the sea's visible
character--there is a "pallidness," a "phosphorescence," a "seeming
ignition" (all from p. 123), even "a cemetary" (p. 192) of the sea. It
is here that we encounter "ripplings of some now waveless sea" (p. 416)
and "old tide-rips of diluvian seas" (p. 555). So there is, for the
first time in the sea novels, modification of sea when it is in the
objective slot. There is, also for the first time, the use of sea to
introduce the "of" phrase--"a sea of sounds"--where sea is, incidentally,
an appositive metaphor for a "long-rolling chant" Taji hears on the
island of Oro.

The prepositional constructions of sea in Redburn are more tempered
and less excessive than those in Mardi. They are hardened, refined, and
a bit mysterious. Initially, the curious ship La Reine is called the
"mistress of a green, glassy sea" (p. 9), and finally, "the bottomless
profound of the sea" is described as "frightful" (p. 288). Between those
references, Melville tells what is on the surface of the sea: "the
trough of a calamitous sea" (p. 9), "phosphorescent sparkles of the damp
night sea" (p. 245); what is within the sea: "the depths of the deep
blue sea" (p. 64), "the vaults of the sea" (p. 127); what shape the sea
takes: "a certain wonderful rising and falling of the sea" (p. 64); and
what it exudes: "the cool air of the sea" (p. 47). From the
prepositional constructions, the description of the sea in this novel is
complete, even running to what it implies for that portion of humanity
that would live on it: "the discipline of the sea" (p. 29), "Miserable
dog's life is this of the sea" (p. 66). A fine syntactical tie between
Mardi and Redburn (and another between Redburn and White-Jacket, as we
shall see) is that those two novels both contain one construction in
which sea introduces an "of" phrase; no other novels do that except
Moby-Dick, which contains four such constructions (on pp. 4, 162, 227, and
339). What is more coincidental is that both of those references
associate sea metaphorically with "sound." In Redburn "some thronged
Italian air" which Carlo plays on his organ, Redburn, captivated, calls
"a mixed and liquid sea of sound, that dashes spray in my face" (p. 250).

A syntactic tie joining Redburn and White-Jacket is Redburn's final
prepositional sea construction, "the bottomless profound of the sea"
(p. 288), which contains the whole of the first such construction in
White-Jacket ("the bottom of the sea"--p. 72) and a good deal of the last
("the speechless profound of the sea"--p. 392). Between those two
references, the sea's appearance is highlighted ("the spray of the sea"--
pp. 83, 191; "the sudden swells of the calm sea"--p. 392; "occasional
phosphorescence of the yeasting sea"--p. 106), though there is also
reference to human interaction with the sea--"a snuff of the sea" (p. 271)
and assertion of human emotion about the sea--"the combined fury of the
sea and wind" (p. 108).

The majority of the prepositional sea constructions that appear in
Moby-Dick are either animal, human, or forcefully and provocatively
inanimate. Not surprisingly, most of the animal references refer to the

White Whale--"the great prize ox of the sea" (p. 255), "this vast dumb
brute of the sea" (p. 298), "the utmost monster of the seas" (p. 300),
"a dragon of the sea" (p. 305), "a high hill of the sea" (p. 320), and
"the gliding great demon of the seas of life" (p. 162). Regal roles
associate humanity with the sea--"a king of the sea" (p. 114), "a diademed
king of the sea" (p. 282), "the throne of the seas" (p. 117), "the monarch
of the seas" (p. 118). And, most provocative within the animate category,
are those expressly human characteristics relegated to the sea--"the open
independence of her sea" (p. 97), "those occasional caprices of the sea"
(p. 267), "the universal cannibalism of the sea" (p. 235), "the salt
breath of the newfound sea" (p. 400), "the fair face of the pleasant sea"
(p. 262), and "the vast blue eye of the sea" (p. 190).
    Both the animate and the inanimate characteristics of the prepositional
sea constructions in Moby-Dick amount to less of an actual description of
the sea than previous novels have given us. Instead, the character of
the sea, its deepest nature, is being sounded, and what so often emerges
is ominous (or at least mysterious), something only dimly perceived by
mankind, unapproachable, alien, and, more often than not, hostile.
    Something of the sea's color (whether black or white) renders it
physically impenetrable, first of all: "the shuddering cold and
blackness of the sea" (p. 50), "the dead wintry bleakness of the sea"
(p. 111), "muffled rollings of a milky sea" (p. 169), "the blackness of
the sea and the night" (p. 353). It is also psychologically impenetrable,
possessing what we can never know: "the secrets of the currents in the
seas" (p. 158), "the subtlest secrets of the seas" (p. 326), "subtleness
of the sea" (p. 235), "the profundity of the sea" (p. 239), "the vast
swells of the omnipotent sea" (p. 193), "sweet mystery about this sea"
(p. 399). The sea is mesmerizing and not a little deceptive: "the
infinite series of the sea" (p. 136), "the widely contrasting serenity of
those seductive seas" (p. 139), "dreaminess . . . over the ship . . .
over the sea" (p. 185), "the fancied security of the middle of solitary
seas" (p. 316), "the wide trance of the sea" (p. 242). Finally, the
implication of both transient and everlasting doom accompanies the sea--
"an elemental strife at sea" (p. 110), "the full awfulness of the sea"
(p. 235), "the great shroud of the sea" (p. 469).
    Another grammatical technique that Melville uses for implying
association with (or involvement of) the sea and another entity is joining
the two with a copula. Although a simple technique, Melville does not
use it often; in fact, it does not appear until the third novel, and
there it occurs only once. Furthermore, sea is not in that case in its
pure form, but in compound, and refers not to a body of water but to a
bird--"the daring 'Diver,' or sea-kite" (M, p. 136).
    There seem to be no occurrences of a copula joining sea to another
object in Redburn, but in White-Jacket it happens five times, in a pattern
that begins and ends with a compounded form of sea regularly alternating
with phrases which use the pure form of the word. Furthermore, all of
the compounded forms involve some element of humanity: "sea-kings and
sea-lords" (p. 28), "corsairs, captives, dungeons, and sea-fights"
(p. 168), "my sea-tutor and sire" (p. 396). The two occasions when the
pure word sea combines with something else go considerably farther in
illuminating the nature of the sea. The first is also a personification--
"the combined fury of the sea and wind" (p. 108), and the second combines
with an item created for the destruction of humanity--"The gallows and
the sea refuse nothing" (p. 377). All of this casts a vengeful,
destructive light on the sea which, as we have seen and which will be
further substantiated, is intensified in Moby-Dick.

On nearly a dozen occasions in Moby-Dick, sea combines with very elemental things--with the land (pp. 125, twice on 235), with the air (p. 442), with the night (p. 353), with the ship (p. 185), with the whale (p. 49), but most often and most variously with the sky. Both sea and "sky" are associated with a sunrise (p. 317) and modified by "the lonely sunset" (p. 409). Both can be mild ("that smiling sky, and this unsounded sea"--p. 445) and violent ("sky and sea roared and split with the thunder, and blazed with the lightening"--p. 413). But perhaps the most significant and explicit description of this sort of the sea occurs in a polysyndeton that generalizes from the particulars we have already witnessed: "seas, or winds, or whales, or any of the ordinary irrational horrors of the world" (p. 104).

Perhaps more important than what we can deduce from the subtle syntactic connections Melville makes with the sea is what he more overtly and expressly makes known about the sea, what the sea signifies to the characters of his books--by simile, metaphor, or conscious description apart from simple modification. Every single novel presents the sea as something that inexplicably draws the souls and bodies of men to it. In Typee Tommo fervently expresses an "impatience . . . to reach the sea" (p. 119) and by the end of Omoo "the impulse urging me to sea once more" (p. 315) is still with him. In the next book Taji notices how "passion "passionately fond of the sea" (p. 283) the local natives are, and the protagonist in Melville's fourth novel extolls, "give me this . . . salt-sea life" (R, p. 66). Attraction to the sea is voiced by Jack Chase in the fifth book, "A snuff of the sea . . . is inspiration" (WJ, p. 271). Finally, symptoms of longing for the sea are indicated to Ishmael in a variety of ways: he begins to be "over conscious" of his lungs, he grows "grim about the mouth" and "hazy about the eyes," and his "hypos" get the upper hand of him. It is, in short, "a damp, drizzly November" in his soul (MD, pp. 12-14).

Neither that attraction nor the object of it is fully explained or defined. In fact, our not fully understanding the sea may be the reason for a good deal of its charm for us. Early in Moby-Dick Ishmael conjectures that the sea is "an everlasting terra incognita" (p. 235), which he later further elaborates: "There is, one knows not what sweet mystery about this sea, whose gently awful stirrings seem to speak of some hidden soul beneath; like those fabled undulations of the Ephesian sod over the buried Evangelist St. John" (p. 399). And the fact that the sea is such a mystery may be one reason Melville uses a variety of similes and metaphors in attempting a description of it. He would have his audience approach the sea by what is familiar to them, remembering that any one metaphorical route in isolation would not be sufficient. Only with the aggregate of the things the metaphorical language implies (though some of them may seem paradoxical), and then with that mysterious ontology which is more than the sum of them, does Melville begin to present the sea in its completeness and complexity for his readers.

One thing to bear in mind, which Melville does not make plain until the final sea novel, is that the sea exaggerates things. "Wild . . . fabulous rumors" become credible at sea, and a sailor at sea is "wrapped by influences all tending to make his fancy pregnant" (MD, p. 156). Belief is then, for the sea time, suspended by immediate sensation.

The immediate sensations are, as the figurative language that attends sea reveals, highly energetic, with a vitality that is nearly alive. In Mardi, the sea is compared to "ten thousand [boiling] caldrons" (p. 118), "fountains of [spouting] fire" (p. 121), "a [glowing] burnished shield" (p. 149). In Moby-Dick, likewise, the seas "seethe like a boiling pan"

(p. 3), are "spangled . . . like gold-beater's skin" (p. 346), and
"bubblingly leap" with light and heat like "a crucible of molten gold"
(p. 423).

Imagery in the four final novels intensifies the activity of the sea
with an animation that is animal. The sea is "charger-like" (M, p. 553),
it "neighs and snorts" (R, p. 66). It resembles "a savage tigress that
tossing in the jungle overlays her own cubs" when it "dashes even the
mightiest whales against the rocks" (MD, p. 235). It is also the "stable"
of such "brute monsters," and of "moral monsters" as well (WJ, p. 377).

On a higher stratum of animation, the sea is personified. In its
depth it is like Hautia (M, p. 647). It is capable of thought (M, p. 303),
of refusal (WJ, p. 101), of rebellion (MD, p. 48). "Like giants' palms
outspread" (MD, p. 423) the sea pushes the Pequod on its way. It is a
great leveler of character: "it knocks the false keel right off a
pretender's bows, it tells him just what he is, and makes him feel it,
too" (WJ, p. 271). And it is also a leveler in a more devastating sense,
swallowing up ships and crews (MD, p. 235): "But not only is the sea
such a foe to man who is an alien to it, but it is also a fiend to its
own offspring; worse than the Persian host who murdered his own guests;
sparing not the creatures which itself hath spawned."

A paradox emerges from the similes and metaphors that surround the
sea. On one hand it takes on connotations of a creator/provider--it is
"the place to cradle genius" (WJ, p. 271). Over "all four continents"
rise and flow "sea-pastures, wide-rolling watery prairies and Potters'
Fields" (MD, p. 399). The sea is a prairie, home of the "prairie cock"
Nantucketer (MD, p. 63); it is a "harvest plain," stacked with the
dolphins' "glittering sheaves of spray" (M, p. 644). It is, in the words
of Obed Macy, the historian, "a green pasture where our children's
grand-children will go for bread" (MD, p. 8).

But if it sustains life, it also destroys it. It resembles "a great,
black gulf" (R, p. 78), "a shroud" (M, p. 123), a "sepulcher" (M, p. 300).
White Jacket calls it "the true Tophet and bottomless pit of many workers
of iniquity" (WJ, p. 377). Ishmael, however, implies that man in part
deserves the terrors of the sea:

    . . . for ever and for ever, to the crack of doom, the sea
    will insult and murder him [baby man], and pulverize the
    stateliest, stiffest frigate he can make; nevertheless . . .
    man has lost that sense of the full awfulness of the sea
    which aboriginally belongs to it (MD, p. 235).

The sea is, then, as Melville's language indicates to us, beyond the
understanding of man, and far more powerful than man. It is a force that,
for no reason other than whim or chance, holds the sustenance and the
destruction of man in its rise and fall, and yet man does not falter in
his allegiance to or affection for it. An attraction which puzzles him
nevertheless enthralls him.

Notes

1. W. H. Smyth, The Sailor's Word-Book: An Alphabetical Digest of Nautical Terms (London: Blackie and Son, 1867), p. 102.

2. The reference is to the first example in Typee of a sentence containing billows. See the list of sentences following, in Appendix E. Subsequent references indicate a sea novel by its first letter and the number of the sentence containing the sea term under discussion within that book.

3. According to Merton M. Sealts, Jr., Melville's Reading: A Check-list of Books Owned and Borrowed (Madison: The University of Wisconsin Press, 1966), pp. 51, 68, and 86, Melville had read Pope's translations of Homer and Ovid in 1849, but did not acquire a three-volume set of Pope's poetry until 1856. We do know from Sealts, p. 73, that Melville read Lamb in 1848-1849 and was delighted with him (see also Melville's letter of 1 May 1850 to Dana, The Letters of Herman Melville, ed. Merrell R. Davis and William H. Gilman [New Haven: Yale University Press, 1960], p. 108). Both Pope and Lamb customarily use such phrases as "finny tribes."

4. Smyth, The Sailor's Word-Book, p. 674.

5. C. Hugh Holman, A Handbook to Literature, 3d ed. (New York: The Odyssey Press, 1972), p. 261, defines "hypallage" as "a figure of speech in which an epithet is moved from the more natural to the less natural one of a group of nouns, as when Virgil writes of 'the trumpet's Tuscan blare' when the normal order would be 'the Tuscan trumpet's blare.'"

6. George Steiner, in reviewing a recent two-volume compilation of J.M.W. Turner's paintings (see his "Fires at Sea," The New Yorker 54 [June 5,]978]: 110-16) believes that the sea on fire epitomizes Romantic iconography: "the equation between energy and delight, between the titanic forces in nature and the dynamics of the ego, seemed to find specific expression in a symbiosis of fire and water, of flame and sea foam." For as long ago as Shakespeare's age (both Shakespeare and Melville, incidentally, apply the word "yeasty" to the sea) writers have, says Steiner, sought a "verbal correlative" for juxtaposing the fire with the sea. He describes the merger of those two phenomena in Turner's paintings, "the sense of heat, of fermentation, of pulsing combustion" and then quotes Turner, "lashed to the mast, sketch pad in hand," observing and then painting--"'the water, like a witch's oils,/ Burnt green, and blue, and white,'" or "incendiary gashes of sunlight on . . . smoking seas," or shadows of ships burning a "still and awful red" into the sea.

7. Although neither Melville, Dana, nor Smyth defines this concept, Melville explains it scientifically ("the presence of large quantities of putrescent animal matter") and superstitiously ("a commotion among the mermaids, whose golden locks, all torn and disheveled, do irradiate the waters"--both quotations are from Mardi, p. 123). It is more completely (and probably more accurately) defined by Gershom Bradford, The Mariner's Dictionary (New York: Weathervane Books, 1952), p. 193:
> Phosphorescent sea: a phenomenon of glowing light frequently
> seen at sea at some point of agitation such as the breaking

crest of a wave, the bow wave and wake of a vessel, or
the dipping of an oar. It is supposed to be caused by
the oxidation of a secretion emitted by jellyfish and
other animalculae when agitated by some disturbance.
The jellyfish causing this condition have been found
in a wide variety of forms. The pale light of
phosphorescence sometimes attains considerable brilliancy,
one shipmaster reporting that a bucket of the water from
overside at such a time was sufficient to cause a glow
of illumination in the cabin. Another reported great
difficulty in making out the lights of vessels until
close aboard owing to the brilliance of the sea.

8.   Smyth, The Sailor's Word-Book, p. 618.

9.   Ibid, p. 602.

10. Ibid, p. 362.

THE GLOSSED CONCORDANCE

For sailors have their own names, even for things that are
familiar ashore; and if you call a thing by its shore name,
you are laughed at for an ignoramus and a land-lubber.
                                              --Redburn

     The concordance which follows offers definitions of the sea terms
that Herman Melville used, all citations of them which I have recorded
from his first six novels, and the parts of speech of the words in each
citation. The responsibility for the completeness and accuracy of the
references as recorded rests with me, and there is bound to exist a
definite margin of human error. The editions of Melville's novels which
I used are the most authoritative to date, volumes produced by
Northwestern University Press and the Newberry Library for Typee, Omoo,
Mardi, Redburn, and White-Jacket, and, since that edition of Moby-Dick
is still several years away from the press, Harrison Hayford and Hershel
Parker's Norton Critical Edition of Melville's final sea novel.
     My definitions were adopted, whenever possible, from lexicographies
written by mariners who were contemporaries of Melville, notably W. H.
Smyth's The Sailor's Word-Book: An Alphabetical Digest of Nautical Terms
(1867), Richard Henry Dana's The Seaman's Friend (1857), and W. Clark
Russell's Sailors' Language: A Collection of Sea-Terms and their
Definitions (1883). When none of those books included a sea term that
Melville used, I consulted other sources, including Webster's 1828
American Dictionary of the English Language, Gersholm Bradford's The
Mariner's Dictionary, and, rarely, a passage in one of Melville's novels
where he provides a definition himself. When those sources failed to
yield a needed definition, I have gone to the OED, or, for an occasional
term, to Van Nostrand's Scientific Encyclopedia, Larousse's Encyclopedia
of World Geography, and Professor John B. Owen of the Department of
Biology, University of North Dakota.
     The definitions I recorded are usually, but not exclusively,
verbatim. At times I have shortened the original definitions to only
that portion which is applicable to Melville's uses; at other times I
have retained phrases which may not apply directly, but which are
linguistically curious or which aid in preserving the peculiar flavor of
the time or of the jargon of sailors.

The concordance is alphabetized by sea term, each entry consisting of the word, its definition (with the source indicated by the author's last name in parentheses following the definition—the bibliography may be consulted for the complete citation), the contextual references by novel in which the word appears (preceded by page number and part of speech). For example, in the case of the first word, the glossary reads:

ABEAM. In a line at right angles to the vessel's length; opposite the centre of a ship's side. (Smyth)

> White-Jacket--p. 44 (adv.) with the wind astern or abeam.

The vocabulary terms may be grouped in a variety of ways, some of which are used in the appendices. Appendix A gives the alphabetical word-list and assigns the number(s) of the semantic class(es) in which each term participates in the sea novel canon, and then groups the words according to those respective classes. Appendix B does the same thing for the syntactic categories. Appendix C indicates the compounds Melville uses novel by novel. The final two appendices involve the words in their contexts, Appendix D displaying various brands of metaphorical activity in which the sea language participates, and the final appendix quoting those sentences containing the six vocabulary words examined in Chapter III.

ABEAM. In a line at right angles to the vessel's length; opposite the centre of a ship's side. (Smyth)

> White-Jacket--p. 96 (adv.) with the wind astern, or abeam.

ABYSS. A deep mass of waters; in hydrography it was synonymous with gulf. (Smyth)

> Typee--p. 30 (n.) We plunged headlong into the seething abyss.

> Mardi--p. 63 (n.) I inclined myself over towards the abyss.

ADRIFT. Floating at random; the state of a boat or vessel broken from her moorings; and driven to and fro without control by the winds and waves. Cast loose; cut adrift. (Smyth)

> Mardi--p. 27 (adv.) the lashings adrift; p. 120 (adv.) cutting adrift the last fragments; p. 425 (adv.) turn not adrift prematurely.

> White-Jacket--p. 378 (adv.) or set themselves adrift on the wide ocean.

> Moby-Dick--p. 448 (adv.) the sheets of their sails adrift.

AFLOAT. Borne up and supported by the water; buoyed clear of the ground; also used for being on board ship. (Smyth)

> Omoo--p. 41 (adv.) afloat, they are absolutely mad after it; p. 216 (adv.) it had never been afloat.

Mardi--p. 6 (adv.) we'll be all afloat; p. 7 (adj.) some ugly craft still afloat; p. 32 (adv.) afloat or suspended; p. 120 (adv.) once more afloat in our shell; p. 167 (adv.) we were once more afloat; p. 256 (adv.) Among other decanters set afloat; p. 484 (adv.) morning's twilight found us once more afloat; p. 581 (adv.) must needs go round to keep afloat.

Redburn--p. 104 (adv.) He was a Cain afloat; p. 158 (adv.) so great a number of ships afloat; p. 166 (adv.) the idea of a Mivart's or Delmonico's afloat; p. 309 (adv.) so clever ashore and so craven afloat.

White-Jacket--p. 17 (adv.) Though bowing to naval discipline afloat; p. 21 (adv.) may be he was the wandering Jew afloat; p. 23 (adv.) a Harry the Eighth afloat; p. 34 (adv.) but afloat it will not do; p. 53 (adv.) when a rumor was set afloat; p. 84 (adv.) may they and their descendents--ashore or afloat; p. 175 (adv.) a sort of State Prison afloat; p. 224 (adv.) thought it was me that set afloat that yarn; p. 226 (adv.) I have taken an oath to keep afloat to the last letter; p. 234 (adv.) was as much a monarch afloat; p. 295 (adv.) Afloat or wrecked the martial law; p. 329 (adv.) how long I had been afloat; p. 388 (adv.) never again catch old Boombolt afloat; p. 390 (adv.) were the greatest curmudgeons afloat; p. 390 (adv.) is but this old-fashioned world of ours afloat.

Moby-Dick--p. 48 (adv.) come nigh to drowning while yet afloat; p. 56 (adv.) Hiding his canoe, still afloat; p. 106 (adv.) this earthly air; whether ashore or afloat; p. 405 (adj.) afloat all day upon smooth, slow heaving swells.

AFT. A Saxon word contradistinctive of fore, and an abbreviation of abaft--the hinder part of the ship, or that nearest the stern.--Right aft is in a direct line with the keel from the stern.--To haul aft a sheet is to pull on the rope which brings the clue or corner of the sails more in the direction of the stern.--The mast rakes aft when it inclines toward the stern. (Smyth)

Omoo--p. 7 (adv.) instead of extending fore and aft; p. 59 (adv.) washed clean aft; p. 69 (adv.) four or five rushed aft.

Mardi--p. 33 (adv.) the wind being from aft; p. 70 (adv.) hauled aft the sheet; p. 86 (adj.) to the fore and aft-stays.

Redburn--p. 53 (adv.) So I scrubbed away fore and aft; p. 69 (adv.) standing round the windlass looking aft; p. 75 (adv.) showed her decks fore and aft; p. 112 (adv.) the captain had him called aft; p. 283 (adv.) went aft to the mate; p. 293 (adv.) let them have an occasional run fore and aft.

White-Jacket--p. 10 (adv.) These have aft the fore and main-sheets; p. 34 (adv.) he is braced up fore and aft; p. 40 (adv.) or reefing top-sails fore and aft; p. 44 (adv.) gunner's gang were at work fore and aft; p. 47 (adj.) divisions of the frigate, fore and aft; p. 55 (adj.) Next day, fore and aft; p. 69 (adv.) galley cooks would be going fore and aft; p. 72 (adv.) I went aft to get a squint at 'em; p. 85 (adv.) is spread with hammocks, fore and aft; p. 97 (adv.) fore

and aft set t'-gallant-sails; p. 102 (adv.) were ridden fore and aft
on a rail; p. 172 (adv.) of having a clear stroll fore and aft;
p. 184 (adv.) among all hands fore and aft; p. 189 (adv.) to prey
upon honest seamen, fore and aft; p. 198 (adv.) D'ye hear there, fore
and aft; p. 202 (prep.) The cry ran fore and aft the ship; p. 225
(adv.) D'ye hear there, fore and aft; p. 255 (adv.) the whole extent
aft to the bulk-head; p. 279 (adv.) who, as I came aft, eyed me in
such a manner; p. 281 (adv.) sauntered aft into his cabin; p. 288
(adv.) and, marching aft, endeavors to; p. 323 (adv.) the awnings
were spread fore and aft; p. 356 (adv.) D'ye hear there, fore and
aft; p. 357 (adv.) D'ye hear there, fore and aft; p. 361 (adv.) D'ye
hear there, fore and aft; p. 372 (adv.) A cry went fore and aft;
p. 388 (adv.) D'ye hear there, fore and aft; p. 399 (prep.) Glance
fore and aft our flush decks.

Moby-Dick--p. 48 (adv.) [wave] runs roaring fore and aft; p. 60 (adj.)
completely sweeping the entire after part of the deck; p. 93 (adv.)
Muster 'em aft here--blast 'em; p. 94 (adv.) Aft here, ye sons of
bachelors; p. 141 (adv.) ordered Starbuck to send everybody aft.

ALBATROS(S). A large, voracious, long-winged sea-bird, belonging to the
genus Diomedea; very abundant in the Southern Ocean and the Northern
Pacific; though said to be rarely met with within the tropics. (Smyth)
There was formerly a superstition that the soul of a departed sailor
animated the albatross and for this reason seamen were reluctant to kill
them. (Bradford)

Omoo--p. 35 (n.) the gray albatros, peculiar to these seas; p. 74
(n.) plucked from a distended albatros' wing.

White-Jacket--p. 7 (n.) it looks like a white albatross' wing; p. 7
(n.) was taken for an albatros himself; p. 116 (n.) Unnumbered white
albatros were skimming the sea.

Moby-Dick--p. 164 (n.) Bethink thee of the albatros; p. 165 (n.)
goney was some seaman's name for albatros; p. 202 (n.) The Albatros;
p. 202 (n.) a sail loamed ahead, the Goney (Albatros) by name;
p. 421 (n.) the shivered remnants of the jib and fore and main-top-
sails . . . went eddying away to leeward, like the feather of an
albatross; p. 451 (n.) stretching it with stun-sails, like the
double-jointed wings of an albatross.

ALBICORE. A fish of the family Scomberidae, found in shoals in the
ocean; it is about 5 or 6 feet long, with an average weight of nearly
100 lbs. when fine. (Smyth's spelling is "albacore.")

Typee--p. 10 (n.) Then you would see the superb albicore; p. 23 (n.)
A vast shoal of bonetas and albicores.

Omoo--p. 13 (n.) fishing for albicores with a bone hook; p. 15 (n.)
the bonettas and albicores frolicking round us.

Mardi--p. 41 (n.) watched the darting albicore.

ALEWIFE.   The Clupea alosa, a fish of the herring kind, which appears in
the Philosophical Transactions for 1678, as the aloofe; the corruption
therefore was a ready one.   (Smyth)

Redburn--p. 265 (n.) Bologna sausages, Dutch herrings, alewives and
other delicacies.

Moby-Dick--p. 119 (n.) sharks and shad, alewives and herring.

ALLIGATOR.   [from the Spanish lagarto.]   The crocodile of America.   The
head of this voracious animal is flat and imbricate; several of the under
teeth enter into and pass through the upper jaw; the nape is naked; on
the tail are two rough lateral lines.   (Smyth)

Mardi--p. 31 (n.) even the alligator dies in his mail; p. 40 (n.) as
the alligator thrusts; p. 225 (n.) like alligators, or Hollanders;
p. 417 (n.) patriarchs of crocodiles and alligators.

ALOFT.   [Anglo-Saxon, alofte, on high.]   Above; over-head; on high.
Synonymous with up above the tops, at the mast-head, or anywhere about
the higher yards, masts, and rigging of ships.--Aloft there!   the hailing
of people in the tops.--Stay aloft!   the command to the people in the
rigging to climb to their stations.   Also, heaven: "Poor Tom is gone
aloft."   (Smyth)

Moby-Dick--p. 14 (adv.) I go as a simple sailor, aloft there to the
royal mast-head.

AMBERGRIS.   A fragrant drug floating on sea-coasts, the origin and
production of which was long a matter of dispute, although now known to
be a morbid product developed in the intestines of the spermaciti whale
(Physeter macrocephalus).   It is of a grayish colour, very light, easily
fusible, and is used both as a perfume and a cordial, in various
extracts, essences, and tinctures.   (Smyth)

Mardi--p. 374 (n.) more like ambergris than amber; p. 374 (n.) you
know all about ambergris; p. 374 (n.) Ambergris is found both on land
and at sea; p. 374 (n.) But what is this ambergris; p. 375 (n.)
Ambergris is the petrified gallstones of crocodiles; p. 375 (n.)
comes sweet scented ambergris from those musky; p. 375 (n.) theology,
or amber, or ambergris, it's all the same; p. 375 (n.) ambergris is a
morbid secretion of the Spermaciti whale; p. 375 (n.) a quarter-
quintal of ambergris was more valuable.

Moby-Dick--p. 336 (n.) In vain it was to rake for Ambergriese in the
paunch of this Leviathan; p. 338 (n.) something worth a good deal more
than oil; yes, ambergris; p. 340 (n.) had not the slightest suspicion
concerning the ambergris; p. 342 (n.) And this, good friends, is
ambergris, worth a gold guinea; p. 342 (n.) Ambergris; p. 342 (n.)
Now this ambergris is a very curious substance; p. 342 (n.) the
precise origin of ambergris remained, like amber itself, a problem;
pp. 342-3 (n.) By some, ambergris is supposed to be the cause, and by
others the effect, of the dyspepsia in the whale; p. 343 (n.) that

the incorruption of this most fragrant ambergris should be found in
the heart of such decay.

ANCHO**R.** A large and heavy instrument in use from the earliest times for
holding and retaining ships, which it executes with admirable force.
With few exceptions it consists of a long iron shank, having at one end
a ring, to which the cable is attached, and the other branching out into
two arms, with flukes or palms at their bill or extremity. A stock of
timber or iron is fixed at right angles to the arms, and serves to guide
the flukes perpendicularly to the surface of the ground.--At anchor, the
situation of a ship which rides by its anchor.--To anchor, to cast or let
go the anchor, so that it falls into the ground for the ship to ride
thereby.--Up anchor, pipe to weigh; every man to his station.--Anchor is
also used figuratively for anything which confers security or stability.--
Anchorage, ground which is suitable, and neither too deep, shallow, or
exposed for ships to ride in safety upon; also the set of anchors
belonging to a ship; also a royal duty levied from vessels coming to a
port or roadstead for the use of its advantages. It is generally marked
on the charts by an anchor, and is described according to its attributes
of good, snug, open, or exposed.--Bower-Anchors, those at the bows and in
constant working use. They are called best and small, not from a
difference in size, but as to the bow on which they are placed; starboard
being the best bower, and port the small bower.--Sheet-anchor, one of
four bower anchors supplied, two at the bows, and one at either chest-tree
abaft the fore-rigging; one is termed the sheet, the other the spare
anchor; usually got ready in a gale to let go on the parting of a bower.
(Smyth)

> Typee--p. 5 (n.) riding snugly at anchor in some green cove; p. 12
> (n.) was the anchorage we desired to reach; p. 13 (n.) pilot the ship
> to a good and secure anchorage; p. 15 (n.) after we had come to an
> anchor; p. 18 (n.) immediately upon coming to an anchor; p. 24 (n.)
> Viewed from our ship as she lay at anchor; p. 25 (n.) dropped her
> anchor in its waters beneath; p. 270 (v.) to a whale ship which was
> anchored near the shore; p. 271 (n.) captain came forward and
> ordered the anchor weighed.

> Omoo--p. 14 (n.) he might one day find his anchor down; p. 14 (n.) do
> not come to an anchor for eighteen or twenty months; p. 19 (n.) She
> was riding to her anchor in the bay; p. 19 (n.) was not to let go an
> anchor; p. 19 (v.) anchored alongside of her; p. 20 (n.) sometimes
> customary when lying at an anchor; p. 26 (n.) as far as safe
> anchorage is concerned; p. 50 (n.) The captain's anchor is pretty
> nigh atrip; p. 70 (n.) eventually be brought to her anchors; p. 76
> (n.) the ship must let go her anchor; p. 81 (n.) the anchor takes
> hold of the bottom; p. 83 (v.) to have the ship snugly anchored;
> p. 100 (n.) until the anchor was down; p. 100 (n.) proceeded to
> bring us to an anchor; p. 102 (n.) her rusty little anchor was
> caught; p. 149 (n.) as they catted the anchor; p. 153 (n.) for the
> anchor was weighing; p. 153 (n.) The anchor was soon up; p. 216 (n.)
> dropped overboard the native contrivance for an anchor; p. 270 (n.)
> vessels enter to their anchorage; p. 289 (n.) Going from Po-Po's
> house toward the anchorage; p. 299 (n.) In a grove near the
> anchorage; p. 299 (n.) she drops her anchor in its waters; p. 316
> (n.) The anchors came up cheerily.

Mardi--p. 64 (n.) foul anchors, skewered hearts; p. 69 (v.) brig lay
anchored; p. 161 (n.) how weigh the isle's coral anchor; p. 178 (n.)
profoundly at anchor; p. 432 (v.) In this arbor we anchored; p. 498
(n.) Bello's great navy were riding at anchor; p. 554 (v.) a line-of-
battle-ship . . . anchored in the sea; p. 620 (n.) our only
anchorage is when we founder.

Redburn--p. 4 (n.) and old anchors and chain-cable piled on the walk;
p. 31 (n.) came to anchor; p. 31 (n.) I'll do the yawing after the
anchor's up; p. 32 (n.) all hands were called to up anchor; p. 32 (n.)
The anchor being secured; p. 33 (n.) we passed ships lying at anchor;
p. 41 (n.) had gold anchors in his ears; p. 93 (n.) her starboard
anchor was gone; p. 96 (n.) through fleets of fishermen at anchor;
p. 122 (n.) to pound the rust off the anchor; p. 127 (n.) came to
anchor in the stream; p. 128 (v.) Not long after anchoring; p. 130
(n.) we hove up the anchor; p. 134 (n.) sailor-scrawls of foul
anchors, lovers' sonnets; p. 138 (n.) till he hove up anchor for the
world to come; p. 143 (n.) But what does this anchor here; p. 143 (n.)
that anchor, ship, and Dibdin's ditty; p. 147 (n.) and warehouses,
and bales, and anchors; p. 175 (n.) inscriptions, crowns, anchors,
eagles; p. 189 (n.) gilded emblems outside--an anchor, a crown;
p. 196 (n.) As soon as we came to anchor; p. 218 (n.) the sign of the
Gold Anchor in Union-street; p. 225 (n.) Arrived at the Gold Anchor;
p. 237 (n.) to the sign of the Gold Anchor; p. 240 (n.) as the crews
catted their anchors; p. 245 (n.) where they never weigh anchor;
p. 300 (n.) though scores of ships were here lying at anchor; p. 301
(n.) down goes our old anchor; p. 303 (n.) from the sign of the
Golden Anchor; p. 309 (n.) here they all came to anchor before the
bar.

White-Jacket--p. 4 (n.) as if I were weighing the anchor; p. 6 (n.)
All hands up anchor; p. 7 (n.) All hands up anchor; p. 7 (n.) in the
shape of our ponderous anchor; p. 9 (n.) in tacking ship, coming to
anchor; p. 9 (n.) there are Sheet-Anchor-men--old veterans all; p. 9
(n.) the fore-yard, anchors, and all the sails; p. 17 (n.) cried a
growling old sheet-anchor-man; p. 18 (n.) the frigate came to anchor;
p. 25 (n.) sport long coats and wear the anchor-button; p. 27 (n.)
crowns and anchors worked on the sleeves; p. 47 (n.) the old sheet-
anchor-men, who spent their time; p. 54 (n.) roared an old sheet-
anchor-man; p. 72 (n.) cried Scrimmage, a sheet-anchor-man; p. 72 (n.)
cried the sheet-anchor-man; p. 72 (n.) In addition to the Bower-
anchors carried; p. 72 (n.) a frigate carries large anchors . . .
called Sheet-anchors; p. 72 (n.) the old seamen . . . are called
Sheet-anchor-men; p. 73 (n.) cried Scrimmage, the sheet-anchor-man;
p. 86 (n.) One rheumatic old sheet-anchor-man . . . was driven;
p. 90 (n.) inquired an Irish waister of an old Spanish sheet-anchor-
man; p. 109 (n.) fine weather we encountered after first weighing
anchor; p. 157 (n.) a sheet-anchor-man . . . once touched his hat;
p. 159 (n.) As we glided on toward our anchorage; p. 160 (v.) fast
anchored in the bay; p. 160 (n.) behold now the Neversink at her
anchors; p. 169 (n.) from Broadbit, a sheet-anchor-man; p. 170 (n.)
stitching picturesque eagles, and anchors; p. 170 (n.) to order a
palm-tree, an anchor, a crucifix; p. 176 (v.) though his vessel be
anchored; p. 178 (n.) and moor them to the frigates' anchor-buoy;
p. 180 (n.) A knowing old sheet-anchor-man; p. 180 (n.) but the
sheet-anchor-man's integrity is like a rock; p. 180 (n.) the sheet-

anchor-man goes to his confidants; p. 195 (n.) lie at anchor in one
port; p. 198 (n.) by the man-of-war's-man while lying at anchor;
p. 202 (n.) You venerable sheet-anchor-men; pp. 202-3 (n.) cried an
old sheet-anchor-man; p. 211 (v.) ere Noah . . . anchored his ark;
p. 211 (v.) there lay anchored in you all these green . . . isles;
p. 212 (n.) these flag-ships might all come to anchor; p. 213 (n.)
ere we weighed anchor for home; p. 214 (n.) keep us always tethered
at anchor; p. 219 (n.) little boys wearing best-bower anchors on
their lapels; p. 227 (n.) in 1782 sunk at her anchors at Spithead;
p. 229 (n.) not yet weighed their anchors; p. 239 (n.) when an old
sheet-anchor-man, standing by; p. 244 (n.) he with the anchor-button;
p. 245 (n.) came to anchor within a biscuit's toss; p. 265 (n.) the
English frigate, weighing her anchor; p. 268 (n.) All hands up anchor,
ahoy; p. 306 (n.) ramblings of some old sheet-anchor-man; p. 311 (n.)
Tawney, a sheet-anchor-man; p. 324 (n.) He was a sheet-anchor-man;
p. 339 (n.) ten best-bower-anchors wouldn't sink this 'ere top-man;
p. 353 (n.) companions--the old sheet-anchor-men around him; p. 357
(n.) Where are you, sheet-anchor-men; p. 358 (n.) emblazoning every
anchor-button on the coat; p. 363 (n.) was carved all over with . . .
anchors; p. 366 (n.) hoarsley whispered an old sheet-anchor-man;
p. 366 (n.) he heard . . . the ship swing to her anchor; p. 372 (n.)
one of a squadron at anchor; p. 382 (n.) weigh the ponderous anchor;
p. 384 (n.) His anchor's strip when his money's all spent; p. 388 (n.)
cried a sheet-anchor-man; p. 395 (n.) Cable and Anchor all clear;
p. 396 (n.) for our anchor still hangs from our bows.

Moby-Dick--p. 21 (adj.) when this corner-anchored old ark rocked so
furiously; p. 27 (n.) he's come to anchor somewhere; p. 49 (n.) And
now behold Jonah taken up as an anchor and dropped; p. 63 (n.) when
the little Moss came snugly to anchor; p. 84 (n.) By the great anchor,
what a harpoon he's got there; p. 94 (n.) for a considerable time
after heaving up the anchor; p. 94 (n.) the next thing to heaving up
the anchor; p. 94 (n.) looking over the bows for the approaching
anchor; p. 94 (n.) sink the ship before the anchor could be got up;
p. 150 (n.) a jig or two before we ride to anchor; p. 233 (n.) with
a frigate's anchors for my bridle-bits and fasces of harpoons for
spurs; p. 248 (n.) all hands were preparing to cast anchor; p. 256
(n.) upon Stubb setting the anchor-watch; p. 281 (n.) the jaw is
dragged on board, as if it were an anchor; p. 364 (n.) it was like
sitting in the fluke of an anchor; p. 418 (n.) The anchors are
working, sir; p. 419 (n.) take your leg off from the crown of the
anchor here.

AQUATIC. Inhabiting or relating to the water. (Smyth)

Omoo--p. 217 (adj.) when the motion of our aquatic cot awakened us;
p. 266 (adj.) taking the girls on an aquatic excursion.

ARCHIPELAGO. A corruption of Aegeopelagus, now applied to clusters of
islands in general. Originally the Aegean Sea. An archipelago has a
great number of islands of various sizes, disposed without order; but
often contains several subordinate groups. Such are the Aegean, the
Corean, the Caribbean, Indian, Polynesian, and others. (Smyth)

Typee--p. 147 (n.) throughout the whole Polynesian Archipelago;
p. 227 (n.) among the inhabitants of the Polynesian Archipelago.

Omoo--p. 63 (n.) all over this Archipelago; p. 210 (n.) in the whole
Polynesian Archipelago.

Mardi--p. 137 (n.) in the paradisiacal archipelago of the Polynesians;
p. 164 (n.) in another quarter of the Archipelago; p. 167 (n.) the
extent of the Archipelago grew; p. 175 (n.) in the whole Archipelago;
p. 175 (n.) the kings of the Archipelago; p. 176 (n.) to the people
of the Archipelago; p. 190 (n.) other quarters of the Archipelago;
p. 197 (n.) the tour of the Archipelago; p. 206 (n.) throughout the
archipelago of Mardi; p. 219 (n.) in this part of the Archipelago;
p. 221 (n.) in the free air of the Archipelago; p. 231 (n.) throughout
the Archipelago; p. 276 (n.) the dominion of the entire Archipelago;
p. 287 (n.) famous throughout the Archipelago; p. 323 (n.) drawing
near the archipelago; p. 334 (n.) tongues spoken throughout the
Archipelago; p. 363 (n.) but the whole Archipelago has; p. 398 (n.)
throughout the Archipelago; p. 462 (n.) In a certain quarter of the
Archipelago; p. 471 (n.) baring the outer reef of the Archipelago;
p. 472 (n.) the last island discovered in the Archipelago; p. 472 (n.)
kings and emperors of the Archipelago; p. 476 (n.) the groups and
clusters of the Archipelago; p. 520 (n.) Of all nations in the
Archipelago.

Redburn--p. 165 (n.) rather, it is a small archipelago.

White-Jacket--p. 193 (n.) emperor of the whole oaken archipelago;
p. 211 (n.) Archipelago Rio!

Moby-Dick--p. 318 (n.) from the thickly studded oriental archipelagoes;
p. 393 (n.) with a general chart of the oriental archipelagoes; p. 396
(n.) to be floated away to the starry archipelagoes; p. 400 (n.)
float . . . low-lying, endless, unknown Archipelagoes, and
impenetrable Japans.

ARGOSY. A merchant ship or carrack of burden, principally of the Levant;
the name is by some derived from Ragusa, but by others with more
probability from the Argo. Shakespeare mentions "argosies with portly
sail." Those of the Frescobaldi were the richest and most adventurous of
those times. (Smyth)

Moby-Dick--p. 447 (n.) rising from the painted hull of an argosy.

ARK. The sacred and capacious vessel built by Noah for preservation
against the flood. It was 300 cubits in length, 50 in breadth, and 30
in height; and of whatever materials it was constructed, it was pitched
over or pay'd with bitumen. (Smyth)

White-Jacket--p. 211 (n.) ere Noah on old Ararat anchored his ark.

Moby-Dick--p. 21 (n.) when this corner-anchored old ark rocked so
furiously; p. 319 (n.) Well, boys, here's the ark; pp. 384-5 (n.) In
Noah's flood he despised Noah's Ark.

ASHORE. Aground on land.--To go ashore, to disembark from a boat.
Opposed to aboard. (Smyth)

Typee--p. 17 (adv.) The animal . . . had been taken ashore; p. 16
(adv.) there were about one hundred soldiers ashore; p. 25 (adv.)
When ashore they would try to frighten us; p. 26 (adv.) should you
like to be shoved ashore there, eh; p. 28 (adv.) I became so
impatient to get ashore; p. 33 (adv.) was to be sent ashore on
liberty; p. 33 (adv.) when ashore we should run no chance; p. 34 (adv.)
I suppose you want to go ashore; p. 34 (adv.) Ten to one, men, if you
go ashore; p. 34 (adv.) Plenty of white men have gone ashore here;
p. 35 (adv.) I would go ashore if every pebble on the beach; p. 35
(adv.) preparatory to going ashore; p. 35 (adj.) he for one preserved
his go-ashore traps; p. 36 (adv.) and commenced pulling us ashore;
p. 74 (adv.) leaps ashore with the goods intended for barter; p. 255
(adv.) he sent his first-lieutenant ashore with a letter.

Omoo--p. 8 (adv.) and sent a boat ashore; p. 14 (adv.) and send a
boat ashore to trade; p. 15 (adv.) had stepped ashore there; p. 21
(adv.) they pulled rapidly ashore; p. 23 (adv.) sailors . . . had
recently gone ashore there; p. 23 (adv.) got in readiness to go
ashore; p. 24 (adv.) the rest of the pigmies stepped ashore; p. 27
(adv.) chuckling at the prospect of going ashore; p. 27 (adv.) plans
for swimming ashore from the wreck; p. 27 (adv.) He had gone ashore
as a sovereign power; p. 34 (adv.) sporting under the bows like pups
ashore; p. 41 (adv.) lovers of fun sailors are ashore; p. 45 (adv.)
had either of them been ashore; p. 48 (adv.) when they ought to be
ashore; p. 51 (adv.) after a run ashore; p. 53 (adv.) taking the
place of that sneaking rascal, nobody, ashore; p. 69 (adv.) intended
to set himself ashore; p. 70 (adv.) he was going ashore with the
captain; p. 73 (adv.) they were to go ashore again; p. 74 (adv.)
should be prepared and sent ashore; p. 75 (adv.) as soon as the mate
went ashore; p. 75 (adv.) general dissatisfaction ashore; p. 79 (adv.)
I shall have sent ashore; p. 79 (adv.) rather than go ashore and be
buried; p. 79 (adv.) I might be sent ashore; p. 81 (adv.) Captain Guy
will remain ashore for the present; p. 82 (adv.) must have been
concerted ashore; p. 87 (adv.) bent the men were upon going ashore;
p. 96 (adv.) when he went ashore at Tahiti; p. 98 (adv.) on the part
of those ashore; p. 102 (adv.) Captain Guy's ashore; p. 104 (adv.) of
the two to be set ashore; p. 110 (adv.) an occasional opportunity to
run ashore; p. 112 (adv.) They Take Us Ashore; p. 112 (adv.) and
pulled ashore; p. 122 (adv.) eventually put them ashore at Wallis'
island; p. 125 (adv.) the first day they went ashore; p. 128 (adv.)
Going ashore, to my surprise; p. 133 (adv.) We had not been many days
ashore; p. 146 (adv.) giving balls of an evening to the ladies ashore;
p. 147 (adv.) there was no lack of idle sailors ashore; p. 148 (adv.)
the authorities refusing to let him be put ashore; p. 148 (adv.) was
left ashore at the sailor hospital; p. 150 (adv.) the laughing-stock
of all the foreigners ashore; p. 151 (adv.) for having all our chests
sent ashore; p. 152 (adv.) to carry its owner ashore on an errand;
p. 153 (adv.) and upon going ashore; p. 158 (adv.) who had just
stepped ashore; p. 159 (adv.) they bore an equivocal character ashore;
p. 159 (adv.) No sailor steps ashore; p. 164 (adv.) people from the
Duff came ashore; p. 166 (adv.) many worthy foreigners ashore; p. 182
(adv.) sent ashore on a holyday; p. 200 (adv.) introducing the
amorous Frenchmen to the ladies ashore; p. 215 (adv.) he towed a

rotten old water-cask ashore; p. 228 (adv.) he waded ashore; p. 235
(adv.) except in one or two tramps ashore; p. 246 (adv.) and very few
foreigners were living ashore; p. 252 (adv.) after swimming a few
yards, waded ashore; p. 269 (adv.) by a stroll ashore; p. 285 (adv.)
Put ashore from his ship; p. 289 (adv.) and the skipper's ashore
kitching 'em; p. 289 (adv.) jist be after sailing ashore in a jiffy;
p. 290 (adv.) and paddled ashore; p. 292 (adv.) and went ashore;
p. 312 (adv.) like all sailors ashore; p. 312 (adv.) when they came
ashore; p. 313 (adv.) The next time the Vineyarder came ashore; p. 313
(adv.) Ashore, these fellows are equally riotous; p. 315 (adv.) and
stepped ashore with my advance.

Mardi--p. 3 (adv.) I had stepped ashore; p. 6 (adv.) put me ashore;
p. 6 (adv.) putting you ashore; p. 10 (adv.) ashore he would avoid
the plague; p. 68 (adv.) there drifted ashore; p. 68 (adv.) put her
ashore; p. 162 (adv.) "Come ashore!" cried Jarl; p. 312 (adv.) who,
while ashore, had expressed; p. 482 (adv.) at Constantinople, he
foremost sprang ashore.

Redburn--p. 14 (adv.) From the boat's bow, I jumped ashore; p. 25 (adv.)
I resolved to go ashore; p. 28 (adv.) Ashore with you, you young
loafer; p. 29 (adv.) ordered this drunken rascal ashore; p. 29 (adv.)
that is, men living ashore; p. 31 (adv.) surfeited with eating and
drinking ashore; p. 32 (adv.) in which they had been indulging ashore;
p. 45 (adv.) For when ashore; p. 46 (adv.) after laying idle ashore;
p. 48 (adv.) in the habit of going to church, when he was ashore;
p. 57 (adv.) how they went reeling ashore; p. 58 (adv.) when he slept
ashore there; p. 65 (adv.) for things that are familiar ashore; p. 68
(adv.) who had always lived ashore; p. 68 (adv.) whether I was
dressing to go ashore; p. 71 (adv.) while ashore, a gentleman on
false pretenses; p. 79 (adv.) when the ship's company went ashore;
p. 80 (adv.) all my pleasant, sunny Sundays ashore; p. 83 (adv.) a
sad profligate and gay deceiver ashore; p. 89 (adv.) invidious
observations of people ashore; p. 101 (adv.) and ashore at Marseilles;
p. 112 (adv.) the little hero went ashore by himself; p. 113 (adv.)
he was permitted to go ashore at last; p. 115 (adv.) swept ashore in
a gale; p. 117 (adv.) it may possibly drift ashore; p. 130 (adv.) the
crew were told to go ashore; p. 130 (adv.) they must get their meals
ashore; p. 130 (adv.) taking their salt junk ashore; p. 131 (adv.)
when we all sprang ashore; p. 137 (adv.) used to smuggle himself
ashore; p. 137 (adv.) had an hour to go ashore to breakfast; p. 137
(adv.) They lived ashore on the fat of the land; p. 152 (adv.) when
the crew went ashore to supper; p. 153 (adv.) after breakfast, jumped
ashore; p. 185 (adv.) the heaps of rubbish carried ashore; p. 186
(adv.) in the buckets of rubbish carried ashore; p. 188 (adv.) The
first morning I went ashore; p. 196 (adv.) as a security against their
carrying it ashore; p. 196 (adv.) which they smuggled ashore; p. 218
(adv.) necessity of boarding them ashore; p. 242 (adv.) they could
precisely define, ashore, the difference; p. 265 (adv.) who had been
a grocer ashore; p. 301 (adv.) demanded for carrying them ashore;
p. 301 (adv.) was triumphantly rowed ashore; p. 301 (adv.) they
bounded ashore; p. 302 (adv.) proposed that we should go ashore;
p. 303 (adv.) and sallied ashore; p. 309 (adv.) who were so clever
ashore.

White-Jacket--p. 9 (adv.) who, when ashore, at an eating house; p. 10
(adv.) talking over their lover affairs ashore; p. 10 (adv.) when
going ashore after a long cruise; p. 17 (adv.) yet ashore, he was a
stickler; p. 32 (adv.) Though you may go ashore; p. 54 (adv.) they
could no longer gratify their thirst ashore; p. 61 (adv.) who had
once kept an oyster-cellar ashore; p. 84 (adv.) may they and their
descendents--ashore or afloat; p. 87 (adv.) The same number of men
ashore would expand; p. 112 (adv.) As in the camp ashore; p. 123
(adv.) full as a sail-maker's loft ashore; p. 146 (adv.) if he
tarries ashore in time of danger; p. 153 (adv.) In trying to raft them
ashore; p. 154 (adv.) fought many Brandywine battles ashore; p. 160
(adv.) of a line-of-battle ship transplanted ashore; p. 161 (adv.)
when pulled ashore by his barge-men; p. 161 (adv.) to be carrying a
Lieutenant ashore; p. 165 (adv.) But we plain people ashore; p. 167
(adv.) a clerk in a Post-Office ashore; p. 178 (adv.) encountered at
the Palace-landing ashore; p. 180 (adv.) having drank somewhat freely
ashore; p. 183 (adv.) saying that the Purser was ashore; p. 184 (adv.)
Inquiries were made ashore; p. 184 (adv.) had his confidential agents
ashore; p. 189 (adv.) seldom went ashore without the cane; p. 190
(adv.) More than once a master-at arms ashore has; p. 192 (adv.) when
I'm ashore, I myself am part of the public; p. 196 (adv.) he was able
to hobble ashore on crutches; p. 205 (adv.) for the purpose of selling
them ashore; p. 207 (adv.) like schoolboys playing ball ashore; p. 209
(adv.) expecting to be sent ashore; p. 213 (adv.) one day's "liberty"
to go ashore; p. 214 (adv.) And what do you want to go ashore for;
p. 222 (adv.) which ashore employ the eyes, tongues, and thoughts;
p. 225 (adv.) get ready to go ashore on liberty; p. 226 (adv.) we
were pulled ashore; p. 226 (adv.) I went ashore on the first day;
p. 227 (adv.) our officers frequently went ashore for pleasure;
p. 228 (adv.) this Surgeon's mate must needs go ashore; p. 228 (adv.)
fallen in the way of temptations ashore; p. 234 (adv.) as he himself
was ashore; p. 241 (adv.) and keeping late hours ashore; p. 242 (adv.)
all strangers are ordered ashore; p. 246 (adv.) had been prohibited
from going ashore; p. 246 (adv.) he proposed paddling himself ashore;
p. 250 (adv.) Cuticle chanced to be ashore; p. 264 (adv.) to being
taken ashore for burial; p. 264 (adv.) rowed his remains ashore;
p. 269 (adv.) not get recovered from its night's dissipation ashore;
p. 274 (adv.) practiced by connoisseurs ashore; p. 294 (adv.) who
happens to be dwelling ashore; p. 304 (adv.) inadmissible in any
master ashore; p. 317 (adv.) and his going ashore; p. 324 (adv.) he
had often partaken ashore; p. 325 (adv.) answers to a public hospital
ashore; p. 329 (adv.) how long I had been ashore; p. 351 (adv.) what
they could have fairly earned ashore; p. 366 (adv.) was rowed ashore;
p. 375 (adv.) by the fire-side hatreds . . . ashore; p. 375 (adv.)
What too many seamen are when ashore; p. 378 (adv.) in a State Prison
ashore; p. 381 (adv.) three thousand seamen . . . fled ashore; p. 384
(adv.) as in the sailor dance-houses ashore; p. 388 (adv.) Once more
ashore; p. 389 (adv.) to keep themselves ashore; p. 390 (adv.) not
three days after getting ashore; p. 390 (adv.) is derived from his
behavior ashore; p. 390 (adv.) ashore he is no longer a sailor.

Moby-Dick--p. 6 (adv.) which some Asiatics had killed, and were then
towing ashore; p. 6 (adv.) when either thrown ashore or caught near
the coast; p. 24 (adv.) than bachelor Kings do ashore; p. 36 (adv.)
how long each one had been ashore; p. 36 (adv.) has tarried whole
weeks ashore; p. 58 (adv.) he carried such a troublesome thing with

him ashore; p. 106 (adv.) this earthly air, whether ashore or afloat;
p. 153 (adv.) when brave hearts snap ashore.

ASTERN. Any distance behind a vessel; in the after-part of the ship; in
the direction of the stern, and therefore the opposite of ahead.--To
drop astern, is to be left behind,--when abaft a right angle to the keel
at the mainmast, she drops astern. (Smyth)

Omoo--p. 153 (adv.) twenty shallops towering astern.

Mardi--p. 27 (adv.) its towing astern; p. 27 (adv.) of the breaker
astern; p. 30 (adv.) the ship left miles astern; p. 41 (adv.) farther
and farther astern; p. 52 (adv.) the wind being astern; p. 58 (adv.)
to drop it astern; p. 71 (adv.) breeze from astern; p. 74 (adv.)
leaving the island astern; p. 85 (adv.) dropping the islands astern;
p. 96 (adv.) have the wind from astern; p. 121 (adv.) for many rods
astern; p. 126 (adv.) leaving these sights astern; p. 127 (adv.) and
astern an arched cabin; p. 141 (adv.) farther and farther astern; p.
p. 145 (adv.) instead of astern as before; p. 148 (adv.) For astern
the rear was brought up; p. 149 (adv.) this poor little Boneeta
astern; p. 149 (adv.) for the Boneeta left far astern; p. 150 (adv.)
with the spear there, astern; p. 214 (adv.) Pile them high astern;
p. 423 (adv.) if the arrow yet remain astern; p. 503 (adv.) Porpheero
far astern.

Redburn--p. 49 (adv.) the man astern rang his bell; p. 64 (adv.)
ahead and astern; p. 66 (adv.) with an eternal breeze astern; p. 164
(adv.) drop astern of the Undaunted; p. 171 (adv.) These officers
lived astern in the cabin; p. 171 (adv.) the fancy piece astern
comprised; p. 219 (adv.) looking astern where they stood.

White-Jacket--p. 44 (adv.) too remarkable to be left astern; p. 96
(adv.) with the wind astern, or abeam; p. 109 (adv.) with the wind
astern; p. 109 (adv.) after it is astern; p. 112 (adv.) till that
perilous promontory should be far astern; p. 116 (adv.) with the wind
astern; p. 272 (adv.) Out of sight, astern, to be sure, sir; p. 394
(adv.) Being now astern of the frigate; p. 398 (adv.) The port we
sail from is forever astern.

Moby-Dick--p. 15 (adv.) head winds are far more prevalent than winds
from astern; p. 94 (adv.) Captain Peleg ripped and swore astern;
p. 111 (adv.) ice and icebergs all astern.

ATLANTIC. The sea which separates Europe and Africa from the Americas,
so named from the elevated range called the Atlas Mountains in Marocco.
(Smyth)

Typee--p. 3 (n.) a fourteen-days' passage across the Atlantic.

Mardi--p. 7 (n.) between the Atlantic and Pacific; p. 104 (n.)
frequenting the North Atlantic; p. 122 (n.) both in the Atlantic and
Pacific; p. 122 (n.) In the Atlantic, there is very seldom; p. 296
(n.) The wide Atlantic can rush in; p. 367 (n.) when these Atlantics
and Pacifics.

Redburn--p. 5 (n.) had several times crossed the Atlantic on business affairs; p. 16 (n.) crossed the Atlantic several times; p. 33 (n.) as having crossed the Atlantic Ocean; p. 33 (n.) we must cross the great Atlantic Ocean; p. 34 (n.) stretches the great Atlantic Ocean; p. 68 (n.) so far away on the wide Atlantic Ocean; p. 76 (n.) here I am on the Great Atlantic Ocean; p. 76 (n.) the great Atlantic Ocean was a puddle; p. 98 (n.) to keep warm the North Atlantic; p. 107 (n.) in transatlantic trips; p. 112 (n.) after stealing a passage across the Atlantic; p. 129 (n.) the whole broad Atlantic being between them; p. 139 (n.) across the Atlantic; p. 139 (n.) a bridge of boats across the Atlantic; p. 163 (n.) after her passage across the Atlantic; p. 218 (n.) gallantly crossed the Atlantic as a sailor; p. 219 (n.) the pleasure of your society across the Atlantic; p. 248 (n.) to pay this passage over the Atlantic; p. 261 (n.) that ever stepped over the Atlantic; p. 285 (n.) made the run across the Atlantic; p. 293 (n.) during the long voyage across the Atlantic.

White-Jacket--p. 97 (n.) hitherto made merry runs across the Atlantic; p. 115 (n.) than a passage undertaken from the Atlantic; p. 378 (n.) were born east of the Atlantic.

Moby-Dick--p. 7 (n.) Not a mightier whale than this/ In the vast Atlantic is; p. 38 (n.) brave houses and flowery gardens came from the Atlantic, Pacific, and Indian oceans; p. 75 (n.) when the Atlantic was an almost unknown sea; p. 95 (n.) Spite of this frigid winter night in the boisterous Atlantic; p. 97 (n.) blindly plunged like fate into the lone Atlantic; p. 121 (n.) often descried by passengers crossing the Atlantic; p. 210 (n.) he had long followed our austere Atlantic; p. 285 (n.) though the Sperm Whale . . . mixed the Atlantic with the Pacific; p. 326 (n.) amid the tornadoed Atlantic of my being; p. 369 (n.) but only in the North and South Atlantic; p. 446 (n.) in the moonlit Atlantic and Indian oceans.

ATOLL. An Indian name for those singular coral formations known as lagoon-islands, such as the Maldive cluster, those in the Pacific, and in other parts within the tropics, where the apparently insignificant reef-building zoophytes reside. (Smyth)

Mardi--p. 374 (n.) all over the atolls and reefs; p. 549 (n.) atolls all, or coral carcanets.

BALEEN. The scientific term for the whalebone of commerce, derived from balaena, a whale. It consists of a series of long horny plates growing from each side of the palate in place of teeth. (Smyth)

Moby-Dick--p. 5 (n.) did afford 500 weight of baleen; p. 121 (n.) commonly known as whalebone or baleen; p. 121 (n.) in his baleen, the Fin-back resembles; p. 122 (n.) From having the baleen in his mouth; p. 122 (n.) denominated Whalebone whales, that is, whales with baleen; p. 122 (n.) classification . . . founded upon either his baleen, or hump; p. 122 (n.) The baleen, hump, back-fin, and teeth.

BARGE. A boat of a long, slight, and spacious construction, generally carvel-built, double-banked, for the use of admirals and captains of ships of war.--Barge, in boat attacks, is next in strength to the launch. It is likewise a vessel or boat of state, furnished and equipped in the most sumptuous style;--and of this sort we may naturally suppose to have been the famous barge or galley of Cleopatra, which, according to the beautiful description of Shakespeare--

> Like a burnished throne
> Burnt on the water: the poop was beaten gold,
> Purple her sails; and so perfumed, that
> The winds were love-sick with them; the oars were silver,
> Which to the tune of flutes kept time, and made
> The water which they beat to follow faster
> As amorous of their strokes.

The barges of the lord-mayor, civic companies, &c., and the coal-barges of the Thames are varieties. Also, an early man-of-war, of about 100 tons. Also, an east-country vessel of burden, used on rivers for conveying goods from one place to another, and loading and unloading ships: it has various names, as a Ware barge, a west-country barge, a sand barge, a row-barge, a Severn trough, a light horseman, &c. They are usually fitted with a large sprit-sail to a mast, which, working upon a hinge, is easily struck for passing under bridges. Also, the bread-barge or tray or basket, for containing buscuit at meals. (Smyth)

Typee--p. 36 (n.) eye happened to light on the bread-barge and beef-kid.

Mardi--p. 200 (n.) so many barges and shallops; p. 213 (n.) Bow-Paddler of the royal barge; p. 285 (n.) each barge of Odo courteously flanked; p. 334 (n.) until embarking in his barge; p. 370 (n.) seated apart, on both sides of the barge; p. 482 (n.) oft embarked in his gilded barge; p. 483 (n.) look well to thy barge of state; p. 482 (n.) do thou with thy barge!

White-Jacket--p. 161 (n.) She also carried a Commodore's Barge; p. 161 (n.) the officers see to it that the Commodore's Barge; p. 161 (n.) when pulled ashore by his barge-men; p. 161 (n.) a great honor to be a Commodore's barge-man; p. 161 (n.) while our Commodore's barge floated by; p. 161 (n.) But the barge never stopped; p. 179 (n.) The cockswain of the Commodore's barge; p. 179 (n.) procures to be discharged from the barge; p. 179 (n.) this cockswain of the Commodore's barge; p. 179 (n.) the barge carries the Commodore across the bay; p. 180 (n.) which is always kept in the barge; p. 180 (n.) now descending into the barge; p. 180 (n.) The barge is ordered out to the booms; p. 180 (n.) is in your barge at the booms; p. 180 (n.) that you, or any of your barge-men; p. 180 (n.) offer to enter that barge before morning; p. 180 (n.) shall enter the barge before morning; p. 233 (n.) He came in a splendid barge; p. 309 (n.) alongside a three-decker in his barge.

BARK, BARQUE. [from barca, low Latin.] A general name given to small ships, square-sterned, without head-rails; it is, however, peculiarly appropriated by seamen to a three-masted vessel with only fore-and-aft

sails on her mizen-mast.--Bark-rigged. Rigged as a bark, with no square
sails on the mizen-mast. (Smyth)

Typee--p. 252 (n.) the barque was about to get under weigh; p. 252
(n.) Karakoee . . . again repaired aboard the barque.

Omoo--p. 9 (n.) She was a small barque of a beautiful model; p. 59
(n.) the barque, diving her bows under; p. 95 (n.) as officers of the
bark Jane.

Mardi--p. 200 (n.) our barks may drown; p. 256 (n.) ruling like barks
before a breeze; p. 361 (n.) the place of debarkation was in sight;
p. 556 (n.) That voyager steered his bark through seas.

Moby-Dick--p. 14 (n.) to take care of myself, without taking care of
ships, barques, brigs.

BARNACLE. (Lepas anatifera). A species of shell-fish, often found
sticking by its pedicle to the bottom of ships, doing no other injury
than deadening the way a little:

Barnacles, termed soland geese
In th' islands of the Orcades.--Hudibras

They were formally supposed to produce the barnacle-goose! (vide old
cyclopedias): the poet, however, was too good a naturalist to believe
this, but here, as in many other places, he means to banter some of the
papers which were published by the first establishers of the Royal Society.
The shell is compressed and multivalve. The tentacula are long and
pectinated like a feather, whence arose the fable of their becoming geese.
They belong to the order of Cirripeds. (Smyth)

Typee--p. 5 (n.) what an unsightly bunch of those horrid barnacles;
p. 22 (n.) Her hull was incrusted with barnacles; p. 103 (n.) a
garden spot for barnacles.

Mardi--p. 83 (n.) in the great green barnacles; p. 83 (n.) the more
the barnacles grow; p. 83 (n.) the clearing away of barnacles; p. 83
(n.) these barnacles oftentimes troubled her; p. 126 (n.) all over
green barnacles; p. 149 (adj.) paddling along by our barnacled sides;
p. 149 (adj.) monster fish with the barnacled sides; p. 181 (n.)
denuded of the minute green barnacles.

White-Jacket--p. 71 (n.) The whole buoy was embossed with barnacles;
p. 125 (n.) round spectacles, which he called his barnacles; p. 153
(n.) so covered with minute barnacles; p. 153 (n.) Upon clearing away
the barnacles and moss.

Moby-Dick--p. 61 (n.) From that hour I clove to Queequeg like a
barnacle; p. 116 (adj.) with the barnacled hulls of the leviathan;
p. 230 (adj.) drawing alongside the barnacled flank of a large running
Right Whale; p. 282 (adj.) this green, barnacled thing, which the
Greenlanders call the crown.

BAY. An inlet of the sea formed by the curvature of the land between two capes or headlands, often used synonymously with gulf; though, in strict accuracy, the term should be applied only to those large recesses which are wider from cape to cape than they are deep. Exposed to sea-winds, a bay is mostly insecure. A bay has proportionately a wider entrance than either a gulf or haven; a creek has usually a small inlet, and is always much less than a bay. (Smyth)

Typee--p. 7 (n.) was rendezvousing in the bay of Nukuheva; p. 11 (n.) was denominated Massachusetts Bay; p. 11 (n.) dwelling about the shores of the other bays; p. 12 (n.) in the bay of Nukuheva was the anchorage; p. 12 (n.) as the bay we sought lay on its farther side; p. 12 (n.) and entered the bay of Nukuheva; p. 12 (n.) floating in that lovely bay; p. 12 (n.) as soon as we entered the bay; p. 13 (n.) As we slowly advanced up the bay; p. 14 (n.) of the foot of the bay; p. 15 (n.) for the whole period that she remained in the bay; p. 23 (n.) The bay of Nukuheva in which we were then lying; p. 24 (n.) The imposing scenery of this bay; p. 24 (n.) Besides this bay the shores of the island; p. 25 (n.) the inhabitants of our bay were as arrant cannibals; p. 25 (n.) imprudently venturing into this bay; p. 25 (n.) sought to enter the bay of Nukuheva; p. 25 (n.) who had thus weighed her into their fatal bay; p. 25 (n.) passing slowly by the entrance of this bay; p. 26 (n.) not as yet visited the bay of Typee; p. 26 (n.) landed in boats and canoes at the head of the bay; p. 28 (n.) when we entered the bay of Tior; p. 30 (n.) acquired all the knowledge concerning the bay; p. 30 (n.) the whole population of the bay would be immediately; p. 37 (n.) through a rather populous part of the bay; p. 39 (n.) lofty elevations that encompassed the bay rose; p. 40 (n.) The lonely bay of Nukuheva; p. 41 (n.) we should be enabled to view the large bays; p. 43 (n.) not descending into the bay until the ship's departure; p. 54 (n.) divided as we were from the bay; p. 66 (n.) we might easily regain the bay of Nukuheva; p. 74 (n.) ships never enter this bay; p. 74 (n.) some intrepid captain will touch in the skirts of the bay; p. 79 (n.) six men-of-war lying in the hostile bay; p. 98 (n.) probably still lay in the bay of Nukuheva; p. 98 (n.) from making any visit to the bay; p. 99 (n.) by which the bay might be reached; p. 104 (n.) that there were boats approaching the bay; p. 108 (n.) with the boats which had visited the bay; p. 119 (n.) seen at a great distance approaching the bay; p. 120 (n.) whether any boats visited the bay; p. 127 (n.) those of the adjoining bay of Happar; p. 137 (n.) their hostile visits to the surrounding bays; p. 139 (n.) How long you been in this bay? You like this bay; p. 141 (n.) although admitted into the bay on a friendly footing; p. 143 (n.) taking place in the different bays of the island; p. 180 (n.) of the neighboring bay of Nukuheva; p. 181 (n.) presented by its inhabitants with those of the bay; p. 182 (n.) those who have merely touched at Nukuheva Bay; p. 194 (n.) in my visit to the Bay of Tior; p. 205 (n.) to hold at bay the intruding European; p. 205 (n.) voyagers are lured into smiling and treachous bays; p. 206 (n.) some distance from the bay; p. 223 (n.) Of its effects in the bay of Tior; p. 239 (n.) The French could not long defer a visit to the bay; p. 241 (n.) Suppose you no like this bay, why you come; p. 245 (n.) in a boat which had just entered the bay; p. 246 (n.) evident that a boat had entered the bay; p. 247 (n.) had for some cause or other entered the bay; p. 249 (n.) the very act of pulling out from the bay; p. 251 (n.) a jutting point of the bay round which we had to pass;

p. 252 (n.) in the neighboring bay of Typee; p. 252 (n.) off the
entrance to the Typee bay; p. 261 (n.) the report had spread that
boats had touched at the bay; p. 263 (n.) coming off in his canoe to
the ships in the bay; p. 264 (n.) although he seldom came into the
bay; p. 264 (n.) he was sometimes employed to come round to the bay;
p. 265 (n.) he then intended to bring into the bay; p. 268 (n.) we
taboo men have wives in all the bays; p. 270 (n.) They came upon the
valleys of Nukuheva on one side of the bay; p. 271 (n.) turning the
headland and entering the bay; p. 271 (n.) he was going to visit the
bay again in a French boat.

Omoo--p. 3 (n.) in a boat which visited the bay; p. 3 (n.) hove to
off the mouth of the bay; p. 5 (n.) made good our escape from the
bay; p. 8 (n.) before daylight we arrived off the bay of Nukuheva;
p. 14 (n.) in some outlandish bay or other; p. 19 (n.) She was riding
to her anchor in the bay; p. 21 (n.) The bay was as calm as death;
p. 21 (n.) The bonus of a musket to the King of the Bay; p. 23 (n.)
a shady glen opening from a deep bay; p. 24 (n.) riding pertly over
the waves of the bay; p. 26 (n.) was the large and populous bay of
Hannamanoo; p. 26 (adj.) the embayed waters were gentle as a lake;
p. 26 (n.) came full upon the bay of Hannamanoo; p. 27 (n.) which was
coming out of the bay; p. 31 (n.) from one hostile bay to another;
p. 71 (n.) shipping at the Bay of Islands; p. 83 (n.) snugly anchored
in Papeetee Bay; p. 95 (n.) at the Bay of Islands in New Zealand;
p. 98 (n.) Papeetee Bay is considered a ticklish one; p. 98 (n.)
After stretching across the bay; p. 98 (n.) the barrier directly
facing the bay; p. 101 (n.) Lying in a semi-circle around the bay;
p. 101 (n.) A site on one side of the bay; p. 101 (n.) the
picturesqueness of the bay; p. 102 (n.) at the bottom of Papeetee Bay;
p. 140 (n.) in sending a boat into the bay; p. 152 (n.) away he
paddled for the head of the bay; p. 153 (n.) away we went out of the
bay; p. 159 (n.) among the vessels in the bay; p. 162 (n.) the bay is
so shallow; p. 215 (n.) touching at an adjoining bay; p. 224 (n.)
accompanied me to Afrehitoo--a neighboring bay; p. 238 (n.) more
healthful than the inhabitants of the bays; p. 245 (n.) Upon one
shore of the bay; p. 264 (n.) upon the southern shore of Papeetee Bay;
p. 288 (n.) lying land-locked, far up the bay; p. 288 (n.) an
importation from the Bay of Islands; p. 289 (n.) A bay, considered by
many voyagers; p. 289 (n.) catch a peep of the widening mouth of the
bay; p. 289 (n.) The open space lies at the head of the bay; p. 291
(n.) staggered out of the bay of Papeetee; p. 297 (n.) presenting a
semicircular sweep to the bay; p. 299 (n.) a ship is descried coming
into the bay; p. 316 (n.) we slowly glided down the bay.

Mardi--p. 104 (n.) at the bottom of Callao Bay; p. 353 (n.) we put
into a little bay; p. 402 (n.) Voyaging on, we entered a bay; p. 475
(n.) sweeping into a fine broad bay; p. 498 (n.) the storm-swept
surges in Naples' bay; p. 547 (n.) A vast and silent bay.

Redburn--p. 33 (n.) carried us further and further down the bay;
p. 33 (n.) instead of sailing out of the bay; p. 33 (n.) when I
thought of really entering that bay; p. 101 (n.) sunned himself in
the Bay of Naples; p. 107 (n.) in the Bay of Islands; p. 193 (n.) the
bitter blasts from Baffin's Bay; p. 300 (n.) Now rose the city from
out the bay; p. 310 (n.) we looked out over the bay.

<u>White-Jacket</u>--p. 9 (n.) fellows that sing you "The Bay of Biscay Oh";
p. 43 (n.) colored illustrations of the harbors and bays; p. 159 (n.)
one of the most magnificent bays in the world; p. 159 (n.) the
charming Bay of Botafogo; p. 160 (n.) fast anchored in the bay;
p. 172 (n.) in an amphitheatrical bay like Rio; p. 179 (n.) the barge
carries the Commodore across the bay; p. 210 (n.) The Bay of all
Beauties; p. 210 (n.) the Bay of All Saints; p. 210 (n.) Rio is the
Bay of all Rivers--the Bay of all Delights--the Bay of all Beauties;
p. 211 (n.) they roll cannonades down the bay; p. 212 (n.) in this
abounding Bay of Rio; p. 212 (n.) the sole inlet to the bay; p. 212
(n.) poised over that magnificent bay; p. 217 (n.) on the shores of
Chesapeake Bay; p. 245 (n.) moved further up the bay; p. 264 (n.) in
plain sight from the bay; p. 265 (n.) when we should leave the bay;
p. 268 (n.) vessels may emerge from the bay; p. 268 (n.) we dropped
and dropped down the bay; p. 314 (n.) off the Bay of Valparaiso;
p. 318 (n.) The Bay was covered with masts; p. 318 (n.) to the bottom
of the bay; p. 372 (n.) at anchor in the Bay of Naples; p. 372 (n.)
the Bay of Naples . . . not being deemed.

<u>Moby-Dick</u>--p. 56 (n.) A Sag Harbor ship visited his father's bay.

<u>BEACH</u>. A littoral margin, or line of coast along the sea-shore, composed
of sand, gravel, shingle, broken shells, or a mixture of them all: any
gently sloping part of the coast alternately dry and covered by the tide.
(Smyth)

<u>Typee</u>--p. 14 (n.) We were still some distance from the beach; p. 17
(n.) in the shelter of a grove near the beach; p. 17 (n.) at full
speed over the hard sand beach; p. 18 (n.) lofty staff planted
within a few yards of the beach; p. 25 (n.) facilitated his escape
by night along the beach; p. 28 (n.) she shot two-thirds of her
length along the beach; p. 35 (n.) if every pebble on the beach was
a live coal; p. 36 (n.) which stood hard by the beach; p. 40 (n.) We
had left the beach early in the morning; p. 74 (n.) nearly its whole
population down to the beach; p. 105 (n.) fearful of arriving too
late upon the beach; p. 106 (n.) the hope of reaching the beach in
time; p. 106 (n.) let me go with them to the beach; p. 107 (n.) began
to return from the beach; p. 119 (n.) the path that conducted to the
beach; p. 119 (n.) impulse was to hurry down to the beach; p. 120 (n.)
the return of the natives from the beach; p. 121 (n.) procured some
time or other in traffic on the beach; p. 193 (n.) had died . . . in
a house near the beach; p. 205 (n.) standing upon the beach; p. 206
(n.) spread to dry upon the beach at Nukuheva; p. 207 (n.) a general
rush of the men towards the beach; p. 223 (n.) announced his landing
on the beach; p. 233 (n.) who must have been massacred on the beach;
p. 247 (n.) until we should have arrived upon the beach; p. 247 (n.)
that there were no boats at the beach; p. 248 (n.) the roar of the
surf breaking upon the beach; p. 248 (n.) shouts of the crowd upon
the beach were distinctly audible; p. 250 (n.) moved towards the now
almost deserted beach; p. 261 (n.) eager as Toby was to gain the
beach; p. 263 (n.) anxious to learn what was going on at the beach;
p. 264 (n.) The moment he saw the old rover on the beach; p. 264 (n.)
scarcely ever went back from the beach; p. 265 (n.) fruit would be
heaped up in stacks on the beach; p. 265 (n.) even if we get him down
to the beach; p. 265 (n.) they would not hear of his stirring from

the beach; p. 266 (n.) if he remained much longer on the beach;
p. 266 (n.) if I leave you here on the beach; p. 266 (n.) how do you
know they will bring him down to the beach; p. 270 (n.) They soon
descended towards the beach; p. 271 (n.) if he did not find me on
the beach.

Omoo--p. 21 (n.) turned up like tortoises on the beach; p. 21 (n.)
foot of theirs should never touch the beach; p. 24 (n.) the tiny
craft shot up the beach; p. 24 (n.) paused about its length from the
beach; p. 24 (v.) but beach their boat; p. 32 (n.) before the palace,
on the beach; p. 66 (n.) from beach to mountain top; p. 81 (n.) I'm
nothing more nor a bloody beach-comber; p. 101 (n.) extends a wide,
smooth beach; p. 102 (n.) lay bilged upon the beach; p. 112 (n.) as
we struck the beach; p. 116 (n.) spreading themselves upon a beach of
small, sparkling shells; p. 146 (v.) The alarmed islanders, beaching
their canoe; p. 147 (n.) idle sailors ashore, mostly Beach-combers;
p. 148 (n.) by assuring the beachcombers solemnly; p. 148 (n.) a
small place upon the beach; p. 149 (n.) The beach was quite near;
p. 159 (n.) recommended by the commodore of the beachcombers; p. 175
(n.) to the little marine villas upon the beach; p. 176 (n.) The
canoes are hauled up on the beach; p. 198 (n.) that he had gone down
to the beach; p. 199 (n.) we stole down to the beach; p. 200 (v.) and
beached the boat; p. 201 (n.) the only one back from the beach; p. 215
(n.) The doctor suggested a walk to the beach; p. 224 (n.) a few yards
from the beach; p. 226 (n.) Zeke's hailing us loudly from the beach;
p. 227 (n.) they were to be lugged down to the beach; p. 227 (n.) we
arrived at the beach together; p. 228 (n.) we managed to shamble down
to the beach; p. 228 (n.) drove them before him, down to the beach;
p. 229 (n.) We hurried down to the beach; p. 231 (n.) romantic
articles of commerce;--beach-de-mer; p. 235 (n.) we decided . . . to
strike the beach again; p. 246 (n.) and marched off to the beach;
p. 246 (n.) then going round by way of the beach; p. 250 (n.) to walk
along the beach as we paddled; p. 250 (n.) all we had to do was to
follow the beach; p. 251 (n.) repairing to the beach; p. 252 (n.) was
the damp and slightly yielding beach; p. 252 (n.) hopping, skipping,
and jumping along the beach; p. 253 (n.) the beach contracted to
hardly a yard's width; p. 253 (n.) Turning round a bold sweep of the
beach; p. 255 (n.) A fine walk along a beach of shells; p. 263 (n.)
prevented from breaking on the beach; p. 266 (n.) Right on the beach
was a mighty old cocoa-nut tree; p. 268 (n.) they stood upon the
beach; p. 270 (n.) following the beach; p. 271 (n.) A stone's cast
from the beach; p. 275 (n.) going round by the beach to Partoowye;
p. 289 (n.) you all at once find yourself upon the beach; p. 291 (n.)
each man stepped upon the beach.

Mardi--p. 8 (n.) laving a beach of shells; p. 70 (n.) upon the sharp
coral beach; p. 120 (n.) strown upon ocean's beach; p. 137 (n.) in
good time was cast upon the beach; p. 143 (n.) till it kisses the
beach at Orodia; p. 161 (n.) hauled up on the silent beach; p. 162
(n.) danced about the beach; p. 166 (n.) I pushed my shallop its
golden beach; p. 168 (n.) The beach was lined with expectant natives;
p. 168 (n.) carried us up the beach; p. 187 (n.) there landed on the
beach; p. 191 (n.) dwelt hard by the beach; p. 194 (n.) returning
billows on a beach long bared; p. 198 (n.) Media, on the beach;
p. 201 (n.) Within several paces of the beach; p. 201 (n.) The beach
gained; p. 217 (n.) we swept toward the beach; p. 219 (n.) fight of

clubs on the beach; p. 262 (n.) The beach gained, we embarked; p. 273
(n.) whose base was as the sea-beach; p. 273 (n.) Ranged on the beach;
p. 286 (n.) to touch the beach of Mondoldo; p. 286 (n.) ere we yet
touched the beach; p. 302 (n.) were drawn up on the beach; p. 305
(v.) beached on its seaward shore; p. 314 (n.) Soft lap the beach the
billows there; p. 326 (v.) in silence we beached our canoes; p. 358
(n.) Quitting the beach; p. 364 (n.) canoe was missing from the beach;
p. 394 (n.) over the beach,/ The soft sand beach; p. 401 (n.) As we
neared the beach; p. 411 (n.) and proceeding to the beach; p. 437 (n.)
Hurled up on the beach; p. 481 (n.) we departed for the beach; p. 492
(n.) for a smooth, clear beach; p. 513 (n.) we rapidly gained the
beach; p. 524 (n.) great crowds ran down to the beach; p. 531 (n.)
our keels grated the beach; p. 536 (n.) which they tossed upon the
beach; p. 548 (n.) regains the beach; p. 548 (n.) our prows lie
rotting on the beach; p. 549 (v.) whenever a canoe is beached; p. 553
(n.) coasting on by barbarous beaches; p. 589 (n.) as we keeled the
beach; p. 611 (n.) The beach was strewn with scoria and cinders;
p. 623 (n.) as we neared the beach; p. 632 (n.) thoughtfully we
strolled along the beach; p. 632 (n.) laved the beach with a fire
that cooled it; p. 637 (n.) At sunrise, we stood upon the beach;
p. 638 (n.) And from the beach, he wended; p. 645 (v.) our prows were
beached; p. 653 (n.) I flitted on the damp and weedy beach; p. 653
(v.) where a prow was beached.

Redburn--p. 115 (n.) remind one of the sea-beach; p. 145 (n.) on the
beach is the figure of a small man; p. 149 (n.) multitudinous as
pebbles on the beach; p. 299 (n.) along whose eastern beach.

White-Jacket--p. 12 (adj.) his gales off Beachy Head; p. 159 (n.) a
noble tract of beach; p. 180 (n.) When the Commodore comes down to
the beach; p. 246 (n.) from a party at the Beach of the Flamingoes;
p. 264 (n.) hard by the Beach of the Flamingoes; p. 295 (n.) and
scramble to the beach; p. 393 (n.) moaning as of low waves on the
beach.

Moby-Dick--p. 13 (n.) or invest his money in a pedestrian trip to
Rockaway Beach; p. 62 (n.) all beach, without a background; p. 100
(n.) by the beaches of unrecorded, javelin islands; p. 131 (n.) on
the white coral beach; p. 321 (n.) Ahab's brow was left gaunt and
ribbed, like the black sand beach; p. 410 (n.) waves . . . gently
chafed the whale's broad flank, like soft surf upon a beach.

BILLOWS. The surges of the sea, or waves raised by the wind; a term more
in use among poets than seamen. (Smyth)

Typee--p. 3 (n.) I tossed on the billows of the wide-rolling Pacific;
p. 248 (n.) I saw the flashing billows themselves.

Omoo--p. 33 (n.) cast over the heaving billows; p. 312 (n.) I at last
pined for the billows.

Mardi--p. 8 (n.) the cadence of mild billows; p. 25 (n.) where
prowling sharks come not nor billows roll; p. 30 (n.) toy we were to
the billows; p. 49 (n.) making ringed mountain billows; p. 85 (n.)
bounding over the billows; p. 118 (n.) immense, long-extended, and

long-rolling billows; p. 160 (n.) rising up from the billows to greet
us; p. 160 (n.) The billows rolled listlessly by; p. 194 (n.) over me
like returning billows; p. 214 (n.) to the billows' throng; p. 214
(n.) in billows black; p. 216 (n.) surged toward Juan in enormous
billows; p. 216 (n.) the blue billows seemed swallowed up; p. 273 (n.)
where the wild billows from seaward; p. 273 (adj.) in billowy
battalions charge they; p. 273 (n.) So charged the bright billows;
p. 293 (n.) they wait for a billow that suits; p. 273 (n.) as the
overgrown billow bursts; p. 283 (n.) and swore by wave and billow;
p. 303 (n.) to the low moan of the billows; p. 314 (n.) Soft lap the
beach the billows there; p. 368 (n.) I roll down by billow from afar;
p. 414 (n.) Over silvery billows we glided; p. 512 (n.) Billows beat
against its base; p. 545 (n.) Over bowling billows are gliding;
p. 554 (n.) by foam-white, breaking billows; p. 554 (n.) but the
billows smote them as they reared; p. 586 (n.) Long we rocked upon
the circling billows; p. 593 (n.) In hairy billows, his great mane
tossed like the sea; p. 623 (n.) The palm plumes wave,/ The billows
lave; p. 644 (n.) the blue billows gush; p. 654 (n.) the combing
billows must break over.

Redburn--p. 127 (n.) with the solemn roll of the billows; p. 147 (n.)
They braved the billows for precarious food; p. 193 (n.) whose every
billow is bound for the main; p. 289 (n.) on the windlass, watching
the billows; p. 292 (n.) They die, like the billows that break on the
shore.

White-Jacket--p. 14 (n.) may be now rolling over the blue billows;
p. 97 (n.) while the heedless craft is bounding over the billows;
p. 105 (n.) in milk-white billows of foam; p. 108 (n.) suspended
right over the rampant billows; p. 214 (n.) But who can always on the
billows lie; p. 268 (n.) rolled by the smooth, sliding billows;
p. 270 (n.) But how we boom through the billows; p. 380 (n.) the
man-of-war's-man rolls round the world like a billow; p. 393 (n.)
death flooded over me with the billows.

Moby-Dick--p. 45 (adj.) How billow-like and boisterously grand; p. 48
(n.) he is sprung upon by a panther billow; p. 50 (n.) whom all the
waves of the billows of the seas; p. 63 (n.) folds her wings and is
rocked to sleep between billows; p. 126 (n.) they invariably come
from the breezy billows to windward; p. 144 (n.) the billow lifts
thee; p. 146 (n.) The envious billows sidelong swell; pp. 158-9 (n.)
in unensanguined billows hundreds of leagues away; p. 192 (n.) like
the confused scud from white rolling billows; p. 225 (n.) distended
tusked mouth into which the billows are rolling; p. 237 (n.) undulated
there on the billows; p. 258 (n.) answered by a helping heave from
the billows; p. 298 (n.) still at every billow that broke; p. 327 (n.)
as if lifted by half spent billows from afar; p. 409 (n.) the billows
have still rolled on speechless and unspoken to; p. 410 (n.) ye
billows are my foster-brothers; p. 423 (n.) rolled in long slow
billows of mighty bulk; p. 423 (n.) Yoke on the further billows;
p. 427 (n.) jerkingly raised and lowered by the rolling billows;
p. 449 (n.) thrusting his oblong white head up and down in the
billows; p. 450 (n.) the but half baffled channel billows only
recoil; p. 462 (n.) I feel now like a billow that's all one crested
comb; p. 468 (n.) ye bold billows of my whole foregone life; p. 469
(n.) over the destroying billows they almost touched.

BINNACLE. A wooden case or box, which contains the compass, and a light
to illuminate the compass at night; there are usually three binnacles on
the deck of a ship-of-war, two near the helm being designed for the man
who steers, weather and lee, and the other midships, 10 or 12 feet before
these, where the quarter-master, who conns the ship, stands when steering
or going with a free wind. (Smyth)

> Mardi--p. 71 (n.) planted full before him on the binnacle; p. 101 (n.)
> reflected in the glass of the binnacle; p. 109 (n.) turned toward the
> light of the binnacle; p. 110 (n.) notwithstanding the syren face in
> the binnacle; p. 114 (n.) abstraction of the compass from the
> binnacle; p. 114 (n.) at the emptiness of the binnacle.

> Redburn--p. 70 (n.) with his little bell in the binnacle; p. 108 (n.)
> in the vicinity of the binnacle; p. 118 (n.) I liked to peep in at
> the binnacle; p. 118 (n.) Our binnacle, by the way; p. 119 (n.) so as
> to overrun this binnacle.

> Moby-Dick--p. 114 (adj.) Lighting the pipe at the binnacle lamp;
> p. 130 (n.) after a grave peep into the binnacle; p. 138 (adj.) the
> local attraction of all binnacle magnets; p. 192 (n.) seemed as two
> visible needles in two unerring binnacle compasses; p. 354 (adj.) by
> the steady binnacle lamp illuminating it; p. 451 (n.) pacing the
> deck, binnacle-watch in hand.

BLOW. Applied to the breathing of whales and other cetaceans. The
expired air from the lungs being highly charged with moisture, which
condenses at the temperature of the atmosphere, appears like a column of
steam. (Smyth)

> Moby-Dick--p. 9 (v.) There she blows; was sung out from the mast-head;
> p. 9 (v.) There she blows! . . . There she blows! there-there-thar
> she blows.

BLUBBER. The layer of fat in whales between the skin and the flesh,
which is flinched or peeled off, and boiled for oil, varying from 10 to
20 inches in thickness. (Smyth)

> Mardi--p. 32 (n.) and a blubber-spade.

> Redburn--p. 100 (n.) blubber-boilers, as they contemptuously style;
> p. 107 (n.) vast masses of unctuous blubber.

> Moby-Dick--p. 139 (n.) seeking sentiment in tar and blubber; p. 139
> (n.) Ten thousand blubber-hunters sweep over thee in vain; p. 206 (n.)
> repeat gamesome stuff about spouters and blubber-boilers; p. 258 (adj.)
> to this block the great blubber hook . . . was attached; p. 258 (n.)
> as the blubber envelopes the whale precisely as the rind does an
> orange; p. 259 (n.) into an unfurnished parlor called the blubber-
> room; p. 285 (n.) how the blubber wraps the body of the whale; p. 343
> (n.) cutting up the fresh blubber in small bits; p. 344 (n.) to
> afford a place for the blubber of the Dutch whale fleet to be tried
> out; p. 349 (n.) here and there adhering to the blanket of blubber;
> p. 350 (n.) at once to descend into the blubber-room; p. 351 (n.) in

mincing the horse-pieces of blubber for the pots; pp. 252-3 (n.) the crisp, shrivelled blubber, now called scraps or fritters.

BOAT. A small open vessel, conducted on the water by towing or sailing. The construction, machinery, and even the names of boats, are very different, according to the various purposes for which they are calculated, and the services on which they are employed. (Smyth)

Typee--p. 9 (n.) and tumbling into their boat; p. 10 (n.) and Boatswain, the dog, leaped up; p. 12 (n.) came alongside of us in a whale-boat; p. 13 (n.) in getting into the weather-quarter boat; p. 13 (n.) amicably engaged in disentangling their boats; p. 15 (n.) or reclined at full length upon the boats; p. 25 (n.) venturing into this bay in an armed boat; p. 26 (n.) landed in boats and canoes at the head of the bay; p. 28 (n.) by water in the ship's boat; p. 28 (n.) I stood up in the bow of the boat; p. 28 (n.) attended by all the boats of his squadron; p. 35 (n.) At two bells the boat will be manned; p. 36 (n.) for the liberty-men to get into the boat; p. 36 (n.) where I found all the party in the boat; p. 74 (adj.) with two or three armed boats' crews; p. 74 (n.) while the boats . . . lie just outside the surf; p. 74 (n.) one of the boats pulls in under cover; p. 98 (n.) returning . . . in one of the boats of the squadron; p. 98 (adj.) persuading the Frenchmen to detach a boat's crew; p. 104 (n.) that there were boats approaching the bay; p. 106 (n.) should I succeed in getting down to the boats; p. 106 (n.) as soon as the boats should leave the shore; p. 108 (n.) Toby had gone away with the boats; p. 109 (n.) that he was waiting for the sailing of a boat; p. 119 (n.) that boats had been seen at a great distance; p. 120 (n.) whether any boats visited the bay; p. 132 (n.) There was no boat on the lake; p. 224 (adj.) obliged to call together his boat's crew; p. 245 (n.) long-lost companion had arrived in a boat; p. 246 (n.) It was evident that a boat had entered the bay; p. 247 (n.) that there were no boats at the beach; p. 249 (n.) object that met my view was an English whale-boat; p. 249 (n.) the boat was only hanging off to keep out of the surf; p. 249 (n.) waving him off to his boat; p. 250 (n.) and take him into the boat; p. 250 (n.) I found myself safe in the boat; p. 251 (n.) before it was over the boat was under full way; p. 251 (n.) it was not until the boat was above fifty yards from the shore; p. 251 (n.) Karakoee, who was steering the boat; p. 251 (n.) I seized the boat-hook; p. 252 (adj.) proved so fatal to many a boat's crew; p. 252 (n.) capsize the boat; p. 252 (n.) I dashed the boat-hook at him; p. 252 (n.) rise to the surface in the wake of the boat; p. 252 (n.) one other of the savages reached the boat; p. 252 (n.) The whale-boat, manned by the tabooed crew; p. 261 (n.) the report had spread that boats had touched at the bay; p. 263 (n.) No sign of a boat; p. 265 (n.) in readiness for the boats which he then intended; p. 265 (n.) I will bring him round to Nukuheva in the boats; p. 270 (n.) Toby begged hard for an armed boat; p. 270 (n.) Jimmy and the Typee started in two of the ship's boats; p. 270 (n.) and descried the boats turning the headland; p. 271 (n.) he was going to visit the bay again in a French boat; p. 271 (n.) he had the satisfaction of seeing the French boat start; p. 271 (n.) Hardly was the boat out of sight.

Omoo--p. 3 (n.) he escaped in a boat which visited the bay; p. 3 (n.)
This boat belonged to a vessel; p. 3 (n.) the boat, manned by "Taboo"
natives; p. 3 (n.) The boat having gained the open sea; p. 5 (n.) The
four boats hanging from her sides; p. 5 (adj.) To say nothing of the
savage boat's crew; p. 8 (n.) and sent a boat ashore; p. 10 (n.) Even
the three junior mates who had headed the whale boats; p. 14 (n.) and
send a boat ashore to trade; p. 19 (n.) As soon as a boat could be
lowered; p. 20 (n.) to show two boats gone from the side; p. 20 (n.)
ordered him to clear away another boat; p. 20 (n.) It was the Mowree
and the boat; p. 20 (n.) The boat having at nightfall been hoisted up;
p. 21 (n.) There was another boat remaining; p. 21 (adj.) There was a
whistling of a boatswain's pipe; p. 21 (n.) towing the two whale
boats; p. 23 (n.) so a boat was at once got in readiness; p. 24 (n.)
When the boat neared the head of the inlet; p. 24 (n.) the boat spun
round; p. 24 (n.) for the boat paused about its length; p. 24 (n.)
but reach their boat; p. 25 (n.) the boat returned to the ship; p. 26
(n.) by the time the boat came alongside; p. 27 (n.) so two boats were
at once lowered; p. 27 (n.) assisted by the boats we were soon out of
danger; p. 35 (n.) known among seamen as the boatswain; p. 69 (n.) in
the stern-sheets of the captain's boat; p. 70 (n.) the boat was
lowered and brought to the gangway; p. 70 (n.) lowering him into the
boat; p. 70 (n.) adjusting matters in the boat; p. 70 (n.) He then
sprang into the boat; p. 71 (n.) A dead whale, or a stove boat; p. 71
(n.) stands erect in the head of the boat; p. 72 (n.) the boat was
still chasing him; p. 72 (adj.) the bitterest disappointment to a
boat's crew; p. 72 (n.) the boat sped like an arrow; p. 72 (adj.)
hand was on the boat's gunwhale; p. 75 (n.) On return of the boat;
p. 75 (n.) in the morning a shore boat; p. 81 (n.) to man three boats;
p. 84 (n.) coming on deck to enter his boat; p. 84 (n.) ordered the
cook and steward into his boat; p. 86 (n.) in the stern of his boat;
p. 86 (n.) Tumbled into the quarter-boat; p. 94 (n.) to come off in a
shore boat; p. 95 (n.) The boats, however, were saved; p. 95 (n.) The
three boats, commanded respectively; p. 95 (n.) in the captain's boat
went crazy; p. 95 (n.) the boat capsized; p. 95 (n.) the other boats
being separated; p. 96 (n.) the remaining boats taking in all sail;
p. 96 (n.) the third mate's boat, in all probability; p. 96 (n.) the
boat, drifting fast to leeward; p. 96 (n.) the boat touched, for
fruit, at an island; p. 96 (n.) he finally escaped in the boat; p. 98
(n.) No sign, however, of boat or pilot; p. 102 (n.) when a boat came
alongside; p. 103 (n.) The boat was painted a pirate black; p. 106
(adj.) whom we supposed a boatswain's mate; p. 106 (adj.) The
boatswain's mate went to work; p. 106 (adj.) The boatswain's mate
only hit out at them; p. 110 (n.) those belonging to the boats; p. 110
(n.) manoeuvering with the boats; p. 128 (n.) we sent a boat off to
see whether; p. 140 (n.) in sending a boat into the bay; p. 146 (n.)
lowering a boat instantly; p. 146 (adj.) the ship's ensign flying in
the boat's stern; p. 173 (n.) they had much to say about steamboats;
p. 199 (n.) were expected to visit Papeetee in their boat; p. 199 (n.)
the boat was waiting; p. 200 (n.) and beached the boat; p. 224 (n.) A
trim little sail-boat was dancing; p. 226 (n.) in bringing them down
to his sail-boat; p. 227 (n.) flinging his potatoes into the boat;
p. 229 (n.) The boat at last loaded; p. 229 (n.) and saw the boat
gliding toward us; p. 289 (adj.) One boat's crew of 'em is gone;
p. 290 (n.) and four chubby boats hanging at the breast; p. 291 (n.)
they clubbed, and purchased a sail-boat; p. 292 (n.) instinctively
kept the boat before the wind; p. 292 (n.) the adventurers sold the
boat for a trifle; p. 313 (n.) She dropped her boats into the brine.

Mardi--p. 4 (n.) sending a boat; p. 7 (n.) in an open boat; p. 7 (n.)
of the boat to be obtained; p. 12 (n.) One of the ship's boats; p. 16
(n.) in one of her boats; p. 17 (n.) and a boat sail; p. 19 (n.) a
boat was to be abstracted; p. 19 (n.) the boats of a South Sea-man;
p. 19 (adj.) the settling of the boat's middle; p. 19 (n.) the boats
are in plain sight; p. 20 (n.) one of these boats; p. 20 (n.) eyed
the boats like a cornet; p. 20 (n.) the bow boat was, perforce,
singled out; p. 21 (n.) where our boat; p. 22 (n.) boats-crew-watches;
p. 22 (adj.) composed of a boat's crew; p. 22 (n.) oar of the boat;
p. 23 (n.) boats-crew-watch; p. 23 (adj.) the starboard-quarter-
boat's-watch; p. 27 (n.) placed in the boat; p. 27 (n.) the boat was
to windward; p. 27 (n.) lift it into the boat; p. 27 (adj.) to the
boat's stern; p. 27 (n.) the boat fairly suspended; p. 28 (n.) the
boat bounded; p. 28 (n.) the good boat headed round; p. 28 (n.) Quick
to the boats; p. 28 (n.) those other boats; p. 28 (n.) leaped into
the boats; p. 28 (n.) lifted into the boat; p. 29 (n.) in an open
boat; p. 29 (n.) in our frail boat; p. 32 (n.) and converted the
boat-hook; p. 32 (n.) when the boat rolled; p. 32 (n.) the boat-
hatchet for cutting; p. 32 (n.) strain upon the boat; p. 33 (n.)
launched into the boat; p. 33 (n.) or seat of the boat; p. 33 (n.)
stern of the boat; p. 33 (adj.) almost lifted the light boat's stern;
p. 37 (n.) in an open Boat; p. 37 (n.) in an open Boat; p. 39 (n.) to
an open boat; p. 41 (n.) flew into our boat; p. 44 (n.) in the middle
of the boat; p. 44 (n.) in the bottom of the boat; p. 44 (adj.) in
the boat's quiet stern; p. 46 (n.) When in the boats; p. 46 (n.) And
the boats lying motionless; p. 47 (n.) most elevated part of the boat;
p. 47 (n.) at the other end of the boat; p. 49 (n.) planking of the
boat; p. 49 (n.) of the swiftest pilot-boat; p. 50 (n.) as our boat,
like a bird; p. 54 (adj.) less than a boat's length; p. 54 (n.)
mostly toward our boat; p. 55 (n.) were observed close to the boat;
p. 57 (n.) we but a boat; p. 58 (n.) with the oars of our boat; p. 58
(n.) our boat was still towing; p. 58 (n.) had no boats; p. 59 (n.)
sent him into the boat; p. 70 (n.) when the boat was completely;
p. 72 (n.) the boat drew nearer; p. 72 (n.) the boat still gaining;
p. 72 (n.) dragged into the boat; p. 72 (n.) turn the boat around;
p. 72 (n.) careening of the boat; p. 72 (n.) past the ill-fated boat;
p. 72 (n.) leaving in the boat; p. 72 (n.) anew upon the boat; p. 73
(n.) spun the boat round; p. 73 (n.) canting the boat over; p. 74 (n.)
sunk the boat; p. 85 (n.) of them in our boat; p. 86 (n.) strange
object was a boat; p. 89 (n.) in an open boat; p. 90 (n.) in our
marvelous boat; p. 107 (n.) ere rigging the life-boat; p. 116 (n.) A
long calm in the boat; p. 120 (n.) Samoa and I were in the boat;
p. 121 (n.) Slumbering in the bottom of the boat; p. 121 (n.) a
cadaverous gleam upon the boat; p. 122 (n.) coming into close contact
with our boat; p. 122 (n.) pushed the boat away from it; p. 125 (n.)
ranks as a sea boat; p. 126 (n.) was it a boat; p. 127 (n.) whether
it was indeed a whale-boat; p. 127 (n.) we had provided our boat;
p. 129 (n.) to give the boat a sheer; p. 132 (n.) hostile entrance
into our boat; p. 132 (adj.) in the boat's head; p. 132 (n.) swear to
depart in our boat forthwith; p. 132 (n.) for us to regain the boat;
p. 133 (n.) dashed side by side for the boat; p. 134 (adj.) lengthwise
across the boat's seats; p. 135 (n.) Standing foremost in the boat;
p. 135 (n.) they were passed into the boat; p. 135 (n.) bound hand
and foot in the boat; p. 147 (n.) Had a plank dropped out of our boat;
p. 150 (n.) hugged the vilified boat; p. 151 (n.) Hugging the boat to
desperation; p. 151 (n.) the Chevalier might despise our boat; p. 166
(n.) quickly toward the boat.

Redburn-- p. 6 (n.) a fat-looking, smoky fishing-boat; p. 7 (n.) and three boats sailing after it; p. 7 (n.) where the steamboat was to leave for New York; p. 11 (n.) At last gaining the boat we pushed off; p. 12 (n.) owing to the other boats not running; p. 12 (n.) The boat was off; p. 13 (n.) and the boat touched the wharf; p. 14 (adj.) From the boat's bow; p. 28 (n.) clean out that pig-pen in the long-boat; p. 28 (n.) for another boat called the jolly-boat was capsized; p. 28 (n.) was capsized right over the long-boat; p. 28 (n.) These two boats were in the middle of the deck; p. 28 (n.) to crawl inside of the long-boat; p. 29 (n.) to throw these shavings into the long-boat; p. 31 (n.) came off, one by one, in Whitehall boats; p. 31 (n.) as they rolled out of their boats; p. 32 (n.) a steam tug-boat with a strong name; p. 33 (n.) passed . . . small boats with ladies in them; p. 36 (n.) the steamboat left us; p. 36 (n.) took hold of a little boat on her deck; p. 37 (n.) and got into the boat; p. 40 (adj.) and keep the key of the boatswain's locker; p. 50 (n.) Then they lowered a boat; p. 66 (n.) the beds of the pigs in the long-boat; p. 103 (n.) thought the captain would lower a boat; p. 103 (n.) did not send off a boat; p. 112 (n.) looked like a juvenile boatswain's-mate; p. 121 (n.) for lashings to the boats; p. 123 (n.) steamboat alongside waiting; p. 125 (n.) presently a fishing-boat drew near; p. 125 (n.) it was a very ordinary looking boat; p. 125 (n.) at the receding boat; p. 126 (n.) the pilot boat that brought him; p. 126 (n.) plethoric looking sloop-rigged boat; p. 128 (n.) several boats came off; p. 139 (adj.) though the Boatswain's Mate; p. 139 (n.) they are a bridge of boats across the Atlantic; p. 144 (n.) Boat on the river; p. 147 (n.) Their nets and little boats their only store; p. 166 (n.) not much bigger than a pilot-boat; p. 171 (n.) the three mates, master, and boatswain; p. 171 (adj.) to the music of the boatswain's pipe; p. 198 (n.) so unlike the American boats; p. 242 (n.) jammed among the boats; p. 248 (n.) an old sail spread on the long-boat; p. 259 (n.) in a steamboat for Liverpool; p. 260 (n.) sunning himself in the long boat; p. 268 (adj.) would be standing on the boatswain's locker; p. 277 (n.) Under the Lee of the Long-Boat; p. 277 (n.) come you with me under the lee of the long-boat; p. 278 (n.) under the tarry lee of our long-boat; p. 284 (n.) upon the pig-pen in the boat; p. 296 (n.) and man the boat; p. 296 (n.) our jolly-boat would have taken; p. 296 (n.) we had but two boats; the long-boat and the jolly-boat; p. 296 (n.) The long-boat, by far the largest; p. 296 (n.) Over this the jolly-boat was capsized; p. 296 (n.) keeps its boats; p. 299 (n.) a white wing from the shore--the pilot-boat; p. 300 (n.) yet no boat came off to us; p. 300 (n.) ships, brigs, schooners, and sail boats; p. 301 (n.) The Whitehall boats were around us; p. 310 (n.) seated in the stern of the boat; p. 311 (n.) He accompanied me to the steamboat; p. 312 (adj.) the boat's crew that boarded our vessel; p. 312 (adj.) we lost a boat's crew; p. 312 (n.) who had never entered the boats.

White-Jacket--p. 6 (n.) then let the gruffest of Boat-swains; p. 6 (n.) All was ready; boats hoisted in; p. 11 (adj.) we say nothing here of Boatswain's mates; p. 12 (adj.) The Boatswain's mates whistle round him; p. 15 (n.) eternally talking of . . . sperm oil, stove boats, and Japan; p. 16 (n.) concerning stove boats on the coast of Japan; p. 21 (adj.) in the gun-boat actions on the Lakes; p. 25 (n.) consisting of the Boatswain, Gunner, carpenter; p. 25 (n.) Go and tell the boatswain I want him; p. 27 (adj.) that is, the

Boatswain's . . . mates; p. 33 (n.) like the Chinese boatmen in
Canton River; p. 41 (adj.) ship's corporals, and boatswain's mates;
p. 46 (n.) who so moody as . . . steam-boat engineers; p. 58 (n.) Oh!
I los' my boot in a pilot-boat; p. 58 (adj.) is the shrill pipe of
the boatswain's mate; p. 58 (n.) And if the boatswain's mate is not
by; p. 60 (n.) The boatswain and his mates had piped the hands to
dinner; p. 73 (n.) the three boats were down; p. 73 (n.) cried the
officer of our boat; p. 73 (n.) the boats were hoisted up; p. 94
(adj.) the boatswain's mates bellowed themselves hoarse; p. 102 (n.)
the appearance of the Boatswain, with his silver whistle; p. 102 (n.)
The Boatswain and his mates are the town-criers; p. 105 (adj.) the
boatswain's whistle was heard; p. 113 (n.) forward officers--
Boatswains, Gunners, &c.; p. 117 (n.) to tell the boatswain that he
was wanted; p. 125 (n.) to the boatswain or carpenter; p. 134 (n.) by
the dread summons of the boatswain; p. 137 (n.) the boatswain stood
solemnly on the other side; p. 137 (n.) and the first boatswain's-mate
advanced; p. 138 (n.) The fourth boatswain's-mate advanced; p. 138
(n.) What are you stopping for, boatswain's-mate; p. 140 (adj.) most
boatswain's mates carry the colt; p. 146 (n.) even as the boatswain's
mates are often called upon; p. 156 (n.) Often the boatswain's-mates
were obliged; p. 159 (n.) The Boats . . .; p. 160 (n.) you happen to
belong to one of the numerous boats; p. 160 (n.) of the numerous
boats employed in harbor; p. 160 (n.) Our frigate carried a very
large boat; p. 161 (n.) she carried four boats of an arithmetical
progression; p. 161 (n.) All these boats, except the dinghy; p. 161
(n.) while the other boats--commissioned for genteeler duties; p. 161
(n.) fond of belonging to the boats; p. 161 (n.) our boat laying
motionless on the water; p. 161 (n.) but from another boat; p. 163
(n.) to look out for all boats approaching; p. 163 (adj.) This
proceeded from a boatswain's mate; p. 163 (adj.) the boatswain
himself--not a boatswain's mate; p. 163 (adj.) with the rude whistle
of a boatswain's subaltern; p. 163 (n.) to get rid of my appointment
in his boat; p. 176 (n.) no shore-boat whatever is allowed to
approach; p. 177 (n.) Even the bum-boats, the small craft licensed;
p. 177 (n.) everyone of the numerous ship's boats; p. 177 (n.)
sometimes each boat twenty times in the day; p. 177 (n.) The boat
being descried by the quarter-master; p. 177 (adj.) as the boat's
crew . . . come up the side; p. 177 (adj.) till the whole boat's
crew are examined; p. 177 (n.) then descends into the boat; p. 177
(n.) and reports the boat clean; p. 178 (n.) in hailing all boats
that approach; p. 178 (n.) to fire into a strange boat; p. 178 (n.)
out of a boat just from shore; p. 178 (n.) procured from a knavish
bum-boat; p. 179 (n.) the Gunner, Boatswain, &c., have much greater
opportunities; p. 179 (n.) Yarn, our boatswain, in some inexplicable
way; p. 179 (adj.) perceived by one of the boat's crew; p. 179 (adj.)
stole into the boatswain's room; p. 179 (n.) liquor the boatswain
himself had smuggled; p. 180 (n.) pretense of filling the boat-keg
with water; p. 180 (n.) carries it down to the boat; p. 180 (adj.)
the boat's crew are overhauled; p. 183 (n.) when the market-boat
came off; p. 183 (n.) one of the ship's boats regularly deputed;
p. 183 (n.) when this boat came off; p. 184 (n.) by whom the box had
been brought down to the market-boat; p. 184 (adj.) at the sight of
the boatswain's mates; p. 184 (n.) brought them down to the frigate's
boats; p. 198 (adj.) suddenly the Boatswain's whistle was heard;
p. 213 (adj.) a quarter-gunner, or boatswain's mate; p. 219 (n.) he
went by the name of Boat Plug; p. 223 (adj.) Boatswain's mate, where's

your colt; p. 223 (adj.) the boatswain's mate looked into the crowd
aghast; p. 224 (adj.) Now go on, boatswain's mate; p. 224 (adj.) that
boatswain's mate, too, had a spite agin me; p. 225 (adj.) presently
the boatswain's voice was heard; p. 226 (n.) then the boats were
manned; p. 228 (n.) go ashore in his blue cloth boat-cloak; p. 242
(n.) to waive off all boats drawing near; p. 245 (n.) a boat which,
from its size; p. 245 (n.) perhaps, this boat would be plying; p. 245
(n.) Frank entered the boat with his hat slouched; p. 245 (n.) One
was the officer of his boat; p. 245 (n.) The boat being loaded;
p. 246 (n.) was dragged into the boat; p. 251 (n.) and, calling for a
boat, was not seen again; p. 265 (n.) as a pilot-boat distributes her
pilots; p. 269 (n.) still where the little boat was; p. 276 (adj.) Do
your duty, boatswain's mate; p. 278 (adj.) the announcement made by
the boatswain's mates; p. 278 (adj.) I heard the boatswain's mates
bawling my name; p. 278 (adj.) the boatswain's mate at the fore-
hatchway; p. 278 (adj.) thundered forth by the other boatswain's
mate; p. 279 (n.) the boatswain with his green bag of scourges;
p. 280 (adj.) the boatswain's mate stood curling his finger; p. 280
(adj.) through that dimness the boatswain's mate; p. 319 (n.) ought
to have seen the boat-load of Turkish flags; p. 328 (adj.) under the
scourge of the boatswain's mate; p. 328 (n.) Let the boatswain blow;
p. 337 (n.) when the Boatswain and his mates mustered round; p. 340
(n.) the boatswain and his four mates stood; p. 341 (adj.) roared a
boatswain's mate; p. 345 (n.) all hands were piped down by the
Boatswain; p. 349 (adj.) thundered forth by the boatswain's mates;
p. 356 (adj.) by the Boatswain's mate there stationed; p. 356 (n.)
But directly the Boatswain came rushing; p. 358 (n.) the Boatswain
. . . repeated the previous day's order; p. 358 (adj.) drove the two
boatswain's mates; p. 358 (adj.) Boatswain's mate, ship that ladder;
p. 361 (adj.) parodying the style of the boatswain's mates; p. 365
(adj.) boatswain's mates, do your duty; p. 365 (adj.) you, boatswain's
mate; p. 366 (n.) the old man . . . hired a boat; p. 371 (adj.) a
fresh boatswain's mate is called; p. 371 (n.) he is put into a boat;
p. 371 (adj.) inflicted by the boatswain's mates; p. 371 (n.) the
launch--the largest of the boats; p. 377 (n.) than that dramatic
boat-scene; p. 378 (n.) a boat was lowered; p. 388 (adj.) roared the
boatswain's mates at the gangway; p. 389 (n.) and buy a serving-
mallet-boat; p. 394 (n.) I helplessly sunk into the bottom of the
boat.

Moby-Dick--p. 5 (n.) tow it with a boat as near the shore as it will
come; p. 6 (n.) carry . . . other articles of the same nature in
their boats; p. 8 (n.) The quantity of line withdrawn from the
different boats; p. 8 (n.) he rushes at the boats with his head; p. 9
(n.) the furious monster at length rushed on the boat; p. 10 (n.) It
was not till the boats returned from the pursuit; p. 11 (n.) Cruise
in a Whale Boat; p. 11 (n.) a large Sperm Whale close to the head of
the boat; p. 23 (n.) They had just landed from their boat; p. 40 (adj.)
Forming one of the boats' crews of the ship ELIZA; p. 40 (n.) Who in
the bows of his boat was killed by a Sperm Whale; p. 41 (n.) a stove
boat will make me an immortal by brevet; p. 41 (n.) come a stove boat
and stove body when they will; p. 42 (n.) in mounting a ship from a
boat at sea; p. 48 (n.) But now when the boatswain calls all hands;
p. 57 (n.) get into the same watch, the same boat, the same mess with
me; p. 61 (n.) while the hands were clearing away the stern boat;
p. 84 (n.) did you ever stand in the head of a whale-boat; p. 85 (n.)

Nat Swaine, once the bravest boat-header out of all Nantucket; p. 89
(n.) Hence, the spare boats, spare spars, and spare lines and harpoons,
and spare everythings, almost; p. 93 (n.) Charity had come off in a
whaleboat; p. 95 (n.) The stout sail-boat that had accompanied us;
p. 96 (n.) Don't stave the boats needlessly, ye harpooners; p. 97 (n.)
Ship and boat diverged; p. 107 (n.) is always accompanied by his
boat-steerer or harpooner; p. 141 (n.) A dead whale or a stove boat;
p. 159 (n.) when amid the chips of chewed boats; p. 186 (n.) the
three boats swung over the sea like three samphire baskets over high
cliffs; p. 187 (n.) with a wallow, the three boats dropped with the
sea; p. 190 (n.) started the boat along the water like a horizontal
burst boiler; p. 193 (n.) all the boats tore on; p. 193 (n.) the
brief suspended agony of the boat; p. 193 (n.) the ivory Pequod
bearing down upon her boats; p. 193 (n.) The boats were pulled more
apart; p. 193 (n.) the boat going with such madness through the water;
p. 194 (n.) the boat was still booming through the mist; p. 194 (n.)
A short rushing sound leaped out of the boat; p. 240 (n.) because the
boat is rocking like a cradle; p. 244 (n.) The boat now flew through
the boiling water like a shark all fins; p. 291 (n.) You sail round
his vast head in your jolly-boat; p. 296 (n.) With one intent all the
combined rival boats were pointed for this one fish; p. 299 (n.) the
perpendicular strain from the headlined chocks of the boats; p. 299
(n.) As the three boats lay there on that gently rolling sea; p. 300
(n.) the boats gave a sudden bounce upward; p. 301 (n.) when the
boats pulled upon this whale; p. 301 (n.) As the boats now more
closely surrounded him; p. 316 (n.) No ribs of man or boat can
withstand it; p. 322 (n.) word was passed to spring to the boats;
p. 323 (n.) our beset boat was like a ship mobbed by ice-isles in a
tempest; p. 328 (n.) but the boats still lingered in their wake;
p. 341 (n.) Seizing his sharp boat-spade; p. 345 (n.) the boat
paddled upon the whale; p. 346 (n.) came all foaming up to the chocks
of the boat; p. 350 (n.) The gaff is something like a boat-hook;
p. 385 (n.) He had lighted with such energy upon a thwart of his boat;
p. 400 (adj.) shaping their various weapons and boat furniture; p. 407
(n.) while suspended in an ornamented boat; p. 409 (n.) watching his
final wanings from the now tranquil boat; p. 411 (adj.) the slumbering
crew arose from the boat's bottom; p. 413 (n.) in the higher hoisting
and firmer lashing of the boats; p. 447 (n.) soon all the boats but
Starbuck's were dropped; all the boat-sails set; p. 456 (n.) yet all
three boats were plain as the ship's three masts to his eye; p. 457
(n.) dragged the more involved boats of Stubb and Flask toward his
flukes; dashed them together like two rolling husks on a surf-beaten
beach; p. 457 (n.) Ahab's yet unstricken boat seemed drawn up towards
Heaven by invisible wires; p. 466 (n.) the tremendous rush of the
sea-crashing boat; p. 467 (n.) the temporarily disabled boat lay
nearly level with the waves.

BOBSTAY. Rope or chain used to confine the bowsprit downward to the stem
of cut-water. Their use is to counteract the strain of the foremast-
stays, which draw it upwards. (Smyth)

   Typee--p. 14 (n.) catching at the bob-stays.

BONEETA. The <u>Thynnus pelamys</u>, a fish of the scomber family, commonly about two feet long, with a sharp head, small mouth, full eyes, and a regular semi-lunar tail. (Smyth's spelling is "Bonito.")

<u>Typee</u>--p. 23 (n.) A vast shoal of bonetas and albicores.

<u>Omoo</u>--p. 15 (n.) the bonettas and albicores frolicking round us.

<u>Mardi</u>--p. 148 (n.) The came the Boneetas; p. 149 (n.) befallen this poor little Boneeta; p. 149 (n.) the poor Boneeta is seen no more; p. 149 (n.) No mourning they wear for the Boneeta.

BOOBY. A well-known tropical sea-bird fond of resting out of the water at night, even preferring an unstable perch on the yard of a ship. The name is derived from the way in which it allows itself to be caught immediately after settling. The direction in which they fly as evening comes often shows where land may be found. (Smyth)

<u>Mardi</u>--p. 126 (n.) aquatic fowls, . . . seldom found far from land: . . . reef-pigeons, boobies, gulls, and the like.

BOOM. A long spar run out from different places in the ship, to extend or boom out the foot of a particular sail; as, jib-boom, flying jib-boom, studding-sail booms, driver or spanker boom, ringtail-boom, main-boom, square-sail boom, &c. Boom also denotes a cable stretched athwart the mouth of a river or harbour, with yards, top-masts, or stout spars of wood lashed to it, to prevent the entrance of an enemy. (Smyth)

<u>Omoo</u>--p. 20 (n.) to the end of the flying jib boom; p. 35 (n.) setting right ahead of our boom.

<u>Mardi</u>--p. 116 (n.) by help of a spare boom; p. 118 (n.) we lifted our dangling jib-boom.

<u>Redburn</u>--p. 8 (n.) sitting astride of the spanker-boom; p. 65 (n.) and the sailors were fastening them to the booms; p. 93 (n.) we heard our jib-boom thumping; p. 93 (n.) with another jib-boom we had; p. 93 (adv.) coming together with another jib-boom-and-jib-boom; p. 97 (n.) along to the end of the jib-boom; p. 171 (n.) lost overboard from the flying-jib-boom; p. 300 (n.) almost bringing our jib-boom over.

<u>White-Jacket</u>--p. 108 (n.) the stun'-sail-booms greatly assisted in securing; p. 116 (n.) who that night went forward of the booms; p. 135 (n.) eager to obtain a good place on the booms; p. 177 (n.) whereupon she is hauled out to the booms; p. 180 (n.) The barge is ordered out to the booms; p. 180 (n.) is in your barge at the booms; p. 239 (n.) about the forward part of the booms; p. 271 (n.) Jib-boom, there; p. 272 (n.) the look-out on the jib-boom was hailed; p. 308 (n.) top your boom and sail large, now; p. 310 (n.) must rig out that stun'-sail boom; p. 341 (n.) Damn you! off those booms; p. 384 (n.) under the lee of the booms.

<u>Moby-Dick</u>--p. 60 (n.) the tremendous boom was now flying from side to side; p. 61 (n.) to attempt snatching at the boom to stay it; p. 61

(n.) stood eyeing the boom as if it were the lower jaw of an
exasperated whale; p. 281 (n.) with his [whale's] prodigious jaw . . .
for all the world like a ship's jib-boom; p. 339 (n.) All their noses
upwardly projected from their faces like so many jib-booms.

BOW. The fore-end of a ship or boat; being the rounding part of a vessel
forward, beginning on both sides where the planks arch inwards, and
terminating where they close, at the rabbet of the stern or prow, being
larboard or starboard from that division. (Smyth)

Typee--p. 10 (n.) scared from the water under the bows; p. 15 (n.) or
running out upon the bow; p. 28 (n.) I stood by in the bow of the
boat; p. 249 (n.) lying with her bow pointed from the shore.

Omoo--p. 13 (n.) Part of his time he spent out on the bowsprit; p. 23
(n.) while the foam flaked under her bows; p. 34 (n.) sporting under
the bows like pups ashore; p. 38 (n.) part of the deck about the
bowsprit; p. 38 (n.) planted right in the bows; p. 39 (n.) denominated
in marine architecture "bowsprit Bitts"; p. 39 (n.) the spray heaved
over the bows; p. 51 (n.) with the South East Trades strong on our
bow; p. 65 (n.) running out upon the bowsprit; p. 72 (n.) mad bubbles
that burst under the bows; p. 74 (adj.) nailed against the bowsprit
bitts; p. 95 (n.) swept her down under our bows; p. 102 (n.) seemed
to lock their leafy boughs over its bowsprit; p. 104 (n.) as we swept
under the bows; p. 104 (n.) sat quietly in the bow of the cutter;
p. 149 (n.) standing up on the bowsprit; p. 152 (n.) it was secured
by a line to the bowsprit; p. 153 (n.) standing alone and motionless
in the bow; p. 160 (n.) with a paddle in the bow; p. 161 (n.) Dropping
silently under her bows; p. 216 (n.) in we sprang--the doctor into
the bow; p. 229 (n.) and Zeke standing up in the bows.

Mardi--p. 3 (n.) the coral-hung anchor swings from the bow; p. 19 (n.)
by the bow and stern; p. 22 (n.) of which I was bowsman; p. 23 (n.)
waves against the bow; p. 47 (n.) a triangular little platform in the
bow; p. 50 (n.) sea under our bow; p. 63 (n.) the spare end of a
bowline; p. 65 (n.) under her bows; p. 69 (n.) captive of her bow;
p. 70 (n.) from the bob-stays to the bow-sprit; p. 80 (n.) he was
innocent as the bowsprit; p. 91 (n.) bravadoes broad on their bows;
p. 101 (n.) a view far beyond the bowsprit; p. 104 (n.) most solid
part of her hull, the bow; p. 126 (n.) broad off from our bow; p. 127
(n.) swept right across our bow; p. 128 (n.) mad spray from the bow;
p. 129 (n.) brought the bow, where I stood; p. 132 (n.) laid the bow
of the Chamois; p. 135 (n.) indicating a line near the bow; p. 213
(n.) foremost, or Bow-Paddler; p. 285 (n.) projecting over the bow of
the largest canoe; p. 306 (n.) when the Chamois was fleeing from
their bow; p. 436 (n.) Our bows! our bows!/ The thousand bows of Narvi;
p. 461 (n.) walk we to the bow; p. 582 (n.) I will nail it to our bow;
p. 615 (n.) across our bows, between two isles; p. 618 (n.) thus
hummed to himself our bowsman; p. 618 (n.) the merry bowsman, too
gleefully reaching forward; p. 618 (n.) that in which the bowsman
fell; p. 650 (n.) A bow-shot from the sea.

Redburn--p. 6 (n.) like pagodas, in the bow and stern; p. 6 (n.) for
the white spray was about the bows; p. 9 (n.) waves were breaking
over her bow; p. 9 (n.) a calamitous sea under the bows; p. 14 (n.)

From the boat's bow; p. 25 (n.) in the bow of the ship; p. 31 (n.)
their chests in the bow; p. 36 (n.) schooner running across our bows;
p. 50 (n.) the shrieking man jumped over the bows; p. 52 (n.) the dull
beating against the ship's bows; p. 63 (n.) a strange, musical noise
under her bows; p. 63 (n.) have let me go out on the bowsprit; p. 64
(n.) scattering them under our broad bows; p. 65 (n.) such as the
starboard-main-top-gallant-bow-line; p. 66 (n.) shaking off the foam
from her bows; p. 82 (n.) with the sea breaking over the bows; p. 92
(n.) saw the mate standing on the bowsprit; p. 93 (n.) heard our
jib-boom thumping against our bows; p. 100 (n.) nothing but a bowline
round the mid-ships; p. 116 (n.) I and the figure-head on the bow;
p. 122 (n.) swang me over the bows in a bowline; p. 126 (n.) with
flat bows, that went sheering; p. 164 (n.) cast off your bow-line . . .;
p. 164 (n.) get out a bow-line; p. 166 (n.) with broad bows painted
black; p. 171 (n.) while forward, on the bows; p. 174 (n.) but on a
bow-line; p. 175 (n.) clipper-built about the bows; p. 196 (n.)
darting under a ship's bows; p. 220 (n.) the figure-head on our bows;
p. 239 (n.) with the bow against the water-gate; p. 239 (n.) no one
could board us except by the bowsprit; p. 239 (n.) Staggering along
that bowsprit; p. 244 (n.) behind the bowsprit-bitts; p. 253 (n.)
they pursued you from bowsprit to mainmast; p. 259 (n.) running out a
little way on the bowsprit; p. 260 (n.) looking straight off from the
bows; p. 260 (n.) porpoises under the bows; p. 268 (n.) in the
vessel's bows; p. 268 (n.) standing right in the extreme bows of the
ship; p. 269 (n.) after it without a bowline; p. 294 (n.) we turned
over two broad, blue furrows from our bows; p. 298 (n.) the emigrants
clustered around the bows.

White-Jacket--p. 7 (n.) up to our bows came several thousand pounds;
p. 9 (n.) and all the sails on the bowsprit; p. 71 (n.) fished it up
from the bows; p. 72 (n.) I came near pitching off the bowsprit;
p. 73 (n.) In addition to the Bower-anchors carried on her bows;
p. 83 (n.) facing the taffrail instead of the bowsprit; p. 94 (n.)
squall was coming down on the weather-bow; p. 105 (n.) the spray
dashed over the bows; p. 106 (n.) The ship's bows were now butting,
battering, ramming; p. 110 (n.) the contrary course presents to it
your bows; p. 110 (n.) like the ribbed bows of a frigate; p. 135 (n.)
the seas broke heavily against the bows; p. 152 (n.) three points off
our lee-bow; p. 159 (n.) our bowsprit pointing for it straight;
p. 178 (n.) suspended over the bows; p. 178 (n.) should succeed in
getting under the bows; p. 269 (n.) broad on our weather-bow; p. 270
(n.) with its broad bows like a ram; p. 271 (n.) right off a
pretender's bows; p. 272 (n.) Her bows were rooting in the water;
p. 272 (n.) yet still not a bow was to be seen; p. 273 (n.) will lay
his two hands on the bow-chasers of the Neversink; p. 324 (n.)
captain of the starboard bow-chaser; p. 324 (n.) this captain of the
starboard bow-chaser was; p. 325 (n.) charged upon it with our gallant
bowsprit; p. 325 (n.) the triangular area in the bows; p. 348 (n.)
Her bowsprit is gone; p. 388 (n.) come plump on the enemy's bows; p.
p. 394 (n.) a soft ripple at her bows; p. 395 (n.) believed to be
broad on our bow; p. 396 (n.) our anchor still hangs from our bows;
p. 397 (n.) Haste, point our bowsprit for yon shadowy shore.

Moby-Dick--p. 9 (n.) Three points off the lee bow, sir; p. 17 (n.)
nigh enough to risk a harpoon from the bowsprit; p. 40 (n.) who in
the bows of his boat was killed by a sperm whale; p. 43 (n.) in the

likeness of a ship's bluff bows; p. 44 (n.) the bow must bear the
earliest brunt; p. 44 (n.) kneeling in the pulpit's bows; p. 48 (n.)
aghast Jonah sees the rearing bowsprit pointing high; p. 59 (n.) the
little Moss tossed the quick foam from her bows; p. 60 (n.) the Moss
. . . ducked and dived her bows as a slave before the Sultan; p. 60
(n.) as we stood by the plunging bowsprit; p. 61 (n.) those on deck
rushed toward the bows; p. 67 (n.) Her venerable bows looked bearded;
p. 70 (n.) take a peep over the weather-bow; p. 70 (n.) Going forward
and glancing over the weather bow; p. 90 (n.) actively engaged in
looking over the bows; p. 95 (n.) vast curving icicles depended from
the bows; p. 97 (n.) when . . . the Pequod thrust her vindictive bows
with the cold malicious waves; p. 146 (n.) men that man the deathful
whaleboat's bow; p. 148 (n.) shoots on the gay, embattled, bantering
bow; p. 199 (n.) in advance of the white bubbles at the bow; p. 299
(n.) the gunwhales of the bows were almost even with the water;
p. 300 (n.) Not eight inches of perpendicular rope were visible at
the bows; p. 320 (n.) land soon loomed on the starboard bow; p. 363
(n.) carelessly reclining in his own boat's bow; p. 407 (n.) hanging
captive from the bowsprit was seen the long lower jaw; p. 448 (n.)
its bow, by anticipation, was made to face the whale's head while yet
under water; p. 452 (adv.) broken bow to shattered stern; p. 467 (n.)
the before whale-smitten bow-ends of two planks burst through.

BRAIL. Rope passing through leading-blocks on the hoops of the mizzen-
mast and gaff, and fastened to the outermost leech of the sail, in
different places, to truss it close up as occasion requires; all try-
sails and several of the stay-sails also have brails. (Smyth)

Mardi--p. 116 (n.) hanging loose in the brails.

BREACH. The act of leaping out of the water; applied to whales. (Smyth)

Moby-Dick--p. 455 (n.) this breaching is his act of defiance; p. 455
(v.) There she breaches! there she breaches; p. 455 (v.) Aye, breach
your last to the sun, Moby Dick.

BREAKER. Small barrels for containing water or other liquids; they are
also used in watering the ship as gang-casks. Also, those billows which
break violently over reefs, rocks, or shallows, lying immediately at, or
under, the surface of the sea. They are distinguished both by their
appearance and sound, as they cover that part of the sea with a perpetual
foam, and produce loud roaring, very different from what the waves usually
have over a deeper bottom. (Smyth)

Omoo--p. 89 (n.) was a long line of breakers; p. 89 (n.) so as to
close with the breakers; p. 90 (n.) Breakers! breakers close aboard;
p. 98 (n.) by the time the breakers were roaring; p. 266 (n.) darted
their spears in the very midst of the breakers; p. 270 (n.) the
breakers looked, in the distance; p. 270 (n.) diversifying the long
line of breakers.

Mardi--p. 4 (n.) creamy breakers frothing round its base; p. 27 (n.)
to manhandle our clumsy breaker; p. 27 (n.) a long rope to the

breaker; p. 27 (n.) the breaker, acting as a clog; p. 27 (n.) our
dropping overboard the breaker; p. 27 (n.) dead weight of the
breaker; p. 28 (n.) by the touring breaker; p. 28 (n.) rope attached
to the breaker; p. 32 (n.) the precious breaker we lashed firmly;
p. 44 (n.) at the invaluable breaker; p. 44 (n.) the breaker lay on
its bilge; p. 44 (n.) the breaker must be leaking; p. 44 (n.) then
lift one end of the breaker; p. 44 (n.) that the breaker was in all
respects; p. 44 (n.) thou and thy breaker were a study; p. 44 (n.)
Besides the breaker; p. 44 (n.) we came to the breaker; p. 44 (n.)
from the breaker; p. 44 (n.) bung-hole of the breaker; p. 49 (n.)
water in the breaker; p. 49 (n.) piled upon the breaker; p. 49 (n.)
bailed out the breaker; p. 102 (n.) near by, in a breaker; p. 654
(n.) the breakers dashed ghost-white.

Moby-Dick--p. 43 (n.) a lee coast of black rocks and snowy breakers;
p. 168 (n.) if by night he hear the roar of breakers; p. 178 (n.) but
the gods shipwrecked him again upon unknown rocks and breakers;
p. 396 (n.) and so form the white breakers of the milky way.

BRIG. A two-masted square-rigged vessel, without a square main-sail, or
a trysail-mast abaft the main-mast. (Smyth) An hermaphrodite brig has a
brig's foremast and a schooner's mainmast. (Dana) The ship's prison.
(Bradford)

Omoo--p. 27 (n.) who had deserted from a trading brig; p. 35 (n.)
when commanding a small brig; p. 96 (n.) caught sight of a brig;
pp. 298-9 (n.) he had lost a colonial armed brig; p. 299 (n.) and
report the loss of his brig.

Mardi--p. 65 (n.) showing the desolate brig; p. 69 (n.) the fated
brig lay; p. 80 (adj.) in the brig's case.

Redburn--p. 4 (n.) The coppered and copper-fastened brig Leda; p. 4
(n.) A brig; p. 4 (n.) on board a coppered and copper-fastened brig;
p. 4 (n.) Plenty more brigs and any quantity of ships; p. 164 (n.)
She was a dark little brig; p. 166 (n.) A black brig from Glasgow;
p. 174 (n.) was a little brig from the Coast of Guinea; p. 175 (n.)
The brig, heavily loaded; p. 300 (n.) while thick and more thick,
ships, brigs.

White-Jacket--p. 55 (n.) they were ordered into the brig, a jail-
house; p. 90 (n.) confined in the ship's prison--the brig; p. 134
(n.) found themselves prisoners in the brig; p. 136 (n.) of the
marine sentry at the brig; p. 144 (n.) kept a seaman confined in the
brig; p. 158 (n.) in the case of sloops of war and armed brigs;
p. 183 (n.) have that box put into the brig; p. 184 (n.) return the
box to the brig; p. 185 (n.) for several weeks were confined in the
brig; p. 187 (n.) while he was lying ironed in the brig; p. 212 (n.)
of Perry's war-brigs; p. 237 (n.) though in double-darbles in the
brig; p. 302 (n.) to be taken down and put into the brig; p. 303 (n.)
The well-known case of a United States brig; p. 307 (n.) collared,
and dragged into the brig; p. 364 (n.) put that man into the brig;
p. 364 (n.) Put him into the brig; p. 366 (n.) take that man back to
the brig; p. 366 (n.) And now you go into the brig; p. 374 (n.) over
the brig or jail; p. 399 (n.) we have a brig for traspassers.

Moby-Dick--p. 14 (n.) without taking care of ships, barques, brigs;
p. 80 (n.) a short whaling-voyage in a schooner or a brig; p. 353 (n.)
So the pitch and sulphur-freighted brigs.

BRIGANTINE. A square-rigged vessel, with two masts. A term variously
applied by the mariners of the different European nations to a peculiar
sort of vessel of their own marine. (Smyth)

Mardi--p. 57 (n.) in short, a brigantine; p. 58 (n.) now the silent
brigantine; p. 58 (n.) brought the brigantine to the wind; p. 58 (n.)
the brigantine had no boats; p. 62 (n.) that the brigantine was
untenanted; p. 62 (n.) that we were alone in the brigantine; p. 63
(adj.) to throw the brigantine's head; p. 63 (n.) misgivings about
the brigantine; p. 63 (n.) regard to the character of the brigantine;
p. 68 (n.) What Befel the Brigantine; p. 69 (n.) accompanied in the
brigantine; p. 69 (n.) coming off to the brigantine; p. 69 (n.) where
lay the brigantine; p. 69 (n.) from where the brigantine; p. 70 (n.)
low chains of the brigantine; p. 70 (n.) to wreck the brigantine;
p. 70 (n.) the brigantine, now gliding; p. 71 (n.) and the brigantine
heading right out; p. 71 (n.) Capture of the brigantine; p. 71 (n.)
badly did the brigantine steer; p. 72 (n.) gaining on the brigantine;
p. 72 (n.) hove to the brigantine; p. 74 (n.) to overhaul the
brigantine; p. 80 (n.) the brigantine drifting hither; p. 80 (n.) in
managing the brigantine; p. 81 (n.) brigantine was saved; p. 86 (n.)
bent upon boarding the brigantine; p. 87 (n.) our first boarding the
brigantine; p. 89 (n.) in rescuing the brigantine; p. 90 (n.) with
respect to the brigantine; p. 93 (adj.) hunt up the brigantine's log;
p. 100 (n.) prying about our little brigantine; p. 101 (n.) left the
brigantine to the guardianship; p. 108 (n.) quitted the chamois for
the brigantine; p. 109 (n.) in the brigantine there were many sources;
p. 110 (n.) that whoever steered the brigantine; p. 116 (n.) another
in the brigantine; p. 117 (adj.) to cast the brigantine's head;
p. 117 (adj.) the brigantine's black hull, shaggy; p. 120 (n.) love
for our poor brigantine; p. 125 (n.) overtaken us in the brigantine.

Redburn--p. 174 (n.) crowds of . . . part French brigantines.

BRINE. Water replete with saline particles, as brine-pickle for salt
meat. The briny wave. (Smyth)

Typee--p. 14 (n.) where they clung dripping with the brine; p. 14
(adj.) luxuriant locks . . . were freed from the briny element.

Omoo--p. 72 (n.) a red whirlpool of blood and brine; p. 313 (n.) She
dropped her boats into the brine.

Mardi--p. 3 (n.) reelingly cleave the brine; p. 27 (n.) clove the
brine; p. 45 (n.) in the brine; p. 49 (n.) moistened with brine;
p. 49 (n.) had fallen into the brine; p. 71 (n.) bravely breasted
the brine with the double distilled soul of the precious grape;
p. 117 (n.) drops of brine fell; p. 122 (n.) as we parted the pallid
brine; p. 123 (n.) to kindle a fire in the brine; p. 138 (n.) which
streaming over upon the brine; p. 192 (n.) but dust to brine; p. 214
(n.) in the brine our paddles dip; p. 375 (n.) from flowery cliffs

into the brine; p. 432 (n.) a swallow of brine will help thee; p. 511 (n.) to mix their freshness with the foreign brine; p. 539 (n.) brimmed over upon the brine; p. 540 (n.) instead of this pestilent brine; p. 568 (n.) dragging another, dripping, from the brine; p. 615 (n.) with the brine he mixed the dew of leaves.

Redburn--p. 66 (adj.) give me . . . this briny, foamy life; p. 268 (n.) diving together in the brine; p. 302 (adj.) with the continual flavor of briny beef.

White-Jacket--pp. 96-7 (n.) steeps in a still saltier brine the saltest [about Cape Horn]; p. 116 (n.) and floods of brine descended.

Moby-Dick--p. 242 (n.) as the great fish slowly and regularly spouted the sparkling brine into the air; p. 244 (n.) His tormented body rolled not in brine but in blood; p. 450 (n.) the white brine caking in his wrinkles.

BRIT. A red or sometimes a yellowish organism which floats in vast quantities on some parts of the sea, and serves as a food for whales; a very small fish an inch or so long. (Bradford)

Moby-Dick--p. 182 (n.) none of that peculiar substance called brit is to be found; p. 234 (n.) Brit; p. 234 (n.) we fell in with vast meadows of brit; p. 234 (n.) sluggishly swam through the brit; p. 273 (n.) by its [the sea's] occasional patches of yellow brit; p. 282 (n.) open-mouthed he goes through the seas of brit in feeding time.

BROACH-TO. To fly up into the wind. It generally happens when a ship is carrying a press of canvas with the wind on the quarter, and a good deal of after-sail set. The masts are endangered by the course being so altered, as to bring it more in opposition to, and thereby increasing the pressure of the wind. (Smyth)

White-Jacket--p. 92 (v.) Or, perhaps, the ship broaches to.

BUBBLE. A small bladder or vesicle of water inflated with air. (Webster)

Mardi--p. 209 (v.) the Lagoon beneath, . . . bubbling with the moisture that dropped.

Moby-Dick--p. 199 (n.) far in advance of the white bubbles at the bow; p. 223 (n.) he would bury him in bubbles and foam; p. 296 (v.) causing the waters bchind him to upbubble; p. 300 (n.) not so much as a ripple or a bubble; p. 470 (n.) Round and round, then, and ever contrasting towards the button-like black bubble at the axis of that slowly sheeling circle, like another Ixion I did revolve. Till, gaining that vital centre, the black bubble upward burst.

BUCANIER. A name given to certain piratical rovers, of various European nations, who formerly infested the coasts of Spanish America. They were originally inoffensive settlers in Hispaniola, but were inhumanly driven from their habitations by the jealous policy of the Spaniards; whence originated their implacable hatred to the nation. (Smyth's spelling, "buccaneer")

Mardi--p. 21 (n.) not so much of a bucanier; p. 269 (n.) to Ohonoo all the bucaniers.

Redburn--p. 175 (adj.) The crew were a bucaniering looking set.

BULKHEAD. A partition built up in several parts of a ship, to form and separate the various cabins from each other. Some are particularly strong, as those in the hold, which are mostly built with rabetted or cyphered plank; others are light, and removable at pleasure. Indeed the word is applied to any division made with boards, to separate one portion of the 'tween decks from another. (Smyth)

Typee--p. 92 (n.) decorate the bulkhead of a man-of-war's cabin.

Omoo--p. 38 (n.) partitioned off by a bulkhead.

Mardi--p. 75 (n.) mirror paneled in the bulkhead.

Redburn--p. 238 (n.) extending from the cabin bulkhead; p. 287 (n.) That bulkhead must come down; p. 292 (n.) through the little glass in the cabin bulk-head.

White-Jacket--p. 34 (n.) His broad chest is a bulk-head; p. 67 (n.) placed behind glazed glass gull's-eyes inserted in the bulk-head; p. 68 (n.) every bulk-head in a man-of-war is knocked down; p. 110 (n.) are as bulkheads to dam off an onset; p. 124 (n.) Through low arches in the bulk-head beyond; p. 127 (n.) barred and bolted in dingy bulk-heads; p. 255 (n.) included the whole extent aft to the bulk-head.

BULWARK. The wood work around a vessel, above her deck, consisting of boards fastened to stanchions and timber-heads. (Dana)

Typee--pp. 3-4 (n.) the inside of our bulwarks is painted green; p. 10 (n.) leaning up against the bulwarks; p. 15 (n.) flung themselves lightly over the bulwarks; p. 31 (n.) one of the ship's company leaning over the bulwarks; p. 33 (n.) leaning . . . against the bulwarks and buried in thought.

Omoo--p. 5 (n.) Leaning carelessly over the bulwarks; p. 9 (n.) even the bulwarks were quite rotten; p. 17 (n.) to stand leaning over the bulwarks; p. 23 (n.) jumping up on the bulwarks; p. 29 (n.) the poor savage leaned over the bulwarks; p. 45 (n.) on a plank laid across the bulwarks; p. 59 (n.) One side of the rotten head-bulwarks came in; p. 60 (n.) no help for the demolished bulwarks; p. 68 (n.) leaning over the bulwarks; p. 89 (n.) under the lee of the bulwarks; p. 92 (n.) partly flung over the bulwarks; p. 98 (n.) he sprang upon the bulwarks; p. 99 (n.) standing conspicuously on the bulwarks.

Mardi--p. 19 (n.) to the ship's bulwarks; p. 64 (n.) flitting across
the bulwarks; p. 65 (n.) or posts of the bulwarks; p. 70 (n.) sprang
over the bulwarks; p. 72 (n.) muskets on the bulwarks; p. 11 (n.) to
the bulwarks near by.

Redburn--p. 4 (n.) with high, cozy bulwarks; p. 5 (n.) their woolen
caps above the high bulwarks; p. 9 (n.) He was leaning against the
bulwarks; p. 38 (n.) now lounged against the bulwarks; p. 55 (n.) out
to windward over the bulwarks; p. 93 (n.) a great part of the
starboard bulwark; p. 103 (n.) The bulwarks were pretty much gone;
p. 255 (n.) to mount over the bulwarks; p. 257 (n.) never mounted
about the bulwarks; p. 292 (n.) you see no corpses thrown over the
bulwarks; p. 308 (n.) strung along the top of the bulwarks.

White-Jacket--p. 4 (n.) swabbing bone-dry the very bulwarks I leaned
against; p. 10 (n.) or venture above the bulwarks; p. 28 (n.) conveys
a feeling of the lee bulwarks; p. 69 (n.) Then our bulwarks might
look like the walls; p. 82 (n.) running round the top of the bulwarks;
p. 93 (n.) and the bulwarks round about were draperied; p. 104 (n.)
the strange sail was descried from our bulwarks; p. 106 (n.) mostly
clinging to the weather bulwarks; p. 107 (n.) Above the bulwarks . . .
the gale was horrible; p. 137 (n.) close to the ship's bulwarks;
p. 173 (n.) comfortable stand-up against the bulwarks; p. 173 (n.) is
to lean over the bulwarks; p. 245 (n.) two midshipmen leaning against
the bulwarks; p. 294 (n.) Do not hang back there by the bulwarks;
p. 319 (n.) the dust of the powdered bulwarks; p. 322 (n.) from the
three mast-heads to the bulwarks; p. 323 (n.) would crawl over the
bulwarks; p. 371 (n.) by the blood on the bulwarks of every ship;
pp. 373-4 (n.) flat on their faces behind the bulwarks.

Moby-Dick--p. 12 (n.) some looking over the bulwarks of ships from
China; p. 20 (n.) reminding one of the bulwarks of some condemned old
craft; p. 48 (n.) a panther billow leaping over the bulwarks; p. 61
(n.) secured one end to the bulwarks; p. 67 (n.) open bulwarks were
garnished like one continuous jaw; p. 83 (n.) leaning stiffly over
the bulwarks; p. 95 (n.) The long rows of teeth on the bulwarks
glistened in the moonlight; p. 114 (n.) Ahab stood for a while
leaning over the bulwarks; p. 338 (n.) rejoined a Guernsey-man from
the bulwarks.

BUOY. A floating cask, or piece of wood, attached by a rope to an anchor,
to show its position. Also, floated over a shoal, or other dangerous
place as a beacon. (Dana)

Redburn--p. 126 (n.) we passed immense buoys; p. 127 (n.) this was
the famous Bell-Buoy; p. 289 (n.) rose and fell like some vast buoy.

White-Jacket--p. 71 (n.) that we picked up a life-buoy; p. 71 (n.)
The whole buoy was embossed with barnacles; p. 71 (n.) while even the
life-buoy itself had drifted; p. 71 (n.) that the ship's life-buoys
are kept in good order; p. 72 (n.) two life-buoys are kept; p. 72 (n.)
and drop the buoys overboard; p. 72 (n.) ordered the life-buoy sentries
sentries; p. 72 (n.) make us a brace of life-buoys like that; p. 72
(n.) going down with buoys under you; p. 72 (n.) the life-sentries
there had cut away the buoys; p. 73 (n.) Man or buoy, do you see

either; p, 73 (n.) seen no sign even of the life-buoys; p. 73 (n.)
I told him his buoys wouldn't save a drowning man; p. 178 (n.) and
moor them to the frigate's anchor-buoy; p. 178 (n.) The buoy gained;
p. 393 (n.) at last I bounded up like a buoy; p. 394 (n.) one of the
life-buoys which had been cut away.

Moby-Dick--p. 302 (n.) ere long every boat was a buoy; p. 323 (n.)
they fasten buoys to him; p. 409 (v.) I am buoyed by breaths of once
living things, exhaled as air, but water now; p. 429 (n.) The life-
buoy--a long slender cask--was dropped from the stern; p. 430 (n.)
The lost life-buoy was now to be replaced; p. 430 (n.) A life-buoy of
a coffin; p. 441 (n.) the life-buoy-coffin still lightly swung;
p. 470 (n.) the coffin life-buoy shot lengthwise from the sea;
p. 470 (v.) Buoyed up by that coffin.

CABIN. A room or compartment partitioned off in a ship, where the
officers and passengers reside. In a man-of-war, the principal cabin,
in which the captain or admiral lives, is the upper-after part of the
vessel. (Smyth)

Mardi--p. 6 (n.) he entered his cabin; p. 58 (n.) down in the cabin;
p. 59 (n.) explore the cabin; p. 59 (n.) explore the cabin; p. 59
(adj.) unfastening the cabin scuttle; p. 59 (n.) through the bulk-
head of the cabin; p. 60 (n.) used in a ship's cabin; p. 64 (n.)
while in the cabin; p. 69 (n.) in his cabin; p. 70 (adj.) toward the
cabin scuttle; p. 70 (n.) In the cabin; p. 71 (adj.) from the cabin
skylight; p. 74 (n.) pillage the Cabin; p. 74 (n.) the recesses of
the cabin; p. 75 (adj.) strown about the cabin floor; p. 75 (n.)
slippery grew the cabin deck; p. 81 (n.) den of a cabin; p. 81 (n.)
breaking into the cabin; p. 86 (n.) descent into the cabin; p. 87 (n.)
going on in the cabin; p. 87 (n.) emerged from the cabin; p. 93 (n.)
Descending into the cabin; p. 95 (n.) from the forecastle to the
cabin; p. 95 (n.) after vainly searching the cabin; p. 101 (n.) I
descended to the cabin; p. 127 (n.) astern an arched cabin or tent.

Redburn--p. 15 (n.) and found the captain in the cabin; p. 15 (n.) He
was promenading up and down the cabin; p. 15 (n.) at his comfortable,
and almost luxurious cabin; p. 18 (n.) as we were about leaving the
cabin; p. 18 (n.) to open the cabin-door; p. 40 (adj.) off the
leavings of the cabin table; p. 67 (n.) Making a Social Call on the
Captain in His Cabin; p. 67 (n.) invite me down into the cabin;
p. 68 (adj.) help me plentifully to the nice cabin fare; p. 68 (n.)
to drop into the cabin to pay my respects; p. 69 (n.) walking
straight toward the cabin-door; p. 69 (n.) to call on the captain in
the cabin; p. 69 (n.) I never saw the inside of the cabin; p. 70 (n.)
watch the proceedings in the cabin; p. 70 (n.) my attempt to drop in
at the cabin; p. 71 (n.) the captain rushed out of the cabin; p. 83
(n.) visited the captain in the cabin; p. 107 (n.) the mahogany and
bird's-eye maple cabin; p. 107 (adj.) accommodations for cabin
passengers; p. 107 (n.) the solitary cabin-passenger; p. 108 (n.)
criticize cabin-passengers more than cabin-passengers are . . . aware;
p. 108 (n.) the mysterious cabin-passenger went his way; p. 108 (n.)
adventure befell his cabin-passenger; p. 109 (n.) only one poor
fellow of a cabin-passenger; p. 109 (n.) but the figure of our cabin-
passenger; p. 110 (n.) sort of an occupant of the cabin; p. 110 (n.)

she issued from her cabin; p. 112 (adj.) and the mysterious cabin-
passenger contributing; p. 117 (adj.) the cabin passengers would
never find out; p. 136 (n.) For company over the cabin-table; p. 166
(n.) These craft have each a little cabin; p. 167 (n.) small, low,
and narrow as the cabin is; p. 171 (n.) I was condoling with a young
English cabin-boy; p. 171 (n.) These officers lived astern in the
cabin; p. 196 (n.) the tobacco must remain in the cabin; p. 219 (n.)
I had first accosted him in the cabin; p. 238 (adj.) extending from
the cabin-bulkhead; p. 239 (adj.) the appearance of the cabin-
passenger; p. 241 (n.) with ladies and gentlemen in the cabin; p. 242
(n.) The cabin-passengers of the Highlander; p. 242 (n.) And the
cabin-passengers themselves; p. 260 (n.) with a message from the
cabin; p. 260 (adj.) for the benefit of the cabin occupants; p. 261
(n.) some censorious gentlemen cabin-passengers; p. 261 (n.) these
cabin-people were all ready enough; p. 261 (n.) regard the inmates of
the cabin; p. 261 (n.) a feeling toward the cabin-passengers; p. 261
(n.) they happened to be cabin-passengers; p. 262 (adj.) Another of
the cabin inmates; p. 262 (n.) through the windows of the upper cabin;
p. 265 (n.) called the second cabin; p. 265 (n.) the comforts of the
first cabin; p. 265 (n.) that this second cabin was comprised; p. 265
(adj.) the dandy glances of the cabin bucks; p. 266 (n.) of an opera-
glass from the cabin; p. 269 (n.) and reviewed by the cabin-
passengers; p. 269 (n.) among these magnanimous cabin-passengers;
p. 283 (n.) obliged to issue a ukase from the cabin; p. 284 (n.)
excursions from the cook to the cabin; p. 286 (n.) to the medicine-
chest in the cabin; p. 286 (n.) alleged physician among the cabin-
passengers; p. 286 (n.) from extending into the cabin itself; p. 288
(n.) The panic in the cabin was now very great; p. 288 (adj.) the
cabin passengers would fain have made; p. 288 (n.) which communicated
with the cabin; p. 288 (n.) the cabin, perhaps, presented a scene;
p. 289 (n.) a woman in the cabin; p. 289 (n.) officers, cabin-
passengers, and emigrants; p. 290 (n.) As for the passengers in the
cabin; p. 291 (n.) The cabin passenger who had used to read prayers;
p. 292 (adj.) through the little glass in the cabin bulk-head; p. 298
(n.) the impatient cabin-passengers were arrayed; p. 299 (adj.) beset
by the captain and cabin people for news; p. 301 (adj.) our cabin
passengers were all off; p. 305 (n.) We were told to enter the cabin;
p. 306 (n.) interview with you in this very cabin; p. 307 (n.)
Quitting the cabin; p. 308 (n.) He knocked at the cabin-door; p. 308
(n.) the captain sallied from the cabin; p. 309 (n.) slowly returned
into his cabin.

White-Jacket--p. 6 (n.) in his grand, inaccessible cabin; p. 18 (n.)
being shown into the cabin; p. 19 (n.) was summoned into the cabin;
p. 22 (n.) invited into his cabin over a social bottle; p. 22 (n.)
stationed at our commodore's cabin-door; p. 23 (n.) as kingly in his
cabin; 23 (n.) to repair to the captain's cabin; p. 32 (n.) by
working out a problem in the cabin; p. 33 (n.) when the Captain would
emerge from his cabin; p. 69 (n.) broken chairs and tables in the
Commodore's cabin; p. 75 (n.) by the palace of the Commodore's cabin;
p. 75 (n.) where the commander has a whole cabin to himself; p. 80
(n.) by an express edict from the Captain's cabin; p. 94 (n.) the
captain darted from his cabin; p. 106 (n.) Captain Claret, bursting
from his cabin; p. 111 (n.) held his peace, and stayed in his cabin;
p. 117 (n.) he was wanted in the captain's cabin; p. 128 (n.) their
spacious and curtained cabins; p. 136 (n.) the captain came forward

from his cabin; p. 163 (n.) made his ceremonious way to the cabin;
p. 163 (adj.) called upon to scrub his cabin floor; p. 173 (n.) best
to get back into his cabin; p. 204 (n.) he was called into the
Commodore's cabin; p. 215 (n.) the Commodore had been in his cabin;
p. 222 (n.) the same in cabin-boy and commodore; p. 229 (n.) when
Virtue is crowned in the cabin; p. 255 (n.) to the bulk-head of the
Commodore's cabin; p. 258 (n.) the armed sentry at the Commodore's
cabin-door; p. 266 (n.) from our Commodore's cabin; p. 289 (n.)
slowly emerges from his cabin; p. 290 (n.) half of the Commodore's
cabin had been . . . yielded; p. 291 (n.) the common God of commodore
and cabin-boy; p. 323 (n.) entered from the Captain's cabin; p. 358
(n.) taking a nap in his cabin; p. 374 (adj.) the Commodore's and
Captain's cabin doors; p. 388 (n.) private life of the Commodore in
his cabin; p. 398 (n.) the smallest cabin-boy is as wise as the
Captain.

Moby-Dick--p. 46 (n.) to see its Captain in the cabin; p. 84 (adj.)
had retreated towards the cabin gangway; p. 109 (n.) into the now
sacred retreat of the cabin; p. 421 (n.) The isolated subterraneousness
of the cabin made a certain humming silence.

CABOOSE. The cook-room or kitchen of merchantmen on deck; a diminutive
substitute for the galley of a man-of-war. It is generally furnished
with cast-iron apparatus for cooking. (Smyth)

Mardi--p. 77 (n.) in the little caboose, or cook-house.

CACHALOT. A cetaceous fish, the physeter or spermaciti whale. The
principal species are, the black headed with a dorsal fin, and the round-
headed, without a fin on the back, and with a fistula in the snout. From
this whale is obtained the spermaceti. (Webster)

Mardi--p. 5 (n.) of the Cachalot; p. 6 (n.) for the gentlemanly
Cachalot; p. 6 (n.) of aught but Cachalot; p. 121 (n.) where an
immense shoal of Cachalots; p. 122 (n.) invests the body of the
Cachalot; p. 206 (n.) and the imperial Cachalot-whale.

Moby-Dick--p. 9 (n.) The Cachalot (Sperm Whale) is not only better
armed than the True Whale (Greenland or Right Whale); p. 384 (n.) as
perhaps fifty of these whale-bone whales are harpooned for one
Cachalot.

CALM. There being no wind stirring it is designated flat, dead, or stark,
under each of which the surface of the sea is unruffled. (Smyth)

Omoo--p. 36 (n.) during the frequent calms; p. 73 (n.) toward noon it
fell a dead calm; p. 264 (n.) But after the long morning calms.

Mardi--p. 9 (n.) there was a calm; p. 9 (n.) a calm is no joke; p. 10
(n.) the stillness of the calm; p. 10 (n.) out of the calm; p. 10 (n.)
there is a calm; p. 10 (n.) where the calm leaves him; p. 10 (n.) get
away from the calm; p. 10 (n.) for calm or for gale; p. 10 (n.) is a
calm; p. 17 (n.) calms and currents may; p. 41 (n.) in the profoundest

calms; p. 43 (n.) if a long calm came on; p. 44 (n.) calms fell fast;
p. 48 (v.) They are becalmed; p. 48 (n.) there was a calm; p. 48 (n.)
so in a calm; p. 48 (n.) This calm lasted; p. 49 (n.) second day of
the calm; p. 49 (n.) so long as the calm lasted; p. 51 (n.) In that
long calm; p. 51 (n.) and frequent intermitting calms; p. 51 (n.)
spite of past calms and currents; p. 52 (n.) during the calm; p. 52
(n.) the calm gone by; p. 108 (n.) Calms, light breezes, and currents;
p. 116 (n.) A long calm in the boat; p. 116 (n.) in that hot calm;
p. 116 (n.) owing to the calm; p. 118 (n.) Such was the storm that
came after our calm; p. 160 (n.) trail of a great fish in a calm;
p. 265 (n.) the lagoon a calm; p. 267 (n.) In a Calm, Hautia's
Heralds approach; p. 306 (n.) In long calms, in vain; p. 306 (n.) The
calm still brooded; p. 306 (n.) The breeze which followed the calm;
p. 367 (n.) In my tropical calms; p. 370 (n.) Do you show a tropical
calm without; p. 372 (n.) it's a calm on the waters, and a calm in
our hearts; p. 424 (n.) there fell a calm; p. 424 (n.) Vee-Vee,
impatient of the calm; p. 500 (n.) if calms breed storms, so storms
calms; p. 543 (n.) like porpoises to vessels tranced in calms; p. 558
(n.) By noon, down came a calm; p. 567 (n.) Let us dream out the calm.

Redburn--p. 88 (n.) used to mutter over during a calm; p. 116 (n.)
except during a calm; p. 119 (n.) sometimes in a calm; p. 127 (n.) In
a calm, it [Bell-Buoy] is dumb; p. 295 (n.) from mere dull work in a
calm; p. 298 (n.) this profound, pervading calm seemed suited; p. 298
(n.) and tranced in one common calm.

White-Jacket--p. 14 (n.) And one hot afternoon, during a calm; p. 80
(n.) One extremely warm night, during a calm; p. 102 (n.) The calm
had commenced in the afternoon; p. 104 (n.) Ere the calm had yet left
us; p. 104 (n.) two ships in a calm, and equally affected; p. 104 (n.)
in our own vicinity the calm still reigns; p. 109 (n.) that
treacherous calm immediately preceding it; p. 222 (n.) accompanied by
foul weather, calms, or head-winds; p. 223 (n.) baffled by light head
winds and frequent . . . calms; p. 223 (n.) might have been doing
that to pass away a calm; p. 325 (n.) Had it only been a gale instead
of a calm; p. 326 (n.) In a calm there was none; p. 332 (n.) the first
day of the long, hot calm; p. 336 (n.) the heat of the night calm was
intense; p. 337 (n.) proclaiming through the calm the expiration;
p. 337 (v./n.) here lie becalmed, in the last calm of all; p. 396 (n.)
been tranced in the last calm.

Moby-Dick--p. 4 (n.) the motion of whose [whales'] vast bodies can in
a peaceful calm trouble the ocean; p. 67 (n.) in the typhoons and
calms of all four oceans; p. 152 (n.) this is worse than pulling
after whales in a calm; p. 263 (n.) An intense copper calm, like a
universal yellow lotus, was more and more unfolding its noiseless
measureless leaves upon the sea; p. 313 (n.) when tranquilly swimming
through the mid-day sea in a calm; p. 324 (n.) we were now in that
enchanted calm which they say lurks at the heart of every commotion;
p. 327 (n.) Yes, the long calm was departing; p. 338 (n.) the faint
air had become a complete calm; p. 406 (n.) would to God these
blessed calms would last; p. 406 (n.) calms crossed by storms, a
storm for every calm; p. 409 (n.) the wide-slaughtering Typhoon and
the hushed burial of its after calm; p. 415 (n.) they will swear in
the trance of the calm.

CANAL. A passage for water; a water course; properly a long trench or
excavation in the earth for conducting water, and confining it to narrow
limits. It is chiefly applied to artificial cuts or passages for water,
used for transportation; whereas channel is applicable to a natural water
course. (Webster)

> Mardi--p. 122 (n.) through the spouting canal of the whales; p. 268
> (n.) while two additional canals afforded; p. 288 (n.) by a third
> canal with four branches.

CANOE. A peculiar boat used by several uncivilized nations, formed of
the trunk of a tree hollowed out, and sometimes of several pieces of bark
joined together, and again of hide. They are of various sizes, according
to the uses for which they are designed, or the countries to which they
belong. Some carry sail, but they are commonly rowed with paddles,
somewhat resembling a corn-shovel; and instead of rowing with it
horizontally, as with an oar, they manage it perpendicularly. (Smyth)

> Typee--p. 5 (n.) carved canoes dancing on the flashing blue waters;
> p. 13 (n.) numerous canoes pushed off from the surrounding shores;
> p. 13 (n.) threatening to capsize the canoes; p. 13 (n.) scattered
> here and there among the canoes; p. 14 (n.) the use of canoes in all
> parts of the island is rigorously prohibited; p. 14 (n.) at the risk
> of swamping their canoes; p. 16 (adj.) Congreve rockets to set fire
> on a few canoe sheds; p. 18 (n.) fled by night in a canoe to Emio;
> p. 25 (n.) was met by a large canoe filled with natives; p. 25 (n.)
> the canoe paddled on and the ship followed; p. 26 (n.) landed in
> boats and canoes at the head of the bay; p. 26 (n.) first descry the
> big canoe of the European; p. 36 (n.) under cover of an immense
> canoe-house; p. 36 (n.) throwing themselves here and there upon the
> large war-canoes; p. 36 (n.) stealing out of the canoe-house; p. 37
> (n.) Since leaving the canoe-house; p. 127 (n.) But whether fishing,
> or carving canoes; p. 132 (n.) brought up a light and tastefully-
> carved canoe; p. 132 (n.) while I paddled about in my light canoe;
> p. 132 (n.) unless the canoe was removed; p. 132 (n.) I not only
> wanted the canoe to stay where it was; p. 133 (n.) should not have as
> much right to enter a canoe as a man; p. 133 (n.) skimmed over its
> surface in their canoes; p. 133 (n.) Fayaway and I reclined in the
> stern of the canoe; p. 134 (n.) paddled the canoe to the windward
> side; p. 134 (n.) As I turned the canoe; p. 134 (n.) with upraised
> arms in the head of the canoe; p. 134 (n.) and the canoe glided
> rapidly; p. 138 (n.) with five war-canoes and hundreds of men; p. 150
> (n.) produced their spears, paddles, canoe-gear; p. 163 (adj.)
> elaborately carved canoe-shaped vessels; p. 172 (n.) seated in the
> stern of a canoe; p. 172 (n.) The canoe was about seven feet in
> length; p. 172 (n.) which crowned the prow of the canoe; p. 173 (n.)
> sometime or other he would go in his own canoe; p. 172 (n.) I see thy
> canoe cleaving the bright waves; p. 175 (n.) hollowed out in the
> likeness of a canoe; p. 176 (n.) tucks the canoe under his arm and
> marches off with it; p. 183 (n.) in rude procession, about seventy
> canoes; p. 183 (n.) two lads paddling their canoes; p. 224 (n.) law
> which forbids a female to enter a canoe; p. 238 (n.) which resembled
> in shape a small canoe; p. 238 (n.) pointing at the same time to the
> canoe; p. 241 (n.) then I take you my canoe Nukuheva; p. 263 (n.) for
> ever coming off in his canoe; p. 266 (n.) who seated herself beside

him on the canoe; p. 267 (n.) all by himself, seated upon the broken
canoe; p. 270 (n.) they entered a canoe.

Omoo--p. 21 (n.) a still gliding canoe stole out; p. 27 (n.) we
awaited the arrival of a canoe; p. 27 (n.) the canoe came alongside;
p. 29 (n.) the farewell shouts from the canoe; p. 63 (n.) to load one
of the large sea-canoes; p. 95 (n.) a small canoe was launched; p. 99
(n.) a canoe, coming out from among them; p. 99 (n.) brought the
canoe quite near; p. 100 (n.) darted the canoe right up to the
gangway; p. 102 (n.) palm-trees and elms--canoes and skiffs--; p. 146
(n.) he took umbrage at a canoe full of natives; p. 146 (n.) The
alarmed islanders, beaching their canoe; p. 152 (n.) coming off from
the shore in their canoes; p. 152 (n.) his canoe came alongside;
p. 152 (n.) his canoe came gliding slowly; p. 153 (n.) his canoe,
loaded down to the gunwhale; p. 153 (n.) in the bow of his canoe;
p. 160 (n.) foragers borrowing Captain Bob's canoe; p. 160 (n.) a
canoe is the most ticklish of navigable things; p. 160 (n.) But a
word about the canoes; p. 160 (n.) of seventeen hundred and twenty
large war-canoes; p. 160 (n.) floating alongside, parallel to the
canoes; p. 160 (n.) the canoe can not be overturned; p. 161 (n.)
when the canoe gave a roll; p. 161 (n.) Depressing one end of the
filled canoe; p. 161 (n.) to urge the canoe along by myself; p. 163
(n.) As my canoe drew scarcely three inches of water; p. 163 (n.) I
at last dashed the canoe right up to the wall; p. 176 (n.) The canoes
are hauled up on the beach; p. 203 (n.) napping on the shady side of
a canoe; p. 210 (n.) to an opposite village in their canoes; p. 213
(n.) Zeke called this the canoe-tree; p. 214 (n.) for canoe-building,
the wood is; p. 216 (n.) It was an old war-canoe; p. 216 (n.) The
canoe was at least forty feet long; p. 216 (n.) the creature darted
into the canoe; p. 216 (n.) had attacked his own end of the canoe;
p. 216 (n.) so a small fishing canoe; p. 226 (n.) Dozing in our canoe
the next morning; p. 226 (n.) he told us that a canoe had arrived;
p. 238 (n.) Several small canoes, moored here; p. 242 (n.) Rartoo
fairly dragged us away to a canoe; p. 246 (n.) sprang into a canoe
before the door; p. 250 (n.) round the island in a canoe; p. 250 (n.)
The idea of journeying in a canoe; p. 250 (n.) fall in with a canoe
going our way; p. 255 (n.) where a fleet of canoes was dancing up and
down; p. 262 (n.) and cords for his canoes; p. 262 (n.) He impels his
canoe through the water; p. 263 (adj.) We might then . . . join a
small canoe party; p. 268 (n.) sprang into a sort of family canoe;
p. 268 (n.) about the old men who managed the canoe; p. 269 (n.) We
encountered another canoe; p. 269 (n.) a kind of royal mail-canoe;
p. 269 (n.) forcing our canoe among the bushes; p. 270 (n.) As the
canoe turned a bluff; p. 289 (n.) we jumped into the canoe; p. 289
(n.) harl the poor divils' canow alongside; p. 290 (n.) we dropped
into our canoe; p. 292 (n.) came off to them in their canoes; p. 305
(n.) paddled over to Imeeo, in a canoe; p. 316 (n.) and the canoe
came alongside.

Mardi--p. 40 (n.) through a Caribbean canoe; p. 70 (n.) some in
canoes; p. 70 (n.) concealed in the canoes; p. 71 (n.) some in canoes;
p. 71 (n.) paddling a canoe therein; p. 85 (n.) they took for a canoe;
p. 127 (n.) proving a large double-canoe; p. 127 (n.) we headed away
for the canoe; p. 127 (adj.) and the canoe's wide yawing; p. 127 (n.)
a pair of parallel canoes; p. 128 (n.) prow of that canoe; p. 128
(n.) prostrate inclination of the twin canoes; p. 128 (n.) few

minutes' uproar in the canoe; p. 129 (n.) again stopped their canoe;
p. 129 (n.) a sheer toward the canoe; p. 129 (n.) one of their sacred
canoes; p. 130 (n.) I dropped into the canoe; p. 132 (adj.) against
the canoe's quarter; p. 132 (n.) As we boarded the canoe; p. 133 (n.)
to push us from the canoe; p. 133 (n.) the line that held us to the
canoe; p. 133 (n.) rapidly shot from the canoe; p. 134 (n.) we rowed
for the canoe; p. 134 (n.) As we drew near the canoe; p. 134 (n.) on
the sea, the ill-fated canoe; p. 135 (adj.) brought round to the
canoe's stern; p. 138 (n.) Yillah was to descend in a canoe; p. 140
(n.) her tent into my own canoe; p. 141 (n.) stern of their canoe;
p. 141 (n.) to regain their canoe; p. 141 (n.) dropped the evil-boding
canoe; p. 148 (n.) a day or two after parting with the canoe; p. 152
(n.) of the people of the canoe; p. 157 (n.) where the canoe was in
waiting; p. 160 (n.) no sign of paddle or canoe; p. 161 (n.) A canoe!
a canoe; p. 161 (n.) enlivened by fleets of canoes; p. 161 (n.)
whither all the canoes were now hastening; p. 161 (n.) passing canoe
after canoe; p. 164 (n.) fleet canoes had been dispatched; p. 165 (n.)
navigated by canoes; p. 168 (n.) designating a canoe-house hard by;
p. 177 (n.) because it is unlike a canoe; p. 181 (n.) we journeyed to
the canoe-house; p. 188 (n.) sufficient to float a canoe; p. 189 (n.)
dim glimpses of a canoe; p. 192 (n.) not hearses but canoes; p. 196
(n.) three canoes were selected; p. 199 (n.) what monsters of canoes;
p. 199 (n.) the canoes were odoriferous; p. 199 (n.) likeness of the
foremost canoe; p. 199 (n.) in the head of the canoe; p. 200 (n.) Of
these canoes; p. 200 (n.) by the more swan-like canoes; p. 201 (n.)
our canoes keeled the bottom; p. 213 (n.) So the three canoes were
brought; p. 213 (n.) the canoes at last shooting; p. 215 (n.)
overtaken by a swift gliding canoe; p. 217 (n.) Our canoes were
secured; p. 261 (n.) determined to depart for our canoes; p. 267 (n.)
That still canoe drew nigh; p. 273 (n.) repaired to their canoes;
p. 285 (n.) greeted by six fine canoes; p. 285 (n.) these canoes
floated with ours; p. 285 (n.) of the largest canoe of the six;
p. 286 (n.) for the occupants of our canoes; p. 286 (n.) so that no
canoe could sail; p. 295 (n.) placing him in their canoe; p. 300 (n.)
Let no canoes put to sea; p. 302 (n.) By torch light, numerous canoes;
p. 302 (n.) the canoes all headed toward the openings; p. 303 (n.)
the canoes were disposed in a circle; p. 306 (n.) to the Motoo one of
his fleetest canoes; p. 306 (n.) the canoe that was going to Tedaidee;
p. 306 (n.) the canoe, the canoe of Aleema; p. 307 (n.) a mighty
canoe, full of beings; p. 308 (n.) stealing from their great canoe;
p. 308 (n.) the maiden in yonder canoe; p. 311 (n.) and a canoe of
Mondoldo being about to proceed; p. 321 (n.) found dead in the canoe;
p. 312 (n.) shark's mouth of Media's canoe; p. 312 (n.) eyeing the
receding canoes; p. 313 (n.) As the canoes now glided; p. 316 (n.) we
descried a sharp-prowed canoe; p. 316 (n.) he has swamped three
canoes; p. 317 (n.) quickly turning about his canoe; p. 318 (n.) did
that devil Tribonnora swamp your canoe; p. 318 (n.) If we had had a
canoe; p. 318 (n.) who daily runs down canoes; p. 326 (n.) trappings
of our canoes were removed; p. 326 (n.) in silence we beached our
canoes; p. 327 (n.) one canoe-load of bread-fruit and yams; p. 334
(n.) swimming beside his canoe; p. 354 (n.) highly lucrative business
of canoe-building; p. 354 (n.) neglecting his images, for his canoes;
p. 354 (n.) to three long rows of canoes; p. 354 (n.) Hevaneva's
canoes were in as high repute; p. 354 (n.) of the hollow part of the
canoes; p. 354 (n.) for my images, than for my canoes; p. 355 (n.)
Having taken to our canoes once again; p. 358 (n.) putting out in his

canoe; p. 361 (n.) just after leaving the canoes; p. 364 (n.) But a
fleet canoe was missing; p. 364 (n.) the three canoes had been
reversed; p. 370 (n.) our gloomy canoe seemed a hearse; p. 383 (n.)
torn asunder by Swift-Going Canoes; p. 398 (n.) The canoes sailed on;
p. 399 (n.) elaborately carved canoes; p. 402 (n.) carved work of
certain fantastic canoes; p. 402 (n.) paddlers in charge of our
canoes; p. 414 (n.) the canoes were put about; p. 422 (n.) tracking
the course of a low canoe; p. 432 (n.) our three canoes seemed
baiting by the way; p. 444 (n.) our canoes had been dragged out of
the water; p. 452 (n.) the embargo laid upon our canoes; p. 453 (n.)
In a canoe-fight, after performing; p. 461 (n.) My sire had a canoe
launched; p. 465 (n.) all by himself, in a solitary canoe; p. 466 (n.)
over to Dominora in a canoe; p. 469 (n.) his numerous fleets of war-
canoes; p. 469 (n.) meeting upon the broad lagoon certain canoes;
p. 469 (n.) dragged into the canoes of Dominora; p. 469 (n.) fitting
our several double-keeled canoes; p. 469 (n.) down upon the canoes of
the men; p. 470 (n.) found the canoes of Vivenza much larger; p. 470
(n.) the canoes of Vivenza, locking their yard-arms; p. 471 (n.) The
three canoes still gliding on; p. 471 (n.) he dispatched canoes to
the spot; p. 477 (n.) his navy of three large canoes; p. 478 (n.)
laden down with heavy-freighted canoes; p. 482 (n.) each possessed
long state canoes; p. 482 (n.) often boxed about his canoes; p. 499
(n.) multitudes pushing off wildly in canoes; p. 509 (n.) The canoes
were passing a long, white reef; p. 512 (n.) The canoes drew near;
pp. 517-8 (n.) His canoe-yards are all in commotion; p. 524 (n.) in
wait for canoes periodically bringing; p. 536 (n.) swarms of laborers
discharging from canoes; p. 536 (n.) they pay a price for every canoe-
load; p. 543 (n.) the three canoes raced on; p. 543 (n.) a snow-
hillock, eacn canoe; p. 549 (n.) whenever a canoe is beached; p. 567
(n.) we launched our three canoes; p. 568 (n.) Sleep reigned
throughout the canoes; p. 568 (n.) glided a second canoe; p. 573 (n.)
by giving each canoe a vigorous triple-push; p. 618 (n.) our speeding
canoes were reversed; p. 622 (n.) the three canoes lurched heavily;
p. 622 (n.) floating from the east, a lone canoe; p. 642 (n.) voyaged
in gala canoes all round the lagoon; p. 644 (n.) and keels of canoes.

White-Jacket--p. 58 (n.) Oh! I los' my shoe in an old canoe; p. 212
(n.) of the war-canoes of the Polynesian kings; p. 246 (n.) with the
view of gaining a canoe; p. 246 (n.) In this canoe he proposed.

Moby-Dick--p. 17 (n.) did those aboriginal whalemen, the Red-Men,
first sally out in canoes; p. 396 (n.) like a whale-boat these
coffin-canoes were without a keel.

CANVAS(S). A cloth made of hemp, and used for the sails of ships. It is
purchased in bolts, and numbered from 1 to 8, rarely to 9 and 10. Number
1 being the coarsest and strongest, is used for the lower sails, as fore-
sail and main-sail in large ships. When a vessel is in motion by means
of her sails she is said to be under canvas. (Smyth)

Mardi--p. 3 (n.) Out spreads the canvas--slow, aloft--boom-stretched;
p. 71 (n.) brave show of canvas.

White-Jacket--p. 106 (n.) the enormous horizontal strain on the canvas;
p. 107 (n.) laid out to stow the shattered canvas; p. 120 (adj.) as a

pair of canvas pants spread to dry; p. 195 (n.) piling up the
ponderous folds of canvass; p. 195 (n.) violently treading down the
canvass; p. 202 (n.) How many fathoms of canvass in it; p. 261 (n.)
in a sort of shroud of white canvass; p. 311 (n.) so that the canvass
on the main-mast; p. 311 (n.) immense area of snow-white canvas;
p. 338 (n.) carrying some canvass; p. 338 (n.) after fitting the
canvass to it; p. 338 (adj.) in the foot of the canvass shroud;
p. 339 (n.) That last thing you do to the canvass; p. 339 (n.)
palsied hands were quivering over the canvass.

CAPE. A projecting point of land jutting out from the coastline; the
extremity of a promontory. It differs from a headland, since a cape may
be low. The Cape of Good Hope is always familiarly known as "The Cape."
(Smyth)

Typee--p. 21 (n.) We had left both law and equity on the other side
of the Cape; p. 21 (n.) the longevity of Cape Horn shaling voyages;
p. 155 (n.) from the North Pole to the parallel of Cape Horn; p. 223
(n.) off the pitch of Cape Horn; p. 223 (n.) he would bring down
albatrosses, Cape pigeons, jays.

Omoo--p. 81 (n.) dreaming of ever doubling Cape Horn again; p. 164
(n.) by way of the Cape of Good Hope; p. 164 (n.) vessels coming
round Cape Horn; p. 202 (n.) of Peru, near Cape Blanco; p. 315 (n.)
would be going round Cape Horn.

Mardi--p. 511 (n.) From cape to cape; p. 543 (n.) They round the
stormy Cape of Capes; p. 653 (n.) as fierce as headwinds off capes.

Redburn--p. 57 (n.) by an English cruiser off Cape Verde; p. 90 (n.)
doctor themselves with calomel off Cape Horn; p. 104 (n.) farder off
dan de Cape of Dood Hope; p. 107 (n.) of harpooneers round Cape Horn;
p. 111 (n.) when we made Cape Clear; p. 200 (n.) just as long in
Liverpool as at Cape Horn; p. 259 (n.) showed as Cape Clear; p. 285
(n.) We had been outside of Cape Clear; p. 294 (n.) Off Cape Cod;
p. 294 (n.) Off Cape Cod!

White-Jacket--p. 3 (n.) being bound for Cape Horn; p. 4 (n.) in which
to weather Cape Horn; p. 4 (n.) of scudding round Cape Horn in my
shirt; p. 32 (n.) outward-bound, off Cape Horn; p. 33 (n.) off Cape
Horn or Hatteras; p. 48 (n.) who had been shipped at the Cape De Verd
islands; p. 62 (adj.) called themselves the Cape Horn Snorters and
Neversink Invincibles; p. 78 (n.) Cape Horn is at hand; p. 83 (n.)
Off Cape Horn; p. 84 (n.) off Cape Horn; p. 89 (n.) from the frigid
latitudes of Cape Horn; p. 92 (n.) CAPE HORN THEATRE; p. 92 (n.) The
managers of the Cape Horn Theatre beg leave; p. 96 (n.) Introductory
to Cape Horn; p. 96 (n.) drew nearer . . . to the squally Cape; p. 96
(n.) Cape Horn, Cape Horn; p. 96 (n.) first navigators' weathering of
that terrible cape; p. 96 (n.) to the Cape of Good Hope; p. 96 (n.)
And that stormy cape; p. 96 (n.) Impracticable Cape; p. 96 (n.) still
Cape Horn is Cape Horn. Cape Horn it is that takes; p. 97 (n.)
oftentimes, off Cape Horn, receives a lesson; p. 97 (n.) rashly
conclude that the Cape, after all; p. 97 (n.) he who goes oftenest
round Cape Horn; p. 97 (n.) toward the latitude of the Cape; p. 98
(n.) some who seem to regard the genius of the Cape; p. 98 (n.) they

<u>polish</u> the Cape; p. 98 (n.) who weathered Cape Horn; p. 98 (n.) which
gave its name to the Cape; p. 98 (n.) The next navigator round the
Cape was; p. 99 (n.) But if you want the best idea of Cape Horn;
p. 99 (n.) His chapters describing Cape Horn; p. 99 (n.) the horrors
of the Cape have somewhat abated; p. 100 (n.) The dog-days off Cape
Horn; p. 100 (n.) we are drawing nigh to the Cape; p. 101 (n.) coming
up with the latitude of the Cape; p. 101 (n.) becalmed off Cape Horn;
p. 104 (n.) The Pitch of the Cape; p. 104 (n.) these remote seas off
Cape Horn; p. 105 (n.) was Cape Horn so audaciously insulted; p. 105
(n.) Look out for Cape Horn; p. 106 (n.) by single combat with the
spirit of the Cape; p. 109 (n.) without encountering Cape Horn;
p. 109 (n.) there is some sort of a Cape Horn for all; p. 109 (n.)
your Cape Horns are placid as Lake Lemans; p. 109 (n.) had the Spirit
of the Cape said the word; p. 111 (n.) off the pitch of the Cape;
p. 112 (n.) But with Cape Horn before him; p. 115 (n.) a passage from
the Pacific round the Cape; p. 116 (n.) Cape Horn was said to be
somewhere; p. 116 (n.) The land near Cape Horn . . . is well worth
seeing; p. 116 (n.) After leaving the latitude of the Cape; p. 117
(n.) found many phenomena off Cape Horn; p. 119 (n.) Though leaving
the Cape behind us; p. 121 (n.) Jacketless so near Cape Horn; p. 121
(n.) consequent on leaving Cape Horn; p. 121 (n.) One word more about
Cape Horn; p. 122 (n.) in the cars at Cape Cod for Astoria; p. 122
(n.) by going round Cape Horn; p. 131 (n.) while we were yet running
away from the Cape; p. 200 (n.) Twas on a winter evening, off Cape
Horn; p. 202 (n.) on either side of Cape Horn; p. 228 (n.) used it as
a counterpane off Cape Horn; p. 270 (adj.) shortly after the Cape
Horn theatricals; p. 328 (n.) we were driving near to Cape Horn;
p. 330 (n.) off the pitch of Cape Horn; p. 330 (n.) What sailors call
the Cape Horn Fever; p. 330 (n.) that off Cape Horn; p. 353 (n.)
previous to our weathering Cape Horn; p. 353 (n.) Off Cape Horn it
looked; p. 391 (n.) now somewhere off the Capes of Virginia; p. 395
(n.) the blessed Capes of Virginia are believed to be.

<u>Moby-Dick</u>--p. 16 (n.) I . . . started for Cape Horn and the Pacific;
p. 20 (n.) The picture represents a Cape-Horner in a great hurricane;
p. 21 (n.) a whale, years afterwards slain off the Cape of Blanco;
p. 22 (n.) the full glass--the Cape Horn measure, which you may gulp
down for a shilling; p. 52 (n.) twenty thousand miles from home, by
the way of Cape Horn, that is; p. 75 (n.) to founder the largest ship
that ever sailed round Cape Horn; p. 76 (n.) to carry Queequeg and me
round the Cape; p. 100 (n.) Until the whale fishery rounded Cape Horn;
p. 103 (adj.) far-away domestic memories of his [Starbuck's] young
Cape wife and child; p. 105 (n.) Stubb . . . was called a Cape-Cod-
man; p. 160 (n.) that dreary, howling Patagonian Cape.

<u>CAPSTAN</u>. A mechanical arrangement for lifting great weights. There is a
variety of capstans, but they agree in having a horizontal circular head,
which has square holes around its edge, and in these long bars are
shipped; beneath is a perpendicular barrel, round which is wrapped the
rope or chain used to lift the anchor or other great weight, even to the
heaving a ship off a shoal. (Smyth)

<u>Typee</u>--p. 22 (n.) and led to the capstan or windlass.

Omoo--p. 33 (n.) was leaning against the capstan; p. 36 (n.) draughts
were mixed on the capstan; p. 48 (n.) which was served out at the
capstan; p. 147 (n.) were laid on the capstan-head.

Redburn--p. 117 (n.) Then the magnificent capstan; p. 175 (n.) as
they did about the capstan.

White-Jacket--p. 6 (n.) Man the capstan; p. 6 (n.) capstan-bars in
their places; p. 7 (n.) and heaved round that capstan; p. 16 (n.)
mustering round the capstan; p. 31 (n.) to carry the strain of the
cable to the capstan; p. 31 (n.) cable itself going round the
capstan; p. 93 (adj.) The capstan bars were placed on shot-boxes;
p. 94 (adj.) overturned the capstan bars; p. 156 (n.) but the great
gun-runners and capstan-bars; p. 171 (n.) he looked like a capstan;
p. 226 (n.) the quarter-watch mustered round the capstan; p. 226 (n.)
piled up on the capstan; p. 258 (n.) placing it on the gun-deck
capstan; p. 290 (n.) to gain her own quarters at the capstan; p. 292
(n.) Monthly Muster round the Capstan; p. 292 (n.) we had a grand
muster round the capstan; p. 357 (n.) Muster round the capstan;
p. 396 (n.) We have mustered our last round the capstan.

Moby-Dick--p. 94 (n.) Man the capstan! Blood and thunder!--jump;
p. 388 (n.) Teeth he accounted bits of ivory; heads he deemed but
top-blocks; men themselves he lightly held for capstans.

CAPTAIN. This title is said to be derived from the eastern military
magistrate Katapan, meaning "over everything." The captain, strictly
speaking, is the officer commanding a line-of-battle ship, or a frigate
carrying twenty or more cannon. It is also a title, though incorrectly,
given to the masters of all vessels whatever, they having no commissions.
It is also applied in the navy itself to the chief sailor of particular
gangs of men; in rank, captain of the forecastle, admiral's coxswain,
captain's coxswain, captain of the hold, captain of the maintop, captain
of the foretop, &c. (Smyth)

Typee--p. 4 (n.) devoured by the Captain's pig; p. 4 (n.) laid out
upon the captain's table next Sunday; p. 4 (n.) the captain will
never point the ship for land; p. 4 (n.) the captain will come to his
senses; p. 4 (n.) when the captain found fault with his steering;
p. 4 (n.) why, d'ye see, Captain Vangs; p. 7 (n.) between one of
their captains and our worthy commodore; p. 10 (n.) The captain,
darting on deck; p. 11 (n.) when they were discovered by Captain
Ingraham; p. 11 (n.) Captain Porter refitted his ships; p. 11 (n.) by
Captain Porter was denominated Massachusetts Bay; p. 13 (n.) Our
captain, however, rather distrusted his ability; p. 21 (n.) The
captain was the author of these abuses; p. 21 (n.) the unmitigated
tyranny of the captain; p. 21 (n.) the united influences of Captain
Marryat and hard times; p. 22 (n.) obstacle . . . is overcome by
head-strong captains; p. 25 (n.) The captain, unacquainted with the
localities; p. 30 (n.) our worthy captain, who felt such a paternal
solicitude; p. 34 (n.) our worthy captain, standing in the cabin
gangway; p. 35 (adj.) in spite of the captain's croakings; p. 36 (n.)
immediately communicated it to the captain; p. 74 (n.) some intrepid
captain will touch on the skirts of the bay; p. 95 (n.) A baked baby,
by the soul of Captain Cook; p. 140 (n.) by the captain of a trading

vessel; p. 140 (n.) the captain had, at his own request; p. 223 (n.)
our worthy captain formed one of the party; p. 252 (n.) The captain
of an Australian vessel; p. 255 (n.) especially upon Captain Charlton;
p. 255 (n.) Captain Charlton, insultingly forbidden to leave the
islands; p. 255 (n.) to intimate to the British Captain that he could
not; p. 256 (n.) and captain of the fort; p. 270 (n.) The captain
professed great pleasure at seeing Toby; p. 270 (n.) But this the
captain would not hear of; p. 270 (n.) The captain was unwilling to
give them; p. 271 (n.) when the captain came forward and ordered.

Omoo--p. 3 (n.) where the captain had been informed; p. 6 (n.) I was
sent for into the cabin by the captain; p. 6 (n.) more like a sickly
counting-house clerk than a bluff sea-captain; p. 6 (n.) not . . .
that the captain felt any great compassion; p. 10 (n.) The captain
was a young cockney; p. 10 (n.) had been given his captain in charge;
p. 10 (n.) the silent captain had more to do with the men; p. 11 (n.)
plain that the captain stood in awe of him; p. 11 (n.) plays cards
with the captain; p. 11 (n.) the doctor and the captain lived
together as pleasantly; p. 12 (n.) left the captain on the floor
literally silenced; p. 12 (n.) would not live any longer with the
captain; p. 13 (n.) The captain, having for some time past; p. 14 (n.)
the captain should be willing to keep the sea; p. 15 (n.) Nor was the
captain without hope; p. 15 (n.) that Captain Guy was resolved upon
retrieving the past; p. 17 (n.) It was the captain; p. 18 (n.) Jump
down here, Captain Guy; p. 18 (n.) Come on, Captain Guy; p. 18 (n.)
As the captain once more dipped his head; p. 18 (n.) above the low,
smooth voice of the captain; p. 18 (n.) the captain finally assured
him; p. 19 (n.) This pleased our captain exceedingly; p. 20 (n.) to
tell the captain the news; p. 21 (n.) when Captain Guy made his
appearance; p. 23 (n.) Captain Guy caused the ship to be got underway;
p. 23 (n.) deliberation on the part of the captain and mate; p. 24
(n.) followed over the side by the invalid captain; p. 24 (n.) the
captain started to his feet; p. 24 (n.) when the captain standing up
in its head; p. 24 (n.) The captain declined; p. 25 (n.) Not unusual
on the part of sea captains; p. 27 (n.) the speechless fright of the
captain; p. 28 (n.) as the captain could have no reason to suppose;
p. 34 (n.) the captain again relapsed; p. 45 (n.) before the captain
should demand it; p. 47 (n.) The captain--a mere cipher--was an
invalid; p. 47 (adj.) the captain's nautical knowledge being
insufficient; p. 50 (n.) that Captain Guy was reported as fast
declining; p. 50 (adj.) Tne captain's anchor is pretty nigh atrip;
p. 51 (n.) that if the captain died; p. 51 (n.) that if Captain Guy
was no better in twenty-four hours; p. 51 (n.) The captain was no
better; p. 53 (n.) on the way he is met by the captain; p. 53 (n.)
calls upon the captain to save him; p. 68 (n.) should the captain
leave the ship; p. 69 (adj.) in the stern-sheets of the captain's
boat; p. 69 (n.) the captain, doubtless, intended to set himself
ashore; p. 69 (n.) Invalid whaling captains often adopt a plan;
p. 70 (n.) the captain should have his own way; p. 70 (n.) The
captain was helped on deck; p. 70 (n.) he was going ashore with the
captain; p. 70 (n.) For the nonce, Bembo was captain; p. 73 (n.)
After the captain left; p. 73 (n.) having left the captain at
Papeetee; p. 73 (n.) of what Captain Guy seemed bent upon; p. 75 (n.)
he and Captain Guy were as sociable as could be; p. 78 (n.) formerly
belonging to Captain Guy; p. 81 (n.) As Captain Guy will remain
ashore; p. 82 (n.) for your captain; p. 82 (n.) between him and the

captain; p. 84 (n.) to see how the captain did; p. 87 (adj.) occupying
the captain's arm-chair; p. 87 (n.) our not coming back for the
captain; p. 89 (adj.) since the captain's departure; p. 94 (adj.) in
the captain's state-room; p. 94 (n.) by the captain, Jermin, and the
third mate; p. 95 (adj.) a Lascar in the captain's boat went crazy;
p. 102 (n.) Captain Guy's ashore; p. 103 (n.) of the agreement made
with Captain Guy; p. 107 (n.) had been captain of the foretop; p. 110
(n.) such a devil of a fellow for a captain; p. 113 (n.) with dislike
by his captain; p. 113 (n.) Little as I had seen of Captain Guy;
p. 117 (n.) he went by the name of Capin Bob (Captain Bob); p. 117
(n.) Captain Bob proceeded to "hannapar"; p. 117 (n.) Captain Bob now
bustled about; p. 118 (n.) Captain Bob and his friends lived in a
little hamlet; p. 119 (n.) big man when Capin Tootee (Captain Cook)
heavey in sight; p. 120 (n.) Captain Bob waddled up to us; p. 128 (n.)
for the humanity of sea captains; p. 128 (n.) as our captain was
inexorable; p. 130 (n.) reflections on the consul and Captain Guy;
p. 131 (n.) indulgence on the part of Captain Bob; p. 131 (n.) which
we obtained from Captain Bob; p. 132 (n.) As Captain Bob insensibly
remitted his watchfulness; p. 138 (n.) We Are Carried before the
Consul and Captain; p. 138 (n.) Captain Bob, coming from the bath;
p. 139 (n.) a couch, where Captain Guy reclined; p. 139 (n.) was the
deposition of the captain himself; p. 139 (n.) Captain Guy there,
knows as well as we; p. 140 (n.) the bench of judges communed with
Captain Guy; p. 140 (n.) Hereupon the consul and captain exchanged
glances; p. 140 (n.) no thanks to the benevolence of its captain;
p. 140 (adj.) he summed up Captain Guy's character; p. 140 (n.)
taking the consul and the captain back to the Calabooza; p. 140 (n.)
ordering Captain Bob and his friends to escort us; p. 144 (adj.) much
to Captain Bob's consternation; p. 145 (n.) addressed his invalid
friend, the captain; p. 146 (adj.) tapping the captain's quarter-casks;
p. 146 (n.) the consul and Captain Guy were having a quiet game;
p. 146 (n.) the captain dared not object; p. 147 (n.) that Captain
Guy had gone on board his vessel; p. 148 (n.) they were hard against
Captain Guy; p. 148 (n.) as for the captain; p. 148 (n.) the conduct
all along, of the consul and captain; p. 149 (n.) when Captain Bob,
waddling into the Calabooza; p. 149 (n.) stood Captain Guy; p. 150
(n.) On this hand, Captain Bob could tell us nothing; p. 150 (adj.)
no better place than Captain Bob's; p. 151 (n.) Captain Bob going
along; p. 159 (n.) invariably told by the captains; p. 159 (adj.)
settling down quietly at Captain Bob's; p. 159 (n.) against both
consul and captain; p. 160 (adj.) the foragers borrowing Captain
Bob's canoe; p. 160 (adj.) Captain Bob's gig was exceedingly small;
p. 163 (n.) by captains of British armed ships; p. 165 (n.) certain
man-of-war and merchant captains; p. 166 (adj.) life at Captain Bob's
was pleasant enough; p. 178 (adj.) not fifty rods from Captain Bob's;
p. 179 (adj.) applauded Captain Bob's spirit; p. 182 (n.) A bachelor
friend of Captain Bob; p. 183 (n.) as described to me, by Captain Bob;
p. 186 (n.) Captain Beechey says; p. 187 (n.) under the command of
Captain F. W. Beechey; p. 188 (n.) The excellent Captain Wilson . . .
affirms; p. 188 (n.) Captain Beechey, in alluding to the "Polynesian
Researches" of Ellis; p. 191 (n.) Captain Cook estimated the
population of Tahiti; p. 193 (n.) This voucher, endorsed by Captain
Guy; p. 197 (n.) all the natives but good old Captain Bob; p. 197
(adj.) Captain Bob's men raised the most outrageous cries; p. 198 (n.)
hurriedly addressing Captain Bob in Tahitian; p. 215 (n.) a whaling
captain, touching at an adjoining bay; p. 235 (n.) but Captain Bob

had often shown us one; p. 245 (n.) and found a festival in honor of
Captain Cook; p. 255 (n.) So told me, Captain Bob; p. 259 (n.) A
pompous captain of a man-of-war; p. 265 (n.) like Captain Bob, he was,
in some things; p. 289 (n.) called after its discoverer, Captain
Cook; p. 299 (n.) but Captain Crash, as they called him; p. 299 (n.)
the next day, Captain Crash entertains the sailors; p. 299 (n.)
dismissed every body but Captain Crash; p. 299 (n.) the captain and
girl were first tried together; p. 300 (n.) Captain Crash might have
been seen; p. 303 (n.) whaling captains, and the like; p. 304 (n.)
from the captains of the vessels lying in Papeetee; p. 304 (n.)
Captain Bob once told me the story; p. 312 (n.) But I had seen the
captain; p. 313 (n.) the captain was the finest man in the world;
p. 313 (n.) so as to oblige the captain; p. 313 (n.) that American
sea captains, in the Pacific; p. 313 (n.) was pointed out by the
captain; p. 314 (n.) I found the captain smoking a pipe; p. 314 (n.)
I could not help loving the free-hearted captain; p. 315 (n.) that
the captain, having made good the number.

Mardi--p. 5 (n.) some despot of a captain; p. 6 (n.) of my captain;
p. 6 (n.) Captain; p. 7 (n.) my fine captain; p. 7 (n.) the captain
well knew; p. 10 (adj.) the captain's competency; p. 16 (n.) with
the captain; p. 19 (n.) captain, mates, crew; p. 28 (n.) cried the
captain; p. 28 (n.) again shouted the captain; p. 28 (n.) hoarse
shout of the captain; p. 29 (n.) from all efforts of the captain;
p. 68 (n.) captain included; p. 68 (n.) the captain having bargained;
p. 69 (n.) the Parki's Captain; p. 69 (n.) dining with the captain;
p. 69 (n.) prevailed upon the captain; p. 69 (n.) in whom the captain
much confided; p. 70 (adj.) until the captain's return; p. 70 (adj.)
the captain's three loaded muskets; p. 75 (adj.) found in the
captain's chests; p. 75 (n.) like the valiant captains; p. 76 (adj.)
upon the captain's arms; p. 81 (adj.) in the captain's state room;
p. 87 (n.) which the captain of the Parki; p. 93 (adj.) the captain's
writing desk; p. 94 (n.) Better we, than the captain; p. 95 (n.)
appropriation by the Captain; p. 95 (n.) honest captain sketched this
cenotaph; p. 97 (n.) by his side like a captain; p. 101 (adj.) jaunty
shorecap of the captain's; p. 106 (n.) the ill-fated captain of the
Parki; p. 106 (n.) immediately connected with the unfortunate captain;
p. 107 (n.) the departed captain had very wisely kept; p. 110 (n.)
because the captain well knew that strict watchfulness; p. 110 (n.)
for that period was captain; p. 127 (n.) provided for barter by the
captain.

Redburn--p. 4 (n.) with sunburnt sea-captains going in and out; p. 8
(adj.) in a story-book about Captain Kidd's ship; p. 9 (n.) while the
captain in a glass cup was smoking; p. 12 (adj.) going to the
captain's office to pay my passage; p. 12 (adj.) the captain's clerk,
a slender young man; p. 15 (n.) and found the captain in the cabin;
p. 15 (n.) As soon as I clapped my eye on the captain; p. 15 (n.) he
was just the captain to suit me; p. 15 (n.) said the captain; p. 15
(n.) said the captain, blandly; p. 16 (n.) said the captain to my
friend; p. 16 (n.) said the captain, looking funny; p. 16 (n.) echoed
the captain; p. 16 (n.) said the captain, looking grave and bland
again; p. 16 (n.) the handsome captain looked ten times more funny;
p. 16 (n.) Pray, captain, how much do you generally pay; p. 16 (n.)
said the captain, looking grave and profound; p. 17 (n.) Why,
captain, . . . that won't pay for his clothing; p. 17 (n.) replied

the captain; p. 17 (n.) said the captain smiling; p. 17 (n.) said the captain smiling; p. 17 (n.) to purchase it, captain, to shoot gulls; p. 17 (n.) said the captain; p. 17 (n.) Well, then, captain, you can only give; p. 17 (n.) said the captain; p. 17 (n.) said the captain, with a bow; p. 17 (n.) accosted the captain on my own account; p. 18 (n.) we bade the captain good-morning; p. 26 (n.) he had arranged with the captain; p. 27 (n.) at last the captain came up the side; p. 31 (n.) baskets of wine and fruit for the captain; p. 35 (n.) an old sea-captain; p. 35 (n.) that he was with Captain Langsdorff; p. 35 (n.) when Captain Langsdorff crossed over by land; p. 35 (n.) he was the very first sea-captain; p. 36 (n.) giving orders instead of the captain; p. 37 (n.) stood apart talking with the captain; p. 39 (n.) not deemed company at any time for the captain; p. 40 (n.) accountable to nobody but the captain; p. 43 (n.) as if the captain had sent his cheese-parings; p. 46 (n.) Some sea-captains, before shipping a man; p. 52 (n.) I ever dreamed of becoming a captain; p. 54 (n.) just as captains of fire engines, love to point; p. 58 (n.) always saved the captain for the last; p. 61 (n.) I thought of going to the captain about it; p. 61 (n.) for the captain would only have called me a fool; p. 67 (n.) He Contemplates Making a Social Call on the Captain; p. 67 (n.) the widely altered manner of the captain toward me; p. 67 (n.) some sea-captains are fathers to their crew; p. 67 (n.) I thought that Captain Riga; p. 68 (n.) from the captain to my brother; p. 68 (adj.) without the captain's speaking to me; p. 69 (n.) to pay my respects to the captain; p. 69 (n.) the captain has some nuts and raisins for him; p. 69 (n.) I would complain to my friend the captain; p. 69 (n.) how I had found the captain; p. 69 (n.) for sailors to call on the captain; p. 70 (n.) or the captain was lounging over a decanter; p. 70 (n.) when the captain suddenly made his appearance; p. 70 (n.) both by him and Captain Riga; p. 70 (n.) to lift my hat to the captain; p. 70 (n.) of the dignity of the captain; p. 70 (n.) I resolved to let the captain alone; p. 70 (n.) the captain rushed out of the cabin; p. 71 (n.) Yes, Captain Riga, thought I; p. 72 (adj.) I have been speaking of the captain's old clothes; p. 75 (n.) Mr. Jones had hinted to the captain; p. 75 (n.) and the captain in a green jacket; p. 76 (n.) Our captain, who had put on; p. 76 (n.) To which the other captain rejoined; p. 76 (n.) the manner of the two sea-captains; p. 83 (n.) visited the captain in the cabin; p. 83 (n.) cast-off suits of the captain of a London liner; p. 88 (n.) used to be dunning a sea-captain; pp. 95-6 (n.) pitched upon by an ingenious sea-captain; p. 97 (n.) for the captain to inspect; p. 97 (n.) proved by the captain in person; p. 103 (n.) the captain in the mizzen-top; p. 103 (adj.) I saw the captain's glass; p. 103 (n.) I surely thought the captain would lower a boat; p. 103 (n.) that our captain did not send off a boat; p. 107 (n.) now accommodates a bluff Quaker-captain; p. 107 (n.) in place of the packet-captain; p. 107 (n.) previously unacquainted with the captain; p. 107 (n.) the captain seldom spoke to him; p. 109 (n.) never attempt it in the presence of the captain; p. 110 (n.) Captain Riga was her most devoted; p. 110 (adj.) under the captain's charge; p. 110 (n.) the captain proved an attentive father; p. 110 (n.) as if he thought the captain was audacious; p. 110 (n.) I thought the captain behaved ungallantly; p. 110 (n.) But this Captain Riga was no Raleigh; p. 110 (n.) between this hoydenish nymph and the ill-dressed captain; p. 111 (n.) and the captain followed after; p. 111 (n.) accosting the captain; p. 111 (n.) The captain refused to give it;

p. 112 (n.) the captain had him called aft; p. 112 (n.) the captain,
officers, and mysterious cabin passenger; p. 117 (n.) observe the
captain scolding them often; pp. 118-9 (n.) Had I been the captain;
p. 119 (n.) a particular favorite of the captain; p. 119 (adj.) This
formed the captain's smoking-seat; p. 119 (n.) took much solid
comfort, Captain Riga; p. 119 (adj.) This was the captain's lounge;
p. 131 (n.) if their captains treated them; p. 136 (n.) we saw little
of the captain; p. 136 (n.) would have four or five whiskered sea-
captains; p. 137 (n.) there is no shame in some sea-captains; p. 137
(n.) During the many visits of Captain Riga; p. 143 (n.) into the
hands of some tarry captain; p. 171 (n.) The captain of the vessel
was an Englishman; p. 172 (n.) much to the wrath of Captain Riga;
p. 175 (n.) so particular was the captain; p. 184 (n.) asked for one
of the captains; p. 218 (n.) in an application to the captain; p. 218
(n.) captains interested in the ownership; p. 219 (n.) Captain Riga
was in fact a Russian by birth; p. 219 (n.) yet Captain Riga was a
niggard to others; p. 219 (n.) Captain Riga would gladly close with
him; p. 219 (adj.) I perceived in the captain's face; p. 219 (n.) the
captain expressed a sympathetic concern; p. 220 (n.) at so urbane and
gentlemanly a sea-captain; p. 225 (n.) I well knew that Captain Riga
would not; p. 238 (n.) although the captain might now legally refuse;
p. 238 (n.) Captain Riga and I were flattering ourselves; p. 238 (n.)
the captain . . . has been aware of my absence; p. 238 (n.) The
captain coming on board soon after; p. 241 (n.) every captain of an
emigrant ship; p. 255 (n.) As for the captain; p. 255 (n.) no
gentlemanly and complaisant Captain Riga; p. 255 (n.) Captain Riga
never noticed him now; p. 256 (n.) Captain Riga, Captain Riga; p. 257
(n.) could not get speech of the captain; p. 261 (n.) assured the
attentive Captain Riga; p. 261 (n.) said the captain, bowing; p. 263
(n.) by the despotic ordinances of the captain; p. 263 (n.) no appeal
lies beyond the captain; p. 265 (n.) complaints to the captain were
unheeded; p. 283 (n.) This was told to the captain; p. 284 (n.) that
the Grand Russian, Captain Riga; p. 284 (n.) which the captain caused
to be inflicted; p. 286 (n.) the captain himself went to see them;
p. 287 (n.) no sooner reported to the captain; p. 287 (adj.) to
accomplish the captain's order; p. 288 (n.) but the captain did not
again go down to them; p. 288 (n.) made a prisoner of the captain;
p. 290 (n.) the captain himself at his elbow; p. 290 (n.) with the
generous charity of the captain; p. 292 (n.) a captain will state the
case in the most palliating light; p. 293 (n.) obligatory upon the
captain of a ship; p. 294 (n.) where the captain had just been taking
his noon observation; p. 294 (n.) but so impatient was the captain to
make his port; p. 295 (n.) Of reminding the captain of his existence;
p. 295 (n.) from the captain to the child in the steerage; p. 296 (n.)
in which too many sea-captains indulge; p. 299 (n.) was beset by the
captain; p. 299 (n.) The captain now abdicated in the pilot's favor;
p. 299 (n.) some sea-captains take good heed; p. 300 (n.) Captain
Riga, telescope in hand; p. 305 (n.) sat Captain Riga, arrayed in his
City Hotel suit; p. 305 (n.) while the captain held the ship-papers;
p. 306 (n.) while the captain, throwing aside his accounts; p. 306
(n.) both looked at this incomprehensible captain; p. 306 (n.) The
captain laughed; p. 306 (n.) Captain Riga! . . . Captain Riga; this
won't do; p. 306 (n.) Captain Riga . . . do you not remember; p. 306
(n.) Well, Captain Riga, I have gone out; p. 306 (n.) said the
captain; p. 307 (n.) the state of my account with Captain Riga;
p. 307 (n.) But Captain Riga was a bachelor of expensive habits;

p. 307 (n.) said the captain; p. 307 (n.) There, Captain Riga, you
may keep your tin; p. 307 (n.) said the captain; p. 308 (n.) though
Captain Riga had not been guilty; p. 308 (n.) which should forcibly
impress Captain Riga; p. 308 (n.) was deputed to summon the captain;
p. 308 (n.) requested the steward to inform Captain Riga; p. 308 (n.)
the captain sallied from the cabin; p. 309 (n.) Captain Riga only
lifted his hat.

White-Jacket--p. 5 (n.) Said old Brush, the captain of the paint-room;
p. 6 (n.) On the poop, the captain was looking to windward; p. 11 (n.)
We say nothing here of . . . Captains of the Forecastle, Captains of
the Fore-top, captains of the Main-top, Captains of the Mizen-top,
captains of the After-Guard, Captains of the Main-Hold, captains of
the Fore-Hold, captains of the Head . . . Captain's Steward . . .
Captain's cook; p. 13 (n.) Jack Chase, our noble First Captain of the
Top; p. 13 (n.) even when the captain spoke to him; p. 14 (n.) of one
of the Captains of the fore-top; p. 14 (adj.) the fore-top captain's
most cursory remarks; p. 14 (n.) the fore-top captain meant a ship;
pp. 14-5 (n.) when the fore-top captain, like many others; p. 15 (n.)
I discovered that Jack Chase, our captain; p. 15 (n.) this it was
that so engaged our noble captain; p. 16 (n.) sailed with lords and
marquises for captains; p. 17 (n.) cried the captain; p. 18 (n.) most
courteously to our captain; p. 18 (n.) But Captain Claret must be
obeyed; p. 18 (n.) now inquired for the Peruvian captain; p. 18 (n.)
The foreign captain curled his mustache; p. 18 (n.) who had so
courteously doffed his chapeau to our captain; p. 19 (n.) a most
gentlemanly friend and captain; p. 19 (n.) stepped up to Captain
Claret; p. 19 (n.) said the captain; p. 19 (n.) Your most devoted and
penitent captain of the Main-top; p. 19 (n.) is yet proud to call
Captain Claret his commander; p. 19 (n.) shouted Captain Claret; p. 2
p. 21 (n.) is but a senior captain; p. 21 (n.) no permanent rank . . .
above his captaincy; p. 22 (n.) as the frigate had a captain; p. 23
(n.) Captain Claret was a large, portly man; p. 23 (n.) the captain
is its king; p. 23 (adj.) The captain's word is law; p. 23 (adj.) to
repair to the captain's cabin; p. 23 (n.) replies the captain; p. 23
(n.) when the captain visits the deck; p. 23 (n.) as the captain of a
man-of-war at sea; p. 24 (n.) By the captain he is held responsible;
p. 27 (n.) the Captains of the Tops; p. 27 (n.) So too with the
Captain; p. 27 (n.) So, too, with the Captain; p. 28 (n.) the captain
about three; p. 29 (n.) rejected by modern Commodores and Captains;
p. 29 (n.) Not even the Captain; p. 29 (n.) a Captain once ventured
to dine at five; p. 29 (n.) that Captain received a private note;
p. 32 (n.) who thought of proposing to the captain; p. 33 (n.) when
the captain would emerge from the cabin; p. 41 (n.) My noble captain,
Jack Chase, rather patronized; p. 43 (n.) armed with a warrant from
the captain; p. 49 (n.) without attaining a captaincy and wearing two
epaulets; p. 54 (n.) said a captain of the Hold; p. 62 (n.) numbering,
among the rest, my noble Captain Jack Chase; p. 66 (n.) The name was
bestowed by the captain of the gun; p. 67 (n.) swayed by the captain
in person; p. 67 (n.) Such a sea-martinet was our Captain; p. 68 (n.)
each captain of his gun at his post; p. 68 (n.) A captain combining a
heedful patriotism with economy; p. 71 (n.) cried the Captain of the
Head; p. 72 (n.) the Captains of the surviving ships ordered; p. 73
(n.) cried the Captain of the Head; p. 78 (n.) an order on Brush, the
captain of the paint room; p. 80 (adj.) by an express edict from the
Captain's cabin; p. 84 (n.) The Commodore, Captain . . . have all

night in; p. 84 (n.) to the immortal honor of some captains; p. 88
(n.) solely in the hands of the Captain; p. 88 (n.) of the roll of
American navy-captains; pp. 89-90 (n.) some Captains augment the din;
p. 90 (n.) even had the Captain felt disposed; p. 90 (n.) But how
could Captain Claret . . . behold the grief; p. 91 (n.) upon making
an application to the Captain; p. 91 (adj.) under the Captain's
personal patronage; p. 91 (n.) dragged out while Captain Claret had
the sway; p. 91 (n.) after the indulgence had been granted by the
Captain; p. 92 (n.) Captain Spy-glass . . . Ned Brace, of the After-
Guard; p. 92 (n.) Patrick Flinegan, Captain of the Head; p. 93 (n.)
Captain Claret, enacting the part of censor; p. 93 (n.) the
consequential Captain of the Band himself; p. 93 (n.) neither
Commodore nor Captain honored the people; p. 94 (n.) the Captain
darted from his cabin; p. 95 (n.) sung by the Irish Captain of the
Head; p. 95 (n.) officers there assembled with the captain; p. 97
(n.) your Mediterranean captain, who with a cargo of oranges; p. 97
(n.) But, Captain Rash, those sails of yours; p. 97 (n.) if . . .
Captain Rash is not swept over-board; p. 98 (n.) Among sea-captains,
there are some; p. 101 (n.) a humane proceeding of the Captain;
p. 102 (n.) under the very nose of the most mighty captain; p. 106
(n.) shouted Captain Claret, bursting from his cabin; p. 110 (adj.)
countermanded the Captain's order; p. 110 (adj.) that the Captain's
order was an unwise one; p. 110 (n.) orders, given by the captain and
his Lieutenant; p. 110 (n.) the captain was for scudding; p. 111 (n.)
Captain Claret was hurried forth from his disguises; p. 111 (adj.)
peculiarly lustreless repose of the Captain's eye; p. 111 (n.) the
fact that Captain Claret, while carefully shunning; p. 111 (n.) had
Captain Claret been an out-and-out temperance man; p. 111 (n.) did
the Captain ever venture to reprimand him; p. 111 (n.) Captain Claret
was exempted from personal interposition; p. 113 (n.) no one has a
right to be a naval captain unless; p. 113 (n.) now 68 Captains in
the American navy; p. 113 (n.) petty officers--Captains of the Tops,
&etc.; p. 117 (adj.) he was wanted in the captain's cabin; p. 117 (n.)
It became the duty of the captain; p. 120 (n.) some slight order to
the captains of the tops; p. 121 (n.) supplicated the unexorable
Brush, captain of the paint-room; p. 124 (n.) While the . . . captains
of the tops . . . receive; p. 128 (n.) relics of by-gone old
Commodores and Post-captains; p. 128 (n.) habitations of the living
commodore and captain; p. 131 (n.) formal communication with the
captain and officers; p. 134 (adj.) a flogging, at the captain's
pleasure; p. 135 (n.) from the corpulent Captain himself; p. 136 (n.)
Presently the Captain came forward; p. 136 (n.) during which the
captain, now clothed in his most dreadful attributes; p. 136 (n.)
said the captain; p. 136 (n.) done to propitiate the captain; p. 136
(n.) as most captains love to see a tidy sailor; p. 136 (n.) the
captain turned a deaf ear; p. 136 (n.) said the Captain; p. 137 (n.)
At a sign from the Captain; p. 137 (n.) another sign from the
Captain; p. 137 (adj.) The Captain's finger was now lifted; p. 137
(n.) swearing to have the life of the Captain; p. 138 (n.) cried the
captain; p. 138 (n.) cried the captain; p. 138 (n.) when some captains
in the Navy say; p. 139 (n.) captains in the Navy . . . inflict the
scourge; p. 140 (n.) at the merest wink from the captain; p. 140 (n.)
solely to captains and Courts Martial; p. 141 (n.) a law prohibiting
a captain from inflicting; p. 141 (n.) informed us that their captain
sometimes inflicted; p. 141 (n.) though the captain of an English
armed ship; p. 143 (n.) puts the scourge into the hands of the

captain; p. 143 (n.) the captain is made a legislator; p. 143 (n.)
there is no law to restrain the captain; p. 144 (n.) the Captain of
an American sloop of war; p. 144 (n.) creating the absolute one-man
power in the Captain; p. 144 (n.) the Captain . . . is an absolute
ruler; p. 144 (n.) at the discretion of the Captain; p. 145 (n.) an
American Captain may, and frequently does; p. 145 (n.) yet both
sailor and captain are American citizens; p. 146 (n.) condemning to
the lash a transgressing captain; p. 147 (n.) Commodores and
Captains of the navy; p. 148 (n.) many American captains, who, after
inflicting; p. 150 (n.) another captain to rule over us; p. 150 (n.)
that captain who ever marches at the head; p. 152 (n.) cried Captain
Claret; p. 153 (n.) censorious observations upon the captain; p. 153
(n.) the Commodore and Captain had laid in a goodly stock; p. 153 (n.)
yet Captain Claret was a portly gentleman; pp. 153-4 (n.) that
Captain Claret himself had fought; p. 154 (n.) on the ungenerous
conduct of Captain Claret; p. 154 (n.) while Captain Claret himself,
with an inexhaustible cellar; p. 156 (n.) the most mighty Commodore
and Captain sat before him; p. 156 (n.) Captain Claret would
frequently unite; p. 157 (n.) once touched his hat to the captain;
p. 157 (n.) said the Captain, haughtily; p. 157 (n.) the Captain was
perfectly right; p. 158 (n.) wherein the Captain himself is a moral
man; p. 158 (n.) when their Captain would read the . . . service;
p. 161 (adj.) She also carried . . . a Captain's Gig; p. 161 (adj.)
and the Captain's Gig are manned by gentlemanly youths; p. 161 (n.)
for the eyes of the Commodore or Captain; p. 161 (n.) pulling off his
High Mightiness, the Captain; p. 161 (n.) Captain Claret removed his
chapeau; p. 161 (adj.) It was now Captain Claret's turn to be honored;
p. 162 (n.) while the Captain only nodded; p. 162 (n.) put a question
to an Irish captain of a gun; p. 162 (n.) ceremonious reception of
our captain; p. 162 (n.) the Captain was received with the usual
honors; p. 163 (adj.) was thus honoring the Captain's return; p. 163
(n.) The Captain then slowly mounted the ladder; p. 163 (n.) the
Captain made his ceremonious way; p. 163 (n.) besides the Captain
himself; p. 163 (n.) this was the tune that our Captain always
hinted; p. 163 (adj.) a complimentary appreciation, on the Captain's
part; p. 163 (n.) a sort of body-servant to Captain Claret; p. 172
(n.) for it is not every navy captain who will allow; p. 172 (n.) as
for Captain Claret; p. 172 (n.) yet I will say for Captain Claret
that; p. 173 (adj.) But Captain Claret's leniency in permitting
checkers; p. 173 (n.) were exasperated against the Captain; p. 173
(n.) showed that Captain Claret was a man of a ready understanding;
pp. 177-8 (n.) such as the Commodore himself, the Captain; p. 179 (n.)
of captain of the ship's executioners; p. 182 (n.) excited the
surprise and vexation of the Captain; p. 182 (adj.) So strict were
the Captain's regulations; p. 182 (n.) harangued at the mast by the
Captain in person; p. 182 (n.) assured the Captain that he would still
continue; p. 183 (n.) returned the Captain; p. 183 (adj.) was a
favorite of the Captain's; p. 184 (n.) at once reported to the
captain; p. 184 (n.) Scriggs fell on his knees before the Captain;
p. 184 (n.) the Captain must have thought this a good opportunity;
p. 186 (n.) so many captains of tops; p. 187 (n.) Save my noble
captain, Jack Chase; p. 189 (n.) But this did Captain Claret; p. 189
(n.) Perhaps Captain Claret had read the Memoirs; p. 189 (adj.)
bearing the Captain's name and rank; p. 189 (n.) presented these
articles to the Captain; p. 189 (n.) and the Captain had received
them; p. 189 (n.) with some Captains, a sense of propriety; p. 189

(n.) it was not Captain Claret who would inflict; p. 189 (n.) Now
had Captain Claret deemed himself; p. 189 (n.) of the subordinates
of a man-of-war captain; p. 189 (n.) when Captain Claret received
his snuff-box and cane; p. 190 (n.) in the vivid language of the
Captain of the Fore-top; p. 193 (n.) one of the captains of the
mizzin-top; p. 193 (adj.) surrounded by his post-captain satraps;
p. 195 (n.) belongs to the first captain of the top; p. 200 (n.)
Yours, Captain of the Waist; p. 206 (n.) short of Captain or
Commodore; p. 213 (n.) . . . with the Commodore and the Captain;
p. 213 (n.) the mighty soul of my noble captain of the Top; p. 213
(n.) that is, a captain of the top; p. 213 (n.) waiting till Captain
Claret drew nigh; p. 213 (n.) your trusty sea-warriors, valiant
captain; pp. 213-4 (n.) we poor fellows, valiant Captain; p. 214 (n.)
Will Captain Claret vouchsafe one day's liberty; p. 214 (n.) he
saluted the captain with a gallant flourish; p. 214 (n.) He seemed to
say, Magnanimous Captain Claret; p. 214 (n.) asked the captain,
evasively; p. 214 (n.) is not this Rio a verdant spot, noble captain;
p. 214 (n.) it is a weary thing, Captain Claret; p. 214 (n.) Ah!
Captain Claret . . .; p. 214 (n.) Compared with such a prisoner,
noble Captain; p. 214 (n.) Attracted by the scene between Captain
Claret; p. 215 (n.) turning to Captain Claret; p. 215 (n.) To your
duty, captain of the main-top; p. 215 (n.) said the captain; p. 215
(adj.) cast down by the Captain's coldness; p. 215 (n.) valiant
Commodore and Captain; p. 216 (n.) after . . . Jack's interview with
the . . . captain; p. 217 (n.) a cardinal principle with a Navy
Captain; p. 217 (n.) he should then complain to the Captain; p. 217
(n.) the captain . . . should be thoroughly convinced; p. 217 (n.)
when Captain of a line-of-battle ship; p. 218 (n.) what must be
expected from other Captains; p. 219 (n.) a Navy Captain can not, of
his own authority; p. 220 (n.) which the Captain . . . observes or
disregards; p. 220 (n.) insults inflicted by some captains; p. 220
(n.) pursued by Captains in the English Navy; p. 220 (n.) Captain
Claret himself had no special fondness; p. 220 (n.) Captain Claret
promenaded to and fro; p. 220 (n.) the captain demanded to know;
p. 220 (n.) Captain Claret . . . you know what that is, sir; p. 220
(n.) Captain Claret, I have a purse lashed up here; p. 220 (n.) said
the Captain; pp. 220-1 (n.) fully laid before the Captain; p. 221 (n.)
though the captain permits himself to domineer; p. 222 (n.) The
Effects of this upon a Man-of-war Captain; p. 223 (n.) even the
captain of a frigate is; p. 223 (n.) Never sail under a navy captain
whom you suspect; p. 223 (n.) visible in the deportment of the
Captain; p. 223 (adj.) if there arn't a dozen in that ere captain's
top-lights; p. 223 (n.) the Captain, who had been impatiently walking
the deck; p. 224 (n.) touching and retouching his cap to the captain;
p. 224 (n.) cried the Captain; p. 224 (n.) when the Captain raised
his finger; p. 228 (n.) the Captain ordered them to be sewed up;
p. 231 (n.) repugnance of many Commodores and Captains; p. 239 (n.)
The Captain of the Main-Hold . . . made a polite bow; p. 240 (n.)
sighed the captain of the Fore-top; p. 242 (n.) degraded before the
mast by the captain; p. 246 (adj.) no favorite of the Captain's;
p. 250 (n.) the captain contented himself with privately; p. 265 (n.)
our captain would have no objections; p. 270 (n.) was once a captain
of the forecastle; p. 271 (n.) great men in the world besides
Commodores and Captains; p. 271 (n.) we Homers who happen to be
captains of tops; p. 271 (n.) the Captain's on the poop; p. 272 (n.)
said the Lieutenant, approaching the Captain; p. 272 (n.) roared the

captain; p. 272 (n.) the means adopted by the captain; p. 272 (n.)
Thenceforward all her Captains; p. 272 (n.) made use of by Captain
Claret; p. 272 (adj.) for fear of marring the Captain's plans; p. 272
(n.) cried the captain; p. 272 (n.) when a navy captain does not
happen to be; p. 275 (n.) as patronized by Captain Claret; p. 275 (n.)
was an especial favorite with the Captain; p. 275 (adj.) for the
benefit of the Captain's health; p. 275 (n.) the Captain must be
obeyed; p. 275 (n.) verbally unexpressed applause of the Captain;
p. 275 (adj.) bumping one evening to the Captain's content; p. 275
(n.) The Captain advanced; p. 276 (n.) said the Captain; p. 276 (n.)
said the Captain; p. 276 (adj.) the fact of the Captain's not showing
any leniency; p. 276 (n.) especially the case with Captain Claret;
p. 276 (n.) would have deemed Captain Claret the indulgent father;
p. 276 (n.) would have deemed Captain Claret a fine illustration;
p. 276 (n.) comparisons between a sea-captain and a father; p. 276
(n.) between a sea-captain and the master of apprentices; p. 278 (n.)
Captain Claret came forward to see; p. 278 (n.) the Captain desired
to know; p. 278 (n.) Captain wants ye at the mast; p. 278 (n.) what
the Captain desired of me; p. 279 (n.) found myself standing before
Captain Claret; p. 279 (n.) asked the Captain; p. 279 (n.) at every
sentence they address to the captain; p. 279 (n.) of a personal
interview with Captain Claret; p. 279 (n.) Glancing at the Captain,
the First Lieutenant now produced; p. 279 (n.) known it before this
moment, Captain Claret; p. 280 (n.) The Captain stood on the weather-
side; p. 280 (adj.) right down to the level of the Captain's feet;
p. 280 (n.) Captain Claret . . . showed with an awful vividness;
p. 280 (n.) that Captain Claret was about to degrade me; p. 280 (n.)
no scourge of Captain Claret could cut; p. 280 (n.) I meant to drag
Captain Claret from this earthly tribunal; p. 280 (n.) said Captain
Claret; p. 280 (n.) Captain Claret; p. 281 (n.) had a marine dared to
speak to the Captain; p. 281 (n.) that the Captain . . . did not in
any way reprimand him; p. 281 (n.) Captain Claret looked from Chase
to Colbrook; p. 281 (n.) though supreme Captain of a frigate; p. 288
(n.) to catch the eye of the Captain; p. 289 (n.) sometimes the
Captain feels out of sorts; p. 289 (n.) Captain Claret would
pertinaciously promenade; p. 289 (n.) as the Captain would turn
toward him; p. 289 (n.) the Captain was off again; p. 289 (n.)
Captain Claret, thinking . . . his dignity must; p. 289 (n.) the
Captain, nodding his acceptance; p. 289 (n.) the Captain makes a
profound salutation; p. 289 (n.) that the Captain is at perfect
liberty; p. 289 (n.) Captain Claret at last halts; p. 290 (n.) with
the Commodore, and Captain . . . unite; p. 292 (n.) in solemn review
before the Captain and officers; p. 292 (adj.) by the reading . . .
by the Captain's clerk; p. 292 (n.) before my lord and master,
Captain Claret; p. 293 (adj.) nearly every Article read by the
Captain's clerk; p. 295 (n.) you may, at a wink from the captain;
p. 300 (n.) addressed by a merchant-captain to his crew; p. 300 (n.)
but the merchant-captain does not live under; p. 300 (n.) I honestly
declare that Captain Claret; p. 301 (n.) I must once more cite
Captain Claret; p. 301 (n.) observed or violated at the caprice of
the captain; p. 301 (n.) which invests the Captain with so much
judicial; p. 301 (n.) between the American Captain and the American
sailor; p. 301 (n.) Or is the Captain a creature of; p. 301 (n.) The
law was not made for the Captain; p. 302 (n.) from the decision of
the Captain; p. 302 (n.) the penal power in the Captain; p. 302 (n.)
The Captain smiled; p. 302 (n.) said the captain; p. 303 (adj.) in

the Captain's judgment; p. 304 (n.) concerning a Gothland sea-captain;
p. 305 (n.) But the Captain . . . permitted them; p. 309 (n.) than
the captain of the Forecastle; p. 312 (n.) respectfully accosted the
captain; p. 312 (n.) the Captain leveled it at the heads; p. 312 (n.)
Captain Cardan ordered his . . . quarter-master; p. 314 (n.) order
given by the English Captain; p. 314 (n.) if some brainless bravo be
Captain; p. 314 (n.) the American Captain continued to fight; p. 315
(n.) reputation which the American captain might have; p. 315 (n.)
when the Captain of the Macedonian . . . gave the word; p. 315 (n.)
Had he been captain; p. 316 (n.) The captain of the next gun; p. 316
(n.) presented to him . . . by Captain Hallowell; p. 317 (n.) those
of Jack Chase, our captain; p. 318 (n.) suspected of being the
slaughtered captain; p. 318 (n.) he had been a captain; p. 319 (n.)
flags one of our captains carried home; p. 319 (adj.) glancing at our
captain's maimed hand; p. 319 (n.) by the Second Captain of the Top;
p. 323 (adj.) entered from the captain's cabin; p. 324 (n.) This man
was captain of the . . . bow-chaser; p. 324 (n.) this captain of the
bow-chaser was; p. 324 (n.) in being captain of that gun; p. 325 (n.)
with our five hundred men, Commodore and Captain; p. 328 (n.) protest
against it formally to the captain; p. 328 (n.) at swords' points
with its captain; p. 329 (n.) let the Captain of your gun hunt you up;
p. 332 (n.) poor Baldy, captain of the mizzen-top; p. 341 (n.) the
captain himself stood bareheaded; p. 351 (n.) chiefly for the Captain;
p. 351 (n.) what did the captain pay; p. 353 (n.) the captain of the
Forecastle, old Ushant; p. 355 (n.) But as Captain Claret said
nothing; p. 356 (adj.) Perhaps the Captain's generosity; p. 356 (adj.)
the Captain's beard did not exceed the limits; p. 356 (n.) entered
into the heart of our Captain; p. 356 (n.) words in which the Captain
meditated; p. 356 (adj.) must have been the Captain's cogitations;
p. 356 (n.) The Captain was made; p. 357 (n.) Captain Claret! . . .
were we going into action, Captain Claret . . . Then, Captain Claret;
p. 357 (n.) But now, Captain Claret; p. 357 (n.) this is too bitterly
bad, Captain Claret; p. 357 (n.) Captains of the tops; p. 358 (adj.)
the Captain's eye was observed to wander; p. 358 (n.) Captain Claret
summoned the midshipmen; p. 358 (n.) The Captain was in earnest;
p. 358 (n.) fulminating their displeasure against the Captain; p. 358
(n.) Captain Claret happened to be taking a nap; p. 359 (n.) if the
sayings imputed to the captain were true; p. 360 (n.) Captain Claret!
how can you rest; p. 360 (n.) My noble captain, Jack Chase, was
indignant; p. 360 (n.) he had received from Captain Claret; p. 361
(n.) the noble captain of this frigate's main-top; p. 362 (adj.) had
complied with the Captain's commands; p. 362 (n.) where the Captain
stood ready; p. 363 (n.) Even Captain Claret they ought to have;
p. 363 (n.) Old Ushant's, the ancient Captain of the Forecastle;
p. 363 (n.) most beloved by my glorious captain; p. 364 (n.) said the
captain, eying them severely; p. 364 (n.) said the Captain of the
Forecastle; p. 364 (n.) It is but a few days, Captain Claret; p. 364
(n.) cried the Captain of the Forecastle; p. 364 (n.) addressing the
Captain, said; p. 365 (n.) There the Captain stood; p. 365 (n.)
roared the Captain; p. 365 (adj.) the Captain's excitement had a
little time; p. 365 (n.) the Captain seemed to relent; p. 365 (n.)
Captain Claret . . . you may flog me; p. 365 (n.) roared the Captain
in a sudden fury; p. 365 (n.) cried the captain; p. 366 (n.) said the
captain; p. 366 (n.) cried the captain; p. 366 (n.) you have been
Captain of the Forecastle; p. 367 (n.) As for Captain Claret; p. 367
(n.) deemed Captain Claret a lenient officer; p. 367 (n.) with the

conduct of other Navy Captains; p. 367 (n.) whatever acts Captain
Claret might have; p. 374 (adj.) at the . . . Captain's cabin doors;
p. 375 (n.) If a Captain have a grudge against; p. 380 (n.) By a
statement of Captain Marryat's; p. 382 (n.) This writer was . . .
himself a Captain in the British fleet; p. 385 (n.) blessed with
patriarchal, intellectual captains; p. 386 (n.) the dubbed post-
captains of old Athens; p. 388 (n.) cried the old captain of gun
No. 1; p. 388 (n.) cried the captain of gun No. 1; p. 388 (n.) about
the captain, in his; p. 389 (n.) cried the Captain of the Head;
p. 389 (n.) said the Captain of the Waist; p. 389 (n.) cried the
Captain of the Waist; p. 389 (n.) In that sense, cried the captain of
the waist; p. 390 (n.) You, Captain of the Waist; p. 391 (n.) while
our captain often broke in; p. 392 (n.) when our Captain of the Top;
p. 396 (n.) my liege lord and captain of my top; p. 396 (n.) the
grand Commodore and Captain drove off; p. 398 (n.) is as wise as the
captain; p. 399 (n.) do we appeal to the captain.

Moby-Dick--p. 5 (adj.) Captain Cowley's Voyage round the Globe,
AD 1729; p. 9 (n.) Where away demanded the captain; p. 14 (n.) nor . . .
do I ever go to sea as a . . . captain, or a cook; p. 15 (n.) What of
it, if some old hunks of a sea-captain orders me; p. 15 (n.) however
the old sea-captains may order me about; p. 42 (n.) The wife of a
whaling captain had provided the chapel with; p. 46 (n.) as he steps
on board to see its captain in the cabin; p. 59 (n.) a very stately
punctilious gentleman, at least for a sea captain; p. 60 (n.) the
Captain, a gaunt rib of the sea; p. 94 (n.) many captains never show
themselves on deck; p. 109 (n.) first vague disquietude touching the
unknown captain; p. 392 (n.) Then, a short, little old body like me,
should never undertake to wade out into deep waters with tall, heron-
built captains; p. 441 (n.) replied the hollow-cheeked captain from
his taffrail; p. 458 (n.) Accursed fate! that the unconquerable
captain in the soul should have such a craven mate.

CARIBBEAN. Certain West Indian isles, and the sea between them and the
mainland. (OED)

Mardi-- p. 40 (adj.) through a Caribbean canoe.

CASTAWAY. A person belonging to a vessel stranded by stress of weather.
Men who have hidden themselves, or who are purposely left behind, when
their vessel quits port are castaways. (Smyth)

Mardi--p. 45 (n.) to any future castaway or sailaway; p. 95 (n.)
sailors are mostly foundlings and castaways.

Redburn--p. 275 (adj.) nothing but a castaway sailor.

Moby-Dick--p. 50 (n.) woe to him who . . . while preaching to others
is himself a castaway; p. 198 (adj.) the ships themselves often pick
up such queer castaway creatures; p. 344 (n.) The Castaway; p. 347
(n.) another lonely castaway, though the loftiest and the brightest;
p. 450 (n.) instant destruction of the jeopardized castaways.

CAT-HEAD. Large timbers projecting from the vessel's side, to which the anchor is raised and secured. (Dana)

Redburn--p. 93 (n.) jerked out the bolt near the Cat-head.

CEPHALASPIS. Fossil fishes. (Van Nostrand)

Mardi--p. 417 (n.) sturgeon-forms, cephalaspis, glyptolepesis.

CETOLOGY. The doctrine or natural history of whales. (Webster)

Moby-Dick. p. 2 (n.) must not . . . take the higgledy-piggledy whale statements . . . for veritable gospel cetology; p. 101 (n.) Cetus is a constellation in the South; p. 117 (n.) No branch of Zoology is so much involved as that which is entitled Cetology; p. 117 (n.) the true method of dividing the cetacea into groups; p. 117 (n.) Impenetrable veil covering our knowledge of the cetacea; p. 117 (n.) with cetology, or the science of whales; p. 118 (n.) to project the draught of a systematization of cetology; p. 118 (n.) unsettled condition of this science of cetology; p. 119 (n.) in this ground-plan of cetology; p. 119 (n.) their passports to quit the Kingdom of Cetology; p. 122 (n.) afford the basis for a regular system of Cetology; p. 127 (adj.) But I now leave my Cetological System standing thus unfinished; p. 233 (n.) joined the chase against the starry Cetus; p. 380 (adj.) the most wonderful of all cetacean relics.

CHART. A hydrographical map, or a projection of some of the earth's superficies in plano, for the use of navigators, to aid in the investigation of surface currents. (Smyth)

Mardi--p. 17 (n.) without chart or quadrant; p. 17 (n.) the chart, to be sure, I did not.

CHEVALIER. From Melville we know it is a "dread fish of prey"; Webster and the OED associate it with a horse or a cavalry.

Mardi--p. 150 (n.) Grim death, in the shape of a Chevalier; p. 151 (n.) the Chevalier devours them; p. 151 (n.) dreading lest the Chevalier.

CHONDROPTERYGII. An ancient and famous tribe of sharks. (Melville)

Mardi--p. 39 (n.) of the chondropterygii; p. 40 (n.) ancient and famous tribe of the Chondropterygii.

CHRONOMETER. A valuable time-piece fitted with a compensation-balance, adjusted for the accurate measurement of time in all climates, and used by navigators for the determination of the longitude. (Smyth)

Omoo--p. 61 (n.) Not that the chronometer in the cabin was seldom to be relied on.

Redburn--p. 95 (n.) The chronometer pronounced it noon.

Moby-Dick--p. 103 (n.) [Starbuck's temperament] like a patent chronometer, his interior vitality was warranted to do well in all climates.

CLAM. A well-known bivalve shell-fish. "As happy as a clam at high-water," a figurative expression for otiose comfort. (Smyth)

Mardi--p. 573 (n.) served in great clam-shells.

White-Jacket--p. 389 (n.) I mean to steer a clam-cart.

Moby-Dick--p. 27 (n.) ushered into a small room, cold as a clam; p. 62 (n.) to their very chairs and tables small clams will sometimes be found adhering; p. 64 (N./n./n./adj.) Clam or cod . . . A clam for supper? a cold clam . . . that's a rather cold and clammy reception; p. 65 (n.) It was made of small juicy clams; p. 65 (n.) The area before the house was paved with clam-shells.

CLIPPER. A fast sailer, formerly chiefly applied to the sharp-built raking schooners of America, and latterly to Australian passenger-ships. Larger vessels now built after their model are termed clipper-built: sharp and fast; low in the water; rakish. (Smyth)

Mardi--p. 125 (n.) who contend with the gale is a clipper.

Redburn--p. 130 (n.) at the Sign of the Baltimore Clipper; p. 131 (n.) before the sign of a Baltimore Clipper; p. 153 (n.) Entering the sign of the clipper; p. 160 (n.) at the sign of the Baltimore Clipper to supper; p. 175 (adj.) low, black, clipper-built; p. 180 (n.) the sign of the Baltimore Clipper; p. 204 (n.) except at the sign of the Baltimore Clipper; p. 204 (n.) the proceedings at the sign of the Clipper; p. 216 (n.) encountered him at the sign of the Baltimore Clipper; p. 253 (n.) saw near the sign of the Clipper; p. 272 (n.) the Neversink gained the name of a clipper.

COAST. The sea-shore and the adjoining country; in fact, the sea-front of the land. (Smyth)

Typee--p. 11 (n.) This island . . . has three good harbors on its coast; p. 12 (n.) The reality is very different; bold rock-bound coasts; p. 23 (n.) previous to going on the coast of Japan; p. 205 (n.) shipwrecked on some barbarous coast.

Omoo--p. xiii (n.) along the lawless western coast of South America; p. 6 (n.) well known along the whole western coast of South America; p. 80 (n.) On the coast of Massachusetts; p. 211 (n.) Hilo, a village upon the coast; p. 234 (n.) the village was so remote from the coast; p. 292 (n.) On the coast of Barbaree; p. 299 (n.) on the coast of New Zealand; p. 313 (n.) hurrah for the coast of Japan.

Mardi--p. 6 (n.) on the Nor'-west coast; p. 68 (n.) on the coast of
Mowee; p. 123 (n.) Save twice on the coast of Peru; p. 138 (n.) on
whose coast gurgled up in the sea; p. 140 (n.) to her fate on the
coast of Tedaidee; p. 157 (n.) on the coast of Tedaidee; p. 269 (n.)
Brethren of the coast; p. 289 (n.) harpooned on the coast of Japan;
p. 374 (n.) picked up on the spicy coasts of Jovanna; p. 539 (n.) not
far from its coast; p. 543 (n.) we voyaged along that coast; p. 545
(v.) Northward coasting along Kolumbo's Western shore; p. 552 (v.)
yet on, and on we coasted; counting not the days; p. 553 (v.) Coasting
on by barbarous beaches.

Redburn--p. 5 (n.) from the coast of Africa or New Zealand; p. 57 (n.)
in Portuguese slavers on the coast of Africa; p. 97 (n.) seamen
impute the fogs on the coast; p. 98 (n.) off the coast of Florida;
p. 99 (n.) we ar'n't off the coast of Greenland; p. 100 (n.) on the
coast of Madagascar; p. 121 (adj.) great deal of severe coasting
service; p. 127 (n.) It beats the coast of Afriky, all hollow;
p. 166 (n.) from Iceland or the coast of New-Guinea; p. 174 (n.)
Galliots, Coast-of-Guinea-Man; p. 174 (n.) a little brig from the
Coast of Guinea.

White-Jacket--p. 3 (n.) in Callao, on the coast of Peru; p. 16 (n.)
concerning stove boats on the coast of Japan; p. 18 (n.) the frigate
came to anchor on the coast; p. 55 (n.) selling it . . . to the
people of the coast; p. 98 (n.) on the coasts of Chili and Peru;
p. 109 (n.) after first weighing anchor on the pleasant Spanish coast;
p. 113 (n.) solvers of logarithms in the Coast Survey; p. 122 (n.)
vessels bound to the Nor'-west Coast; p. 123 (n.) away from the
bitter coast of Patagonia; p. 200 (n.) yet I remembered the American
coast; p. 208 (n.) on what coast we adjoin; p. 317 (n.) receiver of
smuggled goods upon the English coast; p. 317 (n.) in midnight coves
upon a stormy coast; p. 357 (n.) to the chill air of the Yankee coast;
p. 395 (n.) till we gained a precise latitude of the coast.

Moby-Dick--p. 5 (n.) Several whales have come in upon this coast;
p. 6 (n.) when either thrown ashore or caught near the coast; p. 16
(n.) I love to sail forbidden seas, and land on barbarous coasts;
p. 23 (n.) or whether caught off the coast of Labrador; p. 38 (n.)
in as howling condition as the coast of Labrador; p. 40 (n.) was
killed by a Sperm Whale on the coast of Japan; p. 43 (n.) against a
terrible storm off a lee coast of black rocks; p. 45 (n.) Joppa . . .
is on the most easterly coast of the Mediterranean; p. 100 (n.)
opulent Spanish provinces on the Pacific coast; p. 102 (n.) though
born on an icy coast; p. 383 (n.) if one coast is no longer enlivened.

COCKLE. A common bivalve mollusc (Cardium edule), often used as food.
(Smyth)

Mardi--p. 573 (n.) the second, lobsters, . . . crabs, cockles.

COD. The Gadus morrhua, one of the most important of oceanic fishes.
The cod is always found on the submerged hills known as banks; as the
Dogger Bank, and banks of Newfoundland. (Smyth)

Moby-Dick--p. 62 (n.) they pushed off in boats and captured cod;
p. 64 (n.) Clam or cod . . . What's that about cods, ma'am; p. 65 (n.)
Mrs. Hussey wore a polished necklace of codfish vertebrae.

COFFER-DAM. A coffer-dam consists of two rows of piles, each row boarded
strongly inside, and being filled with clay within well rammed, thereby
resists outward pressure and is impenetrable by the surrounding water.
(Smyth)

Moby-Dick--p. 23 (n.) with noble shoulders, and a chest like a
coffer-dam.

COMPASS. An instrument employed by navigators to guide the ship's course
at sea. It consists of a circular box, containing a fly or paper card,
which represents the horizon, and is suspended by two concentric rings
called gimbals. This card is attached to a magnetic needle, which,
carrying the card round with it, points north. (Smyth)

Typee--p. 92 (n.) toes, like the radiating lines of the mariners'
compass.

Mardi--p. 27 (n.) at the top of my compass; p. 33 (n.) containing a
small compass; p. 33 (n.) and removed the compass; p. 33 (n.) puzzled
to fix our compass; p. 51 (n.) Sun, compass, stout hearts; p. 65 (n.)
containing the compass; p. 114 (n.) abstraction of the compass from
the binnacle; p. 556 (n.) with compass and the lead, we had not
found; p. 617 (n.) as three printed points upon the compass-card.

Redburn--p. 118 (n.) with learning the compass; p. 118 (n.) the place
that holds a ship's compass.

White-Jacket--p. 270 (n.) knew how to box the compass, my land;
p. 378 (n.) without compass or rudder.

Moby-Dick--p. 13 (n.) Tell me, does the magnetic virtue in the needles
of the compasses of all those ships attract them thither?

CONCH. A large univalve, used as a horn by pilots, fishermen &c., in
fogs: a strombus, triton, or sometimes a murax. (Smyth)

Typee--p. 150 (n.) canoe-gear, battle-clubs, and war-conches; p. 150
(n.) especially the war-conches.

Omoo--p. 32 (n.) By sound of conch-shell it was proclaimed; p. 170
(n.) blast of the war-conch had often resounded.

Mardi--p. 275 (n.) his voice grew sonorous as a conch; p. 326 (n.) to
lay aside his conch; p. 466 (adj.) for one thousand conch shells to
be blown; p. 475 (n.) clamorous with his conch; p. 620 (n.) strike
up, conch and cymbal; p. 649 (n.) Vee-Vee's conch I heard no more.

White-Jacket--p. 46 (n.) a conch-shell might stand on your mantel;
p. 159 (n.) to resemble his lordship's conch shell.

CORAL. A name applied to the hard calcareous support or skeleton of many
species of marine zoophytes. The coral-producing animals abound chiefly
in tropical seas, sometimes forming, by the aggregated growth of countless
generations, reefs, barriers, and islands of vast extent. (Smyth)

Typee--p. 5 (adj.) groves of cocoa-nut--coral reefs--tatooed chiefs;
p. 155 (adj.) cannot be imputed to the coral insect; p. 198 (adj.) in
picturesque and prettily-furnished coral-rock villas.

Omoo--p. 62 (adj.) ascribed to the coral insect; p. 62 (n.) the
inequalities of the coral collect all floating bodies; p. 63 (adj.)
numberless naked, detached coral formations; p. 63 (adj.) The coral
islands are principally visited; p. 64 (adj.) chasing each other in
and out of the coral cells; p. 64 (adj.) catching their long hair in
the coral twigs; p. 89 (adj.) It was the coral reef; p. 90 (adj.) to
the very brink of the coral rampart; p. 98 (adj.) by the coral reef;
p. 98 (n.) grate their keels against the coral; p. 101 (n.) and
fragments of coral; p. 102 (adj.) caught in the coral groves; p. 153
(n.) antlers of red coral; p. 161 (n.) we were just over a ledge of
coral; p. 162 (adj.) It is of coral formation; p. 162 (adj.) you see
coral plants of every hue; p. 163 (n.) of hewn blocks of coral;
p. 250 (n.) surrounded by a regular breakwater of coral; p. 253 (n.)
we had sharp fragments of broken coral; p. 255 (n.) walled in with
coral; p. 266 (adj.) chasing our prey over the coral rocks; p. 266
(adj.) leaped at midnight upon the coral ledges; p. 266 (adj.)
marking the course of the coral barrier; p. 270 (adj.) Dashing
forever against their coral rampart; p. 270 (adj.) But the coral
barriers answer another purpose; p. 270 (n.) resist the formation of
the coral; p. 286 (adj.) A broad pier of hewn coral rocks; p. 292
(n.) and shot upon a ledge of coral; p. 297 (n.) The chapel is built
of hewn blocks of coral; p. 297 (n.) the coral darkens with age.

Mardi--p. 3 (adj.) the coral-hung anchor swings from the bow; p. 70
(adj.) the sharp coral beach; p. 161 (adj.) how weigh the isles'
coral anchor; p. 161 (n.) upon a jutting buttress of coral; p. 178
(adj.) within their coral harbor; p. 188 (adj.) in the branching
boughs of the coral grove; p. 199 (adj.) the coral-rimmed basin;
p. 212 (n.) petrified into white ribs of coral; p. 220 (n.) The-
Heart-of-Black-Coral; p. 236 (n.) surrounded by a mosaic of corals;
p. 236 (adj.) the father of these Coral Kings; p. 238 (adj.) And over
the Coral Kings; p. 250 (n.) hast thou a piece of this coral; p. 253
(n.) imbedded among the corals at his feet; p. 258 (adj.) the ghosts
of the Coral Monarchs; p. 273 (n.) wide banks of coral shelve off;
p. 282 (adj.) rove about in the coral groves; p. 282 (adj.) often
with coral files in their hands; p. 294 (n.) that submerged wall of
coral; p. 294 (adj.) peering into the coral honeycomb; p. 307 (n.)
cheeks were the color of the red coral; p. 352 (adj.) and over many a
coral rock; p. 417 (adj.) The coral wall which circumscribes; p. 418
(adj.) the Chalk, or Coral sandwich; p. 470 (adj.) gallanted them
into their coral harbors; p. 471 (n.) about any detached shelf of
coral in the lagoon; p. 549 (adj.) atolls all, or coral carcanets;
pp. 549-50 (n.) where the glittering coral seemed bones; p. 644 (adj.)
forcing themselves underneath the coral ledge; p. 651 (adj.) with
sparkling, coral ledges.

Moby-Dick--p. 12 (adj.) [Manhattan] belted round by wharves as Indian isles by coral reefs; p. 194 (adj.) the suspended craft seemed a coral boat; p. 223 (n.) which seemed to have touched at a low isle of corals; p. 347 (adj.) Pip saw the multitudinous, God-omnipresent, coral insects; p. 400 (adj.) while all between float milky-ways of coral isles.

CORSAIR. A name commonly given to the piratical cruisers of Barbary, who frequently plundered the merchant ships indiscriminately. (Smyth)

White-Jacket--p. 212 (n.) of all the Barbary Corsairs captured by Bainbridge.

CORVETTE. A flush-decked ship, equipped with one tier of guns; a fine vessel for warm climates, from admitting a free circulation of air. The Bermuda-built corvettes were deemed superior vessels, swift weatherly, "lie to" well, and carry sail in a stiff breeze. The cedar of which they are chiefly built is very buoyant, but also brittle. (Smyth)

Typee--p. 16 (n.) three corvettes to frighten a parcel of naked heathen.

Omoo--p. 19 (n.) proved to be a French corvette; p. 19 (n.) counting upon the assistance of the corvette; p. 21 (n.) swim to the corvette for a cutter; p. 21 (n.) the party from the corvette menacing them; p. 21 (n.) according to the commander of the corvette.

CRAB. A crustaceous fish, the cray-fish, Cancer, a genus containing numerous species. They usually have ten feet, two of which are furnished with claws; two eyes, pedunculated, elongated and movable. (Webster)

Mardi--p. 573 (n.) the second, lobsters, cuttle-fish, crabs.

Moby-Dick--p. 62 (n.) They first caught crabs and quohogs in the sand; p. 282 (n.) when you watch those live crabs that nestle here on this bonnet.

CRAFT. A term in sea-phraseology for every kind of vessel, especially for a favourite ship. Also, all manners of nets, lines, hooks, &c., used in fishing. (Smyth)

Typee--p. 132 (n.) The prohibited craft, guarded by the edicts; p. 134 (n.) was never shipped aboard of any craft.

Omoo--p. 5 (n.) turned out to be a small slatternly looking craft; p. 19 (n.) hull of a small man-of-war craft; p. 24 (n.) the tiny craft shot up the beach; p. 60 (n.) our dauntless craft went along; p. 74 (n.) this here craft goes to sea with us; p. 102 (n.) a very old craft; p. 107 (n.) accounted the "crack" craft in the French navy; p. 231 (n.) was that of building a small craft; p. 312 (n.) the Leviathan was not the craft to our mind; p. 312 (n.) a cosier old craft never floated; p. 313 (n.) thus to deny the dashing little craft; p. 315 (n.) as the Leviathan was so comfortable a craft.

Mardi--p. 3 (n.) your craft may not fly; p. 3 (n.) of our monotonous craft; p. 6 (n.) aboard his craft; p. 7 (n.) on board that very craft; p. 7 (n.) for some ugly craft; p. 11 (n.) in a craft; p. 19 (n.) lashes the craft; p. 20 (n.) selecting my craft; p. 24 (n.) maternal craft; p. 25 (n.) a very old craft; p. 27 (n.) straining the craft; p. 27 (n.) dragged the craft horizontally; p. 30 (adj.) divested our craft's wild motions; p. 32 (n.) our little craft was soon; p. 32 (n.) that our craft was well supplied; p. 33 (n.) belonging to our craft; p. 37 (n.) our solitary craft; p. 39 (n.) as your craft glides; p. 40 (n.) since the good Craft Essex; p. 56 (n.) looked like a far-off craft; p. 57 (n.) a small, two-masted craft; p. 57 (n.) the craft must be a gold-huntress; p. 58 (n.) securing our craft; p. 58 (n.) the craft could; p. 58 (n.) liberty to examine the craft; p. 64 (n.) quit the ill-starred craft; p. 65 (n.) the features of the craft; p. 66 (n.) what craft is this; p. 66 (n.) what craft this was; p. 71 (n.) as the craft drew; p. 71 (n.) point his craft; p. 72 (n.) The craft widely yawed; p. 74 (n.) forced round his craft; p. 75 (n.) gallantly carried his craft; p. 82 (n.) Samoa's little craft; p. 83 (n.) thus to encase your craft; p. 83 (n.) in that lonely craft; p. 86 (n.) a white man's craft; p. 89 (n.) their capturing his craft; p. 93 (n.) on the previous history of the craft; p. 96 (n.) restoring the ill-fated craft; p. 97 (n.) commander of the craft I sailed; p. 101 (n.) the craft being so small; p. 101 (adj.) dozing to the craft's light roll; p. 109 (n.) conduct in all on board our craft; p. 109 (n.) in the night-watch in a craft like ours; p. 110 (n.) once more in a double-decked craft; p. 110 (n.) The mere steering of the craft; p. 114 (n.) shut up in this little oaken craft; p. 117 (n.) the stunned craft, giving one lurch; p. 118 (n.) our almost water-logged craft; p. 127 (n.) the sail of some island craft; p. 127 (n.) Their craft was about thirty feet long; p. 128 (n.) by which the craft was steered; p. 128 (n.) the windward side of the craft; p. 128 (n.) threw their craft into the wind; p. 128 (n.) forcing round their craft; p. 129 (n.) the craft could be no other than; p. 132 (n.) from boarding his craft; p. 132 (n.) demonstration toward our craft; p. 141 (n.) Their craft, our fleet chamois outleaped; p. 145 (n.) in a craft built with hands; p. 149 (adj.) neither scared by our craft's surging; p. 152 (n.) as our craft glides along; p. 161 (n.) we pointed our craft; p. 168 (n.) ordered our craft to be deposited; p. 172 (n.) our craft high and dry; p. 200 (n.) claw-keeled, dragon-prowed crafts; p. 306 (n.) the same double-keeled craft; p. 316 (n.) before it, were several small craft; p. 470 (n.) Bello dispatched a few of his smaller craft; p. 470 (n.) Bello's crafts . . . found the canoes . . . much larger; p. 481 (n.) in the fine craft Bis Taurus that he sailed; p. 482 (n.) And in this craft, Doge-like; p. 483 (n.) without heedful tending, any craft will decay.

Redburn--p. 4 (n.) of a black, sea-worn craft; p. 96 (n.) They were very small craft; p. 97 (n.) that closes over their craft; p. 106 (n.) are the very best of sea-going craft; p. 125 (n.) put his little craft before the wind; p. 166 (n.) these comical little craft are about level with the water; p. 166 (n.) Though his craft was none of the largest; p. 166 (n.) These craft have each a little cabin; p. 172 (n.) in the shrouds of the neighboring craft; p. 174 (n.) another very curious craft; p. 174 (n.) gaze my fill at some outlandish craft; p. 175 (n.) a deal of swearing on board of this craft; p. 289 (n.) the doomed craft beat on; p. 312 (n.) and that the good craft Huntress.

White-Jacket--p. 14 (n.) continual were his allusions to this craft;
p. 15 (n.) we heard no more of the craft; p. 68 (n.) Imagine some
midnight craft sailing down; p. 96 (n.) has sent many a fine craft to
the bottom; p. 97 (n.) while the heedless craft is bounding over the
billows; p. 167 (n.) on board their craft in harbor; p. 177 (n.) the
small craft licensed by the officers; p. 179 (n.) and sink any small
craft; p. 186 (n.) was as eligible a round-sterned craft; p. 211 (n.)
the flag-ship of all the Greek and Persian craft; p. 211 (n.) of all
the musquito craft of Abba Thule; p. 265 (n.) was accounted the
fleetest keeled craft; p. 266 (n.) this fine craft was an American
born; p. 266 (n.) a British-born craft which had once sported; p. 328
(n.) of fire ships and hornet craft; p. 329 (n.) hardly left enough
of that craft; p. 398 (n.) she is but one craft in a Milky-Way fleet;
p. 399 (adj.) do our craft's shabby work; p. 399 (n.) still trim our
craft to the blast; p. 399 (n.) Outwardly regarded, our craft is a
lie; p. 399 (n.) We have both a quarter-deck to our craft.

Moby-Dick--p. 17 (n.) For my mind was made up to sail in no other
than a Nantucket craft; p. 19 (n.) a worse howling than ever it did
about poor Paul's tossed craft; p. 20 (n.) reminding one of the
bulwarks of some condemned old craft; p. 20 (n.) an exasperated whale,
purposing to spring clean over the craft; p. 21 (adj.) that you would
almost fancy you trod some old craft's cockpits; p. 37 (n.) besides
the wild specimens of the whaling-craft; p. 46 (n.) that he paid the
fare thereof ere the craft did sail; p. 67 (n.) you never saw such a
rare old craft as this same rare old Pequod; p. 67 (n.) A cannibal of
a craft, tricking herself forth in the chased bones of her enemies;
p. 68 (n.) A noble craft, but somehow a most melancholy; p. 83 (n.)
that he at no cannibals on board that craft; p. 90 (n.) Queequeg and
I often visited the craft; p. 94 (n.) for he never piloted any other
craft; p. 95 (n.) as the old craft deep dived into the green seas;
p. 110 (n.) like his dismantled craft; p. 138 (n.) the name of
Captain Sleet's good craft; p. 194 (n.) the suspended craft seemed a
coral boat; p. 200 (n.) the piled-up craft rolled down before the
wind; p. 201 (n.) as though they deemed our ship some drifting,
uninhabited craft; p. 203 (n.) this craft was bleached like the
skeleton of a stranded walrus; p. 233 (n.) but the savage craft bore
down on him; p. 244 (n.) you would have thought the craft had two
keels--one cleaving the water, the other the air; p. 244 (n.) the
vibrating, cracking craft canted over her spasmodic gunwhale into the
sea; p. 245 (n.) the imperilled craft, instantly dropping astern;
p. 263 (n.) with the strained craft steeply leaning over to it;
p. 344 (n.) in providing the sometimes madly merry and predestinated
craft; p. 363 (n.) without quitting his little craft; p. 448 (n.)
Ahab whirled the craft aside; p. 449 (n.) as the whale dallied with
the doomed craft.

CREST. The summit of a sea-wave. (Smyth)

Mardi--p. 30 (n.) shouldered us from crest to crest; p. 37 (n.) and
you chip upon one of their lordly crests; p. 50 (n.) ermined with
wave crests; p. 340 (n.) and sparkle in the crests of the waves;
p. 367 (n.) under the light frothy wave-crests of Anacreaon; p. 432
(n.) each curling wave-crest a flume.

White-Jacket--p. 108 (n.) curling their [billows'] very crests under the feet of . . . us.

Moby-Dick--p. 242 (n.) The waves, too, nodded their indolent crests; p. 385 (n.) rearing upon the topmost crest of the equatorial flood.

CREW. Comprehends every officer and man on board-ship, borne as complement on the books. There are in ships of war several particular crews or gangs, as the gunner's, carpenter's, sailmaker's, blacksmith's, armourer's, and cooper's crews. (Smyth)

Omoo--p. 26 (n.) of the character of our crew; p. 27 (n.) what a disappointment for our crew; p. 35 (n.) and a slumbering crew; p. 35 (n.) a mere device to lull the crew; p. 39 (n.) the crews of which after a hard fight; p. 44 (n.) Death and Burial of Two of the Crew; p. 44 (n.) the subsequent conduct of the crew; p. 45 (n.) to have gone among the crew; p. 46 (n.) carried off nearly half the crew; p. 47 (n.) seldom or never occurred to the crew; p. 51 (n.) the crew would be sent home; p. 52 (n.) going among the crew and taking his place; p. 68 (n.) the crew were no longer bound; p. 68 (n.) the state of both vessel and crew; p. 69 (n.) in supposing that such a crew would, in any way; p. 70 (n.) whispered maledictions of his crew; p. 71 (n.) he seldom went among the crew; p. 72 (n.) bitterest disappointment to a boat's crew; p. 73 (n.) to diffuse the right spirit among the crew; p. 75 (n.) as it went among the crew; p. 84 (n.) to regain the favor of the crew; p. 93 (n.) fraternally disposed toward the crew; p. 95 (n.) hearing the maudlin cries of our crew; p. 98 (n.) imputed to the conduct of the crew; p. 110 (n.) to promote dissatisfaction among the crew; p. 140 (n.) his crew was reduced; p. 147 (n.) for the purpose of shipping a new crew; p. 148 (n.) that a new crew was finally obtained; p. 148 (n.) composed part of the Julia's new crew; p. 151 (n.) the worshipful crew of the Julia looked on; p. 159 (n.) their crews frequently visited us; p. 231 (n.) with a native crew; p. 289 (n.) One boat's crew of 'em is gone; p. 29 p. 299 (n.) the crew of the Leviathan made so prodigious a tumult; p. 312 (n.) if her crew were to be credited; p. 315 (n.) compose part of a whaler's crew; p. 315 (n.) having made good the number of his crew.

Mardi--p. 4 (n.) nor its crew; p. 12 (n.) among the crew; p. 14 (n.) among the Acturion's crew; p. 19 (n.) captain, mates, crew; p. 19 (n.) by her crew; p. 22 (n.) boats-crew-watches; p. 22 (n.) composed of a boat's crew; p. 23 (n.) boats-crew-watch; p. 24 (n.) with such a motley crew; p. 29 (n.) which the Acturion's crew; p. 57 (n.) abandoned by her crew; p. 58 (n.) of the crew; p. 58 (n.) abandoned of her crew; p. 62 (adj.) for the crew's hiding away; p. 68 (n.) with a mixed European and native crew; p. 70 (n.) attacked the aghast crew; p. 90 (n.) forming part of the crews; p. 97 (n.) the character of my crew; p. 111 (n.) announced the fact to the startled crew.

Redburn--p. 31 (n.) Every thing . . . was on board but the crew; p. 55 (n.) would corrupt the whole crew; p. 57 (n.) the weakest man, bodily, of the whole crew; p. 59 (n.) no mark or influence among the crew; p. 62 (n.) growing up in me against the whole crew; p. 67 (n.) some sea-captains are fathers to their crew; p. 79 (n.) the best

natured man among the crew; p. 93 (n.) and all her crew felt sure;
p. 93 (n.) of Larry, one of our crew; p. 103 (n.) fastened there by
the crew for a signal; p. 106 (n.) the crew have terrible hard work;
p. 107 (n.) now carries a crew of harpooners; p. 108 (n.) One of the
crew said he was; p. 109 (n.) to the great satisfaction of the crew;
p. 117 (n.) that of the crew, all the men; p. 121 (n.) in which a
ship's crew hold the knowledge; p. 130 (n.) the crew were told to go
ashore; p. 130 (n.) in a large crew remaining at Liverpool; p. 130
(n.) regarded with immeasurable disdain by the crews; p. 133 (n.)
several old guests among our crew; p. 136 (n.) of the life led by our
crew; p. 137 (n.) to proceed with the crew; p. 152 (n.) when the crew
went ashore to supper; p. 166 (n.) with its crew of sober Scotch caps;
p. 166 (n.) though his crew might only consist of himself; p. 170
(n.) flagellating the crew with the flat of his saber; p. 175 (n.)
the crew were a bucaniering looking set; p. 186 (n.) crews of
hundreds and hundreds of ships; p. 196 (n.) when the crew went to
meals; p. 204 (n.) mustering the various crews; p. 218 (n.) three of
our crew had left us; p. 218 (n.) a new crew is easily procured;
p. 220 (n.) further admonished my friend concerning our crew; p. 238
(n.) on board before the rest of the crew; p. 238 (adj.) it became
the crew's business; p. 240 (n.) and passed forward by the crew;
p. 240 (n.) as the crews catted their anchors; p. 245 (n.) strict
orders were given to the crew; p. 253 (n.) mingling with the
Highlander's crew; p. 253 (n.) one of their homeward-bound crew;
p. 254 (n.) polite refinement in the mates and crew; p. 255 (n.) in
the hands of his officers and crew; p. 257 (n.) the crew now
reckoned him fair play; p. 257 (n.) becoming as a hunted hare to the
merciless crew; p. 268 (n.) the crew would throw it overboard for her;
p. 270 (n.) when the crew were about two weeks out; p. 270 (n.) zest
with which the Highlander's crew now shuffled; p. 271 (n.) the crew
became absent, moody; p. 276 (n.) outrageous became his treatment of
the crew; p. 278 (n.) to sing his songs to this ruffian crew; p. 278
(n.) the treatment of the crew threw Harry; p. 283 (n.) where the
crew were assembled; p. 290 (n.) now joined a band of the crew;
p. 305 (n.) set apart for paying off the crew; p. 309 (n.) the last
movements of this remarkable crew; p. 312 (n.) the boat's crew that
boarded our vessel; p. 312 (n.) we lost a boat's crew.

White-Jacket--p. 8 (n.) into which a Man-of-war's Crew is divided;
p. 9 (n.) a man-of-war's crew would be nothing but a mob; p. 10 (n.)
and least sailor-like of the crew; p. 10 (n.) They are the tag-rag
and bob-tail of the crew; p. 11 (n.) into which a man-of-war's crew
is divided; p. 15 (n.) sections of a man-of-war's crew; p. 20 (n.)
into which our crew was divided; p. 27 (n.) all men in common with
the crew; p. 39 (n.) among the crew of a man-of-war; p. 39 (n.) to
instill more virtuous principles into their crew; p. 45 (n.) such
effects produced upon some of the crew; p. 51 (n.) the same view of
the thing that another of the crew did; p. 58 (n.) for the cooking
for the crew is all done; p. 64 (n.) indispensable that the crew
should be duly instructed; p. 66 (n.) Among our gun's crew, however;
p. 73 (n.) the second, third, and fourth cutters' crews; p. 74 (n.)
from a frigate's crew might be culled out men; p. 74 (n.) a man-of-
war's crew could quickly found an Alexandria; p. 81 (n.) suspected of
being an informer among the crew; p. 84 (n.) vouch-safed the morning
hammocks to their crew; p. 87 (n.) over-neat vessels are Tartars to
the crew; p. 88 (n.) may easily inflict upon the crew; p. 88 (n.)

when the crew had washed that part; p. 88 (n.) the crew kneeled down
to their task; p. 90 (n.) Captain Claret, the father of his crew;
p. 91 (n.) having theatricals was allowed to the crew; p. 91 (n.) the
stage-struck portion of the crew had . . . rehearsed; p. 93 (n.)
against lawful authority among the crew; p. 99 (n.) of preserving the
health of the crews; p. 102 (n.) is always regarded by the crew;
p. 107 (n.) About . . . the shouts of the crew; p. 111 (n.) desire to
strike subjection among the crew; p. 111 (n.) so far as any of the
crew ever knew; p. 115 (n.) what care the jolly crew; p. 125 (n.)
used at the martial exercises of the crew; p. 127 (n.) containing an
alphabetic list of all the crew; p. 135 (n.) the crew crowded round
the main-mast; p. 136 (n.) fixed his eyes severely upon the crew;
p. 137 (n.) some of the crew whispered among themselves; p. 137 (n.)
went among the crew with a smile; p. 138 (n.) wept Peter, going among
the crew; p. 138 (n.) and the crew slowly dispersed; p. 138 (n.) the
administration of corporal punishment upon the crew; p. 141 (n.) seem
to be less disliked by their crews; p. 141 (n.) invariably proves a
tyrant to his crew; p. 144 (n.) with its crew of 800 or 1000 men;
p. 148 (n.) showing to the crew with what terrible attributes; p. 148
(n.) with such crews as Lord Collingwood's; p. 149 (n.) through the
insubordination of the crew; p. 155 (n.) to summon the crew to
devotions; p. 155 (n.) were but ill calculated to benefit the crew;
p. 157 (n.) to the officers and crew; p. 158 (n.) papers were
circulated among the crew; p. 158 (n.) he makes a far better chaplain
for his crew; p. 158 (n.) I have known one crew; p. 161 (n.) She also
carried . . . a small yawl, with a crew; p. 161 (n.) All these boats
. . . had their regular crews; p. 162 (n.) the gig's crew were
conducted below; p. 162 (n.) the English crew went to quarters;
p. 172 (n.) he was rather indulgent to his crew; p. 177 (n.) as the
boat's crew . . . come up the side; p. 177 (n.) till the whole crew
are examined; p. 179 (n.) perceived by one of the boat's crew; p. 179
(n.) takes his crew apart, one by one; p. 179 (n.) are numbered among
his crew; p. 180 (n.) kept in the barge to refresh the crew; p. 180
(n.) the boat's crew are overhauled; p. 180 (n.) one of his crew is a
weak-pated fellow; p. 180 (n.) nor any of his crew; p. 183 (n.)
examining both her and her crew; p. 190 (n.) seized by night by an
exasperated crew; p. 197 (n.) without the loss of some of her crew
from aloft; p. 198 (n.) the crew were listlessly lying around; p. 204
(n.) all his accounts with the crew; p. 205 (n.) permitted to be
served out to the crew; p. 205 (n.) are circulated among the crew;
p. 206 (n.) a favorite with many of the crew; p. 216 (n.) soon
forgotten by the crew at large; p. 219 (n.) not at all disliked by
the crew; p. 245 (n.) called away the First-Cutter's crew; p. 265
(n.) the respective efficiency of the crews; p. 274 (n.) authorized
play-time for the crews; p. 274 (n.) his crew seldom amuse themselves;
p. 276 (n.) the indulgent father of his crew; p. 281 (n.) upon the
packed and silent crew; p. 295 (n.) In all cases where the crews of
the ships; p. 300 (n.) addressed by a merchant-captain to his crew;
p. 307 (n.) sly, knavish faces among the crew; p. 307 (n.) yet certain
of the crew; p. 313 (n.) valor displayed by the British crew; p. 314
(n.) presumed to prevail among the crew; p. 314 (n.) by permitting
his hopeless crew to be butchered; p. 314 (n.) that crew must consent
to be slaughtered; p. 316 (n.) dashed dead two thirds of a gun's crew;
p. 318 (n.) My gun's crew carried small flags; p. 328 (n.) to the
healthfulness of the crew; p. 352 (n.) prevailing upon many of the
crew; p. 353 (n.) in the boisterous sports of the crew; p. 354 (n.)

But there were others of the crew; p. 354 (n.) our crew seemed a
company of Merovingians; p. 361 (n.) oh crew of the Neversink; p. 363
(n.) Nestor of the crew; p. 367 (n.) the majority of the Neversink's
crew; p. 371 (n.) to the crews of the other vessels; p. 374 (n.) the
character of the officers and crew; p. 375 (n.) the moral well-being
of the crew; p. 375 (n.) the crowded crew mutually decay; p. 378 (n.)
enlisted with the crew of an American frigate; pp. 378-9 (n.) such
was his name among the crew; p. 379 (n.) degradation of the Caucasian
crew; p. 379 (n.) a proportion to the rest of the crew; p. 380 (n.)
the greater part of her crew be; p. 381 (n.) a full third of all the
crews; p. 382 (n.) reduce the number of a man-of-war's crew; p. 385
(n.) docile and Christianized crews; p. 387 (n.) there were others of
the crew; p. 388 (n.) touching the crew themselves; p. 389 (n.) of
every ten of the Neversink's crew; p. 389 (n.) at least nine tenths
of a crew; p. 390 (n.) let some of the crew of the Neversink; p. 399
(n.) What a swarming crew.

Moby-Dick--p. 6 (n.) Soon to the sport of death the crews repair;
p. 10 (n.) in bloody possession of the savages enrolled among the
crew; p. 11 (n.) out of the crews of whaling vessels (American) few
ever return; p. 23 (n.) That's the Grampus's crew; p. 40 (n.) Forming
one of the boat's crews of this ship ELIZA; p. 94 (n.) and the crew
sprang for the handspikes; p. 108 (n.) to augment their crews from
the hardy peasants; p. 111 (n.) he was everyday visible to the crew;
p. 148 (n.) to sail with such a heathen crew; p. 153 (adj.) here
there's none but the crew's cursed day; p. 449 (n.) but the tiger-
yellow crew were tumbling over each other's heads; p. 467 (n.) its
half-wading, splashing crew, trying hard to stop the gap.

CROCODILE. An amphibious animal of the genus Lacerta or lizard, of the
largest kind. It inhabits the large rivers in Africa and Asia, and lays
its eggs, resembling those of a goose, in the sand, to be hatched by the
heat of the sun. (Webster)

Mardi--p. 375 (n.) Amergris is the petrified gall-stones of
crocodiles; p. 415 (n.) guanos, serpents, tongueless crocodiles;
p. 417 (n.) old patriarchs of crocodiles and alligators; p. 482 (n.)
crusading centaurs, crocodiles, and sharks.

CROW'S-NEST. A small shelter for the look-out man: sometimes made with
a cask, at the top-gallant mast-head of whalers, whence fish are espied.
(Smyth)

Moby-Dick--p. 137 (n.) with those enviable little tents or pulpits,
called crow's nests; p. 138 (n.) recently invented crow's-nest of the
Glacier; p. 138 (n.) He called it the Sleet's crow's-nest; p. 138 (n.)
the Sleet's crow's-nest is something like a large tierce or pipe;
p. 138 (n.) stood his mast-head in this crow's-nest of his; p. 138
(n.) all the little detailed conveniences of his crow's-nest; p. 138
(n.) of his experiments in this crow's-nest.

CRUISE. A voyage in quest of an enemy expected to sail through any
particular tract of the sea at a certain season. The parts of seas

frequented by whales are called cruising grounds of whalers. (Smyth--
Melville also spells it "cruize.")

Typee--p. 5 (adj.) during our passage from the cruising ground; p. 5
(v.) cruising in quest of some region of gold; p. 6 (n.) Journal of
the Cruise of the U.S. frigate Essex; p. 7 (v.) we had been cruising
on the line; p. 22 (v.) a ship unlucky in falling in with whales
continues to cruize after them; p. 22 (v.) cruizing along as leisurely
as ever; p. 34 (n.) as we are just off a six months' cruise.

Omoo--p. 6 (n.) would allow me to enter for one cruise; p. 9 (n.)
captured at sea by a British cruiser; p. 23 (n.) we were fairly
embarked for a long cruise; p. 28 (n.) volunteered for a cruise; p.
p. 34 (n.) to what particular cruising-ground we were going; p. 35
(n.) lent an interest to this portion of the cruise; p. 35 (adj.) we
were bound to a fine cruising ground; p. 42 (n.) gibbeted at sea by a
cruiser; p. 68 (n.) Going into harbor, after a cruise; p. 81 (n.) for
a short cruise in a whaler; p. 82 (n.) for a three months' cruise; p.
p. 86 (n.) to a short cruise under him; p. 100 (n.) whose cruising-
grounds lie in the vicinity; p. 103 (n.) the cruise being virtually
at an end; p. 103 (n.) the fag end of a cruise; p. 109 (n.) the
present her maiden cruise; p. 118 (n.) been a cruise or two in a
whaling-vessel; p. 128 (n.) here we are--started on a six months'
cruise; p. 140 (n.) The Julia sails on a cruise this day week; p. 148
(n.) will only ship for one cruise; p. 158 (n.) flush from a lucky
whaling-cruise; p. 159 (n.) which have their regular seasons for
Cruising; p. 231 (v.) take turns cruising over the tranquil Pacific;
p. 298 (adv.) went off after a whale, last cruise; p. 291 (n.)
shipped for a single cruise; p. 291 (n.) Their cruise was a famous
one; p. 315 (n.) was now bound on her last whaling cruise; p. 315
(n.) I merely stipulated for the coming cruise.

Mardi--p. 3 (n.) on a cruise.

Redburn--p. 57 (n.) being chased by an English cruiser; p. 126 (v.)
cruising about the Irish Sea; p. 193 (n.) going on particular
cruises; p. 312 (n.) shipped . . . at Callao, for the cruise.

White-Jacket--p. 3 (n.) toward the end of a three years' cruise;
p. 10 (n.) when going ashore after a long cruise; p. 12 (n.) who think
of cruising in men-of-war; p. 14 (n.) to refer to last cruise; p. 17
(n.) On this present cruise; p. 19 (n.) discharge that well to the
end of the cruise; p. 22 (n.) during a three years' cruise; p. 33 (n.)
and this cruise over; p. 43 (n.) persons who kept journals of the
cruise; p. 43 (n.) The Cruise of the Neversink; p. 63 (n.) attended
to that business during the entire cruise; p. 63 (n.) three times
every day for a three years' cruise; p. 89 (n.) to have been
previously intoxicated during the cruise; p. 91 (n.) had frequently
during the cruise rehearsed; p. 138 (n.) became silent and sullen for
the rest of the cruise; p. 141 (n.) on the cruise now written of;
p. 171 (n.) during the entire cruise; p. 171 (adv.) besides being on
the smart the whole cruise; p. 197 (n.) a man-of-war returning home
after a cruise; p. 206 (n.) upon her return from a cruise extending;
p. 223 (n.) In the earlier part of the cruise; p. 250 (adv.) I was in
New Zealand last cruise; p. 257 (n.) in nearly three years' cruise;
p. 272 (n.) being on a cruise in the Mediterranean; p. 272 (n.) all

her captains, on all cruises; p. 298 (n.) struck terror into the
cruisers of France; p. 314 (n.) with the two English cruisers; p. 316
(n.) sailed with him in many cruises; p. 351 (adv.) who nearly the
whole cruise sat; p. 351 (adv.) All the cruise they were hard at work;
p. 353 (n.) during the whole three years' cruise; p. 355 (n.)
Throughout the cruise; p. 357 (n.) when after our long, long cruise;
p. 367 (n.) in previous cruises habituated to . . . misusage; p. 378
(n.) during the present cruise; p. 389 (n.) expiration of the present
cruise; p. 389 (n.) with all the experiences of that cruise; p. 390
(adv.) yet, cruise after cruise; p. 390 (n.) men who, during the
cruise; p. 396 (n.) who had lived too fast during the cruise; p. 396
(n.) betokens the end of a cruise that is passing.

Moby-Dick--p. 11 (n.) Cruise in a Whale Boat; p. 59 (n.) all
betokening that new cruises were on the start; p. 121 (adj.)
designated by them Right Whale Cruising Grounds; p. 470 (adj.) It
was the devious-cruising Rachel.

CURRENT. A certain progressive flowing of the sea in one direction, by
which all bodies floating therein are compelled more or less to submit to
the stream. (Smyth)

Typee--p. 46 (n.) for the current of water extended very nearly;
p. 229 (n.) sitting upon a rock in the midst of the current.

Omoo--p. 27 (n.) we got into a strong current; p. 27 (n.) Unexpectedly
a counter-current befriended us; p. 95 (n.) the current swept her
down; p. 98 (n.) from the baffling winds, currents, and sunken rocks.

Mardi--p. 3 (n.) of the many wild currents; p. 17 (n.) calms and
currents may; p. 43 (n.) the more wind, and the less current; p. 51
(n.) whether might not the currents have swept; p. 51 (n.) spite of
past calms and currents; p. 81 (n.) the set of the currents; p. 108
(n.) Calms, light breezes, and currents; p. 111 (n.) the rapid
currents we encountered; p. 111 (n.) counteracted the glide of the
currents; p. 111 (n.) The equatorial currents; p. 111 (n.) these
currents are forever shifting; p. 111 (n.) by reason of the currents;
p. 217 (n.) evading the dangerous currents; p. 234 (n.) much pleasanter
than the currents beneath; p. 258 (n.) in currents full slow; p. 306
(n.) still struggling against strange currents; p. 370 (n.) then, be
sure a thousand contrary currents whirl and eddy within; p. 491 (n.)
the current too strong for our paddlers; p. 492 (n.) the currents
were sweeping us over a strait; p. 511 (n.) by the hostile meeting of
two currents; p. 543 (n.) in amphitheaters undermined by currents;
p. 554 (n.) a current seized us; p. 644 (n.) sleek currents our
coursers; p. 645 (n.) Swifter and swifter the currents now ran;
p. 646 (n.) Then two wild currents met; p. 653 (n.) Conflicting
currents met, and wrestled; p. 653 (n.) but the currents were as
fierce as headwinds; p. 654 (n.) the currents sweep thee oceanward.

Redburn--p. 97 (n.) the temperature of this current; p. 98 (n.) from
whence this current comes.

White-Jacket--p. 48 (n.) to stir the stagnant current in our poor old
Commodore's torpid veins; p. 104 (n.) and equally affected by the

currents; p. 115 (n.) gales are mostly from the westward, also the
current; p. 393 (n.) Some current seemed hurrying me away.

Moby-Dick--p. 158 (n.) as the secrets of the currents in the seas
have never yet been divulged; p. 171 (n.) Ahab was threading a maze
of currents and eddies; p. 171 (n.) who knew the sets of all tides
and currents; p. 296 (n.) because the white-bone or swell at his
broad muzzle was a dashed one, like the swell formed when two hostile
currents meet; p. 461 (n.) however the baser currents of the sea may
turn and tack.

CUTTER. A small single-masted, sharp-built broad vessel, commonly
navigated in the English channel, furnished with a straight running
bowsprit, occasionally run in horizontally on the deck; except for
which, and the largeness of the sails, they are rigged much like
sloops. The name is derived from their fast sailing. (Smyth)

Omoo--p. 21 (n.) swim to the corvette for a cutter; p. 21 (n.) and
then a large cutter pulled out; p. 21 (n.) Another cutter . . . soon
followed; p. 103 (n.) the first-cutter of the Reine Blanche; p. 104
(n.) ordering the delinquent into the cutter; p. 104 (n.) accompanied
us into the cutter; p. 104 (n.) sat quietly in the bow of the cutter;
p. 112 (n.) escorted into a cutter alongside.

White-Jacket--p. 18 (n.) So off went the cutter; p. 19 (n.) and
entering the cutter; p. 71 (n.) Away! Second, Third, and Fourth
Cutters, away; p. 73 (n.) Clear away the cutters; p. 73 (adj.) call
away the second, third, and fourth cutters' crews; p. 152 (n.) a
cutter was lowered; p. 161 (n.) known as the first cutter, the second
cutter, then the third and fourth cutters; p. 161 (n.) from another
boat, the second cutter; pp. 161-2 (n.) The cutter lay still; p. 178
(n.) a fore-top man, belonging to the second cutter; p. 179 (n.)
coming alongside one night in a cutter; p. 219 (n.) when you see an
English cutter; p. 245 (n.) as an oarsman in the First-Cutter; p. 245
(adj.) called way the First-Cutter's crew; p. 246 (n.) near the ship
in one of her cutters; p. 264 (n.) the second cutter was called away;
p. 265 (n.) when the second cutter pulled about; p. 317 (n.) fights
with his British majesty's cutters; p. 394 (n.) one of the cutters
picked me up.

DAVIT. A piece of timber or iron, with sheaves or blocks at its end,
projecting over a vessel's quarter or stern, to hoist up and suspend one
end of a boat. (Smyth)

Mardi--p. 19 (n.) to curved timbers called "davits"; p. 19 (n.)
besides the "davits."

DECK. The platform laid longitudinally over the transverse beams; in
ships of war they support the guns. (Smyth)

Typee--p. 3 (n.) which once decorated our stern and quarter-deck;
p. 7 (n.) and passing along the quarter-deck; p. 9 (adj.) never to be
seated while keeping a deck watch; p. 10 (n.) The captain, darting on

deck from the cabin; p. 12 (n.) to navigate his body across the deck;
p. 15 (n.) quickly frolicking about the decks; p. 15 (n.) the deck
was illuminated with lanterns; p. 22 (n.) old salts, who just managed
to hobble about deck; p. 31 (n.) the recollection of her narrow desks;
p. 31 (n.) that being upon deck, revolving over in my mind; p. 32 (n.)
as smart a looking sailor as ever stepped upon a deck; p. 43 (n.) the
starboard watch were mustered upon the quarter-deck; p. 36 (n.) as I
was about to ascend to the deck; p. 36 (n.) and I sprung upon the
deck; p. 229 (n.) coiled away like a rope on a ship's deck; p. 271
(n.) he grappled Jimmy as he struck the deck.

Omoo--p. 5 (n.) On the quarter-deck was one whom I took; p. 5 (n.) a
low cry ran fore and aft the deck; p. 6 (n.) Immediately on gaining
the deck; p. 6 (n.) Helping me on deck; p. 8 (n.) and let me go on
deck; p. 13 (n.) ran about the decks making himself heard; p. 16 (n.)
there was something to be done on deck; p. 17 (n.) "Tumble on deck,"
he then bellowed; p. 17 (n.) Now, come on deck; p. 17 (n.) happening
to ascend to the quarter-deck; p. 18 (n.) come on deck; come on deck;
p. 18 (n.) have the kindness to come on deck, sir; p. 18 (n.) Let Mr.
Jermin come on deck; p. 18 (n.) retreated to the quarter-deck; p. 19
(n.) coming on deck; p. 20 (n.) he mounted to the deck with a flask
of spirits; p. 20 (n.) Springing on deck again; p. 21 (n.) Dashing
his hat upon deck; p. 21 (n.) By this time the officer of the deck;
p. 21 (n.) our sick men limped about the deck; p. 33 (n.) I ascended
to the deck; p. 38 (n.) embraces the forward part of the deck; p. 38
(n.) it was not five feet from deck to deck; p. 39 (n.) which was a
mere hole in the deck; p. 40 (n.) all who were able darted on deck;
p. 41 (n.) when they fell asleep on deck; p. 42 (n.) some of those on
deck would come below; p. 42 (n.) Suddenly an order was heard on deck;
p. 42 (n.) returned to the deck; p. 43 (n.) the jokers on deck
strained away; p. 43 (n.) when we hurried on deck; p. 44 (n.) carried
on deck; p. 45 (n.) unable to crawl on deck; p. 46 (n.) Many stayed
on deck until broad morning; p. 51 (n.) I happened to go on deck;
p. 55 (n.) is pummeled on deck; p. 56 (n.) rolled about deck, day
after day; p. 59 (n.) secured one end to a ring-bolt in the deck;
p. 59 (n.) The water then poured along the deck; p. 59 (n.) The few
men on deck having sprung; p. 61 (n.) he went staggering about deck;
p. 62 (n.) he came running on deck; p. 68 (n.) The sick . . . were on
deck; p. 68 (n.) The quarter-deck, however, furnished; p. 70 (n.) the
captain was helped on deck; p. 73 (n.) On gaining the deck; p. 74 (n.)
several now ran on deck; p. 75 (n.) No sooner did the consul touch
the deck; p. 76 (n.) to muster on the quarter-deck; p. 79 (n.) to the
other side of the deck; p. 80 (n.) straight down to a seam in the
deck; p. 81 (n.) walked across the deck; p. 83 (adj.) just as the
quarter-deck gathering dispersed; p. 83 (n.) I came on deck quite
incensed; p. 84 (n.) upon Wilson's coming on deck; p. 84 (n.) ran
about deck like madmen; p. 86 (n.) carried across the deck; p. 87 (n.)
secured to the deck; p. 87 (n.) Upon deck every thing looked so quiet;
p. 87 (n.) was left in charge of the deck; p. 88 (n.) both came to
the deck; p. 88 (n.) writhing on the deck; p. 88 (n.) Having remained
upon deck; p. 88 (n.) went on deck; p. 89 (n.) the deserted decks and
broad white sails; p. 89 (n.) casting their shadows upon the deck;
p. 90 (n.) streamed fore and aft the deck; p. 91 (n.) They both fell
to the deck; p. 91 (n.) he was dragged along the deck; p. 91 (n.) he
came staggering on deck; p. 92 (n.) stood upon deck; p. 95 (n.) of
the natives on her decks; p. 95 (n.) made his appearance on deck;

p. 95 (n.) some confusion on the schooner's decks; p. 96 (n.) the instant he touched the deck; p. 97 (n.) leaving the deck to the steward; p. 98 (n.)   those   on deck; p. 100 (n.) in two bounds, stood on deck; p. 102 (n.) as he touched the deck; p. 102 (n.) Muster the mutineers on the quarter-deck; p. 103 (n.) allow nothing superfluous to litter up the deck; p. 105 (n.) down the ladders to the berth-deck; p. 106 (n.) bolted down to the deck; p. 106 (n.) orders the man on deck; p. 109 (n.) But come to tread the gun-deck; p. 109 (n.) On the spar-deck; p. 110 (n.) on the deck of a thoroughly disciplined armed vessel; p. 114 (n.) Escaped from the confined decks; p. 123 (n.) dictated to the chiefs on the gun-deck; p. 146 (n.) on being hailed from the deck; p. 149 (n.) The decks were all life and commotion; p. 153 (n.) I went on deck to take my place; p. 616 (n.) by any one from the quarter-deck; p. 290 (n.) for some one to come on deck; p. 290 (n.) broad in the beam, flush decks.

Mardi--p. 5 (adj.) no quarter-deck dignity; p. 6 (n.) on the deck; p. 19 (n.) from all parts of the deck; p. 20 (n.) from the quarter-deck; p. 20 (n.) traversed the deck; p. 22 (n.) alternately on deck; p. 23 (n.) turn on deck; p. 23 (n.) on the quarter-deck; p. 23 (n.) the mariners on deck; p. 23 (n.) summoned on deck; p. 25 (n.) her familiar decks; p. 26 (n.) aft toward the quarter-deck; p. 28 (n.) just springing to the deck; p. 37 (n.) on a ship's deck; p. 58 (n.) the deck was a complete litter; p. 58 (n.) we went about deck; p. 59 (n.) bundling them on deck; p. 61 (n.) we ascended to the deck; p. 62 (n.) on the quarter-deck; p. 64 (n.) we had brought on deck; p. 64 (n.) in the middle of the quarter-deck; p. 65 (n.) thrusting itself through the deck; p. 66 (n.) dropped it to the deck; p. 66 (n.) having gained the deck; p. 71 (n.) Samoa flew on deck; p. 74 (n.) on the deck; p. 74 (n.) the decks were still cumbered; p. 74 (n.) the decks were washed down; p. 75 (n.) slippery grew the cabin deck; p. 81 (n.) Rushing to the deck; p. 86 (n.) eating and drinking on the quarter-deck; p. 91 (n.) one of their three-deckers; p. 92 (n.) returned to the deck; p. 96 (n.) I repaired to the quarter-deck; p. 97 (n.) walked up and down on the quarter-deck; p. 103 (n.) high and dry on the Parki's deck; p. 105 (n.) brought my brave gentleman to the deck; p. 110 (adj.) once more in a double-decked craft; p. 111 (n.) a violent stamping on the deck; p. 111 (n.) spread every evening on the quarter-deck; pp. 116-7 (n.) used on the forecastle-deck; p. 117 (n.) drops of brine fell upon the deck; p. 117 (n.) sliding across the aslant deck; p. 119 (n.) floated the lighter casks upward to the deck; p. 115 (n.) all awash as her decks would soon be; p. 120 (n.) putting her decks in order; p. 120 (n.) from the deck of the Acturion; p. 123 (n.) And rushing on deck; p. 123 (n.) Now pour it along the deck; p. 367 (n.) running shouting across my decks; p. 481 (n.) Cleopatra was throned on the cedar quarter-deck; p. 554 (adv.) tiers of galleries within, deck on deck.

Redburn--p. 4 (n.) with contempt for the vile deck-loads of hay; p. 8 (n.) all along her two decks; p. 9 (n.) smoking a glass cigar on the quarter-deck; p. 12 (n.) to avoid them, went on deck; p. 12 (n.) one incessant storm raged on deck; p. 13 (n.) I then turned on my heel, and . . . marched on deck; p. 24 (n.) When I reached the deck; p. 25 (n.) to a sort of hole in the deck; p. 25 (n.) I was glad to get on deck; p. 26 (n.) that I had to go on deck; p. 28 (n.) These two boats were in the middle of the deck; p. 29 (n.) some shavings, which lay

about the deck; p. 29 (n.) from several bunches lying on deck; p. 39
(n.) if one drop falls on deck; p. 30 (n.) incautiously looked down
toward the deck; p. 30 (n.) recollect my safe return to the deck;
p. 31 (n.) and swaggered on deck; p. 34 (n.) and putting the decks in
order; p. 36 (n.) took hold of a little boat on her deck; p. 38 (n.)
the sailors were ordered on the quarter-deck; p. 39 (n.) during the
scene on the quarter-deck; p. 40 (n.) watch . . . was called on deck;
p. 45 (n.) kept walking up and down the quarter-deck; p. 47 (n.)
walking briskly up and down the deck; p. 48 (n.) one of them laid on
deck apart; p. 49 (n.) a little bell was rung on the quarter-deck;
p. 50 (n.) the sailors came running up on deck; p. 50 (n.) he had
rushed on deck; p. 53 (n.) He Helps Wash the Decks; p. 53 (n.)
thumping of a handspike on deck; p. 53 (n.) when we got on deck;
p. 53 (n.) to wash down the decks; p. 53 (n.) to splash about all
over the decks; p. 54 (n.) chased a chip all over the deck; p. 54
(n.) I thought this washing down the decks; p. 55 (n.) I ran on deck;
p. 55 (n.) I now ran on deck again; p. 57 (n.) before washing down
the decks; p. 59 (n.) used to run up on deck; p. 60 (n.) where the
light came down from deck; p. 63 (n.) the decks being washed down;
p. 65 (n.) all tumbled upon the deck; p. 68 (n.) I used to pass by
the places on deck; p. 69 (n.) and coming on deck; p. 69 (n.) toward
the cabin-door on the quarter-deck; p. 70 (n.) set in the house on
deck; p. 70 (n.) making fast a rope on the quarter-deck; p. 74 (n.)
made me slip and slide about the decks; p. 74 (n.) from lying down on
deck in it; p. 75 (n.) shambling round the deck in my rags; p. 75 (n.)
showed her decks fore and aft; p. 77 (n.) the fifth and highest sail
from deck; p. 79 (n.) I got down rapidly on deck; p. 80 (n.) The
decks were dripping with wet; p. 85 (n.) inserted into the deck to
give light; p. 85 (n.) in walking the deck; p. 88 (adj.) at one of
the quarter-deck carronades; p. 90 (n.) then go on deck into a rain
storm; p. 92 (n.) sent the whole ship's company flying on deck; p. 92
(n.) when we got on deck; p. 92 (n.) the trampling of feet on the
deck; p. 97 (n.) the after part of the quarter-deck; p. 100 (n.)
during our watch on deck; p. 101 (n.) who went by the name of "Gun-
Deck"; p. 101 (n.) when we washed down decks; p. 101 (n.) according
to Gun-Deck; p. 101 (n.) Gun-Deck had touched at Cadiz; p. 102 (n.)
could hardly carry it off the decks; p. 103 (n.) which broke clear
over the deck; p. 103 (n.) about ten feet above the deck; p. 107 (n.)
The broad quarter-deck, too; p. 107 (n.) sometimes sitting on the
quarter-deck; p. 108 (n.) he glided about the deck; p. 109 (n.)
Spread a mattress on deck; p. 111 (n.) suddenly appeared on deck;
p. 112 (n.) stowing himself away in the between-decks; p. 114 (n.)
turning one side of the deck; p. 115 (n.) and slept down on deck by
the bare stays; p. 118 (adj.) Quarter-Deck Furniture; p. 119 (n.) of
the standing furniture of the quarter-deck; p. 119 (n.) full in the
middle of the quarter-deck; p. 120 (n.) and sending it down on deck;
p. 122 (n.) during their watch on deck; p. 122 (n.) after walking the
deck for four full hours; p. 122 (n.) hurried on deck again; p. 123
(n.) the men on deck, exhilarated; p. 123 (n.) fine shower-bath here
on deck; p. 123 (n.) we on deck became the wits; p. 124 (n.) one
morning I came on deck; p. 126 (n.) who sat grouped together on deck;
p. 137 (n.) and the decks were washed down; p. 139 (n.) sermons to
them on the gun-deck; p. 166 (n.) its quarter-deck elastic from much
dancing; p. 166 (adj.) all the airs of an admiral on a three-decker's
poop; p. 166 (n.) little round glasses placed in the deck; p. 171
(n.) Lascars were on the forecastle-deck; p. 171 (n.) with

Christianity on the quarter-deck; p. 175 (n.) her decks in a state of
most piratical disorder; p. 175 (n.) so that its deck was at least;
p. 198 (n.) here you see the decks turned into pens; p. 198 (n.)
Irish deck-passengers, thick as they can stand; p. 219 (n.) one fine
morning, on the quarter-deck; p. 124 (n.) down the hatchway into the
between-decks; p. 238 (n.) to clear away the between-decks; p. 239
(n.) boxes were already littering the decks; p. 239 (n.) besides the
usual number of casks on deck; p. 239 (n.) all along the between-
decks; p. 249 (n.) reclining all over the decks; p. 241 (n.) to
escape the uncomfortable and perilous decks; p. 421 (n.) in their
exposed galley on deck; p. 242 (n.) the most holy precincts of the
quarter-deck; p. 243 (n.) commanding his instant presence on deck;
p. 243 (n.) the mate retired to the quarter-deck; p. 245 (n.) who had
just come on deck; p. 245 (n.) during the next four hours on deck;
p. 246 (n.) for the watches on deck; p. 249 (n.) were gathered on
deck; p. 253 (n.) once came on deck in a brocaded dressing-gown;
p. 255 (n.) of the rigging about decks; p. 255 (n.) pulling the
proper ropes on deck; p. 257 (n.) even to us, down on deck; p. 260
(n.) some of them came on deck; p. 260 (n.) for Carlo to repair to
the quarter-deck; p. 261 (n.) marching forward from the quarter-deck;
p. 261 (n.) took place during my watch on deck; p. 262 (n.) on the
shady side of the deck; p. 264 (n.) and go to groping over the deck;
p. 267 (n.) made her way to the capacious deck-tub; p. 268 (adj.) in
the deck-tub performances of the O'Regans; p. 268 (n.) purposely came
on deck every morning; p. 269 (n.) all six were invited to the
quarter-deck; p. 271 (n.) during a night-watch on deck; p. 271 (n.)
They were obliged to repair on deck; p. 284 (n.) scores of emigrants
went about the decks; p. 284 (n.) fitted to one of the large deck-
tubs; p. 285 (n.) made their appearance on deck; p. 286 (n.) emigrant
would climb to the deck; p. 286 (n.) would fain now have domiciled on
deck; p. 288 (n.) upon the wet and unsheltered decks; p. 290 (n.) The
decks were cleared; p. 290 (n.) poured themselves out on deck;
p. 290 (n.) sending on deck; p. 293 (n.) to give them more room on
deck; p. 294 (n.) coming forward from the quarter-deck; p. 294 (n.)
settling away the halyards on deck; p. 295 (n.) which generally
attracts every soul on deck; p. 296 (n.) by the whole upward-gazing
crowd on deck; p. 296 (n.) was permanently bolted down to the deck;
p. 299 (n.) forth came an order from the quarter-deck; p. 301 (n.)
the greater part of the night walking the deck; p. 308 (n.)
congregated on the forecastle-deck.

White-Jacket--p. 3 (n.) which, laying on deck, I folded double; p. 7
(n.) it was on the gun-deck that our dinners were spread; p. 7 (n.)
penned up here and there along the deck; p. 8 (n.) are particular
bands stationed on the three decks; p. 9 (n.) and below it to the
deck; p. 9 (n.) there is the After-guard, stationed on the Quarter-
deck; p. 10 (n.) and being stationed on the Quarter-deck; p. 10 (n.)
always stationed on the gun-deck; p. 10 (n.) on the gun-deck of a
frigate; p. 10 (adv./n.) Three decks down--spar-deck, gun-deck, and
berth-deck; p. 10 (n.) they seldom come on deck to sun themselves;
p. 11 (n.) On the gun-deck, a thousand scythed chariots; p. 12 (n.)
and the strange noises under decks; p. 15 (n.) standing still and
yawning on the spar-deck; p. 15 (n.) sneaking about the deck; p. 15
(n.) he sent me down on deck; p. 16 (n.) What knew you of gun-deck;
p. 17 (n.) Jack Chase on a Spanish Quarter-deck; p. 18 (n.)

promenading the Quarter-deck of the stranger; p. 18 (n.) had
disappeared from the Quarter-deck; p. 19 (n.) where that gentleman
stood on the quarter-deck; p. 19 (n.) carried him in triumph along
the gun-deck; p. 20 (adj.) The Quarter-deck Officers . . . and Berth-
deck Underlings; p. 21 (n.) His appearance on the Quarter-deck; p. 23
(n.) When he stands on his Quarter-deck at sea; p. 23 (n.) reports
twelve o'clock to the officer of the deck; p. 23 (n.) when the
captain visits the deck; p. 24 (n.) comprises the after part of the
berth-deck; p. 25 (n.) when . . . the deck swarms with men; p. 25 (n.)
cries an officer of the deck; p. 26 (n.) is on the same deck with it;
p. 26 (n.) On the berth-deck he reigns supreme; p. 26 (n.) designated
in the nomenclature of the quarter-deck; p. 29 (n.) including, to one
watch, eight hours on deck; p. 31 (adj.) One of these two quarter-
deck lords; p. 32 (n.) For upon a frigate's quarter-deck; p. 32 (n.)
the deck is the field of action; p. 33 (adj.) which is the hedge of
the deck officers; p. 33 (n.) to prolong his predecessor's stay on
deck; p. 35 (n.) in the midst of the twilight of the berth deck;
p. 37 (n.) The scoundrels on deck detected me; p. 37 (n.) when it was
my quarter watch on deck; p. 39 (n.) strolling along the benighted
berth-deck; p. 40 (n.) a very different thing on the gun-deck of a
frigate; p. 42 (n.) the long twenty-four-pounders on the main-deck;
p. 45 (n.) and drove us on deck; p. 47 (n.) above the . . .
paltrinesses of the decks below; p. 47 (n.) in the tarry cellars and
caves below the berth-deck; p. 47 (n.) The "steady-cooks" on the
berth-deck; p. 50 (n.) the main-deck is generally filled with crowds;
p. 52 (n.) out from between the guns for a walk on the main-deck;
p. 54 (n.) what consternation and dismay pervaded the gun-deck; p. 55
(n.) a jail-house between two guns on the main-deck; p. 57 (n.) sup
together . . . between the guns on the main-deck; p. 57 (n.) Upon the
berth-deck he has a Chest; p. 59 (n.) set out on deck between the
guns; p. 62 (n.) of the headmost men of the gun-deck; p. 63 (n.) very
seldom to be seen on the spar-deck; p. 64 (n.) to their stations at
the guns on the several decks; p. 65 (n.) to hurry about the decks;
p. 65 (n.) on the starboard side of the quarter-deck; p. 65 (n.) the
quarter-deck is one of the most dangerous posts; p. 65 (adj.) The
quarter-deck armaments of most modern frigates; p. 66 (n.) dangerous
predicament the quarter-deck . . . was; p. 66 (n.) at the guns of
that quarter-deck; p. 67 (n.) And now it is "Fire! fire! fire!" on
the main-deck; p. 67 (n.) The entrance to the magazine on the berth-
deck; p. 69 (n.) might be lying about decks; p. 69 (n.) the gun-deck
might resemble a carpenter's shop; p. 69 (n.) amputating arms and
legs on the berth-deck; p. 69 (n.) the decks would be washed down;
p. 72 (n.) you lopers that live about the decks; p. 74 (n.) you see
every trade in operation on the gun-deck; pp. 74-5 (n.) The quarter-
deck is a grand square; p. 75 (n.) the first floor, or deck, being
rented by a lord; p. 75 (n.) a whole cabin to himself on the spar-
deck; p. 78 (n.) I tore off the jacket; and threw it on the deck; p.
p. 79 (n.) on a frigate berth-deck; p. 80 (n.) lowered myself gently
to the deck; p. 80 (n.) I shall have the whole berth-deck to myself;
p. 81 (n.) was fast asleep on the berth-deck; p. 81 (n.) found a man
lying on the deck; p. 82 (n.) Having then been on deck for twice four
hours; pp. 82-3 (n.) somewhere along the batteries on the gun-deck;
p. 83 (n.) to recline on the larboard side of the gun-deck; p. 83 (n.)
who have been on deck eight hours; p. 83 (n.) I have sometimes slept
standing on the spar-deck; p. 83 (n.) we were given the privilege of
the berth-deck; p. 83 (n.) kept the planks of the berth-deck itself

constantly wet; p. 84 (n.) after battling out eight stormy hours on
deck at night; p. 84 (n.) they are only on deck four hours; p. 84 (n.)
to the picturesque effect of the spar-deck; p. 85 (n.) Every deck is
spread with hammocks; p. 85 (n.) on the already flooded deck; p. 86
(n.) Then on all three decks the operation . . . begins; p. 86 (n.)
over the wet and sanded decks; p. 86 (n.) the decks are remorselessly
thrashed with dry swabs; p. 86 (n.) upon the damp and every-way
disagreeable decks; p. 86 (n.) invariable daily flooding of the three
decks; p. 86 (n.) to drop the crumb of a biscuit on deck; p. 86 (n.)
sick of this daily damping of the decks; p. 87 (n.) pass dry-shod,
like the Israelites, over the decks; p. 87 (n.) you see all the decks
clear; p. 87 (n.) The American sailors mess on the deck; p. 87 (n.)
they sleep any where about the decks; p. 88 (n.) the business of
holy-stoning the decks was often prolonged; p. 88 (n.) concerning the
whiteness of the quarter-deck; p. 88 (n.) this officer came on deck;
p. 88 (n.) in keeping the decks spotless at all times; p. 89 (n.)
reel about, on all three decks; p. 90 (n.) frequent conferences were
held on the gun-deck; p. 91 (n.) The half-deck was set apart for the
theatre; p. 91 (n.) tacked against the main-mast on the gun-deck;
p. 93 (adj.) Lemsford, the gun-deck poet; p. 93 (n.) halyards and
running ropes about the spar-deck; p. 93 (n.) all . . . hurried to
the half-deck; p. 94 (adj.) with true quarter-deck grace; p. 94 (n.)
the trumpet of the officer-of-the-deck; p. 95 (adj.) shipped their
quarter-deck faces again [officers have]; p. 96 (adj.) our wet-decked
frigate drew nearer; pp. 97-8 (n.) lashes every thing on deck
securely; p. 102 (n.) at the main hatchway of the gun-deck; p. 102
(n.) upon the very quarter-deck and poop; p. 103 (n.) who rushed him
along the deck; p. 103 (n.) the man was walking about the deck;
p. 103 (adj.) the officers shipped their quarter-deck faces; p. 104
(n.) altogether out of sight from the deck; p. 105 (n.) climb the
ladders leading to the upper deck; p. 105 (adj.) The main-deck guns
had several days previous; p. 105 (n.) but the lee carronades on the
quarter-deck; pp. 105-6 (n.) By this time the deck was alive; p. 106
(n.) happens then to be officer of the deck; p. 106 (n.) The gale
came athwart the deck; p. 106 (n.) round the double-wheel on the
quarter-deck; p. 107 (n.) which, on the gun-deck, had broken loose;
p. 107 (n.) much protection to those on deck; p. 108 (n.) sent up by
the officer of the deck; p. 111 (n.) and pace the quarter-deck at
night; p. 112 (n.) so on the quarter-deck at sea; p. 113 (n.) some of
the Lieutenants have the deck at night; p. 115 (n.) weight of metal
upon the spar and gun decks; p. 115 (n.) the ship's company messed on
gun-deck; p. 116 (n.) to take our meals upon the berth-deck; p. 116
(n.) every thing on the berth-deck . . . were tossed; p. 116 (n.) was
nothing but the bare deck to cling to; p. 116 (n.) the windows of the
deck opened; p. 116 (n.) a considerable quantity laid upon the decks;
p. 117 (n.) The officer of the deck had sent him; p. 117 (n.)
relieving the uppermost deck of its load of snow; p. 117 (n.) when he
saw the deck covered all over; p. 118 (n.) wandering about the gun-
deck in his barbaric robe; p. 119 (n.) All along the decks; p. 120
(n.) halting and limping across the decks; p. 120 n.) when it was my
quarter-watch on deck; p. 120 (n.) went skulking and "sogering" about
the decks; p. 121 (n.) I scoured the deck with it; p. 121 (n.) never
permitted us to lay down on deck; p. 124 (n.) beneath the berth-deck;
p. 127 (n.) mysterious circles beneath the lowermost deck; p. 129 (n.)
inspected every deck to see that his order; p. 130 (adj.) when
preparing the main-deck batteries for a . . . salute; p. 131 (n.) the

space on the uppermost deck; p. 131 (n.) waiting the pleasure of the
officer of the deck; p. 132 (n.) said the Lieutenant of the Deck,
advancing; p. 136 (n.) were yesterday found fighting on the gun-deck;
p. 137 (n.) One of these squares was now laid on the deck; p. 141
(adj.) quarter-deck authority sits more naturally on them; p. 144 (n.)
a three-decker is a city on the sea; p. 147 (n.) fight you . . . on
your own quarter-deck; p. 153 (n.) They were struck into the gun-deck;
p. 153 (n.) an order now came from the quarter-deck; p. 155 (n.) yea,
and on the gun-deck; p. 155 (n.) standing behind a gun-carriage on
the main-deck; p. 156 (n.) who preached on the quarter-deck of Lord
Nelson; p. 157 (n.) not to attend service on the half-deck; p. 158
(n.) goes his rounds on the berth-deck; p. 160 (n.) but a few decks
of a line-of-battle ship; p. 162 (n.) by order of the officer of the
deck; p. 162 (n.) all along the main-deck; p. 163 (n.) report the
same to the officer of the deck; p. 163 (n.) are marshalled on the
quarter-deck; p. 167 (n.) in a large cask on the berth-deck; p. 171
(n.) belaying pins scattered about the decks; p. 172 (n.) promenading
up and down the gun-deck; p. 172 (n.) at least on the gun-deck;
p. 172 (n.) canvass checkercloths spread upon the deck; p. 174 (n.)
to select a soft plank on the gun-deck; p. 174 (n.) emerge to that
with the sailors on deck; p. 177 (n.) without permission from the
officer of the deck; p. 177 (n.) she is reported to the deck-officer;
p. 177 (n.) touches his hat to the deck-officer; p. 178 (n.)
ascending to the deck out of a boat; p. 179 (n.) on gaining the deck;
p. 180 (n.) goes about the gun-deck throwing out; p. 180 (n.) to the
officer of the deck; p. 180 (n.) to be reported to the deck-officer;
p. 182 (n.) to be reported to the deck-officers; p. 183 (n.) reported
them to the deck-officer; p. 183 (n.) sharpened the vigilance of the
deck-officer; p. 183 (n.) Let it remain on deck; p. 183 (n.) it was
again brought up before the deck-officers; p. 185 (n.) His cook's
mess-chest being brought on deck; p. 186 (n.) standing and consideration on the gun-deck; p. 186 (n.) some of us, of the gun-deck, were
at times condemned; p. 188 (n.) by the aristocratic awning of our
quarter-deck; p. 189 (n.) fore and aft all three decks; p. 191 (adj.)
young Lemsford, the gun-deck bard; p. 191 (n.) of a particular gun on
the main-deck; p. 191 (n.) just as he touched the gun-deck; p. 196
(n.) Baldy came, like a thunder-bolt, upon the deck; p. 196 (n.) on
each side of the quarter-deck; p. 196 (n.) there the officer of the
deck usually stands; p. 196 (n.) right down to the deck in a
thousand splinters; p. 196 (n.) buried his ankle-bones in the deck;
p. 197 (n.) while safely standing on the deck themselves; p. 197 (n.)
thus do the people of the gun-deck suffer; p. 198 (n.) Purser's
auction on the spar-deck; p. 201 (n.) on the gun-deck below; p. 201
(n.) endeavors to rub it black on the decks; p. 205 (n.) Upon the
berth-deck he has a regular counting-room; p. 205 (n.) sat at his
little window on the berth-deck; p. 208 (n.) with the officers of the
quarter-deck; p. 208 (n.) between the forecastle and the quarter-deck;
p. 213 (n.) . . . with the commodore and the Captain on the Quarter-
deck; p. 213 (n.) In his intercourse with the quarter-deck; p. 214
(n.) month after month on the gun-deck; p. 214 (n.) setting sun,
streaming along the deck; p. 217 (adj.) to all the quarter-deck
subordinates; p. 219 (n.) that the majority of quarter-deck officers;
p. 223 (n.) who had been impatiently walking the deck; p. 224 (n.)
slid from the top of his head to the deck; p. 224 (n.) Candy dropped
it on deck; pp. 225-6 (n.) smashed it like a pancake on the deck;
p. 226 (n.) leaping down into the berth-deck after his bag; p. 226

(n.) were immediately dropped on the gun-deck; p. 227 (n.) the gun-
deck resounded with frantic fights; p. 229 (n.) and show the gun-deck
what virtue was; p. 231 (n.) all the prejudices of the quarter-deck;
p. 238 (n.) and the marvelous whiteness of the decks; p. 239 (n.) if
you had to holy-stone the deck yourselves; p. 239 (n.) if you dropped
a grease-spot on deck; p. 239 (n.) company scattered over the decks;
p. 239 (n.) they made the circuit of the berth-deck; p. 239 (n.)
commenced the ascent to the spar-deck; p. 239 (n.) leading from the
berth-deck to the gun-deck; p. 240 (n.) being assisted to the spar-
deck; p. 241 (adj.) A Quarter-deck Officer before the Mast; p. 242
(n.) when he had the deck of a line-of-battle ship; p. 242 (n.)
leaving the deck without a commanding officer; p. 243 (n.) abruptly
accosted me on the gun-deck; p. 245 (n.) looked round for Frank on
the spar-deck; p. 245 (n.) turning anxiously toward the quarter-deck;
p. 245 (n.) ordered down to the main-deck; p. 252 (n.) They assembled
on the half-deck; p. 253 (n.) they returned to the half-deck; p. 255
(n.) immediately descended to the half-deck; p. 258 (adj.) packing it
on the gun-deck capstan; p. 264 (n.) now ascended to the quarter-deck;
p. 269 (n.) giving three cheers from decks; p. 271 (n.) but all the
officers were on deck; p. 272 (n.) Some were sent forward on the
spar-deck; p. 272 (n.) distributed along the gun and berth decks;
p. 272 (n.) from the beams of the main-deck; p. 272 (n.) said the
officer of the deck; p. 275 (n.) is sent flying along the deck;
p. 276 (adj.) had shipped their quarter-deck faces; p. 276 (adj.) it
is this shipping of the quarter-deck face; p. 276 (adj.) if this
quarter-deck face you wear at all; p. 278 (n.) for a bed on the main-
deck; p. 278 (n.) I was on the gun-deck below; p. 278 (n.) and along
all three decks; p. 279 (n.) as I touched the spar-deck; p. 280 (n.)
stood on the weather-side of the deck; p. 280 (n.) a sudden rush
against him, along the slanting deck; p. 282 (n.) forward of the
main-hatchway, on the gun-deck; p. 283 (n.) There is a stout rail on
deck; p. 284 (adv.) oaken dug, deck under deck; p. 284 (n.)
perambulate all the decks of a man-of-war; p. 285 (n.) awaits the
pleasure of the officer of the deck; p. 286 (n.) the officer of the
deck draws near; p. 286 (n.) that officer of the deck may be sure;
p. 287 (n.) the Sunday devotions on the half-deck; p. 287 (n.)
scattered over all three decks; p. 287 (n.) some up the deck-ladders,
some down; p. 287 (n.) approach the First Lieutenant on the quarter-
deck; p. 288 (n.) from one of the lower decks; p. 288 (n.) stiff as a
pike-staff on the quarter-deck; p. 289 (n.) descends from her perch
to the quarter-deck; p. 289 (n.) By those stationed on the quarter-
deck; p. 290 (adj.) but the quarter-deck gun division; p. 290 (n.)
are below, on the main-deck; p. 290 (n.) railing of the Neversink's
quarter-deck; p. 294 (n.) meeting that may be held on the gun-deck;
p. 301 (n.) when he touches his quarter-deck; p. 302 (adj.) before
the bar of quarter-deck officers; p. 305 (n.) the players, scattered
about the decks; p. 306 (n.) is generally the berth-deck; p. 307 (n.)
prowling about on all three decks; p. 307 (n.) lurking round the
fore-mast on the spar-deck; p. 307 (adv.) he is three decks down;
p. 308 (n.) abounding in decks, tops, dark places; p. 309 (n.) were
coming alongside a three-decker; p. 312 (adj.) stationed at the
quarter-deck battery; p. 312 (n.) having been shot away to the deck;
p. 312 (n.) As he touched the deck; p. 313 (n.) The Neversink's main-
deck-batteries; p. 315 (n.) buckets of grog were passed along the
decks; p. 315 (n.) they fell dead to the deck; p. 315 (adj.) escort
me along our main-deck batteries; p. 316 (n.) I was walking with him

along the gun-deck; p. 316 (n.) A pig that ran about the decks; p.
p. 318 (adj.) captain of one of the main-deck guns; p. 322 (n.)
occasional contention of the gun-deck; p. 325 (n.) the decks were
kept constantly sprinkled; p. 325 (n.) the sick-bay . . . was on the
berth-deck; p. 325 (n.) the third deck from above; p. 325 (n.) in the
extreme forward part of that deck; p. 326 (n.) the floor of the berth-
deck; p. 326 (n.) divided our sick-bay from the rest of the deck;
p. 326 (n.) did you see him on deck; p. 326 (n.) the general tumult
of the spar-deck; p. 328 (n.) the continual dampness of the decks;
p. 328 (adj.) been commanded by the deck officer; p. 329 (n.) with
which I returned to the deck; p. 329 (adj.) let the deck officer
bellow; p. 330 (n.) a mouthful of fresh air on the spar-deck; p. 335
(n.) pervaded the entire frigate through all her decks; p. 335 (n.)
on the same deck with the invalid; p. 336 (n.) and lay motionless on
the deck; p. 336 (n.) in the airy vacancies of the half-deck above;
p. 337 (n.) to carry the body up to the gun-deck; p. 337 (n.) we
deposited it on the gun-deck; p. 337 (n.) On deck there, below;
p. 338 (n.) They laid the body on deck; p. 340 (n.) coming down from
the spar-deck; p. 346 (n.) the Professor assembled his pupils on the
half-deck; p. 347 (n.) placed upright on the gun-deck; p. 350 (n.)
coming on deck when all hands are called; p. 351 (n.) sat cross-legged
on the half-deck; p. 351 (n.) making coats . . . for the quarter-deck
officers; p. 351 (n.) in different parts of the gun-deck; p. 355 (n.)
echoed through all her decks and tops; p. 356 (n.) to an observer on
the quarter-deck; p. 356 (n.) made at the main-hatchway of the gun-
deck; p. 356 (n.) that had issued from the quarter-deck; p. 357 (n.)
were the vile barbers of the gun-deck; p. 357 (n.) were scattered
about all the decks; p. 357 (n.) The long area of the gun-deck;
p. 358 (n.) communication between the gun and spar decks; p. 359
(adj.) the gun-deck barbers were observed; pp. 360-1 (n.) as an
officer on the quarter-deck; p. 361 (n.) long, sad beard almost
grazed the deck; p. 363 (n.) consequent upon sleeping on deck;
p. 365 (n.) was escorted along the gun-deck; p. 366 (n.) and gaining
the deck, exclaimed; p. 376 (adj.) from which the deck officer would
turn away; p. 379 (n.) circulating about the decks in citizen's
clothes; p. 379 (n.) cried the deck-officer; p. 383 (n.) yet he paced
the gun-deck as if it were; p. 386 (n.) . . . with Scenes on the Gun-
deck; p. 386 (n.) the Galley, or Cookery, on the gun-deck; p. 389 (n.)
the poet of the gun-deck; p. 390 (n.) driven back to the spirit-tub
and the gun-deck; p. 392 (n.) a straight plumb-line right down to
the deck; p. 392 (n.) that I should not be dashed on the deck; p. 394
(n.) had unrove and fallen to the deck; p. 395 (adj.) Lemsford, the
gun-deck bard; p. 396 (n.) paid us all off on the quarter-deck;
p. 398 (adj.) to the supersitious, gun-deck gossip; p. 399 (n.)
Glance fore and aft our flush decks; p. 399 (n.) hear little of their
tribulations on deck; p. 399 (n.) is the clean-swept deck; p. 399 (n.)
we have both a quarter-deck to our craft; p. 399 (n.) we have both a
quarter-deck . . . and a gun-deck; p. 399 (n.) our gun-deck is full
of complaints.

Moby-Dick--p. 15 (n.) orders me to get a broom and sweep down the
decks; p. 15 (n.) because of the wholesome exercise and pure air of
the forecastle deck; p. 15 (n.) the Commodore on the quarter-deck
gets his atmosphere at second hand; p. 43 (n.) a distinct spot of
radiance upon the ship's tossed deck; p. 46 (n.) arrested ere he
touched a deck; p. 48 (n.) stumbling to the deck; p. 67 (n.) Her

ancient decks were worn and wrinkled, like the pilgrim-worshipped
flagstone in Canterbury Cathedral where Becket bled; p. 93 (n.) were
going it with a high hand on the quarter-deck; p. 107 (n.) moved
about the decks in all the pomp of six feet five in his socks;
p. 108 (n.) when sent for, to the great quarter-deck on high; p. 111
(n.) on the at last sunny deck; p. 112 (n.) to visit the night-
cloaked deck; p. 114 (n.) planting the stool on the weather side of
the deck; p. 136 (n.) a hundred feet above the silent decks; p. 140
(n.) ascended the cabin-gangway to the deck; p. 165 (n.) I ascended
to the overclouded deck; p. 170 (n.) on the hallowed precincts of the
quarter-deck; p. 264 (n.) when tossed by the pirates from the midnight
deck; p. 356 (n.) perilously scoot across the slippery deck; p. 356
(n.) on the sacred quarter-deck enormous masses of the whale's head;
p. 387 (n.) inserting bull's eyes in the deck; p. 426 (n.) where the
deck, with the oblique energy of the wind, was now almost dripping
into the creamy, sidelong-rushing sea.

DEEP. A word figuratively applied to the ocean. Also, only depth over
10 fathoms. (Smyth)   •

Typee--p. 10 (n.) some shapeless monster of the deep.

Mardi--p. 24 (n.) on the broad deep; p. 39 (n.) the Cathays of the
deep; p. 40 (n.) vultures of the deep; p. 58 (n.) monsters of the
deep; p. 109 (n.) between us and the deep; p. 111 (n.) most mysterious
of the mysteries of the deep; p. 140 (n.) though he had sunk in the
deep; p. 211 (n.) the unseen foundations of the deep; p. 273 (n.)
like an army from the deep; p. 436 (n.) catch we heads as fish from
the deep; p. 557 (n.) better to sink in boundless deeps.

Redburn--p. 100 (n.) familiar with the wonders of the deep; p. 127
(n.) at the bottom of the deep; p. 299 (n.) to be committed to the
deep.

White-Jacket--p. 43 (n.) the book was committed to the deep; p. 203
(n.) and committing it to the deep; p. 268 (n.) broad out upon the
deep; p. 295 (n.) when you would be committed to the deep; p. 341
(n.) we commit this body to the deep; p. 376 (n.) wooden-walled
Gomorrahs of the deep; p. 393 (n.) vibrating in the mid-deep; p. 396
(n.) with brooding darkness on the face of the deep.

Moby-Dick--epigram (n.) Leviathan, . . . in the deep/ Stretch'd like
a promontory sleeps or swims; p. 2 (n.) One would think the deep to
be hoary; p. 4 (n.) Leviathan, . . . in the deep/ Stretch'd like a
promontory sleeps or swims; p. 6 (n.) with those that take up their
abode in the deep; p. 48 (n.) but [bowsprit] soon beat downward again
towards the tormented deep; p. 63 (n.) to draw their living from the
bottomless deep itself; p. 104 (n.) Where, in the bottomless deeps,
could he find the torn limbs of his brother; p. 116 (n.) Already we
are boldly launched upon the deep; p. 124 (n.) is so well known as
denizen of the deep; p. 130 (n.) plucked at from the skies, and dived
for in the deep; p. 136 (n.) striding along the deep, as if the masts
were gigantic stilts; p. 196 (n.) consequent bivouacks on the deep;
p. 230 (n.) all the while the thick-lipped leviathan is rushing
through the deep; p. 234 (n.) you can hardly regard any creatures of

the deep with the same feelings that you do those of the shore;
p. 248 (n.) all hands were preparing to cast anchor in the deep;
p. 305 (n.) instead of doing battle with the great monster of the
deep; p. 310 (n.) the great whales should have been . . . sprinkling
and mistifying the gardens of the deep; p. 316 (n.) when he is about
to plunge into the deeps; p. 326 (n.) We saw young Leviathan amours
in the deep; p. 356 (n.) how he [leviathan] is . . . slaughtered in
the valleys of the deep; p. 429 (n.) that man was swallowed up in the
deep; p. 443 (n.) for forty years to make war on the horrors of the
deep; p. 454 (n.) these Nantucketers time that other Leviathan of the
deep; p. 464 (n.) then fell swamping back into the deep.

DELTA. It is well known that rivers which deposit great quantities of
matter, do also very often separate into two or more branches, previous
to their discharge into the sea; p. thus forming triangular spaces, aptly
called deltas from their resemblance to the Greek letter Δ. All deltas
appear by their section to be formed of matter totally different from
that of the adjacent country. They are the creation of the rivers
themselves, which, having brought down with their floods vast quantities
of mud and sand from the upper lands, deposit them in the lowest place,
the sea; at whose margin, the current which has hitherto impelled them
ceasing, they are deposited by mere action of gravity. (Smyth)

   Mardi--p. 256 (n.) At three-fold mouths that Delta-grot.

DELUGE. Any overflowing of water; a swell of water over the natural
banks of a river or shore of the ocean, spreading over the adjacent land.
But appropriately, the great flood or overflowing of the earth by water,
in the days of Noah; according to the common chronology, Anno Mundi,
1656. (Webster)

   Mardi--p. 297 (n.) I was at the subsiding of the Deluge.

   White-Jacket--p. 101 (n.) becalmed at the climax of the Deluge.

DEPTH. The sea, the ocean; The depth closed me round about. Jonah ii.
The abyss; a gulf of infinite profundity: When he set a compass on the
face of the depth. Prov. viii. (Webster)

   Typee--p. 134 (n.) then down into the transparent depths below.

   Mardi--p. 24 (n.) into the calm depths; p. 138 (n.) descending into
   depths unknown; p. 636 (n.) rising from vast depths to the sea's
   surface; p. 651 (n.) from those bottomless depths.

   Redburn--p. 64 (n.) from the depths of the deep blue sea.

   White-Jacket--p. 123 (n.) concerning the subterranean depths of the
   Neversink's hold; p. 342 (n.) sailing far up into the depths of the
   sky.

   Moby-Dick--p. 50 (n.) where the eddying depths sucked him ten
   thousand fathoms down; p. 300 (n.) as not a single groan or cry of

any sort; nay, not so much as a ripple or a bubble came up from its
depths; p. 306 (n.) Vishnoo . . . sounding down in him to the
uttermost depths; p. 347 (n.) Rather carried down alive to wondrous
depths; p. 415 (n.) But as this conductor must descend to considerable
depth; p. 448 (n.) suddenly he peered down into its depths; p. 467
(n.) Slope downwards to thy depths, O sea; p. 468 (n.) the rope's
heavy end smiting the sea, disappeared in its depths.

DINGY. A small boat of Bombay, propelled by paddles, and fitted with a
settee sail, the mast raking forwards. Also, a small extra boat in men-
of-war and merchant ships. (Smyth's spelling is "dinghey.")

White-Jacket--p. 161 (n.) She also carried . . . a "dinghy"; p. 161
(n.) All these boats, except the "dinghy."

DIVE. To ascend or plunge voluntarily head-foremost under the water. A
ship is said to be "diving into it" when she pitches heavily against a
head-sea. (Smyth)

Typee--p. 131 (v.) at one moment they dived deep down; p. 177 (v.)
dive down to the bottom of the sea.

Mardi--p. 182 (adj.) by the deepest diving mermen; p. 267 (v.) diving
deep as high soars the lark; p. 273 (v.) and diving under the swells;
p. 282 (v.) would dive down into the sea; p. 294 (n.) his corps of
sea-divers to repair; p. 294 (v.) by diving far down under; p. 294
(n.) As the king's divers were thus employed; p. 294 (n.) method
adopted by these divers; p. 294 (n.) the diver shot up for the
surface; p. 295 (n.) the diver was borne to a habitation; p. 295 (n.)
the diver was found to be dead; p. 300 (adj.) day of the diver's
decease; p. 301 (n.) the wife of the diver; p. 303 (adj.) the close
of the diver's career; p. 393 (n.) the relatives of the diver;
p. 303 (n.) the last, long plunge of the diver; p. 317 (n.) Devils
are divers; p. 317 (n.) as devils are divers, divers are the devils
in men; p. 380 (adj.) bones of a Pearl-Shell-diver's leg inside;
p. 385 (v.) thou didst dive into the deeps of things; p. 394 (v.)
Diving deep in the sea; p. 422 (v.) dived like red-hot bars beneath
the waves; p. 438 (v.) though Yoomy soars, and Babbalanja dives;
p. 650 (v.) did'st ever dive in deep waters, Taji; p. 651 (v.) where
she dived, the flambeaux clustered; p. 651 (n.) all these may be had
for the diving; p. 651 (v.) Dive thou, and bring up one pearl; p. 651
(n.) for thee, bootless deep diving; p. 651 (v.) dive with me:--join
hands; p. 651 (v.) and I will dive with thee.

Redburn--p. 8 (v.) were trying to dive down and get the treasure;
p. 268 (v.) dunking and diving together; p. 295 (n.) plunged like a
diver into the sea.

White-Jacket--p. 115 (n.) until the old frigate dipped and went into
it like a diving-bell.

Moby-Dick--p. 7 (v.) In the free element, beneath me swam,/ Floundered
and dived . . ./ Fishes; p. 13 (n.) crowds, pacing straight for the
water, and seemingly bound for a dive; p. 61 (v.) dived down and

disappeared; p. 61 (n.) till poor Queequeg took his last long dive;
p. 95 (v.) as the old craft deep dived into the green seas.

DOCK. An artificial receptacle for shipping, in which they can discharge
or take in cargo, and refit.--A dry dock is a broad and deep trench,
formed on the side of a harbour, or on the banks of a river, and
commodiously fitted either to build ships in or to receive them to be
repaired or breamed. They have strong flood-gates, to prevent the flux
of the tide from entering while the ship is under repair. There are
likewise docks where a ship can only be cleaned during the recess of the
tide, as she floats again on the return of the flood. (Smyth)

Omoo--p. 6 (n.) parting with him at Prince's Dock Gates.

Redburn--p. 15 (n.) accompanied me down to the decks; p. 28 (n.)
longed for the ship to be leaving the dock; p. 48 (n.) I had seen
lying off the dock; p. 93 (n.) ship that lay near us in the docks;
p. 102 (n.) like chips in a dock; pp. 109-10 (n.) at Prince's Dock
Gates in Liverpool; p. 110 (n.) the daughter of one of the Liverpool
dock-masters; p. 111 (n.) found floating in the docks; p. 111 (n.)
while straying along the docks; p. 112 (n.) the daughter of the dock-
master gave him; p. 112 (n.) vast crowds thronging the docks of
Liverpool; p. 119 (adj.) belonging to the dock-master's daughter;
p. 130 (n.) working up to a berth in Prince's Dock; p. 130 (n.)
necessary regulations of the Liverpool docks; p. 130 (n.) feed their
luckless tars in dock; p. 136 (n.) remained in Prince's Dock over six
weeks; p. 136 (n.) during our stay in the dock; p. 137 (n.) nearly
all the time we lay in the dock; p. 138 (n.) Corinthian haunts in the
vicinity of the docks; p. 138 (n.) content to lie in Prince's Dock;
p. 139 (n.) launched into the docks; p. 140 (n.) that fellow
staggering along the dock; p. 144 (n.) and the docks irregularly
scattered; p. 147 (n.) its docks, and ships, and warehouses; p. 152
(n.) before entering dock; p. 152 (adj.) tavern, near the Prince's
Dock's walls; p. 153 (n.) I was rapidly walking along the dock;
p. 153 (n.) one of the dock-police, stationed at the gates; p. 153
(n.) the police stationed at the gates of the docks; p. 158 (n.)
upon a passage concerning "The Old Dock"; p. 158 (n.) "The Old Dock"
must be standing; p. 158 (n.) strikes the stranger in coming to this
dock; p. 158 (n.) that this fabulous dock should seem to have; p. 158
(n.) place in that neighborhood called the "Old Dock"; p. 158 (n.)
this pool was made into the "Old Dock"; p. 161 (n.) the ship
Highlander lay in Prince's Dock; p. 161 (n.) I made sundry excursions
to the neighboring docks; p. 161 (n.) the sight of these mighty docks
filled my young mind; p. 161 (n.) a succession of granite-rimmed
docks; p. 161 (n.) originated the model of the Wet Dock; p. 161 (n.)
This term--Wet Dock--did not originate; p. 161 (n.) in order to
distinguish these docks; p. 161 (n.) from the Dry-Dock, where the
bottoms of ships; p. 162 (n.) the docks of Liverpool, even at the
present day; p. 162 (n.) The first dock built by the town; p. 162
(n.) was the "Old Dock"; p. 162 (n.) that long line of dock-masonry;
p. 162 (n.) passing dock after dock; p. 162 (n.) upon their noble
docks; p. 162 (n.) Among the few docks mentioned above; p. 163 (n.)
of any one of these Liverpool docks; p. 163 (n.) to give some account
of Prince's Dock; p. 163 (n.) This dock, of comparatively recent
construction; p. 163 (n.) This dock was built like the others; p. 163

(n.) Prince's Dock is protected by a long pier of masonry; p. 163
(n.) The area of the dock itself; p. 163 (n.) the whole dock is shut
up like a house; p. 163 (n.) when the level of the dock coincides;
p. 163 (n.) as the level of the dock is always at that mark; p. 163
(n.) Prince's Dock is generally so filled; p. 164 (n.) The dock-
masters, whose authority is declared; p. 164 (n.) unavoidable
inconveniences of inclosed docks; p. 164 (n.) a sort of ante-chamber
to the dock itself; p. 164 (v.) it would be impossible to "dock" a
ship; p. 164 (n.) from thence into the docks; p. 164 (n.) concerning
the cost of the docks; p. 164 (n.) that the King's Dock . . . was
completed; p. 164 (n.) a curious story concerning this dock; p. 164
(n.) entered the King's Dock on the first day; p. 164 (n.) dock-
masters are shouting; p. 165 (n.) each Liverpool dock is a walled
town; p. 165 (n.) A Liverpool dock is a grand caravansary inn; p. 165
(n.) ships lying in the very middle of the docks; p. 166 (n.) at the
shipping in Prince's Dock; p. 168 (n.) hardly anything I witnessed in
the docks; p. 168 (n.) from the lofty walls of the docks; p. 170 (n.)
Among the various ships lying in Prince's Dock; p. 172 (n.) well-
dressed people came down to the dock; p. 172 (n.) I was passing
through the Dock Gate; p. 172 (n.) as the regulation of the docks
prohibit; p. 172 (n.) take a stroll along the docks; p. 172 (n.)
strange vessel entered Prince's Dock; p. 176 (n.) found in some of
the docks; p. 176 (adj.) dock laborers of all sorts; p. 176 (n.) And
several times on the docks; p. 177 (n.) It stands very near the docks;
p. 177 (n.) after our arrival in the dock; p. 178 (n.) the swarms of
laborers about the docks; p. 179 (n.) recovery of persons falling
into the docks; p. 179 (n.) constantly prying about the docks; p. 180
(n.) in the vicinity of the docks; p. 183 (n.) I ran down toward the
docks; p. 184 (n.) When I arrived at the docks; p. 184 (adj.) the
Dock Police was distinct from that of the town; p. 185 (adj.) the
Dock-Wall Beggars; p. 185 (n.) so I return to the docks; p. 185 (adj.)
to be seen within the dock walls; p. 185 (n.) enforced by the dock-
masters; p. 186 (n.) paupers that beset the docks; p. 186 (adj.)
issue in crowds from the dock gates; p. 187 (adj.) some inducement to
infest the dock-walls; p. 188 (n.) who thronged the docks as the
Hebrew cripples; p. 188 (n.) turn the waters of the docks into an
elixir; p. 189 (adj.) along the dock walls at noon; p. 190 (n.) on
leaving the dock to go to supper; p. 192 (n.) observation concerning
the Liverpool docks; p. 192 (adj.) upon the flagging round the dock
walls; p. 192 (adj.) in haunting the dock walls; p. 194 (n.) rascals
prowling about the docks; p. 194 (n.) to blow up the Liverpool docks;
p. 195 (adj.) driven out of the dock gates; p. 195 (n.) among the
narrow lanes adjoining the dock; p. 196 (n.) before reaching the
dock; p. 196 (n.) while the ship lay in dock; p. 196 (n.) the great
crowds pouring out of the dock-gates; p. 196 (n.) Along the docks
they sell; p. 196 (n.) Among all the sights of the docks; p. 197 (n.)
valuable information touching the docks; p. 197 (n.) majestic,
magisterial truck-horses of the docks; p. 198 (n.) from a low window
fronting a dock; p. 198 (n.) silence falls upon the docks; p. 198
(adj.) just emerged from Brunswick Dock gates; p. 202 (n.) Liverpool,
away from the docks; p. 203 (n.) walking into some dock hitherto
unexamined; p. 215 (n.) plodding my solitary way to the same old
docks; p. 216 (n.) among the tarry docks; p. 218 (n.) at once betook
himself to the docks; p. 218 (n.) during our stay in the docks;
p. 225 (adj.) and along the dock walls; p. 233 (n.) fast asleep in my
old bunk in Prince's Dock; p. 236 (n.) toward Prince's Dock and the

Highlander; p. 238 (n.) walking along the quay of Prince's Dock;
p. 239 (n.) close into the outlet of Prince's Dock; p. 239 (n.) the
ordinary clamor of the docks; p. 239 (n.) the loud orders of the
dock-masters; p. 240 (n.) we now glided out of the dock; p. 240 (n.)
holding wind-bound in the various docks; p. 243 (adj.) had been
brought on board at the dock gates; p. 248 (n.) he had landed in
Prince's Dock; p. 307 (n.) from dock to dock we have been.

White-Jacket--p. 152 (n.) Some superior old "London Dock"; p. 297
(n.) from the dock-yards of a republic; p. 306 (n.) vaults of the
West India Docks on the Thames; p. 309 (n.) a fellow yawing about
the docks; p. 382 (n.) these dock-lopers of landsmen.

Moby-Dick--p. 18 (n.) a dim sort of out-hanging light not far from
the docks; p. 37 (n.) In thorough fares nigh the docks.

DOLPHIN. Naturalists understand by this word numerous species of small
cetaceous animals of the genus Delphinus, found in nearly all seas. They
greatly resemble porpoises, and are often called by this name by sailors;
but they are distinguished by having a longer and more slender snout.
The word is also generally, but less correctly, applied to a fish, the
dorado (Coryphoena hippuris), celebrated for the changing hues of its
surface when dying. (Smyth)

Typee--p. 132 (n.) like a shoal of dolphins.

Mardi--p. 27 (n.) she quivered like a dolphin; p. 380 (n.) Preserved
between fins of the dolphin; p. 394 (n.) As of dolphins a throng;
p. 551 (n.) long the radiant dolphins fly before the sable sharks;
p. 644 (n.) dolphins were leaping over floating fragments; p. 644
(n.) But what cared the dolphins.

Redburn--p. 9 (n.) among a crowd of glass dolphins and sea-horses;
p. 175 (adj.) fashioned into a dolphin's head; p. 189 (n.) a ship, a
windlass, or a dolphin; p. 220 (n.) seeing the dazzling rays of the
dolphins there.

White-Jacket--p. 29 (n.) dreamy dolphins gliding in the distance;
p. 71 (n.) Dolphins were sporting and flashing around it; p. 168 (n.)
puddinging the dolphin; p. 318 (n.) we were like dolphins among the
flying-fish.

Moby-Dick--p. 44 (n.) As on a radiant dolphin borne; p. 381 (n.)
abounding in centaurs, griffins, and dolphins.

DRIFT. The altered position of a vessel by current or falling to leeward
when hove-to or lying-to in a gale, when but little headway is made by
the action of sails. (Smyth)

Mardi--p. 18 (v.) we drifted north or south.

DROGHER. A small craft which goes round the bays of the West India
Islands, to take off sugars, rum, &c., to the merchantmen. (Smyth)

Redburn--p. 165 (n.) The Salt-Droghers, and German Emigrant Ships; p. 166 (n.) with a multitude of little salt-droghers; p. 167 (n.) to go on board a salt-drogher.

DROWN. To be suffocated in water; to perish in water. "Methought what pain it was to drown."--Shakespeare. (Webster)

Mardi--p. 24 (n.) the drowning eddies did their work; p. 200 (v.) our barks may drown.

Redburn--p. 312 (adj.) drowned persons floating in the harbor.

DUCK. A water-fowl, so called for its plunging. (Webster)

Typee--p. 229 (n.) natural for a human being to swim as it is for a duck.

EDDY. Sometimes used for the dead-water under a ship's counter. Also, the water that by some interruption in its course, runs contrary to the direction of the tide or current, and appears like the motion of a whirlpool. Eddies in the sea not unfrequently extend their influences to a great distance, and are then merely regarded as contrary or revolving currents. It is the back-curl of the water to fill a space or vacuum formed sometimes by the faulty build of a vessel, having the after-body fuller than the fore, which therefore impedes her motion. It also occurs immediately after a tide passes a strait, where the volume of water spreads suddenly out, and curves back to the edges. (Smyth)

Typee--p. 134 (v.) circled and eddied about their summits.

Omoo--p. 27 (n.) the eddies were whirling upon all sides; p. 201 (v.) the musquitoes [sic] here fairly eddied round us; p. 219 (v.) making the air eddy in their wake.

Mardi--p. 3 (n.) of the many wild currents and eddies; p. 24 (n.) the drowning eddies did their work; p. 118 (n.) through eddy, wave, and surge; p. 120 (n.) carry us down in the eddies; p. 155 (n.) by perpetual eddying; p. 234 (n.) after many an eddy and whirl; p. 644 (n.) inveigled by the eddies; p. 653 (n.) a gleaming form slow circled in the deepest eddies; p. 653 (n.) the eddies whirled as before.

White-Jacket--p. 393 (adj.) through the eddying whirl and swirl.

Moby-Dick--p. 50 (adj.) where the eddying depths sucked him ten thousand fathoms down; p. 99 (n.) the sperm whale's vast tail, fanning into eddies the air over his head; p. 159 (n.) oars and men both whirling in the eddies; p. 171 (n.) Ahab was threading a maze of currents and eddies; p. 244 (n.) A continual cascade played at the bows; a ceaseless whirling eddy in her wake; p. 337 (adj.) and by the eddying cloud of vulture sea-fowl that circled; p. 378 (n.) when within the eddyings of his angry flukes; p. 421 (v.) the shivered remnants of the jib and fore and main-top-sails . . . went eddying away to leeward; p. 450 (n.) still they dared not pull into the eddy to strike.

EEL. A well-known fish (<u>Anguilla</u> <u>vulgaris</u>), of elongated form, common in
rivers and estuaries, and esteemed for food. (Smyth)

> <u>Mardi</u>--p. 149 (n.) clinging thereto like the snaky eels; p. 149 (n.)
> But what curious eels these are; p. 150 (n.) And as for the eels
> there above.
>
> <u>Redburn</u>--p. 88 (adj.) to boil in some eel soup.
>
> <u>Moby-Dick</u>--p. 228 (adj.) such is then the outlandish, eel-like,
> limbered, varying shape of him [whale]; p. 348 (n.) my fingers felt
> like eels, and began, as it were, to serpentine and spiraline.

EMBARK. To go on board, or to put on board a vessel. (Smyth)

> <u>Mardi</u>--p. 3 (v.) now was embarked; p. 26 (v.) we embarked upon this
> western voyage; p. 52 (v.) upon which he had embarked; p. 96 (v.) we
> might afterward embark.

FATHOM. The space of both arms extended. A measure of 6 feet, used in
the length of cables, rigging, &c., and to divide the lead (or sounding)
lines, for showing the depth of water. (Smyth)

> <u>Omoo</u>--p. 28 (n.) one thousand fathoms of fine tappa.
>
> <u>Mardi</u>--p. 33 (n.) over two hundred fathoms in length; p. 39 (adv.)
> fathoms down in the sea; p. 54 (n.) about half a fathom; p. 626 (n.)
> violet fathoms down, on that soft, pathetic, woman eye.
>
> <u>Redburn</u>--p. 97 (n.) upward of three hundred fathoms in length; p. 250
> (n./adj.) let me gaze fathoms down into thy fathomless eye; p. 301
> (adv.) fathoms down into the free and independent Yankee mud.
>
> <u>White-Jacket</u>--p. 176 (adv.) would steep themselves a thousand fathoms
> down; p. 202 (n.) How many fathoms of canvas in it; p. 318 (adv.) but
> they sank fifty fathoms.
>
> <u>Moby-Dick</u>--p. 50 (adv.) where the eddying depths sucked him ten
> thousand fathoms down; p. 75 (n.) thy conscience may be drawing ten
> inches of water, or ten fathoms; p. 159 (adj.) to reach the fathom-
> deep life of the whale; p. 281 (adv.) when fathoms down in the sea;
> p. 296 (adv.) many fathoms in the rear; p. 299 (n.) a whale bearing
> on his back a column of two hundred fathoms of ocean; p. 311 (adv.)
> for an hour or more, a thousand fathoms in the sea; p. 311 (adv.)
> when sailing a thousand fathoms beneath the sunlight; p. 326 (n.)
> that from the tub has reeled hundreds of fathoms of rope; p. 360 (n.)
> both [Starbuck and Ahab] with faces which I should say might be
> somewhere within nine fathoms long; p. 374 (adj.) stripped of its
> fathom-deep enfoldings; p. 404 (n.) A coil of new tow-line was then
> unwound, and some fathoms of it taken to the windlass.

FELUCCA. A little vessel with six or eight oars, frequent in the
Mediterranean; its helm may be applied in the head or stern, as occasion

requires. Also, a narrow decked galley-built vessel in great use there, of one or two masts, and some have a small mizen; they carry lateen sails. (Smyth)

   Mardi--p. 482 (n.) in a stout sea-fight, Ziani defeated . . . Otho, sending his feluccas all flying.

FERRY. A passage across a river or branch of the sea by boat. (Smyth)

   Mardi--p. 43 (n.) if we were crossing a ferry.

FIGURE-HEAD. A carved bust or full-length figure over the cut-water of a ship; the remains of an ancient superstition. The Carthaginians carried small images to sea to protect their ships, as the Roman Catholics do still. (Smyth)

   Typee--p. 172 (n.) The spectoral figure-head, reversed in its position; p. 219 (n.) shuddering at the ruin he might inflict upon my figure-head.

   Redburn--p. 9 (n.) and her figure-head, a gallant warrior; p. 116 (n.) when I and the figure-head on the bow; p. 116 (n.) that figure-head was a passenger; p. 116 (n.) a figure-head-builder there, amputated his left leg; p. 116 (n.) Then this figure-head-surgeon gave him another nose; p. 171 (n.) was a sort of devil for a figure-head; p. 220 (n.) invoking wooden Donald, the figure-head on our bows; p. 275 (n.) for the doomed vessel's figure-head.

   White-Jacket--p. 236 (n.) I'll fetch you such a swat over your figure-head.

   Moby-Dick--p. 307 (n.) some vessel with a whale for a figure-head; p. 338 (n.) the word rose, and the bulbous figure-head put together, sufficiently explained the whole.

FIN. The fin of a fish consists of a membrane supported by rays, or little bony or cartilaginous ossicles. The fins of fish serve to keep their bodies upright, and to prevent wavering or vacillation. (Webster)

   Omoo--p. 27 (n.) nothing but fins from head to tail.

   Mardi--p. 40 (n.) with a careless fin; p. 42 (n.) their dorsal fins; p. 42 (adj.) of the finny tribes; p. 42 (adv.) fighting, fin for fin; p. 54 (n.) nibbling at his ventral fin; p. 123 (adj.) of the larger varieties of the finny tribes; p. 148 (adj.) incredible multitude of finny creatures; p. 148 (n.) from their quaint dorsal fins; p. 148 (n.) a wing in the air for every fin in the sea; p. 149 (n.) sea-kelp clinging to its fins; p. 149 (n.) The myriad fins swim on; p. 149 (n.) light hearts and light fins; p. 149 (n.) my merry fins all; p. 149 (n.) that goes without fins; p. 149 (n.) they behold our limber fins; p. 150 (n.) merry fins, swim away; p. 150 (n.) our fins are stout; p. 150 (n.) our fins are stout; p. 151 (n.) as the thousand fins audibly patted; p. 267 (n.) of the bright and twittering fin; p. 288

(adj.) virtuous principles into his finny flock; p. 316 (adj.) a
fiery fin-back whale; p. 374 (n.) find little fishes' fins; p. 380
(n.) preserved between fins of the dolphin; p. 417 (adj.) and other
finny things; p. 418 (n.) fins and flippers fricasseed; p. 420 (n.)
have fins or wings for arms; p. 482 (n.) finned-lions, winged
walruses; p. 570 (n.) furnished with feelers or fins.

Redburn--p. 99 (n.) they ar'n't Fin-backs, for you won't catch a
Fin-back.

Moby-Dick--p. 7 (adj.) Io! Paean! Io! sing/ To the finny people's
king; p. 121 (n.) by the various names of Fin-back, Tall-spout, and
Long-John; p. 121 (n.) the Fin-back resembles the right whale; p. 121
(n.) His grand distinguishing feature, the fin; p. 121 (n.) This fin
is some three or four feet long; p. 121 (n.) this isolated fin will
. . . be seen plainly projecting; p. 121 (n.) this gnomon-like fin
stands up and casts shadows; p. 122 (n.) The Fin-Back is not
gregarious; p. 122 (n.) the Fin-Back is sometimes included with the
right whale; p. 122 (n.) founded upon either his baleen, or hump, or
back-fin, or teeth; p. 122 (n.) The baleen, hump, back-fin and teeth;
p. 140 (n.) every dimly-discovered, uprising fin of some undiscernible
form; p. 143 (adv.) till he spouts black blood and rolls fin out;
p. 174 (n.) His broad fins are bored; p. 203 (n.) small harmless fish
. . . darted away with what seemed shuddering fins; p. 296 (n.) in
the unnatural stump of his starboard fin; p. 296 (n.) Whether he had
lost that fin in battle; p. 298 (n.) while his one poor fin beat his
side in an agony of fright; p. 298 (n.) sideways rolled towards the
sky his one beating fin; p. 301 (n.) impotently flapped with his
stumped fin; p. 310 (adj.) the finny tribes in general breathe the
air; p. 315 (n.) His side-fins only serve to steer by; p. 325 (n.)
The delicate side-fins . . . still freshly retained the plaited
crumpled appearance of a baby's ears newly arrived; p. 329 (n.) the
deep scars of these encounters,--furrowed heads, broken teeth,
scolloped fins; p. 381 (n.) we find the unmistakable print of his own
fin-bone; p. 451 (n.) he seemed to have treble-banked his every fin.

FISH. A general name for a class of animals subsisting in water, which
breathe by means of gills, swim by the aid of fins, and are oviparous.
Cetaceous animals, as the whale and dolphin, are, in popular language,
called fishes; but they breathe by lungs, and are viviparous like
quadrupeds. (Webster)

Typee--p. 6 (n.) vessels engaged in the extensive whale fisheries of
the Pacific; p. 10 (n.) Every now and then a shoal of flying fish;
p. 14 (n.) to be produced by a shoal of fish; p. 22 (v.) her spars
fished with old pipe staves; p. 43 (v.) which were fished up from the
bottom of the now empty; p. 83 (n.) covered all over with representations of birds and fishes; p. 84 (n.) which in length and slightness
resembled a fishing-pole; p. 110 (n.) catching in a little net a
species of diminutive shell-fish; p. 127 (v.) But whether fishing, or
carving canoes; p. 132 (n.) attacked on all sides by a legion of
sword-fish; p. 183 (n.) representations of fishes and other devices;
p. 189 (n.) formed principally of raw fish, bad brandy; p. 206 (adj.)
manner they conducted their great fishing parties; p. 206 (n.)
passionately fond of fish; p. 206 (adj.) that the fishing parties

were formed; p. 206 (n.) nothing talked of but "pehee, pehee" (fish, fish); p. 207 (n.) in readiness for the reception of the fish; p. 207 (n.) The fish were all quite small; p. 207 (n.) The fish were under a strict Taboo; p. 207 (n.) intelligence contained in the words "pehee pemi" (fish come); p. 208 (n.) devouring fish much in the same way that a civilized being; p. 208 (n.) The fish is held by the tail; p. 208 (n.) Raw fish; p. 208 (n.) swallowing great vulgar-looking fishes; p. 208 (n.) a delicate, little, golden-hued fish; p. 208 (n.) But, alas! it was after all a raw fish; p. 209 (n.) to regale myself with raw fish; p. 263 (adj.) He sported a fishing rod in his hand; p. 265 (adj.) The fishing parties met there; p. 268 (n.) A meal of fish, bread-fruit, and bananas.

Omoo--p. xiii (n.) engaged in the Sperm Whale Fishery; p. xiii (n.) to give any account of the whale-fishery; p. 10 (n.) only two fish had been brought alongside; p. 13 (v.) fishing for albicores; p. 14 (v.) having been fished up out of the pickle; p. 15 (n.) what luck in the fishery might yet be in store; p. 34 (n.) and other fish sporting under the bows; p. 36 (n.) Pills and powders . . . were thrown to the fish; p. 63 (n.) visited by the pearl-shell fishermen; p. 71 (n.) performed in the sperm-whale fishery; p. 71 (n.) Bembo was a wild one after a fish; p. 71 (n.) was always pulled up to his fish; p. 72 (n.) the fish sounded; p. 72 (n.) as long as the fish is in sight; p. 76 (n.) what could we expect to do in the fishery; p. 114 (n.) abounding with delicious fish; p. 129 (n.) that of making fish-hooks and gimblets; p. 201 (n.) the few fishermen and their families; p. 202 (n.) We had a good breakfast of fish; p. 202 (n.) Tonoi, the chief of the fishermen; p. 203 (n.) Tonoi's men, the fishermen of the grove; p. 203 (n.) As for fishing, it employed; p. 214 (n.) only poor pehe kannaka (fishermen) left; p. 216 (n.) darted into the canoe like a small sword-fish; p. 216 (adj.) so a small fishing canoe; p. 234 (n.) which abounded in such delicious fish; p. 238 (n.) and one solitary fisherman was paddling; p. 250 (adj.) besides lonely fishermen's huts; p. 252 (n.) before the fishermen were even stirring; p. 253 (adj.) with a fisherman's dwelling in the distance; p. 258 (n.) in each was a small fish, baked in the earth; p. 258 (n.) Laying before his guest one of the packages of fish; p. 258 (n.) an indefinite number of "Pehee Lee Lees" (small fish); p. 259 (n.) The fish were delicious; p. 262 (n.) their fibres are twisted into fishing-lines; p. 266 (n.) p. 266 (n.) Often we went fishing; p. 266 (n.) Spearing fish is glorious sport; p. 266 (n.) you may see the fish-hunters pursuing their sport; p. 266 (n.) The wild fishermen, flourishing their weapons; p. 266 (n.) But fish-spearing was not the only sport; p. 271 (n.) cleaning fish in the brook; p. 272 (n.) But the fish and Indian turnip being none of the best; p. 310 (n.) rolls of old tappa and matting, paddles and fish-spears; p. 310 (n.) ate fish and poee out of her native calabashes; p. 313 (n.) was a luckless ship in the fishery.

Mardi--p. 24 (n.) ruthless blade of the swordfish; p. 31 (n.) the swordfish never surrenders; p. 32 (n.) by the regulations of the fishery; p. 39 (n.) you have seen the "Devil Fish"; p. 40 (n.) of these prolific fish; p. 41 (n.) ghost of a fish; p. 41 (n.) the fish with the chain-plate armor; p. 41 (n.) many flying fish fall a prey; p. 42 (n.) we spied Black Fish; p. 42 (n.) waylaying peaceful fish; p. 48 (n.) not a fish was to be seen; p. 50 (n.) painted fish rippling

past; p. 53 (n.) There is a fish in the sea; p. 53 (n.) dainty little
creatures called Pilot fish; p. 53 (n.) of several small luminous
fish; p. 53 (n.) there were no ray-fish; p. 53 (n.) between the Pilot
fish above mentioned; p. 53 (n.) the Pilot fish seem to act; p. 54
(n.) marveled full as much as those Pilot fish; p. 54 (n.) was about
to dart it at the fish; p. 54 (n.) four or five Remoras, or sucking-
fish; p. 54 (n.) The Remora has little power in swimming; p. 54 (n.)
on the backs of larger fish; p. 54 (n.) the nimble Pilot fish darted;
p. 54 (n.) the little Pilot fish darted; p. 55 (n.) swam the terrified
Pilot fish; p. 78 (n.) fowls of the air nor fishes; p. 83 (n.) The
little flying-fish got used to; p. 103 (n.) followed by shoals of
small fish; p. 103 (n.) the little, steel-blue Pilot fish; p. 103 (n.)
it is not with the Pilot fish; p. 103 (n.) shoals of fish were
darting; p. 103 (n.) their deadly foe the Sword fish; p. 103 (n.)
free-booters, and Hectors, and fish-at-arms; p. 103 (n.) the Indian
Sword fish is by far; p. 104 (n.) the fish here treated is a very
different creature; p. 104 (n.) from the Sword fish frequenting;
p. 104 (n.) he is denominated the Indian Sword fish; p. 104 (n.)
commonly known as the Bill fish; p. 104 (n.) the Sword fish excepted;
p. 105 (n.) our fellow-voyagers, the little fish alongside; p. 121
(n.) small, round, refulgent fish; p. 122 (n.) taken our chamois for
a kindred fish; p. 122 (n.) often done in the fishery; p. 122 (n.)
the rapid darting of fish; p. 123 (n.) There are many living fish,
phosphorescent; p. 123 (n.) divers species of sharks, cuttle-fish;
p. 124 (n.) for the poor little fire-fish; p. 126 (n.) It perceives
the little flying-fish; p. 126 (n.) You see the fish falling through
the air; p. 133 (n.) the sharp spine of a fish; p. 148 (n.) a curious
retinue of fish; p. 148 (n.) by the rank and file of the Trigger-fish;
p. 148 (n.) turn we to the fish; p. 149 (n.) as the first fish that
swam in Euphrates; p. 149 (n.) every fish for itself; p. 149 (n.) any
fish for Samoa; p. 149 (n.) Strange fish; p. 149 (adj.) all is glee,
fishy glee; p. 149 (n.) let us follow this monster fish; p. 149 (n.)
this strange-looking fish; p. 149 (n.) what fish can it be; p. 149
(n.) What a curious fish! What a comical fish; p. 149 (n.) slide on
the back of the Sword fish; p. 150 (n.) We fish, we fish, we merrily
swim; p. 150 (n.) Fish, fish, we are fish with red gills; p. 150 (n.)
Being many, each fish is a hero; p. 150 (n.) We fish, we fish, we
merrily swim; p. 150 (n.) But how now, my fine fish; p. 150 (n.) Pipe
away, merry fish; p. 151 (n.) onslaught of the dread fish of prey;
p. 151 (n.) transfixing the fish on his weapon; p. 151 (n.) the poor
fish fai ly crowded themselves; p. 151 (n.) and in pursuing the fish;
p. 154 (n.) and baskets of fish; p. 160 (n.) like the trail of a
great fish; p. 166 (v.) or comst thou to fish; p. 166 (v.) or come
you to fish; p. 182 (n.) polished white bones of the Ray-fish; p. 211
(n.) beheld a lonely fisherman; p. 267 (n.) Like the fish of the
bright and twittering fin; p. 267 (n.) Bright fish; p. 282 (n.) prying
about with the star-fish; p. 282 (n.) stole upon slumbering swordfish;
p. 283 (n.) the transparent wings of the flying fish; p. 285 (n.) and
of the Fish-ponds, and the Hereafters of Fish; p. 287 (n.) and conduct
us to his fish-ponds; p. 287 (n.) we should have a glimpse of our
fish; p. 288 (n.) that our trip to the fish-ponds; p. 288 (n.) and
the young fish taken from the sea; p. 288 (n.) Fresh-water fish are
only to be obtained; p. 288 (n.) Borabolla's fish, passing through;
p. 288 (n.) the fish darted in a shoal; p. 288 (n.) fish are the most
unchristian; p. 288 (n.) strove after the conversion of fish; p. 289
(n.) any creature, fish, flesh, or fowl; p. 291 (n.) with one of his

favorite cuttle-fish; p. 291 (n.) what of the banquet of fish; p. 305
(v.) to the Motoo to fish; p. 305 (n.) first amazement of the
fishermen; p. 318 (n.) to be at large with the fish; p. 353 (n.)
Arbino the god of fishing; p. 374 (adj.) nothing more than gold-
fishes' brains; p. 374 (adj.) do we not find little fishes' fins;
p. 374 (adj.) Amber is gold-fishes' brains, I say; p. 375 (n.) the
fish that dropped such treasures; p. 380 (n.) A quaint little Fishhook; p. 380 (n.) being the bony blades of nine sword-fish; p. 383
(adj.) King Kroko, and the Fisher Girl; p. 417 (n.) imbedding the
first course of fish; p. 436 (n.) no rods for fishermen; p. 436 (n.)
catch we heads as fish from the deep; p. 456 (n.) as fishermen for
sport, throw two lumps; p. 482 (adj.) dog-like holding a sword-fish
blade; p. 509 (n.) That fishermen/ With lonely spear; p. 536 (n.) in
other words, a species of cuttle-fish; p. 545 (n.) scaring the fish
from before them; p. 545 (n.) The gold-fish fly in golden flashes;
p. 573 (n.) the second, lobsters, cuttle-fish, crabs, cockles, cray-
fish; p. 610 (n.) Fishes rippled, and canaries sung; p. 635 (n.) As
silver-fish in vases; p. 635 (n.) like the fish that's mocked with
wings; p. 641 (n.) three radiant pilot-fish swam in advance; p. 645
(n.) The pilot-fish transformed.

Redburn--p. 6 (n.) a fat-looking, smoky fishing-boat; p. 43 (adj.)
Sometimes it [coffee] tasted fishy; p. 63 (n.) and looks over at the
fish in the water; p. 83 (n.) handsome young oyster boys and gallant
fishermen; p. 96 (n.) It is like a fisherman's walk; p. 100 (n.)
concerning all strange fish; p. 107 (n.) during the prosecution of
the fishery; p. 125 (n.) Presently a fishing-boat drew near; p. 125
(n.) replied the fisherman; p. 128 (n.) and curing of flying-fish;
p. 147 (n.) A band of fishers chose their humble seat; p. 273 (n.)
What outlandish fish may have nibbled; p. 281 (n.) when even a fish
has no foot at all; p. 312 (n.) while we were cutting the fish in.

White-Jacket--p. 71 (v.) The forecastle-men fished it up; p. 153 (n.)
so covered with minute barnacles and shell-fish; p. 153 (n.) a flat
sort of shell-fish was found; p. 153 (n.) Doubtless this shell-fish
had there taken up his quarters; p. 187 (n.) like a disarmed sword-
fish among ferocious white-sharks; p. 295 (adj.) though all her guns
were spiked by sword-fish blades; p. 318 (n.) we were like dolphin
among the flying-fish; p. 323 (n.) gazed down to the gold-fish and
silver-hued flying-fish; p. 393 (n.) some inert, coiled fish of the
sea.

Moby-Dick--p. 1 (n.) by what name a whale-fish is to be called in our
tongue; p. 2 (n.) Now the Lord had prepared a great fish to swallow
up Jonah; p. 3 (n.) The Indian Sea breedeth the most and the biggest
fishes that are; p. 6 (n.) If you should write a fable for little
fishes; p. 6 (n.) requires vast address and boldness in the fishermen;
p. 6 (n.) Edmund Burke's reference in Parliament to the Nantucket
Whale-Fishery; p. 6 (n.) A tenth branch of the king's ordinary
revenue . . . is the right to royal fish; p. 7 (n.) Colnett's Voyage
for the Purpose of Extending the Spermacetti Whale Fishery; p. 7 (n.)
Fishes of every color, form, and kind; p. 7 (n.) Not a father fish
then he,/ Flounders round the Polar Sea; p. 11 (n.) Miriam Coffin or
the Whale-Fisherman; p. 17 (n.) from the bright red windows of the
"Sword-Fish Inn"; p. 18 (n.) But "The Crossed Harpoons," and "The
Sword-Fish Inn"; p. 20 (n.) does it not bear a faint resemblance to a

gigantic fish; p. 27 (adj.) there was a parcel of outlandish bone
fish hooks; p. 37 (n.) all athirst for gain and glory in the fishery;
p. 38 (n.) and joins the great whale-fishery; p. 39 (n.) and few are
the moody fishermen; p. 40 (n.) so many are the unrecorded accidents
in the fishery; p. 45 (n.) And God had prepared a great fish to
swallow up Jonah; p. 45 (adj.) What a noble thing is that canticle in
the fish's belly; p. 49 (adj.) Then Jonah prayed unto the Lord out of
the fish's belly; p. 50 (n.) Then God spake unto the fish; p. 60 (n.)
him bery small-e fish-e; Queequeg no kill-e so small-e fish-e; p. 65
(adj.) Fishiest of all fishy places was the Try Pots; p. 65 (n.) till
you began to look for fish-bones coming through your clothes; p. 65
(adj.) There was a fishy flavor to the milk; p. 65 (adj./adj.) along
the beach among some fishermen's boats, I saw Hosea's brindled cow
feeding on fish remnants; p. 84 (n.) did you ever strike a fish;
p. 89 (n.) the numerous articles peculiar to the prosecution of the
fishery; p. 101 (n.) By old English statutory law, the whale declared
a royal fish; p. 103 (n.) as careful a man as you'll find anywhere in
this fishery; p. 118 (n.) whether a whale be a fish; p. 119 (n.) I
hereby separate the whales from the fish; p. 119 (n.) that the whale
is a fish; p. 119 (n.) all other fish are lungless and cold blooded;
p. 119 (n.) whale is a spouting fish; p. 119 (n.) but the walrus is
not a fish; p. 119 (n.) all the fish familiar to landsmen; p. 119
(n.) among spouting fish; p. 119 (n.) nor, . . . link with it any
fish; p. 119 (n.) spouting, and horizontal tailed fish; p. 119 (n.)
the fish styled Lamatins and Dugongs (Pig-fish and Saw-fish); p. 119
(n.) as these pig-fish are a nosy, contemptible set; p. 120 (n.) when
his oil was only accidentally obtained from the stranded fish; p. 121
(n.) Among the fishermen, he is discriminately designated; p. 121 (n.)
the American fishermen have long pursued; p. 122 (adj.) are the
fishermen's names for a few sorts; p. 124 (n.) I give the popular
fishermen's names for all these fish; p. 124 (n.) used like the blade
of the sword-fish and bill-fish; p. 128 (n.) In the British Greenland
Fishery; p. 139 (n.) those seductive seas in which we Southern fishers
mostly float; p. 139 (n.) enlisting in your vigilant fisheries;
p. 148 (n.) as the small gold-fish has its glassy globe; p. 261 (n.)
your cold-blooded, lungless fish, whose very bellies are refrigerators;
p. 285 (n.) as ordinary fish possess what is called a swimming
bladder; p. 296 (n.) all the combined rival boats were pointed for
this one fish; p. 300 (n.) canst thou fill his skin with barbed iron?
or his head with fish-spears; p. 305 (adj.) this whole story will
fare like that fish, flesh, and fowl idol of the Philistines; p. 323
(n.) the stricken fish darted blinding spray in our faces; p. 329 (n.)
for, alas! all fish bed in common; p. 331 (n.) Fast-fish and Loose-
fish; p. 331 (n.) I. A Fast-Fish belongs to the party fast to it;
II. A Loose-Fish is fair game for anybody who can soonest catch it;
p. 331 (n.) What is a Fast-Fish? Alive or dead a fish is technically
fast, when it is connected with an occupied ship or boat; p. 331 (n.)
What are the sinews and souls of Russian serfs and Republican slaves
but Fast-Fish; p. 334 (n.) What is the great globe itself but a Loose-
Fish? And what are you, reader, but a Loose-Fish and a Fast-Fish,
too; p. 336 (n.) There are two royal fish so styled by the English
law writers; p. 345 (n.) as the fish received the darted iron; p. 361
(n.) with Pisces, or the Fishes, we sleep; p. 364 (adj.) Ahab, putting
out his ivory leg, and crossing the ivory arm (like two sword-fish
blades); p. 365 (n.) free the fast-fish--and old trick; p. 366 (n.)
I . . . clung to that like a sucking fish; p. 406 (adv.) And Stubb,

fish-like, with sparkling scales, leaped in that same golden light;
p. 422 (n.) It's a fair wind that's only fair for that accursed fish;
p. 422 (n.) in the bottomless blue, rushed . . . sword-fish; p. 444
(n.) why should any one give chase to that hated fish; p. 453 (n.)
when night obscures the fish; p. 459 (n.) Shall we deep chasing this
murderous fish till he swamps the last man?

FLEET. A general name given to the royal navy. Also, any number of
ships, whether designed for war or commerce, keeping in company. A fleet
of ships of war is usually divided into three squadrons, and these, if
numerous, are again separated into subdivisions. The term in the navy
was any number exceeding a squadron, or rear-admiral's command, composed
of five sails-of-the-line, with any amount of smaller vessels. (Smyth)

Mardi--p. 186 (n.) in fleets and flotillas flocked round; p. 483 (n.)
straightway after her with all his fleets.

White-Jacket--p. 33 (n.) live in flotillas and fleets; p. 146 (n.) no
matter if we have to dismantle our fleets; p. 147 (n.) certain seamen
of the fleet; p. 148 (n.) to man his majesty's fleets; p. 148 (n.)
when the masts of her multiplied fleets; p. 149 (n.) at the gangways
of his victorious fleets; p. 150 (n.) the English fleet could be
manned without resource; p. 152 (n.) orders to tow the fleet of
strangers; p. 211 (n.) represented by the flag-ships of fleets;
p. 211 (n.) sailed the Acapulco fleets of the Spaniards; p. 211 (n.)
of all the Venetian, Genoese, and Papal fleets; p. 217 (n.) the
principle that pervades the fleet; p. 229 (n.) he was Commodore of
the fleet; p. 248 (n.) The Surgeon of the Fleet; p. 248 (n.) was our
Surgeon of the Fleet; p. 251 (adj.) misery coming under a fleet-
surgeon's eye; p. 251 (n.) Cadwallader Cuticle, our Surgeon of the
Fleet; p. 252 (n.) It seems customary for the Surgeon of the Fleet;
p. 254 (n.) what you have remarked, Mr. Surgeon of the Fleet; p. 254
(n.) by your scientific treatment, Mr. Surgeon of the Fleet; p. 254
(n.) my view of the case, Mr. Surgeon of the Fleet; p. 256 (n.) is
your only resource, Mr. Surgeon of the Fleet; p. 258 (n.) the
conversational tones of the Surgeon of the Fleet; p. 259 (n.) Now
the Surgeon of the Fleet and the top-man presented; p. 260 (n.) Mr.
Surgeon of the Fleet; p. 262 (n.) the Surgeon of the Fleet began;
p. 264 (n.) then Admiral of the fleets of this very country; p. 298
(n.) whose fleets struck terror; p. 313 (n.) appears to be quiet in
the fleet; p. 318 (n.) attacked and vanquished . . . an Ottoman fleet;
p. 319 (n.) It was the Admiral of the Fleet; p. 320 (n.) of the
combined fleets of England, France; p. 346 (adj.) in the theory of
frigate and fleet tactics; p. 347 (n.) composed a quarto treatise on
fleet-fighting; p. 347 (adj.) diagrams of great fleet arrangements;
p. 347 (n.) he discovered part of the French fleet; p. 347 (n.) and
extricate the British fleet by himself; p. 348 (n.) the whole British
fleet is giving chase to her; p. 359 (n.) Lord Bridport, the Admiral
of the Fleet; p. 369 (n.) Flogging through the Fleet; p. 370 (n.)
flogging through the fleet; p. 370 (n.) flogging through the fleet;
p. 371 (n.) thus he is carried through the fleet; p. 371 (n.) They
are rowed through the fleet; p. 371 (n.) that after being flogged
through the fleet; p. 372 (n.) condemned to be flogged through the
fleet; p. 372 (n.) was flogged through the fleet; p. 373 (n.) and the
floggings through the fleet; p. 381 (n.) of all the crews of his

Majesty's fleets; p. 381 (n.) again goes to war with its fleets;
p. 382 (n.) a Captain in the British fleet; p. 388 (adj.) into a
grand fleet engagement; p. 398 (n.) but one craft in a Milky Way fleet.

Moby-Dick--p. 66 (n.) instead of our going together among the whaling-
fleet in harbor; p. 99 (n.) why did the Dutch in De Witt's time have
admirals of their whaling fleets; p. 369 (n.) had in large fleets
pursued that Leviathan.

FLIPPER. The fin-like paw or paddle of marine mammalia; it is also
applied to the hand, as when the boatswain's mate exulted in having
"taken a lord by the flipper." (Smyth)

Mardi--p. 294 (n.) snatching at a flipper when seen; p. 418 (n.)
fins and flippers fricasseed.

FLOAT. A place where vessels float. Also, the inner part of a ship-
canal. In wet-docks ships are kept afloat while loading and discharging
cargo. Also, a raft or quantity of timber fastened together, to be
floated along a river by a tide or current. (Smyth)

Typee--p. 10 (v.) floating on the surface; p. 12 (v.) floating in
that lovely bay; p. 13 (v.) cocoa nuts floating closely together;
p. 16 (adj.) by their dread of the floating batteries; p. 28 (v.) I
felt as if floating in some new element; p. 132 (v.) floated there
as gracefully as a swan; p. 134 (v.) We floated about thus for
several hours.

Omoo--p. 7 (v.) juice of such stalks as one finds floating therein.

Mardi--p. 12 (v.) should float me thither; p. 25 (v.) the Acturion
still floated; p. 51 (adj.) no floating bough; p. 59 (v.) the tallest
frigate that floats; p. 108 (v.) to float out of sight of land;
p. 121 (v.) floated on the sea; p. 137 (v.) floating a rosy mist in
the air; p. 141 (v.) seemed floating before; p. 145 (v.) So away
floated the Chamois; p. 165 (n.) Brave the floating of dyed mantles;
p. 178 (v.) And floating away, these vapors; p. 188 (v.) sufficient
to float a canoe; p. 226 (adj.) were as floating isles in the sea;
p. 256 (adj.) and floating islands of flowers; p. 259 (v.) sideways
floating off; p. 265 (v.) a Moslem turban by us floats; p. 266 (v.)
as we floated on; p. 268 (v.) Then the damsels floated on; p. 285
(v.) these canoes floated with ours; p. 303 (v.) fast it floated away;
p. 456 (v.) to albatrosses floating on the sea; p. 461 (v.) spoil the
best wine ever floated; p. 467 (adj.) flourishing colonies among the
floating ice-bergs; p. 482 (adj.) a floating Juggernaut; p. 539 (adj.)
like the mouth of floating cornucopias; p. 540 (v.) would that we
floated in this glorious stuff; p 551 (v.) sparkling scales that
float along the sea; p. 552 (v.) in rafts thy murdered float; p. 557
(v.) that float on vulgar shores; p. 622 (v.) floating from the east,
a lone canoe; p. 635 (v.) But a sadness glorified . . . floating o'er
them; p. 644 (adj.) over floating fragments of wrecks; p. 651 (v.)
each a lotus floated.

Redburn--p. 100 (v.) that happened to float by us; p. 102 (v.) every

thing floating about; p. 111 (v.) oranges and lemons found floating;
p. 163 (v.) hundreds of immense ships floating; p. 165 (adj.) a
floating colony of the tribe to which it belongs; p. 174 (adj.)
Coast-of-Guinea-Man, and Floating Chapel; p. 175 (adj.) alongside
the Floating Chapel; p. 176 (adj.) The floating chapels which are
to be found; p. 177 (adj.) the floating chapel recalls to mind;
p. 250 (v.) before me float innumerable queens; p. 268 (adj.) from
a floating pulpit; p. 299 (v.) that limberly floated on the waves;
p. 312 (v.) drowned persons floating in the harbor.

White-Jacket--p. 29 (adj.) with all his floating families and farm-
yards; p. 33 (v.) but float his good ship higher; p. 71 (v.) a life-
buoy, descried floating by; p. 96 (v.) that are found floating by;
p. 97 (v.) his sails are floating in the air; p. 108 (v.) as if to
float us from our place; p. 152 (v.) dark objects floating on the
sea; p. 175 (v.) floating in a vast ocean herself; p. 175 (v.) having
a Mediterranean floating in her; p. 193 (adj.) each of whom in his
own floating island is king; p. 247 (v.) was floating on the water;
p. 266 (adj.) never beheld any of these floating trophies.

Moby-Dick--p. 5 (adj.) While the whale is floating at the stern of
the ship; p. 7 (adj.) Gather'd in shoals immense, like floating
islands; p. 16 (v.) in the wild conceits that swayed me to my purpose,
two and two there floated into my inmost soul; p. 20 (v.) three blue,
dim, perpendicular lines floating in a nameless yeast; p. 23 (v.) in
the deep shadows of his eyes floated some reminiscences; p. 43 (v.)
there floated a little isle of sunlight; p. 49 (v.) when instantly an
oily calmness floats out from the east; p. 139 (v.) in which we
Southern fishers mostly float; p. 160 (v.) the ship . . . floated
across the tranquil tropics; p. 325 (v.) floated the forms of the
nursing mothers of the whales; p. 341 (adj.) whereupon Stubb quickly
pulled to the floating body; p. 400 (v.) while all between float
milky-ways of coral isles; p. 409 (v.) All thy unnamable imminglings
float beneath me here; p. 411 (v.) The sky looks lacquered; clouds
there are none; the horizon floats; p. 448 (v.) the three boats now
stilly floated; p. 470 (v.) floating on the margin of the ensuing
scene; p. 470 (v.) the coffin life-buoy . . . floated by my side.

FLOOD. The flux of the tide, or the time the water continues rising.
When the water begins to rise, it is called a young flood, next it is
quarter-flood, half-flood, and top of flood, or high water. Also as
flood-tide. (Smyth)

Typee--p. 38 (n.) the perspiration starting from our bodies in
floods; p. 59 (n.) poured along the deck like a flood.

Mardi--p. 149 (n.) Let us roam the flood; p. 150 (n.) we, that roam
the flood; p. 233 (n.) to join floods with the streams; p. 258 (n.)
Flood-tide, and soul-tide to the brim; p. 265 (n.) Noon-tide rolls
its flood; p. 272 (n.) facing a flood-gate in the barrier; p. 374 (n.)
laws of the tribes before the flood; p. 380 (n.) flourished his tools
before the flood; p. 469 (v.) might have flooded their scattered
proas; p. 488 (v.) flood them over, then; p. 499 (v.) flooding the
forests from their fastnesses; p. 516 (n.) before that fine flood of
old wine; p. 516 (adj.) standing in the Nile at flood tide; p. 525

(v.) And thus, Romara flooded all Mardi; p. 541 (n.) monarchs
survived the flood; p. 635 (n.) came a flood of fragrance.

Redburn--p. 126 (n.) took the first of the flood; p. 169 (n.) our
blood is as the flood of the Amazon; p. 241 (v.) seas would instantly
flood; p. 249 (n.) that ever rolled its flood-tide of harmony.

White-Jacket--p. 33 (n.) if another flood came and overflowed; p. 86
(n.) against this invariable daily flooding; p. 86 (n.) goes
barefooted through the flood with the chillblains; p. 106 (n.) The
spray flew over the ship in floods; p. 115 (v.) as this was now
flooded almost continually; p. 116 (n.) and floods of brine descended;
p. 210 (n.) such a flood of scented reminiscences steals over me;
p. 212 (n.) swing round in concert to the first of the flood; p. 214
(adj.) glittering in the flooding sunset; p. 328 (v.) upon flooding
them with salt water.

Moby-Dick--p. 7 (n.) Montgomery's World before the Flood; p. 16 (n.)
the great flood-gates of the wonder-world swung open; p. 45 (n.) we
feel the floods surging over us; p. 70 (n.) I perceived that the ship
swinging to her anchor with the flood-tide, was now; p. 95 (n.) Sweet
fields beyond the swelling flood; pp. 384-5 (n.) In Noah's flood he
despised Noah's Ark; p. 385 (v./n.) if ever the world is to be again
flooded, like the Netherlands, to kill off its rats, then the eternal
whale will still survive, and rearing upon the topmost crest of the
equatorial flood; p. 395 (n.) vainly warning the infatuated old world
from the flood; p. 396 (n.) and the ocean's invisible flood-tide
lifted him higher and higher towards his destined heaven; p. 410
(adj.) by the gloom of the night they seemed the last men in a
flooded world; p. 462 (n.) Some men die at ebbtide; some at low water;
some at the full of the flood.

FLOTILLA. A fleet or squadron of small vessels. (Smyth)

Typee--p. 13 (n.) in the midst of quite a flotilla of them.

Mardi--p. 186 (n.) in fleets and flotillas flocked round; p. 200 (n.)
our flotilla disposed in the following order; p. 256 (n.) the whole
flotilla of trenchers.

White-Jacket--p. 33 (n.) live in flotillas and fleets.

FLOUNDER. A well-known pleuronect, better to fish for than to eat.
Called also floun-dab. (Smyth)

Mardi--p. 394 (n.) did you sup on flounders last night.

Redburn--p. 74 (n.) made my feet feel flat as flounders.

FLUID. Any substance whose parts easily move and change their relative
position without separation, and which yields to the slightest pressure;
a liquid. Water, flood, chyle, are fluids. (Webster)

Mardi--p. 122 (n.) to the originally luminous fluid contracting still more brilliancy; p. 123 (n.) that the fluid itself becomes charged with the luminous principle.

FLUKE. One of two parts which constitute the large triangular tail of the whale. Flukes, or palms, are also the broad triangular plates of iron on each arm of the anchor, inside the bills of extreme points, which having entered the ground, hold the ship. Seamen, by custom, drop the k and pronounce the word flue. (Smyth)

Moby-Dick--p. 349 (n.) from the thicker portions of his flukes; p. 364 (n.) it was like sitting in the fluke of an anchor; p. 365 (v.) instead of the other whale's that went off to windward, all fluking; p. 366 (n.) and, flukes first, the white hump backed through the wreck; p. 378 (n.) the weighty and majestic, but boneless flukes; p. 446 (n.) There go flukes! No, no; only black water; p. 448 (n.) warningly waving his bannered flukes in the air; p. 457 (n.) feeling with his flukes from side to side.

FOAM. The white froth produced by the collision of the waves, or by the bow of a ship when acted on by the wind; and also by their striking against rocks, vessels, or other bodies. (Smyth)

Typee--p. 62 (adj.) contrasted beautifully with the foamy waters; p. 252 (v.) till it foamed again.

Omoo--p. 23 (n.) while the foam flaked under her bows; p. 24 (n.) borne on what seemed a long flake of foam; p. 64 (n.) which was margined with foam; p. 72 (n.) all was foam and fury; p. 266 (n.) with a long, misty line of foam; p. 270 (n.) and bridling with foam.

Mardi--p. 50 (n.) sporting and frothing in frolicsome foam; p. 54 (n.) in the foam he made away with the bait; p. 117 (n.) this line of surging foam; p. 117 (n.) panting on its flank in the foam; p. 118 (n.) pawing the ocean into foam; p. 118 (n.) its mad, tearing foam; p. 121 (n.) a line of rushing illuminated foam; p. 125 (n.) so recently one sheet of foam; p. 140 (v.) in exultations its surface foamed up; p. 150 (n.) making a foam; p. 150 (n.) a hubbub of scales and of foam; p. 192 (n.) white reef's rack and foam; p. 194 (n.) A rush, a foam of recollections; p. 200 (n.) a sheaf of foam borne upright; p. 213 (v.) waves wide-foaming around us; p. 258 (adj.) bright tide at the foam beaded rim; p. 259 (n.) a young form of foam; p. 273 (n.) He was pointed out in the foam; p. 294 (n.) from whose foamy coping; p. 303 (n.) the white foam lighting up the last; p. 317 (n.) threw up a high fountain of foam; p. 366 (n.) hovering 'twixt breezing and foaming; p. 543 (adj.) ten thousand foam-flaked dromedary-humps uprose; p. 549 (adj.) all over flaked with foamy fleeces; p. 554 (adj.) lit up by foam-white, breaking billows; p. 562 (n.) its margin frothy-white with foam; p. 586 (adj.) leaving braided, foaming wakes; p. 586 (n.) the Death-cloud grazed us with its foam; p. 616 (n.) will that name ever lash thee into foam; p. 633 (n.) Foam played before them as they darted on; p. 644 (n.) the glittering foam all round its white marge; p. 646 (n.) and dashed me into foam; p. 654 (n.) churned in foam.

Redburn--p. 9 (n.) for it looked like the foam and froth; p. 63 (n.)
little fleeces of foam all over the sea; p. 64 (n.) into rolling
avalanches of foam; p. 66 (n.) shaking off the foam from her bows;
p. 66 (n.) like foam from a bridle-bit; p. 66 (adj.) give me . . .
this briny, foamy life; p. 102 (n.) a streak of illuminated foam in
her wake; p. 116 (v.) as the ship went foaming on her way; p. 166 (n.)
I have seen them flying through the foam; p. 289 (n.) Often tumbled
the white foam.

White-Jacket--p. 105 (n.) in milk-white billows of foam; p. 106 (n.)
rolling in the trough of the foam; p. 196 (n.) he became a mere
dislocated skeleton, white as foam; p. 270 (n.) through a cream-
colored ocean of illuminated foam; p. 393 (adj.) through a soft,
seething, foamy lull.

Moby-Dick--p. 3 (n.) beating the sea before him into a foam; p. 59
(n.) the little Moss tossed the quick foam from her bows; p. 60 (n.)
At the same foam-fountain, Queequeg seemed to drink and reel with me;
p. 61 (n.) revealing his brawny shoulders through the freezing foam;
p. 123 (n.) making more gay foam and white water generally; p. 159
(n.) leaving a milky-way wake of creamy foam; p. 201 (n.) like
showers of silver chips, the foam-flakes flew over her bulwarks;
p. 222 (n.) through a blinding foam that blent two whitenesses
together; p. 223 (n.) he would bury him in bubbles and foam; p. 257
(adj.) But in the foamy confusion of their mixed and struggling hosts;
p. 298 (adj.) while stretching from them on both sides, was the
foaming swell that he made; p. 299 (n.) Blinding vapors of foam and
white-fire; p. 309 (n.) wrapt in fleecy foam, the towing whale is
forty feet ahead; p. 346 (adj.) poor Pip came all foaming up to the
chocks of the boat; p. 365 (adv.) this old great-grandfather, with
the white head and hump, runs all afoam into the pod; p. 365 (n.) I
was blind as a bat--both eyes out--all befogged and bedeadened with
black foam; p. 414 (v.) The scud all a flyin',/ That's his [Ocean's]
flip only foamin'; p. 447 (n.) continually set in a revolving ring of
finest, fleecy, greenish foam; p. 450 (n.) Ahab half smothered in the
foam of the whale's insolent tail; p. 455 (n.) piling up a mountain
of dazzling foam; p. 467 (n.) smiting his jaws and fiery semicircular
foam before him as he rushed.

FORE. The distinguishing character of all that part of a ship's frame and
machinery which lies near the stem, or in that direction, in opposition
to aft or after. (Smyth)

Omoo--p. 7 (adv.) instead of extending fore and aft; p. 42 (n.)
dropped down the scuttle from the fore-top; pp. 44-5 (n.) Laying the
body out on the fore-hatch; p. 56 (n.) by descending into the fore-
hold; p. 58 (n.) sometimes stood in the fore-chains; p. 107 (n.) had
been captain of the foretop; p. 149 (n.) loosing the fore-royal.

Mardi--p. 5 (n.) be the Acturion's fore; p. 70 (n.) boarded the fore-
tack; p. 86 (adj.) to the fore and aft-stays; p. 101 (n.) in the
fore-top; p. 110 (n.) a parenthetical pull at the fore-brace.

Redburn--p. 8 (n.) a second was in the fore-top; p. 8 (n.) was
splitting wood near the fore-hatch; p. 53 (adv.) So I scrubbed away

fore and aft; p. 55 (n.) eating his breakfast on the fore-hatch;
p. 75 (adv.) showed her decks fore and aft; p. 82 (n.) his cook-house
was right behind the fore-mast; p. 239 (adj.) except through the fore
and after hatchways; p. 241 (n.) to hold your head down the fore
hatchway; p. 293 (adv.) let them have an occasional run fore and aft;
p. 296 (n.) haul back the fore-yard.

White-Jacket--p. 9 (adj.) and fore, main, and mizen-top-men of each
watch; p. 9 (n.) the fore-yard, anchors, and all the sails; p. 10
(adj.) These haul aft the fore and main-sheets; p. 19 (adj.) between
the fore and main hatches; p. 11 (n.) We say nothing here of . . .
Captains of the Fore-tops, . . . Captains of the Fore-Hold; p. 14
(n.) of one of the Captains of the fore-top; p. 14 (adj.) invariable
ex ordium to the fore-top Captain's . . . remarks; p. 14 (adj.) the
fore-top captain meant a ship; pp. 14-5 (n.) when the fore-top
captain, like many others; p. 16 (n.) you are full of the fore-peak
and the fore-castle; p. 27 (n.) in a tar-cellar down in the fore-hold;
p. 27 (adj.) and of the Fore and Main holds; p. 34 (adv.) he is
braced up fore and aft; p. 40 (adv.) or reefing top-sails fore and
aft; p. 44 (adv.) the gunner's gang were at work fore and aft; p. 47
(adj.) than the top-men of the fore, main, and mizen masts; p. 47
(adj.) divisions of the frigate, fore and aft; p. 55 (adj.) Next day,
fore and aft; p. 62 (n.) made up entirely of fore-top-men; p. 66 (n.)
happens to send overboard your fore-mast; p. 67 (n.) a loud cry is
heard . . . in the fore-top; p. 69 (adv.) galley-cooks would be going
fore and aft; p. 72 (n.) a frigate carries large anchors in her fore-
chains; p. 73 (n.) recall-signal at the frigate's fore-t'-gallant-
mast-head; p. 81 (n.) hem of a pair of white trowsers vanished up one
of the ladders at the fore-hatchway; p. 85 (adv.) is spread with
hammocks, fore and aft; p. 90 (n.) roared a Hollander of the fore-top;
p. 92 (n.) COMMODORE BOUGEE . . . TOM BROWN, of the Fore-top; p. 97
(adv.) fore and aft set t'-gallant-sails; p. 97 (adj.) give her the
fore-top-mast stun'-sail; p. 98 (n.) they drop the fore-sail; p. 102
(adv.) were ridden fore and aft on a rail; p. 102 (n.) one of the
fore-top-men--an ugly-tempered devil; p. 104 (n.) discerned from the
fore-top-mast-head; p. 105 (n.) drenched the men who were on the
fore-yard; p. 117 (n.) an experienced natural philosopher belonging
to the fore-top; p. 124 (n.) you went to it by way of the Fore-
passage; p. 152 (n.) A man at the fore-top-sail-yard; p. 171 (n.) we
had one fore-top-man on board; p. 171 (n.) This fore-top-man paid
eighteen pence; p. 172 (adv.) Of having a clear stroll fore and aft;
p. 174 (n.) He belonged to the fore-hold; p. 178 (n.) a fore-top-man
. . . paid down the money; p. 178 (n.) the fore-top-man slips out of
his hammock; p. 184 (adv.) among all hands, fore and aft; p. 189 (n.)
to prey upon honest seamen, fore and aft; p. 190 (n.) language of the
Captain of the Fore-top; p. 195 (n.) eagerness to vanquish the fore-
mast; p. 198 (adv.) D'ye hear there, fore and aft; p. 202 (n.) you,
gallant fore-top-men; p. 202 (n.) exclaimed a fore-top-man; p. 202
(prep.) The cry ran fore and aft the ship; p. 225 (adv.) d'ye hear
there, fore and aft; p. 239 (n.) tripped him . . . down into the
fore-passage; p. 240 (n.) sighed the Captain of the Fore-top; p. 242
(n.) I place you in the fore-top; p. 246 (n.) a seaman belonging to
the fore-top; p. 278 (n.) the boatswain's mate of the fore-hatchway;
p. 298 (n.) insultingly carried a broom at his fore-mast; p. 307 (n.)
lurking round the fore-mast on the spar-deck; p. 308 (n.) both fore-
tacks over the main-yard; p. 312 (adj.) lost her fore and main-top-

masts; p. 312 (n.) her fore-yard lying in two pieces; p. 322 (n.) in
the sequestered fore-chains of the Neversink; p. 325 (adv.) the
awnings were spread fore and aft; p. 332 (n.) fate of the amputated
fore-top-man; p. 338 (n.) Ar'n't this the fore-top-man, Shenly; p.
p. 338 (n.) than ever he was at the fore-truck; p. 348 (n.) I would
haul back the fore-top-sail; p. 348 (n.) you can't haul back your
fore-top-sail; p. 348 (n.) your fore-mast is lying across your
forecastle; p. 353 (n.) mounting the fore-yard in a gale; p. 353 (n.)
to the hare-brained tenants of the fore-top; p. 356 (adv.) D'ye hear
there, fore and aft; p. 357 (adv.) D'ye hear there, fore and aft;
p. 358 (adj.) from their stations at the fore and main hatchways;
p. 361 (adv.) D'ye hear, fore and aft; p. 363 (n.) coming down the
rigging from the fore-top; p. 372 (adv.) A cry went fore and aft;
p. 383 (n.) a fore-top-man by the name of Landless; p. 388 (n.)
roared a roystering fore-top-man; p. 388 (adv.) D'ye hear there, fore
and aft; p. 389 (n.) fly at my fore; p. 390 (n.) you, seamen of the
fore-top; p. 399 (prep.) Glance fore and aft our flush decks; p. 399
(adj.) we have gallant fore, main, and mizen top-men.

Moby-Dick--p. 48 (adv.) [wave] runs roaring fore and aft; p. 448
(adj.) soon the fore part of him slowly rose from the water.

FORECASTLE. The part of the upper deck foward of the fore mast; or, as
some say, forward of the after part of the fore channels. Also, the
forward part of the vessel, under the deck, where the sailors live, in
merchant vessels. (Dana)

Typee--p. 9 (n.) spreading an awning over the forecastle; p. 31 (n.)
recollection of her narrow decks and gloomy forecastle; p. 35 (n.)
there was a general move towards the forecastle; p. 36 (n.) I lingered
behind in the forecastle; p. 170 (n.) to spin tough yarns on a ship's
forecastle.

Omoo--p. 7 (n.) Going below into the forecastle just after dark; p. 7
(n.) no man who has lived in forecastles is at all fastidious; p. 11
(n.) he lived in the forecastle with the men; p. 13 (n.) all by
himself on the forecastle; p. 16 (adj.) shouted Jermin down the
forecastle scuttle; p. 17 (n.) ever dreams of entering a ship's
forecastle; p. 17 (n.) made his appearance on the forecastle; p. 20
(adj.) showed itself above the forecastle scuttle; p. 20 (n.) he dove
down into the forecastle; p. 24 (n.) somewhat strange in a ship's
forecastle; p. 33 (n.) finding the heat of the forecastle unpleasant;
p. 34 (n.) crouching apart in the forecastle; p. 36 (n.) professional
calls in the forecastle were sometimes made; p. 36 (n.) It was in the
forecastle chiefly; p. 36 (n.) of the democracy in the forecastle;
p. 38 (n.) Most persons know that a ship's forecastle; p. 38 (n.) The
general aspect of the forecastle was dungeon-like; p. 39 (adj.) swung
the forecastle lamp; p. 39 (n.) in the forecastle it looked like the
hollow of an old tree; p. 41 (n.) Ascending from the forecastle; p.
p. 42 (n.) I lay awake in the forecastle; p. 42 (n.) than Julia's
forecastle at midnight; p. 42 (n.) a shadow glided across the
forecastle; p. 45 (n.) all started at a cry from the forecastle;
p. 47 (n.) his men languishing in the forecastle; p. 47 (n.) In the
forecastle, Flash Jack; p. 48 (n.) were set down into the forecastle;
p. 48 (n.) the "Cods," or leaders of the forecastle; p. 52 (n.) and

returned to the forecastle; p. 53 (n.) bids him be off to the
forecastle; p. 54 (n.) crosses the forecastle, tin can in hand; p. 59
(n.) planted on the larboard side of the forecastle; p. 68 (adj.)
This was the opinion of our forecastle Cokes; p. 70 (n.) went into
council upon the forecastle; p. 74 (adj.) addressed the forecastle
parliament in the following strain; p. 74 (n.) formed an ornament of
the forecastle; p. 76 (n.) a "cod" in the forecastle; p. 82 (n.)
borne along to the forecastle; p. 85 (n.) dancing a hornpipe on the
forecastle; p. 86 (adj.) down the forecastle scuttle; p. 88 (n.)
retired into the forecastle; p. 88 (n.) atmosphere of the forecastle
so close; p. 90 (n.) the old cook thundered on the forecastle; p. 97
(n.) when we were wakened in the forecastle; p. 104 (n.) looking over
at us from the forecastle; p. 119 (n.) acquired what he knew of it in
the forecastle; p. 149 (n.) the sailors on the forecastle singing;
p. 289 (n.) sailors lounging about the forecastle; p. 290 (n.) lying
in the kid in the forecastle; p. 316 (n.) a sharp voice hailed the
forecastle.

Mardi--p. 5 (adj.) by our full forecastle choir; p. 12 (adj.)
forecastle chronology; p. 13 (n.) in the Lingua-Franca of the
forecastle; p. 14 (n.) among the "kids" in the forecastle; p. 23
(adj.) the forecastle lamp; p. 26 (n.) into the forecastle; p. 59 (n.)
in the forecastle reigned; p. 60 (n.) busy in the forecastle; p. 61
(n.) rubbish in the forecastle; p. 74 (n.) carronade on the forecastle;
p. 80 (n.) boldly demanded the forecastle; p. 81 (adj.) to her
forecastle boudoir; p. 87 (n.) descended into the forecastle; p. 87
(adj.) over the open forecastle scuttle; p. 87 (n.) it came into the
forecastle; p. 92 (n.) below into the forecastle; p. 93 (n.) carried
down into the forecastle; p. 94 (n.) in a dark hole of the forecastle;
p. 95 (n.) from the forecastle to the cabin; p. 102 (n.) lounging
quietly in the forecastle; p. 114 (n.) descended into the forecastle;
pp. 116-7 (n.) boom, used on the forecastle-deck.

Redburn--p. 24 (n.) go forward to the forecastle; p. 25 (n.) groped
my way down into the forecastle; p. 25 (n.) sleep out the night in
the forecastle; p. 25 (n.) in that damp and dark forecastle; p. 26
(n.) we went below into the forecastle; p. 31 (n.) handed down into
the forecastle; p. 42 (n.) so going down into the forecastle; p. 49
(n.) a large bell which hung on the forecastle; p. 50 (n.) by a horrid
groaning noise down in the forecastle; p. 54 (n.) passed down into
the forecastle; p. 60 (n.) between the two sailors in the forecastle;
p. 68 (n.) and hard biscuit of the forecastle; p. 68 (n.) or sending
word into the forecastle; p. 68 (n.) I went down into the forecastle;
p. 68 (n.) at least for a forecastle; p. 69 (n.) As I was about leaving
the forecastle; p. 75 (n.) sailors grouped upon the forecastle; p. 77
(n.) from the forecastle looked no bigger; p. 82 (n.) he lived round
the corner of Forecastle-square; p. 93 (n.) of the look-out men on
the forecastles; p. 112 (adj.) half way up on the forecastle ladder;
p. 122 (n.) from which you descended into the forecastle; p. 128 (n.)
and going down into the forecastle; p. 130 (n.) are supposed to sleep
in the forecastle; p. 143 (n.) of some tarry captain of the forecastle;
p. 164 (n.) mount the poops and forecastles of the various vessels;
p. 166 (n.) its forecastle echoing with songs; p. 168 (n.) gathered
on the forecastle to sing and pray; p. 171 (n.) The Lascars were on
the forecastle-deck; p. 171 (n.) and paganism on the forecastle;
p. 196 (n.) coming down into the forecastle; p. 196 (n.) our forecastle

was often visited; p. 219 (n.) as I stood upon the forecastle; p. 220
(n.) to the Queen's drawing-room than a ship's forecastle; p. 231 (n.)
in the filthy forecastle of the Highlander; p. 238 (n.) from the cabin
bulkhead to the forecastle; p. 240 (n.) put him likewise into a bunk
in the forecastle; p. 240 (n.) from many a forecastle; p. 243 (n.)
shouting down the forecastle-scuttle; p. 244 (n.) seldom let any
thing be done in the forecastle; p. 244 (n.) in the extreme angle of
the forecastle; p. 244 (n.) a strange odor in the forecastle; p. 244
(n.) the forecastle had been smoked out; p. 245 (n.) would stay alone
in the forecastle; p. 271 (n.) would often be driven out of the
forecastle; p. 271 (adj.) eying the forecastle lamp; p. 272 (n.) from
the opposite corner of the forecastle; p. 273 (n.) has ever supped in
a forecastle; p. 283 (n.) was peeping down into the forecastle;
p. 284 (n.) they hung round the forecastle; p. 295 (n.) Jackson came
up from the forecastle; p. 295 (n.) from his dark tomb in the
forecastle; p. 301 (n.) Harry and I sat on a chest in the forecastle;
p. 302 (n.) to eat in the forecastle; p. 308 (n.) congregated in the
forecastle-deck; p. 308 (n.) debated by the assembly on the forecastle.

White-Jacket--p. 9 (n.) whose place is on the forecastle; p. 11 (n.)
We say nothing here of . . . Captains of the Forecastle; p. 13 (n.)
No one could be better company in the forecastle; p. 16 (n.) you are
full of the fore-peak and the forecastle; p. 27 (n.) the Captains of
the Tops, of the Forecastle; p. 47 (n.) bracing sea-air, and broad-
cast sunshine of the forecastle; p. 71 (n.) The forecastle-men fished
it up; p. 90 (n.) cried a forecastle-man; p. 92 (n.) Mayor . . .
Seafull, of the Forecastle; p. 105 (n.) on the quarter-deck and
forecastle; p. 106 (n.) several of the forecastle-men, were swarming;
p. 117 (n.) his perilous duty on the forecastle; p. 130 (n.) one of
the great guns was discharged from the forecastle; p. 133 (n.) the
empty pan knocking about the forecastle; p. 141 (n.) one of her
forecastle-men told me; p. 161 (n.) manned by the old Tritons of the
forecastle; p. 172 (n.) when going forward to the fore-castle; p. 173
(n.) when he was walking round the forecastle; p. 208 (n.) contrast
between the forecastle and the quarter-deck; p. 215 (n.) carried the
grateful news . . . to them on the forecastle; p. 218 (n.) some
venerable six-footer of a forecastle-man; p. 245 (n.) hurried forward
to the forecastle; p. 270 (n.) was once a captain of the forecastle;
p. 271 (n.) an amateur forecastle-man, White-Jacket; p. 309 (n.) than
the Captain of the Forecastle himself; p. 312 (n.) in two pieces on
her shattered forecastle; p. 324 (n.) two long twenty-four-pounders
on the forecastle; p. 326 (n.) robust old sea-dogs on the forecastle;
p. 348 (n.) your fore-mast is lying across your forecastle; p. 353
(n.) sea grenadiers on the forecastle; p. 353 (n.) the Captain of the
Forecastle, old Ushant; p. 355 (n.) the Old Guard on the Forecastle
still; p. 360 (n.) ere long an old forecastle-man was discovered;
p. 360 (n.) This forecastle-man was ever afterward known; p. 360 (n.)
the contempt hurled on our forecastle-man; p. 363 (n.) the ancient
Captain of the Forecastle; p. 364 (n.) said the Captain of the
Forecastle; p. 366 (n.) you have been Captain of the Forecastle;
p. 374 (n.) at both gangways and forecastle; p. 388 (n.) captain of
gun No. 1 on the forecastle; p. 388 (adj.) cried a forecastle-man;
p. 389 (n.) cried the forecastle-man.

Moby-Dick--p. 14 (n.) I go as a simple sailor, . . . plumb down into
the forecastle; p. 15 (adj.) because of the wholesome exercise and

pure air of the forecastle deck; p. 15 (n.) at second hand from the
sailors on the forecastle; p. 108 (n.) On the grim Pequod's forecastle;
p. 127 (adj.) I shall enumerate them by their forecastle appellations;
pp. 256-7 (adj.) Queequeg and a forecastle seaman came on deck;
p. 370 (adj.) though the savage salt spray bursting down the
forecastle scuttle; p. 384 (n.) some philosophers of the forecastle
have concluded; p. 388 (n.) during the midnight watch on the bearded
forecastle of Noah's ark; p. 404 (n.) looking on from the forecastle.

FRIGATE. In the Royal Navy, the next class vessel to a ship of the line;
formerly a light nimble ship built for the purpose of sailing swiftly.
The English were the first who appeared on the ocean with these ships,
and equipped them for war as well as for commerce. (Smyth)

Typee--p. 6 (n.) Journal of the Cruise of the U.S. frigate Essex;
p. 7 (n.) to shove off from the side of one of the French frigates;
p. 16 (n.) Four heavy, double-banked frigates; p. 18 (n.) in the
Reine Blanche frigate; p. 18 (n.) The frigate . . . got springs on
her cables; p. 18 (n.) and in full view of the frigate; p. 26 (n.)
sailors and marines from the frigate Essex; p. 184 (n.) Commodore
David Porter of the U.S. frigate Essex; p. 254 (n.) which peeped out
of the portholes of the frigate; p. 255 (n.) dispatched by the
admiral in the Carysfort frigate; p. 256 (n.) benignant spirit which
marked the discipline of his frigate; p. 257 (n.) the Dublin frigate,
. . . entered the harbor of Honolulu; p. 258 (n.) the crews of two
frigates . . . gave the crowning flourish.

Omoo--p. 69 (n.) two rows of teeth proclaiming a frigate; p. 99 (n.)
As we held on toward the frigate; p. 103 (n.) going aboard the French
frigate; p. 103 (n.) should we go aboard the frigate; p. 105 (adj.)
we were paraded in the frigate's gangway; p. 109 (n.) of the heavy
sixty-gun frigates now in vogue; p. 112 (n.) we were aboard the
frigate; p. 114 (n.) from the confined decks of the frigate; p. 117
(n.) loss of rest on board the frigate; p. 123 (n.) on the gun-deck
of Du Petit Thouar's frigate.

Mardi--p. 126 (n.) species which are seldom found far from land:
terns, frigate-birds; p. 367 (n.) And like a frigate, I am full with
a thousand souls.

Redburn--p. 129 (n.) did not have a whole frigate-full of wives;
p. 138 (n.) old frigates are converted into chapels; p. 190 (adj.) in
falling from a frigate's mast-head; p. 193 (n.) the frigate Thetis
may be announced; p. 273 (n.) stout masts of seventy-fours and
frigates.

White-Jacket--p. ix (n.) on board of a United States frigate; p. ix
(n.) After remaining in this frigate for more than a year; p. 3 (n.)
when our frigate lay in Callao; p. 8 (adj.) every man of a frigate's
five-hundred-strong; p. 10 (n.) on the gun-deck of a frigate; p. 13
(n.) the frigate gliding through the water; p. 14 (n.) near him,
though under him, in the frigate; p. 15 (n.) the tops of a frigate
are quite spacious and cosy; p. 17 (n.) On this present cruise of the
frigate Neversink; p. 17 (n.) He abandoned the frigate; p. 18 (n.)
the frigate came to anchor; p. 19 (n.) of right you belong to the

frigate Neversink; p. 19 (n.) as there is no resisting the frigate;
p. 19 (n.) was pulled back to the frigate; p. 22 (n.) as the frigate
had a captain; p. 24 (n.) who filled that post aboard of our frigate;
p. 24 (n.) The First Lieutenancy of a frigate; p. 24 (n.) In a
frigate it comprises the after part; p. 24 (n.) in a frigate six or
seven in number; p. 25 (n.) Hence, in a crowded frigate; p. 26 (n.)
In frigates, the ward-room . . . is on the same deck; p. 31 (n.) In
frigates, and all large ships of war; p. 32 (adj.) For upon a
frigate's quarter-deck; p. 32 (n.) with the story of the English
frigate Alceste and the French frigate Medusa; p. 33 (n.) Every man
and every boy in the frigate knows; p. 40 (n.) on the gun-deck of a
frigate; p. 40 (n.) In a frigate, you cannot . . . meander off your
sonnets; p. 43 (n.) harbors and bays at which the frigate had
touched; p. 43 (n.) comical incidents on board the frigate itself;
pp. 46-7 (n.) by my experiences on board our frigate; p. 47 (n.)
being on the loftiest yard of the frigate; p. 47 (n.) The Holders of
our frigate, the Troglodytes; p. 47 (n.) in all divisions of the
frigate; p. 50 (n.) unreservedly consorted while on board the frigate;
p. 50 (n.) Though I was above a year in the frigate; p. 53 (adj.) the
frigate's supply of the delectable beverage; p. 55 (n.) having no
customers on board the frigate; p. 55 (n.) the whole frigate smelled
like a lady's toilet; p. 57 (n.) The common seamen in a large frigate;
p. 58 (n.) In our frigate, this personage; p. 65 (n.) while on board
the frigate; p. 65 (n.) The quarter-deck armaments of most modern
frigates; p. 67 (n.) in less than five minutes the frigate is ready
for action; p. 72 (n.) the frigate was going fast; p. 72 (n.) a frigate
carries large anchors; p. 73 (adj.) recall-signal at the frigate's
fore-t'gallant-mast-head; p. 74 (adj.) from a frigate's crew might be
culled out men; p. 75 (n.) For even thus is it in a frigate; p. 79
(adj.) on a frigate berth-deck; p. 83 (n.) snatch a nap during daytime
in a frigate; p. 85 (adj.) spotless hammocks exposed in a frigate's
nettings; p. 86 (n.) flooding of the three decks of a frigate; p. 91
(n.) had served in other American frigates; p. 96 (n.) our wet-decked
frigate drew nearer; p. 101 (n.) peopled frigates, echoing with the
voices; p. 104 (n.) now perceptibly nearing the frigate; p. 105 (n.)
what frigate's that; p. 105 (n.) we found the frigate leaning over to
it so steeply; p. 108 (n.) our noble frigate seemed thrice its real
length; p. 110 (n.) like the ribbed bows of a frigate; p. 111 (n.)
was the discipline of the frigate; p. 113 (n.) worthily to command
even a frigate; p. 114 (n.) to command a squadron of frigates; p. 115
(n.) going before the wind in a frigate; p. 115 (n.) until the old
frigate dipped and went into it; p. 116 (adj.) as if there were a
volcano in the frigate's hold; p. 116 (n.) sea-nymphs outside the
frigate; p. 123 (n.) less painful sights to be seen in a frigate;
p. 124 (n.) and in a frigate thirty-five dollars per month; p. 127
(n.) to be met with on board our frigate; p. 127 (n.) some remote,
dark corner of the bowels of the frigate; p. 129 (adj.) during a
frigate engagement in the last war; p. 131 (adj.) In frigate phrase;
p. 134 (adj.) through every manly heart in a frigate; p. 135 (n.) the
frigate, staggering under whole top-sails; p. 141 (n.) the seamen
belonging to another American frigate; p. 141 (n.) that this frigate
was vastly admired by the shore ladies; p. 142 (n.) to scourge him
round the world in your frigates; p. 145 (n.) How is it in an American
frigate; p. 153 (n.) had commanded the well-known frigate; p. 155 (n.)
on board this particular frigate of ours; p. 159 (n.) The Frigate in
Harbor; p. 160 (n.) Our frigate carried a very large boat; p. 169 (n.)

My book experiences on board of the frigate; p. 177 (n.) precautions
are taken by most frigate-executives; p. 178 (adj.) and moor them to
the frigate's anchor-buoy; p. 180 (n.) Arrived alongside the frigate;
p. 182 (n.) upon . . . every under-strapper official in the frigate;
p. 184 (adj.) brought them down to the frigate's boats; p. 185 (adj.)
honored upon the frigate's arrival home; p. 186 (n.) our frigate, bad
as it was, was homeward-bound; p. 192 (n.) just as you are aboard the
frigate here; p. 194 (n.) though two American frigates . . . came from
the opposite Poles; p. 205 (adj.) head clerk of the frigate's fiscal
affairs; p. 206 (n.) on board of the old frigate Java; p. 211 (n.) of
all the frigate-merchantment; p. 222 (n.) a frigate houses and homes
five hundred mortals; p. 222 (n.) inmates of a frigate are thrown
upon themselves; p. 223 (n.) even the captain of a frigate is . . .
induced; p. 226 (n.) the rest remaining to garrison the frigate;
p. 226 (n.) had been safe on board the frigate; p. 227 (n.) more like
a mad-house than a frigate; p. 227 (n.) our frigate presented a very
different scene; p. 229 (adj.) high aloft on a frigate's poop; p. 234
(n.) the gold lace of our barons of the frigate; p. 239 (n.) to show
the . . . strangers the bowels of the frigate; p. 239 (n.) from so
great a depth in a frigate; p. 245 (n.) between the store ship and
our frigate; p. 246 (adj.) swimming in the frigate's shadow; p. 247
(n.) was soon on board the frigate; p. 258 (n.) with the slow, slight
roll of the frigate; p. 265 (n.) she passed several foreign frigates;
p. 265 (n.) the English frigate, weighing her anchor; p. 265 (n.)
were the more anxious to race with this frigate; p. 266 (n.) lay the
frigate President; p. 266 (n.) was the frigate Macedonian; p. 267 (n.)
what is the American frigate Macedonian; p. 267 (n.) what is the
English frigate President; p. 268 (n.) that our frigate would at last
ground; p. 268 (n.) the tall main-mast of the English fighting-
frigate; p. 269 (n.) all three frigates were irregularly abreast;
p. 269 (n.) to behold those fine frigates; p. 270 (n.) lost at sea in
the Aurora frigate; p. 272 (n.) friskness and oscillating buoyancy to
the frigate; p. 277 (n.) when I first came on board the frigate;
p. 278 (n.) in getting the frigate round on the other tack; p. 279
(n.) advanced to the dread tribunal of the frigate; p. 279 (n.) on
board the frigate upward of a year; p. 281 (n.) to speak to the
Captain of a frigate; p. 281 (n.) though supreme Captain of a frigate;
p. 282 (n.) There is no part of a frigate; p. 284 (n.) their water-
rimmed, cannon-sentried frigates; p. 287 (n.) now and then taking
place in our frigate; p. 288 (n.) from all quarters of the frigate;
p. 290 (n.) while on board the frigate; p. 290 (n.) in the bosom of
his home, the frigate; p. 294 (n.) serving on board this very frigate;
p. 295 (n.) though this frigate laid her broken bones; p. 301 (n.) he
is cast into an American frigate; p. 305 (n.) one game was allowable
in the frigate; p. 308 (n.) guardo moves and maneuvres of a frigate;
p. 311 (n.) the frigate itself was a glorious sight; p. 312 (n.) The
ship . . . was an English frigate; p. 312 (n.) the English frigate
was reduced; p. 312 (n.) of the very frigates now crippled; p. 312
(n.) This is a seventy-four, not a frigate; p. 313 (n.) of the
frigate-action here spoken of; p. 314 (n.) Captain of a frigate in
the action; p. 314 (n.) between the American frigate Essex; p. 315
(n.) did this American frigate, one iota; p. 315 (n.) was so on board
of the English frigate; p. 318 (n.) an Ottoman fleet of . . . twenty-
five frigates; p. 318 (n.) bowled down the Turkish frigates like nine-
pins; p. 322 (n.) of the gun-deck of our frigate; p. 325 (n.) As with
most frigates, the sick-bay; p. 326 (n.) In a sea-going frigate that

has; p. 327 (adj.) far up into the frigate's main-top; p. 329 (n.)
the Surgeon of a frigate is to be found; p. 335 (n.) the calm
pervaded the entire frigate; p. 345 (n.) There were two academies in
the frigate; p. 346 (adj.) in the theory of frigate and fleet tactics;
p. 350 (n.) and five hundred beards of a frigate; p. 361 (n.) the
mast-head of this same gallant frigate; p. 361 (adj.) captain of this
frigate's main-top; p. 365 (n.) which had bowed at the guns of the
frigate; p. 367 (n.) I know not in what frigate you sail now; p. 378
(n.) with the crew of an American frigate; p. 378 (n.) said about the
frigate that carried him to Russia; p. 379 (n.) while I served on
board the frigate; p. 381 (n.) British frigates, in friendly or
neutral harbors; p. 381 (n.) the night previous to the sailing of the
frigate; p. 382 (n.) in the notorious idleness of a frigate; p. 384
(n.) In drinking success to our frigate; p. 384 (n.) when our frigate
was lying in harbor; p. 386 (n.) whether on board a frigate; p. 388
(n.) The interior affairs of the frigate; p. 388 (n.) when the
frigate was reported to be; p. 391 (n.) our good frigate, now
somewhere off the capes; p. 393 (n.) the frigate slowly gliding by;
p. 394 (n.) Being now astern of the frigate; p. 395 (n.) when our
noble frigate . . . wound her stately way; p. 396 (n.) whitherward
our frigate now glides; pp. 396-7 (n.) wrong in our frigate will be
remembered no more; p. 397 (n.) our frigate strikes soundings at
last; p. 398 (n.) on board a fast-sailing, never-sinking world-
frigate; p. 398 (n.) our world-frigate is bound to no final harbor;
p. 398 (n.) how can this world-frigate prove our eventual abiding
peace; p. 399 (n.) our world-frigate rushes by; p. 399 (n.) while on
board our world-frigate.

Moby-Dick--p. 149 (adj.) gay as a frigate's pennant; p. 264 (n.)
where in her murderous hold this frigate earth is ballasted; p. 353
(n.) bore down upon the Turkish frigates.

FROG. An amphibious animal of the genus Rana, with four feet, a naked
body, and without a tail. (Webster)

Typee--p. 38 (n.) but a bull-frog might as well have tried to make a
passage through the teeth of a comb; p. 229 (n.) I took to be an
uncommonly large species of frog.

Omoo--p. 272 (n.) had a frog leaped from his mouth.

Mardi--p. 507 (n.) gradual metamorphosis into frogs; p. 507 (n.) Have
frogs any tails, old man?

Moby-Dick--p. 29 (n.) as if a parcel of dark green frogs were running
up the trunks of young palms.

GAFF. A spar used in ships to extend the heads of fore-and-aft sails
which are not set on stays. The foremost end of the gaff is termed the
jaw, the outer part is called the peak. (Smyth)

Omoo--p. 60 (n.) our spanker-gaff came down by the run.

Redburn--p. 74 (n.) call them my "gaff-topsail-boots."

White-Jacket--p. 105 (n.) ran up our ensign to the gaff.

GALE. Of wind. Implies what on shore is called a storm, more particularly
termed a hard gale or strong gale; number of force, 10. A stiff gale is
the diminutive of the preceding, but stronger than a breeze.--A fresh
gale is a still further diminutive, and not too strong for a ship to
carry single-reefed topsails when close-hauled. A top-gallant gale, if a
ship can carry her top-gallant sails. (Smyth)

Typee--p. 9 In.) the good ship and the steady gale did the rest;
p. 65 (n.) dismal moaning of the gale through the trees.

Omoo--p. 10 (n.) no gale could bow her over; p. 58 (n.) We Encounter
a Gale; p. 58 (n.) a spicy gale in the tropic latitudes; p. 59 (n.)
what he called his "gale-suit"; p. 96 (n.) it blew a heavy gale;
p. 96 (n.) During the gale; p. 292 (n.) it blew quite a gale.

Mardi--p. 24 (n.) in some distant gale; p. 24 (n.) troubled mists of
midnight gales; p. 431 (n.) And as in tropic gales; p. 482 (n.) in
her [sea's] mad gales of passions; p. 516 (n.) those boisterous gales,
blo ing from out the mouths; p. 532 (n.) ends of ships' royal-yards
in gales; p. 543 (n.) bringing down the gale; p. 557 (n.) still fly
before the gale; p. 605 (n.) to ride out the gale with complacency;
p. 623 (n.) To these, our shores, soft gales invite.

Redburn--p. 9 (n.) raised by the terrible gale; p. 104 (n.) you'll
only go from one gale of wind; p. 115 (n.) swept ashore in a gale;
p. 116 (n.) in a gale of wind; p. 117 (n.) when you are drowned in
the next gale; p. 120 (n.) sending it down on deck in a gale; p. 127
(n.) but in a gale, it is an alarum; p. 165 (n.) sometimes, in heavy
gales, ships lying; p. 248 (n.) as spoon-drift in a gale; p. 273 (n.)
who can say in what gales it may have been; p. 289 (n.) the weather
merged into a gale; p. 289 (n.) we gave to the gale the blackened
bodies; p. 289 (n.) whom the plague, panic and gale had hurried;
p. 295 (n.) leaning backward to the gale; p. 295 (n.) as they hang in
the gale; p. 298 (n.) After the uproar of the breeze and the gale.

White-Jacket--p. 9 (n.) more ungovernable stripping the canvass in a
gale; p. 11 (n.) they issue forth into the gale; p. 12 (n.) like
hawks screaming in a gale; p. 12 (n.) his gales off Beachy Head;
p. 25 (n.) In a gale of wind; p. 32 (n.) when the sails were furled
in a gale; p. 32 (n.) prepare for . . . living gales; p. 32 (n.) you
will have whole months of rains and gales; p. 33 (n.) with the man
who was born in a gale; p. 34 (n.) is a bulk-head, that dams off the
gale; p. 42 (n.) crammed to the very lid with hurricanes and gales;
p. 55 (n.) went about snuffing up the gale; p. 93 (n.) who had
predicted a gale of wind; p. 97 (n.) the whole ship is brewed into
the yeast of the gale; p. 98 (n.) The gale sings as hoarsely as
before; p. 98 (n.) Other ships, without encountering these terrible
gales; p. 98 (n.) encountered a series of tremendous gales; p. 106
(n.) In a sudden gale; p. 106 (n.) The gale came athwart the deck;
p. 107 (n.) in such a gale; p. 107 (n.) of a cessation of the gale;
p. 107 (n.) Above the bulwarks . . . the gale was horrible; p. 108
(n.) but in the gale, he seemed to be whispering; p. 108 (n.) At
length the first fury of the gale began to abate; p. 108 (n.) the

gale so moderated that we shook; p. 110 (n.) in the case of Mad Jack,
during the gale; p. 110 (n.) for flying away from the gale; p. 110
(n.) cases of similar hard squalls and gales; p. 110 (n.) Scudding
exposes to the gale your stern; p. 112 (n.) The leading incident of
the gale; p. 115 (n.) the gales are mostly from the westward; p. 325
(n.) Had it only been a gale instead of a calm; p. 326 (n.) while in
a severe gale; p. 353 (n.) mounting the fore-yard in a gale; p. 384
(n.) whether ordered to the main-truck in a gale; p. 397 (n.) . . .
how mild the balmy gale.

Moby-Dick--p. 11 (n.) Oh, the rare old whale, mid storm and gale;
p. 20 (n.) It's the Black Sea in a midnight gale; p. 38 (n.) how
bitterly will burst those straps in the first howling gale; p. 49 (n.)
the indignant gale howls louder; p. 49 (n.) as Jonah carries down the
gale with him; p. 50 (n.) Woe to him who seeks to pour oil upon the
waters when God has brewed them into a gale; p. 68 (n.) from his
continual sailings in many hard gales; p. 135 (n.) in the dread gale
of God's wrath; p. 135 (n.) though well capable of facing out a stiff
gale; p. 138 (n.) to keep to windward of your head in a hard gale;
p. 160 (n.) he swung to the mad rockings of the gales; p. 202 (n.)
but passively to await the issue of the gale; p. 370 (n.) reefed fast
in the howling gale; p. 374 (n.) after an unusually long raging gale;
p. 393 (n.) in this life's howling gale; p. 398 (n.) mere sickness
could not kill him: nothing but a whale, or a gale; p. 413 (n.) Oh!
jolly is the gale,/ And a joker is the whale; p. 414 (n.) The gale
that now hammers at us to stave us; p. 421 (n.) during the violence
of the gale.

GALLANT. Designates any flag borne on the mizen-mast. (Smyth)

Moby-Dick--p. 51 (adj.) Delight,--top-gallant delight is to him, who
acknowledges no law or lord, but the Lord his God.

GALLEON. A name formerly given to ships of war furnished with three or
four batteries of cannon. It is now retained only by the Spaniards, and
applied to the largest size of their merchant ships employed in West
India and Vera Cruz voyages. (Smyth)

Mardi--p. 104 (n.) anchor-stocks of ancient galleons.

GALLEY. A low, flat-built vessel with one deck, and propelled by sails
and oars, particularly in the Mediterranean. There are also half-galleys
and quarter-galleys, found by experience to be of little utility except
in fine weather. They generally hug the shore, only sometimes venturing
out to sea for a summer cruise. Also, an open boat rowing six or eight
oars, and used on the river Thames by custom-house officers, and formerly
by press-gangs. Also the name of a ship's hearth or kitchen, being the
place where the grates are put up and the victuals cooked. In small
merchantment it is called the caboose; and is generally abaft the
forecastle or forepart of the ship. (Smyth)

Typee--p. 10 (n.) thrust his woolly head from the galley.

Omoo--p. 14 (n.) Like galley-slaves, they are only to be governed.

Mardi--p. 481 (n.) prided themselves upon some holiday galley.

Redburn--p. 239 (n.) the "passengers'-galley" was solidly lashed down;
p. 239 (n.) This galley was a large open stove; p. 263 (n.) I have
made some mention of the "Galley"; p. 264 (n.) over the uncovered
"galley"; p. 284 (n.) cooked them at the public galley; p. 285 (n.)
made in the public galley; p. 293 (n.) to place the galley, or
steerage-passengers' stove; p. 299 (n.) dried with pans of coals from
the galley.

White-Jacket--p. 27 (n.) at a distinct part of the great galley;
p. 34 (n.) lying exposed near the galley; p. 55 (n.) hot water begged
from the galley-cooks; p. 69 (n.) the galley-cooks would be going;
p. 86 (adj.) wearisome, dog-like, galley-slave employment; p. 90 (n.)
blubbered Sunshine, the galley-cook; p. 211 (n.) the flag-ships of
the Phoenician armed galleys; p. 211 (n.) of all the Roman and
Egyptian galleys; p. 227 (n.) than those in the ship's galley; p. 386
(n.) the Galley, or Cookery, on the gun-deck; pp. 386-7 (n.) in the
neighborhood of the galley alone; p. 387 (n.) they hied to the galley
and solaced their souls; p. 387 (n.) at the galley of the Neversink;
p. 388 (n.) for the gossiping smokers of the galley; p. 390 (n.)
registering your solemn vows at the galley; p. 395 (n.) the iron
throats of the guns round the galley.

GALLIOT. A small galley designed only for chase, generally carrying but
one mast, with sixteen or twenty oars. All the seamen on board act as
soldiers, and each has a musket by him ready for use on quitting his oar.
Also, a Dutch or Flemish vessel for cargoes, with very rounded ribs and
flattish bottom, with a mizen-mast stept far aft. (Smyth)

Redburn--p. 174 (n.) Galliots, Coast-of-Guinea-Man, and Floating
Chapel; p. 174 (n.) is the Dutch galliot; p. 174 (n.) The construction
of the galliot; p. 174 (n.) They seldom paint the galliot.

White-Jacket--p. 246 (n.) attached by a rope to a Dutch galiot.

Moby-Dick--p. 67 (n.) mountainous Japanese junks; butter-box galliots;
p. 243 (n.) to transform himself [whale] from a bluff-bowed sluggish
galliot into a sharp-pointed New York pilot-boat; p. 281 (adj.) the
Right Whale's head bears a rather inelegant resemblance to a gigantic
galliot-toed shoe.

GALLIPAGOS (GALAPAGOS) ISLANDS. A group of islands 650 miles west of the
coast of Ecuador, consisting of 24 islands, and more than 60 islets and
rocks. (Larousse) [For a thorough-going description of their
appearance, see Melville's "Sketch First" in The Encantadas.]

Typee--p. 211 (n.) on an uninhabited island of the Gallipagos.

Mardi--p. 3 (n.) Gallipagos, otherwise called the Enchanted Islands.

Moby-Dick--p. 432 (n.) I've heard that the Isle of Albemarle, one of
the Gallipagos, is cut by the Equator right in the middle.

GALLY. To gally, or gallow, is to frighten excessively,--to confound
with fright. It is an old Saxon word. It occurs once in Shakspere:--

> the wrathful skies
> Gallow the very wanderers of the dark,
> And make them keep their caves.
>   --Lear, Act iii. sc. 11.

To common land usages, the word is now completely obsolete. When the
polite landsman first hears it from the gaunt Nantucketer, he is apt to
set it down as one of the whaleman's self-derived savageries. (Melville)

Omoo--p. 72 (v.) he was frightened, or "gallied."

Moby-Dick--p. 322 (v.) they say he is gallied; p. 322 (v.) to gally,
or gallow, is to frighten excessively; p. 322 (adj.) at the strangely
gallied whales before us; p. 323 (adj.) It is chiefly among gallied
whales that this drugg is used.

GAM. A social meeting of two (or more) whale-ships, generally on a
cruising-ground; when, after exchanging hails, they exchange visits by
boats' crews; the two captains remaining, for the time, on board of one
ship, and the two chief mates on the other. (Melville)

Moby-Dick--p. 206 (n.) She has a "Gam"; p. 206 (n.) But what is a Gam;
p. 206 (n.) GAM. Noun--A Social meeting of two (or more) Whale-ships;
p. 207 (n.) There is another little item about Gamming; p. 370 (n.)
It was a fine gam we had . . . And that fine gam I had.

GANGWAY. The platform on each side of the skid-beams leading from the
quarter-deck to the forecastle, and peculiar to deep-waisted ships, for
the convenience of walking expeditiously fore and aft; it is fenced on
the outside by iron stanchions and ropes, or rails, and in vessels of war
with a netting, in which part of the hammocks are stowed. Also, that
part of a ship's side, and opening in her bulwarks, by which persons
enter and depart. (Smyth)

Typee--p. 7 (n.) and pull directly for our gangway; p. 8 (n.) The
ship's company crowding into the gangway; p. 12 (n.) by the aid of
some benevolent persons at the gangway.

Omoo--p. 45 (n.) it was borne to the gangway; p. 75 (n.) advanced to
the gangway to receive them; p. 76 (n.) standing in the cabin gangway;
p. 87 (n.) We tumbled up the gangway; p. 100 (n.) darted the canoe
right up to the gangway; p. 105 (n.) we were paraded in the frigate's
gangway; p. 112 (n.) Being then mustered in the gangway.

Mardi--p. 70 (n.) Samoa stood in the gangway.

White-Jacket--p. 88 (n.) the marine sentry at the gangway; p. 95 (n.)
the same old scene was enacted at the gangway; p. 103 (n.) paid the
penalty of his rashness at the gangway; p. 138 (n.) had never been
degraded at the gangway; p. 140 (n.) at the gangway for petty
offences; p. 142 (n.) cases wherein to be flogged at the gangway is

no dishonor; p. 142 (n.) while his back bleeds at the gangway; p. 144
(n.) were scourged at the gangway till he recanted; p. 149 (n.) was
known at the gangways; p. 163 (n.) standing at the gangway; p. 163
(n.) make an imposing display at the gangway; p. 177 (n.) the
degradation of the gangway; p. 177 (n.) now stations himself at the
gangway; p. 179 (n.) standing over the robber at the gangway; p. 180
(n.) overhauled, as usual, at the gangway; p. 182 (n.) previous to
flogging at the gangway; p. 185 (n.) scourged at the gangway; p. 187
(n.) the seamen whom he had brought to the gangway; p. 188 (n.) from
being seized up at the gangway; p. 214 (n.) happened to emerge from
the after-gangway; p. 216 (n.) the flogging of a man at the gangway;
p. 217 (n.) have been flogged at the gangway; p. 226 (n.) when they
first cross the gangway; p. 233 (n.) At the gangway; p. 239 (n.)
besides getting a dozen at the gangway; p. 241 (n.) mustered in
starboard gangway; p. 244 (n.) may be flogged at the gangway; p. 245
(n.) looking toward the gangway; p. 276 (n.) As in the matter of the
scene at the gangway; p. 279 (n.) As I passed through the gangway;
p. 280 (n.) the opening of the lee-gangway; p. 280 (n.) seen through
the opening at the gangway; p. 282 (n.) Let us forget the scourge and
the gangway; p. 301 (n.) by which the sailor is scourged at the
gangway; p. 305 (n.) under penalty of the gangway; p. 320 (n.) when a
man has been flogged at the gangway; p. 328 (n.) is being scourged at
the gangway; p. 341 (n.) brought his body to the same gangway; p. 345
(n.) Life comes in at one gangway; p. 352 (n.) like the marine
sentries at the gangways in port; p. 364 (n.) Old Ushant at the
Gangway; p. 373 (n.) But the floggings at the gangway; p. 374 (n.) at
both gangways and forecastle; p. 375 (n.) to have him degraded at the
gangway; p. 378 (n.) cut into dog's meat at the gangway; p. 380 (n.)
the special obnoxiousness of the gangway; p. 381 (n.) degraded her
own guardians at the gangway; p. 384 (n.) poor Landless danced quite
as often at the gangway; p. 388 (n.) roared the boatswain's mates at
the gangway; p. 396 (n.) our last man scourged at the gangway; p. 399
(n.) a cat-o'-nine-tails and a gangway.

Moby-Dick--p. 44 (n.) Starboard gangway, there . . . larboard gangway
to starboard; p. 140 (n.) ascended the cabin-gangway to the deck.

GIG. A light narrow galley or ship's boat, clincher-built, and adapted
for expedition either by rowing or sailing; the latter ticklish at times.
(Smyth)

Typee--p. 7 (n.) a gig, gaily bedizened with streamers.

Omoo--p. 160 (n.) Captain Bob's "gig" was exceedingly small.

White-Jacket--p. 161 (n.) She also carried . . . a Captain's Gig;
p. 161 (n.) and the Captain's Gig are manned by gentlemanly youths;
p. 161 (n.) when pulled ashore by his . . . gig-men; p. 161 (n.) one
of the gig-men fell sick; p. 161 (adj./n.) that's the gig's uniform
. . . you are a gig-man; p. 161 (n.) I heard the bugler call away the
"gig"; p. 162 (adj.) the gig's crew were conducted below; p. 163 (n.)
As soon, then, as the gig touched the side; p. 163 (n.) To return to
the gig; p. 163 (n.) since his gig men were often called upon.

GILL. The organ of respiration in fishes, consisting of a cartilaginous
or bony arch, attached to the bones of the head, and furnished on the
exterior convex side with a multitude of fleshy leaves, or fringed
vascular fibrils, resembling plumes, and of a red color in a healthy
state. (Webster)

Typee--p. 208 (n.) scales, bones, gills, and all the inside.

Mardi--p. 149 (n.) with gills showing purple; p. 150 (n.) we are fish
with red gills; p. 288 (n.) mixed to suit any gills.

Moby-Dick--epigram (n.) and at his [Leviathan's] gills/ Draws in;
p. 4 (n.) and at his gills/ Draws in.

GLYPTOLEPIS. An ancient fish with a solid bony carapace, or shell. (Owen)

Mardi--p. 417 (n.) sturgeon-forms, cephalaspis, glyptolepis.

GRAMPUS. A corruption of gran pisce. An animal of the cetacean or whale
tribe, distinguished by the large pointed teeth with which both jaws are
armed, and by the high falcate dorsal fin. It generally attains a length
of 20 to 25 feet, and is very active and voracious. (Smyth)

Typee--p. 10 (n.) but the occasional breathing of the grampus.

Mardi--p. 41 (n.) ponderous sigh of the grampus; p. 255 (n.) humps of
grampuses; p. 290 (n.) sighing like a grampus; p. 418 (n.) seals,
grampuses, and whales.

Moby-Dick--p. 23 (adj.) That's the Grampus' crew; p. 120 (n.) of the
OCTAVO, the Grampus.

GULF. A capacious bay, and sometimes taking the name of a sea when it is
very extensive. A gulf is, strictly speaking, distinguished from a sea
in being smaller, and from a bay in being larger and deeper than it is
broad. It is observed that the sea is always most dangerous near gulfs,
from the currents being penned up by the shores. (Smyth)

Typee--p. 44 (n.) what . . . do you expect to find at the bottom of
that gulf; p. 53 (n.) penetrate to the bottom of every yawning gulf;
p. 60 (n.) hanging over the gulf like so many dark icicles; p. 61 (n.)
fell in fragments against the side of the gulf; p. 212 (n.) been
precipitated into the gulf beneath [down his throat].

Mardi--p. 6 (n.) her hold a gulf; p. 653 (n.) though thou glidest to
gulfs of blackness.

Redburn--p. 67 (n.) I thought the Gulf Stream was in my head; p. 78
(n.) the sea looked like a great, black gulf; p. 97 (n.) to make
mention of the Gulf Stream; p. 97 (n.) In the absence of the Gulf-
weed; p. 98 (n.) such ugly weather in the Gulf; p. 98 (n.) in a
bucket full of the Gulf-Stream; p. 98 (n.) as if the Gulf of Mexico.

White-Jacket--p. 77 (n.) For an instant I thought the Gulf Stream in my head.

Moby-Dick--p. 50 (n.) swallowed him down to living gulfs of doom.

GUNWHALE. That horizontal plank which covers the heads of the timbers between the main and fore drifts. The gunwhale of a boat is a piece of timber going round the upper sheer-strake as a binder for its top-work. When a boat sails with a free wind, and rolls each side, or gunwhale, to the water's edge, she rolls gunwhale-to. (Smyth)

Typee--p. 252 (n.) seizing hold of the gunwhale; p. 252 (n.) He seized the gunwhale.

Omoo--p. 71 (n.) balancing himself right on the gunwhale; p. 72 (n.) on the boat's gunwhale; p. 153 (n.) loaded down to the gunwhale.

Mardi--p. 19 (n.) passed round both gunwhales; p. 32 (n.) along our gunwhales inside; p. 48 (n.) my arms over the gunwhale; p. 49 (n.) clinging to the gunwhale; p. 54 (n.) dozing over the gunwhale; p. 72 (n.) a limb above the gunwhale; p. 122 (n.) against the Chamois' gunwhale; p. 127 (n.) lashed across the four gunwhales; p. 128 (n.) beam, crossing the gunwhales; p. 162 (n.) fifty hands were on the gunwhale; p. 167 (n.) perched upon the gunwhale; p. 199 (n.) The gunwhale was ornamented; p. 212 (n.) glance over the gunwhale; p. 213 (n.) side-ways on the gunwhales; p. 469 (adv.) fleets . . . were fighting, gunwhale and gunwhale; p. 486 (n.) he is musing over the gunwhale; p. 618 (n.) over the six gunwhales all now leaned.

Redburn--p. 296 (n.) without a thole-pin in the gunwhales.

Moby-Dick--p. 186 (n.) while one foot was expectantly poised on the gunwhale; p. 190 (n.) with the whole part of his body above the gunwhale; p. 299 (n.) the gunwhales of the bows were almost even with the water; p. 365 (n.) by sitting all their sterns on the outer gunwhale; p. 365 (adv.) Mountop's boat . . . was gunwhale and gunwhale with mine; p. 415 (n.) so that its [the craft's] gunwhale violently jammed his hand; p. 449 (n.) while both elastic gunwhales were springing in and out; p. 449 (n.) the frail gunwhales bent in, collapsed, and snapped.

GURRY. The dark, glutinous substance which is scraped off the back of the Greenland or right whale, and much of which covers the decks of those inferior souls who hunt that ignoble Leviathan. (Melville)

Moby-Dick--p. 350 (n.) Gurry, so called, is a term properly belonging.

HALYARD. One of the ropes or tackles usually employed to hoist or lower any sail upon its respective yards, gaffs, or stay, except the cross-jack and spritsail-yard, which are always slung. (Smyth's spelling is "Halliard.")

Typee--p. 95 (n.) with the exception of the signal halyards.

Omoo--p. 97 (n.) ordering a pull at the jib-**halyards**.

Redburn--p. 48 (n.) to take a "swig at the halyards"; p. 48 (n.) this swigging at the halyards; p. 121 (n.) to sing out at the halyards; p. 253 (n.) on the maintop-sail halyards; p. 256 (n.) unreeve the short signal halyards; p. 256 (n.) and the thin signal halyards . . . were flying; p. 281 (n.) his late pulling and hauling of halyards; p. 294 (n.) were settling away the halyards on deck.

White-Jacket--p. 7 (n.) scrambled up the ladder to the braces and halyards; p. 7 (n.) away we ran with the halyards; p. 33 (n.) **hands by the halyards**; p. 78 (n.) they had lowered the halyards in affright; p. 93 (n.) at the various halyards and running ropes; p. 95 (n.) settle away the halyards; p. 97 (n.) Hands by the halyard; p. 106 (n.) though the halyards were let go; p. 121 (n.) some at the halyards, some at the braces; p. 176 (n.) he craves . . . a more sturdy swig at the halyards; p. 223 (n.) reprimanding the crowd of seamen at the halyards; p. 235 (n.) on the main-topsail-halyards; p. 391 (n.) the halyards not being rove; p. 391 (n.) this reefing of the halyards; p. 394 (n.) to reeve anew the stun'-sail-halyards.

Moby-Dick--p. 107 (n.) [Daggoo's earrings] so large that the sailors called them ring-bolts, and would talk of securing the top-sail halyards to them; p. 154 (n.) Hands by the halyards; p. 456 (n.) by the isolated backstays and halyards.

HARBOR. A general name given to any safe sea-port. The qualities requisite in a good harbor are, that it should afford security from the effects of the wind and sea; that the bottom be entirely free from rocks and shallows, but good holding ground; that the opening be of sufficient extent to admit the entrance or departure of large ships without difficulty. (Smyth)

Typee--p. 6 (n.) put into the commodious harbor; p. 11 (n.) It has three good harbors on its coast; p. 12 (n.) we drew abreast the entrance to the harbor; p. 13 (n.) he had been appointed pilot of the harbor; p. 20 (n.) Our ship had not been many days in the harbor; p. 24 (n.) at anchor in the middle of the harbor; p. 31 (n.) I should command a view of the entire harbor; p. 31 (n.) as she was working her way out of the harbor; p. 257 (n.) entered the harbor at Honolulu; p. 257 (n.) thunders of the five men-of-war in the harbor; p. 265 (n.) lying in the other harbor; p. 270 (n.) The men-of-war were still lying in the harbor.

Omoo--p. xiii (n.) the only harbors accessible are among the barbarous . . . islands; p. 3 (n.) recently touched at a neighboring harbor; p. 3 (n.) manned by "Taboo" natives from the other harbor; p. 14 (n.) that by lying in harbor; p. 26 (n.) the only harbor of any note; p. 27 (n.) forming one side of the harbor; p. 66 (n.) refitted their vessels in its harbors; p. 68 (n.) Going into harbor; p. 69 (n.) descried lying in the harbor; p. 75 (n.) After holding our ground off the harbor; p. 82 (n.) lying off and on the harbor; p. 94 (n.) a little to leeward of the harbor; p. 95 (n.) a small schooner came out of the harbor; p. 96 (n.) three days hence, in Papeetee harbor; p. 97 (n.) We Enter the Harbor; p. 97 (n.) up to the entrance of the harbor; p. 98

(n.) the Julia was destined for the harbor; p. 98 (n.) to windward of the mouth of the harbor; p. 98 (n.) what he remembered of the harbor; p. 98 (n.) to the harbor; p. 100 (n.) the regular pilot of the harbor; p. 100 (n.) whale-spouts seen from the harbor; p. 100 (adj.) The harbor dues; p. 101 (n.) at the farther end of the harbor; p. 103 (n.) his intention to enter the harbor; p. 139 (n.) down to our arrival in the harbor; p. 140 (n.) a small Australian schooner, lying in the harbor; p. 147 (n.) after our arrival in the harbor; p. 149 (n.) about three weeks after entering the harbor; p. 158 (n.) officers of several ships in harbor; p. 160 (n.) every vessel in the harbor we visited; p. 162 (n.) Right in the middle of Papeetee harbor; p. 162 (n.) Commanding the harbor as it does; p. 185 (n.) vessels of all kinds now enter the harbor; p. 235 (n.) a harbor on the opposite side of the island; p. 246 (n.) the only frequented harbor of Imeeo; p. 246 (n.) reported to be lying in the harbor; p. 278 (n.) that the ship lying in the harbor was the reason; p. 286 (n.) in the very next ship that touched at the harbor; p. 289 (n.) toward the anchorage of the harbor of Taloo; p. 289 (n.) All alone in the harbor; p. 291 (n.) prowling about the village and harbor; p. 306 (n.) the officers of ships touching in her harbors; p. 313 (n.) to lie longer in a pleasant harbor.

Mardi--p. 7 (n.) as one mighty harbor; p. 105 (n.) managed to swim into a Tahitian harbor; p. 178 (n.) within their coral harbor; p. 297 (n.) in the Old Commonwealth's harbor; p. 470 (n.) gallanted them into their coral harbor; p. 586 (n.) we sailed by many tranquil harbors; p. 587 (n.) maelstrŏms, of these harbors.

Redburn--p. 34 (n.) the entrance to New York Harbor from sea; p. 107 (n.) people of Nantucket, New Bedford, and Sag Harbor; p. 115 (n.) whereas, in harbor; p. 115 (n.) and a ship in harbor; p. 115 (n.) in the "Sailors'-Snug-Harbor" on Staten Island; p. 157 (n.) The very harbor of Liverpool is gradually filling up; p. 245 (n.) He's gone to the harbor; p. 273 (n.) at the bottom of strange harbors; p. 285 (n.) Highlander Puts into No Harbor As Yet; p. 299 (n.) from emigrant ships nearing the harbor; p. 302 (n.) Redburn and Harry, Arm in Arm, in Harbor; p. 312 (n.) floating in the harbor of New York.

White-Jacket--p. ix (n.) then lying in a harbor of the Pacific Ocean; p. 3 (n.) her last harbor in the Pacific; p. 43 (n.) various colored illustrations of the harbors and bays; p. 89 (n.) if the ship happen to be lying in harbor; p. 90 (n.) the monotony of lying in foreign harbors; p. 91 (n.) in a Peruvian harbor; p. 129 (n.) it pertained to him, while in harbor; p. 130 (n.) while lying in harbor; p. 158 (n.) the crew of the Neversink, while in harbor; p. 159 (n.) The Frigate in Harbor; p. 159 (n.) the bands of the various men-of-war in harbor; p. 160 (n.) she is tranquilly lying in harbor; p. 160 (n.) in a man-of-war in harbor; p. 160 (n.) of the numerous boats employed in harbor; p. 167 (n.) on board their craft in harbor; p. 170 (n.) Killing Time in a Man-of-war in Harbor; p. 170 (n.) the long, tedious hours in harbor; p. 171 (n.) a solitary, volcanic island in the harbor; p. p. 173 (n.) Still another way of killing time in harbor; p. 174 (n.) whenever employed in killing time in harbor; p. 176 (n.) while lying in harbor; p. 177 (n.) to approach a man-of-war in a foreign harbor; p. 193 (n.) especially manifested in harbor; p. 194 (n.) while away his leisure in harbor; p. 195 (n.) belonging to the

American squadron then in harbor; p. 198 (n.) taking place while in
harbor; p. 207 (n.) While lying in the harbor of Callao; p. 210 (n.)
all emptying into the harbor; p. 211 (n.) this grand harbor of Rio
lay hid in the hills; p. 212 (n.) Diversified as the harbor of
Constantinople; p. 213 (n.) this Rio is a charming harbor; p. 227 (n.)
introducing women on board, in harbor; p. 229 (n.) moor your boys
fast to that best of harbors, the hearth-stone; p. 233 (n.) making a
circuit of the harbor; p. 242 (n.) is about to be inflicted in harbor;
p. 245 (n.) reported a sail entering the harbor; p. 247 (n.) other
American ships of war in harbor; p. 265 (n.) at the mouth of the
harbor; p. 265 (n.) among all the men-of-war in harbor; p. 285 (n.)
enthroned on his poop in a foreign harbor; p. 289 (n.) At sea or in
harbor; p. 326 (n.) But in a smooth harbor; p. 366 (n.) the ship
being now in harbor; p. 372 (n.) and in that harbor; p. 378 (n.) in a
whaling ship lying in a harbor; p. 381 (n.) British frigates, in
friendly or neutral harbors; p. 384 (n.) when our frigate was lying
in harbor; p. 390 (n.) fairly adrift in harbor; p. 395 (n.) concerning
the precise harbor for which we were bound; p. 395 (n.) into the
innermost harbor of Norfolk; p. 398 (n.) our world-frigate is bound
to no final harbor.

Moby-Dick--p. 56 (adj.) A Sag Harbor ship visited his father's bay;
p. 57 (n.) Arrived at last in Old Sag Harbor; p. 89 (n.) replacing
them at the remote harbors usually frequented; p. 99 (n.) men-of-war
now peacefully ride in once savage harbors; p. 107 (n.) the pagan
harbors most frequented by whalemen; p. 116 (adj.) soon we shall be
lost in its [the deep's] unshored, harborless immensities; p. 353
(n.) issuing from their midnight harbors.

HARPOON. A spear or javelin with a barbed point, used to strike whales
and other fish. The harpoon is furnished with a long shank, and has at
one end a broad and flat triangular head, sharpened at both edges so as
to penetrate the whale with facility, but blunt behind to prevent its
cutting out. To the other end a fore-ganger is bent, to which is
fastened a long cord called the whale-line, which lies carefully coiled
in the boat in such a manner as to run out without being interrupted or
entangled. The instant the whale is struck the men cant the oars, so
that the roll may not immerse them in the water. The line flies like
lightning   and is intensely watched. Seven or eight coils have been run
out before the whale "sounds," or strikes bottom, when he rises again to
breathe, and probably gets a similar dose. (Smyth)

Omoo--p. 10 (n.) of the four harpooners; p. 13 (n.) Bembo, the New
Zealand harpooner; p. 34 (n.) by virtue of his being a harpooner;
p. 71 (n.) Being a harpooner; p. 71 (n.) generally selected for
harpooners; p. 71 (n.) the harpooner, of course, stands erect; p. 72
(n.) He darted his harpoon, and missed; p. 72 (n.) He darted both
harpoons; p. 72 (n.) harpoon in hand; p. 81 (n.) that you have two
more harpooners; p. 99 (n.) or I'll dart a harpoon at ye; p. 148 (n.)
three good whalemen for harpooners; p. 313 (n.) but lance and harpoon
almost invariably drew.

Mardi--p. 6 (n.) submitting to the harpoon; p. 6 (n.) keeping his
harpoon; p. 22 (n.) including Mark, the harpooner; p. 23 (n.) Mark,
our harpooner; p. 26 (n.) our harpooner; p. 27 (n.) Mark, the

harpooner; p. 32 (n.) were six harpoons; p. 58 (n.) who had snatched his harpoon; p. 59 (n.) barbed end of his harpoon; p. 59 (n.) preferred his harpoon; p. 66 (n.) Jarl's harpoon was presented; p. 122 (n.) from darting his harpoon; p. 127 (n.) with his long tangled hair and harpoon; p. 132 (n.) equipped with his harpoon; p. 134 (n.) His harpoon was his all; p. 135 (n.) honest Jarl dropped his harpoon; p. 135 (n.) seeing Jarl's harpoon quivering; p. 289 (adj.) this day harpooned on the coast.

Redburn--p. 7 (n.) a great whale . . . stuck full of harpoons; p. 107 (n.) now carries a crew of harpooners; p. 196 (v.) as to harpoon a speckled porpoise.

White-Jacket--p. 188 (adj.) the Devil in his horns and harpooner's tail; p. 394 (n.) that barbed bunch of harpoons pierced through.

Moby-Dick--p. 5 (n.) One of our harpooners told me that he caught once a voyage to Greenland; p. 11 (v.) The Whale is harpooned to be sure; p. 11 (n.) while the bold harpooner is striking the whale; p. 17 (n.) in order to discover when they were nigh enough to risk a harpoon; p. 17 (n.) I paced the streets, and passed the sign of "The Crossed Harpoons"; p. 18 (n.) But "The Crossed Harpoons" and "The Sword-Fish"; p. 21 (n.) Mixed with these were rusty old whaling lances and harpoons; p. 21 (n.) And that harpoon--so like a corkscrew now--was flung in Javan seas; p. 22 (adj.) you haint no objections to sharing a harpooner's blanket, have ye; p. 22 (n.) it would depend upon who the harpooner might be; p. 22 (n.) if . . . the harpooner was not decidedly objectionable; p. 22 (n.) that aint the harpooner, is it; p. 22 (n.) the harpooner is a dark complexioned chap; p. 22 (n.) Where is the harpooner; p. 22 (n.) I began to feel suspicious of this "dark complexioned" harpooner; p. 24 (n.) and that stranger a harpooner; p. 24 (n.) The more I pondered over this harpooner; p. 24 (n.) being a harpooner; p. 24 (n.) any decent harpooner ought to be home; p. 24 (n.) I've changed my mind about that harpooner; p. 25 (n.) The devil fetch that harpooner, thought I; p. 25 (n.) the harpooner might be standing in the entry; p. 25 (n.) unwarrantable prejudices against this unknown harpooner p. 25 (n.) yet no sight of my harpooner; p. 25 (n.) that this harpooner is actually engaged; p. 26 (n.) if that ere harpooneer hears you a slanderin' his head; p. 26 (n.) the other half belongs to a certain harpooneer; p. 27 (n.) and a tall harpoon standing at the head of the bed; p. 35 (n./v.) he takes the harpoon from the bed corner, and . . . begins a vigorous scraping, or rather harpooning of his cheeks; p. 35 (n.) of what fine steel the head of a harpoon is made; p. 35 (n.) sporting his harpoon like a marshal's baton; p. 36 (n.) and harpooners, and ship keepers; p. 38 (n.) Go and gaze upon the iron emblematical harpoons round yonder lofty mansion; p. 42 (n.) He had been a sailor and a harpooneer in his youth; p. 57 (n.) They had made a harpooneer of him; p. 58 (adj.) stopping to adjust the sheath on his harpoon barbs; p. 84 (n.) aghast at the close vicinity of the flying harpoon; p. 85 (n.) Pious harpooneers never make good voyagers . . . no harpooneer is worth a straw who ain't pretty sharkish; pp. 106-7 (n.) even as the harpooneers were flingers of javelins; p. 107 (n.) always accompanied by his boat-steerer or harpooneer; p. 107 (n.) the unerring harpoon of the son fitly replacing the infallible arrow of the sires; p. 109 (n.) though the harpooneers . . . were a far more barbaric, heathenish, and motley

set; p. 133 (adv.) by darting a fork at his back, harpoon-wise;
p. 194 (n.) Queequeg, harpoon in hand, sprang to his feet; p. 332
(v.) though the gentleman had originally harpooned the lady; p. 332
(v.) when a subsequent gentleman re-harpooned her; p. 332 (n.) along
with whatever harpoon might have been found sticking in her; p. 353
(n.) the harpooneers wildly gesticulated with their huge pronged
forks and dippers; p. 417 (n.) Ahab's harpoon, the one forged at
Perth's fire, remained firmly lashed in its conspicuous crotch;
p. 418 (n.) As the silent harpoon burned there like a serpent's
tongue; p. 456 (n.) thy hour and thy harpoon are at hand; p. 469 (n.)
while fixed by infatuation, or fidelity, or fate, to their once lofty
perches, the pagan harpooneers still maintained their sinking
look-outs.

HATCH, HATCHWAY. Hatch, a half-door. Hatchway, a square or oblong
opening in the middle of the deck of a ship, of which there are generally
three--the fore, main, and after--affording passages up and down from one
deck to another, and again descending into the hold. The coverings over
these openings are called hatches. (Smyth)

Omoo--p. 39 (n.) you may seal up every hatchway; p. 56 (n.) were kept
down the after-hatchway; p. 59 (n.) high and dry on the after-hatch.

Mardi--p. 6 (n.) to the combings of her hatch; p. 58 (n.) to secure
the hatches; p. 74 (n.) piled up on the main-hatch; p. 102 (n.) when
the hatch was removed.

Redburn--p. 103 (n.) her open main-hatchway yawned into view; p. 104
(n.) when some shark gulps you down his hatchway; p. 111 (n.) emerged
from the fore hatchway; p. 119 (n.) and speak of the booby-hatch;
p. 166 (n.) cargo snugly secured under hatches; p. 175 (n.) its
hatchways looked like the entrance; p. 224 (n.) and sprang down the
hatchway; p. 239 (n.) except through the fore and after hatchways;
p. 239 (n.) covered with little houses called "booby-hatches"; p. 239
(n.) Upon the main-hatches; p. 241 (n.) from the two "booby-hatches"
came the steady hum; p. 241 (n.) to hold your head down the fore
hatchway; p. 248 (n.) looking down the hatchway where it was; p. 259
(n.) emigrants came rushing up the hatchway; p. 263 (n.) which was
planted over the main hatches; p. 286 (n.) the hatchways on the
steerage were; p. 290 (n.) placed near the opening of the hatchway.

White-Jacket--p. 10 (n.) attending to the drainage and sewerage below
hatches; p. 10 (n.) between the fore and main hatches; p. 26 (n.)
driving the laggards up the hatches; p. 27 (n.) dropped down the
hatchways near them; p. 81 (n.) vanished up one of the ladders at the
fore-hatchway; p. 83 (n.) the spray, coming down the hatchways; p. 93
(n.) ward-room officers emerged from the after-hatchway; p. 94 (n.)
bellowed themselves hoarse at the main-hatchway; p. 102 (n.) at the
main hatchway of the gun-deck; p. 115 (n.) The hatchways of some
armed vessels are but; p. 127 (n.) The Gunner under Hatches; p. 127
(n.) several parts of the ship under hatches; p. 134 (n.) at the
principal hatchway; pp. 136-7 (n.) sometimes placed over the hatchways;
p. 141 (n.) and the combings of the hatchways; p. 162 (n.) musician,
who stood at the main hatchway; p. 183 (n.) seeing the box going down
the hatchway; p. 187 (n.) they had dropped shot down the hatchways;

p. 207 (n.) while pitching the shot up the hatchway; p. 225 (n.) was heard at the main-hatchway; p. 239 (n.) has been tumblin' down the hatchway; p. 239 (n.) against the newly-painted combings of the hatchway; p. 278 (n.) made by the boatswain's mates at the hatchways; p. 278 (n.) bawling my name at all the hatchways; p. 278 (n.) the boatswain's mate at the fore-hatchway; p. 282 (n.) just forward of the main-hatchway; p. 285 (n.) would slowly emerge from the main-hatchway; pp. 287-8 (n.) emerging through the hatchway; p. 295 (n.) serving to embellish the hatchways; p. 295 (n.) and at her yawning hatchways; p. 316 (n.) About the hatchways it looked like a butcher's stall; p. 318 (n.) tear open hatchways in their Moslem sides; p. 337 (n.) with it toward the main hatchway; p. 337 (n.) the corpse reached the hatchway; p. 337 (n.) mustered round the hatchway; p. 338 (n.) out of sight below hatches; p. 341 (n.) stood round the main hatchway; p. 356 (n.) announcement made at the main-hatchway; p. 356 (n.) The Boatswain came rushing to the hatchway; p. 358 (n.) their stations at the fore and main hatchways; p. 379 (n.) disappeared beyond the hatchway; p. 390 (n.) charged to the combings of her hatchways; p. 394 (n.) he'll have that man down his hatchway; p. 398 (n.) the hypochondriac dwellers below hatches; p. 399 (n.) however they may groan beneath hatches.

Moby-Dick--p. 50 (n.) how gladly would I . . . sit on the hatches [i.e., benches, pews] there where you sit; p. 90 (n.) roaring at the men down the hatchways; p. 108 (n.) nothing above hatches was seen of Captain Ahab; p. 352 (n.) at top completely covered by a large, sloping, battened hatchway; p. 395 (n.) you should have stooped over the hatchway; p. 407 (n.) and bolted down her bursting hatches.

HAWSE. This is a term of great meaning. Strictly, it is that part of a vessel's bow where holes are cut for her cables to pass through. It also denotes any small distance between her head and the anchors employed to ride her, as "he anchored in our hawse." If a vessel drives at her anchors into the hawse of another she is said to "foul the hawse" of the vessel riding there.--Hawse-holes, cylindrical holes cut through the bows of a ship on each side of the stern, through which the cables pass, in order to be drawn into or let out of the vessel, as the occasion requires. --Hawser, a large rope or cablet, which holds the middle degree between the cable and towline. (Smyth--Melville sometimes spells it "hauser.")

Typee--p. 4 (n.) from her hawse-holes once more.

Redburn--p. 33 (n.) at work coiling away the hawsers; p. 120 (n.) clearing a foul hawse; p. 130 (n.) The hawsers and tow-lines being then coiled; p. 173 (n.) suitable for large cables and hawsers; p. 273 (n.) it may have lain, as a hawser.

White-Jacket--p. 7 (n.) every tendon a hawser; p. 25 (adj.) they come in at the hawse holes; p. 31 (n.) As the cable enters the hawse-hole; p. 123 (n.) Where the great hawsers and chains are piled; p. 171 (n.) like a capstan with a hawser coiled round; p. 366 (n.) he heard the chain rattle out of the hawse-hole.

Moby-Dick--p. 378 (n.) the whale's intestines . . . lie in him like great cables and hausers coiled away; p. 459 (n.) know that Ahab's hawser tows his purpose yet.

HEAVE. To throw anything overboard. To cast, as heaving the log or the lead. Also, to drag, prize, or purchase, as heaving up the anchor.-- Heave to. To put a vessel in a position of lying-to, by adjusting her sails so as to counteract each other, and thereby check her way, or keep her perfectly still. (Smyth)

> Omoo--p. 316 (v.) Presently, we hove to.

> Redburn--p. 126 (v.) we "hove-to" near the mouth; p. 130 (v.) we hove up the anchor; p. 138 (v.) till he hove up anchor for the world to come.

> White-Jacket--p. 98 (v.) furling every rag and heaving to.

> Moby-Dick--p. 94 (v.) for a considerable time after heaving up the anchor; p. 94 (v.) the next thing to heaving up the anchor; p. 95 (v.) Is that the way they heave in the marchant service; p. 231 (n.) the vessel . . . hove over to the monster as if to a quay; p. 452 (v.) he'a making a passage now, and may heave-to a while.

HEEL. The after end of a ship's keel, and the lower end of the stern-post to which it is connected. Also, the lower end of any mast, boom, bowsprit, or timber.--To heel. To lie over, or incline to either side out of the perpendicular; usually applied to a ship when canted by the wind, or by being unequally ballasted. (Smyth)

> Moby-Dick--p. 47 (v.) the ship, heeling over towards the wharf.

HELM. The machinery by which a vessel is steered, including the rudder, tiller, wheel &c. Applied more particularly, perhaps, to the tiller. (Dana)

> Typee--p. 4 (n.) I'm as good a helmsman as ever put hand in spoke; p. 4 (n.) when I put the helm down so gently.

> Omoo--p. 33 (n.) even the man at the helm nodded; p. 36 (n.) an occasional "trick" at the helm; p. 89 (n.) Bembo was at the helm; p. 89 (n.) was Bembo at the helm; p. 89 (n.) we tore him from the helm; p. 89 (n.) I steadied the helm; p. 90 (n.) the instant I had the helm; p. 98 (n.) ordered the helm up; p. 100 (n.) by the man at the helm; p. 149 (n.) By the man of the helm; p. 229 (n.) with a dozing islander at the helm; p. 292 (n.) the commodore, at the helm.

> Mardi--p. 4 (n.) up helm; p. 5 (n.) at the helm; p. 23 (n.) moving the helm; p. 24 (n.) helm manned; p. 26 (n.) my turn at the helm; p. 26 (n.) at the helm; p. 27 (n.) causing the helm to work; p. 28 (n.) Down helm; p. 33 (n.) exposed at the helm; p. 47 (n.) hand upon helm; p. 57 (n.) though the helm was left; p. 58 (n.) seeing the helm thus lashed; p. 70 (n.) managing the helm aright; p. 71 (n.) managing the helm aright; p. 71 (n.) old graybeard at the helm; p. 71 (n.) clutching wildly at the helm; p. 71 (n.) an instant from the helm; p. 71 (n.) stood at the helm; p. 72 (n.) yielding the helm; p. 81 (n.) helm was instantly shifted; p. 97 (n.) old Jarl at the helm; p. 101 (n.) somebody should stand at the helm; p. 101 (n.) my own turn at

the helm; p. 101 (n.) officiate as helmsman; p. 110 (n.) Annatoo took her turn at the helm; p. 111 (n.) when she was at the helm; p. 114 (n.) being at the helm at dawn; p. 120 (n.) Standing at her vibrating helm; p. 144 (n.) leaving me at the helm; p. 145 (n.) One sweep of the helm; p. 172 (n.) learned in hemp and helm; p. 488 (n.) I am finished off at the helm very much as other Mardians; p. 620 (adj.) Like helmless vessels, tempest-tossed; p. 653 (n.) Mobi at the helm; p. 654 (n.) Give me the helm, old man; p. 654 (n.) The helm! By Oro, I will steer my own fate; p. 654 (n.) He's seized the helm.

Redburn--p. 58 (n.) He was standing at the ship's helm; p. 70 (n.) just before the helm; p. 70 (n.) for the helmsman to strike the half hours by; p. 116 (n.) never would let me go to the helm; p. 116 (n.) if the helmsman be a clumsy, careless fellow; p. 116 (n.) want of quickness at the helm; p. 117 (n.) all the men who came to the helm; p. 118 (n.) right in front of the helm; p. 119 (n.) Nor must I omit the helm; p. 119 (n.) the helm would fetch a lurch; p. 119 (n.) and send the helmsman revolving round; p. 119 (n.) our best steersman at the helm; p. 290 (n.) by the observant steersman at the helm; pp. 291-2 (n.) say, going to the helm.

White-Jacket--p. 36 (n.) Who so moody as . . . helmsmen; p. 106 (n.) for the whole helm and galvanized keel were; p. 106 (n.) hard up the helm; p. 110 (n.) countermanded the captain's order at the helm; p. 110 (n.) By putting the helm hard up; p. 111 (n.) imprudent order to hard up the helm; p. 111 (n.) and thundered forth "Hard down the helm!"

Moby-Dick--p. 43 (n.) and bear a hardy helm; p. 168 (adv.) heart and helm they both go down; p. 354 (n.) drowsiness which ever would come over me at a midnight helm; p. 354 (n.) Never dream with thy hand on the helm; p. 468 (n.) thou firm deck, and haughty helm.

HERMAPHRODITE. A square-rigged vessel with a brig's foremast and a schooner's mainmast. (Smyth)

Redburn--p. 166 (n.) would be replaced by a jovial French hermaphrodite.

HERRING. A common fish--the Clupea harengus. (Smyth)

Typee--p. 207 (n.) generally about the size of a herring.

Mardi--p. 482 (n.) they made a commotion like shoals of herring; p. 575 (n.) a census of the herring would find us far in the majority.

Redburn--p. 43 (n.) as if it was a decoction of Dutch herrings.

White-Jacket--p. 78 (n.) when but one dab of point would make . . . a Mackintosh of a herring-net; p. 202 (n.) A reg'lar herring-net.

Moby-Dick--p. 5 (n.) that [whale] had above a barrel of harrings in his belly; p. 119 (n.) herring . . . were still found dividing . . . the same seas; p. 172 (n.) found to correspond . . . to those of the herring-shoals; pp. 191-2 (n.) nor any sign of a herring, would have been visible.

HOLD. The whole interior cavity of a ship, or all that part comprehended between the floor and the lower deck throughout her length. (Smyth)

Omoo--p. 144 (n.) down they thrust him into the hold; p. 148 (n.) down in the hold.

Mardi--p. 290 (n.) twenty steps down into their holds.

Redburn--p. 8 (n.) get the treasure out of the hold.

White-Jacket--p. 11 (n.) We say nothing here of . . . Captains of the Main-Hold, Captains of the Fore-Hold; p. 24 (n.) down in the hold; p. 27 (n.) and of the Fore and Main holds; p. 41 (n.) a ship of war, above her hold, least abounds; p. 54 (n.) said a Captain of the Hold; p. 68 (n.) are tumbled down into the hold; p. 116 (n.) as if there were a volcano in the frigate's hold; p. 123 (n.) concerning the subterranean depths of the Neversink's hold; p. 123 (n.) a cellar down in the after-hold; p. 123 (n.) tanks for fresh water in the hold; p. 153 (n.) strike the strangers down into the main-hold; p. 174 (n.) He belonged to the fore-hold; p. 175 (n.) emptied into from tanks in the hold; p. 239 (n.) The captain of the Main-Hold; pp. 282-3 (n.) connecting with the immense water-tanks in the hold.

Moby-Dick--p. 145 (n.) nor yet the low laugh from the hold; p. 264 (n.) where in her murderous hold this frigate earth is ballasted; p. 344 (n.) after completely filling her hold with oil; p. 394 (n.) the casks last struck into the hold were perfectly sound; p. 395 (n.) finally descend into the gloom of the hold.

HULL. The Gothic hulga meant a husk or external covering, and hence the body of a ship, independent of masts, yards, sails, rigging, and other furniture, is so called. (Smyth)

Typee--p. 12 (n.) whose black hulls . . . proclaimed their warlike character; p. 22 (n.) Her hull was incrusted with barnacles; p. 40 (n.) dotted . . . with the black hulls of the vessels.

Omoo--p. 5 (n.) her hull and spars a dingy black; p. 9 (n.) thought of her patched sails and blistered hull; p. 19 (n.) waspish hull of a small man-of-war craft; p. 39 (n.) fumigate the hull till the smoke; p. 39 (n.) as they did in her crazy old hull; pp. 73-4 (n.) that the old hull fairly echoed; p. 101 (n.) the condemned hull of a large ship; p. 102 (n.) the hull was then stripped and sold.

Mardi--p. 24 (n.) through the Christian hull; p. 53 (n.) to gambol about his grim hull; p. 58 (n.) in the poisoned hull; p. 64 (n.) from her ghostly hull; p. 83 (n.) her familiar, loitering hull; p. 90 (n.) plundering her hull; p. 92 (n.) the Parki had a hull; p. 100 (n.) whose tragic hull was haunted; p. 101 (n.) no small portion of the hull; p. 104 (n.) penetrated through the most solid part of her hull;

p. 117 (n.) the brigantine's black hull, shaggy; p. 118 (n.) ringing
hollow against her hull; p. 120 (n.) hull rolled convulsively.

Redburn--p. 8 (n.) if I could but once pry open the hull; p. 57 (n.)
received three shots in her hull; p. 92 (n.) the great black hull of
a strange vessel; p. 166 (n.) alongside of those lofty Yankee hulls;
p. 174 (n.) owing to their broad hulls and flat bottoms; p. 175 (n.)
This was the hull of an old sloop-of-war; p. 175 (n.) with the pitchy
smell of the old hull; p. 300 (n.) pointing out a vast black hull.

White-Jacket--p. 69 (n.) would send a shot, meant for the hull;
p. 106 (n.) our whole hull was rolling in the trough; p. 106 (n.)
perhaps the hull itself; p. 110 (n.) the weakest part of your hull;
p. 192 (v.) hull the blockheads; p. 270 (n.) see our black hull
butting the white sea; p. 309 (n.) with a slew of his hull; p. 312
(v.) having been hulled with round shot; p. 318 (n.) pitched into the
old Asia's hull; p. 318 (n.) We dragged his hull to one side; p. 322
(n.) the small platform outside of the hull; p. 338 (n.) His hull
here will soon be going out of sight; p. 348 (n.) she has one hundred
round shot in her hull; p. 370 (n.) scraping the ship's hull under
water; p. 393 (n.) Her vast hull loomed out of the night.

Moby-Dick--p. 67 (adj.) her old hull's complexion was darkened; p. 97
(n.) the two hulls wildly rolled; p. 116 (n.) ere the Pequod's weedy
hull rolls side by side with the barnacled hulls of the leviathan;
p. 153 (n.) and keeled hulls split at sea; p. 181 (n.) an unseen
whale vertically bumping the hull from beneath; p. 248 (n.) the whale
now lies with its black hull close to the vessel's; p. 274 (n.) So
close did the monster come to the hull; p. 289 (n.) the suddenly
relieved hull rolled away from it; p. 319 (n.) while other hulls are
loaded down with alien stuff; p. 355 (n.) in the pitchiest night the
ship's black hull still houses an illumination; p. 393 (n.) for who
can find it in the deep-loaded hull; p. 395 (n.) the hollow hull
echoed underfoot, as if you were treading over empty catacombs;
p. 400 (n.) his ringing cry ran through the vaulted hull; p. 412 (n.)
graceful masts erectly poised upon her long, ribbed hull; p. 415 (n.)
that its end may avoid all contact with the hull; p. 433 (n.) all
life fled from the smitten hull; p. 442 (n.) some of the flying
bubbles might have sprinkled her hull with their ghostly baptism;
p. 447 (n.) like to some flag-staff rising from the painted hull of
an argosy; p. 455 (n.) ran into each other in the one concrete hull;
p. 466 (n.) catching sight of the nearing black hull of the ship;
p. 468 (n.) thou uncracked keel; and only god-bullied hull.

ICHTHYOLOGY. The science of fishes, or that part of zoology which treats
of fishes, their structure, form, and classification, their habits, uses,
&c. (Webster)

Mardi--p. 39 (n.) the student of Ichthyology.

INLET. A term in some cases synonymous with cove and creek, when speaking
of the supply and discharge of lakes and broad waters, or an opening in
the land, forming a passage to any inclosed water. (Smyth)

Typee--p. 24 (n.) indented by several other extensive inlets; p. 25
(n.) She was soon conducted to a beautiful inlet; p. 252 (n.) pulled
towards the head of the inlet.

ISLAND, ISLE. Island may be simply described as a tract of land entirely
surrounded with water; but the whole continuous land of the Old World
forms one island, and the New World another; while canals across the
isthmuses of Suez and Panama would make each into two. The term properly
only applies to smaller portions of land; and Australia, Madagascar,
Borneo, and Britain are among the larger examples. Their materials and
form are equally various, and so is their origin; some having evidently
been upheaved by volcanic eruption, others are the result of accretion,
and still more revealing by their strata that they were formerly attached
to a neighboring land. The sudden emergence of Sabrina, in the Atlantic,
has occasioned wonder in our own day. So has that of Graham's Island,
near the south coast of Sicily; and the Archipelago is daily at work.
Isle, a colloquial abbreviation of island. Islet, smaller than an island,
yet larger than a key; an insular spot about a couple of miles in circuit.
(Smyth)

Typee--p. xiv (n.) descriptive of the islands in the Pacific; p. xiv
(n.) lately occurring at the Sandwich, Marquesas, and Society Islands;
p. 5 (n.) an irresistible curiosity to see those islands; p. 5 (n.)
these isles had sprung up like a scene; p. 5 (n.) these islands,
undisturbed for years, relapsed; p. 6 (n.) some interesting
particulars concerning the islanders; p. 6 (n.) which there is in one
of the islands; p. 6 (n.) despaired of reclaiming these islands from
heathenism; p. 6 (n.) to establish a branch Mission upon certain
islands; p. 6 (n.) The islanders at first gazed in mute admiration;
p. 7 (adj.) Not thus shy . . . was the Island Queen herself; p. 7 (n.)
to touch at these islands; p. 7 (n.) The King of the Cannibal Islands;
p. 9 (n.) silently sweeping us towards the islands; p. 11 (n.) This
island, although generally called; p. 11 (n.) comprising the islands
of Ruhooka, Ropo, and Nukuheva; p. 11 (n.) lie in the immediate
vicinity of the other islands; p. 11 (n.) after the discovery of the
adjacent islands; p. 11 (n.) Nukuheva is the most important of these
islands; p. 11 (n.) This island is about twenty miles in length;
p. 11 (n.) known by the name bestowed upon the island itself; p. 11
(n.) residing in the more remote sections of the island; p. 12 (n.)
we found ourselves close in with the island; p. 12 (n.) are surprised
at the appearance of the islands; p. 12 (n.) the principal features
of these islands; p. 12 (n.) The whole group of islands had just been;
p. 13 (n.) wandering among the islands of the Pacific; p. 13 (n.) you
would have thought the islanders were on the point of; p. 14 (n.)
nothing else than the head of an islander; p. 14 (n.) some of the
islanders . . . directed our attention; p. 15 (n.) inhabiting some
yet undiscovered islands; p. 16 (n.) that we arrived at the islands;
p. 16 (n.) The islanders looked upon the people; p. 17 (n.) purposely
calculated to dazzle the islanders; p. 17 (n.) at the period of our
arrival at the islands; p. 17 (n.) unanimously pronounced by the
islanders; p. 18 (n.) the rightful sovereign of the entire island;
p. 18 (n.) set sail for the doomed island; p. 18 (n.) wide alarm
spread over the island; p. 20 (n.) to risk my fortunes among the
savages of the island; p. 22 (n.) touched at some of those unstable
islands; p. 23 (n.) somewhere off Buggerry Island; p. 23 (n.) having

touched at the Sandwich Islands; p. 23 (n.) relating to the island
and its inhabitants; p. 23 (n.) flanked on either side by two small
twin islets; p. 24 (n.) the shores of the island are indented; p. 24
(n.) inspire the other islanders with unspeakable terrors; p. 25 (n.)
prodigious notoriety all over the islands; p. 25 (n.) as any of the
other tribes on the island; p. 25 (n.) unacquainted with the
localities of the island; p. 26 (n.) When the inhabitants of some
sequestered island; p. 26 (n.) upon some of the inoffensive islanders;
p. 27 (n.) whose course from island to island; p. 27 (n.) bloodthirsty
disposition of some of the islanders; p. 29 (n.) while the simple
islander; p. 30 (n.) among the natives of a barbarous island; pp. 30-1
(n.) that the islanders, from motives of precaution; p. 32 (n.) seen
him since our arrival at the island; p. 33 (n.) after remaining upon
the island; p. 35 (n.) you need not blame me if the islanders make a
meal; p. 36 (n.) I fully relied upon the fruits of the island; p. 36
(n.) happened to be the rainy season of the islands; p. 37 (n.) as it
drove the islanders into their houses; p. 39 (n.) As we looked down
upon the islanders; p. 40 (n.) what seemed to be the highest land on
the island; p. 44 (n.) the interior of the island having apparently
been; p. 46 (n.) a track formed by the islanders; p. 47 (n.) instead
of rambling about the island; p. 48 (n.) abandon vessels in romantic
islands; p. 48 (n.) all the islands of Polynesia enjoy the reputation;
p. 48 (n.) in common with the Hibernian isle; p. 51 (n.) that there
were several such upon the island; p. 67 (n.) that might indicate the
vicinity of the islanders; p. 70 (n.) to redouble the astonishment of
the islanders; p. 72 (n.) every announcement on the part of the
islanders; p. 72 (n.) among the Marquese islanders is manufactured;
p. 73 (n.) especially on a South-Sea island; p. 74 (n.) from visiting
that section of the island; p. 74 (n.) to designate the Islanders;
p. 74 (n.) A "Tabooed Kannaka" is an islander whose person; p. 76 (n.)
fair appearances the islanders conveyed; p. 78 (n.) remarkable in the
appearance of the splendid islander; p. 79 (n.) re-entered the house
with an aged islander; p. 81 (n.) peculiarity . . . in many other of
the islanders; p. 83 (n.) to write thus of the poor islander; p. 87
(n.) maidens of the island were passionately fond of flowers; p. 90
(n.) the indolent disposition of the islanders; p. 92 (n.) terminates
among the warriors of the island; p. 94 (n.) as the forms of four of
the islanders were seen; p. 95 (n.) there never was a calf on the
island till you landed; p. 96 (n.) Last of all came a burly islander;
p. 98 (n.) sacrificed by those ferocious islanders; p. 101 (n.)
suddenly I saw three of the islanders; p. 101 (n.) perceived the
three islanders standing a little distance off; p. 104 (n.) some
caprice on the part of the islanders; p. 105 (n.) had we seen the
islanders in such a state of bustle; p. 106 (n.) made up his mind to
accompany the islanders; p. 106 (n.) The islanders were now to be
seen hurrying along; p. 107 (n.) Towards sunset the islanders in
small parties; p. 109 (n.) The conduct of the islanders appeared
inexplicable; p. 111 (n.) The islander, placing the larger stick;
p. 116 (n.) the islanders assemble in harvest groups; p. 117 (n.) the
islanders chiefly depend upon the supplies; p. 117 (n.) rarely met
with upon the Sandwich Islands; p. 120 (n.) During my whole stay on
the island; p. 121 (n.) to show the islanders with what facility;
p. 122 (n.) during my stay in the island; p. 123 (n.) change in the
conduct of the islanders towards me; p. 124 (n.) Let the once smiling
and populous Hawaiian islands; p. 125 (n.) four or five Marquesan
Islanders sent to the United States; p. 126 (n.) number of Americans

despatched to the Islands; p. 127 (n.) the islanders were not entirely
exempt; p. 128 (n.) The islanders were now to be seen running past;
p. 129 (n.) they were worked by the islanders; p. 130 (n.) must occur
very rarely among the islanders; p. 133 (n.) high time the islanders
should be taught a little gallantry; p. 134 (adj.) but my island
beauty's began at the waist; p. 135 (n.) only to be seen in the South
Sea Islander; p. 136 (n.) He advanced surrounded by the islanders;
p. 138 (n.) a sad deceiver among the simple maidens of the island;
p. 138 (n.) Of no little consequence among the islanders; p. 139 (n.)
never before remarked in any part of the island; p. 139 (n.) a
singular custom among the islanders; p. 140 (n.) access to all the
valleys in the island; p. 140 (n.) at a subsequent visit to the
island; p. 141 (n.) of the unchangeable determination of the
islanders; p. 143 (n.) in the different bays of the island; p. 147
(n.) generally worn on the Marquesan Islands; p. 148 (n.) the
renowned conqueror and king of the Sandwich Islands; p. 148 (n.) is
unknown upon the Marquesan Islands; p. 149 (n.) The islanders are
somewhat abstemious; p. 150 (n.) The islanders, who only smoke a
whiff or two; p. 151 (n.) the delight of the islanders was boundless;
p. 155 (n.) in high estimation by the islanders; p. 155 (n.) buried
in the green nook of an island; p. 155 (n.) They establish the great
age of the island; p. 155 (n.) The origin of the island of Nukuheva;
p. 155 (n.) dwellings of the islanders were almost invariably built;
p. 155 (n.) in nearly all the valleys of the island; p. 156 (n.)
whenever an enterprising islander chooses; p. 161 (adj.) confronted
for a moment by this band of Island girls; p. 164 (n.) a single plant
growing on the island; p. 165 (n.) Upon the Sandwich Islands it has
been employed; p. 169 (n.) treating of the Washington, or Norhtern
Islands; p. 170 (n.) a man who . . . was only at one of the islands;
p. 170 (n.) practiced upon the Marquesas Islands; p. 170 (n.)
officiates as showman of the island; p. 171 (n.) he knows as little
as the islanders do; p. 171 (n.) As the islanders always maintained a
discreet reserve; p. 171 (adj.) I christened the scene of our island
yachting; p. 173 (n.) to the fanciful superstition of the islanders;
p. 173 (n.) the religious theories of the islands; p. 175 (n.) was
the "crack god" of the island; p. 177 (n.) to take the whole island
of Nukuheva in his mouth; p. 177 (n.) intercourse with the South Sea
islanders; p. 177 (n.) while I remained upon the island; p. 177 (n.)
the islanders in the Pacific; p. 180 (n.) to my general knowledge of
the islanders; p. 180 (n.) that these islanders derived no advantage;
p. 181 (n.) Nothing in the appearance of the islanders; p. 181 (n.)
as it ever does among the South Sea islanders; p. 182 (n.) like the
wretched inhabitants of the Sandwich Islands; p. 182 (n.) without
visiting other portions of the island; p. 183 (n.) All the islanders
are more or less in the habit; p. 183 (n.) The first of these islands
seen by Mendanna; p. 183 (n.) dwelling on that and the other islands
of the group; p. 183 (n.) The islanders are still the same; p. 184
(n.) the Marquesans are by far the most splendid islanders; p. 184
(n.) distinguishing characteristic of the Marquesan islanders; p. 184
(n.) rendered the young islanders who wore them very distinguished;
p. 184 (n.) they held with vessels touching the island; p. 185 (n.)
might have been left on the island by Wallace, Carteret; p. 186 (n.)
The civil institution of the Marquesas Islands; p. 186 (n.) At the
Sandwich Islands; p. 188 (n.) rapidly refining the natives of the
Sandwich Islands; p. 188 (n.) In the progress of events at these
islands; p. 189 (n.) puppet of a chief magistrate in the Sandwich

Islands; p. 191 (n.) polygamy exists among the islanders; p. 191 (n.)
This holds true of many of the islands of Polynesia; p. 192 (n.) The
contrast exhibited between the Marquesans and other islanders; p. 192
(n.) spread universal licentiousness over the island; p. 192 (n.)
even upon those islands seldom or never desolated; p. 192 (n.) to
prevent the overstocking of the islands; p. 193 (n.) decrease the
population of the Sandwich Islands; p. 193 (n.) swell the ordinary
mortality of the islands; p. 193 (n.) the same with those of all
other tribes on the island; p. 194 (n.) The islanders understand the
art of embalming; p. 195 (n.) that the Marquesas Islands have been
converted to Christianity; p. 195 (n.) Heaven help the "Isles of the
Sea"; p. 195 (n.) How little do some of these poor islanders
comprehend; p. 195 (n.) Among the islands of Polynesia; p. 196 (n.)
Honolulu, the metropolis of the Sandwich Islands; p. 196 (n.) a little
go-cart drawn by two of the islanders; p. 198 (n.) apostolic functions
upon the remote islands; p. 198 (adj.) in the practical operations of
the Sandwich Islands Mission; p. 198 (n.) to go to the Sandwich
Islands and see the missionaries; p. 198 (n.) present deplorable
condition of the Sandwich Islands; p. 199 (n.) to the cause of
Christianity in the Sandwich Islands; p. 200 (n.) tempted to say that
none existed on the island; p. 200 (n.) These islanders were heathens;
p. 201 (n.) Each islander reposed beneath his own palmetto thatching;
p. 201 (n.) inhabitants of nearly all the Polynesian Islands; p. 201
(n.) contradiction in the moral character of the islanders; p. 202
(n.) there were none on the island; p. 202 (n.) Today I see an
islander; p. 203 (n.) The islanders, while employed in erecting this
tenement; p. 204 (n.) During my whole stay on the island; p. 204 (n.)
feuds they carry on against their fellow-islanders; p. 205 (n.) less
guilty, then, are our islanders; p. 206 (n.) All the South Sea
Islanders are passionately fond; p. 207 (n.) did not repress the
impatience of the islanders; p. 208 (adj.) when I first saw my island
beauty devour one; p. 211 (n.) on an uninhabited island of the
Gallipagos; p. 212 (n.) At the Sandwich Islands and at two or three
of the Society group; p. 212 (n.) no wild animals of any kind on the
island; p. 213 (n.) when an islander bound on some expedition; p. 213
(n.) never any of that "remarkable weather" on the island; p. 213 (n.)
agility and ingenuity of the islanders; p. 217 (n.) tattooing as
performed by these islanders; p. 221 (n.) the religious institutions
of most of the Polynesian islands; p. 221 (n.) after residing for
years among the islands in the Pacific; p. 223 (n.) for the religious
prejudices of the islanders; p. 224 (n.) on the neighboring island of
Ropo; p. 224 (n.) consider the slight disparity of condition among
the islanders; p. 224 (n.) over the various clans on a single island;
p. 224 (n.) prevails upon all the northern Marquesas Islands; p. 224
(n.) opposed to the ordinary customs of the islanders; p. 225 (n.) on
Mowee, one of the Sandwich Islands; p. 226 (n.) after the universal
practice of these islanders; p. 229 (n.) No wonder that the South Sea
Islanders are so amphibious; p. 231 (n.) on the behavior of the islanders
toward me was as kind; p. 233 (n.) Two of the three were heads of the
islanders; p. 233 (n.) studiously concealed them from the islanders;
p. 234 (n.) The excessive unwillingness betrayed by the Sandwich
Islanders; p. 234 (n.) there was living on the island of Mowee; p. 23
p. 235 (n.) when a tumultuous crowd of islanders emerged; p. 236 (n.)
The excited throng of islanders; p. 241 (n.) he waved his spear in
adieu to the islanders; p. 242 (n.) before the islanders should
discover my absence; p. 242 (n.) that the islanders were nearly as

irritable; p. 243 (n.) might have roused the suspicions of the
islanders; p. 243 (n.) thousands of miles from the savage island;
p. 245 (n.) The startled islanders sprang from their mats; p. 246 (n.)
we were met by a party of some twenty islanders; p. 247 (n.) I heeded
not the assurances of the islanders; p. 249 (n.) It was manned by
five islanders; p. 249 (n.) tabooed in all the valleys of the island;
p. 249 (n.) the islanders had threatened to pierce him with their
spears; p. 250 (n.) several of the islanders now raised a simultaneous
shout; p. 252 (n.) The athletic islander . . . was dashing the water
before him; p. 252 (n.) sailed to that part of the island; p. 253 (n.)
or perished at the hands of the islanders; p. 254 (n.) scruples of
the more conscientious islanders; p. 254 (n.) proceedings of the
English at the Sandwich Islands; p. 255 (n.) by the native authorities
of the Sandwich Islands; p. 255 (n.) insultingly forbidden to leave
the islands; p. 255 (n.) tendered to his acceptance the provisional
cession of the islands; p. 256 (n.) endeared himself to nearly all
orders of the islanders; p. 256 (n.) misrule to which these poor
islanders are subjected; p. 256 (n.) the laws at the Sandwich Islands
are subject to; p. 256 (n.) restoration of the islands to their
ancient rulers; p. 258 (n. natives of the surrounding islands flocked
to Honolulu; p. 258 (n.) some of the islanders caught in the very act
of stealing; p. 258 (n.) reveal in their true colors the character of
the Sandwich islanders; p. 258 (n.) never had any idea of appropriating
the islands; p. 261 (n.) and the Islanders halted; p. 264 (n.) two
natural prodigies which . . . were then on the island; p. 264 (n.)
was the terror of all the island round; p. 265 (n.) asked Toby whether
he wished to leave the island; p. 265 (n.) I cannot leave the island
unless my comrade goes with me; p. 265 (n.) He was still struggling
with the islanders; p. 266 (n.) mixed up with the mysterious customs
of the islanders; p. 268 (n.) where the island ridges are comparatively
low; p. 269 (n.) The island-punch--arva--was brought in; p. 271 (n.)
upbraiding me for leaving you on the island.

Omoo--p. xiii (n.) among the barbarous or semi-civilized islands of
Polynesia; p. xiv (n.) in various parts of the islands of Tahiti and
Imeeo; p. xiv (n.) from the dialect of the Marquesas Islands; p. xiv
(n.) a person wandering from one island to another; p. 3 (n.) visited
the Marquesas Islands; p. 3 (n.) At the island of Nukuheva he left
his vessel; p. 3 (n.) neighboring harbor of the same island; p. 6 (n.)
concerning my residence on the island; p. 12 (n.) to leave the vessel
clandestinely at one of the islands; p. 14 (n.) among the savages of
the islands; p. 15 (n.) a village on the island of St. Christina;
p. 19 (n.) the blue, looming island of St. Christina greeted us;
p. 20 (n.) reverend the clergy of the island; p. 21 (n.) was a
shouting rabble of islanders; p. 22 (n.) the islanders have no idea
of taking part; p. 23 (n.) an island just north of the one we had
quitted; p. 24 (n.) that the islanders should draw near; p. 25 (n.)
landing at islands comparatively unknown; p. 25 (n.) the islanders
coming down to the shore; p. 26 (n.) On the other side of the island;
p. 26 (n.) dividing the islands of La Dominica and St. Christina;
p. 26 (n.) Of any note about the island; p. 27 (n.) war-god of the
entire island; p. 28 (n.) found quite at home upon the savage islands;
p. 28 (n.) no other white man on the island; p. 29 (n.) were heard
unmoved by our islander; p. 30 (n.) had lived so long on the island;
p. 30 (n.) though of the same group of islands; p. 30 (n.) was
practiced upon the island; p. 34 (n.) in the figurative language of

the island; p. 34 (n.) the air of the island having disagreed; p. 35
(n.) why new islands are still occasionally discovered; p. 35 (n.)
small clusters of islands vaguely laid down; p. 35 (n.) was a small
cluster of islands; p. 45 (n.) a Portuguese, from the Cape-de-Verd
Islands; p. 47 (n.) to be safely landed upon any island; p. 51 (n.)
the sooner we get to those islands of yours; p. 51 (n.) pointed for
the island is Tahiti; p. 51 (n.) a place so famous as the island in
question; p. 51 (n.) The island turned out to be; p. 62 (n.) sometimes
called the Coral Islands; p. 62 (n.) the inclosing island, in such
cases; p. 62 (n.) girdled by numbers of small, green islets; p. 63
(n.) These would appear to be islands; p. 63 (n.) some of the islands
are altogether uninhabited; p. 63 (n.) have settled among the leeward
islands; p. 63 (n.) with which island they always carried on; p. 63
(n.) The Coral Islands are principally visited; p. 63 (n.) Some of
the uninhabited islands; p. 64 (n.) annually exported from the Society
Islands; p. 64 (n.) before we drew near the island; p. 64 (n.) Beyond
it was another and larger island; p. 65 (n.) by far the most famous
island; p. 65 (n.) Unlike many of the other islands; p. 66 (n.) the
French bestowed upon the island; p. 66 (n.) than of any other island
in Polynesia; p. 66 (n.) supposed to have touched at the island;
p. 67 (n.) missions to the neighboring islands; p. 68 (n.) The sight
of the island was right welcome; p. 69 (n.) to touch at the island;
p. 71 (n.) shipping at the Bay of Islands; p. 73 (n.) as is usual
about these islands; p. 75 (n.) born on the island; p. 81 (n.) I
shipped at the Islands about four months ago; p. 89 (n.) girdling the
island; p. 95 (n.) for the adjoining island of Imeeo; p. 95 (n.) now
resident on the island; p. 95 (n.) at the Bay of Islands in New
Zealand; p. 96 (n.) touched, for fruit, at an island; p. 96 (n.) After
staying on the island more than two years; p. 96 (n.) he traded among
the neighboring islands; p. 98 (n.) most northerly point of the island;
p. 99 (n.) a boy and an old man--both islanders; p. 102 (n.) she had
made all sail for the island; p. 114 (n.) rose the still, steep peaks
of the island; p. 114 (n.) has done for the island; p. 114 (n.) crosses
the island in that direction; p. 114 (n.) it fed all the streams on
the island; p. 115 (n.) Like the Sandwich Islanders; p. 118 (n.)
without some . . . plan for leaving the island; p. 118 (n.) visits to
other parts of the island; p. 121 (n.) has been done for these
islanders; p. 122 (n.) I happened to arrive at the island; p. 122 (n.)
put them ashore at Wallis' island; p. 123 (n.) the conduct of the
Sandwich Island missionaries; p. 123 (n.) led to his seizure of the
island; p. 123 (n.) the island was forthwith seized; p. 124 (n.)
During my stay upon the island; p. 124 (n.) concerning the ability of
the island to cope; p. 124 (n.) the island, which before was divided;
p. 124 (n.) the islanders fought desperately; p. 125 (n.) several
speeches were made by the islanders; p. 125 (n.) most of the islanders
still refuse to submit; p. 125 (n.) what islander would venture to
jeopardize his soul; p. 126 (n.) of the thousand unconverted isles of
the Pacific; p. 127 (n.) before the discovery of the islands by the
whites; p. 128 (n.) Roorootoo, a lone island, some two days' sail;
p. 128 (n.) The island is very small; p. 128 (n.) were as famous
among the islands round about; p. 128 (n.) he is better off on the
island; p. 130 (n.) even though she were but an islander; p. 132 (n.)
exhaust the uncultivated resources of the island; p. 132 (n.) The
islanders seldom use salt with their food; p. 140 (n.) Was it not you
that was taken off the island; p. 142 (n.) pity for the ladies of the
island; p. 146 (n.) The alarmed islanders, beaching their canoe;

p. 146 (n.) From New Zealand to the Sandwich Islands; p. 146 (n.)
Upon the missionary islands; p. 150 (n.) so long as we remained on
the island; p. 152 (n.) The islanders are much like the rest of the
world; p. 152 (n.) In the annals of the island; p. 152 (n.) the
practice has continued in some islands; p. 153 (n.) had spread to the
neighboring islands; p. 153 (n.) one of the Society Isles; p. 159 (n.)
gave up all thoughts of leaving the island; p. 160 (n.) Among the
Society Islands; p. 162 (n.) is a bright, green island; p. 162 (n.)
The island is called Motoo-Otoo; p. 163 (n.) to make a fortress of
the island; p. 163 (n.) looked more like the spook of the island;
p. 163 (n.) so considered by the islanders in general; p. 164 (n.)
and the islanders theirs; p. 165 (n.) known to have visited the
island; p. 166 (n.) never stepped on the island; p. 168 (n.) there
were no less than thirty-six on the island; p. 168 (n.) from all
parts of the island; p. 167 (n.) the islanders love to dwell; p. 170
(n.) the rank and fashion of the island; p. 171 (n.) with South Sea
islanders; p. 172 (n.) from the people of the Sandwich Islands;
p. 173 (n.) the island no more yours; p. 173 (n.) this very small
island; pp. 173-4 (n.) Because that island good island; p. 173 (n.)
of the highest chiefs on the island; p. 174 (n.) adapted to the minds
of the islanders; p. 174 (n.) the Great Revival at the Sandwich
Islands; p. 174 (n.) afterward sent to Oahu (Sandwich Islands);
p. 175 (n.) to the selection of their island as the very first field;
p. 175 (n.) the Sandwich Islanders actually knocked out their teeth;
p. 175 (n.) At one of the Society Islands; p. 176 (n.) repose broods
over the whole island; p. 179 (n.) going all over the island; p. 179
(n.) by a late benevolent visitor at the island; p. 180 (n.) previous
to our arrival at the island; p. 180 (n.) the islanders take a sly
revenge; p. 185 (n.) the missionaries now on the island are; p. 185
(n.) At the Sandwich Islands; p. 185 (n.) recognizing the nationality
of the island; p. 185 (n.) the morality of the islanders is . . .
improved; p. 185 (n.) into the language of the island; p. 186 (n.)
moral and religious condition of the island; p. 186 (n.) Account of
the Principal Islands of the South Sea; p. 187 (n.) where the
inhabitants of an island; p. 188 (n.) On the island of Imeeo; p. 188
(n.) went even further at the Sandwich Islands; p. 188 (n.) that the
people of that island had; p. 188 (n.) respecting the Sandwich
Islanders; p. 188 (n.) in both groups of islands; p. 188 (n.) in his
intercourse with the islanders; p. 189 (n.) obsolete in many parts of
the island; p. 190 (n.) of these partially civilized islanders; p.
p. 190 (n.) a plant indigenous to the island; p. 190 (n.) civilization
among the South Sea Islands; p. 190 (n.) the capital of the Sandwich
Islands; p. 191 (n.) of the common people of the island; p. 191 (n.)
upon these poor, untutored islanders, a curse; p. 191 (n.) incredible
depopulation of the Sandwich Islands; p. 191 (n.) from the records
kept on the islands; p. 191 (n.) The Chapter on the Sandwich Islands;
p. 192 (n.) The islanders themselves, are mournfully watching; p. 199
(n.) deserting their ship at Fanning's Island; p. 199 (n.) the island
immediately adjoining; p. 199 (n.) the opportunity for leaving the
island; p. 200 (n.) told about the neighboring islands; p. 202 (n.)
wild cattle and hogs overrunning the island; p. 207 (n.) only open
toward the leeward side of the island; p. 209 (n.) and the way they
came on the island; p. 209 (n.) racing over the island of Imeeo; p.
210 (n.) timid in crossing the island; p. 210 (n.) Vancouver's attempts
to colonize the islands; p. 210 (n.) one of the largest islands;
p. 210 (n.) Ellis' Journal of Visit to the Sandwich Islands; p. 211

(n.) from all the islands of the group; p. 211 (n.) upon the single
island of Hawaii; p. 213 (n.) The wild hogs of the island; p. 213
(n.) the pesky critter's on t'other side of the island; p. 214 (n.)
since the islanders had been Christians; p. 214 (n.) of the plain on
this island; p. 215 (n.) insects were introduced upon the island;
p. 217 (n.) At this part of the island; p. 219 (n.) where myself and
three of the islanders were standing; p. 219 (adj.) my island backers
were roosting among the trees; p. 221 (adj.) our island friends were
now in high spirits; p. 221 (n.) none of the islanders could be
induced; p. 222 (n.) the islanders went along on a brisk trot; p. 227
(n.) such thing as a barrow, or cart, on the island; p. 229 (n.) with
a dozing islander at the helm; p. 231 (n.) of trading among the
neighboring islands; p. 234 (n.) grew the finest fruit of the islands;
p. 235 (n.) a harbor on the opposite side of the island; p. 237 (n.)
the principal circulating medium on the island; p. 237 (n.) in the
very heart of the island; p. 246 (n.) wishing to see as much of the
island as we could; p. 246 (n.) lies on the western side of the
island; p. 247 (n.) Upon islands little visited by foreigners;
p. 247 (n.) one of the Tonga Islands; p. 247 (n.) Upon another island
of the same group; p. 247 (n.) Even upon the Sandwich Islands; p. 248
(n.) practiced his vocation on the Sandwich Islands; p. 249 (n.) But
as friendless wanderers over the island; p. 249 (n.) and much
respected all over the island; p. 250 (n.) The island of Imeeo is
very nearly surrounded; p. 250 (n.) going twenty or thirty miles
round the island; p. 257 (n.) So far round had we skirted the island;
p. 259 (n.) much lively chanting among the islanders; p. 261 (n.)
anticipate its covering the entire island; p. 262 (n.) Upon other
islands which I have visited; p. 262 (n.) the islander reposes
beneath its shade; p. 262 (adj.) it upholds the islander's dwelling;
p. 263 (n.) Upon one of the Tonga Islands; p. 263 (n.) Even upon the
Sandwich Islands; p. 263 (n.) upon islands where the swell of the
sea; p. 264 (n.) I ever saw at the islands; p. 266 (n.) all round the
island; p. 268 (adj.) of that comfortable old island gondola; p. 269
(n.) in a distant part of the island; p. 270 (n.) round a considerable
part of the island; p. 270 (n.) Nearly all the Society Islands;
p. 270 (n.) by little fairy islets, green as emerald; p. 271 (n.) an
old hermit of an islander; p. 273 (adj.) where he manufactured his
island poteen; p. 277 (n.) was an aristocratic-looking islander;
p. 277 (n.) among the people of the Society Islands; p. 279 (n.) by
Society Islanders talking Saxon; p. 279 (n.) The semi-civilization of
the island must have had something to do; p. 280 (n.) any thing like
practical piety, upon these islands; p. 286 (n.) Throughout the
Society Islands; p. 287 (n.) the leeward islands of the group; p. 288
(adj.) had been falling in love with some island coquet; p. 288 (n.)
after being three years a resident of the island; p. 288 (n.) an
importation from the Bay of Islands; p. 289 (n.) admired from the
other side of the island; p. 291 (n.) from another part of the island;
p. 291 (n.) a visit from a certain uninhabited island; p. 292 (n.)
ran over for the opposite island of Imeeo; p. 292 (n.) By the help of
the islanders; p. 292 (n.) some time previous had died on the island;
p. 293 (n.) ignorance of the love vocabulary of the island; p. 295
(n.) the stranger had been on the island about two years; p. 299 (n.)
among the islands of the Pacific; p. 300 (n.) in this quarter of the
island; p. 300 (n.) sentenced to eternal banishment from the island;
p. 302 (n.) extended his rule over the entire island; p. 302 (n.)
defeated, and expelled from the island; p. 303 (n.) an island about

one hundered miles from Tahiti; p. 303 (n.) from one island to another;
p. 304 (n.) to go over to his beggarly island of Imeeo; p. 306 (n.)
that of the American missionaries at the Sandwich Islands; p. 307 (n.)
Embarking at his native island; p. 308 (n.) on the island of Imeeo; p
p. 308 (n.) I found this islander a philosopher; p. 312 (n.) native
of the island of Martha's Vineyard; p. 315 (n.) by shipping several
islanders; p. 316 (n.) to take off the islanders who had accompanied
us; p. 316 (n.) the island had gone down in the horizon.

Mardi--p. 68 (n.) at the Pearl Shell Islands; p. 68 (n.) one of the
Hawaiian isles; p. 68 (n.) in all the Sandwich Islands; p. 68 (n.) of
the Navigator Islands; p. 68 (n.) of a far-off, anonymous island;
p. 69 (n.) fell in with a cluster of islands; p. 69 (n.) at these
islands; p. 69 (n.) their influence over the islanders; p. 69 (n.) on
the thither side of the island; p. 71 (n.) four or five Islanders;
p. 72 (n.) two of the Islanders swam; p. 74 (n.) from the Island;
p. 74 (n.) leaving the island astern; p. 74 (n.) among the Islanders;
p. 80 (adj.) the poor islander's philosophy; p. 81 (n.) a cluster of
low islands; p. 81 (n.) at the Pearl Shell Islands; p. 81 (n.) Of
encountering any Islanders; p. 82 (n.) in approaching the isles;
p. 82 (n.) The Pearl Shell islands excepted; p. 85 (n.) own dear
native island; p. 85 (n.) sighted a cluster of low islands; p. 85 (n.)
dropping the islands astern; p. 89 (n.) of having seen the islands;
p. 89 (n.) those islands could form; p. 90 (n.) on the shore of some
island; p. 90 (n.) faith in the Islander; p. 90 (n.) upon the rude
Islander; p. 93 (n.) I closely questioned the Islander; p. 96 (n.)
sailing out of the Hawaiian Islands; p. 96 (n.) peace of those
islands was wholly unknown; p. 96 (n.) of falling in with islands
whereat; p. 99 (n.) my Islander had a soul in his eye; p. 99 (n.)
native designation of the islands; p. 99 (n.) otherwise known as the
Navigator Islands; p. 99 (n.) island of Upolua; p. 125 (n.) of the
chain of islands we sought; p. 127 (adj.) sail of some island craft;
p. 127 (n.) passages between distant islands; p. 128 (n.) the
Islanders threw their craft; p. 129 (n.) the Islanders again stopped;
p. 129 (n.) still nearer to the Islanders; p. 129 (n.) the Islander,
who caught it; p. 129 (n.) the country to which the Islanders
belonged; p. 131 (n.) from the island of Amma to the gods of Tedaidee;
p. 132 (n.) the Islanders slowly retreated; p. 132 (n.) the Islanders
completely surrounded us; p. 132 (n.) several of the Islanders making
a rush; p. 133 (n.) Jarl battling with two Islanders; p. 135 (n.)
signed the Islanders to retire beyond it; p. 136 (n.) outburst of
voices from the Islanders; p. 137 (n.) unlike those of the Islanders;
p. 137 (n.) Oroolia, the Island of Delights; p. 137 (n.) To this isle,
while yet an infant; p. 137 (n.) upon the beach of the Island of Amma;
p. 139 (adj.) the strange arts of the island priesthood; p. 139 (n.)
revisiting the islands of Paradise; p. 141 (n.) yell going up from
the Islanders; p. 141 (n.) Islanders once more lifted; p. 142 (n.)
from the hands of the Islanders; p. 142 (n.) in the blessed isle of
Oroolia; p. 142 (n.) away from your isle in the sea; p. 143 (n.) from
isle to isle; p. 144 (n.) destination was still the islands; p. 145
(n.) voyaging for the island Tedaidee; p. 145 (n.) destination was
the fairy isle; p. 153 (n.) in those islands where human sacrifices;
p. 157 (n.) the island of Amma was no longer; p. 158 (n.) reminiscences
of her shadowy isle; p. 160 (n.) It was innumerable islands; p. 160
(n.) the islands grew more distinct; p. 160 (n.) from our vicinity to
the isles; p. 161 (n.) in the broad shadows of the isles; p. 161 (n.)

was a little island; p. 161 (n.) and fly away, island and all; p. 161
(n.) how weigh the isle's coral anchor; p. 161 (n.) but all the
islands seemed slumbering; p. 161 (n.) the Islanders retreated;
p. 161 (n.) they all made for one island; p. 161 (n.) pointed our
craft for the island; p. 161 (adj.) outer line of the isle's shadow;
p. 162 (n.) went up from the Islanders; p. 162 (n.) the Islanders ran
up to their waists; p. 163 (n.) What saw the Islanders; p. 163 (n.)
the Islanders regarding it as sacred; p. 164 (n.) those of the islands
adjacent; p. 164 (n.) the Islanders regarded me; p. 164 (n.) their
islands were known; p. 166 (n.) On my island of Odo; p. 167 (n.) as
we rounded isle after isle; p. 168 (n.) A small island, of moderate
elevation; p. 171 (n.) entered the Islanders; p. 174 (n.) ancestors
came on the island; p. 176 (n.) with the exception of certain islands;
p. 176 (n.) no certain knowledge of any isles; p. 178 (n.) lay the
Mardian fleet of isles; p. 182 (adj.) The crown of the island prince;
p. 183 (n.) palm trees on an isle; p. 186 (n.) visits from the
neighboring islands; p. 188 (n.) a little green tuft of an islet;
p. 188 (n.) all round the island; p. 188 (n.) Between these islets
and the shore; p. 188 (n.) One of these islets was wooded; p. 189
(n.) people of the neighboring islands; p. 190 (n.) description of
the island; p. 190 (n.) Now comes his isle; p. 190 (n.) where islands
close adjoining; p. 191 (adj.) the island's throbbing heart; p. 191
(n.) the whole isle looked carefree; p. 191 (n.) the isle well nigh
surrounding; p. 192 (n.) seen throughout the isle; p. 192 (n.) all
who died upon that isle; p. 192 (n.) when round the isles; p. 192 (n.)
Odo was but a little isle; p. 192 (n.) what follows, said these
Islanders; p. 193 (n.) Yillah and I in our islet; p. 194 (n.) Fleeing
from the islet; p. 194 (n.) to range the isle; p. 194 (n.) dispatched
to the neighboring islands; p. 196 (n.) wandering to the neighboring
islands; p. 196 (n.) to the more distant islands; p. 197 (n.) to
visit every one of the isles; p. 198 (n.) which islands first to
visit; p. 199 (n.) round to my isle came Media; p. 200 (n.) drawing
near to the islands; p. 200 (n.) all her isles; p. 210 (n.) Valopee,
or the Isle of Yams; p. 201 (adj.) double-ridge the island's entire
length; p. 201 (n.) the isle seems divided; p. 201 (n.) the assembled
islanders ran; p. 202 (n.) before the heir to the isle; p. 202 (n.)
elderly chiefs of the island; p. 203 (n.) Tongatona ruled the isle;
p. 203 (n.) nothing permanent but the island itself; p. 206 (n.)
practiced in the Hawaiian Islands; p. 208 (n.) we early withdrew from
the isle; p. 211 (n.) covetous glances upon our blooming isles; p. 21
p. 211 (n.) and seizing the nearest islet; p. 212 (n.) promontory of
a neighboring island; p. 216 (n.) upon one of the largest islands;
p. 216 (n.) upon several wooded isles; p. 217 (n.) sentineled by its
tributary islets; p. 217 (n.) almost cleaving this quarter of the
island; p. 217 (n.) the shouts of the Islanders reverberated; p. 219
(n.) sought to subdue all the isles; p. 220 (n.) the island
acquiesced in the new sovereignty; p. 220 (n.) in the traditions of
the island; p. 221 (n.) the chief priests of the island were present;
p. 221 (n.) In the history of the island; p. 223 (n.) he remembered
the law of his isle; p. 223 (n.) landscapes of the neighboring isles;
p. 226 (n.) we spied many Islanders taking a bath; p. 226 (n.) eyes
were as floating isles; p. 226 (adj.) the Island Kings bound their
foreheads; p. 230 (n.) espied it as an isle in the sea; p. 234 (n.)
buttressing the island to the east; p. 236 (n.) the strange customs
of the isle; p. 245 (n.) those isles of yours; p. 245 (n.) can those
isles; p. 245 (n.) any glen of his own natal isle; p. 248 (n.) sent

Agents to the surrounding Isles; p. 248 (n.) the kings of the
neighboring islands; p. 248 (n.) dispatched to the isles special
agents; p. 249 (n.) to explore the island of Rafona; p. 250 (n.) west
side of the island of Rafona; p. 251 (n.) They visit the Tributary
Islets; p. 251 (n.) among its tributary isles; p. 251 (n.) returned
to their islets; p. 252 (n.) in isles that have viceroys for kings;
p. 254 (n.) distilled in the Philippine isles; p. 256 (n.) and
floating islands of flowers; p. 257 (n.) the Kings and demigods of
the islands; p. 262 (n.) inhabiting the island of Quelquo; p. 262
(n.) the innocent people of which island; p. 262 (n.) the cause of
which the Islanders; p. 263 (n.) pinching and pounding the unfortunate
Islanders; p. 263 (n.) to have been on that very island; p. 263 (n.)
all the herb-leeches on the island; p. 263 (n.) the people of that
island never; p. 264 (n.) that though the people of that island;
p. 265 (n.) Nora-Bamma, Isle of Nods; p. 265 (n.) hard telling sun-
clouds from the isles; p. 265 (n.) spake Braid-Beard, of the isle;
p. 266 (n.) would you wander through the isle; p. 269 (n.) the Origin
of the Isle of Rogues; p. 269 (n.) respecting the isle toward which;
p. 269 (n.) a suspicious appellative for their island; p. 269 (n.)
and malefactors of the neighboring islands; p. 270 (n.) persons to
still another island; p. 272 (n.) the island of Ohonoo was the base;
p. 272 (n.) forming many isles; p. 272 (n.) shores of this same
island; p. 273 (n.) and fall on the isle like an army; p. 274 (n.) at
another quarter of the island; p. 275 (n.) When a certain island
shall stir; p. 275 (n.) then the ruler of that island; p. 276 (n.)
cooked up in this insignificant islet; p. 276 (n.) lord of the whole
island; p. 276 (n.) wandered up and down in this isle; p. 277 (n.)
tutelar deity of the isle; p. 278 (n.) that the islanders venture not;
p. 280 (n.) an islet which according; p. 280 (n.) to know more of the
isle; p. 285 (n.) and that jolly Island of his; p. 286 (n.) could
sail by the island; p. 292 (n.) to remain on the island; p. 300 (n.)
Meanwhile, all over the isle; p. 301 (n.) his spirit in the aerial
isles; p. 302 (n.) torches trailing round the isle; p. 304 (n.)
Returning to the isle; p. 305 (n.) we were prepared to quit his isle;
p. 305 (n.) "Motoos," or little islets of the great reef; p. 305 (n.)
natives of some unknown island; p. 306 (n.) of a low, uninhabited
isle; p. 307 (n.) might stir up the Islanders against me; p. 307 (n.)
touched at our island of Amma; p. 311 (n.) against me the people of
the isle; p. 311 (n.) willing to remain on the island; p. 311 (n.)
whether the islands of Mardi; p. 312 (n.) departing for the other
side of the island; p. 314 (n.) How sweet, how sweet, the Isles from
Hina; p. 316 (n.) belonging to the poorer sort of Islanders; p. 316
(n.) heir to three islands; p. 323 (n.) the great central peak of the
island; p. 324 (n.) grows in all the isle; p. 324 (n.) a Bread-fruit
orchard of the holy island; p. 325 (n.) these Islanders take no
thought of the morrow; p. 326 (n.) Coming close to the island; p. 326
(n.) and behold the isle; p. 327 (n.) to showing strangers the island;
p. 327 (n.) this island was free to all; p. 328 (n.) to lead you
aright over all this island; p. 328 (n.) wealthy chief of a distant
island; p. 332 (n.) Hivohitee, Pontiff of the isle; p. 332 (n.) in
what part of the isle he abode; p. 333 (n.) in the goodliest isle of
Mardi; p. 334 (n.) the Islander regarding the fowl; p. 334 (n.) say
the Islanders; p. 337 (n.) in my native isle; p. 341 (n.) particular
family upon the island; p. 341 (n.) to the innermost wilderness of the
island; p. 341 (n.) In the wild heart of the island; p. 342 (n.)
islanders, who at times penetrated; p. 342 (n.) about the inhabited

portions of the isle; p. 343 (n.) to the opposite quarter of the
island; p. 343 (n.) high western shore of the island; p. 343 (n.) In
this lake were many islets; p. 343 (n.) its many islets greeted us
like a little Mardi; p. 343 (n.) Toward the islet of Dolzono we first
directed; p. 345 (n.) Let us depart, and visit the islet; p. 348 (n.)
and in various islands; p. 348 (n.) as Alma on the isle of Maramma;
p. 349 (n.) everything in this isle strengthens; p. 349 (n.) of what
we have seen in this island; p. 349 (n.) and in this very isle;
p. 350 (n.) Sooner will they yield to you the isles; p. 351 (n.) to
complete the circumnavigation of the island; p. 351 (n.) say these
islanders; p. 351 (n.) Dispatched round the island; p. 353 (n.)
making idols for the surrounding isles; p. 354 (n.) and work of the
sacred island; p. 355 (n.) the great island on which they were born;
p. 358 (n.) we spied a solitary Islander; p. 361 (n.) the inmost
oracle of the isle; p. 367 (n.) and the grinding islands crush the
skulls; p. 373 (n.) especially in the isles toward the East; p. 378
(n.) Pedulla, was but a little island; p. 381 (n.) and curvet in the
isles; p. 391 (n.) the language of the remote island of Bertranda;
p. 399 (n.) Jointly, they purchased an island; p. 401 (n.) the island
of Pimminees came in sight; p. 410 (n.) Taji would leave no isle
unexplored; p. 406 (n.) tour of certain islands in Mardi; p. 413 (n.)
but a rumor in the isles of the East; p. 414 (n.) must be the Isle of
Fossils; p. 416 (adj.) upon the islet's other side; p. 417 (n.) the
origin of all the isles; p. 417 (n.) wall which circumscribes the
isles; p. 420 (n.) came to Mondoldo prove isles afar; p. 422 (n.)
when we pushed from the islet; p. 435 (n.) How the isles grow and
multiply around us; p. 435 (n.) More isles! more isles; p. 439 (n.)
Of the Isle of Diranda; p. 439 (n.) to give us some little account of
the island; p. 439 (n.) nuptuals taking place in the isle; p. 439 (n.)
denude of herbage his portion of the island; p. 440 (n.) throughout
the island, by proclamation; p. 444 (n.) the whole island was in a
state of uproarious commotion; p. 452 (n.) provide for the execution
of an Islander; p. 453 (n.) The vaunt of her isles sleeps deep in the
sea; p. 453 (n.) The vaunt of her isles sleeps deep in the sea;
p. 454 (n.) chanted through all the isles; p. 461 (n.) Of the Sorcerers
in the Isle of Minda; p. 462 (n.) was an island called Minda; p. 463
(n.) the everyday affairs of the isle; p. 465 (n.) whose island of
Dominora is before us; p. 465 (n.) proprietorship of a barren islet;
p. 467 (n.) between the rulers of the most distant islands; p. 467
(n.) Porpheero, a neighboring island; p. 468 (n.) interest in those
of the remotest islands; p. 468 (n.) so with Vivenza, a distant
island; p. 468 (n.) he loved to take . . . the breadth of broad isles;
p. 469 (n.) belonging to the before-mentioned island; p. 471 (n.) and
incidentally, of other isles; p. 471 (n.) eventual existence of an
islet there; p. 471 (n.) in a distant island dwelt a man; p. 472 (n.)
Kolumbo . . . was the last island discovered; p. 473 (n.) all the
isles were proud of him; p. 476 (n.) rose and fell the isles; p. 476
(n.) But another skirmish with the isles; p. 477 (n.) concerning the
disputed islet; p. 478 (n.) the whole island a garden; p. 482 (adj.)
in proportion to the extension of the isle's naval dominion; p. 487
(n.) many aristocrats of our isles; p. 491 (n.) They sail round an
Island without landing; p. 491 (n.) along the western white cliffs of
the isle; p. 492 (n.) toward a deep green island; p. 492 (n.) Alas,
sweet isle; p. 492 (n.) Isle, whose future is in its past; p. 492 (n.)
thrice we circumnavigated the isle; p. 493 (n.) renouncing all claim
upon the isle; p. 496 (n.) The isles are Oro's; p. 499 (n.) The isles

were made to burn; p. 501 (n.) Tis a new, new isle; p. 529 (n.) and
all the isles form one table-land; p. 539 (n.) we passed a cluster of
islets; p. 539 (n.) All these isles were prolific gardens; p. 542 (n.)
She is a rainbow to the isles; p. 543 (n.) among great mountain passes
of ice-isles; p. 547 (n.) were all the isles gold globes; p. 549 (n.)
They seek through the Isles of Palms; and pass the Isles of Myrrh;
p. 549 (n.) bright islets multiplied around; p. 549 (n.) we came to
savage islands; p. 550 (n.) like glow worms, glowed the islets;
p. 551 (n.) Sweet isles of myrrh; p. 550 (n.) our prows sailed in
among these isles; p. 553 (n.) till another island vast, was reached;
p. 553 (n.) This rocky islet passed; p. 556 (n.) Part and parcel of
the Mardian isles; p. 556 (n.) we had not found these Mardian Isles;
p. 566 (n.) In my own isle of Odo; p. 567 (n.) we sailed from sea to
sea; and isle to isle; p. 569 (n.) And now for the Isle of Cripples;
p. 569 (n.) The Isle of Cripples; p. 569 (n.) the islanders of a
neighboring group had long ago; p. 569 (n.) on no account must they
quit the isle; p. 569 (n.) And to the surrounding islanders; p. 570
(n.) Soon, we drew nigh to the isle; p. 576 (n.) the origin of the
isle itself; p. 572 (n.) the people of the isle became greatly
scandalized; p. 572 (n.) embarrassment into which your island is
thrown; p. 574 (n.) lighting his trombone as we sailed from the isle;
p. 575 (n.) odds and ends of the isles; p. 578 (n.) Like pebbles,
were the isles to sink in space; p. 582 (n.) I, Bardianna, of the
island of Vamba; p. 583 (n.) to Bomblum of the island of Adda; p. 583
(n.) resident of the aforesaid island of Vamba; p. 584 (n.) being in
the isle of Vamba; p. 586 (n.) dashed every isle; p. 588 (n.) we drew
nigh to an island; p. 588 (adj.) turn our back on the isle's shadowy
side; p. 590 (n.) and swore the isle was glad; p. 590 (n.) Such the
isle, in which we tarried; p. 593 (n.) sway it o'er your isle; p. 600
(n.) that struck, all the isles shall resound; p. 610 (n.) doubtless
would depart his isle; p. 610 (n.) see you not the isle is hedged;
p. 610 (n.) I mistrust it . . . an imprisoned island; p. 611 (n.)
This isle many pass; p. 615 (n.) waving his plumed bonnet to the
isles; p. 615 (n.) across our bows, between two isles; p. 617 (n.)
Thus far, through myriad islands; had we searched; p. 618 (n.) The
isles hold thee not, thou departed; p. 622 (n.) turn aside to Serenia,
a pleasant isle; p. 623 (n.) we care not to visit thy isle; p. 623
(n.) we will e'en see this wondrous isle; p. 623 (n.) an island
blooming with bright savannas; p. 624 (n.) In this, our isle,/ Bright
flowers smile; p. 625 (n.) in all its tributary isles; p. 625 (n.)
Even in the Holy Island many are oppressed; p. 627 (n.) Tell me of
this island and its people; p. 628 (n.) this isle is all one temple
to his praise; p. 628 (n.) in the islands round about; p. 629 (n.)
Oro we love, this isle; p. 631 (n.) gilded the island round about;
p. 632 (n.) this isle is full of mysteries; p. 633 (n.) what seem
from Mardi's isles, the glow-worm stars; p. 636 (n.) Nearing the
isles, thus breathed my guide; p. 637 (n.) yet from this isle; p. 638
(n.) more isles, thou say'st, are still unvisited; p. 638 (n.) point
our prows for Odo's isle; p. 638 (n.) More isles we visited; p. 638
(n.) seek, through all the isles and stars; p. 641 (n.) rose the isle
of Hautia; p. 642 (n.) and every island a canto; p. 642 (n.) hunted
them from island to island; p. 642 (n.) to the number of islands;
p. 642 (n.) singing upon each isle; pp. 642-3 (n.) Flozella being the
lost isle in their circuit; p. 643 (n.) now ruling the isle; p. 643
(n.) was this isle . . . the last place of my search; p. 644 (n.) all
the isle, as a hanging-garden soars; p. 644 (n.) And round about the

isle; p. 645 (n.) This orchard was the frontlet of the isle; p. 649
(n.) a strait flows between this isle and Odo.

Redburn--p. 32 (n.) rounded the green south point of the island; p. 32
(n.) and passed Governor's Island; p. 33 (n.) passed the green shore
of Staten Island; p. 64 (n.) not the smallest island; p. 94 (n.) and
the Falkland Islands at the other; p. 107 (n.) in the Bay of Islands;
p. 116 (n.) in the "Sailors-Snug-Harbor" in Staten Island; p. 165 (n.)
each ship is an island; p. 178 (n.) waiting for a passage to the Isle
of Man; p. 199 (n.) marveling at the fertility of an island; p. 231
(n.) dug up on the ancient island of Capreae; p. 259 (n.) was their
own native island; p. 299 (n.) on the shores of Staten Island; p. 300
(n.) On Staten Island side; p. 300 (n.) pointing out to the
passengers, Governor's Island.

White-Jacket--p. 14 (adj.) A finer specimen of the island race of
Englishmen; p. 32 (n.) looked at Hermit Island through an Opera-glass;
p. 48 (n.) who had been shipped at the Cape De Verd islands; p. 98
(n.) land now called Terra Del Fuego was an island; p. 98 (n.) is a
cluster of small islands; p. 98 (n.) between which and the former
island are; p. 117 (n.) he had engaged at the Society Islands; p. 122
(n.) making the voyage to and from the Spice Islands; p. 159 (n.) or
Isle of the Snakes; p. 160 (adj.) But what is an insular fortress;
p. 168 (n.) that the Islanders bitterly lamented to Knox; p. 171 (n.)
a solitary, volcanic island in the harbor; p. 172 (n.) palace, square,
island, fort; p. 193 (n.) each of whom in his own floating island is
king; p. 193 (n.) as the Sultan of the Isles of Sooloo; p. 211 (n.)
lay anchored in you all these green, rocky isles; p. 211 (n.) But God
did not build on you, isles; p. 315 (n.) savoring of the Feejee
Islands; p. 323 (n.) in quest of the Solomon Islands; p. 347 (n.) the
north end of the Island of Dominica.

Moby-Dick--p. 4 (n.) Waller's Battle of the Summer Islands; p. 7 (n.)
[fish] Gathered in shoals immense, like floating islands; p. 9 (n.)
The Whale-ship Globe . . . belonged to the island of Nantucket; p. 12
(n.) there is now your insular city of the Manhattoes, belted round
by wharves as Indian isles by coral reefs; p. 16 (adj.) the wild and
distant seas where he rolled his island bulk; p. 17 (n.) there was a
fine boisterous something about everything connected with that famous
old island; p. 39 (n.) and there these silent islands of men and
women sat; p. 39 (n.) Near the Isle of Desolation, off Patagonia;
p. 43 (n.) there floated a little isle of sunlight; p. 57 (n.) He at
once resolved to accompany me to that island; p. 59 (n.) The people
of his island of Kokovoko; p. 62 (n.) they [people] are . . . made an
utter island of by the ocean; pp. 96-7 (n.) If ye touch at the islands,
Mr. Flask, beware of fornication; p. 100 (n.) by the beaches of
unrecorded javelin islands; p. 100 (n.) The uncounted isles of all
Polynesia confess the same truth; p. 108 (n.) Islanders seem to make
the best whalemen; p. 108 (n.) An Anacharsis Clootz deputation from
all the isles of the sea; p. 134 (adj.) How could he forget that in
his Island days; p. 162 (n.) the calculating people of that prudent
isle; p. 209 (n.) They contain round archipelagoes of romantic isles;
p. 210 (adj.) pointing her prow for her island haven; p. 318 (n.)
stretch the long islands of Sumatra, Java, Bally, and Timor; p. 318
(n.) lurking among the low-shaded cove and islets of Sumatra; p. 323
(n.) our beset boat was like a ship mobbed by ice-isles; p. 384 (n.)

and all the Isles of the sea combined; p. 393 (n.) representing the
long eastern coasts of the Japanese islands; p. 396 (n.) not only do
they believe that the stars are isles; p. 445 (n.) in drawing nigh to
some barbarous isle.

ISTHMUS. A narrow neck of land which joins a peninsula to its continent,
or two islands together, or two peninsulas, without reference to size;
(Smyth)

> Omoo--p. 65 (n.) connected by a low, narrow isthmus.

> White-Jacket--p. 98 (n.) beholding . . . from the Isthmus of Darien;
> p. 122 (n.) shall have penetrated the Isthmus of Darien.

JIB. A large triangular sail, set on a stay, forward. The jib is a sail
of great command with any side wind, in turning her head to leeward.
(Smyth). --Flying-jib sets outside of the jib.--Jib-boom: the boom,
rigged out beyond the bowsprit, to which the tack of the jib is lashed.
(Dana)

> Omoo--p. 20 (adj.) to the end of the flying jib boom; p. 35 (adj.)
> sitting right ahead of our jib boom; p. 60 (n.) our flying jib-boom
> snapped off; p. 69 (n.) with her jib-boom pointing out; p. 73 (n.)
> haul up the courses; run down the jib; p. 90 (n.) the jib-sheets,
> lashed the stays; p. 95 (n.) capsized from the sails' "jibing";
> p. 97 (n.) ordering a pull at the jib-halyards.

> Mardi--p. 14 (n.) or jib-boom-end; p. 32 (n.) into a handy boom for
> the jib; p. 57 (n.) the foresail, main sail and jib being set; p. 57
> (n.) jib was hoisted.

> Redburn--p. 93 (adj.) one of our flying-jib guys jerked out; p. 93
> (n.) we heard our jib-boom thumping; p. 93 (n.) with another jib-boom
> we had; p. 93 (adv.) coming together, jib-boom-and-jib-boom; p. 97
> (n.) along to the end of the jib-boom; p. 171 (n.) lost overboard
> from the flying-jib-boom; p. 300 (n.) bringing our jib-boom over one
> of the forts.

> White-Jacket--p. 105 (n.) flying-jib taking quick leave; p. 105 (n.)
> the flying-jib was swept into the air; p. 271 (n.) Jib-boom, there;
> p. 272 (n.) the look-out on the jib-boom was hailed.

> Moby-Dick--p. 143 (n.) he fan-tails like a split jib in a squall;
> p. 151 (n.) Split jibs! tear yourselves; p. 154 (n.) there goes the
> jib-stay; p. 339 (n.) All their noses upwardly projected from their
> faces like so many jib-booms.

JUNK. The Chinese junk is the largest vessel built by that nation, and
at one period exceeding in tonnage any war-vessels then possessed by
England. The extreme beam is one-third from the stern; it shows no stem.
The bow on deck is square, over which the anchors slide fore and aft.
Having no keel, and being very full at the stern, a huge rudder is
suspended, which at sea is lowered below the depth of the bottom. The

masts are immense, in one piece. The cane sails are lug and heavy. The
hull is divided into water-tight compartments, like tanks.--Junk is also
any remnants or pieces of old cable, or condemned rope, cut into small
portions for the use of making points, mats, swabs, gaskets, sinnot,
oakum, and the like. (Smyth)

Mardi--p. 482 (n.) Emperor of Japan, had a dragon-beaked junk.

Redburn--p. 114 (n.) odds and ends of old rigging called "junk";
p. 115 (n.) This "junk" is bought at the junk shops along the
wharves.

Moby-Dick--p. 67 (n.) square-toed luggers, mountainous Japanese
junks; p. 248 (n.) four or five laborers . . . will draw a bulky
frighted junk.

KEEL. The lowest and principal timber of a vessel, running fore-and-aft
its whole length, and supporting the whole frame. It is composed of
several pieces, placed lengthwise, and scarfed and bolted together.
(Dana).—To keel, when a ship rolls on her keel. (Smyth)

Omoo--p. 7 (n.) at right angles to the keel; p. 90 (n.) the Julia,
with her short keel; p. 98 (n.) ships now and then grate their keels.

Mardi--p. 4 (n.) every time her keel crossed; p. 17 (n.) to his
utmost keel; p. 19 (n.) under the keel; p. 55 (n.) one was under our
keel; p. 103 (n.) racing along close to the keel; p. 104 (n.) some
ship's keel crossing his road; p. 122 (n.) which shot from about our
keel; p. 141 (n.) our keel left no track; p. 200 (adj.) claw-keeled,
dragon-prowed crafts; p. 201 (v.) our canoes keeled the bottom;
p. 306 (adj.) the same double-keeled craft; p. 367 (n.) with their
Himmaleh keels; p. 469 (n.) that all . . . prowling keels . . . were
invaders; p. 469 (adj.) fitting out several double-keeled canoes;
p. 482 (n.) so swift was its keel; p. 483 (n.) the dry-rot may be
eating into its keel; p. 531 (n.) our keels grated the beach; p. 551
(n.) Whitherward rush . . . ten thousand keels; p. 554 (n.) our keels
sped eastward; p. 555 (n.) we seekers now curved round our keels;
p. 586 (n.) chase the flying Malay keels; p. 589 (v.) as we keeled
the beach; p. 618 (n.) the rush of the waves by our keels; p. 644
(n.) and keels of canoes.

Redburn--p. 163 (n.) the keels of the ships inclosed by the quays;
p. 244 (n.) rooted in the ship's keel; p. 296 (n.) as much a fixture
as the vessel's keel.

White-Jacket--p. 34 (n.) that divides it in two, like a keel; p. 45
(n.) whereunto the moldering keels of shipwrecked vessels; p. 106 (n.)
helm and galvanized keel were . . . feverish; p. 121 (n.) take the
measure of the ship's entire keel; p. 211 (n.) of all the Danish
keels of the Vikings; p. 265 (adj.) was accounted the fleetest keeled
craft; p. 371 (n.) put a piece of a keel on the fire; p. 371 (n.) it
knocks the false keel right off; p. 298 (n.) of all the keels of a
Dutch Admiral; p. 348 (n.) nail my flag to the keel, if there was no
other place; p. 370 (n.) a punishment . . . called keel-hauling;
p. 370 (n.) is even worse than keel-hauling; p. 374 (n.) both
clinging to one keel.

Moby-Dick--p. 51 (n.) can never shake from this sure Keel of the
Ages; p. 97 (n.) one touch of land though it but graze the keel;
p. 297 (n.) the Pequod's keels had shot by the three German boats
last lowered; p. 299 (n.) sailed over by the three flying keels;
p. 308 (n.) as though diligently seeking to insure a crop of hair
from the craft's bald keel; p. 322 (n.) did the herd . . . become
notified of the three keels that were after them; p. 337 (v.) I
thought they would keel up before long; p. 393 (n.) my conscience is
in this ship's keel; p. 433 (adj.) this fourth boat--the swiftest
keeled of all; p. 439 (n.) all rib and keel was solid Ahab; p. 454
(n.) for by live-oaks! my spine's a keel; p. 455 (n.) both balanced
and directed by the long central keel; p. 455 (n.) to that one fatal
goal which Ahab their one lord and keel did point to; p. 461 (adj.)
something so unchangeable, and full as strong, blow my keeled soul
along; p. 468 (n.) ye three unsurrendered spires of mine; thou
uncracked keel.

KELP. Marine growth that accumulates on rocks. It is valuable in the
manufacture of iodine. It is also a warning of rocks beneath. (Bradford)

Typee--p. 113 (n.) filled with different descriptions of kelp.

Mardi--p. 283 (n.) sporting musky girdles of sea-kelp.

Moby-Dick--p. 45 (adj.) we sound with him to the kelpy bottom of the
waters.

KELSON. A timber placed over the keel on the floor-timbers, and running
parallel with it. (Dana's spelling is "keelson.")

Moby-Dick--p. 51 (n.) Is not the main-truck higher than the kelson is
low; p. 364 (n.) drop it half way down to the kelson.

KENTLEDGE. Pigs of iron cast for permanent ballast, laid over the
kelson-plates. (Smyth)

Omoo--p. 45 (n.) some "kentlege" [sic] being placed at the feet
instead of shot.

Moby-Dick--p.319 (n.) She is ballasted . . . not altogether with
unusable pig-lead and kentledge.

KNIGHT-HEADS. Two large oak timbers, one on each side of the stern,
rising up sufficiently above it to support the bowsprit, which is fixed
between them. Also, formerly, in many merchant ships, two strong frames
of timber fixed on the main-deck, a little behind the fore-mast, which
supported the ends of the windlass. (Smyth)

Typee--p. 10 (n.) leaped up between the knight-heads.

Omoo--p. 100 (n.) jumping up between the knight-heads.

Redburn--p. 268 (n.) laid before her between the knight-heads; p. 268 (n.) if she went between the knight-heads again with her book.

Moby-Dick--p. 412 (n.) Standing between the knight-heads.

KNOT. A division on the long line, bearing a similar proportion to a mile. Indeed, in nautical parlance, the words "knot" and "mile" are synonymous, alluding to the geographical mile of 60' to a degree of latitude. (Smyth)

Mardi--p. 51 (n.) the loose estimation of the knots; p. 54 (n.) hardly three knots an hour; p. 108 (n.) computation of the knots run hourly; p. 461 (n.) never sailed faster than three knots.

KRAKEN. The fictitious sea-monster of Norway. (Smyth)

Redburn--p. 96 (n.) regular krakens, that made it high tide.

LAGOON. An inland broad expanse of salt water, usually shallow, and connected with the sea by one or more channels, or washes over the reef. (Smyth)

Omoo--p. 62 (n.) surrounding a smooth lagoon; p. 62 (n.) Some of the lagoons; p. 62 (n.) Other lagoons still; p. 63 (n.) The oysters are found in the lagoons; p. 64 (n.) Within, nestled the still, blue lagoon.

Mardi--p. 69 (n.) within a deep, smooth, circular lagoon; p. 70 (n.) beach of the lagoon; p. 161 (n.) the still, green waters of the wide lagoon; p. 162 (n.) like a gull over a smooth lagoon; p. 167 (n.) urging us over the lagoon; p. 178 (n.) how tranquil the wide lagoon; p. 189 (n.) gazing intently into the lagoon; p. 193 (n.) Fairy bower in the fair lagoon; p. 196 (n.) the tour of the lagoon; p. 198 (n.) a rude map of the lagoon; p. 199 (n.) the lagoon within; p. 200 (n.) As we gained the open lagoon; p. 201 (n.) with the green of the lagoon; p. 209 (n.) a cavernous shadow upon the lagoon beneath; p. 216 (n.) crossing the lagoon; p. 216 (n.) but throughout the lagoon; p. 216 (n.) bursting into the lagoon; p. 217 (n.) currents here ruffling the lagoon; p. 217 (n.) beneath that of the lagoon; p. 262 (n.) in a remote corner of the lagoon; p. 265 (n.) the lagoon a calm; p. 272 (n.) here and there fell into the lagoon; p. 273 (n.) hotly into the lagoon; p. 275 (n.) remove Ohonoo to the center of the lagoon; p. 286 (n.) it radiated far out upon the lagoon; p. 288 (n.) the salt waters of the lagoon; p. 313 (n.) glided across the lagoon; p. 317 (n.) into the paddock of the lagoon; p. 325 (n.) one fertile waste in the lagoon; p. 334 (n.) swarming throughout the lagoon; p. 343 (n.) but a portion of the smooth lagoon; p. 351 (n.) running out into the lagoon; p. 369 (n.) proceeded with the tour of the lagoon; p. 399 (n.) toward the extreme west of the lagoon; p. 401 (n.) fine breezy air of the open lagoon; p. 408 (n.) from various quarters of the lagoon; p. 414 (n.) far and near illuminating the lagoon; p. 415 (n.) gradually washing into the lagoon; p. 415 (n.) from the lower-most vaults of the lagoon; p. 424 (n.) becalming the water of the wide lagoon;

p. 432 (n.) the lagoon, here and there, seemed on fire; p. 453 (n.)
sunk to the bottom of the lagoon; p. 453 (n.) Lachrymose riverlets,
and inconsolable lagoons; p. 458 (n.) in the tides of the lagoon;
p. 465 (n.) in a very remote quarter of the lagoon; p. 467 (n.)
situated to the north of the lagoon; p. 469 (n.) swore that the
entire lagoon was his; p. 469 (n.) deeming the lagoon their old
monarch's . . . domain; p. 469 (n.) meeting upon the broad lagoon
certain canoes; p. 471 (n.) detached shelf of coral in the lagoon;
p. 482 (n.) did King Bello stand up and wed with the lagoon; p. 482
(n.) in due time embraced the entire lagoon; p. 497 (n.) gaining the
more open lagoon; p. 498 (n.) Hitherto the lagoon had been smooth;
p. 511 (n.) currents, one from over the lagoon; p. 512 (n.) a lofty
ridge, jutting out into the lagoon; p. 517 (n.) Across this wide
lagoon he casts his serpent eyes; p. 523 (n.) till at length, from
over the lagoon; p. 536 (n.) abounding at the bottom of the lagoon;
p. 549 (n.) due west, across the blue lagoon; p. 553 (n.) we launched
upon the calm lagoon; p. 556 (n.) Morning dawned upon the same mild,
blue lagoon; p. 558 (n.) and the lagoon all tossed with white, flying
manes; p. 562 (n.) The lagoon was calm, as we landed; p. 567 (n.) the
lagoon, still, as a prairie of an August moon; p. 568 (n.) a dark
form bounded into the lagoon; p. 575 (n.) the abounding lagoon being
its two-thirds; p. 618 (n.) had fallen into the lagoon; p. 642 (n.)
all round the lagoon; p. 649 (n.) which sped far out into the lagoon;
p. 654 (n.) the Lagoon, black with the still shadows of the mountains.

LANDSMAN, LAND-LUBBER. Landsman: the rating formerly of those on board
a ship who had never been at sea, and who were usually stationed among
the waisters or after-guard. Some of those used to small craft are more
ready about the decks than in going aloft. The rating is now Second-
class Ordinary. Land-Lubber: a useless long-shorer; a vagrant stroller;
Applied by sailors to the mass of landsmen, especially those without
employment. (Smyth)

Omoo--p. 52 (n.) joined the ship as a landsman; p. 52 (n.) lazy,
good-for-nothing land-lubber; p. 53 (n.) so the land-lubber, afraid
to refuse; p. 53 (adj.) The land-lubber's spirits often sink. p. 53
(n.) Alas! I say again, for the land-lubber at sea; p. 53 (n.) of all
land-lubbers, the most lubbery; p. 54 (n.) he shipped as landsman
aboard the Julia; p. 54 (n.) seats himself beside the land-lubber;
p. 57 (n.) Do you deny it, you lubber; p. 78 (n.) Land-lubber that he
was; p. 104 (n.) to the poor land-lubber; p. 106 (n.) a great lubber
of a fellow; p. 107 (adj.) it was a lubbery piece of business
throughout; p. 110 (n.) while the landsmen; p. 120 (n.) well was it
for the land-lubber.

Redburn--p. 60 (n.) a green-hand, a landsman on his first voyage;
p. 62 (n.) superiority to greenhorns and landsmen; p. 65 (n.) for an
ignoramus and a land-lubber; p. 79 (n.) the last person . . . is a
landsman; p. 108 (adj./n.) any lubberly landsman of a passenger;
p. 257 (n.) Few landsmen can imagine; p. 302 (n.) like royal
landsmen, we were masters.

White-Jacket--p. 10 (n.) they are composed chiefly of landsmen; p. 38
(n.) may seem strange to those landsmen; p. 53 (n.) forlorn
individuals, shipping as landsmen; p. 92 (n.) Police-officers,

Soldiers, Landsmen generally; p. 109 (n.) But, sailor or landsman,
there is some sort; p. 114 (n.) Any American landsman may hope to
become; p. 121 (n.) Pull--pull! you lazy lubbers; p. 143 (n.) hardly
credible to landsmen; p. 145 (n.) What would landsmen think; p. 216
(n.) one of those wretched landsmen; p. 222 (n.) employ the eyes,
tongues, and thoughts of landsmen; p. 231 (n.) however salutary they
may appear to landsmen; p. 231 (n.) to be fully comprehended by
landsmen; p. 231 (n.) what does this landsman know; p. 276 (n.) For
any landsman to have beheld; p. 276 (n.) that landsman would have
deemed Captain Claret; p. 300 (n.) language which no landsman would
ever hearken to; p. 303 (n.) We moderns, who may be landsmen; p. 309
(n.) take the best specimen of a seaman for a landsman; p. 367 (n.)
Had he been a mere landsman; p. 369 (n.) most landsmen will probably
regard; p. 369 (n.) to what landsmen would deem excessive cruelties;
p. 375 (n.) can hardly be imagined by landsmen; p. 376 (n.) The
landsman who has neither read; p. 376 (n.) let that landsman guardedly
remain; p. 380 (n.) her mustering a crowd of landsmen; p. 381 (n.)
the crews . . . consisted of landsmen and boys; p. 382 (n.) these
"dock-lopers" of landsmen; p. 382 (n.) hopelessly depraving the
volunteer landsmen; p. 390 (n.) no longer a sailor, but a landsman.

Moby-Dick--p. 12 (n.) But these are all landsmen; p. 60 (adj.) the
jeering glances of the passengers, a lubber-like assembly; p. 98 (n.)
somehow come to be regarded among landsmen as . . . unpoetical and
disreputable; p. 98 (n.) I am all anxiety to convince ye, ye landsmen,
of the injustice hereby done; p. 117 (n.) Many are the men . . .
landsmen and seamen; p. 119 (n.) all the fish familiar to landsmen;
p. 124 (n.) has furnished a proverb to landsmen; p. 191 (n.) To a
landsman, no whale . . . would have been visible; p. 253 (adj.) by
crawling through the lubber's hole; p. 255 (n.) landsmen seem to
regard the eating of him with abhorrence; p. 298 (n.) while this
clumsy lubber was striving to free his white-ash; p. 364 (n.)
abjectly reduced to a clumsy landsman again; p. 376 (adj.) to make
him at all budge to any landsman's imagination.

LANYARD. A rope rove through dead-eyes for setting up rigging. Also, a
rope made fast to anything to secure it, or as a handle, is sometimes
called a lanyard. (Dana)

Omoo--p. 292 (n.) and hack away the lanyards of the rigging.

LARBOARD. The left side of a ship, when the spectator's face is towards
the bow. The Italians derive starboard from questa borda, "this side,"
and larboard from quella borda, "that side"; abbreviated sta borda and la
borda. Their resemblance caused so many mistakes that, by order of the
admiralty, larboard is now thrown overboard, and port substituted. (Smyth)

Typee--p. 36 (n.) while the poor larboarders shipped their oars.

Omoo--p. 48 (adj.) and the other for the larboard; p. 51 (adj.) braced
sharp up on the larboard tack; p. 59 (adj.) was planted on the
larboard side of the forecastle.

Mardi--p. 52 (adv.) to starboard or larboard.

Redburn--p. 38 (adj.) He is Put into the Larboard Watch; p. 39 (adj.) that is the larboard watch; p. 92 (adj.) It was the larboard watch's turn.

White-Jacket--p. 8 (adj.) watches--starboard and larboard; p. 9 (adj.) men of each watch--starboard and larboard; p. 9 (adj.) They relieve the whole Larboard Watch of top-men; p. 62 (adj.) On the Larboard hand was Mess No. 31; p. 83 (adj.) on the larboard side of the gun-deck; p. 130 (adj.) first from the larboard side; p. 172 (adj.) for the whole larboard side is kept clear; p. 231 (n.) He does not know starboard from larboard.

Moby-Dick--p. 44 (adv./adj.) side away to larboard--larboard gangway to starboard; p. 63 (n.) [land direction] till we opened a white church to the larboard.

LAUNCH. The largest or long-boat of a ship of war. (Smyth)

White-Jacket--p. 160 (n.) carried a very large boat . . . called a launch; p. 161 (n.) The launch was manned by the old Tritons; p. 175 (n.) the launch would come alongside with water-casks; p. 371 (n.) the launch--the largest of the boats.

LAY. When a man is paid in proportion to the success of the voyage, instead of by the month. This is common in whalers. (Smyth)

Omoo--p. 51 (n.) The men were shipped "by the lay."

Moby-Dick--p. 73 (n.) received certain shares of the profits called lays; p. 73 (n.) these lays were proportioned to the degree of importance; p. 73 (n.) my own lay would not be very large; p. 73 (n.) was what they call a rather long lay: p. 74 (n.) I thought that the 275th lay would be about the fair thing; p. 74 (v./n.) well, old Bildad, you are determined that I, for one, shall not lay up many lays here below; p. 84 (n.) Look ye, Quohog, we'll give ye the ninetieth lay.

LEE. The side opposite to that from which the wind is blowing; as, if a vessel has the wind on her port side, that side will be the weather, and the starboard will be the lee side.--A-lee, the position of the helm when its tiller is borne over to the lee-side of the ship, in order to go about or put her head to windward. (Smyth).--Leeward, the lee side. In a direction opposite to that from which the wind blows, which is called windward. The opposite of lee is weather, and of leeward is windward; the two first being adjectives. (Dana)

Omoo--p. 63 (adj.) settled among the leeward islands; p. 89 (n.) under the lee of the bulwarks; p. 89 (adv.) flew to leeward, thus; p. 90 (adj.) Let go the leeward fore-brace; p. 94 (adv.) we remained a little to leeward; p. 96 (adv.) the boat, drifting fast to leeward; p. 98 (adj.) the leeward entrance is preferred; p. 287 (adj.) the leeward islands of the group.

Mardi--p. 4 (n.) to leeward; p. 17 (n.) under our lee; p. 26 (n.)
under the lee; p. 27 (adj.) from the ship's lee side; p. 27 (adv.)
brought it to leeward; p. 28 (adv.) with prow to leeward; p. 28 (adv.)
dead to leeward; p. 30 (adv.) far to leeward; p. 74 (adv.) lashed the
tiller alee; p. 118 (adv.) for to leeward was soon; p. 206 (adv.)
blown far to leeward.

Redburn--p. 70 (n.) I ran to the lee-scuppers where it fell; p. 103
(n.) there was a wreck on the lee-beam; p. 103 (n.) ran into it with
the lee-roll; p. 112 (n.) a thorough washing in the lee-scuppers;
p. 117 (n.) bring her by the lee; p. 141 (n.) under the lee of the
rock; p. 174 (n.) they make leeway at a sad rate; p. 262 (n.) under
the lee of the spanker; p. 277 (n.) Under the lee of the Long-Boat;
p. 277 (n.) come you with me under the lee of the long-boat; p. 278
(n.) under the tarry lee of our long-boat; p. 286 (adj.) to shun the
leeward side of the vessel; p. 289 (adv.) lamentations were driven to
leeward.

White-Jacket--p. 21 (adv.) invariably shrunk over to leeward; p. 28
(adj.) conveys the feeling of the lee bulwarks; p. 97 (n.) or is
brought by the lee; p. 105 (adj.) but the lee carronades on the
quarter-deck; p. 105 (adv.) with every lurch to leeward; p. 108 (adv.)
scarcely hear the man to lee-ward; p. 108 (n.) clinging to the lee-
yard-arm; p. 118 (adj.) with us, upon the extreme leeward side;
p. 111 (n.) under the enticing lee of his decanter; p. 116 (n.)
simultaneously with a violent lee-roll; p. 123 (n.) come under the
lee of my white jacket; p. 130 (n.) rapidly drifted away to leeward;
p. 152 (n.) three points off our lee-bow; p. 160 (n.) close under the
lee of that . . . mass of rock; p. 238 (n.) having also rolled off to
leeward; p. 270 (adj.) gliding on the leeward side; p. 275 (n.) were
repeatedly summoned into the lee waist; p. 276 (adj.) to have beheld
him in the lee waist; p. 280 (n.) was the opening of the lee-gangway;
p. 341 (adj.) assembled in the lee waist; p. 347 (n.) becalmed under
the lee of the land; p. 384 (n.) under the lee of the booms; p. 389
(n.) swab up the lee-scuppers.

Moby-Dick--p. 9 (adj.) Three points off the lee bow, sir; p. 13 (n.)
loitering under the shady lee of yonder warehouses will not suffice;
p. 43 (adj.) ship beating against a terrible storm off a lee coast;
p. 75 (n.) the squall's gone off to leeward; p. 97 (adj.) storm-
tossed ship, that miserably drives along the leeward land; p. 97 (n.)
than to be ingloriously dashed upon the lee; p. 130 (adj.) sitting in
the lee quarter-boat; p. 186 (n.) on the lee-beam, about two miles
off; p. 256 (adv.) lash the helm a'lee; p. 354 (n.) the fatal
contingency of being brought to the lee; p. 396 (n.) uncertain
steering, and much lee-way adown the dim ages; p. 414 (n.) yonder, to
windward, all is blackness of doom; but to leeward, homeward; p. 418
(adj.) and the lee lift is half-stranded; p. 421 (n.) the shivering
remnants . . . went eddying away to leeward; p. 447 (n.) with rippling
swiftness, shooting to leeward; p. 448 (n.) towards the dim blue
spaces and wide wooing vacancies to leeward.

LEECH. A blood-sucker; an animal of the genus Hirudo, a species of
aquatic worm, which is used in the medical art for topical bleeding.
(Webster)

Mardi--p. 181 (n.) like so many leeches.

LEVIATHAN.   1. An aquatic animal, described in the book of Job, ch. xii,
and mentioned in other passages of the Scripture. In Isaiah, it is called
the crooked serpent. It is not agreed what animal is intended by the
writers, whether the crocodile, the whale, or a species of serpent.
2. The whale, or a great whale.--Milton. (Webster)

Omoo--p. 289 (n.) All alone in the harbor lay the good ship Leviathan;
p. 290 (n.) The appearance of the Leviathan herself [a ship]; p. 296
(n.) occupied by three sailors from the Leviathan; p. 299 (n.) the
crew of the Leviathan made so prodigious a tumult; p. 312 (n.) the
Leviathan was not the craft to our mind; p. 312 (adj.) we had rather
avoided the Leviathan's men; p. 313 (n.) when darted by the men of
the Leviathan; p. 315 (n.) as the Leviathan was so comfortable a craft.

Mardi--p. 32 (n.) also employed in hunting the leviathan; p. 42 (n.)
assailing leviathan himself; p. 42 (n.) if leviathan gets but one
sweep; p. 122 (n.) the Leviathans might destroy us; p. 289 (n.) that
the leviathan this day harpooned.

Redburn--p. 100 (n.) those who hunt the leviathan.

Moby-Dick--p. i (n.) There Leviathan,/ Hugest of living creatures . . .
sleeps or swims; p. 2 (n.) what has been promiscuously said, thought,
fancied and sung of Leviathan; p. 2 (n.) Leviathan maketh a path to
shine after him; p. 2 (n.) there is that Leviathan whom thou hast
made to play therein; p. 2 (n.) the Lord . . . shall punish Leviathan
the piercing serpent, even Leviathan that crooked serpent; p. 3 (n.)
if it is not Leviathan dsecribed by the noble prophet Moses; p. 3 (n.)
the great Leviathan that maketh the seas to seethe like a boiling pan;
p. 4 (n.) by art is created that great Leviathan, called a
Commonwealth; p. 4 (n.) That sea beast/ Leviathan, which God of all
his works/ Created hugest; p. 4 (n.) There Leviathan,/ Hugest of
living creatures . . . sleeps or swims; p. 4 (n.) lie/ The huge
Leviathans to attend their prey; p. 7 (n.) from dread Leviathan/ To
insect millions peopling every wave; p. 17 (n.) first sally out in
canoes to give chase to the Leviathan; p. 20 (n.) does it not bear a
faint resemblance to a gigantic fish . . . even the great Leviathan
himself; p. 72 (adj.) spilled tuns upon tuns of leviathan gore;
p. 100 (n.) who wrote the first account of our leviathan; p. 106 (n.)
seemed to think that the great Leviathans had personally and
hereditarily affronted him; p. 114 (n.) a great lord of Leviathans
was Ahab; p. 116 (n.) ere the Pequod's weedy hull rolls side by side
with the barnacled hulls of the Leviathan; p. 116 (adj.) the more
special leviathanic revelations and allusions; p. 118 (adj.)
Reference to nearly all the leviathanic allusions; p. 118 (n.) to
hook the nose of this leviathan; p. 119 (n.) with the Leviathan;
p. 119 (adj.) I do by no means exclude from the leviathanic
brotherhood; p. 120 (n.) this is the most venerable of the leviathans;
p. 122 (n.) this leviathan seems the banished and unconquerable Cain;
p. 122 (n.) to attempt a clear classification of the leviathan;
p. 123 (n.) descend into the bowels of the various leviathans; p. 124
(n.) possessing all the grand distinctive features of the leviathan;
p. 127 (n.) suspecting them for mere sounds, full of Leviathanism,

but signifying nothing; p. 157 (n.) as fearfully distinguished from all other species of the leviathan; p. 157 (n.) whose sole knowledge of the leviathan is restricted; p. 171 (n.) fully acquainted with the ways of the leviathans; p. 177 (n.) thou famed leviathan, scarred like an iceberg; p. 178 (n.) carried down to the bottom of the sea by the sounding leviathan; p. 226 (n.) let us glance at those pictures of leviathan purporting to be sober; p. 227 (n.) pictures of the different species of the Leviathan; p. 227 (n.) the living Leviathan has never yet fairly floated himself for his portrait; p. 228 (n.) difference in contour between a young sucking whale and a full-grown Platonian Leviathan; p. 228 (adj.) could be inferred from any leviathan's articulated bones; p. 228 (n.) the great Leviathan is that one creature in the world which must remain unpainted to the last; p. 230 (n.) all the while the thick-lipped leviathan is rushing through the deep; p. 233 (n.) have I chased Leviathan round and round the Pole; p. 249 (n.) sharks, swarming round the dead leviathan; p. 262 (n.) previous to completely stripping the body of the leviathan; p. 275 (n.) of having to do with so ignoble a leviathan; p. 291 (n.) To scan the lines of his face, or feel the bumps on the head of this Leviathan; p. 295 (adj.) he slewed round his boat and made after the leviathan lamp-feeders; p. 296 (n.) it is not customary for such venerable leviathans to be at all social; p. 299 (n.) this it is that often torments the Leviathan into soon rising again; p. 300 (n.) by three such thin threads the great Leviathan was suspended like the big weight to at eight day clock; p. 300 (n.) Leviathan had run his head under the mountains of the sea; p. 304 (n.) as Leviathan was in the very act of carrying her off; p. 304 (n.) inasmuch as this Leviathan was slain at the very first dart; p. 311 (n.) For not by hook or by net could this vast leviathan be caught; p. 315 (adj.) the Leviathan's tail acts in a different manner; p. 316 (n.) in the ordinary floating posture of the leviathan; p. 317 (adj.) as the mightiest elephant is but a terrier to Leviathan, so, compared with Leviathan's tail, his trunk is but the stalk of a lily; p. 322 (n.) Had these leviathans been but a flock of simple sheep; p. 326 (n.) Starbuck saw long coils of the umbilical cord of Madame Leviathan; p. 326 (adj.) We saw young Leviathan amours in the deep; p. 328 (adj.) while he is always of the largest leviathanic proportion; p. 329 (n.) Should any unwarrantably pert young Leviathan coming that way; p. 330 (n.) warning each young Leviathan from his amorous errors; p. 330 (n.) a lone whale--as a solitary Leviathan is called; p. 330 (n.) the young males . . . are by far the most pugnacious of all Leviathans; p. 336 (n.) In vain it was to rake for Ambergriese in the paunch of this Leviathan; p. 350 (n.) those inferior souls who hunt that ignoble Leviathan; p. 350 (adj.) cut from the tapering part of Leviathan's tail; p. 356 (n.) how the great leviathan is afar off descried; p. 357 (n.) the entire ship seems great leviathan himself; p. 369 (n.) had in large fleets pursued that Leviathan; p. 371 (adj.) During my researches in the Leviathanic histories; p. 373 (n.) discoursing upon the joists and beams; the rafters, ridge-pole, sleepers, and under-pinnings, making up the framework of leviathan; p. 375 (adj.) There is a Leviathanic Museum, they tell me, in Hull, England; p. 378 (n.) Applied to any other creature than the Leviathan; p. 378 (n.) But where Leviathan is the text, the case is altered; p. 380 (adj.) to some utterly unknown Leviathanic species; p. 380 (adj.) among these mighty Leviathan skeletons, skulls, tusks, jaws; p. 380 (n.) affinities of the annihilated ante-chronical Leviathans; p. 380 (n.) who can

show a pedigree like Leviathan; p. 381 (n.) Gliding above them, old
Leviathan swam as of yore; p. 381 (n.) Inasmuch, then as this
Leviathan comes floundering down upon us; p. 383 (n.) whether
Leviathan can long endure so wide a chase; p. 383 (n.) peremptorily
forbids so inglorious an end to the Leviathan; p. 383 (n.) these
Leviathans; in small pods, were encountered much oftener; p. 384 (n.)
concerning these last mentioned Leviathans; p. 442 (n.) in the
bottomless blue, rushed mighty leviathans; p. 454 (n.) as the mighty
iron Leviathan of the modern railway is so familiarly known in its
every pace; p. 454 (n.) these Nantucketers time that other Leviathan
of the deep.

LIGHTHOUSE. A sort of tower, erected upon a headland, islet, or rock,
whose lights may be seen at a great distance from the land to warn
shipping of their approach to these dangers. (Smyth)

   Redburn--p. 6 (n.) a tumble-down gray lighthouse surmounting it;
   p. 126 (n.) might have been a fort, or a light-house.

   White-Jacket--p. 45 (adj.) beware of . . . lonely light-house men;
   p. 45 (n.) people living in arsenals and light-houses.

   Moby-Dick--p. 62 (n.) more lonely than the Eddystone lighthouse.

LINER. A line-of-battle ship. Also, a designation of such packet or
passenger ships as trade periodically and regularly to and from ports
beyond sea, in contradistinction to chance vessels. Also, a term applied
by seamen to men-of-war and to their crews. (Smyth)

   Redburn--p. 83 (n.) of the captain of a London liner; p. 106 (n.) was
   not a Liverpool liner; p. 106 (n.) vessels which are neither liners
   nor regular traders; p. 106 (n.) that the Highlander was not a liner;
   p. 106 (n.) for aboard of those liners; p. 107 (n.) So, not being a
   liner; p. 166 (n.) perhaps, a magnificent New York liner.

LIQUID. A fluid or flowing substance; a substance whose parts change
their relative position on the slightest pressure, and which flows on an
inclined plane; as water, wine, milk &c. (Webster)

   Mardi--p. 85 (adj.) far sloping down the liquid sphere.

LOBSTER. A well-known marine crustacean, Astacus marinus. (Smyth)

   Mardi--p. 507 (n.) witness the lobster and the turtle; p. 507 (n.) I
   think of him more of a lobster; p. 507 (n.) I am a lobster; p. 573
   (n.) the second, lobsters, cuttle-fish, crabs.

LUGGER. A small vessel with quadrilateral or four-cornered cut sails,
set fore-and-aft, and may have two or three masts. (Smyth)

   Moby-Dick--p. 67 (n.) square-toed luggers; mountainous Japanese junks.

MACKEREL. The Scomber vulgaris, a well-known sea-fish. (Smyth)

Mardi--p. 507 (n.) I am a . . . mackerel.

Moby-Dick--p. 62 (n.) they waded out with nets for mackerel.

MAELSTROM. A famous whirlpool in the Arctic Ocean on the west coast of
Norway, formerly supposed to suck in and destroy all vessels within a
long radius. Also, a great whirlpool. (OED)

Moby-Dick--p. 222 (n.) The whale rushed round in a sudden maelstrom;
p. 457 (n.) diving down into the sea, disappeared in a boiling
maelstrom, in which, for a space, the odorous cedar chips of the
wrecks danced round and round, like the grated nutmeg in a swiftly
stirred bowl of punch.

MAIN. Figuratively, the ocean. (Smyth)

Typee--p. 35 (n.) preserved his go-ashore traps for the Spanish main.

Omoo--p. 14 (n.) in the lawless ports of the Spanish Main; p. 69 (n.)
throwing down the main-braces.

Mardi--p. 113 (n.) hidden away in the main-top; p. 113 (n.) chain
plates under the starboard main-channel; p. 511 (n.) From cape to
cape, this whole main we see.

Redburn--p. 24 (n.) who was calking [sic] down the main-hatches.

White-Jacket--p. 77 (n.) [stars] sailing in heaven's blue, as we on
the azure main.

Moby-Dick--p. 4 (n.) Like as the wounded whale to shore flies thro'
the maine; p. 203 (adv.) the wind now rising amain; p. 470 (n.) I
floated on a soft and dirge-like main.

MAN-OF-WAR. Any vessel in the royal navy.--Man-of-war's man, a seaman
belonging to the royal navy. (Smyth)

Typee--p. 79 (n.) we had seen six men-of-war lying in the hostile bay;
p. 92 (adj.) decorate the bulkhead of a man-of-war's cabin; p. 203
(n.) I have been one of the crew of a man-of-war; p. 257 (n.) to the
thunders of the five men-of-war in the harbor; p. 270 (n.) The men-
of-war were still lying in the harbor.

Omoo--p. 6 (n.) One was that of an old man-of-war's man; p. 19 (adj.)
of a small man-of-war craft crept into view; p. 21 (adj.) pulled out
from the man-of-war's stern; p. 100 (n.) that a man-of-war is drawing
near; p. 108 (n.) of the imperfect discipline of a French man-of-war;
p. 108 (n.) practiced in men-of-war; p. 165 (adj.) to come from
certain men-of-war and merchant captains; p. 182 (n.) on a holyday
from a man-of-war; p. 247 (n.) an old man-of-war's man fills the post
of barber; p. 259 (n.) A pompous captain of a man-of-war; p. 299 (n.)

smuggled over from the man-of-war; p. 304 (n.) when an American man-of-war was lying at Papeetee.

Redburn--p. 6 (n.) represented three old-fashioned French men-of-war; p. 88 (n.) about a man-of-war's man; p. 99 (n.) A Whaleman and a Man-of-war's-Man; p. 101 (adj.) was a young man-of-war's man we had; p. 101 (adj.) always dressed in man-of-war style; p. 101 (adj.) like a romantic man-of-war's man; p. 112 (adj.) a comical little pair of man-of-war's man's trowsers; p. 175 (n.) about the capstan on a man-of-war; p. 188 (adj.) He was an old man-of-war's man; p. 190 (n.) dressed like a man-of-war's man; p. 219 (adj.) in a Guernsey frock and man-of-war trowsers.

White-Jacket--p. ix (adj.) My man-of-war experiences and observations are incorporated; p. 8 (adj.) into which a Man-of-war's Crew is divided; p. 8 (n.) This plan is followed in all men-of-war; p. 8 (n.) But in all men-of-war; p. 9 (adj.) a man-of-war's crew would be nothing but a mob; p. 11 (adj.) the principal divisions into which a man-of-war's crew; p. 11 (n.) subdivision of duties in a man-of-war; p. 11 (n.) unused to the tumult of a man-of-war; p. 12 (n.) who think of cruising in men-of-war; p. 13 (n.) in all things pertaining to a man-of-war; p. 14 (n.) It is often the custom of men-of-war's men; p. 15 (adj.) various sections of a man-of-war's crew; p. 15 (adj.) unmitigated detestation of a true man-of-war's man; p. 16 (n.) but when Tubbs came down upon men-of-war; p. 16 (n.) do you pretend to vilify a man-of-war; p. 16 (n.) a man-of-war is to whalemen; p. 16 (n.) to high life in a man-of-war; p. 16 (n.) the prevailing prejudice of men-of-war's-men; p. 20 (n.) . . . and Berth-deck Underlings of a Man-of-war; p. 20 (n.) serpentine streamer worn by all men-of-war; p. 23 (n.) as the captain of a man-of-war at sea; p. 26 (n.) the usage of a man-of-war thrusts various subordinates; p. 27 (adj.) the criterion of rank in our man-of-war world; p. 28 (n.) a criterion of rank on board a man-of-war; p. 29 (adj.) we men-of-war's men . . . largely partake in the immortality; p. 29 (adj.) natural hour for us men-of-war's men to dine; p. 29 (n.) the dinner hour on board a man-of-war; p. 30 (n.) in those instances where men-of-war . . . have encountered; p. 31 (n.) Having glanced at the grand divisions of a man-of-war; p. 35 (n.) the living on board a man-of-war is like; p. 36 (n.) in which to put any thing in a man-of-war; p. 38 (adj.) romantic notions of the man-of-war's man's character; p. 39 (n.) among the crew of a man-of-war; p. 39 (n.) all the minor pilferings on board a man-of-war; p. 40 (n.) not even all the tar and tumult of a man-of-war; p. 42 (adj.) Quoin was a little man-of-war's man; p. 44 (adj.) The Good or Bad Temper of Men-of-war's men; p. 44 (n.) the gunner's gang of every man-of-war; p. 47 (adj.) impartial account of our man-of-war world; p. 48 (n.) the First Lieutenants I saw in other men-of-war; p. 50 (adj.) A Man-of-war Hermit in a Mob; p. 51 (adj.) that his list of man-of-war friends was already made up; p. 51 (n.) what could have induced such a man to enter a man-of-war; p. 51 (adj.) even among our man-of-war mob; p. 52 (n.) most high-bred castaways in a man-of-war; p. 57 (n.) A Salt-Junk Club in a Man-of-war; p. 58 (n.) against that immemorial rule of men-of-war; p. 62 (n.) a dashing, blaze-away set of men-of-war's men; p. 64 (n.) General Training in a Man-of-war; p. 64 (n.) a proceeding in all men-of-war called "general quarters"; p. 64 (n.) the specific object for which a man-of-war is built; p. 65 (n.) one of the most dangerous posts of a man-of-war;

p. 68 (n.) every bulk-head in a man-of-war is knocked down; p. 68 (n.)
of which all men-of-war carry a large supply; p. 69 (n.) And men-of-
war's-men understand it, also; p. 72 (n.) In men-of-war, night and
day; p. 72 (n.) are the regulations of men-of-war; p. 72 (n.) the old
seamen stationed in that part of a man-of-war; p. 74 (n.) A Man-of-war
Full as a Nut; p. 74 (n.) lost to their trades and the world by
serving in men-of-war; p. 74 (adj.) a man-of-war's crew could quickly
found an Alexandria; p. 74 (n.) a man-of-war is a city afloat; p. 75
(n.) a man-of-war is a lofty, walled, and garrisoned town; p. 75 (n.)
a man-of-war resembles a three-story house; p. 77 (n.) he means not
life in a man-of-war; p. 79 (n.) How they Sleep in a Man-of-war;
p. 82 (n.) why Men-of-war's-men are, generally Short-lived; p. 82 (n.)
In a man-of-war at sea; p. 82 (n.) But in a man-of-war you can do no
such thing; p. 84 (n.) men-of-war's-men are not allowed the poor boon;
p. 84 (n.) the uniformity of daily events in a man-of-war; p. 84 (n.)
should be legally guaranteed to the man-of-war's-man; p. 85 (n.)
Wash-day, and House-cleaning in a Man-of-war; p. 86 (n.) as a man-of-
war's-man, White-Jacket . . . protests; p. 87 (n.) makes a wash-house
of a man-of-war; p. 87 (n.) especially this unobstructedness of a
man-of-war; p. 87 (n.) Of all men-of-war, the American ships; p. 87
(n.) And of all men-of-war, the general discipline; p. 87 (n.) what
more does a man-of-war's-man absolutely require; p. 87 (n.) Among all
men-of-war's-men; p. 88 (n.) The abhorrence which men-of-war's-men
have; p. 89 (n.) Theatricals in a Man-of-war; p. 90 (n.) disposed to
indulge his man-of-war's-men; p. 91 (n.) a man-of-war is that theatre;
p. 95 (n.) began to think a man-of-war a man-of-peace-and-good-will;
p. 95 (adj.) this was an old man-of-war's-man's phrase; p. 102 (n.)
are the town-criers of a man-of-war; p. 118 (n.) In our man-of-war,
this semi-savage; p. 123 (n.) at the Subterranean Ports of a Man-of-
war; p. 124 (n.) the lower grade of officers in a man-of-war; p. 125
(n.) keen sense of my situation as a man-of-war's-man; p. 130 (n.)
all men-of-war are great bullies on the high seas; p. 131 (n.) In
men-of-war, the space on the uppermost deck; p. 132 (n.) well known
by men-of-war's-men; p. 135 (n.) to all men-of-war's-men this summons
conveys; p. 135 (n.) hundreds of men-of-war's-men have been made proof;
p. 137 (adj.) privilege accorded to every man-of-war culprit; p. 141
(n.) the Lieutenants of the Watch in American men-of-war; p. 141 (n.)
that on board of the American man-of-war; p. 141 (n.) that American
men-of-war's-men have often observed; p. 142 (adj.) for to a man-of-
war's-man's experienced eye; p. 142 (n.) to the general depravity of
the man-of-war's-man; p. 144 (n.) the condition on shipboard of an
American man-of-war; p. 145 (n.) every American man-of-war's-man
would be . . . justified; p. 149 (n.) on board an American man-of-war;
p. 153 (n.) as is often the case with men-of-war; p. 155 (n.) The
Chaplain and Chapel in a Man-of-war; p. 156 (adj.) eminently
illustrated in our man-of-war world; p. 156 (n.) man-of-war's-men, in
general, make but poor auditors; p. 157 (n.) chaplains are to be found
in men-of-war; p. 158 (n.) the Christianity of man-of-war's men;
p. 159 (n.) the bands of the various men-of-war in harbor; p. 160 (n.)
the world in a man-of-war; p. 160 (n.) looks like another man-of-war;
p. 160 (n.) men-of-war from their youth; p. 160 (n.) in a man-of-war
in harbor; p. 164 (n.) most of us man-of-war's-men harmoniously dove-
tail; p. 164 (n.) the greatest puzzle in the world--this man-of-war
world itself; p. 165 (n.) Some of the Ceremonies in a Man-of-war;
p. 165 (n.) The ceremonials of a man-of-war; p. 165 (n.) there still
lingers in American men-of-war; p. 167 (adj.) A Man-of-war Library;

p. 167 (n.) than with most man-of-war's-men on board; p. 170 (n.)
Killing Time in a Man-of-War in Harbor; p. 170 (n.) as it is called
in a man-of-war; p. 171 (n.) in men-of-war, every sailor has; p. 172
(adj.) even in our man-of-war world; p. 172 (n.) the checker-men and
man-of-war's-men included; p. 173 (n.) their officers used these man-
of-war's-men; p. 175 (n.) thought it applicable to a man-of-war;
p. 175 (n.) we shall have exchanged this State's Prison man-of-war;
p. 176 (n.) Smuggling in a Man-of-war; p. 176 (n.) the man-of-war's-
man is exposed to the most temptations; p. 176 (n.) Immured as the
man-of-war's-man is; p. 177 (n.) concerning no one thing in a man-of-
war; p. 177 (n.) is allowed to approach a man-of-war; p. 178 (n.) do
man-of-war's-men contrive to smuggle; p. 179 (n.) compound interest
in a man-of-war; p. 181 (adj.) there is little among man-of-war
smugglers; p. 182 (n.) A Knave in Office in a Man-of-war; p. 182 (n.)
pervading nearly all ranks in some men-of-war; p. 184 (adj.) the
common necessaries of a man-of-war life; p. 185 (n.) when some man-
of-war's-men crave liquor; p. 186 (adj.) our man-of-war world itself
was as eligible; p. 186 (adj.) revealed to our man-of-war world;
p. 188 (adj.) in defining a man-of-war villain; p. 188 (n.) essential
criminality of any man-of-war's-man; p. 188 (n.) man-of-war's-men
will not be judged; p. 188 (adj.) I will stand by even a man-of-war
thief; p. 189 (adj.) of the subordinates of a man-of-war captain;
p. 190 (n.) upon the discharge of our man-of-war's-men at home;
p. 190 (n.) the people of a man-of-war have been guilty of; p. 191
(n.) Publishing Poetry in a Man-of-war; p. 193 (n.) thins the locks
of most man-of-war's-men; p. 193 (adj.) ponderous man-of-war and
navy-regulation tarpaulin hat; p. 194 (n.) as every man-of-war
furnished with a signal-book; p. 195 (n.) When several men-of-war of
one nation; p. 196 (n.) Aboard of most large men-of-war; p. 196 (n.)
in the last repose of the man-of-war's-men; p. 197 (n.) Hardly ever
will you hear of a man-of-war returning home; p. 197 (n.) The death
of most of these man-of-war's-men lies at the door; p. 198 (n.) An
Auction in a Man-of-war; p. 198 (n.) the weariness experienced by the
man-of-war's-man; p. 202 (adj.) call it a white-washed man-of-war
schooner; p. 204 (n.) Purser, Purser's Steward, and Postmaster in a
Man-of-war; p. 204 (n.) on board of all men-of-war; p. 204 (n.) of
all the non-combatants of a man-of-war; p. 204 (n.) all the financial
affairs of a man-of-war; p. 205 (n.) Lucky is it for man-of-war's-men;
p. 207 (n.) this the man-of-war's-man knows; p. 208 (n.) between the
man-of-war's-man and his officer; p. 208 (n.) ever hope to prevail in
a man-of-war; p. 208 (n.) as the very object of a man-of-war; p. 208
(n.) so long as a man-of-war exists; p. 211 (n.) Judgment-day of the
whole world's men-of-war; p. 213 (n.) no sailor in a man-of-war ever
presumes; p. 216 (n.) a common event--at least in a man-of-war;
p. 219 (n.) a phrase which a man-of-war's-man peculiarly applies;
p. 219 (n.) leads a lord's life in a man-of-war; p. 222 (adj.) The
Effects of this upon a Man-of-war Captain; p. 222 (n.) spiteful
practices against the man-of-war's-man; p. 222 (n.) the higher the
rank in a man-of-war; p. 226 (adj.) my man-of-war world alone must
supply me; p. 226 (n.) invariably permitted to man-of-war's-men;
p. 226 (n.) as man-of-war's-men will know this to be the case; p. 227
(n.) been enacted in American men-of-war; p. 227 (n.) releasing "the
people" of a man-of-war from . . . discipline; p. 228 (n.) the records
of the steerages of men-of-war; p. 229 (adj.) came down to redeem our
whole man-of-war world; p. 233 (n.) A Shore Emperor on board a Man-
of-war; p. 233 (n.) visiting all the men-of-war in rotation; p. 243

(adj.) A Man-of-war Button divides two Brothers; p. 246 (n.) A Man-of-war's-man Shot at; p. 252 (adj.) A Consultation of Man-of-war Surgeons; p. 256 (n.) whose important functions in a man-of-war will; p. 258 (n.) of the crowd of man-of-war's-men outside; p. 265 (adj.) Man-of-war Trophies; p. 265 (n.) dropping the surgeons aboard the American men-of-war; p. 265 (n.) gliding about among all the men-of-war in harbor; p. 268 (adj.) A Man-of-war Race; p. 270 (adj.) It's the man-of-war epic of the world; p. 270 (n.) on board the old Romney man-of-war; p. 272 (adj.) of the rulers of our man-of-war world; p. 274 (n.) Fun in a Man-of-war; p. 274 (n.) the race (our man-of-war Derby); p. 277 (n.) every seaman in a man-of-war; p. 279 (n.) generally the custom with man-of-war's-men; p. 281 (n.) describing killing time in a man-of-war; p. 282 (adj.) A Man-of-war Fountain, and other Things; p. 282 (adj.) things pertaining to our man-of-war world; p. 282 (n.) when man-of-war shall be no more; p. 282 (n.) to show to the people . . . what a man-of-war was; p. 283 (n.) had but served on board a man-of-war; p. 283 (n.) so, in a man-of-war, there are a variety; p. 284 (adj.) in his moated old man-of-war castle of Warwick; p. 284 (n.) perambulate all the decks of a man-of-war; p. 285 (n.) the sailors in a man-of-war are the most . . . anxious; p. 286 (n.) Thus, in a man-of-war, the lords may be said; p. 288 (n.) between officers on board a man-of-war; p. 290 (n.) exceedingly grateful to a man-of-war's-man; p. 299 (n.) a grand re-christening of the men-of-war; p. 301 (n.) a proverb, familiar to man-of-war's-men; p. 302 (n.) illustrates the ideas that man-of-war's-men . . . have; p. 303 (n.) punishment inflicted upon a man-of-war's-man; p. 303 (n.) to the entire body of American man-of-war's-men; p. 304 (n.) with the interior life of a man-of-war; p. 304 (n.) under which the man-of-war's-man lives; p. 305 (n.) Night and Day Gambling in a Man-of-war; p. 305 (n.) man-of-war's-men are perhaps the most inclined; p. 305 (n.) And gambling . . . in a man-of-war operates; p. 306 (adj.) operations by man-of-war gamblers; p. 306 (n.) when man-of-war's-men desire to gamble; p. 307 (n.) most thrives in a man-of-war; p. 307 (n.) On board of most men-of-war; p. 307 (adj.) In man-of-war parlance; p. 308 (adj.) the mysteries of man-of-war vice are wonderful; p. 309 (n.) for what man-of-war's-men call; p. 309 (adj.) is this man-of-war world of ours; p. 311 (n.) with British man-of-war's-men; p. 314 (n.) valor of a man-of-war's-man can never assume; p. 315 (n.) generally the case in a man-of-war; p. 316 (adj.) to snap this man-of-war world's sword; p. 317 (n.) being drafted on board a man-of-war; p. 320 (n.) Some man-of-war's-men have confessed to me; p. 322 (n.) to which the seamen in a man-of-war are condemned; p. 323 (n.) and stern-gallery of a man-of-war; p. 323 (adj.) a good thing with you in this man-of-war world; p. 324 (n.) The omission of this rite in a man-of-war; p. 324 (adj.) the best righteousness of our man-of-war world; p. 324 (n.) The Hospital in a Man-of-war; p. 325 (n.) we were a most puissant man-of-war; p. 325 (n.) is that part of a man-of-war; p. 329 (n.) in which a man-of-war is far better for the sea; p. 330 (adj.) any true man-of-war invalid; p. 330 (n.) On board of every American man-of-war; p. 335 (n.) How Man-of-war's-men Die at Sea; p. 335 (adj.) according to man-of-war usage; p. 337 (n.) the man-of-war's-men would cry out; p. 338 (n.) in men-of-war the sail-maker is the undertaker; p. 341 (n.) How they Bury a Man-of-war's-man at Sea; p. 341 (n.) In a man-of-war, everything proceeds; p. 343 (n.) What remains of a Man-of-war's-man after his Burial; p. 343 (n.) among the sailors on board a man-of-war; p. 345 (adj.) A Man-of-war College; p. 345 (adj.) In our

man-of-war world; p. 345 (adj.) under the man-of-war scourge; p. 345
(adj.) This man-of-war life has not left me unhardened; p. 345 (adj.)
the task of portraying our man-of-war world; p. 350 (adj.) Man-of-war
Barbers; p. 350 (n.) connected with the domestic affairs of a man-of-
war; p. 350 (adj.) while a man-of-war barber is having his customers;
p. 351 (adj.) the implements of these men-of-war barbers; p. 352
(adj.) does a man-of-war barber have; p. 352 (n.) trouble for a man-
of-war's-man to keep; p. 352 (n.) that make up an efficient man-of-
war's-man; p. 355 (n.) the ruthless barbers of a man-of-war; p. 358
(n.) no knowing what man-of-war's-men will . . . do; p. 359 (n.) vast
magnitude in our man-of-war world; p. 360 (n.) love-curls and man-of-
war ringlets; pp. 360-2 (n.) on the quarter-deck of a Peruvian man-
of-war; p. 363 (n.) He was a man-of-war's-man; p. 367 (n.) the
feelings which man-of-war's-men sometimes cherish; p. 367 (n.) unheard
of in most American men-of-war; p. 368 (n.) our man-of-war's-men were
right; p. 369 (n.) Man-of-war's-men are so habituated; p. 369 (adj.)
certain enormities in this man-of-war world; p. 370 (n.) still
employed by man-of-war's-men; p. 370 (n.) inflicted by an American
man-of-war; p. 373 (n.) The Social State in a Man-of-war; p. 373 (n.)
smugglings, and tipplings of a man-of-war; p. 374 (n.) to the seamen
in all large men-of-war; p. 374 (n.) surely these man-of-war's-men
must be; p. 374 (n.) that the man-of-war's-man casts but an evil eye;
p. 374 (adj.) interior of a man-of-war's discipline; p. 375 (n.) in
most men-of-war there runs a sinister vein; p. 375 (n.) iron etiquette
of a man-of-war; p. 375 (n.) the domestic interior of a man-of-war;
p. 375 (n.) that the man-of-war's-man is so vicious; p. 376 (n.)
There are evils in men-of-war; p. 377 (n.) are men-of-war familiarly
known; p. 377 (n.) and man-of-war's-men especially; p. 378 (n.) with
three French men-of-war alongside; p. 378 (n.) owing to this scarcity
of man-of-war's-men; p. 379 (n.) my condition as a man-of-war's-man;
p. 380 (n.) but the man-of-war's-man . . . the man-of-war's-man rolls
round the world; p. 380 (n.) the general discipline of a man-of-war;
p. 380 (n.) the circumstances of a man-of-war admit; p. 382 (n.)
scoundrels of all sorts in a man-of-war; p. 382 (adj.) reduce the
number of a man-of-war's crew; p. 382 (n.) a man-of-war . . . must
feed at the public cost; p. 382 (n.) by both English and American
man-of-war's-men; p. 383 (n.) to think that man-of-war's-men are;
p. 383 (n.) the iniquities of a man-of-war; p. 384 (n.) enables some
man-of-war's-men to coax jolly; p. 385 (n.) He has no business in a
man-of-war; p. 385 (n.) apply to all men-of-war; p. 385 (n.) more
than one noble man-of-war's-man; p. 386 (n.) Smoking-club in a Man-of-
war; p. 386 (n.) In men-of-war, the Galley, or Cookery; p. 387 (n.)
in the man-of-war's-man permitted to regale; p. 388 (n.) domestic
by-play of a man-of-war; p. 389 (n.) Know ye not, man-of-war's-men;
p. 389 (n.) a crew of five hundred man-of-war's-men; p. 390 (n.) alas
for the man-of-war's-man; p. 390 (n.) A Man-of-war's-man is only a
man-of-war's-man at sea; p. 390 (n.) a man-of-war is but this old-
fashioned world; p. 398 (n.) As a man-of-war that sails through the sea.

Moby-Dick--p. 99 (n.) If American and European men-of-war now
peacefully ride; p. 262 (n.) Espied by some timid man-of-war.

MARINE, MARINER. Marine, belonging to the sea. It is a general name for
the royal or mercantile navy of any state; also the whole economy of
nautical affairs.--Mariner, one who obtains his living on the sea, in
whatever rank. (Smyth)

Typee--p. 7 (adj.) the marine guard presented arms; p. 26 (n.) a
considerable detachment of sailors and marines; p. 92 (adj.) the toes,
like the radiating lines of the mariner's compass; p. 155 (adj.) may
have been thrown up by a submarine volcano; p. 184 (n.) Fanning, a
Yankee mariner of some reputation; p. 223 (adj.) albatrosses, Cape
pigeons, jays, petrels, and divers other marine fowl; p. 223 (n.)
talk taboo to the marines.

Omoo--p. 39 (adj.) denominated in marine architecture; p. 63 (n.)
hospitality is seldom taxed by the mariner; p. 64 (adj.) far below
the reach of the mariner's lead; p. 68 (adj.) sanctioned by the
Marine Courts of Law; p. 79 (n.) the two mariners at the bottom of
the sea; p. 110 (n.) they have no marines; p. 110 (n.) building up a
great military marine; p. 124 (n.) The French sailors and marines;
p. 146 (n.) a rude hut of entertainment for mariners; p. 162 (adj.)
to admire the marine gardens; p. 175 (n.) to the little marine villas
upon the beach; p. 182 (n.) the uniform of a parcel of drunken
marines; p. 270 (n.) fully appreciated by the mariner.

Mardi--p. 3 (n.) whence, and whither wend ye, mariners; p. 13 (n.)
that an old marine like him; p. 23 (n.) marines on deck; p. 24 (n.)
as old marines believe; p. 44 (n.) ye marines who list; p. 60 (n.)
tell that to the marines; p. 64 (n.) drawn by old Finnish mariners;
p. 68 (adj.) and its submarine mysteries; p. 91 (n.) in most military
marines; p. 95 (n.) the effects of a mariner; p. 122 (adj.)
exhibitions of marine phosphorescence; p. 127 (n.) being in what
marines denominate; p. 147 (n.) upon the arm of the wonderful marine;
p. 191 (adj.) fancying a marine vicinity; p. 192 (n.) above the
shipwrecked marine; p. 200 (adj.) stage of marine architecture;
p. 367 (n.) many mariners rush up from; p. 418 (adj.) marine mammalia;
p. 461 (n.) The mariners never sailed faster; p. 471 (adj.) of the as
yet nearly sub-marine territory; p. 506 (adj.) Polyp, despising its
marine existence.

Redburn--p. 114 (n.) Of my becoming a rare mariner; p. 121 (n.) To
distinguish such a mariner; p. 127 (n.) warning all mariners to flee;
p. 131 (n.) kept by a broken-down American mariner; p. 138 (n.) make
the hapless mariner their prey; p. 172 (n.) among the crowds of
mariners; p. 175 (adj.) converted into a mariner's church; p. 177 (n.)
St. Nicholas, the patron of mariners; p. 193 (n.) In the British armed
marine; p. 289 (n.) the marine Jackson, who seemed elated.

White-Jacket--p. 11 (n.) he hears the tread of armed marines; p. 16
(n.) to that much-maligned class of mariners; p. 24 (n.) playing
chess with the Lieutenant of Marines; p. 24 (adj.) purser, chaplain,
Surgeon, Marine officers; p. 24 (adj.) the Marine officers talk of
storming fortresses; p. 26 (adj.) including . . . ship's corporals,
marine sergeants; p. 27 (adj.) The marine sergeants are generally
tall fellows; p. 48 (adj.) Lieutenants, Purser, Marine officers;
p. 54 (n.) asked a Corporal of Marines; p. 55 (adj.) the marine sentry
who stood guard over them; p. 62 (adj.) Opposite, was one of the
marine messes; p. 62 (adj.) mustering the aristocracy of the marine
corps; p. 88 (adj.) the marine sentry at the gangway turned his back;
p. 92 (n.) Sailors, Marines, Bar-keepers, Crimps; p. 94 (adj.) At the
discharge of a marine's musket; p. 97 (n.) A veteran mariner is never
deceived; p. 112 (n.) But in that gallant marine; p. 112 (n.) fact in

the history of a kindred marine; p. 113 (n.) in so renowned a marine
as England's; p. 120 (n.) to find out who those "horse-marines" and
"sogers" were; p. 136 (n.) on one side, and an armed marine on the
other; p. 136 (adj.) obtaining the permission of the marine sentry;
p. 150 (n.) flogging in the British armed marine; p. 163 (adj.) the
whole marine guard, except the sentries on duty; p. 167 (adj.)
custody of one of the marine corporals; p. 172 (n.) was chiefly
patronized by the marines; p. 184 (n.) to be an old superannuated
marine; p. 184 (n.) who did the cooking for the marine-sergeants;
p. 184 (n.) This marine was one of the most villainous-looking
fellows; p. 184 (adj.) insinuated himself into the honorable marine
corps; p. 184 (n.) This terrified marine was at length forced; p. 185
(n.) The miserly marine, Scriggs, with the pick-lock eye; p. 185 (n.)
Scriggs, the marine, coming in for one third; p. 202 (n.) came among
the bags of deceased mariners; p. 213 (n.) and we poor mariners;
p. 223 (n.) my name is horse-marine; p. 227 (n.) many an old mariner
. . . called upon the Flag-staff; p. 234 (adj.) the marine guard
presented arms; p. 239 (adj.) detached from the marine corps; p. 255
(n.) of which the marine-orderly paced; p. 257 (n.) From having no
military marine herself; p. 280 (n.) handsome and gentlemanly corporal
of marines; p. 281 (n.) had a marine dared to speak to the Captain;
p. 298 (n.) (L'Ord. de la Marine); p. 299 (n.) possible efficiency of
a military marine; p. 301 (n.) which so hems in the mariner by law;
p. 303 (n.) forefathers who happened to be mariners; p. 304 (n.) in
the merchant service of the national marine; p. 307 (n.) especially
certain of the marines; pp. 308-9 (n.) you may sometimes hear/ even
marines jerk; p. 315 (n.) These mariners seized the buckets; p. 318
(n.) our marines sent their leaden pease; p. 345 (n.) by an invalid
corporal of marines; p. 352 (adj.) like the marine sentries at the
gangways; p. 357 (n.) let the marines fix their bayonets; p. 357 (n.)
gunner's mates! mariners, all; p. 359 (n.) should at once have
summoned the marines; p. 362 (n.) They were old and venerable mariners;
p. 370 (n.) remains in the French national marine; p. 373 (n.) carry
soldiers, called marines; p. 373 (n.) to have a marine to each gun;
p. 373 (n.) Our marines had no other; p. 373 (n.) her marines generally
lie flat; p. 374 (n.) are these marines of any essential service;
p. 374 (n.) why have marines at all; p. 374 (n.) these marines are to
the seamen; p. 374 (n.) but an evil eye on a marine; p. 374 (n.) To
call a man a "horse-marine"; p. 374 (n.) antagonism between the marine
and the sailor; p. 374 (n.) for the marine to thrust his bayonet;
p. 374 (n.) if the marine revolts; p. 374 (n.) in which the marine
and sailor stand toward; p. 381 (n.) narrative of "John Nichol,
Mariner"; p. 396 (n.) How the Lieutenant of Marines sheathed his
sword; p. 399 (n.) a sword-belted Officer of Marines.

Moby-Dick--p. 7 (n.) Which language cannot paint, and mariner/ Had
never seen; p. 8 (n.) A mariner sat in the shrouds one night; p. 23
(n.) and in rolled a wild set of mariners enough; p. 37 (n.)
Mediterranean mariners will sometimes jostle the affrighted ladies;
p. 46 (n.) Strong intuitions of the men assure the mariners; p. 48
(n.) till the mariners come nigh to drowning; p. 48 (n.) The eager
mariners ask him who he is; p. 49 (n.) the mariners become more and
more appalled; p. 97 (n.) one Bulkington was spoken of, a tall, new-
landed mariner; p. 100 (n.) that Cook with all his marines and
muskets would not willingly have dared; p. 104 (n.) If then, to
meanest mariners; p. 126 (n.) Their appearance is generally hailed

with delight by the mariner; p. 327 (adj.) the submarine bridal-
chambers and nurseries vanished; p. 334 (n.) It seems that some honest
mariners of Dover or Sandwich; p. 335 (n.) Now when these poor sunburnt mariners, bare-footed, and with their trowsers rolled high up;
p. 335 (n.) Upon this the poor mariners in their respectful
consternation; p. 393 (n.) the mariners readily detect any serious
leakage in the precious cargo; p. 400 (n.) excited the curiosity of
the mariners; p. 413 (n.) the mariner encounters the direst of all
storms; p. 418 (n.) many of the mariners did run from him in a terror
of dismay; p. 424 (adj.) as developed in the mariner's needle; p. 429
(n.) most mariners cherish a very superstitious feeling about seas;
p. 454 (n.) of what present avail to the becalmed or windbound mariner.

MARITIME. Pertaining to sea affairs: all but synonymous with marine.
(Smyth)

Omoo--p. 109 (adj.) not being essentially a maritime people; p. 263
(adj.) The true delights in a maritime situation.

Mardi--p. 481 (adj.) even so have maritime potentates ever prided
themselves.

White-Jacket--p. 304 (adj.) recognized by all writers on maritime law.

Moby-Dick--p. 42 (adj.) imputable to that adventurous maritime life
he had led.

MARLING-SPIKE. An iron pin, tapering to a point, and principally used to
separate the strands of a rope, in order to introduce the ends of some
other through the intervals in the act of knotting or splicing; it is
also used as a lever in marling, fixing seizings, &c. (Smyth's spelling
is "marline-spike.")

Omoo--p. 80 (n.) Here the mate looked marlingspikes; p. 151 (n.)
sewing utensils, marling-spikes, strips of calico; p. 200 (n.) called
by our companions, "the Marling-spike"; p. 212 (n.) the "Marling-
spike" lifted its finger; p. 289 (n.) and among these, the same
silent Marling-spike.

MAST. A long cylindrical piece of timber elevated perpendicularly upon
the keel of a ship, to which are attached the yards, the rigging, and
the sails. It is either formed of one piece, and called a pole-mast, or
composed of several pieces joined together and termed a made mast.
MAST-HEAD. The upper part of a mast above the rigging. (Smyth)

Typee--p. 10 (n.) in still louder accents hailed the mast-head;
p. 134 (n.) but a prettier little mast than Fayaway; p. 271 (n.)
Descending from the mast almost distracted.

Omoo--p. 3 (n.) as a sailor before the mast; p. 9 (n.) The lower
masts were said to be unsound; p. 19 (n.) the masts and yards lined
distinctly; p. 27 (n.) might leap upon it from the mast-head; p. 28
(n.) a dog before the mast; p. 33 (n.) flung themselves around the

foremast; p. 34 (n.) relieve the "lookouts" at the mast-heads; p. 43
(n.) striking against the mast; p. 46 (n.) nailed as a charm to the
foremast; p. 48 (n.) the men came down from the mast-heads; p. 58 (n.)
It was the main-t'-gallant-mast; p. 76 (n.) he called the main-mast
to witness; p. 84 (n.) flapping against the mast with every roll;
p. 84 (n.) Mast-head, there; p. 91 (n.) standing doggedly by the
mizen-mast; p. 96 (n.) as a man before the mast; p. 113 (n.) A man of
any education before the mast; p. 292 (n.) the two masts going over
the side about midnight.

Mardi--p. 7 (n.) at the mast-head; p. 7 (n.) high upon the mast;
p. 14 (n.) to truck of main-mast; p. 14 (n.) to look at the mast-head;
p. 16 (n.) at the fore-mast-head; p. 26 (n.) lee of the mizzen-mast;
p. 30 (n.) we made shrouds to the mast; p. 49 (n.) we unshipped the
mast; p. 60 (n.) wheezings of the masts and yards; p. 62 (n.) to the
mainmast; p. 63 (n.) swore by the mainmast; p. 70 (n.) full at the
foremast; p. 70 (n.) decline a ship's mast; p. 72 (n.) to the mast;
p. 76 (n.) upon the foremast and mainmast; p. 78 (n.) hung it aloft
from the topmast-stay; p. 101 (n.) from one mast to the other; p. 102
(n.) almost strong enough to sustain the mainmast; p. 117 (n.) The
masts rose, and swayed; p. 117 (n.) snatched from its rack against
the mainmast; p. 117 (n.) the wounded mast snapped in twain; p. 117
(n.) the mainmast carried over with it the foremast; p. 118 (n.) were
the shattered fragments of the masts; p. 120 (n.) in the splintered
stub of the mainmast; p. 128 (n.) supported obliquely in the crotch
of a mast; p. 128 (n.) in which the mast was placed; p. 128 (n.)
leading up to the head of the mast; p. 161 (n.) than to plant our
mast; p. 213 (n.) occupying the place of the foremast; p. 268 (n.)
Yoomy sang, leaning against the mast; p. 354 (n.) with paddles, out-
riggers, masts; p. 372 (n.) to run them up toward the mast-head;
p. 377 (n.) its colors at half mast; p. 482 (n.) its masts young
Zetland firs; p. 354 (n.) flag-staffs, like an admiral's masts.

Redburn--p. 4 (n.) with high, cozy bulwarks, and rakish masts; p. 4
(adj.) from the wooden, one-masted, green-and-white painted sloops;
p. 5 (n.) of the masts bending like twigs; p. 6 (n.) snug little
turrets on top of the mast; p. 8 (n.) because the masts, yards, and
ropes were made; p. 8 (n.) Not to speak of the tall masts; p. 27 (n.)
and Slushing Down the Top-Mast; p. 29 (n.) slush down the main-top
mast; p. 30 (n.) to slush down the main-top mast; p. 30 (n.) dab this
slush all over the mast; p. 30 (n.) I was to ascend a ship's mast;
p. 33 (n.) when I looked up at the high, giddy masts; p. 42 (n.)
you'll feel as strong as the mainmast; p. 45 (n.) a little higher up
on the mast; p. 66 (n.) Every mast and timber seemed to have a pulse;
p. 78 (n.) holding on might and main to the mast; p. 82 (n.) his cook-
house was right behind the foremast; p. 103 (n.) The foremast was
snapt off; p. 103 (n.) At the head of the stump of the mainmast;
p. 108 (n.) flitting from mast to mast; p. 119 (n.) the fife-rail
round the mainmast; p. 120 (n.) about striking a top-gallant-mast;
p. 121 (n.) to make a jury-mast out of a yard; p. 159 (n.) it will . . .
be your ship's mainmast; p. 161 (n.) tangled thicket of masts along
the East River; p. 165 (n.) in a grand parliament of masts; p. 166
(n.) have lost their top-gallant-masts; p. 166 (n.) with nothing
visible but the mast and sail; p. 173 (n.) And the loss of a foretop-
mast; p. 175 (n.) a steeple took the place of a mast; p. 190 (n.) in
falling from a frigate's mast-head; p. 220 (n.) he had often climbed

the masts; p. 242 (n.) athwart-ships, by the main-mast; p. 266 (n.)
upon getting as far as the mainmast; p. 273 (n.) How many stout masts
of seventy-fours; p. 288 (n.) from going forward beyond the mainmast;
p. 294 (n.) though the light mast sprung like a switch; p. 300 (n.)
We saw the Hartz Forest of masts.

White-Jacket--p. 9 (n.) orders pertaining to the main-mast; p. 9 (n.)
the main-mast belongs to another detachment; p. 33 (n.) Then would
masts surmount spires; p. 47 (n.) than the top-men of the fore, main,
and mizzen masts; p. 34 (n.) They were brought up to the mast; p. 66
(n.) happens to send overboard your fore-mast; p. 69 (n.) Our stout
masts and yards might be lying; p. 69 (n.) splicing and fishing the
shattered masts and yards; p. 73 (n.) hailing the main-mast-head;
p. 73 (n.) recall-signal at the frigate's fore-t'gallant-mast-head;
p. 74 (n.) to muster at the main-mast; p. 75 (n.) in the shape of the
main-mast; p. 86 (n.) the by-ways and corners about the masts and
guns; p. 91 (n.) found tacked against the main-mast; p. 92 (n.) JACK
CHASE . . . PERCY ROYAL-MAST; p. 92 (n.) PERCY ROYAL-MAST . . . JACK
CHASE; p. 94 (n.) in the chivalric character of "Percy Royal-Mast";
p. 94 (n.) where Percy Royal-Mast rescues fifteen oppressed sailors;
p. 96 (n.) or the tall masts, imbedded in icebergs; p. 97 (n.) give
her the fore-top-mast stun'-sail; p. 97 (n.) The masts are willows;
p. 97 (n.) In all probability his three masts have gone; p. 99 (n.)
my friend Dana's unmatchable "Two Years Before the Mast"; p. 102 (n.)
Swings were rigged from the tops, or the masts; p. 104 (n.) discerned
from the fore-top-mast-head; p. 106 (n.) The gigantic masts seemed
about to snap; p. 107 (n.) This saved the main-mast; p. 131 (n.) the
space . . . round about the main-mast; p. 131 (n.) to be brought up
to the mast; p. 131 (n.) which sailors . . . too often experience at
the mast; p. 131 (n.) The main-mast, moreover, is the only place;
p. 131 (n.) straight to the main-mast he repairs; p. 135 (n.) the
crew crowded round the main-mast; p. 135 (n.) on the starboard side
of the main-mast; p. 136 (n.) took up their stations at the mast;
p. 136 (n.) against being summoned to the mast; p. 147 (n.) to come
down from the lofty mast-head of an eternal principle; p. 148 (n.)
when the masts of her multiplied fleets; p. 182 (n.) were publicly
harangued at the mast; p. 189 (n.) he was summoned to the mast;
p. 195 (n.) so that the main-mast is all eagerness; p. 195 (n.) to
vanquish the fore-mast; p. 195 (n.) the mizzen-mast to vanquish them
both; p. 195 (n.) on all three masts were soon climbing; p. 196 (n.)
The royal-yard forms a cross with the mast; p. 198 (n.) and mustered
round the main-mast; p. 198 (n.) which were deposited at the base of
the mast; p. 201 (n.) again summoned round the main-mast; p. 213 (n.)
Jack . . . made his appearance . . . at the mast; p. 217 (n.) when
the man is brought to the mast; p. 220 (n.) punishment of sending
them to the mast-head; p. 220 (n.) as sending them before the mast;
pp. 220-1 (n.) laid before the Captain at the mast; p. 223 (adj.) we
were hoisting the main-top-mast stun'-sail; p. 224 (n.) in his
audience at the mast; p. 232 (n.) the great body of men before the
mast; p. 236 (n.) yet, by the mast; p. 241 (n.) A Quarter-deck Officer
before the Mast; p. 242 (n.) degraded before the mast; p. 255 (n.)
stretched across the ship by the main-mast; p. 259 (n.) with an arm
like a royal-mast; p. 268 (n.) came the tall main-mast; p. 275 (n.)
brought them up to the mast; p. 277 (n.) White-Jacket arraigned at
the Mast; p. 278 (n.) Captain wants ye at the mast; p. 279 (n.) I saw
the quarter-master rigging the gratings; p. 281 (n.) in behalf of a

seaman at the mast; p. 283 (n.) is the office of mast-man; p. 283 (n.)
on deck, at the base of each mast; p. 283 (n.) It is the sole duty of
the mast-man; p. 283 (n.) The main-mast-man of the Neversink; p. 284
(n.) so sits our old mast-man on the coat of the mast; p. 284 (n.)
you would almost think this old mast-man had; p. 285 (n.) Advancing
to the main-mast; p. 289 (n.) at last halts near the main-mast;
p. 294 (n.) By the main-mast; p. 298 (n.) insultingly carried a broom
at his fore-mast; p. 307 (n.) lurking round the fore-mast on the
spar-deck; p. 309 (n.) black ribbon flying from his mast-head; p. 310
(adj.) leaning against the top-mast shrouds; p. 311 (n.) the canvass
on the main-mast and fore-mast; p. 311 (n.) The three shrouded masts
looked like; p. 312 (n.) lost her fore and main-top-masts; p. 312
(n.) her mizzen-mast having been shot away; p. 316 (n.) he paused
abreast of the main-mast; p. 316 (n.) in order to hurl over the mast;
p. 316 (n.) dug out of the main-mast; p. 316 (n.) where he sleeps in
his moldering mast; p. 318 (n.) to nail to the mast in case; p. 318
(n.) covered with masts and yards; p. 319 (n.) brought down the
Turkish Admiral's main-mast; p. 322 (n.) leading down from the three
mast-heads; p. 342 (n.) hovering over the main-mast during the
service; p. 348 (n.) I'd nail my colors to the main-royal-mast;
p. 348 (n.) your main-mast has gone by the board; p. 348 (n.) your
fore-mast is lying across your forecastle; p. 348 (n.) your main-mast,
also, has gone; p. 358 (n.) forward of the main-mast; p. 359 (n.)
substitute miniature main-masts; p. 361 (n.) at the mast-head of this
same gallant frigate; p. 361 (n.) that Nature herself has nailed to
the mast; p. 362 (n.) The Rebels brought to the Mast; p. 362 (n.)
summoned in a body to the mast; p. 363 (n.) to brace his main-mast;
p. 364 (n.) now stood in silence at the mast; p. 364 (n.) then paraded
themselves at the mast; p. 365 (n.) up the ladder to the main-mast;
p. 374 (n.) the uttermost point on their main-mast; p. 376 (n.)
complaints were made at the mast; p. 377 (n.) should have converted
the ship's masts; p. 392 (adj.) I was mounting the top-mast shrouds;
p. 393 (n.) I had fallen in a line with the main-mast; p. 393 (n.)
nearly abreast of the mizzen-mast; p. 396 (n.) round our mast we
circle; p. 397 (n.) when down from our main-mast comes; p. 399 (n.)
a bar by our main-mast.

Moby-Dick--p. 2 (n.) hie aloft to the royal-mast with your hearts;
p. 5 (n.) They frequently climb up the masts; p. 9 (n.) sung out from
the mast-head; p. 9 (n.) Mast-head ahoy; p. 10 (n.) with look-outs at
the mast-heads; p. 14 (n.) I go as a simple sailor, right before the
mast; p. 14 (n.) aloft there to the royal mast-head; p. 20 (n.) with
its three dismantled masts alone visible; p. 21 (n.) impaling himself
upon the three mast-heads; p. 50 (n.) how gladly would I come down
from this mast-head; p. 60 (n.) the two tall masts buckling like
Indian canes; p. 67 (n.) Her masts-- . . . her masts stood stiffly up
like the spines of the three old kings; p. 83 (adj.) you'd better
ship for a missionary, instead of a fore-mast hand; p. 85 (n.) with
all three masts making such an everlasting thundering; p. 85 (n.) how
to rig jury-masts; p. 90 (n.) roaring up to the riggers at the mast-
head; p. 94 (n.) as the sailors lingered at the main-mast; p. 110
(adj./n.) like his dismasted craft, he shipped another mast without
coming home for it; p. 111 (n.) he seemed as unnecessary there as
another mast; p. 135 (n.) my first mast-head came round; p. 135 (n.)
the mast-heads are manned almost simultaneously; p. 135 (n.) as the
business of standing mast-heads; p. 135 (n.) the earliest standers of

mast-heads; p. 135 (n.) intended to rear the loftiest mast-head in
all Asia; p. 135 (n.) as that great stone mast of theirs; p. 135
(adj.) the Egyptians were a nation of mast-head standers; p. 135 (n.)
remarkable instance of a dauntless stander-of-mast-heads; p. 135 (n.)
Of modern standers-of-mast-heads; p. 136 (n.) high aloft on his
towering main-mast in Baltimore; p. 136 (n.) Admiral Nelson . . .
stands his mast-head in Trafalgar; p. 136 (n.) to couple in any
respect the mast-head standers of the land; p. 136 (n.) to the one
proper-mast-head, that of a whale-ship at sea; p. 136 (n.) The three
mast-heads are kept manned; p. 136 (n.) as if the masts were gigantic
stilts; p. 137 (n.) your most usual point of perch is the head of the
t'gallant-mast; p. 138 (n.) all standers of mast-heads are furnished
with; p. 143 (v.) it was Moby Dick that dismasted me; p. 184 (n.) his
voice was now often heard hailing the three mast-heads; p. 210 (adj.)
they are swept by Borean and dismasting blasts; p. 236 (n.) her three
tall tapering masts mildly waved; p. 257 (n.) firmly lashed to the
lower mast-head; p. 258 (n.) nods her frighted mast-heads to the sky;
p. 295 (n.) when whales were almost simultaneously raised from the
mast-heads of both vessels; p. 331 (n.) a mast, an oar, a nine-inch
cable, a telegraph wire, or a strand of cobweb, it is all the same;
p. 338 (n.) get more oil by chopping up and trying out these three
masts of ours; p. 352 (n.) planted between the foremast and the main-
mast; p. 356 (n.) afar off descried from the mast-head; p. 382 (n.)
the almost omniscient look-outs at the mast-heads of the whale-ships;
p. 407 (adj.) in her top-mast cross-trees; p. 412 (n.) her three
firm-seated graceful masts erectly poised; p. 413 (n.) showed the
disabled masts fluttering here and there; p. 415 (n.) each of the
three tall masts was silently burning; p. 416 (adj./n.) I take that
mast-head flame we saw for a sign of good luck, for those masts are
rooted in a hold; p. 416 (n.) our three masts will yet be as three
spermaceti candles; p. 455 (n.) The mast-heads, like the tops of tall
palms; p. 461 (n.) instantly from the three mast-heads three shrieks
went up; p. 462 (n.) Good by, mast-head--keep a good eye upon the
whale.

MATE. An officer under the master. (Dana)

Typee--p. 10 (n.) the mate in still louder accents hailed; p. 61 (n.)
Mate, do me the kindness not to fall.

Omoo--p. 5 (n.) whom I took for the chief mate; p. 6 (n.) The mate
was now called below; p. 6 (n.) the mate stretched me out on the
windlass; p. 8 (n.) "Here, shipmate," said I; p. 8 (n.) the mate says
it's in a devil of a way; p. 10 (n.) Even the three junior mates who
had headed; p. 10 (n.) he left every thing to the chief mate; pp. 10-11
(n.) So the bluff mate . . . was occasionally/made a tool of; p. 11
(n.) the mate had every thing his own way; p. 11 (n.) Such was our
mate; p. 13 (n.) The mate, however, was as hearty; p. 13 (n.) little
intercourse with any body but the mate; p. 16 (n.) whom the mate had
never decidedly got the better of; p. 16 (n.) prided himself upon
talking up to the mate; p. 16 (n.) This insolence flung the fiery
little mate into a mighty rage; p. 17 (n.) shouted the mate; p. 18
(n.) cried the mate; p. 18 (n.) this quarrel's between the mate and
me; p. 18 (adj.) where the mate's rough tones were heard; p. 20 (n.)
The mate at once went out to the end; p. 20 (n.) the mate and the

Mowree were to stand; p. 20 (n.) the mate snored most strangely;
p. 21 (n.) The mate leaped into her; p. 23 (n.) roared the mate; p.
p. 23 (n.) deliberation on the part of the captain and the mate;
p. 29 (n.) between our new shipmate and his countrymen; p. 33 (n.)
and the mate himself, with arms folded; p. 34 (n.) The mate put an
end to the discussion; p. 34 (n.) headed respectively by the mate and
the Mowree; p. 34 (n.) succeeding to the place of the second mate;
p. 35 (n.) entertained by my reckless shipmates; p. 35 (n.) For what
reason the mate was so reserved; p. 42 (n.) their shipmates often
amused themselves; p. 44 (n.) The mate was then called; p. 45 (n.)
The mate, who was far from being sober; p. 45 (n.) we had tossed a
shipmate to the sharks; p. 46 (n.) his shipmate swore that a wet
hammock; p. 47 (n.) no one but the mate seemed to know; p. 48 (n.)
the mate would say; p. 48 (n.) the mate carelessly observed; p. 50
(n.) the mate was perfectly sober; p. 51 (n.) the mate in duty bound;
p. 51 (adj.) Every thing forbade the mate's plan; p. 53 (n.) if the
mate sends him after his quadrant; p. 58 (n.) the mate carried sail
without stint; p. 61 (n.) The mate, however, in addition to; p. 62
(n.) though the mate alone might have been; p. 62 (adj.) The mate's
tremulous attempts to level; p. 69 (n.) cried the mate; p. 69 (n.)
leaving the vessel under the mate; p. 70 (n.) helped on deck by the
mate; p. 70 (n.) the mate, after a private interview; p. 70 (adj.)
contrary to the mate's advice; p. 71 (n.) every body but the mate
more or less distrusted; p. 73 (n.) the mate, having left the captain;
p. 75 (n.) as soon as the mate went ashore; p. 75 (n.) The mate was
now assailed by a hundred questions; p. 76 (n.) as Wilson and the
mate went below; p. 76 (adj.) of the mate's intemperate habits; p. 78
(n.) By the side of Wilson was the mate; p. 80 (n.) to say against
your mate, Mr. Jermin; p. 80 (n.) Here the mate looked marlingspikes;
p. 81 (adj.) Upon the mate's assuring him; p. 81 (n.) the mate was
holding his peace; p. 81 (n.) your mate, Mr. Jermin, will command;
p. 84 (n.) the mate ordered the cook and steward; p. 84 (n.) happy in
the affection of his shipmates; p. 86 (n.) the mate came off; p. 88
(n.) the mate had in vain endeavored; p. 89 (n.) ordered by the mate;
p. 91 (adj.) immediately over the mate's head; p. 92 (n.) shouted the
mate; p. 92 (n.) cried the mate; p. 92 (adj.) in answer to the mate's
repeated questions; p. 92 (n.) the mate but dimly understood; p. 94
(n.) who had promised the mate; p. 94 (n.) The mate must have known
this; p. 94 (n.) that the mate had said so; p. 94 (n.) the mate had
locked him up; p. 95 (n.) the mate was justly incensed; p. 95 (n.) an
old shipmate of Jermin's; p. 95 (n.) by the captain, Jermin, and the
third mate; p. 96 (adj.) the third mate's boat, in all probabilities;
p. 96 (n.) our mate had sailed from that port; p. 96 (n.) hearing of
his lost shipmates; p. 96 (n.) when Viner, the lost third mate; p. 96
(n.) promising his old shipmate to see him; p. 97 (n.) the mate, with
Baltimore and the Dane; p. 97 (n.) the mate, no longer relying upon
the consul; p. 98 (n.) the mate seemed more reckless than ever; p. 98
(n.) the mate was not to be daunted; p. 99 (n.) was all addressed to
the mate; p. 100 (n.) he then strode up to the mate; p. 103 (n.) The
mate also--who had always been friendly; p. 103 (n.) After a talk
with the mate; p. 103 (n.) according to our most experienced shipmates;
p. 106 (n.) whom we supposed a boatswain's mate; p. 106 (n.) The
boatswain's mate went to work; p. 106 (n.) The boatswain's mate only
hit out at them; p. 110 (n.) to some less fortunate shipmate; p. 139
(n.) the manifold derelictions of the mate himself; p. 139 (n.) we
all looked round for the mate; p. 142 (n.) In most of my shipmates;

p. 145 (n.) we had caught no glimpse of the mate; p. 146 (n.) fled
through the village, the mate after them; p. 146 (adj.) the mate's
delinquencies being summarily passed over; p. 148 (n.) with a steady
New Englander for second mate; p. 290 (n.) the mate of the vessel
called out; p. 309 (n.) formerly the mate of a merchant vessel;
p. 312 (n.) We became acquainted with the third mate.

Mardi--p. 19 (n.) Captain, mates, crew; p. 23 (n.) our solitary
watch-mate; p. 26 (n.) our solitary watchmate; p. 28 (n.) from the
chief mate; p. 95 (n.) the chief mate, whose duty.

Redburn--p. 19 (n.) I say, maty--look here; p. 27 (n.) the first and
second mates of the ship; p. 27 (n.) to make friends with the second
mate; p. 27 (n.) I should have offered my box to the chief mate;
p. 28 (n.) the chief mate approached in a great hurry; p. 29 (n.) But
just then the mate came along; p. 29 (n.) the mate observing me,
exclaimed; p. 29 (adj.) when I heard the chief mate's voice; p. 30
(n.) But the mate had turned on his heel; p. 31 (n.) muttered the
chief mate; p. 37 (n.) he left the giving orders to the chief mate;
p. 38 (n.) The chief mate began by selecting; p. 38 (adj.) the second
mate's turn came to choose; p. 38 (n.) both of the mates never so
much as looked; p. 39 (adj.) it was the chief mate's next turn to
choose; p. 39 (n.) said the chief mate; p. 39 (n.) speaking to the
second mate; p. 39 (n.) said the chief mate; p. 39 (n.) said the
second mate again; p. 39 (adj.) they put me in the chief mate's
division; p. 39 (n.) the second mate called one of the sailors; p. 39
(n.) as if the second mate was a "born gentleman"; p. 39 (n.) when I
heard the chief mate call him; p. 39 (n.) so far as the second mate
is concerned; p. 39 (n.) though the chief mate occasionally is;
pp. 39-40 (n.) the second mate has to breakfast; p. 40 (n.) very
civilly to the chief mate; p. 45 (n.) The chief mate kept walking up
and down; p. 45 (n.) the mate suddenly stopped; p. 46 (n.) the mate
would always say; p. 46 (n.) of popularity among his shipmates; p. 47
(n.) any such good sailors among my ship-mates; p. 48 (n.) where the
chief mate could not see them; p. 50 (n.) the chief mate ran forward;
p. 50 (n.) as the chief mate called it; p. 53 (n.) So I went to the
chief mate; p. 54 (n.) the mate began heaving buckets; p. 56 (n.)
Some Account of One of His Shipmates; p. 63 (n.) and the mate set us
to work; p. 65 (n.) the mate ordered me to do a great many simple
things; p. 65 (n.) for fear of the mate; p. 65 (n.) the mate having
ordered me to draw some water; p. 69 (n.) the mate had set me to
tarring; p. 69 (n.) when the chief mate met me; p. 69 (n.) aboard a
ship that he was mate of; p. 70 (n.) when the mate came running up;
p. 70 (n.) Indeed this chief mate seemed to have; p. 74 (n.) the mate
asked me once; p. 78 (n.) I knew it was the mate hurrying me; p. 85
(n.) when all my messmates were asleep; p. 89 (n.) He would often ask
his shipmates; p. 92 (n.) we saw the mate standing; p. 92 (n.) that
our own mate was raising; p. 93 (n.) terribly reprimanded by the mate;
p. 109 (n.) as for the mates; p. 109 (n.) said the mate, who was a
bit of a wag; p. 112 (n.) he told the mate to send him forward; p.
p. 112 (n.) looked like a juvenile boatswain's-mate; p. 114 (n.) the
mate entertained good hopes; p. 119 (adj.) and the chief mate's
secretary; p. 122 (n.) I received from the chief mate; p. 125 (n.)
the mate accordingly backed the main yard; p. 125 (n.) the mate asked
him why he did not; p. 125 (n.) cried the mate, shaking his fist;
p. 127 (n.) soon learned from my ship-mates; p. 133 (n.) while my

shipmates were now engaged; p. 134 (n.) drunk by most of my shipmates;
p. 136 (n.) his Prime Minister and Grand Vizier, the chief mate;
p. 137 (n.) and tucked in by the two mates; p. 137 (n.) and the chief
mate was often put to it; p. 139 (n.) though the Boatswain's Mate;
p. 153 (n.) My shipmates, of course, made merry; p. 171 (n.) as were
also the three mates; p. 175 (n.) The mate had a wooden leg; p. 186
(n.) of the second mate of a merchant ship; p. 188 (n.) went ashore
with my shipmates; p. 189 (n.) chance to stumble upon a shipmate;
p. 195 (n.) a shipmate of mine purchased it; p. 196 (n.) under
custody of the chief mate; p. 204 (n.) but my shipmates did; p. 216
(n.) He was speaking to one of my shipmates; p. 224 (n.) at which
business the mate had set me; p. 238 (n.) the mate seemed to know
nothing about it; p. 238 (n.) and the mate perceiving me, said;
p. 238 (n.) added the mate; p. 243 (n.) the chief mate at last came
forward; p. 243 (n.) giving the mate to understand; p. 243 (n.) the
mate retired to the quarter-deck; p. 244 (n.) It's a water-rat,
shipmates, that's dead; pp. 244-5 (n.) from the scuttle by the mate;
p. 245 (n.) the mate sprang down in a rage; p. 254 (n.) cried the
mate; p. 254 (adj.) in the mate's [estimation]; p. 254 (n.) I suppose
your Hottentot of a mate; p. 254 (n.) polite refinement in the mates
and crew; p. 255 (n.) ignoring the fact that his shipmates; p. 256
(n.) the mate singled him out; p. 256 (n.) said the mate; p. 256 (n.)
cried the mate; p. 256 (n.) making a dash at the mate; p. 256 (n.)
said the mate; p. 256 (n.) cried the mate; p. 257 (n.) cried the mate;
p. 257 (n.) he went to the mate; p. 257 (n.) the mate gave him a
blunt denial; p. 257 (n.) Harry then told the mate solemnly; p. 264
(adj.) at the mate's command; p. 266 (n.) the mate would accost him;
p. 269 (n.) one good thing on the part of the mate; p. 269 (n.) cried
the mate; p. 270 (n.) my shipmates disposed of their tobacco; p. 270
(n.) inducing the mate to surrender; p. 273 (n.) when solicited by a
shipmate for a "chaw"; p. 275 (n.) the more sneaking and cowardly of
my shipmates; p. 277 (n.) who with his watchmates requested him;
p. 283 (n.) at last went aft to the mate; p. 284 (n.) said the mate;
p. 286 (n.) in the face of the chief mate; p. 286 (n.) than the mate
promptly repaired; p. 287 (n.) that the mate succeeded in getting the
sailors below; p. 287 (n.) cried the mate; p. 287 (n.) roared the
mate; p. 287 (n.) Further efforts were made by the mate; p. 288 (n.)
the mate attended them with his medicines; p. 288 (n.) induced him to
tell the two mates; p. 290 (n.) and even tender care of the mate;
p. 296 (n.) which had closed over the head of our shipmates; p. 296
(n.) from the mate; p. 302 (n.) but the mate and the rats; p. 308 (n.)
by the looks of our shipmates; p. 309 (n.) well, maties; p. 309 (n.)
our shipmates departed.

White-Jacket--p. 4 (n.) my heartless shipmates ever used to stand up;
p. 11 (n.) We say nothing here of Boatswain's mates, Gunner's mates,
Carpenter's mates, Sail-maker's mates, Armorer's mates; p. 12 (n.)
The Boatswain's mates whistle round him; p. 13 (n.) on the best
possible terms with my top-mates; p. 14 (n.) was voted a bore by his
shipmates; p. 16 (n.) Topmates; p. 27 (n.) Carpenter's, and Sail-
maker's mates; p. 29 (n.) let us candidly confess it, shipmates;
p. 36 (n.) regarded as needless by one of my top-mates; p. 36 (adj.)
My top-mate's contrivance was this; p. 37 (n.) I told my good top-mate;
p. 41 (n.) made by the less learned of his shipmates; p. 41 (n.) ship's
corporals, and boatswain's mates; p. 44 (n.) including the two gunner's
mates; p. 44 (n.) Priming, the nasal-voiced gunner's mate; p. 45 (n.)

A fine top-mate of ours; p. 45 (n.) My top-mates thought that this
remarkable metamorphose; p. 47 (n.) especially him who had once been
our top-mate; p. 57 (n.) are served out by one of the master's mates;
p. 58 (n.) is the shrill pipe of the boatswain's mate; p. 60 (n.)
The boatswain and his mates had piped the hands to dinner; p. 60 (n.)
My messmates were assembled; p. 67 (n.) a gunner's mate . . . thrusts
out the cartridges; p. 69 (n.) the surgeon and his mates would be
amputating; p. 70 (n.) would answer for some poor shipmate; p. 77 (n.)
who are shipmates and fellow-sailors or ours; p. 77 (n.) my watchmates
had hied to their hammocks; p. 9. (n.) Think of it, shipmates; p. 94
(n.) the boatswain's mates bellowed themselves hoarse; p. 101 (n.)
subjects for the surgeon and his mates; p. 102 (n.) serves to collect
round him . . . his four mates; p. 102 (n.) The Boatswain and his
mates are; p. 121 (n.) accosting a mess-mate with a sort of . . .
assumption; p. 124 (n.) to reflect credit on the yeoman and his mates;
p. 128 (n.) which one of his mates once told me; p. 134 (n.) summons
of the boatswain and his mates; p. 136 (n.) two of his young mess-
mates had gone to his bag; p. 137 (n.) he gave one to each of his
mates; p. 137 (n.) and the first boatswain's-mate advanced; p. 137
(adj.) to applause of their ship-mate's nerve; p. 138 (n.) The fourth
boatswain's-mate advanced; p. 138 (n.) what are you stopping for,
boatswain's-mate; p. 140 (n.) most boatswain's mates carry the colt;
p. 146 (n.) even as the boatswain's mates . . . are often called upon;
p. 156 (n.) the boatswain's-mates were obliged to drive; p. 161 (n.)
which a messmate doffed for my benefit; p. 163 (n.) This proceeded
from a boatswain's mate; p. 163 (n.) the boatswain himself--not a
boatswain's mate; p. 170 (n.) the only method adopted by my shipmates;
p. 173 (n.) as a philosophical shipmate observed; p. 174 (n.) seen so
many of my shipmates all employed; p. 175 (n.) in the books of the
master's mate; p. 178 (n.) vigilance of the master-at-arms and his
mates; p. 180 (n.) I have stationed two of my mess-mates; p. 184 (n.)
at the sight of the boatswain's mates; p. 185 (n.) he had induced a
mess-mate of ours; p. 186 (n.) But whatever we mess-mates thought;
p. 193 (n.) a sad accident befell a mess-mate of mine; p. 195 (n.)
the story of my poor mess-mate Baldy; p. 196 (n.) has fallen upon his
own shipmates in the tops; p. 205 (n.) epistles of their more
fortunate shipmates; p. 208 (n.) buried heads of killed comrades and
mess-mates; p. 213 (n.) a quarter-gunner, or boatswain's mate; p. 213
(n.) favor for himself and shipmates; p. 214 (n.) you and your
shipmates are after some favor; p. 215 (n.) cried his shipmates;
p. 223 (n.) taking off old Priming, the gunner's mate; p. 223 (n.)
Boatswain's mate, where's your colt; p. 223 (n.) the boatswain's mate
looked into the crown aghast; p. 224 (n.) Now go on, boatswain's mate;
p. 224 (n.) that boatswain's mate, too, had a spite again me; p. 225
(n.) the liberty his shipmates so earnestly coveted; p. 226 (n.) we
were pulled ashore by our shipmates; p. 227 (n.) But one of our
Surgeon's mates; p. 228 (n.) this Surgeon's mate must needs go ashore;
p. 236 (n.) He may well wear a green one, top-mates; p. 236 (n.) I say,
top-mates; p. 242 (n.) entered the merchant-service as a chief mate;
p. 246 (n.) a mess-mate, though not a top-mate of mine; p. 258 (n.)
Carpenter's mate, . . . will you never get through; p. 258 (n.) in
the arms of two of his mess-mates; p. 258 (n.) one of the mess-mates
was obliged to keep; p. 259 (n.) said his mess-mates; p. 259 (n.)
addressing the two mess-mates; p. 261 (n.) cried the two mess-mates;
p. 261 (n.) Stand by, now, you mess-mates; p. 261 (n.) his mess-mates
pinioned him; p. 264 (n.) the mess-mates of the top-man rowed; p. 276

(n.) Do your duty, boatswain's mate; p. 277 (n.) all my shipmates
were liable to that; p. 278 (n.) the announcement made by the
boatswain's mates; p. 278 (n.) I heard the boatswain's mates bawling
my name; p. 278 (n.) the boatswain's mate at the fore-hatchway;
p. 278 (n.) by the other boatswain's mate; p. 280 (n.) the boatswain's
mate stood curling his fingers; p. 280 (n.) the boatswain's mate,
scourge in hand; p. 293 (n.) stand bareheaded among my shipmates;
p. 295 (n.) Can your shipmates so much as drink; p. 306 (n.) the
master-at-arms, assisted by his mates; p. 310 (n.) Here comes Aurora;
top-mates, see; p. 316 (n.) perceiving an old mess-mate; p. 318 (n.)
a mess-mate shoved in the dead man's . . . cap; p. 328 (n.) under the
scourge of the boatswain's mate; p. 329 (n.) can be answered by your
mess-mates; p. 332 (n.) that a mess-mate of mine, by the name of
Shenly; p. 332 (n.) An old gunner's mate of the mess . . . this
gunner's mate; p. 332 (n.) another mess-mate of ours . . . also a
mess-mate; p. 333 (n.) My dear mess-mate; p. 333 (n.) Gunner's mate
. . . Gunner's mate; p. 333 (n.) For God's sake, gunner's mate;
p. 333 (n.) you will mess alone, gunner's mate; p. 333 (n.) you are
an old bear, gunner's mate; p. 333 (n.) the murder of one of my
shipmates; p. 335 (n.) Shenly, my sick mess-mate; p. 335 (n.) we, his
mess-mates, were officially notified; p. 335 (n.) that our poor mess-
mate was run down; p. 335 (n.) went down to relieve one of my mess-
mates; p. 336 (n.) whispered my mess-mate; p. 336 (n.) Good-by, good-
by, mess-mate; p. 336 (n.) the well-known features of my mess-mate;
p. 336 (n.) to rouse . . . four or five of my mess-mates; p. 337 (n.)
directly myself and mess-mates; p. 337 (n.) when the Boatswain and
his mates mustered; p. 337 (n.) A mess-mate of the other watch;
p. 339 (n.) I never yet sewed up a shipmate; p. 339 (n.) their mess-
mates sticks their spoons in the rack; p. 340 (n.) for all the world
like a hammock-mate; p. 340 (n.) that have Death for a hammock-mate;
p. 340 (n.) cried one of the sail-maker's mates; p. 340 (n.) As the
mate and his man departed; p. 341 (n.) the boatswain and his four
mates stood round; p. 341 (n.) the mess-mates of Shenly brought his
body; p. 341 (n.) roared a boatswain's mate; p. 341 (n.) Shenly's
mess-mates tilted the board; p. 349 (n.) thundered forth by the
boatswain's mates; p. 351 (n.) two of them (the mates) at nineteen
dollars; p. 353 (n.) the begrimed gunner's mates . . . sported . . .
beards; p. 356 (n.) by the Boatswain's mate there stationed; p. 356
(n.) after soundly rating his tipsy mate; p. 357 (n.) gunner's mates!
mariners, all; p. 358 (n.) now attended by all four of his mates;
p. 358 (n.) drove the two boatswain's mates; p. 358 (n.) Boatswain's
mate, ship that ladder; p. 359 (n.) until deserted by their own mess-
mates; p. 361 (n.) parodying the style of the boatswain's mates;
p. 365 (n.) boatswain's mates, do your duty; p. 365 (n.) said a top-
mate; p. 365 (n.) you, boatswain's mate; p. 366 (n.) a mess-mate of
Ushant's; p. 370 (n.) his own shipmates are then made; p. 371 (n.) a
fresh boatswain's mate is called; p. 371 (n.) inflicted by the
boatswain's mates; p. 374 (n.) served out by the Master's mate;
p. 380 (n.) patriotism in many of my shipmates; p. 388 (n.) roared
the boatswain's mates at the gangway; p. 389 (n.) Shipmates! take me
by the arms; p. 389 (n.) Start my soul-bolts, maties; p. 389 (n.) Ay,
maties, ten of us waisters; p. 389 (n.) Blast the sea, shipmates;
p. 389 (n.) venerate it so highly, shipmates; p. 397 (n.) Hand in
hand we top-mates stand; p. 399 (n.) When a ship-mate dies; p. 399
(n.) Oh, shipmates and world-mates, all round; p. 400 (n.) yet,
shipmates and world-mates! let us never forget.

Moby-Dick--p. 8 (n.) By Owen Chase of Nantucket, first mate of said
vessel; p. 11 (n.) "Stern all!" exclaimed the mate; p. 35 (n.) nearly
all whalemen; chief mates, and second mates, and third mates; p. 85
(adv.) that same voyage when thou went mate with Captain Ahab; p. 90
(adj.) another time with a bunch of quills for the chief mate's desk;
p. 93 (n.) the riggers bestirred themselves; the mates were actively
engaged; p. 102 (n.) The chief mate of the Pequod was Starbuck;
p. 106 (n.) Now these three mates . . . were momentous men; p. 108
(n.) The mates regularly relieved each other at the watches; p. 111
(n.) needing supervision the mates were fully competent to; p. 393
(n.) said the reddening mate; p. 418 (adj.) For the moment all the
aghast mate's thoughts seemed theirs.

MERCHANT, MERCHANTMAN.--Merchant, A ship in trade. (Webster indicates
that this sense of the term is "not used," though Melville certainly uses
it.)--Merchantman, a trading vessel employed in importing and exporting
goods to and from any quarter of the globe. (Smyth)

Redburn--p. 170 (n.) these merchantmen were nearly the largest in the
world; p. 240 (n.) a vast fleet of merchantmen.

White-Jacket--p. 8 (n.) that in merchantmen the seamen are divided
into watches; p. 130 (n.) They domineer over the poor merchantmen;
p. 148 (n.) but boarded their own merchantmen; p. 278 (n.) as in a
merchant upon similar occasions; p. 312 (n.) out of a New England
merchant; p. 329 (n.) better for the sailor than a merchant; p. 380
(n.) the necessities of a merchant; p. 381 (n.) a berth in an outward-
bound merchant.

Moby-Dick--p. 15 (adj.) after having repeatedly smelt the sea as a
merchant sailor; p. 59 (adj.) Now a certain grand merchant ship once
touched at Kokovoko.

MERMAID. A fabulous sea-creature of which the upper half was said to
resemble a woman, the lower half a fish. (Smyth)

Typee--p. 14 (n.) could be nothing else than so many mermaids; p. 14
(n.) very like mermaids they behaved too; p. 15 (n.) were completely
in the hands of the mermaids; p. 132 (n.) in the absence of the
mermaids.

Omoo--p. 64 (n.) Think of those arch creatures, the mermaids.

Mardi--p. 123 (n.) caused by a commotion among the mermaids; p. 182
(n.) by the deepest diving mermen of Mardi; p. 282 (n.) making love
to the mermaids; p. 283 (n.) about the beautiful and bountiful
mermaids; p. 374 (n.) congealed tears of broken-hearted mermaids;
p. 380 (adj.) A long tangled lock of Mermaid's Hair; p. 380 (adj.) A
mermaid's comb for the toilet; p. 380 (n.) particularly curious
concerning Mermaids; p. 394 (n.) what mermaid is this; p. 394 (adj.)
to the flatness of the mermaid's foot; p. 394 (n.) mermaids are all
vertebrae below the waist; p. 482 (n.) and mermen, and mermaids, and
Neptune only knows all; p. 645 (n.) as seines-full of mermaids.

Redburn--p. 88 (n.) singing songs about susceptible mermaids; p. 299 (n.) couches for all mermaids who were not fastidious.

Moby-Dick--p. 115 (n.) a sort of badger-haired old merman, with a hump on his back, takes me by the shoulders; p. 402 (n.) the thousand mermaids sing to them.

MIZ(Z)EN. The aftermost mast of a ship, correctly mizen-mast, but commonly only the epithets of fore, main, or mizen distinguish them from each other. (Smyth)

Omoo--p. 19 (adj.) examined her from the mizzen rigging; p. 98 (n.) the ensign was set at the mizen-peak.

Mardi--p. 28 (n.) from the mizzen-top.

Redburn--p. 76 (n.) Hoisted at her mizzen-peak; p. 97 (n.) through a block in the mizen-rigging; p. 103 (n.) the captain in the mizzen-top; p. 109 (adj.) half way up the mizzen rigging; p. 255 (n.) he carried two mizen-peaks at his stern.

White-Jacket--p. 9 (n.) the fore, main, and mizen-top-men of each watch; p. 11 (n.) we say nothing here of . . . captains of the Mizen-top; p. 46 (n.) at sea, it ought to be in the mizzen-top; p. 47 (adj.) than the top-men of the fore, main, and mizzen-masts; p. 105 (n.) held on with the other to the mizzen-shrouds; p. 136 (n.) belonging to the mizzen-top; p. 138 (adj.) Peter, the mizzen-top lad; p. 184 (n.) one of the boys of the mizzen-top was flogged; p. 193 (n.) one of the captains of the mizzen-top; p. 194 (n.) that may be exhibited at the mizzen-peak; p. 195 (n.) and the mizzen-mast to vanquish them both; p. 195 (n.) What are you 'bout there, mizzen-top-men; p. 202 (n.) echoed a mizzen-top-man; p. 225 (n.) a young mizzen-top-man . . . whipped the tarpaulin; p. 257 (adj.) fell from the mizzen-top-sail yard; p. 307 (n.) the boys of the mizzen-top are generally chosen; p. 312 (n.) her mizzen-mast having been shot away; p. 332 (n.) poor Baldy, captain of the mizzen-top; p. 348 (n.) Mizzen-top-sail; p. 348 (n.) your mizzen-top-mast . . . was shot down; p. 353 (n.) and the giddy lads in the mizzen; p. 363 (n.) which the wags of the mizzen-top called; p. 393 (n.) nearly abreast of the mizzen-mast; p. 399 (adj.) we have gallant fore, main, and mizen top-men.

MOLLUSCA. In zoology, a division or class of animals whose bodies are soft, without an internal skeleton, or articulated covering. Some of them breathe by lungs, others by gills; some live on land, others in water. (Webster)

Mardi--p. 123 (n.) the myriads of microscopic mollusca; p. 417 (n.) sandwiching strange shapes of mollusks; p. 536 (n.) subsisting among the mollusca of the Tunicata order; p. 537 (n.) the Tunicata order of mollusca; p. 537 (n.) to such creatures as those mollusca; p. 538 (n.) In kings, mollusca, and toad-stools.

MOLLYMEAUX. A bird which follows in the wake of a ship rounding the Cape. It is a small kind of albatross. (Smyth's spelling is "molly-mawk.")

Mardi--p. 126 (n.) aquatic fowls . . . seldom found far from land: terns, frigate-birds, mollymeaux.

MOOR. To secure a ship with anchors, or to confine her in a particular station by two chains or cables, either fastened to the mooring chains or to the bottom; a ship is moored when she rides by two anchors. (Smyth)

Typee--p. 45 (v.) we ought to be mooring ourselves for the night.

Omoo--p. 59 (n.) tore it from its moorings; p. 224 (n.) A trim little sail-boat was dancing out at her moorings; p. 238 (v.) Several small canoes, moored here; p. 316 (v.) ordered the ship unmoored.

Mardi--p. 69 (v.) had been moored.

Redburn--p. 175 (v.) when she came to moor alongside.

White-Jacket--p. 160 (v.) moored in the deep-green water; p. 178 (v.) and moor them to the frigate's anchor-buoy; p. 229 (v.) moor your boys fast to that best of harbors, the hearth-stone.

Moby-Dick--p. 19 (v.) more wonderful than that an iceberg should be moored to one of the Moluccas; p. 46 (v.) the spile . . . to which the ship is moored; p. 58 (v.) the little Nantucket packet schooner moored at the wharf; p. 59 (v.) the world-wandering whale ships lay silent and safely moored; p. 248 (v.) the vast corpse itself, not the ship, is to be moored; p. 250 (v.) around a dead sperm whale, moored by night to a whale-ship at sea; p. 337 (v.) no cupidity could persuade them to moor alongside of it.

MULLET. A well-known fish, of which there are several species. The gray mullet, mugil capito, and the red mullet, mullus surmuletus, are the most common on the British coast. (Smyth)

Mardi--p. 282 (n.) plucking the reverend mullets by the beard.

MUSSEL. A bivalvular shell fish of the genus Mytilus. (Webster's spelling is "muscle.")

Typee--p. 151 (n.) using a piece of mussel-shell for tweezers.

MUTINY, MUTINEER. Mutiny, revolt or determined disobedience of regular authority by sailors, and punishable with death. Shakespeare makes Hamlet sleep "worse than the mutines in the bilboes." (Smyth)--Mutineer. A person in military or naval service, who rises in opposition to the authority of the officers, who openly resists the government of the army or navy, or attempts to destroy due subordination. (Webster)

Omoo--p. 66 (n.) Here the memorable mutiny of the Bounty; p. 69 (n.) volunteered to head a mutiny; p. 73 (n.) breathing nothing but downright mutiny; p. 81 (n.) we're all a parcel of mutineers and pirates; p. 82 (adj.) In the midst of this mutinous uproar; p. 83 (n.)

NAUTILUS. The pearly nautilus, N. pompilius, is a marine animal belonging to the same class (Cephalopoda) as the cuttlefish, but protected by a beautiful, chambered, discoid shell. (Smyth)

Mardi--p. 179 (n.) each seemed a pearly, scroll-prowed nautilus; p. 283 (adj.) embark thereon in nautilus shells; p. 380 (adj.) Stork's Leg, supporting a nautilus shell; p. 647 (adj.) to me, a nautilus shell.

Moby-Dick--p. 447 (adj.) Like noiseless nautilus shells, their light prows sped through.

NAVIGATE. Conducting vessels on the sea.--Navigation, the art of navigating, not only by the peculiar knowledge of seamanship in all its intricate details, but also by such a knowledge of the higher branches of nautical astronomy as enables the commander to hit his port, after a long succession of bad weather, and an absence of three or four months from all land.--Navigator, a person skilled in the art of navigation.--Circumnavigation, the term for making a voyage round the world. (Smyth)

Typee--p. 5 (n.) under whose auspices the navigator sailed; p. 11 (n.) is by some navigators considered as forming; p. 27 (v.) many a petty trader that has navigated the Pacific; p. 177 (n.) Although this prince of navigators; p. 183 (n.) a small volume entitled "Circumnavigation of the Globe"; p. 234 (n.) reposed the "remains" of the great circumnavigator; p. 234 (adj.) the man who had eaten the great navigator's great toe.

Omoo--p. viii (v.) the vessels navigating those remote waters; p. 35 (v.) navigating this vast ocean; p. 47 (n.) we would be left without a navigator; p. 51 (v.) bound to navigate the ship; p. 61 (n.) Jermin, as navigator, kept our reckoning; p. 66 (n.) and other illustrious navigators; p. 87 (n.) the whole art and mystery of navigation; p. 119 (n.) personal acquaintance with the great navigator; p. 160 (adj.) a canoe is the most ticklish of navigable things; p. 186 (n.) Kotzebue, the Russian navigator, says; p. 231 (v.) to navigate the future schooner; p. 231 (n.) He enlarged upon the science of navigation; p. 302 (adj.) who, in that navigator's time.

Mardi--p. 10 (v.) to navigate the ship; p. 11 (adj.) that of the Navigator's islands; p. 68 (adj.) a native of the Navigator Islands; p. 69 (n.) Samoa, the Navigator; p. 81 (n.) to the navigator; p. 93 (v.) or aid in navigating her homeward; p. 96 (n.) possessed no instruments of navigation; p. 99 (adj.) known as the Navigator Islands; p. 100 (v.) necessary to navigating the Parki; p. 164 (n.) sad fate of an eminent navigator; p. 165 (v.) deep foliage of woodlands navigated; p. 174 (n.) The celebrated navigator referred to; p. 256 (n.) adapting them to easy navigation; p. 290 (v.) circumnavigated by hatchet-faced knaves; p. 351 (n.) to complete the circumnavigation of the island; p. 461 (n.) the circumnavigator meanwhile pleasantly going; p. 492 (v.) thrice we circumnavigated the isle.

Redburn--p. 67 (n.) and teach me problems in navigation; p. 90 (n.) at the end of Bowditch's Navigator; p. 133 (v.) continually

without a downright mutiny; p. 102 (n.) Muster the mutineers on the
quarter-deck; p. 102 (n.) a list was made out of the "mutineers";
p. 159 (n.) for desertion, or alleged mutiny; p. 313 (n.) Is there a
mutiny on board a ship.

Mardi--p. 58 (n.) unscrupulous mutineers; p. 91 (n.) in quest of the
mutineers.

Redburn--p. 52 (n.) and stir up a mutiny.

White-Jacket--p. 149 (n.) developed themselves at the great mutiny of
the Nore; p. 149 (n.) these terrific mutinies . . . were almost
universally attributed; p. 358 (n.) recognizing no attempt at mutiny;
p. 359 (n.) charged upon the "mutineers"; p. 359 (n.) to avert an
incontestable act of mutiny; p. 359 (n.) could prevail upon the
Spithead mutineers; p. 359 (n.) of a tragical mutiny; p. 374 (v.)
that if the sailor mutinies; p. 400 (v.) let us not mutiny with
bloody pikes in our hands.

Moby-Dick--p. 9 (n.) Narrative of the Globe Mutiny, by Lay and Hussey
survivors, A.D. 1828; p. 9 (n.) Life of Samuel Cornstock (the
mutineer), by his brother.

NAUTICAL.   Relating to navigation, sailors, or maritime affairs in general.
(Smyth)

Typee--p. 201 (adj.) forays made upon them by their nautical visitors;
p. 223 (adj.) "Oh, hang your taboo," says the nautical sportsman.

Omoo--p. 16 (adj.) known by his nautical cognomen of "Chips"; p. 34
(adj.) bestowing upon him the nautical appellation of "Luff"; p. 47
(adj.) the captain's nautical knowledge being insufficient; p. 70
(adj.) familiarity with most nautical names and phrases; p. 235 (adj.)
driven him to don the nautical garb.

Mardi--p. 15 (adj.) my nautical reminiscences; p. 18 (adj.) for
nautical instruments; p. 91 (adv.) must be nautically submissive;
p. 93 (adj.) and nautical instruments; p. 93 (adj.) nautical
instruments had been clandestinely; p. 123 (adj.) notion of one of my
nautical friends; p. 384 (adj.) And works of nautical poets.

Redburn--p. 120 (adj.) in the approved nautical style; p. 139 (adj.)
clever religious tracts in the nautical dialect; p. 187 (adj.) dressed
in the nautical garb; p. 270 (adj.) has a Jackish and nautical flavor;
p. 272 (adj.) if they adopted this nautical method; p. 273 (adj.) of
an epicure in nautical fragrancies.

White-Jacket--p. 168 (adj.) nothing to say about nautical phrases;
p. 232 (adj.) performing other nautical maneuvres; p. 329 (adj.) long
familiarity with nautical invalids; p. 343 (adj.) In place of these
they substitute nautical names; p. 347 (adj.) also originated a
nautical maneuvre.

circumnavigating the apartment; p. 198 (v.) they have to navigate
the boisterous Narrow Seas; p. 294 (v.) like a dandy circumnavigating
the dress-circle.

White-Jacket--p. 10 (v.) They may circumnavigate the world fifty
times; p. 12 (n.) all previous circumnavigations of this terraqueous
glo^be; pp. 76-7 (n.) still accompanied by those old circumnavigators,
the stars; p. 96 (n.) than the first navigator's weathering of that
terrible cape; p. 98 (n.) the first navigators who weathered Cape
Horn; p. 98 (n.) The next navigator round the Cape was; p. 238 (v.)
mincingly circumnavigating a shotbox; p. 284 (n.) reading Bowditch's
Navigator; p. 345 (v.) great ships-of-the-line were navigated; p. 346
(n.) the application of mathematics to navigation; p. 398 (n.) will
prove an endless circumnavigation of space.

Moby-Dick--p. 5 (n.) Schouten's Sixth Circumnavigation; p. 62 (n.)
put an incessant belt of circumnavigations round it; p. 361 (n.) so
far as the Massachusetts calendar, and Bowditch's navigator, and
Daboll's arithmetic go.

NAVY. Any assembly of ships, whether for commerce or war. More
particularly the vessels of war which, belonging to the government of any
state, constitute its maritime force. (Smyth)

Typee--p. 29 (adj.) all the paraphernalia of his naval rank.

Omoo--p. 14 (adj.) auction sale of condemned navy stores in Sydney;
p. 42 (n.) Immediately, Navy Bob, a stout, old Triton; p. 76 (n.)
exclaimed Navy Bob; p. 85 (n.) sung out Navy Bob; p. 99 (adj.) dressed
in an old naval frock-coat; p. 104 (n.) cried Navy Bob; p. 107 (n.)
regarded with infinite scorn by Navy Bob; p. 107 (n.) they did things
differently in the English navy; p. 108 (n.) As long, however, as
navies are needed; p. 109 (adj.) that true criterion of naval courage;
p. 109 (n.) the "crack" craft in the French navy; p. 109 (adj.) In
exchanging naval courtesies; p. 110 (n.) In the French navy; p. 110
(adj.) one of those horrid naval bores; p. 134 (n.) turning this time
to old Navy Bob; p. 191 (n.) an intelligent surgeon in the United
States Navy; pp. 213-4 (n.) it supplied the navies of the Kings of
Tahiti.

Mardi--p. 289 (n.) ploughed by navies of mortals; p. 374 (n.) But no
navies could buy it; p. 452 (adj.) being of a naval description;
p. 477 (n.) as the addition to his navy of three large canoes; p. 482
(adj.) the extension of the isle's naval dominion; p. 482 (n.) and
led his navies a very boisterous life; p. 498 (n.) all Bello's great
navy were riding at anchor; p. 518 (n.) In navies his forests are
being launched.

Redburn--p. 88 (adj.) These high-sounding naval names; p. 100 (n.)
talking of sailor life in the navy; p. 139 (n.) to man the navies of
the moon; p. 162 (adj.) patriotic gratitude to those naval heroes;
p. 171 (n.) something as work is done in the navy; p. 193 (n.) and
embark in her Majesty's navy; p. 193 (n.) as in the American navy.

White-Jacket--p. 6 (adj.) or else--in the navy phrase; p. 7 (adj.)
More rural than naval were the sounds; p. 10 (n.) which drove them . . .
into the hard-hearted navy; p. 14 (n.) meant a ship in the English
navy; p. 17 (adj.) To avoid naval discipline; p. 17 (adj.) Though
bowing to naval discipline afloat; p. 18 (adj.) a fine, mixed martial
and naval step; p. 20 (n.) recognized in the American navy; p. 20 (n.)
about creating great officers of the navy; p. 25 (n.) in the navy it
has become a proverb; p. 27 (n.) in the American navy are only
distinguished; p. 27 (n.) But in the English navy they wear; p. 27
(n.) In the French navy they are known by; p. 30 (n.) Mr. Secretary
of the Navy, . . . you should interpose; p. 32 (adj.) whom the sight
of a trim-fitting naval coat; p. 32 (adj.) Take that to heart, all ye
naval aspirants; p. 43 (adj.) or a Paixhan Shot into Naval Abuses;
p. 43 (n.) forbidding any person in the Navy to bring any other
person in the Navy; p. 53 (n.) equally unprecedented remissness in
the Naval-store-keeper at Callao; p. 53 (n.) In the American Navy;
p. 53 (n.) inducement which keeps many men in the Navy; p. 54 (n.)
they incontinently entered the navy; p. 65 (n.) found mounted in the
batteries of the English and American navies; p. 67 (n.) Are our
officers of the Navy utterly unacquainted; p. 74 (n.) The Navy is the
asylum for the perverse; p. 84 (n.) was hardly ever heard of in the
navy; p. 84 (adj.) the fact is upon navy record; p. 78 (n.) In the
English navy; p. 87 (n.) In the Turkish navy; p. 88 (n.) of the roll
of American navy-captains; p. 89 (n.) sometimes the custom in the
American Navy; p. 112 (n.) are there incompetent officers in the
gallant American Navy; p. 113 (adj.) an accomplished and skillful
naval generalissimo; p. 113 (adj.) no one has a right to be a naval
captain; p. 113 (n.) not a few Selvagees and Paper Jacks in the
American navy; p. 113 (n.) According to the last Navy Register (1849);
p. 113 (n.) 68 Captains in the American navy; p. 113 (n.) owing to
the Navy Department being well aware; p. 113 (n.) who live on the
navy without serving it; p. 113 (n.) nor against the able seamen in
the navy; p. 114 (n.) the rank of a commissioned officer in our navy;
p. 114 (n.) some incompetent officers in our navy; p. 124 (adj.) as
the naval cat-o'-nine-tails; p. 125 (adj.) with a wonderful zeal for
the naval service; p. 129 (n.) but not observed at all in the Turkish
navy; p. 130 (n.) including the acting Secretary of the Navy; p. 130
(adj.) for the deceased head of the naval department; p. 135 (adj.)
the naval summons to witness punishment carries a thrill; p. 138 (n.)
when some captains in the Navy say; p. 139 (n.) arguments advanced by
officers of the Navy; p. 139 (n.) captains in the Navy . . . inflict
the scourge; p. 140 (n.) punishments for very trivial offences in the
Navy; p. 140 (n.) to the cause of temperance in the Navy; p. 140 (n.)
when the historian Bancroft, Secretary of the Navy; p. 140 (n.) the
Lieutenants in the Navy bitterly rail against; p. 140 (n.) in the
breaking up of all discipline in the Navy; p. 140 (n.) for the
government of the Navy; p. 140 (n.) no similar abuses were known in
the English Navy; p. 141 (n.) as much flogging at present in the
English Navy; p. 141 (adj.) who happens to rise to high naval rank;
p. 141 (n.) According to the present laws and usages of the Navy;
p. 142 (adj.) the marks of a naval scourging with the cat; p. 143 (n.)
all the Commodores in the American Navy are obnoxious; p. 143 (n.)
committed by persons belonging to the Navy; p. 144 (n.) In the American
Navy there is an everlasting suspension; p. 144 (n.) against the laws
of the Russian Navy; p. 144 (n.) because the laws of that Navy;

p. 144 (n.) were he transferred to the Russian Navy; p. 144 (adj.)
that though the naval code comes under the head; p. 144 (n.) if any
person in the Navy negligently perform; p. 145 (adj.) stands a good
part of the naval laws; p. 145 (n.) laws involving flogging in the
Navy do not render; p. 146 (adj.) as the boatswain's mates, the navy
executioners; p. 146 (adj.) Or will you say that a navy officer is;
p. 146 (n.) we assert that flogging in the navy is opposed; p. 146
(n.) Commodores and captains of the navy; p. 147 (adj.) after these
navy rebels had been imprisoned; p. 148 (n.) knocked down and dragged
into the navy; p. 148 (n.) in the American navy, where corporal
punishment; p. 148 (n.) effects of government abuses in the navy;
p. 149 (n.) jeopardized the very existence of the British navy;
p. 149 (adj.) of all advocates of navy flogging; p. 149 (adj.) who
may happen to be navy officers; p. 149 (n.) insubordination of the
men in the navy; p. 150 (n.) the law of the English navy; p. 157 (n.)
introduction of chaplains into the Navy; p. 158 (n.) by the regulation
of the Navy; p. 158 (adj.) warmly attached to a naval commander;
p. 160 (n.) the ingenuity of any First Lieutenant in the Navy; p. 162
(adj.) This naval etiquette is very much like; p. 165 (n.) The general
usages of the American Navy; p. 165 (n.) usages that prevailed in the
Navy; p. 166 (adj.) that a naval officer should be surrounded; p. 166
(adj.) And by bringing down naval officers; p. 171 (n.) in her British
majesty's Navy; p. 172 (adj.) for it is not every navy captain who
will allow; p. 188 (adj.) of the honorable Board of Commodores and
Navy Commissioners; p. 189 (adj.) though long-established naval
customs; p. 193 (adj.) navy-regulation tarpaulin hat; p. 194 (n.)
contains the Masonic signs and tokens of the navy; p. 199 (n.) he was
Purser's steward in the Navy; p. 204 (adj.) above that of his equals
in navy rank; p. 206 (n.) There are Pursers in the Navy; p. 208 (n.)
much more extensive than the American Navy; p. 209 (adj.) so vast an
augmentation of her naval force; p. 209 (adj.) among crowds of the
British naval officers; p. 209 (adj.) Had they not been naval officers;
p. 209 (n.) Standing navies as well as standing armies; p. 216 (n.)
sometimes driven into the Navy; p. 127 (adj.) a cardinal principle
with a Navy Captain; p. 217 (n.) for the navies of Constitutional
Monarchies; p. 218 (n.) the tacit principle in the Navy seems to be;
p. 218 (n.) have regarded flogging in the Navy with the deepest
concern; p. 219 (n.) the midshipmen in the English Navy are not
permitted; p. 219 (n.) little boys wearing best-bower anchors in the
American Navy; p. 219 (adj.) a Navy Captain can not, of his own
authority; p. 220 (n.) pursued by Captains in the English Navy;
p. 221 (n.) In the American Navy; p. 227 (n.) discontinued, both in
the English and American Navy; p. 229 (n.) not yet weighed their
anchors for the Navy; p. 230 (n.) Midshipmen entering the Navy early;
p. 230 (n.) at which some of the midshipmen enter the Navy; p. 230
(adj.) the British military and naval services were kept distinct;
p. 230 (adj.) before he entered the naval service; p. 231 (n.)
Midshipmen sent into the Navy; p. 231 (n.) matters connected with the
general welfare of the Navy; p. 231 (n.) to the opinions of the
officers of the Navy; p. 231 (n.) perpetuated in the Navy many evils;
p. 231 (n.) but the Navy goes down from generation to generation;
p. 231 (n.) when a Secretary of the Navy ventures; p. 231 (adj.) you
hear some of the Navy officers say; p. 231 (adj.) cheerfully leave to
navy officers; p. 242 (n.) had entered the Navy when very young;
p. 242 (n.) he re-entered the Navy at Pensacola; p. 244 (n.) sailing
from the Brooklyn Navy-yard; p. 248 (n.) of being the foremost Surgeon

in the Navy; p. 249 (adj.) he always hung his Navy cap; p. 255 (adj.)
were arrayed in their blue navy uniforms; p. 257 (n.) when the army
and navy furnish no inducements; p. 257 (adj.) exchange your Navy
commissions; p. 257 (n.) for the amputation-tables of foreign navies;
p. 266 (n.) Thus, in the English Navy; p. 272 (n.) one of the slowest
vessels in the American Navy; p. 274 (adj.) when a navy captain does
not happen to be; p. 283 (adj.) except according to Navy regulations;
p. 285 (n.) In modern navies this custom is reversed; p. 292 (adj.)
whether they were according to the Navy cut; p. 294 (n.) No private
in the navy shall disobey; p. 294 (n.) If any person in the navy
shall sleep; p. 294 (n.) while hostile navies are playing cannon-ball
billiards; p. 297 (n.) the penal laws of the American Navy; p. 297
(n.) as heard of in the American Navy; p. 298 (n.) was at the head of
the Navy; p. 298 (n.) deemed so glorious to the British Navy; p. 298
(adj.) The first Naval Articles of War in the English Language;
p. 298 (n.) better Government of his Majesty's Navies; p. 298 (n.) in
force in the British Navy; p. 298 (adj.) directly sanctioning naval
scourging; p. 298 (adj.) the above-mentioned British Naval Code;
p. 298 (n.) now governing the American Navy; p. 298 (n.) for better
government of the Navy; p. 299 (n.) the English Navy . . . was full
of officers; p. 300 (n.) The present usages of the American Navy;
p. 300 (n.) No person in the Navy shall quarrel with any other person
in the Navy; p. 300 (n.) Officers of the Navy, answer me; p. 300 (n.)
no officer or other person in the Navy; p. 301 (n.) let me ask you,
officers of the Navy; p. 301 (adj.) throughout the whole naval code;
p. 301 (n.) unwritten laws of the American Navy; p. 302 (adj.) treat
of the naval courts martial; p. 302 (n.) In the English Navy, it is
said; p. 302 (n.) in the English Navy, it is said; p. 303 (adj.) the
whole nature of this naval code; p. 303 (n.) to the war exigencies of
the Navy; p. 303 (adj.) for the operation of the naval code; p. 304
(n.) Compare the sea-laws of our Navy; p. 304 (n.) unusualness of the
laws of the American Navy; p. 304 (adj.) for clothing . . . naval
courts-matrial with powers; p. 314 (n.) If any person in the Navy
shall . . . cry for quarter; p. 314 (adj.) But in a naval officer,
animal courage is; p. 316 (adj.) wrought out by naval heroes in scenes;
p. 328 (adj.) though the Navy regulations nominally vest him; p. 328
(n.) Not a seaman enters the Navy; p. 329 (n.) as with every other
matter in the Navy; p. 335 (n.) must have driven into the Navy;
p. 338 (n.) retained in the Navy more as pensioners; p. 345 (adj.) a
sort of army and navy seminary; p. 346 (n.) the office of Professor
in the Navy; p. 346 (adj.) not required by the Navy regulations;
p. 350 (n.) professors of polite trades in the Navy; p. 355 (n.) it
was disgraceful to the Navy; p. 356 (n.) the limits prescribed by the
Navy Department; p. 357 (adj.) according to the Navy regulations;
p. 358 (adj.) of a standard violating the Navy regulations; p. 359
(n.) prevented the disgrace to the American Navy; p. 365 (n.)
prescribed by the Navy Department; p. 366 (adj.) he was beyond the
reach of naval law; p. 367 (adj.) compared with the conduct of other
Navy Captains; p. 367 (n.) the usages of the Navy had made him;
p. 369 (n.) the subject of punishment in the Navy; p. 370 (n.) a
punishment inflicted . . . in the American Navy; p. 370 (n.) abolished
from the English and American navies; p. 370 (n.) is known in the
Navy as; p. 371 (n.) himself once a surgeon in the Navy; p. 372 (adj.)
than the Navy cat-o'-nine-tails; p. 372 (adj.) exhibition of American
naval law; p. 374 (n.) why have marines at all in the Navy; p. 374
(adj.) or else the naval service must be; p. 374 (adj.) held by most

Navy officers; p. 374 (adj.) the perfection of Navy discipline; p. 375 (n.) to most vessels in the Navy; p. 375 (adj.) the operation of the Naval code; p. 375 (adj.) organic to a Navy establishment; p. 377 (n.) The manning of Navies; pp. 377-8 (n.) is the sailor saying in the American Navy; p. 378 (n.) a far worse servitude in the Navy; p. 378 (n.) Sailors wanted for the Navy; p. 378 (n.) prohibiting slaves in the Navy; p. 378 (n.) the American Navy is not altogether; p. 379 (n.) foreigners in the American Navy; p. 379 (n.) it is not in the American Navy; pp. 379-80 (n.) though in no navy, perhaps, have they ever; p. 380 (n.) How it is in the French Navy; p. 380 (n.) introduction of foreigners into any Navy; p. 380 (n.) to deter the navies of all countries; p. 380 (n.) men employed in the English Navy; p. 381 (n.) appalled at the discipline of the Navy; p. 381 (adj.) according to an English Navy officer; p. 382 (adj.) a pamphlet on Naval Subjects; p. 382 (n.) so galling . . . as the Navy; p. 382 (n.) men who enter the Navy to draw their grog; p. 382 (n.) if they did not find a home in the Navy; p. 383 (n.) during a ten years' service in the Navy; p. 385 (n.) wherever . . . the American Navy . . . has formed; p. 385 (n.) the American Navy needs no eulogist; p. 387 (n.) throw in a naval sketch from Cruikshank; p. 389 (n.) Let the Navy go by the board; p. 389 (n.) What, then, must the Navy be; p. 390 (n.) the foremost in denouncing the Navy; p. 390 (n.) Thus, in part, is the Navy manned; p. 399 (adj.) to the indefinite Navy Commissioners.

Moby-Dick--p. 99 (n.) sail a navy of upwards of seven hundred vessels; p. 151 (n.) to think of the green navies and the green-skulled crews; p. 264 (n.) Where unrecorded names and navies rust; p. 347 (n.) the same ruthless detestation peculiar to military navies and armies; p. 369 (adj.) Commanded by a naval Post-Captain; p. 417 (n.) though thou [fire] launchest navies of full-freighted worlds.

NEPTUNE. A mythical god of the sea. (Bradford)

Mardi--p. 149 (n.) upon some green, mossy province of Neptune; p. 482 (n.) and Neptune only knows all.

White-Jacket--p. 77 (n.) intercede for me with Neptune, O sweet Amphitrite; p. 152 (n.) from the Wine-coolers of Neptune; p. 353 (n.) his long beard streaming like Neptune's.

NIPPERS. A whaleman's nipper is a short firm strip of tendinous stuff cut from the tapering part of Leviathan's tale: it averages an inch in thickness, and for the rest, is about the size of the iron part of a hoe. Edgewise moved along the oily deck, it operates like a leathern squilgee; and by nameless blandishments, as of magic, allures along with it all impurities. (Melville)

Moby-Dick--p. 350 (n.) Nippers. Strictly the word is not indigenous to the whale's vocabulary.

OAKUM. The state into which old ropes are reduced when they are untwisted and picked to pieces. It is principally used in calking the seams, for stopping leaks, and for making into twice-laid ropes. (Smyth)

Omoo--p. 53 (n.) who orders him to pick some oakum.

Redburn--p. 115 (n.) with yellow beards like oakum; p. 122 (n.) they set me to picking oakum; p. 137 (n.) or picked oakum; p. 224 (n.) I was engaged picking oakum; p. 272 (n.) When in picking oakum; p. 303 (n.) rubbing them hard with a bit of oakum.

White-Jacket--p. 42 (n.) brushing out their touch-holes with a little wisp of oakum; p. 94 (n.) strands of rope and bunches of oakum; p. 290 (n.) with his teeth through a bunch of oakum.

Moby-Dick--p. 275 (n.) he's always wanting oakum to stuff into the toes of his boots; p. 339 (n.) Some thinking they would catch the plague, dipped oakum in coal-tar; p. 362 (n.) oakum in the toes of his pumps as usual; p. 432 (n.) He's looking this way--come, oakum; quick.

OAR. A slender piece of timber used as a lever to propel a boat through the water. The blade is dipped into the water, while the other end within board, termed the loom, is small enough to be grasped by the rower. (Smyth)

Typee--p. 28 (n.) propelled by three or four strong strokes of the oars; p. 36 (n.) the poor larboarders shipped their oars; p. 74 (n.) with their oars shipped; p. 78 (n.) the other [end] flattened like an oar-blade; p. 251 (n.) our natives pulled till their oars bent again; p. 252 (n.) They would grapple the oars; p. 252 (n.) he would have seized one of the oars.

Omoo--p. 20 (adj.) for a couple of oar men; p. 70 (n.) with only the cook and steward as oarsmen; p. 96 (n.) made bundles of their oars; p. 199 (n.) we shipped the oars; p. 228 (n.) from the middle of a stout oar; p. 228 (n.) he politely rested the blade of the oar; p. 228 (n.) the springing and buckling of the clumsy oar.

Mardi--p. 28 (n.) our oars were out; p. 28 (n.) resuming our oars; p. 33 (n.) dropping his oar; p. 40 (n.) at our steering oar; p. 43 (n.) over the midship oar; p. 43 (n.) take to our oars; p. 43 (n.) Take to our oars; p. 51 (n.) loom of the Skyeman's oar; p. 52 (n.) to dry on oars peaked; p. 56 (n.) Jarl's oar showed sixteen notches; p. 56 (n.) I shipped the oars; p. 57 (n.) we added oars; p. 57 (n.) we lay on our oars; p. 57 (n.) using our oars; p. 58 (n.) barred down with the oars; p. 71 (n.) buckling to their oars; p. 72 (n.) tugged at their oars; p. 72 (n.) oar in hand; p. 72 (n.) two of their oars; p. 73 (n.) seizing the solitary oar; p. 117 (n.) as a sweep or great oar; p. 122 (n.) we at last out oars; p. 122 (n.) away from it with our oars; p. 128 (n.) we lay on our oars; p. 128 (n.) I bade Jarl and Samoa out oars; p. 128 (n.) Samoa dropped his oar; p. 128 (n.) pulling also at our oars; p. 129 (n.) to the blade of our long mid-ship oar; p. 481 (n.) its silver plated oars, musical as flutes.

Redburn--p. 250 (n.) like silver oars in bubbling brooks.

White-Jacket--p. 73 (n.) each man look out along his oar; p. 73 (n.) and look along your oars; p. 73 (n.) But the sixteen oarsmen still continued their talk; p. 102 (n.) others, mounted upon oars; p. 103

(n.) the Portuguese was straddling an oar; pp. 152-3 (n.) The men
sprang to their oars; p. 161 (n.) the cockswain suddenly cried,
"Oars"; p. 161 (n.) every oar was suspended in the air; p. 161 (n.)
presently I heard "Oars"; p. 225 (n.) Lay on your oars a while;
p. 233 (n.) rose upright to their oars at every stroke; p. 245 (n.)
from his place as an oarsman; p. 245 (n.) attempts to get rid of his
oar; p. 245 (n.) gained his oar.

Moby-Dick--p. 345 (n.) Stubb's after-oarsman chanced so to sprain his
hand; p. 387 (n.) reforming the shape of clumsy-bladed oars; pp. 387-8
(n.) An oarsman sprains his wrist; p. 388 (n.) Stubb longs for
vermillion stars to be painted upon the blade of his every oar;
p. 448 (n.) with oars speak.

OCEAN. This term, in its largest sense, is the whole body of salt water
which encompasses the globe, except the collection of inland seas, lakes,
and rivers: in a word, that glorious type of omnipotent power, whether
in calm or tempest:--"Dark, heaving, boundless, endless, and sublime,/
The image of Eternity." (Smyth)

Typee--p. xiii (n.) by the author tossing about on the wide ocean;
p. 12 (n.) little elevated above the surrounding ocean; p. 15 (n.)
some yet undiscovered island in the midst of the ocean; p. 27 (n.) to
traverse thousands of miles of ocean; p. 28 (n.) upon the long smooth
swell of the ocean; p. 248 (n.) Oh glorious sight and sound of ocean.

Omoo--p. 5 (n.) that broke the broad expanse of the ocean; p. 6 (n.)
many a league of ocean had been traversed; p. 33 (p.) on the rim of
the ocean; p. 35 (n.) navigating this vast ocean; p. 63 (n.) just
emerging, as it were, from the ocean; p. 65 (n.) above the level of
the ocean; p. 96 (n.) alone upon the ocean; p. 188 (n.) Voyage to the
South Pacific Ocean; p. 259 (n.) surrounded by an ocean of catsup;
p. 266 (n.) the sullen ocean, thundering; p. 270 (n.) was the blending
blue sky and ocean.

Mardi--p. 4 (n.) did the ocean appear so monotonous; p. 4 (n.) through
the ocean; p. 7 (n.) he regards that ocean; p. 7 (n.) rolled the ocean
beneath; p. 22 (n.) across the ocean; p. 29 (n.) I had regarded the
ocean as a slave; p. 39 (adj.) and the ocean moors of the Pacific;
p. 43 (adj.) no ocean leagues to traverse; p. 47 (n.) headless of the
wide ocean; p. 48 (n.) the ocean, upon its surface; p. 50 (n.)
rustling robe of the ocean; p. 50 (n.) Oh, Ocean; p. 108 (adj.) aspect
of the skies near the ocean's rim; p. 109 (adj.) by reason of the
ocean streams; p. 109 (n.) place upon the ocean was always known;
p. 111 (adj.) a specific cause for the ocean streams; p. 111 (n.) For,
that the ocean, according; p. 117 (n.) milk-white crest upon the
surface of the ocean; p. 118 (n.) pawing the ocean into foam; p. 118
(n.) when the furrowed ocean all round; p. 120 (adj.) once strown
upon ocean's beach; p. 121 (n.) we beheld the ocean of a pallid white
color; p. 121 (n.) in the South Seas and the Indian Ocean; p. 122 (n.)
any portion of the ocean luminous; p. 123 (n.) from the phosphorescent
ocean; p. 127 (n.) that part of the ocean upon which; p. 156 (n.) one
of those ever moaning of oceans; p. 178 (n.) surged the jet-black
ocean; p. 192 (adj.) the myriads that were ocean-tombed; p. 222 (adj.)
and breathe the free ocean air; p. 267 (adj.) in still ocean's dark;

p. 272 (n.) where eastward the ocean rolls; p. 278 (n.) sound the
ocean-haze at your feet; p. 303 (n.) gazing down into the ocean;
p. 303 (n.) by sliding into the ocean; p. 366 (n.) all round me, long
rushing oceans; p. 366 (n.) bleak and wild the ocean; p. 367 (n.) and
high over my ocean; p. 373 (n.) is sometimes thrown up by the ocean;
p. 420 (n.) our great reef is surrounded by an ocean; p. 435 (n.)
round all is heaving that infinite ocean; p. 482 (n.) should sport a
brave ocean-chariot; p. 488 (n.) mountains, vales, plains, and oceans;
p. 498 (n.) as if the land were the ocean; p. 511 (n.) which at their
mouths dam back the ocean; p. 529 (n.) Oro has poured out an ocean;
p. 540 (n.) every ocean a wine-vat; p. 540 (n.) Inland, the woodlands
stretched an ocean; p. 551 (n.) whitherward in mid-ocean; p. 554 (n.)
upon a smooth expanse, an inland ocean; p. 565 (n.) can not fathom
the ocean at his feet; p. 577 (n.) the ocean we would sound is
unfathomable; p. 580 (n.) the ocean a puddle; p. 595 (n.) sat within
view of the ocean; p. 629 (adj.) My soul sets back like ocean streams;
p. 651 (n.) till we come up in oceans unknown; p. 654 (adv.) the
currents sweep thee oceanward; p. 654 (n.) that outer ocean lashed
the clouds.

Redburn--p. 5 (n.) how I thought of their crossing the great ocean;
p. 16 (n.) my father has crossed the ocean; p. 33 (n.) as having
crossed the Atlantic Ocean; p. 33 (n.) if we had crossed the ocean
and returned; p. 33 (n.) we must cross the great Atlantic Ocean;
p. 34 (n.) many thousand miles of foaming ocean; p. 34 (n.) stretches
the great Atlantic Ocean; p. 34 (n.) had said he had crossed the
ocean; p. 54 (n.) there was plenty of water in the ocean; p. 63 (n.)
could hardly imagine that this was the same ocean; p. 64 (n.) the
sight of the great ocean itself; p. 64 (n.) did I realize till now
what the ocean was; p. 64 (n.) swelling and sinking all over the
ocean; p. 66 (n.) give me this glorious ocean life; p. 68 (n.) so far
away on the wide Atlantic Ocean; p. 72 (n.) warm and pleasant upon
the ocean; p. 76 (n.) come out of the infinite blue ocean; p. 76 (n.)
here I am on the great Atlantic Ocean; p. 76 (n.) the great Atlantic
Ocean was a puddle; p. 78 (n.) I could not see far out upon the ocean;
p. 93 (n.) sink down into the ocean; p. 94 (n.) sailing along on the
ocean; p. 95 (n.) and Beholds a Herd of Ocean-Elephants; p. 96 (n.)
had suddenly jetted out of the ocean; p. 97 (n.) the multitudinous
ships crossing the ocean; p. 97 (n.) degrees higher than that of the
ocean; p. 97 (n.) the temperature of the ocean; p. 98 (n.) flowing
through the ocean; p. 100 (n.) about the wild places in the Indian
Ocean [Gulf Stream]; p. 100 (n.) of the free and easy Indian Ocean;
p. 122 (n.) repeating Lord Byron's Address to the Ocean; p. 127 (n.)
with the savage places of the Indian Ocean; p. 129 (n.) on either
side of the ocean; p. 134 (adj.) of foul anchors, lovers' sonnets,
and ocean ditties; p. 164 (n.) from a voyage across the ocean; p. 168
(n.) to the roll of the great ocean-organ; p. 240 (n.) make the run
across the ocean; p. 248 (n.) on life's ocean was swept along; p. 252
(adj.) part of the way to that ocean grave; p. 253 (adj.) those ocean
barbarians; p. 259 (n.) all the rest was broad ocean; p. 286 (n.)
most elemental principles of ocean-life; p. 288 (n.) were dropped
into the ocean; p. 298 (adj.) in the soft, subdued ocean swell.

White-Jacket--p. ix (n.) lying in a harbor of the Pacific Ocean;
p. 12 (n.) as he advances along the files of old ocean-warriors;
p. 16 (n.) turning . . . the ocean into a whale-pen; p. 34 (n.) so

that he might cross the ocean sober; p. 47 (n.) when the face of the
ocean was black; p. 56 (n.) cheered with the grateful smell, old
Ocean smiled; p. 76 (n.) wherever we ocean-wanderers rove; p. 90 (n.)
approaching a most perilous part of the ocean; p. 90 (adj.) behold
the grief of his ocean children; p. 92 (n.) to inform the inhabitants
of the Pacific and Southern Oceans; p. 96 (n.) has been driven across
the Southern Ocean; p. 130 (n.) with a hissing hot ball sent bowling
across the ocean; p. 175 (n.) floating in a vast ocean herself;
p. 214 (n.) Are we not but just from the ocean Sahara; p. 227 (n.) in
the Pacific or Indian Ocean; p. 269 (n.) the ocean pawed its white
hoofs to the spur; p. 270 (n.) through a cream-colored ocean of
illuminated foam; p. 270 (n.) round the East Cape into the Indian
Ocean; p. 271 (n.) and he was an ocean-rover, too; p. 271 (n.) how
bid the ocean heave and fall; p. 271 (n.) there's no gammon about the
ocean; p. 280 (n.) pitch him headforemost into the ocean; p. 284 (n.)
enact on the ocean the proud part; p. 311 (n.) gigantic Turkish Emirs
striding over the ocean; p. 337 (n.) a bucket of water which I drew
from the ocean; p. 353 (n.) battling out watches on the ocean;
p. 377 (n.) with the ocean for a background; p. 378 (n.) set themselves
adrift on the wide ocean; p. 383 (n.) breathe the very poetry of the
ocean; p. 389 (n.) the ocean was held sacred; p. 389 (adj.) snuffing
the ocean air; p. 397 (n.) Appeased, old ocean now shall rage no more.

Moby-Dick--p. 4 (n.) can in a peaceful calm trouble the ocean till it
boil; p. 4 (adj.) which God of all his works/ Created hugest that
swam the Ocean stream; p. 5 (n.) In their way they saw many whales
sporting in the ocean; p. 7 (n.) The ocean serves on high; p. 8 (n.)
who had been killed by a whale in the Pacific ocean; p. 8 (n.)
destroyed by a large Spermwhale in the Pacific Ocean; p. 19 (n.) The
voyages of the Dutch and English to the Northern Ocean; p. 10 (n.) It
is impossible to meet a whale-ship on the ocean without being struck
by her mere appearance; p. 10 (n.) Tales of a Whale Voyager to the
Arctic Ocean; p. 11 (adj.) In his ocean home will be/ A giant in
might; p. 12 (n.) almost all men in their degree, sometime or other,
cherish very nearly the same feelings towards the ocean with me;
p. 12 (adj.) Posted like silent sentinels all round the town, stand
thousands upon thousands of mortal men fixed in ocean reveries; p. 14
(n.) But that same image [the ungraspable phantom of life], we
ourselves see in all rivers and oceans; p. 38 (n.) gardens came from
the Atlantic, Pacific and Indian oceans; p. 39 (n.) fishermen, shortly
bound for the Indian Ocean or Pacific; p. 50 (adj.) when the whale
bounded upon the ocean's utmost bones; p. 50 (n.) his ears--like two
sea-shells--still multitudinously murmuring of the ocean; p. 57 (n.)
he proposed to sail about, and sow his wild oats in all four oceans;
p. 62 (n.) that they are . . . made an utter island of by the ocean;
p. 62 (n.) and in all seasons and all oceans declared everlasting war
with the mightiest animated mass that has survived the flood; p. 62
(n.) parcelling out among them the Atlantic, Pacific, and Indian
oceans; p. 67 (n.) Long seasoned and weather-stained in the typhoons
and calms of all four oceans; p. 70 (n.) I perceived that the ship . . .
was now obliquely pointing towards the open ocean; p. 72 (adj.) but
all his subsequent ocean life . . . had not moved this native born
Quaker one single jot; p. 89 (n.) whaling, which necessitates a three-
years' housekeeping upon the wide ocean; p. 95 (n.) we found ourselves
almost broad upon the wintry ocean; p. 98 (n.) Up from the spray of
thy ocean-perishing--straight up, leaps thy apotheosis; p. 118 (n.)

and sailed through oceans; p. 121 (n.) have long pursued in the Indian
Ocean; p. 139 (n.) Roll on, thou deep and dark blue ocean, roll;
p. 140 (n.) takes the mystic ocean at his feet for the visible image
of that deep, blue bottomless soul; p. 171 (n.) with the charts of
all four oceans before him; p. 171 (n.) in the unhooped oceans of
this planet; p. 172 (n.) continuing their way along a given ocean-
line; p. 173 (n.) only his casual stopping-places and ocean inns, so
to speak; p. 174 (n.) in the broad, boundless ocean; p. 177 (adj.)
you may call it ocean-wide renown; p. 179 (n.) The dark ocean and
swelling waters were nothing; p. 194 (n.) grown up to us from the
bottom of the ocean; p. 202 (n.) By night the same muteness of
humanity before the shrieks of the ocean prevailed; p. 210 (adj.)
Steelkilt was wild-ocean born, and wild-ocean nurtured; p. 234 (n.)
does the ocean furnish any fish that in disposition; p. 235 (n.) That
same ocean rolls now; that same ocean destroyed the wrecked ships of
last year; p. 235 (n.) Panting and snorting like a mad battle steed
that has lost its rider, the masterless ocean overruns the globe;
p. 236 (n.) For as this appalling ocean surrounds the verdant land,
so in the soul of man there lies one insular Tahiti, full of peace
and joy, but encompassed by all the horrors of the half known life;
p. 272 (n.) That unsounded ocean you gasp in, is Life; p. 299 (n.)
bearing on his back a column of two hundred fathoms of ocean; p. 316
(n.) kitten-like, he plays on the ocean as if it were a hearth;
p. 320 (n.) they have been hunted over all four oceans; p. 347 (n.) a
whole mile of shoreless ocean was between Pip and Stubb; p. 347 (n.)
to swim in the open ocean is as easy to the practiced swimmer as to
ride in a spring-carriage ashore; p. 353 (adj.) the wild ocean darkness was intense; p. 355 (n.) The sun hides not the ocean; p. 396
(adj.) and the ocean's invisible flood-tide lifted him higher and
higher towards his destined heaven; p. 399 (n.) that serene ocean
rolled eastwards from me a thousand leagues of blue; p. 399 (n.) the
Indian Ocean and Atlantic being but its arms; p. 402 (n.) to the
death-longing eyes of such men, who still have left in them some
interior compunctions against suicide, does the all-contributed and
all-receptive ocean alluringly spread forth his whole plan of
unimaginable, taking terrors, and wonderful, new-life adventures;
p. 405 (adj.) beholding the tranquil beauty and brilliancy of the
ocean's skin, one forgets the tiger heart that pants beneath it; and
would not willingly remember, that this velvet paw conceals a
remorseless fang; p. 411 (adj.) That unblinkingly vivid Japanese sun
seems the blazing focus of all glassy ocean's immeasurable burning-
glass; p. 412 (n.) Old man of oceans! of all this fiery life of thine,
what will at length remain but one little heap of ashes; p. 413 (n.)
Such a funny, sporty, gamy, jesty, joky, hoky-poky lad, is the Ocean,
oh; p. 414 (n.) Such a funny, sporty, gamy, jesty, joky, hoky-poky
lad, is the Ocean, oh; p. 437 (n.) Ahab . . . seemed to have chased
his foe into an ocean-fold; p. 443 (adv.) away, whole oceans away,
from that young girl-wife I wedded past fifty; p. 447 (n.) the ocean
grew still more smooth; seemed drawing a carpet over its waves;
seemed a noon-meadow, so serenely it spread; p. 457 (n.) he pushed
his pleated forehead through the ocean; p. 459 (n.) 'Twas rehearsed
by thee and me a billion years before this ocean rolled.

OFFING. Implies to seaward; beyond anchoring ground. (Smyth) --
Distance from the shore. (Dana)

Omoo--p. 26 (n.) stood away from an offing.

Moby-Dick--p. 60 (n.) and our offing gained, the moss did homage to the blast; p. 95 (n.) At last we gained such an offing.

ORK. "Orca" is a classical name for a large voracious sea-animal, probably a grampus. Anglicized as ork or orc; thus in the second song of Drayton's strange Polyolbion--"The ugly orks, that for their lord the ocean woo." And Milton afterwards introduces them--"An island salt and bare,/ The haunt of seals and orcs, and sea-mews clang." (Smyth)

Moby-Dick--p. 3 (n.) Touching that monstrous bulk of the whale or ork.

ORLOP. The lowest deck, formerly called "over-lop," consisting of a platform laid over the beams in the hold of ships of war, whereon the cables were usually coiled, and containing some cabins as well as the chief store-rooms. (Smyth)

Mardi--p. 367 (n.) mariners rush up from the orlop below.

White-Jacket--p. 16 (n.) What knew you of gun-deck, or orlop.

OUTRIGGER. A spar rigged out to windward from the tops or crosstrees, to spread the breast-backstays. (Dana hyphenates the word.)

Typee--p. 13 (n.) occasionally the projecting outriggers.

Omoo--p. 160 (n.) what sailors call an outrigger; p. 160 (n.) The outrigger was a mere switch; p. 161 (n.) the outrigger flew overhead.

Mardi--p. 354 (n.) with paddles, outriggers.

OYSTER. A bivalvular testaceous animal, found adhering to rocks or other fixed substances in salt water which is shallow, or in the mouths of rivers. Oysters are deemed nourishing and delicious food. (Webster)

Omoo--p. 63 (n.) The oysters are found in the lagoons; p. 231 (n.) beach-de-mer, the pearl-oyster.

Mardi--p. 58 (adj.) were pearl oyster shells; p. 68 (adj.) and pearl oyster shells; p. 68 (adj.) business of oyster diving; p. 69 (n.) for seeking the oysters; p. 78 (n.) or oystermen, oysters; p. 130 (n.) as the opening of pearl oysters; p. 353 (n.) the precious pearl within the shaggy oyster.

Redburn--p. 88 (adj.) fell in love with handsome young oyster boys; p. 167 (n.) like a couple in a box at an oyster-cellar; p. 304 (n.) spending his money freely at the oyster-saloons; p. 305 (n.) invested it in a grand, underground oyster-cellar.

White-Jacket--p. 61 (n.) who had once kept an oyster-cellar ashore; p. 173 (n.) of flying to the first oyster-cellar; p. 173 (n.) nothing but a plate of stewed oysters.

Moby-Dick--p. 41 (n.) we are too much like oysters observing the sun through the water; p. 363 (n.) with bedded oysters for the shaggy bark; p. 437 (n.) oysters come to join me.

PACIFIC. The Pacific Ocean was the name given by the Spaniards to the "Great Ocean," from the fine weather they experienced on the coast of Peru. Other parts, however, prove this a misnomer. (Smyth)

Typee--p. xiv (n.) descriptive of the islands in the Pacific; p. 3 (n.) tossed on the billows of the wide-rolling Pacific; p. 6 (n.) Journal of the Cruise of the U.S. frigate Essex, in the Pacific; p. 6 (n.) extensive whale fisheries of the Pacific; p. 19 (n.) long, measured, dirge-like swell of the Pacific; p. 13 (n.) wandering among the islands of the Pacific; p. 21 (n.) for a pleasure excursion to the Pacific; p. 22 (n.) those unstable islands in the far Pacific; p. 23 (n.) she still continues in the Pacific; p. 27 (n.) many a petty trader that has navigated the Pacific; p. 97 (n.) do not probably exist in the Pacific; p. 126 (n.) depravity of a certain tribe in the Pacific; p. 170 (n.) among the barbarous tribes of the Pacific; p. 177 (n.) that the islanders in the Pacific; p. 184 (n.) who visit the principal groups in the Pacific; p. 192 (n.) and other islanders of the Pacific; p. 205 (n.) several of the primitive tribes in the Pacific; p. 221 (n.) residing for years among the islands in the Pacific; p. 255 (adj.) the English commander-in-chief on the Pacific station.

Omoo--p. xiii(n.) among the crews of ships in the Pacific; p. 10 (n.) more commonly called in the Pacific; p. 28 (n.) upon the savage islands of the Pacific; p. 33 (n.) into the immense flank of the Western Pacific; p. 35 (n.) the Pacific has been principally sailed over in known tracts; p. 48 (n.) whalemen in the Pacific never think of carrying spirits; p. 58 (n.) in the tropic latitudes of the Pacific; p. 62 (n.) most remarkable and interesting in the Pacific; p. 81 (n.) among sailors in the Pacific; p. 81 (n.) wedded to the Pacific; p. 103 (n.) for the English squadron in the Pacific; p. 126 (n.) of the thousand unconverted isles of the Pacific; p. 128 (n.) those in the Pacific have little enough of the virtue; p. 159 (n.) This is customary all over the Pacific; p. 187 (n.) Narrative of a Voyage to the Pacific; p. 188 (n.) A Missionary Voyage to the South Pacific; p. 231 (n.) take turns cruising over the tranquil Pacific; p. 235 (n.) In the free and easy Pacific; p. 257 (n.) upon the mild, blue, endless Pacific; p. 270 (n.) were the vast swells of the Pacific to break; p. 299 (n.) among the islands of the Pacific; p. 313 (n.) that American sea captains, in the Pacific; p. 316 (n.) all before us the wide Pacific.

Mardi--p. xvii (n.) voyages in the Pacific; p. 7 (n.) in the Pacific; p. 7 (n.) between the Atlantic and Pacific; p. 39 (n.) ocean moors of the Pacific; p. 39 (n.) who crosses the Pacific; p. 42 (n.) The Pacific is populous as China; p. 83 (n.) In the tropical Pacific; p. 104 (n.) by seamen in the Pacific; p. 109 (n.) in this quarter of the Pacific; p. 111 (n.) vicinity of the line in the Pacific; p. 116 (n.) over the equatorial latitudes of the Pacific; p. 122 (n.) both in the Atlantic and Pacific; p. 122 (n.) whereas, in the Pacific, all instances; p. 144 (n.) peculiar balm of the mid-Pacific near land;

p. 153 (n.) among the people of the Pacific; p. 289 (n.) that Paradise
is one vast Pacific; p. 367 (n.) when these Atlantics and Pacifics
thus undulate.

Redburn--p. 107 (n.) round Cape Horn into the Pacific; p. 312 (n.) I
found myself a sailor in the Pacific; p. 312 (n.) been in the Pacific
several years.

White-Jacket--p. ix (n.) in a harbor in the Pacific Ocean; p. 92 (n.)
inform the inhabitants of the Pacific and Southern Ocean; p. 96 (n.)
that way to seek a passage to the Pacific; p. 98 (n.) passages had
been made to the Pacific; p. 98 (n.) first sailed through them into
the Pacific; p. 115 (n.) a passage from the Pacific round the Cape;
p. 149 (n.) governing the American squadron in the Pacific; p. 372
(n.) while the Neversink was in the Pacific; p. 378 (n.) lying in a
harbor of the Pacific.

Moby-Dick--p. 8 (n.) who had been killed by a whale in the Pacific
ocean; p. 8 (n.) attacked and finally destroyed by a large sperm
whale in the Pacific Ocean; p. 16 (n.) I . . . started for Cape Horn
and the Pacific; p. 38 (n.) gardens came from the Atlantic, Pacific,
and Indian oceans; p. 39 (n.) shortly bound for the Indian Ocean or
Pacific; p. 40 (n.) on the off-shore Ground in the Pacific; p. 126
(n.) He is only found, I think, in the Pacific; p. 210 (n.) he had
long followed our austere Atlantic and your contemplative Pacific;
p. 285 (n.) though the Sperm Whale . . . mixed the Atlantic with the
Pacific; p. 295 (n.) you still occasionally meet with their flag in
the Pacific; p. 319 (n.) descending upon the Line in the Pacific;
p. 393 (n.) tropical outlets from the China waters into the Pacific;
p. 399 (n.) this serene Pacific . . . must ever after be the sea of
his adoption; p. 402 (n.) and from the hearts of infinite Pacifics,
the thousand mermaids sing to them; p. 443 (n.) nor did all the
Pacific contain such wealth as that one wee drop.

PACKET. A vessel making regular voyages between the same ports with mails,
passengers, and express freight; a liner of the sailing ship days. (Bradf
(Bradford)

Moby-Dick--p. 17 (n.) learning that the little packet for Nantucket
had already sailed; p. 58 (adj.) the little Nantucket packet schooner
moored at the wharf; p. 121 (n.) in the New York packet-tracks.

PADDLE. A kind of oar, used by the natives of India, Africa, America,
and by most savages; it is shorter and broader in the blade than the
common oar.--To paddle, is to propel a boat more purely by hand, that is,
without a fulcrum or rowlock. (Smyth)

Typee--p. 14 (n.) she puts in requisition the paddles of her own fair
body; p. 25 (v.) the canoe paddled on and the ship followed; p. 92
(n.) a great variety of rude spears and paddles; p. 132 (v.) while I
paddled about in my light canoe; p. 132 (v.) paddle with me about the
lake; p. 133 (v.) should be obliged to paddle about in the water;
p. 133 (n.) my trusty valet plied the paddle; p. 34 (v.) after we had
been paddling about for some time; p. 134 (v.) and paddled the canoe

to the windward side; p. 134 (n.) I directed its course with my
paddle; p. 150 (n.) warriors produced their spears, paddles; p. 172
(v.) the chief was paddling his way to the realms of bliss; p. 173
(v.) Aye, paddle away, brave chieftain; p. 174 (n.) instead of
terminating in a paddle; p. 183 (v.) two lads paddling their canoe;
p. 229 (v.) paddling about as if it had just risen to the surface;
p. 265 (n.) supported by four upright paddles; p. 270 (v.) and
paddled off to a whale ship.

Omoo--p. 99 (v.) Both were paddling with might and main; p. 99 (n.)
tearing his paddle out of the water; p. 99 (n.) flourishing his
paddle; p. 99 (n.) with suspended paddle; p. 99 (v.) Paddle away with
ye; p. 100 (n.) Jim, seizing his paddle; p. 146 (v.) got frightened,
and paddled for the shore; p. 152 (v.) away he paddled for the head
of the bay; p. 160 (n.) meant for a solitary paddler; p. 160 (n.)
with a paddle in the bow; p. 161 (n.) that my paddler made such
clumsy work; p. 161 (v.) and then paddled away; p. 162 (v.) have I
often paddled; p. 163 (v.) I could paddle close up; p. 163 (v.)
succeeded in paddling out of harm's reach; p. 163 (v.) running about
the place as I paddled; p. 216 (n.) fanning himself wildly with an
old paddle; p. 216 (v.) paddling a good distance off; p. 226 (v.)
Upon paddling up; p. 238 (v.) one solitary fisherman was paddling;
p. 242 (v.) paddling over to the village; p. 246 (v.) paddled with
might and main; p. 250 (v.) to walk along the beach as we paddled;
p. 262 (n.) with a paddle of the wood; p. 266 (v.) paddling off to
the reef; p. 268 (v.) As we paddled away; p. 269 (v.) paddling with
might and main; p. 269 (n.) for them to cease paddling; p. 270 (n.)
they seized the paddles from the hands; p. 270 (n.) as the paddle is
only waved thus; p. 289 (v.) and paddled off to her; p. 289 (v.)
paddle away wid yees for dear life; p. 290 (v.) and paddled ashore;
p. 305 (v.) Tanee was privately paddled over to Imeeo; p. 310 (n.)
tappa and matting, pad les and fish-spears; p. 315 (v.) The next day
I paddled off to the ship; p. 315 (v.) she would herself paddle me off.

Mardi--p. 165 (n.) paddle-blades reversed under arms; p. 167 (n.) six
of his paddlers; p. 189 (v.) slowly paddling; p. 200 (n.) and six
vivacious paddlers; p. 200 (n.) their broad paddle-blades carved;
p. 200 (n.) and paddles playing; p. 209 (n.) our paddlers only threw
back their heads; p. 213 (n.) Minstrel leads off with a Paddle-Song;
p. 213 (n.) the Paddle-Chant of the warriors; p. 213 (n.) and paddles
in hand; p. 213 (n.) our paddlers seated themselves; p. 213 (n.)
foremast, or Bow-Paddler; p. 213 (n.) the six rows of paddle-blades
being uplifted; p. 213 (n.) Our paddles fly; p. 214 (n.) in the brine
our paddles dip; p. 215 (n.) signing our paddles to desist; p. 268
(n.) ply paddles all; p. 284 (n.) Opaque as this paddle; p. 302 (n.)
with paddlers standing by; p. 316 (n.) running down innocent paddlers;
p. 317 (n.) his steering-paddle between his legs; p. 318 (n.) each
with a paddle; p. 318 (v.) we would have to paddle it; p. 318 (v.) we
have only our bodies to paddle; p. 326 (n.) our paddlers also stripped
to the waist; p. 354 (n.) being furnished with paddles; p. 378 (n.)
About prows there, ye paddlers; p. 378 (n.) having heard the shouts
of our paddlers; p. 402 (n.) from the paddlers in charge of our canoes;
p. 411 (n.) the paddles quietly urging us along; p. 421 (n.) Ho,
paddlers! we depart; p. 424 (n.) our paddlers plied their broad stout
blades; p. 424 (n.) with respect to one of our paddlers; p. 435 (n.)
the paddlers suddenly altered our course; p. 469 (n.) the paddlers of

the hump-backed king; p. 469 (n.) these paddlers seized upon several
of their occupants; p. 469 (n.) these luckless paddlers were dragged;
p. 469 (v.) commanded to paddle home their captors; p. 475 (n./v.)
our paddles paddling; p. 482 (n.) that dipping their paddles in the
sea; p. 491 (n.) the current too strong for our paddlers; p. 504 (n.)
one of our silliest paddlers burst into . . . mirth; p. 545 (n.)
sails wide-spread, and paddles plying; p. 562 (n.) all our paddlers
gazed; p. 567 (n.) One of ye paddlers, watch; p. 611 (n.) A chorus!
there, ye paddlers; p. 611 (n.) ply paddles; p. 612 (n.) that our
paddles seem thus muffled; p. 618 (n.) with paddle plying; p. 618 (n.)
Ho! merrily ho! we paddlers sail; p. 618 (n.) Drop paddles all, and
list; p. 620 (n.) each dip of the paddles in the now calm water;
p. 644 (n.) and paddles suspended.

Redburn--p. 311 (n.) we almost counteracted the play of the paddles.

White-Jacket--p. 178 (v.) paddles along under the surface; p. 246 (v.)
he proposed paddling himself ashore.

Moby-Dick--p. 56 (v.) he paddled off to a distant strait; p. 56 (n.)
he sat down in the stern, paddle low in hand; p. 345 (v.) the boat
paddled upon the whale; p. 448 (n.) with oars speak, and paddles down.

PASSAGE. A voyage, is generally supposed to comprise the outward and
homeward passages. (Smyth)

Typee--p. 3 (n.) about a fourteen-day's passage across the Atlantic;
p. 5 (n.) during our passage from the cruising ground; p. 31 (n.)
effect unperceived a passage to the mountains; p. 38 (n.) a bull-frog
might as well have tried to work a passage; p. 39 (n.) speedily
opening a passage towards it.

Omoo--p. 61 (n.) on our passage to Tahiti.

Mardi--p. 68 (n.) touching there on a passage; p. 111 (n.) prolonged
our passage; p. 122 (n.) more brilliancy from its passage; p. 127 (n.)
in making passages between; p. 262 (n.) a rather long passage being
now before us.

Moby-Dick--p. 46 (n.) I seek a passage in this ship to Tarshish;
p. 46 (adj.) the passage money, how much is that; p. 47 (n.) Jonah is
put down for his passage.

PEARL. A beautiful concretion found in the interior of the shells of
many species of mollusca, resulting from the deposit of nacreous
substance round some nucleus, mostly of foreign origin. The Meleagrina
margaritifera, or pearl oyster of the Indian seas, yields the most
numerous and finest specimens. (Smyth)

Typee--p. 115 (adj.) by means of a piece of mother-of-pearl shell;
p. 116 (adj.) sharp teeth of the mother-of-pearl shell; p. 218 (adj.)
cruel-looking mother-of-pearl-handled things; pp. 232-3 (adj.) filled
with oval bits of mother-of-pearl shell.

Omoo--p. 63 (adj.) visited by the pearl-shell fishermen; p. 231 (n.) beach-de-mer, the pearl-oyster; p. 310 (n.) inlaid with silver and mother-of-pearl.

Mardi--p. 68 (n.) in quest of pearls; p. 68 (adj.) and pearl oyster shells; p. 81 (adj.) at the Pearl Shell islands; p. 82 (adj.) The Pearl Shell islands excepted; p. 95 (n.) some Cleopatra pearls; p. 96 (adj.) a considerable quantity of pearl shells; p. 103 (adj.) Ever since leaving the Pearl Shell islands; p. 119 (adj.) with the pearl shells on board; p. 130 (adj.) as the opening of pearl oysters; p. 136 (n.) a rose-colored pearl on her bosom; p. 137 (adj.) a spell unlocking its pearly casket; p. 138 (n.) and a rose-colored pearl on her bosom; p. 179 (adj.) a pearly, scroll-prowed nautilus; p. 182 (n.) fillet of the most precious pearls; p. 193 (n.) Nor did the pearl on her bosom; p. 194 (n.) tearful pearls beneath life's sea; p. 199 (adj.) rows of pearly human teeth; p. 280 (adj.) true pearl shells rang musically; p. 283 (n.) brimful of seed-pearls; p. 283 (n.) sporting pearls in their ears; p. 300 (adj.) castanets of pearl shells; p. 346 (n.) holding pearl-shells on their heads; p. 352 (n.) the precious pearl within the shaggy oyster; p. 359 (n.) decorated with pearl-shells suspended; p. 360 (n.) and its pearl-shells jingled; p. 380 (n.) bones of a Pearl-shell-diver's leg; p. 391 (adj.) smitten with the pearly mouth of Hohora; p. 391 (n.) the same for whose pearls; p. 436 (adj.) Barbed with sharp pearl shells; p. 438 (n.) I unfold its petals, and disclose a pearl; p. 458 (adj.) when you strike a pearl shell; p. 509 (n.) Her sweet, sweet mouth!/ The peach-pearl shell; p. 645 (n.) torquoise-hyacinths, ruby-roses, lily-pearls; p. 650 (n.) Did'st ever see where pearls grow; p. 651 (n.) Hautia ros rose; hands, full of pearls; p. 651 (n.) bring up one pearl if thou canst; p. 651 (n.) Pearls, pearls! thy pearls; p. 652 (n.) Yillah's rose-pearl danced before me; p. 652 (n.) hast mosses? sea-thyme? pearls; p. 653 (n.) passed Hautia's cave of pearls.

White-Jacket--p. 22 (adj.) ivory-handled hair-brushes and mother-of-pearl combs; p. 294 (n.) you turn a dumb diver after pearl-shells.

PENINSULA. A tract of land joined to a continent by a comparatively narrow neck termed an isthmus. (Smyth)

Omoo--p. 65 (n.) great central peaks of the larger peninsula; p. 114 (n.) encompasses the larger peninsula; p. 114 (n.) Taiarboo, or the lesser peninsula; p. 124 (n.) Upon the peninsula of Taraiboo; p. 302 (n.) king of the larger peninsula of Tahiti.

Moby-Dick--p. 318 (n.) In a continuous line from that peninsula.

PERIWINKLE. The *win-winde* of the Anglo-Saxons, a favorite little shell-fish, the pin-patch, or *Turbo Littoreus*. (Smyth's spelling is "perriwinkle.")

Mardi--p. 417 (n.) then snails, and periwinkles.

PIER. A quay; also a strong mound projecting into the sea, to break the violence of the waves. (Smyth)

Omoo--p. 297 (n.) it stands upon an artificial pier; p. 308 (n.) he
conducted us along the pier.

Redburn--p. 4 (n.) and rounding the head of the pier; p. 23 (n.) I
walked out to the end of the pier; p. 111 (n.) in an empty hogshead
on the piers; p. 134 (n.) only land upon wharves and pier-heads;
p. 139 (n.) harangue them from the pier-heads; p. 161 (n.) slip-shod,
shambling piers of New York; p. 161 (n.) vast piers of stone; p. 163
(n.) solidified again as materials for the quays and piers; p. 163
(n.) by a long pier of masonry; p. 164 (n.) through a narrow entrance
between pier-heads; p. 164 (n.) glides into the ante-chamber between
the pier-heads; p. 217 (n.) we rambled about St. George's Pier;
p. 231 (n.) In the principal pier; p. 243 (n.) four or five hours
after quitting the pier; p. 301 (n.) knotted our old ship . . . to
the pier; p. 308 (n.) that some gentlemen were on the pier-head.

White-Jacket--p. 46 (n.) It should be placed on a bracket in the
pier; p. 148 (n.) and boarded foreign pier-heads; p. 396 (n.) drove
off from the pier-head.

Moby-Dick--p. 12 (n.) some seated upon the pier-heads.

PIRATE. A sea-robber, yet the word pirata has been formerly taken for a
sea-captain. (Smyth)

Omoo--p. 42 (n.) like a parcel of pirates gibbeted at sea; p. 50 (n.)
some of those pirates there for'ard may; p. 74 (n.) A History of the
Most Atrocious and Bloody Piracies; p. 81 (adv.) stepping forward
piratically; p. 81 (n.) a parcel of mutineers and pirates; p. 92 (n.)
ye blood-thirsy pirates; p. 95 (n.) must have taken us for a pirate;
p. 99 (n.) you piratee (pirate); p. 103 (adj.) The boat was painted a
pirate black.

Redburn--p. 58 (n.) full of piracies, plagues, and poisonings; p. 104
(n.) no more than a Malay pirate; p. 175 (adj.) in a state of most
piratical disorder; p. 190 (n.) terrific stories of pirates and sea
murders.

White-Jacket--p. 372 (n.) that harbor, once haunted by pirates.

Moby-Dick--p. 6 (n.) guarding and protecting the seas from pirates
and robbers; p. 62 (adj.) parcelling out . . . the . . . oceans, as
the three pirate powers did; p. 318 (adj.) Time out of mind the
piratical proas of the Malays; p. 321 (n.) the bloodthirsty pirates
chasing him; p. 321 (n.) after steadily dropping and dropping the
pirates astern.

PITCH. The plunging of a ship's head in a sea-way; the vertical vibration
which her length makes about her centre of gravity; a very straining
motion. (Smyth)

Omoo--p. 52 (v.) one day when the ship was pitching.

Moby-Dick--p. 450 (n.) This motion is peculiar to the sperm whale.
It receives its designations (pitch-poling) from its being likened to

that preliminary up-and-down poise of the whale-lance, in the exercise called pitch-poling, previously described.

PLANK. One of the thick, strong boards, used for covering the sides and decks of vessels. (Dana)

Typee--p. 21 (n.) the particular vengeance of this Lord of the Plank.

Omoo--p. 39 (n.) you entered by a plank.

Mardi--p. 7 (n.) to the brown planks; p. 24 (n.) her fated planks; p. 49 (n.) upper planking of the boat; p. 49 (n.) one of the plank-ends started; p. 49 (n.) to secure the rebellious plank; p. 92 (n.) screw-bolts which held together the planks; p. 181 (n.) had fastened to our planks; p. 483 (n.) plank be put for plank; p. 586 (n.) dragged down every plank and soul; p. 654 (n.) though every plank breaks up beneath me.

Redburn--p. 26 (n.) stretched ourselves out on the planks.

White-Jacket--p. 69 (n.) strewn with jagged splinters from our wounded planks; p. 69 (n.) take out the shambles' smell from the planks; p. 83 (n.) kept the planks of the berth-deck . . . constantly wet; p. 86 (n.) squeeze the last dribblings of water from the planks; p. 91 (n.) and her planks are the boards indeed; p. 174 (n.) select a soft plank on the gun-deck; p. 399 (n.) oft-painted planks comprised above the water-line.

Moby-Dick--p. 114 (n.) Ahab lurchingly paced the planks; p. 130 (n.) takes a few turns along the planks; p. 324 (n.) On both sides the sea came in at the wounded planks.

POLYNESIA. A group of islands; a name generally applied to the islands of the Pacific Ocean collectively, whether in clusters or straggling. (Smyth)

Typee--p. xiv (adj.) In the polynesian words used in this volume; p. 6 (adj.) Ellis, in his Polynesian Researches; p. 27 (n.) in all cases of outrages committed by Polynesians; p. 48 (n.) all the islands of Polynesia enjoy; p. 49 (adj.) the peculiar charm of every Polynesian landscape; p. 112 (adj.) that food which the children of a Polynesian father; p. 135 (adj.) standing for the statue of the Polynesian Apollo; p. 147 (adj.) throughout the whole Polynesian Archipelago; p. 157 (adj.) rise and fall of Polynesian Stock; p. 164 (adj.) soothing the cares of Polynesian life; p. 169 (adj.) with the horrible descriptions of Polynesian worship; p. 170 (n.) concerning the religious institutions of Polynesia; p. 175 (adj.) is in nearly all the Polynesian dialects used; p. 184 (n.) their great superiority over all other Polynesians; p. 191 (n.) This holds true of many of the islands of Polynesia; p. 192 (adj.) The ratio of increase among all the Polynesian nations; p. 195 (n.) to ameliorate the spiritual condition of the Polynesians; p. 195 (n.) Among the islands of Polynesia; p. 201 (adj.) the inhabitants of nearly all the Polynesian Islands; p. 203 (adj.) friendships of some of the Polynesian nations;

p. 206 (n.) The Polynesians seldom use a hook and line; p. 221 (adj.)
religious institutions of most of the Polynesian islands; p. 227
(adj.) among the inhabitants of the Polynesian Archipelago; p. 234
(n.) The Polynesians are aware of the detestation; p. 258 (adj.) It
was a sort of Polynesian saturnalia.

Omoo--p. xiii (n.) barbarous or semi-civilized islands of Polynesia;
p. xiii (n.) account of the present condition of the converted
Polynesians; p. xiv (adj.) one or two imperfect Polynesian vocabularies
have been published; p. xiv (adj.) from the Polynesian Researches of
Ellis; p. 99 (n.) to many of the natives of Polynesia; p. 124 (n.)
(no favorites, by the way, throughout Polynesia); p. 142 (n.)
throughout all the protestant missionary settlements in Polynesia;
p. 144 (n.) many jolly proselytes may he make in Polynesia; p. 152
(n.) all the Polynesians are in the habit of making bosom friends;
p. 152 (n.) the Polynesians could not testify the warmth; p. 160 (n.)
the Tahitians, like all Polynesians; p. 165 (n.) in all Polynesia;
p. 169 (adj.) the chapel of the Polynesian Solomon; p. 170 (n.)
pervading every considerable edifice in Polynesia; p. 170 (n.) for
Christian worship in Polynesia; p. 171 (n.) with the peculiar
animation of the Polynesians; p. 174 (n.) to designate the natives of
Polynesia; p. 175 (n.) a quality inherent in Polynesians; pp. 178-9
(adj.) so apparent in all Polynesian converts; p. 184 (n.) the
intercourse of foreigners with the Polynesians; p. 184 (n.) the
missionaries in Polynesia must always . . . struggle; p. 186 (n.)
subject of Christian mission in Polynesia; p. 186 (n.) Polynesia; or
an Historical Account; p. 187 (n.) have conversions in Polynesia been
in most cases; p. 188 (n.) and morals among the converted Polynesians;
p. 188 (n.) the depravity among the Polynesians; p. 188 (adj.) in
alluding to the Polynesian Researches of Ellis; p. 190 (n.) an indolent
people like the Polynesians; p. 202 (n.) all uneducated foreigners,
residing in Polynesia; p. 204 (n.) Farming in Polynesia; p. 205 (n.)
used in any part of Polynesia; p. 209 (n.) in any part of Polynesia;
p. 210 (adj.) in the whole Polynesian Archipelago; p. 245 (adj.)
deliver lectures on Polynesian antiquities; p. 247 (adj.) In the
train of many Polynesian princes; p. 254 (n.) The Polynesians carry
their hospitality to an amazing extent; p. 255 (n.) In Polynesia, it
is esteemed a great hit; p. 260 (n.) How different from the volatile
Polynesian in this; p. 261 (n.) the improvident Polynesian had thought
of his posterity; p. 262 (n.) To the Polynesian; p. 269 (n.) but among
the Polynesians; p. 278 (n.) familiar to foreigners, throughout
Polynesia; p. 280 (n.) among all the natives of Polynesia; p. 295 (n.)
whether I could possibly be in Polynesia; p. 296 (n.) the most
beautiful white woman I ever saw in Polynesia; p. 297 (n.) Holding
court in Polynesia; p. 297 (n.) several churches in Polynesia now
look almost as sooty; p. 299 (n.) Thus, in Polynesia as elsewhere;
p. 305 (adj.) the Saturn of the Polynesian mythology.

Mardi--p. xvii (adj.) a romance of Polynesian adventure; p. 67 (adj.)
Of a Polynesian sailor; p. 70 (n.) these Polynesians will climb palm
trees; p. 74 (n.) cupidity of the Polynesian; p. 77 (n.) In Polynesia,
every man; p. 107 (n.) the Upoluan, like all Polynesians; p. 127 (n.)
like those used by the Polynesians; p. 137 (n.) questioned her in
Polynesian; p. 137 (n.) addressed her in Polynesian; p. 137 (n.)
paradisiacal archipelago of the Polynesians.

Redburn--p. 173 (n.) much the same way as in Polynesia.

White-Jacket--p. 117 (adj.) had a Polynesian servant on board; p. 118 (n.) had we been Polynesians and he an American; p. 212 (adj.) of the war-canoes of the Polynesian kings.

POLYP. The common name of all those small gelatinous animals, whose mouth is surrounded by tentacula or feelers (whence the name), and conducts to a simple stomach, or one followed by intestines in the form of vessels. They constitute a distinct class or order of zoophytes, and include those compound animals, with a fixed and solid stem, which were formerly regarded as marine plants (Lithophytes). (Webster)

Mardi--p. 506 (n.) A fresh-water polyp, despising its marine existence; p. 506 (n.) the Polyp at last turned itself inside out; p. 506 (n.) the Polyp will live turned inside out; p. 507 (n.) what is undeniable of the Polyp.

PONTOON. A kind of portable boat specially adapted for the formation of the floating bridges required by armies. (Smyth)

Mardi--p. 256 (n.) to bridge the lake with pontoons.

Redburn--p. 110 (n.) by converting it into a pontoon over a puddle.

POOP. The aftermost and highest part of a large ship's hull. Also, a deck raised over the after-part of a spar-deck, sometimes called the round-house. A frigate has no poop, but is said to be pooped when a wave strikes the stern and washes on board. (Smyth)

Typee--p. 22 (n.) of the signal halyards and poop-down-haul.

Redburn--p. 300 (n.) Captain Riga . . . stood on the poop.

White-Jacket--p. 6 (n.) On the poop, the captain was looking; p. 21 (n.) on the weather side of the poop; p. 33 (n.) pacing the poop with long, bold, indefatigable strides; p. 34 (n.) where he stands on the poop; p. 72 (n.) darting a glance toward the poop; p. 102 (n.) upon the very quarter-deck and poop; pp. 162-3 (n.) is always stationed on the poop; p. 163 (n.) the whole brass band, elevated upon the poop; p. 177 (n.) descried by the quarter-master from the poop; p. 193 (n.) The Commodore on the Poop; p. 194 (n.) on the poop of his flag-ship; p. 197 (n.) that the Commodore on the poop may be glorified; p. 217 (n.) as if proceeding from the Commodore on the poop; p. 223 (n.) walking the poop; p. 229 (n.) sits high aloft on a frigate's poop; p. 234 (n.) The brazen band on the poop struck up; p. 245 (n.) The vessel was hailed from our poop; p. 269 (n.) the stately officers on the poops stiffly saluted; p. 271 (n.) the Captain's on the poop; p. 285 (n.) of a Commodore enthroned on his poop; p. 289 (n.) promenade up and down the poop; p. 311 (n.) The whole band would be assembled on the poop; p. 348 (n.) and blow my brains out on the poop; p. 396 (n.) sheathed his sword on the poop.

PORPOISE. The phocoena communis. One of the smallest of the cetacean
or whale order, common in the British seas. (Smyth)

Omoo--p. 20 (n.) splashing the water like porpoises; p. 34 (n.) No
sign of life was perceptible but the porpoises; p. 59 (n.) who went
breaching along like a porpoise.

Mardi--p. 42 (n.) little larger than a porpoise; p. 283 (adj.)
bracelets of wee little porpoise teeth; p. 374 (n.) fins, porpoise-
teeth, sea-gulls' beaks; p. 374 (n.) the fat porpoise frozen and
tombed in an iceberg; p. 543 (n.) like porpoises to vessels tranced
in calms.

Redburn--pp. 87-8 (n.) he looked like a fat porpoise; p. 97 (n.)
hauling up a fat porpoise; p. 196 (n.) as to harpoon a speckled
porpoise; p. 260 (n.) the occasional appearance of porpoises.

Moby-Dick--p. 38 (n.) portion off their nieces with a few porpoises
a-piece; p. 120 (n.) of the DUODECIMO, the Porpoise; p. 126 (n.)
DUODECIMOES.--These include the smaller whales. I The Huzza porpoise.
II The Algeriae porpoise. III The Mealy-mouthed porpoise; p. 126
(adj.) porpoise meat is good eating, you know; p. 184 (n.) and not
omit reporting even a porpoise; p. 254 (n.) an admirable sauce to be
eaten with barbacued porpoises.

PORT. An old Anglo-Saxon term still in full use. It strictly means a
place of resort for vessels, adjacent to an emporium of commerce, where
cargoes are bought and sold, or laid up in warehouses, and where there
are docks for shipping. Port is also in a legal sense a refuge more or
less protected by points and headlands, marked out by limits, and may be
resorted to as a place of safety, though there are many ports but rarely
entered. The left side of the ship is called port, by admiralty order,
in preference to larboard, as less mistakable in sound for starboard.
Port-holes, the square apertures in the sides of a ship through which to
point and fire the ordnance. (Smyth)

Typee--p. 13 (n.) in one of the principal ports on the main; p. 21
(n.) in some of the ports of Chili or Peru; p. 34 (n.) and have got
through most all our work in port; p. 254 (n.) which peeped out of
the portholes of the frigate.

Omoo--p. 6 (n.) to discharge me, if I so desired, at the next port;
p. 9 (n.) Fitted for a privateer out of a New England port; p. 10 (n.)
from a long sojourn in a dissipated port; p. 14 (n.) picked up in the
lawless ports of the Spanish Main; p. 51 (n.) to navigate the ship to
the nearest civilized port; p. 56 (n.) Bound into port; p. 69 (n.)
are we not going into port; p. 80 (n.) a well known sea-port on the
coast; p. 95 (n.) run out of the side-ports; p. 96 (n.) our mate had
sailed from that port; p. 97 (n.) to take the ship into port; p. 110
(n.) In port, he kept them constantly; p. 147 (n.) the gang controlled
the port; p. 148 (n.) as a charge of the port; p. 291 (n.) to be
discharged at the next port.

Mardi--p. 6 (n.) I make no port; p. 7 (n.) waits not for port; p. 49
(n.) from the day she left port; p. 68 (n.) sailed from her port;

p. 69 (n.) they left their port; p. 74 (n.) at one side of the ports;
p. 554 (n.) through a thousand port-holes.

Redburn--p. 4 (n.) will sail from the above port; p. 8 (n.) I used
to try to peep in at the portholes; p. 45 (n.) with most seamen the
first night out of port; p. 48 (n.) and our being just out of port;
p. 63 (n.) The second day out of port; p. 68 (n.) while yet in port;
p. 71 (n.) when Mr. Jones and I called upon him in port; p. 77 (n.)
on the second night out of port; p. 93 (n.) are never heard of after
leaving port; p. 106 (n.) at stated intervals between the two ports;
p. 108 (n.) we were but a few days from port; pp. 108-9 (n.) that
before arriving in port; p. 112 (n.) when we got to that port;
p. 115 (n.) than while lying in port; p. 116 (n.) to make a bee-line
from port to port; p. 122 (n.) by gazing through a port-hole; p. 128
their having wives and sweethearts in every port; p. 128 (n.) So long
as we laid in port; p. 138 (n.) of all sea-ports in the world; p. 138
(n.) extolling it above all other sea-ports; p. 138 (n.) they are set
adrift in a foreign port; p. 164 (n.) called the Port-a-Ferry; p. 166
(n.) arrived from the most distant ports; p. 172 (n.) along the docks
of a great commercial port; p. 198 (n.) when the Highlander arrived
in port; p. 216 (n.) smoky sailor-lanes and by-ways of a seaport;
p. 218 (n.) through the crimps of the port; p. 239 (n.) had left us
for good, while in port; p. 240 (n.) sailing to the Yankee ports from
Liverpool; p. 241 (n.) bound for any port in America; p. 273 (n.)
previous to our arrival in port; p. 289 (n.) an inch of progress
toward her port; p. 290 (n.) the hopeful thought of soon reaching
their port; p. 294 (n.) impatient was the captain to make his port;
p. 297 (n.) to their now drawing near to their port; p. 298 (n.) all
bound to one common port; p. 307 (n.) His politeness, while in port;
p. 309 (n.) his imperturbable politeness while in port; p. 312 (n.)
made all the haste I could to the seaport.

White-Jacket--p. 13 (n.) The first night out of port was a clear,
moonlight one; p. 17 (n.) to riot in some abandoned sea-port; p. 33
(n.) steady! port! world ho; p. 34 (n.) while in port; p. 42 (n.) He
would sometimes get outside of the port-holes; p. 53 (n.) we were not
many days out of port; p. 55 (n.) were sent flying out of the ports;
p. 67 (n.) to help run in and out of the port-hole that . . . mass of
metals; p. 75 (adj.) with its long rows of port-hole casements; p. 83
to their smoking-room at the bridle-port; p. 96 (n.) of ships that
have sailed from their ports; p. 105 (n.) and the port-holes closed;
p. 112 (n.) in merely running in and out a gun at a port-hole; p. 123
(n.) A Peep through a Port-hole at the Subterranean Ports; p. 130 (n.)
after rolling in at the port-holes; p. 141 (n.) while the Neversink
was dying in a South American port; p. 160 (n.) with its port-holes
and lofty flag-staffs; p. 160 (n.) whereas, in port, . . . they lead
the laziest of lives; p. 162 (n.) In the first place, while in port;
p. 171 (n.) of passing time while in port; p. 172 (n.) admiring the
shore scenery from the port-holes; p. 172 (n.) not much room, while
in port; p. 175 (n.) difficulty we had in killing time while in port;
p. 176 (n.) in working his calamities in port; p. 178 (n.) thrust
through the lower port-holes at night; p. 178 (n.) gains a port-hole;
p. 180 (n.) two of my mess-mates at the port-holes; p. 191 (n.)
crawling partly out of the port-hole; p. 195 (n.) lie at anchor in
one port; p. 202 (n.) Look at the port-holes; p. 227 (n.) in some far
away, outlandish port; p. 242 (n.) took place while we lay in port;

p. 245 (n.) gazing out of a port-hole; p. 264 (n.) pointing shoreward, out of a port-hole; p. 272 (n.) she happened to sail out of Port Mahon; p. 275 (n.) have bumped him out of a port-hole; p. 280 (n.) where the side-ladders are suspended in port; p. 283 (n.) they station no sentries at the port-holes; p. 295 (n.) Every morning, in port; p. 305 (n.) very soon have been pitched out of the ports; p. 307 (n.) while laying in port; p. 307 (n.) so that, in port, the diversion of gambling; p. 316 (n.) A shot entering one of the port-holes; p. 318 (n.) knocked three port-holes into one; p. 318 (n.) cried it out from the Turkish port-holes; p. 318 (n.) thrusting his neck out of the port-hole; p. 319 (n.) A shot struck the side of my port-hole; p. 322 (n.) I have often retreated to a port-hole; p. 324 (n.) I stole through a port-hole; p. 330 (n.) chicken-coop was replenished at every port; p. 339 (n.) looking out at your port-hole much longer; p. 352 (n.) marine sentries at the gangways in port; p. 356 (n.) sun, streaming in at the port-holes; p. 360 (n.) tossed it out of the port-hole behind him; p. 363 (n.) with grandchildren in every port; p. 370 (n.) in any American sea-port; p. 378 (n.) along the wharves of our sea-ports; p. 388 (n.) as we drew nearer and nearer to our port; p. 391 (n.) gliding toward our still invisible port; p. 398 (n.) The port we sail from is forever astern.

Moby-Dick--p. 17 (n.) ere I could embark from my destined port; p. 37 (n.) any considerable seaport will frequently offer to view; p. 38 (n.) the comical things he does upon reaching the seaport; p. 57 (n.) as being the most promising port for an adventurous whaleman to embark from; p. 94 (n.) marquee was never pitched except in port; p. 97 (n.) The port would fain give succor; the port is pitiful; in the port is safety; p. 97 (n.) But in that gale, the port, the land, is that ship's direct jeopardy; p. 118 (n.) in all but some few scientific retreats and whale-ports; p. 318 (n.) This rampart is pierced by several sally-ports; p. 334 (n.) some honest mariners of . . . some one of the Cinque Ports; p. 334 (n.) Now the Cinque Ports are partially or somehow under the jurisdiction of a sort of policeman.

PRIVATEER. A man-of-war equipped by individuals for cruising against the enemy. (Smyth)

Omoo--p. 9 (n.) Fitted for a privateer out of a New England port.

PROA. The larger war-vessels among the Malays, remarkable for their swiftness. (Smyth)

Mardi--p. 70 (n.) piled up in their proas; p. 161 (n.) as three proas showed themselves; p. 161 (n.) other proas pushed off; p. 161 (n.) occupants of the proas that had landed; p. 305 (n.) perceived a strange proa; p. 305 (n.) The murderer's proa outsailing theirs; p. 306 (n.) perceiving that strange proa in tow; p. 469 (n.) might have flooded their scattered proas; p. 552 (n.) Luzianna hither sent her proas.

Moby-Dick--p. 318 (n.) Time out of mind the piratical proas of the Malays.

PROW. Generally means the foremost end of a vessel. Also, a name for
the beak of a xebec or felucca. (Smyth)

Typee--p. 172 (n.) which crowned the prow of the canoe.

Omoo--p. 9 (n.) when she dashed the waves from her prow; p. 26 (n.)
against our coppered prow; p. 60 (n.) with her splintered prow
dripping; p. 152 (n.) platform just behind the prow; p. 216 (n.) The
prow terminated in a high, blunt beak.

Mardi--p. 28 (n.) which prow to leeward; p. 109 (n.) dragon rudely
carved on our prow; p. 120 (n.) lifted its sharp prow; p. 127 (n.) a
yoke of huge clumsy prows; p. 128 (n.) The high, beaked prow; p. 128
(n.) This prow was railed off; p. 129 (n.) he inferred from the
altar-like prow; p. 140 (n.) suddenly borne into my prow; p. 141 (n.)
fruit, hanging from the altar-prow; p. 141 (n.) Foremost in the prow;
p. 143 (n.) My prow shall keep kissing the waves; p. 144 (n.) our
prow was kept pointing; p. 145 (n.) our light prow headed round;
p. 148 (n.) far in advance of our prow; p. 160 (n.) we turned our
prow due west; p. 162 (n.) I pointed our prow for the shore; p. 167
(n.) Springing out of our prow; p. 179 (adj.) scroll-prowed nautilus;
p. 189 (n.) the near ripple of a prow; p. 199 (n.) black prows curling
aloft; p. 199 (n.) The prow of the foremost; p. 200 (adj.) claw-keeled,
dragon-prowed crafts; p. 200 (n.) shark's-mouth of our prow; p. 200
(n.) from one side of the prow; p. 200 (n.) borne upright at our prow;
p. 214 (n.) Our sharp prows fly; p. 214 (n.) our prow a blow; p. 215
(n.) Seated in the prow; p. 267 (n.) the Iris in its prow; p. 316
(adj.) we descried a sharp-prowed canoe; p. 318 (n.) he pointed ahead
of our prow; p. 354 (n.) including on the prow a duodecimo idol;
p. 378 (n.) About prows there, ye paddlers; p. 431 (n.) till her
gilded prow was perceived; p. 432 (n.) with their shaded prows thrust
in among the flowers; p. 469 (n.) very swell under its thousand prows;
p. 481 (n.) its prow a leveled spear; p. 482 (n.) its prow a seal;
p. 482 (n.) But from another sort of prow; p. 483 (n.) though its
prow be renewed every spring; p. 497 (n.) pointed our prows for
Porpheero; p. 509 (n.) three abreast, with snorting prows; p. 545 (n.)
we spied prow after prow; p. 545 (adj.) Before our prows' resistless
dashes; p. 548 (n.) our prows lie rotting on the beach; p. 549 (n.)
our prows we turned due west; p. 550 (n.) our prows sailed in among
these isles; p. 554 (n.) our three prows lifted themselves in
supplication; p. 557 (n.) oft been circled by ten thousand prows;
p. 558 (n.) till the three prows neighed to the blast; p. 569 (n.)
Keep all three prows, for yonder rock; p. 586 (n.) a thousand prows
sped by; p. 586 (n.) whirling in upon the thousand prows beyond;
pp. 586-7 (n.) whence fled those thousand prows; p. 587 (n.) to which
the thousand prows . . . had been fastened; p. 588 (n.) thither our
prows were pointed; p. 617 (n.) toward the West our three prows were
pointed; p. 622 (n.) our arching prows reared up; p. 622 (n.) Our
shattered prows seemed gilded; p. 622 (n.) holding amaranth and
myrtles, his slender prow; p. 622 (n.) we but need to repair our
prows; p. 623 (n.) tide sang round our splintered prows; p. 638 (adj.)
each prow's ripplings were distinctly heard; p. 638 (n.) to point our
prows for Odo's isle; p. 639 (n.) our storm-worn prows, now pointed
here; p. 639 (n.) and striking 'gainst our prow; p. 641 (n.) in a
mist the siren prow went on before; p. 645 (n.) our prows were beached;
p. 653 (n.) where a prow was beached; p. 653 (n.) as wild waves before

a prow inflexible; p. 654 (n.) turning my prow into the racing tide;
p. 654 (n.) three fixed specters leaning o'er the prow.

Redburn--p. 174 (n.) with hollow waist, high prow and stern.

White-Jacket--p. 96 (n.) driven before the prows of more fortunate
vessels; p. 211 (n.) eagle-like, with blood-dripping prows.

Moby-Dick--p. 44 (n.) the pulpit is its [the world's] prow; p. 110
(n.) beyond the ship's ever-pitching prow; p. 201 (n.) vacating
itself of life before our urn-like prow; p. 407 (n.) previous to
pointing her prow for home; p. 411 (n.) impatient for the order to
point the ship's prow for the equator; p. 447 (n.) Like noiseless
nautilus shells, their light prows sped through the sea.

PTERICHTHYS. Fossil fishes. (Van Nostrand)

Mardi--p. 417 (n.) cephalaspis, glyptolespsis, pterichthys.

QUADRANT. A reflecting instrument used to take the altitude above the
hrizon of the sun, moon, or stars at sea, and thereby to determine the
latitude and longitude of the place, &c. &c. (Smyth)

Omoo--p. 53 (n.) if the mate sends him after his quadrant; p. 61 (n.)
At noon, he brought out his quadrant; p. 62 (n.) to play a sort of
second quadrant to Jermin's first; p. 87 (n.) the gratuitous use of
his quadrant; p. 95 (n.) some provisions, also, a quadrant, and a
few other articles.

Mardi--p. 17 (n.) without chart or quadrant; p. 17 (n.) but a
quadrant; p. 19 (n.) thoughts of sextants and quadrants; p. 60 (n.)
belonged to a quadrant; p. 93 (n.) log, quadrant, and ship's papers;
p. 93 (n.) bits of a quadrant or a sextant; p. 93 (n.) sextant and
quadrant were both.

Redburn--p. 294 (n.) sweeping the vast horizon with his quadrant.

QUAY. A long wharf, usually built of stone, by the side of a harbour,
and having posts and rings, cranes, and storehouses, for the convenience
of merchant ships. (Smyth's spelling is "key.")

Redburn--p. 163 (n.) as materials for the quays and piers; p. 163 (n.)
exclusive of the inclosed quays surrounding it; p. 163 (n.) of the
ships inclosed by the quays; p. 164 (n.) along the edge of the quays
are ranges of iron sheds; p. 164 (n.) displayed along these quays
during the day; p. 172 (n.) who stood on the quay; p. 175 (n.)
transferred it to the quay; p. 176 (n.) from the corners of the quays;
p. 185 (n.) every vessel that unlades at the quays; p. 198 (n.) left
his vehicle standing on the quay; p. 215 (n.) between the quay and
the Highlander; p. 225 (n.) As we hurried across the quay; p. 238
(n.) walking along the quay of Prince's Dock; p. 239 (n.) which
overhung the quay; p. 239 (n.) swinging her broadside more toward
the quay.

Moby-Dick--p. 231 (n.) the vessel . . . hove over to the monster as
if to a quay.

REEF. A certain portion of a sail comprehended between the head of a
sail and any of the reef-bands. The intention of each reef is to reduce
the sail in proportion to the increase of the wind; there are also reefs
parallel to the foot or bottom of large sails, extended upon booms.--
Close-reefed is when all the reefs of the top-sails are taken in.--Reef
is also a group or continuous chain of rocks, sufficiently near the
surface of the water to occasion its breaking over them. (Smyth)

Typee--p. 5 (n.) groves of cocoa-nut--coral reefs--tatooed chiefs.

Omoo--p. 35 (n.) existence of certain shoals, and reefs; p. 46 (v.)
When top-sails were to be reefed; p. 63 (n.) found in the lagoons,
and about the reefs; p. 89 (n.) It was the coral reef; p. 89 (n.) we
were running straight for the reef; p. 90 (n.) owing to a curve of
the reef; p. 90 (n.) little more than a biscuit's toss of the reef;
p. 95 (n.) they struck one night upon an unknown reef; p. 98 (n.) by
the coral reef; p. 98 (n.) between the reef and the shore; p. 98 (n.)
extremely variable inside the reef; p. 102 (n.) than when outside the
reef; p. 149 (n.) Soon the ship drew near the reef; p. 167 (n.) from
the spray of the reef; p. 199 (n.) pulling outside of the reef;
p. 200 (n.) the roar of the Imeeo reef; p. 202 (n.) speared by the
natives, before sunrise, on the reef; p. 217 (n.) the encircling reef
was close to the shore; p. 217 (n.) Pointing to the reef; p. 263 (n.)
by an encircling reef; p. 266 (n.) between the reef and the shore;
p. 266 (n.) and, at low water, the reef itself; p. 266 (n.) going out
upon the great reef itself; p. 266 (n.) paddling off to the reef;
p. 269 (n.) the white reef on one hand; p. 270 (n.) the reef-belt
still accompanied us; p. 270 (n.) the openings in the reefs; p. 289
(n.) the break in the reef by which ships enter; p. 292 (n.) straight
through an opening in the reef; p. 297 (n.) Very nearly white when
hewn from the reefs; p. 316 (n.) swept through the opening in the reef.

Mardi--p. 18 (n.) as for intervening shoals or reefs; p. 24 (n.) upon
some treacherous reef; p. 46 (n.) of a condemned reefing-jacket;
p. 51 (n.) no tern, noddy, nor reef-bird; p. 63 (n.) unawares upon
reefs; p. 71 (n.) shot by the reef; p. 82 (n.) guarded by outpost
reefs; p. 91 (n.) she wrecked on a reef; p. 109 (n.) might have run
close to shoal or reef; p. 144 (n.) the sail taken up by a reef;
p. 160 (n.) within a milk-white zone of reef; p. 160 (n.) while
gleamed the white reef; p. 161 (n.) Near by the break in the reef;
p. 166 (n.) I had picked off a reef; p. 178 (n.) by a frothy luminous
reef; p. 178 (n.) over the circumvallating reef; p. 192 (n.) beyond
the outer reef; p. 192 (adj.) flew the white reef's rock; p. 199 (n.)
playing all round the reef; p. 211 (n.) not very remote from our
outer reef; p. 211 (n.) strode over the reef; p. 216 (n.) now lay
along the reef; p. 216 (n.) through an adjoining breach in the reef;
p. 240 (adj.) sea-girt, reef-sashed, mountain-locked; p. 250 (n.) a
specimen of the famous reef-bar; p. 250 (n.) I have seen this same
reef at Rafona; p. 257 (n.) slew the giants of the reef; p. 272 (n.)
comprise all the groups in the reef; p. 272 (n.) surging against the
outer reef of Mardi; p. 273 (n.) Without the break in the reef;
p. 294 (n.) section of the great Mardian reef; p. 294 (n.) his summer

grotto in the reef; p. 295 (n.) a projection of the reef; p. 302 (n.)
toward the opening in the reef; p. 303 (n.) Passing the reef; p. 303
(n.) in the brooding cells of the Turtle Reef; p. 305 (n.) or little
islets of the great reef; p. 343 (n.) made separate by an arm of
wooded reef; p. 343 (n.) the low reef-side of the lake; p. 367 (n.)
shoreing the white reef of the Milky Way; p. 373 (n.) being plentifully
found on the reefs; p. 374 (n.) all over the atolls and reefs in the
eastern; p. 380 (n.) Picked off the reef at low tide; p. 420 (n.) our
great reef is surrounded; p. 435 (n.) embrace all Mardi like its reef;
p. 471 (n.) here and there baring the outer reef; p. 477 (n.) here
and there clinging to Mardi's circle reef; p. 482 (n.) Dominora was
circled by a reef; p. 509 (n.) canoes were passing a long, white reef;
p. 509 (n.) with lonely spear/ On the reef ken; p. 537 (n.) in clear
weather about the reefs; p. 539 (n.) she loudly vaunts she'll span
the reef; p. 551 (n.) Concentric, inward, with Mardi's Reef; p. 556
(adj.) through the groups in white-reefed Mardi's zone; p. 586 (n.)
they laved all Mardi's reef; p. 611 (n.) Then we have circled not the
round reef wholly; p. 629 (n.) our wide arms embrace all Mardi like
its reef; p. 638 (n.) though she lead me beyond the reef; p. 649 (n.)
The reef is rounded; p. 653 (n.) lived to hunt me round all Mardi's
reef; p. 654 (n.) on the circumvallating reef.

Redburn--p. 40 (v.) when topsails are reefed; p. 102 (n.) taking in
our canvas to double-reefed-top-sails; p. 115 (v.) the first time we
reefed top-sails; p. 115 (n.) I tied my reef-point as quickly; p. 120
(v.) and reefing topsails; p. 121 (v.) those who merely hand, reef,
and steer; p. 121 (v.) how to reef a topsail; p. 283 (n.) without a
glimpse of shore or reef; p. 294 (n.) By night it was a reef-topsail-
breeze; p. 294 (n.) clap a reef into all three top-sails; p. 294 (n.)
before they had begun to haul out the reef-tackles; p. 295 (n.) had
made fast the reef-tackle; p. 295 (n.) which in reefing is accounted
the post of honor; p. 295 (n.) each man griping [sic] his reef-point;
p. 295 (adj.) to confine the reef corner to the yard; p. 296 (n.)
Clutching our reef-points; p. 296 (v.) Bear a hand, and reef away, men.

White-Jacket--p. 8 (v.) in tacking ship, reefing top-sails; p. 25 (n.)
now come the reefers; p. 25 (n.) as much in the way as a reefer;
p. 26 (adj.) running about with double-reefed night-gowns; p. 40 (v.)
or reefing top-sails fore and aft; p. 95 (v.) Stand by to reef all
three top-sails; p. 95 (v.) aloft, top-men! and reef away; p. 96
(adj.) under damp, double-reefed top-sails; p. 97 (v.) top-sails
cautiously reefed; p. 97 (n.) out reefs, my hearties; p. 98 (n.)
deprecate her wrath with double-reefed-top-sails; p. 100 (adj.)
reefing jackets, storm jackets, oil jackets; p. 106 (v.) better to
admit of close-reefing the top-sails; p. 107 (v.) were also clewed
down and close reefed; pp. 108-9 (n.) we shook two reefs out of the
top-sails; p. 220 (adj.) Seeing a reefer's hammock in the quarter-
netting; p. 220 (n.) said the unabashed reefer; p. 244 (adj.) he must
have got a reefer's warrant; p. 244 (n.) must consort . . . with our
chuckle-headed reefers; p. 295 (n.) hidden reefs and rocks, arise;
p. 347 (n.) responded a rather confident reefer; p. 347 (n.) said the
reefer; p. 349 (v.) All hands reef top-sails; p. 388 (n.) about the
reefers in the steerage; p. 391 (v.) the halyards not being rove;
p. 391 (n.) this reeving of the halyards; p. 392 (v.) Having reeved
the line; p. 394 (v.) was ordered to reeve anew the stun'-sail-
halyards; p. 394 (v.) had unrove and fallen to the deck; p. 396 (v.)
we have reefed the last top-sail.

Moby-Dick--p. 12 (n.) belted round by wharves as Indian isles by
coral reefs; p. 152 (n.) Stand by for reefing, hearties; p. 185 (n.)
each silent sailor seemed resolved into his own invisible reef;
p. 370 (v.) we hung there, reefed fast in the howling gale.

RIB. A figurative term for one of a vessel's timbers. (Dana)

Mardi--p. 367 (n.) with their Himmaleh keels and ribs.

Moby-Dick--p. 11 (n.) A Chapter on Whaling in Ribs and Trucks.

RIG, RIGGING. To rig is to fit the shrouds, stays, braces, and running-
rigging to their respective masts, yards and sails. Riggers are men
employed on board ships to fit the standing and running rigging, or to dismantle them. Rigging is a general name given to all the ropes or chains
employed to support the masts, and arrange the sails according to the
direction of the wind. Those are termed "standing" which are comparative
fixtures, and support the masts, &c.; and those "running" which are in
constant use, to trim the yards, and make or shorten sail, &c. (Smyth)

Typee--p. 22 (n.) her rigging knotted and spliced in every possible
direction; p. 35 (v.) bear a hand and rig yourselves; p. 35 (v.)
while the rest were rigging themselves out.

Omoo--p. 5 (n.) rigging all slack and bleached nearly white; p. 9 (n.)
the standing rigging was much worn; p. 19 (n.) he examined her from
the mizzen rigging with his glass; p. 42 (n.) and the hauling of
rigging; p. 46 (n.) was nearly pushed from the rigging; p. 52 (n.) as
clumsy among the crockery as in the rigging; p. 58 (n.) and held there
by the rigging; p. 59 (n.) sprung into the main-rigging; p. 103 (n.)
seized into the rigging, and flogged; p. 290 (n.) as for the running
rigging; p. 292 (n.) and hack away the lanyards of the rigging.

Mardi--p. 14 (n.) or ascend the rigging; p. 23 (n.) coils of rigging;
p. 32 (n.) from the spare rigging; p. 32 (n.) in accordance with the
customary rigging; p. 59 (n.) coils of rigging; p. 63 (v.) we rigged
a substitute; p. 63 (n.) to ascend the fore-rigging; p. 63 (n.) with
hands full of rigging; p. 64 (n.) creaking of the spars of rigging;
p. 65 (n.) The rigging; p. 66 (n.) down from the rigging; p. 66 (n.)
one hand to the rigging; p. 70 (n.) scrambled for the rigging; p. 71
(n.) down the rigging; p. 76 (n.) upon the spare rigging; p. 87 (n.)
tossed out of the rigging; p. 92 (n.) after descending from the
rigging; p. 96 (n.) spare sails and rigging; p. 97 (n.) new running-
rigging was rove; p. 101 (n.) snug nooks in the ship's rigging;
p. 101 (n.) all the wilderness of her rigging; p. 102 (n.) hollow
heart of a coil of rigging; p. 107 (v.) ere rigging the life-boat;
p. 114 (n.) to handle the same piece of rigging; p. 118 (n.) cutting
the rigging that held them; p. 132 (n.) sections of a ship's rigging.

Redburn--p. 8 (n.) of the tall masts, and yards, and rigging; p. 8
(n.) and were mounting up the rigging; p. 8 (n.) with a coil of glass
rigging over his shoulder; p. 16 (n.) I afterward said to one of the
riggers; p. 27 (n.) ordering about a good many men in the rigging;
p. 29 (n.) as for the men at work in the rigging; p. 29 (n.) I found

out that they were riggers; p. 29 (n.) to the kind blandishment of
one of these riggers; p. 30 (n.) and go up the rigging; p. 30 (n.)
Upon getting into the rigging; p. 38 (n.) in jumping into the rigging;
p. 40 (n.) for the sailors when at work in the rigging; p. 41 (n.)
entangled every now and then in the rigging; p. 52 (n.) stumbled
about in the rigging near him; p. 66 (n.) its bones being the stiff
standing-rigging; p. 69 (n.) tarring some strips of canvas for the
rigging; p. 70 (n.) he would tie me into the rigging; p. 73 (n.)
straddling the rigging; p. 74 (n.) tripping me in the rigging; p. 78
(n.) but jumped into the rigging; p. 78 (n.) curling my feet round
the rigging; p. 79 (n.) to fall overboard from the rigging; p. 93 (n.)
we found pieces of strange rigging; p. 97 (n.) rove through a block
in the mizen-rigging; p. 108 (n.) of tying fast in the rigging;
p. 109 (n.) half way up the mizzen rigging; p. 114 (n.) He Begins to
Hop About in the Rigging; p. 114 (n.) as they worked at the rigging;
p. 114 (n.) use odds and ends of old rigging; p. 115 (n.) as nimble
as a monkey in the rigging; p. 115 (n.) running up the rigging at sea;
p. 115 (n.) makes more of a stairs of the rigging; p. 115 (n.) with
one foot in the rigging; p. 121 (n.) to set dead-eyes in the standing
rigging; p. 121 (n.) in working at the rigging; p. 121 (n.) but is an
artist in the rigging; p. 122 (n.) was going on in the rigging;
p. 137 (n.) after which we worked at the rigging; p. 166 (v.) rigged
like sloops; p. 171 (n.) heightened by the rigging of kayar, or
cocoa-nut fiber; p. 172 (n.) to drive all strangers out of the
Highlander's rigging; p. 173 (n.) The rigging, also was of native
manufacture; p. 173 (n.) as well for ropes and rigging as for mats
and rugs; p. 173 (n.) for the running rigging of a ship; p. 173 (n.)
for the shrouds and standing-rigging of a ship; p. 173 (n.) setting
up or slacking off her standing rigging; p. 220 (n.) unless he was
somewhat accustomed to the rigging; p. 220 (n.) an expert tumbler in
the Highlander's rigging; p. 255 (n.) coiling away the slack of the
rigging; p. 255 (n.) to spring into the rigging; p. 255 (n.) acquit
yourself well in the rigging; p. 256 (n.) made one bound into the
rigging; p. 256 (n.) Max went up the rigging; p. 257 (n.) his legs
seemed shaking in the rigging; p. 284 (n.) the same shall be tied
into the rigging; p. 295 (n.) Jackson was cottering up the rigging;
p. 300 (n.) masts and black rigging stretching.

White-Jacket--p. 15 (n.) Tubbs quickly mounted the rigging; p. 16 (n.)
rapidly descending by the rigging; p. 47 (n.) to expatiate themselves
all over the rigging; p. 77 (n.) thought I, as I ran down the rigging,
p. 104 (adj.) pronounced her a full-rigged ship; p. 106 (n.) either
sails, rigging, or sticks; p. 107 (n.) the rigging was coated with a
thin glaze of ice; p. 107 (n.) sprang for the rigging; p. 107 (n.)
the wind flattened us to the rigging; p. 108 (n.) and scramble down
the rigging; p. 173 (n.) just come from tarring down the rigging;
p. 191 (n.) ran down the rigging to the batteries; p. 192 (n.) as he
slowly returned up the rigging; p. 195 (n.) the men sprang into the
rigging; p. 212 (n.) I sprang into the rigging; p. 236 (n.) coming up
the t'-gallant rigging; p. 245 (n.) foremost in the rigging to observe
it; p. 269 (n.) their tall spars and wilderness of rigging; p. 319
(n.) did good service . . . in the torn rigging; p. 320 (n.) with one
hand, in the rigging; p. 363 (n.) as the old man was slowly coming
down the rigging; p. 371 (n.) are then called to man the rigging;
p. 373 (n.) they never put foot in rigging; p. 374 (n.) a seaman or
two in the rigging.

Moby-Dick--p. 12 (n.) some high aloft in the rigging; p. 88 (n.) new
sails were coming on board, and bolts of canvas, and coils of rigging;
p. 90 (n.) roaring up to the riggers at the mast-head; pp. 91-2 (n.)
the hatches were all on, and lumbered with coils of rigging; p. 92
(n.) found only an old rigger there, wrapped in a tattered pea-jacket;
p. 130 (n.) The second Emir lounges about the rigging awhile; p. 139
(n.) I used to lounge up the rigging very leisurely; p. 200 (n.) as
if some winged spirit had lighted in the rigging; p. 248 (n.) three
lights up and down in the Pequod's main-rigging dimly guided our way;
p. 275 (n.) I've seen him lay of nights in a coil of rigging; p. 275
(n.) he coils **it [his tail]** down, do you see, in the eye of the
rigging; p. 400 (n.) at his accustomed place beside the mizen rigging;
p. 414 (n.) let the Typhoon sing, and srtike his harp here in our
rigging; p. 416 (n.) from the arched and overhanging rigging; p. 440
(n.) in such a wilderness of running rigging; p. 455 (n.) The rigging
lived.

RIPPLE.   The small waves raised on the surface of the water by the passage
of a slight breeze, or current, caused by foul bottom.   (Smyth)

Typee--p. 10 (n.) and the rippling at the cut-water.

Mardi--p. 49 (n.) instead of ripples; p. 50 (v.) just rippling the
sea; p. 50 (v.) painted fish rippling past; p. 149 (n.) What rippling
is that; p. 615 (v.) that rippled before his brown and bow-like chest;
p. 638 (n.) each prow's ripplings were distinctly heard; p. 638 (adv.)
ripple after ripple; p. 646 (adj.) their feet made music on the
rippling grass.

Moby-Dick--p. 121 (n.) When the sea is . . . slightly marked with
spherical ripples.

ROLL.   That oscillatory motion by which the waves rock a ship from side
to side.   The larger part of this disturbance is owing to the depth of
the center of gravity below the center of figure, the former exercising
a violent reaction when disturbed from its rest by passing seas;
therefore it is diminished by raising the weights.   (Smyth)

Mardi--p. 155 (v.) far away to where the sea rolled in the sun.

White-Jacket--p. 115 (v.) We rolled and rolled on our way.

Moby-Dick--p. 1 (v.) the Dut. and Ger. Wallen; A.S. Walw-ian, to roll,
to wallow; p. 8 (v.) the infuriated Sperm Whale rolls over and over;
p. 16 (v.) the wild and distant seas where he rolled his island bulk;
p. 44 (v.) while all God's sun-lit waves rolled by; p. 97 (v.) the
two hulls wildly rolled; p. 111 (v.) the Pequod now went rolling
through the bright Quito spring; p. 116 (v.) ere the Pequod's weedy
hull rolls; p. 137 (v.) The tranced ship indolently rolls; p. 139 (v.)
Roll on, thou deep and dark blue ocean, roll; p. 140 (adj.) rocking
life imparted by a gently rolling ship; p. 143 (v.) till he spouts
black blood and rolls fin out; p. 191 (n./v.) the noble negro to
every roll of the sea harmoniously rolled his fine form; p. 411 (n.)
swinging his seated form to the roll of the ship.

ROW. To propel a boat or vessel by oars or sweeps, which are managed in
a direction nearly horizontal. (Smyth)

> Typee--p. 250 (n.) the rowers pulled in as near as they dared; p. 250
> (n.) who told the rowers at once to give way; p. 251 (n.) Our rowers
> got out their knives; p. 252 (n.) the knives of our rowers so mauled
> his wrists.

> Mardi--p. 28 (v.) we had desisted from rowing; p. 28 (v.) we rowed and
> sailed till morning; p. 56 (v.) both rowing; p. 57 (v.) while rowing;
> p. 69 (v.) going along to row; p. 134 (v.) we rowed for the canoe.

ROYAL. The name of a light sail spread immediately next above the top-
gallant sail, to whose yard-arms the lower corners of it are attached; it
used to be termed top-gallant royal, and is never used but in fine
weather. (Smyth)

> Redburn--p. 115 (n.) in furling the top-gallant sails and royals;
> p. 220 (n.) and could furl a royal in a squall; p. 256 (adj.) At last
> he gained the royal yard.

> White-Jacket--p. 7 (n.) top-sails, top-gallants, and royals; p. 7 (n.)
> It was White-Jacket that loosed that main-royal; p. 8 (n.) to loose
> the main-royal; p. 9 (n.) office as looser of the main-royal; p. 36
> (n.) started from my studies to the main-royal-yard; p. 47 (n.)
> loftiest yard of the frigate, the main-royal-yard; p. 72 (n.) than
> the light hand that looses the main-royal; p. 77 (n.) high up on the
> main-royal-yard I reclined; p. 77 (n.) a tremulous voice hailing the
> main-royal-yard; p. 92 (n.) JACK CHASE . . . PERCY ROYAL-MAST; p. 92
> (n.) PERCY ROYAL-MAST . . . JACK CHASE; p. 94 (n.) in the chivalric
> character of Percy Royal-Mast; p. 94 (n.) where Percy Royal-Mast
> rescues fifteen oppressed sailors; p. 196 (n.) the royal-yard forms a
> cross with the mast; p. 212 (n.) furl the t'-gallant-sails and royals;
> p. 234 (n.) A top-man next me on the main-royal-yard; p. 236 (n.)
> Can't you behave yourself, royal-yard-men; p. 255 (n.) covered with
> an old royal-stun'-sail; p. 259 (n.) with an arm like a royal-mast;
> p. 269 (n.) swore by our top-sails and royals; p. 270 (n.) with even
> our main-royal set; p. 311 (n.) with the light copestone of the
> royals; p. 348 (n.) I'd nail my colors to the main-royal-mast.

> Moby-Dick--p. 2 (n.) But gulp down your tears and lie aloft to the
> royal-mast with your hearts; p. 14 (adj.) aloft there to the royal
> mast-head; p. 446 (adj.) reserved for swaying him to the main royal
> mast head; p. 452 (n.) Down royals and top-gallant stun-sails.

RUDDER. The machine by which a vessel or boat is steered. (Dana)

> Omoo--p. 33 (n.) with one foot resting on the rudder.

> White-Jacket--p. 66 (n.) another to unship your rudder; p. 348 (n.)
> her rudder is torn away.

RUN. The after part of a vessel's bottom, which rises and narrows in
approaching the stern-post. (Dana)

Omoo--p. 60 (n.) our spanker-gaff came down by the run.

SAIL. Sailing is the movement of a vessel by means of her sails along the surface of the water. (Smyth) -- Sails are of two kinds: square sails, which hang from yards, their foot lying across the line of the keel, as the courses, topsails, &c.; and fore-and-aft sails, which set upon gaffs, or on stays, their foot running with the line of the keel, as jib, spanker, &c. (Dana)

Typee--p. 5 (v.) The missionaries . . . had sailed by their lovely shores; p. 5 (v.) under whose auspices the navigator sailed; p. 10 (v.) Then you would see the superb albicore sailing aloft; p. 10 (v.) would sail up into the air; p. 10 (v.) sailing under the enemy's flag in the surrounding seas; p. 12 (v.) we were obliged to sail some distance; p. 14 (v.) when we sailed right into the midst; p. 16 (n.) constructed of the old sails and spare spars; p. 17 (v.) The expedition . . . had sailed from Brest; p. 18 (n.) set sail for the doomed island; p. 22 (v.) urgent letters to him to sail for home; p. 22 (n.) her sails all bepatched and bequilted; p. 22 (n.) not a yard was braced or a sail set; p. 27 (v.) sailing away from the scene of devastation; p. 31 (n.) until the sailing of the ship; p. 42 (v.) The Dolly would not sail perhaps for ten days; p. 109 (n.) he was waiting for the sailing of a boat; p. 134 (n.) spreading it out like a sail; p. 152 (v.) either sailing on the little lake with Fayaway; p. 215 (v.) they go sailing through the air in starry throngs; p. 252 (v.) which in a few hours sailed to that part of the island; p. 252 (n.) threw her main-top-sail aback; p. 270 (v.) Our own had sailed some time before; p. 271 (n.) when he came to himself, the sails were set.

Omoo--p. 3 (v.) which afterward sailed without him; p. 3 (v.) he sailed round thither; p. 5 (n.) lay with her main-top-sail aback about a league; p. 6 (v.) touched the ship in which I sailed from home; p. 6 (n.) rolled it up in a piece of an old sail; p. 8 (n.) we made sail again; p. 9 (n.) all this had nothing to do with her sailing; p. 9 (n.) you never thought of her patched sails; p. 10 (v.) sailing to windward; p. 10 (v.) The day they sailed out of Sydney Heads; p. 20 (n.) Dragging the Mowree out of an old sail; p. 25 (n.) but a day's sail from Tahiti; p. 26 (n.) A fresh land-breeze filled our sails; p. 30 (n.) leaving Little Jule to sail away by herself; p. 33 (v.) thinking of the strange objects we might be sailing over; p. 35 (n.) with all sail set; p. 38 (n.) Rude hammocks made out of old sails; p. 45 (n.) by hauling aback the main-top-sail; p. 46 (n.) When top-sails were to be reefed; p. 46 (n.) to furl the main-top-gallant-sail; p. 46 (v.) with whom I have sailed at different times; p. 58 (n.) the mate carried sail without stint; p. 59 (n.) while the sail streamed in ribbons; p. 60 (v.) were sailing along as pleasantly as ever; p. 61 (v.) How far we sailed to the westward; p. 62 (n.) darn a rent in the fore-top-sail; p. 62 (n.) within a day's sail of that place; p. 64 (n.) The Trades scarce filled our swooning sails; p. 67 (v.) have sailed successive missions; p. 69 (n.) with all our light sails wooingly spread; p. 71 (v.) who had sailed with the Mowree; p. 74 (n.) Out stun-sails; p. 84 (n.) our main-top-sail flapping; p. 89 (n.) broad white sails were gleaming; p. 89 (n.) keeping the sails just lifting; p. 90 (n.) Main-sail haul; p. 90 (v.) we were sailing away from the land; p. 90 (n.) with every sail

distended; p. 95 (v.) they had sailed together; p. 95 (n.) then set
sail for a small English settlement; p. 95 (adj.) the boat capsized
from the sail's jibing; p. 96 (n.) boats taking in all sail; p. 96
(v.) our mate had sailed from that port; p. 97 (n.) under short sail;
p. 97 (n.) all sail set; p. 100 (n.) more than one hundred and fifty
sails have annually touched at Tahiti; p. 102 (n.) she had made all
sail for the island; p. 102 (n.) The sails were yet unfurled; p. 103
(v.) was to sail for Valparaiso; p. 110 (n.) exercising yards and
sails; p. 112 (v.) she sailed for Valparaiso; p. 122 (n.) the riots
which preceded the sailing; p. 123 (v.) the rear-admiral sailed;
p. 128 (adv.) some two days' sail from Tahiti; p. 134 (n.) directing
attention to a sail at sea; p. 140 (v.) will sail for that place in
the course of ten days; p. 140 (v.) The Julia sails on a cruise this
day week; p. 140 (v.) a week would elapse ere the Julia sailed;
p. 145 (v.) Little Jule Sails without us; p. 149 (n.) Ah--my boy--
shippy you, harree-maky sail; p. 149 (n.) top-gallant-sails hoisting;
p. 152 (adv.) not many days' sail from Tahiti; p. 152 (n.) the full-
leaved bough of a tree for a sail; p. 153 (n.) At last the day came
for sailing; p. 159 (n.) after the Julia's sailing; p. 164 (n.) by
thus sailing to the eastward; p. 164 (v.) and I'm going to sail round
to Tahiti; p. 194 (n.) About three weeks after the Julia's sailing;
p. 199 (n.) pulling outside of the reef, set the sail; p. 210 (v.)
preferring rather to sail round; p. 224 (n.) A trim little sail-boat
was dancing; p. 226 (n.) in bringing them down to his sail-boat;
p. 229 (n.) at once hoisted sail; p. 231 (n.) to a dissertation on
Mercator's Sailing; p. 269 (n.) we set our sail of matting; p. 286
(v.) who sailed away from his creditors; p. 289 (v.) jist be after
sailing ashore in a jiffy; p. 290 (n.) Her sails were furled loosely;
p. 291 (n.) they clubbed, and purchased a sail-boat; p. 291 (v.) Away
they sailed; p. 292 (v.) Sailing down, sailing down; p. 299 (n.) But,
sail ho; p. 303 (v.) the greater portion of her time sailing about;
p. 313 (n.) but sit on the windlass and sail; p. 313 (v.) when
informed of our desire to sail with him; p. 315 (v.) had determined
upon sailing with the land breeze; p. 316 (n.) the sails were soon
set; p. 316 (n.) Crowding all sail.

Mardi--p. 3 (n.) many a stun' sail; p. 3 (n.) with our sails; p. 3
(v.) we sail for the Gallipagos; p. 4 (v.) as we sailed; p. 4 (v.)
westward sailing; p. 5 (n.) at sailing; p. 5 (n.) In the bunts of the
sails; p. 5 (n.) after some time sailing; p. 7 (n.) when neither sail
nor shore; p. 8 (v.) spirit must have sailed; p. 11 (v.) to be sailed
over; p. 12 (v.) sailed over the salt German sea; p. 14 (v.) in which
I have sailed; p. 16 (v.) swiftly sailing; p. 17 (n.) and a boat sail;
p. 23 (n.) a strange sail is almost a prodigy; p. 23 (n.) of the
still sails aloft; p. 24 (n.) her storm-sails set; p. 28 (n.) set our
sail; p. 32 (n.) we set this sail; p. 32 (n.) wing-and-wing with the
main-sail; p. 32 (n.) thereby much improving our sailing; p. 33 (v.)
management of the main-sail; p. 38 (v.) sailing steadily on; p. 45
(n.) castaway or sailaway as the case may be; p. 50 (n.) until it
struck our sails; p. 51 (v.) we must have sailed due west; p. 52 (v.)
sail blithely through life; p. 56 (n.) a sail, invisible; p. 56 (n.)
our sails were struck; p. 57 (n.) we reset our sail; p. 57 (n.) her
sails were in a state; p. 57 (n.) only the foresail, mainsail; p. 57
(n.) striking our sails once more; p. 57 (v.) and still sailed on;
p. 58 (n.) the rent sails like to blow; p. 65 (n.) here and there the
sails; p. 58 (v.) had sailed from her port; p. 69 (n.) little or no

wind for a sail; p. 70 (n.) the fore-sail; p. 71 (n.) beholding the
foresail set; p. 71 (n.) to descend to the topsail-yard; p. 71 (n.)
after loosening the topsail; p. 71 (n.) The foresail and fore-topsail
were; p. 71 (n.) soon the main-topsail was; p. 71 (n.) loosing the
smaller sails; p. 71 (n.) filling the ill-set sails; p. 71 (n.) of
her ill-adjusted sails; p. 72 (n.) laid his fore-topsail; p. 74 (v.)
Sailing from the Island; p. 81 (n.) picked up by some passing sail;
p. 82 (n.) to hoist the small top-sails; p. 83 (n.) impede the ship's
sailing; p. 89 (v.) might have sailed by; p. 92 (v.) sailing by which;
p. 96 (n.) spare sails and rigging; p. 96 (v.) few vessels sailing
out of; p. 96 (n.) of encountering a friendly sail; p. 97 (n.)
tattered sails were replaced by others; p. 97 (n.) dragged up from
the sail-room below; p. 97 (v.) commander of the craft I sailed;
p. 101 (n.) stretched out on a pile of old sails; p. 109 (v.)
remained some one hundred leagues to sail; p. 109 (v.) in the joyous
sunlight, sailing through; p. 110 (n.) unintelligible orders about
trimming the sails; p. 111 (n.) any unusual flapping of the sails;
p. 111 (n.) doze on a pile of old sails; p. 116 (n.) we proceeded to
furl the sails; p. 125 (n.) And sailing smoothly over a sea; p. 125
(v.) we must have sailed past; p. 125 (n.) perched upon the peak of
our sail; p. 126 (v.) Sailing on, we gradually broke; p. 126 (adj.)
broke in upon immense low-sailing flights; p. 126 (v.) upon sailing
nearer; p. 126 (v.) sail ho; p. 126 (n.) plainly a sail; p. 127 (n.)
As the sail drew nigh; p. 127 (n.) that it must be the sail; p. 127
(n.) then setting the sail; p. 127 (v.) now sailing at right angles;
p. 127 (n.) immense sprawling sail holding; p. 127 (n.) inviting them
to furl their sails; p. 128 (n.) spreading a yellow sail; p. 128 (n.)
to counterbalance the pressure of the sail; p. 128 (n.) with all
haste we set our sail; p. 141 (n.) they soon set their mat-sail;
p. 141 (v.) instead of sailing southward; p. 141 (v.) left no track
as it sailed; p. 144 (n.) the sail taken up by a reef; p. 148 (v.)
And slow sailing overhead were; p. 156 (v.) and sailed to and fro;
p. 157 (n.) And setting sail quickly; p. 160 (n.) our sail faintly
distended; p. 161 (adj.) our mast, sail-set; p. 161 (v.) Instantly
we sailed for them; p. 165 (v.) sailing through the leaves; p. 166
(v.) and hither sailed before its level rays; p. 200 (n.) corners of
our sails displayed; p. 200 (n.) with bellied sails; p. 200 (v.) be
this voyage full gayly sailed; p. 206 (n.) as a man-of-war's main-
sail; p. 209 (v.) And thus did we sail; p. 211 (v.) Sailing past
Pella; p. 213 (n.) their sails rolled up; p. 215 (n.) lowered its
sail when close by; p. 216 (v.) Sailing nearer, we perceived; p. 256
(v.) Sailing high out of water; p. 256 (v.) from hand to hand the
trenchers sailed; p. 256 (v.) for a time sailing deep; p. 256 (v.)
that sailed about; p. 266 (n.) their winnowing sails all swoon;
p. 268 (n.) a breeze! up sails; p. 269 (v.) toward which we were
sailing; p. 278 (n.) sail on; but soft; look down; p. 286 (v.) so
that no canoe could sail; p. 289 (v.) though none have sailed through;
p. 303 (v.) sailing a little distance therefrom; p. 305 (n.) distant
three days' sail; p. 305 (v.) proa outsailing theirs; p. 306 (n.) at
times counteracting their sailing; p. 311 (v.) previous to sailing
for Odo; p. 312 (n.) with that curse in our sails; p. 316 (n.)
pressure of an immense triangular sail; p. 348 (v.) Sailing to and
fro in the lake; p. 354 (n.) with paddles, out-riggers, masts, sails;
p. 355 (v.) we were silently sailing along; p. 364 (v.) Slowly sailing
on; p. 365 (n.) but crowding sail we left them; p. 378 (v.) we have
sailed by Padulla; p. 384 (adj.) Sky-Sail-Pole Lyrics; p. 393 (v.)

Sailing from Padulla; p. 398 (v.) The canoes sailed on; p. 401 (n.)
A long sail over; p. 403 (n.) slender as sky-sail-poles; p. 424 (v.)
still we onward sailed; p. 424 (n.) though our sails were useless;
p. 431 (adj.) 'to ye, too, sailing Cygnus; p. 431 (n.) like a gray,
distant sail before the wind; p. 432 (v.) Noon came as we sailed;
p. 452 (n.) that we set sail from Diranda; p. 461 (v.) the mariners
never sailed faster; p. 465 (v.) sailed over to have audience of
Media; p. 469 (v.) the very clouds of heaven never sailed over
Dominora; p. 475 (n.) Our sails were set; p. 481 (v.) Wherein to sail
over the sea; p. 481 (v.) in the fine craft Bis Taurus that he sailed;
p. 491 (v.) They sail round an Island without landing; p. 499 (n.) Up
sails! and westward to our course; p. 509 (n.) our mat-sails panting
to the breeze; p. 511 (n.) In good time, after many days' sailing;
p. 539 (v.) Sailing south from Vivenza; p. 543 (v.) we sailed in
among great mountain passes; p. 544 (v.) and sailing on, long waited
for the day; p. 545 (n.) sails widespread, and paddles plying; p. 550
(v.) our prows sailed in among these isles; p. 551 (v.) Over balmy
waves, still westward sailing; p. 553 (v.) But as we northward sailed;
p. 554 (v.) Still on we sailed; p. 554 (v.) Over that tideless sea we
sailed; p. 556 (v.) Sailing on; p. 556 (n.) fill their own sails;
p. 557 (n.) though essaying but a sportive sail; p. 565 (v.) Sailing
on, with open eyes; p. 567 (v.) we sailed from sea to sea; p. 574 (v.)
lighting his trombone as we sailed; p. 586 (v.) A Death-cloud sweeps
by them, as they sail; p. 586 (n.) Down sails; drop paddles; p. 586
(v.) we sailed by many tranquil harbors; p. 605 (n.) At dinners, 'tis
not till you take in sail; p. 610 (v.) Sailing on, the next land we
saw; p. 611 (n.) spread all your sails; p. 611 (n.) Set all sail
there, men; p. 617 (v.) We sailed upon an angry sea; p. 617 (n.) When
we set sail from Odo; p. 618 (v.) we paddlers sail; p. 622 (v.) They
sail from Night to Day; p. 623 (n.) 'tis breezing; set the sails;
p. 624 (v.) Though hence he sail with swiftest wings; p. 633 (n.) as
voyagers pass far sails; p. 633 (v.) where worlds had sailed before;
p. 635 (v.) the spirits sailed; p. 638 (v.) and as we sailed away;
p. 638 (v.) On we sailed; p. 639 (n.) their half-rent sails, still
courting every breeze; p. 644 (n.) sails idly flapping; p. 653 (v.)
through that tumult Media sailed serene.

Redburn--p. 4 (v.) will sail for the above port; p. 4 (v.) Will sail
Tuesday the 20th of May; p. 4 (n.) that the time of sailing was fixed
upon so long; p. 6 (v.) All three were sailing through; p. 7 (v.)
three boats sailing after it as fast as they could fly; p. 18 (v.)
you won't get home-sick before you sail; p. 19 (v.) the ship was
advertised to sail; p. 24 (n.) I've shipped to sail in this ship;
p. 25 (v.) the ship would not sail till the next day; p. 28 (v.) sail
away, I tell you, with that shooting-jacket; p. 31 (n.) hoisted the
signal for sailing; p. 33 (n.) instead of sailing out of the bay;
p. 34 (v.) had ever sailed out of these Narrows; p. 35 (v.) sailed
right through the sky and water line; p. 35 (v.) who used to sail to
a place called Archangel; p. 36 (v.) as we sailed through the Narrows;
p. 36 (n.) and the sails were loosed, and hoisted; p. 36 (n.) she
suddenly lowered her sails; p. 37 (n.) then the schooner made sail;
p. 40 (n.) he has to run aloft when top-sails are reefed; p. 45 (n.)
hoisting one of the sails a little higher; p. 50 (n.) to yell out his
orders about the sails; p. 51 (v.) and sail straight away into the
interior; p. 63 (v.) I could hardly believe that I was sailing; p. 63
(n.) with her sails all still; p. 64 (v.) as we sailed in among them;

p. 64 (n.) now getting some stun'-sails ready; p. 64 (n.) these stun'-
sails are light canvas; p. 65 (n.) while the stun-sails were lying
all tumbled; p. 65 (n.) or the larboard-fore-top-sail-clew-line;
p. 66 (n.) At last we hoisted the stun'-sails up; p. 66 (adj.) up to
the top-sail yards; p. 69 (n.) the whole interval that elapsed from
our sailing; p. 72 (v.) in the month of June that we sailed; p. 74
(n.) call them my gaff-topsail-boots; p. 75 (n.) and the wreck of my
gaff-topsail-boots; p. 75 (n.) with all her sails spread wide; p. 77
(n.) Sent up to Loose the Main-Skysail; p. 77 (n.) to loose the main-
skysail; p. 77 (n.) which is the fifth and highest sail; p. 77 (n.)
It was a very small sail; p. 77 (n.) some ships carry still smaller
sails; p. 77 (n.) still smaller sails, above the skysail; p. 77 (n.)
called moon-sails; p. 77 (n.) a skysail seems high enough; p. 77 (n.)
to loose the skysail; p. 78 (n.) found myself hanging on the skysail-
yard; p. 78 (n.) gaskets, or lines typing up the sail; p. 78 (n.) me
too along with the yard and sail; p. 83 (v.) whom he had sailed with;
p. 92 (n.) we heard the flap of her topsails; p. 93 (n.) crowding all
sail before a fresh breeze; p. 94 (v.) find yourself sailing along on
the ocean; p. 94 (n.) without having seen a sail; p. 95 (n.) we
shorten sail for fear of accidents; p. 96 (v.) while sailing through
the fog; p. 96 (v.) found ourselves sailing through fleets; p. 99 (v.)
had sailed out of Nantucket; p. 100 (n.) eyeing the wreck of my gaff-
topsail-boots; p. 101 (n.) about sailing up the rivers; p. 102 (n.)
taking in our canvas to double-reefed-top-sails; p. 103 (v.) So away
we sailed; p. 104 (n.) wouldn't you like to take a sail with them;
p. 106 (v.) sailing upon no fixed days; p. 106 (v.) from those who
had sailed in them; p. 106 (n.) their carrying such a press of sail;
p. 111 (n.) previous to the ship's sailing; p. 114 (n.) the Highlander
may as well make sail; p. 114 (n.) in loosing the main-skysail; p. 11
p. 114 (n.) mending sails; p. 115 (n.) and take in sail; p. 115 (n.)
we reefed top-sails; p. 115 (n.) in furling the top-gallant sails;
p. 116 (n.) The sail would fill out like a balloon; p. 120 (n.) and
reefing topsails; p. 121 (n.) to darn and mend the sails; p. 121 (n.)
that is, run aloft, furl sails, haul ropes; p. 121 (n.) how to reef a
topsail; p. 124 (n.) not a very fast sailer; p. 124 (v.) and the ship
sailed nearer; p. 126 (v.) we sailed on till next day; p. 127 (v.) As
we sailed ahead; p. 133 (n.) By way of a pictorial mainsail; p. 145
(n.) In a ship under full sail; p. 152 (v.) to which I, his son
Wellingborough was sailing; p. 166 (n.) carrying red sails; p. 166
(n.) nothing visible but the mast and sail; p. 168 (n.) several days
before their sailing; p. 173 (n.) and hoisted sail for London; p. 174
(v.) still sail the salt seas; p. 174 (v.) Before the wind, they sail
well; p. 192 (adj.) superior, fast-sailing, coppered and copper-
fastened ships; p. 193 (v.) as about to sail under the command;
p. 193 (v.) the regiments wanting recruits are about to sail; p. 219
(n.) the day previous to the sailing of the ship; p. 220 (n.) handled
the sails in a gentlemanly . . . way; p. 238 (v.) been advertised to
sail in two days' time; p. 239 (v.) who had been shipped to sail with
us; p. 240 (n.) The white sails glistened; p. 240 (v.) of ships
sailing to the Yankee ports; p. 248 (n.) He was reclining upon an old
sail; p. 253 (n.) Before the day of our sailing; p. 253 (adj.) on the
maintop-sail halyards; p. 254 (n.) douse that mainsail now; p. 255
(n.) clewing up a t'-gallant-sail; p. 255 (n.) ropes . . . that
wrapped to sail up; p. 273 (v.) in what remote seas it may have
sailed; p. 285 (adj.) Although fast-sailing ships; p. 288 (v.) the
sea, over which we were sailing; p. 289 (n.) to a storm-staysail;

p. 290 (n.) stun'-sails alow and aloft; p. 294 (n.) it was a reef-
topsail-breeze; p. 294 (n.) even yet we carried a main-top-gallant-
sail; p. 294 (n.) to douse the top-gallant-sail; p. 294 (n.) clap a
reef into all three top-sails; p. 295 (n.) at the extreme weather-end
of the top-sail-yard; p. 295 (n.) all strung along the main-top-sail-
yard; p. 295 (n.) dragging the sail over toward Jackson; p. 295 (n.)
the bellying sail was spattered with a torrent of blood; p. 296 (n.)
with the blood that trickled from the sail; p. 300 (n.) we set sail
for the Narrows; p. 300 (n.) still visible on the topsail; p. 300 (v.)
on we sailed; p. 300 (adj.) ships, brigs, schooners, and sail boats;
p. 300 (n.) covered with white sloop-sails.

White-Jacket--p. 6 (n.) take the wings of the morning, or the sails
of a ship; p. 6 (n.) stun'-sail gear rove; p. 6 (n.) to pay their
creditors with a flying fore-top-sail; p. 7 (n.) unship your bars,
and make sail; p. 7 (n.) the sail-loosers ran out on those broad
boughs; p. 7 (n.) down fell the sails like white clouds from the
ether--top-sails, top-gallants; p. 8 (n.) in tacking ship, reefing
top-sails; p. 9 (n.) when all hands were called to make sail; p. 9
(n.) and all the sails on the bowsprit; p. 9 (n.) attend to the main-
sail and spanker; p. 11 (adj.) we say nothing here of . . . Sail-
maker's mates; p. 15 (n.) cushioning themselves on old sails and
jackets; p. 16 (v.) I have sailed with lords and marquises; p. 68 (n.)
just the chap to make sail on the sly; p. 23 (n.) For when the
sailing-master . . . touches his hat; p. 23 (n.) of the respectful
suggestion of the sailing-master; p. 24 (n.) the Sailing-master,
Purser, Chaplain; p. 25 (n.) consisting of the Boatswain . . . and
Sail-maker; p. 25 (n.) the carpenter and sail-maker practically
understand; p. 26 (n.) the cloth goes to the sail-maker; p. 27 (adj.)
that is, . . . Carpenter's and Sail-maker's mates; p. 32 (n.) when
the sails were furled in a gale; p. 33 (n.) advice as to taking in,
or making sail; p. 33 (n.) wrapped up in a caul, as in a main-sail;
p. 34 (n.) those fellows on the main-topsail-yard; p. 40 (n.) or
reefing top-sails fore and aft; p. 48 (n.) Purser, Marine Officers,
Sailing-master; p. 55 (v.) It was as if we were sailing by some
odoriferous shore; p. 59 (v.) so sail away out of this, and let me
clear up the wreck; p. 68 (v.) Imagine some midnight craft sailing
down; p. 68 (n.) are dragged forth from the sail-room; p. 69 (n.)
would probably "bend" his old topsails; p. 72 (n.) All hands about
ship and shorten sail; p. 76 (v.) we sailors sail not in vain; p. 77
(v.) [stars] sailing in heaven's blue, as we on the azure main; p. 83
(n.) is occupied by the carpenters, sail-makers, barbers; p. 90 (n.)
some weeks prior to the Neversink's sailing from home; p. 94 (n.)
that almost took the main-top-sail aback; p. 94 (n.) Commanding the
top-gallant sails to be taken in; p. 95 (n.) Stand by to reef all
three top-sails; p. 96 (n.) under damp, double-reefed top-sails;
p. 96 (v.) of ships that have sailed from their ports; p. 97 (n.)
without so much as furling a t'-gallant-sail; p. 97 (n.) top-sails
cautiously reefed; p. 97 (n.) fore and aft set t'-gallant-sails;
p. 97 (n.) give her the fore-top-mast stun'-sail; p. 97 (n./adj.)
those sails of yours were much safer in the sail-maker's loft; p. 97
(n.) The masts are willows, the sails ribbons; p. 97 (n.) his sails
are floating in the air; p. 97 (n.) He bends his strongest storm-
sails; p. 98 (n.) they come along under easy sail; p. 98 (n.) woo the
Jezebel with a t'-gallant-studding-sail; p. 98 (n.) deprecate her
wrath with double-reefed-top-sails; p. 98 (n.) they set a spencer or

try-sail; p. 98 (n.) drop the fore-sail; p. 98 (v.) who first sailed
through them; p. 98 (v.) to sail an English ship thereon; p. 101 (n.)
swaddling themselves in old sails; p. 101 (n.) obliged us to furl
most of the sails; p. 104 (n.) a sail had been discerned; p. 104 (n.)
before the strange sail was descried; p. 104 (n.) as a sail, seen as
a mere speck; p. 104 (n.) with all sail set; p. 104 (n.) sent aloft
to loose the sails; p. 105 (n.) Stun'-sails alow and aloft; moon
sails; p. 105 (adj.) our sail-proud braggadocio of an Indiaman;
p. 105 (n.) his t'-gallant stun'-sails . . . taking quick leave;
p. 105 (n.) All hands take in sail; p. 105 (v.) seemed to be sailing
on her side; p. 106 (n.) when a large quantity of sail is . . . to be
furled; p. 106 (n.) every sail seemed bursting with its [the gale's]
wild breath; p. 106 (n.) to admit of close-reefing the top-sails;
p. 106 (n.) strain of the three entire top-sails; p. 106 (n.)
something must go--either sails; pp. 106-7 (n.) there was a rent in
the main-top-sail; p. 107 (n.) the vast sail was rent up and down;
p. 107 (n.) two remaining top-sails were also clewed down; p. 107
(n.) was to furl the main-sail; p. 107 (n.) For to furl this enormous
sail; p. 107 (n.) and furl the main-sail; p. 108 (n.) the sail itself
was flying about; p. 108 (n.) come down and leave the sail to blow;
p. 108 (n.) the stun'-sail-booms greatly assisted in securing our
hold; p. 108 (n.) to help secure what was left of the sail; pp. 108-9
(n.) we shook two reefs out of the top-sails; p. 116 (v.) the ship in
which I then happened to be sailing; p. 123 (adj.) of the sail room,
full as a sail-maker's loft; p. 123 (n.) piled up with great top-
sails and top-gallant-sails; p. 135 (n.) staggering under whole top-
sails; p. 152 (n.) A man at the fore-top-sail-yard; p. 152 (n.) the
man on the fore-top-sail-yard reported; p. 152 (n.) Sail was now
shortened; p. 173 (v.) Soon after the ship had sailed from home;
p. 189 (n.) within a few days' sail of home; p. 193 (n.) with which
his men can handle the sails; p. 194 (n.) exercising yards and sails;
p. 195 (n.) simultaneously loosened their sails to dry; p. 195 (n.)
who shall first have his sails stowed; p. 195 (n.) in furling top-
sails or courses; p. 195 (n.) hard at work at the main-topsail-yard;
p. 195 (n.) the sail being well piled up; p. 196 (n.) brought his
whole weight to bear on the rebellious sail; p. 196 (n.) Baldy jumped
down upon the sail; p. 196 (n.) after Baldy's accident in furling
sails; p. 199 (adj.) mounted the pedestal of the main-top-sail;
p. 202 (n.) The sail-maker was the tailor; p. 211 (v.) King Solomon's
annual squadrons that sailed to Ophir; p. 211 (v.) perhaps, sailed
the Acapulco fleets; p. 211 (n.) of the forty-seven French and
Spanish sail-of-the-line; p. 212 (n.) furl the t'-gallant-sails and
royals; p. 223 (v.) Never sail under a navy captain whom; p. 223 (n.)
hoisting the main-top-mast stun'-sail; p. 223 (n.) for the sail was
but just crawling up; p. 231 (n.) the sole conduct of making and
shortening sail; p. 235 (n.) on the main-topsail-halyards; p. 236
(adj.) from the top-sail-yard; p. 236 (v.) is sailing under false
colors; p. 244 (n.) announcement of the sailing from the Brooklyn
Navy-yard; p. 245 (n.) reported a sail entering the harbor; p. 245
(v.) perhaps the brother had not sailed; p. 255 (n.) covered with an
old royal-stun'-sail; p. 257 (adj.) a man fell from the mizzen-top-
sail yard; p. 265 (n.) These vessels often loosed their sails; p. 265
(n.) the English frigate . . . made all sail; p. 265 (n.) She was
inviting us to a sailing-match; p. 265 (v.) the fleetest keeled craft
sailing under the American long-pennant; p. 266 (v.) she now sailed
the salt seas; p. 266 (v.) sailing under the stars and stripes;

p. 269 (n.) we Yankees swore by our top-sails; p. 269 (n.) we crowded
all sail on St. George; p. 270 (v.) I've sailed over the very track
that Camoens sailed; p. 272 (v.) she happened to sail out of Port
Mahon; p. 272 (v.) she sailed like a shooting-star; p. 278 (n.) when
main-top-sail haul; p. 305 (v.) were sailing homeward over the . . .
sea; p. 308 (v.) top your boom and sail large now; p. 310 (n.) so far
as . . . the ship's sailing were concerned; p. 310 (adj.) must rig
out that stun'-sail boom; p. 311 (n.) her stun'-sails set on both
sides; p. 311 (v.) That ever sailed the sea; p. 312 (v.) the ship in
which we were sailing; p. 316 (v.) who had sailed with him; p. 318
(n.) thirty-two sail of Englishmen, Frenchmen; p. 323 (v.) sailing
over summer seas; p. 326 (n.) as the ordinary wind-sail was the only;
p. 326 (n.) in a severe gale the wind-sail had to be; p. 328 (n.)
among the Lieutenants, Sailing-master; p. 336 (n.) The wind-sail had
collapsed; p. 338 (adj.) two of the sail-maker's gang drew near;
p. 338 (n.) the sail-maker is the undertaker; p. 338 (n.) as if
mending an old sail; p. 339 (v.) as soon as you sails over 'em;
p. 339 (adj.) with a sail-maker's needle through his nose; p. 340
(adj.) cried one of the sail-maker's mates; p. 340 (n.) the foot of
the main-sail wants mending; p. 342 (v.) sailing far up into the
depths of the sky; p. 346 (n.) how to splice a rope or furl a sail;
p. 348 (n.) I would haul back the fore-top-sail; p. 348 (n.) you can't
haul back your fore-top-sail; p. 348 (n.) Haul back the main-top-sail;
p. 348 (n.) Mizzen-top-sail; p. 349 (n.) All hands reef top-sails;
p. 367 (v.) I know not in what frigate you sail now; p. 372 (n.) the
squadron made sail for Algiers; p. 380 (v.) I have repeatedly sailed
with English seamen; p. 381 (n.) the night previous to the sailing of
the frigate; p. 382 (n.) hoist the enormous top-sails; p. 384 (v.)
I've sailed in many Andrew Millers; p. 385 (v.) To sail in such ships
is; p. 388 (v.) reported to be twenty-four hours' sail from the land;
p. 388 (n.) I mean to settle down in a sail-loft; p. 389 (adj.) if
any more . . . sailing signals fly; p. 391 (n.) to set the main-top-
gallant-stun'-sail; p. 392 (n.) I thought it was the sail that had
flapped; p. 392 (n.) relying upon the sail itself; p. 394 (n.) to
reeve anew the stun'-sail-halyards; p. 394 (n.) The sail was soon set;
p. 396 (n.) at last stripped of spars, shrouds, and sails; p. 396 (n.)
we have reefed the last top-sail; p. 397 (n.) ye Lusians spread the
sail; p. 398 (v.) As a man-of-war that sails through the sea; p. 398
(v.) so this earth that sails through the air; p. 398 (adj.) we
mortals are all on board a fast-sailing, never-sinking world-frigate;
p. 398 (v.) The port we sail from is forever astern; p. 398 (v.) we
continue to sail with sealed orders; p. 398 (v.) Thus sailing with
sealed orders.

Moby-Dick--p. 5 (n.) we set sail from the Elbe; p. 10 (n.) The vessel
under short sail, with look-outs at the mast-heads; p. 12 (v.) I
thought I would sail about a little and see the watery part of the
world; p. 16 (v.) I love to sail forbidden seas; p. 17 (v.) in
learning that the little packet for Nantucket had already sailed;
p. 17 (v.) For my mind was made up to sail in no other than a
Nantucket craft; p. 22 (n.) He was trying his hand at a ship under
full sail; p. 45 (v.) as Jonah could possibly have sailed in those
ancient days; p. 46 (v.) how soon sail ye, sir; p. 46 (v.) all sail
with the next coming tide; p. 46 (v.) I'll sail with ye; p. 46 (v.)
ere the craft did sail; p. 57 (v.) For the nonce, however, he proposed
to sail about; p. 59 (n.) Hoisting sail, it glided down the Acushnet

river; p. 60 (n.) The prodigious strain upon the main-sail had parted
the weather-sheet; p. 68 (n.) from his continual sailings in many
hard gales; p. 85 (n.) very quietly overlooking some sail-makers who
were mending a top-sail in the waist; p. 90 (v.) that some time the
next day the ship would certainly sail; p. 95 (n.) At last the anchor
was up, the sails were set; p. 95 (n.) The stout sail-boat that had
accompanied us; p. 96 (n.) Oh! the sail-needles are in the green
locker; p. 97 (n.) with all her might she crowds all sail off shore;
p. 99 (n.) sail a navy of upwards of seven hundred vessels; p. 99 (v.)
where no Cook or Vancouver had ever sailed; p. 113 (v.) he's about
the queerest old man Stubb ever sailed with; p. 118 (v.) But I have
swam through libraries and sailed through oceans; p. 135 (n.) not
till her skysail-poles sail in among the spires of the port; p. 154
in top-gallant sails! Stand by to reef topsails; p. 193 (n.) bearing
down upon her boats with outstretched sails; p. 195 (n.) the sail
collapsed and exploded; p. 234 (v.) we seemed to be sailing through
boundless fields of ripe and golden wheat; p. 318 (n.) do not demand
the obsequious homage of lowered top-sails; p. 320 (n.) Crowding all
sail the Pequod pressed after them; p. 321 (n.) So with stun-sail
piled on stun-sail; p. 337 (n.) whose furled sails betokened that
some sort of whale must be alongside; p. 353 (n.) with broad sheets
of flame for sails; p. 354 (n.) in my ears was the low hum of sails;
p. 358 (v.) away we sail to fight some other world; p. 370 (n.) being
a very fast sailer and a noble craft every way; p. 370 (n.) we
ignorantly furled the skirts of our jackets into the sails; p. 385
(v.) prior to the Pequod's sailing from Nantucket; p. 394 (n.) Furl
the t'-gallant-sails, and close-reef the top-sails; p. 397 (n.) a
piece of sail-cloth being rolled up for a pillow; p. 408 (v./n.)
fortune's favorites sail close by us, we . . . joyfully feel our
bagging sails fill out; p. 421 (n.) The three corresponding new sails
were now bent and reefed; p. 423 (n.) The strong, unstaggering breeze
abounded so, that sky and air seemed vast out-bellying sails; p. 433
(n.) the boastful sails all fell together as blank bladders that are
burst; p. 434 (n./adv.) she crowded all sail--stunsail on stunsail;
p. 441 (v.) you sail upon their tomb; p. 444 (n.) to catch the first
glimpse of his father's sail; p. 454 (n.) The wind that made great
bellies of their sails; p. 461 (n.) The sails shake.

SAILOR. A man trained in managing a ship, either at sea or in harbor. A
thorough sailor is the same with mariner and seaman, but as every one of
the crew is dubbed a sailor, there is much difference in the absolute
meaning of the term. (Smyth)

Typee--p. xiii (n.) Sailors are the only class of men; p. xiii (n.)
the familiarity of sailors with all sorts of curious adventure;
p. xiii (n.) less familiar than the sailor with a life of adventure;
p. 3 (n.) Oh! ye state-room sailors; p. 4 (n.) yet the sailors pray
every minute; p. 10 (n.) that peculiar prolongation of sound that a
sailor loves; p. 15 (n.) what a sight for us bachelor sailors; p. 20
(n.) the concise, point-blank phrase of the sailors; p. 22 (adj.) of
the quality of sailors' fare; p. 26 (adj.) they don't like sailor's
flesh, it's too salt; p. 26 (n.) a considerable detachment of sailors
and marines; p. 32 (n.) he was as smart a looking sailor as ever
stepped; p. 35 (adj.) where the tie of a sailor's neckerchief might
make; p. 134 (n.) we American sailors pride ourselves; p. 140 (n.)

worth while to notice a poor sailor; p. 223 (n.) The sailors were
struck aghast at his impiety; p. 223 (n.) previously shown for the
superstitions of the sailors; p. 252 (n.) that an American sailor was
detained by the savages; p. 255 (n.) Paulet, a bluff and straightforward sailor; p. 257 (n.) an English sailor hauled down the red
cross; p. 263 (n.) He was an old grizzled sailor; p. 265 (n.) Toby
now conjured the sailor to go after me alone; p. 265 (n.) Well must
the old sailor have known, too; p. 265 (n.) The old sailor then went
off; p. 266 (n.) This old woman, the sailor afterwards said; p. 266
(n.) Then there is no hope for you, exclaimed the sailor; p. 266 (n.)
But the sailor had many reasons; p. 266 (n.) that the old sailor,
after all, might possibly be deceiving him; p. 267 (n.) "keep close
to my side," said the sailor; p. 268 (n.) said the sailor; p. 269 (n.)
But the sailor would not listen to him; p. 269 (n.) its effects were
just as the sailor had predicted; p. 270 (n.) for the sailor would be
faithful to his word; p. 270 (n.) but the sailor told him that if he
did; p. 271 (n.) with what the old sailor told him.

Omoo--p. xiii (n.) are the proverbial characteristics of sailors
shown; p. xiv (n.) As a roving sailor, the author spent about three
months; p. 3 (n.) as a sailor before the mast; p. 3 (n.) a fellow-
sailor who accompanied him; p. 5 (n.) leaning carelessly over the
bulwarks were the sailors; p. 6 (n.) coincidences which often befall
the sailor; p. 6 (adj.) frequently met in a sailor boarding-house;
p. 6 (n.) I might have been taken for a sailor with the gout; p. 7
(n.) an old sailor on a chest just under me; p. 7 (adj.) The attention
was sailor-like; p. 9 (n.) Little Jule, as the sailors familiarly
styled her; p. 12 (n.) went forward with his chests among the sailors;
p. 14 (n.) of what sailors call small stores we had but little; p. 14
(n.) a sailor might have made a satisfactory meal; p. 17 (n.) must
wait patiently until the sailor is willing; p. 23 (n.) to procure, if
possible, several English sailors; p. 25 (n.) the light in which many
sailors regard these naked heathens; p. 28 (n.) so many of whom are
found among sailors; p. 38 (adj.) bestowed upon the sailors' sleeping-
quarters; p. 38 (n.) as sailors say; p. 39 (adj.) by the sailors'
chests; p. 39 (adj.) was a locker, or sailors' pantry; p. 39 (n.) a
freak of some drunken sailors; p. 39 (n.) the sailors being mere
tenants; p. 41 (n.) what lovers of fun sailors are ashore; p. 42 (n.)
the sailor pressed softly the chest of his victim; p. 45 (n.) the
dead sailor stitched up as before; p. 46 (n.) Behold here the fate of
a sailor; p. 46 (n.) they have great influence among sailors; p. 47
(n.) that among sailors as a class; p. 47 (n.) first intercourse with
them as a sailor; p. 48 (n.) a thoroughbred sailor deems scarcely any
price too dear; p. 52 (n.) to try and make a sailor of him; p. 52 (n.)
a sailor has no bowels of compassion; p. 53 (n.) a sailor comes along
and wants to know; p. 53 (n.) The sailors perhaps ought to make
allowances; p. 54 (n.) sailors newly waked are no cherubs; p. 57 (adj.)
had a true sailor admiration for Lord Nelson; p. 58 (n.) as every
sailor knows; p. 59 (adv.) sprung into the main-rigging, sailor-like;
p. 68 (n.) and the sailor is apt to indulge; p. 69 (n.) A slight hint
suffices for a sailor; p. 71 (n.) held superior to the sailors; p. 72
(n.) if it do not make him a little peevish, he is no sailor; p. 73
(n.) that sailors seldom obtain justice; p. 74 (n.) uproarious the
comments of the sailors; p. 78 (n.) the sailors ranged themselves;
p. 78 (n.) But among the sailors; p. 78 (adj.) an unsailor-like
article of dress; p. 80 (n.) he looked sharply among the sailors;

p. 80 (n.) into which the cooper's poltroonery had thrown the sailors; p. 81 (n.) he abruptly addressed the sailors; p. 81 (n.) among sailors in the Pacific; p. 83 (n.) on making common cause with the sailors; p. 84 (n.) The sailors ran about deck like madmen; p. 87 (n.) that he was no sailor; p. 87 (n.) long enough among sailors; p. 88 (adj.) after rating him in sailor style; p. 90 (n.) Up came the sailors; p. 91 (n.) as the infuriated sailors came on; p. 91 (adj.) the sailor's heart was beating against the Mowree's; p. 92 (n.) dashing two or three of the sailors aside; p. 92 (n.) Giving the sailors no time to recover; p. 94 (n.) the sailors, for the present, seemed in no hurry; p. 97 (n.) the sailors absolutely refused; p. 99 (adj.) with a sailor's blessing; p. 99 (n.) among sailors of all nations; p. 103 (n.) manned by eighteen or twenty sailors; p. 105 (n.) to half-a-dozen sailor-soldiers; p. 106 (n.) whom we took for an English sailor; p. 109 (n.) they are no sailors; p. 110 (n.) are sailors one moment, soldiers the next; p. 110 (adj.) to any thing like proper sailor pride; p. 110 (n.) being a true sailor; p. 110 (n.) letting the sailors fill their teeth; p. 110 (n.) the sailors asked for meat; p. 110 (n.) Some old merchant sailors had been seized; p. 111 (n.) I say the French are no sailors; p. 114 (n.) A sailor of my acquaintance; p. 116 (n.) house of confinement for his refractory sailors; p. 119 (adj.) he talked little else than sailor phrases; p. 124 (n.) The French sailors and marines; p. 128 (n.) a poor fellow, a sailor, whom I afterward saw; p. 128 (n.) No ship would receive him as a sailor; p. 129 (n.) A sailor, with a cheek like the breast of a roast turkey; p. 132 (n.) a monkey bag (so called by sailors); p. 134 (n.) yes, said the sailor dolefully; p. 134 (n.) plays the deuce with you sailors; p. 134 (n.) The sailors, one and all, made a snatch at the collection; p. 135 (n.) Johnson must have known enough of sailors; p. 139 (adj.) not a little mortified by the old sailor's bluntness; p. 140 (n.) the sailors canvassed the motives of the consul; p. 140 (n.) yet this is the gratitude of a sailor, Mr. Wilson; p. 140 (n.) he merely wished to procure the sailor; p. 140 (n.) as the sailors became riotous; p. 143 (n.) as land beavers are called by sailors; p. 143 (n.) with all the ardor of a sophomorean sailor; p. 145 (n.) don't worry yourself now about those rascally sailors; p. 146 (n.) known among sailors as "Old Mother Tot"; p. 147 (n.) there was no lack of idle sailors ashore; p. 148 (n.) as sailors and congenial spirits; p. 148 (n.) and a sailor every inch; p. 148 (adj.) was left ashore at the sailor hospital; p. 148 (n.) demanded by every sailor; p. 149 (n.) the sailors on the forecastle singing; p. 151 (adj.) the love of a Tahitian for a sailor's trunk; p. 158 (n.) the sailors, like the doctor and myself; p. 158 (n.) in love at first sight with a smart sailor; p. 159 (n.) with the proverbial restlessness of sailors; p. 159 (n.) No sailor steps ashore; p. 160 (n.) for the sailors invariably linked us; p. 160 (n.) for he was no sailor; p. 160 (n.) attach to them what sailors call an "outrigger"; p. 160 (n.) the sailors christened it the Pill Box; p. 160 (n.) upon the strength of my being a sailor; p. 161 (adj.) and a famous sailors' pudding; p. 164 (n.) the sailors keep their Sabbath; p. 164 (n.) upon course suggested by a knowing sailor; p. 166 (n.) better behaved sailors never stepped; p. 173 (n.) in the person of an intelligent Hawaiian sailor; p. 173 (n.) No good sailors living; p. 173 (n.) no run after sailors; p. 177 (adj.) adjusted over a pair of white sailor trowsers; p. 177 (n.) imported in the chest of some amorous sailor; p. 179 (n.) The sailors in the calabooza; p. 182 (n.) The young sailor, for whom

Kooloo deserted me; p. 190 (n.) who would rather pay a drunken
sailor; p. 193 (adj.) obtained for it the sailors' signs manual;
p. 198 (n.) the sailors now deputed the doctor to step forward;
p. 206 (n.) is quite efficacious among sailors; p. 235 (n.) after a
fashion peculiar to sailors; p. 235 (n.) sailors seldom wear shoes;
p. 236 (n.) what sailors call a Scotch cap; p. 237 (n.) of what sailors
call "plug" tobacco; p. 244 (adj.) a musty old pair of sailor trowsers
was drawn forth; p. 254 (adj.) with the most classic sailor phrases;
p. 279 (adj.) two suits of new sailor frocks and trowsers; p. 281
(adj.) swinging overhead in a sailor's hammock; p. 282 (adj.)
furniture consisted of three or four sailor chests; p. 282 (n.) of
the kind which sailors sew into the frame; p. 283 (adv.) streaming
behind, sailor-fashion; p. 287 (n.) sailors, even, attended her
levees; p. 289 (n.) we found four or five sailors lounging; p. 289
(n.) cried a curly-pated little Belfast sailor; p. 290 (n.) It
betokened a true sailor; p. 292 (n.) two sailors got tranquilly over
the side; p. 292 (n.) which had been found in the chest of a sailor;
p. 293 (n.) she knows very well what graceless dogs sailors are;
p. 296 (n.) the other was occupied by three sailors; p. 299 (n.)
Captain Crash entertains the sailors in his grove; p. 299 (n.) The
sailors fought like tigers; p. 307 (n.) Embarking at his native
island, as a sailor; p. 312 (n.) like all sailors ashore, I at last
pined for the billows; p. 312 (n.) a sailor, and no tyrant; p. 313
(n.) got up by the sailors for the purpose of frightening; p. 313
(n.) sailors belong to no nation in particular; p. 313 (n.) an American
sailor is generally distinguished by his red frock; p. 315 (n.) on
second thought, he was no sailor; p. 316 (n.) a mad, merry night
among the sailors; p. 316 (adj.) Once more the sailor's cradle rocked
under me.

Mardi--p. 4 (n.) The sailors were good fellows all; p. 5 (n.) for a
sailor; p. 7 (n.) the bold sailor . . . waits not; p. 13 (n.) in
which sailors should be adepts; p. 14 (n.) for some young sailor;
p. 14 (n.) in the fellowship of sailors; p. 14 (n.) chummying among
sailors; p. 22 (n.) instead of the sailors being divided; p. 23 (n.)
Sailors are quite lively; p. 23 (n.) of the dreaming sailors; p. 24
(n.) every sailor at his post; p. 25 (adj.) eluded a sailor's grave;
p. 28 (n.) shouting of the sailors; p. 28 (n.) impatiently cried the
sailors; p. 29 (n.) the final indifference of sailors; p. 30 (n.) to
sailors, as a class; p. 33 (n.) ordinary tanning of the sailor; p. 40
(n.) so called by sailors; p. 40 (n.) a stray sailor; p. 40 (n.)
sailors denounce them; p. 53 (n.) called Pilot fish by sailors; p. 59
(adj.) was a sailor's chest; p. 62 (n.) from a couple of sailors;
p. 63 (adj.) full of sailors' ghosts; p. 67 (n.) phraseology of a
Polynesian sailor; p. 86 (adj.) he was, sailor-like; p. 94 (n.) upon
the decease of a friendless sailor; p. 94 (n.) sailors reason thus;
p. 95 (n.) sailors are mostly foundlings; p. 101 (n.) to a sailor;
p. 123 (n.) sailors love marvels; p. 132 (adj.) representing some
hundreds of sailor boys; p. 289 (n.) some sailors are slow believers;
p. 289 (n.) the sailors draw a rash inference; p. 467 (n.) a fearless
sailor of his frigid seas.

Redburn--p. 3 (n.) to send me to sea as a sailor; pp. 4-5 (n.) I
remembered the yo heave ho! of the sailors; p. 5 (n.) that that very
ship, and those very sailors; p. 8 (n.) as beautiful little glass
sailors as any body ever saw; p. 8 (n.) Four or five of these sailors

were very nimble; p. 8 (n.) Another sailor was sitting astride; p. 15
(n.) he has long wanted to be a sailor; p. 15 (n.) So you want to be
a sailor; p. 16 (n.) he will go to sea as a sailor; p. 19 (n.) I met
a great crowd of sailors; p. 24 (n.) to see what sort of a looking
sailor I was going to make; p. 24 (n.) one of the sailors who was
going; p. 25 (n.) to belong to the sailors; p. 27 (adj.) in which I
had put a piece of cavendish tobacco, to look sailor-like; p. 28 (n.)
I was going out in the ship as a sailor; p. 28 (n.) "A sailor!" he
cried, "a barber's clerk you mean"; p. 28 (n.) a drunken sailor
peeped in; p. 29 (n.) I saw none of the sailors on board; p. 29 (adj.)
thinking to secure a sailor friend; p. 30 (n.) the salt beef used by
the sailors; p. 31 (n.) Several of the sailors were very drunk; p. 31
(n.) And two other sailors; p. 31 (n.) But though the sailors,
surfeited with eating; p. 32 (n.) that sailors breathe nothing about
such things; p. 33 (n.) to hear some of the sailors; p. 34 (n.) I did
not know what to make of these sailors; p. 34 (n.) at the sailors
standing by me; p. 36 (n.) in the way of becoming a miserable sailor
for life; p. 37 (n.) to me and the sailors; p. 38 (n.) the sailors
were ordered on the quarter-deck; p. 38 (n.) selecting a stout good-
looking sailor; p. 38 (n.) also chose a stout good-looking sailor;
p. 38 (n.) But the sailors, especially the stout good-looking ones;
p. 39 (n.) the second mate called one of the sailors; p. 40 (n.) for
the sailors when at work; p. 40 (n.) asking the rough sailors to let
me drink; p. 40 (n.) I told one of the sailors how it was; p. 40
(adj.) did not outwardly resent the sailor's words; p. 41 (n.) a sort
of lady's sailor; p. 42 (n.) I wondered how the sailors could really
like; p. 45 (n.) The Sailors Becoming a Little Social; p. 45 (n.) as
the sailors they command; p. 46 (n.) the sailors never touched a rope
without using it; p. 46 (n.) It is a great thing in a sailor; p. 46
(n.) the sailors sat on the windlass; p. 46 (n.) for some sailors
always provide little delicacies; p. 46 (n.) finding the sailors all
very pleasant; p. 46 (n.) heard in church in behalf of sailors; p. 47
(adj.) in a magazine, called the Sailors' Magazine; p. 48 (n.) whether
there were any such good sailors; p. 48 (n.) When I heard this poor
sailor; p. 49 (n.) might sit uneasily upon this sailor; p. 49 (n.)
some one of the sailors forward struck a large bell; p. 49 (n.) I
inquired of this Floating Chapel sailor; p. 49 (n.) to laugh and joke
about me, with the other sailors; p. 50 (n.) the Sailors Abuse Him;
p. 50 (n.) I thought one of the sailors must be murdered; p. 50 (n.)
the sailors came running up on deck; p. 50 (n.) he was one of the
sailors; p. 51 (n.) the way in which the sailor spoke; p. 51 (n.) the
sailors who spoke it seemed; p. 51 (adj.) the hardships of a sailor's
life; p. 52 (n.) out of the mouth of honest sailors; p. 54 (n.) a
good many things that a sailor needs; p. 54 (n.) that sailors had no
table to sit down to; p. 54 (n.) Every sailor went to the cook-house;
p. 55 (n.) one of the sailors perceiving what I was about; p. 55 (n.)
the sailors sitting cross-legged; p. 56 (n.) Of this sailor, I shall
have something; p. 56 (n.) just such a looking man was this sailor;
p. 56 (n.) he despised the ordinary sailor rig; p. 58 (n.) He would
talk of sailors being poisoned; p. 59 (n.) though the sailors were
always very bitter; p. 59 (n.) was not much of a sailor; p. 60 (n.)
For sailors are of three classes; p. 60 (n.) the dispute between the
two sailors; p. 60 (adj.) I can tell a sailor's age just like a
horse's; p. 60 (n.) the first man was the oldest sailor; p. 60 (adj.)
could tell a sailor's age like a horse's; p. 61 (n.) that all the
sailors were alike; p. 61 (n.) plot against him among the other

sailors; p. 62 (n.) For merchant sailors have a great idea of; p. 65
(n.) and the sailors were fastening them to the boom; p. 65 (n.) and
the sailors would laugh and wink to each other; p. 65 (n.) for the
first time as sailors; p. 65 (n.) For sailors have their own names;
p. 67 (n.) the difference between me and the rude sailors; p. 68 (n.)
when the sailors saw me thus employed; p. 69 (n.) Meanwhile the
sailors were all standing; p. 69 (n.) returning among the sailors;
p. 69 (n.) not customary for sailors to call; p. 70 (n.) the great
amusement of the sailors; p. 72 (n.) long togs, as the sailors call
them; p. 73 (adv.) owing to their not being cut sailor-fashion; p. 73
(n.) the sailors made a great deal of fun; p. 74 (n.) The sailors
used to call them; p. 75 (n.) going to sea as a sailor; p. 75 (n.) I
saw the strange sailors grouped; p. 76 (n.) while the sailors were
obeying; p. 77 (n.) an old Dutch sailor came up to me; p. 79 (n.)
made good the saying of old sailors; p. 79 (n.) Max was an old
bachelor of a sailor; p. 79 (adj.) in some of the sailor saloons; p.
p. 80 (n.) several of the sailors had twinges of the rheumatism;
p. 85 (n.) in dividing the effects of the sailor; p. 86 (adj.) in the
sailor book-stalls about Fulton Market; p. 86 (n.) to be going to sea
as a common sailor; p. 87 (n.) I must tell of Jack Blunt the sailor;
p. 88 (n.) whose house was much frequented by sailors; p. 88 (adj.)
was an old sailor landlord in Marseilles; p. 90 (n.) this is nothing
to other sailors; p. 90 (n.) the most simple sailor could teach it;
p. 91 (n.) I overheard two of the sailors debating; p. 92 (n.) among
sailors at sea; p. 93 (n.) The sailor who had the look-out; p. 93 (n.)
Sailors can not be too wakeful; p. 94 (n.) such as sailors generally
are; p. 96 (adj.) I perceived the force of that sailor saying; p. 97
(n.) the cry of the sailors ceasing; p. 97 (n.) one of the sailors
carried the lead; p. 97 (n.) but the sailors did not seem; p. 101
(adj.) always talking of sailor life; p. 102 (n.) the sailors only
laughed at me; p. 103 (n.) These were sailors, who long ago; p. 103
(n.) On the part of the sailors; p. 104 (adj.) that's a sailor's
coffin; p. 104 (n.) all sailors are saved; p. 106 (n.) among sailors
come under the general head; p. 108 (n.) The sailors, who are always
curious; p. 108 (n.) One observing sailor was of opinion; p. 108 (n.)
still in vogue among some merchant sailors; p. 109 (n.) one of the
perquisites of sailors; p. 109 (adj.) was our Greenland sailor's
attention called; p. 109 (n.) acquiescence in the demands of the
sailor; p. 110 (n.) To the curious questions of the sailors; p. 111
(n.) which one of the sailors declared "spandangalous"; p. 112 (n.)
to send him forward among the sailors; p. 112 (n.) The sailors
received him with open arms; p. 112 (n.) The sailors took the warmest
interest in him; p. 112 (n.) and the sailors and poor steerage
passengers; p. 114 (n.) in learning the duties of a sailor; p. 114
(n.) the sailors are continually engaged; p. 116 (n.) in the "Sailors'-
Snug-Harbor" on Staten Island; p. 118 (n.) where there are few
inducements to attract a sailor; p. 119 (n.) The sailors, however,
did not like it; p. 120 (n.) A Sailor a Jack of All Trades; p. 120
(adj.) As I began to learn my sailor duties; p. 120 (n.) The business
of a thorough-bred sailor; p. 121 (n.) A thorough sailor must
understand; p. 121 (n.) A sailor, also, in working; p. 121 (n.) they
say he is "a sailor-man"; pp. 122-3 (adj.) to the other sailors' one;
p. 125 (n.) Ah, my fine sailors, from Ameriky; p. 125 (n.) my beautiful
sailors; p. 127 (n.) without thinking of the sailors who sleep; p. 12
p. 128 (n.) coming forward among the sailors; p. 129 (n.) whether he,
a poor sailor; p. 130 (n.) though the sailors are supposed to sleep;

p. 131 (n.) filled with boarding-houses, spirit-vaults, and sailors;
p. 131 (n.) conciliating American sailors; p. 131 (n.) I asked a
sailor standing by; p. 131 (n.) for the lady, and not the sailor;
p. 131 (n.) The sailors took her part; p. 133 (n.) of ballad-singers,
bawling women, babies, and drunken sailors; p. 133 (n.) nothing but a
poor sailor boy; p. 133 (n.) prospects of seeing the world as a
sailor; p. 133 (n.) sailors only go round the world; p. 134 (n.)
covered with sailor-scrawls; p. 134 (n.) Was it possible that sailors
fared thus; p. 134 (n.) the sailors, who at sea live; p. 136 (n.)
Concerning the Prospects of Sailors; p. 137 (n.) the life led by
sailors of American ships; p. 138 (n.) sailors love this Liverpool;
p. 138 (n.) of ameliorating the condition of sailors; p. 138 (n.) the
very fact of their being sailors; p. 138 (n.) the case of sailors, as
a class; p. 139 (n.) condition of the great bulk of sailors; p. 139
(n.) because the sailor, who today steers; p. 139 (n.) from the
exaggerated sailors of Smollett; p. 139 (n.) sailors from one of
these wheels; p. 140 (n.) And yet, what are sailors; p. 140 (n.) to
accommodate sailors already broken down; p. 140 (n.) low estimation
in which sailors are held; p. 140 (n.) can sailors, one of the wheels
of this world; p. 140 (n.) not altogether despair for the sailor;
p. 153 (n.) three parts sportsman, and two soldier, to one of the
sailor; p. 153 (n.) a drunken sailor passing, exclaimed; p. 154 (n.)
visit Liverpool as a poor friendless sailor boy; p. 159 (n.) you are
but a sailor-boy; p. 163 (n.) is well known to American sailors;
p. 164 (n.) irritates and exasperates the sailors; p. 164 (n.) sailors
of all nations are singing out; p. 175 (n.) call the strolling sailors
to their devotions; p. 176 (n.) men, who, like sailors; p. 176 (n.)
to which sailors are most addicted; p. 177 (n.) to which all pious
sailors made offerings; p. 178 (n.) I saw a sailor stretched out;
p. 182 (n.) whom the sailors called <u>Brandy-Nan</u>; p. 183 (adj.) to a
mean little sailor tavern; p. 186 (n.) in the streets frequented by
sailors; p. 187 (n.) thus, at least, it was with the sailors; p. 187
(n.) example of the caprice of sailors; p. 187 (n.) tost into his
poor-box by the sailors; p. 188 (adj.) who wore old sailor hats;
p. 189 (adj.) where the sailor boarding-houses are kept; p. 189 (n.)
especially when the sailors are gathered; p. 189 (n.) exchanged
between old sailors; p. 190 (adj.) the number of sailor ballad-singers;
p. 190 (adj.) happening in the sailor quarters of the town; p. 190
(n.) by a drunken Spanish sailor from Cadiz; p. 191 (n.) neighborhoods
frequented by sailors; p. 191 (n.) from which sailors sometimes
disappear; p. 193 (n.) the command of that fine old sailor; p. 195
(n.) going among the sailors and privately exhibiting; p. 195 (n.)
who practiced upon the sailors in Liverpool; p. 195 (n.) saw sailors
in a state of intoxication; p. 196 (n.) The sailors were then given
to understand; p. 196 (n.) often visited by foreign sailors; p. 202
(n.) interest with which negro-sailors are regarded; p. 207 (n.) I'm
a poor, friendless sailor-boy; p. 213 (n.) I declared myself a Yankee
sailor; p. 216 (n.) among the . . . smoky sailor-lanes and by-ways;
p. 218 (n.) gallantly crossed the Atlantic as a sailor; p. 218 (n.)
not at all indisposed to let their sailors abscond; p. 219 (n.) the
voyage thither, as a sailor; p. 220 (n.) to a sort of treatment from
the sailors; p. 220 (n.) degree in which he was a practical sailor;
p. 221 (n.) he was bent upon going as a sailor; p. 226 (n.) through
crowds of frolicking sailors and fiddlers; p. 234 (adj.) most squalid
haunts of sailor iniquity; p. 237 (adj.) once more in our sailor
habiliments; p. 238 (n.) to know nothing of the proceedings of the

sailors; pp. 349-50 (n.) this stupified sailor . . . was lowered on
board; p. 243 (n.) But the sailors answered for their new comrade;
p. 244 (n.) So the sailor still lay; p. 244 (adj.) he dragged forth
the sailor's arm; p. 245 (n.) the sailors seemed familiar with such
things; p. 245 (n.) no one sailor but Jackson would stay; p. 252 (n.)
how my friend, Harry, got along as a sailor; p. 253 (n.) those
unimpressible, uncivilized sailors of ours; p. 253 (n.) But even
sailors are not blind; p. 253 (n.) acquaintance with the sea-life and
sailors; p. 254 (n.) The sailors took a special spite; p. 254 (n.)
thrown out by the sailors; p. 254 (n.) the sailors almost invariably
impute; p. 256 (n.) cried the mate to the Dutch sailor; p. 257 (n.)
Once a sailor . . . and always a sailor; p. 262 (n.) when disturbed
by the sailors; pp. 264-5 (n.) by sailors burgoo [what oatmeal is
known as]; p. 268 (n.) The sailors took much pleasure; p. 268 (n.)
the rebuke and threat of the sailor; p. 270 (n.) one of the favorite
pursuits of sailors; p. 271 (n.) especially if they chance to be
sailors; p. 271 (n.) on which sailors so much rely; p. 271 (n.) thrown
aside by sailors; p. 272 (n.) generally adopted by sailors; p. 273
(n.) among the sailors was the most eagerly sought; p. 273 (n.) But
the sailors seemed to like it; p. 273 (n.) when the sailors would be
seated inconsolable; p. 275 (n.) nothing but a castaway sailor;
p. 278 (n.) delighted with the rudest minstrelsy are sailors; p. 278
(n.) from the ribald jests so common to sailors; p. 283 (n.) come and
see the sailors eating out of little troughs; p. 284 (n.) they beset
the sailors; p. 287 (n.) succeeded in getting the sailors below;
p. 287 (n.) But the sailors fell back; p. 288 (n.) The sailors
peremptorily refused to go; p. 289 (n.) one of whom was the Greenland
sailor; p. 289 (n.) sailors, officers, cabin-passengers, and emigrants;
p. 295 (n.) Before the sailors had made fast; p. 295 (n.) a moment of
frantic exertion with sailors; p. 296 (n.) the sailors, in my hearing
at least; p. 298 (n.) The sailors whistled and whistled for a wind;
p. 301 (n.) the unknotting of the bonds of the sailors; p. 305 (n.)
the sailors stood deferentially in a semicircle; p. 305 (n.) The
other sailors, after counting their cash; p. 305 (n.) not to be taken
in and cheated, your sailors; p. 305 (n.) the sailors also salaamed;
p. 308 (n.) we found the sailors congregated; p. 308 (n.) of any
particular outrage against the sailors; p. 308 (n.) without speaking
to the sailors on the subject; p. 309 (adj.) till they stopped at a
sailor retreat; p. 309 (n.) pushed them over toward the sailors;
p. 309 (n.) of all men, sailors shake the most hands; p. 312 (n.) I
found myself a sailor in the Pacific.

White-Jacket--p. 3 (adj.) without a grego, or sailor's surtout; p. 4
(n.) So much paint had been stolen by the sailors; p. 9 (n.) who are
always made up of active sailors; p. 10 (adj.) and least sailor-like
of the crew; p. 11 (n.) a sailor has need of a good memory; p. 11 (n.)
consider, now a merchant-sailor altogether unused; p. 15 (n.) forever
to eschew the company of any sailor; p. 16 (n.) deserved the name of
sailors; p. 22 (n.) His cot-boy used to entertain the sailors; p. 25
(n.) and swearing at the sailors; p. 26 (n.) forming the first
aristocracy above the sailors; p. 26 (n.) He it is whom all sailors
hate; p. 31 (n.) went among the sailors by a name; p. 32 (n.) for the
derivation of the name which the sailors applied; p. 32 (n.) who is
not . . . fitted to become a common sailor; p. 33 (n.) The sailors do
not laugh at him outright; p. 34 (n.) but the sailors loved him all
round; p. 34 (n.) than one with a rose-water sailor; p. 35 (n.) that

to a common sailor; p. 35 (n.) with five hundred other sailors diving
into each; p. 35 (n.) many sailors divide their wardrobes; p. 36 (n.)
It must be known, that sailors . . . only cover their hands; p. 38
(n.) sailors, as a class, entertain the most liberal notions; p. 39
(n.) hearing that a sailor has something valuable; p. 43 (n.) to an
admiring circle of the more refined sailors; p. 44 (n.) driving the
sailors away from them; p. 45 (n.) making stinging remarks at the
sailors; p. 51 (n.) For he was no sailor; p. 53 (n.) the sailors
assemble round a large tub; p. 53 (n.) than the sailor does over this
tot; p. 58 (n.) which forbids the sailors to sing out; p. 66 (n.)
Many a poor sailor . . . must have received; p. 66 (n.) manner in
which both sailors and soldiers nowadays fight; p. 68 (adj.) The
sailors' mess-chests are tumbled down; p. 75 (n.) and the mass of
sailors swing their hammocks under all; p. 76 (n.) the sailors used
to fancy that I must be studying astronomy; p. 76 (n.) we sailors
sail not in vain; p. 77 (n.) who are shipmates and fellow-sailors of
ours; p. 78 (adv.) sailor-like, had taken me for the ghost of the
cooper; p. 82 (n.) of a grievance among sailors that ought to be
redressed; p. 82 (n.) the sailors have watch and watch; p. 82 (n.)
did the sailors have a complete night's rest; p. 84 (n.) such a thing
as sailors sleeping in their hammocks in the daytime; p. 86 (adj.) it
keeps the sailor's quarters perpetually damp; p. 86 (n.) let all such
swing their hammocks with the sailors; p. 86 (n.) and every sailor
goes barefooted; p. 87 (n.) and the poor sailors are almost over-
whelmed; p. 87 (adj.) you see no trace of a sailor's dormitory; p. 87
(n.) by the most rigorous edicts . . . with respect to the sailors;
p. 87 (n.) sailors themselves do not often complain; p. 87 (n.) The
American sailors mess on the deck; p. 87 (n.) the sailors roll their
mess-things up; p. 88 (n.) exempts the sailors from a perpetual
annoyance; p. 89 (n.) the intoxicated sailors reel about; p. 90 (n.)
madness to intoxicate the sailors; p. 90 (n.) free permission was
given to the sailors; p. 91 (n.) The sailors who originated this
scheme; p. 91 (adj.) stowed down in the bottom of the sailors' bags;
p. 92 (n.) THE TRUE YANKEE SAILOR; p. 92 (n.) THE TRUE YANKEE SAILOR;
p. 92 (n.) Sailors, Marines, Barkeepers; p. 92 (n.) No sailor permitted
to enter in his shirt-sleeves; p. 93 (n.) the sailors anticipated a
gleeful afternoon; p. 93 (n.) The sailors looked round for the
Commodore; p. 94 (n.) four sailors . . . staggered on the stage;
p. 94 (n.) where Percy Royal-Mast rescues fifteen oppressed sailors;
p. 94 (n.) The sailors pricked their ears at it; p. 95 (n.) But the
sailors never recovered from the disappointment; p. 95 (n.) of not
having the "True Yankee Sailor" sung; p. 95 (n.) once permitted as
sailors to be a little noisy; p. 95 (n.) an old sailor touched my
shoulder; p. 96 (n.) takes the conceit out of fresh-water sailors;
p. 97 (n.) Heaven help the sailors; p. 98 (n.) in the language of
sailors, they polish the Cape; p. 98 (n.) which the gallant sailors
did; p. 101 (n.) where sailors say fire freezes; p. 109 (n.) But,
sailor or landsman, there is some sort; p. 114 (n.) And every American
sailor should be placed; p. 116 (n.) some of the sailors enjoyed the
juvenile diversion; p. 119 (n.) you would see the sailors wrapped in
their jackets; p. 120 (n.) The sailors were so enveloped in monkey
jackets; p. 123 (adj.) where the sailor grog is kept; p. 124 (n.)
when a sailor is ordered one dozen lashes; p. 125 (n.) to retain in
his employment the various sailors; p. 127 (n.) completely inaccessible
to the sailor; p. 129 (n.) The Turkish sailors will sit on their gun-
carriages; p. 131 (n.) which sailors, charged with offences; p. 131

(n.) where the sailor can hold formal communication; p. 132 (n.) salt
beef and pork at the messes of the sailors; p. 132 (n.) the only way
that a sailor could get it cooked; p. 134 (n.) four sailors of the
starboard watch; p. 134 (n.) fights sometimes occurring among sailors;
p. 136 (n.) most captains love to see a tidy sailor; p. 139 (n.)
thereby begetting in the sailor an undue idea; p. 140 (n.) to inflict
chastisement upon a sailor; p. 142 (n.) hurl down the last pride of
some sailor; p. 142 (n.) in whose image the flogged sailor is made;
p. 143 (n.) concerns the punishment of the sailor; p. 143 (n.)
cruelty upon the common sailor; p. 144 (n.) As a sailor, he shares
none; p. 145 (adj.) but in the sailor's case, he is at once condemned;
p. 145 (n.) inflict a severe and degrading punishment upon a sailor;
p. 145 (n.) yet both sailor and captain are American citizens; p. 145
(n.) which is inflicted upon the sailor; p. 146 (n.) by the side of a
transgressing sailor; p. 148 (n.) afterward ruling his sailors by the
mere memory; p. 148 (n.) that his sailors knew this; p. 153 (n.) to
the surprise, grief, and consternation of the sailors; p. 154 (n.)
that the sailors held forth on the ungenerous conduct; p. 155 (adj.)
necessity of every sailor's saving it; p. 156 (n.) and not a sailor
on board but believed; p. 160 (n.) At sea there is more to employ the
sailors; p. 160 (n.) Some sailors are very fond of belonging; p. 166
(n.) how can you make every sailor a commodore; p. 166 (n.)
correspondingly elevate the common sailor; p. 168 (adj.) in a sailor's
estimation; p. 169 (n.) Several other sailors were diligent readers;
p. 170 (n.) The Roman Catholic sailors on board; p. 171 (n.) They
would not fare as Protestant sailors; p. 171 (n.) And many sailors
not Catholic were anxious to have; p. 171 (n.) every sailor has some
brass or steel; p. 172 (n.) that the sailors had much better be
crowded; p. 172 (n.) superintending in person the flogging of a sailor;
p. 173 (n.) as the sailors used their checker-men; p. 173 (n.) whereupon the sailors were exasperated; p. 173 (n.) Some of the sailors
were very precise; p. 174 (n.) emerge to chat with the sailors on
deck; p. 177 (n.) to bring off fruit for the sailors; p. 179 (n.)
sailors who do not draw their government ration; p. 182 (n.) the
number of intoxicated sailors collared and brought up; p. 185 (n.)
clandestinely sold the spirits to the sailors; p. 185 (n.) prices
should have been given by the sailors; p. 185 (n.) The sailors who
became intoxicated; p. 193 (n.) sometimes serves the common sailor
for a bench; p. 195 (n.) the sailors throughout the squadron exert
themselves; p. 198 (n.) after a sailor dies in an armed vessel;
p. 198 (n.) the sailors sprang to their feet; p. 199 (n.) he was
quite a favorite with the sailors; p. 199 (n.) gallant sailors, for
this noble pair of boots; p. 200 (n.) remember, my gallant sailors;
p. 205 (n.) Some disappointed applicants among the sailors; p. 206
(n.) The ideas that sailors entertain of Pursers; p. 206 (n.) Among
sailors, also, Pursers commonly go; p. 206 (n.) whom the sailors
exempt from the insinuations; p. 208 (n.) the majority of the common
sailors of the Neversink; p. 208 (n.) while it held out to the sailor
no promise; p. 213 (n.) no sailor in a man-of-war presumes; p. 217
(n.) said Sir Peter to his sailors; p. 217 (n.) if he but orders a
sailor; p. 218 (n.) in his ordinary intercourse with the sailors;
p. 218 (n.) to a sailor who . . . has chanced to offend him; p. 219
(n.) Imagine an outcast old sailor; p. 220 (n.) to do duty with the
common sailors; p. 221 (n.) between the midshipman and the sailor;
p. 222 (n.) conventionally degraded a being as a sailor; p. 224 (n.)
he advanced toward the sailor; p. 224 (n.) And the sailor received

his dozen; p. 226 (n.) fell in--as all sailors must--with dashing
adventures; p. 227 (n.) some of the sailors must have previously
determined; p. 229 (n.) mixing with its sailors and sinners as equals;
p. 231 (n.) in his intercourse with the sailors; p. 236 (n.) Ringbolt,
the sailor on the other side of him; p. 241 (n.) though all sailors
do certainly keep late hours; p. 242 (n.) I know you henceforth for a
common sailor; p. 242 (n.) re-entered the Navy . . . as a common
sailor; p. 243 (n.) He was one of the few sailors; p. 244 (n.) he an
officer and I a miserable sailor; p. 244 (adj.) with this sailor's
frock on; p. 244 (n.) you are nothing but a sailor; p. 259 (n.) both
sailors and soldiers were subjected; p. 259 (n.) Here was a sailor,
who . . . had stood erect; p. 264 (n.) a sailor of the vessel to which
I was attached; p. 266 (n.) But to some of the sailors; p. 268 (n.)
among the impatient sailors; p. 270 (n.) How many great men have been
sailors; p. 270 (n.) Ulysses, was both a sailor and a shipwright;
p. 270 (n.) Christopher Columbus, was a sailor; p. 270 (n.) Ay,
Camoens was a sailor once; p. 270 (n.) Old Noah was the first sailor;
p. 271 (n.) Shelley, he was quite a sailor; p. 271 (adj.) ought to
have let him sleep in his sailor's grave; p. 271 (n.) And was not
Byron a sailor; p. 271 (adj.) A sailor's life, I say, is the thing;
p. 271 (n.) what are you but a sailor; p. 275 (n.) so the sailors
called him; p. 283 (n.) one of the very rare examples of a sailor;
p. 283 (n.) for, with most sailors, old age comes in youth; p. 285
(n.) the sailors in a man-of-war are the most . . . anxious; p. 287
(n.) The sailors run to and fro; p. 288 (n.) through the long lanes
of sailors at their guns; p. 290 (n.) The sailors said, he looked
like a rat; p. 290 (n.) and the sailors were hurrying to their
stations; p. 293 (n.) to the sailor who infringes these Articles;
p. 298 (n.) the hardihood of the British sailor; p. 298 (n.) governed
Blake's sailors at that period; p. 301 (n.) nearly all those
exclusively referring to the sailors; p. 301 (n.) by which the sailor
is scourged; p. 301 (n.) to which the sailors alone are obnoxious;
p. 301 (n.) involves oppression to the sailor; p. 301 (n.) between
the American Captain and the American sailor; p. 302 (n.) though the
sailor is sometimes tried; p. 302 (n.) in no case do his fellow-
sailors . . . form part; p. 302 (n.) which authorized the sailor to
appeal; p. 304 (n.) sentimental and theoretic love for the common
sailor; p. 304 (n.) which I know that the sailor suffers; p. 304 (adj.)
most of the sailor iniquities practiced therein; p; 306 (n.) trans-
gressed by the unscrupulous sailors; p. 306 (n.) went among the
sailors; p. 308 (n.) who, among the sailors; p. 308 (adj.) the men
who talk the most sailor lingo are the least sailor-like; p. 311 (n.)
Sir Patrick Spens was the best sailor; p. 312 (n.) leveled it at the
heads of the three sailors; p. 314 (n.) but only compel the sailor to
fight; p. 315 (n.) that no sailor will deny; p. 315 (n.) any common-
sense sailors at the guns; p. 315 (n.) those common-sense sailors
must have greatly; p. 316 (n.) the sailors hove the animal overboard;
p. 316 (n.) The sailors who were killed; p. 316 (n.) the heart-stricken
sailor returned to his post; p. 317 (adj.) of sailor frocks and
trowsers; p. 320 (n.) Soldier or sailor; the fighting man is . . . a
fiend; p. 327 (n.) Pills, as the sailors called him; p. 329 (n.)
among the sailors went by the name of The Pelican; p. 329 (n.) a man-
of-war is far better for the sailor; p. 330 (n.) What sailors call
the Cape Horn Fever; p. 330 (n.) some "sogers" of sailors will stand;
p. 330 (n.) whether officers or sailors; p. 330 (n.) only delicacies
given to invalid sailors; p. 330 (n.) into broth for sick sailors;

p. 332 (adj.) rammed home . . . a wad of sailor superstition; p. 334 (n.) of Baldy, the buried sailor in Rio; p. 336 (n.) put into my hand by the sailor; p. 341 (n.) the dead sailor sank in the sea; p. 343 (n.) among the sailors on board a man-of-war; p. 346 (n.) when the sailors were at quarters; p. 349 (n.) scrambling up the ladders with the sailors; p. 350 (n.) rate of pay is fixed for every sailor; p. 350 (n.) which is charged to the sailor; p. 351 (n.) a sort of sleeping partner of a sailor; p. 351 (adj.) nor are the sailor wages he receives; p. 351 (adj.) though knowing little or nothing about sailor duties; p. 352 (n.) if the sailor had any insurance on his life; p. 353 (n.) the more aged sailors . . . sported . . . beards; p. 353 (n.) The long night-watches of the sailor; p. 353 (adj.) especially the genteel young sailor bucks; p. 353 (n.) Many sailors prided themselves; p. 358 (n.) operated upon the sailors like magic; p. 359 (n.) both soldiers and sailors are irresistible; p. 362 (n.) These were chiefly old sailors; p. 362 (n.) the sailors went sullenly to their guns; p. 365 (n.) not a single sailor who complied; p. 367 (n.) oblige their sailors to run up large bills; p. 367 (n.) should provoke such hostility from the sailors; p. 370 (n.) One act of a sailor may be construed; p. 370 (n.) a sailor . . . may legally be flogged to death; p. 371 (n.) before the sailor is sufficiently recovered; p. 372 (n.) an American sailor . . . was flogged; p. 373 (n.) they stood watches like the sailors; p. 374 (n.) the sailors are sometimes ordered; p. 374 (n.) the crowd of sailors . . . are thus additionally guarded; p. 374 (n.) antagonism between the marine and the sailor; p. 374 (n.) that if the sailor mutinies; p. 374 (n.) the pike of the sailor is impatient to charge; p. 374 (n.) in which the marine and sailor stand toward; p. 375 (n.) bears a grudge against a sailor; p. 375 (n.) facts touching the common sailor; p. 375 (n.) as it affects the common sailors; p. 377 (n.) are men-of-war familiarly known among sailors; p. 377 (n.) Nor are sailors . . . at all blind; p. 377 (adj.) is the sailor saying in the American Navy; p. 378 (n.) some repentant sailors have actually jumped; p. 378 (n.) when two French sailors were picked up; p. 378 (n.) these sailors . . . fought like tigers; p. 378 (n.) Sailors wanted for the Navy; p. 380 (n.) evinced by our sailors as a body; p. 380 (n.) many sailors, all the world over, are like; p. 381 (n.) the old sailor . . . tells of his skulking like a thief; p. 381 (n.) pressed into their service foreign sailors; p. 381 (adj.) from claiming his sailor countrymen; p. 383 (n.) Rum and tobacco . . . what more does a sailor want; p. 383 (n.) favorite song was "Dibdin's True English Sailor"; p. 384 (n.) And this is the life of a sailor; p. 384 (adj.) as in the sailor dance-houses; ashore; p. 386 (n.) gossip and news among the sailors; p. 390 (n.) insight into the character of sailors; p. 390 (n.) whole boarding-house of sailors; p. 390 (n.) the popular conceit concerning a sailor; p. 390 (n.) ashore he is no longer a sailor.

Moby-Dick--p. 14 (n.) when I go to sea, I go as a simple sailor; p. 14 (n.) The transition is a keen one, I assure you, from a school-master to a sailor; p. 15 (n.) Again, I always go to sea as a sailor; p. 15 (n.) Finally, I always go to sea as a sailor; p. 15 (n.) at second hand from the sailors on the forecastle; p. 15 (n.) after having repeatedly smelt the sea as a merchant sailor; p. 21 (n.) dearly sells the sailors deliriums and deaths; p. 24 (n.) why I as a sailor should sleep two in a bed; p. 24 (n.) for sailors no more sleep two in a bed at sea; p. 37 (n.) In these last-mentioned haunts

you see only sailors; p. 38 (n.) girdled with a sailor-belt and
sheath-knife; p. 39 (adj.) their sailor sweethearts smell them miles
off shore; p. 39 (n./adj.) scattered congregation of sailors, and
sailors' wives and widows; p. 42 (n.) He had been a sailor and a
harpooner in his youth; p. 42 (adj.) with a truly sailor-like but
still reverential dexterity; p. 46 (n.) all the sailors for the moment
desist; p. 46 (n.) when the sailors find him not to be the man; p. 48
(n.) The sailors mark him; p. 57 (n.) They put him down among the
sailors; p. 86 (adj.) among some of us old sailor chaps, he goes by
that name; p. 88 (n.) both commenting, after each other's fashion,
upon this ragged old sailor; p. 110 (n.) no white sailor seriously
contradicted him when he said; p. 185 (n.) each silent sailor seemed
resolved into his own invisible reef; p. 187 (n.) the sailors, goat-
like, leaped down the rolling ship's side; p. 202 (n.) as if manned
by painted sailors in wax; p. 227 (adj.) breakfasting on three or
four sailortarts; p. 257 (n.) every sailor a butcher; p. 351 (n.)
Look at the sailor, called the mincer; p. 352 (n.) some cynical old
sailors will crawl into them; p. 388 (n.) A sailor takes a fancy to
wear shark-bone ear-rings; p. 409 (n.) the Spanish land-breeze,
wantonly turned sailor, had gone to sea; p. 415 (n.) To sailors, oaths
are household words; p. 429 (n.) for sailors sometimes go aloft in a
transition state.

SALMON. The well-known fish, _Salmo salar_. It is partly oceanic and
partly fluviatile, ascending rivers in the breeding season. (Smyth)

Moby-_Dick_--p. 455 (adj.) as in his immeasurable bravadoes the white
whale tossed himself salmon-like to Heaven.

SALT. A weather-beaten sailor. One of the old seamen who not only have
known but have felt what war was. (Smyth)

Typee--p. 8 (n.) She singled out from their number an old salt; p. 22
(n.) twenty venerable Greenwich-pensioner-looking old salts.

Mardi--p. 46 (n.) an old salt is very much of an old maid.

White-_Jacket_--p. 309 (adj.) even marines jerk out more salt phrases.

Moby-_Dick_--p. 14 (n.) though I am something of a salt.

SAMPSON-POST. A movable pillar which rests on its upper shoulder against
a beam, with the lower tenons into the deck, and standing at an angle of
15° forward. To this post, at 4 feet above the deck, a leading or snatch-
block is hooked, and any fore-and-aft purchase is led by it across the
deck to one similar. The whole crew can then apply their force for
catting and fishing the anchor, or hoisting in or out of boats. (Smyth's
spelling is "Samson's Post.")

Redburn--p. 95 (n.) the top of the Sampson-Post; p. 96 (n.) Seated on
my Sampson-Post.

SAND-BAR. An accumulated shoal or bank of sand, shingle, gravel, or other uliginous substances, thrown up by the sea to the mouth of a river or harbor, so as to endanger, and sometimes totally prevent, the navigation into it. (Smyth, under "bar.")

Mardi--p. 546 (n.) Sand-bars! rise, and stay the tide.

SCALE. The small shell or crust which composes a part of the covering of a fish, consisting of alternate layers of membrane and phosphate of lime. (Webster)

Mardi--p. 41 (n.) and golden scales.

Moby-Dick--p. 406 (n.) And Stubb, fish-like, with sparkling scales, leaped up in that same golden light.

SCHOONER. Strictly, a small craft with two masts and no tops, but the name is also applied to fore-and-aft vessels of various classes. (Smyth)

Omoo--p. 25 (n.) fired at by trading schooners; p. 63 (n.) who arrive in small schooners; p. 75 (n.) in a schooner belonging to the mission; p. 95 (n.) a small schooner came out of the harbor; p. 95 (adj.) some confusion on the schooner's decks; p. 96 (n.) where he now owned the schooner we saw; p. 122 (n.) carried aboard a small trading schooner; p. 122 (n.) which preceded the sailing of the schooner; p. 140 (n.) A small Australian schooner, lying in the harbor; p. 231 (n.) to navigate the future schooner; p. 292 (n.) the schooner was hove over on her beam-ends.

Redburn--p. 36 (n.) I observed a swift little schooner; p. 37 (n.) they pulled him off to the schooner; p. 37 (n.) then the schooner made sail; p. 57 (n.) how he had been in a slaving schooner; p. 103 (n.) a dismantled, water-logged schooner; p. 103 (n.) find out something about the schooner; p. 103 (adj.) so much as learning the schooner's name; p. 126 (n.) to the little gull of a schooner; p. 300 (n.) ships, brigs, schooners, and sail boats.

White-Jacket--p. 202 (n.) call it a white-washed man-of-war schooner; p. 212 (n.) Of Perry's war-brigs, sloops, and schooners; p. 351 (n.) Mostly making . . . little ships and schooners.

Moby-Dick--p. 14 (n.) without taking care of ships, barques, brigs, schooners; p. 58 (n.) the little Nantucket packet schooner moored at the wharf; p. 59 (n.) we stood on board the schooner; p. 61 (n.) The schooner was run into the wind.

SCUD. The low misty cloud. It appears to fly faster than others because it is very near the earth's surface. When scud is abundant, showers may be expected. (Smyth) -- To scud is to drive before a gale. (Russell)

White-Jacket--p. 98 (v.) square the yards, and scud before it; p. 110 (n.) the Captain was for scudding; p. 110 (n.) Scudding makes you a slave to the blast; p. 110 (n.) Scudding exposes to the gale your stern.

Moby-Dick--p. 43 (n.) But high above the flying scud; p. 192 (n.)
like the confused scud from white rolling billows; p. 194 (n.) the
driving scud, rack, and mist, grew darker with the shadows of night;
p. 419 (n.) this brain-truck of mine now sails amid the cloud-scud;
p. 450 (n.) triumphantly to overleap its summit with their scud.

SCUPPER. A round aperture cut through the water ways and sides of a ship
at proper distances, and lined with metal, in order to carry the water
off the deck into the sea. (Smyth)

Omoo--p. 53 (n.) drag him into the lee-scupper.

Mardi--p. 65 (n.) in the wake of every scupper-hole.

Redburn--p. 54 (n.) sent it flying out of a scupper-hole; p. 70 (n.)
I ran to the lee-scuppers where it fell; p. 102 (adj.) the scupper
holes could hardly carry it; p. 102 (n.) hold it down hard in the
weather-scuppers; p. 112 (n.) a thorough washing in the lee-scuppers.

White-Jacket--p. 23 (n.) a slip of wet, torn paper in a scupper-hole;
p. 69 (n.) The scupper-holes having discharged the last rivulet;
p. 389 (n.) swab up the lee-scuppers.

Moby-Dick--p. 350 (n.) lying along lengthwise in the lee scuppers.

SCUTTLE. A small hole or port cut either in the deck or side of a ship,
generally for ventilation. Scuttle butt, a cask having a square piece
sawn out of its bilge and lashed to a convenient place to hold water for
present use. (Smyth) -- To scuttle is to sink a ship by boring holes in
her. (Russell)

Omoo--p. 8 (n.) a splash of water came down the open scuttle; p. 16
(n.) shouted Jermin down the forecastle scuttle; p. 17 (n.) looking
down the scuttle and storming; p. 18 (n.) dipped his head down the
scuttle; p. 20 (n.) showed itself above the forecastle scuttle; p. 21
(v.) she had been scuttled most ruthlessly; p. 39 (n.) slanting down
from the scuttle; p. 40 (n.) and flung them up the scuttle; p. 42 (n.)
a pulley dropped down the scuttle; p. 42 (n.) a whispered conference
over the scuttle; p. 42 (n.) rope leading out of sight up the scuttle;
p. 43 (n.) flew toward the scuttle; p. 69 (n.) to fasten down the
cabin scuttle; p. 81 (n.) Returning to the cabin-scuttle; p. 82 (n.)
stood fast by the scuttle; p. 82 (n.) drawing over the side of the
scuttle; p. 96 (n.) down the forecastle scuttle; p. 88 (n.) but
descended the scuttle; p. 92 (n.) till they came to the cabin scuttle;
p. 94 (n.) keeping the cabin scuttle secured; p. 97 (n.) a handspike
struck the scuttle.

Redburn--p. 49 (n.) the big bell hung right over the scuttle; p. 50
(n.) came rushing up the scuttle in his shirt; p. 51 (n.) came rushing
and shrieking up the scuttle; p. 60 (n.) step out under the scuttle;
p. 167 (n.) seated at the open little scuttle; p. 167 (n.) irruption
of cherry-cheeked young tars from the scuttle; p. 243 (n.) shouting
down the forecastle-scuttle; pp. 244-5 (n.) shouted down among us
from the scuttle.

White-Jacket--p. 60 (n.) the requisite supply of water from the
scuttle-butt; p. 282 (n.) in the immediate vicinity of the scuttle-
butt; p. 282 (n.) The scuttle-butt is a goodly, round, painted cask;
p. 282 (n.) within the scuttle-butt, itself; p. 283 (n.) The scuttle-
butt is the only fountain; p. 283 (n.) the scuttle-butt may be
denominated; p. 283 (n.) the reading of a "rill" from the scuttle-butt;
p. 295 (n.) but a cup of water at the scuttle-butt.

Moby-Dick--p. 92 (n.) we found the slide of the scuttle open; p. 112
(n.) for an old captain like me to be descending this narrow scuttle;
p. 112 (n.) the silent steersman would watch the cabin-scuttle;
p. 130 (n.) thrusting his pale loaf-of-bread face from the cabin-
scuttle; p. 130 (n.) and descends the scuttle; p. 170 (n.) to the
scuttle-butt near the taffrail; p. 370 (n.) though the savage salt
spray bursting down the forecastle scuttle; p. 438 (n.) they saw him
standing in the cabin-scuttle.

SEA. Strictly speaking, sea is the next large division of water after
ocean, but in its special sense signifies only any large portion of the
great mass of waters almost surrounded by land.--Sea-breeze, a wind from
the sea towards the land.--Seaman, a term seldom bestowed among seafaring
men upon their associates, unless they are known to be pre-eminent in
every duty of the thorough-paced tar; one who never issues a command
which he is not competent to execute himself, and is deemed an authority
on every matter relating to sea-craft. The able seaman is the seafaring
man who knows all the duties of common seamanship; the ordinary seaman
is less qualified.--Seaward, towards the sea, or offing.--Deep-sea-lead,
an instrument for discovering the depth of water. It is a tapered
cylinder of lead attached to a lead-line, which is marked at certain
distances to ascertain the fathoms.--Head-sea, a name given to the waves
when they oppose a ship's course, as the ship must rise over, or cut
through each.--Sea-mark, a point or object distinguishable at sea, as
promontories, steeples, rivers, trees, &c., forming important beacons,
and noted on charts.--Sea-attorney, the ordinary brown and rapacious
shark.--Sea-bear, a large seal found both in the northern and southern
hemispheres, which uses its hind limbs in walking on land.--Sea-lawyer,
an idle litigious long-shorer, more given to question orders than to obey
them. One of the pests of the navy as well as of the mercantile marine.--
Sea-legs, implies the power to walk steadily on a ship's decks,
notwithstanding her pitching and rolling.--Seamanship, the noble practical
art of rigging and working a ship, and performing with effect all her
various evolutions at sea.--Sea-nettle, an immemorial name of several
zoophytes and marine creatures which have the power of stinging.--Sea-pie,
a favorite sea-dish in rough weather, consisting of an olla of fish, meat,
and vegetables, in layers between crusts.--Sea-rovers, pirates and robbers
at sea.--Sea-urchin, an animal of the class Echinodermata, of globular
form, and a hard calcareous outer covering, beset with movable spines, on
the ends of which it crawls about. (Smyth)

Typee--p. xiii (n.) the weariness of many a night-watch at sea; p. 3
(n.) Six months at Sea; p. 3 (n.) the sky above, the sea around, and
nothing else; p. 3 (n.) nothing left us but salt-horse and sea-biscuit;
p. 3 (n.) the privations and hardships of the sea; p. 5 (n.) every
time she rises on a sea; p. 5 (n.) among the earliest of European
discoveries in the South Seas; p. 6 (n.) in the sketches of South-Sea

voyages; p. 6 (n.) entitled "A Visit to the South Seas"; p. 9 (n.)
like a veteran old sea-pacer as she was; p. 10 (n.) like a shower of
silver into the sea; p. 10 (n.) the prowling shark, that villanous
footpad of the seas; p. 10 (n.) the appearance of innumerable sea-fowl;
p. 11 (n.) under the enemy's flag in the surrounding seas; p. 12 (n.)
who for the first time visit the South Seas; p. 12 (n.) when beheld
from the sea; p. 12 (n.) sweeping down towards the sea; p. 12 (adj.)
a genuine South-Sea vagabond; p. 18 (n.) the beautiful, the queen of
the South Seas; p. 21 (n.) together with ample store of sea-bread;
p. 22 (adj.) in each new edition of the South-Sea Charts; p. 23 (n.)
you approach it from the sea; p. 24 (n.) demurely wanders along to
the sea; p. 24 (n.) hidden from the world in these remote seas; p. 24
(n.) two or three thousand feet above the level of the sea; p. 26 (n.)
on their march back to the sea; p. 26 (n.) The enormities perpetrated
in the South Seas; p. 27 (n.) to the bottom of the sea; p. 28 (n.) it
is accessible from the sea at one end; p. 28 (n.) across the open
ground in the vicinity of the sea; p. 32 (n.) rovers you sometimes
meet at sea; p. 33 (n.) spurs extended from them almost into the sea;
p. 35 (n.) as a lying old son of a sea-cook; p. 39 (n.) sweeping down
towards the sea from the heights; p. 40 (n.) we had never once turned
our faces to the sea; p. 40 (n.) three thousand feet above the level
of the sea; p. 42 (n.) covered with soft particles of sea-bread;
p. 42 (n.) just recovered from the bottom of the sea; p. 49 (n.)
Midway toward the sea; p. 50 (n.) extending a considerable distance
from the sea; p. 56 (n.) flow into the valley before they reach the
sea; p. 64 (n.) projected into the sea of verdure with which the
valley waved; p. 73 (adj.) especially on a South-Sea island; p. 74
(n.) The natives who live near the sea; p. 74 (n.) to escape to the
open sea; p. 74 (n.) used in the South Seas by Europeans; p. 84 (n.)
ear-ornaments, fabricated from the teeth of some sea-monster; p. 90
(n.) like the old man of the sea astride Sindbad; p. 102 (n.) no
avenue opened to our escape but the sea; p. 105 (n.) from the sea to
their remotest habitation; p. 106 (n.) along the path which led to
the sea; p. 113 (n.) would hie him away to the sea-shore; p. 113 (n.)
collecting various species of rare sea-weed; p. 114 (n.) probably in
the neighborhood of the sea; p. 119 (n.) lay between it and the sea;
p. 119 (n.) impatience I betrayed to reach the sea; p. 120 (n.)
pursuing the route that conducted to the sea; p. 123 (n.) Toward the
sea my progress was barred; p. 132 (n.) a light and tastefully-carved
canoe from the sea; p. 135 (adj.) expression only to be seen in the
South Sea Islander; p. 140 (n.) he had been carried to sea; p. 155
(n.) creation of the various groups in the South Seas; p. 155 (n.)
three thousand feet above the level of the sea; p. 165 (n.) generally
dispersed over the South Seas; p. 170 (n.) reputed the most ferocious
in the South Seas; p. 170 (adj.) from the retired old South-Sea
rovers; p. 172 (n.) a number of sparkling sea-shells; p. 177 (n.) to
the bottom of the sea with it; p. 177 (adj.) in his intercourse with
the South Sea islanders; p. 181 (n.) as it ever does among the South
Sea islanders; p. 184 (n.) the most splendid islanders in the South
Seas; p. 184 (n.) in his "Scenes in the South Seas," expresses;
p. 186 (n.) towards the sea a number of distinguished chiefs resided;
p. 189 (adj.) remorseless inflictions of South Sea civilization;
p. 193 (n.) to any considerable distance towards the sea; p. 195 (n.)
Heaven help the Isles of the Sea; p. 198 (n.) apostolic functions
upon the remote islands of the sea; p. 201 (adj.) which the reader of
South Sea voyages is too apt; p. 206 (n.) they went out towards the

open sea; p. 206 (adj.) All the South Sea Islanders are passionately
fond of fish; p. 212 (n.) upon some of the natives of the South Seas;
p. 229 (adj.) No wonder that the South Sea Islanders; p. 229 (n.) if
they had been in the sea; p. 245 (n.) to be carried at once to the
sea; p. 246 (n.) that I was going down to the sea to meet Toby;
p. 246 (n.) prohibited from approaching the sea; p. 246 (n.) must
have effected his flight by the sea; p. 247 (n.) I proceeded in the
direction of the sea; p. 248 (n.) to continue my progress towards the
sea; p. 249 (n.) the open space which lay between the groves and the
sea; p. 250 (n.) bent upon driving him into the sea; p. 250 (n.)
actually forced him into the sea; p. 251 (n.) some six or seven other
warriors rushed into the sea; p. 251 (n.) it was one of those chopping
angry seas; p. 252 (n.) fatal to many a boat's crew in these seas;
p. 252 (n.) being in distress for men in these remote seas; p. 256
(n.) which on one side directly overhangs the sea; p. 260 (n.) The
author was more than two years in the South Seas; p. 263 (n.) thinking
all the while that they never would get to the sea; p. 263 (n.) was
then permitted to go down to the sea; p. 265 (n.) when they came in
from the sea; p. 266 (n.) they have promised to carry him down to the
sea; p. 266 (n.) neither of you will ever look upon the sea again;
p. 268 (n.) owing to its being near to the sea; p. 270 (n.) where the
highlands slope off into the sea; p. 271 (n.) he was going to sea.

Omoo--p. xiii (n.) than in the South Seas; p. xiii (n.) to attract
the most reckless seamen of all nations; p. xiv (n.) during his
wanderings in the South Seas; p. xiv (adj.) from the oldest books of
South Sea voyages; p. 3 (n.) in an American South Seaman; p. 3 (n.)
The boat having gained the open sea; p. 5 (adj.) changes the rich
berry-brown of a seaman's complexion; p. 6 (n.) than a bluff sea-
captain; p. 6 (n.) on board whalemen in the South Seas; p. 7 (n.)
wild noise and motion of a ship at sea; p. 8 (n.) the cool, fresh air
of a morning at sea; p. 9 (n.) she had been captured at sea; p. 9 (n.)
as a government packet in the Australian seas; p. 9 (n.) and pawed
the sea; p. 10 (n.) More than half the seamen remaining; p. 10 (n.)
no more meant for the sea than a hair-dresser; p. 11 (n.) So far as
courage, seamanship, and a natural aptitude; p. 14 (n.) we had what
English seamen call "shot soup"; p. 14 (n.) willing to keep the sea
with his ship; p. 14 (n.) the most unruly seamen can at sea be kept;
p. 14 (adj.) that many South Sea whalemen do not come; p. 15 (n.)
nothing for the ship but to keep the sea; p. 15 (n.) for the purpose
of obtaining eight seamen; p. 22 (n.) the capture of a party of
desperate seamen; p. 22 (n.) four of the seamen were pitched upon;
p. 24 (n.) which swept down within a few paces of the sea; p. 25 (adj.)
(adj.) not unusual on the part of sea captains; p. 27 (adj.) a white
man, in the South Sea girdle; p. 28 (n.) launched upon the sea; p. 28
(n.) should be given ten whole sea-biscuits; p. 28 (adj.) breezing
strongly from seaward; p. 29 (adj.) Wymontoo, sad to tell . . . was
terribly sea-sick; p. 33 (n.) and the long sea-day began; p. 34 (n.)
We were now fairly at sea; p. 34 (n.) began to settle down into the
routine of sea-life; p. 34 (n.) Blown along over a smooth sea; p. 35
(n.) peculiar to these seas; p. 35 (n.) known among seamen as the
boatswain; p. 35 (n.) the sea was alive with large whales; p. 38 (n.)
A Sea-Parlor Described; p. 39 (n.) can scarcely befall a vessel in
the South Seas; p. 42 (n.) pirates gibbeted at sea by a cruiser;
p. 42 (n.) for a good comfortable smoke at sea; p. 44 (n.) We had
been at sea about twenty days; p. 45 (n.) and fell with a splash into

the sea; p. 45 (n.) the proverbial indiscretions of seamen; p. 46 (n.)
those marvelous tales of the sea; p. 46 (n.) among ignorant seamen,
Finlanders . . . are regarded with peculiar superstition; p. 46 (n.)
we had one of these sea-prophets aboard; p. 47 (n.) Our keeping the
sea under these circumstances; p. 47 (adj.) the unworthiness of Little
Jule, as a sea vessel; p. 47 (n.) flung away the splinters with some
sea joke; p. 47 (n.) sickness at sea is so heartily detested; p. 48
(n.) inveighed a ainst their being kept at sea; p. 48 (n.) The lively
affection seamen have for strong drink; p. 48 (n.) in the South Seas,
where it is so seldom; p. 48 (n.) the oldest seaman in each claims
the treat; p. 48 (adj.) in sea parlance, Chips and Bungs; p. 52 (n.)
a good seaman, going among the crew; p. 53 (n.) a precept inviolable
at sea; p. 53 (n.) for the land-lubber at sea; p. 54 (n.) aboard the
Julia, South Seaman; p. 54 (n.) the most crabbed and choleric old
seamen; p. 54 (n.) here growled an old sea-bear; p. 58 (n.) In these
generally tranquil seas; p. 58 (n.) floored in the trough of a sea;
p. 58 (n.) Jermin, sea-jockey that he was; p. 59 (n.) went hissing
into the sea; p. 59 (n.) Like most South Seamen, the Julia's caboose;
p. 59 (n.) with the heavy sea running; p. 59 (n.) huge pair of well
anointed sea-boots; p. 59 (n.) if a chance sea washed him off his
feet; p. 59 (n.) fairly dished a tremendous sea; p. 60 (n.) the sea
with it; p. 62 (n.) in what part of the South Seas; p. 62 (n.)
connected by a single opening with the sea; p. 62 (n.) at the bottom
of the sea; p. 63 (n.) enough to load one of the large sea-canoes;
p. 63 (n.) in different parts of the South Seas; p. 63 (n.) by the
action of the sea; p. 65 (n.) famous island in the South Seas; p. 65
(n.) land radiates on all sides of the sea; p. 66 (n.) Seen from the
sea; p. 66 (adj.) of all readers of South Sea voyages; p. 68 (n.)
Tahiti from the sea; p. 69 (n.) her jib-boom pointing out to sea;
p. 69 (n.) to keep the ship at sea; p. 70 (n.) so far as mere
seamanship was concerned; p. 70 (n.) In truth, a better seaman never
swore; p. 71 (adj.) according to sea usages; p. 71 (n.) At sea, the
best English they speak; p. 71 (adj.) is the South Seaman's slogan;
p. 72 (n.) The taunts of the seamen may have maddened; p. 74 (n.)
this here craft goes to sea with us; p. 76 (n.) ship's head soon
pointed out to sea; p. 76 (n.) besides being an able seaman; p. 78
(n.) he looked like a land crane blown off to sea; p. 78 (n.) his
outfit of sea-clothing had long since been confiscated; p. 79 (n.)
two mariners at the bottom of the sea; p. 80 (n.) we can't say
anything against Mr. Jermin's seamanship; p. 80 (n.) a wellknown
sea-port; p. 82 (n.) you will go to sea; p. 82 (n.) go to sea in her
they would not; p. 82 (n.) attention of the exasperated seamen; p. 86
(n.) to take the Julia to sea; p. 88 (n.) but the seamen interposing;
p. 88 (n.) a steady seaman be it remembered; p. 91 (n.) give him a
sea-toss; p. 92 (n.) by the salt seas; p. 92 (n.) addressing the
seamen; p. 95 (n.) a South Seaman; p. 95 (n.) After being at sea
about a week; p. 95 (n.) a considerable sea running at the time;
p. 96 (n.) he had continued to follow the seas; p. 98 (adv.) it is
protected seaward by the coral reef; p. 98 (n.) by seamen generally;
p. 99 (n.) the cleverest specimen of his seamanship; p. 101 (n.) a
green lawn slopes off to the sea; p. 102 (n.) Having sprung a leak at
sea; p. 102 (adj.) Found utterly unseaworthy, however; p. 109 (n.)
makes but an indifferent seaman; p. 109 (n.) How few sea-battles have
the French ever won; p. 110 (n.) To make a man a seaman; p. 110 (n.)
against the rim of a hard sea-biscuit; p. 110 (n.) at sea, they were
forever at quarters; p. 110 (n.) and so sent to sea; p. 111 (n.) gave

to the waves of the sea; p. 114 (n.) fertile lands bordering the sea;
p. 115 (n.) the bright blue sea on one side; p. 116 (n.) trickled
into the sea; p. 119 (adj.) In sea parlance, came into view; p. 128
(adj.) This speaks little for the humanity of sea captains; p. 128
(n.) he is better off on the island than at sea; p. 128 (n.) heard of
this melancholy object, from two seamen; p. 134 (adj.) a sea phrase,
for departing this life; p. 134 (n.) directing attention to a sail
at sea; p. 139 (n.) was that of the seamen remaining aboard; p. 140
(n.) satisfaction of every seaman present; p. 146 (n.) she had been
all over the South Seas; p. 147 (n.) all discharged seamen being
forced; p. 148 (n.) he was carried to sea in irons; p. 151 (n.) that
a seaman could think of; p. 152 (n.) their inferiors accosted the
seamen; p. 153 (adj.) with a sea stock of fruits; p. 157 (n.) All
over these seas; p. 160 (n.) of any in the South Seas; p. 167 (n.)
sitting there, enjoying the sea-breeze; p. 167 (n.) a delightful air
from the sea, ladies; p. 169 (adj.) connected with this South Sea
cathedral; p. 171 (n.) with South Sea islanders; p. 174 (n.) than the
people of the South Sea; p. 185 (n.) places of resort in the South
Seas; p. 186 (n.) Principal Islands of the South Sea; p. 187 (n.) of
the missionary settlements in the South Seas; p. 190 (adj.)
civilization among the South Sea Islands; p. 200 (n.) They had been
sea-faring men; p. 201 (n.) of considerable width at the sea; p. 201
(n.) whose roots were washed by the sea; p. 202 (n.) On the side of
the inclosure, next the sea; p. 202 (n.) consisted of a couple of
sea-chests; p. 210 (n.) apparently pouring over into the sea; p. 210
(n.) seventeen thousand feet above the level of the sea; p. 212 (n.)
the sea lay blue and serene; p. 231 (adj.) This South Sea yachting
was delightful; p. 234 (adj.) with deeper dye than in any of the
seaward valleys; p. 246 (n.) being apprehended as runaway seamen;
p. 246 (n.) the best in the South Seas, perhaps; p. 246 (n.) facilities
presented for going to sea; p. 247 (n.) the first seaman that settles
down; p. 249 (n.) nor yet run away seamen; p. 252 (n.) he went
splashing into the sea; p. 253 (n.) the dense thicket almost dipped
into the sea; p. 255 (n.) on a natural terrace overlooking the sea;
p. 257 (n.) a rustic nut-bowl, half-filled with sea-water; p. 258 (n.)
steeped a morsel of food into his nutful of sea-water; p. 258 (n.)
invariably use sea-water in this way; p. 261 (adv.) protected seaward
by a grove . . . of trees; p. 261 (n.) Alluvial flats bordering the
sea; p. 263 (n.) it is perhaps found right on the sea-shore; p. 263
(n.) where the swell of the sea is prevented; p. 263 (adv.) its tall
stem inclines seaward; p. 264 (n.) the sea-breeze comes in; p. 266
(n.) I, for the most part, kept near the sea; p. 267 (n.) to swing
over sea and land; p. 269 (n.) diversifying the monotony of a sea
voyage; p. 270 (n.) which in many places border the sea; p. 270 (n.)
salts held in solution by the sea; p. 286 (n.) found in the immediate
vicinity of the sea; p. 289 (n.) the most beautiful in the South Seas;
p. 289 (n.) flowing through mountain passes to the sea; p. 289 (n.)
and beyond, the sea; p. 289 (n.) will carry yees both to sea; p. 290
(n.) My sheath-knife never cut into better sea-beef; p. 291 (n.) they
never could think of going to sea; p. 297 (n.) handsomest chapels in
the South Seas; p. 312 (n.) we determined upon going to sea; p. 312
(n.) doubtless the effect of his sea-potations; p. 312 (n.) a Prussian,
and an old merchant seaman; p. 313 (n.) and, at sea, nothing to do
but sit; p. 313 (adj.) that American sea captains, in the Pacific;
p. 313 (n.) on board a ship in the South Seas; p. 314 (n.) He then
insisted upon my going to sea; p. 315 (n.) The impulse urging me to
sea once more.

Mardi--p. 3 (n.) out to sea; p. 3 (n.) we shadow the sea; p. 3 (n.)
isle of the sea; p. 3 (n.) as flies the sea-gull; p. 4 (n.) a dark
object arose out of the sea; p. 4 (n.) down to the sea; p. 5 (n.)
sea-moss is over it; p. 5 (adj.) that old sea hearth-stone; p. 6 (n.)
rafting the sea; p. 6 (n.) in southern and more genial seas; p. 6 (n.)
of the sea-captain; p. 7 (n.) among seamen; p. 7 (adj.) the order of
South Sea Rovers; p. 7 (n.) mild, warm seas before; p. 7 (n.) of
these seas; p. 9 (n.) phenomenon of the sea; p. 9 (n.) the sea was at
least margined; p. 11 (n.) around us one wide sea; p. 11 (n.) over a
pleasant sea; p. 12 (n.) a fine old seaman; p. 12 (n.) over the salt
German sea; p. 12 (n.) origin in the sea-life; p. 13 (n.) with seamen
of all tribes; p. 14 (n.) which overtakes most seamen; p. 14 (n.) at
sea; p. 14 (n.) in sea-parlance; p. 16 (n.) so earnest and upright a
seaman; p. 16 (n.) over the sea; p. 16 (n.) any sea-gull passing by;
p. 19 (n.) at sea; p. 19 (n.) boats of a South Sea-man; p. 22 (n.)
being a stalwart seaman; p. 23 (n.) one of these seamen; p. 23 (n.)
in these seas; p. 23 (n.) what are called at sea; p. 23 (adj.) moonless
sea midnight; p. 23 (n.) An old sea-dog; p. 24 (adj.) to what seagull's
scream; p. 24 (n.) of that summer sea; p. 25 (n.) at the bottom of
the sea; p. 28 (adj.) boat bounded on the sea's back; p. 28 (n.)
several seamen were shouting; p. 29 (n.) at sea; p. 33 (n.) a mere
breath rippled the sea; p. 37 (n.) to the very plane of the sea;
p. 37 (n.) in a high, slow-rolling sea; p. 37 (n.) a sea-chamois;
p. 38 (n.) nothing in sight but the self-same sea; p. 38 (n.) upon
what shoreless sea; p. 38 (n.) naught but an endless sea; p. 39 (n.)
infesting the South Seas; p. 39 (n.) the sea-serpent is not a fable;
p. 39 (n.) and in the sea; p. 39 (n.) down in the sea; p. 40 (n.) to
seamen; p. 40 (n.) have been sunk by sea monsters; p. 40 (n.) there
are more sharks in the sea; p. 40 (n.) Brown Shark, or sea-attorney;
p. 40 (n.) ships in the South Seas; p. 41 (n.) Nimrod of the seas;
p. 42 (n.) on the high seas; p. 42 (n.) thrown the blue rolling sea;
p. 42 (n.) the sights of the great South Sea; p. 44 (n.) more or less
sea-water; p. 44 (n.) this sea-water tasted less brackish; p. 44 (n.)
then that of the sea; p. 44 (n.) rinsed out in the sea; p. 44 (n.) A
sea-toss; p. 45 (n.) seamen in the tropics; p. 45 (n.) dip it in the
sea; p. 48 (n.) as in the sea; p. 49 (n.) instantly the sea burst in;
p. 49 (n.) a sea-gale operates; p. 50 (n.) just rippling the sea;
p. 50 (n.) low humming of the sea; p. 50 (n.) noise of wings as sea
fowls flew by; p. 52 (n.) once again my sea tailor plied needle;
p. 53 (n.) There is a fish in the sea; p. 54 (n.) to trail in the sea;
p. 56 (n.) in bright weather at sea; p. 57 (n.) a far off object at
sea; p. 58 (n.) sort of vessel at sea; p. 59 (n.) among the Islanders
of these seas; p. 60 (n.) though aboard on the sea; p. 60 (n.) old
vessels at sea; p. 64 (adj.) this sea cake-basket; p. 65 (n.) from
sea to sea; p. 66 (n.) instinct of an old seaman; p. 68 (n.) sea-slugs,
and other matters; p. 68 (n.) had long followed the sea; p. 69 (n.)
of matrimony at sea; p. 69 (n.) an outlet to the sea; p. 70 (adv.)
cast the Parki's head seaward; p. 71 (n.) right out to sea; p. 71
(adv.) craft drew seaward; p. 71 (n.) fleeing from sea-hawks; p. 72
(n.) fell into the sea; p. 72 (n.) in the trough of the sea; p. 72
(n.) every swell of the sea; p. 74 (n.) gaining the shoreless sea;
p. 74 (n.) committed to the sea; p. 78 (n.) to burying in the sea;
p. 78 (n.) nor fishes of the sea; p. 78 (n.) what was Anglesea; p. 80
(n.) in sight but the sea; p. 81 (n.) loud roaring of the sea; p. 81
(n.) Samoa's seamanship; p. 81 (n.) resolved to keep open sea; p. 82
(n.) in these seas; p. 83 (n.) The calmer the sea; p. 85 (n.) to and

fro in the sea; p. 85 (n.) they espied our little sea-goat; p. 86 (n.)
upon the open sea; p. 90 (n.) in these seas; p. 91 (n.) to keep the
sea; p. 91 (adj.) fight great sea engagements; p. 92 (n.) proper
position of wives at sea; p. 94 (n.) of a friendless sailor at sea;
p. 95 (n.) brought up from the sea; p. 96 (n.) so long as we kept the
sea; p. 97 (n.) command of a vessel at sea; p. 97 (n.) wild and remote
seas where we were; p. 99 (n.) name had been given him by a sea-
captain; p. 100 (n.) drowsy stillness of the tropical sea-day; p. 101
(n.) keeping Argus eyes on the sea; p. 101 (n.) I gazed broad off
upon the blue boundless sea; p. 103 (n.) fish, pleasantly enlivening
the sea; p. 103 (n.) immortal heroes that swim the seas; p. 104 (n.)
but by seamen in the Pacific; p. 105 (n.) ship I met with at sea;
p. 106 (n.) From the sea monarchs, his ancestors; p. 108 (n.) in one's
latitude at sea; p. 109 (n.) sailing through the sparkling sea;
p. 109 (n.) when by night the seamen were permitted; p. 111 (n.) we
were in reality almost a fixture on the sea; p. 111 (n.) equatorial
currents of the South Seas; p. 111 (n.) commingling and purification
of the sea-water; p. 111 (n.) It is well known to seamen; p. 111 (n.)
that a bucket of sea-water; p. 112 (n.) offensiveness of sea-water
left standing; p. 116 (n.) The sun played upon the glassy sea; p. 117
(n.) fell upon the glassy sea before it; p. 117 (n.) dipped their
trucks in the sea; p. 117 (n.) loud above the roar of the sea; p. 118
(n.) sea boiled like ten thousand caldrons; p. 118 (n.) But the sea
ran high; p. 118 (n.) a moderate sea, a steady breeze; p. 119 (n.) So
soon as the sea permitted; p. 120 (n.) To a seaman, a ship is no
piece; p. 120 (n.) hull rolled convulsively in the sea; p. 121 (n.)
floated on the sea; p. 121 (n.) only to be met with in the South Seas;
p. 121 (n.) the sea all around us spouted in fountains of fire;
p. 122 (n.) more radiant than any portion of the sea; p. 122 (n.)
leaving the sea still more sparkling; p. 122 (n.) The sea retained
its luminosity; p. 123 (n.) unattended with any pallidness of the sea;
p. 123 (n.) beheld the sea white as a shroud; p. 123 (n.) the
phosphorescence of the sea is caused by; p. 123 (n.) contradicted by
many intelligent seamen; p. 123 (n.) with which the sea is well known
to abound; p. 123 (n.) this seeming ignition of the sea; p. 124 (n.)
for the poor little fire-fish of the sea; p. 125 (n.) sailing smoothly
over a sea; p. 125 (adj.) ranks as a sea boat; p. 125 (n.) storms
happening so seldom in these seas; p. 126 (n.) The smaller sort
skimmed the sea; p. 126 (n.) the daring Diver, or sea-kite; p. 126
(n.) the sea-kite, bill foremost; p. 126 (n.) flying downward to the
sea; p. 127 (n.) he looked like a sea-god; p. 133 (n.) fell over like
a brown hemlock into the sea; p. 134 (n.) All the while rose and fell
on the sea; p. 137 (n.) borne by a soft wind to the sea; p. 138 (n.)
gurgled up in the sea an enchanted spring; p. 140 (adj.) in place of
the sea moss; p. 140 (n.) drowned in the sea; p. 140 (n.) that had
come over the sea; p. 141 (n.) our prisoners taking to the sea;
p. 141 (n.) before being picked up from the sea; p. 141 (n.) a great
swell of the sea surged up; p. 141 (n.) none but ourselves on the sea;
p. 142 (n.) from your isle in the sea; p. 143 (n.) into the grotto on
the sea-shore; p. 143 (n.) from sea to sea; p. 144 (adj.) with many
subtle and seamanlike splices; p. 145 (n.) no danger in the balmy sea;
p. 145 (n.) strange Yillah gazed down in the sea; p. 148 (n.) for
every fin in the sea; p. 148 (n.) let the sea-fowls fly on; p. 148
(n.) Locusts of the sea; p. 149 (n.) the whole sea to glow like a
burnished shield; p. 149 (n.) It is tangled sea-kelp; p. 150 (n.)
scour the seas with a wish; p. 150 (n.) As through the seas we go;

p. 154 (adj./n.) like sea groves and mosses beneath the calm sea;
p. 155 (n.) to where the sea rolled in the sun; p. 156 (n.) like a
sea-fowl, went softly to sleep; p. 157 (n.) the maiden was borne to
the sea-side; p. 159 (n.) gazed long and fixedly into the sea; p. 159
(n.) as she sunk in the sea; p. 160 (n.) and looking upon the distant
sea; p. 160 (n.) some new constellation in the sea; p. 161 (n.)
quitting the firmament blue of the open sea; p. 161 (n.) leagues down
in the fathomless sea; p. 162 (n.) up to their waists in the sea;
p. 164 (n.) Of a sudden, from the sea-side; p. 166 (n.) to fish in
the sea; p. 166 (n.) to fish in the sea; p. 167 (n.) borne therein
toward the sea; p. 167 (n.) from the grove to the sea; p. 172 (n.) At
sea, Jarl had been the oracle; p. 172 (n.) an old sea-sage, learned;
p. 181 (n.) and short sea-grass; p. 182 (n.) brought up from the sea;
p. 183 (n.) on an isle in the sea; p. 188 (n.) an arbor in the sea;
p. 192 (n.) and hit it in the sea; p. 192 (n.) made a cemetary of the
sea; p. 194 (n.) groves and gardens in the sea; p. 194 (n.) tearful
pearls beneath life's sea; p. 199 (adj.) like the sea serpent's train;
p. 200 (n.) whence his sea-equipage came; p. 209 (n.) as some sea-
hunters unexpectedly have; p. 211 (n.) sink it, downward, into the
sea; p. 211 (n.) they waded through the sea; p. 213 (n.) From seaward
now came a breeze; p. 214 (n.) The wild sea song; p. 216 (n.) an
extraordinary rolling of the sea; p. 217 (n.) when informed that the
sea-cavern; p. 226 (n.) were as floating isles in the sea; p. 230 (n.)
which, in its seas; p. 230 (n.) as an isle in the sea; p. 232 (n.) or
a grotto in the sea; p. 235 (n.) at the season of high sea; p. 240
(adj.) sea-girt, reef-sashed, mountain-locked; p. 245 (n.) all view
of the sea; p. 246 (n.) journeying to the sea-side; p. 256 (n.)
dispatched over sea to another; p. 256 (n.) ruffling the sociable sea;
p. 266 (n.) as in warm Indian seas; p. 271 (n.) and deepened the old
sea; p. 272 (n.) midway cloven down to the sea; p. 272 (n.) bathing
in the surf of the sea; p. 272 (n.) plains sloping outward to the sea;
p. 273 (adv.) billows from seaward roll in upon; p. 273 (n.) whose
base was as the sea-beach; p. 273 (n.) make straight for the outer
sea; p. 274 (n.) from cliff to sea; p. 278 (n.) From the sea to the
shrine of this god; p. 278 (n.) Had you a deep-sea-lead; p. 282 (n.)
dive down into the sea; p. 282 (n.) worrying the sea-nettle; p. 282
(n.) a mad merry night of it with the sea-urchins; p. 283 (n.)
passionately fond of the sea; p. 285 (adj.) to the side of the Sea
Elephant; p. 288 (n.) and the young fish taken from the sea; p. 288
(n.) all floundering from the sea; p. 288 (adj.) finny flock on the
sea shore; p. 294 (n.) his corps of sea-divers; p. 298 (n.) during
his endless sea-rovings; p. 300 (n.) to their sepulcher, the sea;
p. 300 (n.) no canoes put to sea; p. 303 (n.) we drop our dead in the
sea; p. 303 (n.) The bottomless, bottomless sea; p. 303 (n.) The sea
ne'er gives it a thought; p. 303 (n.) Far down in the bottomless sea;
p. 303 (n.) Down, down in the bottomless sea; p. 303 (n.) Deeper down
in the bottomless sea; p. 305 (adj.) beached on its seaward shore;
p. 306 (n.) were plunged into the sea; p. 308 (n.) suffering at sea
must have maddened; p. 314 (n.) Far off in the sea is Marlena; p. 324
(n.) like the sea after a storm; p. 328 (n.) there came up from the
sea-side; p. 334 (n.) bathing with them in the sea; p. 340 (n.) gods
of sea and of land; p. 343 (n.) leaving a narrow channel to the sea;
p. 346 (n.) long-rolling chant, a sea of sounds; p. 366 (n.) a China
wall, built up from the sea; p. 367 (n.) Throned on my sea-side;
p. 373 (n.) the Froth-of-the-Sea they call it, I think; p. 373 (n.)
so-called Farnoo, or Froth-of-the-Sea; p. 373 (n.) in seasons of high

sea; p. 373 (n.) not a word more of the Froth-of-the-Sea; p. 373 (n.)
smugglers' caves, nigh the sea; p. 374 (n.) waxy, then firm, by the
action of the sea; p. 374 (n.) fins, porpoise-teeth, sea-gulls' beaks;
p. 374 (n.) is found both on land and at sea; p. 375 (n.) growing at
the bottom of the sea; p. 379 (n.) Unja came from the bottom of the
sea; p. 380 (n.) the curling silky fibres of the finer sea-weed;
p. 381 (n.) a scale from a sea-kraken its lens; p. 382 (n.) by a
quill from the sea-noddy; p. 394 (n.) Diving deep in the sea; p. 394
(n.) Down flames in the sea; p. 402 (n.) three menials running from
seaward; p. 404 (n.) those from the sea-side had been running; p. 416
(n.) ripplings of some now waveless sea; p. 417 (n.) and barons of
sea-beeves and walrusses; p. 431 (n.) the sea-storm only blows harder;
p. 436 (n.) Tempered by fierce sea-winds; p. 437 (n.) Hurled up on
the beach by the stormy sea; p. 438 (n.) we ride the sea, we ride the
sky; p. 453 (n.) The vaunt of her isles sleeps deep in the sea;
p. 453 (n.) The vaunt of her isles sleeps deep in the sea; p. 456 (n.)
to albatrosses floating on the sea; p. 461 (adj.) forget not that
calabash with the sea-blue seal; p. 466 (n.) warriors to assemble by
land and by sea; p. 467 (n.) a fearless sailor of his frigid seas;
p. 469 (n.) they sallied out to sea; p. 476 (adj.) a helmet of the
sea-porcupine's hide; p. 476 (n.) Tatooed in sea-blue were all the
groups and clusters; p. 476 (n.) all his victories by sea and land;
p. 479 (n.) ere those waters gained the sea; p. 481 (n.) wherein to
sail over the sea; p. 482 (n.) tough Torf-Egill, the Danish Sea-king;
p. 482 (n.) He called it . . . the Sea-hawk; p. 482 (n.) he burnt
incense to the sea-gods; p. 482 (n.) long state canoes; sea-snakes,
all; p. 482 (n.) dipping their paddles in the sea; p. 482 (n.) the
old sea-king of Mardi; p. 482 (n.) all manner of sea-cavalry; p. 482
(n.) when, in a stout sea-fight; p. 482 (n.) Take this . . . and with
it, the sea for thy bride; p. 482 (n.) if the sea was King Bello's
bride; p. 483 (n.) Now, old sea-king; p. 499 (n.) leaping with them
into the seething sea; p. 502 (n.) Soft-rocked by the sea; p. 502 (n.)
In that fresh-born sea; p. 543 (n.) storm-clouds swept the wintry sea;
p. 543 (n.) Ice-splinters . . . seethed into the sea; p. 544 (n.)
another aspect were the sea; p. 544 (n.) met the whirlpool-column
from the sea; p. 546 (n.) with phosphorescence seas are burning;
p. 547 (n.) gold gloves, set in a quicksilver sea; p. 557 (n.) in
sparkling scales that float along the sea; p. 553 (n.) Here, the sea
rolled high; p. 553 (n.) the seas ran mustering to the call; p. 553
(n.) the sea went down; p. 554 (n.) and anchored in the sea; p. 554
(n.) Over that tideless sea we sailed; p. 555 (n.) like old tide-rips
of diluvian seas; p. 555 (n.) from that inland sea emerged; p. 556
(n.) steered his bark through seas; p. 557 (n.) when now our seas
have oft been circled; p. 560 (n.) Fast fly the sea-ripples,/ Revealing
their dimples; p. 560 (n.) when forth, thou hie'st to the frolicsome
sea; p. 567 (n.) we sailed from sea to sea; p. 586 (n.) As in Sooloo's
seas, one vast water-spout; p. 586 (n.) Let us dive down in the sea;
p. 587 (n.) We die by land, and die by sea; p. 593 (n.) his great
mane tossed like the sea; p. 617 (n.) We sailed upon an angry sea;
p. 618 (n.) Ho! over sea-dingle, and dale; p. 618 (n.) deep Night
dived deeper down in the sea; p. 619 (n.) we are dropped in the sea;
p. 632 (n.) as in violent, tropic seas; p. 633 (n.) voyagers pass far
sails at sea; p. 636 (n.) as, when, in sunny, summer seas; p. 636
(adj.) rising from vast depths to the sea's surface; p. 638 (n.)
beyond the reef, through sunless seas; p. 639 (n.) Then sweet Yillah
called me from the sea; p. 644 (n.) looks flowery Flozella, approached

from the sea; p. 644 (n.) the sea, like a harvest plain; p. 647 (n.)
She [Hautia] is deeper than the sea; p. 650 (n.) A bow-shot from the
sea; p. 652 (n.) hast mosses? sea-thyme? pearls; p. 653 (adv.)
channels, seaward tending; p. 653 (n.) we had parted on the sea;
p. 653 (n.) above the smoke of some sea-fight; p. 654 (n.) over an
endless sea.

Redburn--p. 3 (n.) How Wellingborough Redburn's Taste for the Sea Was
Born and Bred in Him; p. 3 (n.) as you are going to sea; p. 3 (n.)
Upon the eve of my departure for the seaport; p. 3 (n.) to send me to
sea as a sailor; p. 4 (adj.) summoned upon the idea of a black, sea-
worn craft; p. 4 (n.) with sunburnt sea-captains going in and out;
p. 4 (n.) a residence in a seaport during early childhood; p. 5 (adj.)
by the well-remembered sea-coal fire in old Greenwich-street; p. 5
(n.) of the monstrous waves at sea; p. 5 (n.) most of my thoughts of
the sea were connected with the land; p. 6 (n.) Two of these
[paintings] were sea-pieces; p. 6 (n.) were sailing through a bright-
blue sea; p. 7 (n.) of seeking my fortune on the sea; p. 8 (n.) of a
real vessel that could go to sea; p. 9 (n.) among a crowd of glass
dolphins and sea-horses; p. 9 (n.) undisputed mistress of a green
glassy sea; p. 9 (n.) so as to cover all the sea; p. 9 (n.) into the
trough of a calamitous sea; p. 9 (n.) the very day I left home to go
to sea; p. 10 (n.) Yes, I will go to sea; p. 15 (n.) whether you want
a fine young lad to go to sea with you; p. 16 (n.) don't want to go
to sea too; p. 16 (n.) you can't get any milk at sea, you know; p. 16
(n.) and he's only going to sea for the humor of it; p. 16 (n.) but
he will go to sea as a sailor; p. 17 (n.) to shoot gulls with at sea;
p. 18 (adj./n.) that will make you very sea-sick when you get to sea;
p. 19 (n.) chap ain't going to sea in a merchantman; p. 19 (n.)
sweetmeats for ye to take to sea; p. 23 (n.) He purchases His Sea-
Wardrobe; p. 24 (n.) would be no getting to sea that day; p. 27 (n.)
no time for snuff-taking at sea; p. 28 (adj.) to save a few dollars
in seamen's wages; p. 28 (n.) Was this then the beginning of my sea-
career; p. 29 (n.) my first lesson in the discipline of the sea;
p. 29 (n.) I learned that sea-officers never gave reasons; p. 29 (n.)
in getting ships ready for sea; p. 32 (n.) He Gets to Sea, and Feels
Very Bad; p. 33 (n.) of lying down at the bottom of the sea; p. 34
(n.) the entrance to New York Harbor from sea; p. 34 (n.) away over
that wide blank of sea; p. 35 (n.) an uncle of mine, an old sea-
captain; p. 35 (n.) from the sea of Okotsk in Asia; p. 35 (n.) he was
the very first sea-captain; p. 35 (n.) he was lost in the White Sea
some years after; p. 35 (n.) and looking to sea; p. 36 (n.) with no
thought of going to sea; p. 36 (n.) standing on the parapet, gazing
off to sea; p. 38 (adj.) He Is Put into the Larboard Watch, Gets Sea-
Sick; p. 39 (n.) at sea all officers are Misters; p. 39 (n.) if only
seamen presumed to omit; p. 40 (n.) of that dreadful thing, the sea-
sickness; p. 42 (adj.) I was telling about my being sea-sick; p. 42
(n.) to drink spirits in case of sea-sickness; p. 42 (n.) if they
come to go to sea; p. 42 (n.) which they brought along to sea with
them; p. 43 (n.) as if some old horse, or sea-beef; p. 43 (adj.) that
now when I was sea-sick; p. 45 (n.) with most seamen the first night;
p. 45 (n.) many of these sea-officers are as wild; p. 46 (n.) far out
upon the lonely sea; p. 46 (n.) Some sea-captains, before shipping a
man; p. 46 (n.) of their adventures by sea and land; p. 46 (n.) they
never carried any pies and tarts to sea; p. 47 (n.) united with the
cool air of the sea; p. 47 (adj.) the Sailors' Magazine, with a sea-

blue cover; p. 47 (n.) about pious seamen who never swore; p. 47 (n.)
when they were too old to go to sea; p. 50 (n.) jumped over the bows
into the sea; p. 51 (n.) the folly which had sent me to sea; p. 51
(n.) such things happened frequently at sea; p. 52 (n.) a boy like
me, had to go to sea; p. 52 (adj.) and fill a good seaman's place;
p. 52 (n.) first night of his voyage to sea; p. 53 (n.) to swing a
bucket into the sea; p. 54 (n.) out of a scupper-hole into the sea;
p. 54 (n.) what I would want at sea; p. 56 (v.) about who had been
sea-faring the longest; p. 57 (n.) being the best seaman on board;
p. 57 (n.) he had been to sea ever since he was eight; p. 58 (n.)
soon as I became a little used to the sea; p. 59 (n.) to see that one
of the seamen; p. 59 (n.) he had shipped for an able-seaman; p. 60
(n.) when he ships for an able-seaman; p. 60 (n.) three classes--able-
seamen, ordinary-seamen, and boys; p. 60 (n.) will only have five or
six able seamen; p. 60 (n.) by the ordinary seamen and boys; p. 60
(n.) about who had been to sea the longest; p. 60 (n.) from eating so
much hard sea-biscuit; p. 62 (n.) that an able seaman is a great man;
p. 62 (n.) And the able seamen in the Highlander; p. 62 (n.) such
great notions about their seamanship; p. 62 (n.) thought that able
seamen received diplomas; p. 63 (n.) He Has a Fine Day at Sea; p. 63
(n.) little fleeces of foam all over the sea; p. 63 (n.) completely
got over my sea-sickness; p. 64 (n.) though we were at sea; p. 64 (n.)
a certain wonderful rising and falling of the sea; p. 64 (n.) from
the depths of the deep blue sea; p. 65 (n.) people who have never
gone to sea; p. 65 (n.) they never had any pails at sea; p. 65 (n.)
said there were no pegs at sea; p. 66 (adj.) give me . . . this salt-
sea life; p. 66 (n.) when the sea neighs and snorts; p. 66 (n.) let
me rock upon the sea; p. 66 (n.) and an endless sea before; p. 66 (n.)
Miserable dog's life is this of the sea; p. 67 (n.) and good will to
seamen; p. 67 (n.) I had heard that some sea-captains are fathers;
p. 69 (n.) for me to carry to sea; p. 69 (adj.) from my ignorance of
sea usages; p. 71 (n.) while we were at sea; p. 71 (n.) the use of
some kind of dye while at sea; p. 72 (adj.) like a summer excursion
to the sea shore; p. 72 (n.) and oil-skin suits, and sea-boots; p. 72
(n.) which old seamen carry in their chests; p. 72 (adj.) which gave
me a sea outfit; p. 72 (n.) I was not many days at sea; p. 73 (n.)
the very pair I now had at sea; p. 74 (n.) unfitted them the more for
sea-service; p. 74 (n.) entered my mind before going to sea; p. 75
(n.) going to sea as a sailor; p. 75 (n.) in going to sea so ill
provided; p. 75 (n.) most wonderful sights of the sea; p. 76 (n.)
smoke tranquilly mounting up into the sea-air; p. 76 (n.) the manner
of the two sea-captains; p. 77 (n.) of my first going aloft at sea;
p. 77 (n.) when the sea was quite calm; p. 78 (n.) the sea looked
like a great, black gulf; p. 78 (n.) or some sort of sea-fowl; p. 78
(n.) Though there was a pretty smooth sea; p. 79 (n.) prided himself
greatly upon his seamanship; p. 79 (n.) about the duties of boys at
sea; p. 79 (n.) like all European seamen in American ships; p. 81 (n.)
according to the invariable custom at sea; p. 82 (n.) with the sea
breaking over the bows; p. 82 (n.) when a man is hung at sea; p. 83
(n.) He never wore the turban at sea; p. 85 (n.) an account of
Shipwrecks and Disasters at Sea; p. 86 (n.) although I was going to
sea; p. 86 (n.) to be going to sea as a common sailor; p. 87 (adj.)
his sea boots drawn up to his knees; p. 88 (n.) given to looking at
sea-life romantically; p. 88 (n.) about a sort of fairy sea-queen;
p. 88 (n.) used to be dunning a sea-captain; p. 89 (n.) Blunt, while
at sea; p. 89 (n.) while we were at sea; p. 90 (n.) for like many

other seamen; p. 90 (n.) he never went to sea without a good supply;
p. 90 (n.) who at sea will doctor themselves; p. 90 (n.) but at sea
the salt air; p. 92 (n.) among sailors at sea; p. 93 (n.) went to
sea, bound for India; p. 93 (n.) though every seaman has heard; p. 93
(n.) heard of those accidents at sea; p. 94 (n.) on the broad,
boundless sea; p. 94 (n.) careering in pride of canvas over the sea;
pp. 95-6 (n.) was once pitched upon by an ingenious sea-captain;
p. 96 (n.) would look like mountains on the sea; p. 97 (n.) the deep-
sea-lead was heaved; p. 97 (n.) We hove our deep-sea-line by night;
p. 97 (n.) of the bottom of the sea; p. 97 (n.) that many seamen
impute the fogs; p. 99 (n.) shipped as an ordinary seaman; p. 99 (n.)
Larry had been bred to the sea; p. 100 (n.) than any other class of
seamen; p. 100 (n.) merchant seamen generally offed a certain
superiority; p. 101 (n.) ye wouldn't have been to sea here; p. 102
(n.) until we got into the Irish Sea; p. 103 (n.) when the sea and
sky had become blue again; p. 103 (n.) lying almost even with the
sea; p. 103 (n.) she rolled in the trough of the sea; p. 103 (adj.)
but my subsequent sea experiences have shown; p. 106 (adj.) are the
very best of sea-going craft; p. 114 (n.) At sea, the sailors are
continually; p. 115 (n.) involuntarily remind one of the sea-beach;
p. 115 (n.) running up the rigging at sea; p. 115 (n.) in being aloft
in a ship at sea; p. 116 (n.) with many wounds of many sea-fights;
p. 119 (adj.) The harness-cask, also, a sort of sea side-board;
p. 120 (adj.) indispensable part of a seaman's vocation; p. 120 (n.)
other matters familiar to an able seaman; pp. 120-1 (n.) serve a long
apprenticeship to the sea; p. 121 (n.) destroy the great nursery for
British seamen; p. 122 (n.) drop out of my hands into the sea; p. 123
(n.) contemplating a voyage to sea; p. 126 (n.) cruising about the
Irish Sea; p. 126 (adj.) by the side of a blazing sea-coal fire;
p. 126 (n.) is quite an arm of the sea; p. 127 (n.) seemed to come
out of the vaults of the sea; p. 128 (n.) As for the other seamen;
p. 128 (n.) stories about the bigamies of seamen; p. 130 (n.) which
they gave them at sea; p. 134 (n.) among the seamen went by the name
of Handsome Mary; p. 134 (adj.) walls, of what had once been sea-blue;
p. 134 (adj.) who at sea live upon salt beef and biscuit; p. 136 (n.)
would have four or five whiskered sea-captains; p. 137 (n.) there is
no shame in some sea-captains; p. 137 (n.) the men's wages ran on, as
at sea; p. 137 (n.) that an improvident seaman can take; p. 138 (n.)
of all sea-ports in the world; p. 138 (n.) extolling it above all
other sea-ports; p. 139 (n.) to take away from seamen; p. 139 (n.)
rations of grog while at sea; p. 143 (n.) and this sea-ditty of
Dibdin's; p. 145 (adj.) upon a bleak rock on the sea shore; p. 158
(n.) without discovering any connection with the sea; p. 158 (n.) to
have no connection with the sea; p. 158 (n.) Eastern traveler
standing on the brink of the Dead Sea; p. 164 (n.) who had long
followed the seas; p. 166 (n.) in readiness for sea; p. 167 (n.)
smoking together in this little sea-cabinet; p. 168 (n.) They keep up
this custom at sea; p. 169 (n.) and the deep-sea-lead, that first
struck; p. 170 (n.) Lascars, the native seamen of India; p. 171 (n.)
and I was informed made excellent seamen; p. 171 (n.) had been tost
[sic] about in violent seas; p. 171 (n.) the Irrawaddy ploughed the
sea; p. 172 (n.) showing much dexterity and seamanship; p. 174 (n.)
still sail the salt seas; p. 176 (n.) to induce seamen visiting
Liverpool; p. 176 (n.) by a motley crowd of seamen; p. 177 (n.) well
known to the seamen of many generations; p. 186 (n.) to excite the
charity of the seamen; p. 187 (n.) that the seamen did much to relieve;

p. 189 (n.) mix with the songs of the seamen; p. 190 (adj.) terrific
stories of pirates and sea murders; p. 191 (n.) eagerly bought up by
the seamen; p. 192 (n.) informing in the judicious seamen; p. 192
(adj.) who prey upon all seafaring men; p. 193 (n.) inducements to
all seamen; p. 194 (n.) to carry them over the sea; p. 196 (n.) poor
Jack finds more sharks than at sea; p. 198 (n.) navigate the boisterous
Narrow Seas; p. 216 (n.) smoky sailor-lanes and by-ways of a seaport;
p. 218 (adj.) born of his old sea reminiscences; p. 218 (n.) to
continue the wages of their seamen; p. 219 (n.) must have driven
Harry to sea; p. 220 (n.) at so urbane and gentlemanly a sea-captain;
p. 220 (adj.) that gay Lothario of all inexperienced, sea-going
youths; p. 220 (adj.) constant sight of his most unseamanlike person;
pp. 220-1 (n.) whether he had not best cross the sea as a . . .
passenger; p. 225 (n.) and ready for sea; p. 230 (n.) methought I was
slowly sinking in some reluctant sedgy sea; p. 238 (n.) more than
ever resolved upon the sea; p. 238 (n.) There is nothing like the
sea; p. 238 (n.) officers who were so dictatorial at sea; p. 238 (n.)
in getting things ready for sea; p. 239 (n.) permitted to cook their
food while at sea; p. 240 (n.) all steering broad out to sea; p. 240
(n.) the sea most smooth; p. 241 (n.) fairly gained the expanse of
the Irish Sea; p. 241 (n.) That irresistable wrestler, sea-sickness;
p. 241 (n.) the poor emigrant's first storm at sea; p. 241 (n.) for
the drenching seas would instantly flood; p. 241 (n.) we had not been
at sea one week; p. 242 (n.) abused by the seamen; p. 243 (n.) like
most old seamen; p. 244 (adj.) wavered for a moment at the seaman's
motionless mouth; p. 244 (n.) like a phosphorescent shark in a
midnight sea; p. 245 (n.) among the phosphorescent sparkles of the
damp night sea; p. 250 (n.) a mixed and liquid sea of sound; p. 250
(n.) as good as gazing down into the great South Sea; p. 252 (n.)
Harry Bolton at Sea; p. 253 (n.) it was known to the seamen; p. 253
(n.) in the first flush of being at sea; p. 253 (n.) never could have
been at sea before; p. 253 (n.) the slightest acquaintance with the
sea-life; p. 254 (n.) invariably impute his sea-going; p. 254 (n.)
What else can bring them to sea; p. 256 (n.) delerious greenhorns
doing such things at sea; p. 257 (n.) at the beck of illiterate sea-
tyrants; p. 257 (n.) every thing connected with the sea-life; p. 257
(n.) Isaac Newton and Lord Bacon would be sea-clowns; p. 259 (n.)
After the first miserable weather we experienced at sea; p. 259 (n.)
look at the great pigs of the s'a; p. 260 (n.) and gazing out at the
sea; p. 261 (n.) after one of these sea-quadrilles; p. 261 (n.) with
which almost all seamen; p. 263 (n.) as at sea no appeal lies beyond
the captain; p. 265 (n.) were provided with sea-biscuit; pp. 267-8
(n.) pumped up from the sea; p. 269 (n.) the amazed seaman found
himself; p. 270 (n.) during a dog-watch below at sea; p. 271 (n.) so
much rely while at sea; p. 272 (n.) but not altogether new among
seamen; p. 273 (n.) in what remote seas it may have sailed; p. 273
(n.) what uncatalogued sea-fowl may have pecked; p. 273 (n.) supped
in a forecastle at sea; p. 275 (n.) after we had been at sea about
ten days; p. 275 (n.) In any of that master's lowering sea-pieces;
p. 283 (n.) should be given one sea-biscuit; p. 285 (n.) not
recovering, while at sea; p. 285 (n.) from their first attack of sea-
sickness; p. 286 (n.) to toss into the sea; p. 286 (n.) throw any
thing to windward at sea; p. 287 (n.) murmuring something about
merchant seamen; p. 288 (n.) the bottomless profound of the sea, over
which we were sailing, concealed nothing more frightful; p. 289 (n.)
of its father's body in the sea; p. 289 (n.) leaving a long, rolling

sea; p. 289 (n.) this heavy sea subsided; p. 290 (n.) ran our course
over a pleasant sea; p. 292 (n.) of the destitute dead, who die on
the sea; p. 292 (n.) you see no plague-ship driving through a stormy
sea; p. 295 (n.) Like most seamen; p. 295 (n.) plunged like a diver
into the sea; p. 296 (n.) dead, ere he struck the sea; p. 296 (n.) in
which too many sea-captains indulge; p. 296 (n.) in case of a fatal
disaster at sea; p. 298 (n.) mid-day sun shone upon a glassy sea;
p. 298 (n.) the blue sea seemed to flow under them; p. 298 (n.) into
the calm, violet sea; p. 298 (n.) This America's skies must be down
in the sea; p. 299 (adj.) among sea-worn people; p. 299 (n.) the sea
was strewn with stuffed bed-ticks; p. 299 (n.) some sea-captains take
good heed; p. 299 (n.) the true condition of the steerage while at
sea; p. 305 (adj.) the expensive excesses of most sea-faring men;
p. 309 (n.) is the case with most seamen; p. 309 (n.) and like
rootless sea-weed; p. 312 (n.) made all the haste I could to the
seaport; p. 312 (n.) One day at sea; p. 312 (n.) to have a little
sea-chat.

White-Jacket--p. ix (n.) In the year 1843 I shipped as ordinary
seaman; p. 7 (adj.) to provide sea repasts for the officers; p. 8 (n.)
in merchantmen the seamen are divided into watches; p. 9 (n.) with a
number of other seamen; p. 9 (n.) are at sea respectively subdivided;
p. 9 (n.) from the most experienced seamen on board; p. 9 (adj.) grim
sea grenadiers; p. 10 (n.) but little seamanship being expected from
them; p. 10 (n.) they acquire the name of sea-dandies; p. 13 (n.)
whatever the other seamen might have been; p. 13 (n.) He was loved by
the seamen; p. 13 (n.) of his profession as a seaman; p. 14 (n.) This
man, though a good seaman; p. 15 (n.) we accounted ourselves the best
seamen; p. 15 (n.) besides giving us lessons in seamanship; p. 16 (n.)
you sea-tallow strainer; p. 16 (adj.) what are even a merchant-seaman's
sorry yarns; p. 16 (n.) a vile desecrator of the thrice holy sea;
p. 17 (n.) to riot in some abandoned sea-port; p. 23 (n.) when he
stands on his Quarter-deck at sea; p. 23 (n.) as the captain of a
man-of-war at sea; p. 24 (n.) he was an excellent seaman; p. 24 (n.)
The Lieutenants discuss sea-fights; p. 25 (adj.) In sea parlance;
p. 25 (adj.) only placed on board a sea-going ship; p. 25 (n.) a
harder time of it than the seamen themselves; p. 26 (n.) apart from
the seamen; p. 26 (adj.) by the various cooks of the seamen's messes;
p. 27 (n.) none who mess apart from the seamen; p. 27 (n.) are only
distinguished from the common seamen; p. 27 (n.) and the common
seamen; p. 28 (n.) the common seamen are specially designated; p. 28
(n.) while the two estates of sea-kings and sea-lords; p. 28 (n.) the
sea-commoners, or the people, keep up; p. 29 (n.) a summer sea--soft
breezes creeping over it; p. 29 (n.) going to their meals before the
other, at sea; p. 30 (n.) of allotting the government meals at sea;
p. 32 (n.) From what sea-alcove; p. 32 (n.) to waste thy fragrance on
the salt sea-air; p. 32 (n.) if a sea-officer dressed well; p. 32 (n.)
but the mere theory of seamanship forms; p. 32 (n.) Of what makes a
seaman; p. 33 (n.) never more tempt the sea; p. 33 (n.) Mad Jack is
in his saddle on the sea; p. 33 (n.) and find their food in the sea;
p. 34 (n.) far as his efficiency as a sea-officer was concerned;
p. 36 (n.) who showed me a pattern for sea-mittens; p. 37 (n.) But
though for clumsy seamen; p. 45 (n.) elevated from the level of a
mere seaman; p. 46 (n.) at sea, it ought to be in the mizzen-top;
p. 47 (n.) they always looked out upon the blue, boundless, dimpled,
laughing, sunny sea; p. 47 (n.) spent their time in the bracing sea-

air; p. 48 (adj.) burrowing down in the cable-tiers, or sea coal-hole;
pp. 48-9 (adj.) many sea lieutenants grow decrepit from age; p. 50
(n.) In the dog-watches at sea; p. 53 (n.) one gill of spirits per
day to every seaman; p. 57 (n.) The common seamen in a large frigate;
p. 66 (n.) In sea-actions, if by good or bad luck; p. 67 (n.) Such a
sea-martinet was our Captain; p. 70 (n.) many a wounded seaman, with
his arm in a sling; p. 71 (n.) and its sides festooned with sea-weed;
p. 71 (n.) and the seamen thronged round it; p. 72 (n.) after several
thousand French seamen had been destroyed; p. 72 (n.) are nearer the
bottom of the sea; p. 72 (n.) the old seamen in that part of a man-
of-war; p. 73 (n.) in perfect silence, we slid up and down the great
seething swells of the sea, but saw nothing; p. 76 (n.) at sea used
often to mount aloft at night; p. 76 (n.) to study the stars upon the
wide, boundless sea, is divine; p. 77 (n.) Let me feel thee again,
old sea; p. 77 (n.) Let me snuff thee up, sea-breeze; p. 77 (n.)
Forbid it, sea-gods; p. 77 (n.) let me lie down with Drake, where he
sleeps in the sea; p. 82 (n.) In a man-of-war at sea; p. 82 (n.) but
every other night at sea; p. 82 (n.) a merchant seaman goes to his
bunk; p. 83 (n.) the starboard side only is left to the seamen; p. 83
(n.) Drenched through and through by the spray of the sea; p. 84 (n.)
that the common seamen should fare so hard; p. 86 (n.) when the ship
is rolling in a sea-way; p. 87 (n.) like the Egyptians in the Red Sea;
p. 88 (n.) One bitter winter morning at sea; p. 90 (n.) some of the
seamen had clubbed together; p. 92 (n.) Mayor . . . Seafull, of the
Forecastle; p. 93 (n.) At the earnest entreaties of the seamen; p. 95
(n.) applauding a mere seaman like Jack Chase; p. 95 (n.) with which
a sea-officer falls back upon . . . the severity; p. 97 (n.)
encountering a tolerably smooth sea; p. 97 (n.) a black cloud rises
out of the sea; p. 97 (n.) when the first green sea breaks over him;
p. 97 (n.) Thus with seamen; p. 98 (n.) Among sea-captains, there are
some; p. 98 (n.) beholding . . . the goodlie South Sea; p. 101 (n.)
sea-boots, comforters, mittens; p. 101 (n.) I wondered at the liquid
sea which refused to freeze; p. 101 (n.) the usual practice of seamen
in a calm; p. 102 (n.) The din frightened the sea-fowl; p. 103 (n.)
the enraged seaman drew from his bosom; p. 104 (n.) a mere speck on
these remote seas; p. 104 (n.) Behold how mincingly it creeps over
the sea; p. 105 (n.) were plunging through the sea, which undulated;
p. 105 (n.) the yard-arm-ends seemed to dip in the sea; p. 106 (n.)
occasional phosphorescence of the yeasting sea; p. 106 (n.) thundering
over and upon the head seas; p. 107 (n.) of such a sound in a night-
tempest at sea; p. 108 (n.) to the combined fury of the sea and wind;
p. 110 (n.) But every seaman knew, at the time; p. 111 (n.) Hence, at
sea, Mad Jack tried to make; p. 112 (n.) so on the quarter-deck at
sea; p. 113 (n.) seldom taken a line-of-battle ship to sea; p. 113
(n.) officers are seldom or never sent to sea; p. 113 (n.) who are
accomplished practical seamen; p. 113 (n.) nor against the able
seamen in the navy; p. 114 (n.) as a common seaman rising to the
rank; p. 114 (n.) shipping green seas on both sides; p. 116 (n.)
albatross were skimming the sea near by; p. 116 (n.) by some hoydenish
sea-nymphs outside the frigate; p. 120 (n.) catching hold of the
skirts of an old sea-dog; p. 121 (n.) Jacketless at sea; p. 124 (n.)
but little more than a mere able seaman; p. 130 (n.) to bring to some
ship at sea; p. 130 (n.) all men-of-war are great bullies on the high
seas; p. 132 (n.) a few crusty traces of some sort of a sea-pie;
p. 132 (n.) be it said that, at sea; p. 132 (n.) Hence the various
sea-roles; p. 135 (n.) To the sensitive seaman that summons sounds

like; p. 135 (n.) the seas broke heavily against the bows; p. 136 (n.)
a lane formed through the crowd of seamen; p. 140 (adj.) to stop a
seaman's grog for a day or a week; p. 140 (n.) as most seamen so
cling to their grog; p. 140 (n.) But there are some sober seamen that
would; p. 140 (n.) can not exempt a prudent seaman from ignominy;
p. 140 (n.) of being disliked or hated by the seamen; p. 141 (n.) the
seamen belonging to another American frigate; p. 141 (n.) a seaman,
for the most trivial alleged offences; p. 142 (n.) what torments must
that seaman undergo; p. 143 (n.) according to the laws and customs in
such cases at sea; p. 144 (n.) to restrain the Captain from imprisoning
a seaman; p. 144 (n.) kept a seaman confined in the brig; p. 144 (n.)
a three-decker is a city on the sea; p. 145 (n.) one set of sea-
citizens is exempted; p. 146 (n.) entering the service of his country
as a common seaman; p. 147 (n.) his officers reported to him certain
seamen; p. 148 (n.) seeing more active service than any sea-officer
of his time; p. 148 (n.) But these seamen of his must have been;
p. 148 (n.) all standing to the sea; p. 148 (n.) not only boarded
foreign ships on the high seas; p. 149 (n.) instances where the
seamen have ran away; p. 150 (n.) attributed to the impressment of
the seamen; p. 152 (n.) eight or ten dark objects floating on the
sea; p. 153 (n.) five goodly puncheons lay wallowing in the sea;
p. 153 (n.) streaming with sea-weed; p. 153 (n.) must have drifted
off to sea; p. 153 (n.) resemble a section of a sea-serpent; p. 154
(n.) in many bloodless Brandywine actions at sea; p. 155 (adj.) spite
of merchant seamen's maxim; p. 155 (adj.) addressing five hundred
salt-sea sinners; p. 157 (n.) A remarkably serious, but bigoted
seaman; p. 158 (adj.) each seaman's mess on board the Neversink;
p. 158 (adj.) for the purpose of building a seaman's chapel in China;
p. 159 (n.) said by seamen to resemble; p. 160 (n.) but an embattled
land-slide into the sea; p. 160 (n.) from what she presented at sea;
p. 160 (n.) At sea there is more to employ the sailors; p. 161 (adj.)
in addition to their seaman's wages; p. 162 (n.) in a sea-tussle,
these lantern-jawed vartlets; p. 162 (adj.) upon the seaman's
inadvertently saying sir to him; p. 166 (n.) in the hearts of most of
the seamen; p. 166 (n.) subordination to their authority among the
seamen; p. 167 (n.) but miserable reading at sea; p. 168 (n.) of
corsairs, captives, dungeons, and sea-fights; p. 174 (n.) somewhat
aloof from the mass of sea-men; p. 176 (n.) serving out his weary
three years in a sort of sea-Newgate; p. 180 (n.) beyond his pay as
an able seaman; p. 187 (n.) his life had often been secretly attempted
by the seamen; p. 189 (n.) to prey upon honest seamen; p. 190 (n.)
all the old grudges of the seamen under his command; p. 191 (n.) to
keep out the spray of the sea; p. 194 (adj.) with a sea-green bag
swung on his shoulder; p. 196 (n.) in giving his orders at sea;
p. 196 (n.) a seaman fell from the main-royal-yard; p. 199 (n.) for
this superior pair of sea-boots; p. 199 (n.) I solemnly guarantee, my
noble sea-fencibles; pp. 199-200 (n.) this superior pair of sea-boots
vibrating at one dollar; p. 203 (n.) How much, my sea fencibles;
p. 203 (n.) spread itself into a bed at the bottom of the sea; p. 206
(n.) coming into disciplinary contact with the seamen; p. 207 (n.)
the precise remarks made by the seamen; p. 208 (n.) the feelings with
which the common seamen and the officers; p. 208 (n.) battles so
naturally averse to the seamen; p. 212 (n.) what was fabled of the
entrance to that sea; p. 212 (n.) you see naught of the land-locked
sea; p. 213 (n.) a rank superior to a mere able-seaman; p. 213 (n.)
old quarter-masters and other dignified sea-fencibles; p. 213 (n.)

your trusty sea-warriors, valiant Captain; p. 216 (n.) long remembered
by the few seamen; p. 217 (n.) deferentially obeyed by the seamen;
p. 217 (n.) thousands of seamen have been flogged; p. 217 (n.)
complaining of a seaman; p. 218 (n.) For a sea-officer, Collingwood
was; p. 218 (n.) in all important functions at sea; p. 218 (n.) their
overbearing manner toward seamen; p. 218 (n.) contract the ill-will
of the seamen; p. 218 (n.) the seamen can not but betray it; p. 218
(n.) while the noblest-minded and most heroic sea-officers; p. 219
(n.) went by the name of Boat Plug among the seamen; p. 220 (n.) this
is one of those sea-statutes; p. 221 (n.) having seen sufficient
service at sea; p. 221 (n.) The former, upon sea-service; p. 222
(adj.) Sea-faring Persons peculiarly subject to being; p. 222 (n.) At
sea, a frigate houses; p. 223 (n.) the infliction of corporal
punishment upon a seaman; p. 223 (n.) wearied by the torrid,
monotonous sea; p. 223 (n.) standing in the waist among a crowd of
seamen; p. 223 (n.) reprimanding the crowd of seamen; p. 223 (n.)
darting his eyes among the seamen; p. 228 (n.) who prematurely are
sent off to sea; p. 230 (n.) in order to learn the profession of a
sea-officer; p. 230 (n.) a boy can hardly be sent to sea too early;
p. 230 (n.) commanded indifferently either by sea or by land; p. 231
(n.) that the science (seamanship) might be attained; p. 231 (n.)
internal affairs of the national sea-service; p. 234 (adj.) your sea
air is a sworn foe; p. 234 (n.) that the swords of sea-officers have;
p. 241 (n.) between keeping late hours at sea; p. 242 (n.) you shall
be flogged like any other seaman; p. 242 (n.) no other profession
than the sea; p. 242 (n.) he was again cashiered at sea; p. 243 (n.)
There is some charm in the sea; p. 246 (n.) There was a seaman
belonging; p. 255 (n.) used for burials at sea; p. 265 (n.) When we
were nearly ready for sea; p. 265 (n.) made all sail with the sea-
breeze; p. 266 (n.) she now sailed the salt seas as a trophy; p. 266
(n.) down the sea-coast and along the endless banks; p. 266 (n.) of
the twinges we sea-patriots must have felt; p. 268 (n.) the wild
Tartar breezes of the sea; p. 270 (n.) see our black hull butting the
white sea; p. 270 (n.) when he went to sea; p. 270 (n.) who went to
sea with Gama; p. 270 (n.) he himself, poor fellow, was lost at sea;
p. 271 (n.) A snuff of the sea . . . is inspiration; p. 271 (n.) the
sea is the place to cradle genius; p. 271 (n.) Heave and fall, old
sea; p. 272 (n.) supposed to be very bad trim for the sea; p. 274 (n.)
many of the seamen became joyous; p. 274 (n.) for the crews of most
ships at sea; p. 275 (n.) bumped him out of a port-hole into the sea;
p. 276 (n.) with what facility a sea-officer assumes; p. 276 (n.)
poetical comparisons between a sea-captain and a father; p. 276 (n.)
between a sea-captain and the master of apprentices; p. 277 (n.) in
tacking ship every seaman in a man-of-war; p. 277 (adj.) it is every
seaman's duty to be found; p. 278 (n.) very few of the seamen could
tell; p. 278 (n.) generally betokened to other seamen; p. 280 (n.)
showing the far sea beyond; p. 280 (n.) the blue sea seen through the
opening . . . showed with an awful vividness; p. 280 (n.) My eye was
measuring the distance between him and the sea; p. 281 (n.) in behalf
of a seaman at the mast; p. 281 (n.) one of the foremost man among
the seamen; p. 283 (n.) was a very aged seaman; p. 284 (n.) The Lord
Nelsons of the sea; p. 284 (n.) potent is the authority of these sea-
wardens; p. 285 (n.) this prerogative is only his while at sea;
p. 287 (n.) bowls along over a jubilant sea; p. 289 (n.) At sea or in
harbor; p. 291 (n.) at the array of grim seamen around her; p. 292
(n.) offences . . . that a seaman may commit; p. 294 (n.) at the

bottom of the sea; p. 295 (n.) should you come to die at sea; p. 295
(n.) surge all the sea against us; p. 298 (n.) when Robert Blake
swept the Narrow Seas; p. 298 (n.) Ships-of-war, and Forces by Sea;
p. 298 (n.) sanctioning naval scourging at sea; p. 298 (n.) in the
Sea Laws of the absolute monarch; p. 298 (n.) Rights and Duties of
Merchant-Seamen; p. 300 (n.) Herein are the good Ordinances of the
Sea; p. 300 (n.) The consulate of the Sea; p. 301 (n.) I must also
cite . . . nearly all the seamen; p. 301 (n.) provides means for a
seaman deeming himself; p. 301 (n.) guarantees to the mass of seamen;
p. 302 (n.) as well as the seamen; p. 302 (n.) It was an English
seaman who related; p. 304 (n.) Compare the sea-laws of our Navy;
p. 304 (n.) compare them with the Consulate of the Sea; p. 304 (n.)
concerning a Gothland sea-captain; p. 304 (n.) of an officer
commanding at sea; p. 304 (n.) a sea-officer in command should be
clothed; p. 304 (n.) for clothing modern sea-commanders; p. 305 (n.)
over the warm, smooth sea of the tropics; p. 306 (n.) as not to
disturb the sleeping seamen; p. 309 (n.) you would take the best
specimen of a seaman; p. 310 (n.) an enthusiastic admirer of sea-
scenery; p. 310 (n.) stretching his bold hand over the sea; p. 311
(n.) snow-white canvass sliding along the sea; p. 311 (adj.) many
other salt-sea ballads; p. 311 (n.) That ever sailed the sea; p. 311
(n.) And she went to the bottom of the sea--/ The sea, the sea, the
sea; p. 311 (n.) And she went to the bottom of the sea; p. 311 (n.)
He was a staid and sober seaman; p. 312 (n.) been impressed upon the
high seas; p. 312 (n.) frigates now crippled on the sea; p. 313 (n.)
in a frantic sea-fight; p. 313 (n.) candid persons who have been in
sea-fights; p. 313 (n.) that impressed English seamen have not
scrupled; p. 313 (n.) The dissatisfied seamen; p. 314 (n.) where a
seaman . . . impelled by pure fear; p. 314 (n.) of Him who made such
a seaman; p. 314 (n.) run through on the spot the first seaman who;
p. 314 (n.) the secret history of all sea-fights; p. 314 (n.) the
laurels of sea-heroes would turn to ashes; p. 315 (n.) a man hated by
the seamen; p. 322 (n.) gazing broad off upon a placid sea; p. 322
(n.) to which the seamen in a man-of-war; p. 323 (n.) a broad balcony
overhanging the sea; p. 323 (n.) sailing over summer seas in the days
of; p. 323 (n.) with ditty-bags or sea-reticules; p. 324 (n.) I
perceived an aged seaman on his knees; p. 324 (adv.) his face turned
seaward; p. 325 (n.) three days enchanted on the sea; p. 325 (n.)
where the invalid seamen are placed; p. 326 (adj.) In a sea-going
frigate; p. 326 (n.) Before going to sea; p. 326 (n.) of the robust
old sea-dogs on the forecastle; p. 327 (adj.) I always got sea-sick
after taking medicine; p. 328 (n.) Not a seaman enters the Navy;
p. 330 (adj.) the raw sea air, as they will tell you, is not good for
the sick; p. 330 (n.) American man-of-war, bound for sea; p. 335 (n.)
How Man-of-War's-men Die at Sea; p. 335 (n.) was a middle-aged,
handsome, intelligent seaman; p. 336 (n.) at sea cut off from all
ventilation; p. 338 (n.) to that small class of aged seamen; p. 339
(n.) custom generally practiced by most sea-undertakers; p. 341 (n.)
How they Bury a Man-of-war's-man at Sea; p. 341 (n.) the dead sailor
sank in the sea; p. 343 (n.) after his Burial at Sea; p. 343 (n.) to
use the phrase of one of the seamen; p. 344 (n.) for the deceased
seaman had informed him; p. 346 (n.) Every other afternoon, while at
sea; p. 347 (n.) though he had never been to sea; p. 350 (n.) of
standing night-watches at sea; p. 350 (n.) They are rated as able
seamen or ordinary seamen; p. 351 (n.) his wages as a seaman are
still running; p. 351 (n.) stood upon the ship's books as ordinary

seamen; p. 351 (n.) receiving the pay of able seamen; p. 352 (n.) and
shave himself at sea; p. 353 (n.) as the seamen must be shaven;
p. 352 (n.) upon days of high seas; p. 352 (n.) these sea-barbers
pride themselves upon their sea-legs; p. 352 (n.) for going into a
sea-fight; p. 353 (n.) many of the seamen had redoubled; p. 353 (adj.)
embracing the Old Guard of sea grenadiers; p. 353 (adj.) a fine
specimen of a sea sexagenarian; p. 353 (n.) He was a sort of sea-
Socrates; p. 355 (adv.) They said it was unseamanlike; p. 356 (n.)
the beards of both officers and seamen were; p. 358 (n.) a great many
of the older seamen . . . talked; p. 359 (n.) eying the passing
throng of seamen; p. 359 (n.) For some hours the seamen paced; p. 361
(n.) alow and aloft with it at sea; p. 367 (n.) privileges he accorded
to the seamen; p. 370 (n.) raise a mob in any American sea-port;
p. 370 (n.) according to the usages of the sea-service; p. 371 (n.)
is again thrown over the seaman; p. 371 (n.) what many seamen have
seen; p. 372 (n.) One of the seamen sprang overboard; p. 373 (n.) at
sea, they stood watches; p. 374 (n.) may pick off a seaman or two;
p. 374 (n.) these marines are to the seamen; p. 374 (n.) having so
many sea-officers over them; p. 374 (n.) among seamen, one of the
greatest terms; p. 375 (n.) on the part of the common seaman; p. 375
(n.) in one oaken box on the sea; p. 375 (n.) What too many seamen
are when ashore; p. 377 (n./adj.) The gallows and the sea refuse
nothing; is a very old sea saying; p. 377 (n.) as being pushed off to
sea; p. 377 (n.) For the sea is the true Tophet; p. 377 (n.) as the
sea . . . is the stable of brute monsters; p. 378 (n.) sailors have
actually jumped into the sea; p. 378 (n.) along the wharves of our
sea-ports; p. 378 (n.) regularly shipped as a seaman; p. 379 (n.)
envied by many of the seamen; p. 380 (n.) one eighth of the entire
body of seamen; p. 380 (n.) with English seamen who have served;
p. 380 (n.) ready to mix with any sea; p. 380 (n.) the majority of
their best seamen; p. 380 (n.) part of her crew be able seamen;
p. 381 (n.) the great body of English seamen; p. 381 (n.) that might
have carried them beyond sea; p. 381 (n.) a large body of British
seamen; p. 381 (n.) three thousand seamen . . . fled ashore; p. 381
(n.) the kidnapped seamen were far out to sea; p. 382 (n.) the
lamented scarcity of good English seamen; p. 382 (n.) the best seamen
. . . generally succeeded; p. 382 (n.) composed not of regular seamen;
p. 382 (n.) depraving the volunteer landsmen and ordinary seamen;
p. 382 (n.) patriotic verses, full of sea-chivalry; p. 383 (n.) That
man, though a sea-vagabond; p. 384 (n.) they don't fancy sea-lawyers;
p. 384 (n.) that most sea-officers profess to admire; p. 384 (n.) a
seaman who exhibits traits; p. 387 (n.) rising, like Venus from the
sea; p. 388 (n.) Sink the sea; p. 389 (n.) to sea again, I won't;
p. 389 (n.) Blast the sea, shipmates; p. 389 (n.) I venerate the sea;
p. 389 (n.) with all the things of the sea surrounding them; p. 389
(n.) turn their backs on the sea; p. 390 (n.) you, seamen of the fore-
top; p. 390 (n.) is only a man-of-war's man at sea; p. 390 (n.) and
the sea is the place to learn what he is; p. 392 (n.) at sea, . . . a
hundred feet aloft; p. 392 (n.) in the sudden swells of the calm sea;
p. 392 (n.) would sink into the speechless profound of the sea; p. 39
p. 393 (n.) when I struck the sea; p. 393 (n.) As I gushed into the
sea; p. 393 (n.) The blow from the sea must have turned me; p. 393
(n.) some inert, coiled fish of the sea; p. 393 (n.) as of the sea in
the height of a tempest; p. 393 (n.) showing hundreds of seamen in
the hammock-nettings; p. 395 (n.) the white jacket has sunk to the
bottom of the sea; p. 396 (n.) my sea-tutor and sire; p. 396 (n.) .

some reckless, improvident seamen . . . had little or nothing; p. 396
(n.) Let us leave the ship on the sea; p. 396 (adj.) turned out at
the sea-gull call of the watch; p. 398 (n.) As a man-of-war that
sails through the sea; pp. 398-9 (adj.) makes every soul of us
sea-sick.

Moby-Dick--title page (n.) at his breath spouts out a sea; p. 2 (n.)
shall slay the dragon that is in the sea; p. 3 (n.) The Indian Sea
breedeth the most and the biggest fishes; p. 3 (n.) Scarcely had we
proceeded two days on the sea; p. 3 (n.) when about sunrise a great
many whales and other monsters of the sea; p. 3 (n.) beating the sea
before him into a foam; p. 3 (n.) the sea-gudgeon retires into it in
great security, and there sleeps; p. 3 (n.) The great Leviathan that
maketh the seas to seethe like a boiling pan; p. 4 (adj.) That sea
beast/ Leviathan, which God of all his works/ created hugest; p. 4
(n.) and at his [Leviathan's] breath spouts out a sea; p. 4 (n.) The
mighty whales which swim in a sea of water; p. 4 (n.) and have a sea
of oil swimming in them; p. 5 (n.) Whales in the sea/ God's voice
obey; p. 5 (n.) there being more in those southern seas; p. 6 (n.)
when out at sea they are afraid to mention even their names; p. 6 (n.)
his guarding and protecting the seas from pirates and robbers; p. 7
(n.) the sea being then covered with them; p. 7 (n.) Not a fatter
fish than he/ Flounders round the Polar Sea; p. 8 (n.) there--pointing
to the sea--is a green pasture where our children's grand-children
will go for bread; p. 8 (n.) and phosphor gleamed in the wake of the
whale,/ As it floundered in the sea; p. 10 (n.) eight or nine thousand
persons, living here in the sea; p. 11 (n.) And King of the boundless
sea; p. 12 (n.) I account it high time to get to sea as soon as I can;
p. 12 (adj.) as if striving to get a still better seaward peep; p. 13
(n.) Why is almost every robust healthy boy with a robust healthy
soul in him, at some time or other crazy to go to sea; p. 14 (n.) Why
did the Persians hold the sea holy; p. 14 (n.) when I say that I am
in the habit of going to sea whenever I begin to grow hazy about the
eyes; p. 14 (n.) I do not mean to have it inferred that I ever go to
sea as a passenger; p. 14 (n.) Besides, passengers get sea-sick;
p. 14 (n.) nor . . . do I ever go to sea as a Commodore, or a Captain,
or a Cook; p. 14 (n.) when I go to sea, I go as a simple sailor;
p. 15 (n.) What of it, if some old hunks of a sea-captain orders me;
p. 15 (n.) however the old sea-captains may order me about; p. 15 (n.)
Again, I always go to sea as a sailor; p. 15 (n.) Finally, I always
go to sea as a sailor; p. 15 (n.) after having repeatedly smelt the
sea as a merchant sailor; p. 16 (n.) Then the wild and distant seas
where he [whale] rolled his island bulk; p. 16 (n.) I love to sail
forbidden seas; p. 20 (n.) It's the Black Sea in a midnight gale;
p. 21 (n.) And that harpoon--so like a corkscrew now--was flung in
Javan seas; p. 22 (n.) I found a number of young seamen gathered about
a table; p. 23 (adj.) A tramping of sea boots was heard in the entry;
p. 23 (n.) with the arrantest topers newly landed from sea; p. 23 (n.)
since the sea-gods had ordained that he should soon become my shipmate;
pp. 23-4 (n.) till he became my comrade on the sea; p. 24 (n.)
occurred to me just previous to the entrance of the seamen; p. 24 (n.)
sailors no more sleep two in a bed at sea; p. 26 (n.) this here
harpooneer . . . has just arrived from the south seas; p. 27 (adj.)
placing the candle on a crazy old sea chest that did double duty;
p. 27 (adj.) also a large seaman's bag, containing the harpooneer's
wardrobe; p. 29 (n.) However, I had been in the South Seas; pp. 29-30

(n.) shipped aboard of a whaleman in the South Seas; p. 23 (n.) owing
I suppose to his keeping his arm at sea unmethodically in sun and
shade; pp. 35-6 (adj.) sea carpenters, and sea ropers, and sea
blacksmiths; p. 36 (n.) Yes, here were a set of sea-dogs; p. 36 (n.)
had boarded great whales on the high seas; p. 37 (n.) any considerable
seaport will frequently offer to view; p. 38 (n.) the comical things
he does upon reaching the seaport; p. 38 (n.) In bespeaking his sea-
outfit; p. 38 (n.) dragged up hither from the bottom of the sea;
p. 40 (n.) Whether any of the relatives of the seamen whose names
appeared; p. 42 (n.) in mounting a ship from a boat at sea; p. 43 (n.)
borrowed from the chaplain's former sea-farings; p. 43 (n.) was the
pulpit itself without a trace of the same sea-taste; p. 44 (n.) There
was a low rumbling of heavy sea-boots; p. 44 (n.) he seemed kneeling
and praying at the bottom of the sea; p. 44 (n.) in a ship that is
foundering at sea in a fog; p. 45 (n.) yet what depths of the soul
does Jonah's deep sea-line sound; p. 45 (n.) sea-weed and all the
slime of the sea is about us; p. 45 (n.) when the Atlantic was an
almost unknown sea; p. 48 (n.) the uncheered ship for Tarshish, all
careening, glides to sea; p. 48 (n.) But the sea rebels; he will not
bear the wicked burden; p. 48 (n.) He sees no black sky and raging
sea; p. 48 (n.) [whale] even now with open mouth is cleaving the seas
after him; p. 48 (n.) grasps a shroud, to look out upon the sea;
p. 48 (n.) I fear the Lord the God of Heaven who hath made the sea
and the dry land; p. 49 (n.) to take him and cast him forth into the
sea; p. 49 (n.) Jonah taken up as an anchor and dropped into the sea;
p. 49 (n.) and the sea is still; p. 49 (n.) in the eventual deliverance
of him from the sea and the whale; p. 49 (n.) the preacher, who, when
describing Jonah's sea-storm, seemed tossed by a storm himself; p. 50
(n.) tore him along into the midst of the seas; p. 50 (n.) from the
shuddering cold and blackness of the sea; p. 50 (n.) his ears, like
two sea-shells, still multitudinously murmuring of the ocean; p. 50
(n.) Delight is to him, whom all the waves of the billows of the seas
of the boisterous mob can never shake from this sure keel of the Ages;
p. 52 (n.) with the other seamen in the inn; p. 56 (adv.) his canoe,
still afloat, . . . with its prow seaward; p. 57 (adj.) But this fine
young savage--this sea Prince of Wales; p. 57 (n.) He answered, to go
to sea again; p. 58 (n.) though well acquainted with the sea; p. 59
(adj.) a very stately punctilious gentleman, at least for a sea
captain; p. 60 (n.) I . . . turned me to admire the magnanimity of
the sea which will permit no records; p. 60 (n.) the Captain, a gaunt
rib of the sea; p. 62 (n.) that they have to send beyond seas for a
spile; p. 62 (adj.) as to the backs of sea turtles; p. 62 (n.) What
wonder, then, that these Nantucketers, born on a beach, should take
to the sea for a livelihood; p. 62 (adj.) That Himmalehan, salt-sea
Mastodon, clothed with such portentousness of unconscious power;
p. 62 (n.) these naked Nantucketers, these sea hermits, issuing from
their ant-hill in the sea; p. 63 (n.) For the sea is his [the
Nantucketer's]; p. 63 (n.) pirates and privateers, though following
the sea as highwaymen the road; p. 63 (n.) The Nantucketer, he alone
resides and riots on the sea; p. 63 (n.) He lives on the sea, as
prairie cocks in the prairie; p. 67 (n.) but deftly travelled over
sheaves of sea-ivory; p. 68 (n.) he was brown and brawny, like most
old seamen; p. 71 (n.) not unworthy a Scandinavian sea-king; p. 72
(adj.) in his sea-going days, a bitter, hard task-master; p. 73 (n.)
considering that I was used to the sea; p. 76 (n.) leaves her to the
owners till all is ready for sea; p. 85 (n.) Something of the salt

sea yet lingered in Bildad's language; p. 85 (n.) with . . . every
sea breaking over us; p. 89 (n.) nothing should be found wanting in
the Pequod, after once fairly getting to sea; p. 90 (n.) so soon as
the ship sailed out upon the open sea; pp. 93-4 (n.) just as if they
were to be joint-commanders at sea; p. 94 (n.) and steering her well
out to sea; p. 94 (adj.) had placed a small choice copy of Watts in
each seaman's berth; p. 95 (n.) as the old craft deep dived into the
green seas; p. 97 (adj.) [the ship which] fights 'gainst the very
winds that fain would blow her homeward seeks all the lashed sea's
landlessness again; p. 97 (n.) effort of the soul to keep the open
independence of her sea; p. 100 (adj.) All that is made such a
flourish of in old South Sea Voyages; p. 104 (n.) in the conflict
with seas, or winds, or whales, or any of the ordinary irrational
horrors of the spiritual terrors; p. 107 (n.) in the wake of the
great whales of the sea; p. 108 (n.) An Anacharsis Clootz deputation
from all the isles of the sea; p. 109 (n.) the unknown captain, now
in the seclusion of the sea; p. 109 (n.) Three better, more likely
sea-officers and men . . . could not readily be found; p. 110 (n.) in
an elemental strife at sea; p. 110 (n.) the old sea-traditions . . .
popularly invested this old Manxman; p. 110 (n.) this ivory leg had
at sea been fashioned; p. 111 (n.) nothing but the dead wintry
bleakness of the sea had then kept him so secluded; p. 111 (n.) which,
at sea, almost perpetually reigns; p. 112 (n.) Among sea-commanders,
the old greybeards will oftenest; p. 114 (adj.) the thrones of the
sea-loving Danish kings were fabricated of the tusks; p. 114 (n.) a
king of the sea . . . was Ahab; p. 114 (n.) He tossed the still
lighted pipe into the sea; p. 115 (n.) dragging up a lot of seaweed
he had for a clout; p. 117 (n.) Many are the men, . . . landsmen and
seamen; p. 117 (n.) Greenland whale is an usurper upon the throne of
the seas; p. 118 (n.) Greenland whale was to them the monarch of the
seas; p. 118 (adj.) surgeons to English South-Sea whale-ships; p. 118
(n.) To grope down into the bottom of the sea; p. 119 (n.) dividing
the possession of the same seas; p. 119 (adj.) any sea creature
hitherto identified; p. 121 (n.) hunted by the Dutch and English in
the Arctic seas; p. 121 (n.) has been seen almost in every sea;
p. 121 (n.) When the sea is moderately calm; p. 123 (n.) I have never
seen him except in the remoter southern seas; p. 124 (n.) in turning
over the bottom of the sea for food; p. 125 (n.) rising to the surface
of the Polar Sea; p. 125 (adj.) I have gathered that this same sea-
unicorn's horn was in ancient days regarded; p. 125 (n.) He is mostly
found in the circumpolar seas; p. 125 (n.) For we are all killers, on
land and on sea; p. 126 (n.) Both are outlaws, even in the lawless
seas; p. 128 (n.) the grand political maxim of the sea demands;
p. 129 (n.) by no means unobservant of the paramount forms and usages
of the sea; p. 131 (n.) the intense artificialness of sea-usages;
p. 131 (n.) Over his ivory-inlaid table, Ahab presided like a mute,
maned sea-lion on the white coral beach, surrounded by his warlike
but still deferential cubs; p. 134 (adj.) the three salt-sea warriors
would rise and depart; p. 136 (n.) to couple . . . the mast-head
standers of the land with those of the sea; p. 136 (n.) erected lofty
spars along the sea-coast; p. 136 (n.) that of a whale-ship at sea;
p. 136 (n.) the seamen taking their regular turns; p. 136 (n.) swim
the hugest monsters of the sea; p. 136 (n.) There you stand, lost in
the infinite series of the sea; p. 137 (n.) tossed about by the sea;
p. 137 (n.) protected from the inclement weather of the frozen seas;
p. 138 (adj.) stray narwhales, or vagrant sea unicorns; p. 139 (n.)

the widely contrasting serenity of those seductive seas; p. 140 (n.)
by her, borrowed from the sea; by the sea, from the inscrutable tides
of God; p. 140 (n.) you drop through that transparent air into the
summer sea; p. 140 (n.) There most sea-captains usually walk at that
hour; p. 148 (n.) whelped somewhere by the sharkish sea; p. 148 (n.)
Foremost through the sparkling sea; p. 152 (n.) How the sea rolls
swashing 'gainst the side; p. 153 (n.) with storm-lashed guns, on
which the sea-salt cakes; p. 153 (n.) keeled hulls split at sea;
p. 155 (n.) had haunted those uncivilized seas; p. 156 (n.) as the
sea surpasses the land in this matter; p. 156 (n.) whatever is
appallingly astonishing in the sea; p. 158 (n.) as the secrets of the
currents in the seas have never yet been divulged; p. 158 (n.)
harpoons darted in the Greenland seas; p. 159 (n.) even in the limitless, uncharted seas; p. 159 (n.) gliding at high noon through a dark
blue sea; p. 162 (n.) of his undeniable delirium at sea; p. 162 (n.)
he might have seemed the gliding great demon of the seas of life;
p. 165 (n.) in waters hard upon the Antarctic seas; p. 167 (n.) does
the name of the White Sea exert such a spectralness; p. 167 (n.) that
of the Yellow Sea lulls us with mortal thoughts; p. 168 (n.) his ship
sailing through a midnight sea of milky whiteness; p. 168 (n.)
beholding the scenery of the Antarctic seas; p. 169 (n.) the muffled
rollings of a milky sea; p. 171 (adj.) bringing out a large wrinkled
roll of yellowish sea charts; p. 178 (n.) is being carried down to
the bottom of the sea; p. 182 (n.) a great sea-monster was captured
in the neighboring Propontis, or Sea of Marmora; p. 185 (n.) the
seamen were lazily lounging about the decks; p. 185 (n.) so strange a
dreaminess did there then reign all over the ship and all over the
sea; p. 190 (n.) Boat and crew sat motionless on the sea; p. 190 (n.)
silently eying the vast blue eye of the sea; p. 191 (adv.) I can't
see three seas off; p. 191 (n.) by the most riotously perverse and
cross-running seas; p. 193 (n.) Only the infidel sharks in the
audacious seas may give ear; p. 193 (n.) The vast swells of the
omnipotent sea; p. 193 (n.) owing to the increasing darkness of the
dun cloud-shadows flung upon the sea; p. 194 (n.) There we sat up to
our knees in the sea; p. 194 (n.) The rising sea forbade all attempts
to bale out the boat; p. 195 (n.) The mist still spread over the sea;
p. 199 (n.) some plumed and glittering god uprising from the sea;
p. 201 (n.) rend us at last in the remotest and most savage seas;
p. 201 (n.) we rose and fell upon the long, troubled seas; p. 201 (n.)
thick in our rear flew the inscrutable sea-ravens; p. 201 (n.) still
unrestingly heaved the black sea; p. 201 (n.) we found ourselves
launched into this tormented sea; p. 202 (n.) by the perilous seas
that burstingly broke over its bows; p. 203 (n.) they swayed and swung
over a fathomless sea; p. 204 (n.) the wind and sea betokened storms;
p. 210 (n.) to nurse at his maternal sea; p. 210 (n.) as vengeful and
full of social quarrel as the backwoods seaman; p. 210 (n.) in the
solitary and savage seas far from you; p. 221 (n.) shifted and
glistened like a living opal in the blue morning sea; p. 227 (n.)
their deformities floundering in seas of blood and blue paint; p. 227
(n.) The living whale . . . is only to be seen at sea in unfathomable
waters; p. 230 (adj.) Sea fowls are pecking at the small crabs,
shellfish and other sea candies and macaroni, which the Right Whale
sometimes carries on his pestilent back; p. 230 (n.) the glassy level
of a sea becalmed; p. 234 (n.) leaving behind them endless swaths of
blue upon the yellow sea; p. 235 (n.) for ever and for ever, to the
crack of doom, the sea will insult and murder him; p. 235 (n.) man

has lost that sense of the full awfulness of the sea which aboriginally belongs to it; p. 235 (n.) wherein differ the sea and the land; p. 235 (n.) the live sea swallows up ships and crews; p. 235 (n.) not only is the sea such a foe to man . . . but it is also a fiend to its own offspring; p. 235 (n.) Like a savage tigress that tossing in the jungle overlays her own cubs, so the sea dashes even the mightiest whales against the rocks; p. 235 (n.) Consider the subtleness of the sea; p. 235 (n.) Consider, once more, the universal cannibalism of the sea; p. 236 (n.) consider them both, the sea and the land; p. 236 (n.) when a stillness almost preternatural spread over the sea; p. 239 (n.) dragged down after him into the profundity of the sea; p. 241 (n.) the Pequod's crew could hardly resist the spell of sleep induced by such a vacant sea; p. 242 (n.) across the wide trance of the sea; p. 242 (n.) lazily undulating in the trough of the sea; p. 244 (n.) dashed the sea-water into it; p. 244 (n.) The slanting sun playing upon this crimson pond in the sea; p. 249 (n.) Though amid all the smoking horror and diabolism of a sea-fight; p. 255 (n.) He [whale] is the great prize ox of the sea; p. 256 (n.) would have almost thought the whole round sea was one huge cheese, and those sharks the maggots in it; p. 257 (n.) they cast long gleams of light over the turbid sea; p. 260 (n.) those New England rocks on the sea-coast; p. 261 (n.) in those shuddering, icy seas of the North; p. 262 (n.) upon the fair face of the pleasant sea; p. 262 (n.) The sea-vultures all in pious mourning; p. 263 (n.) in a discolored, rolling, and oftentimes tumultous and bursting sea; p. 263 (n.) unfolding its noiseless measureless leaves upon the sea; p. 265 (n.) an incorruptible sea and air rolling and flowing between; p. 267 (n.) by one of those occasional caprices of the seas were tumbling; p. 267 (n.) the crazy sea that seemed leagued with him; p. 268 (n.) a broad white shadow rose from the sea; p. 272 (n.) what the devil is ginger?--sea coal; p. 276 (n.) that you meant to give Fedallah a sea-toss; p. 283 (n.) how this mighty monster is actually a diademed king of the sea; p. 238 (n.) was sinking utterly down to the bottom of the sea; p. 296 (n.) They left a great, wide wake, as though continually unrolling a great wide parchment upon the sea; p. 298 (n.) he spasmodically sank in the sea; p. 298 (n.) but the fear of this vast dumb brute of the sea; p. 300 (n.) As the three boats lay there on that gently rolling sea, gazing down into its eternal blue noon; p. 300 (n.) the utmost monster of the seas was writhing and wrenching in agony; p. 300 (n.) Leviathan had run his head under the mountains of the sea; p. 300 (n.) when a dense herd of white bears are scared from it into the sea; p. 304 (n.) was tied to a rock on the sea-coast; p. 305 (n.) Thou art . . . as a dragon of the sea; p. 312 (n.) No roses, no violets, no cologne water in the sea; p. 313 (n.) swimming through the mid-day sea in a calm; p. 314 (n.) solemnly sailing through a calm tropical sea; p. 315 (adj.) from the tails of all other sea creatures; p. 316 (n.) the fancied security of the middle of solitary seas; p. 317 (n.) during a sunrise that crimsoned sky and sea; p. 318 (n.) the thousand islands of that oriental sea are enriched; p. 320 (n.) as she would rise on a high hill of the sea; p. 323 (n.) as we thus tore a white gash in the sea; p. 324 (n.) In this central expanse the sea presented that smooth satin-like surface, called a sleek; p. 326 (n.) Some of the subtlest secrets of the seas seemed divulged to us; p. 332 (n.) after a hard chase of a whale in the northern seas; p. 332 (n.) wherein a gentleman, after in vain trying to bridle his wife's viciousness, had

at last abandoned her upon the seas of life; p. 336 (n.) we were
slowly sailing over a sleepy, vapory, mid-day sea; p. 336 (n.) A
peculiar and not very pleasant smell was smelt in the sea; p. 337 (n.)
by the eddying cloud of vulture sea-fowl that circled; p. 343 (n.)
those whalemen did not then . . . try out their oil at sea; p. 343
(n.) the shortness of the season in those icy seas; p. 346 (n.) Pip
was left behind on the sea, like a hurried traveller's trunk; p. 346
(n.) the spangled sea calm and cool, and flatly stretching away, all
round, to the horizon, like gold-beater's skin hammered out to the
extremest; p. 346 (n.) Bobbing up and down in that sea; p. 347 (n.)
when sailors in a dead calm bathe in the open sea; p. 347 (n.) The
sea had jeeringly kept his finite body up, but drowned the infinite
of his soul; p. 353 (n.) This served for a sea-sofa; p. 353 (n.) as
the wind howled on, and the sea leaped; p. 353 (n.) steadfastly shot
her [the ship] red hell further and further into the blackness of the
sea and the night; p. 354 (n.) for long hours silently guided the way
of this fire-ship on the sea; p. 356 (n.) this way and that in the
midnight sea; p. 364 (n.) from a boat on the open sea; p. 364 (adj.)
too much of a cripple to use their sea bannisters; p. 366 (n.) sending
me to bed, half seas over, about three o'clock in the morning; p. 372
(n.) pursuing their game in those frigid Polar Seas; p. 373 (adj.) a
sea-side glen not very far distant from what our sailors called
Bamboo-Town; p. 378 (n.) only on the profound unbounded sea; p. 381
(n.) there are rocks that shoot two Miles into the Sea; p. 384 (n.)
and all the Isles of the sea combined; p. 384 (n.) He swam the seas
before the continents broke water; p. 387 (adj.) Like all sea-going
ship carpenters; p. 387 (n.) in uncivilized and far-distant seas;
p. 395 (n.) the hollow hull . . . reeled and rolled in the sea like
an air-freighted demijohn; p. 395 (n.) mount his [whale's] dead back
in a rolling sea; p. 396 (n.) and the rolling sea seemed gently
rocking him to his final rest; p. 396 (n.) their own mild,
uncontinented seas, interflow with the blue heaven; p. 396 (n.)
according to the usual sea-custom; p. 399 (n.) one knows not what
sweet mystery about this sea, whose gently awful stirrings seem to
speak of some hidden south beneath; p. 399 (n.) And meet it is, that
over these sea-pastures, wide-rolling watery prairies and Potter's
Fields of all four continents; p. 399 (n.) this serene Pacific . . .
must ever after be the sea of his adoption; p. 400 (n.) with the other
consciously inhaled the salt breath of the new found sea--the sea in
which the hated White Whale must even then be swimming; p. 405 (n.) a
certain filial, confident, land-like feeling towards the sea; p. 406
(n.) gazing far down from his boat's side into that same golden sea;
p. 407 (n.) while cruising in the same seas; p. 408 (n.) the now
useless brick and mortar were being hurled into the sea; p. 409 (n.)
floating in the lovely sunset sea and sky; p. 409 (n.) in these most
candid and impartial seas; p. 409 (n.) somewhere in the heart of
these unverdured seas; pp. 409-10 (n.) Then hail, for ever, hail, O
sea, in whose eternal tossings the wild fowl finds his only rest!
Born of earth, yet suckled by the sea; p. 411 (n.) Thou sea-mark!
thou high and mighty Pilot; p. 413 (adj.) sea-coal ashes . . . sea-
coal, not your common charcoal; p. 413 (n.) When darkness came on,
sky and sea roared and split with the thunder; p. 413 (n.) A great
rolling sea, dashing high up against the reeling ship's high tetering
side, stove in the boat's bottom at the stern, and left it again, all
dripping through like a sieve; p. 413 (n.) but the sea will have its
way; pp. 414-5 (n.) Now, as the lightening rod to a spire on shore is

intended to carry off the perilous fluid into the soil; so the kindred
rod which at sea some ships carry to each mast, is intended to conduct
it into the water; p. 415 (n.) as a swashing sea heaved up under his
own little craft; p. 415 (n.) when most they teter over to a seething
sea; p. 416 (n.) a number of the seamen, arrested by the glare, now
cohered together, and hung pendulous, like a knot of numbed wasps
from a drooping, orchard twig; p. 418 (n.) but the sea that had stove
its bottom had caused the loose leather sheath to drop off; p. 423
(n.) Next morning the not-yet-subsided sea rolled in long slow billows
of mighty bulk, and striving in the Pequod's gurgling track, pushed
her on like giants' palms outspread; p. 423 (n.) The sea was as a
crucible of molten gold, that bubblingly leaps with light and heat;
p. 423 (n.) a tandem, I drive the sea; p. 426 (n.) where the deck . . .
was now almost dripping into the creamy, sidelong-rushing sea; p. 427
(n.) the mad sea parts the log-line; p. 429 (n.) were the voices of
newly drowned men in the sea; p. 429 (n.) a little tossed heap of
white bubbles in the blue of the sea; p. 431 (n.) there are no caps
at sea but snow-caps; p. 436 (n.) now she beat against a head sea;
p. 440 (n.) Ahab gazed abroad upon the sea for miles and miles;
p. 440 (n.) the hoisted sailor should . . . fall all swooping to the
sea; p. 440 (n.) one of those red-billed savage sea-hawks; p. 442 (n.)
The firmaments of air and sea were hardly separable in that all-
pervading azure; p. 442 (n.) the robust and man-like sea heaved with
long, strong, lingering swells, as Samson's chest in his sleep;
p. 442 (n.) these were the strong, troubled, murderous thinkings of
the masculine sea; p. 442 (n.) Aloft, like a royal czar and king, the
sun seemed giving this gentle air to this gold and rolling sea; even
as bride to groom; p. 443 (n.) Ahab dropped a tear into the sea;
p. 445 (n.) lo! that smiling sky, and this unsounded sea; p. 445
(adj.) snuffing up the sea air as a sagacious ship's clog will;
pp. 445-6 (n.) of a long sleek on the sea directly and lengthwise
ahead; p. 446 (n.) at every roll of the sea revealing his high
sparkling hump; p. 447 (n.) sliding along the sea as if an isolated
thing; p. 447 (n.) broken again by the light toes of hundreds of gay
fowl softly feathering the sea; p. 448 (n.) through the serene
tranquillities of the tropical sea; p. 448 (n.) the white sea-fowls
longingly lingered over the agitated pool that he left; p. 448 (n.)
The breeze now freshened; the sea began to swell; p. 448 (n.) Ahab
could perceive no sign in the sea; p. 448 (n.) his vast, shadowed
bulk still half blending with the blue of the sea; p. 449 (n.) so he
fell flat-faced upon the sea; p. 450 (n.) that moment a breaking sea
dashed on him from Moby Dick; p. 454 (n.) the wind and the sea must
be the whaleman's allies; p. 454 (n.) The ship tore on; leaving such
a furrow in the sea; p. 455 (n.) So suddenly seen in the blue plain
of the sea; p. 457 (adj.) like seals from a sea-side cave; p. 459 (n.)
Shall we be dragged by him to the bottom of the sea; p. 461 (n.)
however the baser currents of the sea may turn and tack; p. 463 (n.)
happening to the whale-boats in those swarming seas; p. 465 (n.)
pursuing his own straight path in the sea; pp. 465-6 (n.) the blades
. . . left small splinters in the sea; p. 466 (n.) the White Whale
darted through the weltering sea; p. 466 (adj.) the tremendous rush
of the sea-crashing boat; p. 467 (n.) Slope downwards to thy depths,
O sea, that ere it be for ever too late; p. 467 (n.) forced their
boat through the sledge-hammering seas; p. 468 (n.) rope's heavy end
smiting the sea, disappeared in its depths; p. 469 (n.) the great
shroud of the sea rolled on as it rolled five thousand years ago;
p. 470 (n.) the savage sea-hawks sailed with sheathed beaks.

<u>SEAL</u>. The well-known marine piscivorous animal. (Smyth)

<u>Omoo</u>--p. 10 (v.) go whither she pleased--whaling, sealing; p. 46
(adj.) who always wore a rude seal-skin cap.

<u>Mardi</u>--p. 211 (n.) solitary as a seal on an iceberg; p. 273 (n.) like
seals at the Orkneys; p. 367 (n.) crush the skulls of the peering
seals; p. 418 (n.) seals, grampuses, and whales; p. 467 (adj.) a
seal-skin cap his crown; p. 482 (n.) its prow a seal; p. 543 (n.)
from icy ledges scaring shivering seals; p. 570 (adj.) more active
than any, seal-like.

<u>Redburn</u>--p. 14 (n.) Dripping like a seal; p. 222 (adj.) a small,
glossy head like a seal's.

<u>White-Jacket</u>--p. 16 (n.) voyages to the Shetlands after seal-skins.

<u>Moby-Dick</u>--p. 29 (adj.) presently pulled out . . . a seal-skin wallet
with the hair on; p. 429 (n.) were the resort of great numbers of
seals; p. 429 (n.) most mariners cherish a very superstitious feeling
about seals; p. 429 (n.) In the sea, under certain circumstances,
seals have more than once been mistaken for men; p. 457 (n.) Ahab and
his men struggled out from under it, like seals from a sea-side cave.

<u>SEINE</u>. The name of a large fishing-net. (Smyth)

<u>Mardi</u>--p. 645 (n.) as seines full of mermaids.

<u>SEXTANT</u>. A mathematical instrument for taking altitudes of, and measuring
the angular distance between, the heavenly bodies. (Smyth)

<u>Mardi</u>--p. 19 (n.) thoughts of sextants.

<u>SHAD</u>. The <u>Clupea</u> <u>alosa</u>, a well-known fish, of very disputed culinary
merit, owing perhaps to its own dietetic habits. (Smyth)

<u>Moby-Dick</u>--p. 119 (n.) sharks and shads . . . were still found dividing.

<u>SHALLOP</u>. A small light fishing vessel, with only a small mainmast and
foremast for lug-sails. They are commonly good sailers, and are
therefore often used as tenders to men-of-war. Also, a small boat rowed
by one or two men. (Smyth)

<u>Typee</u>--p. 13 (n.) the projecting outriggers of their slight shallops.

<u>Omoo</u>--p. 153 (n.) more than twenty shallops towing astern.

<u>Mardi</u>--p. 162 (n.) the light shallop darted in among them; p. 166 (n.)
I pushed my shallop from its golden beach; p. 200 (n.) barges and
shallops had touched there; p. 215 (adj.) The third sat in the
shallop's stern; p. 267 (n.) pointing out a shallop gliding near;
p. 302 (n.) occupancy of the rest of the shallops; p. 364 (n.) we

were overtaken by a shallop; p. 365 (n.) Their shallop glided near;
p. 568 (n.) two figures in a shallop, were espied; p. 568 (n.) quickly
vanished the shallop; p. 638 (n.) Our shallops now refitted; p. 644
(n.) For many shallops . . . were oft dashed to pieces; p. 649 (n.)
hands placed me in a shallop; p. 649 (n.) as the shallop fled one way;
p. 654 (n.) headlong dashed a shallop.

Moby-Dick--p. 462 (adj.) as standing in his shallop's stern.

SHARK. A name applied to many species of large cartilaginous fish of the
family Squalidae. Their ferocity and voracity are proverbial. (Smyth)

Typee--p. 10 (n.) and nearer at hand the prowling shark; p. 22 (n.)
Three pet sharks followed in her wake; p. 122 (adj.) The implement
they usually employ is a shark's tooth; p. 167 (adj.) Their heads
were covered with shark skins; p. 217 (adj.) stick, pointed with a
shark's tooth.

Omoo--p. 11 (adj.) teeth, looked absolutely sharkish when he laughed;
p. 27 (n.) the taper figure of a blue shark; p. 27 (n.) but the blue
shark was a mark indelible; p. 32 (n.) The blue shark, and a sort of
Urim and Thummim; p. 32 (adj.) Tapping, tapping, tapping/ The shark
teeth; p. 45 (n.) we had tossed a shipmate to the sharks; p. 55 (n.)
A shark steak, and be hanged to you; p. 216 (n.) being two sharks
with the talons of hawks.

Mardi--p. 23 (n.) talking about sharks; p. 25 (n.) where prowling
sharks come not; p. 40 (n.) calls it a Bone Shark; p. 40 (n.) for the
sharks; p. 40 (n.) there are more sharks in the sea; p. 40 (n.) in
Christening the sharks; p. 40 (n.) the ordinary Brown Shark; p. 40
(n.) the dandy Blue Shark; p. 40 (n.) savage swagger of the Tiger
Shark; p. 40 (n.) shoals of Tiger Sharks; p. 40 (n.) as a shark;
p. 40 (n.) that sharks are lovable; p. 41 (n.) by two of these
aforesaid Tiger Sharks; p. 41 (n.) of all sharks; p. 41 (n.) from the
ghastly White Shark; p. 41 (n.) with a White Shark; p. 41 (n.) the
White Shark sent many a thrill; p. 42 (n.) we encountered Killers and
Thrashers; p. 42 (n.) the Killers seizing; p. 42 (n.) the Thrashers
fastening; p. 49 (n.) for prowling sharks; p. 53 (n.) My Lord Shark
and his Pages; p. 53 (n.) It is the Shovel-nosed Shark; p. 53 (n.) as
scouts to the shark; p. 54 (n.) pointed out an immense Shovel-nosed
Shark; p. 54 (n.) right under the shark; p. 54 (n.) clinging to the
back of the shark; p. 54 (n.) The shark swam sluggishly; p. 54 (n.)
retreated toward the shark; p. 94 (n.) and was eaten up by a shark;
p. 105 (n.) at the mercy of any caitiff shark; p. 105 (n.) with shark-
hook and line; p. 121 (n.) the tracks of sharks were denoted; p. 123
(n.) as true of divers species of sharks; p. 128 (n.) terminating in
rude shark-tails; p. 199 (adj.) in a large, open, shark's mouth;
p. 199 (adj.) just under the shark's mouth; p. 200 (n.) in the high,
open shark's-mouth; p. 214 (n.) As the upright fin of the rushing
shark; p. 217 (adj.) with sonorous Vee-Vee in the shark's mouth;
p. 275 (n.) strong as the back bone of the shark; p. 288 (n.) humanize
the sharks; p. 289 (n.) one whit better than tiger-sharks; p. 289 (n.)
So, also, the sharks; p. 294 (n.) perceived a Devil-shark, so called;
p. 294 (n.) the shark, undaunted, advanced; p. 300 (adj.) beating
shark-skin drums; p. 312 (adj.) suspended from the shark's mouth;

p. 326 (adj.) to descend from the shark's mouth; p. 334 (adj.) the
bites of the ravenous sharks; p. 334 (n.) by three sharks drawing
near; p. 353 (n.) with dried slips of consecrated shark-skin; p. 380
(n.) Skeleton of an immense Tiger-shark; p. 380 (adj.) basket-hilted
with shark's jaws; p. 424 (adj.) to his crow's nest in the shark's
mouth; p. 437 (n.) buried erewhile in the head of the shark; p. 469
(n.) that all . . . prowling sharks were invaders; p. 475 (adj.) and
Vee-Vee in the shark's mouth; p. 476 (adj.) and from his dyed shark-
skin girdle; p. 482 (n.) crusading centaurs, crocodiles, and sharks;
p. 517 (n.) when we shall have the shark in our midst; p. 537 (n.) if
a prowling shark touches one member; p. 551 (n.) dolphins fly before
the sable sharks; p. 558 (adj.) from his shark's-mouth prayed little
Vee-Vee; p. 564 (n.) didst ever hear of the Shark-Syllogism; p. 564
(n.) A shark seized a swimmer by the leg; p. 564 (n.) well knowing
that sharks seldom were magnanimous; p. 601 (n.) some she-shark must
have been his dam; p. 641 (n.) three ravenous sharks astern.

Redburn--p. 41 (n.) one of the vertibrae bones of a shark; p. 103 (n.)
a playhouse for the sharks; p. 104 (n.) when some shark gulps you
down; p. 112 (n.) toss him overboard as a tit-bit for John Shark;
p. 138 (n.) most abounds in all the variety of land-sharks; p. 244
(n.) precisely like a phosphorescent shark; p. 300 (n.) hull which,
like a shark, showed tiers of teeth.

White-Jacket--p. 171 (n.) among seven hundred and seventy-five
thousand white sharks; p. 177 (n.) no shark-boat whatever is allowed
to approach; p. 187 (n.) like a disarmed sword-fish among ferocious
white-sharks; p. 295 (n.) mouth-yawning sharks swam in and out;
p. 377 (n.) with the snake, the shark, and the worm; p. 394 (n.) See
that white shark; p. 396 (n.) our last man tossed to the sharks.

Moby-Dick--p. 7 (n.) voracious enemies,/ Whales, sharks, and monsters,
arm'd in front or jaw; p. 65 (n.) Hosea Hussey had his account books
bound in superior old shark-skin; p. 69 (n.) thou dost not talk shark
a bit; p. 85 (n./adj.) Pious harpooneers never make good voyagers--it
takes the shark out of 'em; no harpooneer is worth a straw who aint
pretty sharkish; p. 100 (adj.) they, in heathenish sharked waters;
p. 112 (n.) their dreams would have been of the crunching teeth of
sharks; p. 119 (n.) sharks and shad . . . were still found dividing;
p. 125 (n.) For we are all killers, on land and on sea; Bonapartes
and Sharks included; p. 126 (n.) Provoke him, and he will buckle to a
shark; p. 148 (adj.) Whelped somewhere by the sharkish sea; p. 164
(n.) Witness . . . the white shark of the tropics; p. 164 (n.) us the
white-shrouded bear or shark; p. 164 (n.) in allusion to the white,
silent stillness of death in this shark; p. 193 (n.) Only the infidel
sharks in the audacious seas may give ear to such words; p. 235 (n.)
The accursed shark alone can in any generic respect be said to bear
comparative analogy to him; p. 235 (n.) as the dainty embellished
shape of many species of sharks; p. 249 (n.) thousands on thousands
of sharks, swarming round the dead leviathan; p. 249 (n.) sharks will
be seen longingly gazing up to the ship's decks; p. 249 (adj.) a
shocking sharkish business enough for all parties; p. 249 (n.) though
sharks also are the invariable outriders of all slave ships; p. 254
(n.) I'm bressed if he aint more of shark than Massa Shark hisself;
p. 256 (n.) and those sharks the maggots in it; p. 256 (n.) torn and
splashed by the insatiate sharks; p. 262 (n.) the air-sharks all

punctiliously in black or speckled; p. 271 (n.) the sharks now freshly
and more keenly allured; p. 271 (n.) the otherwise miscellaneously
carnivorous shark will seldom touch a man; p. 272 (n.) to the maw of
what seemed a peculiarly ferocious shark; p. 388 (adj.) A sailor takes
a fancy to wear shark-bone ear-rings; p. 396 (n.) tossed like something
vile to the death-devouring sharks; p. 402 (adj.) swathed in a
bristling shark-skin apron; p. 406 (n.) Tell me not of thy teeth-tiered
sharks; p. 410 (n.) sat watching the sharks, that spectrally played
round the whale; p. 416 (adj.) The parted mouth of Tashtego revealed
his shark-white teeth; p. 442 (n.) in the bottomless blue, rushed . . .
sharks; p. 449 (n.) the whale obliquely lying on his back, in the
manner of a biting shark; p. 456 (n.) a sight more savage than the
embattled teeth of sharks; p. 457 (n.) twitching his legs upwards to
escape the dreaded jaws of sharks; p. 463 (n.) numbers of sharks,
seemingly rising from out the dark waters beneath the hull, maliciously
snapped at the blades of the oars; p. 463 (n.) the sharks . . .
apparently following them in the same prescient way that vultures hover
over the banners of marching regiments; p. 463 (n.) therefore their
flesh more musky to the senses of the sharks; p. 465 (n.) the unpitying
sharks accompanied him; p. 466 (adj.) Pull on! 'tis the better rest,
the shark's jaw than the yielding water; p. 470 (n.) The unharming
sharks, they glided by as if with padlocks on their mouths.

SHEER. The act of deviating from the line of the course, so as to form a
crooked and irregular path through the water; this may be occasioned by
the ship's being difficult to steer, but more frequently arises from the
negligence or incapacity of the helmsman. (Smyth)

Omoo--p. 72 (v.) The men sheered off.

SHEET. A rope used in setting a sail, to keep the clew down to its place.
With square sails, they haul the boom over one way and another. They
keep down the inner clew of a studding sail and the after clew of a jib.
Sheet anchor, a vessel's largest anchor; not carried at the bow. (Dana)

Typee--p. 7 (n.) In the stern sheets reclined Mowanna; p. 36 (n.) the
rest of the watch in the stern sheets.

Omoo--p. 69 (n.) he spread out in the stern-sheets; p. 90 (n.) the
jib-sheets lashed the stays.

Mardi--p. 70 (n.) hauled aft the sheet; p. 71 (n.) she strained away
at the sheets; p. 619 (n.) with a viper in our winding-sheets.

White-Jacket--p. 7 (n.) till every sheet was distended; p. 9 (n.)
there are Sheet-Anchor-men--old veterans all; p. 10 (n.) These haul
aft the fore and main-sheets; p. 17 (n.) cried a growling old sheet-
anchor-man; p. 47 (n.) the old sheet-anchor-men, who spent their time;
p. 54 (n.) roared an old sheet-anchor-man; p. 72 (n.) cried Scrimmage,
a sheet-anchor-man; p. 72 (n.) cried the sheet-anchor-man; p. 72 (n.)
large anchors in her fore-chains, called Sheet-anchors; p. 72 (n.)
the old seamen . . . are called Sheet-anchor-men; p. 73 (n.) cried
Scrimmage, the sheet-anchor-man; p. 86 (n.) One rheumatic old sheet-
anchor-man . . . was driven; p. 90 (n.) inquired an Irish waister of

an old Spanish sheet-anchor-man; p. 157 (n.) a sheet-anchor-man . . .
once touched his hat; p. 169 (n.) from Broadbit, a sheet-anchor-man;
p. 180 (n.) A knowing old sheet-anchor-man; p. 180 (adj.) but the
sheet-anchor-man's integrity is like a rock; p. 180 (n.) the sheet-
anchor-man goes to his confidants; p. 199 (n.) pedestal of the main-
top-sail sheet-bitts; p. 202 (n.) you venerable sheet-anchor-men;
pp. 202-3 (n.) cried an old sheet-anchor-man; p. 239 (n.) when an old
sheet-anchor-man, standing by; p. 306 (n.) the ramblings of some old
sheet-anchor-man; p. 311 (n.) Tawney, a sheet-anchor-man; p. 324 (n.)
He was a sheet-anchor-man; p. 353 (n.) ancient companions--the old
sheet-anchor-men around him; p. 357 (n.) Where are you, sheet-anchor-
men; p. 366 (n.) hoarsely whispered an old sheet-anchor-man; p. 388
(n.) cried a sheet-anchor-man.

Moby-Dick--p. 60 (n.) The prodigious strain upon the main-sail had
parted the weather-sheet; pp. 193-4 (n.) still further aft the sheet
of his sail; p. 448 (n.) the sheets of their sails adrift.

SHELL. The hard calcareous external covering of the mollusca, crustacea,
and echinoderms. Shell-fish, a general term applied to aquatic animals
having a hard external covering or shell, as whelks, oysters, lobsters,
&c. These are not, however, properly speaking, fish. (Smyth)

Typee--p. 15 (n.) from a little round shell that passed; p. 110 (n.)
in a little net a species of diminutive shell-fish; p. 110 (n.)
resembling goblets made of tortoiseshell; p. 115 (n.) by means of a
piece of mother-of-pearl shell; p. 116 (n.) sharp teeth of the mother-
of-pearl shell; p. 150 (n.) with pointed bits of shell or flint;
p. 151 (n.) using a piece of mussel-shell for tweezers; p. 172 (n.) a
number of sparkling sea-shells; p. 172 (n.) a belt of the same shells
ram all round it; p. 233 (n.) filled with oval bits of mother-of-pearl
shell.

Omoo--p. 32 (n.) By sound of conch-shell it was proclaimed; p. 63
(adj.) visited by the pearl-shell fisherman; p. 63 (n.) fifty thousand
dollars' worth of shells; p. 116 (n.) a beach of small, sparkling
shells; p. 152 (n.) I was a virtuoso in shells and curiosities;
p. 153 (n.) a heap of yellow bananas and cowree shells; p. 255 (n.) A
fine walk along a beach of shells.

Mardi--p. 8 (n.) a beach of shells; p. 58 (n.) were pearl oyster
shells; p. 68 (adj.) at the Pearl Shell Islands; p. 69 (n.) where the
shells they sought; p. 77 (n.) a flinty, serrated shell; p. 81 (adj.)
at the Pearl Shell islands; p. 82 (adj.) The Pearl Shell Islands
excepted; p. 83 (adj.) craft in shell armor; p. 95 (n.) feloniously
abstracted from the shells; p. 96 (n.) a considerable quantity of
pearl shells; p. 103 (adj.) Ever since leaving the Pearl Shell Islands;
p. 119 (n.) with the pearl shells on board; p. 120 (n.) afloat in our
shell; p. 137 (n.) fell into the opening valve of a shell; p. 153 (n.)
like the lips of a shell; p. 156 (n.) he came to her with a shell;
p. 156 (n.) which in that little shell; p. 156 (n.) Yillah, the bird,
and the shell were inseparable; p. 164 (n.) the blast of numerous
conch shells; p. 192 (n.) left behind bones mixed with shells; p. 199
(n.) of rich spotted Leopard and Tiger-shells; p. 200 (n.) cowrie
shells jingling at its ears; p. 200 (n.) a red conch-shell; p. 201

(n.) string of small, close-fitting, concave shells; p. 280 (n.) true
pearl shells rang musically; p. 283 (n.) embark thereon in nautilus
shells; p. 295 (n.) semi-transparent cup of cocoa-nut shell; p. 300
(n.) castanets of pearl shells; p. 300 (n.) and cutting themselves
with shells; p. 301 (n.) scratched themselves with their shells;
p. 346 (n.) holding pearl-shells on their heads; p. 359 (n.) with
pearl-shells suspended by cords; p. 360 (n.) and its pearl-shells
jingled; p. 380 (adj.) bones of a Pearl-shell-diver's leg; p. 380 (n.)
Stork's Leg, supporting a nautilus shell; p. 403 (n.) adjusting her
necklace of cowrie shells; p. 436 (n.) Barbed with sharp pearl shells;
p. 458 (n.) when you strike a pearlshell; p. 466 (n.) for one
thousand conch shells to be blown; p. 482 (n.) scupllture--shell-work,
medallions, masques; p. 509 (n.) long, white reef, sparkling with
shells; p. 509 (n.) Her sweet, sweet mouth!/ The peach-pearl shell;
p. 510 (n.) A shell! a shell!/ A vocal shell; p. 573 (n.) served in
great clam-shells; p. 623 (n.) where innumerable shells were gently
rolling; p. 647 (n.) to me, a nautilus shell.

Redburn--p. 27 (adj.) I took out an old tortoise-shell snuff-box.

White-Jacket--p. 46 (n.) a conch-shell might stand on your mantel;
p. 153 (n.) closely adhering, like a California-shell; p. 159 (n.) to
resemble his lordship's conch-shell; p. 294 (n.) you turn a dumb
diver after pearl-shells.

Moby-Dick--p. 50 (n.) his ears, like two sea-shells, still
multitudinously murmuring of the ocean; p. 447 (n.) Like noiseless
nautilus shells, their light prows sped through.

SHIP. Any craft intended for the purposes of navigation; but in a
nautical sense it is a general term for all large square-rigged vessels
carrying three masts and a bowsprit.--Line-of-battleship, one carrying
upwards of 74 guns.--Ship of war, one which, being duly commissioned,
wears a pendant. Merchant ship, a vessel employed in commerce to carry
commodities of various sorts from one port to another.--To ship, to
embark men or merchandise.--To ship a sea, a wave breaking over all in a
gale. Ship-mate, a term once dearer than brother, but the habit of short
cruises is weakening it. (Smyth)

Typee--p. xiii (n.) warmest sympathies of the author's shipmates;
p. 4 (n.) will never point the ship for the land; p. 4 (n.) The old
ship herself longs to look out upon; p. 4 (n.) Poor old ship; p. 5
(n.) Poor old ship; p. 7 (n.) as the flag-ship of the American
squadron; p. 8 (adj.) The ship's company crowding into the gangway;
p. 9 (n.) and then the good ship and the steady gale did the rest;
p. 11 (n.) being the only one at which ships are much in the habit of
touching; p. 11 (n.) Captain Porter refitted his ships; pp. 12-3 (n.)
proferred his services to pilot the ship; p. 13 (n.) we swept by the
ships of the squadron; p. 13 (n.) he had deserted his ship; p. 13 (n.)
these cocoa nuts were all steadily approaching towards the ship;
p. 14 (adj.) succeeded in getting up the ship's side; p. 15 (n.) The
ship taken, we could not do otherwise; p. 15 (n.) Our ship was now
wholly given up; p. 20 (n.) Our ship had not been many days in the
harbor; p. 20 (adj.) I signed as a matter of course the ship's
articles; pp. 20-1 (n.) violated on the part of the ship in which I

served; p. 22 (adj.) consumed in due course by the ship's company;
p. 22 (n.) a ship unlucky in falling in with whales; p. 22 (n.) for
their sake to bring back the ship; p. 24 (n.) Viewed from our ship as
she lay at anchor; p. 25 (adj.) recount in pantomime to our ship's
company; p. 25 (n.) the canoe paddled on and the ship followed; p. 28
(adj.) by water in the ship's boat; p. 30 (n.) brought back
ignominiously to the ship; p. 31 (n.) until the sailing of the ship;
p. 31 (n.) my design . . . to any of my shipmates; p. 31 (adj.) I
perceived one of the ship's company leaning; p. 32 (n.) in them my
big-hearted shipmate vented the bile; p. 32 (n.) he entertained a
cordial detestation of the ship; p. 33 (n.) the only individual on
board the ship; p. 33 (n.) is he not the very one of all my shipmates;
p. 33 (n.) Seen from the ship, their summits appeared; p. 33 (n.)
observed its bearings and locality from the ship; p. 34 (n.) only
three of them ever got back to the ship again; p. 35 (n.) and all
back to the ship again before sunset; p. 35 (adj.) the confusion
which always reigns among a ship's company; p. 35 (n.) when our
shipmates wondered at this; p. 36 (n.) thus on our guard with our own
shipmates; p. 36 (adj.) Go by the name of midshipmen's nuts; p. 36
(v.) while the poor larboarders shipped their oars; p. 36 (n.) shortly
after our leaving the ship; p. 41 (n.) would be certain to convey us
back to the ship; p. 42 (n.) of the various articles we had brought
from the ship; p. 43 (adj.) not descending into the bay until the
ship's departure; p. 44 (n.) it looks blacker than our ship's hold;
p. 45 (n.) let us 'bout ship and steer in some other direction; p. 46
(n.) Then, shipmate, my toplights have gone out; p. 56 (n.) as steep
as the sides of a line-of-battle ship; p. 57 (n.) Ah, shipmate; p. 60
(n.) No, shipmate, on the contrary; p. 74 (n.) ships never enter this
bay; p. 74 (v.) with their oars shipped; p. 134 (v.) was never shipped
aboard of any craft; p. 134 (n.) Out of the calico I had brought from
the ship; p. 145 (n.) I had worn, when I quitted the ship; p. 170
(adj.) to spin tough yarns on a ship's forecastle; p. 183 (n.) made
toward the ships by swimming; p. 183 (n.) whose eyes were fixed on
the ship; p. 184 (n.) the chaplain of the U.S. ship Vincennes; p. 192
(n.) the disease introduced among them by De Bougainville's ships;
p. 205 (adj.) the crew of vessels shipwrecked on some barbarous coast;
p. 211 (n.) might have escaped from one of the ships at Nukuheva;
p. 229 (adj.) coiled away like a rope on a ship's deck; p. 234 (adj.)
a strip of ship's copper nailed against an upright post; p. 249 (n.)
the Reine Blanche--the French flag-ship; p. 252 (adj.) in order to
recruit his ship's company; p. 252 (n.) while the ship lay "off and
on" awaiting its return; p. 256 (adj.) which had rendered him the
idol of his ship's company; p. 263 (n.) coming off in his canoe to
the ships in the bay; p. 264 (n.) about our having run away from the
ship; p. 264 (n.) engage fruit for ships lying in Nukuheva; p. 265
(n.) there was a ship in want of men; p. 269 (n.) "If I get you off
to a ship," said he; p. 270 (n.) and paddled off to a whale ship;
p. 270 (v.) However, he agreed to ship him; p. 270 (adj.) Jimmy and
the Typee started in two of the ship's boats; p. 271 (n.) and the
ship fast leaving the land.

Omoo--p. xiii (n.) among the crews of ships in the Pacific; p. 3 (n.)
the ship appeared in the distance; p. 6 (n.) at which place touched
the ship; p. 6 (v.) I was asked whether I desired to ship; p. 6 (v.)
In this way men are frequently shipped on board; p. 6 (adj.) the
ship's articles handed me to sign; p. 7 (n.) Safe aboard of a ship;

p. 7 (n.) the wild noise and motion of a ship at sea; p. 7 (n.) is a matter all ship-owners must settle; p. 7 (adv.) My crib . . . was placid athwartships; p. 8 (n.) "Here shipmate," said I; p. 8 (n.) the natives who had brought me to the ship; p. 8 (n.) and every thing respecting the ship; p. 10 (adj.) the ship's company, all told, numbered; p. 12 (n.) as assistant-surgeon of an emigrant ship; p. 13 (adj.) having sent in a written resignation as the ship's doctor; p. 14 (n.) Hong merchants never had the shipping of it; p. 14 (n.) willing to keep the sea with his ship; p. 15 (n.) there was nothing for the ship; p. 16 (n.) I had scarcely been aboard of the ship; p. 16 (adj.) He was the ship's carpenter; p. 16 (n.) the latter was the only man in the ship; p. 17 (adj.) ever dreams of entering a ship's forecastle; p. 18 (n.) he might look out for his ship himself; p. 20 (n.) to put our ship under a rigorous Taboo; p. 23 (n.) Captain Guy caused the ship to be got under way; p. 23 (v.) desirous of shipping aboard of one of their own country vessels; p. 24 (adj.) looked somewhat strange in a ship's forecastle; p. 25 (n.) the boat returned to the ship; p. 27 (adj.) purpose of pulling the ship's head round; p. 29 (n.) between our new shipmate and his countrymen; p. 29 (n.) The ship was plunging hard; p. 33 (n.) and the ship heading right out; p. 34 (n.) nothing to do but steer the ship; p. 34 (n.) We saw no ships, expected to see none; p. 35 (n.) as if from a plague-ship; p. 35 (n.) by exploring ships and adventurous whalers; p. 35 (n.) of a ship like ours penetrating into these regions; p. 35 (n.) I had heard of ships striking at midnight; p. 35 (n.) entertained by my reckless shipmates; p. 35 (adj.) never revealed to us the ship's place at noon; p. 38 (adj.) Most persons know that a ship's forecastle; p. 38 (n.) in the very eyes of the ship; p. 38 (n.) when the ship rolled; p. 39 (n.) the ship was in a most dilapidated condition; p. 39 (n.) enough will survive to repeople the ship; p. 42 (n.) their shipmates often amused themselves; p. 42 (n.) with the uniform motion of the ship; p. 45 (adj.) the ship's headway was then stopped; p. 45 (n.) and the ship glided on; p. 45 (n.) we had tossed a shipmate to the sharks; p. 46 (n.) in tacking ship, voices called aloud; p. 46 (n.) his shipmate swore that a wet hammock; p. 46 (n.) of our number would remain aboard the ship; p. 47 (adj.) always kept the ship's reckoning; p. 49 (n.) they made a practice of coming round ships; p. 50 (adj.) water from the ship's coppers; p. 50 (n.) consarning the ship; p. 50 (n.) to run off with the ship; p. 51 (n.) bound to navigate the ship; p. 51 (adj.) the ship's head should be pointed for the island; p. 51 (v.) The men were shipped "by the lay"; p. 52 (n.) who had joined the ship as a landsman; p. 52 (n.) one day when the ship was pitching; p. 52 (adj.) a ship's company is by no means disposed; p. 54 (v.) he shipped as landsman; p. 59 (n.) the ship rushed by; p. 59 (v.) now and then shipped green glassy waves; p. 59 (n.) fairly deluged that part of the ship; p. 64 (n.) To return to the ship; p. 68 (n.) should the captain leave the ship; p. 68 (n.) at the other end of the ship; p. 69 (n.) Several ships were descried; p. 69 (n.) to keep the ship at sea; p. 70 (n.) the ship was completely in our power; p. 70 (n.) the ship would eventually be brought; p. 70 (n.) keep the ship at a safe distance from the land; p. 70 (n.) Guy's thus leaving the ship in the men's hands; p. 71 (n.) against his being left in charge of the ship; p. 71 (v.) shipping at the Bay of Islands; p. 73 (n.) returned to the ship; p. 74 (v.) shipped under a feigned cognomen; p. 75 (n.) Mr. Jermin, tack ship; p. 76 (adj.) the ship's head soon pointed out to sea; p. 76 (n.) with which he inveighed

against the ship; p. 76 (n.) the ship must let go her anchor; p. 76
(adj.) tin case containing the ship's papers; p. 76 (adj.) sung out
for the ship's company; p. 79 (adj.) a list of the ship's company;
p. 79 (n.) and so get rid of the ship; p. 81 (v.) I shipped at the
islands; p. 81 (n.) this ship has been placed in my hands; p. 81 (v.)
ship now and then; p. 82 (n.) necessity for taking the ship in; p. 83
necessity for taking the ship in; p. 83 (n.) were to remain in the
ship; p. 83 (n.) to have the ship snugly anchored; p. 84 (n.) I
thought the ship would be seized; p. 84 (n.) happy in the affection
ot his shipmates; p. 87 (n.) if we only stuck to the ship; p. 88 (n.)
in that part of the ship; p. 88 (n.) with the present safety of the
ship; p. 89 (adj.) rising and falling with the ship's motion; p. 89
(adj.) bringing the ship's head to the wind; p. 90 (n.) 'bout ship!
'bout ship; p. 90 (n.) throwing the ship full into the wind; p. 94
(n.) that the ship, after all, would be obliged; p. 95 (n.) an old
shipmate of Jermin's; p. 96 (n.) hearing of his lost shipmates;
p. 96 (n.) promising his old shipmate; p. 97 (n.) the ship--now
standing off shore; p. 97 (n.) to take the ship into port; p. 97 (n.)
refused to assist in working the ship; p. 97 (n.) the ship in the
hands of four or five men; p. 98 (n.) we were now to tack ship; p. 98
(n.) by which ships enter; p. 98 (n.) ships now and then grate their
keels; p. 99 (n.) As we held on toward the frigate and shipping;
p. 99 (n.) produced peals of laughter from the ship; p. 100 (n.) that
the ship was his; p. 100 (n.) for every ship brought in; p. 101 (n.)
the condemned hull of a large ship; p. 102 (n.) to go over this poor
old ship; p. 102 (n.) with nobody to work the ship; p. 102 (n.) you
wished the ship in; p. 103 (n.) my time aboard the ship had expired;
p. 103 (n.) according to our most experienced shipmates; p. 103 (n.)
in one of her majesty's ships; p. 103 (n.) Armed ships allow nothing
superfluous; p. 104 (n.) Shoving clear from the ship; p. 105 (n.) a
meek little midshipman was called; p. 105 (adj.) for one of the ship's
corporals; p. 106 (n.) down comes a midshipman; p. 107 (n.) on board
a line-of-battle ship; p. 108 (n.) In an American or English ship;
pp. 108-9 (n.) on board his own ship; p. 109 (n.) how few ships have
they ever carried; p. 109 (n.) The best of shipwrights; p. 109 (n.)
She was a new ship; p. 109 (n.) to be seen in a fine fighting-ship;
p. 110 (n.) to some less fortunate shipmate; p. 111 (n.) they are not
building their ships; p. 113 (n.) resolution with respect to the ship;
p. 119 (n.) [food] come ship by by; p. 120 (n.) Being extravagantly
fond of ship-biscuit; p. 121 (n.) express the juice to sell to the
shipping; p. 128 (n.) no ship would receive him as a sailor; p. 129
swam round the ships of Wallis; p. 132 (n.) the demands of the
shipping exhaust the uncultivated resources; p. 132 (n.) to bring him
some from the ship; p. 133 (n.) which, on board the ship, he told us
was not needed; p. 134 (adj.) This sudden change from ship fare to
shore living; p. 139 (n.) intended soon to go aboard his ship; p. 139
(adj.) had turned ship's evidence; p. 139 (adj.) solemnly drew forth
the ship's articles; p. 139 (adj.) pointing to the marks of the ship's
company; p. 140 (n.) The ship was the means of my deliverance; p. 142
(n.) In most of my shipmates; p. 143 (n.) unless to go aboard the
ship; p. 143 (n.) they had taken him on board the ship; p. 146 (adj.)
the ship's ensign flying in the boat's stern; p. 147 (adj.) providing
herself with a huge ship's lantern; p. 147 (n.) for the purpose of
shipping a new crew; p. 147 (v.) no member was allowed to ship on
board; p. 148 (n.) Anxious to pack the ship off as soon as possible;
p. 148 (n.) as the best and fastest of ships; p. 148 (adj.) what was

wanting for the ship's larder; p. 148 (n.) with respect to the ship;
p. 148 (v.) by every sailor shipping at Tahiti; p. 148 (v.) the men
. . . will only ship for one cruise; p. 149 (n.) Ah--my boy--shippy
you, harree--maky sail; p. 149 (n.) Soon the ship drew near the reef;
p. 150 (n.) The ship out of the way; p. 152 (n.) seldom visited by
shipping; p. 158 (n.) including the officers of several ships; p. 159
(n.) We Levy Contributions on the Shipping; p. 159 (v.) and offer to
ship; p. 159 (n.) that the whaling-ships . . . began to arrive;
p. 160 (n.) a sly, nocturnal visit aboard his ship; p. 161 (n.) the
ship was at hand; p. 163 (n.) by captains of British armed ships;
p. 163 (n.) the missionaries of the good ship Duff; p. 164 (n.) who
board the shipping for their washing; p. 173 (n.) Beretanee ships of
thunder come; p. 173 (n.) many whale-ships here now; p. 185 (n.) from
the frequent visits of ships-of-war; p. 197 (n.) the arrival of ships
was growing less frequent; p. 198 (n.) no getting away in a ship;
p. 199 (v.) we shipped the oars; p. 202 (n.) among the shipping
touching at Papeetee; p. 202 (n.) deserted from a ship; p. 210 (n.)
Lord Byron's Voyage of H.B.M. Ship Blonde; p. 215 (n.) The ship
belonged to Nantucket; p. 226 (n.) with an order from a ship lying
there; p. 249 (n.) for the apprehension of deserters from ships;
p. 270 (n.) for the purpose of watering his ship; p. 278 (n.) that
the ship lying in the harbor was the reason; p. 285 (n.) Put ashore
from his ship; p. 286 (n.) in the very next ship that touched at the
harbor; p. 288 (n.) we sallied out on an excursion to the ship;
p. 288 (adj.) He turned out to be a runaway ship's carpenter; p. 289
(n.) the break in the reef by which ships enter; p. 289 (n.) lay the
good ship Leviathan; p. 289 (v.) to learn whether we wanted to ship;
p. 289 (adj.) where the rest of the ship's company were; p. 289 (n.)
And it's shipping yer after, my jewels; p. 290 (v.) listening to more
inducements to ship; p. 290 (n.) as it does in some of your dandy
ships; p. 290 (n.) convinced that the good ship never deserved;
p. 291 (v.) they had, six months before, shipped for a single cruise;
p. 299 (n.) when no ships were in Taloo; p. 299 (n.) a ship is descried
coming into the bay; p. 306 (n.) belonging to the officers of ships;
p. 307 (n.) he afterward ran away from the ship; p. 312 (n.) The
account he gave us of the ship; p. 313 (n.) was a luckless ship in
the fishery; p. 313 (n.) Thither the ship was bound; p. 313 (n.) the
first time we visited the ship; p. 313 (n.) Is there a mutiny on
board a ship; p. 314 (adj.) I would find the ship's articles; p. 314
(n.) upon my going to sea in the ship; p. 315 (n.) I paddled off to
the ship; p. 315 (v.) by shipping several islanders; p. 315 (n.)
paddle me off to the ship; p. 316 (n.) ordered the ship unmoored.

Mardi--p. 3 (n.) Ship bound to the northeast; p. 4 (n.) we felt the
ship strike; p. 4 (n.) against that rare old ship; p. 4 (v.) we had
shipped; p. 5 (n.) these shipmates of mine; p. 5 (n.) on ship-board;
p. 5 (adj.) to the ship's dull roll; p. 6 (v.) I shipped; p. 6 (n.)
the ship is hungry; p. 6 (v.) I did not ship; p. 6 (n.) till this
ship is full; p. 7 (n.) Leave the ship; p. 7 (n.) Leave the ship;
p. 7 (n.) of the dull, plodding ship; p. 9 (n.) impatience of the
ship; p. 10 (n.) to navigate the ship; p. 10 (n.) taken the ship to
wife; p. 11 (n.) to outlive great ships; p. 12 (adj.) one of the
ship's boats; p. 14 (n.) his shipmate; p. 14 (n.) No school like a
ship; p. 14 (n.) thus aboard of all ships; p. 14 (n.) never did
shipmate of mine; p. 15 (n.) It is a Fidus-Achates-ship; p. 16 (n.)
to quit the ship; p. 17 (n.) stick to the ship; p. 19 (adj.) fixed to

the ship's sides; p. 19 (adj.) secured to the ship's bulwarks; p. 19
(adj.) above the ship's rail; p. 20 (adj.) our ship's company; p. 20
(adj.) of the ship's company; p. 20 (adj.) in a ship's hold; p. 22
(n.) withdrawing from the ship; p. 22 (adj.) pulled the midship oar;
p. 23 (n.) in some ships; p. 24 (n.) old ship; p. 24 (n.) of missing
ships; p. 25 (n.) sleep my shipmates; p. 25 (n.) the fate of my
shipmates; p. 25 (adj.) of that old ship's end; p. 27 (adj.) which
hung from the ship's lee side; p. 27 (n.) astern of the ship; p. 27
(adj.) diminished the ship's headway; p. 27 (n.) while the ship yet
clove; p. 27 (n.) quitted the ship; p. 28 (n.) the ship dimly showing;
p. 28 (n.) from the ship; p. 29 (n.) it was the ship; p. 29 (n.) of
returning to the ship; p. 30 (n.) the ship left miles astern; p. 30
(n.) to be towed to the ship; p. 32 (adv.) we lashed firmly amidships;
p. 32 (n.) previous to leaving the ship; p. 32 (n.) were on ship-
board; p. 33 (adj.) when suspended to the ship's side; p. 33 (n.) is
kept on shipboard; p. 33 (n.) prolonged absence from the ship; p. 35
(n.) sheer-plank of ship; p. 37 (adj.) on a ship's deck; p. 40 (n.)
great ships steer out; p. 40 (n.) following ships in the South Seas;
p. 43 (adj.) over the midship oar; p. 45 (n.) even on shipboard;
p. 49 (v.) we unshipped the mast; p. 49 (n.) secret of many a stout
ship; p. 51 (adj.) occasionally incident to ship water; p. 56 (adj.)
a ship's uppermost spars; p. 57 (n.) we were due east from the ship;
p. 57 (n.) the chase being a ship; p. 58 (adj.) the entire ship's
company might; p. 60 (n.) buy a house, or a ship; p. 60 (adj.) such
as are used in a ship's cabin; p. 63 (adj.) sounding a ship's well;
p. 63 (n.) a shade of a ship; p. 68 (n.) by the commander of a ship;
p. 69 (n.) long since deserted the ship; p. 70 (adj.) decline a ship's
mast; p. 81 (n.) pleasantest end of the ship; p. 83 (adj.) much
impede the ship's sailing; p. 90 (n.) of the crews of ships; p. 90
(n.) upon their white shipmates; p. 90 (n.) wrecking the ship; p. 91
(n.) there was a British ship; p. 91 (n.) pretty name for a ship;
p. 91 (n.) christening ships of war; p. 91 (n.) fine names for their
fighting ships; p. 92 (n.) Time to tack ship; p. 92 (n.) a stout ship
fell; p. 93 (adj.) log, quadrant, and ship's papers; p. 94 (n.) his
shipmates oftentimes seize; p. 95 (n.) dying on shipboard; p. 95 (n.)
in small ships; p. 95 (adj.) to keep the ship's record; p. 96 (adj.)
ship's stores are originally procured; p. 101 (adj.) nooks in the
ship's rigging; p. 101 (adj.) a ship's ropes are a study; p. 104
(adj.) some ship's keel crossing his road; p. 104 (n.) In the case of
the ship to London; p. 105 (n.) wound dressed by a ship-surgeon;
p. 105 (n.) This ship I met with; p. 106 (n.) share the prize with my
shipmates; p. 107 (n.) by way of advice to all ship-masters; p. 111
(n.) to heave the ship to; p. 115 (n.) shut up in a ship with such a
hornet; p. 120 (n.) a ship is no piece of mechanism merely; p. 120
(n.) I have loved ships; p. 120 (n.) the bones of drowned ships and
drowned men; p. 122 (n.) where's now our old ship; p. 123 (n.) All
hands ahoy! tack ship; p. 123 (n.) from many an old shipmate; p. 125
(n.) reckless souls tenanting a line-of-battle ship; p. 126 (n.) too
small for a ship; p. 127 (n.) a sea-god that boards ships; p. 127
(adj.) within less than two ships'-lengths; p. 129 (adj.) the blade
of our long mid-ship oar; p. 132 (adj.) sections of a ship's rigging;
p. 132 (n.) ascended the shrouds of a ship; p. 192 (adj.) above the
shipwrecked mariner; p. 214 (n.) the fins of our swimming ship;
p. 259 (adj.) like a ship's shrouds in a Typhoon; p. 290 (n.) as
ships from Teneriffe; p. 367 (n.) to save the good ship from the
shoals; p. 367 (n.) when my ship lies tranced; p. 470 (n.) in the

ship-duels that ensued; p. 481 (n.) brave planks of the good ship
Argos he trod; p. 532 (adj.) playing about the ends of ships' royal-
yards; p. 554 (n.) a line-of-battle ship, all purple stone; p. 605
(adj.) all is snug and ship-shape before you begin; p. 632 (n.) ships
leave a radiant-white, and fire-fly wake; p. 653 (n.) headwinds . . .
that beat back ships.

Redburn--p. 3 (adj.) delightedly perusing the long columns of ship
advertisements; p. 4 (n.) any quantity of ships must be lying there;
p. 4 (n.) reminiscences of wharves, and warehouses, and shipping;
p. 4 (n.) when a large ship was getting under way; p. 5 (n.) that
that very ship, . . . so near to me then; p. 7 (n.) a great whale, as
big as a ship; p. 7 (n.) was an old-fashioned glass ship; p. 7 (n.)
the ship was returned to the donor; p. 7 (n.) This ship . . . became
the wonder and delight; p. 8 (n.) for no other purpose than to see
the ship; p. 8 (n.) to be the death of the glass ship; p. 8 (n.) the
ship was placed on the mantle-piece for a time; p. 8 (n.) in a story-
book about Captain Kidd's ship; p. 8 (n.) rigging of this famous ship;
p. 9 (n.) The name of this curious ship was La Reine; p. 9 (n.) in
which the ship was kept; p. 15 (n.) to the docks among the shipping;
p. 15 (n.) we lighted upon a ship for Liverpool; p. 17 (adj.)
sometimes the custom at the shipping offices; p. 19 (n.) I went alone
to the shipping office; p. 19 (n.) the ship was advertised to sail;
p. 24 (n.) Before I reached the ship; p. 24 (n.) to go on board ship;
p. 24 (v./n.) I've shipped to sail in this ship; p. 24 (n.) I didn't
know there were any rats in the ship; p. 24 (n.) who was going in
the ship; p. 25 (n.) in the bow of the ship; p. 25 (n.) that the ship
would not sail; p. 25 (n.) As I went to the ship; p. 26 (n.) I stepped
aboard the ship; p. 26 (n.) from Liverpool in this very ship; p. 26
(n.) I left the ship; p. 27 (n.) By the time I got back to the ship;
p. 28 (n.) saying that I was going out in the ship; p. 28 (v.) I hope
the old man hasn't been shipping any more greenhorns like you; p. 28
(n.) he'll make a shipwreck of it if he has; p. 28 (n.) they think
nothing of shipping a parcel of farmers; p. 29 (n.) longed for the
ship to be leaving; p. 29 (n.) in getting ships ready for sea; p. 30
(adj.) I was to ascend a ship's mast; p. 30 (n.) the bustle of the
ship increased; p. 31 (n.) in keeping the whole ship waiting; p. 32
(n.) we went past the long line of shipping; p. 33 (n.) and we passed
ships lying at anchor; p. 33 (n.) when the ship returned; p. 35 (n.)
as if he were watching for a ship; p. 36 (n.) not on board of a ship;
p. 36 (n.) and here was the ship; p. 36 (n.) I felt the ship roll;
p. 40 (n.) aboard of a ship; p. 41 (n.) and other work on board ship;
p. 46 (n.) of popularity among his shipmates; p. 46 (v.) Some sea-
captains, before shipping a man; p. 47 (n.) and a ship painted on the
back; p. 48 (n.) any such good sailors among my ship-mates; p. 50 (n.)
the ship lay almost still; p. 50 (n.) which kept pulling round the
ship; p. 52 (v.) than to ship aboard my vessel; p. 52 (adj.) the dull
beating against the ship's bows; p. 56 (n.) He Gives Some Account of
One of His Shipmates; p. 57 (n.) when his ship lost a man; p. 58 (n.)
who stopped ships in the straits of Gaspar; p. 58 (n.) more fit for a
hospital than a ship; p. 58 (adj.) He was standing at the ship's helm;
p. 59 (adj.) what it was that made a whole ship's company submit;
p. 59 (v.) he had shipped for an able-seaman; pp. 59-60 (adj.) in the
eyes of a ship's company; p. 60 (v.) when he ships for an able-seaman;
p. 60 (adj.) Generally, a ship's company of twelve men; p. 60 (n.)
persons called boys aboard merchant-ships; p. 60 (n.) In merchant-

ships, a boy means a green-hand; p. 62 (n.) at any time aboard ships,
a boy is expected; p. 62 (n.) who know nothing about a ship; p. 62
(n.) I found myself a sort of Ishmael in the ship; p. 63 (n.) sailing
in the same ship I had been in; p. 63 (n.) the ship made a strange,
musical noise; p. 64 (n.) on both sides of the ship; p. 64 (n.) when
I could shut the ship out; p. 65 (n.) If you have ever seen a ship;
p. 65 (adj.) a grand new naming of a ship's ropes; p. 66 (n.) which
[the human body], indeed, is something like a ship; p. 68 (n.) when
we first visited the ship; p. 68 (n.) though now the ship was so far
away; p. 69 (n.) by playing such tricks aboard a ship; p. 75 (n.)
when the ship pitched violently; p. 76 (n.) that the ship belonged to
Hamburg; p. 76 (n.) actually beholding a ship; p. 76 (n.) I followed
the strange ship; p. 76 (n.) toward the stern of their ships; p. 77
(n.) some ships carry still smaller sails; p. 78 (n.) I could but
just perceive the ship; p. 78 (adj.) the ship's motion was very great;
p. 78 (n.) when the ship rolled one way; p. 79 (n.) like all European
seamen in American ships; p. 79 (adj.) when the ship's company went
ashore; p. 82 (n.) for naming things that way on shipboard; p. 85 (n.)
One was an account of shipwrecks; p. 89 (n.) He would often ask his
shipmates; p. 92 (adj.) sent the whole ship's company flying; p. 92
(n.) in the dark water before the ship; p. 93 (n.) the strange ship,
scraping by us; p. 93 (n.) for all ships carry spare spars; p. 93 (n.)
on the forecastles of both ships; p. 93 (n.) many ships that are
never heard of; p. 93 (n.) a fine ship that lay near us; p. 93 (n.)
had been run against by a strange ship; p. 93 (n.) in ships that have
suffered; p. 94 (n.) as suddenly as the bravest and fleetest ships;
p. 95 (adj.) and tolling the ship's bell; p. 96 (n.) and no doubt
saved the ship; p. 97 (n.) in the track of the multitudinous ships;
p. 97 (n.) carried the lead outside of the ship; p. 99 (v.) though he
had shipped as an ordinary seaman; p. 99 (n.) won't catch a Fin-back
so near a ship; p. 100 (n.) well understood his business aboard ship;
p. 100 (n.) nothing but a bowline round the midships; p. 102 (n.) so
violent was the motion of the ship; p. 102 (n.) that the ship did not
fall overboard; p. 104 (n.) to see the whole ship swallowed down;
p. 106 (n.) not a Liverpool liner, or packet-ship; p. 106 (n.) come
under the general head of transient ships; p. 106 (n.) sustain the
ship's reputation for speed; p. 107 (n.) the ship that once carried
over; p. 107 (n.) while lying with his ship; p. 107 (n.) Thus departs
the pride and glory of packet-ships; p. 109 (adj.) he shall furnish
the ship's company; p. 111 (n.) the casks discharged from West India
ships; p. 111 (n.) recognized her as the very ship; p. 111 (adj.) on
board previous to the ship's sailing; p. 112 (n.) till he thought the
ship must be out of sight; p. 115 (n.) the ship plunging and rearing
like a mad horse; p. 115 (n.) and the ship leans over; p. 115 (n.) in
being aloft in a ship at sea; p. 115 (n.) and a ship in harbor;
p. 116 (n.) as the ship went foaming on her way; p. 116 (n.) steering
a ship is a great art; p. 116 (n.) he keeps the ship going about;
p. 117 (n.) might make the ship lurch to; p. 118 (adj.) the place
that holds a ship's compass; p. 119 (n.) when the sudden swells would
lift the ship; p. 119 (adj.) The pride and glory of the whole ship's
company; p. 121 (n.) carries with him from ship to ship; p. 121 (adj.)
The estimation in which a ship's crew hold; p. 121 (v.) I had only
shipped for this one voyage; p. 121 (n.) only reaped by the next ship;
p. 124 (n.) which some of the packet ships make; p. 124 (n.) and the
ship sailed nearer; p. 124 (n.) I thought of the shipwreck; p. 125
(n.) like to leave the ship; p. 126 (n.) scattered on board of

different ships; p. 127 (n.) I soon learned from my ship-mates;
p. 130 (n.) jamming against other ships; p. 130 (n.) To a ship, the
American merchantmen; p. 130 (n.) Other ships, however . . . feed;
p. 133 (n.) while my shipmates were now engaged; p. 133 (n.) placed
in a wooden ship; p. 133 (n.) to one of these ships; p. 134 (n.) and
drunk by most of my shipmates; p. 136 (n.) The ship remained in
Prince's Dock; p. 136 (n.) after lounging about the ship; p. 137 (n.)
visits of Captain Riga to the ship; p. 137 (n.) at his post on board
ship; p. 137 (n.) a ship-keeper, hired from shore; p. 137 (n.) led by
sailors of American ships; p. 139 (n.) parsimony of ship-owners has
seconded; p. 139 (n.) steers the Hibernia or Unicorn steam-ship;
p. 143 (n.) What does this anchor here? this ship; p. 143 (n.) that
anchor, ship, and Dibdin's ditty; p. 145 (n.) is a ship under full
sail; p. 147 (n.) allusions to the Aeneid and Falconer's Shipwreck;
p. 147 (n.) its docks, and ships, and warehouses; p. 151 (v.) I would
most probably ship on board; p. 152 (n.) as I lay in my berth on ship-
board; p. 152 (n.) where I and my shipmates were standing; p. 153 (n.)
My shipmates, of course, made merry; p. 153 (n.) But I pointed to my
ship; p. 153 (n.) thefts are perpetrated on board the ships; p. 158
(n.) so great a number of ships afloat; p. 158 (n.) for the benefit
of the shipping; p. 159 (adj.) it [your nose] will . . . be your
ship's mainmast; p. 161 (n.) the ship Highlander lay in Prince's
Dock; p. 161 (n.) struck with the long line of shipping; p. 161 (n.)
where the bottoms of ships are repaired; p. 163 (n.) mostly frequented
by the American shipping; p. 163 (n.) the Mobile and Savannah cotton
ships and traders; p. 163 (n.) ingress to ships is only to be had;
p. 163 (n.) the keels of the ships inclosed by the quays; p. 163 (n.)
to see hundreds of immense ships; p. 163 (n.) Prince's Dock is
generally so filled with shipping; p. 164 (n.) it would be impossible
to dock a ship; p. 164 (n.) our old ship-keeper . . . related; p. 164
(n.) one of the ships which carried over troops; p. 164 (n.) for the
goods unladed from the shipping; p. 165 (n.) The Salt-Droghers, and
German Emigrant Ships; p. 165 (n.) each ship is an island; p. 165 (n.)
in the collective spars and timbers of these ships; p. 165 (n.) Here
ships are lodged at a moderate charge; p. 165 (n.) ships lying in the
very middle of the docks; p. 166 (n.) I spent in gazing at the
shipping; p. 166 (n.) would give way to a Sidney emigrant ship;
p. 166 (n.) for ships bound for America; p. 168 (n.) who come on
board the large New York ships; p. 168 (n.) seven or eight hundred in
one ship; p. 168 (n.) reverberating among the crowded shipping;
p. 170 (n.) Among the various ships lying in Prince's Dock; p. 170
(n.) the Irrawaddy, of Bombay, a country ship; p. 171 (n.) my motives
in paying a visit to the ship; p. 171 (n.) where the ship had been
tost [sic] about; p. 171 (n.) while the heathen at the other end of
the ship; p. 171 (n.) the Lascars were set to stripping the ship;
p. 172 (n.) to see this singular ship; p. 172 (n.) who left strict
orders with our old ship-keeper; p. 172 (n.) I was returning to the
ship; p. 172 (n.) sent to Bombay for ship-building; p. 172 (n.)
crooked timbers in the country ships; p. 173 (n.) wholly built by the
native shipwrights of India; p. 173 (n.) for the running rigging of a
ship; p. 173 (n.) for the shrouds and standing-rigging of a ship;
p. 174 (n.) flat-bottomed salf-cellar of a ship; p. 174 (n.) usually
banding round an American ship; p. 175 (adv.) rusty gun, on a swivel,
amid-ships; p. 175 (n.) lay between two large ships in ballast;
p. 177 (n.) upon the arrival of every Liverpool ship; p. 178 (n.) in
loading and unloading the shipping; p. 178 (n.) the multitudes

employed about the shipping; p. 182 (n.) go on board your ship;
p. 183 (n.) lost time to run to the ship; p. 184 (n.) on my way to
the ship; p. 184 (n.) being obliged to repair to the ship; p. 185 (n.)
carried ashore from the holds of the shipping; p. 185 (adj.) after
discharging a ship's cargo; p. 186 (n.) the second mate of a merchant
ship; p. 186 (n.) in large ships, even more; p. 186 (n.) crews of
hundreds and hundreds of ships; p. 188 (n.) went ashore with my
shipmates; p. 188 (n.) of the oak timbers of Nelson's ship; p. 189
(n.) an anchor, a crown, a ship; p. 189 (n.) chance to stumble upon a
shipmate; p. 192 (n.) superior, fast-sailing, coppered and copper-
fastened ships; p. 193 (v.) they do not ship men; p. 193 (n.) but for
particular ships; p. 195 (n.) a shipmate of mine purchased it; p. 196
(n.) while the ship lay in dock; p. 196 (n.) had secret places in the
ship; p. 196 (adj.) one of ten thousand darting under a ship's bows;
p. 202 (n.) the black cooks and stewards of American ships; p. 204
(n.) but my shipmates did; p. 204 (n.) collectively known by the
names of their ships; p. 215 (n.) across the tiers of ships; p. 216
(n.) He was speaking to one of my shipmates; p. 218 (n.) as a
midshipman in the East India service; p. 218 (n.) to examine the
American shipping; p. 218 (n.) to which the American ships long
staying in Liverpool; p. 219 (v.) that he should offer to ship as a
boy; p. 219 (n.) the day previous to the sailing of the ship; p. 220
(adj.) to the Queen's drawing-room than a ship's forecastle; p. 224
(n.) came bounding on board the ship; p. 224 (n.) But how am I to
leave the ship, Harry; p. 225 (n.) Come, sink the ship; p. 225 (n.)
if I quit the ship; p. 225 (adj.) till the ship's bell struck four;
p. 233 (n.) he had accosted me on board the ship; p. 238 (n.) heard
that the ship Highlander had; p. 238 (n.) had now been absent from
the ship; p. 238 (n.) the discipline of the ship was altogether
relaxed; p. 239 (adv.) tierces were lashed amid-ships; p. 239 (adj.)
against the ship's sides; p. 239 (n.) made expressly for emigrant
ships; p. 239 (n.) we worked the ship close into the outlet; p. 239
(n.) ordering the various ships behind us; p. 239 (n.) and the cheers
of the surrounding ships; p. 239 (v.) who had been shipped to sail
with us; p. 239 (n.) the ship now swinging her broadside; p. 240 (n.)
till the ship was away from the land; p. 240 (n.) a multitude of
ships for all parts of the world; p. 240 (n.) owing to the great
number of ships; p. 240 (n.) in which their ships make the run;
p. 241 (n.) every captain of an emigrant ship; p. 241 (n.) has not
deterred mercenary shipmasters; p. 241 (n.) packed like slaves in a
slave-ship; p. 241 (n.) for in some of these ships; p. 242 (n.)
maintained on board some of these ships; p. 242 (n.) only completely
open space on ship-board; p. 242 (n.) crowded in the waist of the
ship; p. 242 (adv.) ropes were passed athwart-ships; p. 243 (adj.) Of
the three newly shipped men; p. 243 (adj.) His name was down on the
ship's papers; p. 244 (adj.) timbers rooted in the ship's keel;
p. 244 (adj.) from the ship's rolling; p. 244 (n.) It's a water-rat,
ship-mates, that's dead; p. 245 (n.) when brought on board the ship;
p. 247 (n.) There was on board our ship; p. 254 (adj.) to form one of
a ship's company; p. 255 (n.) ignoring the fact that his shipmates;
p. 257 (adj.) from the list of the ship's company; p. 257 (n.) Once a
sailor on board a ship; p. 260 (n.) that the ship had played them
false; p. 263 (n.) For the emigrants in these ships; p. 263 (n.)
owing to the pitching of the ships; p. 265 (n.) in some imaginary
section of the ship; p. 268 (n.) for the purpose of washing down the
ship; p. 268 (n.) in the extreme bows of the ship; p. 270 (n.) my

shipmates disposed of their tobacco; p. 273 (n.) when solicited by a
shipmate for a chaw; p. 275 (n.) with a midnight shipwreck in the
distance; p. 275 (n.) the more sneaking and cowardly of my shipmates;
p. 283 (n.) headwinds drove the ship back; p. 283 (adj.) they must be
supplied from the ship's stores; p. 284 (n.) alarmed me for the safety
of the ship; p. 285 (n.) Although fast-sailing ships; p. 286 (n.)
utmost alarm spread through the ship; p. 287 (v.) they had not shipped
to fight fifty to one; p. 288 (n.) in a ship, you are locked and
bolted; p. 289 (n.) to which we stripped our ship; p. 292 (n.) in a
newspaper paragraph, under the shipping-head; p. 292 (n.) you see no
plague-ship driving through a stormy sea; p. 292 (n.) operate
unfavorably to the ship; p. 292 (n.) concerning emigrant ships in
general; p. 293 (n.) restricting ships to a certain number of
emigrants; p. 293 (n.) obligatory upon the captain of a ship; p. 295
(n.) the ship rearing and plunging under us; p. 295 (n.) It was when
the ship had rolled; p. 296 (n.) which had closed over the head of
our shipmate; p. 296 (n.) Like most merchant ships; p. 296 (v.) had
we been shipwrecked; p. 296 (n.) one merchant ship out of three;
p. 298 (n.) The ship lay gently rolling; p. 298 (n.) betokening the
vicinity of scores of ships; p. 299 (n.) and trimming the ship;
p. 299 (n.) tossed overboard from emigrant ships; p. 300 (n.) though
scores of ships were here lying; p. 300 (n.) while thick and more
thick, ships, brigs; p. 300 (n.) that, ladies, is a line-of-battle-
ship; p. 301 (n.) and knotted our old ship; p. 301 (n.) the ship once
fast to the wharf; p. 301 (n.) the ship that we had loathed; p. 302
(n.) only inhabitants of the deserted old ship; p. 304 (n.) I left
him to get his chest from the ship; p. 305 (n.) to draw much of a
salary from the ship; p. 305 (n.) Harry and I made our appearance on
ship-board; p. 305 (n.) while the captain held the ship-papers;
p. 306 (n.) that I was to go out in your ship; p. 307 (n.) By running
away from the ship in Liverpool; p. 307 (n.) ignored my absence from
the ship; p. 307 (n.) after he had been slaving aboard his ship;
p. 307 (v.) you also shipped for three dollars per month; p. 308 (n.)
By the looks of our shipmates; p. 308 (adj.) the cordial dislike of
the whole ship's company; p. 308 (n.) and at one bound, cleared the
ship; p. 309 (n.) our shipmates departed; p. 310 (n.) the bay, varied
with glancing ships; p. 311 (v.) where men are shipped for the
Nantucket whalers; p. 312 (v.) who had shipped in his vessel; p. 312
(n.) she was the most unlucky of ships; p. 312 (n.) was jammed
between the ship, and a whale.

White-Jacket--p. ix (v.) In the year 1843 I shipped as ordinary
seaman; p. 4 (n.) my heartless shipmates even used to stand up against
me; p. 6 (n.) take the wings of a morning, or the sails of a ship;
p. 7 (n.) and the ship with her nose in the water; p. 7 (v.) unship
your bars; p. 8 (adj.) taking their turn at the ship's duty by night;
p. 8 (n.) stationed on the three decks of the ship at such times;
p. 8 (n.) Also, in tacking ship; p. 9 (n.) besides his special offices.
in tacking ship; p. 9 (adj.) grand divisions of the ship's company;
p. 9 (n.) whose society some of the youngster midshipmen much affect;
p. 9 (n.) which is not the case with all midshipmen; p. 10 (n.) foreign
ladies who may chance to visit the ship; p. 10 (adj.) from the rest
of the ship's company; p. 10 (adv.) These are generally placed
amidships; p. 11 (n.) when all hands are called to save ship; p. 11
(adj.) we say nothing here of . . . ship's corporals; p. 11 (adj.)
his ship's number, or the number to which he must answer; p. 14 (n.)

to be going on wrong aboard ship; p. 14 (adv.) every thing was done
ship-shape and Bristol fashion; p. 14 (n.) the fore-top captain meant
a ship; p. 14 (n.) was voted a bore by his shipmates; p. 15 (n.) in
Her Britannic Majesty's ship; p. 15 (n.) the best seamen in the ship;
p. 16 (n.) turning his ship . . . into a fat-kettle; p. 18 (n.) the
midshipmen attending looking ominously wise; p. 18 (n.) belonging to
the United States Ship Neversink; p. 20 (n.) where they Live in the
Ship; p. 20 (n.) their Social Standing on Ship-board; p. 20 (n.) our
ship . . . was the flag-ship; p. 20 (n.) as her ships of war increase;
p. 21 (n.) temporarily commanding a small number of ships; p. 22 (n.)
they do not say a great deal on board ship; p. 23 (n.) never meddled
immediately with the concerns of the ship; p. 23 (n.) For a ship is a
bit of terra firma; p. 23 (n.) that functionary orders a midshipman
to repair; p. 23 (n.) except concerning the ship; p. 24 (n.) in a
part of the ship thus designated; p. 24 (adj.) Marine Officers, and
Midshipmen's Schoolmaster; p. 25 (n.) otherwise middies or midshipmen;
p. 25 (n.) only placed on board a sea-going ship; p. 25 (n.) are
little more, while midshipmen; p. 25 (n.) the usage of a ship of war
is such; p. 25 (n.) the midshipmen are constantly being ordered;
p. 26 (adj.) selected from the ship's company; p. 26 (adj.) including
ship's corporals . . . and ship's yeomen; p. 27 (adj.) The ship's
corporals are . . . deputies; p. 27 (adj.) the ship's yeoman is a
gentleman; p. 27 (n.) the only man of his rank in the ship; p. 27 (n.)
warrant officers, midshipmen; p. 27 (n.) also, the midshipmen; p. 28
(n.) In a flag-ship; p. 29 (n.) let us candidly confess it, shipmates;
p. 29 (n.) no man on board the ship dare to dine; p. 31 (n.) In
frigates, and all large ships of war; p. 32 (n.) read accounts of
shipwrecks; p. 32 (n.) You can not save a ship by working out; p. 33
(n.) for a charmed life against shipwrecks; p. 33 (n.) but float his
good ship higher and higher; p. 34 (adj.) Like so many ship's shrouds;
p. 34 (n.) wise example set by those ships of the desert; p. 38 (n.)
and one often perpetrated on board ship; p. 41 (n.) often made by the
less learned of his shipmates; p. 41 (n.) of all places in the world,
a ship of war; p. 41 (n.) hostility of the whole tribe of ship-
underlings; p. 41 (adj.) master-at-arms, ship's corporals; p. 42
(adj.) Ranged up against the ship's side at regular intervals; p. 44
(n.) attributable to their Particular Stations and Duties aboard Ship;
p. 44 (n.) I visited an English line-of-battle ship; p. 45 (adj.) the
moldering keels of shipwrecked vessels; p. 47 (n.) the entire ship
abounded with illustrations; p. 48 (v.) who had been shipped at the
Cape **De** Verd islands; p. 48 (n.) that should the ship ever go into
action; p. 48 (n.) In ships of war, the members of the "music"; p. 48
(v.) mostly ships . . . that as soon as the vessel comes; p. 51 (n.)
as ignorant of a ship, indeed; p. 53 (n.) their names are called off
by a midshipman; p. 53 (v.) several forlorn individuals, shipping as
landsmen; p. 54 (n.) The ship was like a great city, when some terrible
calamity has overtaken it; p. 55 (n.) clandestinely brought out in
the ship; p. 56 (adj.) the master-at-arms and ship's corporals; p. 58
(adj.) officially called the ship's cook; p. 58 (adj.) Now the ship's
cooking required very little science; p. 58 (adj.) or occupied at any
other ship's duty; p. 58 (adj.) have so polished the ship's coppers;
p. 63 (n.) men of no mark or consideration whatever in the ship;
p. 64 (adj.) The summons is given by the ship's drummer; p. 64 (n.)
Hearts of oak are our ships; p. 65 (n.) that I must consider the ship
blowing up; p. 65 (n.) If we should chance to engage a ship; p. 66
(n.) Besides, ours was a flag-ship; p. 66 (n.) dangerous predicament

the quarter-deck of Nelson's flag-ship was; p. 66 (v.) another to
unship your rudder; p. 67 (n.) assailing all sides of the ship at
once; p. 67 (n.) and the entire ship is in as great a commotion;
p. 68 (n.) the ship itself would here and there present a far
different appearance; p. 69 (n.) the slightest roll of the ship;
p. 69 (n.) the aspect of the ship . . . would . . . be very dissimilar;
p. 70 (n.) would answer for some poor shipmate; p. 71 (adj.) The
ship's cooper strolled by; p. 71 (n.) to see that the ship's life-
buoys are kept; p. 72 (n.) the Captain of the surviving ships ordered;
p. 72 (n.) All hands about ship; p. 76 (n.) In some ships in which I
have done this; p. 77 (n.) who are shipmates and fellow-sailors of
ours; p. 78 (n.) The ship has no paint to spare; p. 86 (n.) the ship
being one vast wash-tub; p. 86 (n.) who so love to see a ship kept
spick and span; p. 86 (n.) when the ship is rolling in a sea-way;
p. 86 (n.) Is a ship a wooden platter; p. 86 (n.) all the while the
ship carries a doctor; p. 87 (n.) Say you go on board a line-of-battle
ship; p. 87 (n.) the American ships are the most excessively neat;
p. 87 (n.) the general discipline of the American ships; p. 87 (adj.)
peck up their broken biscuit, or midshipmen's nuts; p. 87 (n.) this
unobstructedness in an American fighting-ship; p. 87 (n.) when you
see such a ship; p. 88 (n.) as in other national ships; p. 89 (n.) if
the ship happen to be lying in harbor; p. 89 (n.) the whole ship is
converted into a dram-shop; p. 89 (n.) owing to the related discipline
of the ship; p. 90 (adj.) to be confined in the ship's prison; p. 90
(n.) the melancholy prospects before the ship; p. 90 (n.) Think of it,
shipmates; p. 92 (n.) The Master-at-arms and Ship's Corporals; p. 94
(n.) much heightened by the roll of the ship; p. 95 (adj.) temporary
rupture of the ship's stern discipline; p. 95 (v.) they have shipped
their quarter-deck faces again; p. 96 (n.) that has tossed many a
good ship; p. 96 (n.) many an outward-bound ship has been driven;
p. 96 (n.) of ships that have sailed from their ports; p. 97 (n.)
with their souls full of its shipwrecks and disasters; p. 97 (n.) the
whole ship is brewed into the yeast of the gale; p. 97 (n.) Or,
perhaps, the ship broaches to: p. 97 (n.) The ship is then ready for
the worst; p. 98 (n.) all round the dismantled ship the storm howls;
p. 98 (n.) Other ships . . . spend week after week; p. 98 (n.) to
sail an English ship thereon; p. 99 (n.) young Byron, a midshipman in
the same ship; p. 99 (n.) to the improved condition of ships; p. 102
(n.) about to be promulgated through the ship; p. 102 (n.) the wonted
discipline of the ship was broken; p. 103 (v.) the officers shipped
their quarter-deck faces; p. 104 (n.) two ships in a calm, and equally
affected; p. 104 (n.) pronounces her a full-rigged ship; p. 105 (n.)
Ship ahoy; p. 105 (n.) What ship's that; p. 105 (n.) The United States
ship Neversink, homeward bound; p. 105 (n.) jump, men, and save ship;
p. 106 (adj.) the whole strength of the ship's company; p. 106 (n.)
Mad Jack was the saving genius of the ship; p. 106 (adj.) The ship's
bows were now butting, battering; p. 106 (n.) to throw the ship into
the wind; p. 106 (n.) The spray blew over the ship in floods; p. 106
(n.) owing to the slant of the ship; p. 107 (adj.) was heard the
dismal tolling of the ship's bell; p. 107 (n.) the violent rolling of
the ship was occasioning; p. 107 (n.) converted that part of the ship
into an immense bowling alley; p. 107 (n.) the midshipmen who were
ordered; p. 108 (n.) A midshipman . . . had been sent up; p. 110 (n.)
Mad Jack was for running the ship into its teeth; p. 110 (n.) As with
ships, so with men; p. 111 (n.) which every man in the ship had long
suspected; p. 111 (n.) in going about the ship; p. 113 (n.) seldom

taken a line-of-battle ship to sea; p. 113 (n.) 451 Midshipmen
(including Passed-midshipmen); p. 113 (n.) are known to be sent from
ship to ship; p. 115 (n.) a violent rolling, unknown to merchant
ships; p. 115 (v.) shipping green seas on both sides; p. 115 (adj.)
the ship's company messed on the gun-deck; p. 116 (n.) the ship was
seized with such a paroxysm of rolling; p. 116 (n.) we were about
being swamped in the ship; p. 116 (n.) the ship in which I then
happened to be sailing; p. 117 (n.) At daybreak Midshipman Pert went
below; p. 120 (n.) or sent the midshipmen among them; p. 121 (adj.)
take the measure of the ship's entire keel; p. 122 (n.) when a ship-
canal shall have penetrated; p. 123 (adj.) you see them at a large
ship-chandler's on shore; p. 124 (adj.) where the ship's forges and
anvils may be heard ringing; p. 124 (adj.) the ship's yeoman's store-
room; p. 124 (adj.) it was down in the ship's basement; p. 124 (n.)
yeoman in an American line-of-battle ship; p. 127 (n.) there were
several parts of the ship; p. 128 (n.) laying a train of powder to
blow up the ship; p. 129 (n.) extinguish all lights and all fires in
the ship; p. 130 (n.) a ceremony only observed in a flag-ship; p. 130
(n.) to bring to some ship at sea; p. 131 (n.) for the executive of
the ship to know; p. 132 (n.) so far eastward, you know, shippy, that
they have to; p. 132 (adj.) slily going to Old Coffee, the ship's
cook; p. 134 (n.) with violating a well-known law of the ship; p. 134
(n.) sent through the lowermost depths of the ship; p. 135 (adj.) the
attendance of the entire ship's company; p. 135 (n.) All the officers--
midshipmen included; p. 136 (n.) was a great favorite in his part of
the ship; p. 137 (adj.) on the deck, close to the ship's bulwarks;
p. 137 (adj.) a wave broke against the ship's side; p. 137 (adj.) in
applause of their shipmate's nerve; p. 140 (n.) in any part of the
ship; p. 141 (n.) though the captain of an English armed ship; p. 144
(n.) hardly affect one iota the condition on shipboard; p. 144 (n.)
arising between man and man on board ship; p. 147 (n.) no armed ship
can be kept in suitable discipline; p. 147 (n.) was a disciplinarian
on board the ships; p. 148 (n.) when British press-gangs not only
boarded foreign ships; p. 149 (n.) another almost governed his ships
without it; p. 149 (n.) some English ships of war have fallen a prey;
p. 149 (n.) the seamen have ran away with their ships; p. 153 (n.) on
board of some merchant-ship; p. 155 (n.) No Sundays on shipboard;
p. 155 (n.) is not a ship modeled after a church; p. 157 (n.) to obey
the laws of the ship; p. 157 (n.) on board any ship of an enemy;
p. 157 (n.) sunk or destroyed by any United States ship; p. 157 (n.)
paid for sinking and destroying ships; p. 159 (n.) the courteous
etiquette of these ships; p. 160 (n.) a few decks of a line-of-battle
ship; p. 162 (n.) to be a lord on board of this ship; p. 163 (n.) All
the lieutenants and Midshipmen; p. 166 (n.) even down to a midshipman;
p. 168 (n.) in various parts of the ship; p. 170 (n.) the only method
adopted by my ship-mates; p. 171 (n.) no burned-brick was to be had
from the ship's yeoman; p. 173 (n.) in permitting checkers on board
his ship; p. 173 (n.) Soon after the ship had sailed from home;
p. 173 (n.) as a philosophical shipmate observed; p. 174 (n.) seen so
many of my shipmates all employed; p. 175 (adj.) were decanted into
the ship's bowels; p. 177 (adj.) to hold intercourse with the ship's
company; p. 177 (adj.) every one of the numerous ship's boats; p. 177
(adj.) the ship's Chief of Police; p. 177´(adj.) not a man of the
ship's company ever enters; p. 177 (n.) who are permitted to board
the ship; p. 178 (n.) every one of the numerous officers of the ship;
p. 179 (adj.) of captain of the ship's executioners; p. 180 (n.) they

pull off for the ship; p. 180 (adj.) unutterable proceeding on the
ship's anvil; p. 180 (n.) on that side of the ship; p. 180 (n.)
introducing the six brandy bottles into the ship; p. 182 (n.) could
have been spirited into the ship; p. 183 (adj.) one of the ship's
boats regularly deputed; p. 183 (n.) Purser of the United States ship
Neversink; p. 183 (n.) calling a midshipman; p. 184 (n.) most
villainous-looking fellows in the ship; p. 185 (adj.) turned adrift
among the ship's company; p. 185 (n.) the most inglorious division of
the ship; p. 185 (n.) for hardly any other mess in the ship; p. 186
(n.) men of undeniable mark on board ship; p. 187 (adj.) humorous
contrasts between ship and shore life; p. 189 (adj.) had been adrift
among the ship's company; p. 189 (adj.) in his office as the ship's
chief of police; p. 191 (n.) The great guns of an armed ship; p. 191
(n.) It was our own ship; p. 192 (v.) before I shipped aboard here;
p. 193 (n.) perhaps the armed ships of rival nations; p. 194 (n.)
causing the various spars of all the ships; p. 194 (n.) on the poop
of his flag-ship; p. 194 (n.) stands the signal-midshipman; p. 194
(n.) in case the ship should be captured; p. 195 (n.) round their
lord and master, the flag-ship; p. 195 (n.) in obedience to a signal
from our flag-ship; p. 195 (n.) between the First Lieutenants of the
different ships; p. 196 (n.) of an English line-of-battle ship near
us; p. 196 (n.) falling from that lofty cross in a line-of-battle
ship; p. 196 (n.) has fallen upon his own shipmates in the tops;
p. 197 (n.) to show off the excelling discipline of the ship; p. 202
(n.) The cry ran fore and aft the ship; p. 205 (n.) the Purser's
Steward of most ships; p. 205 (n.) the epistles of their more
fortunate shipmates; p. 205 (n.) On board of those ships; p. 206 (n.)
the Purser of an American line-of-battle ship; p. 206 (n.) the Purser
of a line-of-battle ship; p. 206 (n.) the Purser of a line-of-battle
ship receives; p. 211 (n.) represented by the flag-ships of fleets;
p. 211 (n.) the flag-ships of the Phoenecian armed galleys; p. 211
(n.) the flag-ship of all the Greek and Persian craft; p. 212 (n.)
these flag-ships might all come to anchor; p. 213 (adj.) that our
ship's company must have; p. 213 (n.) favor for himself and shipmates;
p. 214 (n.) you and your shipmates are after some favor; p. 215 (n.)
his own supremacy in his ship; p. 215 (n.) cried his shipmates;
p. 216 (n.) Something concerning Midshipmen; p. 216 (n.) at the
complaint of a mid-shipman; p. 216 (n.) spite and unscrupulousness of
the mid-shipman; p. 217 (n.) order of the minutest midshipman; p. 217
(adj.) touch your hat to a midshipman's coat; p. 217 (adj.) subordinates of an armed ship's chief magistrate; p. 217 (n.) However
childish . . . a midshipman; p. 217 (n.) not publically reprimand the
midshipman; p. 217 (n.) the midshipman had done otherwise; p. 217
(adj.) Upon a midshipman's complaining; p. 217 (n.) Captain of a line-
of-battle ship; p. 217 (n.) calling the midshipman aside; p. 218 (n.)
if the corps of American midshipmen; p. 218 (n.) how easy for any of
these midshipmen; p. 218 (n.) a midshipman can do nothing obnoxious;
p. 218 (n.) is often heard from a midshipman; p. 218 (n.) one who has
seen much of midshipmen; pp. 218-9 (n.) seen but few midshipmen who
were not . . . advocates; p. 219 (n.) the midshipmen in the English
Navy; p. 219 (n.) quite so imperious as in the American ships; p. 219
(n.) you see midshipmen who are noble little fellows; p. 219 (n.)
that a midshipman leads a lord's life; pp. 219-20 (n.) can not . . .
legally punish a midshipman; p. 220 (n.) by some captains upon their
midshipmen; p. 220 (n.) no special fondness for midshipmen; p. 220
(n.) A tall, overgrown young midshipman; p. 220 (n.) The midshipman

obeyed; p. 220 (adj.) in full sight of the entire ship's company;
p. 220 (n.) a midshipman attempted to carry the day; p. 220 (n.) what
particular midshipman was the proprietor; p. 220 (n.) The midshipman
started; p. 220 (n.) this midshipman reported his cot-boy; p. 221
(adj.) the midshipman's charge having been heard; p. 221 (adj.)
through the midshipman's instrumentality; p. 221 (n.) permits himself
to domineer over a midshipman; p. 221 (n.) relationship between the
midshipman and the sailor; p. 221 (n.) a midshipman can neither say
nor do any wrong; p. 221 (n.) wherever these chapters treat of
midshipmen; p. 221 (n.) the officers known as passed-midshipmen;
p. 221 (n.) sufficient service at sea as midshipmen; p. 221 (n.)
promoted to the rank of passed-midshipmen; p. 221 (n.) The difference
between a passed-midshipman and a midshipman; p. 221 (n.) There were
no passed-midshipmen in the Neversink; p. 222 (n.) It has been said
that some midshipmen; p. 222 (n.) as these midshipmen are presumed to
have received; p. 225 (n.) the liberty his shipmates so earnestly
coveted; p. 226 (n.) we were pulled ashore by our shipmates; p. 226
(adj.) The ship's company were divided; p. 226 (n.) the midshipmen
and others were engaged; p. 226 (n.) bringing them off in scattered
detachments to the ship; p. 227 (n.) unless a ship, commanded by some
dissolute Captain; p. 227 (n.) The British line-of-battle ship;
p. 227 (adj.) than those in the ship's galley; p. 227 (n.) upon
returning to the ship; p. 228 (n.) As for the midshipmen; p. 228 (n.)
to the more diminutive class of midshipmen; p. 230 (n.) Midshipmen
entering the Navy early; p. 230 (n.) at which some of the midshipmen;
p. 230 (n.) or had ought to do, professionally, with a ship; p. 231
(n.) Midshipmen sent into the Navy; p. 231 (n.) shortening sail,
tacking ship; p. 233 (adj.) almost made the ship's live-oak knees
knock together; p. 239 (adj.) and the ship's company scattered;
p. 241 (n.) an armed Lieutenant and four midshipmen; p. 242 (n.) If
you ever violate the ship's rules; p. 242 (n.) had the deck of a line-
of-battle ship; p. 244 (n.) of a United States Store Ship; p. 244 (n.)
in the list of officers and midshipmen; p. 244 (n.) I have calculated
that the Store Ship may; p. 244 (n.) this midshipman is your own
brother; p. 245 (n.) to be the long-expected store ship; p. 245 (n.)
in carrying ship-stores; p. 245 (n.) would be plying between the
store ship; p. 245 (adj.) he mounted the store ship's side; p. 245
(n.) he spied two midshipmen; p. 245 (n.) the strange midshipman
laughed aloud; p. 245 (n.) perceived two midshipmen lounging; p. 245
(n.) the store ship at last moved further up; p. 246 (adj.) when the
ship's company went; p. 246 (n.) the sentry on that side of the ship;
p. 246 (n.) happened to be drawing near the ship; p. 247 (n.) he was
not far from the ship; p. 247 (n.) The Surgeons of the other American
ships of war; p. 252 (n.) the surgeons of the neighboring American
ships of war; p. 255 (n.) A large garrison-ensign was stretched
across the ship; p. 255 (adv.) two gun-carriages, dragged amidships;
p. 257 (n.) almost wholly confined in this ship; p. 263 (n.) Being
attached to a United States ship; p. 264 (n.) on board your respective
ships; p. 264 (n.) were dropped aboard of their respective ships;
p. 265 (n.) pulled about among the ships; p. 269 (n.) Now it is not
with ships as with horses; p. 269 (n.) the ship that in a light
breeze is outstripped; p. 270 (n.) was both a sailor and a shipwright;
p. 270 (n.) Falconer, whose shipwreck will never founder; p. 271 (n.)
good for a charm against shipwreck; p. 272 (n.) as make-weights, to
trim the ship; p. 273 (adj.) and take his ship's oath that we Yankees;
p. 274 (n.) the discipline of the ship . . . became a little relaxed;

p. 274 (n.) for the crews of most ships at sea; p. 276 (v.) the
officers had shipped their quarter-deck faces; p. 276 (v.) it is this
shipping of the quarter-deck face; p. 276 (v.) then never unship it
for another; p. 277 (n.) all my shipmates were liable to that; p. 277
(n.) in tacking ship every seaman in a man-of-war; p. 278 (n.) All
hands tack ship, ahoy; p. 278 (n.) the First Lieutenant sent a
midshipman; p. 278 (n.) through the furthest recesses of the ship;
p. 279 (n.) in which he kept up the discipline of the ship; p. 279
(n.) the ship was homeward bound; p. 283 (n.) is the only fountain in
the ship; p. 283 (adj.) by the cooks of the ship's messes; p. 283 (n.)
denominated the town-pump of the ship; p. 284 (adj.) master-at-arms
and ship's corporals . . . perambulate; p. 284 (n.) almost the lowest
subalterns in the ship; p. 285 (adj.) the ship's cook of the Neversink
would slowly emerge; p. 286 (adj.) that the ship's cook has faithfully
cooked; p. 287 (n.) over the separate divisions of the ship; p. 289
(adj.) and the ship's company disappear; p. 290 (adj.) but a tenth
part of the ship's company; p. 292 (n.) in some ships, every man is
required; p. 292 (adj.) before the assembled ship's company; p. 292
(n.) on board of the United States ship Neversink; p. 293 (n.) stand
bareheaded among my shipmates; p. 295 (n.) Can your shipmates so much
as drink; p. 295 (n.) and dash the ship to chips; p. 295 (n.) where
the crews of the ships or vessels; p. 295 (n.) to the officers of
such ships or vessels; p. 295 (n.) as if each ship or vessel were not
so wrecked; p. 298 (n.) his Majesty's Navies, Ships-of-war; p. 301
(n.) some eight of the midshipmen; p. 305 (n.) there was little or no
ship-work to be done; p. 305 (n.) upon their condition on ship-board;
p. 306 (adj.) assisted by his mates, the ship's corporals; p. 306 (n.)
reigns supreme in these bowels of the ship; p. 306 (adj.) The two
ship's corporals went along; p. 306 (n.) for some argus-eyed shipmate;
p. 310 (adj.) so far as . . . the ship's sailing were concerned;
p. 310 (n.) more than in any other part of the ship; p. 311 (n.) And
three times around spun our gallant ship; p. 311 (n.) Three times
around spun our gallant ship; p. 311 (n.) one of the best men in the
ship; p. 312 (n.) The ship that impressed him was; p. 312 (n.) the
ship in which we were sailing; p. 312 (n.) But when a ship of any
nation is running; p. 312 (n.) of the hostile meeting of their ships;
p. 313 (n.) on board of all ships; p. 313 (n.) guns in the after part
of the ship; p. 313 (n.) the guns of English armed ships; p. 314 (n.)
continued to fight his crippled ship; p. 316 (n.) This part of the
ship . . . was called; p. 316 (n.) when the ship struck; p. 316 (n.)
the main-mast of the French line-of-battle ship; p. 318 (n.) on board
Admiral Codrington's flag-ship; p. 318 (n.) an Ottoman fleet of three
ships-of-the-line; p. 318 (n.) and a swarm of fire ships; p. 318
(adj.) in case the ship's colors were shot away; p. 318 (n.) looking
at the Turkish line-of-battle ship; p. 319 (n.) sent it flying into
the line-of-battle ship; p. 322 (adj.) the angles of an armed ship's
stern; p. 323 (n.) outside of the ship; p. 324 (n.) in his own part
of the ship; p. 325 (n.) drew the tar from the seams of the ship;
p. 325 (n.) not an unusual one on ship board; p. 324 (n.) some account
of a part of the ship; p. 325 (n.) in the bows of the ship; p. 327
(n.) whether it was the wide roll of the ship; p. 328 (n.) general
sanitary affairs of the ship; p. 328 (n.) a long time to spend in one
ship; p. 332 (n.) the murder of one of my shipmates; p. 336 (n.)
buried in the very bowels of the ship; p. 337 (adj.) regular stroke
of the ship's great bell; p. 339 (n.) I never yet sewed up a shipmate;
p. 339 (n.) in a compass of a Greenland ship; p. 343 (n.) of one of

the seamen, in the midships; p. 343 (adj.) one of the ship's barbers;
p. 345 (n.) problems were solved by the midshipmen; p. 345 (n.) great
ships-of-the-line were navigated; p. 346 (n.) was he known throughout
the ship; p. 347 (n.) making marks . . . for the ships; p. 347 (n.)
till you have saved that crippled French ship; p. 348 (n.) That ship,
young gentlemen, is the Glorieuse; p. 348 (n.) That would not save
your ship, sir; p. 348 (n.) I'd tack ship, any way; p. 348 (n.) that
this ship . . . can not be saved; p. 350 (adj.) The allusion to one
of the ship's barbers; p. 350 (adj.) exempted from all ship's duty;
p. 351 (n.) adj.) stood upon the ship's books as ordinary seamen;
p. 351 (n.) Previous to shipping they had divulged; p. 351 (n.) Mostly
making . . . little ships and schooners; p. 351 (adj.) are set down
on the ship's calendar; p. 352 (adj.) nearly the whole ship's company
patronize the ship's barbers; p. 352 (n.) in every variety of ship-
gossip; p. 352 (n.) swaying their bodies to the motion of the ship;
p. 353 (adj.) it was unseamanlike; not ship-shape; p. 356 (adj.) that
very evening the ship's company were astounded; p. 358 (n.) Captain
Claret summoned the midshipmen; p. 358 (v.) and unshipped the ladders;
p. 358 (v.) Boatswain's mate, ship that ladder; pp. 358-9 (n.)
afterward rumored through the ship; p. 359 (n.) on board the United
States ship Neversink; p. 362 (adj.) The whole ship's company crowded;
p. 363 (n.) was carved all over with ships; p. 363 (n.) isn't that
old Chaucer's seaman; p. 366 (n.) he heard . . . the ship swing to
her anchor; p. 366 (n.) the ship being now in harbor; p. 370 (adj.)
passing the rope under the ship's bottom; p. 370 (n.) his own
shipmates are then made to; p. 370 (adj.) now scraping the ship's
hull; p. 370 (n.) authorizes the authorities of a ship; p. 370 (n.)
to witness punishment in the ship; p. 371 (n.) on board the culprit's
own ship; p. 371 (n.) rowed to the next ship; p. 371 (n.) All hands
of that ship are then; p. 371 (n.) by the boatswain's mates of that
ship; p. 371 (n.) stopping at each ship; p. 371 (n.) on the bulwarks
of every ship; p. 372 (n.) in an American national ship; p. 372 (n.)
that the ship was about to blow up; p. 373 (n.) all large ships of
war carry soldiers; p. 373 (n.) When a ship is running into action;
p. 374 (adj.) usually drawn up in the ship's waist; p. 375 (n.) or a
Lieutenant against a midshipman; p. 375 (n.) if a midshipman bears a
grudge; p. 375 (n.) cling to the very kelson of the ship; p. 375 (n.)
tend to beget in most armed ships; p. 375 (n.) though, in other ships;
p. 377 (n.) with a ship and a gallows in the distance; p. 377 (adj.)
should have converted the ship's masts; p. 378 (n.) story concerns a
French armed ship; p. 378 (n.) the men in an American armed ship;
p. 378 (n.) on board of the United States ship Neversink; p. 378 (v.)
A Virginia slave regularly shipped as a seaman; p. 380 (n.) foreigners
serving in the King's ships; p. 380 (n.) patriotism in many of my
shipmates; p. 380 (n.) man the guns of an English ship; p. 380 (n.)
the protracted confinement on board ship; p. 381 (n.) enthusiasm into
the King's ships; p. 382 (n.) the men on board the King's ships;
p. 382 (n.) the magnitude of most of these ships; p. 384 (v.) who
shipped with us at Valparaiso; p. 384 (n.) "Shippy!" said Landless;
p. 384 (n.) Shippy, I've seen service with Uncle Sam; p. 385 (n.) To
sail in such ships is hardly; p. 387 (adj.) by the knell of the ship's
bell; p. 388 (n.) I tell you what it is, shippies; p. 388 (n.) all
hands tumble up, and 'bout ship; p. 389 (n.) Shipmates! take me by
the arms; p. 389 (adj.) before I go again to a ship's wheel; p. 389
(n.) Blast the sea, shipmates; p. 389 (n.) venerate it so highly;
p. 389 (n.) with a stout ship under foot; p. 390 (n.) on board of the

guardo or receiving ship; p. 391 (n.) on board the English line-of-
battle ship; p. 392 (n.) when the ship gave a plunge; p. 392 (n.) the
ship gave another jerk; p. 394 (n.) I essayed to swim toward the ship;
p. 396 (n.) Let us leave the ship on the sea; p. 398 (n.) of which
God was the shipwright; p. 399 (n.) When a shipmate does; p. 399 (n.)
Oh, shipmates and world-mates, all round; p. 400 (n.) Yet, shipmates
and world-mates! let us never forget.

Moby-Dick--p. 2 (n.) There go the ships; p. 5 (n.) While the whale is
floating at the stern of the ship; p. 5 (n.) for fear they should run
their ship upon them; p. 5 (n.) wind N.E. in the ship called The
Jonas-in-the-Whale; p. 6 (n.) Falconer's Shipwreck; p. 8 (n.)
Narrative of the Shipwreck of the Whale Ship Essex of Nantucket; p. 9
The Whale-ship Globe . . . . belonged to the island of Nantucket;
p. 10 (adj.) Another Version of the whale-ship Globe narrative; p. 10
(n.) It is impossible to meet a whale-ship on the ocean without being
struck; p. 10 (n.) that the whites saw their ship in bloody possession
of the savages; p. 10 (n.) Newspaper Account of the Taking and
Retaking of the Whale-ship Hobomack; p. 11 (n.) few [crews] ever
return in the ships on board of which they departed; p. 12 (n.) with
a philosophical flourish Cato throws himself upon his sword; I quietly
take to the ship; p. 12 (n.) some looking over the bulwarks of ships
from China; p. 13 (n.) Tell me, does the magnetic virtue in the
needles of the compasses of all those ships attract them thither;
p. 13 (n.) when first told that you and your ship were now out of
sight of land; p. 14 (n.) as much as I can do to take care of myself,
without taking care of ships; p. 14 (n.) a cook being a sort of
officer on ship-board; p. 20 (n.) the half-foundered ship weltering
there; p. 22 (n.) He was trying his hand at a ship under full sail;
p. 23 (n.) a three years' voyage, and a full ship; p. 23 (n.) he
seemed desirous not to spoil the hilarity of his shipmates; p. 23 (n.)
sea-gods had ordained that he should soon become my shipmate; p. 24
(n.) he was missed by his shipmates; p. 29 (v.) he must be some
abominable savage or other shipped aboard; p. 30 (adj.) thus laying a
bit of ship biscuit on top; p. 36 (n.) harpooners, and shipkeepers;
p. 40 (n.) Forming one of the boats' crews of the ship Eliza; p. 40
(n.) This marble is here placed by their surviving shipmates; p. 42
(n.) like those used in mounting a ship from a boat at sea; p. 43 (n.)
however convenient for a ship; p. 43 (n.) a large painting representing
a gallant ship; p. 43 (adj.) a distinct spot of radiance upon the
ship's tossed deck; p. 43 (n.) "Ah, noble ship," the angel seemed to
say, "beat on . . . thou noble ship"; p. 43 (adj.) in the likeness of
a ship's bluff bows; p. 43 (adj.) fashioned after a ship's biddle-
headed beak; p. 44 (n.) Yes, the world's a ship on its passage out;
p. 44 (n.) Midships! midships; p. 44 (n.) like the continual tolling
of a bell in a ship; p. 45 (n.) Beloved shipmates, clinch the last
verse of the first chapter of Jonah; p. 45 (n.) Shipmates, this book,
containing only four chapters; p. 45 (n.) He thinks that a ship made
by men, will carry; p. 45 (n.) and seeks a ship that's bound for
Tarshish; p. 46 (n.) prowling among the shipping like a vile burglar;
p. 46 (n.) he finds the Tarshish ship receiving the last items of her
cargo; p. 46 (n.) the spill upon the wharf to which the ship is
moored; p. 46 (n.) while all his sympathetic shipmates now crowded
round Noah; p. 46 (n.) I seek a passage in this ship to Tarshish;
p. 47 (adj.) sunk, too, beneath the ship's water-line; p. 47 (n.) the
ship, keeling over towards the wharf; p. 48 (n.) the ship casts off

her cables; p. 48 (n.) the uncheered ship for Tarshish, all careening, glides; p. 48 (n.) That ship, my friends, was the first of recorded smugglers; p. 48 (n.) the ship is like to break; p. 48 (n.) Jonah was gone down into the sides of the ship; p. 48 (n.) wave after wave thus leaps into the ship; p. 49 (n.) seek by other means to save the ship; p. 50 (n.) by taking ship at Joppa; p. 51 (n.) when the ship of this base treacherous world has gone down beneath him; p. 56 (n.) A Sag Harbor ship visited his father's bay; p. 56 (n.) But the ship, having her full complement of seamen, spurned his suit; p. 56 (n.) a distant strait, which he knew the ship must pass through when she quitted the island; p. 57 (n.) But like Czar Peter content to toil in the shipyards of foreign cities; p. 57 (v.) He at once resolved to . . . ship aboard the same vessel; p. 59 (n.) Now a certain grant merchant ship once touched at Kokovoko; p. 59 (n.) side by side the world-wandering whale ships lay silent and safely moored; p. 63 (n.) Merchant ships are but extension bridges; armed ones floating forts; p. 66 (n.) The Ship; p. 66 (n.) I sallied out among the shipping; p. 68 (adj.) it being noon, and the ship's work suspended; p. 70 (n.) the Pequod was as good a ship as any; p. 73 (adj.) drawing forth the ship's articles; p. 74 (adj.) left nearly the whole management of the ship's offices to the two; p. 75 (n.) I would afore now had a conscience to lug about that would be heavy enough to founder the largest ship; p. 83 (v.) young man, you'd better ship for a missionary, instead of a fore-mast hand; p. 86 (n./v./n.) Shipmates, have ye shipped in that ship; p. 90 (n.) on board a ship in which her beloved brother Bildad was concerned; p. 93 (adj.) upon the final dismissal of the ship's riggers; p. 94 (n.) his presence was by no means necessary in getting the ship under weigh; p. 94 (n.) before they quit the ship for good with the pilot; p. 94 (n.) the station . . . is the forward part of the ship; p. 96 (n.) a ship bound on so long and perilous a voyage . . . a ship in which some thousands of his hard earned dollars were invested . . . a ship, in which an old shipmate sailed as captain; p. 96 (n.) Captain Bildad--come, old shipmate; p. 97 (n.) Ship and boat diverged; p. 97 (n.) it fared with him as with the storm-tossed ship; p. 97 (adj.) But in that gale, the port, the land, is that ship's direst jeopardy; p. 99 (n.) the whale-ship has been the pioneer in ferreting out the remotest . . . parts of the earth; p. 100 (adj.) of being set down in the ship's common log; p. 103 (n.) courage was one of the great staple outfits of the ship, like her beef and her bread, and not to be foolishly wasted; p. 109 (adj.) than any of the tame merchant-ship companies; p. 109 (n.) with a fair wind the ship was rushing through the water; p. 110 (adj.) looking straight out beyond the ship's ever-pitching prow; p. 112 (n.) for fear of disturbing their slumbering shipmates; p. 128 (n.) a little domestic peculiarity on ship-board; p. 131 (n.) the official supremacy of a ship-master; p. 133 (n.) they filled their bellies like Indian ships all day loading with spices; p. 136 (n.) the one proper mast-head, that of a whale-ship at sea; p. 136 (n.) as ships once sailed between the boots; p. 137 (n.) The tranced ship indolently rolls; p. 139 (n.) admonish you, ye ship-owners of Nantucket; p. 139 (v.) who offers to ship with the Phaedon instead of Bowditch in his head; p. 140 (n.) that rocking life imparted by a gently rolling ship; p. 168 (n.) he, shivered and half shipwrecked; p. 186 (n.) One of the men selected for ship-keepers; p. 194 (n.) no sign of the ship could be seen; p. 202 (n.) the silent ship . . . day after day tore on through all the swift madness; p. 227 (n.) afloat the vast bulk of him is out of

sight, like a launched line-of-battle ship; p. 255 (n.) for the
seamen to dip their sea-biscuit into the huge oil-pots; p. 258 (n.)
with a great swash the ship rolls upwards and backwards; pp. 288-9
(n.) till the drunk ship reeled and shook as if smitten by an iceberg;
p. 297 (adj.) Pull now, men, like fifty thousand line-of-battle ship
loads of red-haired devils; p. 300 (adj.) the whale broke water
within two ships' lengths of the hunters; p. 302 (n.) The ship
groaned and gasped; p. 321 (n.) gradually the ship neared them;
p. 322 (n.) helplessly floated [whales] like water-logged dismantled
ships on the sea; p. 323 (n.) our beset boat was like a ship mobbed
by ice-isles; p. 338 (n.) this was the romantic name of this aromatic
ship; p. 344 (n.) Some few hands are reserved called ship-keepers;
p. 348 (n.) the ship under indolent sail; p. 353 (n.) The burning
ship drove on; p. 353 (n.) To every pitch of the ship there was a
pitch of the boiling oil; p. 353 (n.) as . . . the sea leaped, and
the ship groaned and dived; p. 354 (n.) silently guided the way of
this fire-ship on the sea; p. 356 (n.) while, perhaps, the ship is
pitching and rolling this way and that; p. 356 (n.) the bowels of the
ship are thrown open; p. 357 (n.) the entire ship seems great
leviathan himself; p. 362 (n.) Ship, old ship! my old head shakes to
think of thee; p. 363 (adj.) Here's the ship's navel, this doubloon
here; p. 363 (n.) once more hailing a ship showing English colors;
p. 370 (n.) the Samuel Enderby was a jolly ship; p. 387 (adj.) Like
all sea-going ship carpenters; p. 387 (adv.) this bench was securely
lashed athwartship; p. 393 (adj.) my conscience is in this ship's
keel; p. 395 (n.) when the ship was about half disembowelled; p. 405
(n.) blended with the black tragedy of the melancholy ship, and
mocked it; p. 413 (adj.) dashing high up against the reeling ship's
high tetering side; p. 415 (adj.) the lower parts of a ship's
lightening-rods are not always overboard; p. 436 (n.) this ship that
so wept with spray, still remained without comfort; p. 454 (n.) The
ship tore on; leaving such a furrow in the sea as when a cannon-ball,
missent, becomes a ploughshare and turns up the level field; p. 454
(n.) This ship and I are two brave fellows; p. 457 (n.) the attentive
ship having descried the whole fight; p. 461 (n.) the braced ship
sailed hard upon the breeze as she rechurned the cream in her own
white wake; p. 468 (n.) Oh! Ye three unsurrendered spires of mine;
thou uncracked keel; and only god-bullied hull, thou firm deck, and
haughty helm, and Pole-pointed prow,--death-glorious ship.

SHOAL. A danger formed by sunken rocks, on which the sea does not break;
but generally applied to every place where the water is shallow, whatever
be the ground. Also, a great quantity of fishes swimming in company.
Also, a vessel is said to shoalen, or shoal her water, when she comes
from a greater into a less depth. (Smyth)

Typee--p. 10 (n.) a shoal of flying fish . . . would leap; p. 14 (n.)
I imagined it to be produced by a shoal of fish; p. 14 (n.) caused by
a shoal of "whihenies"; p. 23 (n.) A vast shoal of bonetas and
albicores; p. 132 (n.) like a shoal of dolphins.

Omoo--p. 35 (n.) the actual existence of certain shoals, and reefs.

Mardi--p. 7 (n.) far from the farthest shoal; p. 18 (n.) as for
intervening shoal or reefs; p. 40 (n.) shoals of Tiger Sharks; p. 69

(n.) to a shoal on the thither side; p. 70 (n.) the natives in shoals;
p. 81 (n.) head-foremost toward a shoal; p. 81 (n.) irregularity and
extent of the shoal; p. 83 (n.) the escape from the shoal; p. 103 (n.)
followed by shoals of small fish; p. 103 (n.) the shoals of fish were
darting; p. 109 (n.) might have run close to shoal or reef; p. 121
(n.) where an immense shoal of cachalots; p. 122 (n.) rejoining the
shoal; p. 151 (n.) upon the outskirts of the shoal; p. 188 (n.)
strangers came not in shoals as before; p. 286 (v.) Soon the water
shoaled; p. 288 (n.) the fish darted in a shoal; p. 367 (n.) save the
good ship from the shoals; p. 367 (n.) Shoals, like nebulous vapors;
p. 452 (n.) between shoals of web-footed warriors; p. 482 (n.) made a
commotion like shoals of herring; p. 557 (n.) than float on vulgar
shoals; p. 644 (n.) shoals of dolphins were leaping over.

Redburn--p. 290 (n.) made a rapid run across these dreaded shoals.

White-Jacket--p. 346 (n.) were navigated over imaginary shoals.

Moby-Dick--p. 7 (n.) Gather'd in shoals immense, like floating
islands; p. 9 (n.) A shoal of Sperm Whales; p. 140 (n.) there might
have been shoals of them in the far horizon; p. 323 (n.) for some one
lone whale on the outskirts of the shoal; p. 323 (n.) as the swift
monster drags you deeper and deeper into the frantic shoal; p. 324
(n.) we glided between two whales into the innermost heart of the shoal.

SHORE. The general name for the littoral of any country against which
the waves impinge, while the word coast is applied to that part of the
land which only lies contiguous to the sea. (Smyth) -- To prop up a ship
or anything with spars called shores. (Russell)

Typee--p. 4 (n.) didn't every one of her stout timbers grow on shore;
p. 5 (n.) The missionaries . . . had sailed by their lovely shores;
p. 6 (n.) barely touched at their shores; p. 6 (n.) the first white
woman who had ever visited their shores; p. 11 (n.) adverse tribes
dwelling about the shores; p. 12 (n.) we were obliged to sail some
distance along the shore; p. 12 (n.) the green eminences of the shore
looking down; p. 13 (n.) canoes pushed off from the surrounding shores;
p. 14 (n.) entering one when hauled on shore; p. 14 (n.) coming off
from the shore to welcome us; p. 16 (n.) cavalier appropriation of
their shores; p. 18 (n.) and drive the invaders from their shores;
p. 23 (n.) From these the shore recedes on both hands; pp. 23-4 (n.)
The beautiful aspect of the shore; p. 24 (n.) Besides this bay the
shores of the island are indented; p. 25 (n.) beneath the shadows of
the lofty shore; p. 26 (n.) rolling through the blue water towards
their shores; p. 31 (n.) avoided wandering about the more elevated
portions of the shore; p. 32 (n.) gazing wistfully upon the shore;
p. 74 (n.) heading off from the shore; p. 106 (n.) as soon as the
boats should leave the shore; p. 113 (n.) would hie him away to the
sea-shore; p. 173 (n.) on those dimly looming shores of Paradise;
p. 183 (n.) when the Spaniards drew near the shore; p. 196 (n.)
vessels which now touch at their shores; p. 247 (n.) believed Toby to
have arrived on the shore; p. 250 (n.) the two parties who had
accompanied me to the shore; p. 251 (n.) the boat was above fifty
yards from the shore; p. 251 (n.) it blew strong upon the shore;
p. 257 (n.) The excitement that her sudden appearance produced on

shore; p. 264 (n.) After welcoming him to the shore; p. 270 (n.) a
whale ship which was anchored near the shore; p. 271 (n.) impossible
to get me down to the shore that morning.

Omoo--p. 19 (n.) Drawing near the shore; p. 20 (n.) they turned about
and made for the shore; p. 21 (adj.) gazing upon the shore scenery;
p. 24 (n.) again made for the shore; p. 25 (n.) the islanders coming
down to the shore; p. 26 (adj.) we got our off-shore tacks aboard;
p. 26 (n.) any communication with the shore; p. 36 (adj.) Like shore
doctors; p. 64 (n.) within less than a cable's length of the shore;
p. 65 (n.) the bold shore undulating along the horizon; p. 67 (n.)
and from their shores also, have sailed; p. 70 (n.) steered for the
shore; p. 73 (n.) Visitors from Shore; p. 75 (adj.) in the morning a
shore boat; p. 83 (adj.) Doctor Long Ghost, the Shore physician;
p. 94 (adj.) to come off in a shore boat; p. 95 (n.) without any word
even from the shore; p. 97 (n.) now standing off shore; p. 98 (n.) by
a bold sweep of the shore; p. 98 (n.) between the reef and the shore;
p. 102 (n.) thus stranded on a strange shore; p. 124 (n.) of a number
of women from the shore; p. 133 (adj.) the shore doctor had some idea
of allowing us; p. 134 (adj.) This sudden change from ship fare to
shore living; p. 146 (n.) got frightened, and paddled for the shore;
p. 152 (n.) chiefs coming off from the shore in their canoes; p. 152
(n.) came gliding slowly along the shore; p. 217 (n.) the encircling
reef was close to the shore; p. 217 (n.) and beheld Zeke wading
toward the shore; p. 237 (n.) we counted upon reaching the shores of
the lake; p. 238 (n.) It was right on the shore of the lake; p. 240
(n.) we came out upon the farthest shore of the lake; p. 242 (n.)
hauled up on the lake shore; p. 246 (n.) Upon one shore of the bay;
p. 250 (n.) extending within a mile or less of the shore; p. 250 (n.)
there were little hamlets along the shore; p. 263 (n.) it is perhaps
found right on the sea-shore; p. 264 (n.) stands right upon the
southern shore; p. 266 (n.) between the reef and the shore; p. 266
(n.) several yards from the shore; p. 269 (n.) the green shore on the
other; p. 270 (n.) round about the shores of Tahiti; p. 291 (n.)
Weary at last of the shore.

Mardi--p. 7 (n.) when neither sail nor shore; p. 30 (n.) only regarded
him on shore; p. 70 (n.) off from the shore; p. 70 (adv.) to steer
the vessel shoreward; p. 71 (n.) made for the shore; p. 72 (n.) make
for the shore; p. 74 (adj.) gaining the shoreless sea; p. 82 (n.) red
rose, bright shore, and soft heart; p. 85 (n.) to avoid the green
treacherous shores; p. 90 (n.) on the shore of some island; p. 101
(n.) jaunty shore-cap of the captain's; p. 126 (n.) pebbles sent
skipping from the shore; p. 145 (n.) upon any of the shores roundabout;
p. 145 (n.) for the green groves and bright shore; p. 145 (n.) was
not Yillah my shore and my grove; p. 145 (n.) no shore for me yet;
p. 145 (n.) shore was so exceedingly remote; p. 160 (n.) And Yillah
pining for the shore; p. 160 (n.) hovering over these violet shores;
p. 161 (n.) rounding a neighboring shore; p. 161 (n.) from many a
shore roundabout; p. 161 (n.) we gained the shore; p. 161 (n.) whence
they waded to the shore; p. 162 (n.) pointed our prow for the shore;
p. 164 (n.) strangers landing upon their shores; p. 188 (n.) Between
these islets and the shore; p. 194 (n.) I gained the neighboring
shore; p. 201 (n.) in drawing nigh to its shores; p. 217 (n.) long,
verdent, northern shore of Juam; p. 257 (n.) Oh! russet shores of
Rhine and Rhone; p. 265 (n.) shadows, willowy shores, all nod; p. 265

(n.) its wavelets hush the shore; p. 272 (n.) as we drew nigh the
shores; p. 273 (n.) stand dripping upon the shore; p. 280 (n.)
gliding by the pleasant shores; p. 281 (n.) inhabiting the very
shores; p. 286 (n.) little less than a mile from the shore; p. 288
(n.) finny flock on the sea shore; p. 295 (n.) made all haste for the
shore; p. 305 (n.) on its seaward shore; p. 306 (n.) and no shore in
sight; p. 314 (n.) Dark and bold, thy shores, Marlena; p. 323 (n.)
rounding a lofty and insulated shore; p. 324 (n.) remitted from the
neighboring shores; p. 326 (n.) the shores of Maramma were silent;
p. 343 (n.) extending from the high western shore; p. 343 (n.) Its
main-shore was a steep acclivity; p. 343 (n.) long line of images on
the shore; p. 347 (n.) Yillah may have touched these shores; p. 350
(n.) again we approach the shore; p. 367 (v.) shoring the white reef;
p. 375 (n.) than pursuing the Behemoths on shore; p. 435 (n.)
promontory of an uninhabited shore; p. 435 (n.) To the bold shores of
Diranda; p. 439 (n.) the shores of Diranda were in sight; p. 472 (n.)
not so much vanquished Bello, as defended their shores; p. 473 (n.)
from the bold old shores of Dominora; p. 492 (n.) between Dominora
and this unhappy shore; p. 498 (n.) the long winding shores of
Porpheero; p. 499 (n.) Off shore! off shore; p. 499 (n.) The shore
was lined with multitudes; p. 499 (n.) in not touching at its shores;
p. 531 (n.) Through part and parcel of the shore we had left; p. 540
(n.) what a glorious shore we pass; p. 545 (n.) coasting along
Kolumbo's Western shore; p. 548 (n.) who wring their hands on distant
shores; p. 549 (n.) Artless airs came from the shore; p. 551 (n.)
what grand shore is this; pp. 553-4 (n.) we neared Hamora's western
shore; p. 534 (n.) the night-winds from the shore came over us;
p. 554 (n.) Hamora's northern shore gleamed thick; p. 556 (n.) since
leaving Piko's shore of spears; p. 556 (n.) Hug the shore, naught new
is seen; p. 568 (n.) with twinklings of will-o-wisps from neighboring
shores; p. 588 (n.) The shore sloped to the water; p. 589 (adv.) and
shoreward tended; p. 610 (n.) and seek the shore; p. 611 (n.) in the
saffron sunset, we neared another shore; p. 623 (n.) will not be
gained by touching at any shores; p. 623 (n.) Wafted from this shore;
p. 623 (n.) the breeze, likewise, found its shore; p. 623 (n.) To
these, our shores, soft gales invite; p. 624 (n.) Ye left behind our
pleasant shore; p. 642 (n.) the shore now in sight was called.

Redburn--p. 27 (n.) and beef, and vegetables from the shore; p. 33
(n.) passed the green shore of Staten Island; p. 64 (n.) not a single
glimpse of green shore; p. 65 (adj.) if you call a thing by its shore
name; p. 72 (n.) summer excursion on the sea shore; p. 124 (n.) I had
fancied the shore would look like; p. 125 (n.) on the very shore now
in sight; p. 125 (n.) caught sight of distant objects on shore;
p. 127 (n.) not in the direction of the shore; p. 127 (n.) two lofty
land-marks on the Lancashire shore; p. 127 (adv.) Looking shoreward;
p. 128 (adj.) coming with a neat parcel of Max's shore clothes;
p. 137 (n.) a ship-keeper, hired from shore; p. 145 (n.) upon a bleak
rock on the sea shore; p. 147 (n.) Their straggling huts were ranged
along the shore; p. 147 (n.) Where'er his shores the broad Atlantic
waves; p. 159 (n.) how the Abbey was on the Cheshire shore; p. 169
(n.) and the dwellers on the shores of the Mediterranean; p. 193 (n.)
that laves the shore of Old England; p. 196 (n.) But though on shore,
at Liverpool; p. 198 (n.) annually land on the shores of the United
States; p. 219 (n.) invigorating preparative to the landing upon a
shore; p. 221 (n.) as if he were already on the shores of Lake Erie;

p. 238 (n.) by the stevedores and lumpers from shore; p. 239 (n.) he
returned on shore; p. 243 (n.) on quitting the American shore; p. 283
(n.) without a glimpse of shore or reef; p. 292 (n.) like the billows
that break on the shore; p. 292 (n.) should be landed on our American
shores; p. 294 (n.) in the shore-bloom that came to us; p. 299 (n.)
wafting to us a white wing from the shore; p. 299 (n.) not even the
distant sight of the shore itself; p. 299 (n.) deposited on the
shores of Staten Island; p. 300 (n.) full of the glad sights and
sounds of the shore; p. 302 (n.) and then prepared for the shore.

White-Jacket--p. 34 (n.) on shore at least; p. 47 (n.) For even on
shore; p. 55 (n.) as if we were sailing by some odoriferous shore;
p. 74 (n.) wrecked on a desert shore; p. 84 (n.) as if they were
staying at a hotel on shore; p. 123 (n.) at a large ship-chandler's
on shore; p. 129 (n.) we received from shore several barrels of
powder; p. 141 (adj.) frigate was vastly admired by the shore ladies;
p. 160 (n.) beset by all the allurements of the shore; p. 163 (n.)
whenever the commodore arrived from shore; p. 165 (adj.) while the
shore pomp in high places; p. 172 (adj.) admiring the shore scenery
from the port-holes; p. 173 (adj.) Several of my shore friends,
indeed; p. 176 (n.) vessel be anchored a mile from the shore; p. 177
(n.) continually plying to and from the shore; p. 177 (n.) ever
enters the vessel from shore; p. 178 (n.) out of a boat just from
shore; p. 187 (adj.) humorous contrasts between ship and shore life;
p. 191 (adj.) returning the shore salute; p. 217 (n.) on the shores
of Chesapeake Bay; p. 226 (n.) only one of which were on shore at a
time; p. 226 (n.) I have nothing to do with the shore; p. 226 (n.)
out of their hiding-places on shore; p. 227 (n.) All visitors from
shore were kept; p. 231 (adj.) doubtless it was to his shore
sympathies; p. 231 (n.) than people on shore; p. 233 (adj.) A Shore
Emperor on board a Man-of-war; p. 233 (n.) we sometimes had company
from shore; p. 264 (adv.) pointing shoreward, out of a port-hole;
p. 295 (n.) upon the Antarctic shores of Palmer's Land; p. 327 (n.)
like the apothecary's on shore; p. 327 (adj.) that a shore apothecary
should actually charge; p. 351 (adj.) nothing that makes a shore shave
such a luxury; p. 365 (n.) to prevent his escape to the shore; p. 327
(n.) though washing the shores of an absolute king; p. 375 (n.)
completely cut off from shore; p. 381 (n.) the press-gang generally
went to shore; p. 382 (n.) so galling to all shore-manhood as the
Navy; p. 390 (n.) these generous-hearted tars on shore; p. 391 (adj.)
talking about the shore delights; p. 393 (n.) he who stands upon the
Corinthian shore; p. 397 (n.) to believe in that far-distant shore;
p. 397 (adv.) and, pointing shoreward, cries; p. 397 (n.) point our
bowsprit for yon shadowy shore.

Moby-Dick--p. 4 (n.) Like as the wounded whale to shore flies thro'
the maine; p. 5 (n.) tore it with a boat as near the shore as it will
come; p. 6 (n.) Spain--a great whale stranded on the shores of
Europe; p. 11 (n.) within less than a stone's throw of the shore;
p. 12 (n.) having little or no money in my purse, and nothing
particular to interest me on shore; p. 39 (n.) their sailor sweethearts
smelt them miles off shore; p. 40 (adj.) on the off-shore Ground in
the Pacific; p. 93 (adj.) several of the shore people were busy in
bringing various last things on board; p. 94 (adj.) having a farewell
merry-making with their shore friends; p. 97 (adv.) with all her
might she crowds all sail offshore; p. 97 (n.) the wildest winds of

heaven and earth conspire to cast her on the treacherous, slavish
shore; p. 97 (adj.) But as in landlessness alone resides the highest
truth, shoreless, indefinite as God; p. 110 (adj.) soon we shall be
lost in its [the deep's] unshored, harborless immensities; p. 140 (n.)
forming at last a part of every shore the round globe over; p. 179
(n.) when almost despairing of reaching any hospitable shore; p. 402
(n.) to the possibilities of the immense Remote, the Wild, the
Watery, the Unshored; p. 414 (n.) as the lightening rod to a spire on
shore is intended to carry off.

SHRIMP.   The small crustacean Crangon vulgaris, well known as an article
of food.   (Smyth)

   Mardi--p. 573 (n.) The first course was shrimp-soup.

SHROUD.   Designates a set of ropes reaching from the mast-heads to the
vessel's sides, to support the masts.   (Dana)

   Typee--p. 13 (n.) steadied himself by holding on to a shroud.

   Omoo--p. 45 (n.) holding on to a shroud; p. 290 (n.) her shrouds
   swung negligently slack.

   Mardi--p. 128 (n.) answered the purpose of shrouds; p. 128 (n.)
   grasping five shrouds; p. 132 (n.) had ascended the shrouds of a
   ship; p. 259 (n.) like a ship's shrouds in a Typhoon; p. 543 (n.) as
   seated in our shrouds.

   Redburn--p. 53 (n.) behind a band fastened to the shrouds; p. 78 (n.)
   keeping my eyes glued, as it were, to the shrouds; p. 114 (n.)
   repairing the numberless shrouds and stays; p. 115 (n.) old shrouds,
   spars, rusty blocks; p. 115 (n.) by the bare stays instead of the
   shrouds; p. 121 (n.) of hempen lace about the shrouds; p. 172 (n.)
   perched themselves in the shrouds of the neighboring craft; p. 173
   (n.) for the shrouds and standing-rigging of a ship; p. 220 (n.) With
   but one hand on a shroud; p. 255 (n.) were springing into the shrouds;
   p. 255 (n.) starting in a prodigious hurry for the shrouds; p. 256
   (n.) reel, and clutch the shrouds; p. 273 (n.) forming part of a
   lofty stay or a shroud.

   White-Jacket--p. 34 (n.) Like so many ship's shrouds; p. 34 (n.) and
   one hand on a shroud; p. 96 (n.) What signify the broken spars and
   shrouds; p. 105 (n.) held on with the other to the mizzen-shrouds;
   p. 106 (n.) beating his trumpet against one of the shrouds; p. 107
   (n.) every hand seemed congealing to the icy shrouds; p. 108 (n.) in
   order to reach the shrouds; p. 261 (n.) arrayed in a sort of shroud
   of white canvass; p. 262 (n.) of the pale, gaunt man in the shroud;
   p. 271 (n.) holding on to a shroud; p. 310 (n.) leaning against the
   top-mast shrouds; p. 311 (adj.) The three shrouded masts looked like;
   p. 318 (n.) Among their shrouds; p. 322 (n.) at the base of the large
   shrouds leading; p. 323 (n.) forming the pedestals of the shrouds;
   p. 392 (n.) I was mounting the top-mast shrouds; p. 394 (n.) Sink! oh
   shroud! thought I; p. 392 (n.) stripped of spars, shrouds, and sails.

Moby-Dick--p. 8 (n.) A mariner sat in the shrouds one night; p. 48
(n.) grasps a shroud, to look out upon the sea; p. 110 (n.) pretty
close to the mizen shrouds; p. 110 (n.) one arm elevated, and holding
by a shroud; p. 141 (n.) with one hand grasping a shroud, he orcered;
p. 413 (n.) Holding by a shroud; p. 415 (n.) when his Mene, Mene,
Tekel, Upharsin has been woven into the shrouds.

SILVER-HEAD. Webster shows instead silver-fish, a fish of the size of a
small carp, having a white color, striped with silvery lines. (Webster)

Mardi--p. 148 (n.) swam the helmeted Silver-heads.

SKIFF. A familiar term for any small boat; but in particular, one
resembling a yawl, which is usually employed for passing rivers. (Smyth)

Omoo--p. 102 (n.) palm trees and elms--canoes and skiffs.

Moby-Dick--p. 163 (n.) What skiff in tow of a seventy-four can stand
still?

SKIPPER. The master of a merchant vessel. Also, a man-of-war's man's
constant appellation for his own captain. (Smyth)

Typee--p. 35 (n.) so auspiciously announced by the skipper; p. 42 (n.)
our skipper would hold out to them as an inducement; p. 223 (n.) the
skipper directed his steps to a stream.

Omoo--p. 51 (n.) If the skipper dies, all agree to obey; p. 289 (n.)
and the skipper's ashore kitching 'em; p. 289 (n.) the divil of a
skipper will carry yees both to sea.

Mardi--p. 5 (n.) the skipper himself; p. 5 (n.) our skipper had
abandoned; p. 7 (n.) our skipper himself; p. 29 (n.) did not the
skipper suspect the truth; p. 75 (adj.) the poor skipper's wardrobe.

Redburn--p. 69 (n.) to present his best respects to the skipper;
p. 166 (n.) its staid, thrifty-looking skipper; p. 166 (n.) to
observe the self-importance of the skipper; p. 167 (n.) it affords
accommodations to the skipper; p. 167 (n.) fall into conversation
with its skipper.

Moby-Dick--p. 418 (n.) he takes me for the hunch-back skipper of some
coasting smack.

SKRIMSHANDER. Sketches and numerous other ingenious contrivances whalemen
carve on Sperm Whale-teeth, in their hours of ocean leisure. (Melville)

Moby-Dick--p. 22 (n.) examining by a dim light divers specimens of
skrimshander; p. 24 (n.) But wait a bit, Skrimshander; p. 232 (adj.)
and other like skrimshander articles; p. 232 (adj.) specially
intended for the skrimshandering business.

SLOOP. A small vessel with one mast. (Dana)

Omoo--p. 114 (n.) one of an exploring party from an English sloop-of-war.

Redburn--p. 4 (n.) from the wooden, one-masted, green-and-white-painted sloops; p. 4 (n.) the river sloops were not used to make such prospective announcements; p. 126 (adj.) plethoric looking sloop-rigged boat; p. 166 (n.) rigged like sloops; p. 175 (n.) the hull of an old sloop-of-war; p. 300 (n.) covered with white sloop-sails.

White-Jacket--p. 18 (n.) alongside of a Peruvian sloop of war; p. 18 (n.) go on board that sloop of war; p. 18 (n.) on board a Peruvian sloop of war; p. 18 (n.) Gaining the sloop of war; p. 88 (n.) The First Lieutenant of an English sloop of war; p. 144 (n.) the Captain of an American sloop of war; p. 158 (n.) in the case of sloops of war; p. 160 (n.) as big as a small sloop; p. 212 (n.) Of Perry's war-brigs, sloops, and schooners; p. 241 (n.) men from a United States sloop of war.

Moby-Dick--p. 17 (n.) did that first adventurous little sloop put forth; p. 179 (n.) that any whale could so smite his stout sloop-of-war.

SNATCH-BLOCK. A single block, with an opening in its side below the sheave, or at the bottom, to receive the bight of a rope. (Dana)

Typee--p. 22 (n.) we rove through snatch-blocks.

SOUND, SOUNDING. Sounding is the operation of ascertaining the depth of the sea, and the quality of the ground, by means of a lead and line, sunk from a ship to the bottom, where some of the ooze or sand adheres to the tallow of the hollow base of the lead. Also, the vertical diving of a whale when struck. To be in soundings implies being so near the land that a deep-sea lead will reach the bottom, which is seldom practicable in the ocean. (Smyth)

Typee--p. 22 (n.) never again strike Yankee soundings.

Omoo--p. 72 (v.) and the fish sounded; p. 90 (n.) there are no soundings.

Mardi--p. 7 (n.) Off soundings; p. 91 (n.) Pandora and her bandbox off soundings; p. 123 (n.) we feared we were on soundings; p. 123 (n.) well known to swarm off soundings.

Redburn--p. 125 (n.) fairly robbed before striking soundings; p. 169 (n.) that first struck these soundings; p. 256 (n.) till we strike Yankee soundings again.

White-Jacket--p. 155 (n.) there are no Sundays off soundings; p. 155 (n.) there are No Sundays off soundings; p. 208 (n.) reveals to us on what soundings we are; p. 332 (n.) by the time we strike soundings, men; p. 397 (n.) our frigate strikes soundings at last.

Moby-Dick--p. 17 (v.) With anxious grapnels I had sounded my pocket;
p. 45 (v.) what depths of the soul does Jonah's deep sea-line sound;
p. 45 (v.) we sound with him to the kelpy bottom of the waters;
p. 158 (v.) after sounding to a great depth; p. 168 (n.) in vain the
lead assures him he is still off soundings; p. 181 (v.) we cast the
lead, and sounded, but found no ground; p. 186 (v.) sounding with his
head in one direction; p. 191 (n.) The whales might have made one of
their regular soundings; p. 242 (n.) After the full interval of his
sounding had elapsed; p. 272 (adj.) That unsounded ocean you gasp in,
is Life; p. 299 (n.) that this rapid sounding would soon exhaust the
lines; p. 303 (n.) In the shore Whaling, on soundings, among the Bays
of New Zealand; p. 326 (n.) as, after deep sounding; p. 340 (v.)
Sounding him carefully, Stubb further perceived; p. 408 (n.) for that
vial was filled with Nantucket soundings; p. 448 (v.) the grand god
revealed himself, sounded, and went out of sight.

SOU'-WESTER. A useful water-proof hat for bad weather. (Smyth's
spelling is "South-Wester.")

Redburn--p. 19 (adj.) in a great flapping sou'-wester cap.

Moby-Dick--p. 38 (n.) Here comes another with a sou'-wester and a
bombazine cloak.

SPANKER. A fore-and-aft sail, setting with a boom and gaff, frequently
called the driver. It is the aftermost sail of a ship or bark. (Smyth)

Omoo--p. 60 (n.) our spanker-gaff came down by the run.

Redburn--p. 262 (n.) under the lee of the spanker.

White-Jacket--p. 9 (n.) attend to the main-sail and spanker; p. 223
(n.) with the slack of the spanker-out-haul.

SPAR. The general term for any mast, yard, boom, gaff &c. In ship-
building, the name is applied to small firs used in making staging. (Smyth)

Typee--p. 16 (n.) constructed of old sails and spare spars; p. 22 (n.)
her spars fished with old pipe staves; p. 134 (n.) pride ourselves
upon our straight clean spars.

Omoo--p. 5 (n.) her hull and spars a dingy black; p. 8 (n.) how's
that spar of your'n; p. 10 (n.) with spars erect, she looked right up;
p. 19 (n.) the grim, black spars and waspish hull; p. 58 (n.) every
spar buckled; p. 292 (n.) to break clear from the fallen spars.

Mardi--p. 4 (n.) one of our spars; p. 15 (n.) high upon the spars;
p. 56 (n.) a ship's uppermost spars were observed; p. 64 (n.) creaking
of the spars; p. 71 (n.) every spar quivered and sprung; p. 483 (n.)
the wood-worms exploring into its spars.

Redburn--p. 9 (n.) but many of her glass spars and ropes; p. 93 (n.)
replaced the broken spar; p. 93 (n.) for all ships carry spare spars;

p. 115 (n.) old shrouds, spars, rusty blocks; p. 115 (n.) I felt like being jerked off the spar; p. 116 (n.) tying it down like a slave to a spar; p. 165 (n.) in the collective spars and timbers of these ships; p. 171 (n.) to sending down all her spars and ropes; p. 173 (n.) had her heavy Indian spars replaced; p. 174 (n.) scrape and varnish all its planks and spars; p. 242 (n.) among the boats, casks, and spars; p. 255 (n.) as much at home among the spars.

White-Jacket--p. 15 (n.) and yawning on the spar-deck; p. 63 (n.) very seldom to be seen on the spar-deck; p. 75 (n.) a whole cabin to himself on the spar-deck; p. 83 (n.) I have sometimes slept standing on the spar-deck; p. 94 (n.) to the picturesque effect of the spar-deck; p. 93 (n.) halyards and running ropes about the spar-deck; p. 96 (n.) what signify the broken spars; p. 105 (n.) taking quick leave of the spars; p. 108 (n.) managed to crawl upon the spar; p. 115 (adj.) weight of metal upon the spar and gun decks; p. 194 (n.) causing the various spars of all the ships; p. 198 (n.) Purser's auction on the spar-deck; p. 235 (n.) with that thin pair of spars; p. 239 (n.) commenced the ascent to the spar-deck; p. 240 (n.) being assisted to the spar-deck; p. 245 (n.) looked round for Frank on the spar-deck; p. 269 (n.) to look through their tall spars; p. 269 (n.) no sign of a strange spar was to be seen; p. 272 (n.) Some were sent forward on the spar-deck; p. 279 (n.) as I touched the spar-deck; p. 307 (n.) lurking round the fore-mast on the spar-deck; p. 319 (n.) just as our spars are dressed; p. 326 (n.) the general tumult of the spar-deck; p. 330 (n.) a mouthful of fresh air on the spar-deck; p. 340 (n.) coming down from the spar-deck; p. 358 (adj.) cutting off all communication between the gun and spar decks; p. 396 (n.) stripped of spars, shrouds, and sails.

Moby-Dick--p. 14 (n.) they rather order me about some, and make me jump from spar to spar; p. 61 (n.) at the next jerk, the spar was that way trapped; p. 136 (n.) erected lofty spars along the sea-coast; p. 387 (n.) repairing stove boats, sprung spars; p. 422 (n.) Does he not say he will not strike his spars to any gale; p. 433 (n.) all her spars thickly clustering with men; p. 455 (n.) clinging to a spar with one hand; p. 455 (n.) all the spars in full bearing of mortals, ready and ripe for their fate.

SPECKSYNDER. The chief harpooner in a Greenland ship. He also directs the cutting operations in clearing the whale of its blubber and bones. (Smyth's spelling is "specktioneer.")

Moby-Dick--p. 128 (n.) The Specksynder; p. 128 (n.) an officer called the Specksynder. Literally this word means Fat-Cutter; p. 128 (n.) the Specksynder or Chief Harpooneer reigned supreme; p. 128 (n.) under the corrupted title of Specksioneer.

SPERM, SPERMACITI, SPERMACETTI, PARMACETTI. The Sperm Whale, otherwise known as the cachalot, Physeter macrocephalus. A large cetacean, belonging to the division of delphinoid or toothed whales. It is found in nearly all tropical and temperate seas, and is much hunted for the valuable sperm-oil and spermaceti which it yields. When full grown, it may attain the length of 60 feet, of which the head occupies nearly one-third. (Smyth)

Omoo--p. xiii (n.) are engaged in the Sperm Whale Fishery; p. 10 (n.)
Sperm whaling, however, was what she relied on; p. 39 (n.) With Sperm
Whalemen; p. 48 (n.) But where were the sperm whales; p. 51 (n.) five
hundred barrels of sperm oil under hatches; p. 64 (n.) being much
cheaper than the sperm; p. 71 (adj.) performed in the sperm-whale
fishery.

Mardi--p. 6 (n.) sperm and spermaciti; p. 375 (adj.) secretion of the
Sperm Whale; p. 375 (adj.) the Sperm whale was much hunted; p. 375
(n.) than a whole ton of sperm.

Redburn--p. 99 (adj.) They ar'n't sperm whales; p. 107 (n.) by the
enormous head of the sperm-whale.

White-Jacket--p. 15 (n.) externally talking of line-tubs, Nantucket
sperm oil; p. 189 (adj.) fabricated from a sperm-whale's tooth;
p. 363 (adj.) its handle--a sperm whale's tooth.

Moby-Dick--p. 3 (n.) The sovereignest thing on earth is parmacetti
for an inward bruise; p. 4 (adj.) what spermacetti is, men might
justly doubt; p. 5 (adj.) whether I can master and kill this
Spermaceti whale; p. 6 (adj.) The Spermacetti whale . . . is an
active, fierce animal; p. 7 (adj.) In 40 degrees south, we saw
Spermacetti Whales; p. 8 (adj.) Colnett's Voyage for the Purpose of
Extending the Spermacetti Whale Fishery; p. 8 (adj.) which was
attacked and finally destroyed by a large sperm whale; p. 8 (adj.)
the infuriated Sperm whale rolls over and over; p. 9 (n.) so
important an animal (as the Sperm Whale) should have been so entirely
neglected; p. 9 (adj.) Thomas Beale's History of the Sperm Whale,
1839; p. 9 (adj.) A shoal of Sperm Whales; p. 11 (adj.) He saw the
distended jaws of a large Sperm whale; p. 38 (adj.) recklessly burn
their lengths in spermaceti candles; p. 40 (adj.) who in the bows of
his boat was killed by a Sperm Whale; p. 69 (n.) it [Ahab's leg] was
devoured, chewed up, crunched by the monstrousest parmacetty that
ever chipped a boat; p. 87 (n.) they know he's only one leg; and that
a parmacetti took the other off; p. 102 (adj.) parmacetti oil in its
unmanufactured, unpolluted state, the sweetest of all oils; p. 120
(n.) the only creature from which that valuable substance, sperm, is
obtained; p. 120 (n.) sperm . . . was popularly supposed to be derived
from; p. 120 (n.) this same sperm was that quickening humor; p. 120
(n.) sperm was exceedingly scarce; p. 120 (n.) the true nature of
sperm became known; p. 120 (n.) the whale from which this sperm was
really derived; p. 139 (n.) one pint of sperm the richer; p. 188 (adj.)
Hurrah for the gold cup of sperm oil; p. 255 (n.) But the sperm itself,
how bland and creamy that is; p. 284 (adj.) in the ordinary swimming
position of the Sperm Whale; p. 290 (n.) smothered in the very
whitest and dantiest of fragrant spermaciti; p. 293 (adj.) formed by
the cubic-yards of his sperm magazine; p. 293 (adj.) If you unload his
skull of its spermy heaps; p. 297 (n.) Don't ye love sperm; p. 348
(n.) this same sperm was carefully manipulated ere going to the try-
works; p. 348 (n.) in old times this sperm was such a favorite
cosmetic; p. 348 (n.) in that inexpressible sperm, I washed my hands
and my heart of it; I also began to credit the old Paracelsan
superstition that sperm is of rare virtue in allaying the heat of
anger; p. 348 (n.) I squeezed that sperm till I myself almost melted
into it; I squeezed that sperm till a strange sort of insanity came
over me; p. 349 (n.) let us squeeze ourselves universally into the

very milk and sperm of kindness; p. 349 (n.) Would that I could keep
squeezing that sperm for ever; p. 349 (n.) I saw long rows of angels
in paradise, each with his hands in a jar of spermaciti; p. 349 (n.)
while discoursing of sperm; p. 357 (adj.) The unmanufactured sperm
oil possesses a singularly cleansing virtue; p. 369 (n.) with her
hold full of the precious sperm; p. 407 (n.) in each of her three
basketed tops were two barrels of sperm; p. 416 (n.) chock a block
with sperm-oil . . . so, all that sperm will work up into the masts.

SPILE. A stake or piece of wood formed like the frustum of a cone. A
vent-peg in a cask of liquor. Small wooden pins which are driven into
nail-holes to prevent leaking. (Smyth)

Moby-Dick--p. 12 (n.) Some leaning against the spiles; p. 46 (n.) the
bill that's stuck against the spile upon the wharf; p. 62 (n.) send
beyond seas for a spile to stop a leak in an oil cask.

SPOUT. A term applied to the blowing or breathing of whales and other
cetaceans. The expired air, highly charged with moisture from the lungs,
has frequently been mistaken for a stream of water. (Smyth)

Moby-Dick--p. 8 (v.) observing the whales spouting and sporting with
each other; p. 8 (n.) I saw his spout, he threw up a pair of . . .
pretty rainbows; p. 18 (n.) these words underneath--The Spouter-Inn;
p. 18 (n.) Coffin?--Spouter?--Rather ominous in that particular
connexion; p. 20 (n.) Let us scrape the ice from our frosted feet,
and see what sort of place this Spouter may be; p. 20 (n.) THE
SPOUTER-INN; p. 20 (n.) Entering that gable-ended Spouter-Inn; p. 51
(n.) Returning to the Spouter-Inn from the Chapel; p. 119 (adj.) a
whale is a spouting fish; p. 119 (v.) A walrus spouts much like a
whale; p. 119 (adj.) among spouting fish; p. 119 (adj.) all the
smaller, spouting, and horizontal tailed fish; p. 119 (v.) especially
as they do not spout; p. 143 (v.) till he spouts black blood and rolls
fin out; p. 226 (n.) where all manner of spouts, jets d'eau, hot
springs and cold, Saratoga and Baden-Baden, come bubbling up from his
unexhausted brain; p. 229 (n.) half shrouded by the incensed boiling
spout of the whale; p. 282 (n.) look at these two f-shaped spout-holes;
p. 284 (n.) what nose he has--his spout hole; p. 296 (n.) His spout
was short, slow and laborious; p. 298 (n.) sending his spout before
him in a continual tormented jet; p. 301 (n.) while the natural
spout-hold in his head was only at intervals, however rapid, sending
its offrighted moisture; pp. 301-2 (n.) It was most piteous that last
expiring spout . . . so the last long dying spout of the whale;
p. 304 (n.) the only spout in sight was that of a Fin-Back; p. 312
(n.) the whale only breathes through his spout-hole . . . that his
spouts are mixed with water; p. 320 (n.) this host of vapoury spouts;
p. 322 (n.) so that their spouts all looked like flashing lines of
stacked bayonets; p. 322 (n.) by their short thick spoutings; p. 358
(v.) the ghost is spouted up; p. 374 (n.) so that the mystic head
again sent forth its vapory spout; p. 385 (v.) the eternal whale
will . . . spout his frothed defiance to the skies; p. 446 (n.)
regularly jetting his silent spout into the air; p. 446 (n.) it
seemed the same silent spout they had so long ago beheld; p. 451 (n.)
what a leaping spout; p. 451 (n.) the whale's glittering spout was

regularly announced from the manned mast-heads; p. 452 (n./v.) Sing
out for every spout, though he spouts ten times a second; p. 454 (n.)
blow on and split your spout, O whale; p. 455 (n.) For not by any
calm and indolent spoutings; p. 466 (n.) the smoky mountain mist,
which, thrown off from the whale's spout; p. 467 (v.) assassins of as
good a fellow as ever spouted up his ghost.

SPRAT. A small fish of the species Clupea. (Webster)

Moby-Dick--p. 4 (n.) as if it had been a sprat in the mouth of a whale.

SPRAY. The occasional water that is driven from the top of a wave, which
spreads and flies in small particles. (Webster)

Typee--p. 64 (n.) drenched by the spray of the fall.

Omoo--p. 8 (n.) and flung the spray in my face; p. 39 (n.) little
protection from the spray; p. 58 (n.) with the spray every now and
then dashing; p. 167 (n.) from the spray of the reef; p. 266 (n.)
dashed the spray in our faces.

Mardi--p. 200 (n.) Yoomy, standing where the spicy spray flew; p. 216
(n.) the spray came and went unequally; p. 234 (n.) to avoid the
spray of the rejoicing cataract; p. 259 (n.) then paused in its spray;
p. 644 (n.) what flies through the spray; p. 644 (n.) stacked with
their glittering sheaves of spray; p. 645 (n.) beneath an arch of
spray.

Redburn--p. 6 (n.) for the white spray was about the bows; p. 250 (n.)
that dashes its spray [organ music] in my face; p. 263 (n.) and the
heaving of the spray; p. 289 (n.) drenched in rain and spray; p. 77
(n.) Let me . . . whinny in the spray; p. 83 (n.) Drenched through
and through by the spray of the sea; p. 83 (n.) the spray . . . kept
the planks . . . constantly wet; p. 105 (n.) while forward thy spray
dashed; p. 106 (n.) The spray flew over the ship in floods; p. 137
(n.) and dashed the spray over his exposed back; p. 191 (n.) to keep
out the spray of the sea.

Moby-Dick--p. 95 (n.) whose freezing spray cased us in ice; p. 98 (n.)
Up from the spray of thy ocean-perishing; p. 245 (n.) overwrapped
himself in impenetrable, mad, boiling spray; p. 289 (n.) Daggoo,
through a thick mist of spray; p. 323 (n.) the stricken fish darted
blinding spray in our faces; p. 370 (n.) though the savage salt spray
bursting down the forecastle scuttle; p. 419 (n.) how the devil could
the lucifers get afire in this drenching spray here; p. 436 (n.) you
plainly saw that this ship that so wept with spray; p. 450 (n.)
vindictively tossing their shivered spray still higher into the air;
p. 455 (n.) the spray that he raised . . . intolerably glittered and
glared like a glacier.

SQUALL. A sudden gust of wind, frequently occasioned by the interruption
and reverberation of the wind from high mountains. These are very
frequent in the Mediterranean, particularly in the Levant.--A black squall.

One attended with a dark cloud and generally heavy rain.--A white squall.
This furious and dangerous gust occurs in clear weather, without any
other warning than the white foam it occasions on the surface of the sea,
and a very thin haze. When this squall reaches a ship, copious rain
attends it. It is very destructive to the flying-kite school, and many
lives have been sacrificed by it. (Smyth)

Omoo--p. 39 (n.) In a squall; p. 46 (n.) to furl the main-top-gallant-
sail in a squall; p. 100 (n.) made as much fuss as a white squall.

Mardi--p. 4 (n.) in a very sharp squall; p. 7 (n.) exchanged for
cold, fierce squalls; p. 63 (n.) in a supernatural squall.

Redburn--p. 64 (n.) it gave no tokens of squalls or hurricanes;
p. 102 (n.) was the precursor of a hard squall; p. 104 (n.) they have
plenty of squalls here below; p. 115 (n.) especially during a squall;
p. 173 (n.) between the tropics, in a squall; p. 220 (n.) could furl
a royal squall; p. 288 (n.) had it not been for the rains and squalls.

White-Jacket--p. 32 (n.) Prepare for white squalls; p. 33 (n.)
concerning the likelihood of a squall; p. 59 (n.) Then it was, look
out for squalls; p. 94 (n.) A black squall was coming down; p. 96
(adj.) frigate drew nearer . . . to the squally cape; p. 105 (n.)
became a succession of sharp squalls; p. 105 (n.) tossed about in the
squalls like a foot-ball; p. 107 (n.) at the commencement of the
squalls; p. 110 (n.) in almost all cases of similar hard squalls;
p. 121 (n.) How I hailed every snow-squall.

Moby-Dick--p. 70 (n.) there's a squall coming up, I think; p. 75 (n.)
the squall's gone off to leeward, I think; p. 130 (n.) he strikes
into a sharp but noiseless squall of a hornpipe right over the Grand
Turk's head; p. 143 (n.) he fan-tails like a split jib in a squall;
p. 153 (n.) he must always kill a squall; p. 154 (n.) The squall! the
squall; p. 154 (n.) what a squall; p. 154 (n.) But those chaps . . .
are your white squalls, they; p. 166 (n.) the gauntleted ghost of the
Southern Seas has been denominated the White Squall; p. 194 (n.)
tossed helter-skelter into the white curdling cream of the squall;
p. 194 (n.) squall, whale, and harpoon had all blended together;
p. 194 (n.) the whole squall roared, forked, and crackled around us
like a white fire upon the prairie, in which, unconsumed, we were
burning; p. 196 (n.) with your sail set in a foggy squall; p. 196 (n.)
that squalls . . . were matters of common occurrence; p. 196 (n.)
Starbuck's driving on to his whale almost in the teeth of a squall;
p. 370 (n./adj.) and when the squall came (for it's squally off there
by Patagonia); p. 432 (n.) but squalls come sudden in hot latitudes.

SQUID. An animal allied to the cuttle-fish, belonging to the class
cephalapoda; the calamary or loligo of naturalists. (Smyth)

Moby-Dick--p. 182 (n.) food of the sperm whale--squid or cuttle-fish;
p. 237 (n.) the great live squid, which they say, few whale-ships
ever beheld, and returned to their ports to tell of it; p. 237 (n.)
he will disgorge what are supposed to be the detached arms of the
squid; p. 241 (n.) If to Starbuck the apparition of the Squid was a
thing of portents, to Queequeg it was quite a different object;
p. 343 (adj.) pieces of small squid bones embalmed in that manner.

STARBOARD. The opposite of <u>larboard</u> or <u>port</u>; the distinguishing term for the right side of a ship when looking forward. (Smyth)

<u>Typee</u>--p. 33 (adj.) The next day the starboard watch; p. 34 (adj.) Early the next morning the starboard watch were; p. 35 (adj.) upon the countenances of the starboard watch.

<u>Omoo</u>--p. 21 (adj.) hoisted up to its place over the starboard quarter; p. 48 (adj.) one for the starboard watch; p. 102 (adj.) let them go over to the starboard side; p. 289 (adj.) All the starboard watch ran away last night.

<u>Mardi</u>--p. 52 (n.) to starboard or larboard; p. 113 (adj.) chain-plates under the starboard main-channel.

<u>Redburn</u>--p. 93 (adj.) All her starboard side was torn; p. 93 (adj.) All her starboard anchor was gone; p. 93 (adj.) a great part of the starboard bulwarks; p. 93 (adj.) had rushed past her starboard side; p. 123 (adj.) Starboard watch, ahoy.

<u>White-Jacket</u>--p. 8 (adj.) divided into watches--starboard and larboard; p. 9 (adj.) he permanently belonged to the Starboard Watch; p. 9 (adj.) men of each watch--Starboard and Larboard; p. 62 (adj.) On their starboard hand was Mess No. 2; p. 65 (adj.) on the starboard side of the quarter-deck; p. 83 (adj.) the starboard side only is left to the seamen; p. 105 (adj.) when the starboard watch . . . was below; p. 116 (n.) the messes of the starboard-watch were seated here; p. 116 (adj.) on our starboard beam; p. 130 (adj.) first from the larboard side, and then from the starboard; p. 134 (n.) four sailors of the starboard-watch; p. 135 (adj.) on the starboard side of the main-mast; p. 200 (adj.) between the starboard carronades; p. 225 (adj.) all you starboard-quarter watch; p. 231 (n.) He does not know starboard from larboard; p. 241 (adj.) mustered in the starboard gangway; p. 279 (adj.) with that of the starboard main-lift; p. 324 (adj.) Captain of the starboard bow-chaser; p. 337 (n.) All the starboard-watch, ahoy; p. 347 (adj.) were then on the starboard tack.

<u>Moby-Dick</u>--p. 44 (adj.) Starboard gangway, there . . . larboard gangway to starboard; p. 50 (adj.) on the starboard hand of every woe, there is sure delight; p. 63 (n.) about keeping a yellow warehouse on our starboard; p. 142 (adj.) with three holes punctured in his starboard fluke; p. 296 (adj.) in the unnatural stump of his starboard fin.

STATE-ROOM. A sleeping cabin, or small berth, detached from the main cabin of merchantmen or saloon of passenger vessels. (Smyth)

<u>Mardi</u>--p. 59 (n.) wee little state-rooms.

STEAMER. A vessel propelled through the water by steam. (Webster shows "steam-boat" and "steam-vessel.")

<u>Redburn</u>--p. 33 (n.) As the steamer carried us further; p. 34 (n.) as long as the steamer had hold of us; p. 101 (n.) served in the armed

steamers; p. 198 (n.) Here lie the various black steamers; p. 286 (n.)
the poor passengers in a Liverpool steamer.

White-Jacket--p. 199 (n.) He had been a clerk in a steamer.

STEERAGE. The act of steering. Also, that part of a ship next below the
quarter-deck, immediately before the bulkhead of the great cabin in most
ships of war. The portion of the 'tween-decks just before the gun-room
bulkhead. In some ships the second-class passengers are called steerage
passengers. The admiral's cabin on the middle deck of the three-deckers
has been called the steerage. (Smyth)

Redburn--p. 111 (adj.) to speak of the steerage passengers; p. 211
(n.) the only occupants of the steerage; p. 112 (adj.) once a steerage
passenger rose in the night; p. 112 (adj.) a steerage passenger gave
him a jack-knife; p. 112 (adj.) sailors and poor steerage passengers;
p. 119 (adj.) distant admiration to the steerage passengers; p. 221
(adj.) as a steerage passenger; p. 257 (adj.) as a steerage passenger;
p. 261 (n.) almost all seamen and steerage-passengers; p. 263 (adj.)
or great above for the steerage passengers; p. 263 (n.) were so few
occupants of the steerage; p. 265 (adj.) some of the steerage
passengers, however; p. 265 (n.) contingencies of a voyager in the
steerage; p. 265 (n.) the most considerable man in the steerage;
p. 265 (n.) with the cheapness of the steerage; p. 265 (n.) comprised
in the after part of the steerage itself; p. 267 (adj.) Among the
steerage passengers of the Highlander; p. 267 (n.) Mrs. O'Regan
emerged from the steerage; p. 283 (adj.) Thus exclaimed one of the
steerage children; p. 283 (n.) shortsightedness of the passengers in
the steerage; p. 283 (adj.) That every steerage passenger; p. 284 (n.)
there were secret movements in the steerage; p. 285 (n.) domestic
work to be done in the steerage; p. 286 (n.) the hatchways on the
steerage were . . . hermetically closed; p. 286 (n.) descended into
the steerage; p. 286 (n.) refused even to enter the steerage; p. 287
(n.) the pestilent air of the steerage; p. 287 (n.) who slept in the
farther part of the steerage; p. 288 (n.) was all-important now that
the steerage should be purified; p. 288 (adj.) the steerage passengers
would have been ordered above; p. 288 (n.) Horrible as the sights of
the steerage now were; p. 290 (n.) who proceeding into the steerage;
p. 290 (n.) The steerage passengers . . . wore a still, subdued
aspect; p. 293 (n.) to supply the steerage passengers with decent
lodings; p. 293 (adj.) to place the galley, or steerage-passengers
stove; p. 295 (n.) from the captain to the child in the steerage;
p. 299 (n.) The steerage was now as a bedlam; p. 299 (n.) blanket,
bolster, and bundle of straw in the steerage; p. 299 (n.) give the
steerage a final, thorough cleaning; p. 299 (n.) not get a glimpse of
the true condition of the steerage; p. 300 (adj.) The steerage
passengers almost neighed with delight; p. 310 (adj.) only a very few
of the steerage passengers.

White-Jacket--p. 6 (n.) in the steerage, the middies were busy raising
loans; p. 11 (n.) we say nothing here of . . . Steerage Steward;
p. 26 (n.) live by themselves in the steerage; p. 26 (n.) The steerage
buzzes, hums, and swarms like a hive; p. 104 (n.) As yet we hardly
had steerage-way; p. 388 (n.) about the reefers in the steerage.

STEERSMAN. The helmsman or timoneer. (Smyth)

Mardi--p. 71 (n.) The old steersman; p. 109 (n.) I found the steersman, in whose hands.

Redburn--p. 116 (n.) a true steersman keeps her to her work; p. 290 (n.) our best steersman at the helm; pp. 291-2 (n.) engaged by the observant steersman at the helm.

STEM. The foremost piece uniting the bows of a ship; its lower end scarphs into the keel, and the bowsprit rests upon its upper end. From stem to stern--from one end of the ship to the other. (Smyth)

Mardi--p. 7 (n.) from stem to stern; p. 28 (n.) from stem to stern; p. 102 (n.) from stem to stern.

Redburn--p. 301 (adv.) knotted our old ship, stem and stern.

White-Jacket--p. 177 (n.) and walks from stem to stern; p. 396 (n.) from furthest stem to uttermost stern.

Moby-Dick--p. 127 (n.) that line streaks him from stem to stern.

STERN. The after-part of a ship, ending in the taffarel above and the counters below. (Smyth) -- Stern-all! An order to rowers to back the boat. Stern-on, keeping the stern of a boat at the seas rolling after her. Also said of a ship that rounds and presents her stern as she recedes. (Russell)

Typee--p. 3 (n.) which once decorated our stern and quarter-deck; p. 5 (n.) has formed about her stern-piece; p. 7 (adj.) In the stern sheets reclined Mowanna; p. 12 (n.) trailing over the stern of six vessels; p. 36 (adj.) with the rest of the watch in the stern sheets; p. 133 (n.) Fayaway and I reclined in the stern of the canoe; p. 134 (n.) Seated in the stern; p. 172 (n.) Seated in the stern of a canoe.

Omoo--p. 21 (n.) pulled out from the man-of-war's stern; p. 59 (n.) the Julia reared up on her stern; p. 69 (n.) in the stern-sheets of the captain's boat; p. 86 (n.) in the stern of his boat; p. 102 (n.) its stern settled low in the water; p. 102 (n.) when I saw upon her stern; p. 109 (adj.) she carries a stern gallery; p. 160 (n.) leaped into the stern; p. 216 (n.) upon the stern was something which; p. 216 (n.) and I, into the stern.

Mardi--p. 7 (n.) from stem to stern; p. 19 (n.) by the bow and stern; p. 27 (n.) to the boat's stern; p. 28 (n.) from stem to stern; p. 33 (n.) over the stern of the boat; p. 33 (n.) lifted the light boat's stern; p. 41 (n.) long stood in the stern; p. 44 (n.) in the boat's quiet stern; p. 47 (n.) pondering in the stern; p. 57 (n.) then showing her stern; p. 59 (n.) dead lights in the stern; p. 102 (n.) from stem to stern; p. 135 (n.) brought round to the canoe's stern; p. 141 (n.) now vacant stern of their canoe; p. 199 (n.) of canopied Howdah in its stern; p. 200 (adv.) This image looked sternward; p. 215 (n.) The third sat in the shallop's stern; p. 422 (n.) which

struck our stern, and quivered; p. 481 (n.) its stern gloriously
emblazoned; p. 482 (n.) upon its stern a wilderness of sculpture.

Redburn--p. 6 (n.) like pagodas on the bow and stern; p. 9 (n.) which
was painted on her stern; p. 28 (n.) I got along to the stern; p. 31
(n.) themselves lying back in the stern; p. 37 (n.) and glided under
our stern; p. 75 (n.) passed under our stern; p. 76 (n.) toward the
stern of their ships; p. 97 (n.) till it came to the stern; p. 164
(n.) get out a stern-line; p. 174 (n.) with hollow waist, high prow
and stern; p. 255 (n.) carried two mizen-peaks at his stern; p. 301
(n.) seated in the stern of the boat; p. 301 (n.) our old ship, stem
and stern.

White-Jacket--p. 9 (n.) and other ropes in the stern of the vessel;
p. 72 (n.) are kept depending from the stern; p. 105 (n.) She glided
under our stern; p. 110 (n.) Scudding exposes to the gale your stern;
p. 161 (n.) as he tranquilly sits in the stern; p. 177 (n.) and walks
from stem to stern; p. 233 (n.) At the stern waved the Brazilian flag;
p. 265 (n.) running down under the Neversink's stern; p. 272 (n.) her
stern [was] kicking up its heels in the air; p. 272 (n.) nor a stern
[was to be seen] in our van; p. 299 (n.) which still carried on their
sterns; p. 322 (n.) the angles of an armed ship's stern; p. 323 (n.)
the picturesque, delightful stern-gallery; p. 323 (n.) and the stern-
gallery of a man-of-war; p. 366 (n.) throwing himself into the stern;
p. 396 (n.) from furthest stem to uttermost stern.

Moby-Dick--p. 5 (n.) while the whale is floating at the stern of the
ship; p. 11 (n.) Stern all! exclaimed the mate; p. 11 (n.) Stern all,
for your lives; p. 56 (n.) he sat down in the stern, paddle low in
hand; p. 60 (n.) then slightly tapping his stern in mid-somerset;
p. 61 (adj.) while all hands were clearing away the stern boat; p. 69
(n.) I'll take that leg away from thy stern; p. 127 (n.) that line
streaks him from stem to stern; p. 244 (v.) the boat alternately
sterning out of the way; p. 299 (n.) while the three sterns tilted
high in the air; p. 365 (n.) my boat's crew could only trim dish, by
sitting at their sterns on the outer gunwhale; p. 365 (v.) No use
sterning all, then; p. 409 (v.) Ahab, who had sterned off from the
whale; p. 449 (n.) tumbling over each other's heads to gain the
uttermost stern; p. 449 (n.) the crew at the stern-wreck clinging to
the gunwhales.

STEWARD. The commissary of a vessel and the man who has charge of cooks,
waiters, and other personal service men. (Bradford)

Mardi--p. 28 (n.) Steward!

STOVE. Broken in; thus, when violent damage is done to the upper part of
a ship's hull, she is said to be stove. To stave is to break a hole in
any vessel. (Smyth)

White-Jacket--p. 16 (adj.) concerning stove boats on the coast of Japan.

Moby-Dick--p. 8 (v.) we have been stove by a whale; p. 41 (adj.) a
stove boat will make me an immortal by brevet; p. 41 (adj./v.) and

come a stove boat and stove body when they will, for stave my soul,
Jove himself cannot; p. 85 (v.) for fear of after-claps, in case he
got stove and went to Davy Jones; p. 96 (v.) Don't stave the boats
needlessly, ye harpooners; p. 141 (adj.) A dead whale or a stove
boat; p. 182 (v.) that for half a century stave the ships of a Roman
Emperor; p. 228 (v.) you run no small risk of being eternally stove
and sunk by him; p. 285 (v.) Sperm whale stove a passage through the
Isthmus of Darien; p. 387 (adj.) repairing stove boats; p. 413 (v.) A
great rolling sea . . . stove in the boat's bottom at the stern; p.
p. 414 (v.) where is that stove? . . . his stand-point is stove, man;
p. 414 (v.) The gale that now hammers at us to stave us; p. 465 (adj.)
while the oarsmen were rocking in the two staved boats.

STRAIT. A passage connecting one part of the sea with another. This
word is often written in the plural, but without component reason. (Smyth)

Mardi--p. 645 (n.) that seemed the Straits of Ormus; p. 649 (n.) but
a strait flows between this isle and Odo; p. 654 (n.) Through yonder
strait, for thee, perdition lies.

Redburn--p. 58 (n.) stopped ships in the straits of Gaspar.

White-Jacket--p. 98 (n.) by the Straits of Magellan; p. 98 (n.) are
the Straits of Le Mair.

Moby-Dick--p. 45 (n.) just outside the Straits of Gibralter; p. 56
(n.) he paddled off to a distant strait; p. 319 (n.) upon the vessels
sailing through the straits; p. 382 (n.) look-outs . . . now,
penetrating even through Behring's straits.

STRAND. A sea-margin; the portion alternately left and covered by tides.
Synonymous with beach. It is not altered from the original Anglo-Saxon.
(Smyth)

Mardi--p. 192 (n.) waves ran up the strand in glee; p. 265 (n.) none
ere touched its strand; p. 312 (n.) we pushed from the strand; p. 367
(n.) strowing all the strand; p. 550 (n.) Savage men stood naked on
the strand; p. 554 (n.) rolled over from Vivenza's strand; p. 554 (n.)
as the crosses along the opposing strand; p. 567 (n.) from a wild
strand, we launched our three canoes; p. 587 (n.) the waves ran up
their strands; p. 623 (n.) No calmer strands,/ No sweeter land;
p. 625 (n.) as we gained the strand; p. 644 (n.) against that flowery
strand.

Redburn--p. 243 (n.) that our departure from the English strand.

STREAM. Anglo-Saxon for flowing water, meaning especially the middle or
most rapid part of a tide or current. (Smyth)

Typee--p. 46 (n.) their lower ends within a foot of the stream; p. 46
(n.) did I try to elude the incessant streams; p. 56 (n.) the streams
all run in the same direction; p. 58 (n.) obstructions to the course
of the rapid stream; p. 58 (n.) almost to the surface of the stream;

p. 59 (n.) over which the wild stream poured; p. 62 (n.) leaving the
bed of the stream at the very point; p. 64 (n.) over which the dark
stream bounded; p. 89 (n.) down to the waist in the stream; p. 109
(n.) carrying me to the stream; p. 110 (n.) carry me to a particular
part of the stream; p. 146 (n.) to trot off with me on his back to
the stream; p. 147 (n.) laid in the bed of some running stream;
p. 149 (n.) bent my steps towards the stream; p. 150 (n.) or repair
to the stream with small calabashes; p. 151 (n.) or a bath in the
stream at mid-night; p. 152 (n.) or bathing in the water of the
stream; p. 158 (n.) lugging off to the stream enormous hollow bamboos;
p. 164 (n.) These were filled with water from the stream; p. 201 (n.)
have gone off to bathe in the stream; p. 204 (n.) bathed in the
stream--danced--flirted; p. 223 (n.) the skipper directed his steps
to a stream; p. 228 (n.) I had repaired to the stream for the purpose
of bathing; p. 229 (n.) the baby remaining in the stream about a
minute; p. 229 (n.) bringing her child down to the stream regularly;
p. 237 (n.) he offered to accompany me to the stream; p. 243 (n.) was
obliged to carry me daily to the stream; p. 261 (n.) picking up the
stones in the bed of the stream.

Omoo--p. 65 (n.) watered with fine streams; p. 102 (n.) She was from
the noble stream; p. 114 (n.) streams were heard flowing; p. 114 (n.)
it fed all the streams on the island; p. 118 (n.) leading us down to
the stream; p. 158 (n.) we had a grand washing in the stream; p. 169
(n.) the stream murmurs over them; p. 201 (n.) with links of streams
flashing through; p. 210 (n.) chased with streams of fire; p. 235 (n.)
that there were many streams to ford; p. 261 (n.) watered by streams
from the mountains; p. 269 (n.) as if floating upon an inland stream;
p. 270 (n.) opposite the mouths of running streams; p. 284 (n.)
Through the grove flows a stream.

Mardi--p. 109 (n.) by reason of the ocean streams; p. 111 (n.)
collateral action of the Polar streams; p. 111 (n.) a specific cause
for the ocean streams; p. 111 (n.) particles consequent upon the flow
of the streams; p. 233 (n.) to join floods with the streams trained;
p. 234 (n.) the stream, with a hollow ring and a dash; p. 234 (n.)
the cool stream of upland Trades; p. 234 (n.) the stream flowed at
large; p. 256 (n.) when its lavish stream flows by; p. 338 (n.) as
flows the general stream; p. 368 (n.) Ohio, with all his leagued
streams; p. 403 (n.) ordinary fluid of the springs and streams;
p. 437 (n.) are not foul streams often traced to pure fountains;
p. 511 (n.) are haughty, overbearing streams; p. 544 (n.) veined with
silver streams, and silver ores; p. 546 (n.) or down in beds of
golden streams; p. 552 (n.) Down ancient streams; p. 629 (n.) My soul
sets back like ocean streams.

Redburn--p. 31 (n.) swinging out into the stream; p. 69 (n.) that I
thought the Gulf Stream was in my head; p. 97 (n.) to make mention of
the Gulf Stream; p. 98 (n.) in a bucket full of the Gulf Stream;
p. 127 (n.) came to anchor in the stream; p. 145 (n.) a peaceful
stream of shaded line engraving; p. 147 (n.) Where Mersey's stream,
long winding; p. 163 (n.) those of the vessels in the stream; p. 240
(n.) as we shot into the sea.

White-Jacket--p. 77 (n.) For an instant I thought the Gulf Stream in
my head; p. 210 (n.) flow radiating streams.

Moby-Dick--p. 4 (n.) that swim the ocean stream.

STURGEON. Acipenser sturio, a large fish; it has a cartilaginious
skeleton, with a small circular and tubular mouth. It is found in the
European seas and larger rivers. The roes are made into caviare, and the
sounds and muscular parts into isinglass. It is a royal fish in England.
(Smyth)

Mardi--p. 417 (n.) sturgeon-forms, cephalaspis, glyptolepis.

Moby-Dick--p. 6 (n.) royal fish, which are whale and sturgeon; p. 336
(n.) There are two royal fish . . . --the whale and the sturgeon;
p. 336 (n.) the sturgeon must be divided in the same way as the whale.

SURF. The swell and foam of the sea, which breaks upon the shore, or any
rock lying near the surface. The most violent surfs are those which
break upon a flat shore. (Smyth)

Typee--p. 12 (n.) with the surf beating high against the lofty cliffs;
p. 74 (n.) boats . . . lie just outside the surf; p. 248 (n.) when I
first heard the roar of the surf; p. 249 (n.) hanging off to keep out
of the surf; p. 250 (n.) standing nearly to the waist in the surf;
p. 250 (n.) to the edge of the surf.

Mardi--p. 272 (n.) bathing in the surf of the sea; p. 273 (n.) delight
to gambol in the surf; p. 273 (n.) a surf-board is indispensable;
p. 492 (n.) but the rolling surf forbade; p. 623 (n.) shells were
gently rolling in the playful surf; p. 623 (n.) a verdant surf played
against lofty banks of leaves.

Moby-Dick--p. 12 (n.) commerce surrounds it with her surf; p. 410 (n.)
waves . . . gently chafed the whale's broad flank, like soft surf
upon a beach; p. 469 (n.) a sullen white surf beat against its deep
sides.

SWAN. A large aquatic fowl of the genus Anas. The plumage is of a pure
white color, and its long arching neck gives it a noble appearance.
(Webster)

Redburn--p. 300 (n.) covered with white sloop-sails like fleets of
swans.

SWELL. A rolling wave which seldom breaks unless it meets resistance,
generally denoting a continuous heaving, which remains for some time
after the wind which caused it has subsided. (Smyth)

Typee--p. 10 (n.) The long, measured, dirge-like swell of the Pacific;
p. 28 (n.) upon the long smooth swell of the ocean.

Omoo--p. 15 (n.) gliding up and down the long, slow swells; p. 73 (n.)
lay and roll upon the swells; p. 263 (n.) where the swell of the sea
is prevented; p. 270 (n.) were the vast swells of the Pacific.

Mardi--p. 37 (n.) dark, misty spaces, between long and uniform swells; p. 49 (n.) of the vast, smooth swells; p. 71 (n.) parted the long swells; p. 72 (n.) every swell of the sea; p. 126 (n.) every time we rose upon the swells; p. 141 (n.) a great swell of the sea surged up; p. 256 (n.) resist the convivial swell at times ruffling; p. 273 (n.) and diving under the swells; p. 469 (n.) the very swell under its thousand prows; p. 553 (n.) so, sloping from long rolling swells; p. 615 (n.) his antlers dripping on the swell; p. 622 (n.) canoes lurched heavily in a violent swell.

Redburn--p. 119 (n.) when the sudden swells would lift the ship; p. 298 (n.) in the soft, subdued ocean swell.

White-Jacket--p. 73 (n.) we slid up and down the great seething swells of the sea; p. 101 (n.) At first there was a long, gauky swell; p. 392 (n.) in the sudden swells of the calm sea.

Moby-Dick--p. 161 (n.) delirium seemed left behind him with the Cape Horn swells; p. 193 (n.) The vast swells of the omnipotent sea; p. 230 (n.) causing the slight boat to rock in the swells; p. 272 (n.) slacked off the rope to every swell of the sea; p. 296 (n.) because the white-bone or swell at his broad muzzle was a dashed one, like the swell formed when two hostile currents meet; p. 298 (n.) stretching from them . . . was the foaming swell that he made; p. 364 (n.) for the great swells now lift the boat high up; p. 400 (n.) Lifted by those eternal swells; p. 405 (n.) afloat all day upon smooth, slow heaving swells; p. 442 (n.) the robust and man-like sea heaved with long, strong lingering swells; p. 448 (v.) the sea began to swell; p. 449 (n.) the now rising swells, with all their confluent waves, dazzlingly broke against it.

SWIM. To move along the surface of the water by means of the simultaneous movement of the hands and feet. (Smyth)

Typee--p. 14 (v.) dark hair trailing beside them as they swam; p. 14 (adj.) into the midst of these swimming nymphs; p. 15 (v.) when they had swam miles to welcome us; p. 132 (v.) they swam away in every direction; p. 132 (v.) would swim after me shouting and gambolling; p. 183 (n.) made towards the ships by swimming; p. 229 (v.) as natural for a human being to swim; p. 251 (v.) Their intention was evidently to swim off; p. 251 (n.) unlike the feeble swimmers of civilized countries; p. 251 (n.) the crowd of swimmers shot through the water.

Omoo--p. 21 (v.) and swim to the corvette; p. 27 (v.) All their little plans for swimming ashore; p. 72 (v.) Presently, a dark object swam out; p. 252 (v.) After swimming a few yards.

Mardi--p. 149 (v.) and swam one; p. 149 (v.) swims so toilingly on; p. 149 (v.) fins swim on; p. 149 (v.) How prettily they swim; p. 150 (v.) we merrily swim; p. 150 (v.) Swim away, swim away; p. 150 (v.) To swim, it's exceedingly pleasant; p. 150 (v.) So swim away; p. 150 (v.) We only swim under its lee; p. 150 (v.) we merrily swim; p. 151 (v.) the enemy swam away; p. 214 (v.) Swim on the foe; p. 256 (v.) were sent swimming to the further end; p. 259 (v.) Swimming in the

air; p. 267 (n.) doth the maiden swim; p. 273 (n.) that the swimmers
of Ohonoo; p. 273 (n.) An expert swimmer shifts; p. 273 (n.) the
swimmers thread their way out; p. 290 (v.) swimming deep, full of old
wine; p. 294 (v.) and then swimming along horizontally; p. 294 (v.)
swimming wistfully toward him; p. 294 (v.) swam toward the stranger;
p. 334 (v.) swimming beside his canoe; p. 417 (v.) swimming in saffron
sauces; p. 615 (v.) a mighty moose swam stately as a seventy-four;
p. 654 (v.) for our lives we must now swim.

White-Jacket--p. 394 (v.) I essayed to swim toward the ship.

Moby-Dick--epigram (v.) Leviathan . . . sleeps or swims,/ And a
moving land; p. 4 (v.) Leviathan . . . sleeps or swims,/ And a moving
land; p. 4 (v.) The mighty whales which swim in a sea of water, and
have a sea of oil swimming in them; p. 7 (v.) In the free element
beneath me swam/ . . . Fishes of every color, form, and kind; p. 11
(v.) I saw two of these monsters [whales] . . . slowly swimming;
p. 61 (v.) he was seen swimming like a dog; p. 118 (v.) But I have
swam through libraries; p. 122 (n.) gifted with such wonderous power
and velocity in swimming; p. 136 (v.) between your legs . . . swim
the hugest monsters of the sea; p. 159 (v.) when swimming before his
exulting pursuers; p. 284 (adj.) in the ordinary swimming position of
the Sperm Whale; p. 285 (adj.) ordinary fish possess what is called a
swimming bladder; p. 296 (v.) swam a huge, humped old bull; p. 347
(v./n.) to swim in the open ocean is as easy to the practised
swimmer as to ride in a spring-carriage ashore; p. 384 (v.) He swam
the seas before the continents broke water.

TACK. To go about, to change the course from one board to another from
the starboard to the port tack, or vice versa. It is done by turning the
ship's head suddenly to the wind, whereby her head-sails are thrown aback,
and cause her to fall off from the wind to the other back. (Smyth)

Typee--p. 23 (v.) she is still regularly tacking twice.

Omoo--p. 8 (n.) and making short tacks until morning; p. 26 (n.) got
our off-shore tacks aboard; p. 46 (v.) in tacking ship; p. 51 (n.)
braced sharp up on the larboard tack; p. 75 (v.) Mr. Jermin, tack
ship; p. 90 (n.) away from the land on the other tack; p. 97 (v.) was
to be tacked; p. 98 (v.) we were now to tack ship.

Redburn--p. 289 (n.) now on this tack, now on that; p. 300 (n.) and
making short tacks.

White-Jacket--p. 8 (v.) Also, in tacking ship; p. 9 (v.) besides his
special offices, in tacking ship; p. 72 (n.) soon tossed her about on
the other tack; p. 98 (v.) but tack this way and that; p. 98 (n.) and
shift on the other tack; p. 231 (v.) shortening sail, tacking ship;
p. 277 (v.) in tacking ship every seaman in a man-of-war; p. 277 (v.)
when the word is passed to tack or wear; p. 278 (n.) their proper
stations were, at tacking or wearing; p. 278 (v.) All hands tack
ship, ahoy; p. 278 (n.) getting the frigate round on the other tack;
p. 308 (n.) both fore-tacks over the main-yard; p. 347 (n.) were then
on the starboard tack; p. 348 (v.) I'd tack ship, any way; p. 388 (n.)
but the Yankee nation on the other tack.

Moby-Dick--p. 436 (v.) starboard and larboard, she continued to tack.

TADPOLE. A frog in its first state from the spawn; a porwiggle. (Webster)

Mardi--p. 507 (n.) But where are the tails of the tadpoles.

TAFFRAIL. The upper part of a ship's stern, a curved railing, the ends
of which unite to the quarter-pieces. (Smyth)

Typee--p. 15 (n.) others seated themselves upon the taffrail; p. 223
(n.) he used to sit on the taffrail.

Omoo--p. 59 (n.) Striking the taffrail; p. 84 (n.) leaning against
the taffrail by himself.

Mardi--p. 57 (n.) coming from over the taffrail; p. 61 (n.) moved
toward the taffrail.

Redburn--p. 75 (n.) sitting on the taffrail with a speaking-trumpet;
p. 103 (n.) leaning over sideways against the taffrail; p. 103 (n.)
had lashed themselves to the taffrail for safety; p. 126 (n.) with a
good wind over the taffrail; p. 262 (n.) or smoking cigars on the
taffrail; p. 290 (n.) with a fair, cheering breeze over the taffrail.

White-Jacket--p. 83 (n.) facing the taffrail instead of the bowsprit;
p. 394 (n.) cried a horrified voice from the taffrail.

Moby-Dick--p. 109 (n.) soon as I levelled my glance towards the
taffrail; p. 112 (n.) he was measuring the ship from taffrail to
mainmast; p. 170 (n.) to the scuttle-butt near the taffrail; p. 200
(adj.) The strange, upheaving lifting tendency of the taffrail breeze.

TAR. A perfect sailor; one who knows his duty thoroughly. (Smyth)

Typee--p. 3 (n.) those good-for-nothing tars, shouting and tramping.

Omoo--p. 108 (n.) becomes, in time, a thorough-bred tar; p. 110 (n.)
a thorough tar is unfit for any thing else; p. 135 (n.) The old tar
had complained of the effects.

Mardi--p. 115 (n.) the honest old tar could stand it no longer.

Redburn--p. 79 (n.) whereas old tars are less careful; p. 108 (n.)
Blunt, the Dream Book tar; p. 130 (n.) feed their luckless tars in
dock; p. 139 (n.) because the modern tar is not quite so gross;
p. 140 (n.) among tars who can not read; p. 143 (adj.) into the hands
of some tarry captain; p. 167 (n.) irruption of cherry-cheeked young
tars; p. 175 (n.) to see an old pensioner of a tar; p. 187 (n.) where
crowds of tars were always passing; p. 188 (n.) claimed to be
destitute tars; p. 192 (n.) into the astonished hands of the tars;
p. 219 (n.) sixteen dollars a month to a thorough-going tar; p. 239
(n.) leading a drunken tar by the collar; p. 256 (n.) looked around
among the grinning tars; p. 274 (n.) over twelve or fourteen strong,
healthy tars.

White-Jacket--p. 13 (n.) these were a noble set of tars; p. 14 (n.)
none of the boisterousness, so common to tars; p. 19 (n.) among
crowds of admiring tars; p. 33 (n.) expressly created and labelled
for a tar; p. 39 (n.) which many tars wear round their necks; p. 53
(n.) that dreadfully alarmed many tars; p. 64 (n.) jolly tars are our
men; p. 65 (n.) as beneath a true tar and man of valor; p. 67 (n.)
worked by a set of Bowery-boy tars; p. 92 (n.) altered to suit all
American tars; p. 93 (n.) tars who were anxious to procure substitutes;
p. 102 (n.) pulling and hauling the luckless tars about; p. 116 (n.)
The shower was hailed by the reckless tars; p. 127 (n.) that no
enterprising tar had yet thought of; p. 169 (n.) The sad taste of
this old tar; p. 199 (n.) What shall I have now, my noble tars;
p. 199 (n.) I must close the auction, my tars of Columbia; p. 200 (n.)
look, my noble tars, if you have tears; p. 200 (n.) Tars of Columbia
. . . these boots must be sold; p. 202 (n.) How much for it, my
gallant tars of Columbia; p. 202 (n.) Ay, noble tars; p. 202 (n.) How
much for the jacket, my noble tars; p. 235 (n.) said a young New
England tar beside me; p. 270 (n.) They say Homer himself was once a
tar; pp. 274-5 (n.) the only helmets of our tars; p. 283 (n.) of
decrepit or rheumatic old tars; p. 309 (n.) what man-of-war's-men
call a damn-my-eyes-tar; p. 323 (n.) an irruption of tars; p. 353 (n.)
must have done for this fine old tar; p. 354 (n.) a custom peculiar
to tars; p. 362 (n.) the old tars who still sported their beards;
p. 362 (n.) Reverend old tars, one and all; p. 383 (n.) floggings
accumulated by a reckless tar; p. 385 (n.) several more fine tars
that might be added; p. 390 (n.) Ay, these very tars; p. 390 (n.)
Fine fellow! generous-hearted tars; p. 390 (n.) Well, these generous-
hearted tars on shore.

Moby-Dick--p. 22 (n.) At one end a ruminating tar was still further
adorning it; p. 370 (n.) a warning example to all drunken tars.

TEMPEST. A word not much used by seamen. It is, however, synonymous
with storm, gales, &c. (Smyth)

Mardi--p. 24 (n.) in what time of tempest; p. 49 (n.) some tempest
must have been sending.

White-Jacket--p. 107 (n.) Above all the roar of the tempest; p. 107
(n.) such a sound in a night-tempest at sea; p. 108 (n.) You become
identified with the tempest; p. 115 (n.) in a frigate, in such a
tempest; p. 353 (n.) so active in time of tempest; p. 363 (n.) with
many a tempest has his beard be shake; p. 393 (n.) of the sea in the
height of a tempest; p. 397 (n.) though often in tempest-time we
almost refused to believe.

Moby-Dick--p. 19 (adj.) where that tempestuous wind Euroclydon kept
up a worse howling; p. 19 (adj.) In judging of that tempestuous wind,
says an old writer; p. 19 (adj.) yet that would not keep out the
tempestuous Euroclydon; p. 38 (n.) when thou art driven, straps,
buttons, and all, down the throat of the tempest; p. 48 (n.) for
whose cause this great tempest was upon them; p. 49 (n.) for his sake
this great tempest was upon them; p. 97 (adj.) could so unrestingly
push off again for still another tempestuous storm; p. 323 (n.) like
a ship mobbed by ice-isles in a tempest; p. 412 (n.) which the first

fury of the tempest had left for its after sport; p. 415 (n.) they
will swear . . . in the teeth of the tempest; p. 419 (adj.) none but
cowards send down their brain-trucks in tempest time.

TERRAPIN. A fresh-water tortoise, plentiful in America, and much
esteemed for food. (Smyth)

White-Jacket--pp. 10-11 (n.) come out into the day, like terrapins
from their caves.

TIDE. A regular periodical current of waters, setting alternately in a
flux and reflux; it is owing to the attraction of the sun and moon, but
chiefly to the latter. Neaptides, medium tides, in respect to their
opposites, the springs, being neither so high, so low, nor so rapid.
(Smyth)

Typee--p. 251 (n.) and the tide was against us.

Omoo--p. 101 (n.) the fluctuations of the tides being so inconsiderable;
p. 101 (n.) The Newtonian theory concerning the tides.

Mardi--p. 70 (n.) But the tide ebbing; p. 71 (n.) at that turn of the
tide; p. 214 (n.) On the torrent's tide; p. 258 (n.) Flood-tide, and
soul-tide--to the brim; p. 258 (n.) Drain down that bright tide;
p. 265 (n.) Noon-tide rolls its flood; p. 380 (n.) picked off the
reef at low tide; p. 415 (n.) But at every tide the thin soil; p. 458
(n.) on the surface in the tides of the lagoon; p. 471 (n.) During an
unusually low tide; p. 476 (n.) rose and fell the isles, as by a
tide; p. 479 (n.) Take the tide, ere it turns; p. 497 (n.) at the
turn of the tide; p. 523 (n.) information upon the subject of neap
tides; p. 516 (n.) Thence flowed a tide of red wine; p. 516 (n.)
standing in the Nile at flood tide; p. 540 (n.) Hence flowed a tide
of forest sounds; p. 541 (n.) Though revolutions rise to high spring-
tide; p. 543 (n.) Churned and broken in the boiling tide; p. 546 (n.)
Sand-bars! rise, and stay the tide; p. 554 (adj.) Over the tideless
sea we sailed; p. 555 (n.) like old tide-rips of diluvian seas;
p. 622 (n.) That flushed tide rippled toward us; p. 623 (n.) The
dimpled tide sang round our splintered prows; p. 632 (n.) The fiery
tide was ebbing; p. 633 (n.) my soul tossed on its own tides; p. 654
(n.) turning my prow into the racing tide.

Redburn--p. 130 (n.) through a lock at high tide; p. 139 (n.) has but
drifted along with that great tide; p. 163 (n.) about the time of
high tide; p. 163 (n.) So that when it is low tide; p. 239 (n.) to go
out with the tide; p. 249 (n.) that ever rolled its flood-tide of
harmony; p. 300 (n.) seems to pour through you with all his tides.

White-Jacket--p. 153 (n.) a rich purple tide soon settled the question;
p. 270 (n.) The bounding vessel cuts the roaring tide; p. 318 (adj.)
like black-snakes on half-tide rocks; p. 382 (n.) in all weathers,
all times, tides, and ends.

Moby-Dick--p. 46 (n.) we sail with the next coming tide; p. 48 (n.)
And now the time of tide has come; p. 70 (n.) the ship swinging to

her anchor with the flood-tide; p. 140 (n.) from the inscrutable
tides of God; p. 148 (n.) Time and tide flow wide; p. 171 (n.) who
knew the sets of all tides and currents; p. 201 (n.) as if its [the
sea's] vast tides were a conscience; p. 244 (n.) The red tide now
poured from all sides of the monster like brooks down a hill; p. 321
(n.) Ahab's brow was left gaunt and ribbed, like the black sand beach
after some stormy tide has been gnawing it; p. 396 (n.) and the
ocean's invisible flood-tide lifted him higher and higher towards his
destined heaven; p. 400 (adj.) the Pacific . . . seems the tide-
beating heart of earth; p. 446 (n.) the polished metallic-like marks
of some swift tide-rip; p. 462 (n.) Some men die at ebbtide; some at
low water.

TILLER. A bar of wood or iron, put into the head of a rudder, by which
the rudder is moved. (Dana)

Omoo--pp. 50-51 (n.) there's no one at the tiller; p. 292 (n.) by
holding on to the tiller.

Mardi--p. 70 (n.) calmly at the tiller; p. 71 (n.) handling the
tiller; p. 74 (n.) lashed the tiller alee; p. 109 (n.) sleeping
upright against the tiller; p. 109 (n.) Samoa's aspect, sleeping at
the tiller; p. 110 (n.) gave herself mighty airs at the tiller.

TOP, TOPSAIL. Top, a sort of platform placed over the head of the lower
mast, from which it projects like a scaffold.--Top-sails, the second
sails above the decks, extending across the top-masts, by the topsail-
yards above, and by the lower yards beneath, being fastened to the former
by earings and robands, and to the latter by the topsail-sheets. (Smyth)

Typee--p. 3 (n.) which hung suspended from our tops and stays.

Mardi--p. 3 (n.) The courses and topsails are set; p. 66 (n.) what
stirs in the main-top; p. 66 (n.) aloft to the fore-top; p. 86 (n.)
made for the fore-top; p. 86 (n.) to remain in the top; p. 86 (n.)
together in that airy top; p. 86 (n.) to the main-top; p. 87 (n.) the
fore-top being just over; p. 87 (n.) unhooking a top-block; p. 88 (n.)
occupant of the main-top.

TORF-EGILL. The Danish Sea-king. (Melville)

Mardi--p. 482 (n.) tough Torf-Egill, the Danish Sea-king.

TORTOISE, TURTLE. Tortoise--An animal of the genus Testudo, covered with
a shell or crust.--Turtle, the name sometimes given to the common
tortoise. (Webster)

Typee--p. 110 (n.) resembling goblets made of tortoise shell; p. 191
(n.) live together as harmoniously as so many turtles.

Omoo--p. 21 (n.) turned up like tortoises on the beach; p. 226 (n.)
replied the doctor, like a snapping turtle.

Mardi--p. 282 (n.) serenading the turtles in their cells; p. 294 (n.)
of the fine Hawk's bill turtle; p. 294 (n.) These turtles were only
to be obtained; p. 303 (adj.) cells of the Turtle Reef; p. 304 (n.)
Boraballa's banquet of turtle; p. 391 (n.) like a turtle into its
shell; p. 415 (n.) of beetles, turtles, ant-eaters; p. 507 (n.)
witness the lobster and the turtle.

Redburn--p. 27 (adj.) I took out an old tortoise-shell snuff-box;
p. 303 (adj.) something like bits of fine tortoise shell.

White-Jacket--p. 153 (n.) looked like venerable old loggerhead-
turtles; p. 323 (n.) fabled the world to be supported upon four
tortoises.

Moby-Dick--p. 62 (n.) to their very chairs and tables small clams
will sometimes be found adhering, as to the backs of sea turtles;
p. 177 (n.) marked like an old tortoise with mystic hieroglyphics
upon the back.

TRADE (WINDS). Currents of air moving from about the 30th degree of
latitude towards the equator. The diurnal motion of the earth makes them
incline from the eastward, so that in the northern hemisphere they are
from the N.E., and in the southern hemisphere from the S.E. (Smyth)

Typee--p. 9 (n.) the light trade-winds were silently sweeping us
toward the islands.

Omoo--p. 14 (n.) coquetting with the warm, breezy Trades we bowled
along; p. 51 (n.) with the South East Trades strong on our bow; p. 58
(n.) the before mild Trades, like a woman roused, blew fiercely but
still warmly; p. 64 (n.) The Trades scarce filled our swooning sails.

Mardi--p. 4 (n.) we took the trades; p. 7 (n.) the trades behind;
p. 11 (n.) before a reliable Trade-wind; p. 17 (n.) with a fair
trade breeze; p. 23 (n.) mild and constant are the Trades.

TRANSOM. A piece of timber going across the stern-post, to which it is
bolted. (Dana)

Omoo--p. 86 (n.) throwing ourselves along the transom; p. 146 (n.)
playing cards on the transom.

Redburn--p. 137 (n.) rapping on the transom with his knuckles; p. 291
while the rest kneeled against the transoms.

Moby-Dick--p. 70 (n.) Seated on the transom was what seemed to me a
most uncommon and surprising figure.

TRICK. The time allotted to a man on duty at the helm. The same as
spell. (Smyth) -- Two hours at the helm. (Russell)

Omoo--p. 36 (n.) standing an occasional trick at the helm.

TROUGH. The hollow or interval between two waves, which resembles a broad and deep trench perpetually fluctuating. As the set of the sea is produced by the wind, the waves and the trough are at right angles with it; hence a ship rolls heaviest when she is in the trough of the sea. (Smyth)

Omoo--p. 58 (n.) once in a while floored in the trough of a sea.

Mardi--p. 72 (n.) as they sunk in the trough of the sea.

Redburn--p. 9 (n.) pitching head-foremost down into the trough of a calamitous sea.

Moby-Dick--p. 242 (n.) lazily undulating in the trough of the sea.

TROUT. A river fish of the genus Salmo, variegated with spots, and esteemed as most delicate food. (Webster)

Mardi--p. 288 (n.) in trout or other Waltonian prey.

TRUCK. A circular piece of wood, placed at the head of the highest mast on a ship. It has small holes or sheaves in it for signal halyards to be rove through. (Dana)

Mardi--p. 117 (n.) The masts . . . dipped their trucks in the sea.

Redburn--p. 8 (n.) till I grew dizzy at the main-truck.

Moby-Dick--p. 11 (n.) A Chapter on Whaling in Ribs and Trucks; p. 50 (n.) is not the main-truck higher than the kelson is low; p. 135 (n.) ere the final truck was put to it; p. 190 (n.) some ship which had sunk to all but her trucks; p. 407 (n.) nailed to her main truck was a brazen lamp.

TRY-WORKS. Large copper boilers, for boiling the blubber in whalers. (Smyth)

Moby-Dick--p. 351 (n.) The Try-works; p. 351 (n.) an American whaler is outwardly distinguished by her try-works; p. 351 (n.) The try-works are planted between; p. 353 (n.) Removing the fire-board from the front of the try-works; p. 352 (n.) that the Pequod's try-works were first started; p. 352 (n.) the first fire in the try-works has to be fed; p. 353 (n.) By midnight the works were in full operation; p. 353 (n.) The hatch, removed from the top of the works; p. 353 (n.) Opposite the mouth of the works; p. 355 (n.) Had you descended from the Pequod's try-works.

TUG. A vessel for towing in and out of harbors and the like. (Smyth)

Redburn. p. 240 (n.) A steam-tug, the Goliath, now took us.

VESSEL. A general name for all the different sorts of ships, boats, &c.,
navigated on the ocean or on rivers and canals. (Smyth)

Typee--p. 6 (n.) American and English vessels engaged in; p. 9 (n.)
square in the yards and keep the vessel before the breeze; p. 10 (n.)
they would accompany the vessel; p. 12 (n.) trailing over the stern
of six vessels; p. 12 (n.) than the presence of these vessels; p. 14
(n.) in the water ahead of the vessel; p. 14 (n.) being run over by
the vessel in her course; p. 15 (n.) never I will say was vessel
carried before; p. 17 (n.) one of the vessels of the squadron; p. 21
(n.) As the vessel carries out no cargo; p. 22 (n.) they are put on
board a whaling vessel; p. 22 (n.) he will fill his vessel with good
sperm oil; p. 23 (n.) Such was the account I heard of this vessel;
p. 23 (n.) since I left this same identical vessel; p. 25 (n.) I had
heard too of an English vessel; p. 25 (n.) flocked aboard the doomed
vessel by hundreds; p. 27 (n.) to the crews of other vessels; p. 27
(n.) equip armed vessels to transverse; p. 30 (n.) Having fully
resolved to leave the vessel clandestinely; p. 31 (n.) to look down
upon the detested old vessel; p. 31 (n.) my design of withdrawing
from the vessel; p. 33 (n.) until the departure of the vessel; p. 36
(n.) after the departure of our vessel; p. 40 (n.) dotted . . . with
the black hulls of the vessels; p. 48 (n.) youths who abandon vessels
in romantic islands; p. 54 (adj.) unless assured of our vessel's
departure; p. 66 (n.) to ensure the departure of our vessel; p. 74
(n.) where vessels occasionally lie; p. 140 (n.) the captain of a
trading vessel; p. 163 (n.) elaborately carved canoe-shaped vessels;
p. 184 (n.) very restricted intercourse they held with vessels;
p. 196 (n.) or sent on board the numerous vessels; p. 198 (n.)
frequent visits of all descriptions of vessels; p. 205 (n.) the crew
of vessels, shipwrecked; p. 223 (n.) accidentally left there by an
English vessel; p. 252 (n.) The captain of an Australian vessel;
p. 256 (n.) conveyed by stealth on board such vessels; p. 269 (n.)
part of his wages advanced from the vessel; p. 270 (n.) This was the
vessel in want of men; p. 271 (n.) Toby left his vessel at New Zealand.

Omoo--p. xiii (n.) the vessels navigating those remote waters; p. 3
(n.) This boat belonged to a vessel in need of men; p. 5 (n.) The
vessel we sought lay with her main-topsail; p. 7 (n.) and the vessel
going before the wind; p. 10 (n.) had procured the command of the
vessel; p. 12 (n.) undertook . . . to leave the vessel clandestinely;
p. 13 (n.) the vessel was in a state of the greatest uproar; p. 14
(n.) The crews manning vessels like these; p. 15 (n.) filling the
vessel with oil in the shortest space; p. 23 (n.) of one of their own
country vessels; p. 27 (n.) others so eager for the vessel to strike;
p. 35 (n.) notwithstanding the great number of vessels; p. 35 (n.)
the custom aboard of most vessels; p. 39 (n.) two outlandish cross-
timbers bracing the vessel; p. 39 (n.) can scarcely befall a vessel;
p. 39 (n.) In some vessels; p. 39 (n.) infinitely worst than with
other vessels; p. 47 (n.) unworthiness of Little Jule, as a sea
vessel; p. 48 (n.) by what is styled on board of English vessels;
p. 64 (n.) traffic carried on with trading vessels; p. 66 (n.)
refitted their vessels in its harbors; p. 68 (n.) the state of both
vessels and crew; p. 69 (n.) leaving the vessel under the mate; p. 71
(n.) on board the colonial whaling vessels; p. 76 (n.) imprudence of
intrusting the vessel longer; p. 81 (n.) attaching themselves
permanently to any vessel; p. 83 (n.) to work the vessel in; p. 98

(n.) happened to the vessel before morning; p. 100 (adj.) tokens of a
whaling vessel's approach; p. 102 (n.) sent home in another vessel;
p. 103 (n.) when the vessel left Sydney; p. 109 (n.) the most murderous
vessels ever launched; p. 109 (n.) Recently built, this vessel;
p. 110 (n.) Of a thoroughly disciplined armed vessel; p. 119 (n.)
been a cruise or two in a whaling-vessel; p. 124 (n.) belonging to
one of the French vessels of war; p. 139 (n.) of the seamen remaining
aboard the vessel; p. 146 (n.) proprietor made to quit in the first
vessel; p. 147 (n.) Captain Guy had gone on board his vessel; p. 147
(n.) to ship on board a vessel; p. 148 (n.) the damages the vessel
had sustained; p. 148 (n.) before the vessel reaches home; p. 151 (n.)
previous to the vessel's departure; p. 152 (n.) where the vessel
touched; p. 159 (n.) to go boldly among the vessels; p. 160 (n.)
Night after night every vessel; p. 164 (n.) vessels coming round Cape
Horn; p. 185 (n.) vessels of all kinds now enter; p. 187 (n.) in a
vessel of his own; p. 202 (n.) raising supplies for whaling-vessels;
p. 226 (n.) as they must be on board the vessel by noon; p. 270 (n.)
by which alone vessels enter to their anchorage; p. 289 (n.) by the
unpleasant accounts they gave of the vessel; p. 290 (n.) the mate of
the vessel called out; p. 291 (n.) paid off, at Papeetee, from a
whaling vessel; p. 304 (n.) from the captains of the vessels lying in
Papeetee; p. 309 (n.) formerly the mate of a merchant vessel; p. 312
(n.) in order to learn more of the vessel; p. 313 (n.) The only bad
trait about the vessel was this; p. 314 (n.) if I would come on board
his vessel; p. 315 (n.) to remain in the vessel.

Mardi--p. 21 (n.) that side of the vessel; p. 24 (n.) of that lost
vessel; p. 27 (n.) the vessel having been tacked; p. 27 (adj.) to the
vessel's way; p. 27 (adj.) the vessel's progress; p. 56 (n.) the
distant vessel; p. 56 (n.) I divined that vessel; p. 57 (n.) what
kind of a vessel it was; p. 57 (n.) follow after the vessel; p. 57
(n.) the vessel was no whaler; p. 57 (n.) the vicinity of the vessel;
p. 58 (adj.) which accounted for the vessel's yawing; p. 58 (n.)
unusual for any sort of vessel; p. 59 (n.) the other end of the
vessel; p. 60 (n.) of old vessels; p. 62 (n.) previous to boarding
the vessel; p. 63 (adj.) to alter the vessel's position; p. 68 (n.)
The vessel was the Parki; p. 70 (n.) on nearing the vessel; p. 70 (n.)
to steer the vessel shoreward; p. 71 (n.) who left the vessel; p. 86
(adj.) stopping the vessel's headway; p. 87 (n.) her own end of the
vessel; p. 91 (n.) has been bestowed upon vessels; p. 92 (n.) neither
the vessel nor aught therein; p. 94 (n.) as with many small vessels;
p. 96 (n.) for the few vessels; p. 96 (n.) where the vessel belonged;
p. 96 (n.) might better quit the vessel forthwith; p. 97 (n.) command
of the vessel tacitly yielded; p. 97 (n.) the command of a vessel at
sea; p. 109 (n.) that on board of other vessels; p. 113 (n.)
discovering the little vessel to "gripe" hard; p. 119 (adj.) small
danger of the vessel's sinking outright; p. 120 (n.) lest the vessel
should sink; p. 126 (n.) The vessel to which it belonged; p. 256 (n.)
accumulation of empty vessels; p. 266 (n.) as crews of vessels may;
p. 308 (n.) gained the great vessel; p. 543 (n.) like porpoises to
vessels tranced in calms; p. 620 (n.) Like helmless vessels, tempest-
tossed.

Redburn--p. 4 (n.) How different such vessels must be; p. 8 (n.) the
corresponding parts of a real vessel; p. 24 (n.) where the men slept
in the vessel; p. 52 (n.) than to ship aboard my vessel; p. 66 (n.)

as soon as the vessel felt them; p. 75 (n.) a view of the first
vessel we spoke; p. 76 (n.) had this vessel come out; p. 92 (n.)
great black hull of a strange vessel; p. 93 (n.) who had the look-out
on our vessel; p. 93 (n.) sometimes two vessels coming together;
p. 93 (n.) When I looked at this vessel; p. 93 (n.) It seems that
this vessel; p. 94 (n.) that any one vessel upon such a vast highway;
p. 97 (n.) these little vessels are sometimes run down; p. 97 (adj.)
the vessel's headway was stopt; p. 106 (n.) Merchant vessels which
are neither liners; p. 115 (n.) a pleasant sort of vitality to the
vessel; p. 126 (n.) in quest of Liverpool-bound vessels; p. 130 (n.)
are allowed on board the vessels; p. 130 (n.) by the crews of the New
York vessels; p. 133 (n.) an endless succession of vessels of all
nations; p. 153 (n.) who buy shakings, and rubbish from vessels;
p. 163 (n.) above those of the vessels in the stream; p. 164 (n.) of
the various vessels; p. 164 (n.) where vessels lie waiting their
turn; p. 166 (n.) of any of these diminutive vessels; p. 170 (n.)
upon the large native vessels of India; p. 171 (n.) The captain of
the vessel was an Englishman; p. 172 (n.) this luxury on board his
vessel; p. 174 (n.) they have vessels of a more modern kind; p. 174
(n.) Every day, some strange vessel entered; p. 185 (n.) new accessions
from every vessel; p. 195 (n.) saunter back, and board the vessels;
p. 218 (n.) interested in the ownership of their vessels; p. 219 (n.)
from his long service in the vessels of New York; p. 242 (n.) standing
in the way of working the vessel; p. 248 (n.) from a Messina vessel;
p. 249 (n.) when the vessel was just rippling along; p. 268 (adj.) in
the vessel's bows; p. 269 (n.) to the twins throughout the vessel;
p. 275 (adj.) for the doomed vessel's figure-head; p. 285 (n.) it is
not uncommon for other vessels; p. 286 (n.) to shun the leeward side
of the vessel; p. 296 (n.) as much of a fixture as the vessel's keel;
p. 296 (n.) no vessel full of emigrants; p. 312 (n.) crew that
boarded our vessel; p. 312 (n.) who had shipped in his vessel.

White-Jacket--p. ix (adj.) upon the vessel's arrival home; p. 9 (n.)
and other ropes in the stern of the vessel; p. 18 (n.) exchanged
between national vessels; p. 18 (n.) on board his vessel was a person;
p. 30 (n.) the people of the beaten vessels were fighting; p. 43 (n.)
published so soon as the vessel reached home; p. 45 (n.) moldering
keels of ship-wrecked vessels have imparted; p. 48 (n.) as soon as
the vessel comes within long gun-shot; p. 58 (n.) to sing out, as in
merchant-vessels; p. 87 (n.) over-neat vessels are Tartars to the
crew; p. 88 (n.) when the crew had washed that part of the vessel;
p. 96 (n.) before the prows of more fortunate vessels; p. 98 (n.) in
their small, clumsy vessels; p. 98 (n.) Schouten's vessel, the Horne
. . . was almost lost; p. 105 (n.) The vessel seemed to be sailing on
her side; p. 115 (n.) hatchways of some armed vessels are but poorly
secured; p. 122 (n.) vessels bound to the Nor'-west Coast; p. 162 (n.)
on board the vessel he commanded; p. 176 (n.) For though his vessel
be anchored; p. 177 (n.) secret admission of spirits into the vessel;
p. 177 (n.) ever enters the vessel from shore; p. 178 (n.) some
distance from the vessel; p. 193 (n.) when other vessels of his
squadron are near; p. 195 (n.) the various vessels belonging to the
American squadron; p. 195 (n.) between all the officers of each
vessel; p. 198 (n.) after a sailor dies in an armed vessel; p. 213
(n.) to the supreme authority of the vessel; p. 245 (n.) a vessel
drawing near was reported; p. 245 (n.) The vessel was hailed from our
poop; p. 264 (n.) a sailor of the vessel to which I was attached;

p. 265 (n.) These vessels often loosed their sails; p. 266 (n.) in
repairing a captured vessel; p. 268 (n.) by which alone vessels may
emerge; p. 270 (n.) The bounding vessel cuts the roaring tide; p. 272
(n.) accounted one of the slowest vessels; p. 272 (n.) she outstripped
every vessel on the station; p. 294 (n.) those three men on board an
American armed vessel; p. 295 (n.) shall be separated from their
vessels; p. 295 (n.) to the officers of such ships or vessels; p. 295
(n.) as if such ship or vessel were not so wrecked; p. 308 (n.) in
the crowded vessel; p. 308 (n.) in vessels of all kinds; p. 315 (n.)
had his vessel completely in her power; p. 322 (n.) out of vogue
among merchant-vessels; p. 329 (n.) the general discipline of the
vessel; p. 352 (n.) when the vessel pitches and rolls; p. 371 (n.) to
the crews of the other vessels; p. 373 (n.) distributing the soldiers
in vessels; p. 374 (n.) when the vessel is fairly engaged; p. 374 (n.)
when their vessel is attempted to be boarded; p. 375 (n.) And though
there are vessels; p. 375 (n.) apply to most vessels in the Navy;
p. 378 (n.) attempted their escape from their vessel; p. 378 (n.)
when most armed vessels actually are; p. 385 (n.) There are some
vessels blessed with; p. 385 (n.) The peculiar usages of such vessels.

Moby-Dick--p. 3 (n.) whereas all the other things, whether beast or
vessel, that enter into . . . this monster's . . . mouth; p. 8 (n.)
By Owen Chase of Nantucket, first mate of said vessel; p. 9 (n.) on
board of which vessel occurred the horrid transactions; p. 10 (n.)
The vessel . . . has a totally different air from those engaged
currents and whalings; p. 42 (n.) as if ascending the main-top of his
vessel; p. 57 (n.) to . . . ship aboard the same vessel; p. 86 (n.)
levelled his massive forefinger at the vessel in question; p. 89 (n.)
And though this also holds true of merchant vessels; p. 90 (n.)
everything necessary to fit the vessel for the voyage; p. 99 (n.)
sail a navy of upwards of seven hundred vessels; p. 262 (n.) Espied
by some . . . blundering discovery-vessel from afar; p. 295 (n.)
whales were almost simultaneously raised from . . . both vessels;
p. 415 (adj.) more or less impeding the vessel's way in the water.

VORTEX. A whirlwind, or sudden, rapid, or violent motion of air or water
in gyres or circles. (Smyth)

Mardi--p. 138 (n.) plunging into a vortex, went round and round;
p. 157 (n.) by the vortex on the coast; p. 650 (n.) I [Hautia], the
vortex that draws all in.

Moby-Dick--p. 140 (n.) Over Descartian vortices you hover; p. 469 (n.)
spinning, animate and inanimate, all round and round in one vortex,
carried the smallest ship of the Pequod out of sight; p. 470 (n.) I
was then, but slowly drawn towards the closing vortex.

VOYAGE. A journey by sea. It usually includes the outward and homeward
trips, which are called passages. (Smyth)

Typee--p. 5 (n.) which the older voyagers had so glowingly described;
p. 6 (n.) in the sketches of South-Sea voyages; p. 11 (n.) I shall
follow the example of most voyagers; p. 11 (n.) and by all voyagers,
it is generally known; p. 14 (v.) whenever a Marquesan lady voyages

by water; p. 20 (n.) to endure another voyage on board the Dolly;
p. 20 (n.) to serve in a certain capacity for the period of the
voyage; p. 21 (n.) The longevity of Cape Horn whaling voyages; p. 21
(n.) who officiate as caterers for the voyage; p. 22 (n.) obstacle to
the further prosecution of the voyage; p. 22 (n.) begin the voyage
afresh with unabated zeal; p. 23 (n.) touching the usual length of
these voyages; p. 23 (n.) that we should make an unfortunate voyage;
p. 25 (n.) touched at the group on former voyages; p. 27 (n.)
discovered by voyagers or by travellers; p. 170 (n.) when the
scientific voyager arrives at home; p. 172 (n.) as if eager to hurry
on his voyage; p. 173 (n.) God speed, and a pleasant voyage; p. 177
(n.) made by other eminent voyagers; p. 183 (n.) Figueroa, the
chronicler of Mendanna's voyage; p. 183 (n.) Doctor Christoval
Suaverde de Figueroa's History of Mendanna's Voyage; p. 184 (n.) Cook
in the account of his voyages; p. 201 (n.) the reader of South Sea
voyages is too apt to form; p. 205 (n.) unfortunate voyagers are
lured; p. 205 (n.) every book of voyages which purports to give.

Omoo--p. xiii (n.) These voyages, also, are unusually long; p. xiv
(n.) advisable to quote previous voyagers; p. xiv (n.) from the
oldest books of South Sea voyages; p. 8 (n.) I learned the history of
the voyage thus far; p. 9 (n.) dispatched her on the present voyage;
p. 11 (n.) In the early part of the voyage; p. 14 (n.) usually
infesting this article in long tropical voyages; p. 35 (n.) upon a
former voyage; p. 39 (n.) drunken sailors on a voyage long previous;
p. 46 (n.) On a voyage to India; p. 47 (n.) from the commencement of
the voyage; p. 48 (n.) the regular supplies for the voyage; p. 51 (n.)
of the profits of the voyage; p. 61 (v.) how many leagues we voyaged;
p. 66 (n.) diminish the wonder and admiration of the voyager; p. 66
(n.) of all readers of South Sea voyages; p. 69 (n.) to resume her
voyage at once; p. 71 (n.) he had been two or three voyages in Sydney;
p. 71 (n.) on his first voyage; p. 75 (n.) had been several voyages
to Sydney; p. 81 (n.) who have been aboard the whole voyage; p. 81
(n.) why the voyage should not be at once resumed; p. 110 (n.) they
landed from distant voyages; p. 123 (n.) more than hinted at by recent
voyagers; p. 152 (n.) in old voyages we read of chiefs; p. 187 (n.)
The author of a Voyage round the World; p. 187 (n.) Narrative of a
Voyage to the Pacific; p. 188 (n.) A Missionary Voyage to the South
Pacific; p. 188 (n.) See Vancouver's Voyages; p. 191 (n.) Vide A
Voyage round the World; p. 210 (n.) See Lord Byron's Voyage of H.B.M.
Ship Blonde; p. 229 (n.) told us that the voyagers were returning;
p. 263 (n.) as some voyager has said; p. 268 (n.) ever dreamed of
taking the voyage; p. 269 (n.) though our fellow-voyagers shouted;
p. 269 (n.) diversifying the monotony of a sea-voyage; p. 289 (n.) A
bay, considered by many voyagers; p. 302 (n.) Every reader of Cook's
Voyages; p. 315 (n.) for the residue of the voyage.

Mardi--p. xvii (n.) narratives of voyages; p. 7 (n.) of northern
voyaging; p. 18 (n.) on our voyage westward; p. 20 (n.) for this good
voyage; p. 23 (n.) Voyaging in these seas; p. 26 (n.) upon this
western voyage; p. 44 (n.) as our voyage lengthened; p. 52 (n.) for
the long whaling voyage; p. 68 (n.) on a voyage southward; p. 94 (n.)
seldom worn till a subsequent voyage; p. 95 (n.) on long voyages;
p. 96 (n.) prevented our voyaging to the Hawaiian group; p. 103 (n.)
loneliness of our voyage was relieved; p. 105 (n.) our fellow-voyagers,
the little fish; p. 107 (n.) quiet, lazy, ever-present perils of the

voyage; p. 109 (n.) drowsiness of my fellow-voyagers; p. 115 (n.)
since the commencement of the voyage; p. 126 (n.) on its endless
voyage; p. 129 (n.) found on some priestly voyage; p. 131 (n.) and
the object of their voyage; p. 145 (v.) determined upon voyaging;
p. 156 (v.) had voyaged from Oroolia; p. 157 (v.) the way she would
voyage there; p. 157 (n.) And this was the voyage; p. 161 (v.)
Voyaging along the zone; p. 167 (v.) that the strangers had voyaged
far; p. 181 (n.) during our long lazy voyage; p. 196 (n.) Hence the
voyage in prospect; p. 196 (v.) to voyage in the equipage; p. 197 (n.)
for companions on our voyage; p. 197 (n.) As our voyage would embrace;
p. 198 (n.) the plan of our voyage; p. 199 (n.) devour an innocent
voyager; p. 200 (v.) we voyaged in state; p. 200 (n.) be this voyage
full gayly sailed; p. 201 (n.) we voyagers must dismount; p. 206 (n.)
The voyager who records the fact; p. 208 (n.) throughout the voyage;
p. 228 (n.) in the fine old folio voyages of Hakluyt; p. 256 (n.)
their voyages were brief; p. 286 (n.) till the long voyage in prospect;
p. 301 (n.) orders to return with the voyagers; p. 307 (n.) we
encountered on our voyage; p. 311 (n.) was impatient of the voyage;
p. 312 (n.) beginning a voyage like our own; p. 312 (n.) for us a
prosperous voyage; p. 323 (v.) we were now voyaging straight for
Maramma; p. 371 (n.) among the appliances of this voyage; p. 384 (n.)
And books on voyages; p. 402 (v.) Voyaging on, we entered a bay;
p. 427 (n.) at the outset of this voyage; p. 435 (n.) our brief
voyage, may not embrace; p. 461 (n.) It was many moons on the voyage;
p. 466 (n.) voyaging over to Dominora in a canoe; p. 469 (n.) the
distant voyager passing wild rocks; p. 523 (n.) Next day we retraced
our voyage northward; p. 531 (n.) Our coasting voyage at an end;
p. 543 (v.) we voyaged along that coast; p. 544 (v.) as we northward
voyaged; p. 556 (v.) I've chartless voyaged; p. 556 (n.) That voyager
steered his bark through seas; p. 616 (v.) let's voyage to Aldebaran;
p. 623 (n.) Our voyage has an object; p. 623 (n.) Hail! voyagers,
hail; p. 623 (n.) Hail! voyagers, hail; p. 624 (n.) Hail! voyagers,
hail; p. 624 (n.) Hail! voyagers, hail; p. 624 (n.) Hail! voyagers,
hail; p. 633 (n.) as voyagers pass far sails at sea; p. 637 (n.) My
voyage is ended; p. 642 (v.) youths . . . voyaged in gala canoes;
p. 643 (v.) straight to Flozella would I have voyaged; p. 646 (n.) Is
not thy voyage now ended; p. 646 (n.) through all this long, long
voyage; p. 654 (n.) no voyager e'er puts back.

Redburn--p. 4 (n.) what an important voyage it must be; p. 5 (n.)
long reveries about distant voyages and travels; p. 7 (n.) I was
fated . . . to be a great voyager; p. 9 (n.) on this my first voyage;
p. 15 (n.) to let him go for one voyage; p. 16 (adv.) he'll be cracking
his jokes the whole voyage; p. 23 (n.) informing him of the voyage;
p. 26 (n.) in this very ship on her last voyage; p. 28 (n.) has not
been cleaned out since last voyage; p. 29 (n.) thinking to secure a
sailor friend for the voyage; p. 33 (n.) this was only the first day
of the voyage; p. 33 (n.) before the voyage was ended; p. 33 (n.) at
the end of the voyage; p. 34 (n.) out of these Narrows on a long
voyage; p. 41 (n.) in books of voyages; p. 46 (n.) was a volume of
Voyages and Travels round the World; p. 46 (n.) like books of voyages
they often contradicted; p. 47 (n.) though I did afterward upon the
voyage; p. 47 (n.) but always made a voyage himself; p. 51 (n.) I
thought it an ill-omened voyage; p. 52 (n.) on the very first night
of his voyage; p. 59 (adv.) a notorious old soger the whole voyage;
p. 60 (n.) a landsman on his first voyage; p. 64 (n.) who was on my

first voyage; p. 66 (n.) make a speedy end to this abominable voyage;
p. 72 (n.) my voyage would be like a summer excursion; p. 83 (n.)
upon many previous voyages; p. 93 (n.) felt sure of a prosperous
voyage; p. 100 (n.) to float by us during the voyage; p. 100 (n.)
This was Larry's first voyage; p. 100 (n.) during his whaling voyages;
p. 102 (n.) all through the voyage; p. 106 (n.) though in all her
voyages; p. 107 (n.) on this particular voyage; p. 116 (n.) so that
on a voyage to Liverpool; p. 121 (n.) only shipped for this one
voyage; p. 121 (n.) a short voyage too; p. 123 (n.) contemplating a
voyage to sea; p. 128 (n.) had made frequent voyages to Liverpool;
p. 129 (n.) he had been going Liverpool and New York voyages; p. 130
(n.) in the expense of the voyage; p. 137 (n.) these Liverpool
voyages, likewise those; p. 137 (n.) by the time his voyage terminates;
p. 138 (n.) Whereas, upon a long voyage, say to India; p. 138 (n.)
upon long voyages to distant parts; p. 138 (n.) dangers, and privations
of a voyage; p. 143 (n.) on this very voyage to Liverpool; p. 149 (n.)
town, to which I made my first voyage; p. 164 (n.) from a voyage
across the ocean; p. 166 (n.) hardships encountered on the voyage;
p. 166 (n.) concerning their past voyages; p. 171 (n.) to stand the
hardships of northern voyaging; p. 177 (n.) to grant them short and
prosperous voyages; p. 177 (n.) of every Liverpool ship from a foreign
voyage; p. 186 (n.) Upon a six months' voyage; p. 194 (n.) embark
upon a long voyage; p. 202 (n.) like to make voyages to it; p. 216
(n.) contemplated a voyage to my country; p. 218 (n.) He made one
voyage; p. 219 (n.) by the end of the voyage; p. 219 (n.) and that
the voyage thither; p. 240 (n.) auspicious a beginning of their
voyage; p. 140 (n.) would be an uncommonly long voyage; p. 241 (n.)
to whom a first voyage, under the most; p. 245 (n.) never opened
again during the voyage; p. 252 (n.) For this voyage that you want;
p. 254 (n.) who had made voyages to Canton; p. 255 (n.) you had been
two voyages to Bombay; p. 257 (n.) for the residue of the voyage;
p. 257 (n.) he might make the voyage; p. 357 (n.) always a sailor for
that voyage; p. 259 (v.) after newly voyaging so many days; p. 260
(n.) to the delight of his fellow voyagers; p. 263 (n.) at the end of
the voyage; p. 265 (n.) adapted to the contingencies of a voyager;
p. 265 (adv.) was tormented the whole voyage by his wife; p. 271 (n.)
by sailors on some previous voyage; p. 272 (adj.) last-voyage chaws
were soon gone; p. 278 (n.) Now, during the voyage; p. 283 (n.) with
regard to their outfits for the voyage; p. 284 (n.) for the rest of
this starving voyage; p. 293 (n.) during a long voyage across the
Atlantic; p. 294 (n.) greets the eager voyager from afar; p. 295 (n.)
during the greater part of a voyage; p. 299 (n.) made otherwise than
a tidy and prosperous voyage; p. 301 (n.) gratitude at the end of a
voyage; p. 305 (n.) on the profits of my first voyage; p. 305 (n.)
after the voyage is concluded; p. 308 (n.) The voyage was now
concluded; p. 309 (n.) and drink to the last voyage; p. 311 (n.) will
conclude my first voyage; p. 311 (n.) feared he had gone on a whaling
voyage; p. 312 (n.) must indeed have departed on a whaling voyage;
p. 312 (n.) than any narrated in this My First Voyage.

White-Jacket--p. 11 (n.) after a three years' voyage; p. 16 (n.)
sorry yarns of voyages to China after tea-caddies; p. 16 (n.) and
voyages to the West Indies; p. 16 (n.) and voyages to the Shetlands;
p. 76 (n.) and in all our voyages round the world; p. 122 (n.) have
lengthened their voyages some thousands of miles; p. 122 (n.) in
making the voyage to and from; p. 123 (n.) of five hundred men on a

long voyage; p. 153 (n.) making voyages for the benefit; p. 206 (n.)
aggregate wages of the eighty for the voyage; p. 222 (n.) especially
upon long voyages; p. 300 (v.) wise Men, who voyaged round the world;
p. 323 (v.) as they voyaged in quest of; p. 343 (n.) In case I die on
the voyage; p. 389 (n.) last hours of so long a voyage; p. 398 (n.)
our voyage will prove our eventual abiding place; p. 400 (n.) Life is
a voyage that's homeward-bound.

Moby-Dick--p. 5 (n.) Thomas Edge's Ten Voyages to Spitzbergen in
Purchass; p. 5 (n.) Sir T. Herbert's Voyages into Asia and Africa;
p. 5 (n.) A Voyage to Greenland; p. 5 (n.) Captain Cowley's Voyage
round the Globe A.D. 1729; p. 6 (n.) Cook's Voyages; p. 6 (n.) Uno
von Troll's Letters on Banks's and Solander's Voyage to Iceland in
1772; p. 7 (n.) Colnett's Voyage for the Purpose of Extending the
Spermacetti Whale Fishery; p. 9 (n.) Frederick Debell Bennett's
Whaling Voyage Round the Globe, 1840; p. 10 (n.) The Voyages of the
Dutch and English to the Northern Ocean; p. 10 (n.) a totally different
air from those engaged in a regular voyage; p. 10 (n.) Tales of a
Whale Voyager to the Arctic Ocean; p. 11 (n.) Darwin's Voyage of a
Naturalist; p. 13 (n.) Why upon your first voyage as a passenger, did
you yourself feel such a mystical vibration, when first told; p. 15
(n.) now take it into my head to go on a whaling voyage; p. 15 (n.)
my going on this whaling voyage, formed part; p. 16 (n.) WHALING
VOYAGE BY ONE ISHMAEL; p. 16 (n.) the Fates, put me down for this
shabby part of a whaling voyage; p. 16 (n.) the whaling voyage was
welcome; p. 17 (n.) thence to embark on their voyage; p. 23 (n.) a
three years' voyage, and a full ship; p. 29 (n.) this harpooneer, in
the course of his distant voyages; p. 36 (n.) three days landed from
his Indian voyage; p. 41 (n.) on the eve of a Nantucket voyage; p. 44
(n.) the world's . . . not a voyage complete; p. 80 (n.) some sailors
who had just come from a plum-pudding voyage, as they called it (that
is, a short whaling-voyage in a schooner or brig, confined to the
north of the line, in the Atlantic Ocean only); p. 87 (adv.) nothing
about his losing his leg last voyage; p. 89 (n.) besides the great
length of the whaling voyage; p. 90 (n.) to fit the vessel for the
voyage; p. 93 (n.) Here upon the very point of starting for the
voyage; p. 97 (n.) who in mid-winter just landed from a four years'
dangerous voyage.

WADE. An Anglo-Saxon word, meaning to pass through water without
swimming. (Smyth)

Mardi--p. 211 (v.) they [giants] waded through the sea.

WAKE. The transient, generally smooth, track impressed on the surface-
water by a ship's progress. Its bearing is usually observed by the
compass to discover the angle of lee-way. (Smyth)

Typee--p. 22 (n.) Three pet sharks followed in her wake; p. 223 (n.)
who followed chattering in our wake; p. 252 (n.) rise to the surface
in the wake of the boat.

Mardi--p. 121 (n.) our wake was revealed; p. 303 (n.) the white wake
of the corpse; p. 375 (n.) leaving certain fragments in its wake;

p. 422 (n.) beheld a corruscating wake; p. 543 (n.) which leave their
sandy wakes; p. 551 (n.) they leave their wake around the world;
p. 586 (n.) leaving braided, foaming wakes; p. 632 (n.) ships leave a
radiant-white, and fire-fly wake; p. 633 (n.) wild music was their
wake; p. 654 (n.) straight in my white wake.

Redburn--p. 102 (n.) illuminated foam in her wake; p. 245 (n.)
leaving a corruscating wake as it sank.

White-Jacket--p. 394 (n.) leaving a tranquil wake behind.

Moby-Dick--p. 8 (n.) And the phosphor gleamed in the wake of the
whale; p. 23 (n.) No wonder, then, that they made a straight wake for
the whale's mouth; p. 139 (adv.) this sunken-eyed young Platonist
will tow you ten wakes round the world; p. 146 (n.) I leave a white
and turbid wake; p. 148 (n.) buildst over the dead water of the wake;
p. 159 (n.) leaving a milky-way wake of creamy foam; p. 174 (n.) into
the devious zig-zag world-wide of the Pequod's circumnavigating wake;
p. 193 (n.) the whales seemed separating their wakes; p. 230 (n.)
leaving tons of tumultous white curds in his wake; p. 296 (n.) They
left a great, wide wake; p. 296 (n.) Full in this rapid wake; p. 296
(n.) expose the cause of his devious wake in the unnatural stump of
his starboard fin; p. 298 (n.) all four boats were diagonally in the
whale's immediate wake; p. 321 (n.) loudly directing attention to
something in our wake; p. 321 (n.) But still driving on in the wake
of the whales; p. 347 (n.) Because there were two boats in his wake;
p. 402 (n.) they are always flying in thy wake; p. 408 (n.) as the
two ships crossed each other's wakes; p. 423 (n.) how the same yellow
rays were blending with his undeviating wake; p. 435 (n.) Soon the
two ships diverged their wakes; p. 447 (n.) the blue waters
interchangeably flowed over into the moving valley of his steady
wake; p. 451 (n.) the Pequod bore down in the leeward wake of Moby-
Dick; p. 453 (n.) the creature's future wake through the darkness is
almost as established to the sagacious mind of the hunter, as the
pilot's coast is to him; p. 453 (n.) the proverbial evanescence of a
thing writ in water, a wake; p. 460 (n.) In his infallible wake,
though; but follow that wake, that's all; p. 461 (n.) as she rechurned
the cream in her own white wake.

WALRUS. The Trichecus rosmarus, a large amphibious marine animal, allied
to the seals, found in the Arctic regions. Its upper canines are developed
into large descending tusks, of considerable value as ivory. It is also
called morse, sea-horse, and sea-cow. (Smyth)

Mardi--p. 40 (n.) like those of a walrus; p. 417 (n.) barons of sea-
beeves and walruses; p. 482 (n.) finned-lions, winged walruses.

Redburn--p. 88 (n.) a round face, too, like a walrus.

Moby-Dick--p. 63 (n.) while under his very pillow rush herds of
walruses and whales; p. 119 (n.) A walrus spouts much like a whale;
p. 119 (n.) but the walrus is not a fish; p. 203 (n.) this craft was
bleached like the skeleton of a stranded walrus; p. 364 (adj.) Ahab
. . . cried our in his walrus way.

WASH. A surface covered by floods. Also, a shallow inlet or gulf; the east-country term for the sea-shore. (Smyth)

Moby-Dick--p. 12 (v.) the Battery, where that noble mole is washed by waves.

WATER. The ocean; a sea; a lake; a river; any great collection of water. (Webster)

Typee--p. 4 (n.) the brackish water in his little trough; p. 5 (n.) carved canoes dancing on the flashing blue waters; p. 5 (adj.) In the watery path of Mendanna; p. 10 (n.) scared from the water under the bows; p. 10 (n.) disappear on the surface of the water; p. 10 (n.) sink slowly into the blue waters; p. 10 (n.) silence that reigned over sky and water; p. 10 (n.) and the rippling at the cut-water; p. 12 (n.) glimpses of blooming valleys, deep glens, waterfalls; p. 12 (v.) and watered by purling brooks; p. 13 (n.) would become entangled beneath the water; p. 14 (n.) impelled his necklace of cocoa nuts through the water; p. 14 (n.) whenever a Marquesan lady voyages by water; p. 14 (n.) to a singular commotion in the water; p. 14 (n.) right arm bearing above the water; p. 21 (n.) Choice old water top; p. 23 (n.) is an expanse of water not unlike . . . a horseshoe; p. 23 (n.) From the verge of the water the land rises; p. 24 (n.) in larger and more noisy waterfalls; p. 25 (n.) dropped her anchor in its waters; p. 26 (n.) rolling through the blue waters towards their shores; p. 28 (n.) I had come from Nukuheva by water; p. 28 (n.) we had omitted to supply ourselves with water; p. 28 (adj.) the refreshing influence of a cold-water bath; p. 36 (n.) large drops fell bubbling into the water; p. 37 (n.) became completely saturated with water; p. 44 (n.) low murmurings of distant waterfalls; p. 44 (n.) the roar of those waterfalls down there would better; p. 45 (v.) it is roomy, secluded, well watered; p. 46 (n.) for the current of water extended very nearly; p. 46 (n.) the water was continually finding some new opening; p. 47 (n.) A copious draught of the pure water; p. 49 (n.) to the blue waters in the distance; p. 49 (n.) cascades, whose slender threads of water; p. 52 (n.) in quest of the water which flowed so temptingly; p. 53 (n.) impatient as I was to reach the waters; p. 53 (n.) I fairly loathed the water; p. 56 (n.) with what a steep inclination the water descends; p. 58 (n.) The bed of the watercourse was covered with fragments; p. 58 (n.) forming at intervals small waterfalls; p. 58 (n.) but by wading through the water; p. 59 (n.) whilst the unpitying waters flowed over our prostrate bodies; p. 59 (n.) Our progress along the steep watercourse was . . . slow; p. 59 (n.) the noise of falling waters . . . became more distinct; p. 60 (n.) the lowest of them reaching even to the water; p. 61 (n.) splashing at last into the waters beneath; p. 62 (n.) contrasted beautifully with the foamy waters; p. 64 (n.) to the music of the smaller waterfalls; p. 64 (n.) an arched aperture for the passage of the waters; p. 64 (n.) by the gradual descent of the deep watercourse; p. 74 (n.) long before they reach their waters; p. 80 (n.) moistening them [herbs] in water; p. 88 (n.) washed his fingers in a vessel of water; p. 89 (n.) I should repair to the water and wash; p. 89 (n.) wading up to his hips in the water; p. 89 (n.) cooled my blushes in the water it contained; p. 90 (n.) sliding off into the water; p. 95 (n.) Emetics and lukewarm water; p. 98 (n.) in

returning to the valley by water; p. 100 (n.) I seized a calabash of
water; p. 100 (n.) bathed the part repeatedly in water; p. 100 (n.)
from a cocoa-nut shell a few mouthfuls of water; p. 102 (n.) stooping
over me with the calabash of water; p. 103 (n.) plenty of bread-
fruit--plenty of water; p. 109 (n.) bathing me in its refreshing
water; p. 110 (n.) the waters flowed between grassy banks; p. 110 (n.)
several feet above the surface of the water; p. 110 (n.) performed a
thousand antics in the water; p. 110 (n.) standing in the transparent
water; p. 110 (n.) briskly with a small stone in the water; p. 113
(n.) pouring water in judicious quantities; p. 115 (n.) into a vessel
of cold water; p. 117 (n.) mixed with water until it gains a proper
. . . consistency; p. 131 (n.) enjoyed the recreation in the waters;
p. 131 (n.) This lovely sheet of water was almost circular; p. 131
(n.) propelled themselves through the water; p. 131 (n.) they darted
through the water; p. 131 (n.) dived deep down into the water; p. 132
(n.) drag some of them under the water; p. 132 (n.) It was launched
upon the sheet of water; p. 132 (n.) extended the prohibition to the
waters in which it lay; p. 133 (n.) to paddle about in the water;
p. 133 (n.) swept us gently along the margin of the water; p. 134 (n.)
This lovely piece of water was the coolest spot; p. 134 (n.) glided
rapidly through the water; p. 148 (n.) moistened occasionally with
water; p. 149 (n.) The fresh morning air and the cool flowing waters;
p. 150 (n.) by friction with a smooth stone in the water; p. 151 (n.)
standing up to the waist in water; p. 152 (n.) or bathing in the
waters of the stream; p. 153 (n.) The mineral waters of Arva Wai;
p. 153 (n.) translated into Strong Waters; p. 153 (n.) Wai is the
Marquesan word for water; p. 153 (n.) The water is held in high
estimation; p. 153 (n.) had a great love for the waters; p. 154 (n.)
The water tasted like a solution of a dozen disagreeable things;
p. 154 (n.) cannot give a scientific analysis of the water; p. 154
(n.) whether this is always found in the water; p. 155 (n.) a train
of Elnas laid under the water; p. 158 (n.) for the purpose of filling
them with water; p. 159 (n.) the whole carcass thoroughly washed with
water; p. 164 (n.) These were filled with water from the stream;
p. 165 (n.) A cocoa-nut goblet of water was passed around; p. 165 (n.)
water was poured upon the mass; p. 166 (n.) pressed perpendicularly
into the water; p. 202 (n.) so long as grass grows and water runs;
p. 206 (n.) seldom sought it in their waters; p. 229 (n.) sporting in
the water near her; p. 229 (n.) at swallowing a mouthful of water;
p. 229 (n.) when they are thus launched into the water; p. 229 (n.)
invariably washed in fresh water; p. 240 (n.) from thence reach
Nukuheva by water; p. 242 (n.) "Wai (water)," I laconically answered;
p. 243 (n.) placed a calabash of water by my side; p. 249 (n.) Karokoee
stood near the edge of the water; p. 250 (n.) Marheyo and Kory-Kory
. . . followed me into the water; p. 251 (n.) who had retired from
the edge of the water; p. 250 (n.) active savages were already dashing
into the water; p. 251 (n.) more formidable antagonists in the water;
p. 251 (n.) the crowd of swimmers shot through the water; p. 252 (n.)
was dashing the water before him; p. 263 (n.) ran down the path in
the direction of the water; p. 263 (n.) green space between the
groves and the water; p. 266 (n.) I will bring Tommo, as they call
him, by water.

Omoo--p. xiii (n.) the vessels navigating those remote waters; p. 7
(n.) same sun now setting over a waste of waters; p. 8 (n.) a splash
of water came down the open scuttle; p. 12 (n.) and left to meditate

on bread and water; p. 14 (n.) by rolling about in tepid water; p. 14
(n.) notwithstanding the wateriness of the first course; p. 20 (n.)
splashing the water like porpoises; p. 20 (n.) rolling over and over
in the water; p. 21 (n.) and shot across the water; p. 21 (n.) seen
coming down to the water; p. 24 (n.) Leaving one of their number by
the water; p. 26 (n.) Across the water; p. 26 (n.) with wild falls of
water; p. 26 (n.) the embayed waters were gentle as a lake; p. 27 (n.)
which all the waters of Albana and Pharpar; p. 34 (n.) sousing the
poor fellow with a bucket of salt water; p. 35 (n.) upon waters
comparatively little traversed; p. 36 (n.) diluted with water from
the butt; p. 39 (n.) the water fairly poured down; p. 40 (adj.) to
find a watery grave; p. 49 (n.) Thus went the world of waters to us;
p. 50 (n.) and then filled with buckets of water; p. 53 (adj.) the
veriest wretch of watery world over; p. 59 (n.) served as a sort of
breakwater to the inundation; p. 59 (n.) The water then poured along
the deck; p. 64 (n.) did not seem four feet above the water; p. 65
(v.) watered with fine streams; p. 66 (n.) the water-falls flash out
into the sunlight; p. 69 (n.) booming of her guns came over the water;
p. 72 (n.) sped like an arrow through the water; p. 74 (n.) was then
mixed with water; p. 86 (n.) in going plump into the water; p. 88 (n.)
draw a bucket of water; p. 99 (n.) occasionally looking down in the
water; p. 99 (n.) tearing his paddle out of the water; p. 101 (n.)
All round the water; p. 101 (n.) Across the water, the tri-color also;
p. 101 (n.) to express high-water and midnight; p. 102 (n.) its stern
settled low in the water; p. 102 (n.) in whose waters I had a hundred
times bathed; p. 110 (n.) of the juice of water-facets [sic]; p. 114
(n.) over large water-courses; p. 114 (n.) a choice well of water
bottled up among the mountains; p. 116 (n.) until the waters, spreading
themselves upon a beach; p. 144 (n.) on bread and water; p. 148 (adj.)
the Julia's exchequer was a low-water mark; p. 160 (n.) launched into
the water; p. 160 (n.) or lift it entirely out of the water; p. 160
(n.) and then depressed in the water; p. 161 (n.) that the water
splattered; p. 161 (n.) we were both in the water; p. 161 (n.) made
of flour and water; p. 162 (n.) Down in these waters; p. 169 (v.) and
watering the valley; p. 169 (n.) Flowing waters; p. 187 (n.) and
rushed to the waters of baptism; p. 212 (n.) water-falls lifted up
their voices; p. 214 (n.) near a water-course, long since deserted;
p. 215 (n.) he towed a rotten old water-cask ashore; p. 216 (n.) It
was now proposed to try the water; p. 217 (n.) leaving the water
within smooth; p. 217 (n.) the water-sprites had rolled our stone;
p. 238 (n.) moored here and there to posts in the water; p. 238 (n.)
upon the surface of the starlit water; p. 240 (n.) it swept right
down to the water; p. 250 (n.) surrounded by a regular breakwater of
coral; p. 250 (n.) settlements . . . are right upon the water; p. 252
(n.) cooled by its transit over the waters; p. 253 (n.) a knoll which
rolled off into the water; p. 255 (n.) sloping away to the water;
p. 257 (n.) half-filled with sea-water; p. 258 (n.) steeped a morsel
of food into his nutful of sea-water; p. 258 (n.) invariably use sea-
water in this way; p. 261 (v.) watered by streams from the mountains;
p. 262 (n.) He impels his canoe through the water; p. 266 (n.) leaping
right into the water; p. 266 (n.) and at low water; p. 266 (n.)
splashing through the water in all directions; p. 266 (n.) the
darkness of sky and water was streaked; p. 266 (n.) the end of which
swept the water; p. 266 (n.) fifty or sixty feet from the water;
p. 269 (n.) lying partly in the water; p. 270 (n.) These great natural
breakwaters are admirably; p. 270 (n.) for the purpose of watering

his ship; p. 270 (n.) the fresh water of the land; p. 270 (n.) with a
taste in watering-places truly Tahitian; p. 271 (n.) which, dividing
its waters; p. 274 (n.) the "Tee" is stirred up with water; p. 278
(n.) through which we saw the gleam of water; p. 286 (n.) was built
right out into the water; p. 286 (n.) always most luxuriant near the
water; p. 289 (n.) you catch no glimpse of the water; p. 289 (n.) at
its base the waters lie still; p. 292 (n.) where the waters were
tolerably smooth; p. 299 (n.) she drops her anchor in its waters;
p. 316 (n.) hurried down to the water.

Mardi--p. 7 (adj.) to the water's edge; p. 10 (adj.) in the watery
waste; p. 11 (n.) merely an extension of water; p. 13 (adj.) within
which rolled the watery world; p. 18 (n.) a few inches of water;
p. 20 (n.) an abundant supply of water; p. 20 (n.) as for water;
p. 23 (n.) in these lonely waters; p. 25 (adj.) in the lowest watery
zone; p. 27 (n.) the side depressed in the water; p. 27 (n.) in the
water; p. 29 (adj.) the watery world is all before them; p. 30 (adj.)
now buried in watery hollows; p. 32 (n.) a couple of two-gallon water-
kegs; p. 33 (adj.) this was the water-tight keg; p. 35 (n.) insipid
as water after wine; p. 37 (n.) above the water; p. 37 (adj.) from
watery cliff to cliff; p. 41 (n.) like a spirit in the water; p. 42
(n.) round and round in the water; p. 43 (n.) it was water, bright
water, cool, sparkling water; p. 44 (n.) full of water; p. 44 (n.)
the water then getting beyond the reach; p. 44 (n.) never twice
absorb water; p. 44 (n.) of a leathern goblet for water; p. 45 (n.)
dwelling upon the water; p. 48 (n.) firmaments of sky and water;
p. 48 (n.) sky, air, water, and all; p. 49 (n.) the water in the
breaker; p. 49 (n.) our allowance of water; p. 49 (n.) nearly half
full of water; p. 50 (n.) the water would hold out longer; p. 51 (n.)
our water was improving; p. 51 (n.) occasionally incident to ship
water; p. 51 (n.) as our water improved; p. 58 (n.) in search of
water; p. 58 (n.) in search of water; p. 62 (n.) rather low in the
water; p. 63 (n.) us twain in the water; p. 65 (n.) through the water;
p. 70 (n.) up from the water; p. 71 (n.) plunged into the water;
p. 70 (n.) through the water; p. 72 (n.) springing into the water;
p. 72 (n.) slid into the water; p. 82 (n.) in those generally tranquil
waters; p. 83 (n.) adhere to the very cutwater; p. 85 (adj.) in what
watery world she floated; p. 94 (adj.) farther and farther into the
watery wilderness; p. 96 (n.) abundance of fresh water in casks;
p. 103 (n.) mighty commotion in the water; p. 111 (n.) no onward
progress through the water; p. 111 (n.) comingling and purification
of the sea-water; p. 111 (n.) that a bucket of sea-water; p. 112 (n.)
which is not the case with rain-water; p. 112 (n.) offensiveness of
sea-water left standing; p. 113 (n.) as if someone under water were
jerking; p. 113 (n.) towed heavily in the water; p. 114 (adj.) out of
the wooden can at the water cask; p. 118 (adj.) our almost water-
logged craft; p. 119 (n.) the water, spring-like, came bubbling;
p. 119 (n.) as the water of Saratoga; p. 119 (n.) stowed it with
water and provisions; p. 119 (n.) showed that the water; p. 119 (n.)
specifically heavier than water; p. 121 (n.) pervading hue of the
water cast a cadaverous gleam; p. 121 (n.) raising their heads above
water; p. 122 (n.) headlong down into the water; p. 122 (n.) darting
of fish under water; p. 123 (n.) do irradiate the waters at such
times; p. 123 (n.) Draw a bucket of water; p. 126 (n.) the little
flying-fish in the water; p. 126 (n.) swoops into the water; p. 127
(n.) driving through the water; p. 128 (n.) to force down into the

water; p. 128 (n.) elevated high above the water; p. 137 (n.) hardly
had the waters of Oroolia; p. 138 (adj.) flowed on between blue
watery banks; p. 140 (n.) in the deep waters of my soul; p. 141 (n.)
comes he to the water; p. 143 (adj.) over the wide watery world;
p. 148 (n.) the water alive with their hosts; p. 149 (n.) surging in
the water; p. 149 (n.) so high out of water; p. 151 (n.) a terrific
rushing sound under water; p. 155 (n.) an outlet to the waters;
p. 155 (n.) perpetual eddying of the water; p. 159 (n.) in the waters
she saw lustrous eyes; p. 161 (n.) outstretching its arms in the
water; p. 161 (n.) in upon the still, green waters; p. 161 (n.) the
mild waters stretched all around us; p. 161 (n.) away, away, across
the wide waters; p. 161 (n.) Soon the water all round us; p. 161 (n.)
like frighted water-fowls; p. 161 (n.) isle's shadow on the water;
p. 161 (n.) into the water beyond; p. 179 (n.) a light breeze rippled
the water; p. 190 (v.) watered by roving brooks; p. 190 (n.) drew
nourishment from the water; p. 192 (adj.) But why these watery
obsequies; p. 198 (n.) both light and water waned; p. 201 (n.)
islanders ran into the water; p. 209 (n.) drinking of that water had
aired; p. 211 (n.) his motionless line in the water; p. 211 (n.)
gardens under water; p. 212 (n.) looking down into the water; p. 213
(n.) at last shooting through the water; p. 213 (n.) and back the
waters heap; p. 214 (n.) How the waters part; p. 214 (n.) Heap back;
heap back; the waters back; p. 217 (n.) and across the water; p. 226
(n.) their waters received in green mossy tanks; p. 233 (n.) its
waters being caught in a large stone basin; p. 234 (n.) hand-in-hand
with the cool waters; p. 245 (adj.) that in his blue-water opinion;
p. 251 (n.) and crossing the waters; p. 255 (n.) with the living
waters from the cascade; p. 255 (n.) presiding over the head waters;
p. 256 (n.) sailing high out of water; p. 256 (n.) no head waters
will ye find; p. 258 (n.) water sinks down below; p. 259 (n.) one
with a gourd of scented waters; p. 260 (n.) sought to be revived by
watering; p. 267 (n.) intermitted melody in the water; p. 273 (n.)
thundering in water-bolts; p. 273 (adj.) till it races along a watery
wall; p. 273 (n.) Landing in smooth water; p. 275 (n.) in the middle
of the still water; p. 278 (n.) turning round toward the water;
p. 282 (v.) watered them with the early dew; p. 284 (n.) Clear as
this water; p. 286 (n.) Soon the water shoaled; p. 286 (n.) most
hospitable vicinity to the water; p. 288 (n.) close bordering the
water; p. 288 (n.) letting in upon them the salt waters; p. 288 (n.)
the waters could be mixed; p. 288 (adj.) Fresh-water fish are only to
be obtained; p. 288 (n.) some leaping out of the water; p. 294 (n.)
splashing the water; p. 295 (n.) with a gourd of water; p. 326 (n.)
nigh to famishing for water; p. 306 (n.) laid in good store of
cocoanuts and water; p. 307 (n.) through famishing for water; p. 312
(n.) With clenched hands, they stood in the water; p. 314 (n.) Oh,
the waters that flow through Onimoo; p. 318 (n.) to three men in the
water; p. 355 (n.) the bed of a shallow water-course; p. 335 (n.) in
these consecrated waters; p. 336 (n.) and showing through its waters;
p. 343 (n.) reflected in the green, glassy water; p. 343 (n.) long
lines of phantoms in the water; p. 353 (n.) nigh to the margin of the
water; p. 359 (n.) from the polluted waters here flowing; p. 366 (n.)
in whose waters Danae's shower was woven; p. 368 (adj.) the great
Mississippi musters his watery nations; p. 372 (n.) it's a calm on
the waters; p. 380 (n.) Woven from the leaves of the water-lily;
p. 390 (n.) "Water! Water!" cried Media; p. 402 (n.) menials were
standing in the water; p. 403 (n.) Babbalanja made bold to inquire

for water; p. 414 (n.) and watching the sparkling waters; p. 414 (n.)
a whale's hump in blue water; p. 424 (n.) becalming the water; p. 432
(n.) Down sweeping to the water; p. 435 (n.) gazing abstractedly into
the water; p. 444 (n.) canoes had been dragged out of the water;
p. 452 (n.) hand-to-hand contests in the water; p. 458 (n.) when you
pour water, does it not gurgle; p. 469 (n.) passing wild rocks in the
remotest waters; p. 469 (n.) composed some glorious old salt-water
odes; p. 479 (n.) ere those waters gained the sea; p. 482 (n.) In a
broad arbor by the water-side; p. 482 (n.) flying, like frightened
water-fowl; p. 492 (n.) divided by water, we Mardians; p. 499 (n.)
Over the waters came a rumbling sound; p. 501 (n.) across the wide
waters, for that New Mardi; p. 506 (adj.) A fresh-water Polyp,
despising; p. 523 (n.) On all sides was heard the fall of waters;
p. 544 (n.) upon blue lake-like waters; p. 544 (n.) colonnades of
water-spouts were seen; p. 544 (n.) over the waters stalked; p. 544
(adj.) down, sullen, sunk the watery half; p. 546 (n.) from the golden
waters where she lies; p. 550 (n.) Again blank water spread before
us; p. 554 (adj.) we gained the water's limit; p. 558 (n.) like live
waters from a spring in a silver mine; p. 560 (n.) Ringing of waters,
that silvery jar; p. 568 (n.) the canoes, sleeping upon the waters;
p. 573 (n.) plainly suffering from water in the brain; p. 573 (n.)
Returning to the water-side; p. 581 (n.) seldom makes us open our
eyes under water; p. 586 (n.) one vast water-spout will, sudden,
form; p. 588 (n.) The shore sloped to the water; p. 610 (n.) which
growing in the water; p. 610 (n.) half verdure and half water; p. 611
ploughed up with water-courses; p. 614 (n.) which else were weaker
than water; p. 620 (n.) each dip of the paddles in the now calm
water; p. 622 (n.) Day . . . poured red wine upon the waters; p. 623
(n.) and the waters were deep below; p. 630 (n.) oil he poureth on
the waters; p. 650 (n.) did'st ever dive in deep waters, Taji; p. 650
(n.) we saw far gleams of water; p. 651 (n.) into the water the
maidens softly glided; p. 651 (n.) in the clear, sparkling water;
p. 653 (adj.) They dragged me to the water's brink.

Redburn--p. 4 (n.) That fairly smelt of salt water; p. 6 (n.) cows
standing up to the knees in water; p. 14 (n.) to get a drink of
water; p. 14 (n.) but I only gulped down my water; p. 23 (n.) and
threw the penny into the water; p. 25 (n.) by drinking a glass of
water; p. 25 (n.) much ado to get down the water; p. 25 (n.) stopping
to take in some more water; pp. 25-6 (n.) I gulped down another glass
of water; p. 26 (n.) of another glass of water; p. 34 (n.) where the
sky comes down to the water; p. 34 (n.) where the sky comes down to
the water; p. 35 (adj.) sailed right through the sky and water line;
p. 35 (n.) On the side away from the water; p. 36 (n.) as if it were
a great barrel in the water; p. 45 (n.) we were going through the
water; p. 46 (n.) to break off the first shock of the salt water;
p. 50 (n.) The ship lay almost still on the water; p. 51 (n.) Of even
the smallest puddle of rain-water; p. 52 (n.) Then the water began to
splash; p. 52 (adj.) I did not have any water-proof boots; p. 54 (n.)
heaving buckets of water about; p. 54 (n.) running after him with
full buckets of water; p. 54 (n.) there was plenty of water in the
ocean; p. 54 (n.) made of Indian corn meal and water; p. 55 (n.) that
it was getting low water; p. 63 (n.) The sky and water were both of
the same deep hue; p. 63 (n.) and look over at the fish in the water;
p. 64 (n.) nothing was to be seen but water--water--water--; p. 64
(n.) where they overhang the wide water; p. 65 (n.) the mate having

ordered me to draw some water; p. 68 (n.) After drawing a bucket of
water; p. 72 (n.) for the benefit of the salt water; p. 74 (n.) and
the salt water made them shrink; p. 78 (n.) like a long narrow plank
in the water; p. 80 (n.) you could hardly see the water; p. 81 (n.)
he kept the fat skimmed off the water; p. 82 (n.) making a fire in
the water; p. 90 (n.) salt air and water prevent you; p. 92 (n.) to
some one in the dark water; p. 96 (n.) only a few inches out of the
water; p. 97 (n.) obliterated from the face of the waters; p. 97 (n.)
the drawing of a bucket of salt water; p. 98 (n.) a sort of Mississippi
of hot water; p. 102 (n.) with her nose in the water; p. 103 (adj.) a
dismantled, water-logged schooner; p. 103 (n.) as the water ran into
it; p. 112 (n.) between two large casks of water; p. 116 (adj.)
plunging up and down the watery Highlands; p. 126 (n.) just gliding
through the water; p. 126 (n.) that went wheezing through the water;
p. 137 (n.) worse than driving geese to water; p. 159 (n.) none was
in sight from the water; p. 163 (n.) the entrance is through a water-
gate; p. 164 (n.) Just without the water-gate; p. 166 (adj.) take
their ease in their watery inn; p. 166 (n.) are about level with the
water; p. 173 (n.) The wood is specifically heavier than water;
p. 173 (n.) in resisting the action of the salt water; p. 173 (n.)
after being long soaked in water; p. 175 (n.) some twenty feet from
the water; p. 188 (n.) turn the waters of the docks into an elixir;
p. 198 (n.) with its back to the water; p. 198 (n.) precipitating
himself and truck into the water; p. 239 (n.) a far larger supply of
water was needed; p. 239 (n.) placed over the tierces of water;
p. 239 (n.) with the bow against the water-gate; p. 244 (n.) by the
shaking up of the bilge-water; p. 244 (n.) It's a water-rat, shipmates,
that's dead; p. 264 (n.) dash it out with my bucket of salt water;
p. 267 (n.) full of salt water; p. 268 (n.) then ducking in the water
close by; p. 273 (n.) may have nibbled at it in the water; p. 289 (n.)
like some vast buoy on the water; p. 294 (adj.) as we plowed the
watery prairie [sea]; p. 296 (n.) made him strike far out upon the
water; p. 298 (n.) looking down in this water; p. 299 (n.) a final,
thorough cleaning with sand and water; p. 301 (n.) the high price the
watermen demanded; p. 301 (n.) promising the watermen to pay them
with music.

White-Jacket--p. 7 (n.) and the ship with her nose in the water;
p. 13 (n.) the frigate gliding through the water; p. 72 (n.) the
frigate was going fast through the water; p. 96 (adj.) takes the
conceit out of fresh-water sailors; p. 97 (n.) a horrible mist far
and wide spreads over the water; p. 116 (n.) such volumes of water
came cascading down; p. 135 (n.) the sun . . . was now setting over
the dreary waters; p. 137 (n.) though the air was piercing cold, and
the water drenched him; p. 153 (n.) hoisted them out of the water;
p. 153 (n.) What was to come forth? salt-water or wine; p. 160 (n.)
moored in the deep-green water; p. 161 (n.) our boat laying motionless
on the water; p. 178 (n.) on platforms overhanging the water; p. 178
(n.) softly lowers himself into the water; p. 179 (adj.) to a fine
water-side settlement; p. 210 (n.) the place was known as The Hidden
Water; p. 210 (n.) stretches the broad blue of the water; p. 214
(adj.) The watery wilderness yields no supply; p. 226 (n.) to glance
at it, now and then, from the water; p. 235 (n.) when we should once
be in the water; p. 246 (n.) the commotion he made in the water
attracted; p. 247 (n.) was floating on the water; p. 272 (n.) Her
bows were rooting in the water; p. 284 (adj.) in their water-rimmed,

cannon-sentried frigates; p. 316 (n.) held it over the water a moment;
p. 318 (n.) shrieked it forth from the drowning waters; p. 326 (n.)
partly below the surface of the water; p. 326 (adj.) not much above
the water level; p. 328 (n.) upon flooding them with salt water;
p. 370 (n.) scraping the ship's hull under water; p. 374 (n.) stand
guard over the fresh water; p. 378 (n.) was heard from the face of
the waters; p. 389 (n.) after this mean to stick to fresh water;
p. 389 (n.) or, at least, on fresh water; p. 393 (n.) like a black
world in the water; p. 394 (n.) puffed out above my tight girdle with
water; p. 394 (n.) As they dragged me out of the water; p. 394 (n.)
the Neversink once more glided over the water; p. 399 (n.) planks
comprised above the water-line.

Moby-Dick--p. 4 (n.) The mighty whales which swim in a sea of water;
p. 5 (n.) it will be aground in twelve or thirteen feet water; p. 5
(n.) in wantonness fuzzing up the water through their [whales'] pipes
and vents; p. 7 (n.) So fire with water to compare; p. 7 (n.) larger
in the bore than the main pipe of the water-works at London Bridge;
p. 7 (n.) and the water roaring in its passage through that pipe;
p. 9 (n.) comrades only being preserved by leaping into the water;
p. 10 (n.) on the application for the Erection of a Breakwater at
Nantucket 1828; p. 11 (n.) Suddenly a mighty mass emerged from the
water; p. 12 (adj.) sail about a little and see the watery part of
the world; p. 12 (adv.) Right and left, the streets take you waterward;
p. 12 (n.) Look at the crowds of water-gazers there; p. 13 (n.) more
crowds, pacing straight for the water; p. 13 (n.) They must get just
as nigh the water as they possibly can without falling in; p. 13 (n.)
set his feet agoing, and he will infallibly lead you to water if
water there be in all that region; p. 13 (n.) Yes, as everyone knows,
meditation and water are wedded for ever; p. 13 (n.) what is the one
charm wanting?--Water--there is not a drop of water there; p. 18
(adv.) I now by instinct followed the streets that took me waterward;
p. 37 (n.) But New Bedford beats all Water Street and Wapping; p. 41
(n.) we are too much like oysters observing the sun through the water,
and thinking that thick water the thinnest of air; p. 45 (n.) we
sound with him to the kelpy bottom of the waters; p. 45 (n.) as for
by water, from Joppa; p. 47 (n.) sunk, too, beneath the ship's water-
line; p. 49 (n.) leaving smooth water behind; p. 50 (adj.) and all
the watery world of woe bowled over him; p. 50 (n.) woe to him who
seeks to pour oil upon the waters when God has brewed them into a
gale; p. 59 (n.) Gaining the more open water, . . . the little Moss
tossed; p. 61 (n.) Shooting himself perpendicular from the water;
p. 62 (n.) saw their child borne out of sight over the wide waters;
p. 62 (adj.) and at last . . . explored this watery world; p. 62
(adj.) overrun and conquered the watery world like so many Alexanders;
p. 86 (n.) and were sauntering away from the water; p. 86 (n.) A
confluent small-pox had in all directions flowed over his face, and
left it like the complicated ribbed bed of a torrent, when the rushing
waters have been dried up; p. 100 (n.) they, in heathenish sharked
waters; p. 100 (n.) luckily dropping an anchor in their waters;
p. 103 (adj.) the wild watery loneliness of his [Starbuck's] life did
therefore strongly incline him to superstition; p. 109 (n.) with a
fair wind the ship was rushing through the water; p. 117 (n.) Unfitness
to pursue our research in the unfathomable waters; p. 119 (n.) would
fain have banished the whales from the waters; p. 121 (adj.) it may
well be supposed that the watery circle surrounding it; p. 122 (n.)

rising to the surface in the remotest and most sullen waters; p. 123
(n.) making more gay foam and white water generally; p. 132 (n.) on
so long a voyage in such marketless waters; p. 138 (n.) vagrant sea
unicorns infesting those waters; p. 138 (n.) owing to the resistance
of the water; p. 139 (adj.) take a preliminary view of the watery
pastures; p. 142 (n.) look sharp for white water; p. 146 (n.) pale
waters, paler cheeks, where'er I sail; p. 148 (adj.) The hated whale
has the round watery world to swim in; p. 148 (n.) builded over the
dead water of the wake; p. 155 (adj.) sprinkled over the entire
watery circumference; p. 156 (adj.) from the more transit over the
widest watery spaces; p. 165 (n.) in waters hard upon the Antarctic
seas; p. 165 (n.) in those for ever exiled waters; p. 168 (n.) the
shrouded phantom of the whitened waters is horrible to him; p. 168
(n.) he never rests till blue water is under him again; p. 172 (n.)
the sperm whale's resorting to given waters; p. 179 (n.) the dark
ocean and swelling waters were nothing; p. 182 (n.) destroyed vessels
at intervals in those waters; p. 185 (n.) or vacantly gazing over
into the lead-colored waters; p. 185 (n.) idly looking off upon the
water; p. 192 (n.) nothing but a troubled bit of greenish white water;
p. 192 (n.) in keen pursuit of that one spot of troubled water and
air; p. 193 (adj.) the sudden profound dip into the watery glens and
hollows; p. 193 (n.) The dancing white water made by the chase was
now becoming more and more visible; p. 194 (n.) There's white water
again; p. 194 (n.) the water covering every rib and plank; p. 199
(adj.) an unstaked, watery locality, southerly from St. Helena;
p. 199 (n.) while gliding through these latter waters; p. 201 (n.)
strange forms in the water darted hither and thither before us;
p. 208 (adj.) and all the watery region round about there; p. 211 (n.)
with their feet continually overflowed by the rippling clear water;
p. 227 (n.) The living whale, in his full majesty and significance,
is only to be seen at sea in unfathomable waters; p. 236 (n.) when
the long burnished sun-glade on the waters seemed a golden finger
laid across them; p. 241 (n.) and other vivacious denizens of more
stirring waters; p. 244 (n.) The boat now flew through the boiling
water; p. 249 (n.) wallowing in the sullen black waters; p. 261 (n.)
the water round it torn and splashed by the insatiate sharks; p. 264
(n.) in that awful water-land; p. 272 (n.) half hidden by the blood-
muddied water; p. 274 (n.) they saw a great heap of tumultous white
water; p. 274 (n.) the drops fell like bits of broken glass on the
water; p. 284 (n.) presents an almost wholly vertical plane to the
water; p. 296 (n.) though indeed their back water must have retarded
him; p. 296 (n.) causing the waters behind him to upbubble; p. 299
(n.) the pressure of the water is immense; p. 305 (n.) Thou art as a
lion of the waters; p. 306 (n.) these Vedas were lying at the bottom
of the waters; p. 307 (adj.) and so was saved from a watery doom;
p. 309 (n.) Instead of sparkling water, he now spouts red blood;
p. 313 (n.) the water cascading all around him; p. 319 (n.) cruising
northwards, over waters known to be frequented here; p. 321 (adj.)
when he glanced upon the green walls of the watery defile in which
the ship was then sailing; p. 321 (n.) emerging at last upon the
broad waters beyond; p. 325 (adj.) suspended in those watery vaults;
p. 328 (adj.) swimming about over the watery world; p. 329 (n.) they
start for the Oriental waters in anticipation of the cool season
there; p. 330 (n.) her he takes to wife in the wilderness of waters;
p. 346 (n.) when at last plumping into the water; p. 347 (n.) that
out of the firmament of waters heaved the colossal orbs; p. 356 (adj.)

how he is chased over the watery moors; p. 367 (adj.) was there ever
such another Bunger in the watery world; p. 370 (n.) to go on a
testing cruise to the remote waters of Japan; p. 381 (n.) as this
Leviathan comes floundering down upon us from the head-waters of the
Eternities; p. 384 (n.) He swam the seas before the continents broke
water; p. 392 (n.) the water chucks you under the chin pretty quick;
p. 393 (n.) the tropical outlets from the China waters into the
Pacific; p. 393 (n.) and drench the casks with sea-water; p. 395 (n.)
And like circles on the water, which, as they grow fainter, expand;
so his eyes seemed rounding and rounding, like the rings of Eternity;
p. 399 (adj.) wide-rolling watery prairies and Potter's Fields of all
four continents; p. 399 (n.) It rolls the mid-most waters of the
world; p. 400 (n.) Launched at length upon these almost final waters;
p. 402 (n.) to the possibilities of the immense Remote, the Wild, the
Watery, the Unshored; p. 428 (n.) Making so long a passage through
such unfrequented waters; p. 433 (n.) the white hump and head of Moby
Dick had suddenly loomed up out of the water; p. 434 (n.) he saw . . .
a swift gleam of bubbling white water; p. 443 (n.) watched how his
shadow in the water sank and sank to his gaze; p. 444 (n.) let us fly
these deadly waters; p. 446 (adj.) resembling in the pleated watery
wrinkles bordering it; p. 446 (n.) There go flukes! No, no; only
black water; p. 447 (n.) far out on the soft Turkish-rugged waters;
p. 447 (n.) the blue waters interchangeably flowed over into the
moving valley of his steady wake; p. 448 (adj.) his eyes seemed
whirling round in his head as he swept the watery circle; p. 453 (n.)
the proverbial evanessence of a thing writ in water, a wake; p. 462
(n.) Some men die at ebb tide; some at low water; p. 464 (n.)
Suddenly the waters around them slowly swelled in the broad circles;
then quickly upheaved; p. 464 (n.) the waters flashed for an instant
like heaps of fountains; p. 468 (n.) Through the breach, they heard
the waters pour, as mountain torrents down a flume.

WAVE. A volume of water rising in surges above the general level, and
elevated in proportion to the wind. (Smyth)

Typee--p. 10 (n.) with its surface broken by little tiny waves; p. 13
(n.) bobbing up and down with every wave; p. 173 (n.) I see thy canoe
cleaving the bright waves.

Omoo--p. 9 (n.) when she dashed the waves from her prow; p. 24 (n.)
riding pertly over the waves of the bay; p. 26 (n.) every blue wave
broke with a tinkle; p. 58 (n.) found ourselves battling with the
waves; p. 59 (n.) The crest of a great wave then broke over it; p. 59
(n.) now and then shipped green glassy waves; p. 59 (n.) the wave
subsided; p. 89 (n.) white crests of waves; p. 111 (n.) which Nelson
gave to the waves of the sea; p. 141 (n.) between these, glimpses of
blue, sunny waves; p. 199 (n.) the air, warm--the waves, musical;
p. 238 (n.) canoes . . . were dancing upon the waves; p. 252 (n.)
from which the waves seemed just retired; p. 266 (n.) had been
underwashed by the waves.

Mardi--p. 23 (n.) dash of the waves; p. 24 (n.) path upon the waves;
p. 27 (n.) upon striking the wave; p. 28 (n.) in the trough of the
waves; p. 30 (n.) toiling up the long, calm wave; p. 37 (n.) unless
the waves; p. 49 (n.) its last dying waves; p. 49 (n.) The great

September waves; p. 49 (n.) Every wave in my eyes seemed a soul;
p. 50 (adj.) ermined with wave crests; p. 50 (n.) waves chasing each
other; p. 65 (n.) pushed by a wave; p. 91 (n.) have succumbed to the
waves; p. 118 (n.) through eddy, wave, and surge; p. 122 (n.) except
the crests of the waves; p. 143 (n.) My prow shall keep kissing the
waves; p. 166 (n.) it rose and touched the wave; p. 179 (n.) tipping
every wave-crest in its course; p. 192 (n.) the waves ran up the
strand; p. 213 (n.) in unison with the spirited waves; p. 216 (n.)
the great waves chased each other like lions; p. 256 (n.) it subsided
into the grotto, a wave; p. 265 (n.) its wavelets hush the shore;
p. 273 (n.) where the waves muster; p. 273 (n.) their place on the
very crest of the wave; p. 283 (n.) and swore by wave and billow;
p. 286 (n.) for the waves were grown; p. 303 (n.) the body was
committed to the waves; p. 303 (n.) But a wave-crest received it;
p. 340 (n.) sparkle in the crests of the waves; p. 366 (n.) waves,
mounted parthians; p. 367 (n.) under the light frothy wave-crests;
p. 370 (n.) to the roll of the waves; p. 414 (n.) moon on the dancing
waves; p. 416 (n.) ripplings of some now waveless sea; p. 422 (n.)
like red-hot bars beneath the waves; p. 432 (n.) each curling wave-
crest a flame; p. 432 (n.) vines trailed over to the crisp, curling
waves; p. 518 (n.) being launched upon the wave; p. 551 (n.) Over
balmy waves, still westward sailing; p. 562 (n.) a deep, green wood,
slowly nodding over the waves; p. 567 (n.) as the red sun, magnified,
launched into the wave; p. 587 (n.) Serene, the waves ran up their
strands; p. 618 (n.) save the rush of the waves by our keels; p. 622
(n.) At every head-beat wave; p. 632 (n.) The waves were phosphorescent;
p. 649 (n.) where they tossed me to the waves; p. 653 (n.) as wild
waves before a prow inflexible; p. 654 (n.) the salt waves dashing
the tears from his pallid face.

Redburn--p. 5 (n.) Of the monstrous waves at sea; p. 6 (n.) The waves
were toasted brown; p. 9 (n.) some of whose waves were breaking;
p. 33 (n.) with the great waves rolling over me; p. 34 (n.) steering
right out among those waves; p. 64 (n.) and great cascades of waves;
p. 64 (n.) every happy little wave seemed gamboling; p. 64 (n.) I do
not mean the waves themselves; p. 102 (n.) ploughing milk-white waves;
p. 103 (n.) splitting in two the waves which broke; p. 116 (n.)
daring on the waves; p. 127 (n.) according to the agitation of the
waves; p. 147 (n.) when his noble waves, inglorious, Mersey rolled;
p. 147 (n.) where'er the Baltic rolls his wintry waves; p. 164 (n.)
From the turbulent waves; p. 268 (n.) as if addressing the
multitudinous waves; p. 278 (n.) as I watched the waves; p. 289 (n.)
the waves ran in mountains; p. 289 (n.) tumbled the white form of the
wave-crests; p. 290 (n.) we bore down on the waves; p. 296 (n.)
brewed into the common yeast of the waves; p. 296 (n.) to launch into
the waves; p. 299 (n.) that limberly floated on the waves.

White-Jacket--p. 137 (n.) a wave broke against the ship's side;
p. 310 (n.) would direct our attention to the moonlight on the waves;
p. 393 (n.) moaning, as of low waves on the beach; p. 393 (n.) hears
both the Ionian and the Aegean waves; p. 396 (n.) dip their points in
the impatient waves; p. 397 (n.) And over the starry waves . . .
straight out into that fragrant night; p. 397 (n.) How calm the waves.

Moby-Dick--p. 3 (n.) This came toward us, open-mouthed, raising the
waves on all sides; p. 7 (n.) To insect millions peopling every wave;

p. 12 (n.) the Battery, where that noble mole is washed by waves;
p. 44 (n.) While all God's sun-lit waves rolled by; p. 48 (n.) Wave
after wave thus leaps into the ship; p. 50 (n.) whom all the waves of
the billows of the seas; p. 63 (n.) he hides among the waves, he
climbs them as chamois hunters climb the Alps; p. 76 (n.) Ahab's . . .
been used to deeper wonders than the waves; p. 97 (n.) When . . . the
Pequod thrust her vindictive bows into the cold malicious waves;
p. 114 (n.) The fire hissed in the waves; pp. 136-7 (n.) lost in the
infinite series of the sea, with nothing ruffled but the waves;
p. 140 (n.) the blending cadence of waves with thoughts; p. 147 (n.)
the warm waves blush like wine; p. 152 (n.) would all the waves were
women, then I'd go drown; p. 167 (n.) mortal thoughts of long
lacquered mild afternoons on the waves; p. 173 (n.) there the waves
were stories with his deeds; p. 193 (n.) on the knife-like edge of
the sharper waves; p. 194 (n.) the waves curling and hissing around
us like the erected crests of enraged serpents; p. 194 (n.) the waves
dashed their bucklers together; p. 199 (n.) when all the waves rolled
by like scrolls of silver; p. 201 (n.) the ivory-tusked Pequod . . .
gored the dark waves in her madness; p. 202 (n.) the better to guard
against the leaping waves; p. 202 (n.) through all the swift madness
and gladness of the demoniac waves; p. 203 (n.) As if the waves had
been fullers, this craft was bleached like the skeleton of a stranded
walrus; p. 236 (n.) when the slippered waves whispered together as
they softly ran on; p. 242 (n.) The waves, too, nodded their indolent
crests; p. 264 (n.) heart to heart they sank beneath the exulting
wave; p. 265 (n.) by the sudden onset of a large rolling wave; p. 267
(n.) while a succession of riotous waves rolled by; p. 273 (n.) the
second was Aunt Charity's gift, and that was freely given to the
waves; p. 374 (n.) whatever natural wonders, the wonder-freighted
tribute-rendering waves had cast upon his shores; p. 399 (n.) the
waves should rise and fall, and ebb and flow unceasingly; p. 399 (n.)
the ever-rolling waves but made so by their restlessness; p. 399 (n.)
The same waves wash the moles of the new-built Californian towns;
p. 405 (n.) so sociably mixing with the soft waves themselves, that
like hearth-stone cats they purr against the gunwhale; p. 405 (n.)
not through high rolling waves, but through the tall grass of a
rolling prairie; p. 410 (n.) far out upon the midnight waves, which
gently chafed the whale's broad flank, like soft surf upon a beach;
p. 410 (n.) a hearse and its plumes floating over the ocean with the
waves for the pall-bearers; p. 428 (n.) over waves monotonously mild;
p. 441 (n.) the rolling waves and days went by; p. 447 (n.) seemed
drawing a carpet over its waves; p. 448 (n.) among waves whose hand-
clappings were suspended by exceeding rapture; p. 449 (n.) the now
rising swells, with all their confluent waves, dazzlingly broke
against it; p. 455 (n.) the torn, enraged waves he shakes off, seem
his mane; p. 464 (n.) as the head-beat waves hammered and hammered
against the opposing bow; p. 464 (n.) Drive, drive in your nails, oh
ye waves! to their uttermost heads drive them in; p. 466 (n.) rising
to its level on a combing wave.

WHALE. A general term for various marine animals of the order Cetacea,
including the most colossal of all animated beings. From their general
form and mode of life they are frequently confounded with fish, from
which, however, they differ essentially in their organization, as they
are warm-blooded, ascend to the surface to breathe air, produce their

young alive, and suckle them, as do the land mammalia. The cetacea are divided into two sections:--1. Those having horny plates, called baleen, or "whalebone," growing from the palate instead of teeth, and including the right whales and rorquals, or finners, and hump-backs. 2. Those having true teeth and no whale-bone. To this group belong the sperm-whale, and the various forms of bottle-noses, black-fish grampuses, narwhales, dolphins, porpoises, &c. To the larger species of many of these the term "whale" is often applied. (Smyth)

Typee--p. 3 (n.) cruising after the sperm-whale--beneath the scorching sun; p. 6 (adj.) vessels engaged in the extensive whale fisheries; p. 9 (n.) In pursuit of the sperm whale; p. 10 (n.) the lofty jet of the whale might be seen; p. 11 (adj.) he sallied out upon the large whaling fleet; p. 12 (n.) came alongside of us in a whale-boat; p. 21 (adj.) The longevity of Cape Horn whaling voyages; p. 22 (adj.) the abundance in which they are put on board a whaling vessel; p. 22 (n.) unlucky in falling in with whales; p. 22 (n.) I heard of one whaler; p. 78 (adj.) in his ears were two small and finely shaped sperm-whale teeth; p. 127 (adj.) nor yet moving in whalebone corsets; p. 132 (n.) so little chance among them as a cumbrous whale; p. 150 (adj.) fashioned out of a boar's tusks or whale's teeth; p. 172 (adj.) and boars'-tusks and sperm-whale teeth; p. 201 (adj.) Here is a sperm-whale tooth; p. 249 (n.) the first object that met my view was an English whale-boat; p. 252 (n.) The whale-boat, manned by the tabooed crew; p. 270 (adj.) paddled off to a whale ship.

Omoo--p. xiii (adj.) engaged in the Sperm Whale Fishery; p. xiii (n.) not directly connected with the business of whaling; p. xiii (n.) without pretending to give any account of the whale-fishery; p. 5 (n.) proclaimed her a whaler; p. 6 (n.) men are frequently shipped on board whalemen; p. 10 (v.) she might go whither she pleased--whaling, sealing; p. 10 (n.) Sperm whaling, however, was what she relied upon; p. 10 (adj.) Even the three junior mates who had headed the whale boats; p. 11 (n.) All English whalemen are bound by law; p. 14 (n.) many South Sea whalemen do not come to an anchor; p. 21 (adj.) towing the two whale boats; p. 23 (n.) gone ashore there from an American whaler; p. 34 (n.) whaling was out of the question; p. 35 (n.) by exploring ships and adventurous whalers; p. 35 (n.) scarcely known to other whalemen; p. 35 (n.) the sea was alive with large whales; p. 39 (n.) with Sperm Whalemen; p. 48 (n.) Nowadays, American whalemen in the Pacific; p. 48 (n.) All Sydney whalemen, however, still cling; p. 48 (n.) But where were the sperm whales; p. 49 (n.) the whales he had in his eye; p. 64 (adj.) better than the right-whale oil; p. 69 (adj.) Invalid whaling captains often adopt a plan; p. 71 (n.) two or three voyages in Sydney whalemen; p. 71 (adj.) on board the colonial whaling vessels; p. 71 (adj.) performed in the sperm-whale fishery p. 71 (n.) A dead whale, or a stove boat; p. 72 (n.) brought him up to a large, lone whale; p. 72 (n.) In whaling, as long as; p. 72 (n.) when whales are so hard to be got; p. 72 (n.) Bembo's whale was alongside; p. 72 (adj.) he bounded upon the whale's back; p. 72 (n.) the whale was running; p. 81 (n.) for a short cruise in a whaler; p. 96 (n.) in the boat of an American whaler; p. 100 (n.) whale-spouts seen from the harbor; p. 100 (adj.) tokens of a whaling vessel's approach; p. 100 (n.) They are principally whalemen; p. 102 (n.) She was an American whaler; p. 119 (n.) been a cruise or two in a whaling-vessel; p. 148 (n.) and three good whalemen for harpooners; p. 158

(n.) flush from a lucky whaling-cruise; p. 159 (n.) that the whaling-
ships . . . began to arrive; p. 173 (n.) many whale-ships here now;
p. 202 (n.) raising supplies for whaling-vessels; p. 215 (adj.) a
whaling captain, touching at an adjoining bay; p. 246 (n.) A solitary
whaler, however, was reported; p. 246 (n.) for going to sea in the
whaler; p. 247 (n.) who lost his leg by a whale; p. 289 (n.) went off
after a whale; p. 290 (n.) Like all large, comfortable old whalers;
p. 291 (adj.) paid off, at Papeetee, from a whaling vessel; p. 303
(adj.) all foreigners of distinction--whaling captains; p. 307 (n.)
on board of a French whaler; p. 313 (n.) they frequently got fast to
the whales; p. 313 (n.) that we had left a whaler in Tahiti; p. 315
(adj.) very often compose part of a whaler's crew; p. 315 (adj.) was
now bound on her last whaling cruise.

Mardi--p. 3 (n.) for the whale; p. 3 (n.) Sperm whale; p. 4 (n.)
whale, . . . run in veins; p. 5 (n.) by a whale; p. 5 (n.) no sign of
a whale; p. 5 (n.) after whales unattainable; p. 6 (n.) for the Right
Whale; p. 6 (n.) business of whaling; p. 6 (n.) Right whaling on the
Nor'-West Coast; p. 6 (n.) this horrid and indecent Right whaling;
p. 6 (n.) your true whaleman; p. 6 (n.) Sperm whales are not to be
had; p. 7 (n.) a good whale-boat; p. 11 (n.) even by whalemen; p. 11
(n.) of a whale-boat; p. 15 (n.) the ivory tusk of a whale; p. 16 (n.)
for whales never seen; p. 19 (n.) the slender whale-boat; p. 19 (n.)
the fine whale-boat is most delicate; p. 22 (n.) called among whalemen;
p. 23 (n.) of a heedless whaleman; p. 30 (n.) familiarity with the
business of whaling; p. 30 (n.) day-long pulls after whales; p. 32
(n.) customary rig of whale-boats; p. 32 (n.) a whale-boat is
constantly provided; p. 32 (n.) for cutting the whale-line; p. 33 (n.)
the heavy whale-line; p. 33 (adj.) of a whale-boat's furniture; p. 33
(n.) in pursuing the sperm whale; p. 35 (n.) again I launch whale-
boat; p. 40 (n.) large as a whale; p. 40 (n.) remains of a slaughtered
whale; p. 42 (n.) seizing the Right whale; p. 46 (n.) after whales;
p. 52 (adj.) for the long whaling voyage; p. 56 (n.) was a whaler;
p. 57 (n.) vessel was no whaler; p. 57 (n.) on the back of a whale;
p. 65 (n.) in his whale-boat; p. 71 (n.) the whale boat manned; p. 87
(n.) with the presence of the whale-boat; p. 95 (n.) engaged in the
vocation of whaling; p. 95 (n.) logs of certain whalemen are decorated;
p. 95 (n.) when whales are seen; p. 95 (n.) one for every whale slain;
p. 109 (n.) anxiety unknown to me in the whale-boat; p. 109 (n.) With
impunity, in our whale-boat; p. 121 (n.) deep breathing sound of a
sperm whale; p. 122 (n.) the spouting canal of the whales; p. 122 (n.)
steadily pursued by a solitary whale; p. 122 (n.) intimate companion-
ship of the whales; p. 122 (n.) close vicinity of the whale; p. 122
(n.) a thorough-bred whaleman betrays; p. 125 (n.) high as the whale-
shallop ranks; p. 126 (n.) a boat after a whale; p. 127 (n.) doubt
whether it was indeed a whale-boat; p. 143 (n.) over the great ribs
of the stranded whale; p. 206 (n.) and the imperial Cachalot-whale;
p. 209 (n.) beneath the open, upper jaw of a whale; p. 289 (n.) the
only whales frequenting; p. 289 (n.) whales feed upon small things;
p. 289 (n.) wide enough to admit a sperm-whale; p. 289 (n.) the
possible hereafter of the whales; p. 316 (n.) a fiery fin-back whale;
p. 374 (n.) jetted forth his vapors like a whale; p. 375 (n.) morbid
secretion of the Spermaceti whale; p. 375 (n.) the whale is at times
a sort of hypochondriac; p. 375 (n.) the Spermaceti whale was much
hunted; p. 395 (adj.) whose eyes are fixed in its head, like a whale's;
p. 414 (adj.) black as a whale's hump in blue water; p. 418 (n.)

seals, grampuses, and whales; p. 469 (n.) all prowling whales . . .
were invaders; p. 516 (n.) else, the sperm-whale, . . . would
transcend us all; p. 551 (n.) the great whales turn to die; p. 575
(n.) thoroughfares of the whales.

Redburn--p. 7 (n.) above all there was a picture of a great whale;
p. 19 (n.) he's going to shoot whales; p. 66 (n.) the very breath
that the great whales respire; p. 96 (n.) whales! whales close
alongside; p. 96 (n.) A whale! Think of it! whales close to me;
p. 96 (n.) Can these be whales? Monstrous whales; p. 96 (n.) I lost
all respect for whales; p. 96 (n.) the whales . . . might have
expanded; p. 96 (n.) whales greatly fell in my estimation; p. 96
(adj.) surmounting the whale's belly; p. 97 (n.) coiled away in a
tub, like a whale-rope; p. 99 (n.) A Whale-man and a Man-of-War's-Man;
p. 99 (n.) The sight of the whales mentioned; p. 99 (n.) concerning
what kind of whales they were; p. 99 (n.) They ar'n't sperm whales;
p. 99 (n.) them's crinkum-crankum whales; p. 99 (n.) them is whales
that can't be cotched; p. 99 (n.) bred to the sea in a whaler; p. 100
(n.) for whalemen are far more familiar; p. 100 (adj.) touched during
his whaling voyages; p. 107 (adj.) fit them out for the whaling
business; p. 107 (n.) by the enormous head of the sperm-whale; p. 127
(n.) it was different with Larry the whaleman; p. 148 (n.) Greenland
for her its bulky whale resigns; p. 311 (adj.) she feared he had gone
in a whaling voyage; p. 311 (n.) men are shipped for the Nantucket
whalers; p. 311 (n.) throwing himself away in a whaler; p. 312 (adj.)
must have indeed departed on a whaling voyage; p. 312 (n.) on board
of a whaler; p. 312 (n.) we spoke another whaler; p. 312 (n.) chasing
a whale after sundown; p. 312 (n.) was jammed between the ship, and a
whale.

White-Jacket--p. 10 (adj.) as Jonah did on the whale's belly; p. 15
(n.) we suspected of having served in a whaler; p. 15 (n.) Against
all whalers, indeed; p. 15 (n.) Devil take him, he's been in a whaler;
p. 15 (adj.) on account of his whaling experiences; p. 16 (n.) into
tremendous laudations of whalemen; p. 16 (n.) declaring that whalemen
alone deserved; p. 16 (n.) a man-of-war is to whalemen; p. 16 (n.) in
the proper phrase for whaling; p. 16 (n.) turning . . . the ocean
into a whale-pen; p. 16 (n.) of having myself served in a whaler;
p. 72 (adj.) adopted in the merchant or whaling service; p. 189 (adj.)
fabricated from a sperm-whale's tooth; p. 189 (n.) cunningly wrought
in the shape of a whale; p. 363 (adj.) its handle--a sperm whale's
tooth; p. 378 (adj.) I was in a whaling ship.

Moby-Dick--p. 1 (n.) by what name a whale-fish is to be called in our
tongue; p. 1 (n.) WHALE . . . Sw. and Dan. hval. This animal is
named; p. 1 (n.) WHALE . . . It is more immediately from the Dut. and
Ger. Wallen; p. 1 (n.) Given in the following languages:

ק ה,	Hebrew.	WHALE,	Icelandic.
χητοζ,	**Greek.**	WHALE,	English.
CETUS,	Latin.	BALEINE,	French.
WHŒL,	Anglo-Saxon.	BALLENA,	Spanish.
HVALT,	Danish.	PEKEE-NUEE-NUEE,	Fegee.
WAL,	Dutch.	PEHEE-NUEE-NUEE,	Erromangoan.
HWAL,	Swedish.		

p. 2 (n.) picking up whatever random allusions to whales he could
anyways find; p. 2 (adj.) must not . . . take the higgledy-piggledy

whale statements . . . for veritable gospel cetology; p. 2 (n.) And
God created great whales; p. 3 (n.) among which the whales and
whirlpools called Balæne; p. 3 (n.) about sunrise a great many Whales
and other monsters of the sea, appeared; p. 3 (n.) He visited this
country also with a view of catching horse-whales; p. 3 (n.) The best
whales were catched in his own country; p. 3 (adj.) that enter into
the dreadful gulf of this monster's [whale's] mouth; p. 3 (adj.) This
whale's liver was two cart-loads; p. 3 (n.) Touching that monstrous
bulk of the whale or ork; p. 3 (n.) an incredible quantity of oil
will be extracted out of one whale; p. 3 (n.) Very like a whale; p. 4
(n.) Like as the wounded whale to shore flies thro' the maine; p. 4
(n.) Immense as whales, the motion of whose vast bodies; p. 4 (n.)
Sir T. Browne. Of Sperma Ceti and the Sperma Ceti Whale; p. 4 (n.)
as if it had been a sprat in the mouth of a whale; p. 4 (n.) The
mighty whales which swim in a sea of water; p. 5 (n.) while the whale
is floating at the stern of the ship; p. 5 (n.) In their way they saw
many whales sporting in the ocean; p. 5 (n.) Here they saw such huge
troops of whales, that they were forced to proceed; p. 5 (n.) wind
N.E. in the ship called The Jonas-in-the-Whale; p. 5 (n.) Some say
the whale can't open his mouth; p. 5 (n.) to see whether they can see
a whale; p. 5 (n.) I was told of a whale taken near Shetland; p. 5
(n.) that he caught once a whale in Spitzbergen that was white all
over; p. 5 (n.) Several whales have come in upon this coast; p. 5 (n.)
Anno 1652, one eighty feet in length of the whale-bone kind came in;
p. 5 (n.) whether I can master and kill this Spermaceti whale; p. 5
(n.) whales in the sea/ God's voice obey; p. 5 (n.) we saw also
abundance of large whales; p. 5 (n.) and the breath of the whale is
frequently attended with such an insupportable smell; p. 6 (n.) Tho'
stiff with hoops and armed with ribs of whale; p. 6 (n.) The whale is
doubtless the largest animal in creation; p. 6 (n.) you would make
them speak like great whales; p. 6 (n.) it was found to be a dead
whale; p. 6 (n.) They seemed to endeavor to conceal themselves behind
the whale; p. 6 (n.) The larger whales, they seldom venture to attack;
p. 6 (n.) The Spermacetti Whale found by the Nantuckois, is an active,
fierce animal; p. 6 (n.) Edmund Burke's reference in Parliament to
the Nantucket Whale-Fishery; p. 6 (n.) Spain--a great whale stranded
on the shores of Europe; p. 6 (n.) royal fish, which are whale and
sturgeon; p. 7 (n.) Up-spouted by a whale in air; p. 7 (n.) John
Hunter's account of the dissection of a whale; p. 7 (n.) The aorta of
a whale is larger in the fore than the main pipe of the water-works
at London Bridge; p. 7 (adj.) and the water roaring in its passage
through that pipe is inferior in impetus and velocity to the blood
gushing from the whale's heart; p. 7 (n.) The whale is a mammiferous
animal without hind feet; p. 7 (n.) In 40 degrees south, we saw
Spermacetti Whales; p. 7 (adj.) Colnett's Voyage for the Purpose of
Extending the Spermacetti Whale Fishery; p. 7 (n.) voracious enemies,/
Whales, sharks, and monsters, arm'd in front of you; p. 7 (n.) Not a
mightier whale than this/ In the vast Atlantic is; p. 7 (n.) Charles
Lamb's Triumph of the Whale; p. 8 (n.) observing the whales spouting
and sporting with each other; p. 8 (adj.) made a gateway . . . by
setting up a whale's jaw bones; p. 8 (n.) who had been killed by a
whale in the Pacific Ocean; p. 8 (n.) "No, Sir, 'tis a Right Whale,"
answered Tom; p. 8 (n.) we saw in the Berlin Gazette that whales had
been introduced on the stage there; p. 8 (n.) we have been stove by a
whale; p. 8 (adj.) Narrative of the Shipwreck of the Whale Ship Essex
of Nantucket; p. 8 (n.) which was attacked and finally destroyed by a

large Sperm whale; p. 8 (n.) And the phosphor gleamed in the wake of
the whale; p. 8 (n.) the different boats engaged in the capture of
this one whale; p. 8 (n.) Sometimes the whale shakes its tremendous
tail in the air; p. 8 (n.) the infuriated Sperm Whale rolls over and
over; p. 9 (n.) so important an animal (as the Sperm whale) should
have been so entirely neglected; p. 9 (n.) Thomas Beale's History of
the Sperm Whale, 1839; p. 9 (n./n./n./adj.) The Cachalot (Sperm Whale)
is not only better armed that the True Whale (Greenland or Right
Whale) in possessing a formidable weapon . . . the most dangerous to
attack of all the known species of the whale tribe; p. 9 (adj.)
Frederick Debell Bennett's Whaling Voyage Round the Globe, 1840; p. 9
(n.) Do you see that whale now; p. 9 (n.) A shoal of Sperm whales;
p. 9 (adj.) J. Ross Browne's Etchings of a Whaling Cruise, 1846; p. 9
(n.) The whale-ship Globe, on board of which vessel; p. 9 (n.) Being
once pursued by a whale which he had wounded; p. 10 (n./n./adj./adj.)
The whale fell directly over him, and probably killed him in a moment.
The whale and his captors, or the Whaleman's Adventures and the
Whale's Biography; p. 10 (adj.) Another version of the whale-ship
Globe narrative; p. 10 (n.) The voyages of the Dutch and English . . .
laid open the haunts of the whale; p. 10 (n.) for now in laying open
the haunts of the whale; p. 10 (n.) the whalemen seem to have
indirectly hit upon new clews; p. 10 (n.) It is impossible to meet a
whale-ship on the ocean without being struck by her mere appearance;
p. 10 (n.) may perhaps have been told that these were the ribs of
whales; p. 10 (adj.) Tales of a Whale Voyage to the Arctic Ocean;
p. 10 (n.) Newspaper Account of the Taking and Retaking of the
Whaleship Hobomack; p. 11 (adj.) out of the crews of whaling vessels
(American); p. 11 (adj.) Cruise in a Whale Boat; p. 11 (n./adj.) It
was the whale. Miriam Coffin or the Whale Fisherman; p. 11 (n.) The
whale is harpooned to be sure . . . A Chapter on Whaling in Ribs and
Trucks; p. 11 (n.) I saw two of these monsters (whales) probably
male and female; p. 11 (n.) he saw the distended jaws of a large
Sperm whale; p. 11 (adj.) Wharton the Whale Killer; p. 11 (n.) While
the bold harpooner is striking the whale; p. 11 (n.) Oh, the rare old
Whale, mid storm and gale; p. 15 (n.) I should now take it into my
head to go on a whaling voyage; pp. 15-16 (adj.) doubtless, my going
on this whaling voyage, formed part of the grand programme of
Providence; p. 16 (adj.) WHALING VOYAGE BY ONE ISHMAEL; p. 16 (adj.)
the Fates, put me down for this shabby part of a whaling voyage;
p. 16 (n.) chief among these motives was the overwhelming idea of the
great whale himself; p. 16 (n.) the undeliverable, nameless perils of
the whale; p. 16 (adj.) the whaling voyage was welcome; p. 16 (n.) in
the wild conceits that swayed me to my purpose, two and two there
floated into my inmost soul, endless processions of the whale, and,
midmost of them all, one grand hooded phantom, like a snow hill in
the air; p. 17 (n.) As most young candidates for the pains and
penalties of whaling; p. 17 (n.) though New Bedford has of late been
gradually monopolizing the business of whaling; p. 17 (n.) the place
where the first dead American whale was stranded; p. 17 (n.) did
these aboriginal whalemen, the Red Men, first sally out in canoes;
p. 17 (n.) partly laden with imported cobble-stones--so goes the story
--to throw at the whales; p. 19 (v.) But no more of this blubbering
now, we are going a-whaling; pp. 20-21 (n.) and an exasperated whale,
purposing to spring Man over the craft, is in the enormous act of
impaling himself upon the three mast-heads; p. 21 (adj.) Mixed with
these were rusty old whaling lances; p. 21 (n.) did Nathan Swain kill

fifteen whales between a sunrise and a sunset; p. 21 (n.) [harpoon]
was flung in Javan seas, and run away with by a whale; p. 21 (adj.)
the bar--a rude attempt at a right whale's head; p. 21 (adj.) there
stands the vast arched bone of the whale's jaw; p. 22 (v.) I s'pose
you are goin' a whalin'; p. 23 (adj.) No wonder, then, that they made
a straight wake for the whale's mouth; p. 27 (n.) a papered fireboard
representing a man striking a whale; p. 29 (n.) a story of a white
man--a whaleman too; pp. 29-30 (n.) shipped aboard of a whaleman in
the South Seas; p. 35 (n.) They were nearly all whalemen; p. 36 (n.)
I was preparing to hear some good stories about whaling; p. 36 (n.)
had boarded great whales on the high seas; p. 36 (n.) these bashful
bears, these timid warrior whalemen; p. 37 (n.) besides the wild
specimens of the whaling-craft; p. 37 (n.) to drop the axe and snatch
the whale-lance; p. 38 (n.) and joins the great whale-fishery; p. 38
(n.) Had it not been for us whalemen; p. 38 (n.) fathers, they say,
give whales for dowers to their daughters; p. 39 (adj.) In this same
New Bedford there stands a whaleman's Chapel; p. 40 (n.) who were
towed out of sight by a whale; p. 40 (n.) who in the bows of his boat
was killed by a Sperm whale; p. 41 (n.) that darkened, doleful day
read the fate of the whalemen who had gone before me; p. 41 (n.) Yes,
there is death in this business of whaling; p. 42 (n.) the famous
Father Mapple, so called by the whalemen; p. 42 (adj.) The wife of a
whaling captain had provided the chapel with; p. 44 (n.) The ribs and
terrors in the whale; p. 44 (n.) No more the whale did me confine;
p. 47 (n.) when the whale shall hold him in the smallest of his
bowels' wards; p. 48 (n.) little hears he or heeds he the far rush of
the mighty whale; p. 49 (n.) the whale shoots-to all his ivory teeth,
like so many white bolts, upon his prison; p. 49 (n.) in the eventual
deliverance of him from the sea and the whale; p. 50 (n.) God came
upon him in the whale; p. 50 (n.) when the whale grounded upon the
ocean's utmost bones; p. 50 (n.) the whale came breeching up towards
the warm and pleasant sun; p. 56 (n.) to see something more of
Christendom than a specimen whaler or two; p. 57 (n.) They put him
down among the sailors; and made a whaleman of him; p. 57 (n.) the
practices of whalemen soon convinced him; p. 57 (n.) I told him that
whaling was my own design; p. 57 (n.) the most promising port for an
adventurous whaleman to embark from; p. 58 (n.) like me, was wholly
ignorant of the mysteries of whaling; p. 58 (adj.) whether all whaling
ships did not find their own harpoons; p. 58 (n.) [harpoon] deeply
intimate with the hearts of whales; p. 59 (adj.) side by side the
world-wandering whale ships lay; p. 60 (n.) Queequeg kill-e big whale;
p. 61 (n.) stood eyeing the boom as if it were the lower jaw of an
exasperated whale; p. 63 (n.) while under his very pillow rush herds
of walruses and whales; p. 66 (n.) instead of our going together among
the whaling-fleet in harbor; p. 68 (n.) bone taken from the middle
and highest point of the jaws of the right-whale; p. 69 (v.) But what
takes thee a-whaling; p. 69 (n.) was the other one lost by a whale;
p. 70 (adj.) art thou the man to pitch a harpoon down a live whale's
throat; p. 70 (v.) I was a little staggered, but go a-whaling I must;
p. 71 (adj.) People in Nantucket invest their money in whaling vessels;
p. 71 (n.) Like Captain Peleg, Captain Bildad was a well-to-do,
retired whaleman; p. 72 (n.) when he sailed the old Categut whaleman;
p. 76 (n.) fixed his fiery land in mightier, stranger foes than
whales; p. 80 (n.) a short whaling-voyage in a schooner or brig;
p. 84 (n.) did you ever stand in the head of a whale-boat; p. 84
(adj./adj./n.) 'spose him one whale eye . . . spos-ee him whale-e eye;

why, dat whale dead; p. 85 (n.) He got so frightened about his plaguy
soul, that he shrinked and sheared away from whales; p. 87 (n.) only
I've heard that he's a good whale-hunter; p. 89 (n.) so with whaling,
which necessitates a three-years' housekeeping upon the wide ocean;
p. 89 (adj.) For besides the great length of the whaling voyage;
p. 89 (adj.) of all ships, whaling vessels are the most exposed to
accidents; p. 90 (adj.) with a long oil-ladle in one hand, and a
still longer whaling lance in the other; p. 90 (adj.) Peleg came
running out of his whalebone den; p. 93 (n.) after the ever-thoughtful
Charity had come off in a whale-boat; p. 94 (adj.) this whalebone
marquee was never pitched except in port; p. 96 (v.) Don't whale it
too much a' Lord's days, men; p. 98 (n.) As Queequeg and I are now
fairly embarked in this business of whaling; p. 98 (n.) and as this
business of whaling has somehow come to be regarded; p. 98 (n.) the
business of whaling is not accounted on a level with what are called;
p. 98 (n.) if in emulation of the naval officers he should append the
initials S.W.F. (Sperm Whale Fishery) to his visiting card; p. 98 (n.)
why the world declines honoring us whalemen; p. 99 (adj.) would
quickly recoil at the apparition of the spermwhale's vast tail; p. 99
(adj.) though the world scouts at us whale-hunters; p. 99 (adj.) Why
did the Dutch in De Witt's time have admirals of their whaling fleets;
p. 99 (adj.) fit out whaling ships from Dunkirk; p. 99 (n.) how comes
it that we whalemen of America now outnumber; p. 99 (n.) all the rest
of the banded whalemen in the world; p. 99 (n.) How comes all this,
if there be not something puissant in whaling; p. 99 (n.) whaling may
well be regarded as that Egyptian mother; p. 99 (n.) the whale-ship
has been the pioneer in ferreting out; p. 99 (n.) let them fire
salutes to the honor and the glory of the whale-ship; p. 100 (adj.)
Until the whale fishery rounded Cape Horn; p. 100 (n.) It was the
whalemen who first broke through the jealous policy; p. 100 (n.)
Australia, was given to the enlightened world by the whalemen; p. 100
(n.) The whaleship is the true mother of that now mighty colony;
p. 100 (n.) The whale has no famous author, and whaling no famous
chronicler, you will say; p. 100 (n.) The whale has no famous author,
and whaling no famous chronicler, you will say; p. 101 (n.) from
other, the Norwegian whale-hunter of those times; p. 101 (n.) somehow
whaling is not respectable; p. 101 (n.) somehow whaling is not
respectable; p. 101 (n.) Whaling is imperial; p. 101 (n.) I know a
man that, in his lifetime, has taken three hundred and fifty whales;
p. 101 (n.) the bones of the whale . . . were the most conspicuous
object; p. 101 (n.) for a whale-ship was my Yale College and my
Harvard; p. 102 (n.) In behalf of the dignity of whaling; p. 103 (n.)
I will have no man in my boat . . . who is not afraid of a whale;
p. 103 (n.) no fancy for lowering for whales after sun-down; p. 106
(n.) Flask . . . very pugnacious concerning whales; p. 106 (n.) in
his poor opinion, the wondrous whale was but a species of magnified
mouse; p. 106 (adj.) being armed with their long keen whaling spears;
p. 107 (n.) Tashtego now hunted in the wake of the great whales of
the sea; p. 108 (adj.) it is the same with the American whale fishery;
p. 108 (n.) where the outward bound Nantucket whalers frequently
touch; p. 110 (adj.) from the polished bone of the sperm whale's jaw;
p. 114 (n.) thrones . . . were fabricated . . . of the tusks of the
narwhale; p. 114 (n.) as if, like the dying whale, my final jets were
the strongest and fullest of trouble; p. 115 (adj.) what's his leg
now but a cane--a whalebone cane; p. 115 (n.) it was only . . . a
whaleboning that he gave me--not a base kick; p. 116 (n.) There are

whales hereabouts; p. 116 (n.) A white whale--did ye mark that, man;
p. 116 (n.) systematized exhibition of the whale in his broad general;
p. 117 (n.) among historians of this animal (sperm whale); p. 117 (n.)
Thus speak of the whale; p. 117 (n.) with cetology, or the science of
whales; p. 117 (adj.) Of the names in this list of whale authors,
only those following Owen ever saw living whales; p. 117 (n.) subject
of the Greenland or right-whale; p. 117 (n.) says nothing of the
great sperm whale, compared with which the Greenland whale is almost
unworthy mentioning; p. 117 (n.) the Greenland whale is an usurper
upon the throne of the seas; p; 117 (n.) not even by any means the
largest of the whales; pp. 117-8 (n.) the fabulous or utterly unknown
sperm-whale; p. 118 (n.) in all but some few scientific retreats and
whale-ports; p. 118 (n.) the Greenland whale . . . was to them the
monarch of the seas; p. 118 (n.) the Greenland whale is deposed,--the
great sperm whale now reigneth; p. 118 (n.) pretend to put the living
sperm whale before you; p. 118 (n.) surgeons to English South-Sea
whale-ships; p. 118 (n.) The original matter touching the sperm whale;
p. 118 (n.) the sperm whale . . . lives not complete in any literature;
p. 118 (n.) Far above all other hunted whales, his is an unwritten
life; p. 118 (n.) the various species of whales need some sort of;
p. 118 (n.) I have had to do with whales; p. 118 (n.) a moot point
whether a whale be a fish; p. 119 (n.) I hereby separate the whales
from the fish; p. 119 (n.) would Spain have banished the whales from
the waters; p. 119 (n.) the good old fashioned ground that the whale
is a fish; p. 119 (n.) how shall we define the whale; p. 119 (n.) the
whale is a spouting fish with a horizontal tale; p. 119 (n.) A walrus
spouts much like a whale; p. 119 (n.) the definition of what a whale
is; p. 119 (n.) hitherto identified with the whale; pp. 119-20 (adj.)
come the grand divisions of the entire whale host; p. 119 (n.)
included by many naturalists among the whales; p. 119 (n.) I deny
their credentials as whales; p. 120 (n.) I divide the whales into
three primary BOOKS; p. 120 (n.) I The FOLIO WHALE; II the OCTAVO
WHALE; III the DUODECIMO WHALE; p. 120 (n.) As the type of the FOLIO
I present the Sperm whale; p. 120 (n.) FOLIOS. Among these I here
include the following chapters;--I. The Sperm Whale; II. the Right
Whale; III. the Fin Back Whale; IV. the Hump-backed Whale; V. the
Razor Back Whale; VI. the Sulphur Bottom Whale; p. 120 (n.) (Sperm
Whale).--This whale . . . vaguely known as the Trumpa whale, and the
Physeter whale, and the Anvil Headed whale; p. 120 (n.) the most
formidable of all whales to encounter; p. 120 (n.) when the Sperm
whale was almost wholly unknown; p. 120 (n.) then known in England as
the Greenland or Right whale; p. 120 (n.) that quickening humor of
the Greenland whale; p. 120 (n.) BOOK I. (Folio), CHAPTER II. (Right
whale); p. 121 (n.) yields the article commonly known as whale bone
or baleen; p. 121 (n.) the oil especially known as whale oil; p. 121
(n.) by all the following titles: The whale; the Greenland whale;
the Black whale; the Great whale; the True whale; the Right whale;
p. 121 (n.) What then is the whale; p. 121 (n.) the Greenland whale
of the English whalemen; p. 121 (n.) the Baleine Ordinaire of the
French whalemen; p. 121 (n.) It is the whale which for more than two
centuries past; p. 121 (n.) it is the whale which the American
fishermen have long pursued; p. 121 (n.) designated by them Right
whale Cruising Grounds; p. 121 (n.) a difference between the Greenland
whale of the English and the right whale of the Americans; p. 121 (n.)
The right whale will be elsewhere treated of at some length; p. 121
(n.) with reference to elucidating the sperm whale; p. 121 (n.)

commonly the whale whose distant jet; p. 121 (n.) the Fin-back
resembles the right whale; p. 122 (n.) He seems a whale-hater; p. 122
(n.) a theoretic species denominated whalebone whales; p. 122 (n.)
whales with baleen; p. 122 (n.) Of these so called whalebone whales;
p. 122 (n.) Broad-nosed whales and beaked whales; pike-headed whales;
bunched whales; underjawed whales and rostrated whales; p. 122 (n.)
In connexion with this appellative of whalebone whales; p. 122 (n.)
in facilitating allusions to some kind of whales; p. 122 (n.) which
the whale, in his kind, presents; p. 122 (n.) indiscriminately
dispersed among all sorts of whales; p. 122 (n.) the sperm whale and
the humpbacked whale, each has a hump; p. 123 (n.) nothing but to
take hold of the whales bodily; p. 123 (n.) OCTAVOES. These embrace
the whales of middling magnitude; p. 123 (n.) Why this book of whales
is not denominated the Quarto; p. 124 (n.) because blackness is the
rule among almost all whales; p. 127 (n.) But there are a rabble of
uncertain, fugitive, half-fabulous whales, which, as an American
whaleman, I know; p. 127 (n.) The Bottle-Nose whale; the Junk whale;
the Pudding-Headed whale; the Cape whale; the Leading whale; the
Cannon whale; the Scragg whale; the Coppered whale; the Elephant
whale; the Iceberg whale; the Quog whale; the Blue whale; p. 128 (n.)
Concerning the officers of the whale-craft; p. 128 (n.) unknown of
course in any other marine than the whale-fleet; p. 136 (n.) that of
a whale-ship at sea; p. 137 (adj.) that the mast-heads of a southern
whale ship; p. 137 (n.) in which the look-outs of a Greenland whaler;
p. 137 (n.) in quest of the Greenland whale; p. 138 (n.) for the
purpose of popping off the stray narwhales; p. 139 (n.) your whales
must be seen before they can be killed; p. 139 (n.) the whale-fishery
furnishes an asylum for many romantic; p. 139 (n.) they would rather
not see whales than otherwise; p. 140 (n.) thou hast not raised a
whale yet. Whales are scarce as hen's teeth; p. 141 (n.) What do ye
do when ye see a whale, men; p. 141 (n.) A dead whale or a stove
boat; p. 142 (n.) heard me give orders about a white whale; p. 142
(n.) raises me a white-headed whale with a wrinkled brow and a crooked
jaw; p. 142 (n.) raises me a white-headed whale with a wrinkled brow
and a crooked jaw; p. 142 (n.) raises me a white-headed whale with a
wrinkled brow and a crooked jaw; p. 143 (n.) it was that accursed
white whale that razeed me; p. 144 (n.) be the white whale agent, or
be the white whale principal; p. 146 (adj.) ye men that man the
deathful whale boat's bow; p. 148 (n.) The hated whale has the round
watery world to swim in; p. 148 (n.) The white whale is their
demogorgon; p. 149 (n.) A viewing of those gallant whales; p. 152 (n.)
this [dancing] is worse than pulling after whales in a calm; p. 154
(n.) White squalls? white whale; p. 155 (n.) the unaccompanied
secluded white whale had haunted; p. 155 (n.) owing to the large
number of whale-cruisers; p. 159 (n.) so much invested the whale with
natural terror; p. 159 (adj.) they swam out of the white curds of the
whale's direful wrath; p. 159 (n.) seeking with a six inch blade to
reach the fathom; p. 160 (n.) cherished a wild vindictiveness against
the whale; p. 160 (n.) The white whale swam before him as the
monomaniac incarnation; p. 160 (n.) transferring its idea to the
abhorred white whale; p. 160 (adj.) He piled upon the whale's white
hump the sum of all the general rage; p. 162 (n.) full of rage and
wildness as the bloody hunt of whales; p. 162 (n.) chasing with curses
a Job's whale round the world; p. 163 (n.) The Whiteness of the Whale;
p. 163 (n.) What the white whale was to Ahab; p. 163 (n.) It was the
whiteness of the whale that above all things appalled me; p. 170 (n.)

And of all these things the Albino whale was the symbol; pp. 171-2
(adj.) sperm whale's food . . . the sperm whale's resorting to given
waters; pp. 172-3 (n.) Though the gregarious sperm whales have their
regular seasons; p. 179 (n.) a portly sperm whale, that begged a few
moments confidential business with him; p. 179 (n.) the sperm whale
will stand no nonsense; p. 181 (n.) caused by an unseen whale
vertically bumping the hull; p. 181 (n.) of the great power and
malice at times of the sperm whale; p. 181 (n.) the whale towing her
[ship's] great hull through the water; p. 191 (n.) if the sperm whale,
once struck, is allowed time to rally; p. 182 (n.) the food of the
sperm whale--squid or cuttle-fish; p. 182 (adj.) far too wedded to a
fiery whaleman's ways; p. 186 (n.) The sperm whale blows as a clock
ticks; p. 187 (n.) that took every eye from the whale; p. 190 (n.)
Those tiger yellow creatures of his seemed all steel and whale-bone;
p. 191 (n.) The whales might have made one of their regular soundings;
pp. 191-2 (n.) To a landsman, no whale . . . would have been visible;
p. 193 (n.) into the charmed, churned circle of the hunted sperm
whale; p. 193 (n.) the whales seemed separating their wakes; p. 193
(n.) three whales running dead to leeward; p. 194 (n.) Squall, whale,
and harpoon had all blended together; and the whale . . . escaped;
p. 196 (n./adj.) going plump on a flying whale . . . is the height of
a whaleman's discretion; p. 197 (adj.) Among whale-wise people;
p. 198 (n.) in a whaler wonders soon wane; p. 199 (n.) though herds
of whales were seen by night; p. 201 (n.) that unnearable spout was
cast by one self-same whale; and that whale, Moby Dick; p. 214 (n.)
he fell on the hatch spouting blood like a whale; p. 222 (adj.) as he
fell on the whale's slippery back; p. 222 (n.) But the whale rushed
round in a sudden maelstrom; p. 224 (n.) Monstrous Pictures of Whales;
p. 225 (n.) there are the Prodromus whales of old Scotch Sibbald, and
Jonah's whale . . . As for the bookbinder's whale; p. 227 (n.) there
are plates of an alleged whale and a narwhale. I do not wish to seem
inelegant, but this unsightly whale looks much like an amputated sow;
p. 227 (n.) The living whale, in his full majesty and significance,
is only to be seen at sea in unfathomable waters; p. 228 (n.)
difference of contour between a young sucking whale and a full-grown
Platonian Leviathan; p. 228 (n.) from the naked skeleton of the
stranded whale; p. 229 (n.) Less Erroneous Pictures of Whales; p. 230
(n.) the inert mass of a dead whale a conquered fortress; p. 231 (n.)
Of whales in Paint; in Teeth; in Wood; in Sheet-Iron; in Stone; in
Mountains; in Stars; p. 233 (n.) brass whales hung by the tail for
knockers . . . these knocking whales are seldom remarkable; p. 233
(n.) to trace out great whales in the starry heavens; p. 237 (n.)
they believe it to furnish to the sperm whale his only food; p. 237
(n.) the spermaciti whale obtains his whole food in unknown zones,
below the surface; p. 238 (n.) I have here to speak of the magical,
sometimes horrible whale-line; p. 239 (n.) In these instances, the
whale of course is shifted like a mug of ale; p. 240 (adj.) to account
for those repeated whaling disasters; p. 241 (n.) All men live
enveloped in whale-lines; p. 242 (n.) a gigantic sperm whale lay
rolling in the water like the capsized hull of a frigate; p. 242 (n.)
the whale looked like a portly burgher smoking his pipe of a warm
afternoon; p. 242 (n.) But that pipe, poor whale, was thy last;
p. 244 (adj.) sterning out of the way of the whale's horrible wallow;
p. 247 (n.) the instantaneous violent, convulsive running of the
whale upon receiving the first iron; p. 248 (n.) vacantly eyeing the
heaving whale for a moment; p. 248 (n.) the whale now lies with its

black hull close to the vessel's; p. 249 (n.) fond of the whale as a
flavorish thing to his palate; p. 249 (adj.) Nor was Stubb the only
banqueter on whale's flesh; p. 249 (n.) as they scooped out huge
globular pieces of the whale; p. 249 (n.) The mark they thus leave on
the whale, may be likened to the hollow made by a carpenter in
countersinking for a screw; p. 252 (n.) You don't know how to cook a
whale-steak; p. 254 (n.) whale-balls for breakfast--don't forget;
p. 254 (n.) the whale would by all hands be considered a noble dish;
p. 254 (n.) lived for several months on the moldy scraps of whales;
p. 255 (n.) because the whale is so excessively unctious; p. 257 (n.)
darting their long whaling-spade; p. 259 (n.) what and where is the
skin of the whale; p. 259 (n.) which I use for marks in my whale
books; p. 261 (n.) the whale is indeed wrapt up in his blubber as in
a real blanket or counterpane; p. 261 (n.) like man, the whale has
lungs and warm blood; p. 261 (n.) Oh, man! admire and model thyself
after the whale; p. 261 (n.) like the great whale, retain, o man! in
all seasons a temperature of thine own; p. 261 (n.) Of erections, how
few are domed like St. Peter's! of creatures, how few are vast as the
whale; p. 262 (n.) In life but few of them would have helped the
whale, I ween; p. 262 (n.) Oh, horrible vulturism of earth! from
which not the mightiest whale is free; p. 267 (n.) pronouncing the
white whale to be no less a being than the Shaker God incarnated;
p. 271 (n.) attracted by such prey as a dead whale; p. 272 (n.)
flourished over his head a couple of keen whale-spades; p. 274 (n.)
and the whale not sounding very rapidly; p. 274 (n.) But the fagged
whale abated his speed; p. 279 (adj.) the position of the whale's
eyes corresponds to that of a man's ears; p. 280 (n.) extraordinary
vacillations of movement displayed by some whales; p. 280 (n.) But
the ear of the whale is full as curious as the eye; p. 281 (n.) you
see some sulky whale, floating there suspended; p. 282 (n.) A great
pity, now, that this unfortunate whale should be hare-lipped; p. 285
(n.) For unless you own the whale; p. 286 (adj.) so the whale's vast
plaited forehead forms innumerable strange devices; p. 286 (n.) so
the tun of the whale contains by far the most precious of all his
oily vintage; p. 290 (n.) coffined, hearsed, and tombed in the secret
inner chamber and sanctum sanctorum of the whale; p. 291 (n.) A nose
to the whale would have been impertinent; p. 292 (n.) Genius in the
Sperm whale? Has the Sperm whale ever written a book, spoken a
speech; p. 293 (adj.) how may unlettered Ishmael hope to read the
awful chaldee of the Sperm Whale's brow; p. 293 (n.) The whale, like
all things that are mighty, wears a false brow to the common world;
p. 295 (n.) when whales were almost simultaneously raised from the
mast-heads of both vessels; p. 296 (n.) There were eight whales, an
average pod; p. 296 (n.) whether this whale belonged to the pod in
advance; p. 296 (n.) did ever whale yaw so before; p. 296 (n.)
pointing to the whale line near him; p. 296 (n.) not only was he the
largest, and therefore the most valuable whale; p. 296 (n.) the other
whales were going with such great velocity; p. 299 (n.) And the whale
soon ceasing to sound; p. 299 (n.) the longer the stricken whale
stays under water; p. 299 (n.) how vast, then, the burden of a whale;
p. 300 (n.) One whaleman has estimated it at the weight of; p. 300
(n.) how appalling to the wounded whale must have been such huge
phantoms flitting over his head; p. 300 (n.) the life and death throbs
of the whale; p. 301 (n.) the whale now spouting thick blood; p. 302
(n.) the sunken whale being suspended a few inches beneath them by
the chords; p. 302 (n.) in the dead bodies of captured whales; p. 303

(n.) the sunken whale again rises; p. 304 (n.) the first whale
attacked by our brotherhood was not killed with any sordid intent;
p. 305 (n.) which dragon I maintain to have been a whale; p. 305 (n.)
in many old chronicles whales and dragons are strangely jumbled
together; p. 305 (n.) St. George's whale might have crawled up out of
the sea; p. 306 (n.) has for ever set apart and sanctified the whale;
p. 306 (n.) so Vishnoo became incarnate in a whale; p. 306 (adj.) in
reference to . . . the whale's gastric juices; p. 308 (n.) Towards
noon whales were raised; p. 309 (n.) It is only indispensable with an
inveterate running whale; p. 310 (n.) The agonized whale goes into
his flurry; p. 312 (n.) the whale has no voice; p. 317 (adj.) this
peaking of the whale's flukes is perhaps the grandest sight; p. 317
(n.) I once saw a large herd of whales in the east; p. 317 (n.) the
whale, pronouncing him the most devout of all beings; p. 320 (n.) the
sperm whales . . . are now frequently met within extensive herds;
p. 320 (n.) a continuous chain of whale-jets were up-playing and
sparkling; p. 321 (n.) seemed more to grieve that the swift whales
had been gaining; p. 322 (n.) when a general pausing commotion among
the whales; p. 322 (n.) at the strangely gallied whales before us;
p. 322 (n.) Though many of the whales . . . were in violent motion;
p. 323 (n.) each making for some one lone whale on the outskirts of
the shoal; p. 323 (n.) when . . . the towing whale sideways vanished;
p. 324 (n.) we saw successive pods of whales, eight or ten in each,
swiftly going round and round, like multiplied spans of horses in a
ring; p. 324 (n.) Owing to the density of the crowd of reposing
whales; p. 325 (n.) the unborn whale lies bent like a Tartar's bow;
p. 326 (n.) still engaged in drugging the whales on the frontier of
the host; p. 326 (n.) the sight of the enraged drugged whales now and
then blindly darting; p. 326 (n.) when fast to a whale more than
commonly powerful and alert; p. 326 (n.) when overflowing with mutual
esteem, the whales salute more hominum; p. 327 (n.) in more and more
contracting orbits the whales in the more central circles began to
swim in thickening clusters; p. 327 (n.) the entire host of whales
came tumbling upon their inner centre; p. 327 (n.) while standing in
the bows to prick the fugitive whales; p. 329 (n.) my lord whale
keeps a wary eye on his interesting family; p. 329 (n.) As ashore,
the ladies often cause the most terrible duels among their rivals;
just so with the whales, who sometimes come to deadly battle, and all
for love; p. 329 (n.) my Lord Whale has no taste for the nursery;
p. 330 (n.) as the harem of whales is called by the fishermen's
school; p. 330 (n.) the man who first then entitled this sort of
Ottoman whale; p. 330 (n.) Almost universally, a lone whale . . .
proves an ancient one; p. 330 (n.) excepting those wondrous grey-
headed, grizzled whales; p. 331 (n.) a whale may be struck by one
vessel; p. 331 (n.) after a weary and perilous chase and capture of a
whale; p. 331 (adj.) Perhaps the only formal whaling code; p. 332 (n.)
there was a curious case of whale-trover litigated in England; p. 332
(n.) Erskine contended that the examples of the whale and the lady
were reciprocally illustrative of each other; p. 333 (n.) with regard
to the controverted whale, harpoons, and line; p. 334 (n.) succeeded
in killing and beaching a fine whale; p. 335 (n.) the whale was
seized and sold; p. 336 (n.) ye tail is ye Queen's, that ye queen's
wardrobe may be supplied with ye whalebone; p. 337 (n.) that some
sort of whale must be alongside; p. 337 (n.) must be what the
fishermen call a blasted whale, that is, a whale that has died
unmolested on the sea; p. 337 (n.) this second whale seemed even more

of a nosegay than the first; p. 337 (n.) it turned out to be one of
those problematical whales that seem to dry up and die; p. 341 (n.)
by pulling out the lighter whale of the two from the ship's side;
p. 342 (n.) an essence found in the inglorious bowels of a sick
whale; p. 343 (adj.) unloading one of these whale cemeteries; p. 344
(n.) Nor, indeed can the whale possibly be otherwise than fragrant;
p. 344 (n.) What then shall I liken the sperm whale to for fragrance
. . . ? . . . that famous elephant, with jewelled tusks; p. 346 (n.)
We can't afford to lose whales by the likes of you; a whale would
sell for thirty times what you would; p. 346 (n.) when the whale
started to run; p. 347 (n.) the whale was winged; p. 350 (n.) The
whaling-pike is similar to a frigate's boarding-weapon; p. 350 (n.)
a certain juncture of this post-mortemizing of the whale; p. 353 (n.)
the whale supplies his own fuel and burns by his own body; p. 356
(adj.) enormous masses of the whale's head are profanely piled;
p. 357 (n.) from the ashes of the burned scraps of the whale; p. 357
(n.) three men intent on spying out more whales; p. 359 (adj.) the
mariners revered it [doubloon] as the white whale's talisman; p. 365
(n.) I was ignorant of the White whale at that time; p. 365 (n.) we
lowered for a pod of four or five whales; p. 365 (n.) presently up
breaches from the bottom of the sea a bouncing great whale, with a
milky-white head and hump, all crows' feet and wrinkles; p. 365 (n.)
what a noble great whale it was; p. 365 (adj.) the whale's tail
looming straight up out of it, perpendicular in the air, like a marble
steeple; p. 368 (n.) that the digestive organs of the whale are so
inscrutably constructed; p. 368 (adj.) what you take for the White
whale's malice is only his awkwardness; p. 369 (adj.) thus the vast
Sperm whale grounds of the Pacific were thrown open; p. 371 (adj.)
Nor have I been at all sparing of historical whale research; p. 371
(adj./n.) an ancient Dutch volume, which, by the musty whaling smell
of it, I knew must be about whalers; p. 373 (n.) few whalemen have
penetrated very far beneath the skin of the adult whale; p. 376 (n.)
nor, indeed, should inches at all enter into a congenial admeasurement
of the whale; p. 378 (n.) can the fully invested whale be truly and
livingly found out; p. 378 (n.) From his mighty bulk the whale affords
a most congenial theme; p. 379 (adj.) to compile a lexicon to be used
by a whale author like me; p. 379 (n.) Detached broken fossils of
pre-adamite whales; p. 380 (adj.) Then the whole world was the whale's,
and, king of creation, he left his wake along; p. 380 (n.) at this
antemosaic, unsourced existence of the unspeakable terrors of the
whale; p. 381 (n.) strange attestation of the antiquity of the whale;
p. 381 (n.) Temple, the Rafters the Beams of which are made of whalebone, for whales of a monstrous size are oftentimes cast up dead;
p. 381 (n.) In this Afric Temple of the Whale I leave you, reader,
and if you be a Nantucketer, and a whaleman, you will silently worship
there; p. 381 (adj.) Does the Whale's Magnitude Diminish?--Will He
Perish? p. 381 (n.) not only are the whales of the present day
superior; p. 381 (n.) of the whales found in that Tertiary system;
p. 382 (n.) Of all the pre-adamite whales exhumed; p. 382 (n.) while
the whales of the present hour are an advance; p. 382 (n.) Rope Walks
and Thames Tunnels of Whales; p. 382 (n.) the whale of to-day is as
big as his ancestors; p. 383 (n.) Comparing the humped herds of
whales with the humped herds of buffalo; p. 382 (n.) the hunted whale
cannot now escape speedy extinction; p. 383 (adj./n.) because the
so-called whale-bone whales no longer haunt many grounds; p. 384 (n.)
much more may the great whale outlast all hunting; p. 384 (n.) we

account the whale immortal in his species; p. 385 (n.) then the
eternal whale will still survive; p. 387 (n.) At all times except
when whales were alongside; p. 387 (adj.) out of clean shaved rods of
right-whale bone, and cross-beams of sperm whale ivory; p. 395 (n.)
must not only face all the rage of the living whale; p. 398 (n.) mere
sickness could not kill him: nothing but a whale or a gale; p. 400
(n.) that sea in which the hated white whale must even then be
swimming; p. 400 (n.) Stern all! the White whale spouts thick blood;
p. 402 (v.) And so Perth went a-whaling; p. 405 (n.) pulling, or
sailing, or paddling after the whales; p. 409 (n.) sun and whale both
stilly died together; p. 409 (n.) Nor has this thy whale sunwards
turned his dying head; p. 409 (n.) In vain, oh whale, dost thou seek
intercedings with yon all-quickening sun, that only calls forth life,
but gives it not again; p. 413 (n.) Oh! jolly is the gale,/ And a
joker is the whale; p. 416 (n.) the white flame but lights the way to
the white whale; p. 433 (n.) the strangers boats were engaged with a
shoal of whales; p. 446 (n.) to behold the famous whale they had so
long been pursuing; p. 446 (adj.) attuned to the gradual prolongings
of the whale's visible jets; p. 447 (adj.) like to some flag-staff
rising from the painted hull of an argosy, the tall but shattered
pole of a recent lance projected from the white whale's back; p. 447
(n.) A gentle joyousness--a mighty mildness of repose in swiftness,
invested the gliding whale; p. 447 (n.) not that great majesty supreme!
did surpass the glorified white whale as he so divinely swam; p. 447
(n.) on each bright side, the whale shed off enticings; p. 447 (n.)
Yet calm, enticing calm, oh whale! thou glidest on; p. 448 (adj.) he
gazed beyond the whale's place; p. 449 (n.) the whale obliquely lying
on his back, in the manner of a biting shark; p. 449 (n.) the White
whale now shook the slight cedar as a mildly cruel cat her mouse;
p. 449 (n.) as the whale dallied with the doomed craft in this
devilish way; p. 450 (adj.) in the foam of the whale's insolent tail;
p. 454 (n.) blow on and split your spout, o whale; p. 455 (n.) in his
immeasurable bravadoes the white whale tossed himself salmon-like to
Heaven; p. 456 (n.) he told them he would take the whale head-and-
head; p. 457 (n.) arrow-like, shooting perpendicularly from the sea,
the white whale dashed his broad forehead against its bottom; p. 457
(n.) The first uprising momentum of the whale; p. 458 (n.) Nor white
whale, nor man, nor fiend, can so much as graze old Ahab in his own
proper and inaccessible being; p. 464 (n.) leaving the circling
surface creamed like new milk round the marble trunk of the whale;
p. 466 (n.) he darted his fierce iron, and his far fiercer curse into
the hated whale; p. 467 (adj.) the before whale-smitten bow-ends of
two planks burst through; p. 467 (n.) I grin at thee, thou grinning
whale; p. 468 (n.) upon the whale, which from side to side strangely
vibrating his predestinating head; p. 468 (n.) the whale ran quivering
along its keel; p. 468 (n.) Towards thee I roll, thou all-destroying
but unconquering whale; to the last I grapple with thee; from hell's
heart I stab at thee; for hate's sake I spit my last breath at thee;
p. 468 (n.) the stricken whale flew forward.

WHARF. An erection of wood or stone, raised on the shore of a road or
harbor for the convenience of loading or discharging vessels by cranes or
other means. A wharf is of course built stronger or slighter in proportion
to the effort of the tide or sea which it is intended to resist, and the
size of vessels using it. (Smyth)

Omoo--p. 292 (n.) stepping upon an imaginary wharf.

Mardi--p. 120 (n.) to embark from the wreck, as from a wharf.

Redburn--p. 4 (n.) by certain shadowy reminiscences of wharfs; p. 4 (n.) I remembered standing with my father on the wharf; p. 13 (n.) and the boat touched the wharf at New York; p. 23 (n.) Picks Up His Board and Lodging along the Wharfs; p. 24 (n.) as soon as I arrived at the wharf; p. 26 (n.) I thought the groceries on the wharf would be open; p. 32 (n.) past the long line of shipping, and wharfs; p. 33 (n.) had promised to be on the wharf; p. 68 (n.) visited the ship lying at the wharf; p. 82 (n.) For when we lay at the wharf; p. 89 (n.) placards stuck on the posts along the wharfs; p. 111 (n.) the boy wandered about the wharfs; p. 115 (n.) at the junk shops along the wharfs; p. 134 (n.) only land upon wharfs and pier-heads; p. 161 (n.) only seen the miserable wooden wharfs; p. 161 (n.) by those irregular, unsightly wharfs; p. 238 (n.) can not get any further than the wharf; p. 301 (n.) the ship once fast to the wharf; p. 302 (n.) in the paltry shops along the wharfs; p. 308 (n.) while several carts on the wharf; p. 308 (n.) on the side next to the wharf; p. 309 (n.) Harry and I followed them along the wharf; p. 311 (n.) then, standing on the wharf.

White-Jacket--p. 236 (adj.) you'll think a Long wharf truck-horse kicked you; p. 378 (n.) along the wharfs of our sea-ports; p. 381 (n.) impressed . . . sailors . . . from the public wharfs.

Moby-Dick--p. 12 (n.) your insular city of the Manhattoes, belted round by wharfs as Indian isles by coral reefs; p. 45 (n.) He skulks about the wharfs of Joppa; p. 46 (n.) no friends accompany him to the wharf; p. 46 (n.) that's stuck against the spile upon the wharf; p. 47 (n.) the ship, heeling over towards the wharf; p. 48 (n.) from the deserted wharf the uncheered ship . . . glides; p. 58 (n.) the little Nantucket packet schooner moored at the wharf; p. 59 (n.) shoulders the barrow and marches up the wharf; p. 59 (n.) Huge hills and mountains of casks on casks were piled upon her wharves; p. 82 (n.) walking down the end of the wharf; p. 83 (n.) leaving my comrade standing on the wharf; p. 93 (n.) after the Pequod had been hauled out from the wharf; p. 109 (n.) the solemn whimsicalities of that outlandish prophet of the wharves; p. 319 (n.) loaded down with alien stuff, to be transferred to foreign wharves.

WHIRLPOOL. An eddy or vortex where the waters are continually rushing round. In rivers they are very common, from various accidents, and are usually of little consequence. In the sea they are more dangerous, as the classical Charybdis, and the celebrated Mäelstrom and Saltenstrom, both on the coast of Norway. (Smyth)

Omoo--p. 72 (n.) a red whirlpool of blood and brine; p. 97 (n.) with the last whirl of the whirlpool.

Mardi--p. 138 (n.) Into this whirlpool Yillah was to descend; p. 159 (n.) the whirlpool on the coast of Tedaidee; p. 189 (n.) "The whirlpool," she murmured; p. 193 (n.) she murmured of the whirlpool and mosses; p. 544 (n.) till they met the whirlpool-column from the sea.

White-Jacket--p. 295 (n.) cork-screw whirlpools, suck us down.

Moby-Dick--p. 3 (n.) among which the Whales and Whirlpools called
Balæne; p. 222 (n.) so as to drop astern from the whirlpool; p. 289
(n.) the enormous mass dropped into the sea, like Niagara's Table-
Rock into the whirlpool; p. 450 (n.) even in the heart of such a
whirlpool as that.

WINDLASS. The machine used in merchant vessels to weigh the anchor by.
(Dana)

Omoo--p. 6 (n.) the mate stretched me out on the windlass; p. 6 (n.)
with my feet resting on the windlass; p. 8 (n.) Seated upon the
windlass the greater portion of the day; p. 42 (n.) them all to the
windlass; p. 43 (n.) who was as strong as a windlass; p. 50 (n.)
coming forward to the windlass; p. 59 (n.) dashed it against the
windlass; p. 89 (n.) with my jacket under the windlass; p. 153 (n.)
to take my place at the windlass; p. 206 (adj.) somewhat indecorous
windlass chorus; p. 313 (n.) nothing to do but sit on the windlass.

Mardi--p. 82 (n.) led the halyards to the windlass.

Redburn--p. 46 (n.) the sailors sat on the windlass; p. 46 (n.) then
handed it round along the windlass; p. 47 (n.) up and down the deck
before the windlass; p. 53 (n.) and sat down on the windlass; p. 63
(n.) only have sat on the windlass again; p. 69 (n.) were all standing
round the windlass; p. 70 (n.) after he had got me as far as the
windlass; p. 189 (n.) a crown, a ship, a windlass; p. 278 (n.) So one
might, on the windlass; p. 289 (n.) I sat with Harry on the windlass;
p. 295 (n.) with . . . a thigh like a windlass.

Moby-Dick--p. 94 (n.) to cheer the hands at the windlass; p. 258 (n.)
while every gasping heave of the windlass is answered; p. 348 (n.)
after the bitter exertion at the windlass; p. 445 (n.) we are turned
round and round in this world, like yonder windlass, and Fate is the
handspike.

WINDWARD. The weather-side; that on which the wind blows; the opposite
of leeward. Old sailors exhort their neophytes to throw nothing over the
weather-side except ashes or hot water; a hint not mistakable. (Smyth)

Typee--p. 4 (adv.) she won't go any more to windward; p. 134 (adj.)
to the windward side of the lake.

Omoo--p. 10 (adv.) Sailing to windward; p. 68 (adv.) now and then
looking to windward; p. 90 (adv.) spinning to windward like a top;
p. 98 (adv.) being well to windward.

Mardi--p. 27 (adv.) the boat was to windward; p. 29 (adv.) a speck to
windward broke; p. 117 (adv.) cut the lanyards to windward; p. 117 (adv.)
climbed up to windward; p. 128 (adj.) the windward side of the craft.

Redburn--p. 55 (adv.) I used to shake my hair out to windward; p. 107
(adv.) and gaze out to windward; p. 115 (adj.) you always go up on
the windward side; p. 117 (adv.) looking out to windward; p. 220

(adv.) he could look right to windward and beard it; p. 286 (adv.) pitched over a gallon or two of something to windward; p. 286 (adv.) to throw any thing to windward at sea; p. 295 (adv.) Haul out to windward; p. 295 (adv.) when the ship had rolled to windward.

White-Jacket--p. 6 (adv.) the captain was looking to windward; p. 33 (adv.) and an earnest, inquiring eye to the windward; p. 93 (adv.) many anxious glances were cast to windward; p. 108 (adv.) from his being right to windward of me; p. 108 (adv.) to turn round and look to windward; p. 108 (adv.) word passed along the yard from windward; p. 108 (adv.) like climbing a precipice to get to windward; p. 111 (adv.) and keep a sharp eye to windward; p. 194 (adv.) See anything to windward?

Moby-Dick--p. 114 (adv.) ignorantly smoking to windward all the while; to windward; p. 126 (adv.) come from the breezy billows to windward; p. 202 (adv.) Ahab for hours and hours would stand gazing dead to windward; p. 414 (adv.) yonder, to windward, all is blackness of doom.

WRIGGLE-TAIL. From Melville we know that it is a fish; the OED indicates that the characteristic movement is described by the name.

Mardi--p. 148 (n.) the quivering wriggle-tails.

XIPHIUS PLATYPTERUS. A fish akin to the swordfish of the North Atlantic, though larger, and called "Bill fish" by seamen in the Pacific. (Melville)

Mardi--p. 103 (n.) Xiphius Platypterus; p. 104 (n.) by the outlandish appellation of Xiphius Platypterus.

YACHT. A vessel of state or pleasure: the former is usually employed to convey great personages. One of the designs of a yacht being accommodation, they are usually fitted up with great comfort; their propulsion is by sails or steam. Private pleasure-boats, when sufficiently large for a sea voyage, are also termed yachts. (Smyth)

Typee--p. 171 (n.) the scene of our island yachting.

Omoo--p. 231 (n.) This South Sea yachting was delightful.

Mardi--p. 482 (n.) reckoned in his stud, a slender yacht; p. 610 (n.) the day was very fine for yachting.

Redburn--p. 126 (n.) and prepare for another yachting.

White-Jacket--p. 310 (n.) was one delightful yachting.

YARD. A long cylindrical timber suspended upon the mast of a vessel to spread a sail. They are termed square, lateen, or lug: the first are suspended across the masts at right angles, and the two latter obliquely. --Yard-arm generally means the extremity of the yard, and it is fitted with sheave-holes for reeving sheets through.--Yard-arm and yard-arm, the

situation of two ships lying alongside one another, so near that their
yard-arms nearly touch each other, or even cross. The term implies close
action and no mistake. (Smyth)

Typee--p. 7 (n.) all the honors due to royalty;--manning our yards;
p. 9 (n.) all we had to do . . . was to square in the yards; p. 10
(n.) at times alight on our yards and stays; p. 22 (n.) so that not
a yard was braced or a sail set.

Omoo--p. 19 (n.) the masts and yards lined distinctly; p. 42 (n.)
from the tops and lower yardarms; p. 42 (n.) The yards were being
braced; p. 45 (n.) The main-yard swung round; p. 46 (adj.) phantoms
were seen at the yard arm ends; p. 51 (n.) found the yards braced
sharp up; p. 59 (n.) The yard hung by a hair; p. 59 (n.) The yard,
with a snap and a plunge; p. 69 (n.) stand by to haul back the main-
yard; p. 69 (n.) the main-yard swung round; p. 70 (n.) rigged from
the main-yard; p. 90 (n.) Haul back the head-yards; p. 90 (n.) the
after-yards were whirled round; p. 91 (n.) Hang him at the main-yard;
p. 110 (n.) exercising yards and sails; p. 149 (n.) with one leg
thrown over the yard; p. 290 (n.) furled loosely upon the yards;
p. 316 (n.) we braced the yards square.

Mardi--p. 60 (n.) wheezings of the masts and yards; p. 63 (n.) bracing
round the yards; p. 63 (n.) when the fore-yard swung; p. 65 (n.)
shrouds, halyards and all; p. 70 (n.) escaped to the fore-top-gallant-
yard; p. 81 (n.) yards braced about; p. 82 (n.) one hand could brace
the main-yard; p. 82 (n.) led the halyards to the windlass; p. 85 (n.)
squaring their yards; p. 87 (n.) loud creaking of the yards; p. 97
(n.) daintily squaring her yards; p. 101 (n.) in the slings of the
topsail yard; p. 101 (n.) out to the ends of the yards; p. 117 (n.)
cut the lanyards to windward; p. 117 (n.) upon cutting the third
lanyard; p. 117 (n.) The remaining lanyards parted; p. 128 (n.) The
yard, spreading a yellow sail; p. 367 (n.) the great yards swing
round on their axes; p. 532 (n.) playing about the ends of ships'
royal-yards.

Redburn--p. 4 (n.) with high, cozy bulwarks, and rakish masts and
yards; p. 8 (n.) because the masts, yards, and ropes were made; p. 8
(n.) Not to speak of the tall masts, and yards; p. 50 (n.) his orders
about the sails and yards; p. 64 (n.) beyond the ends of the yards;
p. 66 (n.) up to the top-sail yards; p. 78 (n.) found myself hanging
on the skysail-yard; p. 78 (n.) me too along with the yard and sail;
p. 78 (n.) the yard rising under me; pp. 82-3 (n.) done from one of
the lower yard-arms; p. 93 (n.) of the lower yard-arms had been
broken; p. 93 (n.) carried small and unsightly jury-yards; p. 102 (n.)
in bracing the yards we waded about; p. 114 (n.) to sit on one of the
topsail-yards; p. 115 (n.) found myself hanging over the yard; p. 115
(n.) I felt as fearless on the royal yard; p. 115 (n.) required two
hands on the yard; p. 121 (n.) to make a jury-mast out of a yard;
p. 125 (n.) backed the main yard; p. 165 (n.) yard-arm touches yard-
arm in brotherly love; p. 255 (n.) on the yard aloft; p. 256 (n.) At
last he gained the royal yard; p. 295 (n.) the extreme weather-end of
the topsail-yard; p. 295 (n.) strung along the main-topsail-yard;
p. 295 (n.) to confine the reef corner to the yard; p. 295 (adj.) and
he rode the yard-arm end; p. 295 (n.) Jackson fell headlong from the
yard; pp. 295-6 (n.) with the long projection of the yard-arm; p. 296
(n.) to descend, haul back the fore-yard, and man.

White-Jacket--p. 7 (n.) on those broad boughs, our yards; p. 7 (n.)
as he flew out on the giddy yard-arm; p. 8 (n.) assigned to each yard
of the tops; p. 9 (n.) from above the main-yard; p. 9 (n.) For
including the main-yard; p. 9 (n.) the fore-yard, anchors, and all
the sails; p. 34 (n.) those fellows on the main-topsail-yard; p. 36
(n.) started from my studies to the main-royal-yard; p. 40 (n.) such
as bracing round the yards; p. 47 (n.) being on the loftiest yard of
the frigate . . . the main-royal-yard; p. 68 (n.) The yards are slung
in chains; p. 69 (n.) high over the top-gallant-yards; p. 69 (n.) our
stout masts and yards might be lying; p. 69 (n.) splicing and fishing
the shattered masts and yards; p. 73 (n.) the yards braced forward;
p. 76 (n.) seating myself on one of the upper yards; p. 77 (n.) high
up on the main-royal-yards I reclined; p. 77 (n.) of a tremulous
voice hailing the main-royal-yard from the top; p. 77 (n.) when, like
lightening, the yard dropped under me; p. 77 (n.) the yard had
descended to the cap; p. 97 (n.) down come his t'-gallant-yards;
p. 105 (n.) the yard-arm-ends seemed to dip; p. 105 (n.) drenched the
men who were on the fore-yard; p. 106 (n.) impossible to clew down
the yards; p. 107 (n.) for the yard was now clewed down; p. 107 (n.)
required at least fifty men on the yard; p. 107 (n.) Aloft, main-yard-
men; p. 107 (n.) groped our way out on the yard-arms; p. 108 (n.)
threatening to tear us from the yard; p. 108 (n.) four or five of us
clinging to the lee-yard-arm; p. 108 (n.) the word passed along the
yard from windward; p. 108 (n.) Those on the weather yard-arm managed;
p. 108 (n.) the entire yard was now encased in ice; p. 108 (n.) to
throw ourselves prostrate along the yard; p. 108 (n.) was felt by one
man on that yard; p. 120 (n.) summoned to brace the main-yard; p. 152
(n.) A man at the fore-top-sail-yard; p. 152 (n.) the man on the
fore-top-sail-yard reported; p. 194 (n.) Strike top-gallant-yards;
p. 195 (n.) have his sails stowed on the yards; p. 195 (n.) were soon
climbing about the yards; p. 195 (n.) in the bunt, or middle of the
yard; p. 195 (n.) the main top-men are nearly off the yard; p. 195
(n.) the ponderous folds of canvass in the middle of the yard; p. 195
(n.) hard at work at the main-topsail-yard; p. 196 (n.) a seaman fell
from the main-royal-yard; p. 196 (n.) The royal-yard forms a cross
with the mast; p. 196 (n.) a man, hurled thus from a yard; p. 212 (n.)
I hung over that main-royal-yard; p. 233 (n.) we manned the yards;
p. 234 (n.) A top-man next me on the main-royal-yard; p. 236 (n.)
from the top-sail yard; p. 236 (n.) can't you behave yourself, royal-
yard-men; p. 238 (n.) the people were called down from the yards;
p. 257 (n.) fell from the mizzen-top-sail yard; p. 265 (n.) exercised
yards simultaneously with ourselves; p. 269 (n.) giving three cheers
from decks, yards, and tops; p. 278 (n.) aloft when the yards swung
round; p. 278 (n.) to let go the weather-lift of the main-yard;
p. 278 (n.) the yards, unobstructed, came round; p. 295 (n.) liable
at any time to be run up at the yard-arm; p. 303 (n.) were then hung
at the yard-arm; p. 308 (n.) both fore-tacks over the main-yard;
p. 312 (n.) her fore-yard lying in two pieces; p. 318 (n.) covered
with masts and yards; p. 353 (n.) mounting the fore-yard in a gale;
p. 370 (n.) to the two extremities of the main-yard; p. 382 (n.)
hands to brace the heavy yards; p. 391 (n.) on the giddiest of yards;
p. 392 (n.) to the end of the weather-top-gallant-yard-arm; p. 392
(n.) pitching me still further over the yard; p. 392 (n.) I pitched
from the yard; p. 392 (adj.) Having fallen from the projecting yard-
arm end.

Moby-Dick--p. 263 (n.) every yard-arm on that side projecting like a crane over the waves; p. 287 (n.) runs straight out upon the overhanging main-yard-arm; p. 415 (n.) All the yard-arms were tipped with a pallid fire; p. 415 (n.) they will imprecate curses from the topsail-yard-arms; p. 424 (n.) The yards were braced hard up.

YAW. The quick movement by which a ship deviates from the direct line of her course toward the right or left, from unsteady steering. (Smyth)

Mardi--p. 57 (v.) She continually yawed in her course; p. 58 (n.) for the vessel's yawing; p. 72 (v.) craft widely yawed; p. 127 (n.) from . . . the canoe's wide yawing; p. 256 (v.) yawing heavily to the push.

Redburn--p. 31 (v.) yaw about while you may; p. 31 (n.) I'll do the yawing after the anchor's up.

White-Jacket--p. 309 (v.) When you see a fellow yawing about the docks.

Moby-Dick--p. 296 (v.) did ever whale yaw so before; p. 298 (v.) he yawed in his faltering flight; p. 400 (n.) a certain slight but painful appearing yawing in his gait.

YAWL. A man-of-war's boat, resembling the pinnace, but rather smaller; it is carvel-built, and generally rowed with twelve oars. Also, a small fishing-vessel. (Smyth)

White-Jacket--p. 161 (n.) She also carried . . . a small yawl.

YELLOW-BACK. Smyth shows instead yellow-tail, a well-known tropical fish, often in company with whip-rays; it is about 4 feet long, with a great head, large eyes, and many fins. Leiostomas. (Smyth)

Mardi--p. 148 (n.) by endless battalions of Yellow-Backs.

APPENDICES

Semantics

The Sea Vocabulary: An Alphabetical Listing
Denoting Semantic Classification

Abeam--3C

Abyss--1

Adrift--3C

Afloat--3C, 4

Aft--3C

Albatros(s)--3A

Albicore--3A

Alewife--3A

Alligator--3A

Aloft--3C

Ambergris--3A

Anchor--3C

Aquatic--1

Archipelago--2

Argosy--3C

Ark--3C

Ashore--2

Astern--3C

Atlantic--1

Atoll--2

Baleen--3A

Barge--3C

Bark, Barque--3C

Barnacle--3A

Bay--2

Beach--2

Billows--1

Binnacle--3C

Blow--3A

Blubber--3A

Boat--3C

Bob-stay--3C

Boneeta--3A

Booby--3A

Boom--3C

Bow--3C

Brail--3C

Breach--3A

Breaker--1

Brig--3C

Brigantine--3C

Brine--1

Brit--3A

Broach to--3C

Bubble--1

Bucanier--4

Bulkhead--3C

Bulwark--3C

Buoy--3C

Cabin--3C

Caboose--3C

Cachalot--3A

Calm--3B

Canal--2

Canoe--3C

Canvas(s)--3C

Cape--2

Capstan--3C

Captain--4

Caribbean--1

Castaway--4

Cat-Head--3C

Cephalaspis--3A

Cetology--3A

Chart--3C

Chevalier--3A

Chondropterygii--3A

Chronometer--3C

Clam--3A
Clipper--3C
Coast--2
Cockle--3A
Cod--3A
Coffer-dam--3C
Compass--3C
Conch--3A
Coral--3A
Corsair--4
Corvette--3C
Crab--3A
Craft--3C
Crest--1
Crew--4
Crocodile--3A
Crow's-nest--3C
Cruise--3C
Current--1
Cutter--3C
Davit--3C
Deck--3C
Deep--1
Delta--2
Deluge--1
Depth--1
Dinghy--3C
Dive--3A, 3C, 4
Dock--3C
Dolphin--3A
Drift--3C
Drogher--3C
Drown--3C
Duck--3A
Eddy--1
Eel--3A
Embark--4
Fathom--1, 3A, 3C, 4
Felucca--3C
Ferry--3C
Figure-head--3C
Fin--3A
Fish--3A
Fleet--3C
Flipper--3A
Float--3C, 4
Flood--1
Flotilla--3C
Flounder--3A
Fluid--1
Fluke--3A
Foam--1
Fore--3C
Forecastle--3C
Frigate--3C
Frog--3A

Gaff--3C
Gale--3B
Gallant--3C
Galleon--3C
Galley--3C
Galliot--3C
Gallipagos (Galapagos) Islands--2
Gally--3A
Gam--3C
Gangway--3C
Gig--3C
Gill--3A
Glyptolepis--3A
Grampus--3A
Gulf--2
Gunwhale--3C
Gurry--3A
Halyard--3C
Harbor--2
Harpoon--3C, 4
Hatch, Hatchway--3C
Hawse--3C
Heave to--3C
Heel--3C
Helm--3C
Hermaphrodite--3C
Herring--3A
Hold--3C
Hull--3C
Ichthyology--3A
Inlet--2
Island, Isle--2
Isthmus--2
Jib--3C
Junk--3C
Keel--3C
Kelp--3A
Kelson--3C
Kentledge--3C
Knight-Head--3C
Knot--3C
Kraken--3A
Lagoon--2
Landsman, Land-lubber--4
Lanyard--3C
Larboard--3C
Launch--3C
Lay--4
Lee--3C
Leech--3A
Leviathan--3A
Lighthouse--3C
Liner--3C
Liquid--1
Lobster--3A
Lugger--3C

Mackerel--3A
Maelstrom--1
Main--1
Man-of-war--3C
Marine, Mariner--1, 3A, 4
Maritime--1
Marling-Spike--3C
Mast--3C
Mate--4
Merchant, Merchant-Man--3C, 4
Mermaid--4
Miz(z)en--3C
Mollusca--3A
Mollymeaux--3A
Moor--3C
Mullet--3A
Mussel--3A
Mutiny, Mutineer--4
Nautical--1, 3C, 4
Nautilus--3A
Navigate, Navigator--4
Navy--3C, 4
Neptune--4
Nippers--3A
Oakum--3C
Oar--3C
Ocean--1
Offing--3C
Ork--3A
Orlop--3C
Outrigger--3C
Oyster--3A
Pacific--1
Packet--3C
Paddle--3C
Passage--3C
Pearl--3A
Peninsula--2
Periwinkle--3A
Pier--3C
Pirate--4
Pitch--3C
Plank--3C
Polynesia--2
Polyp--3A
Pontoon--3C
Poop--3C
Porpoise--3A
Port--2
Privateer--4
Proa--3C
Prow--3C
Pterichthys--3A
Quadrant--3C
Quay--2
Reef--2

Rib--3C
Rig, Rigging--3C
Ripple--1
Roll--3A, 3C
Row--3C
Royal--3C
Rudder--3C
Run--3C
Sail--3C
Sailor--4
Salmon--3A
Salt--4
Sampson-Post--3C
Sand-bar--2
Scale--3A
Schooner--3C
Scud--1
Scupper--3C
Scuttle--3C
Sea--1, 4
Seal--3A
Seine--3C
Sextant--3C
Shad--3A
Shallop--3C
Shark--3A
Sheer--3C
Sheet--3C
Shell--3A
Ship--3C
Shoal--2, 3A
Shore--2
Shrimp--3A
Shroud--3C
Silver-head--3A
Skiff--3C
Skipper--4
Skrimshander--4
Sloop--3C
Snatch-block--3C
Sound, Sounding--2, 3A, 3C
Sou'-wester--3B
Spanker--3C
Spar--3C
Specksynder--4
Sperm, Spermaciti, Spermacetti,
   Parmacetti--3A
Spile--3C
Spout--3A
Sprat--3A
Spray--1
Squall--3B
Squid--3A
Starboard--3C
State-room--3C
Steamer--3C

Steerage--3C, 4
Steersman--4
Stem--3C
Stern--3C
Steward--4
Stove--3C
Strait--2
Strand--2
Stream--1
Sturgeon--3A
Surf--1
Swan--3A
Swell--1
Swim--3A, 4
Tack--3C
Tadpole--3A
Taffrail--3C
Tar--4
Tempest--3B
Terrapin--3A
Tide--1
Tiller--3C
Top, Top-sail--3C
Torf-Egill--4
Tortoise, Turtle--3A
Trade--3B
Transom--3C
Trick--4
Trough--1
Trout--3A
Truck--3C
Try-works--3C
Tug--3C
Vessel--3C
Vortex--1
Voyage--3C
Wade--4
Wake--1
Walrus--3A
Wash--1
Water--1
Wave--1
Whale--3A
Wharf--2
Whirlpool--1
Windlass--3C
Windward--3C
Wriggle-tail--3A
Xiphius Platypterus--3A
Yacht--3C
Yard--3C
Yaw--3C
Yawl--3C
Yellow-back--3A

Semantic Classification of the Sea Vocabulary

1. <u>PRIMARY SEA TERMS</u>

Abyss
Aquatic
Atlantic
Billows
Breaker
Brine
Bubble
Caribbean
Crest
Current
Deep
Deluge
Depth
Eddy
Fathom
Flood
Fluid
Foam
Liquid
Maelstrom
Main
Marine
Maritime
Nautical
Ocean
Pacific
Ripple
Scud
Sea
Spray
Stream
Surf
Swell
Tide
Trough
Vortex
Wake
Wash
Water
Wave
Whirlpool

2. <u>SECONDARY SEA TERMS</u>

Archipelago
Ashore
Atoll
Bay
Beach
Canal
Cape

Coast
Delta
Gallipagos (Galapagos) Islands
Gulf
Harbor
Inlet
Island, Isle
Isthmus
Lagoon
Peninsula
Polynesia
Port
Quay
Reef
Sand-bar
Shoal
Shore
Sounding
Strait
Strand

3A. <u>TERTIARY SEA TERMS</u>

Albatros(s)
Albicore
Alewife
Alligator
Ambergris
Baleen
Barnacle
Blow
Blubber
Boneeta
Booby
Breach
Brit
Cachalot
Cephalaspis
Cetology
Chevalier
Chondropterygii
Clam
Cockle
Cod
Conch
Coral
Crab
Crocodile
Dive
Dolphin
Duck
Eel
Fathom

Fin
Fish
Flipper
Flounder
Fluke
Frog
Gally
Gill
Glyptolepis
Grampus
Gurry
Herring
Ichthyology
Kelp
Kraken
Leech
Leviathan
Lobster
Mackerel
Marine
Mollusca
Mollymeaux
Mullet
Mussel
Nautilus
Nippers
Ork
Oyster
Pearl
Periwinkle
Polyp
Porpoise
Pterichthys
Roll
Salmon
Scale
Seal
Shad
Shark
Shell
Shrimp
Silver-head
Sound
Sperm, Spermaciti, Spermacetti,
  Parmacetti
Spout
Sprat
Squid
Sturgeon
Swan
Swim
Tadpole
Terrapin
Tortoise, Turtle
Trout
Walrus

Whale
Wriggle-tail
Xiphius Platypterus
Yellow-back

3B. TERTIARY SEA TERMS

Calm
Gale
Sou'-wester
Squall
Tempest
Trade

3C. TERTIARY SEA TERMS

Abeam
Adrift
Afloat
Aft
Aloft
Anchor
Argosy
Ark
Astern
Barge
Bark, Barque
Binnacle
Boat
Bob-stay
Boom
Bow
Brail
Brig
Brigantine
Broach to
Bulkhead
Bulwark
Buoy
Cabin
Caboose
Canoe
Canvas(s)
Capstan
Cat-head
Chart
Chronometer
Clipper
Coffer-dam
Compass
Corvette
Craft
Crow's-nest
Cruise

Cutter
Davit
Deck
Dinghy
Dive
Dock
Drift
Drogher
Drown
Fathom
Felucca
Ferry
Figure-head
Fleet
Float
Flotilla
Fore
Forecastle
Frigate
Gaff
Gallant
Galleon
Galley
Galliot
Gam
Gangway
Gig
Gunwhale
Halyard
Harpoon
Hatch, Hatchway
Hawse
Heave to
Heel
Helm
Hermaphrodite
Hold
Hull
Jib
Junk
Keel
Kelson
Kentledge
Knight-head
Knot
Lanyard
Larboard
Launch
Lee
Lighthouse
Liner
Lugger
Man-of-war
Marling-spike
Mast
Merchant, Merchant-man

Miz(z)en
Moor
Nautical
Navy
Oakum
Oar
Offing
Orlop
Outrigger
Packet
Paddle
Passage
Pier
Pitch
Plank
Pontoon
Poop
Proa
Prow
Quadrant
Reef
Rib
Rig, Rigging
Roll
Row
Royal
Rudder
Run
Sail
Sampson-post
Schooner
Scupper
Scuttle
Seine
Sextant
Shallop
Sheer
Sheet
Ship
Shroud
Skiff
Sloop
Snatch-block
Soundings
Spanker
Spar
Spile
Starboard
State-room
Steamer
Steerage
Stem
Stern
Stove
Tack
Taffrail

```
Tiller
Top, Top-sail
Transom
Truck
Try-works
Tug
Vessel
Voyage
Wharf
Windlass
Windward
Yacht
Yard
Yaw
Yawl
```

4. QUATERNARY SEA TERMS

```
Afloat
Bucanier
Captain
Castaway
Corsair
Crew
Dive
Embark
Fathom
Float
Harpooneer
Landsman, Land-lubber
Lay
Mariner
Mate
Merchantman
Mermaid
Mutiny, Mutineer
Nautical
Navigate, Navigator
Navy
Neptune
Pirate
Polynesian
Privateer
Sailor
Salt
Seaman
Skipper
Skrimshander
Specksynder
Steerage
Steersman
Steward
Swim
Tar
Trick
Wade
```

APPENDIX *B*
Syntactics

The Sea Vocabulary: An Alphabetical Listing
Denoting Syntactic Classification

Abeam--adv
Abyss--n
Adrift--adv
Afloat--adj, adv
Aft--adv, prep
Albatros(s)--n
Albicore--n
Alewife--n
Alligator--n
Aloft--adv
Ambergris--n
Anchor--n, v, adj
Aquatic--adj
Archipelago--n
Argosy--n
Ark--n
Ashore--adj, adv
Astern--adv
Atlantic--n
Atoll--n
Baleen--n
Barge--n
Bark, Barque--n
Barnacle--n, adj
Bay--n, adj
Beach--n, v
Billows--n, adj
Binnacle--n, adj
Blow--v
Blubber--n, adj
Boat--n, adj
Bob-stay--n
Boneeta--n
Booby--n

Boom--n, adv
Bow--n, adj, adv
Brail--n
Breach--n, v
Breaker--n
Brig--n, adj
Brigantine--n, adj
Brine--n, adj
Brit--n
Broach to--v
Bubble--n, v
Bucanier--n, adj
Bulkhead--n
Bulwark--n
Buoy--n, v
Cabin--n, adj
Caboose--n
Cachalot--n
Calm--n, v
Canal--n
Canoe--n, adj
Canvas(s)--n, adj
Cape--n, adj
Capstan--n, adj
Captain--n, adj
Caribbean--adj
Castaway--n, adj
Cat-head--n
Cephalaspis--n
Cetology--n, adj
Chart--n
Chevalier--n
Chondropterygii--n
Chronometer--n

Clam--n, adj
Clipper--n, adj
Coast--n, v, adj
Cockle--n
Cod--n
Coffer-dam--n
Compass--n
Conch--n, adj
Coral--n, adj
Corsair--n
Corvette--n
Crab--n
Craft--n, adj
Crest--n
Crew--n, adj
Crocodile--n
Crow's-nest--n
Cruise--n, v, adj, adv
Current--n
Cutter--n, adj
Davit--n
Deck--n, adj, adv
Deep--n
Delta--n
Deluge--n
Depth--n
Dinghy--n
Dive--n, v, adj
Dock--n, v, adj
Dolphin--n, adj
Drift--v
Drogher--n
Drown--v, adj
Duck--n
Eddy--n, v, adj
Eel--n, adj
Embark--v
Fathom--n, adj, adv
Felucca--n
Ferry--n
Figure-head--n
Fin--n, adj
Fish--n, v, adj
Fleet--n, adj
Flipper--n
Float--n, v, adj
Flood--n, v, adj
Flotilla--n
Flounder--n
Fluid--n
Fluke--n, v
Foam--n, v, adj, adv
Fore--n, adj, adv, prep
Forecastle--n, adj
Frigate--n, adj
Frog--n

Gaff--n
Gale--n
Gallant--adj
Galleon--n
Galley--n
Galliot--n, adj
Gallipagos (Galapagos) Islands--n
Gally--v, adj
Gam--n
Gangway--n
Gig--n, adj
Gill--n
Glyptolepis--n
Grampus--n, adj
Gulf--n
Gunwhale--n, adv
Gurry--n
Halyard--n
Harbor--n, adj
Harpoon--n, v, adj
Hatch, Hatchway--n
Hawse--n, adj
Heave to--v
Heel--v
Helm--n, adj, adv
Hermaphrodite--n
Herring--n
Hold--n
Hull--n, v, adj
Icthyology--n
Inlet--n
Island, Isle--n, adj
Isthmus--n
Jib--n, adj, adv
Junk--n
Keel--n, v, adj
Kelp--n, adj
Kelson--n
Kentledge--n
Knight-head--n
Knot--n
Kraken--n
Lagoon--n
Landsman, Land-lubber--n, adj
Lanyard--n
Larboard--n, adj, adv
Launch--n
Lay--n, v
Lee--n, adj, adv
Leech--n
Leviathan--n, adj
Lighthouse--n, adj
Liner--n
Liquid--adj
Lobster--n
Lugger--n

Mackerel--n
Maelstrom--n
Main--n, adv
Man-of-war--n, adj
Marine, Mariner--n, adj
Maritime--adj
Marling-spike--n
Mast--n, adj
Mate--n, adj, adv
Merchant, Merchant-man--n, adj
Mermaid--n, adj
Miz(z)en--n, adj
Mollusca--n
Mollymeaux--n
Moor--n, v
Mullet--n
Mussel--n
Mutiny, Mutineer--n, v, adj
Nautical--adj, adv
Nautilus--n, adj
Navigate, Navigator--n, v. adj
Navy--n, adj
Neptune--n
Nippers--n
Oakum--n
Oar--n
Ocean--n, adj, adv
Offing--n
Ork--n
Orlop--n
Outrigger--n
Oyster--n, adj
Pacific--n, adj
Packet--n, adj
Paddle--n, v
Passage--n, adj
Pearl--n, adj
Peninsula--n
Periwinkle--n
Pier--n
Pirate--n, adj
Pitch--n, v
Plank--n
Polynesia--n, adj
Polyp--n
Pontoon--n
Poop--n
Porpoise--n, adj
Port--n, adj
Proa--n
Prow--n, adj
Pterichthys--n
Quadrant--n
Quay--n
Reef--n, v, adj
Rib--n

Rig, Rigging--n, v, adj
Ripple--n, v
Roll--n, v
Row--n, v
Royal--n, adj
Rudder--n
Run--n
Sail--n, v, adj, adv
Sailor--n, adj
Salmon--adv
Salt--n, adj
Sampson-Post--n
Sand-bar--n
Scale--n
Schooner--n, adj
Scud--n, v
Scupper--n, adj
Scuttle--n, v
Sea--n, adj, adv
Seal--n, adj, adv
Seine--n
Sextant--n
Shad--n
Shallop--n, adj
Shark--n, adj
Sheer--v
Sheet--n, adj
Shell--n, adj
Ship--n, v, adj, adv
Shoal--n, v
Shore--n, adj, adv
Shrimp--n
Shroud--n, adj
Silver-head--n
Skiff--n
Skipper--n, adj
Skrimshander--n, adj
Sloop--n, adj
Snatch-block--n
Sound, Sounding--n, v, adj
Sou'-wester--n, adj
Spanker--n
Spar--n, adj
Specksynder--n
Sperm, Spermaciti, Spermacetti,
   Parmacetti--n, adj
Spile--n
Spout--n, v, adj
Sprat--n
Spray--n
Squall--n, adj
Squid--n, adj
Starboard--n, adj
State-room--n
Steamer--n
Steerage--n, adj

```
Steersman--n
Stem--n, adv
Stern--n, adj, adv
Steward--n
Stove--v, adj
Strait--n
Strand--n
Stream--n
Sturgeon--n
Surf--n
Swan--n
Swell--n, v
Swim--n, v, adj
Tack--n, v
Tadpole--n
Taffrail--n, adj
Tar--n, adj
Tempest--n, adj
Terrapin--n
Tide--n, adj
Tiller--n
Top, Top-sail--n
Torf-Egill--n
Tortoise, Turtle--n, adj
Trade--n
Transom--n
Trick--n
Trough--n
Trout--n
Truck--n
Try-works--n
Tug--n
Vessel--n, adj
Vortex--n
Voyage--n, v, adv
Wade--v
Wake--n, adv
Walrus--n
Wash--v
Water--n, v, adj, adv
Wave--n
Whale--n, v, adj
Wharf--n
Whrilpool--n
Windlass--n, adj
Windward--adj, adv
Wriggle-tail--n
Xiphius Platypterus--n
Yacht--n
Yard--n, adj
Yaw--n, v
Yawl--n
Yellow-back--n
```

Syntactic Classification of the Sea Vocabulary

a. NOUNS

Abyss
Albatros(s)
Albicore
Alewife
Alligator
Ambergris
Anchor
Archipelago
Argosy
Ark
Atlantic
Atoll
Baleen
Barge
Bark, Barque
Barnacle
Bay
Beach
Billows
Binnacle
Blubber
Boat
Bob-stay
Boneeta
Booby
Boom
Bow
Brail
Breach
Breaker
Brig
Brigantine
Brine
Brit
Bubble
Bucanier
Bulkhead
Bulwark
Buoy
Cabin
Caboose
Cachalot
Calm
Canal
Canoe
Canvas(s)
Cape
Capstan
Captain
Castaway
Cat-head
Cephalaspis

Cetology
Chart
Chevalier
Chondropterygii
Chronometer
Clam
Clipper
Coast
Cockle
Cod
Coffer-dam
Compass
Conch
Coral
Corsair
Corvette
Crab
Craft
Crest
Crew
Crocodile
Crow's-nest
Cruise
Current
Cutter
Davit
Deck
Deep
Delta
Deluge
Depth
Dinghy
Dive
Dock
Dolphin
Drogher
Duck
Eddy
Eel
Fathom
Felucca
Ferry
Figure-head
Fin
Fish
Fleet
Flipper
Float
Flood
Flotilla
Flounder
Fluid
Fluke
Foam

Fore
Forecastle
Frigate
Frog
Gaff
Gale
Galleon
Galley
Galliot
Gallipagos (Galapagos) Islands
Gam
Gangway
Gig
Gill
Glyptolepis
Grampus
Gulf
Gunwhale
Gurry
Halyard
Harbor
Harpoon
Hatch, Hatchway
Hawse
Helm
Hermaphrodite
Herring
Hold
Hull
Ichthyology
Inlet
Island, Isle
Isthmus
Jib
Junk
Keel
Kelp
Kelson
Kentledge
Knight-head
Knot
Kraken
Lagoon
Landsman, Land-lubber
Lanyard
Larboard
Launch
Lay
Lee
Leech
Leviathan
Lighthouse
Liner
Lobster
Lugger
Mackerel

Maelstrom
Main
Man-of-war
Marine, Mariner
Marling-spike
Mast
Mate
Merchant, Merchant-man
Mermaid
Miz(z)en
Mollusca
Mollymeaux
Moor
Mullet
Mussel
Mutiny, Mutineer
Nautilus
Navigate, Navigator
Navy
Neptune
Nippers
Oakum
Oar
Ocean
Offing
Ork
Orlop
Outrigger
Oyster
Pacific
Packet
Paddle
Passage
Pearl
Peninsula
Periwinkle
Pier
Pirate
Pitch
Plank
Polynesia
Polyp
Pontoon
Poop
Porpoise
Port
Proa
Prow
Pterichthys
Quadrant
Quay
Reef
Rib
Rig, Rigging
Ripple
Roll

Row
Royal
Rudder
Run
Sail
Sailor
Salt
Sampson-Post
Sand-bar
Scale
Schooner
Scud
Scupper
Scuttle
Sea
Seal
Seine
Sextant
Shad
Shallop
Shark
Sheet
Shell
Ship
Shoal
Shore
Shrimp
Shroud
Silver-head
Skiff
Skipper
Skrimshander
Sloop
Snatch-block
Sound, Sounding
Sou'-wester
Spanker
Spar
Specksynder
Sperm, Spermaciti, Spermacetti,
   Parmacetti
Spile
Spout
Sprat
Spray
Squall
Squid
Starboard
State-room
Steamer
Steerage
Steersman
Stem
Stern
Steward
Strait

Strand
Stream
Sturgeon
Surf
Swan
Swell
Swim
Tack
Tadpole
Taffrail
Tar
Tempest
Tide
Tiller
Top, Top-sail
Torf-Egill
Tortoise, Turtle
Trade
Transom
Trick
Trough
Trout
Truck
Try-works
Tug
Vessel
Voyage
Wake
Walrus
Water
Wave
Whale
Wharf
Whirlpool
Windlass
Wriggle-tail
Xiphius Platypterus
Yacht
Yard
Yaw
Yawl
Yellow-back

b. VERBS

Anchor
Beach
Blow
Breach
Broach to
Bubble
Buoy
Calm
Coast
Cruise

Dive
Dock
Drift
Drown
Eddy
Embark
Fish
Float
Flood
Fluke
Foam
Gally
Harpoon
Heave to
Heel
Hull
Keel
Lay
Moor
Mutiny
Navigate
Paddle
Pitch
Reef
Rig
Ripple
Roll
Row
Sail
Scud
Scuttle
Seal
Sheer
Ship
Shoal
Sound
Spout
Stove
Swell
Swim
Tack
Voyage
Wash
Water
Whale
Yaw

c.   ADJECTIVES

Afloat
Anchor
Aquatic
Ashore
Barnacle
Bay

Billows
Binnacle
Blubber
Boat
Bow
Brig
Brigantine
Brine
Bucanier
Cabin
Canoe
Canvas(s)
Cape
Capstan
Captain
Caribbean
Castaway
Cetology
Clam
Clipper
Coast
Conch
Coral
Craft
Crew
Cruise
Cutter
Deck
Dive
Dock
Dolphin
Drown
Eddy
Eel
Fathom
Fin
Fish
Fleet
Float
Flood
Foam
Fore
Forecastle
Frigate
Gallant
Galliot
Gally
Gig
Grampus
Harbor
Harpoon
Hawse
Helm
Hull
Island, Isle
Jib

Keel
Kelp
Landsman, Land-lubber
Larboard
Lee
Leviathan
Lighthouse
Liquid
Man-of-war
Marine
Maritime
Mast
Mate
Merchant, Merchant-man
Mermaid
Miz(z)en
Mutiny, Mutineer
Nautical
Nautilus
Navigate, Navigator
Navy
Ocean
Oyster
Pacific
Packet
Passage
Pearl
Pirate
Polynesia
Porpoise
Port
Prow
Reef
Rig, Rigging
Royal
Sail
Sailor
Salt
Schooner
Scupper
Sea
Seal
Shallop
Shark
Sheet
Shell
Ship
Shore
Shroud
Skipper
Skrimshander
Sloop
Sound, Sounding
Sou'-wester
Spar
Sperm, Spermaciti, Spermacetti,
   Parmacetti

Spout
Squall
Squid
Starboard
Steerage
Stern
Stove
Swim
Taffrail
Tar
Tempest
Tide
Tortoise, Turtle
Vessel
Water
Whale
Windlass
Windward
Yard

d.   ADVERBS

Abeam
Adrift
Afloat
Aft
Aloft
Ashore
Astern
Boom
Bow
Cruise
Deck
Fathom
Foam
Fore
Gunwhale
Helm
Jib
Larboard
Lee
Main
Mate
Nautical
Ocean
Sail
Salmon
Sea
Ship
Shore
Stem
Stern
Voyage
Wake
Water
Windward

APPENDIX C
Compounding in the Sea Novels

*=Those compounds which are novel-specific.

1. TYPEE

    go-ashore*
    bread-barge*
    boat-hook
    whale-boat
    bob-stay*
    bowsprit
    bulkhead
    war-canoes
    canoe-house*
    canoe-shaped*
    war-conches
    coral-rock*
    three-deckers
    fishing-pole*
    figure-head
    forecastle
    bull-frog*
    gangway
    gunwhale
    hatch-holes*
    helmsmen
    island-punch*
    knight-heads
    man-of-war
    mast-head
    mussel-shell*
    oar-blade*
    outrigger
    mother-of-pearl
    mother-of-pearl-handled*
    poop-down-haul*

    sea-biscuit
    sea-bread
    sea-captain
    sea-cook
    sea-fowl
    seaman
    sea-monsters
    sea-shell
    sea-shore
    sea-weed
    shell-fish*
    snatch-blocks
    spermaciti-whale*
    stern-sheets
    topsail
    tortoiseshell*
    cut-water*
    waterfalls
    watercourse
    whalebone

2. OMOO

    beach-de-mer*
    beach-comber*
    boatswain
    sail-boat
    steamboat
    bowsprit
    bulkhead
    canoe-building
    canoe-tree*

mail-canoe*
sea-canoe*
war-canoe
capstan-head*
conch-shell
war-conch
cruising-ground*
first-cutter*
berth-deck
gun-deck
three-decker
spar-deck
fisherman
fish-hooks*
fish-hunter*
fish-spear
swordfish
whale-fishery
fore-chain
fore-hatch
fore-royal*
fore-top
forecastle
forecastle-square*
spanker-gaff*
galley-slave
gangway
gunwhale
jib-halyard*
hatchway
after-hatchway
jib-boom
flying-jib-boom
jib-halyards
knight-heads
landsman
landlubber
main-braces
man-of-war
man-of-war's-man
marling-spike
foremast
mast-head
shipmate
oarsmen
outrigger
pearl-oyster*
mother-of-pearl
side-port*
main-rigging
main-sail
topsail
fore-topsail
main-topsail
main-top-gallant-sail*
fellow-sailor

lee-scuppers
cabin-scuttle
sea-bear*
sea-beef
sea-biscuit
sea-breeze
sea-canoe*
sea-chest*
sea-clothing*
sea-day*
sea-faring
sea-life
seaman
sea-parlance
Sea-Parlor*
sea-port
sea-prophets*
sea-shore
sea-toss
sea-voyage
sea-water
seal-skin
jib-sheet
ship-biscuit*
ship-owner*
plague-ship*
off-shore
sloop-of-war
sperm-whale
stern-sheets
whaling-vessel*
fellow-voyager*
breakwater
watercourse
water-falls
high-water*
water-sprite*
right-whale*
whale-spouts*
whaling-cruise*
whirlpool
after-yards*
head-yards*
main-hard

3. MARDI

sea-beach*
bulkhead
blubber-spade*
boat-hook
boat-hatchet*
boats-crew-watches
starboard-quarter-boat's-watch*
life-boat*

pilot-boat
whale-boat
jib-boom
bowline
bow-paddler*
bow-shot*
bowsman*
bowsprit
canoe-building
canoe-fight*
canoe-load
canoe-yards*
war-canoe
castaway
clam-shells
coral-rimmed*
The-Heart-of-Black-Coral*
wave-crest*
quarter-deck
three-decker
Delta-grot*
Pearl-shell-diver's
finned-lions*
cuttle-fish*
fish-at-arms*
Fish-ponds*
flying-fish*
gold-fishes'
pilot-fish*
ray-fish*
star-fish*
sucking-fish*
sword-fish
Trigger-fish*
flood-gate
flood-tide
foam-flaked*
foam-white*
wide-foaming*
fore-brace*
fore-tack*
fore-top
forecastle
frigate-birds*
gangway
gunwhale
hatchway
main-hatch
jib-boom-end*
main-channel*
main-top*
foremast
fore-mast-head*
main-mast
mast-head
mizzen-mast

Royal-mast
topmast-stay*
watch-mate
merchantman
mizzen-top
ocean-chariot*
ocean-tombed*
oceanward*
Bow-Paddler*
paddle-blades*
Paddle-Song*
lily-pearl*
pearl-shell
rose-pearl*
porpoise-teeth*
dragon-prowed*
scroll-prowed*
sharp-prowed*
reef-bird*
reef-sashed*
reef-side*
reefing-jacket*
white-reefed*
fore-rigging
running-rigging*
foresail*
topsail
fore-topsail
main-sail
mat-sails*
sailaway*
sail-room
sail-set*
sky-sail-poles*
storm-sails*
top-sail
topsail-yard*
sand-bar
scupper-hole
deep-sea-lead*
Froth-of-the-Sea*
sea-beeves*
sea-blue
sea-biscuit
sea-captain
sea-cavalry*
sea-cavern*
sea-chamois*
sea-diver*
sea-dogs
sea-equipage*
sea-fight
sea-fowl
sea-gale
sea-girt*
sea-goat*

sea-god
sea-gull
sea-hawks*
sea-kelp*
sea-king
sea-kite*
sea-kraken*
sea-life
seamen
seamonsters
sea-moss*
sea-nettle*
sea-noddy*
sea-pacer*
sea-parlance
sea-porcupine's*
sea-ripples*
sea-rovings*
sea-sage*
sea-serpent
sea-shore
sea-side
sea-slugs*
sea-snakes*
sea-tailor*
sea-thyme*
sea-toss
sea-urchin*
sea-water
sea-weed
sea-winds
Devil-sharks*
shark-skin*
shark's-mouth*
Shark-Syllogism*
she-shark*
tiger-sharks
winding-sheets*
shell-work*
Fidus-Achates-ship*
ship-duels*
ship-shape
ships'-lengths*
shipwrecked
main-shore*
shore-cap*
shrimp-soup
silver-heads*
state-room*
steersman
sturgeon-forms*
surf-board*
flood-tide
noon-tide*
soul-tide*
tide-rips*

fore-top*
main-top*
top-block*
Torf-Egill*
fresh-water
salt-water*
water-bolts*
water-fowls*
water-kegs*
water-logged
water-side*
water-spouts*
water-tight*
wave-crest*
whale-boat*
whale-line
whale-shallop*
whalemen*
whirlpool*
whirlpool-column*
wriggle-tails*
fore-yard*
fore-top-gallant-yard*
main-yard
yellow-backs*

4.   REDBURN

blubber-boilers*
boatswain
fishing-boat
long-boat*
pilot-boat
steamboat
tug-boat*
jib-boom
flying-jib-boom*
spanker-boom*
bowline
bowsprit
bow-sprit-bitts*
starboard-main-top-gallant-
   bow-line*
bulkhead
cabin-boy
cabin-door
cabin-passenger*
cabin-table*
packet-captain*
sea-captain
cat-head
clipper-built*
Coast-of-Guinea-Man*
deck-passengers*
deck-tub*

forecastle-deck*
gun-deck
quarter-deck
between-decks*
dockgates*
dock-master*
dock-police*
Dock-Wall*
Dry-Dock*
salt-drogher*
figure-head
Fin-back
fisherman
flood-tide
fore-hatch
fore-top
fore-yard
forecastle
forecastle-deck*
forecastle-scuttle*
passengers'-galley*
gunwhale
booby-hatch*
hatchway
main-hatch
main-hatchway
helmsmen
jib-boom
flying-jib-boom
knight-heads
lee-beam
lee-scuppers
lighthouse
man-of-war's-man
foremast
jury-mast
mainnast
mainroyalmast
mast-head
one-masted*
top-gallant-mast
messmate
shipmate
merchantman
mizen-peaks*
mizzen-rigging*
mizzen-top
Ocean-Elephants*
ocean-life*
ocean-organ*
ocean-saloons*
oyster-cellar*
pier-head
Port-a-Ferry*
port-hole
sea-port

double-reefed-top-sails
reef-point
reef-tackles*
reef-topsail-breeze*
standing-rigging*
fast-sailing*
gaff-topsail-boots*
larboard-fore-top-sail-clew-
    line*
main-skysail*
moon-sails*
reef-topsail-breeze*
sailboat
sailing-master
sloop-sails*
storm-stay-sail
stun'-sail
t'-gallant-sail
topsail
top-sail-yard*
negro-sailors*
sailor-boy*
sailor-lanes*
sailor-man*
sailor-rig*
sailor-scrawls*
Sailor's-Snug-Harbor*
Sampson-Post*
weather-scuppers*
scuttle-butt
deep-sea-line*
salt-sea
sea-air
sea-beef
sea-biscuit
sea-blue
sea-boots
sea-cabinet*
sea-captain
sea-career
sea-chat*
sea-clowns*
sea-coal
sea-ditty*
sea-faring
sea-fight
sea-fowl
sea-going
sea-horses*
sea-life
seaman
able-seaman
ordinary-seaman*
sea-officer
sea-pieces*
sea-port

seaport
sea-potations*
sea-quadrilles*
sea-queen*
sea-service
sea-sick
sea-sickness*
sea-tyrants*
Sea-Wardrobe*
sea-weed
sea-worn
land-shark
packet-ships*
ship-building*
ship-papers*
shipwreck*
sloop-of-war
sloop-sails*
sperm-whale
steerage-passenger
steersman
stern-line
tortoise-shell
steam-tug*
flood-tide
bilge-water*
water-gate*
water-logged
water-proof*
water-rat*
jury-yards*
skysail-yards*

5. WHITE-JACKET

anchor-buoy*
anchor-button*
best-bower-anchors*
Bower-anchors*
sheet-anchor-man*
barge-men
boat-cloak*
boat-header*
boat-load*
boat-peg*
boatswain
bum-boats*
gun-boat*
market-boat*
shark-boat
shore-boat
steam-boat
stern-boat*
whale-boat
jib-boom

bow-chasers*
bowsprit
lee-bow*
weather-bow
war-brigs*
bulkhead
life-buoy
cabin-bars*
cabin-boy
cabin-door
cabin-floor*
war-canoe
capstan-bars
merchant-captain*
navy-captain*
sea-captain
clam-cart*
conch-shell
First-Cutter's
berth-deck
deck-ladders*
deck-officer*
gun-deck
half-deck*
main-deck*
main-deck-batteries*
quarter-deck
spar-deck
three-decker
dock-lopers*
dock-yards*
figure-head
fish-surgeon's*
flying-fish
gold-fish
shell-fish*
sword-fish
fleet-fighting*
fleet-surgeon's*
forecastle
forecastle-man*
fore-chains
fore-hatchway*
fore-hold*
fore-passage*
fore-peak*
fore-top
fore-t'gallant-mast-head*
fore-top-man*
fore-top-mast*
fore-top-mast-head*
fore-top-sail-yard*
fore-truck*
fore-yard
frigate-action*
frigate-executives*

frigate-merchantmen*
world-frigate*
galley-cook*
galley-slave
gangway
gig-men*
main-topsail-halyard*
stun'-sail-halyard*
hatchway
after-hatchway
main-hatchway
herring-net*
after-hold*
main-hold*
keel-hauling*
landsman
lee-bow*
lee-gangway*
lee-roll*
lee-yard-arm*
lighthouse
man-of-war
man-of-war's-man
horse-marine*
marine-orderly*
marine-sergeant*
fore-mast
main-mast
mast-head
mast-man*
mizzen-mast
quarter-master*
royal-mast
top-mast
boatswain's-mate*
mess-mate
messmate   ·
shipmate
top-mate*
watchmate
mizzen-shrouds*
mizzen-top
mizen-top-men*
mizzen-top-sail*
navy-regulation*
Navy-yard*
oarsman
ocean-wanderer*
ocean-warriors*
ocean-rover*
mother-of-pearl
pearl-shell
pier-head
bridle-port*
port-hole
sea-port

close-reefing*
double-reefed*
double-reefed-top-sail
full-rigged*
main-royal*
main-royal-mast*
main-royal-yard*
Royal-mast*
royal-stun'-sail*
royal-yard-men*
fore-topsail
gallant-sail
gallant-studding-sail
mainsail
main-sail
main-top-sail
main-topsail-yard*
sail-loft*
sail-maker*
Sail-maker's*
sailing-master
sail-of-the-line*
sail-proud*
sail-room
stun'-sail
stun'-sail-booms*
stun'-sail-halyard*
t'-gallant-sail
t'-gallant-studding-sail*
topsail
top-sail
try-sail*
wind-sail*
fellow-sailor
merchant-sailor*
lee-scupper
scupper-hole
scuttle-butt
salt-sea
sea-actions*
sea-air
sea-alcove*
sea-boots
sea-breeze
sea-chivalry*
sea-citizens*
sea-coast
sea-commanders*
sea-dandies*
sea-dog
sea-fencibles*
sea-fight
sea-fowl
sea-going
sea-green*
sea-gull

```
sea-king
sea-laws*
sea-lawyers*
sea-legs*
sea-lord*
seaman
able-seaman
sea-mittens*
sea-Newgate*
sea-numphs*
sea-officer
sea-patriots*
sea-pie*
sea-port
sea-reticules*
sea-rolls*
sea-scenery*
sea-serpent
sea-service
sea-Socrates*
sea-statutes*
sea-tallow*
sea-tussle*
sea-tutor*
sea-undertakers*
sea-vagabond*
sea-wardens*
sea-warriors*
sea-way*
sea-weed
seal-skin
shark-boat*
white-shark
flag-ship*
shipboard
ship-gossip*
ship-shape
ships-of-the-line*
ship-stores*
ship's-yeoman*
ship-underlings*
ship-work*
shipwrecked*
sloop of war
spanker-out-haul*
spar-deck*
sperm-whale
snow-squall*
starboard-quarter
starboard-watch*
steerage-way*
stern-galley*
damn-my-eyes-tar*
tempest-time'
half-tide*
loggerhead-turtles*
```

```
fresh-water
water-line
water-rimmed*
fore-top-sail-yard*
top-gallant-yard*
weather-top-gallant-yard-arm*
whirlpool
```

6. MOBY-DICK

```
alewives*
anchor-watch*
corner-anchored*
binnacle-watch*
blubber-hunter*
blubber-room*
boat-hook
boat-sail*
boat-spade*
boat-steerer*
jolly-boat*
sail-boat
whale-boat
jib-boom
bow-ends*
bowsprit
weather-bow
life-buoy
life-buoy-coffin*
coffin-canoes*
whale-canoe
Cape-Cod-man*
Cape-Horner*
sea-captain
castaway
clam-shell
codfish*
coffer-dam*
whaling-craft*
crow's-nest
quarter-deck
fathom-deep*
figure-head*
back-fin*
Fin-back
side-fin*
Fast-Fish*
fish-bones*
fisherman
fish-like
fish-spear
gold-fish
Gold-fishes'
Loose-Fish*
sword-fish
```

whale-fish*
whale-fishery
whaling-fleet*
flood-gate
flood-tide
foam-flakes*
foam-flaked
foam-fountain*
forecastle
top-gallant*
galliot-toed*
gangway
cabin-gangway*
gunwhale
hatchway
herring-shoals*
Knight-heads
landsman
lee-beam
lee-way
lighthouse
man-of-war
marlingspike
foremast
fore-mast
jury-mast
mast-head
stander-of-mast-heads*
top-mast
oarsmen
after-oarsmen*
ocean-fold*
ocean-inns*
ocean-perishing*
ocean-wide*
packet-tracks*
pier-head
sally-ports*
main-rigging
gallant-sail
main-sail
mainroyalmast
main-royalmast
sail-boat
sail-cloth*
sail-needles*
stun'-sail
t'-gallant-sail
topsail
sailor-belt*
cloud-scud*
cabin-scuttle
salt-sea
sea-boots
sea-coal
sea-coast

sea-commander
sea-crashing*
sea-custom*
sea-dog
sea-farings*
sea-fight
sea-fowl
sea-god
sea-going
sea-gudgeon*
Sea-hawk
sea-ivory*
sea-king
sea-line*
sea-lion
sea-loving*
seaman
sea-mark*
sea-outfit*
sea-pastures*
seaport
sea-port
sea-salt*
sea-shell
sea-sick
sea-side
sea-sofa*
sea-storm*
sea-taste*
sea-toss
sea-traditions*
sea-unicorn's*
sea-usages
sea-water
sea-weed
seal-skin
air-sharks*
shark-bone*
shark-skin
shark-white*
line-of-battle-ship*
ship-board
ship-keeper
ship-master*
ship-owners*
shipyards*
off-shore
sloop-of-war
Spouter-Inn*
spout-hole*
spout-hole's*
stern-wreck*
flood-tide
tide-beating*
tide-rip*
main-truck*

try-works*
discovery-vessel*
breakwater
headwater*
water-gazers*
water-land*
whalebone
whale-craft*
whale-cruisers*
whale-hater*
whale-hunter
whale-lance*
whale-line
whaling-pike*
whale-ports*
whale-spade*
whale-steak*
whale-trover*
whale-wise*
whirlpool

APPENDIX **D**
Metaphorical Activity
of the Sea Vocabulary

Land (Non-Sea) Objects Described in Sea Terms

OMOO

p. 28	one thousand fathoms of fine tappa
p. 201	the musquitoes [sic] here fairly eddied round us
p. 210	chased with streams of fire

MARDI

p. 194	the thought of things broke over me like returning billows
p. 194	A rush, a foam of recollections!
p. 194	tearful pearls beneath life's sea
p. 258	Flood-tide, and soul-tide to the brim! [goblet of wine]
p. 259	The mirth now blew a gale; like a ship's shrouds in a typhoon, every tendon vibrated
p. 265	Noon-tide rolls its flood
p. 516	before that fine flood of old wine
p. 555	Lo, Landmarks! granite continents upon whose flanks Time leaves its traces, like old tide-rips of diluvian seas
p. 558	[Yoomy's verses] came bubbling out of me, like live waters from a spring in a silver mine
p. 635	came a flood of fragrance

REDBURN

p. 141   under the lee of the rock

p. 245   [the grave] the harbor where they never weigh anchor

p. 248   on life's ocean [Carlo] was swept along

p. 249   that ever rolled its flood-tide of harmony

p. 250   let me gaze fathoms down into thy fathomless eye

p. 250   [organ music] a mixed and liquid sea of sound, that dashes its spray in my face. . . . soft, dulcet, dropping sounds, like silver oars in bubbling brooks

WHITE-JACKET

p. 44   in the rapid wake of these chapters [of the book]

p. 53   when a rumor was set afloat

p. 153   But a rich purple tide [port wine] soon settled the question

p. 193   each of whom in his own floating island [ship] is king

p. 210   such a flood of scented reminiscences steals over me

p. 398   We mortals are all on board a fast-sailing never-sinking world-frigate, on which God was the ship-wright; and she is but one craft in a Milky-Way fleet, of which God is the Lord High Admiral. . . . And believe not the hypochondriac dwellers below hatches, who will tell you, with a sneer, that our world-frigate is bound to no final harbor whatever, that our voyage will prove an endless circumnavigation of space.

p. 399   our world-frigate rushes by

p. 399   while on board our world-frigate

MOBY-DICK

p. 4   his restless pain,/ Like as the wounded whale

p. 4   By art is created that great Leviathan, called a Commonwealth

p. 6   Spain--a great whale stranded on the shores of Europe

p. 13   loitering under the shady lee of yonder warehouses

p. 16   the great flood-gates of the wonder-world swung open

p. 20   walls of Spouter Inn reminded one of the bulwarks of some condemned old raft

p. 27   ushered into a small room, cold as a clam

p. 44   the pulpit is its [the world's] prow

p. 44   Yes, the world's a ship on its passage out

p. 50   how gladly would I . . . sit on the hatches [benches, pews]
               there where you sit

p. 50   how gladly would I come down from this mast-head pulpit

p. 62   [Nantucket is] more lonely than the Eddystone lighthouse

p. 62   that to their very chairs and tables small clams will
               sometimes be found adhering, as to the backs of sea turtles

p. 63   [land directions] about keeping a yellow warehouse on our
               starboard

p. 130   he strikes into a sharp but noiseless squall of a horn-pipe
               right over the Grand Turk's head

p. 140   from the inscrutable tides of God

p. 152   this [dancing] is worse than pulling after whales in a calm

p. 233   with a frigate's anchors for my bridle-bits and fasces of
               harpoons for spurs

p. 244   The red tide now poured from all sides of the monster like
               brooks down a hill

p. 264   where in her murderous hold this frigate earth is ballasted

p. 272   That unsounded ocean you gasp in, is Life

p. 332   abandoned her upon the seas of life

p. 388   Teeth he accounted bits of ivory; heads he deemed but top-
               blocks; men themselves he lightly held for capstans

p. 396   and so form the white breakers of the milky way

p. 402   Are these thy Mother Carey's chickens, Perth? they [sparks]
               are always flying in thy wake

p. 409   the Spanish land-breeze, wantonly turned sailor, had gone to
               sea

p. 410   a hearse and its plumes floating over the ocean with the
               waves for the pall-bearers

p. 423   sky and air seemed vast out-bellying sails

p. 454   as the mighty iron Leviathan of the modern railway is so
               familiarly known

p. 458   Accursed fate! that the unconquerable captain in the soul
                should have such a craven mate

Sea Objects (or Men) Described in Land
(or Non-Sea) Terms

OMOO

p. 34   [fish] sporting under the bows like pups ashore

p. 316   Once more the sailor's cradle [ship] rocked under me

MARDI

p. 41   [the White Shark] stealing along like a spirit in the water

p. 256   the great waters chased each other like lions

p. 283   and swore by wave and billow

pp. 316-17   whale, having broken into the paddock/ of the lagoon

p. 367   Shoals, like nebulous vapors, shoreing the white surf of the
                Milky Way, against which the wrecked worlds are dashed

p. 368   I roll down my billow from afar

p. 432   each curling wave-crest a flame

p. 543   ten thousand foam-flaked dromedary-humps uprose

p. 644   the sea, like a harvest plain

REDBURN

p. 66   when the sea neighs and snorts

p. 294   [captain was] like a dandy circumnavigating the dress-circle

p. 294   as we plowed the watery prairie [the sea]

WHITE-JACKET

p. 23   a ship is a bit of terra firma

p. 54   The ship was like a great city, when some terrible calamity
                has overtaken it

p. 64   Hearts of oak are our ships

p. 74   a man-of-war is a city afloat

p. 75   a man-of-war is a lofty, walled, and garrisoned town . . . .
                a man-of-war rexembles a three-story house

p. 86   the ship being one vast wash-tub

p. 91   a man-of-war is that theatre [a continual theatre in the
               world]

p. 144   a three-decker is a city on the sea

p. 229   moor your boys fast to that best of harbors, the hearth-stone

p. 269   the ocean pawed its white hoofs to the spur

p. 270   our black hull butting the white sea with its broad bows
               like a ram

p. 376   wooden-walled Gomorrahs [ships] of the deep

p. 377   For the sea is the true Tophet

p. 377   as the sea . . . is the stable of brute monsters

p. 393   the frigate slowly gliding by like a black world in the water

MOBY-DICK

p. 3   The great Leviathan that maketh the seas to seethe like a
               boiling pan

p. 7   [aorta of the whale] larger in the fore than the main pipe
               of the water-works at London Bridge

p. 16   the wild and distant seas where he [the whale] rolled his
               island bulk

p. 16   the whale, . . . one grand hooded phantom, like a snow hill
               in the air

p. 51   when the ship of this base treacherous world has gone down
               beneath him

p. 60   the two tall masts buckling like Indian canes in land
               tornadoes

p. 63   pirates and privateers, though following the sea as highwaymen
               the road

p. 63   Merchant ships are but extension bridges; armed ones but
               floating forts

p. 63   [the Nantucketer] He lives on the sea, as prairie cocks in
               the prairie, he hides among the waves, he climbs them as
               chamois hunters climb the Alps

p. 67   her masts stood stiffly up like the spines of the three old
               kings of Cologne

p. 147 the warm waves blush like wine

p. 194 the whole squall roared, forked, and crackled around us like
      a white fire upon the prairie, in which, unconsumed, we were
      burning

p. 194 the waves curling and hissing around us like the erected
      crests of enraged serpents

p. 199 when all the waves rolled by like scrolls of silver

p. 203 As if the waves had been fullers, this craft was bleached
      like the skeleton of a stranded walrus

p. 235 like a mad battle steed that has lost its rider, the
      masterless ocean overruns the globe

p. 235 Like a savage tigress that tossing in the jungle overlays
      her own cubs, so the sea dashes even the mightiest whales
      against the rocks

p. 256 would have almost thought the whole round sea was one huge
      cheese, and those sharks the maggots in it

p. 263 An intense copper calm, like a universal yellow lotus, was
      more and more unfolding its noiseless measureless leaves
      upon the sea

p. 274 the drops [from the snapping line] fell like bits of broken
      glass on the water

p. 316 [the whale] kitten-like, he plays on the ocean as if it were
      a hearth

p. 324 we . . . saw successive pods of whales, eight or ten in each,
      swiftly going round and round, like multiplied spans of
      horses in a ring

p. 346 the spangled sea calm and cool, and flatly stretching away,
      all round, to the horizon, like gold-beater's skin hammered
      out to the extremest

p. 347 to swim in the open ocean is as easy to the practised
      swimmer as to ride in a spring-carriage ashore

p. 405 beholding the tranquil beauty and brilliancy of the ocean's
      skin, one forgets the tiger heart that pants beneath it; and
      would not willingly remember, that this velvet paw but
      conceals a remorseless fang

p. 405 the soft waves . . . like hearth-stone cats they purr against
      the gunwhale

p. 412 her three firm-seated graceful masts erectly poised . . .
      seemed as the three Horatii pirouetting on one sufficient
      steed

p. 447   the ocean grew still more smooth, seemed drawing a carpet
over its waves; seemed a noon-meadow, so serenely it spread

p. 447   Like noiseless nautilus shells, their light prows sped
through the sea

p. 448   among waves whose hand-clappings were suspended by exceeding
rapture

p. 449   the white whale now shook the slight cedar as a mildly cruel
cat her mouse

p. 454   The ship tore on; leaving such a furrow in the sea as when
a cannon-ball, missent, becomes a plough-share and turns up
the level field

p. 455   the torn, enraged waves he [Moby-Dick] shakes off, seem his
mane

p. 463   the sharks . . . apparently following them in the same
prescient way that vultures hover over the banners of
marching regiments

p. 464   the waters flashed for an instant like heaps of fountains

Men Described in Sea Terms

TYPEE

p. 191   all three thenceforth live together as harmoniously as so
many turtles [marriage customs]

OMOO

p. 11   teeth, looked absolutely sharkish when he laughed

p. 20   a party of girls . . . splashing the water like porpoises

p. 226   replied the doctor, like a snapping turtle

MARDI

p. 80   he was innocent as the bowsprit

p. 259   The mirth now blew a gale; like a ship's shrouds in a
Typhoon, every tendon vibrated

p. 275   his arm waved strong as the back bone of the shark; yea,
his voice grew sonorous as a conch

p. 307   Their chief . . . was a being, whose cheeks were of the
color of the red coral

p. 482   they [warriors] made a commotion like shoals of herring

p. 507   I am a lobster, a mackerel, any thing you please

p. 620   Like helmless vessels, tempest-tossed, our only anchorage is
              when we founder

p. 650   She [Hautia] is deeper than the sea

p. 650   I [Hautia], the vortex that draws all in

REDBURN

p. 66   [human body] which, indeed, is something like a ship

pp. 87-88   [Jack Blunt] looked/ like a fat porpoise, standing on end.
              He had a round face, too, like a walrus

p. 139   he has but drifted along with that great tide [the evils of
              being a sailor], which, perhaps, has two flows for one ebb

p. 245   "He's gone to the harbor where they never weigh anchor"

p. 250   let me gaze fathoms down into thy fathomless eye

p. 255   They said he [Harry Bolton] carried two mizen-peaks [his
              swallow-tailed coat] at his stern

p. 292   They die, like the billows that break on the shore

p. 309   here they all came to anchor before the bar

p. 309   [sailors] like rootless sea-weed

WHITE-JACKET

pp. 10-11   [crew members, called Troglodites] come out into the day,
              like terrapins/ from their caves

p. 12   Boatswain's mates whistle around White Jacket like hawks
              screaming in a gale

p. 34   [Mad Jack] Like so many ship's shrouds, his muscles and
              tendons are all set true, trim, and taut; he is braced up
              fore and aft, like a ship on the wind. His broad chest is
              a bulk-head, that dams off the gale; and his nose is an
              aquiline, that divides it in two, like a keel.

p. 48   to stir the stagnant current in our poor old commodore's
              torpid veins

p. 59   [the mess-cook, chasing the crew out of his galley] you've
              all had enough; so sail away out of this, and let me clear
              up the wreck

p. 110   our ribbed chests, like the ribbed bows of a frigate, are as
              bulkheads to dam off an onset

p. 187   [Bland, the master-at-arms] his intrepidity, I say, is now
                fearlessly gliding among them, like a disarmed sword-fish
                among ferocious white-sharks

p. 259   a sailor [Dr. Cuticle's patient] with an arm like a royal-
                mast and a thigh like a windlass

p. 308   [the master-at-arms to Leggs] top your boom and sail large,
                now

p. 318   We were like dolphin among the flying-fish

p. 380   the man-of-war's-man rolls round the world like a billow

MOBY-DICK

p. 4   Like as the wounded whale to shore flies thro' the maine

p. 17   with anxious grapnels I had sounded my pocket [Ishmael]

p. 23   with noble shoulders, and a chest like a coffer-dam
                [Bulkington]

p. 27   [Queequeg] he's come to anchor somewhere

p. 29   as if a parcel of dark green frogs were running up the
                trunks of young palms [what Queequeg's legs looked like]

p. 39   and there these silent islands of men and women sat

p. 41   we are too much like oysters observing the sun through the
                water

p. 44   [Father Mapple's voice] like the continual tolling of a bell
                in a ship

p. 45   yet what depths of the soul does Jonah's deep sea-line sound

p. 49   And now behold Jonah taken up as an anchor and dropped

p. 50   [Jonah] his ears, like two sea-shells, still multitudinously
                murmuring of the ocean

p. 51   top-gallant delight is to him . . . whom all the waves of
                the billows of the seas of the boisterous mob can never
                shake from this sure keel of the Ages [God] [Father Mapple's
                sermon]

p. 60   the captain, a gaunt rib of the sea

p. 60   slightly tapping his stern in mid-somerset [Queequeg]

p. 60   Queequeg kill-e big whale [for man]

p. 61   From that hour I clove to Queequeg like a barnacle

p. 62   they [people] are . . . made an utter island of by the ocean

p. 69   I'll take that leg away from thy stern

p. 75   the squall's [Peleg's anger] gone off to leeward, I think

p. 85   no harpooner is worth a screw who ain't pretty sharkish

p. 86   A confluent small-pox had in all directions flowed over his
             [the prophet's] face, and left it like the complicated
             ribbed bed of a torrent, when the rushing waters have been
             dried up

p. 103   like a patient chronometer, his interior vitality was
             warranted to do well in all climates [Starbuck]

p. 103   the wild watery loneliness of his [Starbuck's] life

p. 107   [Daggoo's earrings were] so large that the sailors called
             them ring-bolts, and would talk of securing the top-sail
             halyards to them

p. 110   [Ahab] like his dismasted craft

p. 114   as if, like the dying whale, my [Ahab's] final jets were the
             strongest and fullest of trouble

p. 131   Ahab presided like a mute, maned sea-lion on the white coral
             beach

p. 133   they filled their bellies like Indian ships all day

p. 136   Washington, too, stands high aloft on his towering main-mast
             in Baltimore

p. 136   Admiral Nelson . . . stands his mast-head in Trafalgar Square

p. 149   gay as a frigate's pennant [Stubb about his wife]

p. 191   the noble negro to every roll of the sea harmoniously rolled
             his fine form

p. 241   All men live enveloped in whale-lines

p. 261   like the great whale, retain, o man! in all seasons a
             temperature of thine own

p. 289   the enormous mass [Tashtego and the bucket]

p. 321   Ahab's brow was left gaunt and ribbed, like the black sand
             beach after some stormy tide has been gnawing it

p. 326   amid the tornadoed Atlantic of my being

p. 332   though the gentleman had originally harpooned the lady . . .
             when a subsequent gentleman reharpooned her . . . along with
             whatever harpoon might have been found sticking in her

p. 339   All their noses upwardly projected from their faces like so
                many jib-booms

p. 348   my fingers felt like eels, and began, as it were, to
                serpentine and spiralize

p. 364   Ahab, putting out his ivory leg, and crossing the ivory arm
                (like two sword-fish blades)

p. 365   my boat's crew could only trim dish, by sitting all their
                sterns on the outer gunwhale

p. 366   I clung to that like a sucking fish

p. 395   And like circles on the water, which, as they grow fainter,
                expand, so his eyes seemed rounding and rounding, like the
                rings of Eternity [Queequeg's]

p. 445   we are turned round and round in this world, like yonder
                windlass, and Fate is the handspike

p. 455   to that one fatal goal which Ahab their one lord and keel
                did point to

p. 457   like seals from a sea-side cave [Ahab and men under the boat]

p. 459   I feel strained, half stranded, as ropes that tow dismasted
                frigates in a gale . . . But . . . know that Ahab's hawser
                tows his purpose yet

Sea Objects Described in Terms of Other Sea Objects

OMOO

p. 21   [whale boats] turned up like tortoises on the beach

MARDI

p. 40   tusk-teeth overlap its [the Bone Shark's] jaws like those of
                the walrus

p. 161   fleets of canoes, darting hither and thither like frighted
                water-fowls

p. 162   like a gull over a smooth lagoon [the shallop]

p. 482   [Ziani's feluccas] all flying, like frightened water-fowl
                from a lake

REDBURN

p. 7   a great whale, as big as a ship

p. 165   each Liverpool dock is a walled town . . . or rather, it is
             a small archipelago . . . For, in itself, each ship is an
             island, a floating colony of the tribe to which it belongs

p. 165   each ship is an island

p. 166   a multitude of little salt-droghers, rigged like sloops

p. 181   short sea-grass, . . . like so many leeches, had fastened to
             our planks

p. 289   the Highlander rose and fell like some vast buoy on the water

p. 300   covered with white sloop-sails like fleets of swans

WHITE-JACKET

p. 153   [puncheons] looked like venerable old loggerhead-turtles

p. 193   emperor of the whole oaken archipelago [a commodore over a
             group of ships]

MOBY-DICK

title page
and p. 4   Leviathan . . . at his breath spouts out a sea

p. 7   [fish] Gathered in shoals immense, like floating islands

p. 12   [Manhattan] belted round by wharves as Indian isles by coral
             reefs

p. 21   when, this corner-anchored old ark rocked so furiously

p. 61   stood eyeing the boom as if it were the lower jaw of an
             exasperated whale

p. 62   to their very chairs and tables small clams will sometimes
             be found adhering, as to the backs of sea turtles

p. 63   those on deck stood eyeing the boom as if it were the lower
             jaw of an exasperated whale

p. 116   ere the Pequod's weedy hull rolls side by side with the
             barnacled hulls of the leviathan

p. 127   that line streaks him [mealy-mouthed porpoise] from stem to
             stern

p. 159   to reach the fathom-deep life of the whale

p. 177   thou Chilean whale, marked like an old tortoise with mystic
             hieroglyphics upon the back

p. 177   thou famed leviathan, scarred like an iceberg

p. 227   afloat the vast bulk of him is out of sight, like a launched
                line-of-battle ship

p. 244   The boat now flew through the boiling water like a shark all
                fins

p. 281   with his [the whale's] prodigious jaw . . . for all the
                world like a ship's jib-boom

p. 281   The jaw [whale's] is dragged on board, as if it were an
                anchor

p. 296   the white-bone or swell at his [the whale's] broad muzzle
                was a dashed one, like the swell formed when two hostile
                currents meet

p. 322   [whales] helplessly floated like water-logged dismantled
                ships on the sea

p. 323   our beset boat was like a ship mobbed by ice-isles

p. 337   by the eddying cloud of vulture sea-fowl that circled

p. 364   it was like sitting in the fluke of an anchor [sitting on a
                blubber-hook]

p. 374   When the vast body [the whale] had at last been stripped of
                its fathom-deep enfoldings

p. 378   [the whale's] intestines . . . lie in him like great cables
                and hausers coiled away in the subterranean orlop-deck of a
                line-of-battle-ship

p. 396   and the ocean's invisible flood-tide lifted him higher and
                higher towards his destined heaven

p. 410   waves . . . gently chafed the whale's broad flank, like soft
                surf upon a beach

p. 421   [sails] went eddying away to leeward, like the feathers of
                an albatross

p. 448   soon the fore part of him [Moby-Dick] slowly rose from the
                water

p. 453   the creature's [whale's] future wake through the darkness is
                almost as established to the sagacious mind of the hunter as
                the pilot's coast is to him

p. 455   in his immeasurable bravadoes the white whale tossed himself
                salmon-like to Heaven

p. 457   dragged the more involved boats of Stubb and Flask towards
                his flukes; dashed them together like two rolling husks on
                a surf-beaten beach

p. 469   the great shroud of the sea rolled on as it rolled five
              thousand years ago [final words in the book]

Personification of Sea Objects

MARDI

p. 50   And flung abroad over the visible creation was the sun-
              spangled, azure, rustling robe of the ocean, ermined with
              wave crests

p. 143   My prow shall keep kissing the waters

p. 482   in her [the sea's] mad gales of passions

p. 633   Foam played before them as they darted on

REDBURN

p. 241   That irresistable wrestler, sea-sickness

p. 311   we almost counteracted the play of the paddles

WHITE-JACKET

p. 47   when the face of the ocean was black

p. 47   the blue, boundless, dimpled, laughing, sunny sea

p. 73   Man or buoy, do you see either

p. 295   though this frigate laid her broken bones upon the Antarctic
              shores

MOBY-DICK

p. 48   But the sea rebels; he will not bear the wicked burden

p. 48   a panther billow leaping over the bulwarks

p. 50   when the whale grounded upon the ocean's utmost bones

p. 60   the magnanimity of the sea which will permit no records

p. 97   when . . . the Pequod thrust her vindictive bows into the
              cold malicious waves

p. 100   The uncounted isles of all Polynesia confers the same truth

p. 201   heaved the black sea, as if its vast tides were a conscience;
              and the great mundane soul were in anguish and remorse for
              the long sin and suffering it had bred

APPENDIX E

Six Sea Terms
in Their Sentences

Billows (1)

<u>TYPEE</u>

1) p. 3   Yes, reader, as I live, six months out of sight of land;
           cruising after the sperm-whale beneath the scorching sun of
           the Line, and tossed on the billows of the wide-rolling
           Pacific--the sky above, the sea around, and nothing else!

2) p. 248 Before long I saw the flashing billows themselves through
           the opening between the trees.

<u>OMOO</u>

1) p. 33   But my meditations were soon interrupted by a gray, spectral
           shadow cast over the heaving billows. It was the dawn, soon
           followed by the first rays of the morning.

2) p. 312 It would never do, longer to trespass on Po-Po's hospitality;
           and then, weary somewhat of life in Imeeo like all sailors
           ashore, I at last pined for the billows.

<u>MARDI</u>

1) p. 8   My spirit must have sailed with it [a bird]; for directly,
           as in a trance, came upon me the cadence of mild billows
           laving a beach of shells, the waving of boughs, and the
           voice of maidens, and the lulled beatings of my own dissolved
           heart, all blended together.

2) pp. 24-5 Peacefully may she [the <u>Acturion</u>, which Melville deserted]
             rest⁄ at the bottom of the sea; and sweetly sleep my

shipmates in the lowest watery zone, where prowling sharks come not, nor billows roll.

3) p. 30   What a mere toy we were to the billows, that jeeringly shouldered us from crest to crest, as from hand to hand lost souls may be tossed along by the chain of shades which enfilade the route to Tartarus.

4) p. 49   For as a pebble dropped into a pond ruffles it to its marge; so on all sides, a sea-gale operates as if an asteroid had fallen into the brine; making ringed mountain billows, interminably expanding, instead of ripples.

5) p. 85   But very soon after, they espied our little sea-goat, bounding over the billows from afar.

6) p. 118   Yet the rack and scud of the tempest, its mad, tearing form, was subdued into immense, long-extended, and long-rolling billows; the white cream on their crests like snow on the Andes.

7) p. 160   Gliding on, the islands grew more distinct; rising up from the billows to greet us; revealing hills, vales, and peaks, grouped within a milk-white zone of reef, so vast, that in the distance all was dim.

8) p. 160   The billows rolled listlessly by, as if conscious that their long task was nigh done; while gleamed the white reef, like the trail of a great fish in a calm.

9) p. 194   The thoughts of things broke over me like returning billows on a beach long bared. A rush, a foam of recollections.

10) p. 214   [A Paddle-Song:] All: "The wild sea song, to the billows' throng,/ Rising, falling."

11) p. 214   All: "Heap back; heap back; the waters back!/ Pile them high astern, in billows black;"

12) p. 216   Sailing nearer, we perceived an extraordinary rolling of the sea, which bursting into the lagoon through an adjoining breach in the reef, surged toward Juam in enormous billows.

13) p. 216   But under the brow of a beetling crag, the spray came and went unequally. There, the blue billows seemed swallowed up, and lost.

14) pp.   As at Juam,/where the wild billows from seaward roll in upon
    272-3   its cliffs; much more at Ohonoo, in billowy battalions charge they hotly into the lagoon, and fall on the isle like an army from the deep.

15) p. 273   So charged the bright billows of cuirassiers at Waterloo; so hurled them off the long line of living walls, whose base was as the sea-beach, wreck-strown, in a gale.

16) p. 273   Here, throwing themselves upon their boards, tranquilly they
             wait for a billow that suits.

17) p. 273   At last all is lost in scud and vapor, as the overgrown
             billow bursts like bomb.

18) p. 283   "In short, these stout little manikins were passionately
             fond of the sea, and swore by wave and billow, that sooner
             or later they would embark thereon in nautilus shells, and
             spend the rest of their roving days thousands of inches from
             Tupia."--Yoomy

19) p. 303   The mysterious voice died away; no sign of the corpse was
             now seen; and mute with amaze, the company long listed to
             the low moan of the billows and the sad sough of the breeze.

20) p. 314   Yoomy's song: "Soft sigh the boughs in the stilly air,/
             Soft lap the beach the billows there;"

21) p. 368   And as the great Mississippi musters his watery nations:
             Ohio, with all his leagued streams; Missouri, bringing down
             in torrents the clans from the highlands; Arkansas, his
             Tartar rivers from the plain;--so, with all the past and
             present pouring in me, I roll down my billow from afar.

22) p. 414   It was night. But the moon was brilliant, far and near
             illuminating the lagoon. Over silvery billows we glided.

23) p. 512   It [ridge jutting into lagoon] terminated in a lofty,
             natural arch of solid trap. Billows beat against its base.

24) p. 545   Song of Gold-Hunters: "We rovers bold,/ To the land of
             Gold,/ Over bowling billows are gliding."

25) p. 554   In the deep darkness, here and there, its margin [Hamora's
             western shore] was lit up by foam--white, breaking billows
             rolled over from Vivenza's strand, and down from northward
             Dominora; marking places where light was breaking in, upon
             the interior's jungle-gloom.

26) p. 554   The lightenings forked and flashed; the waters boiled; our
             three prows lifted themselves in supplication; but the
             billows smote them as they reared.

27) p. 586   Long we rocked upon the circling billows, which expanding
             from that center, dashed every isle, till, moons afterward,
             faint, they laved all Mardi's reef.

28) p. 593   Babbalanja: "In hairy billows, his [Lombardo's] great mane
             tossed like the sea; his eyeballs flamed two hells; his paw
             had stopped a rolling world."

29) p. 623   Song of a multitude: "To these, our shores, soft gales
             invite: The palm plumes wave,/ The billows lave."

30) p. 644   For, lo you! the glittering foam all round its white marge
              [Flozella]; where, forcing themselves underneath the coral
              ledge, and up through its crevices, in fountains, the blue
              billows gush.

31) p. 654   Mohi's tale: "The state is tossed in storms; and where I
              stand, the combing billows must break over."

REDBURN

1) pp.   As I stood leaning over the side, and trying to summon up
126-7   some image of Liverpool, to see how the reality would answer
              to my conceit; and while the fog, the mist, and gray dawn
              were investing every thing with a mysterious interest, I was
              startled by the doleful, dismal sound of a great bell, whose
              slow intermitting tolling seemed in unison with the solemn
              roll of the billows.

2) p. 147   Extract from the prologue of the guidebook: "mured to
              hardship, patient, bold and rude,/ They braved the billows
              for precarious food."

3) p. 193   There, as his eye sweeps down the St. Lawrence, whose every
              billow is bound for the main that laves the shore of Old
              England; as he [Canadian soldier] thinks of his long term of
              enlistment, which sells him to the army as Doctor Faust sold
              himself to the devil; how the poor fellow must groan in his
              grief, and call to mind the church-yard still, and his Mary.

4) p. 289   In the first morning-watch, I sat with Harry on the windlass,
              watching the billows; which, seen in the night, seemed real
              hills, upon which fortresses might have been built; and real
              valleys, in which villages, and groves, and gardens, might
              have nestled.

5) p. 292   They [people who die at sea] die, like the billows that
              break on the shore, and no more are heard or seen.

WHITE-JACKET

1) p. 14   Wherever you may be now rolling over the blue billows, dear
              Jack! take my best love along with you; and God bless you,
              wherever you go!

2) p. 97   For now, while the heedless craft is bounding over the
              billows, a black cloud rises out of the sea; the sun drops
              down from the sky; a horrible mist far and wide spreads over
              the water.

3) p. 105   The main-deck guns had several days previous been run in and
              housed, and the port-holes closed, but the lee carronades on
              the quarter-deck and forecastle were plunging through the
              sea, which undulated over them in milk-white billows of foam.

4) p. 108   For about three quarters of an hour we thus hung suspended
             right over the rampant billows, which curled their very
             crests under the feet of some four or five of us clinging to
             the lee-yard-arm, as if to float us from our place.

5) p. 214   Waller's verse: "But who can always on the billows lie?/
             The watery wilderness yields no supply."

6) p. 268   Slowly we dropped and dropped down the bay, glided like a
             stately swan through the outlet, and were gradually rolled
             by the smooth, sliding billows broad out upon the deep.

7) p. 270   Jack Chase: "But how we boom through the billows!"

8) p. 380   "Born under a gun, and educated on the bowsprit," according
             to a phrase of his own, the man-of-war's-man rolls round the
             world like a billow, ready to mix with any sea, or be sucked
             down to death in the Maelstrom of any war.

9) p. 393   As I gushed into the sea, a thunder-boom sounded in my ear;
             my soul seemed flying from my mouth. The feeling of death
             flooded over me with the billows.

MOBY-DICK

1) p. 45   How billow-like and boisterously grand!

2) p. 48   But at that moment he is sprung upon by a panther billow
             leaping over the bulwarks.

3) p. 50   Delight is to him, whom all the waves of the billows of the
             seas of the boisterous mob can never shake from this sure
             Keel of the Ages!

4) p. 63   With the landless gull, that at sunset folds her wings and
             is rocked to sleep between billows; so, at nightfall, the
             Nantucketer, out of sight of land, furls his sails, and lays
             him to his rest, while under his very pillow rush herds of
             walruses and whales.

5) p. 126   Full of fine spirits, they invariably come from the breezy
             billows to windward.

6) p. 144   Ah! constrainings seize thee; I see! the billow lifts thee!

7) p. 146   The envious billows sidelong swell to whelm my track; let
             them; but first I pass.

8) pp.   Forced into familiarity, then, with such prodigies as these;
158-9   and knowing that after repeated, intrepid assaults, the
             White Whale had escaped alive; it cannot be much matter of
             surprise that some whalemen should go still further in their
             superstitions; declaring Moby Dick not only ubiquitous, but
             immortal (for immortality is but ubiquity in time); that
             though groves of spears should be planted in his flanks, he

would still swim away unharmed; or if indeed he should ever
be made to spout thick blood, such a sight would be but a
ghastly deception; for again in unensanguined/billows
hundreds of leagues away, his unsullied jet would once more
be seen.

9) pp.   To a landsman, no whale, nor any sign of a herring, would/
191-2   have been visible at that moment; nothing but a troubled bit
           of greenish white water, and thin scattered puffs of white
           vapour hovering over it, and suffusingly blowing off to
           leeward, like the confused scud from white rolling billows.

10) p. 225 It has a sort of howdah on its back, and its distended
            tusked mouth into which the billows are rolling, might be
            taken for the Traitors' Gate leading from the Thames by
            water into the Tower.

11) p. 237 No perceptible face or front did it have; no conceivable
            token of either sensation of instinct; but undulated there
            on the billows, an unearthly, formless, chance-like
            apparition of life.

12) p. 258 More and more she leans over to the whale, while every
            gasping heave of the windlass is answered by a helping heave
            from the billows; till at last, a swift, startling snap is
            heard; with a great swash the ship rolls upwards and
            backwards from the whale, and the triumphant tackle rises
            into sight dragging after it the disengaged semi-circular
            end of the first strip of blubber.

13) p. 298 Now to this hand, now to that, he yawed in his faltering
            flight, and still at every billow that broke, he spasmodically
            sank in the sea, or sideways rolled towards the sky his one
            beating fin.

14) p. 327 First, the whales forming the margin of our lake began to
            crowd a little, and tumble against each other, as if lifted
            by half spent billows from afar; then the lake itself began
            faintly to heave and swell; the sub-marine bridal-chambers
            and nurseries vanished; in more and more contracting orbits
            the whales in the more central circles began to swim in
            thickening clusters.

15) p. 409 Look! here, far water-locked; beyond all hum of human weal
            or woe; in these most candid and impartial seas; where to
            traditions no rocks furnish tablets; where for long Chinese
            ages, the billows have still rolled on speechless and
            unspoken to, as stars that shine upon the Niger's unknown
            source; here, too, life dies sunwards full of faith; but see!
            no sooner dead, than death whirls round the corpse, and it
            heads some other way.

16) p. 410 Born of earth, yet suckled by the sea; though hill and
            valley mothered me, ye billows are my foster-brothers!

17) p. 423   Next morning the not-yet-subsided sea rolled in long slow
              billows of mighty bulk, and striving in the Pequod's
              gurgling track, pushed her on like giants' palms outspread.

18) p. 423   Yoke on the further billows; hallo! a tandem, I drive the
              sea!

19) p. 427   In turn, jerkingly raised and lowered by the rolling billows,
              the towing resistance of the log caused the old reelman to
              stagger strangely.

20) pp.   Ripplingly withdrawing from his prey, Moby Dick now lay at a
449-50   little distance, vertically thrusting his oblong white head
              up and down in the billows; and at the same time slowly
              revolving his whole spindled body; so that when his vast
              wrinkled forehead rose--some twenty or more feet out of the
              water--the now rising swells, with all their confluent waves,
              dazzlingly broke against it;/ vindictively tossing their
              shivered spray still higher into the air.

21) p. 450   So in a gale, the but half baffled Channel billows only
              recoil from the base of the Eddystone, triumphantly to
              overleap its summit with their scud.

22) p. 462   Some men die at ebbtide; some at low water; some at the full
              of the flood;--and I feel now like a billow that's all one
              crested comb, Starbuck.

23) p. 468   Ho, ho! from all your furthest bounds, pour ye now in, ye
              bold billows of my whole foregone life, and top this one
              piled comber of my death!

24) p. 469   But as the last whelmings intermingly poured themselves over
              the sunken head of the Indians at the mainmast, leaving a
              few inches of the erect spar yet visible, together with long
              streaming yards of the flag, which calmly undulated, with
              ironical coincidings, over the destroying billows they
              almost touched;--at that instant, a red arm and a hammer
              hovered backwardly uplifted in the open air, in the act of
              nailing the flag faster and yet faster to the subsiding
              spar.

Shore (2)

[NOTE: Not all of the SHORE sentences are recorded, only those which contribute in some significant way to the syntax or semantics of the word.]

TYPEE

1) p. 23   From these [two small twin islets] the shore recedes on both hands, and describes a deep semi-circle.

2) pp. 23-4   The beautiful/aspect of the shore is heightened by deep and romantic glens, which come down to it at almost equal distances, all apparently radiating from a common centre, and the upper extremities of which are lost to the eye beneath the shadow of the mountains.

3) p. 24   Besides this bay the shores of the island are indented by several other extensive inlets, into which descend broad and verdant valleys.

4) p. 25   She was soon conducted to a beautiful inlet, and dropped her anchor in its waters beneath the shadows of the lofty shore.

5) p. 26   When the inhabitants of some sequestered island first descry the "big canoe" of the European rolling through the blue waters towards their shores, they rush down to the beach in crowds, and with open arms stand ready to embrace the strangers.

6) pp. 30-31   Having ascertained the fact before alluded to, that the islanders, from/ motives of precaution, dwelt together in the depths of the valleys, and avoided wandering about the more elevated portions of the shore, unless bound on some expedition of war or plunder, I concluded that if I could effect unperceived a passage to the mountains, I might easily remain among them, supporting myself by such fruits as came in my way until the sailing of the ship, an event of which I could not fail to be immediately apprised, as from my lofty position I should command a view of the entire harbor.

7) p. 113   In pursuance of this idea, old Marheyo himself would hie him away to the sea-shore by the break of day, for the purpose of collecting various species of rare sea-weeds; some of which among these people are considered a great luxury.

8) p. 173   To the material eye thou makest but little progress; but with the eye of faith, I see thy canoe cleaving the bright waves, which die away on those dimly looming shores of Paradise.

OMOO

1) p. 21   Meanwhile Doctor Long-Ghost and myself lounged about, cultivating an acquaintance, and gazing upon the shore scenery.

2) p. 26   But as the sun was setting by the time the boat came
             alongside, we got our off-shore tacks aboard and stood away
             for an offing.

3) p. 26   Before we held any communication with the shore, an incident
             occurred which may convey some further idea of the character
             of our crew.

4) p. 36   Like shore doctors, he did not eschew his own medicines, for
             his professional calls in the forecastle were sometimes made
             when he was comfortably tipsy: nor did he omit keeping his
             invalids in good-humour, spinning his yarns to them, by the
             hour, whenever he went to see them.

5) p. 64   On we glided, within less than a cable's length of the shore,
             which was margined with foam that sparkled all round.

6) p. 65   But when the clouds floated away, and showed the three peaks
             standing like obelisks against the sky; and the bold shore
             undulating along the horizon, the tears gushed from his eyes.

7) pp. 66-7 It was to the pagans/ of Tahiti that the first regularly
             constituted Protestant missionaries were sent; and from
             their shores also, having sailed successive missions to the
             neighboring islands.

8) p. 75   After holding our ground off the harbor during the night, in
             the morning a shore boat, manned by natives, was seen coming
             off.

9) p. 83   As for Doctor Long-Ghost, the shore physician, instead of
             extending to him any professional sympathy, had treated him
             very cavalierly.

10) p. 94   During the morning of the day which dawned upon the events
             just recounted, we remained a little to leeward of the
             harbor, waiting the appearance of the consul, who had
             promised the mate to come off in a shore boat for the
             purpose of seeing him.

11) p. 95   Noon came, and no consul; and as the afternoon advanced
             without any word even from the shore, the mate was justly
             incensed; more especially, as he had taken great pains to
             keep perfectly sober against Wilson's arrival.

12) p. 98   Formed by a bold sweep of the shore, it is protected seaward
             by the coral reef, upon which the rollers break with great
             violence.

13) p. 102   Before leaving Tahiti, I had the curiosity to go over this
             poor old ship, thus stranded on a strange shore.

14) p. 133   Being upon the consul's hands, all our expenses were of
             course payable by him in his official capacity; and, therefore,
             as a friend of Wilson, and sure of good pay, the shore doctor
             had some idea of allowing us to run up a bill with him.

15) p. 134   This sudden change from ship fare to shore living, plays the deuse with you sailors, so be cautious about eating fruit.

16) p. 240   At last, after taking a wide circuit, we came out upon the farthest shore of the lake.

17) p. 242   They would give us no more "hevars" that night; and Rartoo fairly dragged us away to a canoe, hauled up on the lake shore; when we reluctantly embarked, and, paddling over to the village, arrived there in time for a good nap before sunrise.

18) p. 246   Upon one shore of the bay stands the village of Partoowye, a missionary station.

19) p. 263   In its greatest perfection, it [the cocoa-palm] is perhaps found right on the sea-shore, where its roots are actually washed.

20) p. 264   The finest orchard of cocoa-palms I know, and the only plantation of them I ever saw at the islands, is one that stands right upon the southern shore of Papeetee Bay.

21) p. 269   A fresh breeze springing up, we set our sail of matting, and glided along as tranquilly as if floating upon an island stream; the white reef on one hand, and the green shore on the other.

MARDI

1) p. 7   Leave the ship when neither sail nor shore was in sight!

2) p. 70   Meanwhile, a gray-headed old chief stood calmly at the tiller, endeavoring to steer the vessel shoreward.

3) p. 74   It was now late in the afternoon; and for the present bent upon avoiding land, and gaining the shoreless sea, never mind where, Samoa again forced round his craft before the wind, leaving the island astern.

4) p. 82   Though once attained, all three--red rose, bright shore, and soft heart--are full of love, bloom, and all manners of delights.

5) p. 85   Still days, days, days sped by; and steering now this way, now that, to avoid the green treacherous shores, which frequently rose into view, the Parki went to and fro in the sea; till at last, it seemed hard to tell, in what watery world she floated.

6) pp. 101-2   I found a jaunty shore-cap of the captain's, hidden away in the hollow heart/ of a coil of rigging; covered over in a manner most touchingly natural, with a heap of old ropes; and near by, in a breaker, discovered several entire pieces of calico, heroically tied together with cords almost strong enough to sustain the mainmast.

7) p. 145   Besides, what cared I now for the green groves and bright
             shore?

8) p. 145   Was not Yillah my shore and my grove?

9) p. 145   Enough: no shore for me yet.

10) p. 145   Yet that shore was so exceedingly remote, and the folly of
             endeavoring to reach it in a craft built with hands, so very
             apparent, that what wonder I really nourished no thought of
             it?

11) p. 160   The jeweled vapors, erewhile hovering over these violet
             shores, now seemed to be shedding their gems; and as the
             almost level rays of the sun, shooting through the air like
             a variegated prism, touched the verdant land, it trembled
             all over with dewy sparkles.

12) p. 161   "A canoe! a canoe!" cried Samoa, as three proas showed
             themselves rounding a neighboring shore.

13) p. 194   Fleeing from the islet, I gained the neighboring shore, and
             searched among the woods; and my comrades meeting, besought
             their aid.

14) p. 201   Valapee, or the Isle of Yams, being within plain sight of
             Media's dominions, we were not very long in drawing nigh to
             its shores.

15) p. 217   Cautiously evading the dangerous currents here ruffling the
             lagoon, we rounded the wall of cliff, and shot upon a smooth
             expanse; on one side, hemmed in by the long, verdant,
             northern shore of Juam; and across the water, sentineled by
             its tributary islets.

16) p. 257   Oh! russet shores of Rhine and Rhone!

17) p. 265   Nid-nods its tufted summit like three ostrich plumes; its
             beetling crags, bent poppies, shadows, willowy shores, all
             nod; its streams are murmuring down the hills; its wavelets
             hush the shore.

18) p. 280   Embarking from Ohonoo, we at length found ourselves gliding
             by the pleasant shores of Tupia, an islet which according to
             Braid-Beard had for ages remained uninhabited by man.

19) p. 281   It is now above ten hundred thousand moons, since there died
             the last of a marvelous race, once inhabiting the very
             shores by which we are sailing.

20) p. 288   Crouching on the bank, the Ranger now called several by name,
             patted their scales, carrying on some heathenish nursery-
             talk, like St. Anthony, in ancient Coptic, instilling
             virtuous principles into his finny flock on the sea shore.

21) p. 305   Going at day break to the Motoo to fish, they preceived a
              strange proa beached on its seaward shore; and presently
              were hailed by voices; and saw among the palm trees, three
              specter-like men, who were not of Mardi.

22) p. 314   Dark and bold, thy shores, Marlena;/ But green, and timorous,
              thy soft knolls,/ Crouching behind the woodlands.

23) p. 323   Soon, rounding a lofty and insulated shore, the great central
              peak of the island came in sight; domineering over the
              neighboring hills; the same aspiring pinnacle, descried in
              drawing near the archipelago in the Chamois.

24) p. 326   At every place, hitherto visited, joyous crowds stood ready
              to hail our arrival; but the shores of Maramma were silent,
              and forlorn.

25) p. 343   The lake was but a portion of the smooth lagoon, made
              separate by an arm of wooded reef, extending from the high
              western shore of the island, and curving round toward a
              promontory, leaving a narrow channel to the sea, almost
              invisible, however, from the land-locked interior.

26) p. 343   Its main-shore was a steep acclivity, with jutting points,
              each crowned with mossy old altars of stone, or ruinous
              temples, darkly reflected in the green, glassy water; while,
              from its long line of stately trees, the low reef-side of
              the lake looked one verdant bluff.

27) p. 367   Shoals, like nebulous vapors, shoreing the white reef of the
              Milky Way, against which the wrecked worlds are dashed;
              strowing all the strand, with their Himmaleh keels and ribs.

28) p. 435   "How the isles grow and multiply around us!" cried Babbalanja,
              as turning the bold promontory of an uninhabited shore, many
              distant lands bluely loomed into view.

29) p. 435   "To the bold shores of Diranda," said Media.

30) p. 473   Did ye not bring it [undoubted valor] with ye from the bold
              old shores of Dominora, where there is a fullness of it left?

31) p. 492   "My lord," said Yoomy, "while we tarried with King Bello, I
              heard much of the fewd between Dominora and this unhappy
              shore."

32) p. 498   The sun was now setting behind us, lighting up the white
              cliffs of Dominora, and the green capes of Verdanna; while
              in deep shade lay before us the long winding shores of
              Porpheero.

33) p. 540   "Look, look! my lord," cried Yoomy, "what a glorious shore
              we pass."

34) p. 545   Now, northward coasting along Kolumbo's Western shore, whence
              came the same wild forest-sounds, as from the Eastern; and

where we landed not, to seek among those wrangling tribes;--
after many, many days, we spied prow after prow, before the
wind all northward bound: sails wide-spread, and paddles
plying: scaring the fish from before them.

35) p. 548   With this bright gold, could we but join our waiting wives,
who wring their hands on distant shores, all then were well.

36) p. 551   What grand shore is this?

37) pp.   This rocky islet passed, the sea went down; and more we
553-4   neared/ Hamora's western shore.

38) p. 554   On our right, Hamora's northern shore gleamed thick with
crescents; numerous as the crosses along the opposing strand.

39) p. 556   Morning dawned upon the same mild, blue lagoon as erst; and
all the lands that we had passed, since leaving Piko's shore
of spears, were faded from the sight.

40) p. 568   But nearer and nearer, low-creeping along, came mists and
vapors, a thousand; spotted with twinklings of will-o-wisps
from neighboring shores.

41) p. 589   At length we gained the sunny side, and shoreward tended.

42) p. 623   Behind, another, and a verdant surf played against lofty
banks of leaves; where the breeze, likewise, found its shore.

43) p. 623   To these, our shores, soft gales invite:/ The palm plumes
wave,/ The billows lave,/ And hither point fix'd stars of
light!

44) p. 624   Time flies full fast; life soon is o'er;/ And he may mourn,/
That hither borne,/ Ye left behind our pleasant shore.

45) p. 642   As if Mardi were a poem, and every island a canto, the shore
now in sight was called Flozella-a-Nina, or The-Last-Verse-
of-the-Song.

REDBURN

1) p. 33   As the steamer carried us further and further down the bay,
and we passed ships lying at anchor, with men gazing at us
and waving their hats; and small boats with ladies in them
waving their handkerchiefs; and passed the green shore of
Staten Island, and caught sight of so many beautiful
cottages all overrun with vines, and planted on the beautiful
fresh mossy hill-sides; oh!

2) p. 64   All round us, on both sides of the ship, ahead and astern,
nothing was to be seen but water--water--water; not a single
glimpse of green shore, not the smallest island, or speck of
moss anywhere.

3) p. 65   For sailors have their own names, even for things that are
              familiar ashore; and if you call a thing by its shore name,
              you are laughed at for an ignoramus and a land-lubber.

4) p. 73   It was very early in the month of June that we sailed; and I
              had greatly rejoiced that it was that time of the year; for
              it would be warm and pleasant upon the ocean, I thought; and
              my voyage would be like a summer excursion to the sea shore,
              for the benefit of the salt water, and a change of scene and
              society.

5) p. 124   Now what, exactly, I had fancied the shore would look like,
              I can not say; but I had a vague idea that it would be
              something strange and wonderful.

6) pp.   I thought of Robert Emmet, and that last speech of his before
124-5   Lord Norbury; I thought of Tommy Moore, and his amatory
              verses; I thought of Curran, Grattan, Plunket, and O'Connell;
              I thought of my uncle's ostler, Patrick Flinnigan; and I
              thought of the shipwreck of the/ gallant Albion, tost to
              pieces on the very shore now in sight; and I thought I
              should very much like to leave the ship and visit Dublin and
              the Giant's Causeway.

7) p. 127   The day came, and soon, passing two lofty landmarks on the
              Lancashire shore, we rapidly drew near the town, and at last,
              came to anchor in the stream.

8) p. 127   Looking shoreward, I beheld lofty ranges of dingy warehouses,
              which seemed very deficient in the elements of the marvelous;
              and bore a most unexpected resemblance to the ware-houses
              along South-street in New York.

9) p. 128   What was my astonishment, therefore, to see this really
              decent, civil woman coming with a neat parcel of Max's shore
              clothes, all washed, plaited, and ironed, and ready to put
              on at a moment's warning.

10) p. 145   Reverentially folding this map, I pass a plate of the Town
              Hall, and come upon the Title Page, which, in the middle, is
              ornamented with a piece of landscape, representing a loosely
              clad lady in sandals, pensively seated upon a bleak rock on
              the sea shore, supporting her head with one hand, and with
              the other, exhibiting to the stranger an oval sort of salver,
              bearing the figure of a strange bird, with this motto
              elastically stretched for a border--"Deus nobis hæc otia
              fecit."

11) p. 159   For the book discoursed of both places, and told how the
              Abbey was on the Cheshire shore, full in view from a point
              on the Lancashire side, covered over with ivy, and brilliant
              with moss!

12) p. 243   It was destined that our departure from the English strand,
              should be marked by a tragical event, akin to the sudden end
              of the suicide, which had so strongly impressed me on
              quitting the American shore.

13) p. 292   Let us waive that agitated national topic, as to whether
              such multitudes of foreign poor should be landed on our
              American shores; let us waive it, with the one only thought,
              that if they can get here, they have God's right to come,
              though they bring all Ireland and her miseries with them.

14) p. 294   Off Cape Cod! and in the shore-bloom that came to us--even
              from that desert of sand-hillocks--methought I could almost
              distinguish the fragrance of the rosebush my sisters and I
              had planted, in our far inland garden at home.

15) p. 300   The steerage passengers almost neighed with delight, like
              horses brought back to spring pastures; and every eye and
              ear in the Highlander was full of glad sights and sounds of
              the shore.

WHITE-JACKET

1) p. 55   It was as if we were sailing by some odoriferous shore, in
              the vernal season of violets.

2) p. 74   Wrecked on a desert shore, a man-of-war's crew could quickly
              found an Alexandria by themselves, and fill it with all the
              things which go to make up a capital.

3) p. 141   It was worth while to state that this frigate was vastly
              admired by the shore ladies for her wonderfully neat
              appearance.

4) p. 160   Whereas, in port, unless some particular service engages
              them, they lead the laziest of lives, beset by all the
              allurements of the shore, though perhaps that shore they may
              never touch.

5) p. 165   And while both England and America have become greatly
              liberalized in the interval; while shore pomp in high places
              has come to be regarded by the more intelligent masses of
              men as belonging to the absurd, ridiculous, and mock-heroic;
              while that most truly august of all the majesties of earth,
              the President of the United States, may be seen entering his
              residence with his umbrella under his arm, and no brass band
              or military guard at his heels, and unostentatiously taking
              his seat by the side of the meanest citizen in a public
              conveyance; while this is the case, there still lingers in
              American men-of-war all the stilted etiquette and childish
              parade of the old-fashioned Spanish court of Madrid.

6) pp.   Still another mode of passing time, was arraying yourself in
171-2   in your best/ "togs" and promenading up and down the gun-
              deck, admiring the shore scenery from the port-holes, which,
              in an amphitheatrical bay like Rio--belted about by the most
              varied and charming scenery of hill, dale, moss, meadow,
              court, castle, tower, grove, vine, vineyard, aqueduct,
              palace, square, island, fort--is very much like lounging
              round a circular cosmorama, and ever and anon lazily peeping
              through the glasses here and there.

7) p. 173   Several of my shore friends, indeed, when suddenly
             overwhelmed by some disaster, always make a point of flying
             to the first oyster-cellar, and shutting themselves up in a
             box, with nothing but a plate of stewed oysters, some
             crackers, the castor, and a decanter of old Port.

8) p. 187   But in his conversations there was no trace of evil; nothing
             equivocal; he studiously shunned on indelicacy, never swore,
             and chiefly abounded in passing puns and witticisms, varied
             with humorous contrasts between ship and shore life, and
             many agreeable and racy anecdotes, very tastefully narrated.

9) p. 191   "Ah!" said a top-man, "returning the shore salute they gave
             us yesterday."

10) p. 231   And doubtless it was to his shore sympathies that the well-
             known humanity and kindness which Blake evinced in his
             intercourse with the sailors is in a large degree to be
             imputed.

11) p. 233   A Shore Emperor on board a Man-of-war.

12) p. 264   "When, upward of twenty years ago, I was with Lord Cochrane,
             then Admiral of the fleets of this very country"--pointing
             shoreward, out of a port-hole--"a sailor of the vessel to
             which I was attached, during the blockade of Bahia, had his
             leg--"

13) p. 295   Nay, White-Jacket, though this frigate laid her broken bones
             upon the Antarctic shores of Palmer's Land; though not two
             planks adhered, and at her yawning hatchways mouth-yawning
             sharks swam in and out; yet, should you escape the wreck and
             scramble to the beach, this Martial Law would meet you still,
             and snatch you by the throat.

14) p. 327   But, then, this pallid young apothecary charged nothing for
             it, and that was no small satisfaction; for is it not
             remarkable, to say the least, that a shore apothecary should
             actually charge you money--round dollars and cents--for
             giving you a horrible nausea?

15) p. 351   No psyche glasses; no hand-mirror; no ewer and basin; no
             comfortable padded footstool; nothing, in short, that makes
             a shore "shave" such a luxury.

16) p. 372   In due time the squadron made sail for Algiers, and in that
             harbor, once haunted by pirates, the punishment was
             inflicted--the Bay of Naples, though washing the shores of
             an absolute king, not being deemed a fit place for such
             exhibition of American naval law.

17) p. 382   Now it may be easily imagined who are the men, and of what
             moral character they are, who, even at the present day, are
             willing to enlist as full-grown adults in a service so
             galling to all shore-manhood as the Navy.

18) p. 390   Seeing this sight, I thought to myself, well, these
              generous-hearted tars on shore were the greatest curmudgeons
              afloat!

19) p. 391   Headed by Jack Chase, the quarter-watch were reclining in
              the top, talking about the shore delights into which they
              intended to plunge, while our captain often broke in with
              allusions to similar conversations when he was on board the
              English line-of-battle ship, the Asia, drawing nigh to
              Portsmouth, in England, after the battle of Navarino.

20) p. 393   Oh soul! thou then heardest life and death: as he who
              stands upon the Corinthian shore hears both the Ionian and
              the Aegean waves.

21) p. 397   And over the starry waves, and broad out into the blandly
              blue and boundless night, spiced with strange sweets from
              the long-sought land--the whole long cruise predestinated
              ours, though often in tempest-time we almost refused to
              believe in that far-distant shore--straight out into that
              fragrant night, ever-noble Jack Chase, matchless and
              unmatchable Jack Chase stretches forth his bannered hand,
              and, pointing shoreward, cries: "For the last time, hear
              Camoens, boys! . . ./ Appeased, old Ocean now shall rage no
              more;/ Haste, point our bowsprit for yon shadowy shore."

MOBY-DICK

1) p. 40   Sacred/ To the Memory/ of/ Robert Long, Willis Elery,/
              Nathan Coleman, Walter Canny,/ Seth Macy, and Samuel Gleig,/
              Forming one of the boats' crews/ of/ The Ship Eliza,/ who
              were towed out of sight by a whale,/ on the off-shore Ground
              in the/ PACIFIC,/ December 31st, 1839./ This Marble/ Is here
              placed by their surviving/ Shipmates.

2) p. 93   Soon the crew came on board in twos and threes; the riggers
              bestirred themselves; the mates were actively engaged; and
              several of the shore people were busy in bringing various
              last things on board.

3) p. 94   And all this seemed natural enough; especially as in the
              merchant service many captains never show themselves on deck
              for a considerable time after heaving up an anchor, but
              remain over the cabin table, having a farewell merry-making
              with their shore friends, before they quit the ship for good
              with the pilot.

4) p. 97   With all her might she crowds all sail off shore; in so
              doing, fights 'gainst the very winds that fain would blow
              her homeward; seeks all the lashed sea's landlessness again;
              for refuge's sake forlornly rushing into peril; her only
              friend her bitterest foe!

5) p. 97   Glimpses do ye seem to see of that mortally intolerable
              truth; that all deep, earnest thinking is but the intrepid

effort of the soul to keep the open independence of her sea;
while the wildest winds of heaven and earth conspire to cast
her on the treacherous, slavish shore?

6) p. 97   But as in landlessness alone resides the highest truth,
shoreless, indefinite as God--so, better is it to perish in
that howling infinite, than be ingloriously clashed upon the
lee, even if that were safety!

7) p. 116   Already we are boldly launched upon the deep, but soon we
shall be lost in its unshored, harborless immensities.

8) p. 179   Here are his reflections some time after quitting the ship,
(footnote)   during a black night in an open boat, when almost despairing
of reaching any hospitable shore.

9) p. 402   Death seems the only desirable sequel for a career like this;
but Death is only a launching into the region of the strange
Untried; it is but the first salutation to the possibilities
of the immense Remote, the Wild, the Watery, the Unshored;
therefore, to the death-longing eyes of such men, who still
have left in them some interior compunctions against suicide,
does the all-contributed and all-receptive ocean alluringly
spread forth his whole plain of unimaginable, taking terrors,
and wonderful, new-life adventures; and from the hearts of
infinite Pacifics, the thousand mermaids sing to them--
"Come hither, broken-hearted; here is another life without
the guilt of intermediate death; here are wonders
supernatural, without dying for them."

Fin (3A)

OMOO

1) p. 27   A broad blue band stretched across his face from ear to ear, and on his forehead was the taper figure of a blue shark, nothing but fins from head to tail.

MARDI

1) p. 40   This dainty shark [the Blue Shark] invariably lounged by with a careless fin and an indolent tail.

2) p. 42   They [Black Fish] seemed to swim by revolving round and round in the water, like a wheel; their dorsal fins, every now and then shooting into view, like spokes.

3) p. 42   Besides all these, we encountered Killers and Thrashers, by far the most spirited and "spunky" of the finny tribes.

4) p. 42   Oh, believe me, God's creatures fighting, fin for fin, a thousand miles from land, and with the round horizon for an arena, is no ignoble subject for a masterpiece.

5) p. 54   One of them [Pilot fish] was right under the shark, nibbling at his ventral fin; another above, hovering about his dorsal appurtenance; one on each flank; and a frisking fifth pranking about his nose, seemingly having something to say of a confidential nature.

6) p. 123   Not to peculiarize this circumstance as true of divers species of sharks, cuttle-fish, and many others of the larger varieties of the finny tribes; the myriads of microscopic mollusca, well known to swarm off soundings, might alone be deemed almost sufficient to kindle a fire in the brine.

7) p. 148   Soon we found ourselves the nucleus of an incredible multitude of finny creatures, most anonymous.

8) p. 148   Then, like a third distinct regiment, wormed and twisted through the water like Archimedean screws, the quivering Wriggle-tails; followed in turn by the rank and file of the Trigger-fish--so called from their faint dorsal fins being set in their backs with a comical curve, as if at half-cock.

9) p. 148   And slow sailing overhead were flights of birds; a wing in the air for every fin in the sea.

10) p. 149 It is tangled sea-kelp clinging to its fins.

11) p. 149 The myriad fins swim on; a lonely waste, where the lost one drops behind.

12) p. 149 No, no; all is glee, fishy glee, and frolicking fun; light hearts and light fins; gay backs and gay spirits.

13) p. 149   Swim away, swim away! my merry fins all.

14) p. 149   Let us roam the flood; let us follow this monster fish with the barnacled sides; this strange-looking fish, so high out of water; that goes without fins.

15) p. 149   No, no; for sure, they behold our limber fins, our speckled and beautiful scales.

16) p. 150   Swim away; merry fins, swim away!

17) p. 150   We fish, we fish, we merrily swim,/ We care not for friend nor for foe:/ Our fins are stout,/ Our tails are out,/ As through the seas we go./ We fish, we fish, we merrily swim,/ We care not for friend nor for foe:/ Our fins are stout,/ Our tails are out,/ As through the seas we go.

18) p. 151   A jacket, rolled up, was kept in readiness to be thrust into the first opening made; while as the thousand fins audibly patted against our slender planks, we felt nervously enough; as if treading upon thin, crackling ice.

19) p. 267   Like the fish of the bright and twittering fin,/ Bright fish! diving deep as high soars the lark,/ So, far, far, far, doth the maiden swim,/ Wild song, wild light, in still ocean's dark.

20) p. 288   Crouching on the bank, the Ranger now called several by name, patted their scales, carrying on some heathenish nursery-talk, like St. Anthony, in ancient Coptic, instilling virtuous principles into his finny flock on the sea shore.

21) pp.   But just then a fiery fin-back whale, having broken into the
316-7   paddock of the lagoon, threw up a high fountain of foam, almost under Tribonnora's nose; who, quickly turning about his canoe, cur-like slunk off; his steering-paddle between his legs.

22) p. 374   Imbedded in amber, do we not find little fishes' fins, porpoise-teeth, sea-gulls' beaks and claws; nay, butterflies' wings, and sometimes a topaz?

23) p. 380   (Preserved between fins of the dolphin.)

24) p. 417   And next, my lord, we have the fine old time of the Old Red Sandstone sandwich, clapped on the underlying layer, and among other dainties, imbedding the first course of fish,-- all quite in rule,--sturgeon-forms, cephalaspis, glyptolepis, pterichthys; and other finny things, of flavor rare, but hard to mouth for bones.

25) p. 418   The second side-course--miocene--was out of course, flesh after fowl:--marine mammalia,--seals, grampuses, and whales, served up with sea-weed on their flanks, hearts and kidneys deviled, and fins and flippers fricasseed.

26) p. 420   They may have some better seeing sense than ours; perhaps,
              have fins or wings for arms.

27) p. 482   In a broad arbor by the water-side, it was housed like Alp
              Arslan's war-horse, or the charger Caligula deified; upon
              its stern a wilderness of sculpture:--shell-work, medallions,
              masques, griffins, gulls, ogres, finned-lions, winged
              walruses; all manner of the sea-cavalry, crusading centaurs,
              crocodiles, and sharks; and mermen, and mermaids, and Neptune
              only knows all.

28) p. 570   Here, helping himself along with two crotched roots, hobbled
              a dwarf without legs; another stalked before, one arm fixed
              in the air, like a lightening rod; a third, more active than
              any, seal-like, flirted a pair of flippers, and went
              skipping along; a fourth hopped on a solitary pin, at every
              bound, spinning round like a top, to gaze; while still
              another, furnished with feelers or fins, rolled himself up
              in a ball, bowling over the ground in advance.

REDBURN

1) p. 99   "They ar'n't sperm whales," said Larry, "their spouts ar'n't
              bushy enough; they ar'n't Sulphur-bottoms, or they wouldn't
              stay up so long; they ar'n't Hump-backs, for they ar'n't got
              any humps; they ar'n't Fin-backs, for you won't catch a Fin-
              back so near a ship; they ar'n't Greenland whales, for we
              ar'n't off the coast of Greenland; and they ar'n't right
              whales, for it wouldn't be right to say so."

MOBY-DICK

1) p. 7   "Io! Paean! Io! sing,/ To the finny people's king."

2) p. 121   Under this head I reckon a monster which, by the various
              names of Fin-Back, Tall-Spout, and Long-John, has been seen
              almost in every sea and is commonly the whale whose distant
              jet is so often descried by passengers crossing the Atlantic,
              in the New York packet-tracks.

3) p. 121   In the length he attains, and in his baleen, the Fin-back
              resembles the Right Whale, but is of a less portly girth,
              and a lighter color, approaching to olive.

4) p. 121   His grand distinguishing feature, the fin, from which he
              derives his name, is often a conspicuous object.

5) p. 121   This fin is some three or four feet long, growing vertically
              from the hinder part of the back, of an angular shape, and
              with a very sharp pointed end.

6) pp.   When the sea is moderately calm, and slightly marked with
121-2   spherical ripples, and this gnomon-like fin stands up and
              casts shadows upon the wrinkled surface, it may well be

supposed that the watery circle surrounding it somewhat resembles a dial, with its style and/wavy hour-lines graved on it.

7) p. 122   The Fin-Back is not gregarious.

8) p. 122   From having the baleen in his mouth, the Fin-Back is sometimes included with the right whale, among a theoretic species denominated <u>whalebone whales</u>, that is, whales with baleen.

9) p. 122   In connexion with this appellative of "Whalebone whales," it is of great importance to mention, that however such a nomenclature may be convenient in facilitating allusions to some kind of whales, yet it is vain to attempt a clear classification of the Leviathan, founded upon either his baleen or hump, or fin, or teeth; notwithstanding that those marked parts or features very obviously seem better adapted to form the basis for a regular system of cetology than any other detached bodily distinctions, which the whale, in his kinds, presents.

10) p. 122   The baleen, hump, back-fin, and teeth; these are things whose peculiarities are indiscriminately dispersed among all sorts of whales, without any regard to what may be the nature of their structure in other and more essential particulars.

11) p. 140   Perhaps they were; or perhaps there might have been shoals of them in the far horizon; but lulled into such an opium-like listlessness of vacant, unconscious reverie in this absentminded youth by the blending cadence of waves with thoughts that at last he loses his identity; takes the mystic ocean at his feet for the visible image of that deep, blue, bottomless soul, pervading mankind and nature; and every strange, half-seen, gliding, beautiful thing that eludes him; every dimly-discovered, uprising fin of some undiscernable form, seems to him the embodiment of those elusive thoughts that only people the soul by continually flitting through it.

12) p. 143   And this is what ye have shipped for, men! to chase that white whale on both sides of land, and over all sides of earth, till he spouts black blood and rolls fin out.

13) p. 174   His broad fins are bored, and scalloped out like a lost sheep's ear!

14) p. 203   At that moment the two wakes were fairly crossed, and instantly, then, in accordance with their singular ways, shoals of small harmless fish, that for some days before had been placidly swimming by our side, darted away with what seemed shuddering fins, and ranged themselves fore and aft with the strangers' flanks.

15) p. 296   As an overladen Indiaman bearing down the Hindostan coast with a deck load of frightened horses, careens, buries,

rolls, and wallows on her way; so did this old whale heave his aged bulk, and now and then partly turning over on this cumbrous rib-end, expose the cause of his devious wake in the unnatural stump of his starboard fin.

16) p. 296   Whether he had lost that fin in battle, or had been born without it, it were hard to say.

17) p. 298   The whale was now going head out, and sending his spout before him in a continual tormented jet, while his one poor fin beat his side in an agony of fright.

18) p. 298   Now to this hand, now to that, he yawed in his faltering flight, and still at every billow that he broke, he spasmodically sank in the sea, or sideways rolled towards the sky his one beating fin.

19) p. 301   For, by this time, so spent was he by loss of blood, that he helplessly rolled away from the wreck he had made; lay panting on his side, impotently flapped with his stumped fin, then over and over slowly revolved like a waning world; turned up the white secrets of his belly; lay like a hog, and died.

20) p. 310   Everyone knows that by the peculiar cunning of their gills, the finny tribes in general breathe the air which at all times is combined with the element in which they swim; hence, a herring or cod might live in a century, and never once raise its head above the surface.

21) p. 315   His side-fins only serve to steer by.

22) p. 325   The delicate side-fins, and the palms of his fluke, still freshly retained the plaited crumpled appearance of a baby's ears newly arrived from foreign parts.

23) p. 329   Not a few are captured having the deep scars of these encounters,--furrowed heads, broken teeth, scolloped fins; and in some instances, wrenched and dislocated mouths.

24) pp.   But not alone has this Leviathan left his pre-adamite traces
380-81   in the stereotyped plates of nature, and in limestone and marl bequeathed his ancient bust; but upon Egyptian tablets, whose/ antiquity seems to claim for them an almost fossiliferous character, we find the unmistakable print of his fin.

25) p. 403   I, too, want a harpoon made; one that a thousand yoke of fiends could not part, Perth; something that will stick in a whale like his own fin-bone.

26) p. 451   But the added power of the boat did not equal the added power of the whale, for he seemed to have treble-bnaked his every fin; swimming with a velocity which plainly showed, that if now, under these circumstances, pushed on, the chase would prove an indefinitely prolonged, if not a hopeless

one; nor could any crew endure for so long a period, such an unintermitted, intense straining at the oar; a thing barely tolerable only in some one brief vicissitude.

Squall (3B)

<u>OMOO</u>

1) p. 39   In a squall, the water fairly poured down in sheets like a cascade, swashing about, and afterward spirting [sic] up between the chests like the jets of a fountain.

2) p. 46   The carpenter himself, going with another man to furl the main-top-gallant sail in a squall, was nearly pushed from the rigging by an unseen hand; and his shipmate swore that a wet hammock was flirted in his face.

3) p. 100   At this time our steerage-way was almost gone; and yet, in giving his orders, the passionate old man made as much fuss as a white squall aboard the Flying Dutchman.

<u>MARDI</u>

1) p. 4   Like favors snappishly conferred, they [the "trades"] came to us, as is often the case, in a very sharp squall; the shock of which carried away one of our spars; also our fat old cook off his legs; depositing him plump in the scuppers to leeward.

2) p. 7   But soon these regions would be past; the mild equatorial breeze exchanged for cold, fierce squalls and all the horrors of northern voyaging.

3) p. 63   Therefore I held my peace; while Jarl went on to declare, that with regard to the character of the brigantine, his mind was now pretty fully made up;--she was an arrant imposter, a shade of a ship, full of sailor's ghosts, and before we knew where we were, would dissolve in a supernatural squall, and leave us twain in the water.

<u>REDBURN</u>

1) p. 64   Never did I realize till now what the ocean was: how grand and majestic, how solitary, and boundless, and beautiful and blue; for that day it gave no tokens of squalls or hurricanes, such as I had heard my father tell of; nor could I imagine, how any thing that seemed so playful and placid, could be lashed into rage, and troubled into rolling avalanches of foam, and great cascades of waves, such as I saw in the end.

2) p. 102   This violent rain was the precursor of a hard squall, for which we duly prepared, taking in our canvas to double-reefed-top-sails.

3) p. 104   "No, no," said Blunt, "all sailors are saved; they have plenty of squalls here below, but fair weather aloft."

4) p. 115   To my amazement, also, I found, that running up the rigging
              at sea, especially during a squall, was much easier than
              while lying in port.

5) p. 173   And the loss of a foretop-mast, between the tropics, in a
              squall, he attributed to this circumstance.

6) p. 220   I told him, that unless he was somewhat accustomed to the
              rigging, and could furl a royal in a squall, he would be
              sure to subject himself to a sort of treatment from the
              sailors, in the last degree ignominious to any mortal who
              had ever crossed his legs under mahogany.

7) p. 288   It was all-important now that the steerage should be
              purified; and had it not been for the rains and squalls,
              which would have made it madness to turn such a number of
              women and children upon the wet and unsheltered decks, the
              steerage passengers would have been ordered above, and their
              den have been given a thorough cleansing.

WHITE-JACKET

1) p. 32   Prepare for white squalls, living gales and Typhoons; read
              accounts of shipwrecks and horrible disasters; peruse the
              Narratives of Byron and Bligh; familiarize yourselves with
              the story of the English frigate Alceste, and the French
              frigate Medusa.

2) p. 33   He encouraged those old Tritons, the Quarter-masters, to
              discourse with him concerning the likelihood of a squall;
              and often followed their advice as to taking in, or making
              sail.

3) p. 59   Then it was, look out for squalls.

4) p. 94   A black squall was coming down on the weather-bow, and the
              boatswain's mates bellowed themselves hoarse at the main-
              hatchway.

5) p. 96   And now, through drizzling fogs and vapors, and under damp,
              double-reefed top-sails, our wet-decked frigate drew nearer
              and nearer to the squally cape.

6) p. 105   With a suddenness by no means unusual in these latitudes,
              the light breeze soon became a succession of sharp squalls,
              and our sail-proud braggadocio of an Indiaman was observed
              to let every thing go by the run, his t'-gallant stun'-sails
              and flying-jib taking quick leave of the spars; the flying-
              jib was swept into the air, rolled together for a few
              minutes and tossed about in the squalls like a football.

7) p. 107   The most terrific job of all was to furl the main-sail,
              which, at the commencement of the squalls, had been chewed
              up, coaxed and quieted as much as possible with the bunt-
              lines and slab-lines.

8) p. 110   It is needless to say that, in almost all cases of similar
             hard squalls and gales, the latter step, though attended
             with more appalling appearances, is, in reality, the safer
             of the two, and the most generally adopted.

9) p. 121   How I hailed every snow-squall; for then--blessings on them!
             --many of the men became <u>white jackets</u> along with myself;
             and, powdered with the flakes, we all looked like millers.

MOBY-<u>DICK</u>

1) p. 70   "Not much," I replied--"nothing but water; considerable
             horizon though, and there's a squall coming up, I think."

2) p. 75   "Whew!" he whistled at last--"the squall's gone off to
             leeward, I think."

3) p. 130   But the third Emir, now seeing himself all alone on the
             quarter-deck, seems to feel relieved from some curious
             restraint; for, tipping all sorts of knowing winks in all
             sorts of directions, and kicking off his shoes, he strikes
             into a sharp but noiseless squall of a hornpipe right over
             the Grand Turk's head; and then, by a dexterous sleight,
             pitching his cap up into the mizen-top for a shelf, he goes
             down rollicking, so far at least as he remains visible from
             the deck, reversing all other processions, by bringing up
             the rear with music.

4) p. 143   "Corkscrew!" cried Ahab, "aye, Queequeg, the harpoons lie
             all twisted and wrenched in him; aye, Daggoo, his spout is a
             big one, like a whole shock of wheat, and white as a pile of
             our Nantucket wool after the great annual sheep-shearing;
             aye, Tashtego, and he fan-tails like a split jib in a squall."

5) p. 153   I heard old Ahab tell him he must always kill a squall,
             something as they burst a water-spout with a pistol--fire
             your ship right into it!

6) p. 154   The squall! the squall! jump, my jollies!

7) p. 154   --Jimmini, what a squall!

8) p. 166   From its snowy aspect, the gauntleted ghost of the Southern
             Seas has been denominated the White Squall.

9) p. 194   The whole crew were half suffocated as they were tossed
             helter-skelter into the white curdling cream of the squall.

10) p. 194   Squall, whale, and harpoon had all blended together; and the
             whale, merely grazed by the iron, escaped.

11) p. 194   The wind increased to a howl; the waves dashed their bucklers
             together; the whole squall roared, forked, and crackled
             around us like a white fire upon the prairie, in which,
             unconsumed, we were burning; immortal in these jaws of death!

12) p. 196   I suppose then, that going plump on a flying whale with your
              sail set in a foggy squall is the height of a whaleman's
              discretion?

13) p. 196   Considering, therefore, that squalls and capsizings in the
              water and consequent bivouacks on the deep, were matters of
              common occurrence in this kind of life; considering that at
              the superlatively critical instant of going on to the whale
              I must resign my life into the hands of him who steered the
              boat--oftentimes a fellow who at that very moment is in his
              impetuousness upon the point of scuttling the craft with his
              own frantic stampings; considering that that particular
              disaster to our own particular boat was chiefly to be imputed
              to Starbuck's driving on to his whale almost in the teeth of
              a squall, and considering that Starbuck, notwithstanding,
              was famous for his great heedfulness in the fishery;
              considering that I belonged to this uncommonly prudent
              Starbuck's boat; and finally considering in what a devil's
              chase I was implicated, touching the White Whale: taking
              all things together, I say, I thought I might as well go
              below and make a rough draft of my will.

14) p. 370   Yes, and we flipped it at the rate of ten gallons the hour;
              and when the squall came (for it's squally off there by
              Patagonia), and all hands--visitors and all--were called to
              reef topsails, we were so top-heavy that we had to swing
              each other aloft in bowlines; and we ignorantly furled the
              skirts of our jackets into the sails, so that we hung there,
              reefed fast in the howling gale, a warning example to all
              drunken tars.

15) p. 432   That was sudden, now; but squalls come sudden in hot
              latitudes.

Anchor (3C)

1) p. 5   But courage, old lass, I hope to see thee soon within a biscuit's toss of the merry land, riding snugly at anchor in some green cove, and sheltered from the boisterous winds.

2) p. 12   In the bay of Nukuheva was the anchorage we desired to reach.

3) pp. 12-13   Although he was utterly unable to stand erect or to navigate his body across the deck, he still magnanimously proffered his services to pilot the/ ship to a good and secure anchorage.

4) p. 15   In the evening after we had come to an anchor the deck was illuminated with lanterns, and this picturesque band of sylphs, tricked out with flowers, and dressed in robes of variegated tappa, got up a ball in great style.

5) p. 18   The frigate, immediately upon coming to an anchor, got springs on her cables, and with her guns cast loose and her men at their quarters, lay in the circular basin of Papeete, with her broadside bearing upon the devoted town; while her numerous cutters, hauled in order alongside, were ready to effect a landing, under cover of her batteries.

6) p. 24   Viewed from our ship as she lay at anchor in the middle of the harbor, it presented the appearance of a vast natural amphitheatre in decay, and overgrown with vines, the deep glens that furrowed its sides appearing like enormous fissures caused by the ravages of time.

7) p. 25   She was soon conducted to a beautiful inlet, and dropped her anchor in its waters beneath the shadows of the lofty shore.

8) p. 270   Here he received another welcome from his Nukuheva wives, and after some refreshments in the shape of cocoa-nut milk and poee-poee, they entered a canoe (the Typee of course going along) and paddled off to a whale ship which was anchored near the shore.

9) p. 271   Hardly was the boat out of sight, when the captain came forward and ordered the anchor weighed; he was going to sea.

1) p. 14   But the truth was, that by lying in harbor, he ran the risk of losing the remainder of his men by desertion; and as it was, he still feared that, in some outlandish bay or other, he might one day find his anchor down, and no crew to weigh it.

2) p. 14   It is for this reason, that many South Sea whalemen do not come to an anchor for eighteen or twenty months on a stretch.

3) p. 19   She was riding to her anchor in the bay, and proved to be a
French corvette.

4) p. 19   His original intention was not to let go an anchor; but,
counting upon the assistance of the corvette in case of any
difficulty, he now changed his mind, and anchored alongside
of her.

5) p. 20   The night of our arrival, the mate and the Mowree were to
stand "watch and watch," relieving each other every four
hours; the crew, as is sometimes customary when lying at
anchor, being allowed to remain all night below.

6) p. 26   This is the only harbor of any note about the island, though
as far as a safe anchorage is concerned it hardly deserves
the title.

7) p. 50   The captain's anchor is pretty nigh atrip; I shouldn't
wonder if he croaked afore morning.

8) p. 70   But the doctor's influence at last began to tell; and, with
a few exceptions, they agreed to be guided by him; assured
that, if they did so, the ship would eventually be brought
to her anchors, without any one getting into trouble.

9) p. 76   It was no use talking; come what come might, the ship must
let go her anchor.

10) p. 81   It is applied to certain roving characters, who, without
(footnote)   attaching themselves permanently to any vessel, ship now and
then for a short cruise in a whaler; but upon the condition
only of being honorably discharged the very next time the
anchor takes hold of the bottom; no matter where.

11) p. 83   All we wanted was to have the ship snugly anchored in
Papeetee Bay; entertaining no doubt that, could this be
done, it would in some way or other peaceably lead to our
emancipation.

12) p. 100   Pulling a greasy silk handkerchief still lower over his
brow, and improving the sit of his frock-coat, with a
vigorous jerk, he then strode up to the mate; and, in a more
flowery style than ever, gave him to understand that the
redoubtable "Jim," himself, was before him; that the ship
was his until the anchor was down; and he should like to
hear what any one had to say to it.

13) p. 100   Our gentleman now proceeded to bring us to an anchor,
jumping up between the knight-heads, and bawling out "Luff!
Luff! keepy off! keepy off!" and insisted upon each time
being respectfully responded to by the man at the helm.

14) p. 102   At last the wishes of many were gratified; and like an
aeronaut's grapnel, her rusty little anchor was caught in
the coral groves at the bottom of Papeetee Bay.

15) p. 149   The decks were all life and commotion; the sailors on the forecastle singing "Ho, cheerly men!" as they catted the anchor; and the gallant Jermin, bareheaded as his wont, standing up on the bowsprit, and issuing his orders.

16) p. 153   Giving him all I could spare from my chest, I went on deck to take my place at the windlass; for the anchor was weighing.

17) p. 153   The anchor was soon up; and away we went out of the bay with more than twenty shallops towing astern.

18) pp. 216-17   It was now proposed to try the water; so a small fishing canoe, hauled up near by, was quickly launched; and paddling a good distance off, we dropped overboard the native contrivance for an anchor--a heavy stone,/ attached to a cable of braided bark.

19) p. 270   Curiously enough, the openings in the reefs, by which alone vessels enter to their anchorage, are invariably opposite the mouths of running streams; an advantage fully appreciated by the mariner who touches for the purpose of watering his ship.

20) p. 289   Going from Po-Po's house toward the anchorage of the harbor of Taloo, you catch no glimpse of the water, until coming out from deep groves, you all at once find yourself upon the beach.

21) p. 299   In a grove near the anchorage, he had a rustic shanty and arbor; where, in quiet times, when no ships were in Taloo, a stray native once in a while got boozy, and staggered home, catching at the cocoa-nut trees as he went.

22) p. 299   Soon, she drops her anchors in its waters; and the next day, Captain Crash entertains the sailors in his grove.

23) p. 316   The anchors came up cheerily; the sails were soon set; and with the early breath of the tropical morning, fresh and fragrant from the hillsides, we slowly glided down the bay, and were swept through the opening in the reef.

MARDI

1) p. 64   Our castle, the Bread-Barge was of the common sort; an oblong oaken box, much battered and bruised, and like the Elgin Marbles, all over inscriptions and carving: foul anchors, skewered hearts, almanacs, Burton-blocks, love verses, links of cable, Kings of Clubs, and divers mystic diagrams in chalk, drawn by old Finnish mariners, in casting horoscopes and prophecies.

2) p. 69   Now, the fated brig lay anchored within a deep, smooth, circular lagoon, margined on all sides but one by the most beautiful groves.

3) p. 161   But alas! how weigh the isle's coral anchor, leagues down
             in the fathomless sea?

4) p. 178   Full before me, lay the Mardian fleet of isles, profoundly
             at anchor within their coral harbor.

5) p. 432   In this arbor we anchored.

6) p. 498   See! spire behind spire, as if the land were the ocean, and
             all Bello's great navy were riding at anchor.

7) p. 554   On our left, Porpheero's southwest point, a mighty rock,
             long tiers of galleries within, deck on deck; and flag-
             staffs, like an admiral's masts: a line-of-battle-ship,
             all purple stone, and anchored in the sea.

8) p. 620   Like helmless vessels, tempest-tossed, our only anchorage is
             when we founder.

REDBURN

1) p. 4   Coenties Slip must be somewhere near ranges of grim-looking
             warehouses, with rusty iron doors and shutters, and tiled
             roofs; and old anchors and chain-cable piled on the walk.

2) p. 31   At last we cast loose, and swinging out into the stream,
             came to anchor, and hoisted the signal for sailing.

3) p. 31   Yaw about while you may, my hearties, I'll do the yawing
             after the anchor's up.

4) p. 32   Every thing at last being in readiness, the pilot came on
             board, and all hands were called to up anchor.

5) p. 32   The anchor being secured, a steam tug-boat with a strong
             name, the Hercules, took hold of us; and away we went past
             the long line of shipping, and wharves, and warehouses; and
             rounded the green south point of the island where the
             battery is, and passed Governor's Island, and pointed right
             out for the Narrows.

6) p. 33   As the steamer carried us further and further down the bay,
             and we passed ships lying at anchor, with men gazing at us
             and waving their hats; and small boats with ladies in them
             waving their handkerchiefs; and passed the green shore of
             Staten Island, and caught sight of so many beautiful
             cottages all overrun with vines, and planted on the beautiful
             fresh mossy hill-sides; oh! then I would have given any
             thing if instead of sailing out of the bay, we were only
             coming into it; if we had crossed the ocean and returned,
             gone over and come back; and my heart leaped up in me like
             something alive when I thought of really entering the bay at
             the end of the voyage.

7) p. 41   His trowsers were of clear white duck, and he sported a
            handsome pair of pumps, and a tarpaulin hat bright as a
            looking-glass, with a long black ribbon streaming behind,
            and getting entangled every now and then in the rigging; and
            he had gold anchors in his ears, and a silver ring on one of
            his fingers, which was very much worn and bent from pulling
            ropes and other work on board ship.

8) p. 93   All her starboard side was torn and splintered; her starboard
            anchor was gone; and a great part of the starboard bulwarks;
            while every one of the lower yard-arms had been broken, in
            the same direction; so that she now carried small and
            unsightly jury-yards.

9) p. 96   On the next day, the fog lifted; and by noon we found
            ourselves sailing through fleets of fishermen at anchor.

10) p. 122 Often furnished with a club-hammer, they swung me over the
            bows in a bowline, to sound the rust off the anchor; a most
            monotonous, and to me a most uncongenial and irksome business.

11) p. 127 The day came, and soon, passing two lofty land-marks on the
            Lancashire shore, we rapidly drew near the town, and at last,
            came to anchor in the stream.

12) p. 128 Not long after anchoring, several boats came off, and from
            one of them stept a neatly-dressed and very respectable-
            looking woman, some thirty years of age, I should think,
            carrying a bundle.

13) p. 130 In the afternoon our pilot was all alive with his orders;
            we hove up the anchor, and after a deal of pulling, and
            hauling, and jamming against other ships, we wedged our way
            through a lock at high tide; and about dark, succeeded in
            working up to a berth in Prince's Dock.

14) p. 134 Three tall brass candlesticks shed a smoky light upon smoky
            walls, of what had once been sea-blue, covered with sailor-
            scrawls of four anchors, lovers' sonnets, and ocean ditties.

15) p. 138 For in Liverpool they find their Paradise--not the well
            known street of that name--and one of them told me he would
            be content to lie in Prince's Dock till he hove up anchor
            for the world to come.

16) p. 143 But what does this anchor here? this ship? and this sea-
            ditty of Dibdin's?

17) p. 143 No: that anchor, ship, and Dibdin's ditty are mine; this
            hand drew them; and on this very voyage to Liverpool.

18) p. 147 It sings of Liverpool and the Mersey; its docks, and ships,
            and warehouses, and bales, and anchors; and after decanting
            upon the abject times, when "his noble waves, inglorious,
            Mersey rolled," the poet breaks forth like all Parnassus
            with:--

19) p. 175   It was an antique, covered with half-effaced inscriptions,
              crowns, anchors, eagles; and it had two handles near the
              trunnions like those of a tureen.

20) p. 189   From the various boarding-houses, each distinguished by
              gilded emblems outside--an anchor, a crown, a ship, a
              windlass, or a dolphin--proceeds the noise of revelry and
              dancing; and from the open casements lean young girls and
              old women, chattering and laughing with the crowds in the
              middle of the street.

21) p. 196   As soon as we came to anchor in the river, before reaching
              the dock, three custom-house underlings boarded us, and
              coming down into the forecastle, ordered the men to produce
              all the tobacco they had.

22) p. 218   Thus determined, he exchanged his trunk for a mahogany
              chest; sold some of his superfluities; and moved his quarters
              to the sign of the Gold Anchor in Union-street.

23) p. 225   Arrived at the Golden Anchor, where Harry put up, he at once
              led me to his room, and began turning over the contents of
              his chest, to see what clothing he might have, that would
              fit me.

24) p. 237   Once more in Liverpool; and wending my way through the same
              old streets to the sign of the Golden Anchor; I could
              scarcely credit the events of the last thirty-six hours.

25) p. 240   The white sails glistened in the clear morning air like a
              great Eastern encampment of sultans; and from many a
              forecastle, came the deep mellow old song Ho-o-he-yo,
              cheerily men! as the crews catted their anchors.

26) p. 245   "He's gone to the harbor where they never weigh anchor,"
              coughed Jackson.

27) p. 300   But though the long rows of white-washed hospitals on the
              hill side were now in plain sight, and though scores of
              ships were here lying at anchor, yet no boat came off to us;
              and to our surprise and delight, on we sailed, past a spot
              which every one had dreaded.

28) p. 301   Hurra! hurra! and ten thousand times hurra! down goes our
              old anchor, fathoms down into the free and independent
              Yankee mud, one handful of which was now worth a broad manor
              in England.

29) p. 303   It reminded me of his manner, when we had started for
              London, from the sign of the Golden Anchor, in Liverpool.

30) p. 309   And here they all came to anchor before the bar, and the
              landlord, a lantern-jawed landlord, bestirred himself behind
              it, among his villainous old bottles and decanters.

WHITE-JACKET

1) p. 4   Soaked and heavy, what a burden was that jacket to carry
               about, especially when I was sent up aloft; dragging myself
               up, step by step, as if I were weighing the anchor.

2) p. 6   All hands up anchor!

3) p. 7   All hands up anchor!

4) p. 7   With a jerk and a jerk, we broke ground; and up to our bows
               came several thousand pounds of old iron, in the shape of
               our ponderous anchor.

5) p. 9   Besides White-Jacket's office as looser of the main-royal,
               when all hands were called to make sail; and besides his
               special offices, in tacking ship, coming to anchor, &c.; he
               permanently belonged to the Starboard watch, one of the two
               primary, grand divisions of the ship's company.

6) pp.   "Jack Chase not to be found?" cried a growling old sheet-
17-18   anchor-man, one of your malicious prophets of past events:
               "I thought so; I know'd it;/ I could have sworn it--just the
               chap to make sail on the sly."

7) p. 18   Months passed away, and nothing was heard of Jack; till at
               last, the frigate came to anchor on the coast, alongside of
               a Peruvian sloop of war.

8) p. 25   Though these worthies sport long coats and wear the anchor-
               button; yet, in the estimation of the ward-room officers,
               they are not, technically speaking, rated gentlemen.

9) p. 27   But in the English navy they wear crowns and anchors worked
               on the sleeves of their jackets, by way of badges of office.

10) p. 47   Whereas, the old sheet-anchor-men, who spent their time in
               the bracing sea-air and broad-cast sunshine of the
               forecastle, were free, generous-hearted, charitable, and
               full of good-will to all hands; though some of them, to tell
               the truth, proved sad exceptions; but exceptions only prove
               the rule.

11) p. 54   "The grog gone!" roared an old Sheet-anchor-man.

12) p. 72   "There, Bungs!" cried Scrimmage, a sheet-anchor-man, "there's
               a good pattern for you; make up a brace of life-buoys like
               that; something that will save a man, and not fill and sink
               under him, as those leaky quarter-casks of yours will the
               first time there's occasion to drop 'em."

13) p. 72   "Don't believe it!" cried the sheet-anchor-man; "you lopers
               that live about the decks here are nearer the bottom of the
               sea than the light hand that looses the main-royal."

14) p. 72   In addition to the <u>Bower-anchors</u> carried on her bows, a
(footnote)   frigate carries large anchors in her fore-chains, called
              <u>Sheet-anchors</u>.

15) p. 72   Hence, the old seamen stationed in that part of a man-of-war
(footnote)   are called <u>Sheet-anchor-men</u>.

16) p. 73   "Bungs, is it?" cried Scrimmage, the sheet-anchor-man; "I
              told him his buoys wouldn't save a drowning man; and now he
              has proved it!"

17) p. 86   One rheumatic old sheet-anchor-man among us was driven to
              the extremity of sewing a piece of tarred canvas on the seat
              of his trowsers.

18) p. 90   "Is this the <u>riglar</u> fruits of liberty?" touchingly inquired
              an Irish waister of an old Spanish sheet-anchor man.

19) p. 109   Thus, all the fine weather we encountered after first
              weighing anchor on the pleasant Spanish coast, was but the
              prelude to this one terrific night; more especially, that
              treacherous calm immediately preceding it.

20) p. 157   A remarkably serious, but bigoted seaman, a sheet-anchor-man
              --whose private devotions may hereafter be alluded to--once
              touched his hat to the captain, and respectfully said, "Sir,
              I am a Baptist; the chaplain is an Episcopalian; his form of
              worship is not mine; I do not believe with him, and it is
              against my conscience to be under his ministry."

21) p. 159   As we glided on toward our anchorage, the bands of the
              various men-of-war in harbor saluted us with national airs,
              and gallantly lowered their ensigns.

22) p. 160   With all her batteries, she is tranquilly lying in harbor,
              surrounded by English, French, Dutch, Portuguese, and
              Brazilian seventy-fours, moored in the deep-green water,
              close under the lee of that oblong, castellated mass of rock,
              Ilha das Cobras, which, with its port-holes and lofty flag-
              staffs, looks like another man-of-war, fast anchored in the
              bay.

23) p. 160   Ay, behold now the Neversink at her anchors, in many respects
              presenting a different appearance from what she presented at
              sea.

24) pp.   I diversified this reading of mine, by borrowing Moore's
168-9   "<u>Loves of the Angels</u>" from Rose-water, who recommended it as
              "<u>de charmingest of</u> volumes;" and a Negro Song-book,
              containing <u>Sittin' on a Rail</u>, <u>Gumbo/Squash</u>, and <u>Jim along
              Josey</u>, from Broadbit, a sheet-anchor-man.

25) p. 170   Still, they had other pursuits; some were expert at the
              needle, and employed their time in making elaborate shirts,
              stitching picturesque eagles, and anchors, and all the stars
              of the federated states in the collars thereof; so that when

they at last completed and put on these shirts, they may be said to have hoisted the American colors.

26) p. 170   They would <u>prick</u> you to order a palm-tree, an anchor, a crucifix, a lady, a lion, an eagle, or any thing else you might want.

27) p. 176   For though his vessel be anchored a mile from the shore, and her sides are patrolled by sentries night and day, yet these things can not entirely prevent the seductions of the land from reaching him.

28) p. 178   Of a certain moonless night, he was to bring off three gallons of spirits, <u>in skins</u>, and moor them to the frigate's anchor-buoy--some distance from the vessel--attaching something heavy, to sink them out of sight.

29) p. 180   A knowing old sheet-anchor-man, an unprincipled fellow, putting this, that, and the other together, ferrets out the mystery; and straightway resolves to reap the goodly harvest which the cockswain had sowed.

30) p. 180   He attempts to bribe the other to secrecy, by promising half the profits of the enterprise; but the sheet-anchor-man's integrity is like a rock; he is no mercenary, to be bought up for a song.

31) p. 180   This done, the sheet-anchor-man goes to his confidants, and arranges his plans.

32) p. 195   When several men-of-war of one nation lie at anchor in one port, forming a wide circle round their lord and master, the flag-ship, it is a very interesting sight to see them all obeying the commodore's orders, who meanwhile never opens his lips.

33) p. 198   Some allusion has been made to the weariness experienced by the man-of-war's-man while lying at anchor; but there are scenes now and then that serve to relieve it.

34) p. 202   "You venerable sheet-anchor-men! and you, gallant fore-top-men! and you, my fine waisters! what do you say now for this superior old jacket?"

35) pp.   "What are you busin' that 'ere garment for?" cried an old
202-3   sheet-/anchor-man.

36) p. 211   Archipelago Rio! ere Noah on old Ararat anchored his ark, there lay anchored in you all these green, rocky isles I now see.

37) pp.   Amphitheatrical Rio! . . ./ of all the Barbary corsairs
211-12   captured by Bainbridge; of the war-canoes of the Polynesian kings, Tammahammaka and Pomare--ay! one and all, with Commodore Noah for their Lord High Admiral--in this abounding Bay of Rio these flag-ships might all come to anchor, and swing round in concert to the first of the flood.

38) p. 213   We had not lain in Rio long, when in the innermost recesses
              of the mighty soul of my noble captain of the Top--
              incomparable Jack Chase--the deliberate opinion was formed,
              and rock-founded, that our ship's company must have at least
              one day's "liberty" to go ashore ere we weighed anchor for
              home.

39) p. 214   Surely you will not keep us always tethered at anchor, when
              a little more cable would admit of our cropping the herbage!

40) p. 219   Nor will you fail to remark, when you see an English cutter
              officered by one of these volunteers, that the boy does not
              so strut and slap his dirk-hilt with a Bobadil air, and
              anticipatingly feel of the place where his warlike whiskers
              are going to be, and sputters out oaths so at the men, as is
              too often the case with the little boys wearing best-bower
              anchors on their lapels in the American Navy.

41) p. 227   The British line-of-battle ship, Royal George, which in 1782
              sunk at her anchors at Spithead, carried down three hundred
              English women among the one thousand souls that were drowned
              on that memorable morning.

42) p. 229   But, hold them fast--all those who have not yet weighed
              their anchors for the Navy--round and round, hitch over
              hitch, bind your leading-strings on them, and, clinching a
              ring-bolt into your chimney-jam, moor your boys fast to that
              best of harbors, the hearth-stone.

43) p. 244   I won't see him, by Heaven, with this sailor's frock on, and
              he with the anchor button!

44) p. 245   The vessel was hailed from our poop, and came to anchor
              within a biscuit's toss of our batteries.

45) p. 265   When we were nearly ready for sea, the English frigate,
              weighing her anchor, made all sail with the sea-breeze, and
              began showing off her pace, by gliding about among all the
              men-of-war in harbor, and particularly by running down under
              the Neversink's stern.

46) p. 268   "All hands up anchor, ahoy!"

47) p. 306   Throughout the night these policemen relieve each other at
              standing guard over the premises; and, except when the
              watches are called, they sit in the midst of a profound
              silence, only invaded by trumpeter's snores, or the ramblings
              of some old sheet-anchor-man in his sleep.

48) p. 311   There was an old negro, who went by the name of Tawney, a
              sheet-anchor-man, whom we often invited into our top of
              tranquil nights, to hear him discourse.

49) p. 324   He was a sheet-anchor-man, an earnest Baptist, and was well
              known, in his own part of the ship, to be constant in his
              solitary devotions in the chains.

50) p. 339   I tell ye, now, ten best-bower-anchors wouldn't sink this
              'ere top-man.

51) p. 353   Indeed, at times he was wont to talk philosophy to his
              ancient companions--the old sheet-anchor-men around him--as
              well as to the hare-brained tenants of the fore-top, and the
              giddy lads in the mizzen.

52) p. 357   Where are you, sheet-anchor-men! Captains of the tops!
              gunner's mates! mariners, all!

53) p. 358   They tumbled up, as commanded; and for the rest of that
              night contented themselves with privately fulminating their
              displeasure against the Captain, and publicly emblazoning
              every anchor-button on the coat of admired Mad Jack.

54) p. 363   His sheath-knife was an antique--a sort of old-fashioned
              pruning hook; its handle--a sperm whale's tooth--was carved
              all over with ships, cannon, and anchors.

55) p. 366   "And now go and cut your own throat," hoarsely whispered an
              old sheet-anchor-man, a mess-mate of Ushant's.

56) p. 366   He remained prisoner till we arrived in America; but the
              very moment he heard the chain rattle out of the hawse-hole,
              and the ship swing to her anchor, he started to his feet,
              dashed the sentry aside, and gaining the deck, exclaimed,
              "At home, with my beard!"

57) p. 372   Some years ago a fire broke out near the powder magazine in
              an American national ship, one of a squadron at anchor in
              the Bay of Naples.

58) p. 382   In the first place, the magnitude of most of these ships
              requires a large number of hands to brace the heavy yards,
              hoist the enormous top-sails, and weigh the ponderous anchor.

59) p. 384   "Jack dances and sings, and is always content,/ In his vows
              to his lass he'll ne'er fail her;/ His anchor's atrip when
              his money's all spent,/ And this is the life of a sailor."

60) p. 388   "Who says the old man at the helm of the Yankee nation can't
              steer his trick as well as George Washington himself?" cried
              a sheet-anchor-man.

61) p. 395   Cable and Anchor all clear

62) p. 396   No! let all this go by; for our anchor still hangs from our
              bows, though its eager flukes dip their points in the
              impatient waves.

MOBY-DICK

1) p. 21   A still duskier place is this, with such low ponderous beams
              above, and such old wrinkled planks beneath, that you would

almost fancy you trod some old craft's cockpits, especially
of such a howling night, when this corner-anchored old ark
rocked so furiously.

2) p. 27   But I stood irresolute; when looking at a clock in the corner,
he exclaimed, "I vum it's Sunday--you won't see that
harpooner to-night; he's come to anchor somewhere--come
along then; do come; won't ye come?"

3) p. 49   And now behold Jonah taken up as an anchor and dropped into
the sea; when instantly an oily calmness floats out from the
east, and the sea is still, as Jonah carries down the gale
with him, leaving smooth water behind.

4) p. 63   It was quite late in the evening when the little Moss came
snugly to anchor, and Queequeg and I went ashore; so we
could attend to no business that day, at least none but a
supper and a bed.

5) p. 84   By the great anchor, what a harpoon he's got there! looks
like good stuff that; and he handles it about right.

6) p. 94   And all this seemed natural enough; especially as in the
merchant service many captains never show themselves on deck
for a considerable time after heaving up the anchor, but
remain over the cabin table, having a farewell merry-making
with their shore friends, before they quit the ship for good
with the pilot.

7) p. 94   As I hinted before, this whalebone marquee was never pitched
except in port; and on board the Pequod, for thirty years,
the order to strike the tent was well known to be the next
thing to heaving up the anchor.

8) p. 94   And here Bildad, who, with Peleg, be it known, in addition
to his other offices, was one of the licensed pilots of the
port--he being suspected to have got himself made a pilot in
order to save the Nantucket pilot-fee to all the ships he
was concerned in, for he never piloted any other craft--
Bildad, I say, might now be seen actively engaged in looking
over the bows for the approaching anchor, and at intervals
singing what seemed a dismal stave of psalmody, to cheer the
hands at the windlass, who roared forth some sort of a chorus
about the girls in Booble Alley, with hearty good will.

9) pp.   I almost thought he would sink the ship before the anchor
94-5   could be got up; involuntarily I paused on my handspike, and
told Queequeg/ to do the same, thinking of the perils we both
ran, in starting on the voyage with such a devil for a pilot.

10) p. 150 Hist, boys! let's have a jig or two before we ride to anchor
in Blanket Bay.

11) p. 233 With a frigate's anchors for my bridle-bits and fasces of
harpoons for spurs, would I could mount that whale and leap
the topmost skies, to see whether the fabled heavens with

all their countless tents really lie encamped beyond my
mortal sight!

12) p. 248   Very soon you would have thought from the sound on the
Pequod's decks, that all hands were preparing to cast anchor
in the deep; for heavy chains are being dragged along the
deck, and thrust rattling out of the port-holes.

13) pp.   Nevertheless, upon Stubb setting the anchor-watch after his
256-7   supper was concluded; and when, accordingly, Queequeg and a/
forecastle seaman came on deck, no small excitement was
created among the sharks; for immediately suspending the
cutting stages over the side, and lowering three lanterns,
so that they cast long gleams of light over the turbid sea,
these two mariners, darting their long whaling-spades, kept
up an incessant murdering of the sharks, by striking the
keen steel deep into their skulls, seemingly their only
vital part.

14) p. 281   With a long, weary hoist the jaw is dragged on board, as if
it were an anchor; and when the proper time comes--some few
days after the other work--Queequeg, Daggoo, and Tashtego,
being all accomplished dentists, are set to drawing teeth.

15) p. 364   This was quickly lowered to Ahab, who at once comprehending
it all, slid his solitary thigh into the curve of the hook
(it was like sitting in the fluke of an anchor, or the
crotch of an apple tree), and then giving the word, held
himself fast, and at the same time he also helped to hoist
his own weight, by pulling hand-over-hand upon one of the
running parts of the tackle.

16) p. 418   The anchors are working, sir.

17) p. 419   First take your leg off from the crown of the anchor here,
though, so I can pass the rope; now listen.

Tar (4)

1) p. 3   Oh! ye state-room sailors, who make so much ado about a
fourteen-days' passage across the Atlantic; who so
pathetically relate the privations and hardships of the sea,
where, after a day of breakfasting, lunching, dining off
five courses, chatting, playing whist, and drinking
champagne-punch, it was your hard lot to be shut up in
little cabinets of mahogany and maple, and sleep for ten
hours, with nothing to disturb you but "those good-for-
nothing tars, shouting and trampling over head."--what would
ye say to our six months out of sight of land?

OMOO

1) pp.   The boy becomes, in time, a thorough-bred tar, equally ready
108-9   to strip and take a dozen on/ board his own ship, or, cutlass
in hand, dash pell-mell on board the enemy's.

2) p. 110 Indeed, a thorough tar is unfit for any thing else; and what
is more, this fact is the best evidence of his being a true
sailor.

3) p. 135 The old tar had complained of the effects of immoderate
eating of fruit.

MARDI

1) p. 115 Ere long, so outrageous became Annatoo's detestation of him,
that the honest old tar could stand it no longer, and like
most good-natured men when once fairly roused, he was swept
through and through with a terrible typhoon of passion.

REDBURN

1) pp.   I only held on/ hard, and made good the saying of old
78-9   sailors, that the last person to fall overboard from the
rigging is a landsman, because he grips the ropes so
fiercely; whereas old tars are less careful, and sometimes
pay the penalty.

2) p. 108 Blunt, the Dream Book tar, swore he was a magician; and took
an extra dose of salts, by way of precaution against his
spells.

3) p. 130 Other ships, however--the economical Dutch and Danish, for
instance, and sometimes the prudent Scotch--feed their
luckless tars in dock, with precisely the same fare which
they give them at sea; taking their salt junk ashore to be
cooked, which, indeed, is but scurvy sort of treatment,
since it is very apt to induce the scurvy.

4) p. 139   Thus, because the sailor, who today steers the Hibernia or
Unicorn steam-ship across the Atlantic, is a somewhat
different man from the exaggerated sailors of Smollet, and
the men who fought with Nelson at Copenhagen, and survived to
riot themselves away at North Corner in Plymouth;--because
the modern tar is not quite so gross as heretofore, and has
shaken off some of his shaggy jackets, and docked his Lord
Rodney queue:--therefore, in the estimation of some observers,
he has begun to see the evils of his condition, and has
oluntarily improved.

5) p. 140   You will do no such thing; but at a distance, you will perhaps
subscribe a dollar or two for the building of a hospital, to
accommodate sailors, already broken down; or for the
distribution of excellent books among tars who can not read.

6) p. 143   The book must have fallen into the hands of some tarry
captain of a forecastle.

7) p. 167   And once, while marveling how a couple like this found room
to turn in, below; I was amazed by a noisy irruption of
cherry-cheeked young tars from the scuttle, whence they came
rolling forth, like so many curly spaniels from a kennel.

8) p. 175   There was a little balcony near the base of the steeple,
some twenty feet from the water; where, on week-days, I used
to see and old pensioner of a tar, sitting on a camp-stool,
reading his Bible.

9) p. 187   I must mention the case of an old man, who every day, and
all day long, through sunshine and rain, occupied a
particular corner, where crowds of tars were always passing.

10) p. 188   Among the paupers were several who wore old sailor hats and
jackets, and claimed to be destitute tars; and on the
strength of these pretensions demanded help from their
brethren; but Jack would see through their disguise in a
moment, and turn away, with no benediction.

11) p. 192   Not content with thus publicly giving notice of their
whereabouts, these indefatigable Sangrados and pretended
Samaritans hire a parcel of shabby workhouse-looking knaves,
whose business consists in haunting the dock walls about
meal times, and silently thrusting mysterious little billets
--duodecimo editions of the larger advertisements--into the
astonished hands of the tars.

12) p. 219   Therefore, as it was agreed between Harry and me, that he
should offer to ship as a "boy," at the same rate of
compensation with myself, I made no doubt that, incited by
the cheapness of the bargain, Captain Riga would gladly
close with him; and thus, instead of paying sixteen dollars
a month to a thorough-going tar, who would consume all his
rations, buy up my young blade of Bury, at the rate of half
a dollar a week, with the cheering prospect, that by the end
of the voyage, his fastidious palate would be the means of

leaving a handsome balance of salt beef and pork in the
harness-cask.

13) p. 239   Staggering along that bowsprit, now came a one-eyed crimp,
leading a drunken tar by the collar, who had been shipped
to sail with us the day previous.

14) p. 256   Harry looked round among the grinning tars with a glance of
terrible indignation and agony; and then settling his eye on
me, and seeing there no hope, but even an admonition of
obedience, as his only resource, he made one bound into the
rigging, and was up at the main-top in a trice.

15) p. 274   The extraordinary dominion of this one miserable Jackson,
over twelve or fourteen strong, healthy tars, is a riddle,
whose solution must be left to the philosophers.

WHITE-JACKET

1) p. 13   Whatever the other seamen might have been, these were a
noble set of tars, and well worthy an introduction to the
reader.

2) p. 14   His manners were easy and free; none of the boisterousness,
so common to tars; and he had a polite, courteous way of
saluting you, if it were only to borrow your knife.

3) p. 19   So Jack went forward among crowds of admiring tars, who
swore by his nut-brown beard, which had amazingly lengthened
and spread during his absence.

4) p. 33   Mad Jack was expressly created and labelled for a tar.

5) p. 39   A gang will be informed, that such a fellow has three or
four gold pieces in the monkey-bag, so called, or purse,
which many tars wear round their necks, tucked out of sight.

6) p. 53   We were not many days out of port, when a rumor was set
afloat that dreadfully alarmed many tars.

7) p. 64   It is a regular tune, with a fine song composed to it; the
words of the chorus, being most artistically arranged, may
give some idea of the air:/ "Hearts of oak are our ships,
jolly tars are our men,/ We always are ready, steady, boys,
steady,/ To fight and to conquer, again and again."

8) p. 65   But to toil and sweat in a fictitious encounter; to squander
the previous breath of my precious body in a ridiculous
fight of shams and pretentions; to hurry about the decks,
pretending to carry the killed and wounded below; to be told
that I must consider the ship blowing up, in order to
exercise myself in presence of mind, and prepare for a real
explosion; all this I despise, as beneath a true tar and man
of valor.

9) p. 67   Meantime, a loud cry is heard of "Fire! fire! fire!" in the
            fore-top; and a regular engine, worked by a set of Bowery-
            boy tars, is forthwith set to playing streams of water aloft.

10) p. 92   [a poster for the Cape Horn Theatre]: To conclude with the
            much-admired song by Dibdin, altered to suit all American
            Tars, entitled "The True Yankee Sailor."

11) p. 93   So the men whose regular turns, at the time of the
            performance, would come round to be stationed in the tops,
            and at the various halyards and running ropes about the
            spar-deck, could not be permitted to partake in the
            celebration, there accordingly ensued, during the morning,
            many amusing scenes of tars who were anxious to procure
            substitutes at their posts.

12) p. 102 Gangs of men, in all sorts of outlandish habiliments, wild
            as those worn at some crazy carnival, rushed to and fro,
            seizing upon whomsoever they pleased--warrant-officers and
            dangerous pugilists excepted--pulling and hauling the
            luckless tars about, till fairly baited into a genial warmth.

13) p. 116 The shower was hailed by the reckless tars with a hurricane
            of yells; although, for an instant, I really imagined we
            were being swamped in the sea, such volumes of water came
            cascading down.

14) p. 127 Also, in losing myself in some remote, dark corner of the
            bowels of the frigate, in the vicinity of the various
            store-rooms, shops, and warehouses, I much lamented that no
            enterprising tar had yet thought of compiling a Handbook of
            the Neversink, so that the tourist might have a reliable
            guide.

15) p. 169 The sad taste of this old tar, in admiring such vulgar stuff,
            was much denounced by Rose-water, whose own predilections
            were of a more elegant nature, as evidenced by his exalted
            opinion of the literary merits of the "Loves of the Angels."

16) p. 199 "What shall I have now, my noble tars, for this superior
            pair of sea-boots?"

17) p. 199 "I must close the auction, my tars of Columbia; this will
            never do."

18) p. 200 "And look!" he exclaimed, suddenly seizing the boot, and
            exhibiting it on high, "look, my noble tars, if you have
            tears, prepare to shed them now."

19) p. 200 "Tars of Columbia," said the auctioneer, imperatively,
            "these boots must be sold; and if I can't sell them one way,
            I must sell them another."

20) p. 202 "How much for it, my gallant tars of Columbia? say the word,
            and how much?"

21) p. 202   "Aye, noble tars," said the auctioneer, "you may well stare
              at it; you will not find another jacket like this on either
              side of Cape Horn, I assure you."

22) p. 235   "I suppose that old gentleman, now," said a young New
              England tar beside me, "would consider it a great honor to
              put on his Royal Majesty's boots; and yet, White-Jacket, if
              yonder Emperor and I were to strip and jump overboard for a
              bath, it would be hard telling which was of the blood royal
              when we should once be in the water."

24) p. 270   They say Homer himself was once a tar, even as his hero,
              Ulysses, was both a sailor and a ship-wright.

25) pp.   But the only helmets of our/ tars were those with which
274-5   nature had furnished them.

26) p. 283   As in all extensive establishments--abbeys, arsenals,
              colleges, treasuries, metropolitan post-offices, and
              monasteries--there are many snug little niches, wherein are
              ensconced certain superannuated old pensioner officials;
              and, more especially, as in most ecclesiastical
              establishments, a few choice prebendary stalls are to be
              found, furnished with well-filled mangers and racks; so, in
              a man-of-war, there are a variety of similar snuggeries for
              the benefit of decrepit or rheumatic old tars.

27) p. 309   When you see a fellow yawing about the docks like a
              homeward-bound Indiaman, a long commodore's pennant of black
              ribbon flying from his mast-head, and fetching up at a grog-
              shop with a slew of his hull, as if an Admiral were coming
              alongside a three-decker in his barge; you may put that man
              down for what man-of-war's-men call a damn-my-eyes-tar, that
              is, a humbug.

28) p. 323   At other times, one of the tattooing artists would crawl
              over the bulwarks, followed by his sitter; and then a bare
              arm or leg would be extended, and the disagreeable business
              of "bricking" commence, right under my eyes; or an irruption
              of tars, with ditty-bags or sea-reticules, and piles of old
              trowsers to mend, would break in upon my seclusion, and,
              forming a sewing-circle, drive me off with their chatter.

29) p. 353   Judge, then, what half a century of battling out watches on
              the ocean must have done for this fine old tar.

30) p. 354   Many sailors, with naturally tendril locks, prided themselves
              upon what they call love curls, worn at the side of the head,
              just before the ear--a custom peculiar to tars, and which
              seems to have filled the vacated place of the old-fashioned
              Lord Rodney cue, which they used to wear some fifty years ago.

31) p. 362   That same evening, when the drum beat to quarters, the
              sailors went sullenly to their guns, and the old tars who
              still sported their beards stood up, grim, defying, and
              motionless, as the rows of sculptured Assyrian kings, who,

with their magnificent beards have recently been exhumed by
Layard.

32) pp.   Reverend old tars, one and all; some of them might have/
362-3   been grandsires, with grandchildren in every port round the
             world.

33) p. 383   There was on board of the Neversink a fore-top-man by the
             name of Landless, who, though his back was cross-barred, and
             plaided with the ineffaceable scars of all the floggings
             accumulated by a reckless tar during a ten years' service in
             the Navy, yet he perpetually wore a hilarious face, and at
             joke and repartee was very Joe Miller.

34) p. 385   And Jack Chase, Old Ushant, and several more fine tars that
             might be added, sufficiently attest, that in the Neversink
             at least, there was more than one noble man-of-war's-man who
             almost redeemed all the rest.

35) p. 390   Ay, these very tars--the foremost in denouncing the Navy;
             who had bound themselves by the most tremendous oaths--these
             very men, not three days after getting ashore, were rolling
             round the streets in penniless drunkenness; and next day
             many of them were to be found on board of the guards or
             receiving-ship.

36) p. 390   Fine fellows! generous-hearted tars!

37) p. 390   Seeing this sight, I thought to myself, well, these
             generous-hearted tars on shore were the greatest curmudgeons
             afloat! it's the bottle that's generous, not they!

MOBY-DICK

1) p. 22   At one end a ruminating tar was still further adorning it
             [the old wooden settle] with his jack-knife, stooping over
             and diligently working away at the space between his legs.

2) p. 370   Yes, and we flipped it at the rate of ten gallons the hour;
             and when the squall came (for it's squally off there by
             Patagonia), and all hands--visitors and all--were called to
             reef topsails, we were so top-heavy that we had to swing
             each other aloft in bowlines; and we ignorantly furled the
             skirts of our jackets into the sails, so that we hung there,
             reefed fast in the howling gale, a warning example to all
             drunken tars.

Bibliography

Allen, Gay Wilson. <u>Melville and His World</u>. New York: The Viking Press, 1971.

The <u>American Heritage Dictionary of the English Language</u>. Boston: Houghton Mifflin Company, 1969.

Anderson, Charles Roberts, ed. <u>Journal of a Cruise to the Pacific 1842-1844</u>. Durham, N.C.: Duke University Press, 1937.

Anderson, Charles Roberts. <u>Melville in the South Seas</u>. New York: Columbia University Press, 1951.

Arvin, Newton. <u>Herman Melville</u>. n.p.: William Sloane Associates, Inc., 1950.

Ball, Alice Morton. <u>Compounding in the English Language</u>: <u>A Comparative Review of Variant Authorities with a Rational System for General Use and a Comprehensive Alphabetic List of Compound Words</u>. New York: The H. W. Wilson Co., 1941.

Bloomfield, Leonard. <u>Language</u>. New York: Holt, Rinehart, and Winston, 1933.

Bradford, Gershon. <u>The Mariners' Dictionary</u>. New York: Weathervane Books, 1952.

Camus, Albert. "Herman Melville." In <u>Lyrical and Critical Essays</u>, pp. 288-294. New York: Alfred A. Knopf, 1969.

Christensen, Francis and Bonniejean. <u>A New Rhetoric</u>. New York: Harper & Row, 1976.

_____. <u>Notes toward a New Rhetoric: Six Essays for Teachers</u>. New York: Harper & Row, 1967.

Dana, Richard Henry. <u>The Seaman's Friend</u>. Boston: Thomas Groom & Co., 1857.

Davis, Merrill R. and William H. Gilman, eds. The Letters of Herman Melville. New Haven: Yale University Press, 1960.

"The Death Craft." The Democratic Press and Lansingburgh Advertiser, 16 November 1839, p. 1.

Emerson, Ralph Waldo. The Journals and Miscellaneous Notebooks of Ralph Waldo Emerson. Ed. Alfred A. Ferguson. Vol. 4. Cambridge: Belknap Press of Harvard University Press, 1964.

"Fragments from a Writing Desk No. 1." The Democratic Press and Lansingburgh Advertiser, 4 May 1839, p. 1.

"Fragments from a Writing Desk No. 2." The Democratic Press and Lansingburgh Advertiser, 18 May 1839, pp. 1-2.

Fries, Charles Carpenter. The Structure of English: An Introduction to the Construction of English Sentences. New York: Harcourt, Brace and Company, 1952.

Funk & Wagnalls New "Standard" Dictionary of the English Language. New York: Harcourt, Brace and World, Inc., 1961.

Gilman, William H. Melville's Early Life and Redburn. New York: New York University Press, 1951.

Hamilton, Frederick W. Compound Words: A Study of the Principles of Compounding, the Components of Compounds, and the Use of the Hyphen. Chicago: Committee on Education, United Typothetae of America, 1918.

Harrison, Rev. Matthew. The Rise, Progress and Present Structure of the English Language. Philadelphia: E. C. and J. Biddle, 1850.

Holman, C. Hugh. A Handbook to Literature, 3rd ed. New York: The Odyssey Press, 1972.

Howard, Leon. Herman Melville: A Biography. Berkeley: University of California Press, 1951.

Jespersen, Otto. A Modern English Grammar on Historical Principles. Vol. 4. Copenhagen: Ejnar Munksgaard, 1949.

_____. A Modern English Grammar on Historical Principles. Vol. 6. Copenhagen: Ejnar Munksgaard, 1942.

Jodrell, Richard Paul. Philology on the English Language. London: Cox and Baylis, 1820.

Knight, Austin M. Modern Seamanship. New York: D. Van Nostrand Co., Inc., 1943.

Larousse Encyclopedia of World Geography, 1964 ed.

Lawrence, D. H. "Herman Melville's 'Typee' and 'Omoo.'" In Studies in Classic American Literature, pp. 129-134. New York: The Viking Press, 1966.

Lawrence, D. H.   "Whitman."   In Studies in Classic American Literature,
    pp. 160-171. New York: The Viking Press, 1966.

Leech, Geoffrey. A Linguistic Guide to English Poetry. London: Longman
    Group Ltd., 1969.

_____. "'This Bread I Break'--Language and Interpretation." A
    Review of English Literature 6 (1965): 66-75.

Lees, Robert B. The Grammar of English Nominalizations. Bloomington:
    Indiana University Press, 1968.

Levin, Harry. The Power of Blackness. New York: Alfred A. Knopf, 1958.

Lewis, Charles Lee. Books of the Sea: An Introduction to Nautical
    Literature. Annapolis, Md.: United States Naval Institute, 1943.

Leyda, Jay. The Melville Log: A Documentary Life of Herman Melville,
    1819-1891. Vol. 1. New York: Harcourt, Brace and Company, 1951.

Matthiessen, F. O. American Renaissance: Art and Expression in the Age
    of Emerson and Whitman. London: Oxford University Press, 1941.

Melville, Herman. "Hawthorne and His Mosses." In Moby-Dick, or The
    Whale, pp. 535-551. Ed. Harrison Hayford and Hershel Parker. New
    York: W. W. Norton & Co., Inc., 1967.

_____. Journal up the Straits. Ed. Raymond Weaver. New York:
    Cooper Square Publishers, Inc., 1971.

_____. Mardi and a Voyage Hither. Ed. Harrison Hayford, Hershel
    Parker, and G. Thomas Tanselle. Evanston and Chicago: Northwestern
    University Press and the Newberry Library, 1970.

_____. Moby-Dick, or The Whale. Ed. Harrison Hayford and Hershel
    Parker. New York: W. W. Norton & Co., Inc., 1967.

_____. Omoo: A Narrative of Adventures in the South Seas. Ed.
    Harrison Hayford, Hershel Parker, and G. Thomas Tanselle. Evanston
    and Chicago: Northwestern University Press and the Newberry Library,
    1968.

_____. Redburn: His First Voyage. Ed. Harrison Hayford, Hershel
    Parker, and G. Thomas Tanselle. Evanston and Chicago: Northwestern
    University Press and the Newberry Library, 1968.

_____. Typee: A Peep at Polynesian Life. Ed. Harrison Hayford,
    Hershel Parker, and G. Thomas Tanselle. Evanston and Chicago:
    Northwestern University Press and the Newberry Library, 1968.

_____. White-Jacket, or the World in a Man-of-War. Ed. Harrison
    Hayford, Hershel Parker, and G. Thomas Tanselle. Evanston and
    Chicago: Northwestern University Press and the Newberry Library, 1970.

Metcalf, Eleanor Melville. Herman Melville: Cycle and Epicycle.
    Cambridge: Harvard University Press, 1953.

Metcalf, Eleanor Melville, ed. Journal of a Visit to London and the
    Continent By Herman Melville 1849-1850. Cambridge: Harvard
    University Press, 1948.

Miles, Josephine. Style and Proportion: The Language of Prose and
    Poetry. Boston: Little, Brown & Co., 1967.

Miller, Edwin Haviland. Melville. New York: George Braziller Inc., 1975.

Miller, Perry. The Raven and the Whale: The War of Words and Wits in
    the Era of Poe and Melville. New York: Harcourt, Brace and
    Company, 1956.

The National Union Catalog: Pre-1956 Imprints. Vol. 159. London:
    Mansell Information/Publishing Ltd., 1971.

Ohmann, Richard. "Literature as Sentences." In Readings in Applied
    Transformational Grammar, pp. 129-140. Ed. Mark Lester. New York:
    Holt, Rinehart and Winston, Inc., 1973.

The Oxford Dictionary of English Etymology, 1966. ed.

The Oxford English Dictionary, 1970 ed.

Owen, Dr. John B. Department of Biology, University of North Dakota,
    Grand Forks, North Dakota. Interview. 3 May 1978.

Quirk, Randolph, Sidney Greenbaum, Geoffrey Leech, and Jan Svartvik. A
    Grammar of Contemporary English. New York: Seminar Press, 1972.

Rosenheim, Frederick. "Flight from Home: Some Episodes in the Life of
    Herman Melville." The American Image 1 (1940): 1-30.

Russell, W. Clark. Sailors' Language: A Collection of Sea-Terms and
    their Definitions. London: Sampson Low, Marston, Searle &
    Rivington, 1883.

_____. "Sea Stories." Contemporary Review 46 (1884): 343-363.

Sealts, Merton J., Jr. Melville's Reading: A Check-List of Books Owned
    and Borrowed. Madison: The University of Wisconsin Press, 1966.

Smyth, W. H. The Sailor's Word-Book: An Alphabetical Digest of Nautical
    Terms. London: Blackie & Son, 1867.

Steiner, George. "Fires at Sea." The New Yorker 54 (June 5, 1978):
    110-116.

Teall, F. Horace. The Compounding of English Words: When and Why Joining
    or Separation is Preferable with Concise Rules and Alphabetical Lists.
    New York: John Ireland, 1891.

Trent, William P. A History of American Literature, 1607-1865. New York:
    D. Appleton, 1903.

Van Nostrand's Scientific Encyclopedia, 2nd ed.

Weaver, Raymond, ed. Billy Budd and Other Prose Pieces by Herman
    Melville. London: Constable and Company Ltd., 1924.

Weaver, Raymond. Herman Melville: Mariner and Mystic. New York:
    George H. Doran Co., 1921.

Webster, Noah. An American Dictionary of the English Language, 2 vols.
    n.p., 1828; reprint ed., New York: Johnson Reprint Corp., 1970.

Young, Gloria L. The Sea as a Symbol in the Work of Herman Melville and
    Joseph Conrad. Ph.D. dissertation, Kent State University, 1971.

About the Author

JILL B. GIDMARK is Assistant Professor of Skills and Writing at University of Minnesota General College in Minneapolis. She is Director of the Reading Laboratory at the General College and has written articles on language and business, English as a second language, communication skills, and American literature.